D0075987

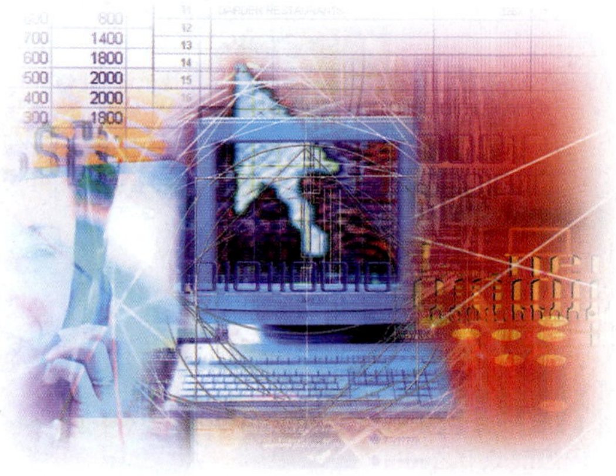

STATISTICS

for Business and Economics

MICROSOFT® EXCEL ENHANCED

HEINZ KOHLER

Willard Long Thorp Professor of Economics
Amherst College

Australia • Canada • Mexico • Singapore • Spain
United Kingdom • United States

SOUTH-WESTERN
THOMSON LEARNING™

Executive Editor: Mike Reynolds
Developmental Editors: Amy Holmes, Patricia Taylor
Marketing Strategist: Charlie Stutesman
Project Editors: Claudia Gravier, Jim Patterson
Art Director: Van Mua
Production Manager: Cindy Young
Manufacturing Manager: Lisa Kelley
Picture & Literary Rights Editor: Linda Blundell
Copy Editors: Leon Unruh, Michele Gitlin
Cover Designer: Van Mua
Cover Images: © Digital Vision
Cover Printer: Lehigh Press, Inc.
Compositor: Clarinda
Printer: R.R. Donnelley Willard

Printed in the United States of America

1 2 3 4 5 6 7 05 04 03 02 01

For more information about our products, contact us at:
Thomson Learning Academic Resource Center
1-800-423-0563

For permission to use material from this text, contact us by:
Phone: 1-800-730-2214
Fax: 1-800-730-2215
Web: www.thomsonrights.com

ISBN: 0-03-029731-1
Library of Congress Catalog Card Number: 2001096628

Microsoft EXCEL screen shots reprinted by permission from Microsoft Corporation.

Photo credit: p. 100, © Bettman Archive/Corbis Images

Asia
Thomson Learning
60 Albert Complex, #15-01
Albert Complex
Singapore 189969

Australia
Nelson Thomson Learning
102 Dodds Street
South Street
South Melbourne, Victoria 3205
Australia

Canada
Nelson Thomson Learning
1120 Birchmount Road
Toronto, Ontario M1K 5G4
Canada

Europe/Middle East/South Africa
Thomson Learning
Berkshire House
168-173 High Holborn
London WC1 V7AA
United Kingdom

Latin America
Thomson Learning
Seneca, 53
Colonia Polanco
11560 Mexico D.F.
Mexico

Spain
Paraninfo Thomson Learning
Calle/Magallanes, 25
28015 Madrid, Spain

PREFACE

***"The future isn't what it used to be"*—YOGI BERRA**

Current business students face a worldwide job market that will demand the most of their abilities. They will face tough decisions in times of extreme uncertainty. Instead of spending all of their hours delving into the intricacies of theoretical mathematics or "number crunching," this generation of business managers will need a solid foundation that will enable them to go to the Internet, pull down relevant information, enter that information into their computers, and know how to interpret the results quickly and accurately. If they are given the statistical tools to make decisions despite uncertainty, they will make sound decisions. So my job here is to develop their statistical reasoning and intuition via the technology that they will use in class and beyond.

Consider this, a business and economics statistics book built from page one around skills, software, and the Internet. Unlike Thomas Edison, who invented the light bulb, and unlike Alexander Graham Bell, who invented the telephone, Henry Ford didn't invent anything. Henry Ford simply improved the way something was already being done. In the same way, I hope that this book will contribute to the next revolution in the way that Business Statistics is taught—and more importantly, *used*—by the next generation of graduates.

This is the 21st century—a world of computers and the Internet. According to the *Computer Industry Almanac,* in late 2000, Americans used 159 million computers, which came to 580 computers per 1,000 people. By 2005, Americans are expected to use 230 million computers! The absolute numbers were equally impressive in Europe, but computer-per-capita *growth rates* were even higher in China, India, Russia, and other parts of the world. No wonder that 350 million people worldwide regularly used the Internet in late 2000, a number that is expected to reach 800 million by 2005!

I have designed this book to give students skills built around computer software and the Internet and have actually made computers the integral tool used to teach the concepts rather than merely providing an occasional screen image of what students should have gotten if they used computer programs.

CREATIVE, COOL APPLICATIONS

Together with its supplements, the book teaches statistics in the context of literally thousands of examples from the business and economic worlds. These examples illustrate vividly how the careful collection, effective presentation, and proper analysis of numerical information enable decision makers to draw important inferences.

This teaching-by-doing approach provides students with a fine appreciation of the power and applicability of statistical methods. Because the sheer volume of important statistical techniques is mind-boggling, and space and time are limited, the text avoids deriving formulas and presenting extended mathematical proofs. The applications approach seeks to teach sound statistical reasoning in a more limited sense: Students learn which techniques can be used under which circumstances and how the results—properly interpreted—can help them make sound decisions.

Look at Chapter 7, for example. EXCEL Example 7.1 on page 227 gives students specific instructions, step-by-step, to retrieve data (downloaded from the Internet) about total profit figures for the top 100 multinational companies of 1997, integrate those data into the computer program, and generate meaningful results immediately—which is the kind of procedure designed to build student confidence. Students learn by doing.

Or look at page 608 and Application 14.1, *Racial Bias in Mortgage Lending?* Here students learn how seemingly sterile formulas can address crucial issues of our times. Consider how often businesses are accused of one kind of discrimination or another and how this story may well aid students' own decision making in the future.

Finally, study Applications 20.1, *Measuring Soviet Economic Growth*, and 20.2, *Comparing U.S. with Soviet Real GNP*, on pages 988–989, Boring historical examples? Hardly. Students learn to appreciate the flaws of index-number formulas and how their own economic comparisons over time or space might succumb to the *index number problem*.

Statistics for Business and Economics: Microsoft® EXCEL Enhanced utilizes EXCEL, already on most computers. Chapter 2, *Learning About EXCEL*, provides a detailed introduction to the statistical analysis tools of EXCEL. Students will refer to this chapter throughout the course and beyond. In addition, Chapters 4–22 feature numerous self-contained EXCEL examples that jointly introduce every nook and cranny of the program. (Look under *EXCEL Examples* in the Subject Index for a complete listing.) Most end-of-chapter Practice Problems and numerous problems in the supplements provide further training in EXCEL. For even more advanced and involved statistical procedures, there is *HKStat,* an EXCEL add-in that ensures the speed and reliability of the statistical computations. *HKStat* which I developed and placed on the CD-ROM that accompanies this text, consists of 54 templates that use EXCEL's own functions and wizards to yield fast and accurate results. A list of these programs follows the Table of Contents. But note: Even though students will do most of their work with EXCEL, on a few occasions, text tables show the computer's invisible computations in detail. This helps students understand the nature of the procedures involved. It also helps them appreciate how lucky they are that computers now take care of the grinding, tedious paper-and-pencil calculations of old.

USING THE INTERNET

This book differs from the typical statistics text in yet another way. Early in the text, Chapter 3, *Finding Existing Data: From Print to Internet,* introduces students to an exciting new way of gathering data. They learn to find masses of data on the World Wide Web, along with ways to import data into software programs. The chapter introduces major U.S. government Web sites, well over 100 foreign government sites, the Web sites of all companies on the Year 2000 *Fortune 500* list, and many other interesting data sources. Appropriate hyperlinks to all of these appear on the student CD-ROM accompanying the text. Students will refer to Chapter 3 throughout the course and beyond.

A FLEXIBLE APPROACH

As I talk with business statistics instructors, I often hear how their courses vary in their topic sequence. Keeping those comments in mind, I have tried to do two things. First, I wrote each chapter so that it can stand on its own—a modular approach that allows instructors to organize the sequence that best fits their needs. Second, realizing that, ultimately, the text needs its own organization, I have structured the text in a logical progression that I think students will find easy to follow. The Contents in Brief show the text's eight-part divisions. Part I features a preview of the text and a discussion of its associated software program. Students then learn how to collect data (Part II), before they learn how to describe them (Part III). In Part IV, they learn about probability, so that they can draw meaningful inferences (Parts V and VI). Their studies are then supplemented by turning to other topics favored by economists and business administrators, respectively (Parts VII and VIII).

But we all have limited time, and no one should look upon this text as a novel that must be read in order, from the first page of Chapter 1 to the last page of Chapter 23. Given the book's modular style, you might instead look upon this text as a treasure trove of raw material that you can shape to your own liking. Depending on the type of course you have in mind, you can focus your attention on some chapters, while ignoring others. You can change the order in which you assign chapters. You can ignore many sections and subsections within chapters (and some of these sections are even designated as *optional*). Students can consult skipped material later in different contexts. Instructors, in short, have *great flexibility* in designing course outlines of their own that are well suited to their personal preferences and, above all, to the needs of their particular students.

CAREFUL PEDAGOGY

I have paid special attention to helping students learn. Features that help them understand and retain material include:

- **Looking Ahead:** A succinct summary at the beginning of each chapter shows students what they can expect to learn. (*Tip:* Want a more elaborate forecast of things to come? Look at the actual chapter *Summary* near the chapter's end.)
- **Preview:** A self-contained real-life example found near the beginning of each chapter is designed to illustrate the essence of the chapter. These examples help students see how they might apply chapter principles later.
- **Typical Problem:** This "teaser" feature helps you focus on the kinds of questions you can answer with techniques discussed in the chapter.
- **Definition Boxes:** These highlight carefully worded definitions of key terms.
- **Caution Boxes:** I point out common errors and misunderstandings to help students avoid typical slip ups.

- **Formula Boxes:** These highlight important formulas and define all the symbols used in writing them down.
- **Technical Detail Boxes:** As the name suggests, these provide finer detail that students may skip without adverse consequences. Some readers may prefer the detail, so we have included it.

- **Example Problems:** Special sections within each chapter that apply new material without the help of the computer.
- **EXCEL® Examples:** Special sections within each chapter that apply new material via the associated computer program.
- **Optional Sections:** Major sections of some chapters could be omitted when class is pressed for time, but students can consult them later.

- **Applications:** Self-contained stories, usually based on journal articles or major statistical studies, illustrate the use of the chapter's techniques in "the real world." Almost 90 free-standing Applications appear throughout the text or on its associated Web site.
- **Graphs:** These are self-contained features by virtue of carefully worded captions, providing a valuable tool for review.
- **Summary:** A review of the chapter's main points appears at the end of each chapter.
- **Key Terms:** An end-of-chapter listing of key terms, all of which appear in boldface in the text when they are first introduced.
- **Practice Problems:** Some 50 end-of-chapter problems are segregated by text section. (Answers for all odd-numbered problems appear on the student CD-ROM; those for all even-numbered problems can be found in the Instructor's Manual.)

SUPPLEMENTS FOR STUDENTS

The CD-ROM. The CD-ROM is filled with a multitude of helpful materials, including:

- Elaborate solutions (in EXCEL as well as MINITAB format) to all 575 odd-numbered end-of-chapter Practice Problems.

- Data files (EXCEL format) for all nontrivial data sets used in the text and its supplements.
- Hyperlinks to data sources on the Internet, notably to U.S. government databases, to almost 150 foreign government statistical offices, to all companies on the Year 2000 *Fortune 500* list, and more.
- *Student Workbook* featuring 360 true-false questions (with answers), 360 multiple-choice questions (with answers), 23 major Achievement Tests (featuring 144 problems with detailed solutions), recognition exercises for all the key terms boldfaced in the text (and listed near the end of each chapter), an alphabetical glossary of all the key terms used in the text, a similar glossary of all symbols used in the text, and a chapter-by-chapter listing of key formulas.
- *HKStat,* an EXCEL add-in featuring 54 templates (listed after the Table of Contents) that produce rapid answers to problems and adds to what EXCEL can do.

The Web Site. Additional useful material appears on the publisher's Web site, which anyone can visit at http://www.harcourtcollege.com/business_stats/kohler. The site also includes:

- Online Quizzing and Testing for each chapter of the text, including 240 interactive multiple-choice questions.
- More than two dozen biographical sketches of historical figures who developed the statistical techniques encountered in the text.
- All sorts of hyperlinks to interesting statistics-oriented Web sites, notably those run by academic institutions.
- *Recommended Readings* for each chapter of the text for further study.
- *Statistics in the News*, featuring numerous examples (keyed to text chapters and frequently updated) of how statistical methods are put to work in our lives.

SUPPLEMENTS FOR INSTRUCTORS

The printed text is associated with two major supplements for instructors: a *Test Bank* and an *Instructor's Kit* (containing the *Instructor's Manual and Instructor's Resource CD-ROM*). I have tried to make these very complete and very helpful, and they are the result of many years of teaching, along with numerous comments and ideas from colleagues. I trust that you will find these useful.

The Test Bank. Along with answers and solutions, the *Test Bank* provides an unduplicated set of

- 528 True-False Questions
- 1,056 Multiple-Choice Questions
- 364 Practice Problems

The Instructor's Kit: Instructor's Manual and Instructor's Resource CD-ROM. The Instructor's Manual features alternative course outlines for courses of different lengths and provides suggestions for those teaching one-semester courses, two-semester courses, or four-quarter courses.

- Teaching tips and additional teaching materials for each chapter of the text.

- Elaborate solutions (in EXCEL as well as MINITAB format) to all 575 even-numbered end-of-chapter Practice Problems (elaborate rather than succinct solutions are provided for those instructors who wish to hand out solutions to students).

The Instructor's Resource CD-ROM features

- Microsoft Word files of the IM
- Microsoft Word files of the Test Bank
- Microsoft PowerPoint slides

ACKNOWLEDGMENTS

A multitude of individuals deserves thanks for helping me with this project. Several years ago, all of the following looked at early parts of the manuscript and gave me good advice: Mary Alguire, University of Arkansas; Ralph Beals, Amherst College; Richard E. Beckwith, California State University–Sacramento; Harry Benham, University of Oklahoma; Georgio Canarella, California State University–Los Angeles; Stephen G. Cecchetti, New York University; Edward Coulson, Pennsylvania State University; George Dery, University of Lowell; Mark Eakin; University of Texas at Arlington; Barry Elledge, Appalachian State University; Douglas Elvers, University of North Carolina at Chapel Hill; John S. Gafar, Long Island University; Joseph Glaz, University of Connecticut; Gerald Goldberg, Florida Institute of Technology; Tarsaim L. Goyal, University of the District of Columbia; Paul W. Guy, California State University–Chico; Stephen Grubaugh, Bentley College; Richard D. Heath, Saint Cloud State University; Hannah Hiles, Wesleyan University; Peter Hoefer, Pace University; Patrick R. Huntley, University of Arkansas; Mel Jameson, University of Rochester; Thomas Johnson, North Carolina State University; Denis F. Johnston, Georgetown University; Robert Karsteter, Mount St. Mary's College; Ronald S. Koot, Pennsylvania State University; David Larson, University of New Orleans; Allen Lee, Northeastern University; Robert C. Marshall, Duke University; G. E. Martin, Clarkson University; Jerrold May, University of Pittsburgh; James McDowell, Rocky Mountain College; Peter H. Michael, California State University–Sacramento; Jeff Mock, Diablo Valley College; Keith T. Poole, Carnegie-Mellon University; Harry O. Posten, University of Connecticut; Lawrence B. Pulley, Brandeis University; David R. Rogers, Purdue University; John D. Scholl, Rio Grande College; Saul Schwartz, Tufts University; Thomas Severini, Northwestern University; Thomas Sexton, SUNY at Stony Brook; Edwin Shapiro, University of San Francisco; Jennifer Snyder, University of Pennsylvania; C. B. Sowell, Berea College; Leonard W. Swanson, Northwestern University; Kathryn Szabat, La Salle University; Stanley A. Taylor, California State University–Sacramento; Willbann D. Terpening, University of Notre Dame; Bulent Uyar, University of North Dakota; Lee J. Van Scyoc, University of Wisconsin–Oshkosh; Bruce Verrnuelen, Colby College; James E. Willis, Louisiana State University; and Allan R. Young, University of Hawaii–Manoa.

More recently, another group of reviewers examined more advanced sections of the manuscript. Again, I wish to express my sincere gratitude for their work: Jana C. Anderson, Colorado State University; Byung Cho, University of Notre Dame; Chia-Shin Chung, Cleveland State University; Robert Escudero, Pepperdine University; Nicholas Farnum, California State University at Fullerton; Richard A. Fentriss, University of South Florida; Gail Heyne Hafter, St. Louis Community College at Meramec; John Hafter, University of Nebraska at Omaha; Mabel T. Kung, California State University at Fullerton; Jay G. Patankar, University of Akron; Louis G. Pol, University of Nebraska at Omaha; Farhad Raiszadeh, University of Tennessee at Chattanooga; Anuj Srivastava, Florida State University; H. F. Williamson, University at Urbana–Champaign; and Mari Yetimyan, San Jose State University.

The CD-ROM associated with the MINITAB edition of this text contains a copy of the Student Edition of MINITAB. I thank the company for its permission to bundle their excellent program with the text. I am equally grateful for innumerable instances of generous help given me during the writing process by Jeff Hartzell, Glenda M. Bartley, and others associated with the Author Assistance Program associated with MINITAB.

Special thanks go to many at Harcourt College Publishers who have jointly helped produce a beautiful book. The list includes Gary L. Nelson, the senior acquisitions editor who brought me into the fold, and Michael Reynolds, executive editor who shepherded the project to completion. It includes Anita Borger, who initially served as developmental editor, and Patricia D. Taylor, senior consulting developmental editor who developed and managed the entire book package and did a truly superb job. It includes the ever-capable in-house developmental editor Amy Holmes, art director Van Mua, project editors Christy Goldfinch, Claudia Gravier, and Jim Patterson; production manager Cindy Young; manufacturing manager Lisa Kelley; permissions editor Linda Blundell, and many others who steered this book through the long process of production.

I dedicate this book to my brother, Professor Günter Köhler, who helped me in countless ways hardly anyone will ever know.

CONTACT INFORMATION I would be grateful to hear from any and all users of this text and its supplements. Your comments and suggestions will make for a better book when the next edition is born. Just write me a letter at hkohler@amherst.edu or leave a note at my publisher's Web site at http://www.harcourtcollege.com.

Heinz Kohler
Amherst College
October 2001

CONTENTS IN BRIEF

Contents

HKStat Programs

PART

I

INTRODUCTION

Chapter 1

THE NATURE OF STATISTICS

LOOKING AHEAD

After reading this chapter, you will know what you can expect to learn from this text. Among other things, you will:

1. come to know *statistics* as a field of study that develops and uses techniques for the careful collection, effective presentation, and proper analysis of numerical information (a fact that is reflected in the titles of Parts II to VI of this text),
2. get a chapter-by-chapter preview of the kinds of business and economic problems you will learn to solve and, in the process, come to see why *statistics* is said to facilitate wise decision making in the face of uncertainty and is viewed as a "universal guide to the unknown,"
3. meet a number of basic statistical concepts, including statistical *populations, samples, variables, data,* and more, and
4. learn to distinguish different types of data (such as *nominal, ordinal, interval,* and *ratio* data) and, thus, develop an awareness of different data qualities, which, in turn, determines what types of arithmetic operations can be performed with these data.

AND HERE IS A TYPICAL PROBLEM YOU WILL BE ABLE TO SOLVE:

You just received *Fortune* magazine's latest *Global 500* report, which provides information on the world's 500 largest corporations. Besides each company's name, country, industry code, and number of employees, the report includes dollar amounts and rankings of each firm's revenues, profits, assets, and stockholders' equity.

a. Identify the elementary units.

b. How many variables can you find in this report? What are they?

c. Identify the variables as quantitative or qualitative.

d. Identify variables as discrete/continuous or binomial/multinomial.

e. Can you find examples of nominal, ordinal, interval, and ratio data in this report? Why would you care?

Preview

You are a film producer and your studio has just spent millions of dollars creating a new soap opera that seems destined to be shown on television. Naturally, you want to make as much money as possible. Thus, it is time to devise a marketing strategy. Several possibilities come to mind:

- First, all rights to the new series *could* be sold to a distributor who is willing to pay $125 million right now, and that could be the end of the story as far as you are concerned.
- Second, the program could be offered to a TV network for review with these possible results (in your judgment): a 60 percent chance of rejection (which ruins all further chances of a sale to anyone and spells a $30 million loss) or a 40 percent chance of getting a contract (which means a $300 million profit).
- Third, you could hire a consulting firm, which is willing to offer advice on the network's likely reaction for a $1 million fee. The consulting firm's "track record" is given in Table 1.1. During the past decade, the consulting firm has issued numerous reports in similar situations. An ultimate rejection—an event here designated as E_1—was preceded by a report predicting rejection, R_1, 80 percent of the time, and by a report predicting a contract offer, R_2, 20 percent of the time. On the other hand, an eventual contract offer—an event here designated as E_2—was preceded by a report predicting rejection 30 percent of the time and by a report predicting a contract offer 70 percent of the time.

What then is your optimal strategy? Should you grasp the sure thing and pocket $125 million now by selling the rights? Should you take the −$30 million versus +$300 million gamble by showing the pilot to network executives? Should you buy the advice and then take the action that maximizes your likely revenue (sell the rights if report R_1 is received; offer the film to the network if report R_2 is received)? Or should you buy the advice now and, after having received your report, rethink the whole matter in light of Table 1.1?

Surely, you can picture yourself now, with report R_1 in hand, about to make that $125 million deal with the distributor, yet thinking about the lost chance of making $300 million if the report is wrong. Surely, you can see yourself fretting all night, with report R_2 in hand, about to contact the network and collect that $300 million prize, while thinking about the very real chance, if the report is wrong, of ending up $30 million in the red instead of pocketing $125 million for sure. . . .

Business executives face decision-making problems like this every day. By the time you have studied the last chapter of this text, you will be able to solve this particular problem in no time. And you will acquire similar skills in every chapter in between.

TABLE 1.1 | Film Consultant's Track Record

	Subsequent Events	
Prior Advice Given	E_1 = rejection	E_2 = contract offer
R_1 = network will reject	80%	30%
R_2 = network will offer contract	20%	70%

1.1 Introduction

Ask anyone to define the nature of *statistics* and, just as in the dictionary, you are likely to get one of three answers. Some, like you perhaps, are about to take a course in the subject. They will naturally think of statistics as a *field of study* that somehow deals with the collection, presentation, and interpretation of numerical data. There will be others, the vast majority of people no doubt, who will instantly think of *masses of data,* seemingly infinite in number, that constantly bombard us in our daily lives. Just think of all those numbers ceaselessly spewing forth from television sets, radios, newspapers, and sites on the World Wide Web: data about the weather and sports events; election results and opinion polls; prices of bonds, stocks, foreign monies, and commodity futures; rates of inflation, unemployment, and economic growth.... Finally, a few other people, already trained in the discipline, will conjure up a highly technical meaning of the term that we, too, will meet in later chapters. The term *statistics* can refer to *summary measures,* such as sample averages and sample proportions, that have been computed from relatively few data gathered by *sampling* a much larger collection of data called a *population.*

In fact, these three definitions are linked. Statistics, viewed as a scientific discipline, inevitably uses as raw material those very masses of data that most people associate with the term. Indeed, statistics courses used to have an ugly reputation precisely because they involved endless, boring hours of manipulating masses of data. But such number crunching is no more. Sophisticated computer software, such as Microsoft's EXCEL or the MINITAB program packaged with one version of this text, can perform powerful magic. As Chapter 2 illustrates, upon starting either program, you encounter a screen that is nicely divided into a series of columns and rows and invites you to enter data, masses of them, if you want. Indeed, in the case of EXCEL, a single Workbook contains 16 blank spreadsheets. Each of these measures 256 columns by 65,536 rows. That comes to 16,777,216 cells, which could be printed on a sheet of paper 19 feet wide and 1,300 feet long! In the case of MINITAB's Professional Version, an eager user can fill in 150 million of those pretty cells (provided there is sufficient computer memory), but even the lower limit of a mere 5,000 entries in the Student Version can keep you busy for quite some time. Relax! You won't have to do that in this course.

Having entered your data into either program, you must specify an appropriate statistical technique. A few well-chosen keystrokes will do, and wham! In a fraction of a second, you have your result. Times have certainly changed. Not so many years ago, some of these calculations might have taken weeks and even months or years of work.

1.2 Collecting Data

Any practical statistical work requires data, data, and more data. A first branch of the discipline of statistics, therefore, focuses on the careful collection of this crucial type of raw material. Such collection can proceed in one of three ways: (1) An investigator can look for data that already exist because others have gathered them in the past. (2) Brand-new data can be generated with the help of so-called observational studies that involve census taking or sampling. (3) Brand-new data can be generated by conducting carefully controlled experiments. These three approaches are explained in Chapters 3, 4, and 5 of this text, respectively.

FINDING EXISTING DATA

When relevant information already exists somewhere, an investigator need only find it. A business administrator, for example, might simply search the firm's internal records for material that quietly resides in filing cabinets or computer memories. Thus, customer records would provide names, addresses, telephone numbers, data on amounts purchased, credit limits, and more. Employee records would provide names, addresses, job titles, years of service, salaries, Social Security numbers, and even numbers of sick days used. Production records would contain lists of products, part numbers, and quantities produced, along with associated labor costs, raw material consumption, and equipment usage. A government economist would, similarly, have access to vast databases held by the Bureau of the Census, the Department of Labor, the Federal Reserve Board, and the Office of Management and Budget, to name but a few. From the point of view of the business administrator or the government economist, respectively, all of the sources just mentioned are *internal* sources.

In addition to scouring internal sources of information, our business administrator or government economist could also look for *external* depositories of already existing data and persuade their owners to share information. Indeed, all kinds of organizations, ranging from Dow Jones and Company to the Dun and Bradstreet Corporation to the Medical Economics Company, routinely gather data and sell them to would-be users in the private sector and in government agencies alike. As a student, you are already familiar with the use of preexisting data. When writing your next paper, you are unlikely to generate brand-new information (although you will learn how to do so in this text). More likely, you will turn to some source of data gathered by someone else. You might check out the *Statistical Abstract of the United States* or one of the numerous other sources listed in its Appendix I, Guide to Sources of Statistics, State Statistical Abstracts, and Foreign Statistical Abstracts, a perusal of which we highly recommend. Better yet, you might check out the Internet's FedStats site (introduced in Chapter 3) that leads you to data collected by over 70 agencies of the U.S. government. Or you might click on the link to any one of almost 200 foreign government sites or visit the sites of any *Fortune 500* company, every one of which is listed on the CD-ROM accompanying this text. Yet, from the point of view of the professional statistician, the matter of collecting data, especially *current* data, is usually much more complicated than checking out internal or external sources of existing data. More often than not, this question arises: How can trustworthy *new* data be generated?

GENERATING NEW DATA

New data about persons or objects possessing characteristics that interest a statistician can be generated either by conducting a complete or sample *survey* or by performing a controlled *experiment.* These two approaches are presented in Chapters 4 and 5, respectively. Here we introduce the general idea, which is conveyed by these definitions:

DEFINITION 1.1 The collection of data about persons or objects by merely recording information about selected characteristics of interest (such as A or B), while paying no attention to possibly widely diverging other characteristics (such as C or D) that may affect the chosen characteristics, is called an **observational study** or **survey.**

DEFINITION 1.2 The collection of data about persons or objects by deliberately exposing them to some kind of change, while leaving all else unchanged, and subsequently recording how identical persons or objects respond to different types of change, or how different types of persons or objects respond to identical change, is called a **controlled experiment.**

GENERATING SURVEY DATA In a *survey,* a characteristic such as the annual salary of workers, for example, may simply be observed and recorded for different workers without regard to factors, like length of service, education, and work experience, that make workers different from one another. These factors may, in fact, be responsible for the observed differences in their salaries. If, by pure accident, a firm employs lots of recently hired women with little education and next to no work experience, while also employing lots of men hired decades ago who are highly educated and have plenty of work experience, you can guess what will happen: A survey of salaries that ignores length of service, education, and work experience can easily create the impression that women are being paid less than men merely because of their sex.

This being said, you can, perhaps, anticipate an answer to the following survey problem:

CHAPTER 4 | Generating New Data: Census Taking and Sampling

Domino's Pizza once was sued by Amstar, maker of Domino sugar, on the grounds that use of this name confused people. Indeed, Amstar had interviewed women shopping in supermarkets, had shown them a Domino's Pizza box, and had asked whether they thought the pizza makers produced any other product. Some 71 percent said "sugar." If you were a statistician hired by Domino's Pizza, how could you help your client?

GENERATING EXPERIMENTAL DATA Experimental data, in contrast to survey data, are generated more carefully. Thus, a firm may divide its 40 new employees into two groups of equal size (with the help of some random device you will learn about in Chapter 4). It may then administer a special training program to one of the groups only. If the 20 employees who went through the program exhibited superior productivity later on, the training program might justifiably be credited with those improvements. After all, other factors that could account for this result, such as group differences in age, motivation, or prior work experience, were effectively equalized by random division of the original group of 40 workers.

Can you anticipate an answer to the following question that you will soon encounter?

CHAPTER 5 | Generating New Data: Controlled Experiments

Pharmaceutical companies can increase their sales by billions of dollars per year if they are lucky enough to come up with a new best-selling drug. No wonder they are always experimenting. One such company selected 100 adults at random and managed to persuade 80 of them to take calcium supplements, which were suspected of lowering blood pressure. A comparison of the subjects' before-and-after blood pressure readings confirmed the suspicion. As a statistician hired by the Food and Drug Administration, evaluate this experiment.

Despite the fact that experimental data tend to be more reliable or "stronger" than survey data, most new data in business, economics, and many other fields, are not generated by controlled experiments. More likely than not, they are generated by (complete or sample) surveys. This happens because it is often impossible, or extremely costly, to carry out experiments. We could not easily divide the country's labor force (or even a segment of it) at random into three groups and then subject each group to different tax rates in order to study the effect of taxes on labor supply. Nor could we simply divide the country's newly born (or even a segment of them) at random into two groups and then subject only one of the groups to a lifetime of smoking in order to study the effect of smoking on health. Nevertheless, as you will learn later in this text, with proper statistical techniques, we can learn a great deal about such matters even from surveys.

Our discussion so far, however, must not be misunderstood. The modern scientific *discipline* of statistics is not very well described by the popular image of statistics as a field of study that is preoccupied with the acquisition and publication of masses of data. Much more so, statistics is about the subsequent description and analysis of data. Indeed, most textbooks, including this one, emphasize the latter two branches of the discipline, that is, *descriptive statistics* and *inferential statistics,* over methods for collecting data.

1.3 Describing Data

Once we have collected data, they become the raw material for those laboring in a second branch of the statistics discipline. The *descriptive* statistician focuses on the postcollection task of effectively *presenting* data, of organizing and condensing them, usually with the help of tables and graphs (Chapter 6) or with the help of numerical summary measures (Chapter 7). As we will see, unlike mere listings of masses of raw data, such as those that the Internet provides, this type of presentation alone makes data understandable and often reveals patterns otherwise hidden in unprocessed data.

DEFINITION 1.3 A branch of the discipline that is concerned with developing and using techniques for effectively presenting numerical information so as to highlight patterns otherwise hidden in data sets is called **descriptive statistics.**

Here are two examples of working with descriptive statistics:

CHAPTER 6 | Presenting Data: Tables and Graphs

Imagine you were working for a chemicals firm that is interested in expanding its fertilizer sales in California and Florida. You are supposed to provide information about current fertilizer usage, and you instantly think of *oranges.* Create a relevant *cross tabulation* for your next staff meeting. (*Hint:* To find current data, visit http://www.fedstats.gov, a site maintained by the federal government's Interagency Council on Statistical Policy.)

CHAPTER 7 | Presenting Data: Summary Measures

Your boss wants to acquire a major software company. You are to gather relevant information. Visit http://www.fortune.com, a site maintained by *Fortune* magazine. Identify the revenues, profits, and numbers of employees of each of the *Fortune 500* companies in the *computer software* industry. Using EXCEL or MINITAB, compute and print out descriptive summary statistics on the three types of data series just noted.

The importance of descriptive statistics is illustrated vividly by numerous other examples found later in this text. As we will show, the effective presentation of data can lead a production engineer to discover the secret behind the recent breakdowns of motors produced by a firm, can help a historian unravel the mystery of a disputed authorship, can aid spies in cracking a secret code, and can enable managers to monitor quality in an ongoing production process.

As useful as it may be, however, descriptive statistics too comprises only a small part of the modern discipline of statistics. Contrary to another common view that identifies data collection *and* descriptive statistics with the entire field of study, another branch of the discipline is nowadays considerably more important.

1.4 Analyzing Data

Modern statisticians direct most of their effort not toward collecting and presenting numerical information but toward analyzing it. They are laboring in a third branch yet of the statistics discipline. They focus on applying reason to data in order to draw sensible conclusions from them. Their chief concern is making reasonable inferences, from the limited information that is available, about matters that are not known. Accordingly, 16 chapters of this book (Chapters 8–23) deal exclusively with *analytical* or *inferential statistics.*

DEFINITION 1.4 A branch of the discipline of statistics that is concerned with developing and using techniques for properly analyzing (or drawing inferences from) numerical information is called **analytical statistics** or **inferential statistics.**

Sometimes a general truth is inferred from particular instances. At other times, statisticians reverse the process and draw conclusions about the particular from their knowledge of the general.

DRAWING INFERENCES BY INDUCTIVE REASONING

Drawing inferences about an unknown whole from a known part is called **inductive reasoning.** Inductive reasoning is at work, for example, when a statistician concludes that between 1 and 3 percent of a firm's total output is defective because 2 percent of an output *sample* did, in fact, not meet quality standards. (As we will learn, even this result may be clouded by uncertainty, because the *method* used to derive this conclusion may provide correct results only 95 percent of the time and incorrect results in the remaining cases.)

DRAWING INFERENCES BY DEDUCTIVE REASONING

On the other hand, drawing inferences about an unknown part from a known whole is **deductive reasoning.** Deductive reasoning is at work, for example, when a statistician concludes that a particular unit of a firm's output (namely, a unit produced at plant 7, during the night shift, and with the help of components supplied by firm X) has 5 chances in 100 of being included in a quality test. This conclusion may reflect the facts that (a) 5 percent of the firm's total output meets the above criteria and (b) the portion of output to be tested is being selected from total output by a random process. Thus, it is likely to reflect the characteristics of total output. As a matter of fact, deductive reasoning and inductive reasoning complement one another. As we will see, before statisticians can safely generalize from the part to the whole, they must study how the part has been generated from the whole.

LOOKING AHEAD

The importance of inferential statistics is illustrated by the rich array of examples found throughout this book and its supplements. Statistical techniques help firms screen job applicants, budget research and development expenditures, determine the quality of raw materials received or of output produced, and decide whether sales personnel are better motivated by salary or commission. Statistical techniques can, similarly, help firms choose the best one among several product designs, leasing arrangements, oil-drilling sites, fertilizer types, or advertising media. And inferential statistics can tell firms precisely how the quantity of their product that consumers demand relates to the product's price, to the prices of substitutes and complements, to consumer income, and, perhaps, even to the consumer's sex.

Government officials are equally avid users of what this text has to teach. Inferential statistics plays an important role in ensuring the reliability of space missions and of more mundane airport lighting systems. And statistical techniques help answer questions such as these: Do motorcycle helmets really reduce accident fatalities? Do nursing homes discriminate against Medicaid recipients? Do the boxes of raisins marketed by this firm truly contain 15 ounces as claimed? Do the firms in this state meet antipollution standards? When is this recession likely to end? What is next year's probable rate of inflation? This list, too, can be expanded at will.

Here, chapter by chapter, are some specific problems you will encounter and learn to solve. Naturally, the list contains terms you haven't yet met. Don't fret. You will learn about them in due course.

CHAPTER 8 | The Theory of Probability

A wine producer has designed a distinctive bottle in the hope of increasing sales. The manager views the probability of success as 50 percent, based on experience, but also orders a survey of customers. The manager knows that when consumers are enthusiastic and sales are about to rise, the type of survey about to be taken will confirm that positive market climate 90 percent of the time. But in 10 percent of the cases, the survey will say the opposite. When consumers are unimpressed and sales prospects look dim, the survey will so indicate 60 percent of the time. But in 40 percent of the cases, it will then say the opposite. The survey is taken and shows great consumer enthusiasm about the bottle. What is the manager's new assessment of the probability of success?

CHAPTER 9 | Discrete Probability Distributions

An automobile manufacturer has fitted all of the firm's cars with an identical pollution-control device, designed to meet government standards. Yet experience shows that 5 percent of cars tested perform below these pollution standards. Assume that 20 cars coming off the assembly line during a given month are selected at random. What is the probability that a government inspector who tests 20 cars a month in the above fashion will unjustly accuse the manufacturer of producing more than 5 percent of all cars below standard?

CHAPTER 10 | Continuous Probability Distributions

The city miles-per-gallon (mpg) rating of cars is a normally distributed random variable with a mean of 25.9 and a standard deviation of 2.45. If an automobile manufacturer wants to build a car with an mpg rating that improves upon 99 percent of existing cars, what must the new car's mpg rating be?

CHAPTER 11 | Sampling Distributions

The manufacturer of batteries for aircraft emergency-locator transmitters claims that the lifetime of these batteries is normally distributed with a mean of 30 months and a standard deviation of 3 months. An aircraft manufacturer checks out 50 batteries and discovers a sample mean of only 29 months. What is the probability that the battery manufacturer's claim is true?

CHAPTER 12 | Estimation

United Parcel Service wants to determine the gasoline savings if all of its trucks were switched from regular to radial tires. Some 150 trucks get new tires. Half of them are regular tires; the others are radial tires. One truck in each group, furthermore, is matched with one in the other group by make, age, region of the world, and other aspects that might affect gasoline consumption. After 3 months, the mileage on trucks with radial tires is found, on average, to be 5 miles per gallon higher than on trucks with regular tires. The sample standard deviation of the differences is 3 mpg. Construct a 98 percent confidence interval for the potential mileage gain if a similar switchover were made on all of the firm's trucks worldwide.

CHAPTER 13 | Hypothesis Testing: The Classical Technique

The Environmental Protection Agency is allowing a plant to dump its waste into a river—as long as the effluent averages no more than 4 parts per million (ppm) of a certain toxic substance. During the course of one week, the EPA randomly samples the effluent and finds, in 64 samples, an average of 4.2 ppm of toxic substance, with a standard deviation of 1 ppm. Is the plant violating EPA standards?

CHAPTER 14 | Hypothesis Testing: The Chi-Square Technique

An advertising agency wants to know whether consumer preferences for three brands of coffee are independent of the person's gender. The answer will determine whether different ads must be created for men's and women's magazines. A simple random sample of 100 persons yields Table 1.2. So, can we say that people's coffee preferences do not depend on their sex?

TABLE 1.2 | Preferences Indicated by Coffee Drinkers

	(B) Brand Preference			
(A) Sex	**A**	**B**	**C**	**Total**
Male	18	25	17	60
Female	32	5	3	40
Total	50	30	20	**100**

CHAPTER 15 | Analysis of Variance

An analyst wants to test whether the average price per share differs among three stock exchanges, A–C. Independent random samples of eight stocks from each market yield the following (in dollars per share):

A: 45, 56, 82, 49, 53, 61, 48, 51
B: 17, 19, 27, 22, 31, 41, 15, 16
C: 30, 19, 82, 49, 31, 19, 16, 51

Perform the desired test.

CHAPTER 16 | Simple Regression and Correlation

A marketing manager wants to establish the relationship between the number of cereal boxes sold, Y, and the shelf space devoted to them, X. Given the data of Table 1.3, determine an appropriate equation relating Y to X.

TABLE 1.3 | Cereal Boxes Sold and Shelf Space

Number of Boxes Sold, Y	Feet of Shelf Space, X	Number of Boxes Sold, Y	Feet of Shelf Space, X
145	3	125	7
151	6	190	5
235	9	210	10
120	5	118	8
272	13	100	7
300	15	390	12
110	2	210	6

CHAPTER 17 | Multiple Regression and Correlation

An executive of a shoe manufacturing company wants to assess the relationship between average daily sales at the firm's factory outlet stores, Y, and a number of possible determinants. These include the number of competitors within a 3-mile radius, X_1, per capita annual income in the county, X_2, and the average price per pair of shoes, X_3. Given the data of Table 1.4 on the next page, compute a multiple regression equation.

CHAPTER 18 | Model Building with Multiple Regression

A textbook publisher has collected the data of Table 1.5 on the next page. Create an economic model that relates copies sold to the review ratio and the Web site availability.

CHAPTER 19 | Time Series and Forecasting

The following time series represents U.S. corporate tax liabilities from 1959 to 1997 (in billions of dollars): 23.6; 22.7; 22.8; 24.0; 26.2; 28.0; 30.9; 33.7; 32.7; 39.4; 39.7; 34.4; 37.7; 41.9; 49.3; 51.8; 50.9; 64.2; 73.0; 83.5; 88.0; 84.8; 81.1; 63.1; 77.2; 94.0; 96.5; 106.5; 127.1; 137.0; 141.3; 140.5; 133.4; 143.0; 165.2; 186.6; 211.0; 226.1; 246.1.

a. Estimate the trend in the form of a 7-year moving-averages series.

b. On the basis of the slope of the trend line between the last two numbers estimated in (a), forecast corporate taxes in 2004.

TABLE 1.4 | Factory Outlet Stores Data

Average Daily Sales ($1,000s), Y	Competitors within 3 Miles (number), X_1	Per Capita Income in County ($1,000/year), X_2	Average Price of Shoes ($/pair), X_3
2.8	0	3.1	28
3.1	0	4.0	31
.6	4	2.9	67
1.9	1	5.9	44
1.9	1	6.9	47
1.4	1	4.9	43
.6	6	2.7	78
2.5	3	4.7	34
1.7	1	4.2	23
2.9	2	6.0	33
4.8	2	7.3	55
3.9	3	7.2	66
5.1	0	8.0	43
8.6	0	14.7	83

TABLE 1.5 | Sample Data on Textbook Sales

Copies Sold (1,000s/year), Y	Favorable-to-Unfavorable Review Ratio, X_1	Web Site (= 0 if unavailable; = 1 if available), D_1
7	5.1	0
11	4.6	0
14	6.0	0
17	2.0	0
29	3.1	1
39	0.2	1
52	0.1	1
6	10.3	0
3	5.0	0
2	12.0	0

CHAPTER 20 | Index Numbers

The manager of an orchard has collected the data of Table 1.6. Compute a 1995 *Laspeyres quantity index* for the orchard's output, based on 1985. Can you see any problem with interpreting the index number?

TABLE 1.6 | Orchard Data

	Output (thousands of bushels)				Price (dollars per bushel)			
Item	1985	1990	1995	2000	1985	1990	1995	2000
Almonds	12	13	15	9	20	19	15	26
Apricots	4	5	8	6	10	10	9	12
Cherries	20	15	16	25	25	28	30	15
Peaches	6	6	6	7	15	12	12	12

CHAPTER 21 | Hypothesis Testing: Nonparametric Techniques

A business school admissions board stands accused of manipulating admissions according to a secret daily quota system based on applicants' sex. The board denies the charge and claims that sex is never even considered during the admission process. Therefore, the order of male/female admissions must be random. Investigators acquire the information given in Table 1.7 for 60 successive admissions. (M = male, F = female, and data are to be read in successive rows.) Make an appropriate hypothesis test and decide whether the board discriminates on the basis of sex.

TABLE 1.7 | Business School Admissions Data

Order of Admission	Sex of Admission
1–10	M M M M M F F M M M
11–20	M M F F F M M M M M
21–30	F F M F M M M M M F
31–40	F F M M M M M M M F
41–50	F F M F M M M M M M
51–60	M M F F M M F F M M

CHAPTER 22 | Quality Control

A production process is designed to fill bottles with 16.5 ounces of liquid detergent on the average. The population of filling weights is normally distributed and has a standard deviation of .8 ounce. Inspectors take periodic samples of 35 bottles. One sample yields a mean filling weight of 16.2 ounces, the next two yield 15.8 ounces and 17.3 ounces. Is the production process running properly?

CHAPTER 23 | Decision Theory

A U.S. firm plans to enter a new market in China. The firm's executives are considering four alternatives: (1) building a plant in China, (2) hiring a Chinese sales force to sell U.S.-made products exported to China, (3) sending mail-order catalogues to Chinese consumers, and (4) teaming up with Chinese firms that would act as sales agents. The executives believe that the profit consequences of each of these approaches will differ, depending on whether demand turns out to be low, moderate, or huge. In millions of dollars, the next year profit predictions are 2, 4, and 10 for (1); 3, 3, and 3 for (2); −5, −1, and +20 for (3); and −2, 0, and 30 for (4). Assuming they want to maximize profits, what should the executives do?

1.5 Statistics—A Universal Guide to the Unknown

All of the previous examples have at least one thing in common. They illustrate dramatically how inferential statistics can facilitate decision making in the face of uncertainty. Indeed, one can argue that such is the main purpose of the entire discipline.

DEFINITION 1.5 The field of study known as **statistics** is a branch of mathematics that is concerned with facilitating wise decision making in the face of uncertainty and that, therefore, develops and uses techniques for the careful collection, effective presentation, and proper analysis of numerical information.

This definition clearly incorporates all of the branches of statistics discussed so far. In addition, by failing to specify who the decision makers are, the above definition quite correctly suggests the universal applicability of what statistics has to offer. As the earlier examples have shown, modern statistical techniques routinely guide business executives, as well as government economic-policy makers, in making reasonable decisions in the face of uncertainty. In addition, the same techniques are just as useful, and are just as frequently applied, outside the fields of business and economics. Like mathematics in general, statistics is a universal type of language that all sciences use regularly. Drawing valid inferences from limited information is just as important to historians and psychologists, to geneticists and medical researchers, to astronomers and engineers as it is to business executives and economists. We shall see examples of this universal use of statistics as well. Among others, questions such as these will be posed and answered: How can we decipher a secret code? How can we resolve the issue of a disputed authorship? Were Mendel's genetics data fudged? Does smoking cause heart disease? Is toothpaste A better than toothpaste B? Is ESP real?

1.6 Basic Statistical Concepts

As is true of practitioners in all scientific disciplines, statisticians have a language all of their own. In this section, we meet some of their favorite terms. This will prove helpful in later chapters when we discuss issues of collecting, describing, and analyzing data more fully.

ELEMENTARY UNITS AND THE FRAME

A statistical investigation invariably focuses on people or things with characteristics in which someone is interested. The persons or objects that have characteristics of interest to statisticians are called **elementary units.** Thus, someone who wanted to learn about the racial composition of a firm's labor force would quickly identify the individual employees of that firm as the elementary units. But someone concerned about the amount of credit extended by that firm might view individual credit accounts as the elementary units to be investigated. Even the flashcubes produced by the firm, the lightbulbs installed in its plants, or the boxes of cereal shipped by one of its divisions could be regarded as elementary units—provided someone was interested in discovering, respectively, the percentage of defective flashcubes produced, the lifetimes of lightbulbs used, or the content weights of cereal boxes sold. A complete listing of all elementary units relevant to a statistical investigation is called a **frame.**

Consider a statistician who is hired to evaluate charges of racial and sex discrimination allegedly occurring in one of those small firms that can be found at any one of thousands of private airports across the United States. (Believe it or not, in 1999 there were over 18,000 operating airports in the United States, and over 13,000 of them were private.) Our airport operator's personnel records might provide the information listed in Table 1.8. In this case, any one entry in column 1 is an elementary unit. All the entries in the shaded portion of that column jointly represent the frame.

VARIABLES AND DATA

In general, any one elementary unit may possess one or more characteristics that interest a statistician. In Table 1.8, five characteristics, ranging from race and sex to annual salary, are listed in the headings of columns 2–6. Such characteristics of elementary units are called **variables,** presumably because observations about these characteristics will likely *vary* from one elementary unit to the next.

Any single observation about a specified characteristic of interest is called a **datum.** It is the basic unit of the statistician's raw material. Any collection of observations about one or more characteristics of interest, for one or more elementary units, is called a **data set.** A data set is **univariate, bivariate,** or **multivariate** depending on whether it contains information on one variable only, on two variables, or on more than two. The 45 entries in columns 2–6 of Table 1.8 (namely, 5 data for each of 9 elementary units), thus, constitute a *multivariate data set.*

QUALITATIVE AND QUANTITATIVE VARIABLES

Table 1.8 teaches us something else: Any given characteristic of interest to the statistician can differ in kind or in degree among various elementary units. A variable that is normally described in words rather than numerically (because it differs in kind rather than degree among elementary units) is called a **qualitative variable.** Table 1.8 contains three qualitative variables: race, sex, and job title. Qualitative variables can, in turn, be *binomial* or *multinomial.* Observations about a **binomial qualitative variable** can be made in only two categories: for example, male or female, employed or unemployed, correct or incorrect, defective or satisfactory, elected or defeated, absent or present. Observations about a **multinomial qualitative variable,** in contrast, can be made in more than two categories; consider job titles, colors, languages, religions, or types of businesses.

On the other hand, a variable that is normally expressed numerically (because it differs in degree rather than kind among the elementary units under study) is called a **quantitative variable.** Table 1.8 contains two of them: years of service and annual salary. Quantitative variables can, in turn, be *discrete* or *continuous.* Observations about a **discrete quantitative variable** can assume values only at specific points on a scale of values, with inevitable gaps between them. Such data differ from each other by clearly defined steps. Consider observing the number of children in families, of employees in firms, of students in classes, of rooms in houses, of cars in stock, of cows in pastures. Invariably, the individual data will be disconnected from each other by gaps on the scale of values. In the above instances, they will look like 1, 2, 3, . . . and 49; never like 3.28 or 20.13. It is impossible to have 3.28 children in a family or to observe 20.13 cows in a pasture because these items come in whole units only. But note that the gaps representing impossible values need not span the entire space between *whole* numbers. Stock prices, for example, are reported in

TABLE 1.8 | Selected Characteristics of All Full-Time Employees of Mountain Aviation, Inc.; December 31, 2000

This table illustrates a number of basic statistical concepts. Thus, column 1 lists nine ***elementary units*** *that jointly constitute the* ***frame*** *(shaded). The headings of columns 2–6 show various characteristics of the elementary units that are called* ***variables.*** *They can be qualitative (race, sex, job title) or quantitative (years of service, annual salary). Any single observation about a given elementary unit is a* ***datum*** *(the plural is* ***data****). This particular table contains a* ***multivariate data set*** *because it records observations about several variables for each elementary unit. All possible observations about a given variable, such as the shaded entries in column 3 or 6, constitute a statistical* ***population.*** *Any subset of a population or frame, such as the boxed data in column 6, is a* ***sample.***

Qualitative variables (Race, Sex, Job Title) — *Quantitative variables* (Years of Service, Annual Salary)

List of Employees (1)	Race (2)	Sex (3)	Job Title (4)	Years of Service (5)	Annual Salary (6)
Abel	White	Male	Pilot	2	$39,000
Cruz	White	Male	Chief Mechanic	10	70,000
Dunn	Black	Male	Chief Pilot	23	85,000
Hill	Black	Female	Secretary	5	17,000
King	White	Male	Janitor	8	21,000
Otis	White	Male	Grounds Keeper	10	21,000
West	Black	Male	Mechanic	2	36,000
Wolf	White	Female	Pilot	7	36,000
Zorn	White	Female	Mechanic	7	40,000

Frame (containing 9 elementary units) — ***Population of employee sexes (containing 9 data)*** — ***Sample of employee salaries (containing 3 data)***

NOTE: As you will learn in Chapter 4, many types of samples exist. Not all of them are equally likely to reflect the makeup of the sampled population. For example, the group of three salaries found in the column 6 box here might be a *convenience sample* that was selected merely for the ease of illustration. It might also be a *simple random sample* that was selected by some procedure such as writing the nine salaries on slips of paper, mixing the slips in a bowl, and pulling out three. In the latter case, as you will learn in Chapter 8, it is possible to select 84 different samples of 3 out of 9. That would give us 1 chance in 84 of selecting the particular sample shown here.

eighths of dollars (or to the nearest $0.125). These discrete figures can take on values of 67 1/8, 67 2/8, 67 3/8 (or equivalent dollar decimals per share) but cannot take on values between these. (The quoting of prices by eighths is a throwback to the old pirate days and the Spanish gold "pieces of eight.")

Observations about a **continuous quantitative variable** can, in contrast, assume values at all points on a scale of values, with no breaks between possible values. Consider height, temperature, time, volume, or weight. Weight, for instance, might be reported as 7 pounds or 8 pounds but also as 7.3 pounds or even 7.3425 pounds, depending entirely on the sensitivity of the measuring instrument involved. No matter how close two values are to each other, it is always possible for a more precise device to find another value between them.

CAUTION

The distinction between qualitative and quantitative variables is visually obvious in Table 1.8. The observations about one type of variable are recorded in words; those about the other type in numbers. Yet that distinction can easily be blurred. Quantitative variables can be converted into seemingly qualitative variables, and the opposite is also true. Thus, a statistician could replace the column 5 and 6 numerical data by words, such as *low, intermediate,* or *high,* although probably nobody would wish to give up the more precise information recorded in Table 1.8. On the other hand, it is common practice to *code* observations about qualitative variables with the help of numbers. Thus, a statistician might turn the verbal entries of Table 1.8 into *numbers* by recording, say, "white" as 1 and "black" as 2 in column 2, by recording "male" as 0 and "female" as 1 in column 3, and by assigning numbers between 0 and 6 to the seven job titles in column 4. Nevertheless, the distinction between qualitative and quantitative variables, although then hidden, would remain.

Being aware of the distinction is important for this reason: Even when qualitative data are encoded numerically, we cannot perform meaningful arithmetic operations with them, whereas we can do so with quantitative data. Thus, it would make no sense to report the "sum of races" in our firm as 12 (using the code just noted), but it would be valid to report the sum of annual salaries as $365,000.

POPULATION VERSUS SAMPLE

We must finally consider two other concepts of particular importance.

DEFINITION 1.6 The set of all possible observations about a specified characteristic of interest is called a statistical **population.**

DEFINITION 1.7 A subset of a statistical population, or of the frame from which it is derived, is called a **sample.**

As Table 1.8 illustrates, it is possible to draw several statistical populations from a given frame. We have one frame (the shaded list of elementary units in column 1), but five variables (the headings of columns 2–6). Hence our table contains five populations. The shaded entries in column 3, for example, make up the population of employee sexes; those in column 6 make up the population of employee salaries; and so on for columns 2, 4, and 5.

Note that a statistical population consists of *all possible* observations about a variable. Because they correspond to *all* the employees of our firm, the entries in column 6 make up the population of employee salaries in our hypothetical study. In a firm of only nine employees, it is easy to observe the entire salary population. But imagine the difficulty of such an undertaking if we attempted to carry out a similar study for the entire aviation industry or even for the entire labor force of the United States!

Under such circumstances, statisticians often make observations concerning selected elementary units only. They observe only n such units out of the larger number N that exist. Naturally, they end up with a subset of all the possible observations about the characteristic of interest, which is then called a *sample.* The boxed entries in column 6 of Table 1.8, for instance, make up one of many possible samples of employee salaries—namely, the sample based on observing the salary characteristics of only Otis, West, and Wolf. These three names themselves can, in turn, be viewed as a sample of the frame.

What constitutes a population or a sample of that population depends entirely on the context in which the question arises. If the goal were to study salaries only at Mountain Aviation, Inc., the data in shaded column 6 of Table 1.8 would, as a group, make up the relevant population. If the goal were to study salaries in the entire aviation industry, however, the identical column 6 data, even as a group, would constitute only a (pitifully small and probably not very representative) sample of the much larger population of salaries in the industry as a whole.

In addition, as you will learn in Chapter 4, it is important to note that several types of samples exist and not all of them provide information of equal quality. The particular sample illustrated in Table 1.8 may well be a *convenience sample,* selected because the three salaries in question just happened to be located next to one another. In fact, however, it would be possible to select 84 different samples of size $n = 3$ from among the $N = 9$ salaries listed in Table 1.8. Thus, if we had used a random process to select a *random sample* of three salaries in Table 1.8, we would have had only 1 chance in 84 to select the particular sample shown there. (More about *that* in Chapter 8!)

1.7 Major Types of Data

No matter how hard they try to do a good job, data gatherers will always come up with data of varying quality. This is so because different data sets are *inherently* different, as another look at Table 1.8 can quickly show: Observations about *qualitative* variables (columns 2–4) are typically made in words but are possibly coded into numbers later on for purposes of data processing. Observations about quantitative variables, in contrast, are numerical at the outset (columns 5–6). Anyone who works with numbers, therefore, must be very clear about their precise meaning.

Consider the numbers in the series 1, 2, 3, . . . 10, 11, 12. They could be house numbers found along a street. They could be numbers on the Beaufort scale, measuring wind velocity. They could be numbers on the Fahrenheit scale, indicating temperature. They could be hourly wages paid different workers in a factory. Believe it or not, despite the fact that we are looking at the same numbers, 1 through 12, these four examples point to radically different *types* of data. We must discuss these data types before we turn, in Chapter 2, to the task of entering data into a computer. Not every data type is suitable for the arithmetic operations that computers can perform so rapidly and well.

In fact, the assignment of numbers to characteristics that are being observed—which is **measurement**—can yield any one of four types of data. In order of increasing sophistication, it can produce *nominal, ordinal, interval,* or *ratio* data, and different statistical concepts and techniques are appropriately applied to each type.

NOMINAL DATA

Suppose you were working, as we will later in this text, with an alphabetic list of the 110 largest multinational firms that maintained headquarters in the United States. (Table 4.1 on page 110 contains such a list.) Continually referring to the actual company names, such as Goodyear Tire & Rubber or Minnesota Mining & Manufacturing, may soon become awkward and unwieldy. So you decide to substitute *numbers* for those company names, ranging from 00 for Abbott Laboratories to 99 for Xerox. These numbers are **nominal data.** They merely *name* or label differences in kind. Thus, they serve the purpose of classifying observations about qualitative variables into mutually exclusive groups where the numbers in each group can then be counted. (Numbers between 00 and 99, for example, might refer to multinational companies, numbers between 100 and 159 to other types of firms, and so on.)

In fact, we meet nominal data every day. House numbers provide a good example. The green house at the corner might be assigned the number 1, the yellow house across the street a 2, the white house in the middle of the block a 6, and so on, until the brick house at the end is labeled with a 12. Similarly, a statistician working with Table 1.8 presented earlier might code "male" as 0 and "female" as 1 for the sake of mere convenience, but alternative labels of "male" = 100 and "female" = 50 would serve as well.

Invariably, nominal data provide the weakest level of measurement in the sense that they contain only the tiniest amount of useful information. More importantly, as the slightest bit of thought about these examples can confirm, it never makes sense to add, subtract, multiply, divide, rank, average, or otherwise manipulate nominal data arithmetically. We can merely *count* them. The presence of 12 numbers on a street denotes the existence of 12 houses. Five 1's, according to one of the above codes, indicates the presence of five females. And that is all.

Consider how *adding* all the house numbers on our street would yield a meaningless number 78. Summing six 0's and three 1's to a total of 3 (because, say, six men and three women are working in a firm) would be equally silly. Ordering nominal numbers by size, or *ranking* them, would be senseless as well. Although 2 is smaller than 6, in what sense is the yellow house numbered 2 smaller than the white house numbered 6? Although 1 is greater than 0, in what sense is "female" greater than "male"? Nor could we assume that equal *differences* or *intervals* between nominal data carry any meaning at all: Just because 12 − 10 = 2 and 10 − 8 = 2 as well, could we assume that the distance between house #12 and house #10 is the same as that between house #10 and house #8? Hardly. And *dividing* one house number by another would be pointless, too. True enough, the ratio of 12/6 is 2, but can we say that house #12 is somehow twice as large or otherwise more important than house #6 down the street?

ORDINAL DATA

The next level of measurement produces **ordinal data.** These are numbers that label differences in kind, as nominal data do, but that, in addition, by their very size also *order* or rank observations on the basis of importance. Consider another list of those 100 multinational companies, but this time let it not be alphabetical. Let the companies be *ranked* from the one with the smallest profit, labeled 00, to the one with the highest profit, labeled 99. We can compare such ordinal numbers meaningfully as greater than, smaller than, or equal to one another. But they contain no information about *how much* greater or smaller one labeled item is compared to the other. Thus, company 99 has a larger profit than company 63, and company 63 has a smaller profit than company 69, but that is all we can say. *Differences* between ordinal numbers or *ratios* of such numbers remain meaningless. Just because 69 − 63 = 6 and 17 − 11 = 6 as well, can we conclude that the profit difference between companies 69 and 63 comes to the same dollar figure as that between companies 17 and 11? Certainly not. Just because (80/20) = 4, can we conclude that the profit of company 80 is four times as large as that of company 20? We cannot.

Just like nominal data, we encounter ordinal data often in our daily lives. The Beaufort wind scale used by weather forecasters provides a good example. It codes a wind velocity of less than 1 mile per hour (mph) as 0 or "calm," a velocity of 1–3 mph as 1 or "light air," a velocity of 4–7 mph as 2 or "light breeze," and so on, until velocities above 75 mph are reached and labeled 12 or "hurricane." Clearly, the order of numbers matters here. The larger the number, the stronger the wind. Yet these data make no statement about *how much* stronger or weaker the assessment becomes as we move along the scale in one direction or another. It may look as if moving along the Beaufort scale from 0 to 12 in equal steps of 1 represents equal increases in velocity, but such is not the case. Codes 1 and 2 represent average wind speeds of 2 and 5.5 mph, respectively. Thus the difference between "light air = 1" and "light breeze = 2" comes to 3.5 mph. Yet codes 10 and 11 represent average wind speeds of 59 and 69.5 mph, respectively. Thus the difference between "whole gale = 10" and "storm = 11" is 10.5 mph.

Similar examples abound. Assessments of a product as *superb, average,* or *poor* might be recorded as 2, 1, 0, as 250, 10, 2, or even as 10, 9, 4.5—the important thing is that larger ordinal numbers denote a more favorable assessment, or a higher ranking, while smaller ones do the opposite. Yet, in such an assessment, a 2 is deemed better than a 1 but not necessarily twice as good. A 250 is deemed better than a 10 but not necessarily 25 times as good. A 4.5 is deemed worse than a 9 but not necessarily half as good. And that is all.

Once again, meaningful arithmetic operations with ordinal data, as with nominal data, are not possible.

INTERVAL DATA

Somewhat more information is contained in **interval data.** These are numbers that possess all the characteristics of ordinal data and, in addition, relate to one another by meaningful *intervals* or distances. This is so because all numbers are referenced to a common (although admittedly arbitrary) zero point. As a result, addition and subtraction are permissible, but multiplication and division continue to make no sense.

Certain scales of calendar time, clock time, and temperatures provide good examples of measurements that start from an arbitrarily located zero point and then use an equally arbitrary but consistent distance unit for expressing intervals between numbers. Consider how the Celsius scale places zero at the water-freezing point, whereas the Fahrenheit scale places it far below the freezing point. Within the context of either scale, the distance unit (degree of temperature) has a consistent meaning. Each degree Celsius equals 1/100 of the distance between water's freezing and boiling points. Each degree Fahrenheit equals 1/180 of that distance. However, the zero point, being arbitrarily located, does not denote the absence of the characteristic being measured. Unlike 0° on the absolute (Kelvin) temperature scale that is familiar to scientists, neither 0°F nor 0°C indicates a complete absence of heat. As a result, any *ratio* of Fahrenheit or Celsius data fails to convey meaningful information. For example, 90°F is *not* twice as hot as 45°F. Indeed, the ratio of the corresponding Celsius figures (32.2° and 7.2°) does not equal 2 : 1 but well over 4 : 1.

RATIO DATA

The highest level of measurement, producing the most useful information, yields **ratio data.** These are numbers that possess all the characteristics of interval data and, in addition, have meaningful *ratios* because they are referenced to an absolute or natural zero point that denotes the complete absence of the characteristic being measured. All types of arithmetic operations, even multiplication and division, can be performed with such data. Unlike in the Fahrenheit/Celsius example, the ratio of any two such numbers is independent of the unit of measurement because each number is a distance measure from the same zero point. For example, the measurement of hourly wages, monthly salaries, age, area, distance, height, volume, or weight produces ratio data. So does a measurement of temperature on the Kelvin scale, the zero point of which is tied to zero molecular speed. Consider hourly wages as a case in point.

Clearly, it makes sense to say that an hourly wage of $12 is larger than one of $9, which is larger than one of $6. (In contrast, when working with those nominal data taking the place of alphabetically ordered company names, it made no sense to say that company 12 is larger than company 9, which is larger than company 6.) Thus, hourly wage data give the kind of information provided by *ordinal* data.

In addition, it makes sense to compare intervals between hourly wage data and to say that the distance between $12 and $9 equals the distance between $9 and $6. (In contrast, the differ-

APPLICATION 1.1

Time in Cyberspace

A perfect example of the birth of *interval data* is provided by the worldwide effort to replace the familiar 24-hour clock with a new type of *universal* time. Such adjustments of our way of measuring time are nothing new. In the United States, for example, different cities used to set their clocks by the sun until the late 1800s. Then the railroads came along and introduced the now-familiar time zones in order to coordinate their schedules and avoid collisions. An 1874 treaty established Greenwich mean time, which later served lots of people very well, including ships and airlines. In 1960, scientists in Paris set up an atomic clock, based on vibrations of the cesium atom. And now there is the Swatch Group, the world's largest watchmaker, which wants us to live on *Internet time.*

Figure 1.A illustrates what is involved.

The new time starts at an arbitrary zero point and beats 000 at midnight over the Swatch building in Biel, Switzerland. It also divides the day into 1,000 *swatch beats,* each equivalent to 86.4 good old seconds. So, if it's 3 P.M. local time, or 15:00 hours, by the old clock, you are at 625 universal time, as the display shows.

As you might have guessed, Swatch is selling an Internet watch around the world ($70 at the time of this writing) and you can even download software at its site to teach your computer a trick or two about the meaning of Internet time.

SOURCES: Adapted from http://www.swatch.com and Amy Harmon, "It's @786. Do You Know Where Your Computer Is?" *The New York Times,* March 7, 1999, Section 4, p. 2.

FIGURE 1.A | Standard Time and Internet Time

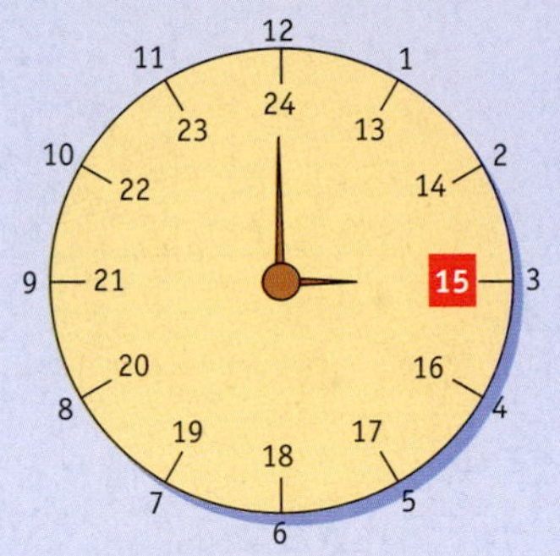

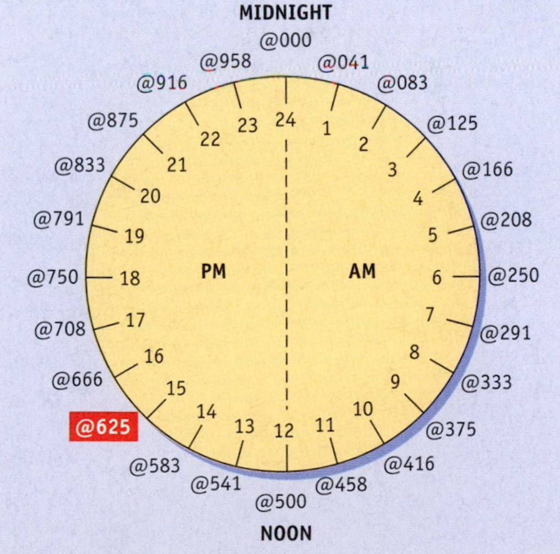

ence between company 12 and 9, or between company 9 and 6, carries no meaning.) Thus, hourly wage data also give the type of information provided by *interval* data.

Further, hourly wage data are *ratio* data because we can safely describe $12 as twice as much money as $6. The ratio (12/6) = 2 tells us so. (In contrast, the ratio between company 12 and company 6 tells us nothing at all. In Table 4.1 on page 110, does dividing company 12 = Archer Daniels Midland by company 6 = American International Group give us company 2 = Alcoa?) So far as hourly wage data are concerned, even a change in the unit of measurement, as from dollars to cents or from dollars to francs (at an exchange rate of, say, 6 francs to the dollar) does not change this conclusion: 1,200 cents still is twice as much money as 600 cents; 72 francs still is twice as much as 36 francs. Ultimately, this is true because zero dollars, zero francs, and zero cents all mean precisely the same thing. (In contrast, 0°F ≠ 0°C ≠ 0°K.)

TABLE 1.9 | Major Data Types

Qualitative variables are usually described verbally. When coded, these verbal descriptions turn into numbers that are nominal or ordinal data. Arithmetic operations with such data—including adding, subtracting, multiplying, dividing, or averaging—yield pure nonsense. In contrast, quantitative variables are always described numerically, either by interval or ratio data. Interval data allow some types of arithmetic operations; ratio data allow all types.

Variable	Associated Data Type	Description of Data	Permitted Operations	Examples
Qualitative	Nominal	Numbers that merely *name* or label differences in kind; their order has no particular meaning, nor do their differences or ratios	Placing numbers into mutually exclusive groups; counting numbers in each group	The two-digit codes from 00 to 99 for an alphabetical list of 100 most admired firms; highway or telephone numbers
Qualitative	Ordinal	Numbers that not only label differences in kind, but that by their size also *order* or rank observations on the basis of importance, while differences between numbers or ratios of such numbers are meaningless	As above plus comparing numbers as greater than, smaller than, or equal to one another	The ranking of college courses as 3 for excellent, 2 for good, and 1 for poor; student class ranks; the ranking of runners at the finish line
Quantitative	Interval	Numbers that not only label differences in kind and by their size rank observations, but that are also referenced to a common (but arbitrary) zero point, which makes their *intervals* or differences comparable, while their ratios are meaningless due to the arbitrariness of the zero point	As above plus adding and subtracting	Fahrenheit and Celsius temperature scales; clock time; calendar time
Quantitative	Ratio	Numbers that not only label differences in kind, by their size rank observations, and are separated by meaningful intervals, but that are also referenced to an absolute or natural zero point, which makes their *ratios* meaningful as well	As above plus multiplying and dividing	The salary data listed in Table 1.8; measures of length, volume, weight

The fact that ratios of numbers convey meaningful information is the advantage of ratio data over interval data. No wonder that statisticians, when they have a choice, prefer ratio data to interval data, interval data to ordinal data, and ordinal data to nominal data. Table 1.9 summarizes our discussion of data types for those who seek a quick review.

Summary

1. The term *statistics* has at least three different meanings to people. Some think of it as a *field of study* that somehow deals with the collection, presentation, and interpretation of numerical data. For others, the term conjures up images of *masses of data,* seemingly infinite in number. Still others attribute a highly technical meaning to the term, thinking of *summary measures*—such as sample averages and sample proportions—that have been computed from relatively few data gathered by sampling a much larger collection of data.
2. Masses of data are, indeed, the statistician's raw material, and a first branch of the discipline of statistics focuses on the careful collection of data. Such collection can proceed in one of three ways:
   - **a.** An investigator can look for data that already exist because others have gathered them in the past.
   - **b.** Brand-new data can be generated with the help of observational studies that involve census taking or sampling.
   - **c.** Brand-new data can be generated by conducting carefully controlled experiments.
3. A second branch of the discipline of statistics, known as *descriptive statistics,* is concerned with developing and using techniques for the effective presentation of numerical information so as to highlight patterns otherwise hidden in a data set.
4. A third branch of the discipline of statistics, undoubtedly the most important one, is concerned with developing and using techniques for properly analyzing (or drawing inferences from) numerical information and is therefore called *analytical statistics* or *inferential statistics.*
5. In the end, the discipline of statistics is, perhaps, best viewed as a branch of mathematics that develops and uses techniques for the careful collection, effective presentation, and proper analysis of numerical information. As such it facilitates wise decision making in the face of uncertainty and becomes a universal guide to the unknown.
6. The process of data collection, a crucial prerequisite for subsequent descriptive and analytical work, employs a number of basic concepts. Thus, a statistical investigation focuses on persons or objects, which are called *elementary units.* These elementary units possess characteristics of interest, called *variables.* Observations about them, which can be qualitative or quantitative, are called *data.* The set of all possible observations about a specified characteristic of interest is called a *population.* A subset of it (or of the *frame* from which the population is derived) is referred to as a *sample.*
7. The assignment of numbers to characteristics that are being observed, which is *measurement,* can yield any one of four types of data. In order of increasing sophistication, it can produce *nominal, ordinal, interval,* or *ratio* data. Different statistical concepts and techniques are appropriately applied to each type. Arithmetic operations with nominal and ordinal data, for example, are out of the question.

Key Terms

analytical statistics
binomial qualitative variable
bivariate data set
continuous quantitative variable
controlled experiment
data set
datum
deductive reasoning
descriptive statistics
discrete quantitative variable
elementary units
frame
inductive reasoning
inferential statistics
interval data
measurement
multinomial qualitative variable
multivariate data set
nominal data
observational study
ordinal data
population
qualitative variable
quantitative variable
ratio data
sample
statistics
survey
univariate data set
variables

Practice Problems

Section 1.1 Introduction

1. This is a fun question that elaborates on this chapter's Preview. It challenges you to do some serious thinking, but you can also learn much by merely looking up the answers on the Student CD-ROM. First, study the solution that is given here to this chapter's Preview problem; then consider the questions that follow.

   If you forgo buying the consulting firm's advice, the optimal action is to sell the rights for $125 million, which is illustrated in Figure 1.1.

   If you do buy the consulting firm's advice, the optimal action, now illustrated in Figure 1.2, is this: If R_1 is received, sell the rights and take the $125 million minus the $1 million fee. If R_2 is received, offer the film to the network and earn an expected $200 million.

   a. Can you guess the meaning of the $102 million number at point *b* in Figure 1.1?

   b. Can you guess the meaning of the $154.4 million number at point *b* in Figure 1.2?

   c. Can you guess what strategy the filmmaker would be well advised to follow: forgoing the advice or buying the advice?

FIGURE 1.1 | The Soap Opera Decision without Advice

Note: *The 60 percent chance of rejection and the 40 percent chance of a contract offer are indicated as probability of event E_1 being .6 and probability of event E_2 being .4.*

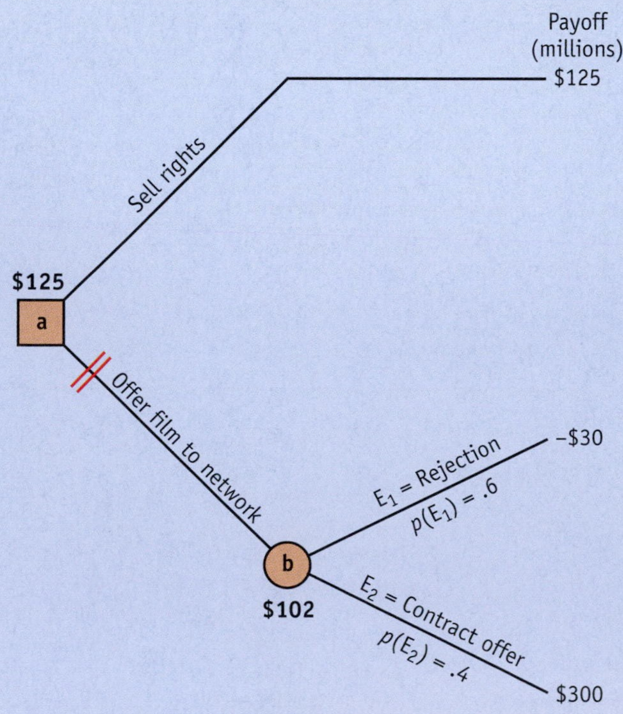

FIGURE 1.2 | The Soap Opera Decision with Advice

Note: You need not fully understand all of the entries in Figure 1.2 at this point.

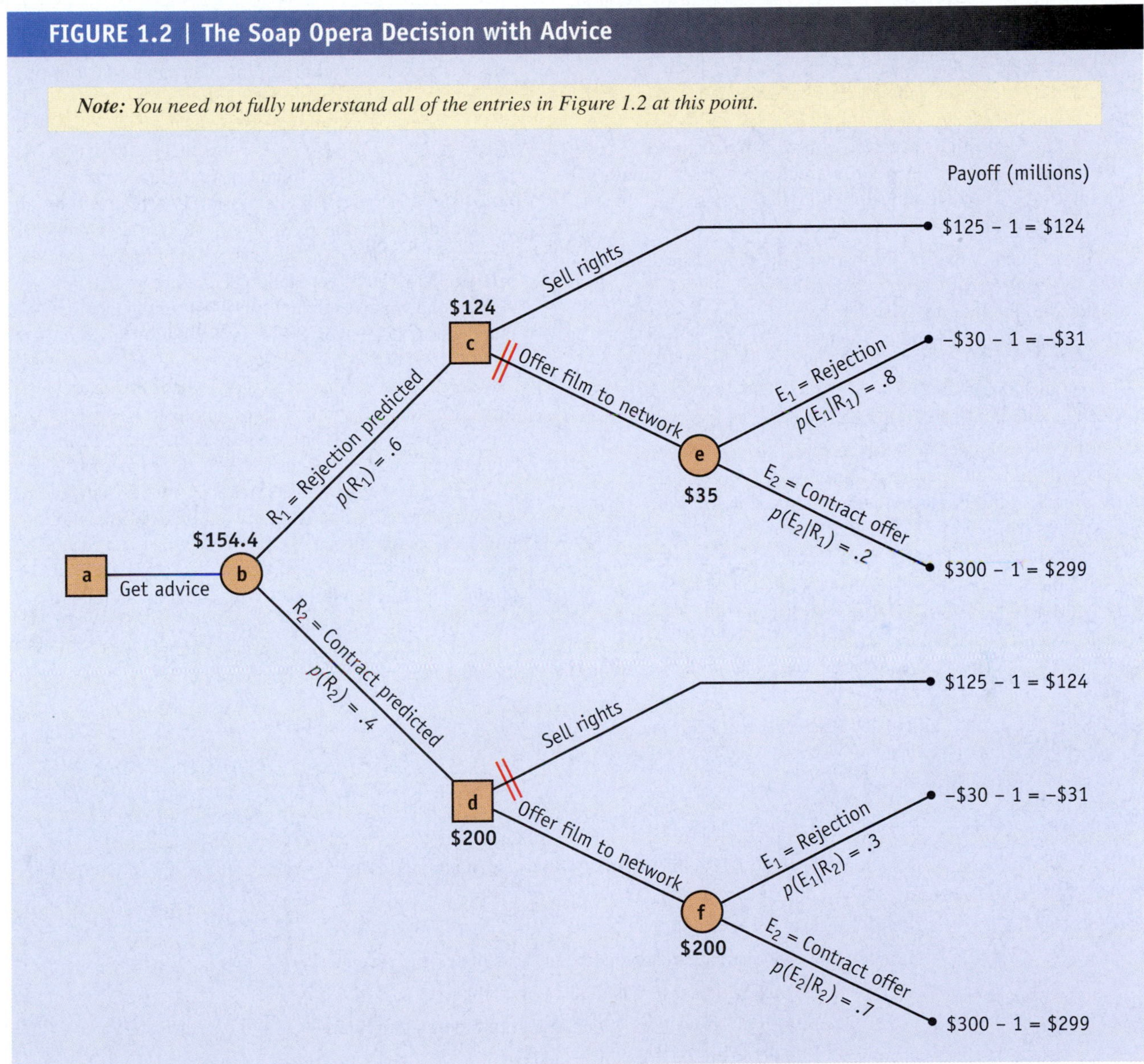

d. What do you think is the maximum amount the filmmaker could be made to pay for the (admittedly imperfect) advice?

SECTION 1.2 THE COLLECTION OF DATA

2. This problem provides a preview of the type of material to be discussed at length in Chapter 3. If you are connected to the Internet, visit http://www.fedstats.gov, a site maintained by the Interagency Council on Statistical Policy. Click on **Agencies** and explore the manifold sources of U.S. federal government statistics. List five agencies that supply data to this site.

3. This problem provides a preview of the type of material to be discussed at length in Chapter 3. If you are connected to the Internet, visit http://www.statcan.ca, a site maintained by Statistics Canada. Click on **English** (unless you prefer French) > **Canadian Statistics** > **The Economy: The Latest Indicators**. Then find the latest monthly Canadian merchandise export figure.

4. This problem provides a preview of the type of material to be discussed at length in Chapter 3. If you are connected to the Internet, visit http://www.inegi.gob.mx, a site maintained by Mexico's National Institute of Statistics, Geography, and Informatics.

   Click on **English** (unless you prefer Spanish) > **Economy** > **Short Term Economic Indicators** > **Financial, Stock Market, and Monetary Indicators**. Then find the latest monthly yield figure for commercial paper.

5. This problem provides a preview of the type of material to be discussed at length in Chapter 4. If you are connected to the Internet, visit http://www.gallup.com, a site maintained by the Gallup Organization. Check it out; then write an essay on what Gallup tells you about its sampling techniques.

6. This problem provides a preview of the type of material to be discussed at length in Chapter 4. If you are connected to the Internet, visit http://www.roper.com, a site maintained by the Roper Organization. Check it out; then write an essay on what Roper tells you about its sampling techniques.

7. This problem provides a preview of the type of material to be discussed at length in Chapter 4. If you are connected to the Internet, visit http://www.louisharris.com, a site maintained by the Harris Organization. Check it out; then write an essay on the latest monthly Harris poll.

8. Section 1.2 briefly anticipates issues that will be discussed at length in later chapters. One of these issues is the difference between *surveys* and *experiments* and the significance of exercising control over elementary units whose characteristics are being scrutinized. Imagine annual salaries of workers in a firm to equal $10,000 for everyone, plus $1,000 for every year of work experience. Salaries are, thus, *totally unrelated to race*. Then imagine that most of a firm's black workers are young (and, therefore, have had little work experience), while most of its white workers are older (and have had many years of experience on the job). Someone merely *surveying* salaries might find an average salary of $15,000 a year among blacks and of $28,000 a year among whites and might conclude, quite incorrectly, that the firm's management is discriminating based on race.

   In contrast, a *controlled* study would divide the firm's workers into groups according to work experience and would compare salaries within each group. Such a study would find identical salaries between (1) the few white and (2) the many black workers in the younger and less experienced group. And it would find identical but higher salaries between (1) the many white and (2) the few black workers in the older and more experienced group. Thus, the controlled study would avoid the false racial discrimination charge.

   Make up a detailed numerical example to corroborate the story told by the numbers given here.

SECTION 1.6 BASIC STATISTICAL CONCEPTS

9. Consider Table 1.10, which contains selected data found in *Fortune* magazine's 1999 *Global 500* report.
   - **a.** Identify the elementary units.
   - **b.** How many variables can you find in this table? Which are they?
   - **c.** Identify the variables as quantitative or qualitative.
   - **d.** Identify variables as discrete/continuous or binomial/multinomial.
   - **e.** What kind of data set does this table contain?

10. In 1999, *Fortune* magazine surveyed more than 10,000 executives, directors, and securities analysts to rank corporate reputations on the basis of eight criteria, including innovativeness, quality of management, employee talent, quality of products/services, long-term investment value, financial soundness, social responsibility, and use of corporate assets. On the basis of their answers, it created something like a report card that ranked U.S. corporations from "most admired" = 1 to "least admired" = 469. Table 1.11 provides information about the top ten.
    - **a.** Identify the elementary units.
    - **b.** How many variables can you find in this table? Which are they?
    - **c.** Identify the variables as quantitative or qualitative.
    - **d.** Identify variables as discrete/continuous or binomial/multinomial.
    - **e.** What kind of data set does this table contain?

11. In 1999, *Fortune* magazine surveyed more than 10,000 executives, directors, and securities analysts to rank corporate reputations. On the basis of their answers, it created something like a report card

TABLE 1.10 | Selected Characteristics of the World's Largest Corporations in 1999

Company (1)	Country (2)	Industry (3)	Revenues ($ billion) (4)	Profits ($ million) (5)	Employees (thousands) (6)
1. General Motors	U.S.	Autos	161.3	2,956	594
2. DaimlerChrysler	Germany	Autos	154.6	5,656	442
3. Ford Motor	U.S.	Autos	144.4	22,071	345
4. Wal-Mart Stores	U.S.	Retail	139.2	4,430	910
5. Mitsui	Japan	Trading	109.4	233	33
6. Itochu	Japan	Trading	108.7	−267	6
7. Mitsubishi	Japan	Trading	107.2	244	36
8. Exxon	U.S.	Oil	100.7	6,370	79
9. General Electric	U.S.	Electrical	100.5	9,296	293
10. Toyota Motor	Japan	Autos	99.7	2,787	184
11. Royal Dutch Shell	Brit./Neth.	Oil	93.7	350	102
12. Marubeni	Japan	Trading	93.6	−921	65
13. Sumitomo	Japan	Trading	89.0	−102	31
14. IBM	U.S.	Computers	81.7	6,328	291
15. AXA	France	Insurance	78.7	1,702	88

SOURCE: *Fortune,* August 2, 1999, pp. F1, F16, F18, F19, and F21.

TABLE 1.11 | *Fortune*'s Most Admired U.S. Companies, 1998

Company Name (1)	Company Rank (2)	Chief Executive (3)	1998 Total Return (4)
General Electric	1	Jack Welch	41.0%
Coca-Cola	2	Doug Ivester	1.3%
Microsoft	3	Bill Gates	114.6%
Dell Computer	4	Michael Dell	248.5%
Berkshire Hathaway	5	Warren Buffett	52.2%
Wal-Mart Stores	6	David Glass	107.6%
Southwest Airlines	7	Herb Kelleher	38.4%
Intel	8	Craig Barrett	69.0%
Merck	9	Raymond Gilmartin	41.3%
Walt Disney	10	Michael Eisner	−8.5%

SOURCE: Author's table based on *Fortune,* March 1, 1999, pp. 68ff.

that ranked U.S. corporations from "most admired" = 1 to "least admired" = 469. Table 1.12 provides information about the bottom ten.

a. Identify the elementary units.

b. How many variables can you find in this table? Which are they?

c. Identify the variables as quantitative or qualitative.

d. Identify variables as discrete/continuous or binomial/multinomial.

e. What kind of data set does this table contain?

TABLE 1.12 | *Fortune*'s Least Admired U.S. Companies, 1998

Company Name (1)	Company Rank (2)	1998 Total Return (3)
Foundation Health	460	−46.6%
Fruit of the Loom	461	−46.1%
Viad	462	+59.4%
Olston	463	−49.9%
U.S. Industries	464	−38.4%
Stone Container	465	+36.2%
Oxford Health Plans	466	−4.4%
MedPartners	467	−76.5%
Shoney's	468	−57.7%
Trump Hotels & Casinos	469	−43.9%

SOURCE: Author's table based on *Fortune,* March 1, 1999, pp. 68ff.

12. Consider the data of Table 1.13.

a. Identify the elementary units.

b. How many variables can you find in this table? Which are they?

TABLE 1.13 | Best Picture Nominees for the 1998 Academy Awards

Title (1)	Distributor (2)	Gross Revenue by February 1999 (3)
Saving Private Ryan	Dreamworks	$196.0 million
Shakespeare in Love	Miramax	37.6 million
Thin Red Line	Fox	31.2 million
Elizabeth	Gramercy	21.6 million
Life Is Beautiful	Miramax	18.8 million

SOURCE: Author's table, based on *Variety,* various issues.

c. Identify the variables as quantitative or qualitative.

d. Identify variables as discrete/continuous or binomial/multinomial.

e. What kind of data set does this table contain?

13. Consider the data of Table 1.14.

a. Identify the elementary units.

b. How many variables can you find in this table? Which are they?

c. Identify the variables as quantitative or qualitative.

d. Identify variables as discrete/continuous or binomial/multinomial.

e. What kind of data set does this table contain?

TABLE 1.14 | Best Picture Winners at 1993 to 1997 Academy Awards

Title (1)	Distributor (2)	Gross Revenue by February 1999 (3)
Schindler's List, 1993	Universal	$96.1 million
Forrest Gump, 1994	Paramount	329.7 million
Braveheart, 1995	Paramount	75.6 million
The English Patient, 1996	Miramax	78.7 million
Titanic, 1997	Paramount	600.8 million

SOURCE: Author's table, based on *Variety,* various issues.

14. Consider the data of Table 1.15.

a. Identify the elementary units.

b. How many variables can you find in this table? Which are they?

c. Identify the variables as quantitative or qualitative.

d. Identify variables as discrete/continuous or binomial/multinomial.

e. What kind of data set does this table contain?

TABLE 1.15 | Best U.S. Video Sales, February 1–7, 1999

Title (1)	Sales Rank (2)	Distributor (3)	Retail Price (4)
Mulan	1	Disney	$26.99
City of Angels	2	Warner	19.95
Tae-Bo Workout	3	Ventura	39.95
U.S. Marshals	4	Warner	19.98
Parent Trap	5	Disney	22.99

SOURCE: Author's table, based on *Videoscan.*

15. Consider the data of Table 1.16.

a. Identify the elementary units.

b. How many variables can you find in this table? Which are they?

c. Identify the variables as quantitative or qualitative.

d. Identify variables as discrete/continuous or binomial/multinomial.

e. What kind of data set does this table contain?

TABLE 1.16 | Best U.S. Video Rentals, February 1–7, 1999

Title (1)	Rental Rank (2)	Distributor (3)	Rentals per Copy (4)
There's Something . . .	1	Fox	3.8
Rush Hour	2	New Line	4.0
The Truman Show	3	Paramount	3.7
Mulan	4	Disney	3.3
Lethal Weapon 4	5	Warner	2.2

SOURCE: Author's table, based on *Video Business Magazine.*

16. Consider the data of Table 1.17.

a. Identify the elementary units.

b. How many variables can you find in this table? Which are they?

c. Identify the variables as quantitative or qualitative.

d. Identify variables as discrete/continuous or binomial/multinomial.

e. What kind of data set does this table contain?

TABLE 1.17 | Best U.S. Business Software Sales (Windows and DOS), December 1998

Title (1)	Sales Rank (2)	Publisher (3)	Retail Price (4)
Turbo Tax	1	Intuit	$18
Windows 98 Upgrade	2	Microsoft	88
Turbo Tax Deluxe	3	Intuit	48
Quicken	4	Intuit	31
Quicken Deluxe	5	Intuit	58

SOURCE: Author's table, based on *PC Data.*

17. Consider the data of Table 1.18.

a. Identify the elementary units.

b. How many variables can you find in this table? Which are they?

TABLE 1.18 | Best U.S. Business Software Sales (Macintosh), December 1998

Title (1)	Sales Rank (2)	Publisher (3)	Retail Price (4)
Mac OS 8.5	1	Apple	$91
Norton Utilities 4.0	2	Symantec	94
Printmaster Gold	3	Learning Co.	25
Norton Antivirus 5.0	4	Symantec	64
Adobe Illustrator 8.0 Upgrade	5	Adobe	114

SOURCE: Author's table, based on *PC Data.*

c. Identify the variables as quantitative or qualitative.

d. Identify variables as discrete/continuous or binomial/multinomial.

e. What kind of data set does this table contain?

18. In each of the following cases, determine whether the data set is *univariate, bivariate,* or *multivariate:*

a. A table contains income data for 50 consumers.

b. A table contains data on quantity produced and total cost for 7 factories.

c. A table contains data on total assets, revenue growth, and management style for 100 firms.

d. A table contains data on job category, sex, years of experience, and performance indexes for 500 employees.

e. A table contains interest rate forecasts by 30 so-called experts for numerous financial instruments.

19. In each of the following cases, determine whether the data set is *univariate, bivariate,* or *multivariate:*

a. A table contains data on last year's dollar purchases, estimated annual income, and geographic location of 1 million customers.

b. A table contains data on the ask and bid prices for 25 different corporate bonds.

c. A table contains data on quality ratings (A = best and E = worst) for 10 types of refrigerators.

d. A table contains data on 100 incoming airline passengers who have been questioned about the reason for their trip (10 categories, ranging from business to honeymoon), the likely length of their stay, their likely expenditures in town, and their type of accommodation (6 categories, ranging from hotel to own home).

e. A table contains data on 50 shoppers concerning the number of CDs bought in the past 12 months, their age, and their favorite type of music (10 categories, ranging from classical to rock).

20. Classify the following variables, first as *qualitative* or *quantitative,* and second as *binomial/multinomial* or *discrete/continuous:*

a. the number of telephone calls made by someone during a day

b. the dollar figures listed on a sheet of paper

c. the sexes of corporate executives

d. the running times of participants in a race

e. the employment/unemployment status of workers

f. the types of hair coloring sold in a drugstore

21. Classify the following variables, first as *qualitative* or *quantitative,* and second as *binomial/multinomial* or *discrete/continuous:*
    - **a.** the weight lost by a dieter
    - **b.** the types of skills found among a firm's employees
    - **c.** the attendance record of students in a class
    - **d.** the ages of applicants for a marriage license
    - **e.** the types of cars seen in a parking lot
    - **f.** the pressure required to fracture a casting
22. Classify the following variables as *qualitative* or *quantitative:*
    - **a.** a firm's average cost of production
    - **b.** a town's tax rate
    - **c.** the religious affiliations of a firm's employees
    - **d.** the national unemployment rate
    - **e.** the brands of gasoline for sale in a city
    - **f.** a listing of the states in which 50 firms achieved their highest sales
23. Classify the following variables as *qualitative* or *quantitative:*
    - **a.** a list of foreign exchange rates
    - **b.** the number of black executives in an industry
    - **c.** the depth of tread remaining on aircraft tires after 1,000 landings
    - **d.** the Dow Jones Industrial Average
    - **e.** the political party affiliations of a firm's employees
    - **f.** the types of sports practiced by a group of people
24. Make a list of 6 variables that are qualitative and binomial.
25. Make a list of 6 variables that are qualitative and multinomial.
26. Make a list of 6 variables that are quantitative and discrete.
27. Make a list of 6 variables that are quantitative and continuous.

SECTION 1.7 MAJOR TYPES OF DATA

28. Identify the *data types* found in
    - **a.** Table 1.10.
    - **b.** Table 1.11.
29. Identify the *data types* found in
    - **a.** Table 1.12.
    - **b.** Table 1.13.
30. Identify the *data types* found in
    - **a.** Table 1.14.
    - **b.** Table 1.15.
31. Identify the *data types* found in
    - **a.** Table 1.16.
    - **b.** Table 1.17.
    - **c.** Table 1.18.
32. Review each of the cases in Practice Problem 18 and identify the *data types* involved.
33. Review each of the cases in Practice Problem 19 and identify the *data types* involved.
34. Review each of the cases in Practice Problem 20 and identify the *data types* involved.
35. Review each of the cases in Practice Problem 21 and identify the *data types* involved.
36. Review each of the cases in Practice Problem 22 and identify the *data types* involved.
37. Review each of the cases in Practice Problem 23 and identify the *data types* involved.
38. Among numbers describing the following, which are *nominal* data?
    - **a.** distances traveled
    - **b.** student I.D. numbers
    - **c.** net assets
    - **d.** room numbers

e. sound levels inside different airplanes

f. drivers' ratings of the handling characteristics of cars

g. football jersey numbers

39. Classify numbers describing the following as *nominal, ordinal, interval,* or *ratio* data:

a. the location of voters by district

b. the ages of employees

c. the order in which cars finish a race

d. models of computers

e. the number of white blood cells found in a cubic centimeter

f. the colors of new cars

40. Classify numbers describing the following as *nominal, ordinal, interval,* or *ratio* data:

a. ratings of colleges

b. temperature readings at the airport

c. the daily receipts of a supermarket

d. consumer brand preferences concerning types of coffee

e. army ranks

f. a corporate hierarchy from president to janitor

g. calendar years

41. A product is produced in six alternative colors: blue, brown, green, red, yellow, and white.

a. Code the colors with the help of nominal data.

b. Show why adding, subtracting, multiplying, dividing, ranking, or averaging such data would be nonsensical.

c. Review Table 1.8 on page 16 and code the column (2) data as "1" for "white" and "2" for "black." Enter the nine data into a calculator and sum them. Comment on the result.

42. Find a list of the names of the 50 states of the United States. (Your telephone book area code listing might be a good start.)

a. Code the names in alphabetical order from Alabama = 1 to Wyoming = 50. What kinds of data do you have?

b. Add the code numbers and divide by 50 to get the average. Interpret your result.

43. List 6 data types that are clearly *nominal* in nature.

44. List 6 data types that are clearly *interval* in nature.

45. List 6 data types that are clearly *ordinal* in nature.

46. Consider the following situations; identify the types of data involved:

a. A quality inspector has classified defective units of a product as 1 and satisfactory units as 2.

b. A hotel manager has labeled rooms on the first, second, or third floors by numbers in the 100's, 200's, or 300's, respectively, while also designating rooms on the north or south side of the building by even or odd last digits. Thus, 102, 104, 106 stand for first-floor rooms to the north; 301, 303, 305 for third-floor rooms facing south.

47. Someone claims that coding Olympic "gold," "silver," and "bronze" as 3, 2, and 1 amounts to creating interval data. What do you think?

48. The *Fujita* or *F scale* measures the intensity of tornadoes, as follows:

0 Wind velocity 40–72 mph; damages chimneys, tree limbs, and sign boards.

1 Wind velocity 73–112 mph; flips cars, mobile homes, peels roofing.

2 Wind velocity 113–157 mph; tears roofs off houses, splinters mobile homes.

3 Wind velocity 158–206 mph; tears roofs and walls off houses, uproots trees.

4 Wind velocity 207–260 mph; levels frame houses, generates missiles.

5 Wind velocity 261–318 mph; hurls houses and cars long distances.

What kind of data are the intensity numbers 0–5?

49. Identify the *types of data* created when the following are coded from 1–5:

a. Movie ratings: G, PG, PG13, R, X

b. Restaurant ratings: *, **, ***, ****, *****

c. Soft-drink sizes: baby, small, medium, large, extra large

d. Employee salary classes: GS1, GS2, GS3, GS4, GS5

e. Staff positions: president, vice president, department head, associate department head, secretary

50. Identify the *types of data* created when the following are coded from 1–5:

a. Method of payment: cash, check, debit card, Visa card, Mastercard

b. The largest energy companies on *Fortune*'s 1999 *Global 500* list: Suez Lyonnaise des Eaux, Enron, RAO Gazprom, Dynegy, Transcanada Pipelines

c. The largest aerospace companies on *Fortune*'s 1999 *Global 500* list: Boeing, Lockheed Martin, United Technologies, Raytheon, AlliedSignal

d. The largest banks on *Fortune*'s 1999 *Global 500* list: Bank of America Corporation, Credit Suisse, Deutsche Bank, HSBC Holdings, ABN AMRO Holding

e. The largest chemicals companies on *Fortune*'s 1999 *Global 500* list: E. I. du Pont de Nemours, Bayer, BASF, Hoechst, Dow Chemical

Chapter 2

LEARNING ABOUT EXCEL

LOOKING AHEAD

By reading this chapter, you will learn to do amazing things with EXCEL. You will

1. become acquainted with the EXCEL workspace, which features menus and tools, the formula bar and the chart wizard, giant worksheets, and more,
2. explore the typical stages of an EXCEL project—from data entry and manipulation to the production of descriptive and inferential statistics and the printing and saving of your work, and
3. become aware of crucial avenues for further study, notably those provided by the program's built-in Help features and by visiting EXCEL on the Web.

AND HERE IS A TYPICAL PROBLEM YOU WILL BE ABLE TO SOLVE:

It has often been argued that chief executive officers who deliver superior returns to shareholders should receive high personal compensation, while others who disappoint shareholders should suffer the consequences and get paid much less. You are given a long list of companies, along with data on the five-year total compensation of their CEOs and the firms' five-year annualized stock return. Based on these data, you are to find out whether this theory works out in practice. Do executives get paid what they deserve?

a. As a first step in your analysis, enter the data into an EXCEL worksheet.

b. Then, using an appropriate EXCEL procedure, determine the strength of association between executive compensation and stock performance.

PREVIEW

You are working for a new Internet company that plans to solicit advertising from multinational corporations headquartered in the United States. Your boss has given you a special assignment: Identify the one hundred largest firms among U.S.-based multinationals (size being measured by their foreign revenues). Make a list of these revenues and note each company's foreign profits as well. Finally, in your report, show the *range* of foreign revenues and foreign profits encountered within this group of firms and also compute the *average* firm's foreign revenue and foreign profit.

Surely yours is not an exceedingly difficult task. Yet, without a computer, you would be saddled with quite a bit of detective work and a considerable amount of computational drudgery. Even if you had those numbers at your fingertips, just adding 100 revenue numbers and again 100 profit figures (and dividing each sum by 100) would not only be boring and time-consuming, but would also produce results of dubious accuracy. Luckily, you live in the 21st century. As you will learn in this chapter and the next, you can capture data such as these on the Internet in no time, enter them into a computer program, such as EXCEL, and have your result in two seconds flat.

First, you might visit http://www.forbes.com, a Web site maintained by *Forbes* magazine, and capture the kinds of data shown in Table 2.1. (More about *that* in Chapter 3.)

TABLE 2.1 | The 100 Largest U.S.-Based Multinationals in 1999

Company	Foreign Revenue (millions of dollars)	Foreign (Net) Profit (millions of dollars)
Abbott Laboratories	4,559	512
Aflac	5,657	621
Alcoa	6,611	1,091
AlliedSignal	3,248	209
American Express	5,400	2,141
.	.	.
.	.	.
Dow Chemical	11,030	1,327
Eastman Kodak	6,989	1,390
EI du Pont de Nemours	11,692	1,672
Electronic Data Sys	6,588	743
Eli Lilly	3,401	818
.	.	.
.	.	.
Morgan Stanley, DW	7,400	3,393
Motorola	13,990	−962
NCR	3,659	−137
Nike	4,101	4
Oracle	3,573	380
.	.	.
.	.	.
Wal-Mart Stores	12,247	8,120
Walt Disney	3,834	759
Warner-Lambert	4,327	611
Whirlpool	4,842	118
Xerox	12,767	556

SOURCE: Data originally published in *Forbes*, July 26, 1999, pp. 202–206.

Second, you might enter the same data into EXCEL, issue a few simple commands, and instantly derive this result (along with other data not reproduced here):

Foreign Revenue (mil$)		Foreign Profit (mil$)	
Mean	9583.96	Mean	1069.967742
Median	5695	Median	520
Minimum	2994	Minimum	−2743
Maximum	80705	Maximum	8120
Count	100	Count	93

With respect to foreign revenue, the computer tells us, $N = 100$ data were analyzed, showing an average or *mean* of $9,583.96 million and ranging from a minimum of $2,994 million to a maximum of $80,705 million. With respect to foreign profits, the computer tells us, $N = 93$ data were analyzed (because $N^* = 7$ data were missing), showing a mean of $1,069.967742 million and ranging from a minimum of −$2,743 million to a maximum of $8,120 million. More than that! The *median* foreign revenue (half of these firms had less, half had more) was $5,695 million, while the median foreign profit was $520 million. Your boss will be pleased.

And here is a secret that might please you as well: Using a computer and EXCEL, it took the author fewer than 10 minutes to capture the data in question at http://www.forbes.com/tool/toolbox/int500/ and derive the results just discussed. Once you have studied this chapter and the next, you can do no worse.

2.1 Introduction

Microsoft EXCEL is a comprehensive and powerful spreadsheet application, originally designed to help businesses organize masses of data. As such, the program was meant to replace those armies of accountants who used to spend their lives recording data and, calculators in hand, subjecting them to endless, boring rounds of computations. Indeed, EXCEL's ability neatly to display data in rows and columns and to link them by formulas so that a change in one column instantly updates linked data in other columns—all of which pleases accountants to no end—remains one of its main beneficial features today. By now, however, EXCEL does much more than take the dread out of old-style accounting. It allows us to explore data with the help of great tables and dazzling graphics. Its built-in functions quickly produce descriptive statistics, such as averages, medians, and modes. Most importantly, the program's latest incarnation, EXCEL 2000, has become an attractive alternative to specialized statistical software applications, which makes it a helpful learning tool for almost every chapter of this text.

Moreover, when built-in functions are not enough, you can call on extra programs, known as *add-ins,* to augment basic EXCEL capabilities. Such useful additives include Solver, Analysis ToolPak, Microsoft Map, and more. You can install only the additional modules you want and do not have to clutter up your computer with anything you do not need. Also, as time passes, you will note that third-party developers continue to create application-specific add-ins—a matter you can check out by occasional visits to the Microsoft Web site. (In later chapters, more likely than not, you will want to use HKStat, an add-in developed by the author of this text and found on the CD-ROM that accompanies it.) This chapter assumes that you know the basics of using your computer—how to start applications, use your mouse, move and close windows, and so on.

It introduces you to major features of EXCEL 2000 and also shows you where to get additional help when you want to learn more about the program's finer details.

2.2 The EXCEL Environment

We begin our EXCEL tour with a brief overview of the environment in which you will do your work.

THE EXCEL SCREEN

After starting EXCEL, you will encounter an opening screen that is vertically split into various sections, as shown in Figure 2.1. The screen as a whole is the **workbook window** and is initially named Book 1. Although the grid of numerous rows and columns dominates the workspace, the remainder of the screen is no less important.

At the very top of the EXCEL workspace is the **title bar.** It displays (at the far left) a menu icon (you can click on it to see the choices), followed by the name of the current workbook, and (at the far right) the usual minimize, maximize, and close-window buttons. Just below the title bar is

FIGURE 2.1 | EXCEL's Opening Screen

Upon starting EXCEL, you encounter an opening screen entitled Book 1. It contains numerous **navigation bars** *and a currently active* **worksheet**. *Eventually, any one EXCEL workbook can contain numerous worksheets, only one of which will be active at any given time.*

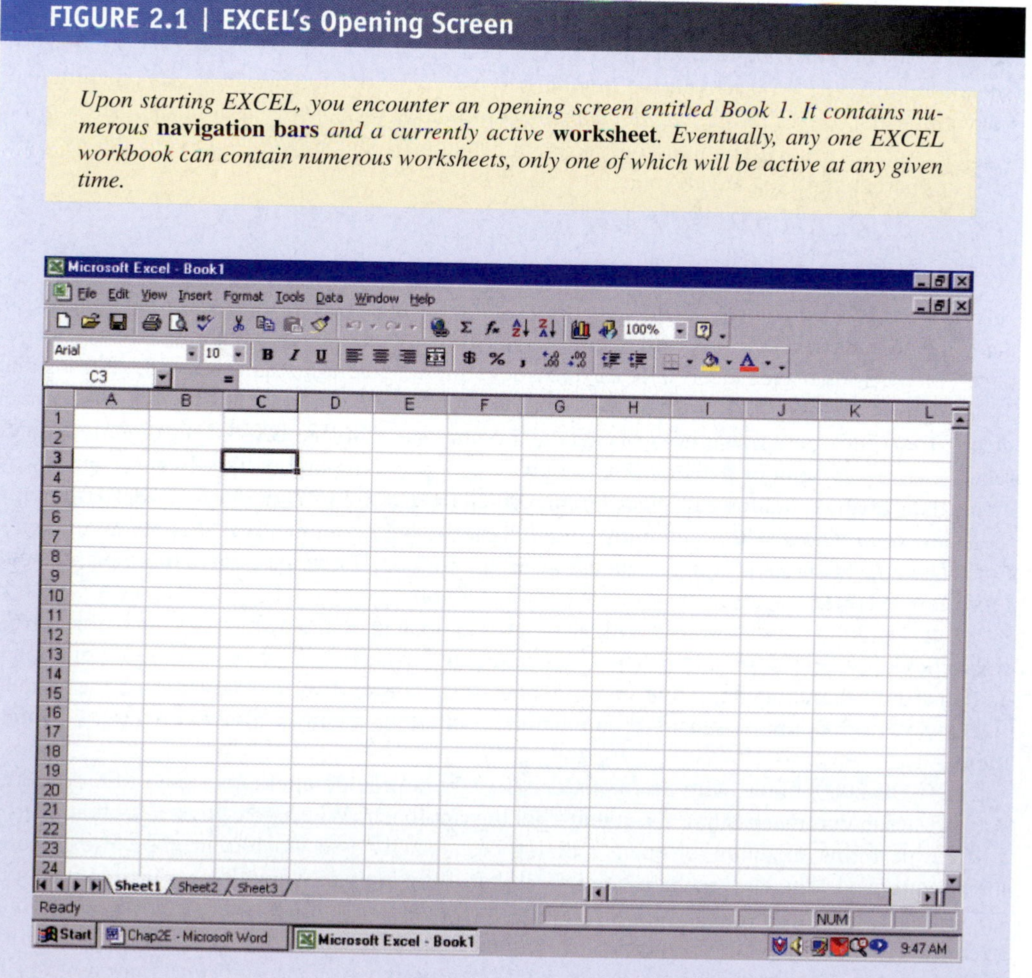

the **menu bar,** where you can select commands to manipulate data you have entered. The two strips of icons below the menu bar are *toolbars,* known as the **standard toolbar** and the **formatting toolbar,** respectively. The last of the strips above the grid, finally, is the **formula bar.** You can recognize it by the equal sign (=) in the shaded section toward the left.

The huge white area of rows and columns is the **worksheet.** It stands ready to receive the data with which you want to work. An EXCEL workbook normally consists of three worksheets (note the three **sheet tabs** just below the last visible row), but you can add more. (The total number of worksheets that you can open is limited only by your computer's memory.) To activate a given worksheet, just click on its tab. However, when there are so many worksheets that there is insufficient space for all the tabs, some tabs are hidden and you may first have to use the four **tab scrolling buttons** to the left of the sheet tabs to find the tab you need to click. The two tab scrolling buttons in the middle scroll the tabs one worksheet at a time in the indicated direction. The two outermost tab scrolling buttons scroll directly to the first or last tab in the workbook. (**Tip:** By default, EXCEL calls the worksheets Sheet 1, Sheet 2, Sheet 3, and so on, but you may want to give them more meaningful names. Simply right-click on the tab, click **Rename** on the menu, Backspace, type your chosen name directly on the tab, and click elsewhere on the sheet. You can use up to 31 characters, including spaces, but excluding square brackets, colons, forward and back slashes, question marks, and asterisks. However, the longer the name you type, the wider the tab becomes and the fewer tabs you can see without scrolling.)

Below the sheet tabs resides the **status bar.** It displays the current condition of your workspace. Most of the time, as in Figure 2.1 on the previous page, you see the word Ready to the left, meaning that the worksheet is ready to accept new information. As you type new information, you may see the word Enter. When you activate the formula bar or double-click a cell that already contains data, you will see the word Edit. After you lock in new information you just typed (for example, by pressing Enter on the keyboard) or after you discard information (for example, by pressing the Esc key), the status bar returns to the Ready mode.

MENUS AND TOOLS

Have another look at Figure 2.1, but this time focus on the **menu bar,** the horizontal bar just below the Microsoft EXCEL—Book 1 title bar. Here you select commands to manipulate the data you have entered in the worksheet. EXCEL provides nine menus: File, Edit, View, Insert, Format, Tools, Data, Window, and Help. You can click on an item in the menu bar to open the associated menu. Then click on a menu item to execute a command. This happens either directly or indirectly—via a submenu or a dialog box. In any case, your command will use data in some way: create data, change existing data, draw graphs based on data, and so on. (**Note:** EXCEL monitors the status of your worksheet and allows you to choose only commands that apply at any given time. The black commands on a menu are available for use. If a menu item is dimmed, it is currently unavailable.)

Although it may be menu overkill, you can also open up many a **shortcut menu,** simply by right-clicking your mouse button. The shortcut menu pops up adjacent to the mouse pointer and contains only the commands that apply to the item indicated by the position of the pointer. Because it offers context-sensitive commands, a shortcut menu is also known as a **context menu.**

EXCEL 2000 comes with 24 toolbars. All of them provide alternative (and often quicker) ways to issue commands than the menu-clicking approach. When you click a toolbar button, EXCEL performs an action, or opens a dialog box, exactly as it would with the corresponding menu command. The bar just below the menu bar, for example, which is also visible in Figure 2.1, is the **standard toolbar.** To see the name of any one of its buttons, place your mouse pointer over the button and let it hover there for a second. You will discover buttons to start a new workbook, open an existing workbook, or save an open workbook. You will find buttons to print, provide a print preview, and check spelling. You will meet the Format Painter, the Chart Wizard, and more. And don't forget to check out that tiny arrow at the very end. It will help you customize your toolbar as you wish.

Just below the standard toolbar resides the **formatting toolbar.** Its buttons let you select a new font or change its size, make text bold, italic, or underlined, align text in various ways, and so much more. (Point to each choice and check it out!)

But the buttons found on existing toolbars constitute only a small part of the total number of buttons supplied with EXCEL. If you are so inclined, you can add any of the unused buttons to existing toolbars. You can also remove buttons you do not need. In the process, you can customize the existing toolbars for the type of work you are most likely to do. You can even create entirely new toolbars of your own design. To add a button, click **View** > **Toolbars** > **Customize,** click the Toolbars tab and check the box of the bar you want to modify, click the Commands tab and select a category, select the desired icon, drag it to the toolbar, and release it when the tiny x attached to your pointer turns into a +. To get rid of an existing button, click **View** > **Toolbars** > **Customize,** then literally drag the offending button off the toolbar and release the mouse button.

Are you sorry you made the changes just described? To get your old built-in toolbar back, again click **View** > **Toolbars** > **Customize,** click the Toolbars tab, select the toolbar in question, and click **Reset.** The original toolbar reappears, looking like new.

(**Note:** Throughout this text, we will follow the typographical convention just introduced in the previous paragraph: Click **View** > **Toolbars** > **Customize** is shorthand for saying "Click **View;** then, on the menu that appears, click **Toolbars;** then, on the submenu, click **Customize.**" You will also encounter more extended abbreviations of multiple commands.)

THE WORKSHEET

Like traditional accounting ledgers, an EXCEL worksheet is a grid of columns and rows. As Figure 2.1 illustrates, columns are identified by letters, while rows are identified by numbers. At any given moment, however, the computer screen shows only a tiny portion of the much larger worksheet. In fact, EXCEL automatically provides 256 columns and 65,536 rows. This makes for 16,777,216 column/row intersections, known as **cells,** that are ready to receive your data. Keep in mind, moreover, that each new workbook starts out with three blank sheets, containing a joint total of 50,331,648 little boxes. And you can add new sheets, too, each providing another 16,777,216 cells!

So, while you won't have any trouble fitting in all of your data, you might have trouble finding them without the program's **cell reference system.** This feature is designed to help you find data quickly in the giant worksheet. Each of those little boxes in the giant grid is given a **cell address** or **cell reference,** consisting of a combination of column letter and row number, such as C3. In Figure 2.1, for instance, the currently active cell, which *is* the intersection of column C and row 3, can be identified in three ways: (1) by the heavy outline of the cell box in the worksheet, (2) by the boldfaced **C** and **3** in the worksheet frame above and to the left of that cell, and (3) by the entry of C3 in the leftmost portion, known as the **name box,** of the formula bar.

It is easy enough, of course, to label worksheet rows by consecutive numbers from 1 to 65,536. An alphabet of 26 letters, on the other hand, does not seem up to the task of labeling 256 columns. EXCEL solves the problem by labeling columns from A to Z and then doubling up letters as needed. Thus, column Z is followed by AA, AB, . . . and AZ, which is followed, in turn, by BA, BB, . . . and BZ, and so on, until the last and 256th column is called IV (which is not to be confused with the Roman 4). The last cell reference in any worksheet, therefore, is IV65536.

The **worksheet scroll bars** along the right and bottom sides of any sheet provide you with the means to view other parts of the mostly hidden sheet. If you click the up or down arrow on the vertical scroll bar, the sheet moves up or down one row at a time. If you click the right or left arrow on the horizontal scroll bar, the sheet moves right or left one column at a time. To speed things up, you can hold down the Shift key and drag the vertical central scroll box up or down (or the horizontal box right or left), while monitoring the pop-up screen tip box. It predicts the position you will see when you release the mouse button. (**Tip:** You can also move to a specific cell address with lightning speed by clicking **Edit** > **GoTo,** typing the desired cell address into the *Reference* box, and clicking **OK.**)

THE FORMULA BAR

Formulas are the heart and soul of a spreadsheet. Armed with a few rules, you can turn your EXCEL worksheet into a powerful calculator. The formula bar, located just above the worksheet, comes in handy. It is divided into three sections.

- The leftmost *name box* section contains the address of the currently active cell (such as C3 in Figure 2.1). When applicable, the drop-down button provides additional information.
- The shaded middle section initially displays only the formula's equal sign (=). The equal sign is also known as the *edit formula button.* However, the moment you type something into a cell, two additional buttons, the *cancel button* and the *enter button,* appear in the middle section, just left of the equal sign.
- The long white area to the right of the equal sign becomes alive as soon as you begin to build your formula (by typing into the formula bar or the active cell).

All **formulas** are equations that analyze data to return some result. Formulas always begin with an equal sign (=). *It is crucial that you type the equal sign when creating your formula.* Without it, EXCEL displays what you type and computes nothing.

The equal sign is followed by **arguments** (which can be values, such as 5.8, or cell references, such as C3).

Different arguments are connected by **arithmetic operators:** + for addition, − for subtraction, * for multiplication, / for division, and ^ for exponentiation. In complicated formulas that contain many arguments and many arithmetic operators, you can avoid confusion and improve readability by creating a line break without affecting the subsequent computations. Simply hold down the Alt key and press Enter.

EXCEL Example 2.1

To illustrate how you can make a formula work for you, enter the following demand function into EXCEL worksheet 1, columns A and B, respectively. Then let EXCEL compute the revenue associated with each price/quantity combination and display it in column C.

Price:	1	2	3	4	5	6
Quantity:	800	700	600	500	400	300

SOLUTION:

1. Click cell A1, type **Price** and press **Enter.** In cell A2, type **1** and press **Enter.** In cell A3, type **2** and press **Enter.** And so on.
2. In similar fashion, enter **Quantity** and the six associated values in column B.
3. Click cell C1, type **Revenue,** and press **Enter.**

FIGURE 2.2 | Using the EXCEL Formula Bar

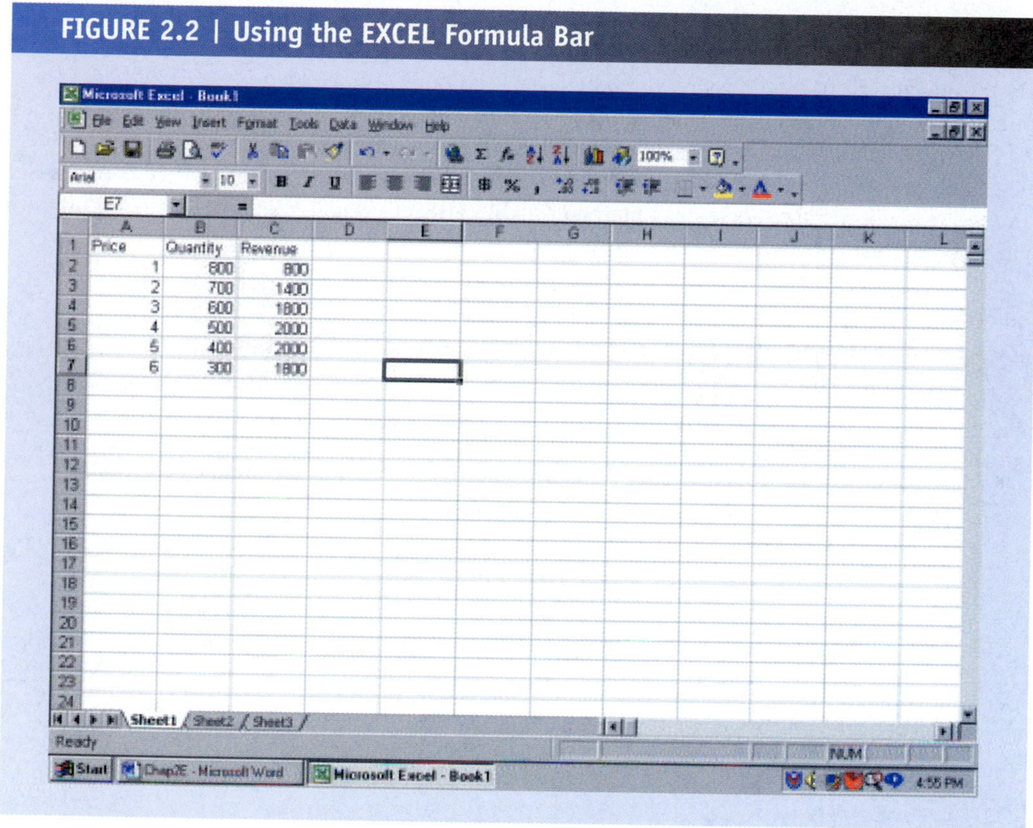

	A	B	C
1	Price	Quantity	Revenue
2	1	800	800
3	2	700	1400
4	3	600	1800
5	4	500	2000
6	5	400	2000
7	6	300	1800

4. Click cell C2, then click the formula bar to the right of the equal sign. Finally, type **= A2*B2** and click the green check mark, which is the formula bar's Enter button. The correct entry of 800 appears in cell C2.
5. To extend the formula to the remainder of column C, point the cursor to the handle in the lower right corner of the C2 active cell. As the cursor changes to a +, depress the left mouse button, and drag the cursor down to include cells C3, C4, C5, C6, and C7. Click anywhere on the worksheet and note the correct entries in column C, as Figure 2.2 shows.

Note: While you have the Figure 2.2 worksheet in front of you, you can learn another important lesson. Successively click on Cells C2, then C3, C4, and so on. Note how the formula bar displays information on how the values were calculated: Click on 800 and you are told that this C2 value =A2*B2. Click on 1400 and you are told that this C3 value = A3*B3. Click on the first 1800 and you are told that this C4 value = A4*B4. Finally, click on the last 1800 and you are told that this C7 value =A7*B7.

The lesson is this: In this example, all of the cell addresses appearing in the formula bar (A2, B2, A3, B3, A4, B4, and, finally, A7, B7) are **relative cell references.** Such relative references give rise to analogous rather than identical computations when an EXCEL formula is placed in another cell. Thus, moving the formula =A2*B2 from C2 to C3 results in C3=A3*B3 (rather than in C3=A2*B2). Even though you typed =A2*B2 in step 4 above, EXCEL interpreted your instructions as relative rather than absolute. It did not make the *identical* calculation (of 1 times 800) repeatedly, but made *analogous* calculations (of 2 times 700, 3 times 600, and so on) in the remaining rows (just as you intended).

There may, however, be occasions when you *want* EXCEL to perform the identical calculation repeatedly. In that case, you must enter **absolute cell references** in the formula. You can do that by inserting a dollar sign ($) before each column and row name. Absolute cell references, such as $A$2 or $B$2, give rise to identical rather than analogous computations when an EXCEL formula is placed in another cell. Thus, moving the formula =$A$2*$B$2 from C2 to C3 results in C3=$A$2*$B$2 (rather than in C3=$A$3*$B$3). You can try it out easily enough: Repeat the above exercise, but enter $A$2*$B$2 in step 4. Column C will fill up with values of 800 in every row!

CAUTION

When formulas contain more than one arithmetic operator, it is crucial to be aware of the order of precedence with which computations are performed. Expressions in parentheses are processed first. Beyond that, exponentiation precedes multiplication and division, which, in turn, precedes addition and subtraction. For example, the formula A1 = 5 +2*3 returns a result of 11 (because multiplication is done first), not the result of 21. To get a 21, one would instead have to write A1 = (5+2)*3.

2.3 The Stages of a Typical Project

Let us consider the major steps involved in carrying out an EXCEL project.

STARTING A NEW PROJECT

As we have already seen, just starting EXCEL will create Book 1, a new and empty workbook file such as Figure 2.1, and signal the program's readiness to work on a new project. However, you can also start a new project in the middle of other work, simply by clicking the **New** button on the standard toolbar or, if you prefer, by going to the menu bar and clicking **File** > **New** > **General** > **OK.** Finally, if you have previously saved a project, you can click **File** > **Open,** select the relevant drive and folder (such as, C: My Documents) and then click on the relevant file in the list of all possible files that the dialog box displays. EXCEL will do the rest, entering all of your saved work into the new project. Thus, you can pick up right where you left off. (*Tip:* If you merely want to open a new worksheet in an already-existing workbook, just click **Insert** > **Worksheet.**)

ENTERING DATA

Unless you have reopened a previously saved project, your worksheet is empty. It is time to enter the raw material that EXCEL is supposed to process. As Section 2.4 will show, data can be entered in a variety of ways: by typing them in, by copying them from some other place and pasting them in, by generating them with EXCEL commands, and, of course, from previously saved files.

MANIPULATING DATA

Once you have data in your worksheet, they can be manipulated in numerous ways, as Section 2.5 will show. For example, you can select individual cells, contiguous groups of cells, or non-contiguous ranges of cells for special consideration. You can edit and sort data, add or delete entire columns or rows, and more.

PRODUCING DESCRIPTIVE STATISTICS

When you are finished preparing your data, you can display information that describes them with the help of tables, graphs, and arithmetic summary measures. In the process, you will learn to use the *Chart Wizard,* a step-by-step approach to the creation of customized graphs. You will also meet the *Function Wizard,* a collection of over 300 preset formulas, known as **built-in functions** that can save you the time and trouble of creating your own equations in the formula bar. Section 2.6 will provide examples.

DRAWING INFERENCES

You can also use a large variety of procedures to draw inferences about things unknown from the data at your disposal. Using HKStat, for example, you can estimate last year's profit of the average *Fortune 500* company from a mere sample of 20 profit data and you can do so with a specified degree of confidence. Or you can conduct hypothesis tests concerning the value of this unknown population average. Again, using Microsoft's Analysis ToolPak, you can compute correlation coefficients, create regression equations, or subject time series to exponential smoothing, to name but a few cases in point. Section 2.7 will introduce this most important aspect of EXCEL.

SAVING YOUR WORK

Whenever you are so inclined, you can save your entire project—the data, the output from commands, graphs, and more—in one fell swoop. Just click **File** > **Save As,** select the drive and folder wherein you want to save your work, type a filename in the dialog box (up to 255 characters, including spaces, are allowed), and click **Save.** (*Tip:* By default, EXCEL saves everything in the *My Documents* folder. If you wish, you can create a new default. Suppose you wanted to save everything in C:\WINDOWS\EXCEL Workbooks. To do so, open Windows Explorer, click **C** > **Windows** > **File** > **New** to create a new folder. Type *EXCEL Workbooks* in the place of the temporary filename and press Enter. Then, in EXCEL, click **Tools** > **Options** > **General;** in the *Default file location* box, type C:\WINDOWS\EXCEL Workbooks, and click **OK.** You are set for life.)

PRINTING YOUR WORK

Numerous ways exist for printing all or part of your work. Just clicking the Print button on the standard toolbar will print the active worksheet, using EXCEL's default settings, which you can change. Instead, you may wish to use the menu approach, clicking **File** > **Page Setup,** which opens a four-tabs dialog box that lets you specify numerous details about the printed page, its margins, headers and footers, and more.

What if you just want to print all or a portion of your worksheet? Click in the upper left cell of the area you have in mind, hold your left mouse button, and drag down and right until the desired area is highlighted in blue and, thus, *selected.* Click **File** > **Print Area** > **Set Print Area.** Then wait for the selected area to be surrounded by a dotted line. **Click File** > **Print** > **OK.**

CONCLUDING YOUR WORK

You can escape your work at any time by simply clicking the close button in the upper right corner on your workbook window. (However, EXCEL will ask you whether you want to save changes made since your last Save.) You can also delete your workbook entirely by clicking **File** > **Open,** right-clicking the filename in the dialog box list, and clicking **Delete** on the shortcut menu that appears. Want to get rid of a single worksheet only? Right-click its sheet tab, click **Delete** on the shortcut menu and then **OK.** (Caution: Deleting a worksheet is one of the few actions in EXCEL that cannot be undone!)

2.4 Entering Data

You can bring data into an EXCEL worksheet in a variety of ways: by typing them in, by copying them from some other place and pasting them in, by generating them with EXCEL commands, and, of course, from previously saved files. We will consider each of these approaches in turn, but before we do, we must become familiar with a bit of EXCEL terminology.

THREE DATA TYPES

EXCEL distinguishes three types of data—text, value, and formula.

- **Text data** (also called *labels*) are strings of characters that can consist of a mix of letters, numbers, spaces, and punctuation symbols (such as "Test Number 4" or "AT&T"). EXCEL always aligns text data at the left side of cells.
- **Value data** can be numbers, dates, or times. They are always aligned at the right side of cells. Typical *numbers* are 14 or 14.567 or $34.23 or 2.3% or even 1.45E+6, which is scientific notation for 1.45 times 10 to the 6th power, or 1,450,000. Typical *dates* are 11/24/00 or 11-24-00 or 24-Nov-00 or 24/Nov/00 and even 24Nov00. But be careful: You need 4 digits for the years 1900–1929 and also for years 2030 and later. Two digits are fine for 1930–2029. Thus 99 is interpreted as 1999, 00 as 2000, and 29 as 2029, but 30 as 1930 rather than 2030. Typical *times* are 2:17 PM or 2:17:22 PM or 14:17 or 14:17:22. (*Tip:* If you ever want to enter the *current* date or time into an active cell, press Ctrl + semicolon (;) for the date. Press Ctrl + Shift + semicolon (;) for the time.)
- **Formula data** are equations that analyze data to return some result. Formulas always begin with an equal sign (=) and were introduced by EXCEL Example 2.1 earlier. You will see plenty of additional examples throughout this text. Formulas can, however, be typed directly into cells instead of the formula bar.

TYPING DATA INTO THE WORKSHEET

In this section, you can learn a few useful skills for typing in your own data.

PICKING A STARTING POINT Picture yourself facing an empty worksheet, such as Figure 2.1. Before you enter columns and rows of data, it pays to anticipate your future need to distinguish different columns and rows of data from one another. Almost surely, you will want to enter labels at the heads of columns or rows. It is well worth it, therefore, to reserve a row at the top (such as row 1) for future column heads and a column on the left (such as column A) for future row heads. Thus, assuming EXCEL is in the Ready mode (glance at the status bar), you may want to position your cell pointer for your first entry by clicking cell B2. (If EXCEL is not in the Ready mode, try pressing the Esc key.)

MAKING FLAWLESS ENTRIES You can enter data *one column at a time* by successively typing an entry and pressing the Enter key. The cell pointer moves down one cell at a time. You can also enter data *one row at a time* by successively typing an entry and pressing the Tab key. The cell pointer moves right one cell at a time. (*Tip:* If you make a mistake while entering data, press

Backspace to correct if you haven't yet pressed Enter or Tab. Otherwise, double-click in the offending cell and place your pointer where needed to retype.)

ADDING HEADERS Eventually, when you do type your column or row heads, they will probably be text, which EXCEL will ignore in future calculations. But what if you need labels consisting of *numbers,* such as the years 2000, 2001, 2002, and so on? Just type an apostrophe (') before each number, and EXCEL will treat it as a label to be ignored in computations. Don't be surprised, however, if the apostrophe remains invisible! (*Tip:* More often than not, labels require multiple lines of text. You can easily enter them, and have EXCEL increase the height of the label row accordingly, by pressing Alt + Enter at the point at which you want the line to break.)

STYLE FORMATTING When entering numbers, you are expected to use normal decimal points. For large numbers you are free to use or not use commas to separate hundreds from thousands, thousands from millions, and so on. (If you do use commas, they will appear in the cells, but not in formulas.) You can also change the style of entries by selecting any part of the worksheet and then clicking **Format > Style,** clicking the arrow on the *Style name* box, clicking on the desired style name, and **OK.** Alternatively, you can apply common styles to selected cells by clicking certain buttons on the formatting bar. Consider the Currency Style button, the Percent Style button, the Comma Style button, or the two buttons that increase or decrease, respectively, the number of decimals by one.

MAKING ROOM What if your entries won't fit into the given cells and spill over into adjacent areas? Position the mouse pointer at the lower right corner of the column header button or of the row header button. When the pointer changes to a double arrow, click and drag the pointer till the column has the width or the row has the height you want. Alternatively, click the column (or row) header button to select the column (or row), then click **Format > Column** (or **Row**) **> AutoFit.**

NAMING SELECTED AREAS By the time you have many data in your worksheet, it will be a good idea to *name* certain sections of it, because EXCEL will then use these names in formulas and all kinds of output that these formulas compute. For example, you may wish to call column A "Price," column B "Quantity," and column C "Revenue." Later on, you will be grateful to read a statement that equates Price times Quantity with Revenue, which makes eminent sense. The equivalent statement that A times B equals C may well leave you bewildered.

To name a cell or range of cells, select it, click the Name box in the formula bar, press Backspace, type your chosen name, and press Enter. (All names must begin with a letter or underscore, have a maximum of 255 characters, and contain no spaces. You may use periods or underscores as word separators.)

EXCEL Example 2.2

Is it worth it to get an MBA? In 2000, *Forbes* magazine sent questionnaires to more than 14,000 persons who had graduated from U.S. business schools in 1994. Table 2.2 on the following pages shows selected results.

a. Enter the data into EXCEL.

b. Name each column.

c. Save your worksheet for later use.

TABLE 2.2 | The Fruits of an MBA

This table shows that B-school is a wise choice for many. Consider the University of Chicago, highlighted in red. Measured in constant dollars, after deducting tuition and forgone compensation, a 1994 Chicago graduate made a 5-year net gain of $55,000 over pre-MBA compensation. It took a mere 3.7 years after graduation to break even. (All data are medians, which means the numbers were smaller for one half of affected individuals and larger for the other half.)

Business School	5-Year Net Gain (thousands of dollars)	5-Year Net Gain (as % of tuition and forgone compensation)	Years to Break Even
Alabama (Manderson)	9	17	4.5
Arizona (Eller)	16	22	4.3
Arizona State	15	22	4.3
BYU (Mariott)	42	62	3.6
Carnegie Mellon	49	46	3.7
Chicago	55	43	3.7
Columbia	58	50	3.7
Connecticut	19	32	4.1
Cornell (Johnson)	37	34	4.0
Dartmouth (Tuck)	87	66	3.5
Denver (Daniels)	3	4	4.8
Duke (Fuqua)	29	24	4.3
Emory (Goizueta)	8	7	4.7
Florida (Warrington)	12	15	4.6
Fordham	5	6	4.8
Georgia (Terry)	29	42	4.0
Georgia State (Robinson)	30	47	3.6
Harvard	101	75	3.3
Illinois Urbana-Champaign	23	35	3.9
Indiana (Kelley)	42	50	3.6
Iowa (Tippie)	1	1	5.0
Maryland (Smith)	38	51	3.5
Michigan	13	11	4.6
Michigan State (Broad)	35	51	3.5

TABLE 2.2 *(continued)*

Business School	5-Year Net Gain (thousands of dollars)	5-Year Net Gain (as % of tuition and forgone compensation)	Years to Break Even
Minnesota (Carlson)	35	47	4.0
MIT (Sloan)	59	45	3.7
Northwestern (Kellogg)	41	32	4.1
Notre Dame	22	25	4.2
NYU (Stern)	23	21	4.4
Ohio State (Fisher)	50	70	3.3
Oklahoma (Price)	16	29	4.2
Penn State (Smeal)	28	33	4.1
Pennsylvania (Wharton)	56	44	3.9
Purdue (Kranert)	36	47	3.7
Rice (Jones)	20	26	4.2
Rochester (Simon)	14	15	4.5
Rollins (Crummer)	2	2	4.9
SMU (Cox)	9	9	4.7
Stanford	74	57	3.5
Texas-Austin	26	29	4.2
UC Berkeley (Haas)	64	64	3.4
UCLA (Anderson)	63	58	3.7
UNC (Kenan-Flagler)	21	22	4.4
USC (Marshall)	7	6	4.8
Vanderbilt (Owen)	17	17	4.5
Virginia (Darden)	54	51	3.6
Wake Forest (Babcock)	53	62	3.4
Washington	13	21	4.4
Washington U (Olin)	35	38	4.0
Wisconsin-Madison	30	38	4.0

SOURCE: *Forbes,* February 7, 2000, pp. 102 and 104.

SOLUTION:

a.

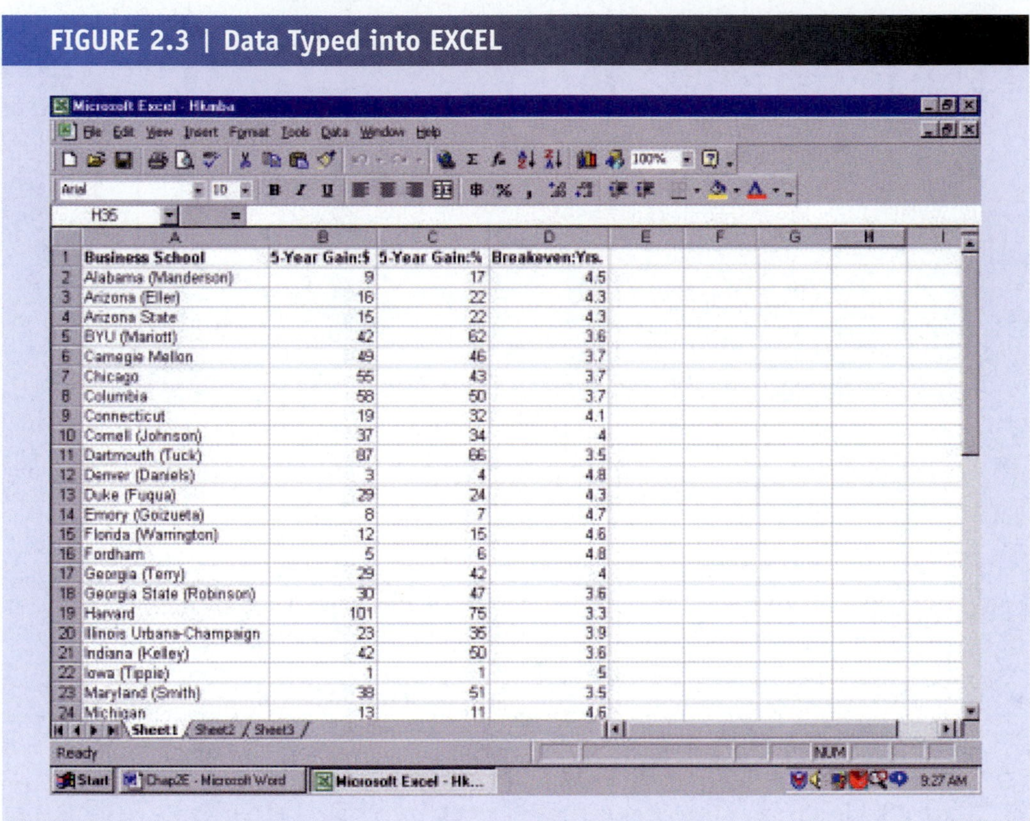

FIGURE 2.3 | Data Typed into EXCEL

	A	B	C	D
1	**Business School**	**5-Year Gain:$**	**5-Year Gain:%**	**Breakeven:Yrs.**
2	Alabama (Manderson)	9	17	4.5
3	Arizona (Eller)	16	22	4.3
4	Arizona State	15	22	4.3
5	BYU (Mariott)	42	62	3.6
6	Carnegie Mellon	49	46	3.7
7	Chicago	55	43	3.7
8	Columbia	58	50	3.7
9	Connecticut	19	32	4.1
10	Cornell (Johnson)	37	34	4
11	Dartmouth (Tuck)	87	66	3.5
12	Denver (Daniels)	3	4	4.8
13	Duke (Fuqua)	29	24	4.3
14	Emory (Goizueta)	8	7	4.7
15	Florida (Warrington)	12	15	4.6
16	Fordham	5	6	4.8
17	Georgia (Terry)	29	42	4
18	Georgia State (Robinson)	30	47	3.6
19	Harvard	101	75	3.3
20	Illinois Urbana-Champaign	23	35	3.9
21	Indiana (Kelley)	42	50	3.6
22	Iowa (Tippie)	1	1	5
23	Maryland (Smith)	38	51	3.5
24	Michigan	13	11	4.6

b. Follow the procedure discussed on page 45. For example, you can select successive columns by clicking on the letter header, then type Business_School, Dollar_Gain, Percent_Gain, and Breakeven_Years, respectively, in the formula bar name box and press Enter.

c. Follow the procedure discussed on page 43. For example, you may click **File** > **Save As,** then put your work into the EXCEL Workbooks folder by typing HKMBA into the File name box and clicking **Save.**

COPYING AND PASTING DATA

Copying and pasting data is a quick way to move data into EXCEL from another application or even from somewhere else within EXCEL. Relatively few simple steps are involved:

1. Highlight the data you want and copy them to the clipboard. Within EXCEL, the copy command is **Edit** > **Copy.**

2. In one of EXCEL's worksheets, select the cell where your first entry is to go and click **Edit > Paste.** (Alternatively, click the Paste button on the standard toolbar.)

Chapter 3 will discuss what may well be the most important source of data for many applications: importing data from the Internet.

GENERATING DATA WITHIN EXCEL

There are numerous ways in which you can generate data within EXCEL. The data you need might be random data, which you can use to take a random sample, as a later chapter will show. Or you may need data that exhibit an obvious pattern, such as 3, 6, 9, 12 to designate certain months of the year. Or you may need something in between these two extremes. You will encounter many examples in special EXCEL boxes throughout this text, notably those employing formulas you create or built-in functions you use. Here we introduce one particularly useful procedure—the generation of *patterned* data.

A common task involves filling a column with words or numbers that follow a sequence; for example, all the months from January to December, all the numbers from 1 to 100, or all the *even* numbers between 1 and 60. Such can be accomplished with a few simple steps:

1. Enter the first two values of your series in a chosen column (or row). The difference between the two starting values determines the change in the series from one cell to the next.
2. Select the two filled-in cells and note the small square, known as the **fill handle,** at the bottom right corner of the active cell. Point to the fill handle and note the pointer turning into crosshairs (+). Right-click and drag the fill handle over the desired range.
3. On the shortcut menu, click on the appropriate choice, such as **Fill Series.**

(*Tip:* If you have trouble with any of the foregoing steps, click **Tools > Options > Edit** and make sure that the *Allow cell drag and drop* box is checked.)

EXCEL Example 2.3

Open a new EXCEL workbook. Create the following patterned data:

a. In column A, all even numbers between 1 and 20.
b. In column C, all even numbers between 20 and 1.
c. In column E, every tenth between −1 and +1.
d. In column G, two sets of weekdays from Monday to Sunday.

SOLUTION: Follow the procedure just explained. The result is Figure 2.4 on the next page. (To make things fit in column G, click on the G header, then **Format > Column > Autofit.**)

FIGURE 2.4 | Generating Patterned Data

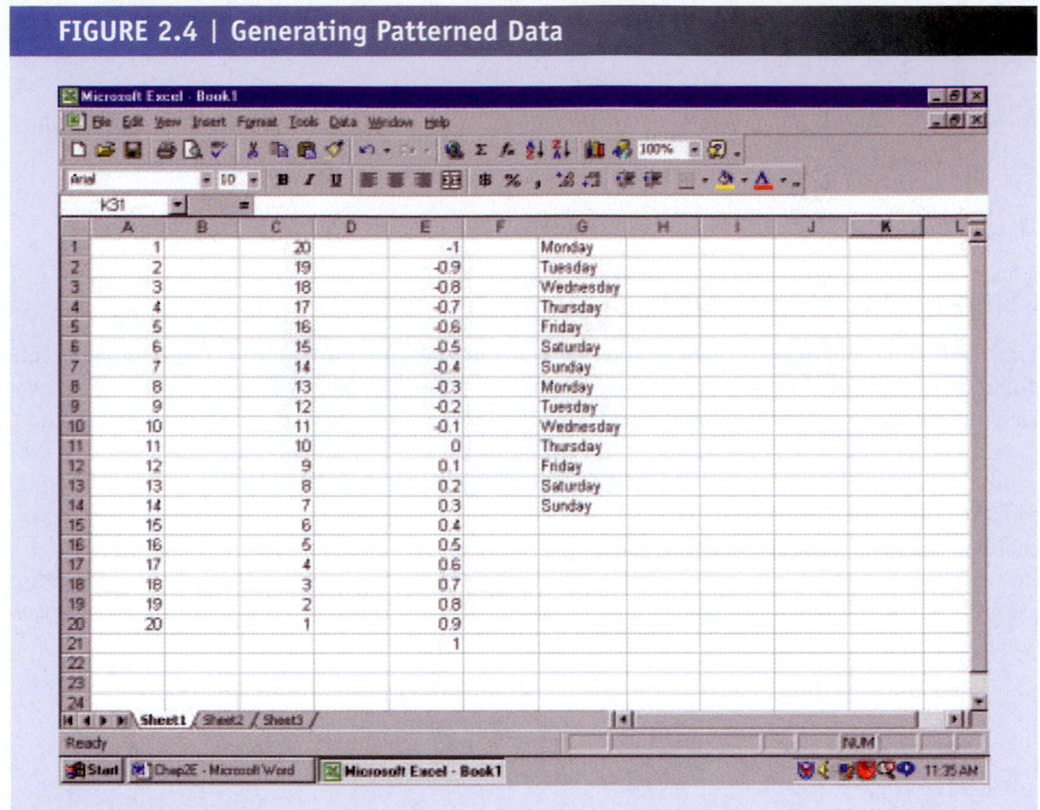

	A	B	C	D	E	F	G
1	1		20		-1		Monday
2	2		19		-0.9		Tuesday
3	3		18		-0.8		Wednesday
4	4		17		-0.7		Thursday
5	5		16		-0.6		Friday
6	6		15		-0.5		Saturday
7	7		14		-0.4		Sunday
8	8		13		-0.3		Monday
9	9		12		-0.2		Tuesday
10	10		11		-0.1		Wednesday
11	11		10		0		Thursday
12	12		9		0.1		Friday
13	13		8		0.2		Saturday
14	14		7		0.3		Sunday
15	15		6		0.4		
16	16		5		0.5		
17	17		4		0.6		
18	18		3		0.7		
19	19		2		0.8		
20	20		1		0.9		
21					1		

OPENING AN EXCEL DATA FILE

You can add data to any project by copying them from an EXCEL file that was previously saved. You only need a few clicks to retrieve it:

1. Click **File** > **Open.**
2. A dialog box appears. Click on the filename and click **Open.** (Or just double-click the filename.)

EXCEL Example 2.4

The CD-ROM associated with this text contains an EXCEL workbook file, HK99F500, which contains selected 1998 data about all companies on the 1999 *Fortune 500* list.

Open a new EXCEL workbook and add the file to it.

SOLUTION: Following the procedure just noted, you will derive Figure 2.5 in an instant:

FIGURE 2.5 | Selected Data About All 1999 *Fortune 500* Companies

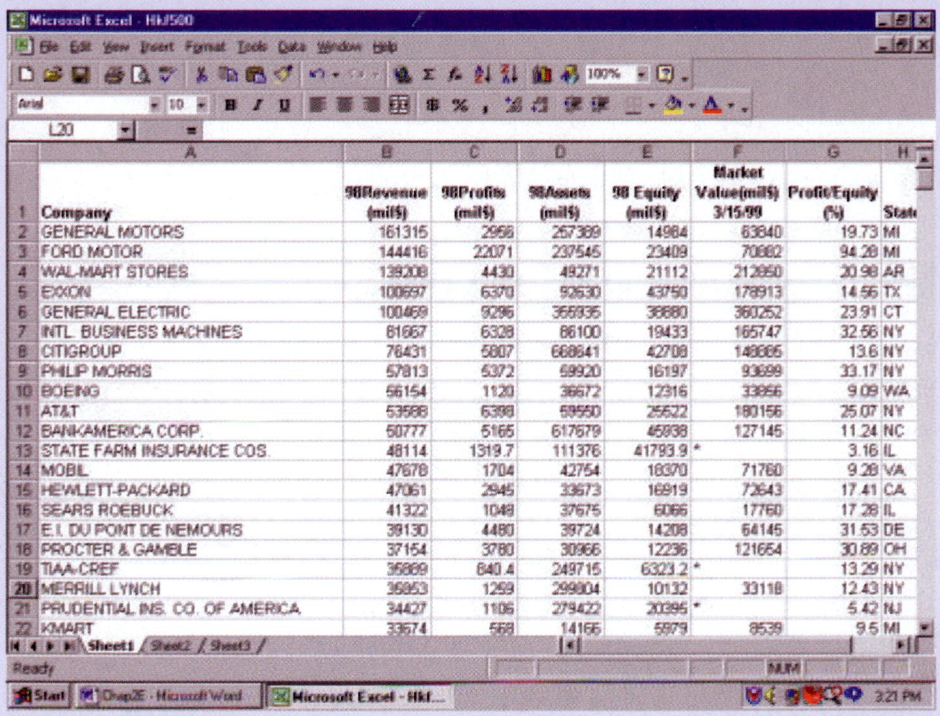

	Company	98Revenue (mil$)	98Profits (mil$)	98Assets (mil$)	98 Equity (mil$)	Market Value(mil$) 3/15/99	Profit/Equity (%)	State
2	GENERAL MOTORS	161315	2956	257389	14984	63840	19.73	MI
3	FORD MOTOR	144416	22071	237545	23409	70882	94.28	MI
4	WAL-MART STORES	139208	4430	49271	21112	212850	20.98	AR
5	EXXON	100697	6370	92630	43750	178913	14.56	TX
6	GENERAL ELECTRIC	100469	9296	355935	38880	360252	23.91	CT
7	INTL. BUSINESS MACHINES	81667	6328	86100	19433	165747	32.56	NY
8	CITIGROUP	76431	5807	668641	42708	148686	13.6	NY
9	PHILIP MORRIS	57813	5372	59920	16197	93699	33.17	NY
10	BOEING	56154	1120	36672	12316	33866	9.09	WA
11	AT&T	53588	6398	59550	25522	180156	25.07	NY
12	BANKAMERICA CORP.	50777	5165	617679	45938	127145	11.24	NC
13	STATE FARM INSURANCE COS.	48114	1319.7	111376	41793.9	*	3.16	IL
14	MOBIL	47678	1704	42754	18370	71760	9.28	VA
15	HEWLETT-PACKARD	47061	2945	33673	16919	72643	17.41	CA
16	SEARS ROEBUCK	41322	1048	37675	6066	17760	17.28	IL
17	E.I. DU PONT DE NEMOURS	39130	4480	39724	14208	64145	31.53	DE
18	PROCTER & GAMBLE	37154	3780	30966	12236	121654	30.89	OH
19	TIAA-CREF	35889	840.4	249715	6323.2	*	13.29	NY
20	MERRILL LYNCH	35853	1259	299804	10132	33118	12.43	NY
21	PRUDENTIAL INS. CO. OF AMERICA	34427	1106	279422	20395	*	5.42	NJ
22	KMART	33674	568	14166	5979	8539	9.5	MI

2.5 Manipulating Data

Once you have data in an EXCEL worksheet, you may want to rearrange or reorganize them before working with them. For example, you can delete rows or columns, convert data from one type to another, and change the way they are displayed (such as displaying a date as 3/17/02 instead of March 17, 2002). You can sort your data, combine columns, create subsets of columns, and fill columns with values that are calculated from values in other columns. The list goes on. We will consider a few of these possibilities.

SELECTING CELLS AND RANGES OF CELLS

Before performing an action, you must *select* the area you want to affect.

- To select a single cell, place the white-cross mouse pointer over it and click.
- To select an entire row (or column), similarly point to the numbered row head (or the letter column head) and click.
- To select a block of cells consisting of several adjacent rows or several adjacent columns, place the white-cross mouse pointer over the cell in the upper left corner of the block, click and hold the left mouse button, while dragging the pointer down and right until the desired area is highlighted. (If you prefer, you can place the white-cross mouse pointer over the cell in the lower right corner of the block, click and hold the left mouse button, while dragging the pointer up and left.)

- To select several blocks of cells that are not contiguous, press and hold Ctrl, while performing the action described in (3) repeatedly.
- To select a very large number of cells in a row or column, you can also click the first cell, hold down Shift, scroll to the last cells, and click on it.
- To select all cells at once, click the Select All button, which is the gray square just above the row 1 label and to the left of the column A label.

(*Tip:* To deselect an area, click anywhere else on the worksheet.)

MANIPULATING CELLS, ROWS, AND COLUMNS

Here are some of the actions you may wish to take, along with their consequences:

- Click **Edit** > **Cut.** The selected cells are surrounded by a moving dotted line and the selection is placed on the clipboard. When you activate another cell and click **Edit** > **Paste,** the selection reappears at the new location and the original selection is gone, as if you had cut it out of the worksheet with scissors.
- Click **Edit** > **Copy.** The selected cells are surrounded by a moving dotted line and the selection is placed on the clipboard. When you activate another cell and click **Edit** > **Paste,** the selection reappears at the new location and the original selection is still there.
- Click **Edit** > **Clear** > **All.** The content of the selected cells disappears as if you had used an eraser; the empty cells remain.
- Click **Edit** > **Delete,** make one of the choices on the submenu and click **OK.** The selected cells are deleted. The following rows or columns move up or left.
- Click a column head letter and then **Insert** > **Columns.** The column in question moves to the right and an empty column appears in its place. (To insert multiple columns, drag across multiple column heads from the intended insertion point.)
- Click a row head number and then **Insert** > **Rows.** The row in question moves down and an empty row appears in its place. (To insert multiple rows, drag across multiple row heads from the intended insertion point.)

SUBSETTING AND SPLITTING DATA

Often you will want to perform analyses or create graphs for a subgroup of observations within a larger data set. For example, you may want to focus only on the females in a study, or only on the sales revenue in a certain quarter. EXCEL can create a worksheet that contains only the subset you want. When you make that worksheet active, subsequent analyses or graphs will be based on the subset only. To split a worksheet on the basis of certain subgroups of a variable,

1. Select the column containing the subgroups in question. (A column labeled *Sex,* for example, will contain entries of *male* and *female.* A column labeled *Quarters* will contain entries of *first, second, third,* and *fourth.*)
2. Click **Data** > **Filter** > **Autofilter.**
3. Click the arrow at the head of the grouping variable's column. You will see a list of subgroups. Clicking on one of these will reveal a new worksheet containing only rows of data pertaining to the chosen subgroup.

EXCEL Example 2.5

Review EXCEL Example 2.4. Then find all the 1999 *Fortune 500* companies that were headquartered in Florida.

SOLUTION: Once again open the file HK99F500. Note that the states in which headquarters were located appear in column H.

1. Select column H.
2. Click **Data** > **Filter** > **Autofilter.**
3. Click the arrow at the head of column H, then click **FL.** The new worksheet reveals 11 companies fitting the chosen criterion, as Figure 2.6 shows.

FIGURE 2.6 | Selected Data about 1999 *Fortune 500* Companies with Headquarters in Florida

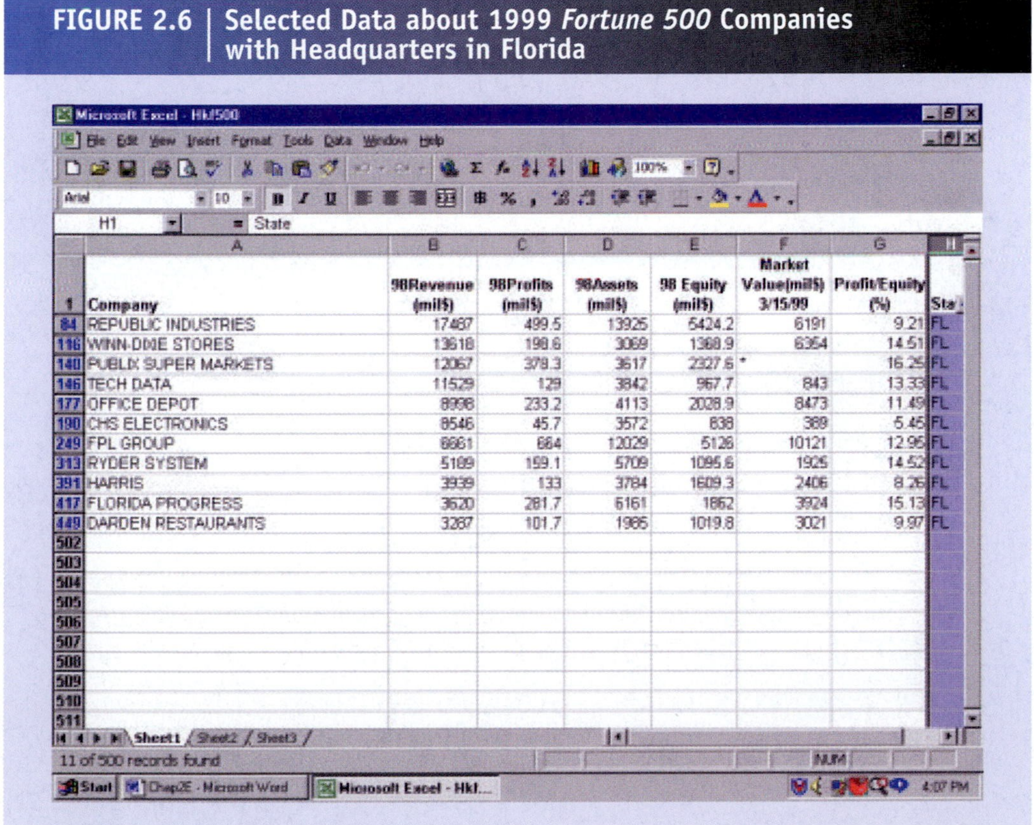

1	Company	98Revenue (mil$)	98Profits (mil$)	98Assets (mil$)	98 Equity (mil$)	Market Value(mil$) 3/15/99	Profit/Equity (%)	State
84	REPUBLIC INDUSTRIES	17487	499.5	13925	5424.2	6191	9.21	FL
116	WINN-DIXIE STORES	13618	198.6	3069	1368.9	6354	14.51	FL
140	PUBLIX SUPER MARKETS	12067	378.3	3617	2327.6	*	16.25	FL
146	TECH DATA	11529	129	3842	967.7	843	13.33	FL
177	OFFICE DEPOT	8998	233.2	4113	2028.9	8473	11.49	FL
190	CHS ELECTRONICS	8546	45.7	3572	838	389	5.45	FL
249	FPL GROUP	6661	664	12029	5126	10121	12.95	FL
313	RYDER SYSTEM	5189	159.1	5709	1095.6	1925	14.52	FL
391	HARRIS	3939	133	3784	1609.3	2406	8.26	FL
417	FLORIDA PROGRESS	3620	281.7	6161	1862	3924	15.13	FL
449	DARDEN RESTAURANTS	3287	101.7	1986	1019.8	3021	9.97	FL

SORTING DATA

Frequently, you will have good reason to arrange column entries in a different order. For example, you may wish to rearrange entries alphabetically in the case of text, in ascending or descending order in the case of numbers, or chronologically in the case of date/time data. Table 2.2 on pages 46-47 is a case in point. Wouldn't it be much more interesting if those business schools were not listed alphabetically, but in descending order from highest 5-Year Dollar Gain to lowest? You can accomplish this easily, as the following example shows.

EXCEL Example 2.6

Review EXCEL Example 2.2 on pages 45-48. Then open a new workbook along with the file HKMBA that was created then. Sort the data from highest to lowest 5-Year Dollar Gain.

SOLUTION:

1. Select columns A–D by clicking the Select All button.
2. Click **Data** > **Sort.**
3. In the *Sort by* box, enter **5-Year Gain:$** and choose *Descending.*
4. Choose *My list has Header row* and click **OK.**

The result is Figure 2.7. It instantly highlights the most lucrative business schools. (Dollar figures are in thousands.)

FIGURE 2.7 | Business Schools Rearranged

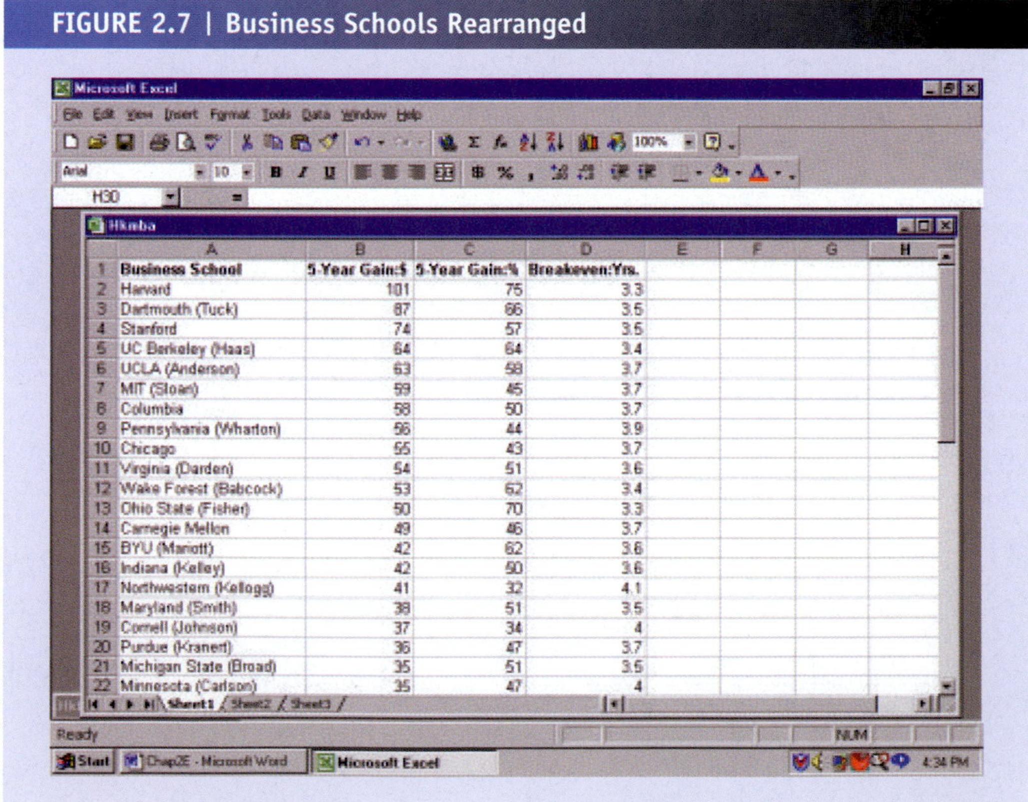

	A	B	C	D
1	Business School	5-Year Gain:$	5-Year Gain:%	Breakeven:Yrs.
2	Harvard	101	75	3.3
3	Dartmouth (Tuck)	87	66	3.5
4	Stanford	74	57	3.5
5	UC Berkeley (Haas)	64	64	3.4
6	UCLA (Anderson)	63	58	3.7
7	MIT (Sloan)	59	45	3.7
8	Columbia	58	50	3.7
9	Pennsylvania (Wharton)	56	44	3.9
10	Chicago	55	43	3.7
11	Virginia (Darden)	54	51	3.6
12	Wake Forest (Babcock)	53	62	3.4
13	Ohio State (Fisher)	50	70	3.3
14	Carnegie Mellon	49	46	3.7
15	BYU (Marriott)	42	62	3.6
16	Indiana (Kelley)	42	60	3.6
17	Northwestern (Kellogg)	41	32	4.1
18	Maryland (Smith)	38	51	3.5
19	Cornell (Johnson)	37	34	4
20	Purdue (Krannert)	36	47	3.7
21	Michigan State (Broad)	35	51	3.5
22	Minnesota (Carlson)	35	47	4

(*Tip:* Are you sorry you did all this sorting? Just click **Edit** > **Undo Sort;** or sort again, this time based on column A business school names, in ascending order from A to Z.)

2.6 Producing Descriptive Statistics

As you will see throughout this text, EXCEL can produce an impressive array of descriptive statistics, ranging from tables and arithmetic summary measures to fanciful graphs. We will illustrate this fact with two examples here.

ARITHMETIC SUMMARY MEASURES

Consider once again the file on your CD-ROM that is filled with information about the *Fortune 500* companies. You could enter the file into an EXCEL worksheet and look at it in detail, but all that information would be pretty overwhelming. In addition to the company names, you would find 500 separate revenue data, 500 profit figures, 500 asset data, 500 equity numbers, 500 company market values, and more. Staring at these lists, it would take you forever just to figure out such simple things as the largest and smallest revenue number or the largest and smallest profit earned. Without a computer, more complicated questions would be even harder to answer. How long, do you think, would it take you to compute the 500 companies' *average* revenue or to determine exactly how many of them took in between $500 million and $750 million in 1998? As the following example suggests, EXCEL can tell you in no time at all.

EXCEL Example 2.7

The CD-ROM associated with this text holds an EXCEL workbook file, HK99F500, which contains selected 1998 data about all companies on the 1999 *Fortune 500* list. Open a new EXCEL workbook and add the file to it. Then ask EXCEL to display descriptive statistics about the companies' revenues.

SOLUTION: You open the file as illustrated in EXCEL Example 2.4 on page 50. Then

1. Click **Tools** > **Data Analysis** > **Descriptive Statistics** > **OK.**
2. A *Descriptive Statistics* dialog box appears. In the *Input Range* box, enter the location of the data you want to describe, here the range **B1:B501.** (*Tip:* Except for a column label, the input range must contain numeric data only, which is the case here. When this is not the case—consider missing-value symbols interspersed with numeric data—you must first remove nonnumeric entries by eliminating the offending cells.)
3. Check *Grouped By columns* and *Labels in First Row.*
4. Under *Output options,* check *New Worksheet Ply.*
5. Check *Summary statistics.*
6. Click **OK.**
7. The result appears on a new worksheet. To make the data fit the columns perfectly, click **Format** > **Column** > **Autofit Selection.**

At this point, the output looks like this:

98Revenue(mil$)	
Mean	11481.222
Standard Error	702.2036152
Median	6621.5
Mode	5482
Standard Deviation	15701.75018
Sample Variance	246544958.6
Kurtosis	39.5775365
Skewness	5.44998244

(continued)

98Revenue(mil$) *(continued)*	
Range	158419
Minimum	2896
Maximum	161315
Sum	5740611
Count	500

You need not understand all of this material right now—that will be your task in Chapter 7. However, a few things are obvious right away:

Your file contains $N = 500$ revenue numbers. Their average, here called the *mean,* was $11,481.222 million. Half the numbers were below and half were above $6,621.5 million, which is what the *median* denotes. The lowest number was $2,896 million; the highest was $161,315 million. A lot of useful information—brought to us in one second flat!

GRAPHS

Graphs are equally useful tools for summarizing masses of data. EXCEL calls them *charts,* and it can produce many types of charts. (Click, for example, the *Chart Wizard* on the standard toolbar to see a list of standard graphs.) Two examples here introduce the subject.

EXCEL Example 2.8

The CD-ROM associated with this text contains an EXCEL worksheet file, HK99F500, which contains selected 1998 data about all companies on the 1999 *Fortune 500* list. Open a new EXCEL workbook and add the above file to it. Then ask EXCEL to display a *histogram* of the companies' revenues.

Note: As you will learn in Chapter 6, such a graph divides the minimum-to-maximum range found in a data set into a number of classes (EXCEL calls them **bins**) and then depicts the frequency of occurrences within each class (here the number of companies with revenues falling into these classes) with the help of differently sized vertical bars. Strictly speaking, a histogram requires that the vertical bars touch one another, but such is not the case in EXCEL unless you edit the graph.)

SOLUTION: Open the file as illustrated in EXCEL Example 2.4 on page 50. Then take these steps:

1. On the basis of the known range of data (EXCEL Example 2.7 shows data ranging from a minimum of $2,896 million to a maximum of $161,315 million), create a column of desired *upper* class limits. Starting at cell J2, for example, enter upper limits of 20,000, 40,000, 60,000, 80,000, 100,000, 120,000, 140,000, 160,000 and 180,000, using the autofill procedure illustrated in EXCEL Example 2.3.
2. Click **Tools** > **Data Analysis** > **Histogram** > **OK.**
3. In the *Histogram* dialog box, under *Input Range,* enter **B2:B501** (and do *not* check the *Labels* box, because you have just excluded the cell B1 label from the range).

4. Under *Bin Range,* enter **J2:J10.** (*Tip:* You can also leave the *Bin Range* box empty. In that case, EXCEL creates evenly distributed intervals using the minimum and maximum values of the input range as end points and making the number of intervals equal to the square root of the number of input values. The result is rarely satisfactory.)
5. Check *New Worksheet Ply* and *Chart Output* and click **OK.**

The output appears as Figure 2.8. It consists of a new worksheet holding a frequency table and (initially) a not-too-pretty chart. (As the following EXCEL example will show, we can make the graph considerably prettier by editing it.)

The left table column lists the previously chosen upper class limits or bin values. In the right-hand column, EXCEL reports the number of revenue data that were equal to or smaller than the same row's bin value but larger than the previous row's bin value (if one exists). For example, there were 49 companies with revenues of $40,000 million or less, but above $20,000 million. Likewise, there was 1 company with revenue of $180,000 million or less, but above $160,000 million.

The frequency table confirms in a general way what our earlier descriptive statistics told us more precisely. As we learned on pages 55-56, one company's revenues were as low as $2,896 million. At least half of all companies had revenues below $6,621.5 million. The average revenue was $11,481.222 million. And one company (General Motors) had the maximum revenue of $161,315 million.

FIGURE 2.8 | A Histogram of *Fortune 500* Companies' 1998 Revenues

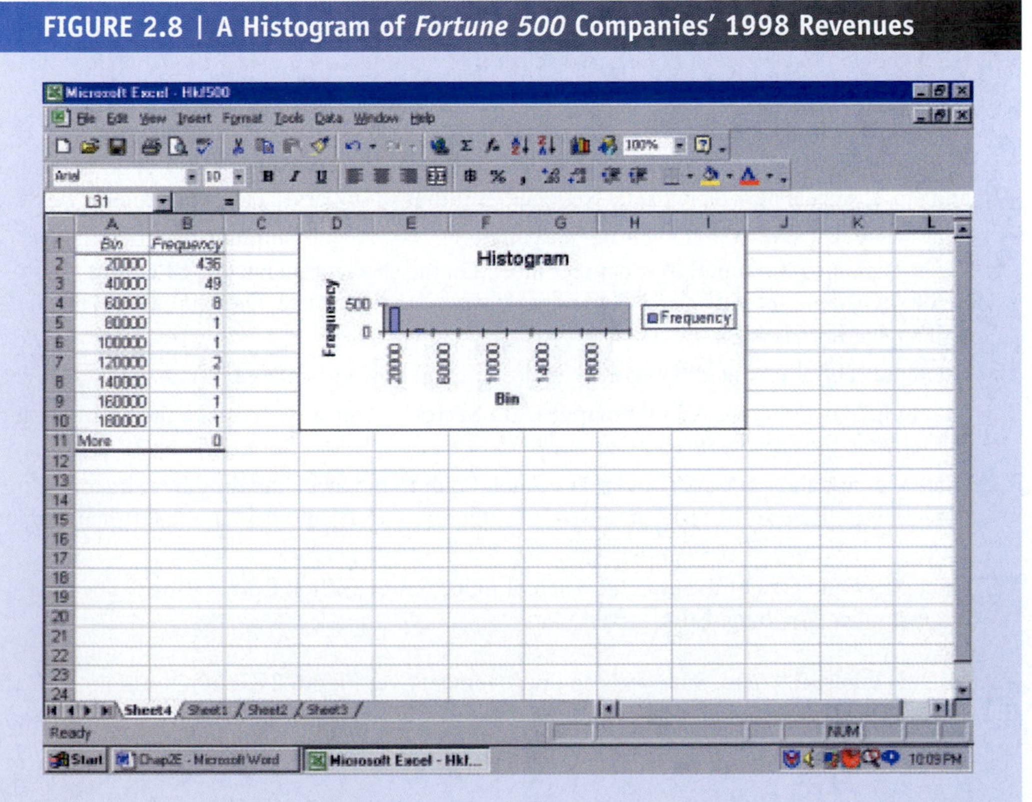

EXCEL Example 2.9

You can edit EXCEL charts, such as that created in Example Problem 2.8, to make them look prettier and much more informative. Do so now with the Figure 2.8 histogram. Then make a separate printout of your new graph.

Note: It is well worth your while to follow this exercise. It teaches you the kind of skills you need to turn ugly charts into beautiful graphs in one minute flat. (Well, almost that. It took the author two minutes, although you will need more time on your first try.)

SOLUTION: Answers can vary. Here is one possibility, which enlarges the graph, improves the labeling throughout, and adds a better title:

1. Select the histogram by clicking once on the white area within its boundaries. Point to the lower right handle and drag it down and right to create a larger graph reaching across 7 columns and 18 rows. (*Tip:* Just for fun, let your mouse pointer hover over any graph feature, such as an individual bar or label. Note the explanation that appears.)
2. Right-click the lower left corner of the graph. On the shortcut menu, click **Format Chart Area** > **Font** > **Regular** > **8** > **OK.**
3. Click the word *Histogram* to select it. Place the I-beam cursor at the end, backspace, and erase. Type a new title (Fortune 500 Companies in 1998) and press Enter.
4. Right-click the new title. On the shortcut menu, click **Format Chart Title** > **Font** > **Bold** > **10** > **OK.**
5. Right-click the legend box. On the shortcut menu, click **Clear** to make it disappear.
6. Right-click the central gray area. On the shortcut menu, click **Format Plot Area.** Then click the **white square** and **OK** to eliminate the gray background.
7. Click the vertical (*Frequency*) label to select it. Drag it up as far as it will go. Then right-click it. On the shortcut menu, click **Format Axis Title** > **Alignment.** Under *Orientation,* change the *Degrees* to 0 and click **OK.** This turns the label to a horizontal position.
8. Click the horizontal (*Bin*) label to select it. Place the I-beam cursor at the end, backspace, and erase. Type a new label [Total Revenue (millions of dollars)] and press Enter. Click the label again and drag it into the lower right corner.
9. Right-click any horizontal-axis number label. On the shortcut menu, click **Format Axis** > **Scale.** In *Number of categories between tick-mark labels,* enter **2,** and click **OK.** The labels will appear horizontal.
10. Click the central plot area. Drag the handles left and down to enlarge it.
11. Right-click any blue bar. Click **Format Data Series** > **Options.** To make the bars contiguous, change the *Gap width* to 0 and click **OK.**
12. Click the plot area. Type **436** and press Enter. Point to the label and drag it to the top of the first column. Repeat the procedure with the other frequency numbers in the left-hand table. (Now you know how to add a label anywhere within any graph!)
13. Click the white area of the graph to select it in its entirety. Click **Edit** > **Copy.** Then, in the target application, click **Edit** > **Paste.**

The result is Figure 2.9 here. Surely it's an improvement over Figure 2.8, but it's still not perfect. (For example, it is not obvious that the horizontal tick-mark labels refer to *upper* class limits.)

FIGURE 2.9 | The Edited Histogram

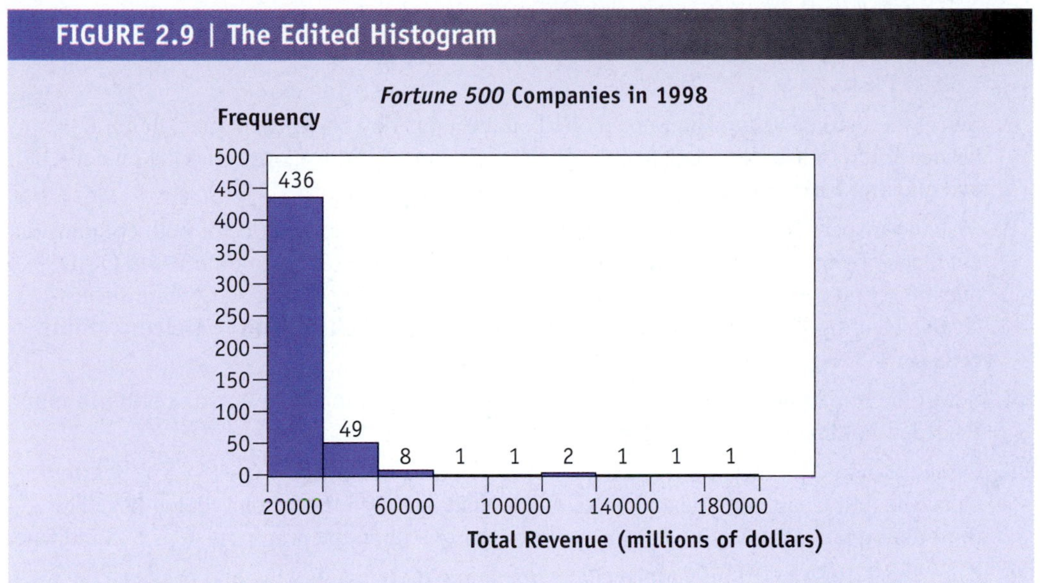

2.7 Drawing Inferences

As you will learn by numerous examples throughout this text, EXCEL (or associated add-ins) can perform hundreds of procedures that allow you to extract information and draw inferences from your data about matters otherwise unknown. Two examples in this section illustrate the point.

EXCEL Example 2.10

Someone has just asserted the existence of a simple relationship between the market values of U.S. corporations and their current profits: "The two variables move together such that the latter always explains the former." You are not so sure about the claim, but you are willing to check it out with recent data about the *Fortune 500* companies. Using the file HK99F500 on your CD-ROM,

a. create a *scatter diagram* that that plots combinations of market value (measured vertically) and profit (measured horizontally).

b. create a *regression equation* that relates the two variables mathematically, assuming market value is the variable to be explained and profit is the explanatory variable.

c. create another scatter diagram that contains a graph of the equation, colored in red.

SOLUTION:

Part (a)

After opening a new worksheet and entering the file, you will notice that market values or profit data are missing for some of the 500 companies—a fact evidenced by asterisks in the affected cells. To eliminate the 38 companies involved from your data set, perform steps 1–3. Then proceed with the remaining steps.

1. Select the profit data to be plotted on the X-axis by clicking on the column C header. Then transfer the data to column P by clicking **Edit > Copy,** clicking on cell P1, and clicking **Edit > Paste.**
2. Select the market-value data to be plotted on the Y-axis by clicking on the column F header. Then transfer the data to column Q by clicking **Edit > Copy,** clicking on cell Q1, and clicking **Edit > Paste.**
3. Visually inspect columns P and Q. Whenever a value is missing in one or both columns (as evidenced by at least one asterisk in some 38 rows), eliminate the column P *and* Q row in question. You can accomplish this feat in one fell swoop by pressing Ctrl while successively selecting the affected column P and Q rows, then clicking **Edit > Delete > Shift cells up > OK.**
4. Select the remaining 462 profit and market-value combinations by clicking on the column P header, holding Ctrl, and clicking on the column Q header.
5. On the standard toolbar, click the **Chart Wizard,** then **Standard Types > XY(Scatter).** Click the first Chart subtype and **Next.** Click **Next** again on the second dialog box. The third dialog box affords you several ways to improve upon the graph, as steps 6–8 indicate.
6. Click the **Titles** tab. Eliminate the *Chart title* completely by clicking and backspacing. Then type the labels shown in Figure 2.10 below in the *Value (X) axis* and *Value (Y) axis* boxes.
7. Click the **Gridlines** tab. Eliminate all check marks (and, thus, the gridlines).
8. Click the **Legend** tab. Eliminate all check marks (and, thus, the legend). Click **Next.**
9. In the fourth dialog box, choose *As object in Sheet 2* and click **Finish.** The graph appears in Sheet 2, but can surely be improved upon. (*Tip:* To view a display of the precise coordinates of any one of the 462 blue dots, let the mouse pointer point to it.)
10. Click the graph and drag its handles to make it larger.

FIGURE 2.10 | 1999 *Fortune 500* Companies Scatter Plot

The scatter plot does not reveal a particularly close relationship between profit and market value.

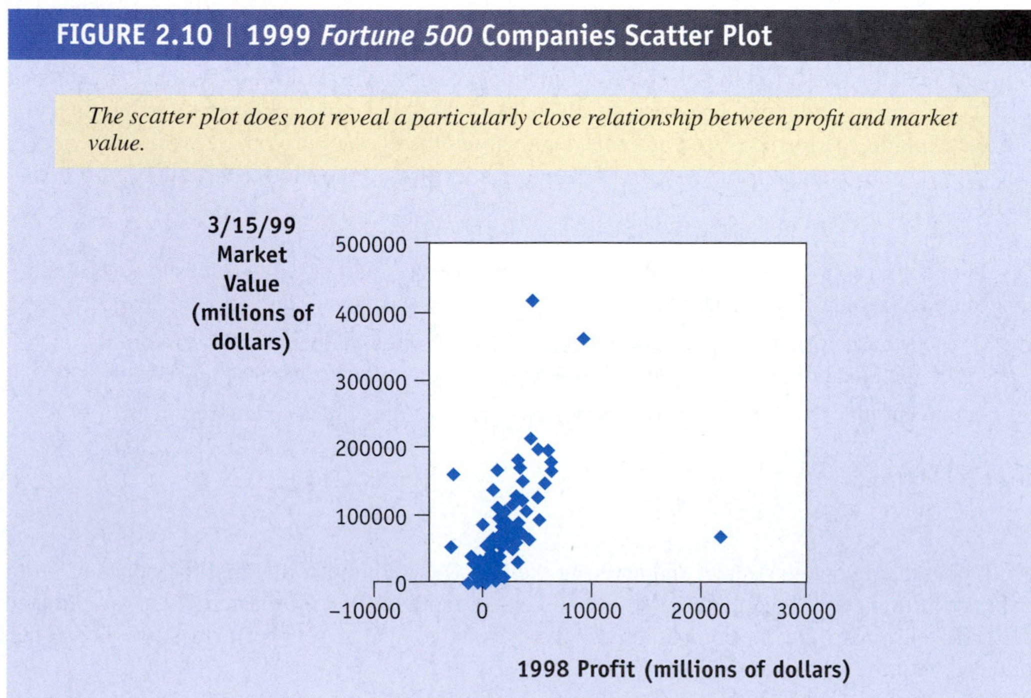

11. To eliminate the graph border and the gray background, right-click the gray area. Click **Format Plot Area.** Under *Pattern* and *Border,* choose *None.* Under *Area,* click the **white square** and **OK.**
12. Right-click the horizontal number labels. Click **Format Axis** > **Font** > **Regular** > **10** > **OK.**
13. Right-click the vertical number labels. Click **Format Axis** > **Font** > **Regular** > **10.** Click **Scale,** check the *Major unit* box, type in 100000, and click > **OK.**
14. Right-click the horizontal X axis. Click **Format Axis** > **Scale,** change the *Value (Y) axis crosses at* to **−5000** and click **OK.** This stops the vertical Y axis from crossing in the midst of all the blue dots. (*Tip:* You can similarly reposition a horizontal X axis by right-clicking the vertical Y axis and making analogous changes.)
15. Right-click the vertical axis title. Click **Format Axis Title** > **Alignment.** Change *Degrees* to zero, click **OK,** and drag the title to the position shown in Figure 2.10.

Part (b)

A few simple steps are involved:

1. Click **Tools** > **Data Analysis** > **Regression** > **OK.**
2. In the *Input Y Range* box, enter **Q1:Q463**
3. In the *Input X Range* box, enter **P1:P463**
4. Check *Labels* (because the first cell of each input column is a text label) and *New Worksheet Ply.* Click **OK.**

Along with all kinds of other things that you need not understand right now, the program provides information to construct the following *regression equation* (in millions of dollars):

$$\text{Market Value} = 9{,}444.22 + 17.42 \text{ Profit}$$

EXCEL suggests that a company's market value can be best estimated as $9,444.22 million plus 17.42 times the company's Profit, also measured in millions of dollars. Thus, at least this much of the claim is correct: Higher profit does lead to higher market value.

Part (c)

1. Repeat the steps noted in (b), but also check *Line Fit Plots* prior to the last (Step 4) **OK.**
2. EXCEL produces one of its really ugly graphs, reproduced as Figure 2.11 here:

FIGURE 2.11 | A Fitted Line Plot

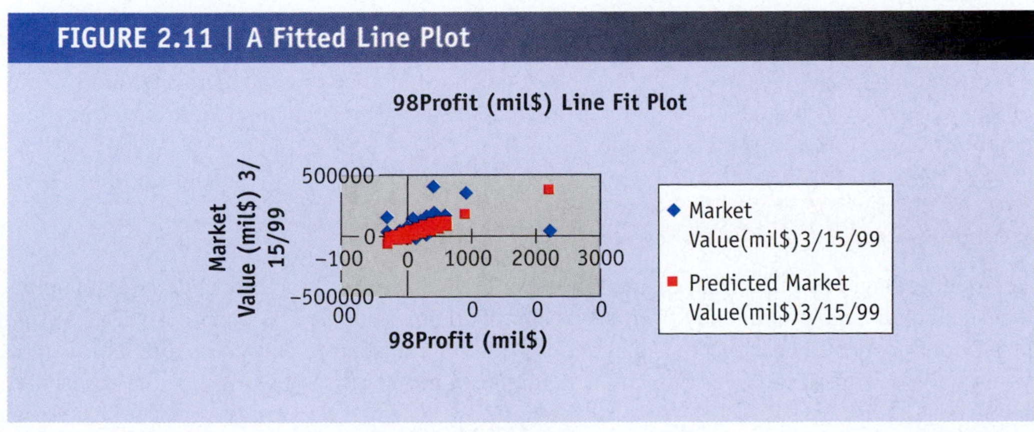

FIGURE 2.12 | *Fortune 500* Companies Scatter Plot with Regression Line

The Figure 2.10 scatter plot is reproduced here, but for each profit figure the market value predicted by the regression equation is indicated as well (by the height of the red line).

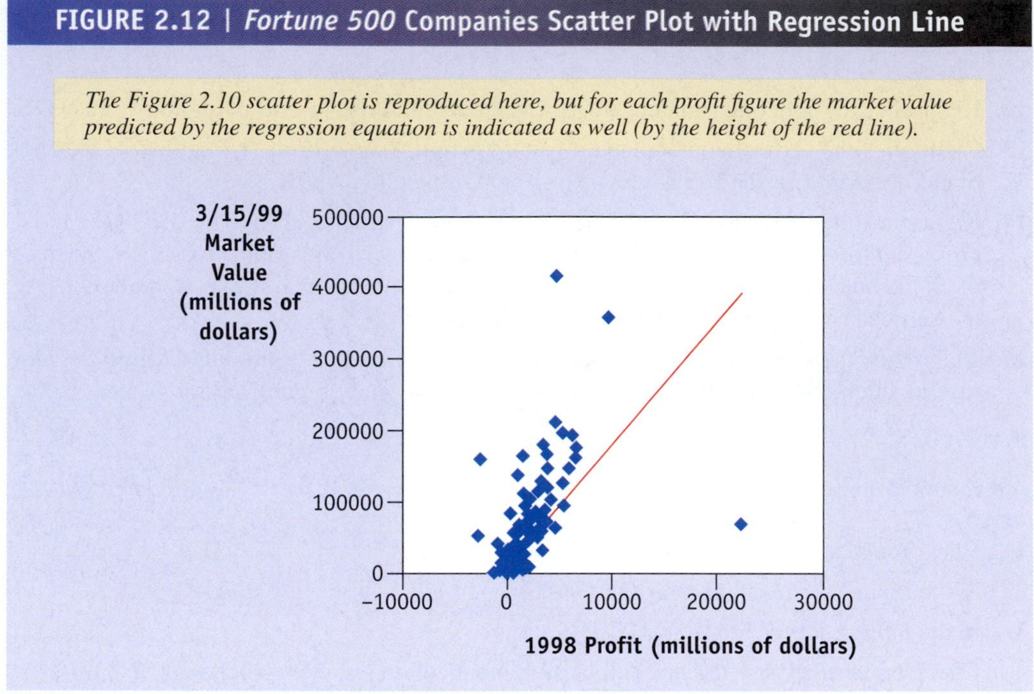

3. Using the techniques described in Part (a), however, we can greatly improve upon Figure 2.11, as indicated in Figure 2.12.

Note: Originally, EXCEL produces individual color dots, called markers, rather than a straight line, to indicate the predicted market value for any given profit. To turn the separate dots into the line shown here,

1. Click on one of the color dots, which selects the entire series.
2. Click **Format** > **Selected Data Series** > **Patterns.**
3. Under *Line,* choose *Automatic.*
4. Under *Marker,* choose *None* and click **OK.**

Comment: The (best-fitting) red regression line hardly seems a good summary of the actual market-value-versus-profit relationships represented by the blue dots. Perhaps the original idea ("profit explains market value") wasn't such a good one after all. (You will learn a lot more about this type of analysis and associated graphs in Chapters 16–18 of this text. Here we are merely demonstrating a few of EXCEL's capabilities.)

EXCEL Example 2.11

The scatter diagrams in EXCEL Examples 2.10 and 2.12 show at least five *outliers,* data points that seem to diverge prominently from the cluster of all other points. These market-value-versus-profit combinations may reflect special and unusual circumstances and you may want to redo your analysis without the five company data in question. As a first step, identify the companies involved.

SOLUTION: While you have your graph on your screen, use your cursor to point to each of the outliers in turn. A *Chart Tip* box appears, giving you these profit/market value coordinates:

−2,669 and 160,654

−2,743 and 53,338

4,490 and 418,579

9,296 and 360,252

22,071 and 70,882

By visually inspecting data columns C and F in workbook file HK99F500, you can find the associated companies in rows 3, 6, 29, 81, and 110 of your EXCEL file. They are Ford Motor, General Electric, Compaq Computer, MCI Worldcom, and Microsoft.

2.8 Getting Help

The best way to learn about EXCEL, no doubt, is to go ahead and work with the program—again and again. Before long, its manifold features will become familiar like old friends. On the way to that happy state of affairs, however, you will want help, and you can get it in a variety of ways. This final section explains.

SCREEN TIPS

The simplest way to get help involves **screen tips.** These are descriptive labels that appear whenever you let the mouse pointer rest over a toolbar button or some other element in an EXCEL window. At a minimum, the pop-up description gives you the name of the element, sometimes more. Earlier, we have already met screen tips associat-ed with various elements in EXCEL charts. EXCEL Example 2.11 provides a case in point.

WHAT'S THIS?

At any time, you can also get *context-sensitive* help—relative to what you are currently doing in a worksheet—by activating the What's This? feature. You can do so in a variety of ways:

- by clicking **Help** > **What's This?** on the menu bar.
- by pressing Shift + F1.
- by clicking on the question mark button in most dialog boxes.

The result is always the same: Your mouse pointer has a question mark beside it, and when you click on any element you want to know more about with the question-mark pointer, an explanation will pop up. (To get rid of the special pointer, press ESC or click outside the explanation box.)

THE OFFICE ASSISTANT

The most elaborate help is available

- by clicking **Help** > **Microsoft Excel Help** on the menu bar.
- by clicking the question mark on the standard toolbar.
- by simply pressing F1.

All of these approaches activate the *Office Assistant,* an animated character who first appears in the form of a paper clip, named Clippit, along with a box asking *What would you like to do?* You can type a question in plain English and click **Search.** The typical response is another box, containing a bulleted list of topics to explore. You can click on any one of these or you can click **See more** and get a further list of relevant topics on which you can click as well. Eventually, a Microsoft EXCEL Help screen appears, filled with all the information you could possibly want.

(*Tip:* The help screen may appear as a small bar in the upper left corner of your worksheet. If it does, just click on its maximize button and, if necessary as the screen fills up, drag the Office Assistant out of the way. In addition, you can left-click on the Office Assistant icon to make the suggestion box go away or reappear, and you can right-click on the icon to activate a shortcut menu. If you click **Hide,** the icon disappears. If you click **Options** > **Gallery,** you meet eight alternative Office Assistant icons that you can install. If you click **Animate!** repeatedly, you can escape your work and make the assistant perform wondrous feats of sight and sound.)

The Microsoft Help window itself also has a toolbar. It is well worth it to explore its buttons by clicking on them. Clicking on the leftmost *Show* button, for example, shrinks the explanation box towards the right and reveals a box on the left with three tabs, labeled *Contents, Answer Wizard,* and *Index.* Clicking on the *Contents* tab reveals a long list of topics (and subtopics) that you can explore and that jointly teach literally *everything* that there is to know about EXCEL. The *Answer Wizard* tab, in turn, like the Office Assistant icon, invites you to type in your own question and click **Search.** The *Index* tab, finally, asks for key words and topics that you care to learn about. In all cases, if you are so inclined, you can print out the answers by clicking the *Print* button.

Interestingly, the Office Assistant is more than willing to answer questions you haven't even asked. If you right-click its icon, for example, and then click **Options,** you can check a box titled *Show Tip of the Day at startup.* You can also let the Office Assistant sit silently in a corner of your screen as you work. He will watch you and let you know whenever there is a more efficient way to perform an operation. In that case, a yellow light bulb appears. Just click the bulb and read the tip. (For example, as you repeatedly click **Edit** > **Copy** and then **Edit** > **Paste** on the menu bar, the Office Assistant may suggest simply clicking the copy and paste buttons on the standard toolbar. Thus, by having the Office Assistant sitting in a corner of the screen, you can constantly learn slightly better ways of doing your work.)

EXCEL ON THE INTERNET

Users all over the globe can access EXCEL information 24 hours a day on the World Wide Web at: http://www.microsoft.com/office/Excel. With just a few keystrokes, visitors can join the EXCEL 2000 Tour, find How-to Articles, learn about Tips and Tricks, Office Bookstore Titles for EXCEL 2000, subscribe to e-mail newsletters, and more.

If you are already connected to the Internet and have EXCEL running, there is an alternative approach. Click **Help** > **Office on the Web,** and you will get connected to http://officeupdate.microsoft.com/welcome/Excel.asp. After trying out the Welcome, Downloads, and Assistance buttons, you will agree that everything you want to know about EXCEL is right there at your fingertips. Articles on working with formulas and charts, information on how to publish worksheets to the Web, third-party EXCEL links, and many more items of interest are all a click away.

(*Tip:* Whenever you are running EXCEL, you can also get quick customer-support information by clicking **Help** > **About Microsoft Excel** > **Tech Support** and then exploring the Microsoft EXCEL Help page, including the *Contents* tab. However, prior to *telephoning* Microsoft representatives, you may want to click **Help** > **About Microsoft Excel** > **System Information** and print out the display of your computer's current system configuration.)

Summary

1. EXCEL is a comprehensive and powerful spreadsheet application, originally designed to help businesses organize masses of data and to take the dread out of old-style accounting. By now, however, EXCEL does much more. It allows us to explore data with the help of great tables and dazzling graphics. Its built-in functions quickly produce numerical descriptive statistics. Most importantly, the program's latest incarnation, EXCEL 2000, has become an attractive alternative to specialized statistical software applications, which makes it a helpful leaning tool for almost every chapter of this text.
2. EXCEL contains a wide range of tools that can be used to describe and analyze data. Work proceeds within a *workbook window* that contains giant gridlike *worksheets* wherein all data are entered and stored. Instructions to the computer are issued by *commands,* usually by clicking an item on the *menu bar,* by clicking a *toolbar* button, or by typing formulas in the *formula bar.*
3. A typical EXCEL project begins with data entry, which can occur by typing data into worksheet cells, copying and pasting data from somewhere else, generating data within EXCEL, or opening a previously saved EXCEL file.
4. Once entered, data can be manipulated in numerous ways. Cells, rows, and columns in the worksheet can be cut, copied, cleared, deleted, and inserted. Data can be split into subsets and sorted. The list goes on.
5. EXCEL is superb at producing descriptive statistics, ranging from numerous arithmetic summary measures to equally numerous types of graphs (which EXCEL prefers to call *charts*).
6. EXCEL (along with its add-ins) can also perform hundreds of procedures that allow you to draw inferences from data about matters otherwise unknown. For example, you can estimate unknown values with specified degrees of confidence, conduct hypothesis tests, create regression equations and then plot them in a graph, to name but a few cases in point.
7. The best way to learn about EXCEL is to go ahead and work with the program. Along the way, two major avenues for enhancing that learning exist: EXCEL's built-in Help features (such as screen tips, the What's This? feature, and the Office Assistant) and EXCEL's Internet site.

Key Terms

absolute cell references
arguments
arithmetic operators
bins
built-in functions
cell address
cell reference
cell reference system
cells
context menu
fill handle
formatting toolbar
formula bar
formula data
formulas
menu bar
name box
relative cell references
screen tips
sheet tabs
shortcut menu
standard toolbar
status bar
tab scrolling buttons
text data
title bar
value data
workbook window
worksheet
worksheet scroll bars

Practice Problems

Section 2.2 The EXCEL Environment

1. The EXCEL worksheet has 256 columns and 65,536 rows. Assume that the typical column is 1 inch wide and the typical row is 1/4 inch high. Use the *formula bar* to compute
   a. the total number of cells in a single worksheet.
   b. the width of the worksheet, measured in feet, if you were to print it on paper.
   c. the height of the worksheet, measured in feet, if you were to print it on paper.
2. When creating formulas, it is crucial to be aware of the precedence rule with which arithmetic operations are performed. In each case below, make the computation in your head, then check the result by using the EXCEL formula bar.
   a. 4 + 10 / 2
   b. (4 + 10) / 2
   c. 4 * 10 + 8 / 4 − 2
   d. (4 * 10) + 8 / (4 − 2)

3. When creating formulas, it is crucial to be aware of the precedence rule with which arithmetic operations are performed. In each case on the right, make the computation in your head. Then check the result by using the EXCEL formula bar.

a. 4 * (10 + 8) / 4 − 2
b. (4 * 10 + 8) / 4 − 2
c. 4 * 10 + 8 / 4 − 2
d. 4 * 10^2 + 8 / 4 − 2

Section 2.4 Entering Data

4. You are a security analyst and your focus today is Internet companies. As a first step in your analysis, enter the Table 2.3 data into an EXCEL worksheet. Then save them in a data file named HKNET.

TABLE 2.3 | Selected Data on Internet Companies in February 2000 (dollars per customer)

Company	Market Cap	Revenue	Profit
SportsLine.com	204	21.82	−3.42
Lycos	244	7.39	1.87
barnesandnoble.com	562	67.66	−22.34
Quokka Sports	735	39.16	−43.08
eToys	1,198	85.29	−138.28
NetZero	1,140	16.28	−24.44
MindSpring	1,373	271.95	115.48
Amazon.com	1,400	160.01	−21.68
eBay	1,952	29.57	9.39
Yahoo!	2,038	18.99	10.31
priceline.com	2,295	178.12	.52
E*Trade	2,660	523.13	42.56
Schwab	4,562	683.27	288.84
AOL	5,781	272.44	89.08
Chemdex	104,903	1,698.04	−1,299.76
VerticalNet	2,827,931	13,917.24	−776.21

SOURCE: *Fortune,* February 21, 2000, p. 198.

5. You are a security analyst and your focus today is the sports industry. As a first step in your analysis, enter the Table 2.4 data into an EXCEL worksheet. Then save them in a data file named HKMLB.

TABLE 2.4 | The Prices of Major League Baseball Teams

Baseball Team	1998 Price (million dollars)	1999 Price (million dollars)
New York Yankees	361	491
Cleveland Indians	321	359
Atlanta Braves	300	357
Baltimore Orioles	322	351
Colorado Rockies	302	311
Arizona Diamondbacks	291	291
Texas Rangers	253	281
Los Angeles Dodgers	237	270
Boston Red Sox	229	256
New York Mets	193	249
Houston Astros	190	239
Seattle Mariners	251	236
Tampa Bay Devil Rays	225	225
Chicago Cubs	204	224
San Francisco Giants	188	213
St. Louis Cardinals	174	205
San Diego Padres	161	205
Anaheim Angels	157	195
Chicago White Sox	214	178
Cincinnati Reds	136	163
Toronto Blue Jays	141	162
Milwaukee Brewers	127	155
Florida Marlins	159	153
Detroit Tigers	137	152
Philadelphia Phillies	131	145
Pittsburgh Pirates	133	145
Oakland Athletics	118	125
Kansas City Royals	108	96
Minnesota Twins	94	89
Montreal Expos	88	84

SOURCE: Adapted from *Forbes,* May 31, 1999, p. 114.

6. You are a security analyst and your focus today is the sports industry. As a first step in your analysis, enter the Table 2.5 data into an EXCEL worksheet. Then save them in a data file named HKNFL.

TABLE 2.5 | The Prices of National Football League Teams

Football Team	1998 Price (million dollars)	1999 Price (million dollars)
Dallas Cowboys	412	663
Washington Redskins	402	607
Tampa Bay Buccaneers	346	502
Carolina Panthers	364	488
New England Patriots	251	460
Miami Dolphins	340	446
Denver Broncos	321	427
Jacksonville Jaguars	293	419
Baltimore Ravens	329	408
Seattle Seahawks	324	399
Pittsburgh Steelers	301	397
Cincinnati Bengals	310	394
St. Louis Rams	322	390
New York Giants	287	376
San Francisco 49ers	254	371
Tennessee Titans	321	369
New York Jets	259	363
Kansas City Chiefs	256	353
Buffalo Bills	251	326
San Diego Chargers	247	323
Green Bay Packers	244	320
Philadelphia Eagles	248	318
New Orleans Saints	242	315
Chicago Bears	237	313
Minnesota Vikings	232	309
Atlanta Falcons	234	306
Indianapolis Colts	228	305
Arizona Cardinals	230	301
Oakland Raiders	235	299
Detroit Lions	312	293

SOURCE: Adapted from *Forbes,* September 20, 1999, p. 177.

7. You are a security analyst and your focus today is the sports industry. As a first step in your analysis, enter the Table 2.6 data into an EXCEL worksheet. Then save them in a data file named HKNHL.

TABLE 2.6 | National Hockey League Data

Hockey Team	1998 Price (million dollars)	1999 Price (million dollars)	1998/99 Revenue (million dollars)
New York Rangers	195	236	84.2
Philadelphia Flyers	187	211	75.5
Boston Bruins	184	197	70.5
Detroit Red Wings	185	194	71.8
Chicago Blackhawks	170	185	65.9
Montreal Canadiens	167	175	64.9
Florida Panthers	105	163	65.0
Colorado Avalanche	138	160	57.2
Toronto Maple Leafs	119	151	62.7
Dallas Stars	118	149	59.4
Washington Capitals	179	145	55.8
New York Islanders	111	142	40.4
St. Louis Blues	154	137	62.2
New Jersey Devils	125	135	51.9
Nashville Predators	*	130	48.3
San Jose Sharks	108	123	51.2
Mighty Ducks of Anaheim	109	117	46.7
Tampa Bay Lightning	101	112	34.1
Los Angeles Kings	105	109	33.9
Pittsburgh Penguins	89	100	41.5
Vancouver Canucks	100	96	38.3
Buffalo Sabres	91	91	53.7
Phoenix Coyotes	86	89	42.5
Ottawa Senators	94	79	46.7
Calgary Flames	78	78	39.1
Edmonton Oilers	67	72	36.1
Carolina Hurricanes	80	70	24.1

SOURCE: Adapted from *Forbes,* December 13, 1999, p. 96.

8. You are a security analyst and your focus today is the sports industry. As a first step in your analysis, enter the Table 2.7 data into an EXCEL worksheet. Then save them in a data file named HKNBA.

TABLE 2.7 | National Basketball Association Data

Basketball Team	1998 Price (million dollars)	1999 Price (million dollars)	1998/99 Revenue (million dollars)	1998/99 Profit (million dollars)
New York Knicks	296	334	92.9	4.0
Chicago Bulls	304	307	66.8	20.4
Los Angeles Lakers	269	282	58.7	−0.9
Portland Trail Blazers	245	257	57.1	−13.5
Phoenix Suns	234	239	58.3	5.8
Philadalphia 76ers	196	231	57.7	1.8
Detroit Pistons	205	226	51.3	−1.7
Utah Jazz	201	215	47.7	−0.7
Washington Wizards	207	209	48.6	−2.8
Boston Celtics	176	187	41.5	2.3
Seattle Supersonics	169	183	43.6	−2.3
Indiana Pacers	152	178	34.2	−19.4
Cleveland Cavaliers	160	170	37.8	−0.1
San Antonio Spurs	122	169	42.3	−6.7
Houston Rockets	166	168	44.3	−3.6
New Jersey Nets	157	166	38.6	−8.6
Miami Heat	145	162	33.1	−20.7
Orlando Magic	134	159	37.9	−9.1
Sacramento Kings	119	151	34.3	−12.5
Atlanta Hawks	140	150	28.8	−19.3
Minnesota Timberwolves	119	146	41.7	4.2
Dallas Mavericks	119	141	26.1	−14.7
Golden State Warriors	130	140	31.8	−7.7
Toronto Raptors	121	138	33.6	−8.0
Charlotte Hornets	124	136	30.3	−2.2
Vancouver Grizzlies	134	127	28.2	−12.4
Denver Nuggets	110	124	23.8	−9.8
Milwaukee Bucks	94	111	25.8	−14.9
Los Angeles Clippers	102	103	23.0	−13.2

SOURCE: Adapted from *Forbes,* December 13, 1999, p. 100.

9. You are a security analyst and your focus today is the recent performance of stock funds. As a first step in your analysis, enter the Table 2.8 data into a EXCEL worksheet. Then save them in a data file named HKSTOCK.

TABLE 2.8 | The Performance of Stock Funds

Stock Fund	Assets 11/30/99 (million dollars)	Median Market Cap (billion dollars)	5-Year Annualized Total Return (percent)	Type of Fund*
Vanguard US Growth	17,801	134.8	30.3	1
Vanguard Growth and Income	8,022	64.4	28.8	1
Fidelity Fund	14,324	53.8	27.9	1
Bridges Investment Fund	62	61.5	26.9	1
Fidelity Growth Company	19,209	17.5	34.7	1
Janus Fund	37,853	61.5	31.2	1
McM Funds-Balanced	173	66.7	18.9	2
Columbia Balanced Fund	1,014	68.0	17.6	2
Vanguard Tax-Managed Balanced	308	38.6	17.1	2
Pax World Fund	1,017	39.8	21.1	2
Janus Balanced Fund	3,078	29.7	23.7	2
Scudder Internat'l Fund-I Shares	4,361	21.7	21.1	3
Fidelity Internat'l Growth & Income	1,209	22.4	18.0	3
T Rowe Price International Stock	11,328	24.7	15.7	3
Vanguard International Growth	8,654	19.9	15.2	3
EuroPacific Growth Fund	30,364	17.6	21.5	3
Janus Worldwide Fund	28,420	52.2	30.9	4
New Perspective Fund	28,980	30.9	23.9	4
Montgomery Global Commun-R	478	15.1	35.8	4
Capital World Growth & Income	10,022	11.5	20.8	4
Citizens Global Equity	170	29.7	28.9	4
Vanguard 500 Index	98,196	78.2	28.5	5
Spartan Market Index	9,813	68.0	28.2	5
T Rowe Price Equity Index	4,760	78.0	28.2	5
Vanguard Balanced Index	2,903	43.6	19.1	5

*1 = U.S.Stock; 2 = U.S.Balanced; 3 = Foreign Stock; 4 = Global Stock; 5 = Index.
SOURCE: Adapted from *Forbes,* February 7, 2000, p. 162.

10. You are working for an advertising agency and plan to solicit the 20 largest foreign companies for business. As a first step in your strategy, enter the Table 2.9 data into an EXCEL worksheet. Then save them in a data file named HK20LFC.

TABLE 2.9 | Selected Data on 20 Largest Foreign Companies

Company	Industry	Country	1999 Revenue (billion dollars)	1999 Employees (thousands)
DaimlerChrysler	autos	Germany	146.5	433.9
Mitsui & Co.	trading	Japan	109.2	10.9
Itochu	trading	Japan	108.6	8.4
Mitsubishi	trading	Japan	107.0	36.0
Toyota Motor	autos	Japan	99.6	183.9
Royal Dutch/Shell	energy	Netherlands	93.7	102.0
Marubeni	trading	Japan	93.4	8.9
Sumitomo	trading	Japan	89.0	30.7
AXA Group	insurance	France	78.7	78.9
Volkswagen Group	autos	Germany	76.3	275.6
Nippon Tel & Tel	telecomm	Japan	76.0	216.8
BP Amoco	energy	United Kingdom	67.7	99.0
Nissho Iwai	trading	Japan	67.6	19.5
Siemens Group	elec & electron	Germany	66.0	401.0
Allianz Worldwide	insurance	Germany	64.9	105.7
Hitachi	elec & electron	Japan	62.3	328.4
Matsushita Electric	appliances	Japan	59.7	282.2
ING Group	financial services	Netherlands	57.2	82.8
Sony	appliances	Japan	53.1	177.0
Metro	retailing	Germany	52.1	181.3

SOURCE: Adapted from *Forbes,* July 26, 1999, p. 160.

11. You are working for an advertising agency and plan to solicit the largest Internet companies for business. As a first step in your strategy, enter the Table 2.10 data into an EXCEL worksheet. Then save them in a data file named HK20LIC.

12. It has often been argued that chief executive officers who deliver superior returns to shareholders should receive high personal compensation, while others who disappoint shareholders should suffer the consequences and get paid much less. Based on the accompanying data, you are to find out whether this theory works out in practice. Do executives get paid what they deserve? As a first step in your analysis, enter the Table 2.11 data into an EXCEL worksheet. Then save them in a data file named HKEXEC.

TABLE 2.10 | Selected Data on Large Internet Companies, Mid-1999

Company	Recent Stock Price (dollars/share)	Market Cap (billion dollars)	Projected 1-Year Sales Growth (percent)
America Online	138	149.8	32
Cisco Systems	119	189.6	36
Microsoft	81	406.3	20
eBay	199	24.0	94
Yahoo!	158	34.5	41
@Home	150	16.8	315
Amazon	143	23.0	57
CMGI	240	11.2	89
Exodus	90	3.6	84

SOURCE: Adapted from *Fortune,* June 7, 1999, pp. 96, 98, and 100.

TABLE 2.11 | Executive Pay Versus Stock Return

Company	Executive	5-Year Total Compensation (thousands of dollars)	5-Year Annualized Stock Return (percent per year)
Integrated Health Services	Robert N. Elkins	43,526	−36
Advanced Micro	Walter J. Sanders III	38,401	−10
Cendant	R. Silverman	134,513	7
United Health Care	William W. McGuire	46,787	2
Occidental Petroleum	Ray R. Irani	125,453	8
Service Corp Int	Robert L. Waltrip	69,053	7
Health South	Richard M. Scrushy	147,869	10
Primark	Joseph E. Kasputys	47,677	8
Engelhard	Orin R. Smith	25,330	1
IBP	Robert L. Peterson	34,369	8
3Com	Eric A. Benhamou	40,414	10
TRW	Joseph T. Gorman	29,286	7
CSX	John W. Snow	21,250	2
Int'l Flavors and Frags	Eugene P. Grisanti	19,881	3
Eastman Kodak	George M. C. Fisher	38,955	11
Microsoft	William H. Gates	2,569	75
PeopleSoft	David A. Duffield	1,711	46
Paychex	Thomas Golisano	2,836	49
Altera	Rodney Smith	3,644	53

(continued)

TABLE 2.11 | Executive Pay Versus Stock Return (continued)

Company	Executive	5-Year Total Compensation (thousands of dollars)	5-Year Annualized Stock Return (percent per year)
Costco Cos	James D. Sinegal	2,167	41
Zions Bancorp	Harris H. Simmons	4,494	51
Sepracor	Timothy J. Barberich	5,485	71
Tellabs	Michael J. Birck	5,438	71
Berkshire Hathaway	Warren E. Buffet	500	35
Sanmina	Jure Sola	6,013	74
Commerce Bancorp	Vernon W. Hill II	3,855	39
Biomet	Dane A. Miller	1,579	34
Reinsurance Group Am	Greig Woodring	3,455	34
Express Scripts	Barrett A. Toan	5,607	43
Popular	Richard L. Carrion	4,091	36

SOURCE: Adapted from *Forbes,* May 17, 1999, p. 204.

13. You work for an advertising agency and are to find out whether recent Super Bowl Internet advertisers got their money's worth. As a first step in your analysis, enter the Table 2.12 data into an EXCEL worksheet. Then save them in a data file named HKBOWL.

TABLE 2.12 | The Year 2000 Super Bowl Effect

Advertiser	Daily Web Site Visitors Before Super Bowl Jan. 9–23 (unduplicated thousands)	Daily Web Site Visitors After Super Bowl Jan. 30–31 (unduplicated thousands)
WebMD.com	254	497
Lifeminders.com	210	491
Monster.com	396	414
ETrade.com	436	412
WWF.com	290	353
Hotjobs.com	83	282
WSJ.com	133	183
Pets.com	38	156
Kforce.com	4	108

SOURCE: Adapted from *The New York Times,* February 2, 2000, p. C10.

14. As a stock market analyst you are aware of the tremendous gains in the Nasdaq Composite Index since its inception in 1971: During the 1970s, the index moved from 100 to 151.14 (a gain of 51.14%). During the 1980s the index moved from 151.14 to 454.82 (a gain of 200.93%). And during the 1990s, the index moved from 454.82 to 3,620.24 (a gain of 695.27%). You want to analyze similarly the movements of the Dow Jones Industrial Average. As a first step in your analysis, enter the Table 2.13 data into an EXCEL worksheet. Then save them in a data file named HKDOW.

TABLE 2.13 | The Dow Jones Industrial Average During the 20th Century

Decade	Beginning Index	Ending Index
1900s	66.08	99.05
1910s	99.05	107.23
1920s	107.23	248.48
1930s	248.48	150.24
1940s	150.24	200.13
1950s	200.13	679.36
1960s	679.36	800.36
1970s	800.36	838.74
1980s	838.74	2,753.20
1990s	2,753.20	11,224.70

SOURCE: Adapted from *The Wall Street Journal,* December 13, 1999, p. C23.

15. As a stock market analyst you are studying the "merger moguls," companies that advise other companies in merger deals. As a first step in your analysis, enter the Table 2.14 data into an EXCEL worksheet. Then save them in a data file named HKMOGULS.

TABLE 2.14 | The Merger Moguls of 1999

Company	1999 Value of Deals (billion dollars)	1999 Number of Deals
Goldman Sachs	1,350.62	419
Morgan Stanley Dean Witter	1,134.66	458
Merrill Lynch	1,098.49	385
Credit Suisse First Boston	529.35	331
J. P. Morgan	516.24	245
Warburg Dillon Read	494.43	285
Salomon Smith Barney	457.87	282
Lazard Houses	376.44	166
Lehman Brothers	311.74	200
Deutsche Bank	293.30	234

SOURCE: Thomson Financial Securities Data

16. According to the National Bureau of Economic Research, the U.S. business cycle during the 20th century included 21 periods of expansion. You want to study them. As a first step in your analysis, enter the Table 2.15 data into an EXCEL worksheet. Then save them in a data file named HKBOOMS.

TABLE 2.15 | 20th-Century Economic Expansions in the United States

Period of Expansion	Number of Months
Dec. 1900–Sept. 1902	21
Aug. 1904–May 1907	33
June 1908–Jan. 1910	19
Jan. 1912–Jan. 1913	12
Dec. 1914–Aug. 1918	44
March 1919–Jan. 1920	10
July 1921–May 1923	22
July 1924–Oct. 1926	27
Nov. 1927–Aug. 1929	21
March 1933–May 1937	50
June 1938–Feb. 1945	80
Oct. 1945–Nov. 1948	37
Oct. 1949–July 1953	45
May 1954–Aug. 1957	39
April 1956–April 1960	24
Feb. 1961–Dec. 1969	106
Nov. 1970–Nov. 1973	36
March 1975–Jan. 1980	58
July 1980–July 1981	12
Nov. 1982–July 1990	96
March 1991–Feb. 2000+	108

17. It is mid-1999. You work for Merrill Lynch, which is just about ready to join the growing ranks of online brokerages. You are asked to analyze the competition, as summarized in the accompanying table. As a first step in your analysis, enter the Table 2.16 data into an EXCEL worksheet. Then save them in a data file named HKBOL.

TABLE 2.16 | U.S. Brokers on Line, Mid-1999

Broker	Assets (billion dollars)	Accounts (thousands)	Average Daily Trades
Schwab	219.0	2,500	138,250
E*Trade	21.1	909	65,800
Waterhouse	38.8	615	57,800
Datek	5.5	205	50,345
Fidelity	160.0	2,300	49,981
Ameritrade	19.5	428	41,252
DLJ Direct	11.2	590	19,062
Discover	5.9	134	13,838

TABLE 2.16 | (continued)

Suretrade	1.3	130	11,000
Nat'l Discount Brokers	6.8	125	6,580
Others	34.0	552	42,166

SOURCE: Adapted from *The New York Times,* June 2, 1999. p. C28.

18. The CD-ROM associated with this text contains an EXCEL worksheet file, HK100MN97, which contains selected 1997 data about the 100 largest U.S.-based multinationals. Open a new EXCEL project and add the file to it.

SECTION 2.5 MANIPULATING DATA

19. Review EXCEL Example 2.4 on page 50. Then find all the 1999 *Fortune 500* companies that were headquartered in Wisconsin.

20. Review EXCEL Example 2.4 on page 50. Then find all the 1999 *Fortune 500* companies that were headquartered in the state of Washington.

21. Review EXCEL Example 2.4 on page 50. Then find all the 1999 *Fortune 500* companies that were headquartered in Virginia.

22. Review EXCEL Example 2.4 on page 50. Then find all the 1999 *Fortune 500* companies that were headquartered in Texas.

23. Review EXCEL Example 2.4 on page 50. Then find all the 1999 *Fortune 500* companies that were headquartered in New York.

24. Review EXCEL Example 2.4 on page 50. Then find all the 1990 *Fortune 500* companies that were headquartered in New Jersey.

25. Review EXCEL Example 2.4 on page 50. Then find all the 1999 *Fortune 500* companies that were headquartered in Michigan.

26. Review EXCEL Example 2.4 on page 50. Then find all the 1999 *Fortune 500* companies that were headquartered in Massachusetts.

27. Review EXCEL Example 2.4 on page 50. Then find all the 1999 *Fortune 500* companies that were headquartered in California.

28. Review Practice Problem 9. Then open the file HKSTOCK, which was created at the time. Create a new worksheet containing the Foreign Stock Funds only.

29. Review Practice Problem 10. Then open the file HK20LFC, which was created at the time. Create a new worksheet containing German firms only.

SECTION 2.6 PRODUCING DESCRIPTIVE STATISTICS

30. The CD-ROM associated with this text holds an EXCEL worksheet file, HK99F500, which contains selected data about all companies on the 1999 *Fortune 500* list. Open a new EXCEL project and add the file to it. Then ask EXCEL to display descriptive statistics about *Pennsylvania* companies only, concerning

a. revenues and **b.** profits.

31. The CD-ROM associated with this text holds an EXCEL worksheet file, HK99F500, which contains selected data about all companies on the 1999 *Fortune 500* list. Open a new EXCEL project and add the file to it. Then ask EXCEL to display descriptive statistics about *Ohio* companies only, concerning

a. revenues and **b.** profits.

32. The CD-ROM associated with this text holds an EXCEL worksheet file, HK99F500, which contains selected data about all companies on the 1999 *Fortune 500* list. Open a new EXCEL project and add the file to it. Then ask EXCEL to display descriptive statistics about *North Carolina* companies only, concerning

a. revenues and **b.** profits.

33. The CD-ROM associated with this text holds an EXCEL worksheet file, HK99F500, which contains selected data about all companies on the 1999 *Fortune 500* list. Open a new EXCEL project and add the file to it. Then ask EXCEL to display descriptive statistics about *Missouri* companies only, concerning

a. revenues and **b.** profits.

34. The CD-ROM associated with this text holds an EXCEL worksheet file, HK99F500, which contains selected data about all companies on the 1999 *Fortune 500* list. Open a new EXCEL project and add the file to it. Then ask EXCEL to display descriptive statistics about *Maryland* companies only, concerning

a. revenues and **b.** profits.

35. Review Practice Problem 5. Then open the file HKMLB that was created at the time. Create a histogram of the 1999 market values of Major League Baseball teams.

36. Review Practice Problem 6. Then open the file HKNFL that was created at the time. Create a histogram of the 1999 market values of National Football League teams.

37. Review Practice Problem 7. Then open the file HKNHL that was created at the time. Create a histogram of the 1998/99 revenues of National Hockey League teams.

38. Review Practice Problem 8. Then open the file HKNBA that was created at the time. Create a histogram of the 1998/99 profits of National Basketball Association teams.

39. The CD-ROM associated with this text holds an EXCEL worksheet file, HK99F500, which contains selected data about all companies on the 1999 *Fortune 500* list. Open a new EXCEL project and add the file to it. Then ask EXCEL to create a histogram of the 500 companies' market values on 3/15/99.

40. You are working for Chase Manhattan. Your company is trying to enter Internet banking in a big way, but first you must learn about the competition. You know the market shares, as of January 2000: Wells Fargo 14.14%, Bank of America 9.55%, Citigroup 4.82%, Bank One 4.01%, Fleet/BankBoston 3.87%, First Union 2.96%, Washington Mutual 2.29%, Wachovia 1.81%. As a first step, try something new: Illustrate these data in a *pie chart.* (**Hint:** Enter the names and percentages into two worksheet columns; perhaps the range A1:B9. Click the **Chart Wizard** on the standard toolbar, followed by **Standard Types** > **Pie,** and respond to the choices.)

SECTION 2.7 DRAWING INFERENCES

41. Someone recently claimed that the current market price of National Hockey League teams could easily be explained by the teams' recent revenues. You find that hard to believe, but then you do have the Table 2.6 data, now stored in EXCEL file HKNHL. Use the 1999 data to check out the claim, creating a scatter-plot/regression-line graph like Figure 2.12.

42. Someone recently claimed that the current market price of National Basketball Association teams could easily be explained by the teams' recent revenues. You find that hard to believe, but then you do have the Table 2.7 data, now stored in EXCEL file HKNBA. Use the 1999 data to check out the claim, creating a scatter-plot/regression-line graph like Figure 2.12.

43. Someone recently claimed that the current market price of National Basketball Association teams could easily be explained by the teams' recent profits. You find that hard to believe, but then you do have the Table 2.7 data, now stored in EXCEL file HKNBA. Use the 1999 data to check out the claim, creating a scatter-plot/regression-line graph like Figure 2.12.

44. As you will learn in Chapter 16, a *correlation coefficient* expresses the strength of association between two variables in a single number. It ranges between 0 and -1, if one variable rises as the other falls. It ranges between 0 and $+1$, if the two variables both rise or fall together. Retrieve the EXCEL file HKEXEC that was created in Practice Problem 12. Then compute a correlation coefficient between executive compensation and stock performance. (**Hint:** Click **Tools** > **Data Analysis** > **Correlation** > **OK** and enter the C2:D31 input range when requested.)

45. Review Practice Problem 17. Then, using a procedure explained in Practice Problem 44, determine the strength of association between

a. assets and number of accounts.

b. number of accounts and average daily trades.

SECTION 2.8 GETTING HELP

46. You are eager to create a *hyperlink* but have no idea whether EXCEL can do it for you. Find the information via EXCEL's built-in Help feature.

47. While working out Practice Problem 46, you have stumbled onto the Microsoft EXCEL Help page. Make use of the Help page to find out all there is to know about EXCEL's *shortcut keys.*

48. While working out Practice Problem 46, you have stumbled onto the Microsoft EXCEL Help page. Make use of the Help page to find out all there is to know about EXCEL's *Analysis ToolPak.*

49. While working out Practice Problem 46, you have stumbled onto the Microsoft EXCEL Help page. Make use of the Help page to find out all there is to know about EXCEL's ability to *create charts.*

50. You have encountered the term *regression* several times in this chapter and have no idea what it means. Nor do you have your textbook on hand to read Chapters 16–18 right now. As a first step, you want EXCEL to teach you about its *regression analysis tool.* Use EXCEL's built-in Help feature to access relevant material.

PART II

COLLECTING DATA

Chapter
3

FINDING EXISTING DATA: FROM PRINT TO INTERNET

LOOKING AHEAD

After reading this chapter, you will know a great deal about finding external data, which are data that already exist in someone else's hands. Among other things, you will learn about:

1. major print sources of business and economic data, which until recently were the only significant external data sources,
2. basic Internet concepts to prepare you for finding data the 21st-century way,
3. important data sites on the World Wide Web, including those of U.S. government agencies, foreign statistical offices, and companies on the year 2000 *Fortune 500* list, and
4. a variety of techniques for grabbing data off the Internet and moving them into the worksheets of statistical computer applications, such as EXCEL or MINITAB.

AND HERE IS A TYPICAL PROBLEM YOU WILL BE ABLE TO SOLVE:

Visit http://www.whitehouse.gov, a site maintained by the White House. Click **Virtual Library** > **Contents of this Web site.** In the *search box,* type *Council of Economic Advisers* and click **Search.** Click **CEA Home Page** > **2000 Economic Report of the President** > **download current year statistical tables in spreadsheet format** > **corporate profit and finance** > **common stock prices and yields** > **xls.** The relevant table appears in EXCEL. If you wish, you can transfer it to MINITAB, with copy-and-paste-cells commands.

PREVIEW

Most people who are about to study business or economic issues are likely to turn, at least initially, to data collected by someone else. Until very recently, this meant turning to data available *in print.* And most of these printed data, in turn, were collected and published by some agency of *government.* There are historical reasons for this state of affairs.

In every country on earth, the earliest statisticians were interested in collecting and displaying information useful to the *state,* which is how *statistics* got its name. These early data gatherers collected data on births and deaths to aid officials in charge of the military draft. They collected data on diseases to aid others concerned with the public health. And to facilitate the collection of taxes, they collected data on the ownership of land and animals, on exports and imports, on incomes and expenditures, and more. Indeed, all this has been going on for a very long time.

As early as 3800 B.C., Babylonians used clay tablets to record agricultural yields and commodity trade, along with associated tax revenues. Ancient Egyptians kept track of population and wealth for similar reasons, and they did so long before the 1st pyramid was built. Books of the Bible, such as Numbers and Chronicles, have preserved data on the population and material belongings of the Israelites. No matter when and where you look—at China ca. 2000 B.C., at the Roman Empire in the 1st century, at the world of William the Conqueror a thousand years later—governments have always busily collected and published data. The English king just noted, for instance, cleverly put together the famous Domesday Book of 1086 (pronounced "Doomsday"—a foreshadowing of April 15 and the IRS?), listing the extent and value of all the landowners' estates and livestock that the supreme ruler could then tax. But as a look at present-day government publications, such as the *Statistical Abstract of the United States* or the *Economic Report of the President,* suggests, that good old tradition of statisticians aiding government has certainly not died out. In fact, nowadays we can do a lot better than record a few precious data on the walls of caves, sticks of wood, dried animal skins, or slabs of stone. Every government on Earth makes masses of data available to masses of people, not only by using paper and ink, but also by producing data-filled CD-ROMs for personal computers and, above all, by maintaining fancy Web sites on the Internet.

The U.S. government, for example, unlike most other governments around the world, does not have a single, centralized statistical office. Nevertheless, the numerous federal agencies that collect and publish data are jointly maintaining a single Internet site that can be visited via http://www.fedstats.gov. When you do, you will encounter the opening screen reproduced as Figure 3.1 on the following page.

From there you can access statistical data collected by over 70 agencies of the U.S. federal government. Elsewhere, you can now find similar sites maintained by the governments of other countries, by international agencies such as the Organization for Economic Cooperation and Development or the United Nations, and, of course, by an ever-growing number of business enterprises throughout the world. In this chapter you will learn where to find those mountains of data and how to bring them into your favorite computer program for analysis.

3.1 Introduction

On occasion, those who wish to study matters relating to business or economics are lucky because they already have the relevant data. A business administrator, for example, can simply search the firm's internal records for material that already resides in filing cabinets or computer memories. Thus, customer records would provide names, addresses, telephone numbers, data on amounts purchased, credit limits, and more. Employee records would provide names, addresses, job titles, years of service, salaries, Social Security numbers, and even numbers of sick days

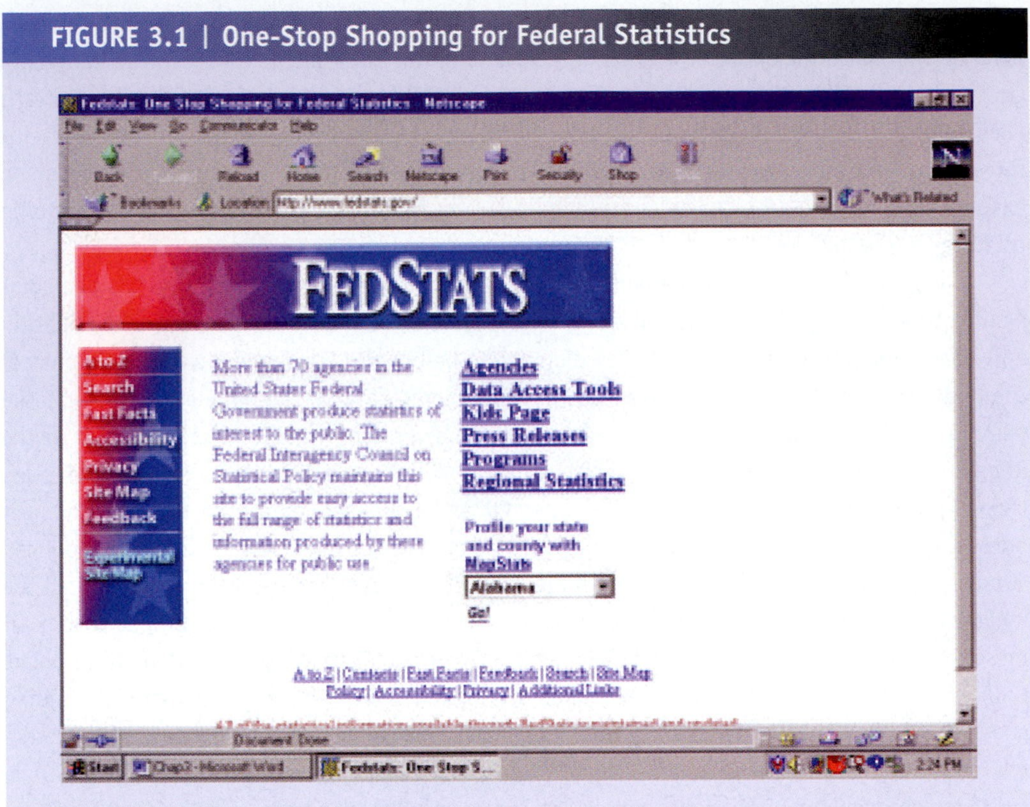

FIGURE 3.1 | One-Stop Shopping for Federal Statistics

used. Production records would contain lists of products, part numbers, and quantities produced, along with associated data on labor costs, raw material consumption, and equipment usage. A government economist could, similarly, access vast databases held by the Bureau of the Census, the Department of Labor, the Federal Reserve Board, and the Office of Management and Budget, to name but a few. From the point of view of the business administrator or the government economist, respectively, all of the data just mentioned are **internal data.** They were naturally created as a by-product of the regular activities of the very person, firm, or government that wants to use the data.

The focus of this chapter, however, is somewhere else. It deals with situations in which investigators know that relevant data exist, but those data are in the hands of others who might be persuaded to share them—just for the asking in some cases and for a hefty fee in others. The chapter, thus, focuses on **external data.** Such data were created by entities other than the person, firm, or government that wants to use them. As a student, you are already familiar with the use of preexisting external data. When writing your next paper, you are unlikely to generate brand-new information (although you will learn how to do so in the very next chapter). More likely, you will turn to data gathered by someone else. You will turn to some book or magazine, place a data-filled CD-ROM in your computer or, perhaps, even search the World Wide Web.

Until recently, data collected by others and made available *in print,* usually for a fee, have been the only type of external data. Such data, of course, continue to be available today. The very next section will identify some sources of them. In the past decade, however, a new and increasingly important source of external data has emerged. Potentially, the *World Wide Web* makes masses of data available to masses of people without the intervention of the printed page. This represents an enormous change from earlier days—even times as recent as the year of your birth. Thus, it makes sense to devote only a small part of this chapter to finding data in print, while devoting most of it to a typical 21st-century task: importing data to your computer from the *Internet.*

3.2 Finding Data in Print

Table 3.1 lists some of the most useful business and economic data sources that are available in print. Many of the publishers in question, however, also provide CD-ROMs containing preformatted data files that you can easily transfer to your favorite statistical computer application, such as EXCEL or MINITAB. More often than not, those CD-ROMs come at a hefty price.

TABLE 3.1 | Major Business and Economic Data Sources in Print

U.S. Federal Government

1. U.S. Bureau of the Census, *Statistical Abstract of the United States* (Washington, D.C.: U.S. Government Printing Office, published annually). Recent editions contain close to 1,500 tables of data. Also very helpful is an appendix containing a Guide to Sources of Statistics, State Statistical Abstracts, and Foreign Statistical Abstracts.
2. Council of Economic Advisers, *Economic Report of the President* (Washington, D.C.: U.S. Government Printing Office, published annually). Recent editions contain over 100 tables of data on all aspects of the economy.

International Organizations

3. International Monetary Fund, *World Economic Outlook* (Washington, D.C.: IMF, published biannually). Recent issues contain about 50 major tables of data on the global economy.
4. Organization for Economic Cooperation and Development, *OECD Economic Surveys* (Paris: OECD, published annually for each of the member countries). Contains numerous tables of data on all aspects of the economy.
5. United Nations, *Human Development Report* (New York: Oxford University Press, published annually). Recent editions contain about 50 major tables of economic and social data.
6. World Bank, *World Development Report* (New York: Oxford University Press, published annually). Recent editions contain about 25 major tables of economic and social data.
7. World Bank, *World Tables* (New York: Oxford University Press, published annually). Contains standardized data for more than 200 economies.

Other

8. *Forbes* (a bimonthly magazine). Contains masses of business data. In particular, look for annually recurring features such as 500 Biggest Private Companies / The Top 800 (executive compensation vs. stock performance) / The International 500 / Mutual Fund Survey / America's 400 Richest People / 200 Hot Small Companies / The Platinum List (America's best big companies) / The *Forbes 500s* / Annual Report on American Industry / The 200 Best Small Companies.
9. *Fortune* (a bimonthly magazine). Contains masses of business data. In particular, look for annually recurring features such as The *Fortune 500* / America's Most Admired Companies / The 100 Best Companies to Work For / The *Global 500* / The 100 Fastest-Growing Companies / The 40 Wealthiest Americans / The *Fortune e-50*.
10. *The Wall Street Journal* (a business-day newspaper). Contains masses of data in every issue.

3.3 Basic Internet Concepts

This chapter's introduction referred to the World Wide Web as well as the Internet. Although many people use the two terms interchangeably, they are not the same thing.

INTERNET VERSUS WORLD WIDE WEB

The **Internet** is larger than the Web. It consists of millions of computers, called **servers,** which are connected by telephone lines. Originally this planetary network of computers facilitated communication via e-mail, newsgroups, and FTP sites. As you probably know, **e-mail** involves a point-to-point transmission of a message in the form of text encoded in standard ASCII and uses addresses with those .com, .edu, .org, .gov and similar endings. In contrast, **newsgroups** are more like community bulletin boards: You post a message to a newsgroup and every member of the group can read it, while you don't even have to know who these members are. An **FTP (file transfer protocol) site,** finally, enables people to post materials not in text format but as binary files, which others with correct passwords can download to their computers.

The Internet is enormous, constantly changing, and forever growing. One of its outgrowths (and, thus, merely a part of it) is the **World Wide Web,** best seen, perhaps, as an enormous collection of computer files, called **Web pages.** These Web pages live on computers all over the world and contain **hyperlinks,** which, when clicked, cause a program known as a **Web browser** to find and display on the screen whatever other document has been specified in the link.

CONVENTIONS GOVERNING THE WEB

The World Wide Web is governed by certain conventions, including a document formatting standard called **hypertext markup language (HTML)** and a file-and-location description known as the **universal resource locator (URL).** The latter specifies the types of data in a file, the path to the data, and sometimes even their location within a document. Those who follow these conventions can easily create and share documents regardless of their physical locations and of computer platform and display requirements.

However, no one has to *register* a new Web page. No central clearinghouse for the ever-changing and ever-growing volume of Web pages exists. As a result, when you look for data on the Web, you cannot turn to some up-to-date, accurate index because no one has remotely succeeded in exhaustively cataloguing the staggering information on hundreds of millions of pages on the Web. What you can do is seek the help of *Web directories* and *search engines.*

SEARCHING THE WEB

So-called **Web directories,** with names such as Yahoo! and Lycos, Excite and Infoseek, Magellan and Starting Point, are partial indexes that enable you to explore the World Wide Web in either broad or finely tuned structures by clicking on lists of (someone else's) key terms again and again. These maps of cyberland are the creation of actual human beings who develop their indexes from Web pages that their owners have voluntarily registered. To keep you from being overwhelmed and help you narrow down your browsing, these editors divide the subject matter into at most 20 main topics. They link each of the main topics to subtopics, and to further subtopics, going down as many as 10 levels. But even at their best, these directories help you explore only a small percentage of existing Web pages.

In contrast, so-called **search engines,** with names such as AltaVista, HotBot, Internet Sleuth, NorthernLight, and Webcrawler, allow you to explore the World Wide Web by typing in key words of your own (rather than clicking on someone else's key words). No human intervention here. Search engines employ computer programs, known as **spiders** or **robots** (nicknamed **bots**) that compile huge indexes of Internet material and then use the indexes to find matches for search requests made by people seeking to explore the World Wide Web. They then present a list of hyperlinks to associated bunches of Web pages, called **Web sites,** containing the key words. Compared to Web directories, search engines have one advantage: They also look at sites that their creators have not registered with anyone. On the other hand, they cannot penetrate sites that are password protected or reside behind a server firewall. Thus, they too cover only a tiny portion of existing material.

BOOLEAN LOGIC AND SUCH

Searching for information on the Web can be a frustrating experience, even with the help of Web directories and search engines. You can help yourself by employing **Boolean logic.** Named after British mathematician George Boole (1815–1864), it supports efficient searches of the Web by the careful employment of logical connectors NOT, AND, OR (and sometimes NEAR or ADJACENT TO) between key words used in search requests.

Thus, if you are looking for information about the Ford Motor Company, merely typing in *Ford* is ill advised. The search engine will provide thousands of links not only to the company, but also to sites dealing with shallow places in bodies of water, the 38th president of the United States (or his wife), various members of the automobile manufacturer's family, the British writer Madox Ford (who examined adulterous relationships), the American filmmaker John Ford (who won an Academy Award for *The Grapes of Wrath*), and many more. So, this is what you can do:

- If your request includes two words linked by NOT, the search will drop all documents containing the word following NOT. If you request information about *Ford* NOT *President,* you automatically exclude all sites dealing with the president (or anything else you type after the word NOT). Unfortunately, using NOT will drop all documents that contain the second term *anywhere.* Thus, an auto company document referring to Henry Ford as company *president* would be excluded as well.
- If your request includes two words linked by AND, the search will only provide the limited set of documents that include both words, no matter how far apart. You might try *Ford* AND *Autos* to produce all documents corresponding to what Chapter 8 will call the *intersection of two events:* the joint appearance of *Ford* and *autos* in the same document.
- If your request includes two words linked by OR, the search will provide a vast set of documents containing either word, not necessarily both words at the same time. Calling for *Ford* OR *Autos,* will get you what Chapter 8 will call the *union of two events:* the appearance of either *Ford* or *autos* in any document, not necessarily both words at the same time.

Note: Some search engines allow you to substitute a plus sign (+) for AND and a minus sign (−) for NOT.

What you can also do—and that is, perhaps, the main advantage of reading this chapter—is to rely on the experience of others who have searched and found. The various sections of this chapter let you share some of that experience—with regard to data in print (nowadays often accompanied with CD-ROMs), numerous interesting Web sites, and special techniques for grabbing data from those sites.

3.4 Finding Data on the World Wide Web

This section identifies selected sources of data on the Web. All of these sources were available at the time of this writing, but keep in mind that the Web is forever evolving. On occasion, when you try to contact one of the addresses noted here, things will have changed.

U.S. GOVERNMENT SOURCES

Table 3.2 lists the author's favorite links to business and economic data published by the U.S. federal government.

Note: Just in case Table 3.2 fails to get you the information you seek, you are almost certain to find it by visiting http://ciir2.cs.umass.edu/Govbot/, the Center for Intelligent Information Retrieval site, which lets you type in key words and search more than 1.5 million Web pages from U.S. government sites.

TABLE 3.2 | Major U.S. Government Data Sources on the Web

Web Address	Comments
http://www.fedstats.gov	Takes you to the home pages of more than 70 federal agencies, ranging from the Bureau of Labor Statistics and the Bureau of the Census to the Environmental Protection Agency and the Occupational Safety and Health Administration. In addition, provides results of periodic censuses, economic profiles by state and county, and more.
http://www.fedworld.gov	The National Technical Information Service's portal to all federal government Web sites and millions of files, containing reports and databases.
http://www.census.gov/sdc/www	Takes you to the Web sites of 51 State Data Centers (50 states plus District of Columbia).
http://www.gpo.gov	Takes you to the Web site of the Government Printing Office, where you can note and order all available print products and also learn about links to documents in GPO databases.
http://www.sec.gov	Takes you to the Web site of the Securities and Exchange Commission, which, in turn, leads you to the EDGAR database of corporate information. (EDGAR stands for Electronic Data Gathering, Analysis, and Retrieval system.)
http://www.house.gov	Takes you to the Web site of the U.S. House of Representatives, with lots of links to data sources.
http://www.senate.gov	Takes you to the Web site of the U.S. Senate, with lots of links to data sources.
http://www.whitehouse.gov	Takes you to the Web site of the White House, with lots of links to data sources, including the *Economic Report of the President*.
http://www.federalreserve.gov	Takes you to the Web site of the Board of Governors of the Federal Reserve System, with lots of data and links to the 12 regional Federal Reserve Bank sites.

FOREIGN GOVERNMENT SOURCES

Table 3.3 lists the author's favorite links to business and economic data published by well over 100 foreign governments or international organizations around the world. (All of the addresses are also found on the CD-ROM that accompanies this text. Most of them lead to a home page in English. A few require you to read French or Spanish.)

TABLE 3.3 | Major Foreign Government Data Sources on the Web

Country	Web Address
Algeria	http://www.ons.dz/
Andorra	http://www.andorra.ad/govern/ministeris/finances/estudis/
Argentina	http://www.indec.mecon.ar/i_default.htm
Armenia	http://www.armstat.am/
Aruba	http://www.arubastatistics.com/
Australia	http://www.abs.gov.au/
Austria	http://www.oestat.gv.at/
Azerbaijan	http://www.azeri.com/goscomstat/
Barbados	http://www.bgis.gov.bb/statistics/
Belarus	http://president.gov.by/Minstat/en/main.html
Belgium	http://www.statbel.fgov.be/
Benin	http://planben.intnet.bj/13a/benin.htm
Bolivia	http://www.ine.gov.bo/
Brazil	http://www.ibge.gov.br/english/default.asp
Bulgaria	http://www.nsi.bg/
Cambodia	http://www.nis.gov.kh/
Canada	http://www.statcan.ca/
Chile	http://www.ine.cl/
China	http://www.stats.gov.cn/english/index.html
Colombia	http://www.dane.gov.co/
Costa Rica	http://www.meic.go.cr/inec/
Croatia	http://www.dzs.hr/
Cyprus	http://www.pio.gov.cy/dsr/index.html
Czech Republic	http://www.czso.cz/
Denmark	http://www2.dst.dk/internet/startuk.htm http://www.hagstova.fo/Welcome_uk.html
Dominican Republic	http://www.estadistica.gov.do/
Ecuador	http://www4.inec.gov.ec/
Egypt	http://interoz.com/economygoveg/index.htm
El Salvador	http://www.minec.gob.sv/presenta.htm/
Estonia	http://www.stat.ee/wwwstat/eng_stat/
European Community	http://europa.eu.int/comm/eurostat/
Fiji Islands	http://www.statsfiji.gov.fj/
Finland	http://www.stat.fi/index_en.html
France	http://www.insee.fr/ http://www.ined.fr/
Germany	http://www.statistik-bund.de/e_home.htm
Greece	http://www.statistics.gr/
Greenland	http://www.statgreen.gl/
Guatemala	http://www.ine.gob.gt/

(continued)

TABLE 3.3 | Major Foreign Government Data Sources on the Web (*continued*)

Country	Web Address
Hong Kong	http://www.info.gov.hk/censtatd/
Hungary	http://www.ksh.hu/eng/homeng.html
Iceland	http://www.stjr.is/statice/Welcome.html
India	http://www.censusindia.net/ http://www.nic.in/stat/
Indonesia	http://www.bps.go.id/
International Organizations	
FAO	http://www.fao.org/
IFC	http://www.ifc.org
ILO	http://www.ilo.org/
IMF	http://www.imf.org
OECD	http://www.oecd.org/
UN	http://www.un.org/Depts/unsd/ http://www.un.org/Pubs/CyberSchoolBus/infonation/e_infonation.htm
World Bank	http://www.worldbank.org
Iran	http://www.sci.iranet.net/
Ireland	http://www.cso.ie/
Israel	http://www.cbs.gov.il/engindex.htm
Italy	http://www.istat.it/homeing.html
Jamaica	http://www.statinja.com/
Japan	http://www.stat.go.jp
Jordan	http://www.dos.gov.jo/
Kazakhstan	http://www.kazstat.asdc.kz/indexe.htm
Korea	http://www.nso.go.kr/
Kuwait	http://www.mop.gov.kw/english/main0.htm
Kyrgyzstan	http://stat-gvc.bishkek.su/
Latvia	http://www.csb.lv/
Lebanon	http://www.cas.gov.lb/
Lithuania	http://www.std.lt/
Luxembourg	http://statec.gouvernement.lu/
Macao	http://www.dsec.gov.mo/
Malawi	http://www.nso.malawi.net/
Malaysia	http://www.statistics.gov.my/
Malta	http://www.magnet.mt/home/cos/
Marshall Islands	http://www.rmiembassyus.org/stats.html
Mauritania	http://www.ons.mr
Mauritius	http://ncb.intnet.mu/cso.htm
Mexico	http://www.inegi.gob.mx/
Moldova	http://www.moldova.md/index_en.html

(continued)

TABLE 3.3 *(continued)*

Country	Web Address
Mongolia	http://www.statis.pmis.gov.mn
Morocco	http://www.statistic.gov.ma/
Mozambique	http://www.ine.gov.mz/
Netherlands	http://www.cbs.nl/en/index.htm
New Zealand	http://www.govt.nz/ps/min/stats
Norway	http://www.ssb.no/www-open/english/
Oman	http://www.moneoman.org
Pakistan	http://www.statpak.gov.pk
Palestinian Authority	http://www.pcbs.org/
Panama	http://www.contraloria.gob.pa/direcciones/estycenso/index.htm
Paraguay	http://www.dgeec.gov.py/
Peru	http://www.inei.gob.pe/
Philippines	http://www.census.gov.ph/ http://www.nscb.gov.ph/
Poland	http://www.stat.gov.pl/english/index.htm
Portugal	http://www.ine.pt/ http://www.ip.pt/srea/
Romania	http://www.cns.ro/indexe.htm
Russia	http://www.gks.ru/eng/
Saint Lucia	http://www.stats.gov.lc/
Singapore	http://www.singstat.gov.sg/
Slovakia	http://www.statistics.sk/webdata/english/index2_a.htm
Slovenia	http://www.sigov.si/zrs/index_e.html
South Africa	http://www.statssa.gov.za/
Spain	http://www.ine.es/ http://www.istac.rcanaria.es
Sri Lanka	http://www.lk/national/census/sl_figures95.html
Sweden	http://www.scb.se/indexeng.htm
Switzerland	http://www.admin.ch/bfs/eindex.htm
Taiwan	http://www.dgbasey.gov.tw/
Thailand	http://www.nso.go.th/eng/index.htm
Tunisia	http://www.ins.nat.tn/
Turkey	http://www.die.gov.tr/ENGLISH/index.html
Ukraine	http://www.ukrstat.gov.ua/
United Arab Emirates	http://www.uae.gov.ae/mop/statistics.htm
United Kingdom	http://www.statistics.gov.uk/
Uruguay	http://www.ine.gub.uy/
Uzbekistan	http://www.gov.uz/mms100fr.html
Venezuela	http://www.ocei.gov.ve/
Yugoslavia	http://www.szs.sv.gov.yu/homee.htm

Note: On occasion, the statistical offices of some countries change their Web addresses and those of other countries add theirs. To get an update, visit http://www.census.gov/main/www/stat_int.html.

And here is a tip: If you can't find a specific country listing in Table 3.3, visit the second of the UN sites listed in the table. This so-called InfoNation site provides neatly organized data for all UN member states.

FORTUNE 500 COMPANY SOURCES

Table 3.4 provides excerpts from a much larger table on the CD-ROM accompanying this text and containing data about all *Fortune 500* companies on the year 2000 list. Click a Web address to visit a company's home page and find additional data. (The list of companies itself, of course, changes over the years. For an update, visit http://www.fortune.com/fortune/fortune500/index.html.)

TABLE 3.4 | *Fortune 500* Company Data Sources on the Web

Company	Industry	State	Web Address
General Motors	Motor vehicles and parts	MI	http://www.gm.com
Ford Motor	Motor vehicles and parts	MI	http://www.ford.com
Wal-Mart Stores	General merchandisers	AR	http://www.wal-mart.com
Exxon	Petroleum refining	TX	http://www.exxon.com
General Electric	Electronics/electrical equipment	CT	http://www.ge.com
Intl. Business Machines	Computers/office equipment	NY	http://www.ibm.com
Citigroup	Diversified financials	NY	http://www.citi.com
Philip Morris	Tobacco	NY	http://www.philipmorris.com/default.asp
Boeing	Aerospace	WA	http://www.boeing.com
AT&T	Telecommunications	NY	http://www.att.com
•	•	•	•
•	•	•	•
H.J. Heinz	Food	PA	http://www.heinz.com
St. Paul Cos.	Property and casualty insurance	MN	http://www.stpaul.com
CBS	Entertainment	NY	http://www.cbs.com
Lear	Motor vehicles and parts	MI	http://www.lear.com
Gap	Specialty retailers	CA	http://www.gap.com
Northwest Airlines	Airlines	MN	http://www.nwa.com
Office Depot	Specialty retailers	FL	http://www.officedepot.com
Colgate-Palmolive	Soaps/cosmetics	NY	http://www.colgate.com
•	•	•	•
•	•	•	•

OTHER INTERESTING DATA SOURCES

The preceding sections have introduced the most obvious data sources that would be of interest to students of business and economics, but there are many others. Consider this sobering fact: At the time of this writing, the World Wide Web contained an estimated 800 million pages and no single search engine indexed more than 16 percent of it. (For an update on these measurements, visit http://www.wwwmetrics.com/.) Ultimately, you have to rely on other people's recommendations to select your favorite data-providing sites. Table 3.5 puts together a number of other interesting data sources that this author recommends.

Note: You can find still other sources on the CD-ROM that accompanies this text. If you want to search for additional sites on your own, here is a place to start: http://dir.yahoo.com/business_and_economy/economic_indicators/.

TABLE 3.5 | Additional Data Sources on the Web

Web Address	Comments
http://netec.wustl.edu/WebEc.html	WebEc, an attempt to categorize free information about business and economics on the Web; in particular, see *Economics Data* and *Business Economics*.
http://rfe.wustl.edu/EconFAQ.html	Resources for Economists on the Internet, a guide sponsored by the American Economic Association; in particular, see *Data*.
http://www.economagic.com/	Economagic, a database with over 100,000 U.S. economic time series. Subscribers can get all data in COPY/PASTE format, in the form of self-updating EXCEL files, and more.
http://www.lexis-nexis.com/business/	The Lexis-Nexis database tells you everything you want to know about business.
http://web.lexis-nexis.com/statuniv	Lexis-Nexis lets you search an index of over 100,000 statistical publications.
http://www.economist.com/	*The Economist* magazine's home page; for data, click the Economist Intelligence Unit.
http://interactive.wsj.com/home.html	*The Wall Street Journal* can lead you to lots of data.
http://www.nytimes.com/yr/mo/day/business/	*The New York Times* provides business data.
http://www.forbes.com/	The Web site of *Forbes* magazine provides lots of data from current and past print editions.
http://www.fortune.com/fortune/	The Web site of *Fortune* magazine provides lots of data from current and past print editions.
http://www.nber.org/data_index.html	The National Bureau of Economic Research provides plenty of online data.
http://www.worldwatch.org/	The Worldwatch Institute provides lots of unusual data series and links to other Web resources.
http://www.interquote.com/main.html	InterQuote provides continuously updating real-time market data for stocks, options, commodity futures, and more.

(continued)

TABLE 3.5 | Additional Data Sources on the Web *(continued)*

Web Address	Comments
http://www.hoovers.com/	Hoover's Online company capsules contain lots of data for thousands of U.S. firms; click on Hoover's Industry Sectors.
http://www.irin.com/	The Investor Relations Information Network provides a worldwide data bank of annual company reports.
http://www.econ-datalinks.org/	A searchable database sponsored by the American Statistical Association.
http://www.companiesonline.com	Dun & Bradstreet lets you search for information on over 100,000 public and private companies.
http://www.inc.com/500/	A site devoted to the 500 fastest-growing private U.S. companies, with a searchable database going back to 1982.
http://www.geoinvestor.com/countryindex.htm	An interesting 40-country database.
http://www.mediametrix.com	A site devoted to measuring everything that happens on the World Wide Web.

3.5 How to Grab Data off the Web

The preceding sections have introduced all kinds of sites at which you might find the data you care to use. One issue remains: How do you get those data onto the worksheet of your favorite software application, such as EXCEL or MINITAB?

COPY AND PASTE

The simplest procedure, which will work most of the time, involves nothing more difficult than the good old copy-and-paste approach.

1. At the Web site where your data are located, *select the data* you want by clicking at the beginning of the upper left number and, while pressing down the left mouse button, dragging the screen pointer right or down till you reach the end of the last number you want to grab. Release the mouse button. The desired block of data should be highlighted. An alternative approach: Just click at the beginning of the first row of your chosen data, scroll to the end of the last row you want, hold down Shift, and click at the end of your desired selection.

   Note: Often, when you merely want to highlight a single column of data, the highlighting still goes across all the columns. To prevent that, and to highlight an individual column only, hold down the Alt key while you drag.
2. Click **Edit** > **Copy** or merely click the **Copy** button on the toolbar to send the selected data to the clipboard.
3. In the target application, such as an EXCEL or MINITAB worksheet, click the first cell wherein you want your data to appear (and thereby activate that cell).
4. Click **Edit** > **Paste** or merely click the **Paste** button on the toolbar to send the selected data to your worksheet.

Note: The aforementioned procedure works in EXCEL, but you may have to use **Edit > Paste Cells** in MINITAB. If you are pasting text into an application that prefers RTF to plain text, you may have to use **Edit > Paste Special** and choose Unformatted text.

POSSIBLE COMPLICATIONS

Sometimes the four-step procedure just discussed does not work. One common reason involves national differences in the way large numbers and decimals are treated. In the United States, it is common practice to separate thousands from millions, millions from billions, and so on, with the help of commas. In other countries, the separation can involve spaces or periods or nothing at all. Thus, the number *one and a half million* would appear as 1,500,000 in the United States, but could look like 1.500.000 or 1 500 000, or even 1500000 elsewhere. Software applications can easily become confused as a result. EXCEL, for example, is happy with the commas. MINITAB refuses to accept them. Both programs would balk at 1.500.000 (seeing two decimal points in a single number) and at 1 500 000 (seeing three separate numbers).

The treatment of decimals can cause similar problems. EXCEL and MINITAB are happy with 34.67 but would misinterpret the German equivalent of 34,67 (as the *two* numbers 34 and 67).

Luckily, problems like these can easily be overcome by introducing an additional procedure after step 2 above:

3a. Instead of pasting your strangely formatted numbers (strange from the U.S. point of view!) into your worksheet directly, paste them into another application, such as Microsoft Word.

3b. Select your numbers as in step 1 above.

3c. Click **Edit > Replace** to activate the Find and Replace dialog box.

3d. What you do next depends on the nature of your problem:

If your problem is *spaces in the middle of large numbers,* enter a space in the *Find what* box (just touch the space bar once; the dialog box *seems* to be unchanged but does in fact contain an invisible space character). Then enter absolutely nothing in the *Replace with* box (that is, ignore the box) and click **Replace All**. A miracle occurs: Your numbers reconstitute themselves without the offending spaces. This is what you should expect. You asked that spaces be replaced with nothing.

If your problem is *periods in the middle of large numbers,* enter a period in the *Find what* box. Then enter absolutely nothing in the *Replace with* box (that is, ignore the box) and click **Replace All**. Your numbers reconstitute themselves without the offending periods.

If your problem is *commas instead of periods to indicate decimals,* enter a comma in the *Find what* box. Then enter a period in the *Replace with* box and click **Replace All**. Your numbers reconstitute themselves with U.S.-type decimal points.

Note: Be careful when using the scary **Replace All** button. You do *not* want to replace spaces or periods or commas anywhere except in your block of selected numbers. If you initially put the offending numbers into a larger document and then answer one of the queries incorrectly, you could lose all spaces, periods and commas throughout that larger document. However, if you do make that error, you can press Ctrl + Z fast to undo everything.

3e. Select your reformatted numbers as in step 1 above; then proceed with original steps 2–4.

SPECIAL PROCEDURES

Sometimes things are too complicated for the copy-and-paste approach. Depending on how data were put on a Web page originally, all kinds of complications can arise when you try to copy them. However, when you encounter problems, help may be close at hand—either on the Web page containing the data you covet or in the program to which you want to transfer them.

WEB AIDS Frequently, the creators of Web pages lend a helping hand. Consider, for example, the FedStats site introduced in this chapter's Preview. If you click Data Access Tools (clearly visible on page 82), you will learn that Web-based tools allow you to use your browser to view predefined reports and generate your own tables with data obtained through searches and queries of summary and microdata files.

The tools provided allow you to select statistical information interactively (for example, making a selection from a scrollable list on a form), to view the data in a variety of formats including HTML tables and graphics, to print data, or to download data into spreadsheets. Most of the tools require at least Netscape 3.x or Internet Explorer 3.x. Some also require you to have an up-to-date unzip program.

EXCEL While running EXCEL, click **Help**, tell the Office Assistant you want to "retrieve data from a Web page," and click **Search**. Read the advice. To get more advice, click the upper left **Show** button on the Help page, click **Contents** > **Using EXCEL to Work with Data on the Web**. There you will find a lengthy tutorial on the subject. Among other things, you can learn about EXCEL's Web Query approach, which allows you to specify which part of a Web page you want to copy and, with some exceptions, how much formatting you want to keep. All you have to do is click **Data** > **Get External Data** > **New Web Query** and follow the directions in the dialog box. Usually, you can have your Web data in moments.

MINITAB While running MINITAB, click **Help** > **Contents** > **Search**, type "importing: data" and click **Display**. Read the information. To learn more, click **Overview**. As you will see by following all the links, MINITAB's capabilities are vast. You can import data from database files by clicking **File** > **Query Database**, which activates the open database connectivity (ODBC) protocol. You can import data from some applications by clicking **File** > **Import Special Text**. This enables you to tell MINITAB how to interpret characters and lines and, thus, to place data into cells correctly. And you can even use the dynamic data exchange (DDE) approach, which establishes a link with another application such that any change of data in the source application automatically updates data in MINITAB.

Summary

1. On occasion, those who wish to study issues relating to business or economics are lucky because relevant data are already in their possession. They can simply mine their *internal* data sources. This chapter, however, focuses on *external* data sources, on situations in which investigators know that relevant data exist, but these data are in the hands of others who might be persuaded to share them.
2. Until recently, data collected by others and made available in print, usually for a fee, were the only type of external data. Major print sources of such external business and economic data are reviewed.
3. Nowadays, a part of the Internet, known as the *World Wide Web,* has the potential to make masses of data available to masses of people—without the intervention of the printed page. To facilitate an understanding of this revolutionary change, basic Internet concepts are reviewed.
4. Business and economic data on the World Wide Web can be found in many places. A number of important sites are introduced, including those of U.S. government agencies, of foreign statistical offices, and of all the companies on a recent *Fortune 500* list.
5. A variety of techniques are discussed for grabbing data off the Internet and moving them into the worksheets of statistical computer applications. The sim-

plest of these procedures is the copy-and-paste approach, but some data have to be reformatted before they can be imported into programs such as EXCEL or MINITAB.

Key Terms

Boolean logic
bots
e-mail
external data
FTP site
hyperlinks
hypertext markup language (HTML)
internal data
Internet
newsgroups
robots
search engines
servers
spiders
universal resource locator (URL)
Web Browser
Web directories
Web pages
Web sites
World Wide Web

Practice Problems

NOTES

1. All of this chapter's problems assume that you are connected to the Internet. Some may require the free Adobe Acrobat Reader to view PDF files. To download it, visit http://www.adobe.com/products/acrobat/readstep.html.
2. Many problems require the use of EXCEL or MINITAB, depending on your version of the text. (The latter program is found on the CD-ROM packaged with the MINITAB version of this text.) The program's major features are explained in text Chapter 2. Plenty of additional advice is available via the program's built-in Help feature.
3. Web sites are forever evolving. The addresses noted in these problems, and the solutions described on the accompanying CD-ROM, were current at the start of 2001. If things have changed in the meantime, you can still learn much about finding and retrieving data by solving a slightly different problem in a slightly different way.

SECTION 3.4 FINDING DATA ON THE WORLD WIDE WEB

SECTION 3.5 HOW TO GRAB DATA OFF THE WEB

1. Visit http://www.fedstats.gov, a site maintained by the Interagency Council on Statistical Policy.
   a. Click on **Agencies** and explore the manifold sources of U.S. federal government statistics. Make a list of five agencies that supply data to this site.
   b. Click on **Bureau of Economic Analysis > Regional Data > Gross state product (GSP) > Current-dollar GSP**. Then capture all the data (in millions of current dollars) for the United States as a whole, Alabama, Alaska, Arizona, Arkansas, and California.
   c. Move the data into your favorite software program, EXCEL or MINITAB. (*Tip:* If the program pastes all data into a single column initially, you can select and copy portions of that column successively and paste them into separate columns.)
2. Visit http://www.fedstats.gov, a site maintained by the Interagency Council on Statistical Policy.
   a. Click on **Agencies** and explore the manifold sources of U.S. federal government statistics. Make a list of five agencies that supply data to this site.
   b. Click on **Bureau of Labor Statistics > Data > Selective Access > National Employment, Hours, and Earnings**. Then answer the queries in succession, choosing Seasonally Ad-

justed, Women Workers (in 1000s), Manufacturing, Years 1990–2000, Format Table, Delimiters Spaces, and so on. Click on the **Retrieve data** button.

   c. Move the data into your favorite software program, EXCEL or MINITAB. (*Tip:* If the program pastes all data into a single column initially, you can select and copy portions of that column successively and paste them into separate columns.)

3. Visit http://www.fedstats.gov, a site maintained by the Interagency Council on Statistical Policy.

   a. Click on **Agencies** > **Bureau of Transportation Statistics** > **Commodity Flow Survey** > **Reports and Products** > **1997 Commodity Flow Survey**, then download a spreadsheet to your desktop showing the 1997 value of state-to-state commodity flows (in million dollars).

   b. Move the data into your favorite software program, EXCEL or MINITAB.

4. Visit http://www.fedstats.gov, a site maintained by the Interagency Council on Statistical Policy.

   a. Click on **Agencies** > **Bureau of the Census**. Under *Business,* click **Foreign Trade** > **Statistics** > **Country by 1-Digit SITC** > **1999** > **Australia** > **Year to Date**. Capture that year's U.S. exports to and imports from Australia (in million dollars).

   b. Move the data into your favorite software program, EXCEL or MINITAB. (*Tip:* Sometimes, when a program insists on placing a small but badly formatted table into a *single* column, you can paste it repeatedly into several columns and then erase irrelevant material in each column.)

5. Visit http://www.fedstats.gov, a site maintained by the Interagency Council on Statistical Policy.

   a. Click on **Agencies** > **Energy Information Administration** > **Historical Data**. In the *Summary Data* box, double-click **Monthly Energy Review**. Then click **Database** > **Energy Overview** > **Go Get It**. Capture the annual data on energy exports, imports, net imports, production, and consumption.

   b. Move the data into your favorite software program, EXCEL or MINITAB. (*Tip:* If the program pastes all data into a single column initially, you can select and copy portions of that column successively and paste them into separate columns.)

6. Visit http://www.fedstats.gov, a site maintained by the Interagency Council on Statistical Policy.

   a. Click on **Agencies** > **National Agricultural Statistics Service** > **Census of Agriculture** > **Rankings of Commodities by Market Value of Agricultural Sales** > **Iowa**. Capture the commodity data on farms, sales, and so forth.

   b. Move the data into your favorite software program, EXCEL or MINITAB. (*Tip:* If the program pastes all data into a single column initially, you can select and copy portions of that column successively and paste them into separate columns.)

7. Visit http://www.fedstats.gov, a site maintained by the Interagency Council on Statistical Policy.

   a. Click on **Agencies** > **National Agricultural Statistics Service** > **Online Database** > **County Data** > **Apple Production** > **Pennsylvania** > **Submit Request**. Download the data for 1998 apple production, saving them, perhaps, on your desktop.

   b. Move the data into your favorite software program, EXCEL or MINITAB. (*Tip:* If necessary, use Windows Explorer to locate the download file and double-click on it.)

8. Visit http://www.fedstats.gov, a site maintained by the Interagency Council on Statistical Policy.

   a. Click on **Programs** and explore the manifold sources of U.S. federal government statistics. Make a list of five programs that supply data to this site.

   b. Click on **National Accounts** > **Foreign Investment Accounts** > **Foreign direct investment in the U.S.** Then capture 3 years of data on different countries' direct invest position (in millions of dollars on a historical cost basis).

   c. Move the data into your favorite software program, EXCEL or MINITAB. (*Tip:* If the program pastes all data into a single column initially, you can select and copy portions of that column successively and paste them into separate columns.)

9. Visit http://www.fedstats.gov, a site maintained by the Interagency Council on Statistical Policy.

   a. Click on **MapStats** > **Alabama** > **State level only** > **Get Profile** > **1992 Economic Census**.

Then capture Alabama data on number of establishments, sales, and so on.

b Move the data into your favorite software program, EXCEL or MINITAB. (*Tip:* Sometimes, when a program insists on placing a small but badly formatted table into a *single* column, you can paste it repeatedly into several columns and then erase irrelevant material in each column.)

10. Visit http://www.sec.gov, a site maintained by the Securities and Exchange Commission. Click **Enforcement Division** > **Insider Trading** and find out all there is to know about bounties you can earn for reporting insider trading.

11. Visit http://www.whitehouse.gov, a site maintained by the White House. Click **Virtual Library** > **Contents of this Website**. In the *search box,* type *Council of Economic Advisers* and click **Search**. Click **CEA Home Page** > **2000 Economic Report of the President** > **download current year statistical tables in spreadsheet format** > **corporate profit and finance** > **common stock prices and yields** > **xls**. The relevant table appears in EXCEL. If you wish, you can transfer it to MINITAB, with copy-and-paste-cells commands.

12. Visit http://www.federalreserve.gov, a site maintained by the Federal Reserve Board. Click **General Information** > **Related Web Sites/Federal Reserve Banks** > **St. Louis** > **Data** > **Monthly Interest Rates** > **Update File**. Then ask for, and paste into your favorite computer program, EXCEL or MINITAB: the federal funds rate, the bank prime loan rate, the 6-month Treasury bill rate (auction average), and the 30-year conventional mortgage rate.

13. Visit http://www.ons.dz, a site maintained by Algeria's Office National des Statistiques. Find data about the country's agricultural production in recent years.

14. Visit http://www.indec.mecon.ar/i_default.htm, a site maintained by Argentina's National Institute of Statistics and Censuses. Find data about the country's foreign trade in recent years.

15. Visit http://www.statbel.fgov.be, a site maintained by the Belgian National Institute of Statistics. Find data about output price indexes in recent years.

16. Visit http://www.statcan.ca, a site maintained by Statistics Canada. Find data about the country's raw material prices in recent years.

17. Visit http://europa.eu.int/comm/eurostat, a site maintained by the European Community. Find out all you can about available databases.

18. Visit http://www.insee.fr, a site maintained by France's National Institute of Statistics and Economic Studies (INSEE). Identify the country's largest corporations, their sales, number of employees, and so forth.

19. Visit http://www.statistik-bund.de/e_home.htm, a site maintained by Germany's Federal Statistical Office. Find out about the makeup of the country's tax revenues.

20. Visit http://www.oecd.org, a site maintained by the Organization for Economic Cooperation and Development (OECD). Find out about the availability of statistical publications in computer readable formats.

21. Visit http://www.sci.iranet.net, a site maintained by the Statistical Center of Iran. Find out about Iran's production of different oil products in recent years.

22. Visit http://www.cbs.gov.il/engindex.htm, a site maintained by Israel's Central Bureau of Statistics. Find out about the site's downloadable zipped files that can be transferred into spreadsheets.

23. Visit http://www.stat.go.jp, a site maintained by the Japanese Statistics Bureau. Find out about the availability of computer readable media.

24. Visit http://www.kazstat.asdc.kz/indexe.htm, a site maintained by the National Statistical Agency of Kazakhstan. Find out about the extent of privatization.

25. Visit http://www.inegi.gob.mx, a site maintained by Mexico's National Institute of Statistics, Geography, and Informatics. Find out about the recent behavior of the Mexican stock market.

26. Visit http://www.gks.ru/eng/, a site maintained by the Russian State Committee for Statistics. Find out about the recent structure of Russia's exports by major commodities.

27. Visit http://www.statssa.gov.za, a site maintained by Statistics South Africa. Find out about the recent behavior of the country's producer prices.

28. Visit http://www.statistics.gov.uk/, a site maintained by the United Kingdom's Office for National Statistics. Find out about StatBase, an online data delivery system.

29. Visit http://www.gm.com, a site maintained by General Motors. Find out about the company's Hungarian operations.

30. Visit http://www.ford.com, a site maintained by Ford. Find out about the company's worldwide operations.

31. Visit http://www.exxon.com, a site maintained by Exxon. Find out about the behavior of the company's dividend payments in recent years.

32. Visit http://www.ge.com, a site maintained by General Electric. Find out about the behavior of the company's mutual funds in recent times.

33. Visit http://www.boeing.com, a site maintained by Boeing. Find out about recent orders and deliveries of commercial jets.

34. Visit http://www.att.com, a site maintained by AT&T. Find out about the recent behavior of Dow Jones Industrial Average components (of which AT&T stock is one).

35. Visit http://www.lear.com, a site maintained by Lear. Find out about the recent value of the company's stock, the number of shares outstanding, and the market cap.

36. Visit http://www.nwa.com, a site maintained by Northwest Airlines. Find out about the company's revenues, expenses, and profits, as listed in its latest quarterly report filed with the Securities and Exchange Commission.

37. Visit http://www.officedepot.com, a site maintained by Office Depot. Find out about the company's recent sales, number of stores, their locations around the world, and so forth.

38. Visit http://www.colgate.com, a site maintained by Colgate-Palmolive. Find out about the company's net income and earnings per share during the past decade.

39. Visit http://www.monsanto.com, a site maintained by Monsanto. Find out about the company's recent revenues (in millions of dollars) from different types of pharmaceuticals. (In 1999, the company's arthritis medication *Celebrex* set industry records on total prescription volume, refills, and cumulative days of patient use.)

40. Visit http://www.sch-plough.com, a site maintained by Schering-Plough. Find a copy of the company's latest balance sheet.

41. Visit http://www.oracle.com, a site maintained by Oracle. Find copies of the company's income statements for recent fiscal periods.

42. Visit http://rfe.wustl.edu/EconFAQ.html, a site sponsored by the American Economic Association. Find annual data for Moody's corporate bond yield averages.

43. Visit http://www.economagic.com, a site maintained by Economagic. Find a time series of the NASDAQ Composite Index.

44. Visit http://www.nytimes.com/yr/mo/day/business, a site maintained by *The New York Times.* Find out about the current activity at the American Stock Exchange.

45. Visit http://www.forbes.com, a site maintained by *Forbes* magazine. Find the latest list of *Forbes 500* companies, ranked by market value.

46. Visit http://www.fortune.com, a site maintained by *Fortune* magazine. Find the latest list of *Fortune 500* companies and identify pharmaceutical companies, along with their revenues, profits, and so forth.

47. Visit http://www.nber.org/data_index.html, a site maintained by the National Bureau of Economic Research. Find out all you can about its online economic data available for downloading.

48. Visit http://www.worldwatch.org, a site maintained by the Worldwatch Institute. Find out all you can about its downloadable data sets.

49. Visit http://www.irin.com, a site maintained by the Investor Relations Information Network. Find out all you can about the behavior of the stock of Adobe Systems during the past three years.

50. Visit http://www.inc.com/500, a site maintained by Inc.com. Find a list of America's fastest growing private companies for the most recent available year.

Generating New Data: Census Taking and Sampling

LOOKING AHEAD

After reading this chapter, you will understand how new data can be generated by census taking or sampling. Among other things, you will learn to:

1. appreciate numerous reasons for taking samples rather than conducting censuses,
2. distinguish useless nonprobability samples from valuable probability samples,
3. take your own simple random samples with the help of a random numbers table or a computer's random-numbers generator,
4. create other types of random samples, including systematic, stratified, and clustered samples,
5. recognize the sources of random error and systematic error in survey data, and
6. avoid selection bias, nonresponse bias, and response bias, all of which can creep into surveys and invalidate their results.

AND HERE IS A TYPICAL PROBLEM YOU WILL BE ABLE TO SOLVE:

Domino's Pizza once was sued by Amstar, maker of Domino sugar, on the grounds that use of this name confused people. Indeed, Amstar had interviewed women shopping in supermarkets, had shown them a Domino's Pizza box, and had asked whether they thought the pizza makers produced any other product. Some 71 percent said "sugar." If you were a statistician hired by Domino's Pizza, how could you help your client?

PREVIEW

In the summer of 1936, the editors of the *Literary Digest* magazine wanted to predict the next U.S. president, just as they had successfully done five times before. They sent out postcards to 10 million Americans and, on the basis of the replies, announced that Alfred M. Landon, then governor of Kansas, would gain 57 percent of the popular vote and, thus, demolish Franklin D. Roosevelt, the incumbent president. In fact, Roosevelt won by a landslide never before seen in U.S. history. He garnered not the predicted 43 percent, but 62.5 percent of the popular vote and all but 8 of 531 electoral votes. The *Digest* never survived the debacle and folded shortly thereafter. What had gone wrong?

The *Digest*'s poll had been flawed in two ways. First, there was *selection bias:* The people in the sample differed in significant ways from those left out of it. The magazine had mailed its questionnaires to 10 million people whose names had been taken from various sources, such as mailing lists of its own subscribers, club membership rosters, telephone directories, and automobile registration rolls. As a result, higher-income people, who typically voted Republican, were well represented in the *Digest*'s sample. On the other hand, lower-income people, who heavily favored the Democrats, were underrepresented. During the Great Depression, fewer working-class folks could afford magazine subscriptions, club memberships, telephones, and automobiles.

Second, the survey suffered from *nonresponse bias:* The people responding to the questionnaires also differed systematically from the nonrespondents. Only 2.4 million of the 10 million questionnaires were mailed back. Although this made the survey the largest sample ever taken, the answers were skewed nevertheless. A large percentage of more educated people mailed back the questionnaires; a much smaller percentage of the less educated did. The former tended to favor the Republicans; the latter, the Democrats. Thus, a much larger percentage of the nonrespondents than of the respondents favored Roosevelt. This nonresponse bias reinforced the selection bias.

Unfortunately, people are slow to learn from history. In 1948, using another dubious procedure (a form of sampling called *quota sampling*), Gallup's organization (along with Crossley's and Roper's) incorrectly predicted the victory of Thomas E. Dewey, then governor of New York, over Harry S. Truman, another incumbent president. Yet Truman won 52.4 percent of the popular vote. Besides having missed last-minute changes in voter attitudes, the pollsters had again used a national sample that underrepresented the relatively poor. The accompanying photo shows a victorious President Truman with an early edition of the *Chicago Daily Tribune,* which had placed a bit too much confidence in the polls.

Are we more enlightened nowadays? You shouldn't bet on it. In the summer of 1992, before Ross Perot decided to run for president, his *electronic town meeting* proposal gained wide popular support: As president, he and various experts would discuss issues and lay out policy options before a national television audience. People would vote instantly by calling an 800 number or sending an e-mail, and the will of the people would be instituted.The idea suggested efficiency and citizen democracy on a huge scale. It appealed to those who felt disenfranchised by politics as usual and wanted to bypass Congress. Yet the perils of this approach surely outweighed its promise. The 800 number would be flooded by people who cared passionately about an issue. Millions of

others would neither watch nor respond, for lack of interest or lack of access to the kind of telephone or home computer needed. The result would be as unrepresentative as the *Digest*'s postcards. In addition, a loaded selection of speakers and a manipulative scripting of questions could easily elicit any predetermined type of response. Consider this case in point: During the same 1992 presidential campaign, *The New York Times* joined *CBS News* to poll the electorate on whether the nation was spending too much, too little, or just the right amount on "assistance to the poor"; 13 percent said *too much* and 64 percent *too little.* When the same people were asked the same question in a different way (was spending "on welfare" too much, too little, or about right), 44 percent said *too much* and 23 percent *too little.* Unless the respondents perceived a major difference between "the poor" and "people on welfare," both answers could hardly have been correct at the same time.

All of these stories neatly illustrate the problem that economists face when they try to predict, say, the onset of a recession or that business executives face when they seek to identify the preferences of potential customers. Almost always, it is simply too complicated, costly, and time-consuming to contact *everyone* who might possess the kind of information that one seeks. Some kind of sampling, similar to that pioneered by the *Digest,* is inevitable. Yet careless sampling can seriously mislead. That is why the collection of *reliable* data is the first priority of every statistician's work. Relevant techniques and the avoidance of error are this chapter's major concerns.[1]

[1]Adapted from Maurice C. Bryson, The *Literary Digest* Poll: Making a Statistical Myth," *The American Statistician,* November 1976, pp. 184–185; Frederick Mosteller et al., *The Pre-Election Polls of 1948* (New York: Social Science Research Council, 1949); "1-800-TROUBLE," *The New York Times,* June 13, 1992, p. 22; and Robin Toner, "Politics of Welfare: Focusing on the Problems," *The New York Times,* July 5, 1992, p. 1.

4.1 Census Taking versus Sampling

In principle, new data can be generated either by an observational study, also called a *survey,* or by an experiment. This chapter focuses on surveys. Two types of surveys exist: complete and partial.

DEFINITION 4.1 A **census** is a *complete* survey in which observations about one or more characteristics of interest are made for every elementary unit that exists.

DEFINITION 4.2 A **sample survey** is a *partial* survey in which observations about one or more characteristics of interest are made for only a subset of all existing elementary units.

Every census aims to collect a data set consisting of at least one statistical population, but possibly several of them (as in columns 2–6 of Table 1.8 on page 16). Unfortunately, when the number of elementary units is very large, complete success in observing the characteristics of all of these units is likely to elude the census takers. Nevertheless, any reasonably successful

APPLICATION 4.1

GREAT CENSUSES OF THE 1990S

Contrary to common belief, a census does not necessarily ensure more reliable results than do sampling techniques, especially when large numbers of elementary units are involved. The great population censuses of the 1990s provide cases in point.

CASE 1. Consider the likelihood of error in the most ambitious census ever undertaken in the world's history, that of mainland China in 1990. Seven million census workers (enumerators, supervisors, coders, data-entry workers, and computer technicians) were organized to find, count, and classify an estimated 1 *billion* people. They combed every house in the great cities, every shack in the countryside, every nomad's tent in faraway Mongolia. Yet many of the respondents had good reasons not to cooperate: By underreporting births, they avoided criticism of their attitude toward family planning (as well as fines and possible sterilization). By not reporting deaths, they assured themselves larger rations of grain, cloth, and housing space. By hiding from census takers, an estimated 50 million illegal migrants avoided being sent back to places they had left. Nevertheless, the Chinese government reported the population at *precisely* 1,133,682,501.

CASE 2. Many statisticians view the U.S. census of 1990 as another bleak landmark in the annals of arithmetic. This census was also based on the idea that the government can count Americans the way a child counts marbles: 1, 2, 3, . . . , and 248,709,873 (the official result). But consider the diversity, mobility, and uncooperativeness of such a large population, which are bound to make the count highly inaccurate. Consider the processing errors that the 350,000 census workers were bound to make.

Initially, fewer than 50 percent of census forms mailed to addresses in large cities were returned. Some people never got them. Others treated them as junk mail or found them too complex and still others were too busy and forgot or suspected some kind of IRS trick. Yet, in the end, the Census Bureau claimed "a very complete, full, and fair count of everyone, including the homeless." Critics merely scoffed. Using their own lists of licensed drivers, registered voters, utility-bill payers, Medicaid recipients, and more, critics checked the official results in selected areas and noted rampant double counting and undercounting. Consider a family counted in New York and again at its Florida vacation home; consider an illegal alien hiding from the authorities. Consider the obvious processing errors: large numbers of 112-year-old parents with 109-year-old children; 14-year-old widowers and divorcees; 27-year-old workers with 42 years of work experience!

Before long, cities like New York, Chicago, Miami, and Los Angeles, all of which argued that their inner-city minority residents had been undercounted, filed suit to correct the census results. Political representation and federal grants depended on population figures, and city governments wanted to have the numbers changed. Yet, after much wrangling, the U.S. Supreme Court ruled in 1996 that the Bureau of the Census was not obligated to make such corrections.

CASE 3. In 1991, Nigeria closed its borders, shut down shops, factories, government offices, and international airlines, and told its citizens to stay home for a week. Backed by a 7 A.M. to 7 P.M. curfew and the threat of six months in jail for citizens who failed to cooperate, 700,000 census workers crisscrossed the West African nation—using Land Rovers and donkeys, horses and canoes. As in the United States, population counts had important implications for electoral representation as well as for the allocation of government funds. Great precautions were taken. Once a person was counted, his or her thumbnail was marked with indelible ink. Yet acrimony, fraud, and violence were common. Some census workers (as in some U.S. cities) were beaten and kidnapped; others were bribed to swell the total. Still others saw villagers fleeing into the bush before them; it was a bad omen to be counted! Provisionally, the government reported a population of 88.5 million, but final data had not been released even by the end of the decade. At that time, the World Bank *estimated* Nigeria's population at over 120 million, Africa's largest.

SOURCES: Adapted from Nicholas D. Kristof, "China Counts Its Billion-Plus Noses," *The New York Times,* July 2, 1990, p. A3; *idem,* "Census by China Finds 1.13 Billion," *The New York Times,* October 31, 1990, p. A8; James Gleick, "The Census: Why We Can't Count," *The New York Times Magazine,* July 15, 1990, pp. 22–26 and 54; Robert Pear, "Leave Census as Is, Republicans Urge," *The New York Times,* July 29, 1990, p. A25; Kenneth B. Noble, "Nigeria, Its Borders Sealed, Sends 700,000 Workers to Take Census," *The New York Times,* November 29, 1991, pp. Al and 15; Linda Greenhouse, "High Court Rules Results Are Valid in Census of 1990," *The New York Times,* March 31, 1996, pp. A1 and 22; and Abraham Okolo, "The Nigerian Census: Problems and Prospects," *The American Statistician,* November 1999, pp. 321–325.

attempt to collect data on an entire statistical population is referred to as a census. Application 4.1, *Great Censuses of the 1990s,* on the preceding page considers three interesting cases in point.

Statisticians use a variety of procedures to collect census data. One possibility is *direct observation* of some ongoing activity by an investigator who might record, say, the net weights of cereal boxes as they are being filled by a machine or the numbers and brands of such boxes as they are being picked up by customers from a supermarket shelf. A census can also proceed by *self-enumeration,* as when people, having read a set of instructions, make written replies on questionnaires that they received in the mail, on the street corner, or, perhaps, when purchasing an appliance. Finally, a census can involve a *personal or telephone interview* in which an investigator asks questions printed on a carefully prepared list or "schedule" and records the verbal answers that people give. More often than not, however, these same procedures are applied to partial surveys. In such cases, the resultant data set consists of one or more samples (as noted in column 6 of Table 1.8 on page 16). Survey takers hope that the sample data mirror the population data in the sense that valid inferences can be drawn from any given sample about the corresponding, but unknown, statistical population. Whether that hope is justified depends very much on the type of sample that is taken (which we discuss in later sections). Application 4.2, *Sampling as Legal Evidence,* illustrates how sampling is becoming ever more acceptable in all sorts of unexpected areas of our lives.

Sampling as Legal Evidence

Judicial procedures in the United States are designed to establish guilt or innocence "beyond a reasonable doubt" (in criminal cases) or by a "preponderance of evidence" (in civil cases). One would think that statistical data would play a large role in this process. Indeed, official publications of census-like counts, such as those published by the Bureau of the Census, have usually been considered admissible evidence, but counts based on sampling have often encountered hurdles. The courts' negative attitude toward sampling has changed recently, partly because modern election polls have established the power of sampling and partly because we now recognize that crucial knowledge oftentimes cannot be secured in any other way. Thus, the courts have accepted estimates of market shares based on store samples, of mineral deposits based on test drillings, and of depreciation based on samples of plant facilities. In one case, involving a tax refund, a court refused to accept sample evidence based on several hundred thousand sales slips; it insisted on a complete count. Yet the census result fell within 1 percent of the sample estimate.

Courts are still reluctant to accept evidence secured through sampling when interviewing is involved because these interviews are considered *hearsay evidence.* This term refers to evidence that is based not on a witness's personal knowledge but on matters told to him or her by another. Courts have, however, allowed exceptions even here, as long as interview responses did not concern the truth of the matters but only the respondents' state of mind. If respondents are asked whether two trademarks represent the same manufacturer, the interviewers know the facts already. Their goal is to find out whether the respondents know these facts. The interviewers in such cases are deemed competent witnesses. Sample surveys conducted under this rubric have been concerned with consumer awareness to establish (1) whether trademarks or advertising slogans were sufficiently established in consumers' minds to grant them continued legal protection, (2) whether a new trademark was sufficiently different from an existing one to allow its registration, (3) whether certain words, such as "English lavender," were taken literally, thus possibly violating truth-in-labeling acts, and (4) whether certain brand names, such as "Thermos" or "Xerox," were still mentally connected with a specific manufacturer or had become generic names that could no longer be protected.

Courts have also allowed sample evidence secured by interviewing to establish the existence or absence of community prejudice against a defendant and the need to postpone the trial or move it to another community where a fair trial would be more likely.

SOURCE: Adapted from Hans Zeisel, "Statistics as Legal Evidence," *International Encyclopedia of Statistics, vol. 2* (New York: Free Press, 1978), pp. 1118–1119.

4.2 The Reasons for Sampling

Statisticians often have good reasons to undertake sample surveys instead of censuses. In one way or another, all the reasons typically cited for preferring sampling to census taking have something to do with (1) reducing information-gathering costs for a given type of information, or (2) increasing the quantity or quality of information received for a given cost. We cite six such reasons.

PROHIBITIVE COST OF A CENSUS

First, the total cost of collecting and processing data can be huge in a census. Even when the per-unit cost of contacting any single elementary unit is low, the total cost becomes a crucial consideration whenever the number of relevant elementary units is very large. The U.S. Bureau of Labor Statistics, for example, gathers its monthly unemployment data not by questioning the more than 140 million members of the labor force, but by contacting a mere 60,000 households. The information so received is, nevertheless, a reliable indicator of what would be known if the BLS took a complete census. Thus, desired information can be gained with a sample survey at a fraction of what a census would cost.

For the same reason, business firms interested in consumer preferences concerning old or new products never survey all existing consumers but only a tiny percentage of them. Firms even answer questions about their *internal* operations by sampling whenever a census would be too unwieldy and costly. Consider a bank that wishes to ascertain the percentage of errors made when crediting monthly interest to 3 *million* savings accounts or when billing 5 *million* credit accounts. The clerical cost of conducting a census of all accounts would be enormous.

PHYSICAL IMPOSSIBILITY OF A CENSUS

Second, a census is sometimes physically impossible (that is, infinitely costly), as when the number of elementary units is infinitely large or when some units are totally inaccessible. Any *process* that is expected to operate indefinitely under identical conditions, for example, generates an infinite number of outcomes. Thus, a census can never observe all the outcomes of this process. It can never record all the defective memory chips likely to be produced by a new and ongoing production process or all the effects ever to be produced by a new drug. In such situations, sampling cannot be avoided. The same is true when some elementary units are practically impossible to contact, such as all the birds in North America or all the airplanes presumed to have crashed in the ocean or in remote mountain regions or even all the people with addresses unknown or temporarily hospitalized in intensive care.

DESTRUCTIVE NATURE OF A CENSUS

Third, a census is senseless (that is, again, infinitely costly) whenever the acquisition of the desired information destroys the elementary units of interest. Consider questions about the lifetime of batteries or about the quality of flashbulbs or seeds produced by a firm. If every battery, flashbulb, or seed were tested, all of the output would be used up and the answers to the original questions would be useless.

LACK OF TIME FOR A CENSUS

Fourth, a census is senseless whenever it produces information that comes too late. Consider political-opinion polling undertaken prior to an election. A census of many millions of registered voters (or even repeated censuses in the face of rapidly fluctuating preferences) would take too long to yield results. Only sampling can provide the desired information in time.

MORE INFORMATION PER DOLLAR WITH SAMPLING

Fifth, for a given cost, sampling can provide *more detailed* information than a census. Consider how many more questions the Bureau of Labor Statistics could ask those 60,000 households if it spent the same amount of money, or even a quarter of the money, that it would have to spend on a census of the entire labor force, more than 140 million persons.

MORE ACCURATE INFORMATION WITH SAMPLING

Sixth, sampling can provide *more accurate* data than a census. This seems paradoxical but is true. Fewer statistical workers are needed, and they can be better trained and more effectively supervised. Thus, a given cost yields higher-quality information.

4.3 Two Basic Types of Samples

Given the frequency with which sample surveys are employed, for all of the reasons noted in the previous section, we must understand a number of basic facts about sampling now, at the very outset of our journey into the world of statistical reasoning. Depending on the method by which elementary units are selected for observation, one of two basic types of sample will emerge: a *nonprobability sample* or a *probability sample.*

DEFINITION 4.3 Whenever a subset of all existing units is selected *haphazardly* from a statistical frame (or from an associated statistical population), without the use of some randomizing device that assures each unit a known and positive probability of selection, the resultant sample is a **nonprobability sample.**

DEFINITION 4.4 Whenever a subset of all existing units is selected from a statistical frame (or from an associated statistical population) with the help of some randomizing device that assures each unit a known and positive (but not necessarily equal) probability of selection, the resultant sample is a **probability sample** or **random sample.**

In general, information gathered with the help of nonprobability samples is highly suspect and should not be trusted. Nevertheless, lots of people do take such samples, which makes it important to discuss them here. Probability samples, on the other hand, provide very reliable data. As noted, the U.S. Bureau of Labor Statistics does not gather its unemployment figures by taking a *census* and questioning more than 140 million members of the labor force each month. The bureau takes a *probability sample* of a mere 60,000 households instead, and the result is almost as good. Why should you believe the latter claim?

Consider an analogy. Suppose we wanted to determine the proportion of green and yellow peas in a given sackful. If the peas were thoroughly mixed, we could surely take a mere cupful from the sack and get our answer by counting the peas in that cup. The result would be almost exactly the same as if we counted all the peas in the sack. And the same would continue to be true if we had not a sackful, but a truckload of peas, or even an entire trainload of them. Even then a sample of a single cupful would answer our question, *provided* the peas were still thoroughly mixed. In the same way, one can learn about the employment/unemployment status of the entire labor force by merely counting the employed (green peas) and the unemployed (yellow peas) in a sample of the labor force, provided the sample is properly selected (and, thus, contains a thorough mixture of the employed and unemployed). Indeed, the same principle is at work whenever you take a blood test. It would never occur to you and your doctor to drain your entire blood supply (that is, to take a census). A tiny sample will do just fine because we know that everything in your blood is thoroughly mixed as a result of the continuous pumping of your heart.

NONPROBABILITY SAMPLES

Many types of nonprobability samples exist. Here we consider:

- the voluntary response sample
- the convenience sample
- the judgment sample

The worst kind of sample, because it leads to the least reliable results, is not even chosen by the statistician who seeks information. It is the **voluntary response sample,** which consists of people who, in response to some general appeal, have selected themselves to participate in a survey. Consider the people who fill out cards often found at hotels or restaurants that ask "How well did we serve you?" Consider the people who write to their representatives in Congress about one issue or another. Consider the people who respond to appeals on their television screens: "Call this number if you are in favor of X; call that other number if you are against X." In all these cases and many more, only those with strong opinions (and, perhaps, the time and money to waste on that telephone call) will *self-select* themselves into the sample. It is very doubtful that their views will represent the population at large.

Another kind of nonprobability sample, which does involve the statistician, is hardly any better. When samples are selected primarily for expediency in the sense that only the most easily accessible elementary units are chosen for observation, the resultant subset of all elementary units, or of an associated statistical population, constitutes a **convenience sample.** Convenience samples seldom if ever represent a statistical population in the sense that valid inferences can be drawn from the sample about the population. The selection procedure based on convenience almost ensures the opposite: The results may tell us nothing about the population at all! Imagine asking the first 10 people who walk out of a factory gate about their salaries and recording the average at $20,000 per year. You could hardly feel confident about your knowledge of worker salaries, given that your pick of individuals was based entirely on your personal convenience and had nothing to do with whether these workers were representative of the firm's labor force as a whole. Quite possibly, you picked all the janitors, who come to work early and leave early as well; quite possibly, the firm's 900 production workers are earning $40,000 per year, a fact that your careless sampling missed entirely! In the same way, a member of Congress who telephones constituents about their opinions, without regard to the opinions of those who do not happen to answer the phone, who do not have a phone, or who have unlisted telephone numbers, is taking a (worthless) convenience sample.

A somewhat more sophisticated, but still questionable, type of sample emerges when the data collector's personal judgment, presumably based on experience, plays a major role in selecting elementary units for observation. Because the "expert" judgment is believed to make the sample representative of the whole, such a subset of the frame, or associated population, is called a **judgment sample.**

Making such a judgment can be next to impossible, however. Consider selecting a "representative" group of 10 persons from among 1,000 people about whom we already know a great deal. If there were 400 males and 600 females, we could select 4 males and 6 females for our sample, and in this sense our sample would be a miniature of the population. But what about all the other characteristics people have, such as age, education, income, and race? If half the males and two-thirds of the females were over 50 years of age, we could, of course, make sure that 2 of our 4 males were under 50 and 2 of them were over 50 and that 2 of our 6 females were under and 4 of them over that age. If the population also contained 20 percent blacks among males and 30 percent blacks among females, however, we couldn't also arrange for 0.8 black males and 1.8 black females to enter our sample. We might choose 1 black male and 2 black females, but already our sample would have ceased being a miniature of the whole. The more characteristics we considered, the worse our problem would get. The more we tried, the more our judgment sample would look like a convenience sample, as if it were determined solely by our personal whim. Nevertheless, "expert" judgment is often used to select samples. One sad result, reported in this chapter's Preview, involved the 1948 presidential election polls (that were based on a type of judgment sampling called *quota sampling*).

Nevertheless, judgment sampling is sometimes used, even by U.S. government agencies. A good example is the construction of the monthly Consumer Price Index (CPI). Someone decides, on the basis of personal judgment, which prices (among literally billions of prices) are sampled and what weights are assigned to them. Determining the CPI involves complex decisions on which stores in which geographic areas are to be surveyed on which days concerning the prices of which products. A price charged many customers in a popular store is surely more important than one charged few customers in a nearly abandoned store. Prices in tiny Hadley, Massachusetts, affect fewer people than prices in Chicago. Fewer people shop on Mondays than on Saturdays (when they take advantage of weekend specials); and automobile tires, fruit, and meat somehow *seem* more important than horseshoes, matches, and tea. On all these matters and more, "expert" judgment is brought to bear. When it is wrong, as is easily possible, the sample ends up unrepresentative of the associated whole. But what would be more accurate, yet still practical? Nobody knows!

PROBABILITY SAMPLES

Most important is the *probability sample* or *random sample* because it avoids the problem of unrepresentativeness. If properly executed, the random selection process allows the investigator no discretion as to which particular units of the frame or population enter the sample. As a result, such a sample tends to maximize our chances of making valid inferences about the totality from which it is drawn. Because random samples are so important, we must look at them in some detail. Four major types of random samples exist:

- the *simple random sample*
- the *systematic random sample*
- the *stratified random sample*
- the *clustered random sample*

Each is appropriate in different circumstances.

4.4 The Simple Random Sample

We introduce the nature of scientific random sampling with a crucial definition.

DEFINITION 4.5 A **simple random sample** is a subset of a frame, or of an associated population, chosen in such a fashion that every possible *subset* of like size has an equal chance of being selected. This procedure implies that each *individual unit* of the frame or population has an equal chance of selection as well.

EXPLORING THE DEFINITION

We can illustrate the definition most easily by considering a sample of size $n = 3$ that is taken from a *finite* frame, containing a countable number of units, $N = 6$. Let the frame consist of elementary units A, B, C, D, E, and F. You may picture these names written on six slips of paper, placed in a bowl, and thoroughly mixed. Now let a sample of 3 be taken *without replacement,* which means that one slip at a time is drawn from the bowl and is *not* returned to the bowl once it has been read. As a result, any given unit can enter the sample only once. In fact, under the stated conditions, any one of the following 20 samples might emerge:

ABC	ACD	ADE	AEF	BCD	BDE	BEF	CDE	CEF	DEF
ABD	ACE	ADF		BCE	BDF		CDF		
ABE	ACF			BCF					
ABF									

TECHNICAL DETAIL

The number of different samples of size n that can be drawn *without replacement* from a list of N elements equals

$$\frac{N!}{(N-n)!n!}$$

which, in this example equals

$$\frac{6!}{(6-3)!3!} = \frac{6!}{3!3!} = \frac{6 \cdot 5 \cdot 4 \cdot 3 \cdot 2 \cdot 1}{(3 \cdot 2 \cdot 1)(3 \cdot 2 \cdot 1)} = \frac{720}{36} = 20$$

The expression $N!$ is pronounced "N factorial." Its meaning is obvious from the example. But note: By definition, $1! = 1$ and $0! = 1$ as well. We discuss factorials in Chapter 8.

Can you see that vastly more than 20 samples of size $n = 3$ could be drawn from a frame of $N = 6$ if sampling *with replacement* occurred? Under such circumstances, each slip of paper, such as the one labeled A, would be immediately returned to the bowl after being drawn and read. As result, even a sample consisting of three A's would be possible.

In order for our sample to qualify as a *simple random sample,* all 20 of the above subsets must have an equal chance (here, 1 in 20) of being selected. If that were the case, each individual unit would have an equal chance of selection as well. Note how the A appears in 10 of the 20 samples and, thus, has a chance of selection of 1 in 2; but the same statement could be made for the B or the C or any of the other letters.

It is important to understand that some sampling procedures might give each *individual* unit of a frame an equal chance to be selected, but still violate Definition 4.5 by not giving *every possible subset* of like size an equal chance. Consider the frame of 6 units just noted. Suppose we divided these units into two categories, a subset of large units (such as firms A, D, E with annual revenues in excess of $1 billion) and a subset of small units (such as firms B, C, F with smaller revenues). One *could* decide to select one of these two subsets as the sample, if a sample of three was desired, and the actual sample could then be selected by simply tossing a coin. Each of the two listed samples would have an equal chance of being selected—namely, 1 out of 2, depending on whether heads or tails appears. The fact that each of these samples would have an equal chance of being selected would imply that each individual unit contained in either one of these two samples, and, therefore, each unit in the frame, would also have an equal chance (1 out of 2). Yet this procedure would not satisfy the prescription for selecting a simple random sample. There would be some possible samples of size three—namely, combinations of large *and* small elementary units (such as A, B, C or C, E, F)—that would have *zero* chance of being selected.

SELECTING THE SAMPLE

Having defined a simple random sample, we are now ready to ask how such a sample might be selected in practice. We can see why a simple random sample of a city's residents, for example, *cannot* be obtained by interviewing people on Main Street at 11 A.M. on a Monday. Such a procedure would surely exclude all kinds of subsets of the city population. Samples including people at work or in hospitals would have no chance of being selected. In fact, the most common procedure of obtaining a simple random sample involves applying a *lottery process* to the relevant frame or population.

Consider the alphabetical listing, in Table 4.1 on the next page, of the 100 largest multinational companies headquartered in the United States in the late 1990s. (In the survey, "largeness" was determined on the basis of companies' foreign revenues.) For a researcher who wanted to investigate characteristics of these companies at that particular point in time, such as their foreign and domestic sales, their profits, or their assets, this listing represents the frame. In order to take a sample of, say, 10 companies, the researcher might record each of the 100 company names on a separate slip of paper, place the slips of paper in a bowl, mix thoroughly, and draw 10 slips. The firms named on the slips drawn could then be investigated with respect to the variables of interest. Historically, this type of procedure has often been followed. It is troublesome, however, when a large number of elements is involved, because it is then difficult to mix them properly. Indeed, more often than not, randomization by physical mixing is next to impossible. Application 4.3, *The 1970 Draft Lottery Fiasco,* on page 117 provides a vivid illustration of this fact.

Because drawing slips from a bowl is so awkward, a somewhat different but analogous approach is used nowadays, and it involves two steps:

1. Every elementary unit in the relevant frame is coded with a number. If the frame consists of 10 units, for example, its units might be represented by single-digit nominal data ranging from 0 to 9. If the frame consists of 100 or 1,000 units, their numerical names might range from 00 to 99 (as in Table 4.1) or from 000 to 999 instead.

2. A sample of size n is selected by randomly choosing n numbers and relating them to those elementary units with like numbers. In the remainder of this section, we will become acquainted with two ways of making that random choice without having to place slips of paper in a bowl. The first of these, still widely used, involves using a ready-made *random-numbers table.* The second approach makes use of a *random-numbers generator* contained in a computer program, such as EXCEL or MINITAB.

TABLE 4.1 | The 100 Largest U.S.-Based Multinationals in 1997

This table shows the names of those 100 U.S.-based multinational companies that had the highest foreign revenues in 1997. Such revenues ranged from $92.54 billion (Exxon) to $3.078 billion (Cigna). Company names have been coded with two-digit numbers.

Code	Company	Code	Company	Code	Company
00	Abbott Laboratories	33	Digital Equipment	66	Merck
01	Aflac	34	Dow Chemical	67	Merrill Lynch
02	Alcoa	35	Dresser Industries	68	Microsoft
03	Allied Signal	36	Eastman Kodak	69	Minnesota Mining & Manufacturing
04	American Express	37	E. du Pont de Nemours	70	Mobil
05	American Home Products	38	Electronic Data Systems	71	Monsanto
06	American International Group	39	Eli Lilly	72	Morgan Stanley
07	American Standard	40	Emerson Electric	73	Motorola
08	Amoco	41	Exxon	74	NCR
09	AMP	42	Fluor	75	Nike
10	AMR	43	Ford Motor	76	Northwest Airlines
11	Apple Computer	44	General Electric	77	PepsiCo
12	Archer Daniels Midland	45	General Motors	78	Pfizer
13	Atlantic Richfield	46	General Re	79	Pharmacia & Upjohn
14	Avon Products	47	Gillette	80	Philip Morris Cos
15	BankAmerica	48	Goodyear Tire & Rubber	81	Procter & Gamble
16	Bankers Trust New York	49	Halliburton	82	RJR Nabisco
17	Baxter International	50	Hewlett-Packard	83	Safeway
18	Bestfoods	51	HJ Heinz	84	Sara Lee
19	Bristol-Myers Squibb	52	Honeywell	85	Seagate Technology
20	Caterpillar	53	IBM	86	Sears, Roebuck
21	Chase Manhattan	54	Ingram Micro	87	Sun Microsystems
22	Chevron	55	Intel	88	Texaco
23	Chrysler	56	International Paper	89	Texas Instruments
24	Cigna	57	ITT Industries	90	Travelers Group
25	Citicorp	58	Johnson & Johnson	91	TRW
26	Coca-Cola	59	Johnson Controls	92	UAL
27	Colgate-Palmolive	60	JP Morgan & Co	93	Unisys
28	Compaq Computer	61	Kimberly-Clark	94	United Technologies
29	Costco Cos	62	Lear	95	Wal-Mart Stores
30	Crown Cork & Seal	63	Lucent Technologies	96	Walt Disney
31	Deere & Co	64	Manpower	97	Warner-Lambert
32	Dell Computer	65	McDonald's	98	Whirlpool
				99	Xerox

SOURCE: Adapted from *Forbes,* July 27, 1988, pp. 163–164.

USING THE RANDOM-NUMBERS TABLE

A **random-numbers table** is a printed listing of numbers generated by a random process in such a way that each possible digit is equally likely to precede or follow any other digit. In such a table, no discernible pattern arises in the way the digits appear. Suppose we wanted to construct our own table of five-digit random numbers. We could write the numbers from 0 to 9 separately on 10 slips of paper, mix the slips in a bowl, and pull out one. We would have the first digit for our first number. After returning the slip we pulled to the bowl, we would once more mix the 10 slips, pull out one, and thus get the second digit; then, repeating the process, we would determine the third, fourth, and fifth digits. We would, thus, have created our first five-digit random number, and if we cared to, we could create 500 of them, such as those listed in Appendix Table A, *Random Numbers.* Actually, the numbers listed there come from a list of 1 million random digits generated by a computer at the Rand Corporation. Because the computer, like an electronic roulette wheel, followed the selection principle outlined above, each value between 00000 and 99999 had an equal chance of appearing at each of the 500 locations given in Appendix Table A.

It is easy to select a simple random sample of the multinational companies with the help of our random-numbers table. For this purpose, the 100 company names have already been coded by two-digit numbers ranging from 00 to 99. We decide which 10 of the companies are to be in the sample simply by entering the random-numbers table at random and reading off two-digit numbers in any predetermined, systematic way. The first 10 two-digit numbers encountered that correspond to *previously unused* company codes tell us what the sample is.

THE STARTING POINT Many random-numbers tables, including the source from which Appendix Table A has been taken, consist of many pages. It is a good idea to begin the process of selecting a simple random sample by first selecting a page of the table and then selecting a number on that page, at random. Any nonpatterned procedure will do. For example, we might simply open the 400-page Rand Corporation table haphazardly and select page 377. (This page has, in fact, been reproduced as Appendix Table A.) Closing our eyes, we might then place a finger on the chosen page and thus determine number 00717 (row 24, column 5) as our starting number.

THE SELECTION PROCEDURE Actually, we should not even go about finding our starting number until we have decided how we will use it and how we will then proceed to find other numbers. If, as in our case, the data consist of two digits, while the random numbers contain five, we must have a plan for extracting two-digit numbers from our chosen page. We could read only the first two digits of each five-digit number; we could read the last two digits only, or even the second and last digits in each number. A multitude of possibilities exists. And having found our first two-digit number, we can go about finding additional numbers (up to the desired sample size) in any predetermined fashion we like: by proceeding along our initial row to the right or to the left, by moving along our initial column down or up, even by reading numbers diagonally. We can follow any self-imposed plan we like, as long as we never read a given location twice.

OUR FIRST SAMPLE Suppose we had decided to select our sample of 10 (different) companies by reading the last two digits of the five-digit random numbers, while proceeding down along (possibly successive) columns. In order not to select a given company twice, we would skip two-digit numbers previously encountered and ultimately match 10 *different* two-digit numbers with identical company codes. Since our initial number was the 24th number in the

5th column of Appendix Table A, our simple random sample would quickly be determined as follows:

007**17**	Baxter International
107**97**	Warner-Lambert
739**35**	Dressser Industries
534**97**	omitted (97 used above)
692**14**	Avon Products
747**74**	NCR
945**82**	RJR Nabisco
151**07**	American Standard
807**56**	International Paper
894**27**	Colgate-Palmolive
433**35**	omitted (35 used above)
830**01**	Aflac

TECHNICAL DETAIL

Two additional matters might be noted:

First, as we have just seen, if you encounter a given value a second time during the sampling procedure (as happened with numbers 97 and 35 in our case), you simply skip to the next number. The same is recommended when the value encountered has no counterpart in the frame or population being sampled. (Consider choosing from a list of 60 companies only and encountering numbers between 61 and 99 in the random-numbers table.)

Second, some argue that the above procedure for finding a starting position (our number 00717) may not be sufficiently random for *frequent* users of a random-numbers table. This may be so because a given book may tend to open to the same page repeatedly and, thus, a frequent user might again and again select page 377, while a person placing a finger on a page tends to choose a number toward the center of the page (as we did). In order to guard against these dangers, you can select a starting position in any number of truly random ways. For example, if you were working with an eight-page table, you might select a page by tossing a coin three times. There are two possible outcomes for the first toss, heads (H) or tails (T). There are two possible follow-ups for each of these two contingencies on the second toss, making for sequences of HH, HT, TH, or TT. And there are two possible follow-ups for each of these four contingencies on the third toss, making for eight conceivable sequences for the three tosses. These sequences might be linked to the choice of a page in the random-numbers table, as shown in Table 4.2.

Having thus found the page by tossing a coin three times, you might determine the starting position by reading two digits at a time along successive rows and letting the first usable set of two digits point you to a row and the second such set to a column. Can you see why, in Appendix

TABLE 4.2 | Random Selection of a Page Number

Coin tossing can facilitate the random selection of a page number in a random-numbers table.

Possible Sequences of Coin Tosses	Page Number Picked
HHH	1
HHT	2
HTH	3
HTT	4
THH	5
THT	6
TTH	7
TTT	8

Table A (which has 50 rows and 10 columns), this procedure would have you start with row 27 and column 01—that is, with number 20545? The possibilities of random selection are truly limitless.

USING A COMPUTER'S RANDOM-NUMBERS GENERATOR

Instead of using a preprinted random-numbers table, you can generate your own table with the help of a computer program and then use that table just as we used Appendix Table A above. Alternatively, having coded all the elementary units in your frame, you can also ask a computer to select a simple random sample for you.

EXCEL Example 4.1

Create a random numbers table with the help of EXCEL.

SOLUTION Fire up EXCEL; then use the RAND function to generate random numbers between 0 and 1 as follows: Activate cell A1 by clicking on it. Type the formula **=RAND()** and press **Enter.** A first random number appears in cell A1. Click on the cell, point to the handle in the lower right corner and drag it to cell A10 to create a column of such random numbers. Highlight the numbers and drag the cell A10 handle to G10 to create 80 random numbers, such as those in Table 4.3 on the next page.

TABLE 4.3 | Random-Numbers Table Created with EXCEL

0.788776	0.614528	0.493369	0.586679	0.985355	0.696496	0.50247	0.79186
0.990592	0.379163	0.975821	0.745884	0.539044	0.966559	0.785352	0.070714
0.812738	0.15837	0.560874	0.553848	0.552294	0.158117	0.074287	0.690424
0.109512	0.292675	0.57739	0.760732	0.362356	0.779336	0.074862	0.868031
0.730074	0.905279	0.952963	0.261387	0.297898	0.43304	0.094293	0.142588
0.264944	0.867606	0.974117	0.013658	0.341877	0.259295	0.747053	0.568165
0.223065	0.781906	0.30663	0.625152	0.828571	0.015695	0.352317	0.163669
0.931718	0.603013	0.401587	0.201438	0.534739	0.315075	0.56512	0.600821
0.610832	0.887085	0.274379	0.887038	0.81283	0.256614	0.421828	0.875102
0.191078	0.017134	0.481011	0.220283	0.614579	0.987743	0.833256	0.592148

Notes:

1. Don't expect to get the *same* random numbers if you repeat the experiment described here. Also note that you can generate different random numbers in your table by simply pressing the F9 key.
2. You can avoid all those zeros and decimal points and create a table of *whole random digits* by repeating the above procedure, but typing the formula **=INT(10*RAND())**

TECHNICAL DETAIL (EXCEL)

You may ask: How does EXCEL create those random numbers?

EXCEL contains a math function that creates a very long string of numbers that appear to be random. Strictly speaking, however, any set of numbers that is created by a mathematical formula should be called *pseudo* random numbers, which is why many statisticians refer to these numbers as "random" numbers, but we can let that go for now. When someone issues the RAND command, EXCEL haphazardly chooses a starting point somewhere on that string and selects the requested number of numbers. Each time the command is issued, the program selects a different starting point and, thus, comes up with a different set of random numbers.

However, if you have an irresistible urge to have EXCEL give you the *same* set of random numbers twice in a row, that can be arranged.

1. Click **Tools > Data Analysis > Random Number Generation > OK.**
2. In the *Number of Variables* box, enter the number of columns you want, such as **3.**
3. In the *Number of Random Numbers* box, enter the number of rows you want; say, **10.**
4. In the *Distribution* box, choose **Uniform** from the drop-down list; and set *Parameters* between **0** and **1.**
5. In the *Random Seed* box, enter any positive integer of your choice, such as **41,** and remember it.
6. Select an *Output Option,* such as *Output Range,* type in the upper left cell of the range that is to receive your output, such as **A1,** and click **OK.**

(continued)

Technical Detail (EXCEL) (continued)

You will note 30 (pseudo) random numbers in range A1–C10. Then, if you repeat steps 1–5 (using the same seed number), but specify E1 in the last step, you will see the identical "random" numbers appearing in range E1–G10.

EXCEL Example 4.2

Select a simple random sample of 10 companies from Table 4.1 on page 110, using the random numbers to the right of the decimal points that were created in EXCEL Example 4.1.

SOLUTION Pick any systematic procedure for pulling two-digit numbers from Table 4.3, such as "starting with the first number in column 1 and, moving downward, using the last two digits in that column and, if necessary, in subsequent columns."

The Numbers: 76, 92, 38, 12, 74, 44, 65, 18, 32, 78

The Sample: Northwest Airlines, UAL, Electronic Data Systems, Archer Daniels Midland, NCR, General Electric, McDonald's, Bestfoods, Dell Computer, Pfizer

EXCEL Example 4.3

Select a simple random sample of 10 companies from Table 4.1 on page 110, using EXCEL's sampling tool, without first creating a random-numbers table.

SOLUTION

1. Fire up EXCEL and create patterned data reaching from 0 to 99 in column A. (Just enter 0, 1, 2 in cells A1–A3, select the three cells, and drag the cell A3 handle down to cell A100, which will contain the value 99.) These data, just as in Table 4.1, can stand for the company names.
2. Click **Tools** > **Data Analysis** > **Sampling** > **OK** to activate the *Sampling* dialog box.
3. Under *Input Range,* enter **A1:A100.**
4. Under *Sampling Method,* choose **Random,** and under *Number of Samples* enter **10.**
5. Under *Output Options,* choose Output Range and enter **C1** as the first cell to receive the output.
6. Click **OK**.
7. Highlight the column C results and click the *AZ Sort Ascending* button on your toolbar to get a sorted list such as that shown on the next page.

With the help of Table 4.1, these numbers can be converted into an alphabetical list of sampled companies: BankAmerica, Bristol-Myers Squibb, Colgate-Palmolive, Dow Chemical, Halliburton, McDonald's, Nike, Sears Roebuck, Warner-Lambert, Whirlpool.

Note: If you repeat the process, you will get a different random sample.

15
19
27
34
49
65
75
86
97
98

Unfortunately, the EXCEL sampling tool that was introduced in EXCEL Example 4.3 samples a given population *with replacement,* making it possible to select a given element more than once. By sheer luck, as Step 7 confirmed, we avoided that fate above, but we can make *sure* to avoid it by using the following procedure after Step 1 above:

2. Type **=RAND()** in cell B1, select the number appearing in B1, and drag to B100.
3. Select the B1 to B100 range, click **Edit>Copy** and **Edit>Paste Special.**
4. In the *Paste Special* dialog box, select *Values* and *None* (which replaces the formulas in the B column with the values they create), and click **OK.**
5. With the B range selected, click **Data>Sort.** (If the *Sort Warning* box appears, expand the selection to sort.)
6. In the *Sort* dialog box, select *Sort by Column B Ascending* and *No Header row* and click **OK.**

The original column A data now appear in random order, without duplication. You can use the first 10 company codes as your sample.

DRAWBACKS

As you now know, the selection of a simple random sample can be very easy, indeed. You probably would have no trouble at all taking a simple random sample of all the students at your school! But despite its ease of execution, this type of sampling can have two drawbacks.

First, even though it is cheaper than a census, simple random sampling can still be very costly to carry out. Imagine trying to take a 60,000-person sample of the millions of U.S. taxpayers. It may be easy to select the names, as we have learned to do. But picture the *expense* of actually contacting people in Seattle, Washington, then in Key West, Florida, then in Bar Harbor, Maine, and then in all sorts of places in between.

Second, simple random sampling can, on occasion, produce questionable results. Remember that such sampling gives each conceivable sample of size n an equal chance of being picked. That leaves open the possibility of picking an unusual sample. Our pick of 10 multinationals, for example—and we have picked three possible samples in this chapter so far—might yield 10 companies that each suffered major losses during the year in question, despite the fact that most companies on the list made huge profits.

For reasons such as these (and others), some investigators prefer to take different kinds of random samples. These are discussed in Section 4.5.

APPLICATION 4.3

The 1970 Draft Lottery Fiasco

During both World Wars I and II, the U.S. government needed to establish the sequence in which men were to be drafted into the military. In 1917, accordingly, 10,500 black capsules, containing numbers previously assigned to eligible men, were drawn from a glass fishbowl. In 1940, a similar procedure was adopted to draw 9,000 numbers, but there were criticisms: The small wooden paddle, made from a piece of rafter traceable to Philadelphia's Independence Hall and used to stir the capsules, would not reach deep enough into the bowl. It also broke open some of the capsules, impeding the mixing process further. In the end, the numbers drawn looked like anything but random ones. They were concentrated in certain clusters of hundreds, apparently reflecting the fact that the numbers had been poured into the bowl in lots of 100 each. The lesson was clear: Thorough physical mixing of a large number of capsules in a bowl is difficult and any resulting sample is likely to be biased.

Apparently, the lesson had been forgotten when the U.S. instituted the 1970 draft lottery. Three hundred sixty-six capsules, containing all the possible birthdates in a year, were poured into a bowl but not stirred. However, the capsules had been mixed a bit during the process of inserting dated slips of paper into them. Then capsules were drawn out, the order of their withdrawal determining the draft priorities by birthday. The observed sequence strongly reflected the order in which the capsules were created (one month at a time), with late-in-the-year birthdays (encapsulated last) being drawn first and early-in-the-year birthdays (encapsulated first) being drawn last. Therefore, men with early birthdays became less subject to the draft. Several young men filed suit in federal court seeking to have the 1970 lottery voided on the basis of the apparent lack of randomization.

Note: A 1971 draft lottery, in response to widespread criticism of the 1970 lottery, made use of random-numbers tables, discussed in the text.

SOURCE: Adapted from Stephen E. Fienberg, "Randomization and Social Affairs: The 1970 Draft Lottery," *Science,* January 22, 1971, pp. 255–261.

4.5 Other Types of Random Samples

This section provides brief introductions to other types of random samples, notably:

- systematic random samples
- stratified random samples
- clustered random samples

THE SYSTEMATIC RANDOM SAMPLE

On occasion, it is *impossible* to take a simple random sample because one cannot number all of the elementary units of the frame prior to sample selection. This may be so because the size of the frame is not known or because it is infinite or so large that one might as well consider it to be infinite for practical purposes. This sort of situation often arises when sampling involves some kind of ongoing process that has no known ending. Consider someone who is interested in finding the average time it takes to serve customers at McDonald's on any day between 11:30 A.M. and 12:30 P.M. Consider a quality inspector who wants to determine the percentage of defective units produced on an assembly line that never shuts down. Or picture a receiving agent examining daily raw material shipments arriving at a factory yard. How many customers, product units, and raw material shipments are there? The *systematic random sample* has the advantage of being usable even when we do not know the size of the frame and, thus, cannot label each elementary unit with a number.

DEFINITION 4.6 A **systematic random sample** is a subset of a frame, or of an associated population, chosen by randomly selecting one of the first k elements and then including every kth element thereafter until the desired sample size has been reached.

If this procedure is employed and the population size is known, k is determined by dividing population size, N, by desired sample size, n. Consider again those $N = 100$ companies listed in Table 4.1. To select a systematic random sample of, say, $n = 5$ companies, one would wish to include every 20th company on the list, because $k = (N/n) = (100/5) = 20$. The procedure, however, requires that the starting point, the first company included, be chosen at random. By drawing a number between 00 and 19 out of a hat, by using a table of random numbers, or by taking a sample of 1 out of those 20 numbers with the help of a computer, we might randomly pick company number 09 as the starting point. Then our entire sample would consist of the companies coded as 09, 29, 49, 69, and 89. Had our initial choice been 01 or 17, the sample would have been different, of course, consisting of firms labeled 01, 21, 41, 61, and 81 or 17, 37, 57, 77, and 97, respectively.

CAUTION

Systematic random sampling has to be used with care whenever the units to be sampled contain some kind of predictable periodic variability. Imagine trying to take a sample of daily sales at a McDonald's restaurant. If you happen to pick $k = 7$, you are likely to create a disaster because sales vary predictably over the course of each week. If your starting point happens to be a Saturday, *all* your sample data will come from Saturdays, and the average sales figure will be relatively high. If your starting point is a Wednesday instead, all your sample data will come from Wednesdays, and the average sales figure will appear low.

THE STRATIFIED RANDOM SAMPLE

Sometimes the frame or population to be sampled is known to contain two or more mutually exclusive and clearly distinguishable subgroups or *strata* that differ greatly from one another with respect to some characteristic of interest, while the elements within each stratum are fairly homogeneous. In such circumstances, one can select yet a different kind of sample.

DEFINITION 4.7 A **stratified random sample** is a subset of a frame, or of an associated population, chosen by taking separate (simple or systematic) random samples from every stratum in the frame or population, often in such a way that the sizes of the separate samples vary with the importance of the different strata.

Suppose we knew that 10 of the 100 companies listed in Table 4.1 accounted for 70 percent of the 100 companies' sales, while the other 90 companies accounted for the remaining 30 percent. If sales were the characteristic of interest to us, we might wish to ensure that our sampling procedure did not miss the 10 giants, as might well happen if we took either a simple or systematic random sample. We could divide our list into two strata (10 giants and 90 dwarfs) and then create our overall sample by selecting some firms from each of these two groups. For a sample of 10 companies, we might select 7 firms from the giant stratum and 3 firms from the dwarf stratum, and these 10 firms could be expected to account for more than half of all sales. (In this case, the division of the sample between the two strata is *proportional* to sales, our variable of interest, but such proportionality is not a necessity. We could also have taken an identically sized sample of 5 from each stratum. This sort of decision is usually made on the basis of cost. A strictly proportional allocation is chosen only if the cost of sampling is the same in all strata.)

The type of procedure described in this section is, in fact, quite common. Some examples from the business world are summarized in Application 4.4, *How Accountants Save Money by Sampling.*

APPLICATION 4.4

HOW ACCOUNTANTS SAVE MONEY BY SAMPLING

Business firms and other organizations used to spend a great deal of time and money on censuses to determine their accounts receivable or payable and to take physical inventories of equipment, raw materials, goods in process, and the like. Dramatic experiments with census taking versus sampling have shown, however, that such censuses are often unnecessary. Relatively small samples of the relevant populations, if carefully drawn, can produce high-quality results, along with dramatic savings in time and money.

CASE 1. Once upon a time, when you could send a whole freight car full of stuff all the way from Boston to New York for $72 (and a year's college tuition was less than $100, too), the Chesapeake and Ohio Railroad faced a problem. It had to allocate total freight and passenger revenues among several carriers when freight or passengers had traveled over lines owned by different companies, a common occurrence. The clerical cost of dividing the revenues could run into several thousand dollars, a big sum at the time. So the railroad company sponsored an experiment. First, it examined the waybills for interline freight shipments that had occurred over a six-month period. (A waybill is a document describing the nature of goods shipped, their routing, and the total freight charges.) As Table 4.A shows, nearly 23,000 waybills were examined, at a cost of $5,000. The shippers owed the Chesapeake and Ohio (rather than other railroads) $64,651. At a much lower cost, a sample was also taken. It was a *stratified sample,* containing only 1 percent of waybills totaling $5 or less, 10 percent of waybills totaling between $5.01 and $10; 20 percent of waybills totaling between $10.01 and $20; 50 percent of waybills totaling between $20.01 and $40; and 100 percent of waybills in excess of $40. The particular waybills included in the sample were selected with the help of a random-numbers table on the basis of the last two serial-number digits.

TABLE 4.A

	Census	Sample
Number of waybills examined	22,984	2,072
Cost of examination	$5,000	$1,000
Amount found due C&O Railroad	$64,651	$64,568

The result was amazing: The amount due was determined within $83 or 1/10 of 1 percent of the much costlier census figure. Similar accuracy was achieved when the railroad studied five months' worth of interline passenger tickets. A census of the 14,109 tickets revealed the amount due the railroad to be $212,164. A 5 percent sample of these tickets yielded a figure of $212,063. The $101 difference was even less than 1/10 of 1 percent of the census figure.

CASE 2. Airlines face the problem of settling accounts with one another concerning passengers traveling on different airlines during a given trip. Each major airline picks up hundreds of thousands of tickets per month that were issued by and initially paid to other airlines. Clerks used to figure out the revenue allocation for each ticket, but this process could be extremely cumbersome and costly. At one time, 60 possible fares were in effect between Chicago and New York! Three airlines (Northwest, United, and TWA), therefore, conducted a four-month test similar to the one by the Chesapeake and Ohio described above. A census was taken, then a stratified sample. The strata used were first-class, coach, military, and other types of tickets. Individual tickets were pulled on the basis of the last digit in their serial numbers with the help of a random-numbers table. The difference in the census and sample results came to less than $700 per $1 million of tickets. After introducing sampling procedures, one major carrier cut clerical expenses by $75,000 per year; the industry as a whole saved $500,000 per year.

(continued)

Application 4.4 (continued)

CASE 3. One firm, Minneapolis-Honeywell, used to take 100 percent inventories of its goods-in-process. Then it conducted two experiments. First, it took a simple random sample of 500 items out of 5,000 items in one department. The estimated size of the inventory came within 1/10 of 1 percent of the full count. Second, it took a stratified random sample, dividing work-in-process lots from all departments into those of high value ($500 or more) and those of low value. All of the former were counted; only 10 percent of the latter were counted. The sample of 4,200 out of 40,000 items yielded an estimate within 8/10 of 1 percent of the full count.

CONCLUSION. Sampling instead of census taking for accounting purposes is now widespread. Firms use it to estimate their bad debts (by estimating the total of accounts owed for more than 60 days) and to gauge the accuracy of their clerical workers (by contacting a sample of customers concerning their billings). The U.S. Air Force uses it when taking a worldwide audit of its motor-vehicle pool. Power companies use it to divvy up the revenues from electricity that has traveled across different companies' power lines. The list could easily be lengthened.

SOURCES: Adapted from John Neter, "How Accountants Save Money by Sampling," in Judith M. Tanur et al., eds., *Statistics: A Guide to the Unknown* (San Francisco: Holden-Day, 1972), pp. 203–211, and Theodore J. Sielaff, *Statistics in Action: Readings in Business and Economic Statistics* (San Jose, Calif.: Lansford Press, 1963), pp. 20–21and 26–27.

THE CLUSTERED RANDOM SAMPLE

Sometimes, the frame or population to be sampled is naturally subdivided into clusters on the basis of physical accessibility. If each cluster contains widely differing elements, but hardly differs from all the other clusters, we can use a *clustered random sample.*

DEFINITION 4.8 A **clustered random sample** is a subset of a frame, or of an associated population, chosen by taking separate censuses in a randomly chosen subset of geographically distinct clusters into which the frame or population is naturally divided.

Someone who wanted to sample the residents or shops of a city, for example, might divide the city into blocks, randomly select a few of these (by any of the methods previously discussed), and then interview every resident or shop owner within the chosen blocks. Because all those interviewed are geographically close by, this procedure would save considerable transportation expenses and time in comparison to a citywide simple random sample of individual residents or shop owners, who would almost certainly be located in a multitude of different places. *Acceptance sampling* by business firms is likely to follow a similar route. Imagine a firm that had just received a shipment of 1 million coffee cups. Its warehouse would be filled, perhaps, with 10,000 sealed cartons, each containing 100 cups. An inspector who wanted to determine the quality of the cups by taking a 10,000-cup sample could take a simple or systematic random sample of them, but might then have to open and unpack nearly all of the 10,000 cartons in order to find the individual cups selected. It would be much easier to regard each carton as a geographic cluster, select 100 cartons randomly, and inspect every single cup in these cartons only. Some 9,900 of the cartons would not have to be opened at all. It should go without saying that those who employ cluster sampling must create clusters that make sense. If that is not the case, all the saving of money and time will come to naught because the result will mean nothing at all.

4.6 Multistage Samples

The procedures described in Sections 4.4 and 4.5 are called *single-stage sampling,* because, in one way or another, a single sample is taken and that is that. On many occasions, this simple type of sampling is replaced by a more complex **multistage sampling,** a procedure that involves the successive sampling of ever-smaller groups and possibly even the use of different sampling methods at each stage.

An example of multistage sampling might be a nationwide household survey conducted as follows: First, a subset of states (primary clusters) is chosen at random; second, a subset of cities, counties, or townships (secondary clusters) is randomly chosen within the previously selected states; third, a subset of census tracts or city blocks (tertiary clusters) is randomly selected within those cities, counties, or townships. Finally, perhaps, simple, systematic, or stratified samples are taken in each of the tertiary clusters.

Biography 4.1, George Horace Gallup, found on the text Web site, takes a closer look at one of the 20th-century pioneers who introduced and perfected many of the sampling techniques described so far.

4.7 Errors in Survey Data

We have noted how data can be acquired by taking a census or by engaging in various forms of sampling. Inevitably, all survey data are subject to error; errors can arise from innumerable, often unexpected, sources. At best, errors obscure the truth only slightly; at worst, they can reduce the value of a survey below zero, for nothing is more potentially damaging than "knowing" something that isn't so. Errors can be generated during the planning stage of a survey; more errors can be created during the later stages of data recording and processing. Indeed, listing all the ways in which surveys can go wrong would be a hopeless task, and we won't attempt it. It is possible, however, to raise our awareness of the problem by focusing on two broad categories of error, random error and systematic error (or bias).

RANDOM ERROR

Suppose we were interested in the average annual salary received by the employees of a particular firm, such as Mountain Aviation, Inc., discussed in Chapter 1. If we had none of the information given in Table 1.8 on page 16, except the listing of employee names, we could take a random sample of this frame, interview the selected employees about their salaries, and let the average of these sample salaries serve as an estimate of the average salary of all employees. Such a sampling approach would be all the more likely, of course, the greater the number of employees in the firm. A random sample of three might consist of Cruz, Hill, and West. On the basis of their salaries, we could estimate the average annual salary of all employees as $41,000 per year. Yet this result clearly depends entirely on the particular elementary units that we happened to select for our sample. One can, in fact, select 84 different samples of three from among our nine hypothetical employees (see the Technical Detail on page 108), and almost every one of these 84 samples would provide us with a different average-salary estimate for the population in question. The sample consisting of the salaries of Otis, West, and Wolf (shown in the box inside column 6 of Table 1.8) would give us an average-salary estimate of $31,000 per year. Yet a sample consisting of the salaries of Hill, King, and Otis would yield an estimate of only $19,667 per year. All these estimates differ from the average annual salary figure a census would reveal, for the average of *all* the column 6 data is $40,556 per year.

Clearly, individual sample estimates will likely differ from a census figure in one direction or the other. However, if we took repeated samples and averaged the resulting estimates of average salary made by all possible samples of three, we would find the census-derived figure! This amazing fact will occupy us at length in Chapter 11; for now, we must remember this:

DEFINITION 4.9 A major type of error associated with random sampling is **random error, chance error,** or **sampling error.** It equals the difference between the value of a variable obtained by taking a single random sample and the value obtained by taking a census (or by averaging the results of all possible random samples of like size).

This type of error, as one of its names suggests, arises only in sample surveys. It results from the operation of chance that determines which particular units of the population happen to be included in a sample. This error can be positive or negative, tiny or huge, but it can always be reduced by increasing the size or number of random samples taken, and it is zero in a census. Most important, the size of this error can *itself* be estimated and is often reported alongside the observed data. Statisticians can state, for example, that the average annual salary in a firm equals $39,000 and that a census would reveal a number within ±$3,000 of the stated one—that is, between $36,000 and $42,000 in our case. However, honest statisticians must also report that their procedure can be wrong and provides correct results only in, say, 95 out of 100 applications. You will learn more about that in Chapters 11 and 12. For now, focus on the left half of Figure 4.1, which illustrates the nature of random error.

SYSTEMATIC ERROR OR BIAS

Unfortunately, random errors are the least of our problems. Even if we had the complete census information given in column 6 of Table 1.8, we could not be certain that the average annual salary in our firm was $40,556. The true value might well equal $38,556, as noted on the right-hand side of Figure 4.1. This surprising statement is true because every type of survey (sampling or census taking) could produce incorrect data if observations were made or recorded in a manner that was subject to some fundamental flaw. Such a flaw might affect every single measurement in the same way, systematically pushing each one either below or above its true value.

Consider the story of the sales clerk who measured yards of cloth with an old, stretched-out cloth tape, thus causing all the recorded lengths to be lower than the true lengths. A similar predicament could befall the survey taker. Unbeknownst to anyone, an incorrectly programmed computer might, for example, deduct $4,000 from every true salary figure entered in it, and it might thus print out an incorrect set of column 6 data (in the case of a census) or an incorrect subset of them (in the case of sampling). The data, mind you, would look precisely like those in Table 1.8, but they would be wrong, nevertheless.

The people who are being interviewed can be at fault, too. Consider the story of the butcher who weighed each piece of meat with a thumb on the scales, thus causing all the recorded weights to be higher than the true weights. An analogous misfortune could befall the survey taker when "shopping" for information. Like the scheming butcher, the employees being interviewed about their salaries might not tell the truth. They might understate their salaries if they suspected the information was being channeled to the tax collector. They might overstate their salaries if they thought the information was about to be used to compute a 20 percent raise.

This sort of problem is the basis for defining the second major type of error that statisticians must consider.

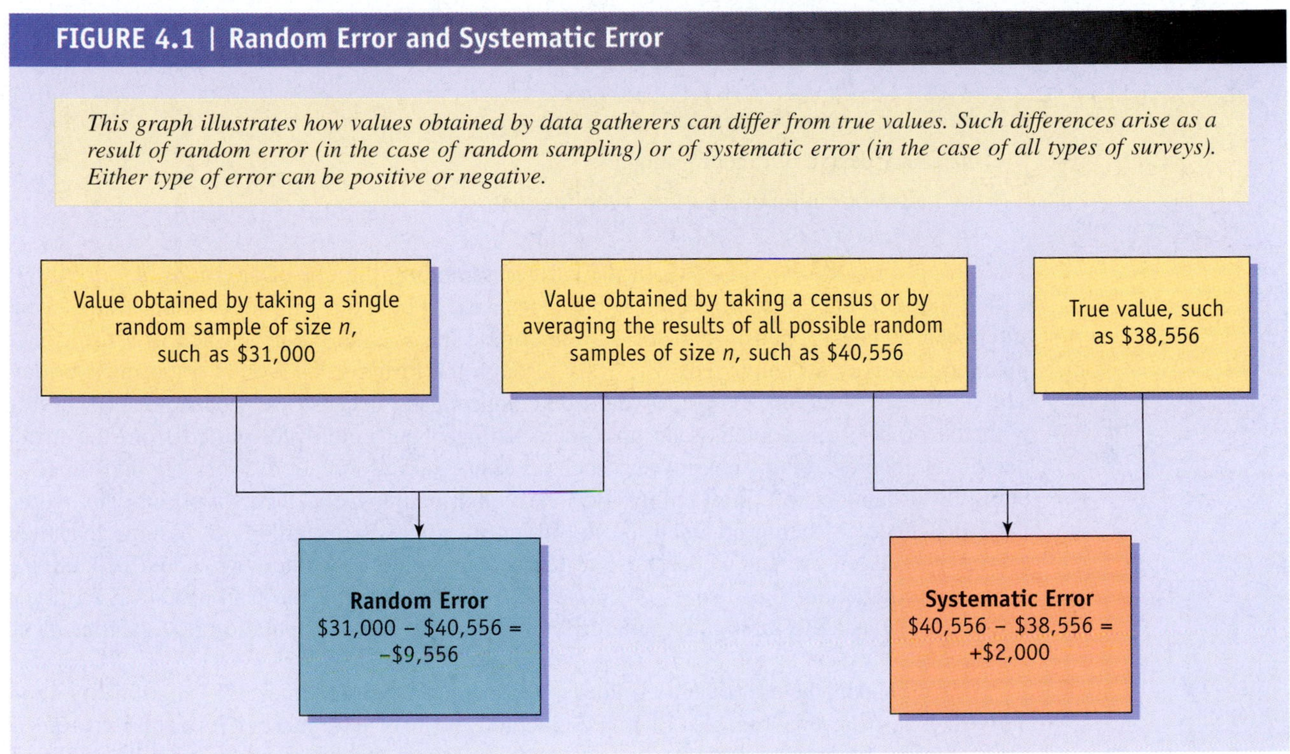

DEFINITION 4.10 A major type of error associated with all surveys is **systematic error, bias,** or **nonsampling error.** It equals the difference between the value of a variable obtained by taking a census (or by averaging the results of all possible random samples of a given size) and the (unknown) true value.

This nature of systematic error or bias is illustrated in the right half of Figure 4.1. Unfortunately, bias can be hard to detect. Further, its size, unlike that of random error, cannot be estimated. For this reason, statisticians who seek to discover the truth must become aware of the major sources of bias and try their best to neutralize them. You can read more about that in this chapter's final section.

4.8 How Bias Creeps into Surveys

If statisticians are not careful, they can literally build systematic error into the very design of their surveys. They can compound it during the survey execution stage. Even the final processing of results can infect a survey with bias. We consider three major types problems here:

- selection bias
- nonresponse bias
- response bias

SELECTION BIAS

Selection bias is a systematic tendency in a survey to favor the inclusion of selected elementary units with particular characteristics, while excluding other such units with other characteristics.

As a result of selection bias, any data that are eventually collected are bound to overrepresent one kind of characteristic and underrepresent another. The sources of selection bias include:

- the use of nonrandom samples
- the faulty design of random samples
- the faulty execution of a perfect sampling plan

TAKING NONRANDOM SAMPLES In the case of sampling, the use of any *nonrandom* sample will almost certainly result in selection bias because it is bound to employ a faulty frame. Consider what would happen in our quest to determine the average salary earned in a firm if we planned to survey all employees who walk through the firm's gates around 5 P.M. next Friday. The accuracy of our survey result would be compromised because we would not be working with the proper frame, such as an up-to-date listing of all employees culled from the firm's personnel records. Many employees, such as those taking vacation, working part-time, or being ill, or janitors working (and leaving) early and, perhaps, executives working late, would have no chance of being included in our survey. It would be hazardous to assume that their salaries would, on average, equal those of the people we do encounter. We would be studying an *actual* population (the salaries of employees who are leaving the firm around 5 P.M. next Friday) that was almost certainly quite different from our *target* population (the salaries of all employees).

Unfortunately, the use of faulty frames is quite common. Sometimes, for lack of better alternatives, it is even unavoidable. Examples include the firm that surveys its actual customers (instead of its potential customers) to assess the prospects for a new product and the political pollster who surveys a group of people whose names were taken from the telephone directory or from car-registration rolls or even from a list of *eligible* voters in order to assess a candidate's chances (when the people who really matter are those *registered* voters who are sure to vote on election day).

BADLY DESIGNED RANDOM SAMPLES Even when a perfect frame is available and *random* sampling is planned, the actual sample taken can turn out to be nonrandom in fact. Consider the attempt to select a *systematic* random sample from a perfect frame that lists all existing elementary units with some type of rhythm. If the frame were a 50-year listing of monthly stock prices, and we selected every 12th number or some multiple thereof, we would end up with a set of data all of which would pertain to the same month, such as December. These selected data could easily differ in some systematic way from all the excluded ones. Or consider an alphabetical listing of names. A systematic random sample might select every 10,000th person on the list. But if most members of some ethnic group had names that began with certain letters—such as Scottish or Irish names that begin with Mc or O'—such a sample could easily miss every one of these people, which would be disastrous if the survey were designed to study ethnic questions. The same sort of problem can occur in badly designed *clustered* random sampling. Because people with similar characteristics, such as education level, ethnic grouping, or income, tend to live close to each other, it is not impossible for cluster sampling to miss a whole range of backgrounds altogether. Such an omission could seriously bias the survey results. (Can you see why such a situation calls for *stratified* random sampling instead?)

FAULTY EXECUTION OF PERFECT SAMPLING PLAN The above examples illustrate how things can go wrong even at the planning stage of a survey, but the same thing can happen at the execution stage. Consider a perfectly planned simple random sample, based on a perfect frame. The survey workers who are to contact the elementary units chosen in the sample may not do a perfect job. If the units to be sampled are people who are to be interviewed and who live in widely scattered places around town, interviewers may just make life easier for themselves by throwing out the sample list. They may simply stay in their hotel rooms and fill out the questionnaires themselves. They may stand at the nearest street corner and interview other people, provided they can find people whose appearance is pleasant enough and whose behavior is conventional. They may knock on doors along the nearest street, provided the neighborhood is attractive enough, there are no dogs in the front yard, and the time of day is right. They may talk to people on the first floor rather than climb the stairs of an apartment building that has no elevators, even though the sampled household resides on the 7th floor. This procedure will, of course, miss all sorts of people, such as those on vacation, those in hospitals or prisons, those at work, those residing in unpleasant parts of town, in trailer camps or dormitories, and, of course, those (often the young) who don't mind living on the 7th floor. Selection bias is the inevitable result, because random sampling doesn't occur unless our interviewers, no matter how hard the task, find specifically named individuals, namely those selected with the help of the random-numbers table or a computer's random-numbers generator. Interviewers who substitute other persons for the randomly selected ones doom the entire survey by turning a *probability* sample into a *convenience* sample. Imagine the biased results in a survey about cosmetics use if the interviewers substituted grandmothers for all the teenagers because the latter were never around. Imagine the misleading results if elderly or working people or vacationers were excluded from surveys that sought to ascertain the demand, respectively, for household help or frozen food or leisure-time products.

NONRESPONSE BIAS

Even the design of a flawless census or random sample, based on a flawless frame, and the employment of the most conscientious survey workers do not guarantee the absence of bias. An additional source of systematic error is **nonresponse bias,** a systematic tendency for selected elementary units with particular characteristics not to contribute data in a survey while other such units, with other characteristics, do. In the presence of this problem, we can reach faulty conclusions because the data actually collected will in fact be based on a convenience sample. The sources of nonresponse bias include:

- the inability to contact the selected elementary units
- badly designed questionnaires

CONTACT PROBLEMS If the elementary units to be surveyed are people (rather than inanimate objects, such as lightbulbs coming off an assembly line), contact can be made in a variety of ways, such as by mail, telephone, or in person. It is all too easy for some people to tear up that mail questionnaire, not to answer the phone or quickly to hang up, or to refuse to cooperate with the surveyor at the door.

BADLY DESIGNED QUESTIONNAIRES Questionnaire features can contribute to nonresponse bias as well. These include physically unattractive designs; hard-to-read print; questions that are boring or intrusive, unclear or long-winded, excessive in number or badly sequenced, forcing respondents to jump back and forth among topics; and, in the case of multiple-choice questions, questions with answers that overlap or that fail to cover all possibilities. Experience shows that low-income people and high-income people, unlike middle-income people, tend not to respond to surveys for reasons such as these. Surely the exclusion of either group is apt to bias survey results.

Application 4.5, *The Politics of Census 2000,* on the next page, provides a dramatic example of how nonresponse bias can affect the world in which we live.

APPLICATION 4.5

THE POLITICS OF CENSUS 2000

The U.S. Constitution mandates a census of the population once per decade. Indeed, such censuses have been held ever since 1790, when Secretary of State Thomas Jefferson sent out 17 U.S. marshals to hire as many assistants as it took to solicit answers to 6 questions from every household across the land: the name of the head of the household, the number of free white males 16 years of age and older, the number of free white males under 16 years of age, the number of free white females, the number of other free persons, and the number of slaves.

THE LEGAL FOUNDATION. Responding to the census takers is required by law, specifically by Title 13 of the *United States Code.* According to the same law, all information is to be kept strictly confidential and is not to be used for taxation, investigation, or regulation. Data may be published, provided specific individuals and businesses are not identified. Nobody may use the *Freedom of Information Act* to acquire data linked with identifiable persons.

THE IMPORTANCE OF CENSUS DATA. Census data have three major uses: First, state population counts are used to apportion seats in the House of Representatives. Second, population totals for counties, cities, and other political subdivisions are used to draw the boundaries of congressional, state, and local legislative districts. Third, population totals are used to apportion federal funds among state, local, and tribal governments. Such funds are disbursed for a multitude of purposes, such as emergency programs for earthquakes, floods, and hurricanes; employment services; highway construction; hospital services; housing assistance; programs for the elderly; and schools.

MISTAKES OF THE PAST. When the Bureau of the Census conducted its Post Enumeration Survey for the 1990 census (a quick series of samples to check the accuracy of the census), it made a shocking discovery: It had undercounted about 1.6% of the total population, but the degree of the undercounting varied widely among specific population groups. The undercount was 5.0% for Hispanics, 4.4% for blacks, 4.5% for American Indians, and a mere 0.7% for non-Hispanic whites. Even though it had been conducted at a steeply higher cost, the 1990 census turned out to be the least accurate one in decades. In plain numbers, it failed to include 8.4 million persons, double-counted another 4.4 million, making for a net undercount of 4 million. Politicians were quick to note that the missed persons tended to be poor, inner-city minority residents who were likely to vote Democratic, while the double-counted persons tended to be affluent, suburban whites who were likely to vote Republican. *And therein lies the basis of what was to happen 10 years hence when plans for the next census were being hatched.*

FIGHTING NONRESPONSE. When formulating its plan for the census of 2000, the Bureau of the Census tried its best to avoid past mistakes. It noted that some 35% of all households had failed to mail back their census forms in 1990. In New York City, the nonresponse rate was even 47%! The uncooperative households had received personal visits by interviewers; yet 20% of them could not be found even after six tries. The Bureau blamed people's increased mobility, limited English skills, and suspicion of government, as well as the fact that ever more parents were both working. And it promised to make an unprecedented effort to reach every person the next time around.

First, argued the Bureau, in the year 2000, it would give everyone multiple opportunities to respond. There would be an initial mailing of census forms to a complete listing of all U.S. addresses (i.e., to a perfect *frame*), put together with the help of the U.S. Postal Service and all state, local, and tribal governments. Reminder cards would go to nonrespondents. Additional forms would be available at public locations. And there would be toll-free telephone numbers to request forms.

Second, once responses had been received from 90% of all addresses in each of 60,000 census tracts, a *simple random sample* of 10% of the remaining nonrespondents would be taken and the result would be multiplied by 10 to account for all of the nonrespondents. As a result, the 2000 census would be the most accurate ever.

A POLITICAL FOOTBALL. The Year 2000 census plan, however, raised a storm of protest from Republican politicians who foresaw a political gain for Democrats once a more accurate count led to redistricting. As they saw it, because legislative districts have to contain roughly equal numbers of persons, many an inner-city district would shrink in geographic size when the previously undercounted were counted. Such a district would vote Democratic. On the other hand, many a suburban district would be combined with a portion of the inner city, once the suburban double-counting disappeared. Such a formerly Republican district might well swing to the Democratic side. As you can guess, the whole matter ended up before the U.S. Supreme Court.

On January 25, 1999, in a split 5-to-4 decision, the Supreme Court banned the proposed use of random sampling for the purpose of getting the state population counts needed to apportion those 435 seats in the House of Repre-

(continued)

Application 4.5 (continued)

sentatives. The Court insisted on the traditional head count. It failed to rule on (and, thus, implicitly approved) the use of sampling to find population figures for redistricting and apportioning federal funds. The Bureau of the Census saw its costs soar by $2 billion, gave up on its hope for greater accuracy with the help of sampling, and revised its plan.

Accordingly, the 2000 census was undertaken with the (unrealistic) goal of making an actual head count of every person at every address in every census tract. Nonrespondents were pursued by numerous personal visits and telephone calls. The resultant figure was 281,421,906. However, it was unlikely to be any more accurate than that of 1990.

POSTSCRIPT. In light of the Supreme Court's vagueness, the Census Bureau also conducted a 300,000-person random sample of the U.S. population to find alternative (and, presumably, more accurate) data that could be used for redistricting or the disbursement of funds. As a result, the politics surrounding the 2000 census produced two different total population figures!

SOURCES: Adapted from Bureau of the Census, *Statistical Abstract of the United States 1998* (Washington, D.C.: 1998), p. 1; Steven A. Holmes, "Census Officials Plan Big Changes in Gathering Data," *The New York Times,* May 16, 1994, pp. A1 and 13; Linda Greenhouse, "In Blow to Democrats, Court Says Census Must Be by Actual Count," *The New York Times,* January 26, 1999, pp. A1 and 20; James Dao, "Census Ruling Reignites Partisan Battle," *The New York Times,* January 27, 1999, p. A13; *idem,* "Two (Many) Choices for 2000 Census," *The New York Times,* February 7, 1999, p. A4; Steven A. Holmes, "Census Director Accuses House Panel of Meddling," *The New York Times,* February 11, 1999, p. A21; *idem,* "The Big Census Issue: Using Sampling in Redistricting," *The New York Times,* February 14, 1999, p. A22; *idem,* "Ruling Said to Raise Census Cost by $2 Billion," *The New York Times,* February 24, 1999, p. A17; and information found on the Bureau of the Census Internet site (http://www.census.gov).

RESPONSE BIAS

Another common type of systematic error is **response bias,** a tendency for answers to survey questions to be wrong in some systematic way. The manifold sources of response bias include:

- the failure to pretest questionnaires
- the failure to motivate truthful answers
- the failure to define terms clearly
- the asking of leading questions
- the inappropriate behavior of interviewers
- the inappropriate behavior of respondents
- the introduction of errors during data processing

FAILURE TO PRETEST QUESTIONNAIRES Nothing, probably, contributes more to response bias than the thoughtless use of seemingly crystal-clear questions that have not been pretested. As a result, data gatherers may look for one thing, while respondents, quite reasonably, provide answers to something else. Students who take exams are familiar with the phenomenon. Consider the frequently told story of the student who answered (c) when confronted with the following:

1. Wind-eroded rocks are most commonly found

a. on mountain tops. **c.** in fertile valleys.
b. on river bottoms. **d.** in outer space.

The teacher had hoped for (a), but the student argued that hardly any people ever *were* on mountain tops, river bottoms, or in outer space; hence, if such rocks were to be *found,* it would most likely happen in (heavily populated) fertile valleys.

Nothing seems easier than to construct similarly inept questions on survey questionnaires. When this happens, survey takers and respondents fail to communicate with one another. Survey results, in turn, become highly questionable.

Failure to Motivate Truthful Answers A good questionnaire contains instructions that explain why the survey is being conducted and how the solicited information will be used. A failure to do so may well bias the answers people give. When asked about their income, for instance, people give different answers depending on whether they suspect that their answer will affect their taxes, their pension, or their bank credit.

The Failure to Define Terms Clearly Survey terms need concrete and specific definitions. For example, is it obvious what it means to live "in poverty" or in a "substandard" home or in a "crime-ridden" neighborhood? Such terms should not be placed on a questionnaire unless they are carefully defined. Nor can people be expected to know what to do when asked to list their hometown (what about soldiers or students?), their employment status (is a retired person *unemployed?*), their trips abroad (does Canada qualify?), their weight (with or without clothes? at morning or at night?), their age (last birthday or nearest birthday?), or their spending plans for next year (next *calendar* year or the next 12 months?).

Asking Leading Questions Most worrisome of all, perhaps, are **leading questions** that lead the respondent, inexorably, to particular, predictable answers. Leading questions can be obvious or extremely subtle. Here are some obvious ones:

1.	As usual, today's food in the dining hall was rotten.	Yes	No
2.	Should we waste further billions to send people into outer space, while there is poverty on earth?	Yes	No
3.	In light of their $3 billion profit, should we reject management's skimpy wage offer?	Yes	No
4.	Does the name *Apple* come to mind when thinking about high-quality computers?	Yes	No

One can safely bet that most answers would be Yes, No, Yes, Yes. Such questions are sure to invite response bias.

There are, however, more subtle ways to ask leading questions. Consider the *sequencing* of different questions in such a way that people answer one question within a frame of reference provided by a (possibly unrelated) earlier question:

10. Which of the following is responsible for making Fruit and Fibre such a superior cereal?

- **a.** It is fruitier.
- **b.** It is nuttier.
- **c.** It is sweeter.
- **d.** It is crunchier.

11. Which of the following do you consider superior?

- **a.** Fruit and Fibre.
- **b.** Bran Chex.
- **c.** Granola.
- **d.** Rice Krispies.

In light of question 10, most people will answer question 11 by choosing (a).

Inappropriate Behavior of Interviewers Even when questionnaires have been designed carefully to avoid all of the preceding problems (and have been pretested to confirm this fact), success is not assured. Interviewers themselves can elicit response bias. For example, interviewers may inadvertently solicit a particular "acceptable" answer to a question by their dress and choice of words (which may betray their social class) or by their tone of voice and demeanor (a gesture of disapproval or surprise at some answers will almost surely affect other answers). Interviewers can also make systematic mistakes when recording answers—for example, by consistently categorizing part-time income or work as full-time. Even the timing of a survey can create response bias. What do you think would happen to all the answers if an interviewer were to conduct a survey on plant safety precisely one day after a rare but major accident? If a survey on hours recently worked were conducted shortly after a major holiday?

Inappropriate Behavior of Respondents Questionnaire designers and interviewers must not receive all the blame, however. Some respondents give false answers despite the most perfect questionnaire and the most proper behavior of interviewers. For example, some respondents may simply not know an answer (do *you* know the brand of tires on your car?) but may give an answer anyway to conceal their ignorance. Others may give whatever answer they think will *please* the interviewer. (It is well known that white and black interviewers get different answers from identical respondents when asking identical questions on racial issues. Likewise, male and female interviewers get different answers on gender issues.) Respondents may give distorted answers in line with some current fad toward optimism or pessimism. And they may tell deliberate falsehoods to mislead competitors or impress interviewers. People are particularly likely to boast of successes and hide failures on "prestige questions" concerning, say, their knowledge of current events or famous people, their reading of books or level of education, their grade-point average or wealth, and even their tooth-brushing and bathing habits. And people simply lie about matters they consider too personal, such as their age, health, and sexual habits, their income, or their tendency to be arrested for drug peddling, drunk driving, or shoplifting.

Data Processing Errors Response bias can even creep into a survey during the data processing stage. Multitudes of people who code, edit, tabulate, print, and otherwise manipulate data have multitudes of opportunities for making noncanceling errors. Those who code answers to **open-ended questions** (which elicit answers in people's own words) may consistently categorize them incorrectly. Editors may consistently introduce high or low values when encountering incomplete or illegible responses and they may fail to eliminate **outliers** or "wild values" (maverick responses that are not believable because they differ greatly from the majority of observed values). Data entry workers may consistently misread 7's as 9's; they may ignore all decimal points, turning every 8.1 into an 81—the list goes on.

Summary

1. Surveys are the most common method of generating data in business and economics. In a complete survey, or *census,* observations are made about one or more characteristics of interest for every elementary unit that exists—by direct observation, self-enumeration, or personal or telephone interview. In a partial survey, or *sample,* such observations are made only for a subset of existing elementary units.
2. A number of reasons for preferring sampling to census taking can be cited. These can include the high cost of a census, its physical impossibility, and, on occasion, its destructive nature. Other reasons may be lack of time for a census and the realization that sampling can provide more information per dollar spent or even more accurate information.
3. Samples of different quality are obtained depending on the method by which the researcher selects elementary units for observation. Two basic types exist. *Nonprobability* samples, such as *voluntary response samples* or interviewer-selected *convenience samples* or *judgment samples,* are not very reliable. *Probability* or *random* samples alone can provide credible information; these include the *simple random sample,* the *systematic random sample,* the

stratified random sample, and the *clustered random sample.*

4. A *simple random sample* is a subset of a frame, or of an associated population, chosen in such a fashion that every possible *subset* of like size has an equal chance of being selected. A truly random selection is next to impossible to achieve when physical elementary units are mixed. Analogous procedures, such as the use of a *random-numbers table* or of a computer's *random-numbers generator,* are much more apt to succeed.
5. A *systematic random sample* is a subset of a frame, or of an associated population, chosen by randomly selecting one of the first k elements and then including every kth element thereafter until the desired sample size has been reached. A *stratified random sample* is a subset of a frame, or of an associated population, chosen by taking separate (simple or systematic) random samples from every stratum in the frame or population, often in such a way that the sizes of the separate samples vary with the importance of the different strata. A *clustered random sample* is a subset of a frame, or of an associated population, chosen by taking separate censuses in a randomly chosen subset of geographically distinct clusters.
6. In many real-life situations, the use of a single sampling technique is abandoned in favor of a more complex *multistage sampling,* a procedure that involves the successive sampling of ever-smaller groups and possibly even the use of different sampling methods at each stage.
7. Whether collected by census or sample, all survey data are subject to error. Values obtained by data gatherers can differ from true values as a result of *random error* (in the case of random sampling) or of *systematic error* or *bias* (in the case of all types of surveys). The size of the former can be estimated, but not so the size of the latter.
8. Systematic error or bias can creep into surveys at the planning stage, during the data collection stage, and even during the data processing stage, and such error can take the form of *selection bias, nonresponse bias,* or *response bias.*

Key Terms

bias
census
chance error
clustered random sample
convenience sample
judgment sample
leading questions
multistage sampling
nonprobability sample
nonresponse bias
nonsampling error
open-ended questions
outliers
probability sample
random error
random-numbers table
random sample
response bias
sample survey
sampling error
selection bias
simple random sample
stratified random sample
systematic error
systematic random sample
voluntary response sample

Practice Problems

NOTES

1. Some problems assume that you are connected to the Internet. The addresses noted in these problems, and the solutions described on the accompanying CD-ROM, were current at the time of this writing. However, Web sites are forever evolving. If things have changed, you can still learn much by solving a slightly different problem in a slightly different way.
2. Some problems require the use of a statistical program such as EXCEL or MINITAB. See Chapter 2 for major program features. Plenty of additional advice is available via the program's built-in Help feature.

SECTION 4.1 CENSUS TAKING VERSUS SAMPLING

The exercises in this section are designed to introduce you to some of the masters in the field of census taking and sampling, including the U.S. Bureau of the Census and the Gallup, Roper, and Harris organizations. By exploring their Web sites and publications, you can learn much about the types of data available as well as the survey methods used to acquire them.

1. Visit http://www.census.gov, a site maintained by the U.S. Bureau of the Census.
   a. Find out the current size of the U.S. population.
   b. Click on **People** and check out the type of information available. List five of the categories.
   c. Find the *poverty threshold* for a single person under the age of 65 for the latest available year.
2. Visit http://www.census.gov, a site maintained by the U.S. Bureau of the Census.
   a. Find out the current size of the U.S. population.
   b. Click on **Business** > **Companies**. Under "Small" Business and Ownership, click **Overview** > **Legal Form of Organization**. Find the number of *individual proprietorships* for the latest available year.
3. Visit http://www.census.gov, a site maintained by the U.S. Bureau of the Census.
   a. Click on **State & County Quick Facts**. On the U.S. map, select **MA**. Create an alphabetical list of the 14 Massachusetts counties and code them for later sampling.
   b. How many congressional districts are there in Massachusetts?
   c. Find the latest census information on total population and median household income in the 1st Congressional District of Massachusetts.
4. Visit http://www.census.gov, a site maintained by the U.S. Bureau of the Census.
   a. Click on **State & County Quick Facts**. On the U.S. map, select **UT**. Create an alphabetical list of the 29 Utah counties and code them for later sampling.
   b. How many congressional districts are there in Utah?
   c. Find the latest census information on total population and median household income in the 1st Congressional District of Utah.
5. Visit http://www.census.gov, a site maintained by the U.S. Bureau of the Census.
   a. Click on **State & County Quick Facts**. On the U.S. map, select **TX**. Find the number of congressional districts in Texas; then find the latest census information on total population and median household income in the 10th Congressional District of Texas.
   b. Click on **State & County Quick Facts**. On the U.S. map, select **HI**. Find the number of congressional districts in Hawaii; then find the latest census information on total population and median household income in the 2nd Congressional District of Hawaii.
6. Visit http://www.census.gov, a site maintained by the U.S. Bureau of the Census. Check out the Latest Economic Indicators with respect to
   a. U.S. International Trade in Goods and Services.
   b. Quarterly Financial Report—Retail Trade.
   c. Household Income.
   d. Poverty.
7. Check out the latest print copy of U.S. Bureau of the Census, *Statistical Abstract of the United States* (Washington, D.C.). Focus on the Appendix, *Guide to State Statistical Abstracts.* Identify (and check out) the Internet sites for
   a. Alaska's Department of Commerce and Economic Development.
   b. California's Department of Finance.
   c. Connecticut's Department of Economic and Community Development.
   d. Idaho's Department of Commerce.
8. Check out the latest print copy of U.S. Bureau of the Census, *Statistical Abstract of the United States* (Washington, D.C.). Focus on the Appendix, *Guide to State Statistical Abstracts.* Identify (and check out) the Internet sites for
   a. Indiana's Business Research Center.
   b. Montana's Department of Commerce, Census, and Economic Information Center.
   c. Nebraska's Department of Economic Development.
   d. Ohio's Department of Development.
9. Check out the latest print copy of U.S. Bureau of the Census, *Statistical Abstract of the United States* (Washington, D.C.). Focus on the Appendix on Metropolitan Areas.
   a. How does the Census Bureau define a Metropolitan Statistical Area (MSA)?
   b. How many MSAs exist?
10. Visit http://www.gallup.com, a site maintained by the Gallup Organization. Check it out; then write an

essay on what Gallup tells you about its sampling techniques.

11. Visit http://www.roper.com, a site maintained by the Roper Organization. Check it out; then write an essay on one of the following:

a. The Roper Reports.

b. The Roper Youth Report.

c. The Roper Reports Worldwide.

d. The Roper Affluent Report.

e. Hot Facts from Roper's Public Pulse.

f. Roper Influentials.

g. Green Gauge.

h. ADD+Impact.

12. Visit http://www.louisharris.com, a site maintained by the Harris Organization. Check it out; then write an essay on one of the following:

a. The latest monthly Harris poll.

b. Issues examined by last year's polls, arranged by category.

Section 4.2 The Reasons for Sampling

13. Consider the following situations and determine whether a census or a sample would be more appropriate:

a. A personnel director who wants to improve labor relations seeks to ascertain the attitudes of the firm's employees.

b. A pharmaceutical firm wants to ascertain the side effects, if any, of a drug that has proven effective against some types of cancer.

c. NASA wants to check the quality of all space shuttle components.

14. Consider the following situations and determine whether a census or a sample would be more appropriate:

a. A manufacturer of wooden matches has discovered that a certain percentage of production always seems to be defective and wants to ascertain what the percentage is.

b. A retail hardware store wants to determine the value of its inventory.

c. Someone wants to predict the outcome of a planned vote on the establishment of no-smoking zones in all public places.

15. In the mid-1990s, the Chinese government wanted to test the attitudes of Chinese citizens toward life, in particular with respect to the teachings of Mao Zedong and Deng Xiaoping. Would a census or a sample have been more appropriate? Why?

Section 4.3 Two Basic Types of Samples

16. Ann Landers, the advice columnist, once asked her readers with children whether they would have children all over again if they could relive their lives. Some 70 percent of 10,000 parents answered with a resounding NO. What type of sample was taken? Evaluate the result.

17. During the O. J. Simpson murder trial of the 1990s, a TV station asked its viewers to spend 50 cents on a 900-number telephone call and indicate whether they thought the one-time football great was guilty or innocent. Evaluate the sampling method used and interpret the result accordingly.

18. Domino's Pizza once was sued by Amstar, maker of Domino sugar, on the grounds that use of this name confused people. Indeed, Amstar had interviewed women shopping in supermarkets, had shown them a Domino's Pizza box, and had asked whether they thought the pizza makers produced any other product. Some 71 percent said "sugar." The court threw out the suit. Can you think of a reason for the court's action?

Section 4.4 The Simple Random Sample

19. How many different samples of 3 might one select from four units (A, B, C, D), and what probability of selection must each of these sets have to make the sample a simple random sample?

20. Consider Table 4.1 on page 110. How many different simple random samples of size $n = 5$ can be drawn without replacement from the list of 100 multinationals? Of size $n = 50$? (*Hint:* See the Technical Detail on page 108 in Section 4.4.)

21. Consider Table 4.1 on page 110. How many different simple random samples of size $n = 4$ can be drawn without replacement from the list of 100 multinationals? Of size $n = 10$? (*Hint:* See the Technical Detail on page 108 in Section 4.4.)

22. Consider Table 1.8 on page 16. How many different simple random samples of size $n = 4$ can be drawn without replacement from the list of 9 employees? Of size $n = 1$? (*Hint:* See the Technical Detail on page 108 in Section 4.4.)

23. Start at the bottom of column 7 of Appendix Table A. By using the first two digits of random numbers and reading upward, select a simple random sample of 10 multinationals from Table 4.1 on page 110. What are their names?

24. Go to Table 4.3 on page 114, which contains computer-generated random numbers. Starting with the row 1, column 1 number and moving down, read the first two digits after each decimal point in column 1 to select a simple random sample of 10 multinationals from Table 4.1 on page 110. What are their names?

25. Go to Table 4.3 on page 114, which contains computer-generated random numbers. Starting with the last number in column 7 and moving up, read the last two digits of each number to select a simple random sample of 10 multinationals from Table 4.1 on page 110. What are their names?

26. Repeat Practice Problem 25, but assume that there are only 50 such multinationals—namely, the ones numbered 00 through 49. If necessary, continue the procedure of selecting the last two digits with the last number in columns 6, 5, and so on. What are the names of sampled firms now?

27. Appendix Table A has 50 rows and 10 columns of 5-digit numbers. Starting at the upper left-hand corner of the table, read two digits at a time along the first row (and possibly along subsequent rows), letting the first usable set of two digits point you to a row and the second usable set to a column where random-number selection is to start. What is your starting number?

28. Given the starting number found in Practice Problem 27, proceed to the right along successive rows, reading the first and last digits of the 5-digit numbers in order to select a sample of six multinationals from Table 4.1 on page 110. What is your sample?

29. Given the starting number found in Practice Problem 27, proceed downward along successive columns, reading the second and third digits of the 5-digit numbers in order to select a sample of five multinationals from Table 4.1 on page 110. What is your sample?

30. Given the starting number found in Practice Problem 27, proceed upward along successive columns, reading the third and fourth digits of the 5-digit numbers in order to select a sample of five multinationals from Table 4.1 on page 110. What is your sample?

31. Use a table of random numbers to select a simple random sample of five doctors from among those listed in the yellow pages of your local telephone directory.

32. Use a table of random numbers to select a simple random sample of five students from among those who are attending your statistics class.

33. You are investigating a firm with 1,967 employees, and you have an alphabetical listing of their names. Select a simple random sample of ten employees

a. with the help of a random-numbers table.

b. with the help of EXCEL or MINITAB.

34. Use EXCEL or MINITAB (with Session Commands) to select a simple random sample of five from

a. the 29 Utah counties found in Practice Problem 4.

b. the 1,200 freshmen enrolled at a university.

c. the latest list of *Fortune 500* companies.

35. Use EXCEL or MINITAB (with Menu Commands) to select a simple random sample of six from

a. the 14 Massachusetts counties found in Practice Problem 3.

b. the numbers 1 though 40 that one can play in a state lottery.

c. the 50 states of the United States.

36. Review Table 1.8 on page 16. Enter its data into columns 1–6 of your computer program, while coding employee names from 1 to 9, race as 1 for *white* and 2 for *black,* sex as 1 for *male* and 2 for *female,* and the job titles, in the order of first mention, from 1 to 7. Then take a simple random sample of 3 employees, along with their associated data, using either EXCEL or MINITAB (with Session Commands).

37. Review Table 1.8 on page 16. Enter its data into columns 1–6 of your computer program, while coding employee names from 1 to 9, race as 1 for *white* and 2 for *black,* sex as 1 for *male* and 2 for *female,* and the job titles, in the order of first mention, from 1 to 7. Then take a simple random sample of 3 employees, along with their associated data, using either EXCEL or MINITAB (with Menu Commands).

SECTION 4.5 OTHER TYPES OF RANDOM SAMPLES

38. Which type of sample was actually taken in each of the following situations?

a. A newscaster reports having taken a random sample of city residents by interviewing people coming out of a supermarket.

b. Between 10 A.M. and 4 P.M., Mondays to Fridays, a pollster calls every 100th number in a city's telephone directory and asks any person who answers to rate various types of detergents. (No effort is made to contact people who do not answer the phone.)

c. The Dow Jones Industrials stock index is constructed by observing the performance of a mere 30 stocks selected by experts as representative of all industrial stocks.

d. The state tourism bureau creates a profile of the "typical" out-of-state tourist by interviewing one evening all out-of-state guests at a single hotel chosen at random.

e. In order to ascertain how well a new product is doing, a pollster checks at known "trendsetters" among retail stores.

f. Using a random-numbers table, a quality inspector selects 20 from among 1,000 numbered boxes containing paper napkins produced during a day, then inspects all the napkins in these boxes.

39. Which of the following are probability samples? How would you characterize the others?

a. Using a table of random numbers, an interviewer selects 10 shopping malls from a list of 200, then interviews the owners of every store in these 10 malls.

b. A farmer throws a pair of dice, comes up with a 7, and then, starting with tree number 7, inspects every peach on every 12th tree in an orchard to ascertain frost damage.

c. A manufacturer sends a questionnaire to all new-car purchasers. The results, based on a 20 percent response, are then tabulated.

d. Representatives of the mayor interview three blacks and seven whites prior to a town meeting concerning a proposed ordinance to close bars at 10 P.M. The proportions chosen reflect the racial makeup of the town.

e. The Equal Employment Opportunity Commission randomly selects 200 men from among 3,000 male faculty members and 200 women from among 800 female faculty members and interviews them.

f. The Equal Employment Opportunity Commission randomly selects 10 full professors, 10 associate professors, 10 assistant professors, and 10 instructors from among 4,567 faculty members at a major university.

40. Select a *systematic random sample* of five firms from Table 4.1 on page 110. What is the value of *k?* Find the starting point for your sample by reading the last row of Appendix Table A and picking the first usable number between 00 and *k.* List your sample.

41. Answer these questions about systematic, stratified, and clustered random samples:

a. How might one select a *systematic* random sample of 200 from among 10,000 bills?

b. How big a sample would one have to take from each stratum if a population was stratified in such a way that each stratum contained completely homogeneous elements and if one desired information equivalent to a census?

c. Imagine that the 100 firms listed in Table 4.1 on page 110 could meaningfully be subdivided into 10 strata, the members of which were, respectively, the firms numbered 00–09, 10–19, 20–29, and so on. Select a *stratified* random sample of one firm from each group, assuming that you picked the following random numbers to represent the last digits of firms to be picked from the strata: 0 8 2 3 3 5 9 5 0 6. List the names.

d. Both stratified and cluster sampling separate a population into groups, yet there are major differences between the two approaches. Explain.

e. Once again consider Table 4.1 on page 110, but now imagine that each successive five firms were a meaningful *cluster.* Select a sample of two from the 20 clusters in which to take censuses. Assume you assigned numbers 00 to 19 to the clusters, then picked the random numbers 17 and 05 from a table. List the firms to be sampled.

SECTION 4.6 MULTISTAGE SAMPLES

42. You are a manager about to expand into a new market (the United States east of the Mississippi). You want to study people's preferences for the goods you want to offer. Prepare a sampling plan.

43. Look at the print edition of U.S. Bureau of the Census, *Statistical Abstract of the United States 1999* (Washington, D.C.: 1999), Appendix III. Write an essay on what the Census Bureau says about its *multistage sampling.*

SECTION 4.7 ERRORS IN SURVEY DATA

44. Look at the print edition of U.S. Bureau of the Census, *Statistical Abstract of the United States 1999* (Washington, D.C.: 1999), Appendix III. Write an essay on what the Census Bureau says about the general nature of *sampling errors* and *nonsampling errors.*

45. Look at the print edition of U.S. Bureau of the Census, *Statistical Abstract of the United States 1999* (Washington, D.C.: 1999), Appendix III. Write an essay on what the Census Bureau says about *sampling errors* and *nonsampling errors* found in its data on

- **a.** population and labor force.
- **b.** education.
- **c.** the federal government.
- **d.** income, expenditures, and wealth.
- **e.** prices.

46. Look at the print edition of U.S. Bureau of the Census, *Statistical Abstract of the United States 1999* (Washington, D.C.: 1999), Appendix III. Write an essay on what the Census Bureau says about *sampling errors* and *nonsampling errors* found in its data on

- **a.** business enterprise.
- **b.** agriculture.
- **c.** construction and housing.
- **d.** manufactures.
- **e.** foreign commerce.

SECTION 4.8 HOW BIAS CREEPS INTO SURVEYS

47. What kinds of errors are likely to occur as a result of each of the following:

- **a.** Consistently reading a wrong column on census forms used as computer input.
- **b.** The inability to interview a family selected as part of a simple random sample.
- **c.** Having only 21 percent of questionnaires returned from a mail survey
- **d.** Judging public opinion from a radio talk show.
- **e.** Asking people about their age rather than their precise birthday.
- **f.** Judging consumer preferences for a product by interviewing people stopped in cars at a red light.
- **g.** Calling 100 people listed in the phone book to rate a new TV show.
- **h.** Taking a random sample of 10 pages of this book to estimate the fractions of the book devoted to text, definition boxes, summaries, practice problems, applications, and the like.
- **i.** Taking a random sample of 10 sentences from the population of sentences found on the second page of Chapter 1 in order to estimate the length of sentences in this book.
- **j.** Asking people how many phone calls they have made (or bars of soap they have used) in the past 24 months.

48. This chapter's Preview casts doubts on the workability of Perot's electronic town meeting idea because of the likelihood of selection bias and nonresponse bias. If these biases could somehow be overcome—and all Americans somehow watched and responded to the TV programs—would problems remain?

49. Response bias is often caused by faulty questionnaires, in particular the use of confusing questions and leading questions. Make up four examples each of

- **a.** confusing questions.
- **b.** leading questions.

50. When all is said and done, what, do you think, can one do to avoid bias in surveys? Make a list.

Chapter 5

GENERATING NEW DATA: CONTROLLED EXPERIMENTS

LOOKING AHEAD

After reading this chapter, you will be able to understand the difference between observational surveys and controlled experiments. Among other things, you will learn:

1. to appreciate why surveys can only reveal an association between two variables, while experiments can also establish causation,
2. to design controlled experiments of your own with the help of randomization or blocking,
3. to set up a variety of complex experiments, such as those using the crossover design, the Latin square design, or the Youden square design, and
4. to distinguish random experimental error from systematic error or bias.

AND HERE IS A TYPICAL PROBLEM YOU WILL BE ABLE TO SOLVE:

Pharmaceutical companies can increase their sales by billions of dollars per year if they are lucky enough to come up with a new best-selling drug. No wonder they are always experimenting. One such company selected 100 adults at random and managed to persuade 80 of them to take calcium supplements, which were expected to lower blood pressure. A comparison of the subjects' before-and-after blood pressure readings confirmed the suspicion. As a statistician hired by the Food and Drug Administration, evaluate this experiment.

PREVIEW

New data about matters unknown can be generated in one of two ways: by conducting a *survey* or by performing an *experiment*. As we saw in the previous chapter, when a census or sample survey is being conducted, statisticians are relatively passive. They merely *observe* elementary units with regard to some characteristic of interest, record what they see, and that is that. Like *Star Trek*'s Captain Picard, they follow the Prime Directive of noninterference and focus on observation, which is why surveys are called *observational studies*. In contrast, statisticians who gather data with the help of experiments take on a more active role. They deliberately introduce some type of change into a situation of interest and then wait breathlessly to record the response. To collect *valid* data, however, experimentation, just like census taking or sampling, has to be conducted with the greatest of care.

Take the case of Dr. O. H. Wangensteen, who once proposed a revolutionary new ulcer treatment: The patient swallows a balloon into which a refrigerant liquid is pumped, which freezes the stomach. In response, the digestive process shuts down temporarily, giving the stomach a chance to heal. The physician had performed this experiment, he said, on 24 patients of his choice and all were cured. But critics scoffed.

Might the good doctor have selected patients that would have become better even without the procedure? Might the doctor have exaggerated the rate of cure? Might the patients have succumbed to the "guinea pig effect," experiencing psychological reductions in symptoms merely because they knew that they were subjects in an experiment? And how long did the cure last? In short, were the data gathered by this "experiment," perhaps, just as worthless as those gathered by a convenience sample?

Before long, another physician, Dr. J. M. Ruffin, performed an alternative and much more rigorous test. He randomly selected 160 ulcer patients and randomly divided them into two groups, a *treatment group* and a *control group*. All of the patients, mind you, were made to swallow that balloon and were given the impression that they underwent the gastric freezing procedure. However, 82 patients in the *treatment* group received the genuine procedure, while 78 patients in the *control* group underwent a fake procedure during which a bypass valve diverted the refrigerant. More than that! The doctors who performed the procedure, just like their patients, had no idea about who belonged to which group. (In such a *double-blind study,* only the statistician knows what is going on.) The results of this controlled experiment were instructive: After the procedure, 76 percent of patients in the treatment group showed improvement or no symptoms; 68 percent of patients in the control group were similarly classified. Over time, patients in both groups relapsed at about the same rate, and at no time was the difference between the two groups significant. Wangensteen's procedure was termed useless.

By now, nearly 40 years have passed since Wangensteen's "experiment." Most modern-day experimenters, just like modern survey takers, have learned how to be much more careful. Take a recent experiment by James Lau and others, also concerned with the control of bleeding ulcers. This time, the question was whether (A) a second endoscopy or (B) outright surgery was the better approach when patients experienced renewed bleeding after an initial endoscopic treatment. (During endoscopy, a flexible fiberoptic tube is passed through the esophagus into the stomach and duodenum to allow the physician to observe an ulcer directly.) From among 1,169 patients who were initially treated, some 100 experienced rebleeding. Of these, 92 patients were randomly assigned either to a second endoscopy (A) or to immediate surgery (B). The remaining 8 patients were excluded from the experiment due to unusual circumstances, including heart attacks, terminal cancer, and such. The result: 25 percent of the A-group and 54 percent of the B-group had complications or died. A second endoscopy to stop bleeding was deemed preferable to surgery.

This chapter tells all about the nature of bad and good experiments such as these—not only in medicine, but in economics and business as well. Indeed, more often than you might think, experiments in these disparate fields are closely linked. Government economists in charge of Medicare, Medicaid, or anti-pollution programs need valid data to make rational decisions, and medical researchers provide those data. And multibillion-dollar pharmaceutical companies, such as Glaxo Wellcome, Merck, or Pfizer, spend huge amounts on medical experiments every year in their never-ending search for better drugs. When they succeed, their profits can rise by a multiple of what they spent.[1]

[1]Adapted from O. H. Wangensteen et al., "Achieving 'Physiological Gastrectomy' by Gastric Freezing," *The Journal of the American Medical Association,* vol. 180, 1962, pp. 439–444; J. M. Ruffin et al., "A Cooperative Double-Blind Evaluation of Gastric 'Freezing' in the Treatment of Duodenal Ulcer," *The New England Journal of Medicine,* vol. 281, 1969, pp. 16–19; and James Y. W. Lau et al., "Endoscopic Retreatment Compared with Surgery in Patients with Recurrent Bleeding after Initial Endoscopic Control," *The New England Journal of Medicine,* vol. 340, 1999, pp. 751–756.

5.1 Association versus Causation

This chapter focuses on how we generate new data with *experiments.* As we will see, properly run experiments can provide more reliable data than surveys do. A survey can highlight an *association* between two variables; that is, it can show that A varies with B, but it can never prove that A *causes* B or the other way around. An experiment, in contrast, can do precisely that. It can establish *causation* between two variables and prove that A causes B.

ASSOCIATION REVEALED BY SURVEYS

On many occasions, one thing appears to be connected to another thing. When we see A, we also see B. When A rises, B rises as well. When A falls, so does B. In circumstances such as these, we may well *suspect* a causal link, but we must be careful not to jump to unwarranted conclusions. The mere observation of such an association proves nothing at all. The observed linkage can be pure coincidence. It can be the result of some third factor, C, that affects both A and B at the same time. And it can, of course, also point to the real thing, the fact that A actually causes B.

A MENTAL EXPERIMENT In order to show how surveys can reveal the existence of association, while being unable to help us choose among the three possible explanations just cited, let us conduct a mental experiment. Consider a firm, Omni Aviation, Inc., about which we make two assumptions:

Assumption 1. The annual salaries of its workers are determined by a simple formula. Without exception, they equal \$10,000 plus \$1,000 for each year of service. Gender, job title, race, or any other factors play no role in setting salary.

Assumption 2. The daily output of its workers can be gauged by a simple formula as well. In units of product, it equals 10 times each worker's years of service. A voluntary training program that the company offers (and that, in fact, has been attended only by highly motivated, more mature workers with many years of service) does not affect productivity at all.

Table 5.1 incorporates the two assumptions just noted and provides additional data about our hypothetical firm. It is the kind of information that survey takers would not possess initially but they could potentially acquire.

Definition 5.1 reviews the nature of a survey and prepares us for a discussion of two possible surveys of our firm.

> **DEFINITION 5.1** The collection of data from elementary units by merely recording information about selected characteristics of interest (such as A or B), while paying no attention to perhaps widely diverging other characteristics, is called an **observational study** or **survey.**

SURVEY #1 First, we imagine survey workers taking a census of the 36 workers in our firm and collecting the data in columns 1, 5, and 6, while paying no attention to all the other variables.

TABLE 5.1 | Selected Data about Omni Aviation, Inc.

All of the information contained in this table is known to us, the readers of this text. However, depending on the questions asked, an investigator who studies this firm may or may not discover all of it.

Number of Workers (1)	Race (2)	Years of Service (3)	Annual Salary (4)	Output per Day (5)	Voluntary Training (6)
16	Black	2	$12,000	20 units	No
2	White	2	$12,000	20 units	No
2	Black	20	$30,000	200 units	Yes
16	White	20	$30,000	200 units	Yes

Their conclusion is fairly obvious: "The daily output of the 18 workers who did not participate in the company's training program comes to 20 units per worker. The daily output of the 18 workers who did participate in the company's training program equals 200 units per worker." So far so good; the survey has established a clear association between participation in the training program and worker output. Many people would, therefore, jump to an additional conclusion: "The training program is highly effective in raising worker productivity." Yet *we* know that this conclusion is wrong.

By Assumption 2 on page 138, the training program is totally *ineffective;* worker productivity is only related to years of service (the causal variable here). Our survey has established an *association* between participation in the training program and productivity, but no one should confuse this association with causation. In fact, the causal variable (years of service in column 3) was totally ignored by the survey takers!

SURVEY #2 Second, we imagine survey workers taking a census of the 36 workers in our firm and collecting the data in columns 1, 2, and 4, while paying no attention to all the other variables. Their conclusion: "The annual salary of the firm's 18 black workers comes to 16 times $12,000, plus 2 times $30,000, or an average $14,000. The annual salary of the firm's 18 white workers comes to 2 times $12,000, plus 16 times $30,000, or an average $28,000." How many people, do you think, would quickly add: "This firm discriminates by race." Yet, again, *we* know this conclusion to be false.

By Assumption 1 on page 138, race is totally ignored when setting salaries; salaries are set on the basis of a color-blind formula that relies on years of service (the causal variable here). Our survey has again established an *association* between race and annual salary, but this is not the same thing as causation. Once again, the causal variable (years of service in column 3) was totally ignored by the census workers.

CAUSATION ESTABLISHED BY EXPERIMENTS

While surveys cannot establish causation, carefully designed experiments can. The reason is easy to see. During a survey, we merely observe what happened, and we never quite know why. During an experiment, we take an active role. We deliberately introduce a single change into a carefully controlled setting; then we observe the consequences, if any. If they do occur, we know the cause because we introduced it. The following definition summarizes the nature of an experiment.

DEFINITION 5.2 The collection of data from elementary units by deliberately exposing them to some kind of change, while leaving all else unchanged, and subsequently recording how identical elementary units respond to different types of change, or how different types of elementary units respond to identical change, is called an **experiment.**

The examples on pages 138–139 should not be misunderstood. Associations detected by surveys do not necessarily mislead on the causation issue. In Survey #1, if researchers had collected information on columns 3 and 5 in Table 5.1, they would have discovered an association between years of service and daily output. These data would, at least, have raised the suspicion of a quite different causal connection. Likewise, in Survey #2, if data on columns 3 and 4 had been gathered, the association between years of service and salary would have become obvious, thus raising the possibility of an entirely different explanation for salary differentials.

Remember this: *Surveys can establish an association between variables, but that association may or may not indicate causation.* But all is not lost. In Chapters 17 and 18, we will meet *multiple regression analysis,* a technique that allows us to use survey data, such as those in Table 5.1, to relate one variable, such as daily output or salary, to lots of different variables simultaneously and then make a pretty good guess about causation as well. Experiments can do even better, as we will see presently.

EXPERIMENT #1 Once again consider the firm discussed in the previous section. Someone who wanted to test the effectiveness of some training program could easily conduct an appropriate experiment. This might involve dividing our firm's 36 workers into two identical groups, such as A and B in Figure 5.1, exposing one group to the program, while leaving the other group alone, and later comparing the daily outputs of the two groups.

Given Assumption 2 on page 138, a training program has no effect on output, which is exactly what the experiment would show. Regardless of the training program, each worker with 2 years of service produces 20 units per day and each worker with 20 years of service produces 200 units per day, making for a daily total of 1,980 units for either group.

EXPERIMENT #2 Someone who wanted to test the effect of race on salary would have a hard time setting up an appropriate experiment, however. It is impossible to *assign* different races to otherwise identical people in the same way that one might require people to take or not to take a training program. *Theoretically,* the experiment in question would have to be set up as shown in Figure 5.2 on page 142. One would start out with two groups of otherwise identical workers. Then, if one could force the Group A workers to be black and otherwise identical Group B workers to be white, one would discover identical group salaries. Given Assumption 1 on page 138, which rules out racial discrimination, this should not be surprising. *In practice,* of course, the race/salary issue could never be resolved in this way, which brings us to a final word about experiments in the next section.

THE LIMITS OF EXPERIMENTATION

Not all issues of interest can be resolved by generating experimental data. This is particularly true in the social sciences. Three major reasons come to mind:

- Experiments can be physically impossible.
- Experiments can be practically impossible.
- Experiments can be ethically unacceptable.

FIGURE 5.1 | A Feasible Controlled Experiment

One can test the effectiveness of a training program by asking two otherwise identical groups of workers either to take or not to take the program and then comparing their output.

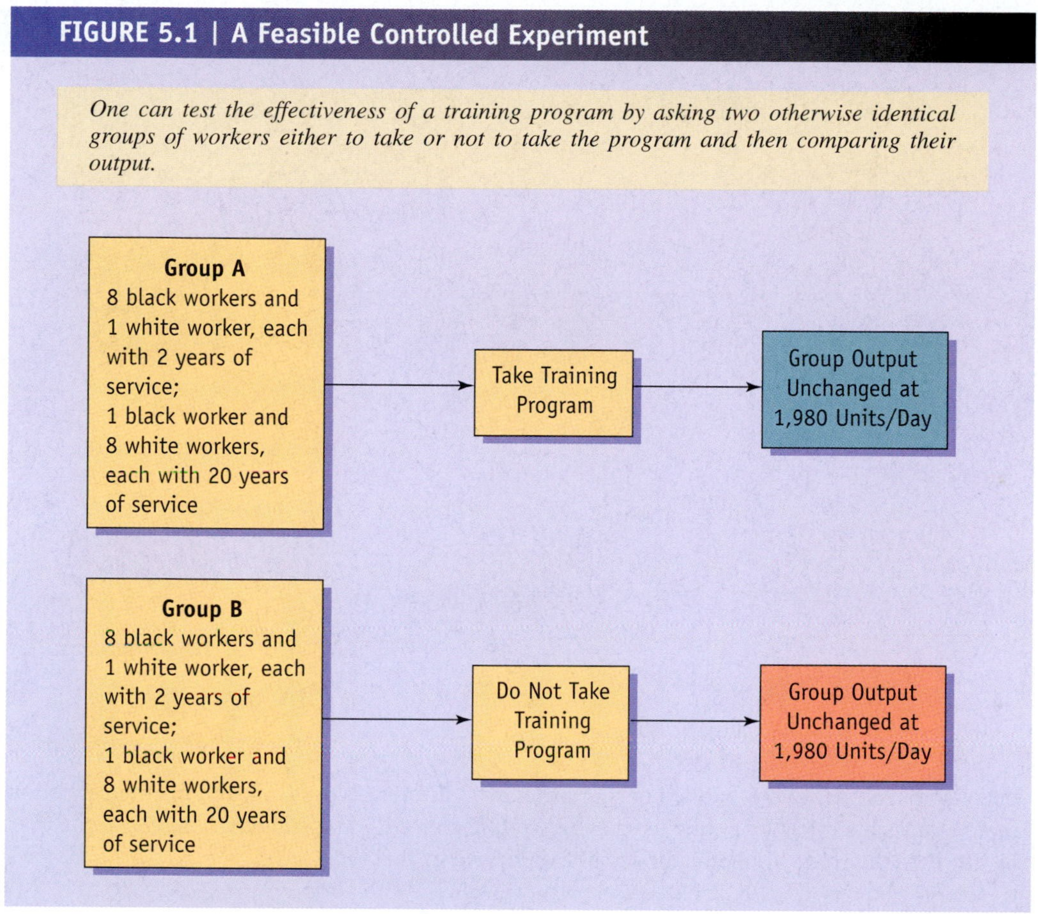

PHYSICALLY IMPOSSIBLE EXPERIMENTS Sometimes, experiments are *physically impossible,* as when the resolution of an issue (such as the alleged effect of sex or race on performance) requires the assignment of different genders or races to otherwise identical groups of people. Our discussion of Experiment #2 on the previous page provides a case in point.

PRACTICALLY IMPOSSIBLE EXPERIMENTS At other times, experiments are, perhaps, physically possible, but *practically impossible* because their execution requires the cooperation of large numbers of people who are not inclined to cooperate. Consider an attempt to measure the deterrent effect of capital punishment by imposing it on a randomly chosen group of 25 states for a few decades, while abolishing it in 25 other states. Or think about measuring the effect of interest rates on the volume of investment and the rate of economic growth and doing so by imposing low rates for one decade, followed by sky-high rates during another.

ETHICALLY UNACCEPTABLE EXPERIMENTS Finally, in some cases practical limitations are reinforced by ethical scruples, and experimentation is avoided for that reason. Imagine testing the effect of college education on lifelong income by arbitrarily assigning half of this year's high school graduates to colleges, while forcing all the others never to go to college at all. Imagine exposing a randomly chosen half of a city's children to a Head Start program prior to first grade and the other half not, and then testing the effect on future academic performance. Many will object even to such limited experimentation with people's lives. How far would one go? Should

Application 5.1 *The Negative Income Tax Experiments*
http://www.harcourtcollege.com/business_stats/kohler/siteresources.html

FIGURE 5.2 | An Impractical Controlled Experiment

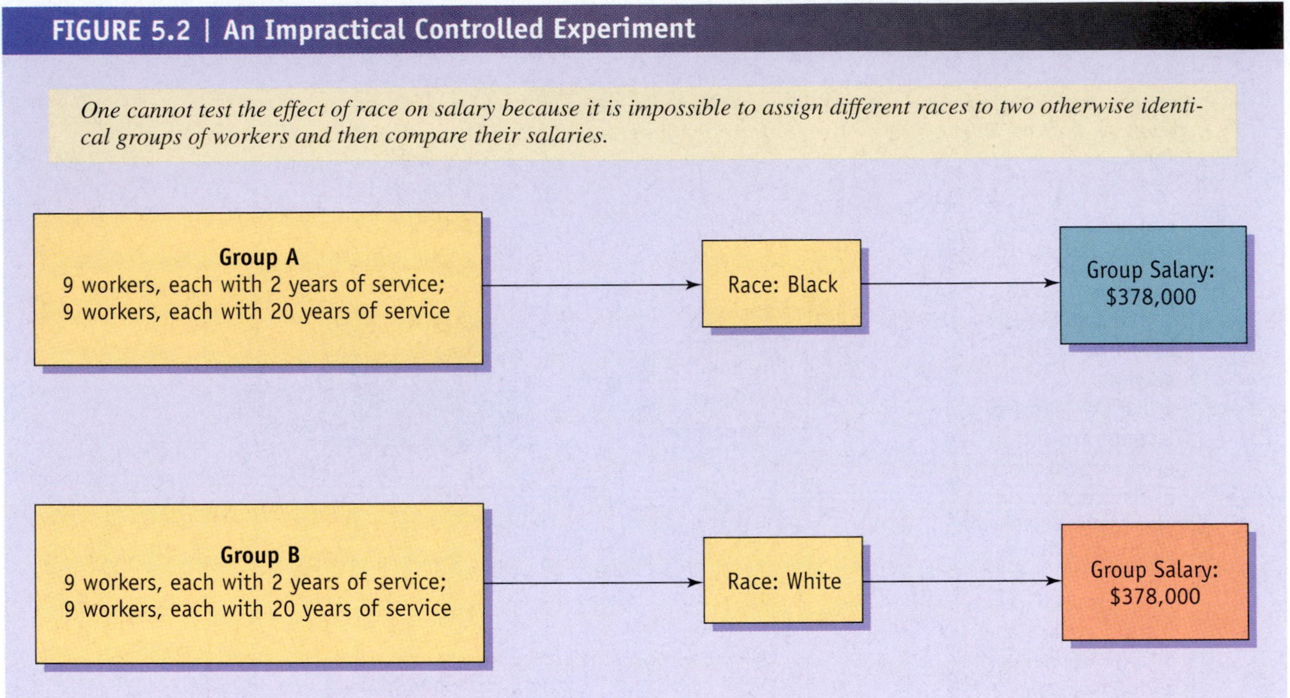

one also experiment with public housing programs, different types of health insurance, and numerous possible types of public assistance? Application 5.1, *The Negative Income Tax Experiments,* tells the story of one major social experiment of this type.

5.2 The Design of Experiments

As we have just seen, carefully designed experiments have one major advantage over census taking and sampling. They can elucidate cause-and-effect relationships, and such knowledge is crucial to economists, business executives, and decision makers in all other fields of endeavor. In this section, we become familiar with the main concepts that the designers of experiments employ.

BASIC CONCEPTS

Experimenters always want to know what kind of effect a change in one variable will have on some other variable. Doctors want to know how gastric freezing or endoscopic treatment or surgery affects bleeding in ulcer patients. Economists want to know how gender or job title or race or years of service affects salaries. Power plant executives want to know how the installation of smokestack scrubbers or the chemical cleaning of coal or the transformation of coal into liquid or gaseous fuel or the purchase of cleaner coal from abroad affects sulfur dioxide emissions. The examples are endless, but statisticians invent a few simple terms to cover all possible cases.

Statisticians designate the variable they expect to be influenced during an experiment as the **response variable** or the **dependent variable** or the **explained variable.** And they call the variable that is to do the influencing the **treatment variable** or the **explanatory variable** or the

independent variable or even the **(experimental) factor.** Oftentimes, a factor can take on alternative values, called **factor levels,** and these can be numerical (such as baking temperatures of 300, 350, or 400 degrees) or verbal (such as the placement of items at the top, middle, or bottom of a supermarket shelf).

STEPS IN VALID EXPERIMENTS

In order to reach valid conclusions, experimenters take four steps:

1. They select persons or objects, called **experimental units,** on which they will perform the experiment. These experimental units correspond to the *elementary units* in surveys and, just like the latter, they can be almost anyone or anything: customers in a store, patients in a hospital, workers in a factory, hamburgers being grilled at McDonald's, and microwave ovens rolling off an assembly line. *Human* experimental units are also referred to as **subjects.**
2. They divide all the experimental units into at least one **experimental group**—the members of which are about to be exposed to some stimulus—and a **control group**—the members of which are *not* to be so exposed.
3. They deliberately apply a different stimulus or **treatment** to the members of each group. (In this context, the deliberate application of *no* stimulus to the control group is regarded as a treatment as well.)
4. They compare the impact of the treatments on the response variable. Control group performance provides a convenient basis by which to compare the performance of all others. Application 5.2, *On Curing the Common Cold and Other Diseases,* on the following page, illustrates how one might come to wrong conclusions in the absence of a control group that is deliberately exposed to *nothing* new.

The following definition summarizes our discussion of comparative experiments.

DEFINITION 5.3 A **comparative experiment** is a four-step procedure consisting of (1) the selection of persons or objects, known as *experimental units,* (2) the division of these units into at least one *experimental group* and one *control group,* (3) the deliberate application of a different stimulus to each experimental group, while withholding any stimulus from the control group, and (4) the comparison of the responses of the different groups to their treatments.

THE CONFOUNDING PROBLEM

One major problem haunts comparative experiments: Extraneous factors (those other than the treatments) may influence the outcome and may lead the experimenter to reach wrong conclusions. Imagine, for example, a group of power plant executives running an experiment that compares traditional methods of electricity production (the control group) with a number of alternative methods (the treatment groups) in order to discover the best way to reduce sulfur dioxide emissions. So they install smokestack scrubbers in one plant, use chemically cleaned coal in another, burn liquid fuel made from coal in a third, place gaseous fuel made from coal in a fourth, and test Indonesia's low-sulfur *enviro-coal* in a fifth. Then they discover that weather influences sulfur dioxide emissions in such a way that high temperatures reduce and low temperatures raise emissions. If Florida plants had tested Indonesia's *enviro-coal* during its relatively warm winter months, while Massachusetts plants, serving as a control, had used American coal during the typical harshness of its winter, a huge observed difference in emissions might be

ON CURING THE COMMON COLD AND OTHER DISEASES

The importance of having a control group in an experiment was highlighted by a three-year study in the 1930s that evaluated a vaccine against the common cold. A homogeneous group of especially susceptible individuals was randomly separated into an experimental group, which received the vaccine, and a control group, which received a saline solution. No group members knew which treatment they received. Table 5.A shows the results.

While the first row seems to indicate that the vaccine had an impressive effect, a comparison with the second row suggests that all the experimental units also received a heavy dose of psychological immunity: Regardless of the treatment type, everyone's colds were reduced substantially, a factor that would not have been obvious in the absence of the control group.

Unfortunately, even modern-day medical decisions are often made on the basis of evidence like that in row 1 alone. Such was the case with the drug diethylstilbesterol, or DES, which was claimed to be effective in preventing miscarriages, all on the basis of five *uncontrolled* trials between 1948 and 1955. Later *controlled* studies, however, showed no difference in the rate of live births between treated and control groups, but the drug was abandoned only in 1973 when some children born to DES-treated mothers developed cancer. Another case is the testing of isoprinosine, introduced in 1972 to treat encephalitis. There were some apparent successes but also 30 deaths within a decade. Even in the 1990s, no one knew whether to praise or blame the drug because no *controlled* study had been made.

SOURCES: H. S. Diehl, A. B. Baker, and D. W. Cowan, "Cold Vaccines: An Evaluation Based on a Controlled Study," *Journal of the American Medical Association* 2 (1938): 1168–1173; and Jerry E. Bishop, "Doctors Debate Use of Controlled Studies to Test Effectiveness of New Treatments," *The Wall Street Journal,* August 8, 1982, p. 21. Table 5.A adapted from Table XLV, "A Study of Vaccination against the Common Cold," in Sir Austin Bradford Hill, *Principles of Medical Statistics,* 8th ed. (New York: Oxford University Press, 1967), p. 276. Copyright © 1966 by The Lancet, Ltd. Reprinted by permission of The Lancet, Ltd.

TABLE 5.A

Group	Treatment	Number of Persons	Average Number of Colds per Year: Before Vaccination	Average Number of Colds per Year: After Vaccination	Reduction in Colds
1. Experimental	Cold vaccine	272	5.9	1.6	73%
2. Control	Saline solution	276	5.6	2.1	63%

entirely due to this extraneous weather factor. Quite possibly, the type of coal had no effect at all! Such mingling of the effects of several explanatory variables (such as the type of coal, deliberately introduced, and the weather accidentally operating at the same time) on a response variable (here sulfur dioxide emissions) is every experimenter's nightmare. The predicament in question is known as the *confounding problem;* the following definition box explains.

DEFINITION 5.4 The problem facing investigators during an attempt to establish a cause-and-effect relationship when the separate influences of several independent variables on a dependent variable are hopelessly intermingled and cannot be distinguished from one another is called the **confounding problem.**

RANDOMIZATION AND BLOCKING

Experimenters can use two major devices to deal with the confounding problem and *control* those extraneous factors. One of these devices is **randomization,** a procedure that lets extraneous factors operate but ensures that each treatment has an equal chance to be enhanced or handicapped by these factors. Randomization requires that experimental units be selected randomly (step 1 on page 143) and also that they be assigned randomly to experimental and control groups (step 2 on page 143). In our power plant example, for instance, we might randomly select plants from many locations to participate in the experiment. Then we might establish six treatment groups—one each for five new methods of power generation plus one (the control) for the traditional method—and randomly assign participating plants to each of these groups. Thus, every one of the treatments would have an equal chance to be administered to a wide selection of plants from many locations and climates.

The other device that experimenters can use to deal with the confounding problem is known as **blocking.** Prior to administering treatments, they can create blocks of experimental units so that all units within any one block are as alike as possible with respect to suspected extraneous factors. In our power plant example, all of the treatments might be administered to Massachusetts plants only (Block 1) and again to Florida plants only (Block 2).

In conclusion, we note two additional concepts that experimenters employ, which leads us, in the next sections, to a more detailed discussion of experimental designs.

DEFINITION 5.5 Any experiment that uses randomization or blocking for the purpose of eliminating the confounding problem is called a **controlled experiment.**

DEFINITION 5.6 Any plan for assigning treatments to experimental units under controlled conditions and, thus, for generating valid data is called an **experimental design.**

5.3 The Randomized Group Design

We begin our study with the simplest of all experimental designs, which parallels the technique of *simple random sampling* that survey takers often choose to employ.

DEFINITION 5.7 An experimental plan that creates one treatment group for each treatment and then randomly assigns each experimental unit to one of these groups is called a **randomized group design** or a **completely randomized design.**

If we had 60 experimental units (coded from 01 to 60) and two treatments (A and B), we might, for example, simply pick the first 30 numbers in the 01 to 60 range that appear in a table of random numbers and assign similarly numbered experimental units to treatment group A. The remaining 30 units would be given treatment B. Or we might ask a computer program, such as EXCEL or MINITAB, to select the first 30 units in the fashion described in Chapter 4.

EXCEL Example 5.1

A publisher plans to conduct an experiment about the effectiveness of a newly created foreign-language teaching device that is to be promoted in a national advertising campaign. The firm's marketing department has recruited 60 college students to serve as experimental units. Treatment A will be the use of the device; treatment B will be traditional teaching methods. The random assignment of 30 students to each of these treatments is expected to control for extraneous factors in this sense: Each group will probably contain similar proportions of very able and not so able students, of highly motivated and totally indifferent students, of well-prepared and ill-prepared students. Accordingly, experimenters expect these very relevant factors of ability, motivation, and preparation to work equally in both groups so that later differences in group performance can be safely attributed to the difference in teaching methods. It is your job to show experimenters how EXCEL might be used to split the 60 students into the two treatment groups.

SOLUTION After coding student names from 1 to 60, you can use the procedure introduced in the page 116 Caution box associated with EXCEL Example 4.3. The first 30 subjects on your random list can receive treatment A; the remaining subjects, treatment B.

1. Fire up EXCEL and create patterned data reaching from 1 to 60 in column A. (Just enter 1, 2, 3 in cells A1–A3, select the three cells, and drag the cell A3 handle down to cell A60, which will contain the value 60.) These data can stand for the student names.
2. Type **=RAND()** in cell B1, select the number appearing in B1, and drag to B60.
3. Select the B1 to B60 range, click **Edit** > **Copy** and **Edit** > **Paste Special.**
4. In the *Paste Special* dialog box, select *Values* and *None* (which replaces the formulas in the B column with the values they create), and click **OK.**
5. With the B range selected, click **Data** > **Sort.** (If the *Sort Warning* box appears, expand the selection to sort.)
6. In the *Sort* dialog box, select *sort by Column B Ascending* and *No header row* and click **OK.**

The original column A data now appear in random order, without duplication. You can use the first 30 student codes as your sample A, the remainder being sample B.

EXCEL Example 5.2

Consider a national experiment on reducing sulfur dioxide emissions in electric power plants. Out of, say, 60 plants, 10 plants are to be randomly assigned to generate power by traditional methods (the control group), while five other groups of 10 plants each are to try out five alternatives. Experimenters want each of these six groups of 10 plants to contain a random selection of plants from Maine, Idaho, Arizona, and Florida, thereby neutralizing extraneous factors like climate or weather. It is your job to show experimenters how EXCEL might be used to split the 60 plants into the six treatment groups.

SOLUTION After coding power plant names from 1 to 60, you can use the procedure introduced in the page 116 Caution box associated with EXCEL Example 4.3. The first 10 subjects on your random list can receive treatment A, the next 10 can receive treatment B, and so on.

1. Fire up EXCEL and create patterned data reaching from 1 to 60 in column A. (Just enter 1, 2, 3 in cells A1–A3, select the three cells, and drag the cell A3 handle down to cell A60, which will contain the value 60.) These data can stand for power plant names.
2. Type **=RAND()** in cell B1, select the number appearing in B1, and drag to B60.
3. Select the B1 to B60 range, click **Edit** > **Copy** and **Edit** > **Paste Special.**

4. In the *Paste Special* dialog box, select *Values* and *None* (which replaces the formulas in the B column with the values they create), and click **OK.**
5. With the B range selected, click **Data** > **Sort.** (If the *Sort Warning* box appears, expand the selection to sort.)
6. In the *Sort* dialog box, select *Sort by Column B Ascending* and *No header row* and click **OK.**

The original column A data now appear in random order, without duplication. You can use the first 10 power plant codes as your sample A, the next 10 as sample B, and so on.

5.4 The Randomized Block Design

We now consider an experimental design that is only slightly more complicated than the randomized group design. It is the equivalent of *stratified random sampling* that survey takers like to use whenever it makes sense to divide existing elementary units into a number of distinct, internally homogeneous strata.

DEFINITION 5.8 An experimental plan that divides all available experimental units into blocks of fairly homogeneous units—each block containing as many units as there are treatments or some multiple of that number—and then randomly matches each treatment with one or more units within each block is called a **randomized block design.**

Recall the above experiment that used the randomized *group* design to test a new foreign-language teaching device. The randomized *block* design provides an alternative way of conducting the same test. Both procedures have the same goal (of evaluating the effectiveness of the foreign-language teaching device); they merely differ in the way they handle the confounding problem.

Under the randomized block design, the language test scores of the 60 students might be examined, and the top two students might be placed in Block 1. Their high scores would suggest that they were very much alike with respect to extraneous factors like ability, motivation, and level of preparation. They would be like a pair of near-twins. If, by the toss of a coin, treatment A (use of the new device) were to be assigned to one of these top two students, and treatment B (continued use of old methods) to the other, the publisher's critics could hardly argue that later differences in test scores were attributable to something other than differences in teaching approach.

Now imagine that the third- and fourth-ranking students were similarly combined to form Block 2, the fifth- and sixth-ranking ones to form Block 3, and so on down the line until the worst two students were placed into Block 30. In each case, one member of the block would receive treatment A; the other one, treatment B. Thus, compared to the randomized group design, the randomized block design would control extraneous influences in a novel way.

Note: When it involves blocks of two experimental units, the randomized block design is often called a **matched-pairs design.** However, as Definition 5.8 indicates, we need not create blocks of precisely two. Even in this example, we could probably just as well create 15 "homogeneous" blocks of four students, rather than 30 blocks of two students. Then we could assign each treatment at random to two students, rather than one student, within each block.

The previous discussion notwithstanding, the randomized block design need not be confined to *human* experimental units. Indeed, the term *blocking* originated in agricultural experiments and first referred to the creation of pieces of land that were as homogeneous as possible with respect to soil, sun, rain, and more. See Application 5.3, *Confounding and Blocking: The Fluorescein Experiment*.

APPLICATION 5.3

Confounding and Blocking: The Fluorescein Experiment

In the 1930s, some researchers alleged that plants grew better when watered with a dilute solution of *fluorescein* rather than plain water. Experimenters predicted the connection because a solution of this yellowish-red crystalline compound ($C_{20}H_{12}O_5$), like plants themselves, responded to light. In one experiment, 54 plants were watered with plain water; another such group was given fluoresce in water(see Figure 5.A). A large effect was observed, as predicted.

Yet no one could replicate the experiment! It turned out that the original experimenter had separated the plots of plants by a wide distance to avoid contamination. As a result, the fluorescein plot differed not only in location but also in fertility. The effect of the treatment with fluorescein water had been *confounded* with that of soil fertility.

In a subsequent experiment, researchers created six homogeneous blocks, each with 18 plants. Within each block, half the plants were given plain water; the other half, fluorescein water—and even that allocation was determined at random, by the toss of a coin. The experimental design is illustrated in Figure 5.B. When the six differences within blocks were compared, no significant effect was noted. Regardless of whether plants received plain water or fluorescein water, their growth was the same.

FIGURE 5.A

× × × × × × × × ×	○ ○ ○ ○ ○ ○ ○ ○ ○
× × × × × × × × ×	○ ○ ○ ○ ○ ○ ○ ○ ○
× × × × × × × × ×	○ ○ ○ ○ ○ ○ ○ ○ ○
× × × × × × × × ×	○ ○ ○ ○ ○ ○ ○ ○ ○
× × × × × × × × ×	○ ○ ○ ○ ○ ○ ○ ○ ○
× × × × × × × × ×	○ ○ ○ ○ ○ ○ ○ ○ ○
Plants watered with plain water	Plants watered with fluorescein water

(continued)

Application 5.3 (continued)

FIGURE 5.B

Block 1		Block 2		Block 3	
× × ×	○ ○ ○	× × ×	○ ○ ○	○ ○ ○	× × ×
× × ×	○ ○ ○	× × ×	○ ○ ○	○ ○ ○	× × ×
× × ×	○ ○ ○	× × ×	○ ○ ○	○ ○ ○	× × ×
P	F	P	F	F	P

Block 4		Block 5		Block 6	
× × ×	○ ○ ○	○ ○ ○	× × ×	○ ○ ○	× × ×
× × ×	○ ○ ○	○ ○ ○	× × ×	○ ○ ○	× × ×
× × ×	○ ○ ○	○ ○ ○	× × ×	○ ○ ○	× × ×
P	F	F	P	F	P

P = plain-water treatment

F = fluorescein-water treatment

SOURCES: William J. Youden, "Chance, Uncertainty, and Truth in Science," *Journal of Quality Technology,* January 1972, p. 8. Figures 5.A and 5.B reprinted with permission from *The Science Teacher,* a publication of the National Science Teachers Association, vol. 35, no. 8, November 1968.

EXAMPLE PROBLEM 5.1

Consider, once again, a hypothetical national experiment to reduce the sulfur dioxide emissions of power plants. How might we compare the effects of six possible treatments without falling prey to the confounding problem introduced by extraneous climate or weather effects? The answer is sketched in the randomized block design of Figure 5.3 on the next page.

As Figure 5.3 shows, we might block out extraneous climate or weather effects by creating separate blocks of plants in Maine and of plants in Florida and then assigning all types of treatments to each block of plants. This allows comparisons within each state, *holding climate or weather constant,* while varying the methods of power generation.

FIGURE 5.3 | Testing Sulfur Dioxide Emissions with a Randomized Block Design

If electric power plants are located in widely different places and if climate and weather are suspected of affecting sulfur dioxide emissions, the comparative testing of alternative emission-reducing power-generation methods can avoid the confounding problem by using a randomized block design.

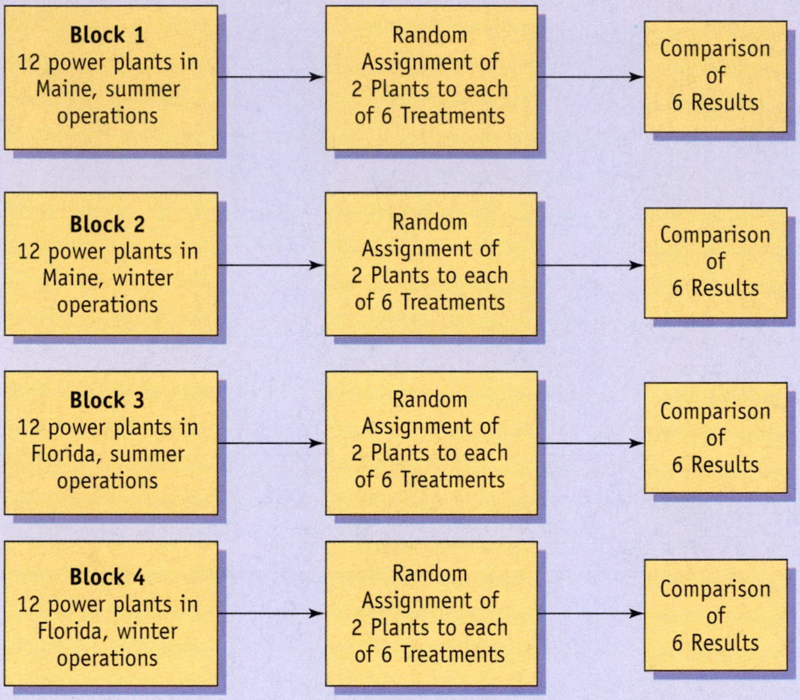

Block 1 12 power plants in Maine, summer operations	→ Random Assignment of 2 Plants to each of 6 Treatments	→ Comparison of 6 Results
Block 2 12 power plants in Maine, winter operations	→ Random Assignment of 2 Plants to each of 6 Treatments	→ Comparison of 6 Results
Block 3 12 power plants in Florida, summer operations	→ Random Assignment of 2 Plants to each of 6 Treatments	→ Comparison of 6 Results
Block 4 12 power plants in Florida, winter operations	→ Random Assignment of 2 Plants to each of 6 Treatments	→ Comparison of 6 Results

5.5 Complex Designs

Experimenters employ a multitude of designs that are considerably more complex than those we have met in the previous sections. They use more complicated designs in more complicated circumstances. Consider cases in which human subjects are known to become tired (or smarter) during the very course of an experiment or in which extraneous influences arise not from a single source but from a multitude of different sources. In all such instances, the experimenter's goal remains the same: to establish the effect of A on B with certainty, without having to worry that experimental outcomes have been compromised by the confounding problem. In this section, we briefly introduce three such complex designs:

- the crossover design
- the Latin square design
- the Youden square design

THE CROSSOVER DESIGN

In a **crossover design,** experimenters create as many groups of experimental units as there are treatments and assign each experimental unit to one of these groups by a random process. Subsequently, they administer every treatment to every experimental unit, but in an order that differs among the groups. Consider an experiment with 90 experimental units, for example, and three treatments (A, B, and C). By a random process, 30 experimental units would be assigned to Group 1, another 30 each to Groups 2 and 3. Yet these groups would not be treatment groups in the sense that each member of a given group receives the same treatment. Instead, every unit, in every group, would get all the treatments. What matters is the *order* in which experimenters apply the treatments. The succession might be A, B, C for Group 1; B, C, A for Group 2; and C, A, B for Group 3. This variation in the order of treatments is designed to counter possible bias that might arise from time trends of fatigue, learning, and the like. If everyone received treatment A first and treatment C last, a consistently worse (or better) performance on C might not indicate any inferiority (or superiority) of C compared to A, but simply the fact that experimental units had become tired (or more skilled) during the course of the experiment.

THE LATIN SQUARE DESIGN

Considerably more complex than the crossover design is the *Latin square design.* It involves randomization and simultaneous blocking in *two* directions because the experimenter suspects the existence of two extraneous sources of variation.

DEFINITION 5.9 The **Latin square design** is an experimental plan that combines randomization with blocking in such a way that two sources of extraneous variation in the data are accounted for at the same time. One extraneous factor is assigned to the columns of the square; another extraneous factor is assigned to the rows. Treatments are then assigned in such a way that each treatment occurs precisely once in each row and in each column.

The square in question refers to an array of letters representing treatments. Letters are arranged so that each appears once in every row and in every column. The rows and columns, in turn, represent extraneous factors that are to be controlled. The square can be of any size; an example of a 3-by-3 square follows:

A	B	C
B	C	A
C	A	B

As complex as it may sound, all this can be easily explained. Consider once more an experiment designed to test the comparative effectiveness of foreign-language teaching devices. This time, treatment A might refer to the conventional book teaching method, treatment B to the use of audiocassettes, and treatment C to the use of computer programs that combine vision and sound. The extraneous factors to be controlled might be the student's initial level of preparation (as measured, perhaps, by a test score) and the type of teacher (as measured, say, by years of teaching experience). Accordingly, the experimental design can be summarized as shown in Table 5.2 on the next page.

It is fairly easy to interpret the table. The row (2), column (3) entry, for example, indicates that a teacher of medium experience would teach a group of highly prepared students with a conventional book (symbol A). The row (1), column (2) entry, in contrast, indicates a run of the

TABLE 5.2 | A Latin Square Design

The Latin square design can control for two types of extraneous factors at the same time, here for teacher experience and student preparation, while making a comparative test of several treatment variables, such as A, B, and C here.

	Student Preparation		
Teacher Experience	Low (1)	Medium (2)	High (3)
(1) Low	A	B	C
(2) Medium	B	C	A
(3) High	C	A	B

experiment involving a teacher of low experience working with students of medium preparation, using audiocassettes (symbol B).

Note that each treatment would be administered three times. (There are three A's in the table, but also three B's and three C's.) Each treatment would also be administered by each type of teacher (an A appears in every row; so does a B, so does a C), and to each type of student (an A as well as a B as well as a C appears in every column). Just as each type of treatment would be administered once to each type of student and once by each type of teacher, so each type of student would be linked with each type of teacher and with each type of treatment, and each type of teacher would administer each type of treatment and teach each type of student! This is enough to take one's breath away. But this somewhat strenuous exertion on the experimenter's part also yields powerful results.

THE RESULTS Assuming that the effect of each of these three factors is independent of the effect of the others, this type of experimental design enables the experimenter to estimate the effects of all three factors from a mere nine observations—namely, the test score changes of nine subjects from before to after the experiment.

First, one can validly estimate the effect of the students' initial level of preparation on subsequent changes in test scores. This can be done by comparing the average of test score changes observed in the three column (1) experiments with similar averages obtained, respectively, from the three column (2) and (3) experiments. This comparison effectively controls for other factors (here type of teacher and type of treatment) by virtue of the fact that each one of the three averages would be based on a one-time association with each teacher and each treatment.

Second, one can validly estimate the effect of the teachers' level of experience on subsequent changes in test scores. This can be done by comparing the average of test score changes observed in the three row (1) experiments with similar averages obtained, respectively, from the three row (2) and (3) experiments. This comparison effectively controls for other factors (now type of student and type of treatment) by virtue of the fact that each one of these three averages would be based on a one-time association with each student and each treatment.

Third, and finally, one can validly estimate the effect of the alternative teaching methods on subsequent changes in test scores. This can be done by comparing the average of test score changes observed when using treatment A with similar averages obtained, respectively, when focusing on the use of treatment B or C. This comparison effectively controls for other factors (now type of student and type of teacher) by virtue of the fact that each one of these three averages would be based on a one-time association with each student and each teacher.

Because the Latin square design allows an experimenter to study simultaneously the effects of several *factors* (here student preparation, teacher experience, and teaching method) on some response variable (here the language test score), this experimental plan is also called a **factorial design.** Moreover, when the experiment is set up to test the effect of every conceivable combination of factors, as in our Table 5.2, it is called a **complete** or **full factorial design,** but when it tests the effects of only a selected number of all possible factor combinations, it is an **incomplete** or **fractional factorial design.** We will meet an example of the latter presently.

THE YOUDEN SQUARE DESIGN

Sometimes experimenters conduct *within-subject tests* during which each person is given different treatments in succession. However, when the number of treatments exceeds the number that can suitably be administered to any one experimental unit, a special design is needed. Such is the **incomplete Latin square design,** also referred to as the **balanced incomplete block design** or **Youden square design.** Consider testing people's preferences concerning half a dozen varieties of coffee (A through F). Almost certainly their tongues will be too insensitive after three tries to tell anything. In this case, experiments might be performed with six individuals, each one of them being asked to rank only three of the brands, with the order of treatment being different for each. Table 5.3 illustrates this design.

TABLE 5.3 | A Youden Square Design

Because each row contains every treatment in this coffee-tasting experiment, every brand (A–F) is once tasted first, once tasted second, and once third. In this manner, the experiment is protected from bias arising from the order of tasting.

Order of Tasting	Person 1	Person 2	Person 3	Person 4	Person 5	Person 6
First	A	B	C	D	E	F
Second	B	C	D	E	F	A
Third	C	D	E	F	A	B

Note: Biography 5.1, *William J. Youden,* found on the Web site associated with this text, tells more about the man who invented this type of experimental design.

5.6 Errors in Experimental Data

Experimental data, like survey data, are subject to error. The types of error are the same as well: random error and systematic error.

DEFINITION 5.10 In controlled experiments, **random error,** also called **experimental error,** equals the difference between the value of a variable obtained by performing a single experiment and the value obtained by averaging the results of a large number of identical experiments.

DEFINITION 5.11 In controlled experiments, **systematic error** or **bias** equals the difference between the value of a variable obtained by averaging the results of a large number of identical experiments and the (unknown) true value.

RANDOM ERROR OR EXPERIMENTAL ERROR

Like sampling procedures, experiments are subject to *random error,* now also called *experimental error.* To understand how this error arises, consider the experiment, based on the randomized group design and noted in EXCEL (or MINITAB) Example 5.1 earlier. It addressed two approaches to teaching foreign languages. The publisher of the new teaching device was interested in the (presumably positive) *test score change* that students using the device could achieve compared to students exposed to traditional teaching methods. If there were no bias and the true test score change (unbeknownst to us) were +18 points, a single experiment might, nevertheless, yield a change of +16 points. Another experiment might yield a change of +22 points, and so on for additional runs of the experiment. These chance variations around the true and unknown value of the variable of interest (here around an assumed +18 points) could be expected to occur, with equal frequency and magnitude, in both directions. Therefore, the true test score change could be discovered only by averaging the results of many repetitions of the experiment.

The left-hand side of Figure 5.4 illustrates the possible occurrence of such random error. Many repetitions of the experiment might reveal an average test score change of +18 points. Yet a single experiment might only show an improvement of +16 points. Thus, this particular single experiment would *understate* the average test score improvement by 2 points; its random error, therefore, would be −2 points. Running any given experiment with many independent repetitions, also known as **replications,** is a good defense against being misled by this type of error.

SYSTEMATIC ERROR OR BIAS

Unfortunately, *systematic error* or *bias* can ruin comparative experiments as well. If the experimenter is not careful, the effects of treatments that are to be measured (say, the test score change associated with two teaching devices) may remain inextricably mixed up or *confounded* with the effects of other factors (say, teacher experience or initial student preparation). As a result, more

FIGURE 5.4 | Errors in Experiments

Experiments are subject to the same type of errors as surveys are. Either type of error can be positive or negative. For a comparison, review Figure 4.1.

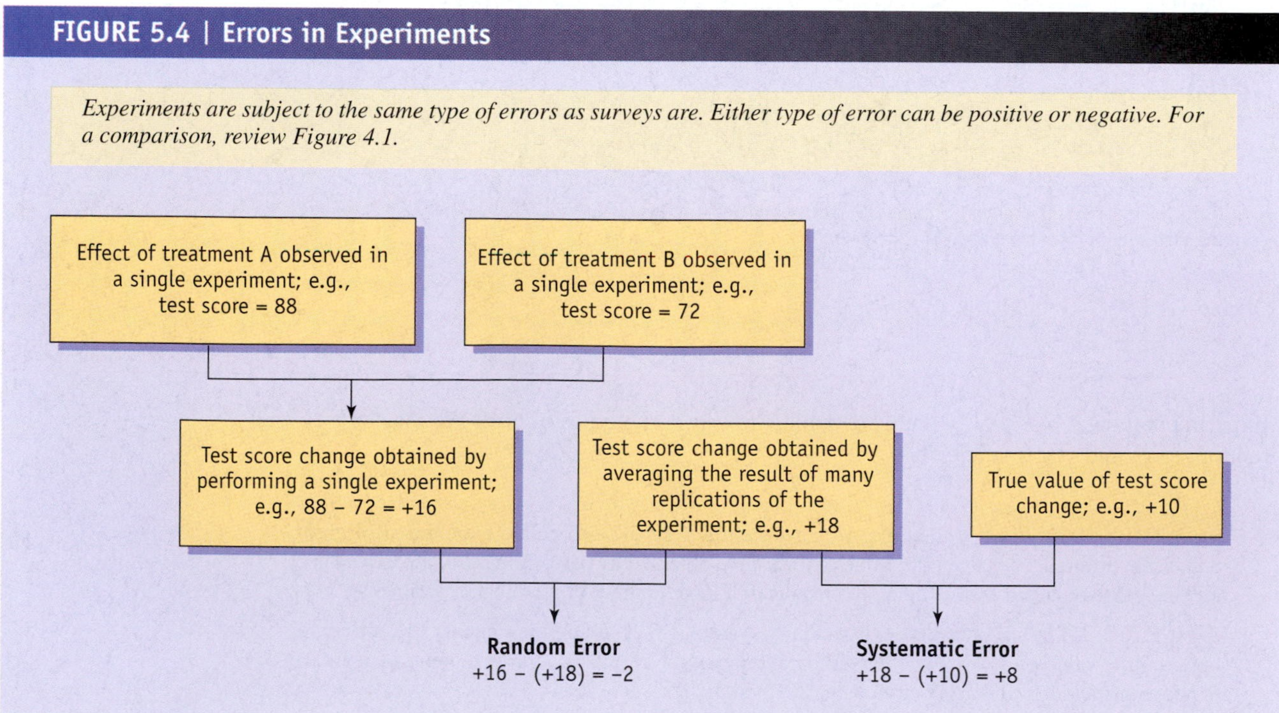

than one cause might be responsible for the observed experimental result. Just imagine what would happen if the students using the new and supposedly superior teaching device were also better prepared initially *and* were taught by more experienced teachers than the control group of students exposed to traditional teaching methods. These other factors alone might raise those students' test scores by 8 points. As indicated in the right-hand side of Figure 5.4, despite the average test score change of +18 points during many replications of the experiment, the true test score change *attributable to the new teaching device* might only be +10 points. The +18 point average test score change observed during many replications of the experiment would thus *overstate* the effects of the new teaching device by our assumed 8 points, which would represent a systematic error.

SELECTION BIAS As in the case of surveys, bias can enter experiments at various stages and in many guises; nothing but eternal vigilance can prevent it. For example, if volunteers are used to form experimental groups and nonvolunteers are used to form control groups, bias is likely to occur because volunteers are rarely like nonvolunteers with respect to relevant factors other than treatments. Application 5.4, *Selection Bias in the Salk Polio Vaccine Trial,* provides a spectacular example of this very point.

APPLICATION 5.4

SELECTION BIAS IN THE SALK POLIO VACCINE TRIAL

In 1954, the biggest public-health experiment to date was carried out in the United States. Researchers sought to determine how effective the Salk poliomyelitis vaccine was in preventing polio. Seemingly, the study was carefully designed. It included nearly 1 million children in grades 1–3. Such a large-scale approach was necessary because the incidence of the disease in the United States then equaled only 50 per 100,000, making an experiment with, say, 10,000 children necessarily inconclusive because only 5 of these could be expected to contract polio. Thus, *any* observed allocation of this number between those vaccinated and those not vaccinated could then be attributed to mere chance. The experiment involved administering the Salk vaccine to about 222,000 second-graders who had their parents' permission and the comparison of this group's experience with that of some 725,000 first- and third-graders who were not vaccinated. The results are shown in Table 5.B.

THE DISCOVERY OF BIAS A comparison of the boldfaced red numbers seemed to indicate that the vaccine was amazingly effective. Yet the study was disastrously *biased.* This comparison of the experimental and control groups was highly unfair! *Only* those second-graders with parental permission had received the vaccine, but *all* first- and third-graders in their schools had been used as controls. Unfortunately, this was a mistake, and here is why:

Poliomyelitis is caused by one of several viruses that appear almost everywhere. However, the disease always hit hardest those children who were better off hygienically and who had better nutrition, better housing, and higher-income,

TABLE 5.B | The First Experiment

School Grade	Treatment	Number of Children	Number Afflicted with Paralytic Polio	Number Afflicted per 100,000
2	Salk vaccine	221,998	38	**17**
1 and 3	None	725,173	330	**46**

(continued)

Application 5.4 (continued)

better-educated parents. Polio was almost unknown in places with the poorest of hygiene. Children living in poor hygienic conditions were exposed to polio early on while they were still protected by immunity passed on by their mothers. At that time, they developed their own immunity, and, henceforth, they contracted polio less often than their hygienically more fortunate peers. As it turned out, higher-income, better-educated parents of second-graders freely gave permission for their children to receive the vaccine; the lesser-educated parents did not. As a result, the second-graders receiving the vaccine were unusually *likely* to contract polio, much more so than their first- and third-grade peers who belonged to all types of parents. (Can you figure how those highlighted Table 5.B numbers might have looked in the *absence* of the bias just noted? Children in both groups would then have been selected so as to be equally at risk. Instead of being high-risk, second-graders would have been of (lower) average risk and the incidence-of-polio number would have been lower than 17. At the same time, instead of being low-risk, first- and third-graders would have been of (higher) average risk and the incidence-of-polio number would have been higher than 46. (Thus, the effectiveness of the vaccine would have been demonstrated more dramatically.)

A Second Experiment A second experiment was designed, involving only children with parental permission (and, thus, presumably, children equally at risk). In this double-blind experiment, each of the volunteers was assigned at random to a group receiving the Salk vaccine or a placebo (a saline solution), but neither the children nor the evaluating physicians knew who got which. To forestall favoritism in the assignment of treatments or prejudice in the appraisal of symptoms, vaccine and placebo vials were identical in appearance and distinguished only by secret code numbers. The results are shown in the first two rows of Table 5.C.

A comparison of the boldfaced red numbers in Table 5.C with those in Table 5.B clearly shows that the Salk vaccine was much *more* effective than the first experiment had demonstrated.

As the last column of Table 5.C indicates, the second experiment also provided evidence for the home-hygiene effect noted above. Unvaccinated children from homes with probably better hygiene had a greater incidence of polio (57) than did those from homes with probably poor hygiene (36).

SOURCES: Adapted from William J. Youden, "Chance, Uncertainty, and Truth in Science," *Journal of Quality Technology,* January 1972, pp. 7–10; Paul Meier, "The Biggest Public Health Experiment Ever: The 1954 Field Trial of the Salk Poliomyelitis Vaccine," in Judith M. Tanur et al., eds., *Statistics: A Guide to the Unknown* (San Francisco: Holden-Day, 1972), pp. 2–13. Tables 5.B and 5.C reprinted with permission from *The Science Teacher,* a publication of the National Science Teachers Association, vol. 35, no. 8, November 1968. Copyright © 1968 by the National Science Teachers Association.

TABLE 5.C | The Second Experiment

Permission Given	Treatment	Number of Children	Number Afflicted with Paralytic Polio	Number Afflicted per 100,000
Yes	Salk vaccine	200,745	33	**16**
Yes	Placebo	201,229	115	**57**
No	None	338,778	121	36

Response Bias Even when randomization and blocking have been used to best advantage to avoid selection bias, response bias can be just as deadly. To cite one example, experimental units or experimenters who are aware of who gets what type of treatment can easily let their prejudices determine the responses they make or record. Thus, people who know they are receiving a new drug that supposedly reduces certain symptoms may report this effect even though they are simply imagining any improvement. Outside observers who are "convinced," even before the experiment, that the drug will work may unconsciously observe what they want to observe and note a reduction in symptoms even in the absence of such an effect. This is why **double-blind**

experiments are preferred in cases where human frailty and suggestibility are likely to play a role. In such experiments, response bias is controlled by letting neither the subjects nor the judges know who is receiving which type of treatment. In the case of drug experiments, for example, all experimental units might receive look-alike pills, half of which are active and half of which are inactive and harmless substances. Such fake substances or procedures that have no physical effect are called **placebos.** Dr. Ruffin's experiment about gastric freezing, noted in this chapter's Preview, is a real-world example of a double-blind experiment using placebos. Most experiments conducted by today's pharmaceutical companies follow Dr. Ruffin's example. Application 5.5, *New Profits from Old Compounds,* tells the story.

APPLICATION 5.5

NEW PROFITS FROM OLD COMPOUNDS

America's pharmaceutical giants, such as Glaxo Wellcome, Merck, Pfizer, and more, continually engage in controlled, comparative, double-blind experiments of the type discussed in this chapter. Before they can market a new drug, they need FDA approval, and the Food and Drug Administration insists on *proof* that the proposed drugs are both safe and effective. An experiment leading to such proof can easily cost $500 million for a single drug. In recent years, therefore, many firms have sought to raise profits by finding *multiple* uses for any given compound. Table 5.D tells an interesting story.

Our table tells by no means the whole story. For example, the American Home Products Corporation's Wyeth-Ayerst Laboratories have long marketed Premarin as an estrogen replacement therapy. Recently, the company has found other uses for the drug, including the possible

TABLE 5.D | Multiple Drug Uses

Firm	Compound	Marketing Strategy	1998 Sales
Abbott Laboratories	divalproex sodium	As Depakote, sold as	
		1. anticonvulsant	$240 million
		2. bipolar disorder drug	$350 million
		3. anti-migraine drug	$25 million
Glaxo Wellcome	buproprion hydrochloride	As Wellbutrin, sold as	
		1. anti-depression drug	$506 million
		As Zyban, sold as	
		2. anti-smoking drug	$151 million
Merck	finasteride	As Proscar, sold as	
		1. drug to counter enlarged prostates	$170 million
		As Propecia, sold as	
		2. drug to fight male baldness	$68 million
Pfizer	sildenafil citrate	As Sildenafil, sold as	
		1. anti-angina drug	n.a.
		As Viagra, sold as	
		2. erectile dysfuntion drug	$788 million

(continued)

Application 5.5 (continued)

prevention of Alzheimer's and tooth loss in women. Eli Lilly & Company has long marketed fluoxetine hydrochloride as Prozac, an antidepressant, but the drug is now also promoted under the name Sarafem for the treatment of severe premenstrual syndrome. Monsanto has long sold Celebrex as an arthritis painkiller; now it is being tested for the prevention of Alzheimer's and colon cancer. The list could easily be lengthened. (But note: So eager are the drug companies to increase profits that they often shade the truth a bit in their advertising campaigns, overdoing the benefits and ignoring the drawbacks. In 1999, the Food and Drug Administration initiated a serious crackdown on numerous firms in the industry for false and misleading commercials.)

SOURCES: Adapted from *Physicians' Desk Reference,* 52nd ed. (Montvale, N.J.: The Medical Economics Company, 1998); "New Profits in Old Bottles," *The New York Times,* March 19, 1999, pp. C1 and 16; and Robert Pear, "F.D.A. Rebuking Drug Companies over Faulty Ads," *The New York Times,* March 28, 1999, pp. A1 and 22.

Summary

1. Properly run experiments can provide more reliable data than surveys do. While surveys can highlight an *association* between two variables, experiments can establish the presence or absence of *causation.* For a variety of reasons, experimentation in the social sciences is particularly difficult.
2. In a *comparative* experiment, persons or objects, known as *experimental units,* are subdivided into at least one *experimental group* that is exposed to some stimulus and one *control group* that is not so exposed. The deliberate stimulus as well as the deliberate withholding thereof is termed a *treatment.* After different experimental units have received one treatment or another, their responses are observed and compared. The resultant data, however, are valid only if all other influences on the response variable remain unchanged during the experiment. Otherwise, the effects of the treatments and of those extraneous factors are intermingled and cannot be distinguished from one another. This *confounding problem* can be minimized by *randomization* or *blocking,* and the use of these devices makes the experiment a *controlled* experiment.
3. Any plan for assigning treatments to experimental units under controlled conditions and, thus, for generating valid data is called an *experimental design.* An experimental plan that creates one treatment group for each treatment and then assigns each experimental unit to one of these groups by a random process is called a *randomized group design* or a *completely randomized design.*
4. An experimental plan that divides the available experimental units into blocks of fairly homogeneous units, each block containing as many units as there are treatments or some multiple of that number, and then randomly matches each treatment with one or more units within each block is called a *randomized block design.*
5. Much more complex designs include the *crossover design,* the *Latin square design,* and the *Youden square design.*
6. Just like survey data, experimental data are subject to different types of *error,* including *random error* (now also called *experimental error*) and *systematic error* (or *bias*).

Key Terms

balanced incomplete block design
bias
blocking
comparative experiment
complete factorial design
completely randomized design
confounding problem
control group
controlled experiment
crossover design
dependent variable
double-blind experiments
experiment
experimental design
experimental error
experimental factor
experimental group
experimental units
explained variable
explanatory variable
factor
factor levels
factorial design
fractional factorial design
full factorial design
incomplete factorial design
incomplete Latin square design
independent variable
Latin square design
matched-pairs design
observational study
placebos
random error

randomization
randomized block design
randomized group design
replications
response variable
subjects
survey
systematic error
treatment
treatment variable
Youden square design

Practice Problems

NOTE

Some problems require the use of the statistical program, EXCEL or MINITAB. The program's major features were explained in Chapter 2. Plenty of additional advice is available via the program's built-in Help feature.

5.1 Association versus Causation

1. Imagine taking a survey of Omni Aviation, Inc., and gathering the data shown in columns 1, 2, and 6 of Table 5.1 on page 139. What wrong conclusions might you reach if you hadn't read this chapter?
2. Imagine taking a survey of Omni Aviation, Inc., and gathering the data shown in columns 1, 3, and 6 of Table 5.1 on page 139. What wrong conclusions might you reach if you hadn't read this chapter?
3. Imagine taking a survey of Omni Aviation, Inc., and gathering the data shown in columns 1, 2, and 5 of Table 5.1 on page 139. What wrong conclusions might you reach if you hadn't read this chapter?
4. Suppose you go to the Internet and visit http://www.fedstats.gov, a site introduced and explored in Chapter 3. Before long, you discover that the consumption expenditures of U.S. households have risen for decades along with the GDP. What could you conclude?
5. Suppose you go to the Internet and visit http://www.fedstats.gov, a site introduced and explored in Chapter 3. Before long, you discover that the volume of gross private domestic investment during the course of the last decade rose and fell whenever interest rates on Treasury securities rose and fell. What could you conclude?
6. Suppose you go to the Internet and visit http://www.fedstats.gov, a site introduced and explored in Chapter 3. Before long, you discover that the federal budget deficit during the last decade rose whenever the volume of imports rose. What could you conclude?

5.2 The Design of Experiments

7. Pharmaceutical companies can increase their sales by billions of dollars per year if they are lucky enough to come up with a new best-selling drug. No wonder they are always experimenting. One such company selected 100 adults at random and managed to persuade 80 of them to take beta-blockers, which were suspected of lowering the pulse rate. A comparison of the subjects' before-and-after pulse rates confirmed the suspicion. Evaluate this experiment.
8. Pharmaceutical companies can increase their sales by billions of dollars per year if they are lucky enough to come up with a new best-selling drug. No wonder they are always experimenting. One such company selected 100 adults at random and managed to persuade 80 of them to take calcium supplements, which were suspected of lowering blood pressure. A comparison of the subjects' before-and-after blood pressure readings confirmed the suspicion. Evaluate this experiment.
9. In 1993, *The Journal of the American Medical Association* reported findings by Dr. E. Giovannucci, who had rummaged through hospital records and discovered this: Of 22,000 men who had a vasectomy, 113 eventually developed prostate cancer. Of 22,000 men who did not have a vasectomy, only 70 were so afflicted. What would you conclude?
10. Imagine yourself being the manager of a company that develops and sells new teaching devices. One new device, called The Genie, has just been created. In preparation for a national ad campaign, one of your employees proposes to test the device by letting one class of students spend a month learning by traditional methods, while a second class uses The Genie, and then to compare their grades. What do you have to say?
11. Imagine yourself being the owner of an airport at which flight training is conducted in four types of single-engine planes. Your manager wants to reduce costs and plans on carefully recording each plane's hours flown and gas consumption for a period of five months. Then you can get rid of the high-cost planes. Evaluate the proposal.
12. Some time ago, a hospital administrator checked the records of hundreds of women who had given birth to children after having had one or more abortions. The health records of the children during their first year of life were then compared to see whether having abortions affects the lives of subsequent children. Evaluate the procedure.

5.3 The Randomized Group Design

13. You work for a pharmaceutical company that always tries to find a new best-seller. A new stimulant drug is a possibility; it is alleged to enhance people's ability to perform a task. Set up an experimental design that will satisfy both the Food and Drug Administration, which must approve the drug, and your marketing manager, who must promote it.

14. You work for Weight Watchers Anonymous and want to test the effectiveness of two diets on people's weight. Set up an experimental design that would provide valid data.

15. You work for a pharmaceutical company that always tries to find new best-sellers. Two new therapies to stop smoking provide one possibility: sustained-release bupropion and a nicotine patch. Set up an experimental design that will satisfy both the Food and Drug Administration, which must approve the therapies, and your marketing manager, who must promote them.

16. As the personnel manager of a company, you wonder whether your workers' job satisfaction could be increased by changing current work schedules (8 to 4:30, five days a week) to staggered start time or to flextime (workers set their own hours). Set up a valid experiment.

17. You work for a pharmaceutical company that always tries to find new bestsellers. Two new therapies provide possibilities: taking aspirin to reduce heart attacks and taking beta-carotene to reduce cancer. Set up an experimental design that will satisfy both the Food and Drug Administration, which must approve the therapies, and your marketing manager, who must promote them.

18. You work for an advertising agency and want to document the effectiveness of TV ads, possibly shown repeatedly and for different lengths of time. Set up an experimental design that will provide valid data.

19. You work for a pharmaceutical company that always tries to find a new best-seller. A new drug, called hydroxyurea, is a possibility; it is alleged to reduce pain among patients suffering from sickle cell disease. Set up an experimental design that will satisfy both the Food and Drug Administration, which must approve the drug, and your marketing manager, who must promote it.

20. As manager of a national string of health clubs, you wonder whether regular exercise can truthfully be promoted as a way to reduce heart attacks. Set up an experimental design that will provide valid data.

21. As manager of a chemical firm, you wonder what might increase the sales of your Japanese beetle traps. Someone has suggested that different *colors* of traps would trap different numbers of beetles. Set up an experimental design that will provide valid data on the subject.

22. As the manager of a national supermarket chain, you wonder whether sales vary with the type of background music you provide. Set up an experimental design that will provide valid data on the subject.

23. As the manager of a factory, you wonder why the quantity of output varies so widely among different shifts. Someone suggests that it all depends on the overseer. Set up an experimental design that will provide valid data on the subject.

24. As the manager of a detergent factory, you wonder whether changing the mere color of your product's packaging could raise sales. Set up an experimental design that will provide valid data on the subject.

5.4 The Randomized Block Design

25. You work for a pharmaceutical company that always tries to find a new best-seller. A long-lasting calcium channel blocker, called nitrendipine, is a possibility. It is alleged to reduce the risk of heart attacks and strokes. However, it is feared that the drug may hurt diabetics. Set up an experimental design that will satisfy both the Food and Drug Administration (FDA), which must approve the drug, and your marketing manager, who must promote it.

26. As a marketing manager, you wonder which of four in-store ads will increase soft drink sales the most. You also suspect that the answer will vary drastically between the U.S. home market and abroad. Set up an experimental design that will provide valid data on the subject.

27. Review Practice Problem 13. Revise the planned experiment on the grounds that the effect is likely to vary substantially between men and women.

28. Review Practice Problem 14. Revise the planned experiment on the grounds that the effect is likely to vary substantially between men and women.

29. Review Practice Problem 15. Revise the planned experiment on the grounds that the effect is likely to vary substantially between men and women.

30. Review Practice Problem 16. Revise the planned experiment on the grounds that the effect is likely to vary substantially between men and women.

31. Review Practice Problem 17. Revise the planned experiment on the grounds that the effect is likely to vary substantially between men and women.

32. Review Practice Problem 18. Revise the planned experiment on the grounds that the effect is likely to vary substantially between blacks and whites.

33. Review Practice Problem 20. Revise the planned experiment on the grounds that the effect is likely to vary substantially between blacks and whites.

34. Review Practice Problem 22. Revise the planned experiment on the grounds that the effect is likely to vary substantially between the young and the old.

35. Review Practice Problem 23. Revise the planned experiment on the grounds that the effect is likely to vary substantially between the young and the old.

36. The manager of a chain of orchards wonders whether the annual yield of apple trees varies with the type of tree. There are three types: Golden Delicious, Macintosh, and Northern Spy. But the manager has no idea how to conduct a test, because the time of the last frost is January for some of the orchards, but it is February, March, April, and even May for others. Thus, the length of the growing season varies widely. Can you help? Set up an experimental design that will produce valid data.

5.5 Complex Designs

37. Review Table 5.2 on page 152.

- **a.** What is the meaning of the row (1), column (2) entry?
- **b.** What is the meaning of the row (3), column (1) entry?

38. A food manufacturer wants to find out which of three types of cold cuts, A–C, customers find the tastiest. Some 90 subjects are available. Create an experimental design that will provide valid data.

39. The text provides an example of a 3-by-3 *Latin square,* which is then embodied in Table 5.2 on page 152. Create a 4-by-4 square.

40. The text provides an example of a 3-by-3 *Latin square,* which is then embodied in Table 5.2 on page 152. Create a 5-by-5 square.

41. Application 5.3, *Confounding and Blocking: The Fluorescein Experiment,* outlines two experiments. An investigator wishes to design a third experiment that simultaneously estimates the effects on plant growth of 3 types of watering (natural rain, N; plain-water irrigation, P; fluorescein-water irrigation, F), 3 types of soil (A, B, and C), and 3 types of fertilizer (a, b, and c). Design such an experiment.

42. An avionics manufacturer is preparing an ad campaign for a new radar altimeter, hoping to gain market share against two competitors. You are to design a simple experiment that simultaneously tests the effects of vibration (Low, Medium, High), temperature (low, medium, high), and brand name (A, B, C) on time-to-failure.

43. A quality engineer is determined to trace the causes of defective items produced. There are three suspects: assembly line speed (.5 mph, .7 mph, .9 mph), worker position (sitting, standing, kneeling), and type of overseer (Greg, Jim, Ruth). You are to design a simple experiment that simultaneously tests these effects on the percentage of defectives produced.

44. An advertising agency wants to test the effects of type of ad (A, B, C), time of day shown on TV (morning, afternoon, evening), and time of hour shown (on the hour, on the half hour, in between) on market response (number of calls made to an 800 number). You are asked to design an experiment.

45. A sales manager wants to test the effects on a product's sales of product display density (loose, tight), store lighting (dim, bright), and background music (classical, rock). You are asked to design an experiment.

46. The manager of a weight-loss clinic wants to test the effects on weight of sex (male, female), diet type (A, B), and exercise regimen (yes, no). You are asked to design an experiment.

47. A Federal Aviation Administration official wants to test the effect on pilot exam performance of sex (male, female), two types of initial basic training (private, military), and two types of advanced instrument training courses (A, B). You are asked to design an experiment.

48. A cereal manufacturer is planning an ad campaign. In preparation for it, people are to taste 6 types of cereal (brands A–F) and rank them. For reasons of cost, only 6 subjects are to be used in a test that you are to design. Do it.

5.6 Errors in Experimental Data

49. Review Practice Problem 48. Why might the experiment involve *random error?* How might one minimize it?

50. Review Practice Problem 48. Why might the experiment involve *systematic error?* How might one minimize it?

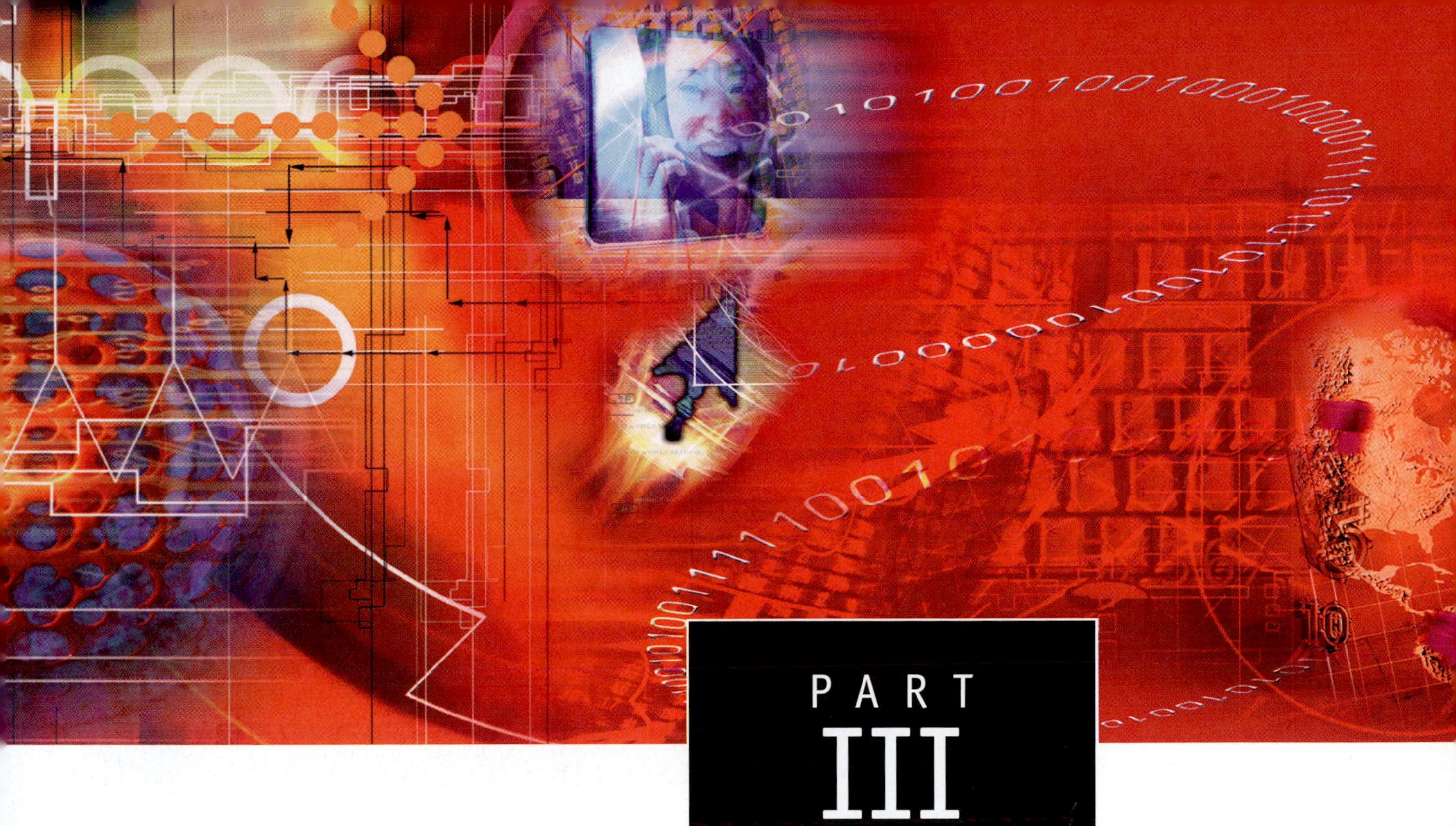

PART III

DESCRIPTIVE STATISTICS

PRESENTING DATA: TABLES AND GRAPHS

LOOKING AHEAD

After reading this chapter, you will be able to present data effectively with the help of tables and graphs. Among other things, you will learn to:

1. make good use of absolute, relative, and cumulative frequency distributions,
2. draw frequency histograms and derivative graphs, such as polygons, frequency curves, and ogives,
3. develop such common graphs as scatter diagrams, time-series line graphs, bar charts, and pie charts, and
4. analyze and draw a number of unusual graphs, including statistical maps, pictograms, stem-and-leaf diagrams, and box-and-whisker diagrams.

AND HERE IS A TYPICAL PROBLEM YOU WILL BE ABLE TO SOLVE:

Imagine you were working for a chemicals firm that is interested in expanding its fertilizer sales in California and Florida. You are supposed to provide information about current fertilizer usage, and you instantly think of *oranges.* Create a relevant *cross tabulation* for your next staff meeting. (*Hint:* To find current data, visit http://www.fedstats.gov, a site maintained by the federal government's Interagency Council on Statistical Policy.)

PREVIEW

If you are running a business, there is one problem you can do without: being accused of racial discrimination. The mere suspicion of such illegal behavior can become very costly, which is what thousands of U.S. banks found out recently.

It all started in 1989, when the Congress amended the 1975 Home Mortgage Disclosure Act, generally known as HMDA. The original act had required lenders to disclose the geographic distribution of their residential mortgage loans in order to discourage *redlining,* a banking practice that routinely denied loans for properties located in certain districts. As subsequent analysis showed, the districts involved tended to be populated by minorities, but the data did not prove discrimination against *individual* applicants. The 1989 amendment sought to produce additional data. It required home mortgage lenders to report information on each applicant's income, race, and sex, and also on the eventual disposition of each mortgage application. Before long, the Federal Reserve, the nation's highest monetary authority, was able to review some 6.3 million mortgage applications that had been processed by 9,300 financial institutions in 1990.

When it comes to buying a home, concluded the Federal Reserve, not all Americans are created equal. Comparing white and black applicants with similar incomes, 85.3 percent of white applicants had been approved, but only 66.6 percent of blacks. The Federal Reserve backed up its claims with volumes of data, such as those in Table 6.1.

Table 6.1 is easy to comprehend, but you must imagine the original table with 9,300 rows! Such masses of data can be pretty confusing. Are the six entries in *our* table merely exceptions, one might ask, or do they represent a wider truth? And this is where *descriptive statistics* can help. For example, one can combine the black/white differentials for all the banks in each state and then present the outcome succinctly in a *statistical map,* such as Figure 6.1 on the next page.

Note how easy it is to identify the black/white differential in each of the 50 states at a glance. The differential was less negative than −10 percent in California and Maine, but it was more negative than −20 percent in the two Carolinas, for example. Such a succinct data presentation with summarizing tables, graphs, or arithmetic measures is the major goal of *descriptive statistics* discussed in this chapter and the next.

But caution is advised: It is one thing to present masses of otherwise confusing data in a form that quickly summarizes what they are all about. It is quite another matter to draw *inferences* about causes and consequences. Looking at Figure 6.1, we *cannot* conclude that racial discrimination in mortgage markets has been proven beyond the shadow of a doubt. True enough, some have thought that the case is strong enough and some banks have paid up. Thus, in 1993, the Shawmut Bank, then New England's third largest, paid $960,000 to black and Hispanic applicants who had been denied loans. And in 1996, the Fleet Financial Group paid $4 million, also to blacks and Hispanics, for "overcharging" these customers on loans they did receive. Yet the issue has remained extremely controversial.

Serious studies have concluded that those Figure 6.1 differentials can be explained by factors *other than* bigotry, that the Federal Reserve's conclusions were marred by the *confounding problem* first noted in

TABLE 6.1 | Federal Reserve Study of U.S. Mortgage Applications in 1990

Lender	Approval Rate for Blacks (%)	Approval Rate for Whites (%)	Black/White Differential (%)
Altus Bank, AL	61.0	88.2	−27.2
Simmons First, AK	42.4	83.0	−40.6
Bank of America, CA	58.5	75.5	−17.0
People's Bank, CT	51.2	88.2	−37.0
.	.	.	.
.	.	.	.
Century Bank, OH	83.3	92.2	−8.9
Meridian Bank, PA	56.1	88.1	−32.0
.	.	.	.
.	.	.	.

FIGURE 6.1 | Black/White Differentials in Mortgage Approvals across the United States in 1990

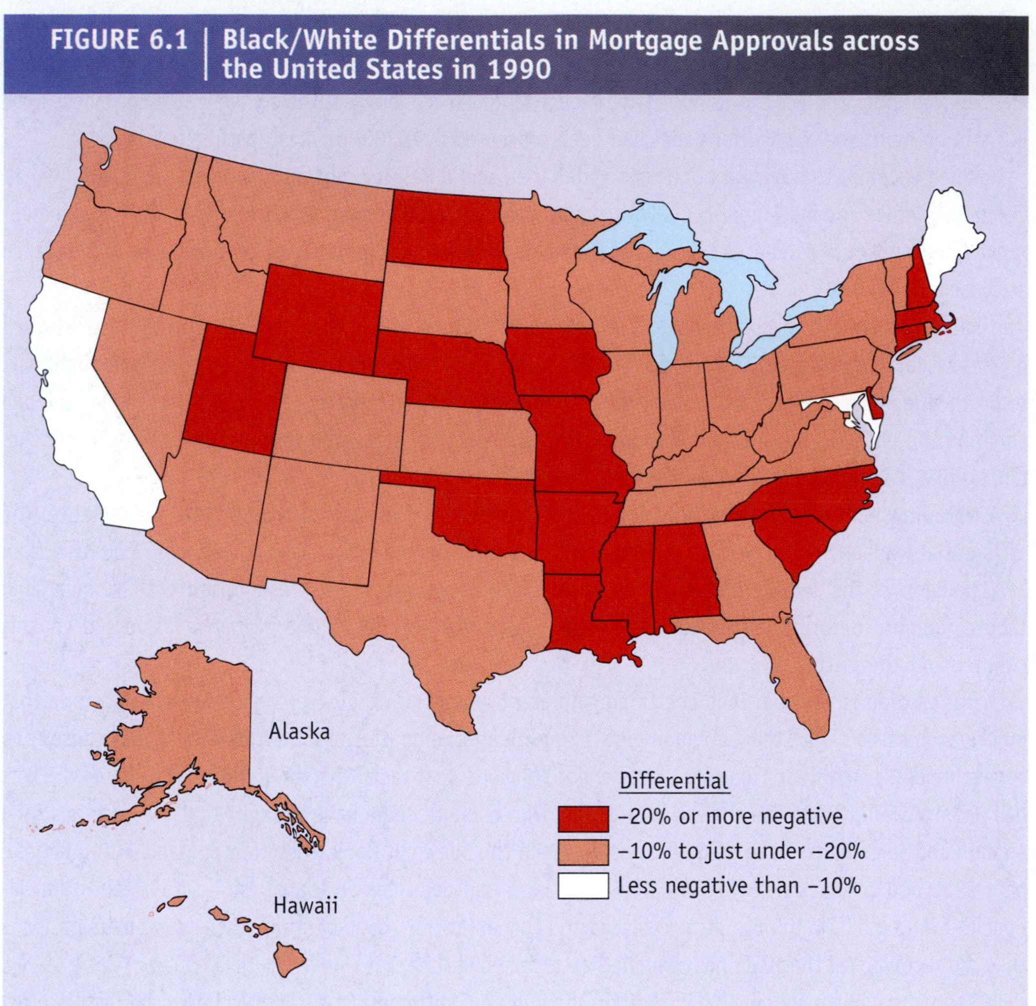

Chapter 5. Some of the observed differentials could be explained by differences in applicant credit histories or wealth or existing debt levels, or even by their banks' inability to *verify* information submitted by applicants—all matters heavily weighed by lenders. Differences could also be attributed to rules laid down by government agencies that subsidize mortgages and that automatically deny applicants whose income is too high to qualify under the law.

The matter is further complicated by the existence of agencies, such as the Federal National Mortgage Association (Fannie Mae) and the Federal Home Loan Mortgage Corporation (Freddie Mac), that buy up mortgages that originating banks later want to sell. Such secondary lenders seek to cut their costs by rejecting *small* mortgages, mortgages in *risky* neighborhoods, and mortgages owed by frequent *job switchers*. The potential inability to resell certain mortgages affects the behavior of banks when they first consider mortgage applications.

With so many variables operating at the same time, mere data summaries, such as Figure 6.1, can tell us nothing about *causal* connections. These are explored by *inferential statistics,* introduced in later chapters of this text. The current chapter takes a first step toward such broader study by showing you how to present data as effectively as possible. In the meantime, you are well advised not to jump to hasty conclusions, even if nicely summarized data seem to suggest them.

SOURCES: Adapted from Paulette Thomas, "Behind the Figures: Federal Data Detail Pervasive Racial Gap in Mortgage Lending," *The Wall Street Journal,* March 31, 1992, pp. A1, 10, and 11; "U.S. Probes Bank Records for Race Bias," *The Wall Street Journal,* May 19, 1992, pp. A2 and 6; Peter Brimelow and Leslie Spencer, "The Hidden Clue," *Forbes,* January 4, 1993, p. 48; Alicia H. Munnell et al., "Mortgage Lending in Boston: Interpreting HMDA Data," *The American Economic Review,* March 1996, pp. 25–53; Peter Passell, "Race, Mortgages, and Statistics," *The New York Times,* May 10, 1996; and Stanley D. Longhofer, "Discrimination in Mortgage Lending: What Have We Learned?" Federal Reserve Bank of Cleveland, *Economic Commentary,* August 15, 1996.

6.1 An Introduction to Table Making

After collecting their data by one or another of the methods introduced in Part II of this text, statisticians turn to an equally important task: presenting the data effectively. This task is particularly crucial when a data collection is large. No human mind is capable of grasping the meaning of any considerable quantity of data unless the information is somehow reduced to a relatively few convenient categories or is condensed with the help of some kind of visual or arithmetic summary. Part III of this text introduces three ways of presenting data: making tables, drawing graphs, and calculating arithmetical summary measures. We begin with tables.

CONFUSING TABLES

The construction of a good statistical table is an art. It involves a great deal more than presenting data in rows and columns *somehow.* Imagine, for example, that a census had been taken of the 100 multinational companies first introduced in Table 4.1 and that data for each of them had been collected on the combined net profit from domestic and foreign operations. Such data are now shown in Table 6.2.

Even though Table 6.2 contains a mere 100 numbers (a far cry from the much larger data sets often encountered in statistical research), it is pretty confusing. To be sure, a comparison of

TABLE 6.2 | A Population of Profits

This table shows the combined 1997 net profits, in millions of dollars, from domestic and foreign operations of each the 100 largest U.S.-based multinationals listed in Table 4.1. Successive rows of numbers correspond to the alphabetical listing of companies in the earlier table.

2094	955	1073	1170	1991	2043	3332	120	3015	458
985	−1045	377	1957	337	3210	866	300	454	3205
2528	3708	3256	2805	1086	3591	4129	740	1855	581
767	956	944	141	1907	355	5	2405	731	−385
1826	8460	146	9163	8203	6645	1352	1427	559	840
3119	302	471	6093	195	6945	−22	114	4777	245
1465	912	481	541	293	1643	4614	1953	3454	2199
3640	294	2586	1180	7	79	606	1491	2223	323
6310	3415	1016	622	1009	658	1188	762	2603	302
5012	−49	1226	−854	1191	6503	1966	870	−162	1452

SOURCE: Adapted from *Forbes,* July 27, 1998, pp. 163–164.

Table 4.1 on page 110 with Table 6.2 here could quickly establish the net profit of Abbott Laboratories (the first company on our list) as $2,094 million and that of Xerox (the last company listed) as $1,452 million, but it would be awkward to look for Chrysler's profit (number 23 on our list) or Pfizer's (number 78). It would be equally awkward to search, say, for the highest and lowest profits in the entire list or for the number of companies that earned more than $3 billion that year.

ORDERED ARRAYS

A listing of data in order of ascending or descending magnitude, which is called an **ordered array,** would certainly be a major improvement. A computer can provide an ordered array in no time.

EXCEL Example 6.1

Enter the data found in Table 6.2 into EXCEL and produce an *ordered array.*

SOLUTION The data have already been entered for you into column E of the file HK100MN97 that is found on the CD-ROM. Thus, you need simply follow these steps:

1. Select column E and click **Edit > Copy.**
2. Activate cell I1 (or the first cell in any other empty column) and click **Edit > Paste.**
3. Select column I and click **Data > Sort.**
4. In the *Sort by* box, enter *Total Profit* and choose *Ascending.*
5. Choose *My list has Header row* and click **OK.**

The sorted values appear in *ascending* order in column I, as they do in Table 6.3.

TABLE 6.3 | The Profit Population Rearranged into an Ordered Array

When the data of Table 6.2 are turned into an ***ordered array*** *from the lowest to the highest number, we can grasp the information more quickly. It is instantly clear, for example, that net profits ranged from −$1,045 million to +$9,163 million. (These extremes referred to Apple Computer and Ford Motor, respectively. The other firms suffering losses were Unisys, Eli Lilly, Whirlpool, TRW, and International Paper.)*

−1045	−854	−385	−162	−49	−22	5	7	79	114
120	141	146	195	245	293	294	300	302	302
323	337	355	377	454	458	471	481	541	559
581	606	622	658	731	740	762	767	840	866
870	912	944	955	956	985	1009	1016	1073	1086
1170	1180	1188	1191	1226	1352	1427	1452	1465	1491
1643	1826	1855	1907	1953	1957	1966	1991	2043	2094
2199	2223	2405	2528	2586	2603	2805	3015	3119	3205
3210	3256	3332	3415	3454	3591	3640	3708	4129	4614
4777	5012	6093	6310	6503	6645	6945	8203	8460	9163

SOURCE: Table 6.2.

An ordered array is clearly an improvement over its unordered counterpart in that a reader is instantly aware of the data set's maximum value (here \$9,163 million), its minimum value (here −\$1,045 million), and the overall range of the data (here the \$10,208 million difference between the maximum and minimum values). Yet, one can surely do better still. As the following sections will show, the comprehension of an otherwise confusing data set can be particularly enhanced with the help of so-called *frequency distributions,* including:

- absolute frequency distributions
- relative frequency distributions
- cumulative frequency distributions

6.2 The Absolute Frequency Distribution

More likely than not, most users of data would not be interested in the detail of either one of the preceding tables and would prefer considerably condensed data. The table maker obliges by carefully dividing the range of available data into collectively exhaustive and mutually exclusive groupings of data, called **classes,** noting how many observations fall into each, and constructing a table on that basis. The absolute number of observations that falls into a given class is referred to as the **absolute class frequency,** which gives the table in question a special name:

DEFINITION 6.1 A tabular summary of a data set showing the *absolute numbers* of observations that fall into each of several collectively exhaustive and mutually exclusive classes is called an **absolute frequency distribution.**

THE NATURE OF DATA CLASSES

It is a matter of personal judgment what kind of data classes best serve the goal of clarity. Inevitably, this judgment will vary with the nature of the raw data in question. If data pertain to a *qualitative* variable, such as types of businesses, the qualitative categories themselves, such as proprietorships, partnerships, or corporations, may well point to the most appropriate types of classes that might be listed in a table. However, alternatives always exist. We could also decide to combine proprietorships and partnerships into a single class and we could split the corporate category into further detail, listing small, medium-sized and large corporations separately.

If data pertain to a *discrete quantitative* variable, such as the number of television sets owned by households, they can, similarly, be classified on the basis of the number of discrete possibilities. Households owning zero television sets can be counted separately from those owning one set, two sets, and so on, but again different classifications are possible. One could combine the counts of households owning two or more sets, for example, into a single class.

Data concerning *continuous quantitative* variables, such as the net profits earned by U.S.-based multinationals, can be classified in any convenient fashion. One thing is certain: A very small number of classes sacrifices too much detail and people learn next to nothing from the tabular presentation; a very large number of classes retains too much information and leaves people confused. As with any presentation, we must always consider the particular needs of our audience. This will help us decide how many and what kinds of classes are most appropriate.

COLLECTIVELY EXHAUSTIVE CLASSES

Whatever choice we make about the types of data classes to use in a table, we must create **collectively exhaustive classes.** As a group, such classes must exhaust all logical possibilities for classifying the available data. If we want to classify data about business types and our table only makes room for partnerships and corporations, we wouldn't know where to put single proprietorship data and our readers would likely wonder about the omission. In one way or another, all of our raw data must find a home. Similarly, if we want to classify our Table 6.3 profit figures, we cannot create one class that ranges from −$2,000 million to $0 million and another that ranges from $2,000 million to $4,000 million and leave it at that. A $355 million profit figure would have no place to go, and the same would be true of any number exceeding $4,000 million.

MUTUALLY EXCLUSIVE CLASSES

Likewise, we must create **mutually exclusive classes.** Such data classes do not overlap and, thus, have no data in common. If they did overlap, many raw data would have more than one home and we could not construct any meaningful table. Thus, the three advertising categories of "television, radio, and mass media" do not make sense, because the last of the three surely includes the first two. Similarly, we should not classify the profits of multinational companies into classes such as −$2,000 million to $0 million, $0 million to $2,000 million, and $2,000 million and more. Where would we place a firm earning $0 profit? In the first category or the second? And where would we place that $2,000 million firm, in the second class or the third? Careful table makers avoid the problem by writing −$2,000 million *to under* $0 million, $0 million *to under* $2,000 million, and $2,000 million and more. Now it is clear that the $0 million firm belongs in the second class and the $2,000 million firm in the third.

THE DESIRABLE NUMBER OF CLASSES

Clarity demands that we feature neither too few classes nor too many. What is the right number? Most statisticians recommend between 5 and 20 classes; some like to use **Sturgess's rule** to determine the desirable number of classes, k. According to this rule, $k = 1 + 3.3 \log n$, where n equals the size of the data set. In our multinational firms example, with $n = 100$ and $\log 100 = 2$, this comes to $k = 1 + 3.3(2) = 7.6$, which might be rounded to 7 or 8. It is rarely desirable, however, to follow such a fixed rule blindly. (What kind of table would we have if we divided our Table 6.3 data, say, into 8 classes and then found *all* of our data fitting into one or two of them?)

THE DESIRABLE WIDTH OF CLASSES

In the case of quantitative data, it is considered desirable to make the **class width,** the difference between the numerical lower and upper limit of a class, the same for all classes. Such uniform width facilitates comparisons among classes, as well as the calculation of summary values (discussed in Chapter 7). Having decided on the desired *number* of classes, we can quickly approximate an appropriate class *width* by dividing the difference between the largest and smallest observation in our data set by the desired number of classes.

If we tentatively decided to condense the Table 6.3 data into eight classes of equal width—a number, perhaps, suggested by Sturgess's rule—we would calculate as follows:

$$\text{approximate class width} = \frac{\text{largest value} - \text{smallest value in data set}}{\text{desirable number of classes}} = \frac{9163 - (-1045)}{8} = 1276$$

For aesthetic reasons, we might round this number to 1,250 and then create whatever number of classes we need to cover the entire range of our data. The result is shown in column 1 of Table 6.4.

TABLE 6.4 | An Absolute Frequency Distribution of Net Profits of the 100 Largest U.S.-Based Multinationals in 1997

An absolute frequency distribution can highlight meaningful patterns otherwise hidden in raw data. Note that the sum of absolute class frequencies necessarily equals the total number of observations.

Class (net profit in millions of dollars) (1)	Absolute Class Frequency (number of companies in class) (2)
−1,250 to under 0	6
0 to under 1,250	49
1,250 to under 2,500	18
2,500 to under 3,750	15
3,750 to under 5,000	3
5,000 to under 6,250	2
6,250 to under 7,500	4
7,500 to under 8,750	2
8,750 to under 10,000	1
	Sum: 100

SOURCE: Table 6.3.

THE FINAL PRODUCT DERIVED

Given the column 1 entries of Table 6.4, we can quickly fill in column 2 by counting relevant numbers in the Table 6.3 ordered array.

Note how the absolute frequency distribution allows us to gather all sorts of intelligence about our multinationals at a glance: Six of them lost money during 1997. Almost half of them earned net profits between \$0 and \$1,250 million. Only three of them enjoyed net profits of \$7,500 million and more. Such succinct information could hardly have been derived, equally rapidly, from the raw data of Table 6.2 and would have been even less possible to derive if the raw data had been more massive in number, as often is the case (except in textbooks).

THE FINAL PRODUCT ASSESSED

Having created our first statistical table, let's pause and become aware of certain aspects of table making that are easy to overlook. Good table making requires us to pay attention to a number of important factors. All of this serves the overriding goal of helping the user understand and interpret information accurately and quickly.

NUMBER AND TITLE When published along with other tables, a table should have a *number* so that readers can find it easily. Often, as in this case, it is convenient to use a chapter number for the purpose; Table 6.4, then, refers to the fourth table in Chapter 6. Sometimes it is useful to use page numbers instead; Table 361a refers to the first table on page 361.

The table number must be followed by a *title* that is as short as possible but also complete. It must focus on *what, where,* and *when:* in this case, the net profits of 100 multinational companies (what), headquartered in the United States (where), during 1997 (when). Consider how useless the entire table would be if any one of these ingredients were left out of the title.

CAPTIONS Often readers appreciate a brief verbal summary that explains what the table is all about. Such a summary can highlight the most important table features, which is particularly useful for later reviews when the table is studied in isolation from its surrounding text. The caption then makes it unnecessary for the user to search the text for detailed explanations about the table's content.

FOOTNOTES Sometimes additional information can be valuable to a user. Such additions often belong in a footnote, designated by letter or symbol to avoid confusion with numbers in the body of the table. When the information contained in the table is based on a *sample survey,* a footnote might include details about:

- sample size
- type of sample taken
- the size of the sampling error (the computation of which we will discuss in a later chapter)
- the likely extent of systematic error or bias (which readers might be able to judge if we provide them with, say, the exact wording of questions asked in a telephone survey or the rate of response encountered to a mail questionnaire)

If a table contains *experimental data,* a footnote can similarly summarize various details, such as the experimental design used to acquire the data.

Indeed, if we wanted to be fussy, we could add a footnote even to the column 2 heading of our Table 6.4: "Strictly speaking, each class frequency refers to the number of *profit figures* from the profit population of Table 6.2 that fit into the designated class, but one can just as well talk about the *number of companies* because each profit figure is linked to a different company."

DECIMALS AND ROUNDING We must inevitably decide how many decimals to retain in the numbers appearing in a table. Should an absolute value of 600.493 be reported as such, as 600.49, or even as 600, with all the decimals dropped? More often than not, retaining many decimals serves no good purpose (in that it adds little information). It may, in fact, do harm (by giving the published data a totally unwarranted air of precision). Having decided on a reasonable number of decimals to retain, we must employ rules for rounding. Typically, decimals from 1 to 4 are eliminated by rounding down (a 5.42 becomes a 5.4); those between 6 and 9 are eliminated by rounding up (a 5.47 becomes a 5.5); and an arbitrary rule is followed with the decimal 5, such as always rounding it to the even possibility (a 5.45 becomes a 5.4 and not a 5.5, and a 5.35 also becomes a 5.4 and not a 5.3). This arbitrary rule serves the purpose of avoiding bias from rounding up more often than down.

ADDED INFORMATION In many cases, the usefulness for later analysis of a summary such as Table 6.4 could be vastly improved by adding another column, showing the *sum* of data pertaining to each class. Thus, the sum of losses made by the 6 companies in class 1 might be given as −$2,517 million, as Table 6.3 attests; the sum of profits of the 49 companies in class 2 might be given as $29,833 million, and similar totals (of $33,249 million, $47,467 million, $13,520 million, $11,105 million, $26,403 million, $16,663 million, and $9,163 million) might be given for the other seven classes. This sort of information could, for example, be used to calculate precise class averages (such as −$2,517 million divided by 6, or −$419.5 million for class 1) and would eliminate the user's need to estimate them. Such estimates are often made by assuming, perhaps incorrectly, that the average pertaining to each class equals the midpoint of the class interval, such as −$625 million for class 1.

The listing of class sums is crucial for **open-ended classes** that have only one stated end point, the upper or lower class limit. Examples are "under $0" or "$7,500 million and above." In cases such as these, users do not even have the option of approximating the class average by the class midpoint. Unfortunately, this desirable practice of listing class sums is rarely followed. As you construct tables, you can make a real contribution to descriptive statistics by considering whether class sums would be useful information for table users.

6.3 The Relative Frequency Distribution

The frequency distribution discussed so far in this chapter is termed an absolute one because it is based on counting absolute *numbers* of observations for each class. On many occasions, however, table users are more interested in the *proportions* of all observations that fall into various classes. Consider a business executive who is preparing an annual report to stockholders. Sure enough, it may be important to note that the company's sales last year were $120,279 million (an absolute number), but stockholders may be considerably more impressed by being told that this number equaled .78 of total industry sales (a proportion). Can you see that this proportion signifies a *market share* of 78 percent? For reasons such as this, we may want to set up entire tables filled with proportions. In a frequency distribution table, any such proportion is called a **relative class frequency** and is the ratio of the number of observations in a particular class to the total number of observations made. Accordingly, we can note another important concept:

DEFINITION 6.2 A tabular summary of a data set showing the *proportions* of all observations that fall into each of several collectively exhaustive and mutually exclusive classes is called a **relative frequency distribution.**

Table 6.5 on the next page illustrates how a relative frequency distribution is derived from an absolute one by simply dividing each of the absolute frequencies, here found in column 2, by the total of observations, here 100, and recording the result in column 3. That third column now shows the *proportion* of all companies in any given class, but one can mentally multiply each of the column 3 entries by 100 and think of *percentages* instead. Thus, focusing on the first row, we

TABLE 6.5 | Deriving the Relative Frequency Distribution of Net Profits of the 100 Largest U.S.-Based Multinationals in 1997

An absolute frequency distribution, such as columns 1 and 2, is easily converted into a relative frequency distribution, as in columns 1 and 3, by successively dividing each absolute frequency by the total number of observations. For example, 6/100 turns into 0.06.

Class (net profit in millions of dollars) (1)	Absolute Class Frequency (number of companies in class) (2)	Relative Class Frequency (proportion of all companies in class) (3)
−1,250 to under 0	6	0.06
0 to under 1,250	49	0.49
1,250 to under 2,500	18	0.18
2,500 to under 3,750	15	0.15
3,750 to under 5,000	3	0.03
5,000 to under 6,250	2	0.02
6,250 to under 7,500	4	0.04
7,500 to under 8,750	2	0.02
8,750 to under 10,000	1	0.01
	Sum: 100	Sum: 1.00

SOURCE: Table 6.3.

notice that the *proportion* of all companies that suffered losses in 1997 came to 0.06, which implies that the *percentage* of companies making losses equaled 6.

CAUTION

In the example illustrated by Table 6.5, the absolute and relative frequency distributions look very much alike, but that is a pure accident due to the fact that there just happen to be 100 observations. If the column 2 values summed to any other number, the two columns of data would look very different from each other. It is no accident, however, that the sum of relative frequencies equals 1.00; such is always the case. Table 6.5A (see top of next page) is a case in point, based on a small company's personnel records.

Relative frequency distributions are particularly useful for comparisons of populations that are similar in type but vastly different in size. We could, for example, compare the racial composition of a single firm's employees versus that of its entire industry. Even though a single firm may have a mere 34 black employees, a tiny number compared to *millions* of black workers in its industry, that firm may, in fact, have made extraordinary efforts to overcome racial imbalance, which only a comparison of *relative* frequencies could show. As in Table 6.5A, the proportion of black employees in this firm may come to 0.046 + 0.096 = 0.142, or 14.2 percent. Yet, at the same time, the corresponding *industry* proportion may equal 0.092, or a mere 9.2 percent.

A dramatic illustration of the usefulness of comparing relative frequency distributions is provided by Application 6.1, *Deciphering Secret Codes,* wherein a small population of letters from the words of a secret message is compared with the vast population of letters that appear in all possible words of the English language.

(continued)

Caution (continued)

TABLE 6.5A | Deriving an Alternative Relative Frequency Distribution

Class (employee race and sex)	Absolute Class Frequency (number of employees in class)	Relative Class Frequency (proportion of all employees in class)
black female	11	(11/239) = 0.046
black male	23	(23/239) = 0.096
white female	59	(59/239) = 0.247
white male	146	(146/239) = 0.611
Total	**239**	**1.000**

APPLICATION 6.1

DECIPHERING SECRET CODES

One of the fastest growing industries in recent years has been e-commerce—buying and selling on the Internet—but merchants have faced one major obstacle. Many people hesitate to supply personal data, such as addresses and credit card numbers, to prospective sellers. What if someone intercepts this information and misuses it? More likely than not, the fear is misplaced; just consider how often *your* credit card is out of your sight in ordinary stores and restaurants and how easy it would be for someone to make copies. Nevertheless, businesses have to take customer security concerns seriously and many of them provide *secure servers* that employ secret codes to scramble sensitive information before it dashes across the Internet.

Interestingly, *frequency distributions* have a lot to do with creating and subsequently reading such secret codes. Such distributions lie at the heart of *cryptanalysis,* the scientific study of converting plain text into unreadable ciphers or codes and of converting the latter into plain text, even if the key is not known. Consider the secret message (presumed to be written in English) contained in Table 6.A.

TABLE 6.A | A Coded Message

IMEUX	ANEMO	MNPKN	EONUC	MOMXB
MJDAM	VNNES	NSXXW	MVSPM	RPMSN
MAMQK	SXNES	NNEMG	SPMMV	AUIMA
CGNEM	DPRPM	SNUPI	DNERM	PNSDV
KVSXD	MVSCX	MPDLE	NONES	NSWUV
LNEMO	MSPMX	DBMXD	CMPNG	SVANE
MTKPO	KDNUB	ESTTD	VMOON	ESNNU
OMRKP	MNEMO	MPDLE	NOLUJ	MPVWM
VNOSP	MDVON	DNKNM	ASWUV	LWMVA
MPDJD	VLNEM	DPZKO	NTUIM	POBPU
WNEMR	UVOMV	NUBNE	MLUJM	PVMA

(continued)

Application 6.1 (continued)

To decipher the message, cryptanalysis first establishes the absolute frequency distribution of the letters in the secret message. Table 6.B provides a count of the number of times each letter occurs and also shows the implied relative frequency distribution. Next, the relative frequency distribution derived from the secret message is compared with a similar distribution of all the letters in a normal English language text, shown in Table 6.C. (Small letters are used in the list of normal English letters to avoid confusion with the capital letters in the coded message.) To make the comparison, the letters of normal English and of the secret message are arranged in Table 6.D in order of decreasing relative frequency.

Although one can hardly expect an immediate letter-for-letter matching in Table 6.D, the juxtaposition can be very helpful in breaking the code. After some trying about, some letters can be identified (for example, *M* as *e* and *N* as *t*), then portions of words, and finally, the whole message. (Note: A good codebreaker looks not only at general letter frequencies, but also considers the preferred associations of one letter with other letters, the order of frequency of the most common doubles, of initial letters, of final letters, of the most frequent one-letter words, and much more.) The key for this particular message is a simple one: The word *SCRAMBLED* is used for the first nine letters of the alphabet, and the remaining code letters, now excluding the letters in the word *SCRAMBLED,* are listed in reverse alphabetical sequence. The first line below shows the plain text and the second line below shows the coded text:

a	b	c	d	e	f	g	h	i	j	k	l	m	n	o	p	q	r	s	t	u	v	w	x	y	z
S	C	R	A	M	B	L	E	D	Z	Y	X	W	V	U	T	Q	P	O	N	K	J	I	H	G	F

As an analysis of Table 6.D can show, even this simple table correctly identifies the meanings of five code letters *(M, N, A, X,* and *B),* and it provides strong hints in the case of a dozen others, the meanings of which are found within a line or two of the code letter. (Thus a *V* is not an *i*, but an *n;* a *D* is not an *r,* but an *i,* and so on). In fact, all but two of the alphabet's 26 letters are decipherable by looking within four lines of the code letter in Table 6.D. The decoded message is an excerpt from the Declaration of Independence:

> We hold these truths to be self-evident, that all men are created equal, that they are endowed by their Creator with certain unalienable rights, that among these are life, liberty and the pursuit of happiness, that to secure these rights, governments are instituted among men, deriving their just powers from the consent of the governed.

TABLE 6.B | Frequency Distribution of 274 Letters in Coded Message

Letter	Absolute Frequency (number)	Relative Frequency (percent)	Letter	Absolute Frequency (number)	Relative Frequency (percent)
A	9	3.3	N	36	13.1
B	5	1.8	O	16	5.8
C	4	1.5	P	21	7.7
D	16	5.8	Q	1	0.4
E	19	6.9	R	5	1.8
F	0	0	S	19	6.9
G	3	1.1	T	4	1.5
H	0	0	U	14	5.1
I	4	1.5	V	18	6.6
J	4	1.5	W	6	2.2
K	8	2.9	X	9	3.3
L	7	2.5	Y	0	0
M	45	16.4	Z	1	0.4
			Totals	**274**	**100.0**

(continued)

Application 6.1 (continued)

TABLE 6.C | Frequency Distribution of 200 Letters of a Normal English Language Text

Letter	Absolute Frequency (number)	Relative Frequency (percent)	Letter	Absolute Frequency (number)	Relative Frequency (percent)
a	16	8	n	14	7
b	3	1.5	o	16	8
c	6	3	p	4	2
d	8	4	q	0.5	0.25
e	26	13	r	13	6.5
f	4	2	s	12	6
g	3	1.5	t	18	9
h	12	6	u	6	3
i	13	6.5	v	2	1
j	1	0.5	w	3	1.5
k	1	0.5	x	1	0.5
l	7	3.5	y	4	2
m	6	3	z	0.5	0.25
			Totals	**200**	**100.0**

SOURCE OF TABLE 6.C: David Kahn, *The Codebreakers: The Story of Secret Writing* (New York: Macmillan, 1967), p. 100.

TABLE 6.D | Comparative Relative Frequency Distributions of Plain and Coded English

Plain English		Coded English		Plain English		Coded English	
Letter	Relative Frequency	Letter	Relative Frequency	Letter	Relative Frequency	Letter	Relative Frequency
e	13	M	16.4	u	3	W	2.2
t	9	N	13.1	f	2	B	1.8
a	8	P	7.7	p	2	R	1.8
o	8	E	6.9	y	2	C	1.5
n	7	S	6.9	b	1.5	I	1.5
i	6.5	V	6.6	g	1.5	J	1.5
r	6.5	D	5.8	w	1.5	T	1.5
h	6	O	5.8	v	1	G	1.1
s	6	U	5.1	j	0.5	Q	0.4
d	4	A	3.3	k	0.5	Z	0.4
l	3.5	X	3.3	x	0.5	F	0
c	3	K	2.9	q	0.25	H	0
m	3	L	2.5	z	0.25	Y	0
				Total	**100.0**	**Total**	**100.0**

(continued)

Application 6.1 (continued)

POSTSCRIPT. In 1976, the National Security Agency (NSA) helped design a code for business that could help in the transmission of sensitive but unclassified data over computer lines. Its Data Encryption Standard (DES) takes a message, translates it into computer language of zeros and ones, and then scrambles it by repeatedly applying any one of 2^{56} mathematical operations. (This number exceeds 72,000 million million!) Although renowned cryptographers the world over had been trying, no one had been able to break the code when the new century dawned. Nevertheless, a cautious U.S. Commerce Department introduced an even more powerful encryption technique late in the year 2000. The new *Rijndael technique* is named after its Belgian creators, Vincent Rijmen and Joan Daemen. Its numeric key to scramble and unscramble messages uses a number of combinations equal to 1,100 followed by 75 zeros. Allegedly, today's best computers would take 149 trillion years to crack the code. (For a bit of perspective, consider that the Big Bang occurred a mere 20 billion years ago!) The NSA, in the meantime, has no comment, which is why some believe the letters stand for *Never Say Anything.*

Biography 6.1, *William and Elizebeth Friedman,* found on the Web site associated with this text, takes a closer look at the fascinating world of cryptography.

6.4 Cumulative Frequency Distributions

Consider once again a business executive who is preparing an annual report to stockholders. The executive could just turn to an absolute or relative frequency distribution and report that the company's $15 billion sales put it in a class containing a mere 4 firms in the 66-firm industry [or containing a proportion of only (4/66) = .06 of all industry firms]. Even though such absolute numbers and proportions can tell important stories, providing the *sums* of various numbers and proportions across several classes in a frequency distribution is usually considerably more instructive. Our executive, for example, may want stockholders to know that 59 companies in the industry had smaller sales than their firm, while only 3 companies had larger sales. Can you see that these numbers imply proportions of (59/66) = .894 for companies with smaller sales and (3/66) = .045 for companies with larger sales? To get numbers such as these, we must to create another kind of frequency distribution table yet.

When variables are quantitative, we can determine a **cumulative class frequency** as the sum of (absolute or relative) class frequencies for all classes up to and including the class in question, beginning at either end of the frequency distribution. If the cumulation process moves from lesser to greater classes, the result is a "less than or equal to upper class limit" type of distribution, which is abbreviated as *LE distribution* (for which we can be grateful). In this kind of distribution, the frequencies counted always pertain to the class in question and all lower ones. If the cumulation process moves from greater to lesser classes, a "more than or equal to lower class limit" type of distribution emerges; it is called an *ME distribution.* In this kind of distribution, the frequencies counted pertain to the class in question and all higher ones. Accordingly, we meet another crucial concept:

DEFINITION 6.3 A tabular summary of a data set showing for each of several collectively exhaustive and mutually exclusive classes the absolute number or proportion of observations that are less than or equal to the upper limits of the classes in question (LE type) or that are more than or equal to their lower limits (ME type) is called a **cumulative frequency distribution.**

We can use the data of Table 6.5 (see page 174) to derive examples of these types of distributions. The results are shown in Tables 6.6 and 6.7 on the next two pages.

TABLE 6.6 | Deriving LE Types of Cumulative Frequency Distributions of the Net Profits of the 100 Largest U.S.-Based Multinationals in 1997

An absolute frequency distribution—columns 1 and 2—is easily converted into a cumulative absolute distribution—columns 1 and 3. Likewise, a relative frequency distribution—columns 1 and 4—can become a cumulative relative distribution—columns 1 and 5. Note how column 2 has been turned into column 3 and how column 4 has been turned into column 5. When cumulation proceeds from lesser to greater classes, as happens here beginning with the bold-faced entries in the first row, an LE type of cumulative frequency distribution emerges. Each member of such a distribution tells us the number or proportion of observations that are less than, or at most equal to, the ***upper*** *limit of the class in question.*

Note: *While it is an accident that the largest cumulative absolute frequency equals 100 in this example, the largest cumulative relative frequency will always equal 1.00.*

Class (net profit in millions of dollars) (1)	Absolute Class Frequency (number of companies in class) (2)	Cumulative Absolute Class Frequency (number of companies in class and lower ones) (3)	Relative Class Frequency (proportion of all companies in class) (4)	Cumulative Relative Class Frequency (proportion of all companies in class and lower ones) (5)
		Start here:		Start here:
−1,250 to under 0	6	**6**	0.06	**0.06**
0 to under 1,250	49	49 + 6 = 55	0.49	0.49 + 0.06 = 0.55
1,250 to under 2,500	18	18 + 55 = 73	0.18	0.18 + 0.55 = **0.73**
2,500 to under 3,750	15	15 + 73 = 88	0.15	0.15 + 0.73 = 0.88
3,750 to under 5,000	3	3 + 88 = **91**	0.03	0.03 + 0.88 = 0.91
5,000 to under 6,250	2	2 + 91 = 93	0.02	0.02 + 0.91 = 0.93
6,250 to under 7,500	4	4 + 93 = 97	0.04	0.04 + 0.93 = 0.97
7,500 to under 8,750	2	2 + 97 = 99	0.02	0.02 + 0.97 = 0.99
8,750 to under 10,000	1	1 + 99 = 100	0.01	0.01 + 0.99 = 1.00

SOURCE: Table 6.5.

It is easy to interpret the entries of either table. Consider Table 6.6. The red entry in column 3 tells us that 91 of our multinational companies made net profits below $5,000 million in 1997, while the red entry in column 5 tells us that 73 *percent* of these multinationals had net profits below $2,500 million in that year.

Now turn to Table 6.7 on the next page. The red entry in column 3 tells us that 9 of our multinational companies had net profits of $5,000 million or more in 1997, while the red entry in column 5 tells us that 27 *percent* of these multinationals made net profits of $2,500 million or more in that year. When you think about it, given that there are 100 companies on our list, the last two statements were implied by the first two statements above!

6.5 Cross Tabulations

All of our tabular presentations so far have involved a single variable, in this case the profits of multinational firms. Oftentimes, however, we may wish to present information about two

TABLE 6.7 | Deriving ME Types of Cumulative Frequency Distributions of the Net Profits of the 100 Largest U.S.-Based Multinationals in 1997

An absolute frequency distribution—columns 1 and 2—is easily converted into a cumulative absolute distribution—columns 1 and 3. Likewise, a relative frequency distribution—columns 1 and 4—can become a cumulative relative distribution—columns 1 and 5. Note how column 2 has been turned into column 3 and how column 4 has been turned into column 5. When cumulation proceeds from greater to lesser classes, as happens here beginning with the boldfaced entries in the last row, an ME type of cumulative frequency distribution emerges. Each member of such a distribution tells us the number or proportion of observations that are more than, or at least equal to, the ***lower*** *limit of the class in question.*

Note: *While it is an accident that the largest cumulative absolute frequency equals 100 in this example, the largest cumulative relative frequency will always equal 1.00.*

Class (net profit in millions of dollars) (1)	Absolute Class Frequency (number of companies in class) (2)	Cumulative Absolute Class Frequency (number of companies in class and higher ones) (3)	Relative Class Frequency (proportion of all companies in class) (4)	Cumulative Relative Class Frequency (proportion of all companies in class and higher ones) (5)
−1,250 to under 0	6	6 + 94 = 100	0.06	0.06 + 0.94 = 1.00
0 to under 1,250	49	49 + 45 = 94	0.49	0.49 + 0.45 = 0.94
1,250 to under 2,500	18	18 + 27 = 45	0.18	0.18 + 0.27 = 0.45
2,500 to under 3,750	15	15 + 12 = 27	0.15	0.15 + 0.12 = **0.27**
3,750 to under 5,000	3	3 + 9 = 12	0.03	0.03 + 0.09 = 0.12
5,000 to under 6,250	2	2 + 7 = **9**	0.02	0.02 + 0.07 = 0.09
6,250 to under 7,500	4	4 + 3 = 7	0.04	0.04 + 0.03 = 0.07
7,500 to under 8,750	2	2 + 1 = 3	0.02	0.02 + 0.01 = 0.03
8,750 to under 10,000	1	**1**	0.01	**0.01**
		Start here: ↗		**Start here:** ↗

SOURCE: Table 6.5.

variables at the same time. Such tabular summaries of data for two variables are called **cross tabulations.** Classes for one variable are represented by the headings of rows, classes for the other variable are represented by column heads, and information pertaining to both variables is entered in various table cells where rows and columns intersect.

Consider, for instance, an advertising agency that wants to steer its clients to the most effective advertising medium. Potential campaign targets might include people engaged in television prime time viewing, radio listening, newspaper reading, and Internet surfing. Those alternatives might become a table's column heads. However, not all people are alike. Potential clients may want to sell their product to a particular group of people; therefore, such factors as people's age, sex, race, educational level, employment status, and income may become relevant. These alternatives might become the row headings of a table. The numbers of people fitting any given combination of column and row categories may then be placed in all the table cells. Table 6.8 is a case in point.

Note how easy it is, with the help of Table 6.8, to target a particular advertising campaign to the right medium. If you have a product designed for the elderly, you certainly would be foolish

TABLE 6.8 | Multimedia Audiences, United States, 1998

Based on a sample taken from 195 million persons 18 years and older, this table shows millions of people who engaged in selected activities within 30 days of the sampling date.

Audience Characteristics	Television Prime Time Viewing	Radio Listening	Newspaper Reading	Internet Surfing
Age				
18 to under 25	18.0	22.4	18.8	6.9
25 to under 35	31.1	37.0	32.5	11.8
35 to under 45	33.1	38.9	36.3	12.3
45 to under 55	25.7	27.9	27.4	9.0
55 to under 65	16.8	16.4	17.6	2.7
65 and older	26.0	19.8	26.2	1.0
Sex				
Male	71.4	79.7	76.4	23.7
Female	79.4	82.8	82.3	19.9
Race				
White	126.9	137.8	135.3	38.2
Black	18.1	18.9	17.4	2.9
Other	5.7	5.8	6.0	2.5
Education				
Some high school	27.8	26.3	23.6	1.3
High school graduate	51.1	53.3	52.3	7.0
Some college	39.9	45.3	44.2	14.7
College graduate	32.0	37.7	38.6	20.7
Employment				
Full time	81.6	97.2	89.6	32.3
Part time	15.0	17.4	16.5	5.2
None	54.3	48.0	52.6	6.1
Household Income				
Under $10,000	12.4	11.3	10.3	0.9
$10,000 to under $20,000	21.4	19.0	19.3	1.5
$20,000 to under $30,000	21.2	21.4	21.3	3.1
$30,000 to under $35,000	9.7	10.3	10.4	1.8
$35,000 to under $40,000	9.8	10.7	10.1	2.2
$40,000 to under $50,000	17.2	19.2	18.3	4.2
$50,000 and more	59.0	70.6	68.9	29.9

SOURCE: Adapted from U.S. Bureau of the Census, *Statistical Abstract of the United States 1998,* p. 573.

to advertise on the Internet, but that may be just the thing to do if you are aiming at college graduates or high-income consumers.

6.6 An Introduction to Drawing Graphs

As the old saying goes, "a picture is worth a thousand words." Well, maybe. It is certainly true that all the information contained in tables can also be graphed and some people find such graphs easier to comprehend. Like table making, creating graphs that *effectively* summarize otherwise confusing masses of raw data is an art. Modern computer programs, such as EXCEL or MINITAB, allow statisticians to create a multitude of excellent graphs; many commonly used graphs are introduced in the following sections.

EXCEL Graphs

EXCEL's graphing capability was introduced briefly in chapter 2 (see pages 56–59 for a quick review). Here are three good ways to familiarize yourself with additional possibilities:

1. Click the *Chart Wizard* that is found on the standard toolbar. The first of four dialog boxes appears. There are two tabs: one for *Standard Types,* another one for *Custom Types* of graphs. Click *Standard Types* and note the drop-down list of 14 types of graphs. Click on *Column* and view the alternative renderings of column charts on the right. Repeat the process for the other types of standard graphs. Then click on *Custom Types* and note the 20 types of graphs available here.
2. For a more comprehensive learning experience, click **Help** > **Microsoft EXCEL Help** on EXCEL's menu bar. The Office Assistant appears, along with a suggestion box. Type *About charts* in the box and click **Search.** Click **About charts;** then maximize the *Microsoft EXCEL Help* screen that probably appears in the upper left corner of your screen.

   Click the upper left **Show** button; then the **Contents** tab; then **Working with Charts** on the drop-down list. Explore the long list of subcategories to learn everything you could possibly want to know about graphing with EXCEL.
3. A third approach to learning about graphing in EXCEL involves clicking **Insert** > **Object** and then selecting an object, such as *Microsoft Map,* from the drop-down list. By experimenting in this way, you can learn to do amazing things (as EXCEL Example 6.2 below will illustrate).

Whatever approach you take, remember that all the good advice given about table making in Section 6.3 applies to graphing as well. EXCEL accommodates your desire to create beautiful graphs by offering a multitude of options that allow you to add clear titles, captions, footnotes, colors, patterns, and whatever else helps those who are meant to look at the graphs.

EXCEL Example 6.2

Review Figure 6.1 in this chapter's Preview. Teach yourself to create an identical graph in EXCEL.

SOLUTION Fire up EXCEL and open the file HKMAP6, which contains two columns of data: the names of the 50 states and a set of nominal data, in which the numbers 25, 15, and 5 represent the three differential categories noted in the Figure 6.1 legend. Select columns A and B and proceed as follows:

1. Click **Insert** > **Object.**
2. In the *Object* dialog box, click the *Create New* tab, then **Microsoft Map** > **OK.**
3. In the *Multiple Maps Available* box, click **United States (AK & HI Inset)** > **OK.** EXCEL displays a tentative map, along with the *Microsoft Map Control* box.

4. Double-click the Column B box in the white area. The *Format Properties* box appears. Click the *Value Shading Options* tab; then change the *Number of value ranges* to **3** and the graph's base *color* to **red.**
5. Select *Equal spread of values in each range* and click **OK.** The graph begins to look like Figure 6.1, but you may want to change title and legend.
6. Double-click on the title and edit it as shown in Figure 6.2.
7. Double-click on the legend and revisit the *Format Properties* box, with the *Legend Options* tab selected. Erase the Title and Subtitle in the box and click **Edit Legend Entries.**
8. In the *Edit Legend Entry* box, successively select each of the computer's legends, erase it, type the legend used in Figure 6.1, and click **OK.**
9. Click **OK** in the *Format Properties* box. Note that EXCEL provides a count of the number of states in each legend category.
10. If you wish, adjust the size and position of the title and legend boxes after double-clicking on them.

FIGURE 6.2 | Black/White Differentials in Mortgage Approvals Revisited in EXCEL

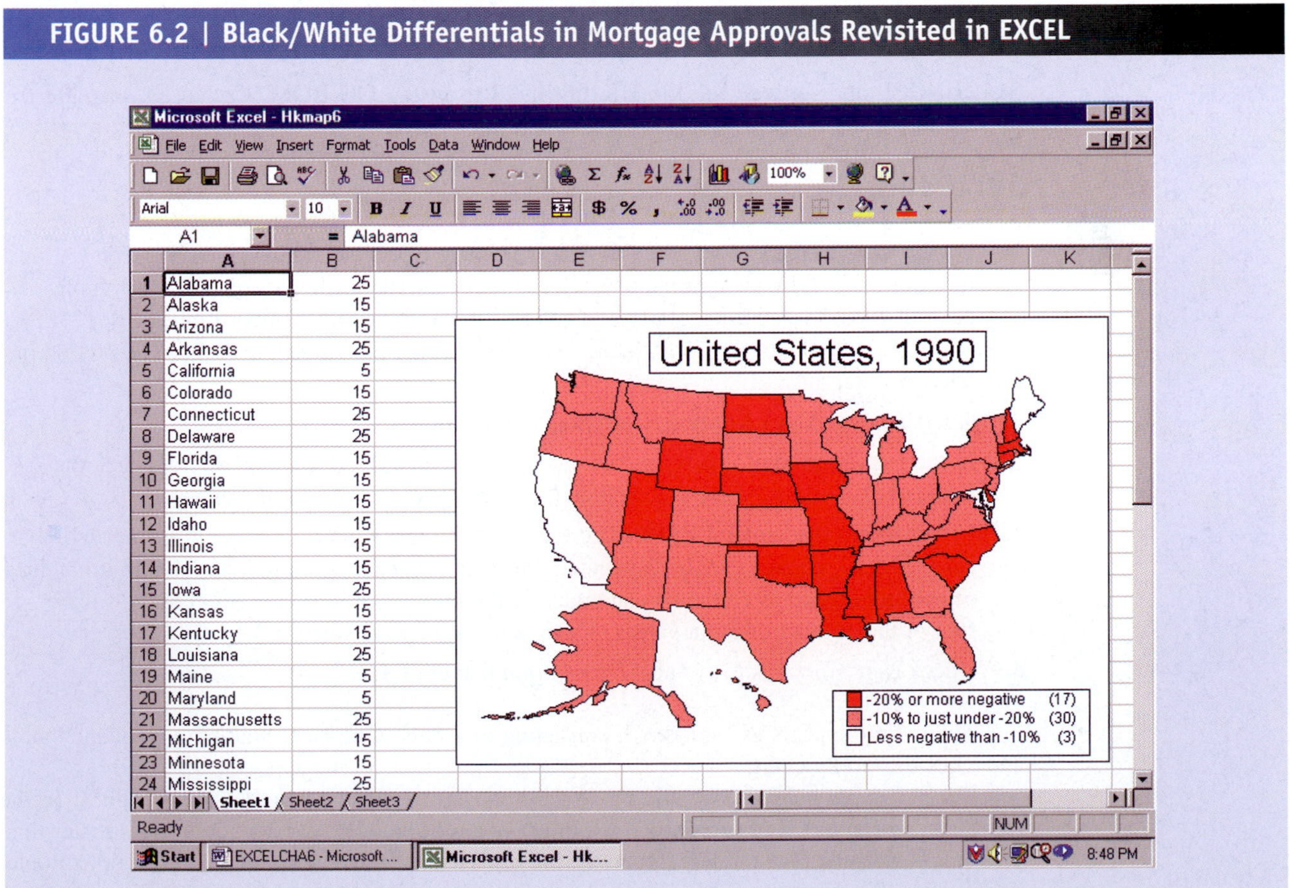

6.7 Frequency Histograms

The kind of information found in absolute or relative frequency distributions, such as those of Table 6.5, can be presented much more dramatically in graphs. Various possibilities exist; statisticians tend to favor the *frequency histogram,* to which we turn next.

DEFINITION 6.4 A **frequency histogram** is a graphical portrayal of an absolute or relative frequency distribution of continuous quantitative data in such a way that lower and upper limits of data classes are identified by tick marks on a horizontal axis, while the corresponding absolute or relative class frequencies are represented by the *areas* of contiguous rectangles that stand on top of each of these class intervals. (Note: If all class intervals are alike, as is true throughout this text and in most computer programs, the absolute or relative class frequencies are also well represented by the *heights* of the contiguous rectangles.)

DEPICTING AN ABSOLUTE FREQUENCY DISTRIBUTION

Consider the net profit figures of those 100 multinational companies first shown in Table 6.2, which we then turned into the ordered array of Table 6.3. With the help of a computer, one can quickly create an absolute frequency histogram of these data, as the following examples illustrate.

EXCEL Example 6.3

Start EXCEL and retrieve the file HK100MN97 from the CD-ROM. Create an *absolute frequency histogram* of the net profit figures found in column E.

SOLUTION

1. On the basis of the known range of data (see Table 6.3, which shows data between a minimum of −$1,045 million and a maximum of $9,163 million), create a column of desired *upper* class limits. Starting at cell J2, for example, enter upper limits of 0, 1250, 2500, 3750, 5000, 6250, 7500, 8750, and 10000, using the autofill procedure illustrated in EXCEL Example 2.3.
2. Click **Tools** > **Data Analysis** > **Histogram** > **OK.**
3. In the *Histogram* dialog box, under *Input Range,* enter **E2:E101** (and do *not* check the *Labels* box, because you have excluded the label in cell E1 from the range).
4. Under *Bin Range,* enter **J2:J10.** (*Tip:* One can also leave the *Bin Range* box empty. In that case, EXCEL creates evenly distributed intervals using the minimum and maximum values of the input range as end points and making the number of intervals equal to the square root of the number of input values. The result is rarely satisfactory.)
5. Check *New Worksheet Ply* and *Chart Output* and click **OK.**

The output appears as Figure 6.3, consisting of a new worksheet holding a frequency table and a not-too-pretty chart.

The left table column lists the previously chosen upper class limits or bin values. In the right-hand column, EXCEL reports the number of profit data that were equal to or smaller than the same row's bin value but larger than the previous row's bin value (if one exists). For example, there were 49 companies with profits above $0 million and at most $1,250 million. The frequency table confirms text Table 6.4 on page 171.

FIGURE 6.3 | EXCEL Printout

Bin	Frequency
0	6
1250	49
2500	18
3750	15
5000	3
6250	2
7500	4
8750	2
10000	1
More	0

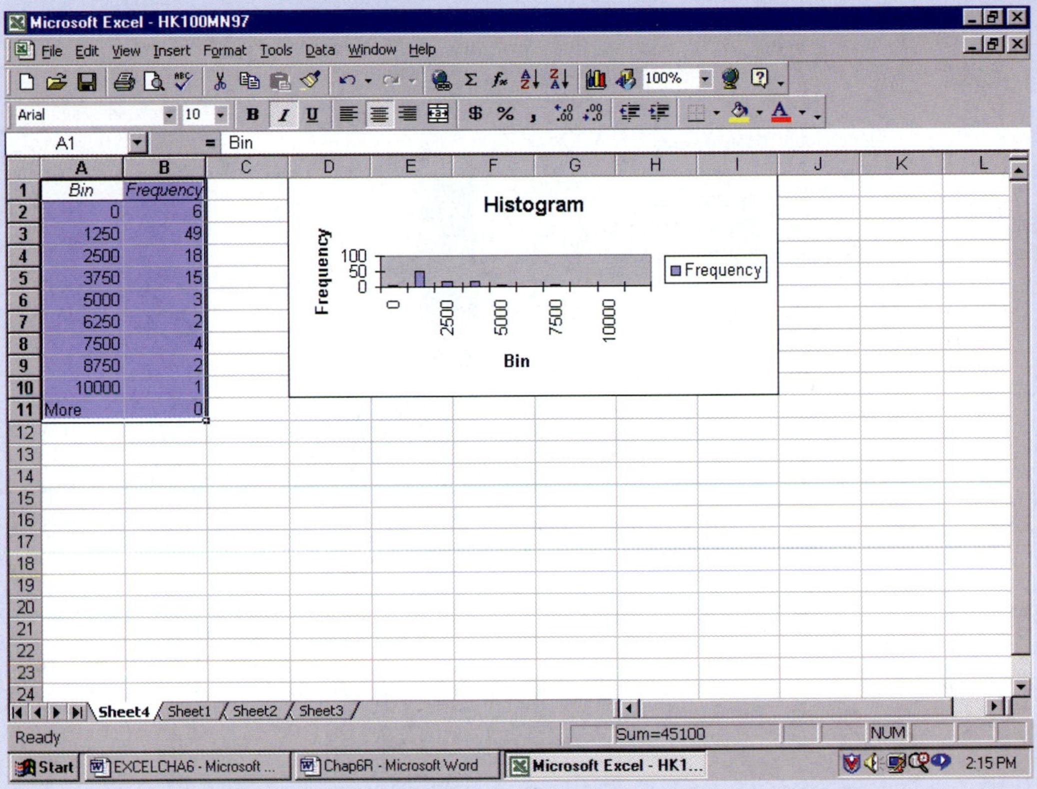

EXCEL Example 6.4

If you encountered the Figure 6.3 EXCEL Printout out of context, you would find it pretty confusing. You might well ask: The frequency of *what* is measured on the vertical axis? The bin label on the horizontal axis stands for *what?* In addition, you could hardly see all those bars in the tiny graph. Using EXCEL, improve upon Figure 6.3 to make it look prettier and more informative.

SOLUTION Use the graph editing procedure illustrated in EXCEL Example 2.9 on pages 58–59. Answers can vary. Figure 6.4 on the next page is one possibility, which enlarges the graph, improves the labels on the two axes, and more.

NOTE Although Figure 6.4 is a clear improvement over Figure 6.3, it is still not perfect. For example, it is not obvious that the horizontal tick-mark labels refer to *upper* class limits and should be moved farther to the right. The precise height of each data column and, thus, the precise absolute frequency (of 6, 49, 18, 15, 3, 2, 4, 2, and 1, respectively) is not obvious, but one can make a close guess. However, as long as the graph resides in EXCEL, you can let your mouse pointer hover over any individual bar and read the height in a screen tip. Try it!

FIGURE 6.4 | Frequency Histogram of 1997 Net Profits of 100 Largest U.S.-Based Multinationals

This graph is a visual representation of columns 1 and 2 of Table 6.5.

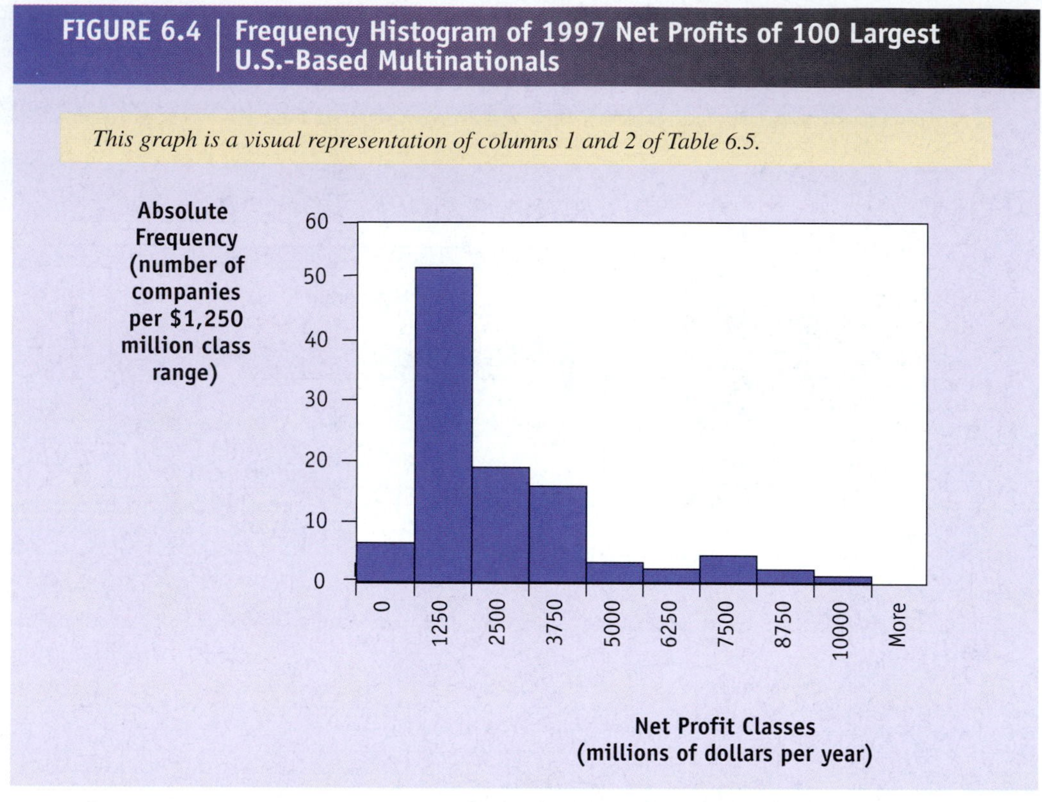

DEPICTING A RELATIVE FREQUENCY DISTRIBUTION

Histograms for relative frequency distributions are constructed on the same principles as those for absolute distributions. A histogram constructed on the basis of columns 1 and 3 of Table 6.5, for example, would have the same shape as that shown in Figure 6.4. The vertical labeling, however, would change to reflect the facts that (1) *relative* frequencies are involved and (2) *proportions* of companies, rather than absolute numbers of the companies, are being measured per $1,250 million range. Indeed, for simplicity's sake statisticians often label the vertical axis of histograms with the term **frequency density,** which equals the ratio of (absolute or relative) class frequency to class width. As long as all classes have the same width (which is the case throughout this text), the terms *absolute frequency* and *absolute frequency density* can be used interchangeably; the same is true for *relative frequency* and *relative frequency density.*

COMMON TYPES OF HISTOGRAMS

All sets of quantitative data can be fitted into some form of frequency distribution that is likely to yield one or another of a relatively few common types of histograms. Figure 6.5 shows some of these histogram shapes, namely those depicting:

- a symmetrical distribution
- a uniform distribution
- a distribution skewed to the left
- a distribution skewed to the right

FIGURE 6.5 | Common Types of Histograms

This graph pictures some of the relative frequency distributions that will be discussed in detail in Chapters 9 and 10. Histograms for relative frequency distributions such as these are always constructed in such a way that the total area covered by a given set of columns equals unity. Therefore, the proportion of the total area taken by any one column (which is indicated throughout) can be readily converted into the percentage of observations falling into the class above which this column has been erected.

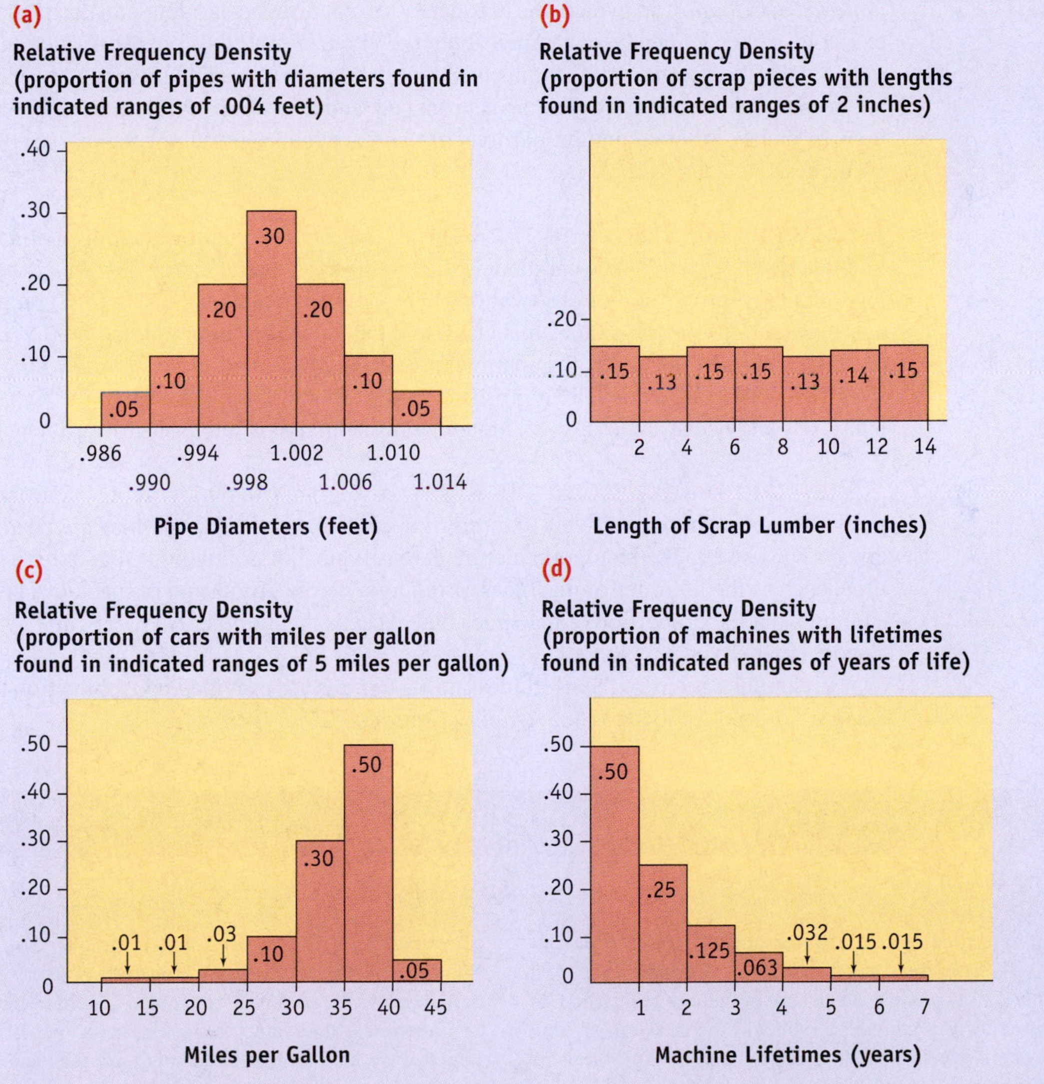

A SYMMETRICAL DISTRIBUTION Histogram (a) pictures the relative frequency distribution of the actual diameters of supposedly 1-foot-wide water pipes produced during a day. This histogram is symmetrical about the interval from 0.998 to 1.002 feet, with the histogram columns to the left and right becoming progressively shorter. The larger the divergence of the actual diameter, in either direction, from the desired diameter of 1 foot, the smaller is the proportion of such pipes produced. Thus, 30 percent of all pipes produced fit in the class on which the central column stands, 20 percent each fit in the two adjacent classes, 10 percent each into the next two, and 5 percent each into the two extreme classes, making for a total of 100 percent. This distribution follows from the fact that the area of the central column takes up .3 times the entire histogram area, the areas of the two adjacent columns each take up .2 times the total area, and so on, as the numbers inside the columns indicate. Naturally, these numbers must add to 1.00. This type of histogram is a rough approximation of the *normal distribution,* which is typical of many (but not all) populations of physical measurements.

A Uniform Distribution Histogram (b), in contrast, approximates a *rectangular* or *uniform distribution* in which the frequency of occurrence is identical in all classes. In this example, someone may be concerned about the waste of materials on a construction job. Lumber may have to be purchased at lengths of 8 feet, while pieces of all sizes from 14 inches to 8 feet are needed. As a result, a lot of scrap is produced, and every one of the scrap pieces measures less than 14 inches. About equal proportions of them are found in each of the classes between 0 and 14 inches.

A Distribution Skewed to the Left Histogram (c) pictures the miles per gallon of gasoline traveled by a year's new car models. It belongs to a general class of *skewed* distributions that feature a large proportion of observations in a dominant class, such as 35 to 40 mpg here, hardly any observations on one side of this class, and lots of observations spread out over a long "tail" of classes on the other side. This particular distribution is said to be *skewed to the left* or *negatively skewed* because there are more observations found to the left than to the right of the dominant class and because moving left along the horizontal axis moves us toward negative values.

A Distribution Skewed to the Right Histogram (d), finally, depicts a distribution that is skewed to the right or positively skewed. It approximates the *exponential distribution,* which is always so skewed. The histogram picture here is typical of populations that exhibit changes over time, such as the lifetimes of machines. A relatively large proportion of machines lasts 1 year, for example, but the proportion of machines that exceeds that number by 1, 2, 3, and more years gets rapidly smaller and smaller.

Vivid illustrations of the usefulness of histograms are provided by Application 6.2, *Deciding Authorship,* and Application 6.3, *Quality Control in Manufacturing.*

APPLICATION 6.2

Deciding Authorship

If you were running one of those auction houses that routinely sells little treasures for millions of dollars each, you would certainly want to make sure of their authenticity. Descriptive statistics can help. Such was the case, not so long ago, when a question arose about the authorship of a piece of writing. At issue was an Elizabethan elegy, published in 1612 and signed "W. S." After indexing all the words in Shakespeare's 36 plays, noting which words appeared 12 times or fewer, and finding the same word frequencies in the elegy, many experts were pretty much convinced of Shakespeare's authorship. Relative frequency distributions have been similarly employed to test the authorship of the Paulines, a set of Christian religious writings possibly written by St. Paul. Another famous case was the Shakespeare-Bacon-Marlowe controversy over who wrote certain plays traditionally attributed to Shakespeare. And then there was the matter of the *Federalist* papers, some of which were claimed simultaneously by Alexander Hamilton and James Madison. Let us consider the latter case to show how *descriptive statistics* can play an important role in solving the puzzle simply by counting something in a systematic way.

After most of them had appeared anonymously in various newspapers, some 85 essays written by Alexander Hamilton, John Jay, and James Madison appeared in book form in 1788. *The Federalist,* as the book was called, has

(continued)

Application 6.2 (continued)

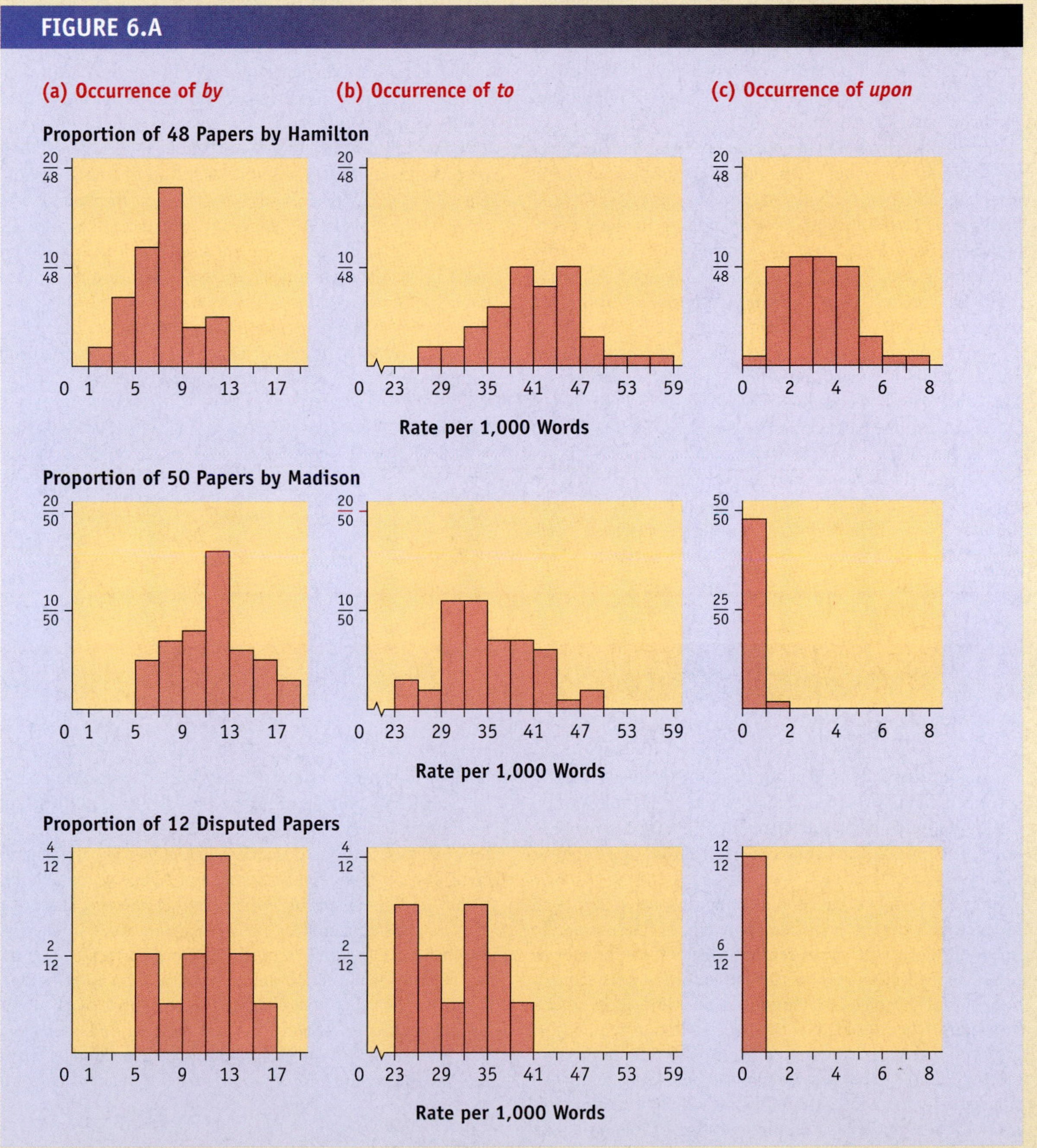

(continued)

Application 6.2 (continued)

ever since been a leading source of information concerning the intent of the framers of the U.S. Constitution, but in the early 1800s a variety of lists appeared with conflicting information about which authors wrote which papers. In particular, 12 papers had been claimed by both Hamilton and Madison after these men had become bitter political enemies. Historians tried in vain to decide authorship on the basis of political content. This line of inquiry led nowhere, partly because both authors wrote these papers as lawyers' briefs in favor of ratifying the Constitution (and not every argument put forward was necessarily their own), partly because the authors' political opinions changed over time (and one couldn't infer their earlier positions from later ones). Nor could average sentence length be used to differentiate the disputed papers. It was 34.5 words in 51 undisputed Hamilton papers and 34.6 words in 14 undisputed Madison papers—the authors wrote in similar styles.

Statisticians, however, employed *rates of word use* to differentiate the two writers' works. They ignored contextual words, such as *law* and *liberty,* that were likely to appear often in all of the papers, simply because of the topic discussed. They focused instead on filler words, such as *by, to,* and *upon*—words that were unrelated to the topic. Three sets of *histograms* depicting rates of word use are shown in panels (a)–(c) of Figure 6.A on the previous page.

Look at the tallest columns in panel (a). In 18 of 48 undisputed Hamilton papers, the word *by* occurred between 7 and 9 times per 1,000 words; yet in 16 of 50 undisputed Madison papers, it occurred between 11 and 13 times per 1,000 words, just as it did in 4 of 12 disputed papers. Compared to Hamilton's, the entire Madison histogram is displaced to the right (as is that of the disputed papers). The more frequent use of *by* suggested Madison authorship.

Similarly, the *less* frequent use of the words *to* and *upon* in Madison's undisputed papers and in the disputed papers lead to the same conclusion. Indeed, the three histogram sets shown here, along with 27 other sets like these, provided overwhelming evidence in favor of Madison being the author of each of the disputed papers.

SOURCES: Adapted from William H. Honan, "A Sleuth Gets His Suspect: Shakespeare," *The New York Times,* January 14, 1996, pp. A1 and 20; and Frederick Mosteller and David L. Wallace, "Deciding Authorship," in Judith M. Tanur et al., eds., *Statistics: A Guide to the Unknown* (San Francisco: Holden-Day, 1972), pp. 164–175. Figure 6.A adapted by permission of Holden-Day, Inc. Copyright © 1972 by Holden-Day, Inc.

APPLICATION 6.3

Quality Control in Manufacturing

A manufacturer of small motors was in trouble. Recently produced motors were breaking down at an unexpected rate. A close look at the manufacturing process was in order. The investigation centered on steel rods that might be too loose in their bearings.

The investigator noted that quality inspectors had been instructed to inspect the inside diameters of the rods and to reject all those with measurements of .9995 centimeter or less. The inspection records of 500 such rods were requisitioned, and the physical measurements were plotted as a histogram. The investigator expected to find a symmetrical histogram, such as histogram (a) in Figure 6.5, because, in the past, errors in either direction from the standard had been equally frequent and smaller errors had been more frequent than larger errors. Yet the investigator found the histogram reproduced as Figure 6.B on the next page, with absolute frequencies of 10, 30, 0, 80, 60, 100, 90, 60, 40, 20, and 10 for the 11 classes of diameters.

The unusual gap just below the lower tolerance limit and the unusually tall column just above it were too obvious to ignore. As it turned out, inspectors had felt pressure to keep scrappage low, because any rod thrown out meant wasted labor, materials, and other costs. As a result, they had misclassified borderline defective rods, with diameters, say, of .9993 centimeter, as borderline acceptable, as if they had diameters of .9995 centimeter. No wonder that too few rods appeared in class 3 and too many in class 4. When their inspection procedures were corrected, not 40, but 105 rods had to be scrapped from the next batch of 500.

The high number of defective rods itself was subsequently traced to a faulty machine setting and corrected. The breakdowns of the motors disappeared. (Chapter 22 of this text is devoted entirely to the issue of quality control.)

SOURCE: Adapted from W. Edwards Deming "Making Things Right," in Judith A. Tanur et al., eds., *Statistics: A Guide to the Unknown* (San Francisco: Holden-Day, 1972), pp. 229–231. Figure 6.B adapted by permission of Holden-Day, Inc. Copyright © 1972 by Holden-Day, Inc.

(continued)

Application 6.3 (continued)

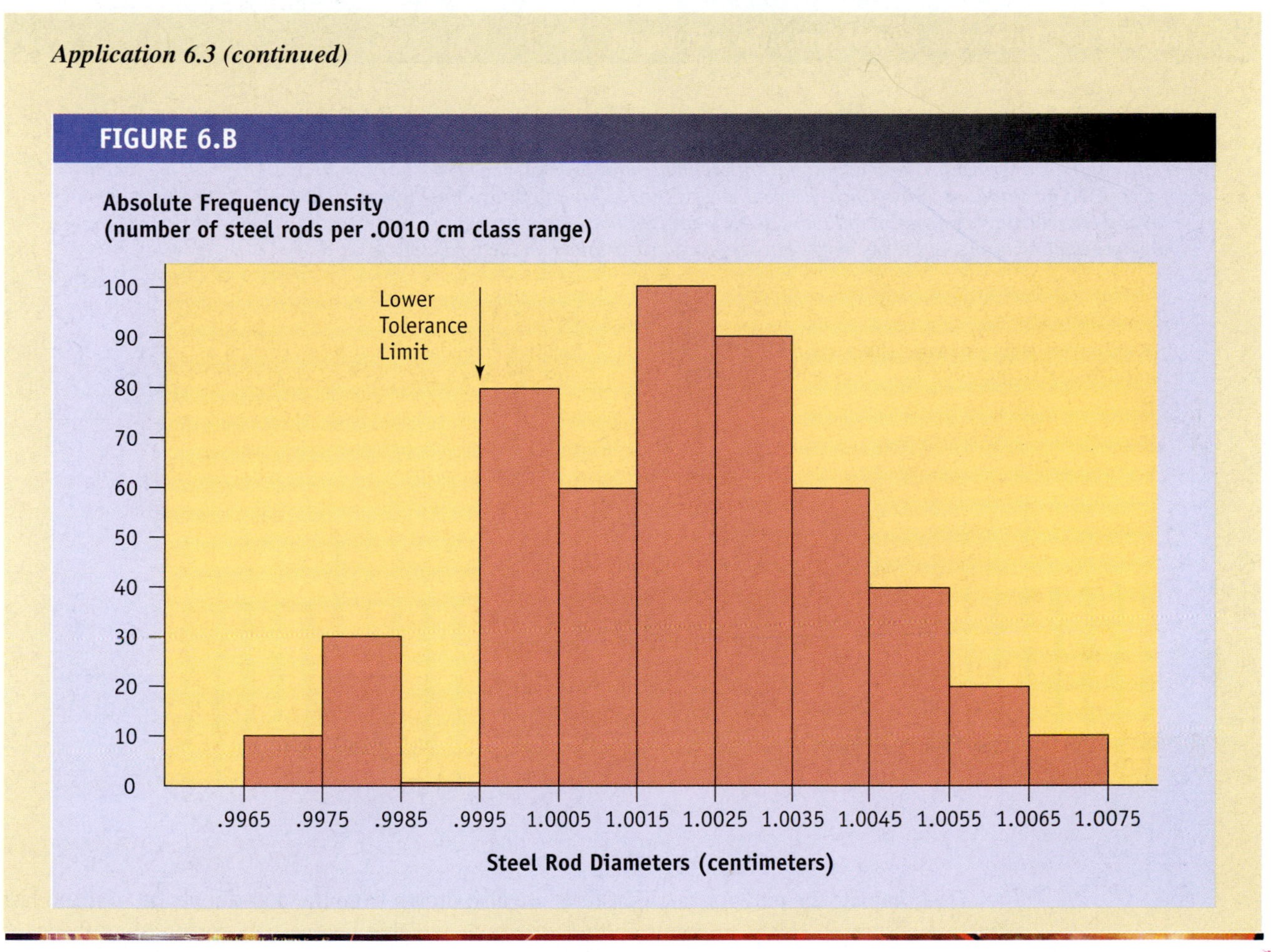

6.8 Frequency Polygon and Frequency Curve

Sometimes it is not necessary to provide all the detail that histograms contain. In such cases, statisticians create streamlined versions of histograms. The following definition suggests two such alternative ways of portraying absolute or relative frequency distributions graphically:

DEFINITION 6.5 A graphical portrayal of an absolute or relative frequency distribution of a continuous quantitative variable as a *many-sided figure* is called a **frequency polygon;** such a portrayal by a smooth *curve* is called a **frequency curve.**

THE FREQUENCY POLYGON

To draw a *frequency polygon,* the same set of coordinates is used as for the histogram, but this time the **class mark,** or midpoint of each class width, is identified as the average of the two class limits, and a dot is positioned above it at a height equal to the absolute or relative frequency density. The dots are then connected by straight lines.

FIGURE 6.6 | Turning a Histogram into a Polygon

Panel (a) depicts the histogram of pipe diameters that was first depicted in Figure 6.5. Fat dots b through h have been placed over the midpoints of every class width at heights equal to that of the histogram columns and thus measure the relative frequency densities. Two additional dots, a and i, have been placed on the horizontal axis, one-half the length of the .004 foot standard unit of measurement, below the lowest and above the highest class limit, respectively. The polygon is created by connecting all these dots by straight lines, here from a to i and back to a. Panel (b) shows the polygon standing alone, but class marks have replaced class limits on the horizontal axis.

(a)

Relative Frequency Density (proportion of pipe diameters per .004 foot class range)

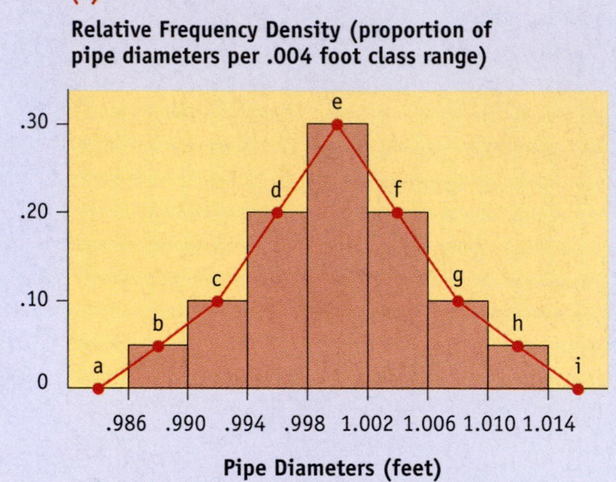

(b)

Relative Frequency Density (proportion of pipe diameters per .004 foot class range)

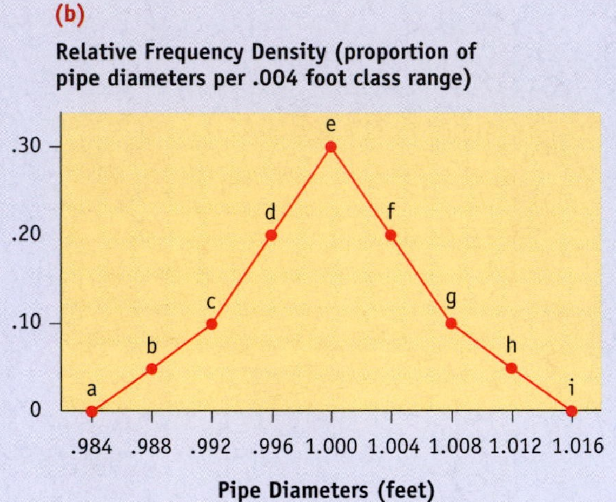

To complete the polygon, straight lines are also drawn from the dots above the first and last class marks, respectively, to points on the horizontal axis that lie one-half the length of the standard unit of measurement below the lowest or above the highest class limit. Figure 6.6 indicates how histogram (a) of Figure 6.5 can be converted into a polygon.

THE FREQUENCY CURVE

The shape of a histogram can also be approximated by a smoothed *frequency curve.*

This approximation can be accomplished by mathematical or graphical techniques and typically serves the purpose of removing irregularities (that arise as a result of sampling error) from a histogram depicting information gathered in a sample survey. The frequency curve can then be viewed as an estimate of the unknown histogram that would emerge if census information were graphed with many classes of tiny widths. Figure 6.7 (see top of nest page) indicates how histogram (c) of Figure 6.5 might be converted into a smoothed frequency curve.

6.9 Ogives

Any cumulative frequency distribution, such as those noted in Tables 6.6 and 6.7 on pages 179 and 180, can be shown graphically as well:

DEFINITION 6.6 A graphical portrayal of a cumulative frequency distribution (LE type or ME type) is called an **ogive** (pronounced "ojive").

FIGURE 6.7 | Turning a Histogram into a Frequency Curve

Panel (a) depicts the histogram of miles per gallon that was first noted in Figure 6.5. A smooth curve is drawn to approximate the shape of this histogram. This frequency curve is shown separately in panel (b).

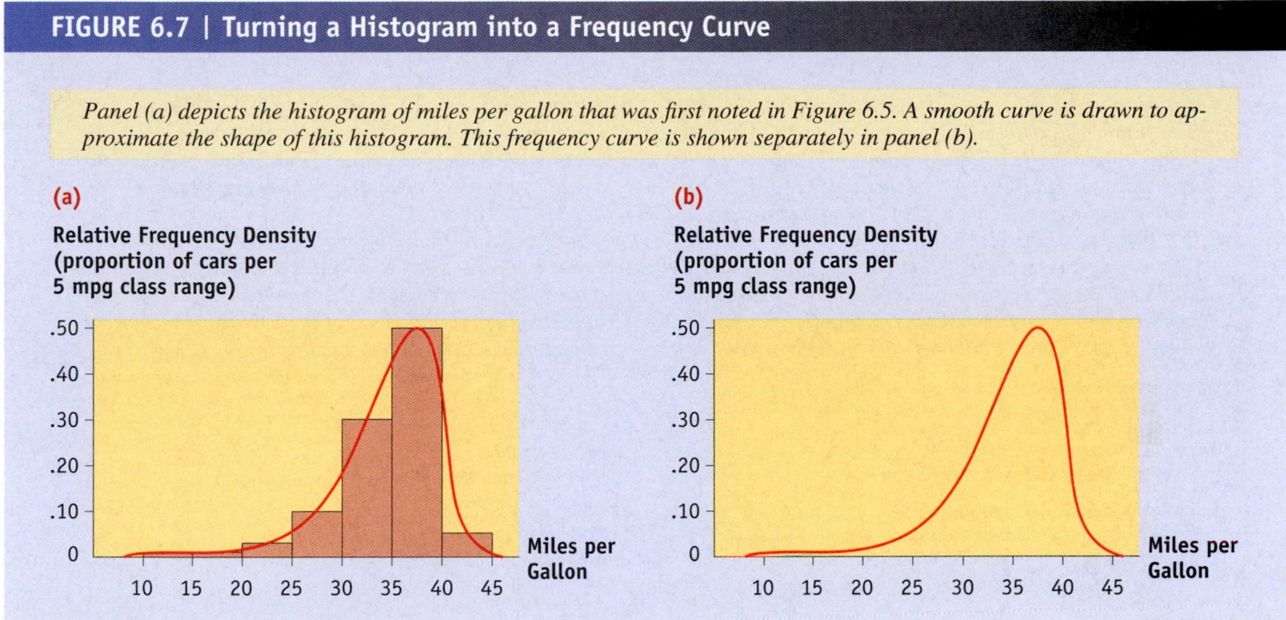

In the case of a less-than-or-equal type of cumulative frequency distribution, each cumulative class frequency is plotted vertically above the *upper* limit of the corresponding class, which, in turn, is measured horizontally. Panel (a) of Figure 6.8 on the next page, for example, shows an ogive based on columns 1 and 3 of Table 6.6. The red column 3 entry of 91 now appears as point *b:* 91 companies had net profits of less than $5,000 million in the year in question.

In the case of a more-than-or-equal type of cumulative frequency distribution, each cumulative class frequency is plotted vertically above the *lower* limit of the corresponding class. Panel (b) of Figure 6.8, for example, shows an ogive based on columns 1 and 3 of Table 6.7. The red column 3 entry of 9 now appears as point *e:* 9 companies had net profits of $5,000 million or more.

6.10 Graphing Two Variables

Sometimes it is desirable to convey information about two variables at the same time. Many graphical procedures exist. In this section, we consider two of the more popular ones: *scatter diagrams* and *time-series line graphs.*

SCATTER DIAGRAMS

A scatter diagram shows the relationship between paired observations of two quantitative variables. But be careful: We are not saying that the relationship has to be close. Nor are we saying that one of the variables must be causally related to the other. These possibilities exist, but when we first draw a scatter diagram, we approach our data with an open mind. We simply want to visualize how they are related to one another and that is that.

DEFINITION 6.7 A graphical display consisting of a scatter of dots, with each dot representing one observation about a variable measured along the horizontal axis and another observation about a different variable measured along the vertical axis, is a **scatter diagram.**

FIGURE 6.8 | Two Types of Ogives

Just as there are two types of cumulative absolute frequency distributions, there are two types of graphs to portray them. Panel (a) is based on columns 1 and 3 of Table 6.6 and represents a less-than type ogive. As did Table 6.6, the panel (a) ogive gives us the number of companies with 1997 net profit less than a certain figure. Thus point a indicates that 0 companies earned less than −$1,250 million, point b shows that 91 companies earned less than $5,000 million, and point c tells us that 100 companies earned less than $10,000 million.

Panel (b) is based on columns 1 and 3 of Table 6.7 and represents a more-than-or-equal type ogive. As did Table 6.7, this ogive gives us the number of companies with 1997 net profit of a certain figure or more. Point d, for example, indicates that all 100 companies earned −$1,250 million or more, point e shows that 9 companies earned $5,000 million or more, and point f tells us that 0 companies earned $10,000 million or more. Clearly, panel (b) is the mirror image of panel (a); in addition, all this information could be shown for relative frequency distributions as well.

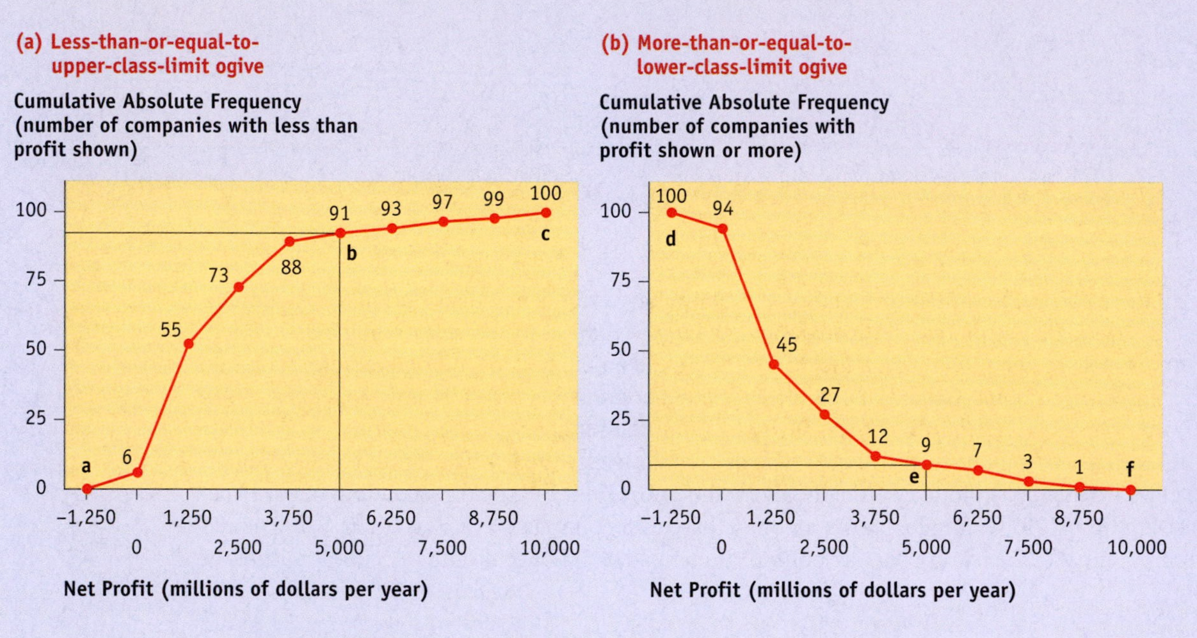

Consider once again the 100 largest U.S.-based multinational companies. Earlier in this chapter, 1997 *net profit* data for these companies were displayed in a variety of tables and graphs. Now imagine collecting additional information about the *total assets* of each of these firms. Instead of displaying the total assets information in tables and graphs of the type we have already encountered, we can create a scatter diagram that shows simultaneously each firm's net profit *and* total asset data by a dot in the usual system of coordinates. The dot's position in relation to the horizontal axis (also known as the *x-axis* or *abscissa*) might indicate the size of a given firm's net profit, while the dot's position with respect to the vertical axis (also known as the *y-axis* or *ordinate*) might indicate the size of the firm's total assets.

Many computer programs are ideally suited to create such a scatter diagram once two columns of quantitative data have been entered into a worksheet, as shown in the following example.

EXCEL Example 6.5

Start EXCEL and retrieve the file HK100MN97 from the CD-ROM. Create a scatter diagram of the companies' total assets, measured vertically, and their net profits, measured horizontally. Comment on the result.

SOLUTION Columns G and E contain the total assets and net profit data, respectively. You can use a procedure similar to that illustrated in part (a) of EXCEL Example 2.10 on pages 59–61. (Because no data are missing, you can skip steps 1–3.) Figure 6.9 is one possible result.

FIGURE 6.9 | 1997 Assets vs. Profits of 100 Largest U.S.-Based Multinationals

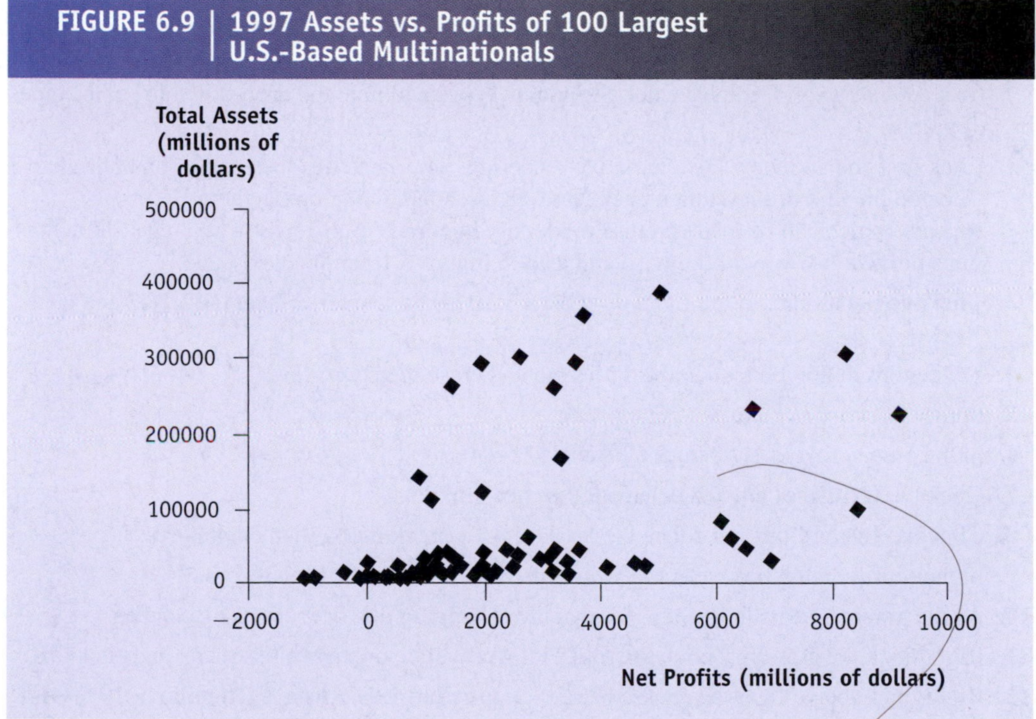

NOTE The graph points to a rather weak relationship between total assets and net profits. Any preconceived notions about large assets inevitably leading to large profits (or small assets leading to small profits) should certainly be questioned.

TIME-SERIES LINE GRAPHS

Frequently, observations about a variable of interest are linked with specific points or intervals of time. Consider a corporate executive who wants to impress stockholders with the movements of the company's stock price over the course of the last year. Consider the economist who has gathered data about the country's price level for the past four decades. Data linked with time are ideally suited to being plotted in a system of coordinates such that measurements of the variable are made on the vertical axis and those of time are made on the horizontal axis.

DEFINITION 6.8 The graphical portrayal, by a continuous line, of data that are linked with time is called a **time-series line graph.**

GRAPHING A SINGLE SERIES Consider graphing data about the movements of the *consumer price index* over the past decades and using a computer for the purpose.

EXCEL Example 6.6

Start EXCEL and retrieve the file HKTSD from the CD-ROM. Column A contains the consumer price index for urban U.S. consumers (CPI-U) for the years 1960–2000, based on 1982–84 = 100. Column B contains labels for the years. Illustrate the data with a time-series line graph.

SOLUTION

1. Select column A; then Click the **Chart Wizard** that is found on the standard toolbar. The first of four dialog boxes appears. There are two tabs; one for *Standard Types,* another one for *Custom Types* of graphs. Click **Standard Types** and note the drop-down list of 14 types of graphs.
2. Click on **Line** and view the alternative renderings of time-series line graphs on the right. Click on the first of these; then click **Next.** In a second dialog box, a tentative graph appears, which can be made prettier in literally hundreds of different ways. The following steps provide *one* way of doing so and lead to Figure 6.10 on the next page.
3. Click the **Series** tab. In the *Category (X) axis labels* box, enter **=Sheet1!B2:B42** and click **Next.**
4. In the third dialog box, click the **Titles** tab and erase the *Chart title.*
5. In the *Category (X) axis* box, enter *Year.*
6. In the *Value (Y) axis* box, enter *CPI-U (1982–84=100).*
7. Click the **Gridlines** tab and delete all the check marks.
8. Click the **Legend** tab and delete the *Show legend* check mark; then click **Next.**
9. In the fourth dialog box, select *As object in Sheet 1* and click **Finish.**
10. As the graph appears in Sheet 1, enlarge it by dragging one or more of its handles.
11. Right-click the gray area, click **Format Plot Area,** click on the white square, and click **OK.**
12. Right-click the vertical-axis tick labels, click **Format Axis** > **Font** > **Regular** > **10** > **OK.**
13. Right-click the horizontal-axis tick labels, click **Format Axis** > **Font** > **Regular** > **10;** then click the **Scale** tab, enter **5** in the *Number of categories between tick-mark labels* box, and click **OK.**
14. Right-click the vertical-axis title, then click **Format Axis Title** > **Font** > **Bold** > **10.**
15. Click the **Alignment tab,** change the *Orientation* to **0** Degrees, and click **OK.**
16. Move the vertical-axis title after clicking it and the plot area to reveal the handles.
17. Right-click the horizontal-axis title, then click **Format Axis Title > Font > Bold > 10 > OK,** and move the title to the spot shown.

By looking at the graph, one can determine that U.S. consumer prices have risen more than fivefold between 1960 and 2000, from an index of roughly 30 to about 170. (The exact numbers were 29.6 and 171.3.)

FIGURE 6.10 | Consumer Price Index for Urban Consumers, United States, 1960–2000

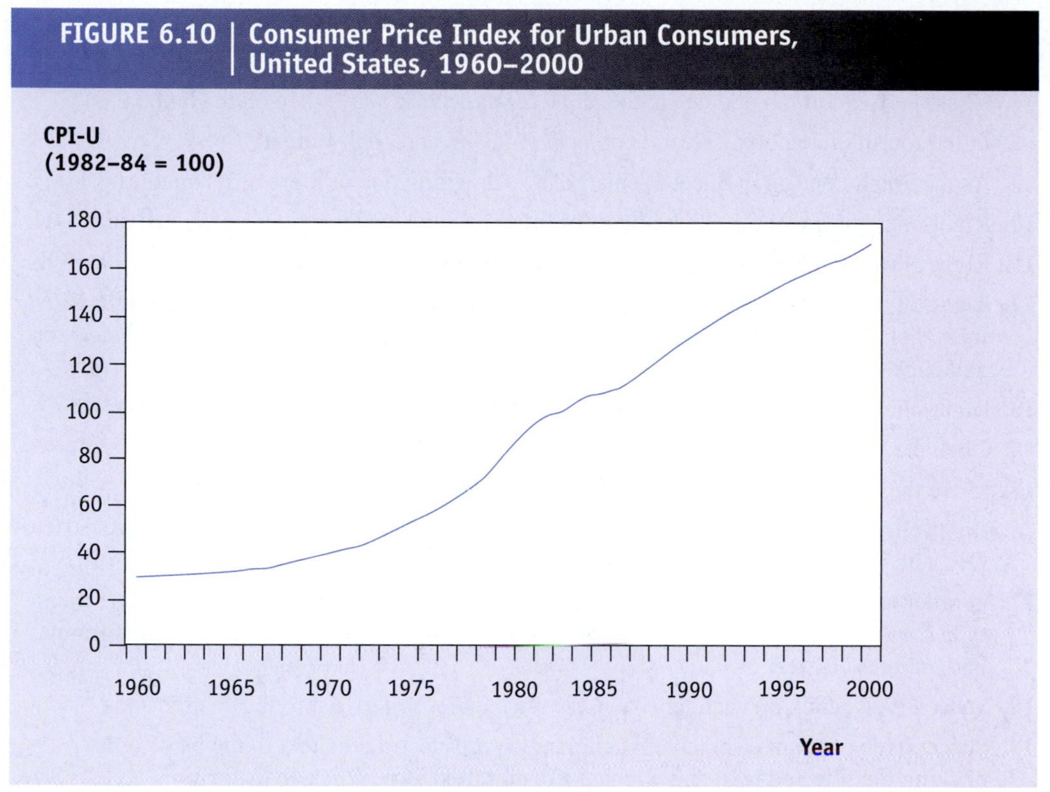

GRAPHING TWO SERIES Consider a display showing the *average weekly earnings* between 1960 and 1999 of Americans working in private nonagricultural industries. We may want to compare two versions of these data in the same graph: *nominal* weekly earnings measured in current dollars and *real* weekly earnings measured in 1982 dollars. Once more, a computer can help.

EXCEL Example 6.7

Start EXCEL and retrieve the file HKTSD from the CD-ROM. Column B contains labels for the years 1960–2000. Columns C and D contain 1960–1999 nominal and real data, respectively, for the average weekly earnings of Americans working in private nonagricultural industries. Illustrate both data series in a single time-series graph.

SOLUTION

1. Select the columns C and D data range; then click the **Chart Wizard** that is found on the standard toolbar. The first of four dialog boxes appears. There are two tabs; one for *Standard Types,* another one for *Custom Types* of graphs. Click **Standard Types** and note the drop-down list of 14 types of graphs.
2. Click on **Line** and view the alternative renderings of time-series line graphs on the right. Click on the first of these; then click **Next.** In a second dialog box, a tentative graph appears, which can be made prettier in literally hundreds of different ways. The following steps provide *one* way of doing so and lead to Figure 6.11 on the next page.
3. Click the **Series** tab. In the *Category (X) axis labels* box, enter **=Sheet1!B2:B42** and click **Next.**
4. In the third dialog box, click **Titles** and in the *Category (X) axis* box, enter *Year.*

5. In the *Value (Y) axis* box, enter *Dollars.*
6. Click the **Gridlines** tab and delete all the check marks.
7. Click the **Legend** tab and delete the *Show legend* check mark; then click **Next.**
8. In the fourth dialog box, select *As object in Sheet 1* and click **Finish.**
9. As the graph appears in Sheet 1, enlarge it by dragging one or more of its handles.
10. Right-click the gray area, click **Format Plot Area,** click on the white square, and click **OK.**
11. Right-click the vertical-axis tick labels, click **Format Axis** > **Font** > **Regular** > **10** > **OK.**
12. Right-click the horizontal-axis tick labels, click **Format Axis** > **Font** > **Regular** > **10;** then click the **Scale** tab, enter **5** in the *Number of categories between tick-mark labels* box, and click **OK.**
13. Right-click the vertical-axis title, then click **Format Axis Title** > **Font** > **Bold** > **10.**
14. Click the **Alignment tab,** change the *Orientation* to **0** Degrees, and click **OK.**
15. Move the vertical-axis title after clicking it and the plot area to reveal the handles.
16. Right-click the horizontal-axis title, then click **Format Axis Title** > **Font** > **Bold** > **10** > **OK,** and move the title to the spot shown.
17. In order to label the two lines, select the chart so the selection handles are showing; then type *current dollars* in the formula bar and press Enter. Type *1982 dollars* in the formula bar and press **Enter.**
18. Successively, click on each label and use the handles to move it to the desired spot.
19. Successively, format each label by clicking on it, selecting the text in the box, right-clicking the selected text, and clicking **Format Text Box.** Click **Regular** Font style > Size **10,** change color if desired, and click **OK.** The result is shown here:

FIGURE 6.11 | Average Weekly Earnings in Private Nonagricultural Industries, United States, 1960–1999

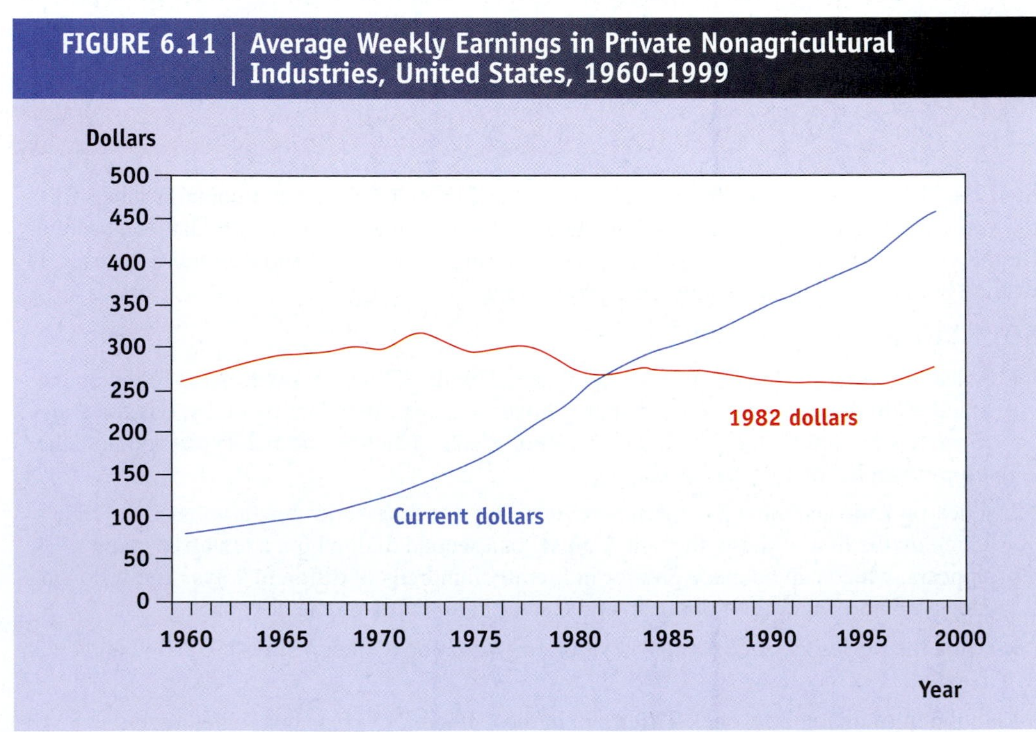

Note what we can learn from the graph: The current-dollar rise in weekly earnings from about \$80 in 1960 to about \$450 in 1999 has not provided extra purchasing power to workers in the affected industries. Indeed, constant-dollar earnings have hardly changed at all, being equal to \$261.92 in 1960 and \$271.25 in 1999. We can't see these *precise* numbers in the graph, but the red line tells the story, nevertheless.

LOGARITHMIC TRANSFORMATIONS Here is another aspect of graphing that you should know about, because it is frequently applied in business and economics applications. Suppose we want to compare on the same graph two series of numbers that move within rather different ranges of values. If a regular arithmetic scale is used on both axes of the graph (which makes it an *arithmetic* chart), the series with the higher range of values (say, the Dow Jones stock market index) will appear to be considerably more volatile than the series with the lower range of values (say, Standard & Poor's stock market index). This volatility, however, can be an illusion. The illusion can be removed by using a *semilogarithmic* chart in which the horizontal scale remains arithmetic, while the vertical scale becomes logarithmic. As a result, equal *percentage* changes in two series of data produce lines of equal slope; the illusion disappears.

A logarithmic scale does not have a zero point because the logarithm of zero equals minus infinity. Such a scale is calibrated in log values in various "cycles" of 1–10, 10–100, 100–1,000, and so on (or, in the other direction, from 1 to 10, 0.1 to 1, 0.01 to 0.1, and so forth). Modern computer programs are ideally suited to draw graphs such as these.

EXCEL Example 6.8

Start EXCEL and retrieve the file HKTSD from the CD-ROM. Column B contains labels for the years 1960–2000. Columns E and F contain 1960–1999 data, respectively, for the Dow Jones Industrial Average and Standard & Poor's Composite stock market indexes. Illustrate both series

a. in the same *arithmetic* chart.

b. in the same *semi-logarithmic* chart.

SOLUTION

a. You can follow the procedure laid out in EXCEL Example 6.7. The result is Figure 6.12 on the next page.

Note how much more volatile the Dow Jones looks in this graph. After all, it crossed the 10,000-line for the first time ever in 1999, at a time when Standard & Poor's index (based on 1941–43 = 10) barely exceeded 1,300. But watch what happens if you draw a semilogarithmic chart.

b. In Step 5, type *Log Index*. In Step 11, just before the OK, click **Scale** and check *Logarithmic Scale*. Ultimately, the semilogarithmic graph looks like Figure 6.13 on the next page. Standard & Poor's index, all along, has moved in tandem with the Dow Jones.

FIGURE 6.12 | The U.S. Stock Market, 1960–99, Arithmetic Scale

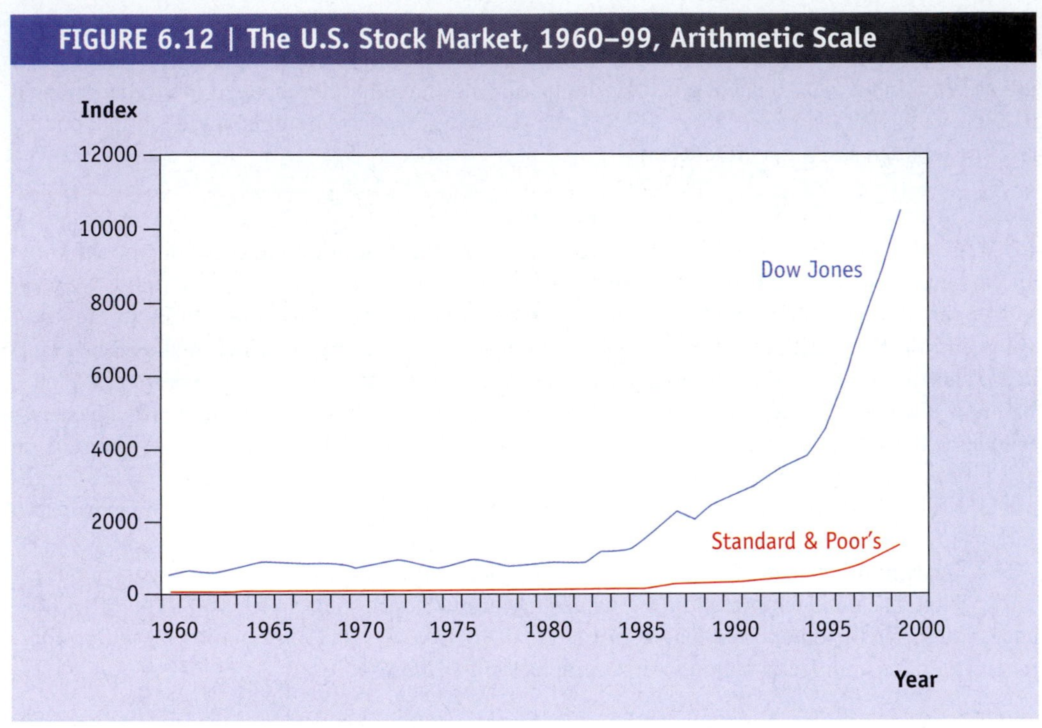

FIGURE 6.13 | The U.S. Stock Market, 1960–1999, Semilog Scale

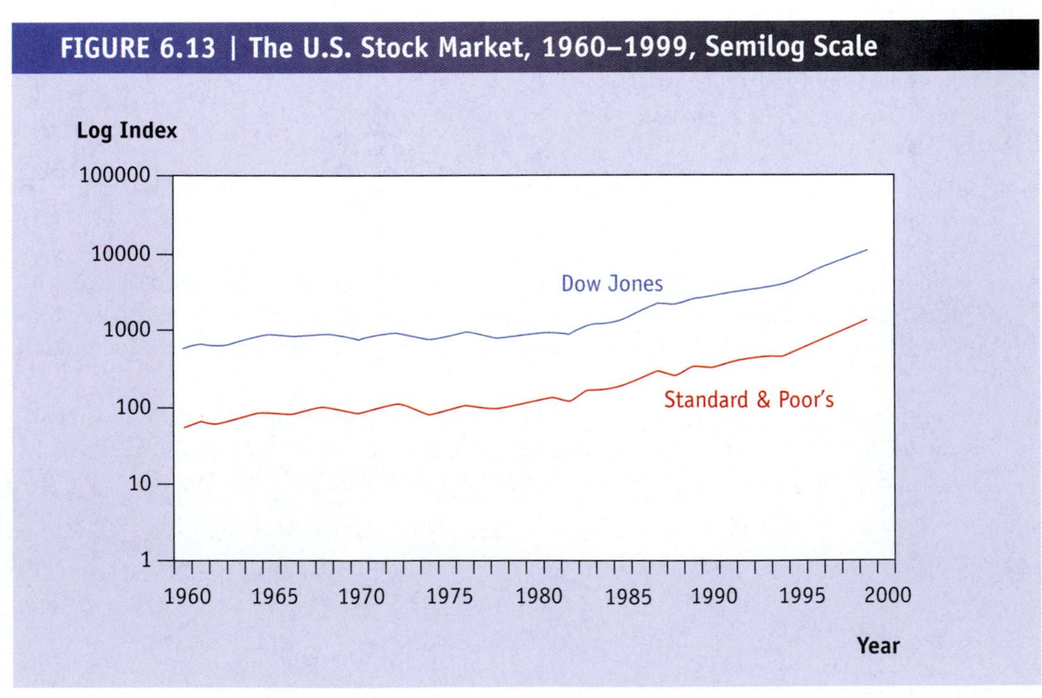

6.11 Bar Charts

We now turn to a type of graph that is, perhaps, the most common one found in the popular press. It is equally effective in presenting data about qualitative and quantitative variables. You may want to use it whenever you seek to communicate a quick comparison of several categories to your readers.

DEFINITION 6.9 A series of horizontal or vertical bars, the lengths of which are proportional to values that are to be depicted, is called a **bar chart.** (On occasion, a chart with vertical bars is called a **column chart.**) Usually, the bars are not contiguous, but sometimes they are drawn to touch each other.

Numerous versions of bar charts exist. Here we show how your computer can draw such charts with:

- horizontal bars
- vertical bars
- clustered and stacked bars

HORIZONTAL BARS First, we consider a single horizontal bar chart.

EXCEL Example 6.9

Suppose you wanted to illustrate the potential for placing ads on the Internet. With the help of relevant data from Table 6.8 on page 181, create a *horizontal bar chart* showing how audience size varies with educational level.

SOLUTION

1. Enter the following Table 6.8 data into an EXCEL worksheet:

A	B
1.3	some high school
7.0	high school graduate
14.7	some college
20.7	college graduate

2. Select column A; then click the **Chart Wizard** that is found on the standard toolbar. The first of four dialog boxes appears.
3. Click **Standard Types > Bar** and view the alternative renderings of bar graphs on the right. Click on the first of these; then click **Next.** In a second dialog box, a tentative graph appears, which can be made prettier in literally hundreds of different ways. The following steps provide *one* way of doing so and lead to Figure 6.14 on the next page.
4. Click the **Series** tab. In the *Category (X) axis labels* box, enter **=Sheet1!B1:B4** and click **Next.**
5. In the third dialog box, click **Titles** and in the *Value (Y) axis* box, enter *Millions of Adults.*
6. Click the **Legend** tab and delete the *Show legend* check mark.

7. Click the **Data Labels** tab, choose *Show value;* then click **Next.**
8. In the fourth dialog box, select *As object in Sheet 1* and click **Finish.**
9. As the graph appears in Sheet 1, enlarge it by dragging one or more of its handles.
10. Right-click the gray area, click **Format Plot Area,** click on the white square, and click **OK.**
11. Right-click the lower left corner of the chart area, click **Format Chart Area > Font > Regular > 10 > OK.**

The graph will look as follows:

FIGURE 6.14 | Millions of Adult Internet Surfers by Level of Education, United States, 1998

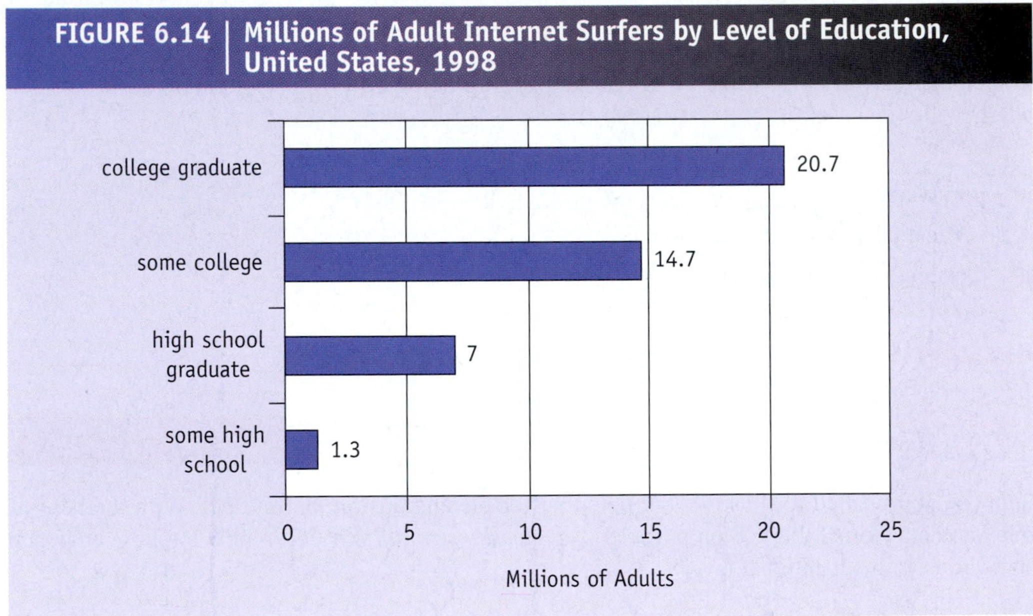

Note how easy it is for anyone to read the graph: During that 30-day sampling period in 1998, some 20.7 million college graduates were surfing the Internet. If you want to reach *them,* an ad on the Net may do the trick. On the other hand, if you want to market a product aimed at high school dropouts, this medium is not for you.

VERTICAL BARS It is easy to use the same data to create a column chart.

EXCEL Example 6.10

Rework EXCEL Example 6.9, but this time create a *column chart.*

SOLUTION Follow the procedure noted in EXCEL Example 6.9, with these exceptions: In Step 3, substitute **Column** for **Bar.** After Step 11, right-click the vertical axis title; then change its alignment and position. You will get a graph like Figure 6.15.

Quite clearly, Figure 6.15 conveys the same information as Figure 6.14.

FIGURE 6.15 | Millions of Adult Internet Surfers by Level of Education, United States, 1998

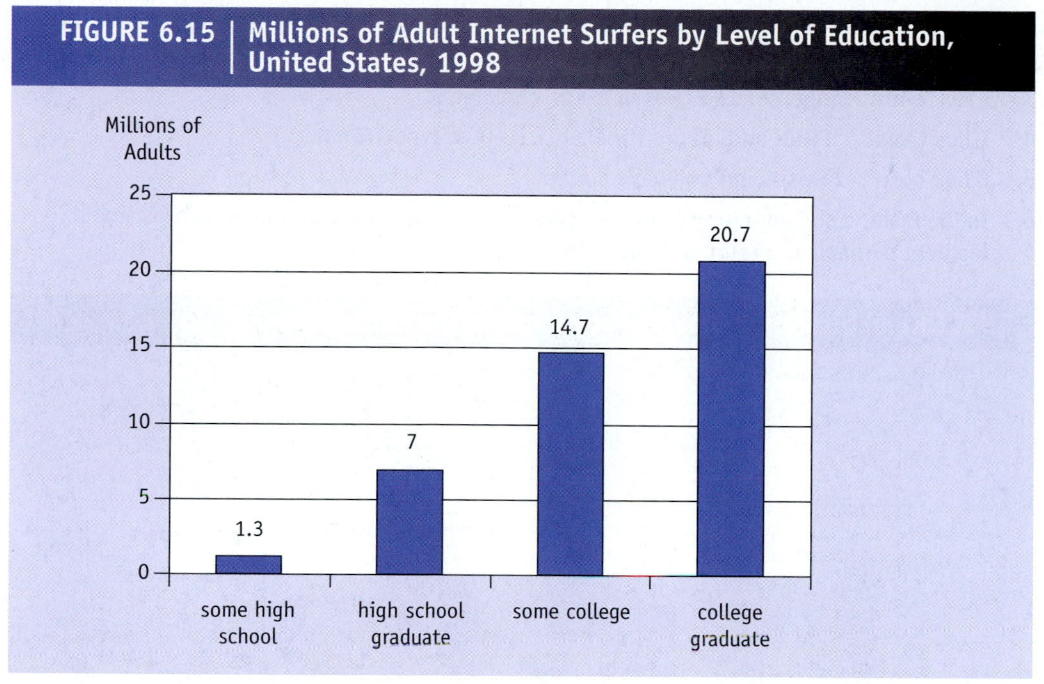

CLUSTERED AND STACKED BARS Computers are equally amenable to the creation of bar charts that show subgroups within the groupings on the x-axis. The technique is called *clustering* when each subgroup is shown as a separate bar. It is called *stacking* when subgroups appear as blocks lying on top of each other within a single bar. The following example explains.

EXCEL Example 6.11

Suppose an economist wants to convey the *reasons* people give for their unemployment and how, if at all, these reasons have changed over time. In the United States in 1978, some 6.201 million people were unemployed; of these, 2.585 million were job losers, 0.874 million were job leavers, 1.857 million were labor force reentrants, and 0.885 million were new labor force entrants. Corresponding numbers for 1988 were 6.7 million, 3.092 million, 0.983 million, 1.809 million, and 0.816 million. And similar numbers for 1998 were 6.208 million, 2.822 million, 0.734 million, 2.132 million, and 0.520 million. Illustrate these data with

a. a clustered column chart.

b. a stacked column chart.

SOLUTION

a. To learn about clustering, take the following steps:

1. Enter the data into an EXCEL worksheet:

A	B	C	D
	1978	**1988**	**1998**
job losers	2.585	3.092	2.822
job leavers	0.874	0.983	0.734
reentrants	1.857	1.809	2.132
new entrants	0.885	0.816	0.52

2. Select columns A–D. Click the **Chart Wizard** > **Standard Types** > **Column,** the first of the graphical choices, and **Next.**
3. Click **Data Range,** select *Series in Rows,* click **Next.**
4. Click **Next** > **Titles** and, in the *Value (Y) axis* box, type *Millions.*
5. Click **Next** > **Finish,** and you have a graph.
6. In the fashion shown in previous examples, you can edit the graph in numerous ways, leading, perhaps, to Figure 6.16 here:

FIGURE 6.16 | Unemployment by Reason, United States

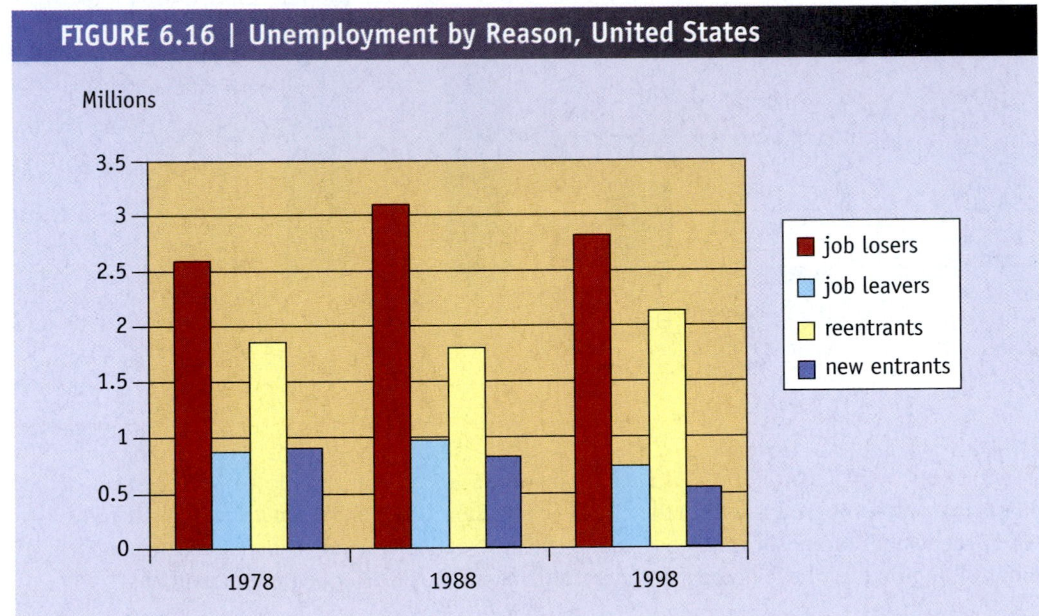

b. Repeat the procedure, except for changing the graph number and choosing the *second* of the graphical alternatives in Step 2. The result is shown here:

FIGURE 6.17 | Unemployment by Reason, United States

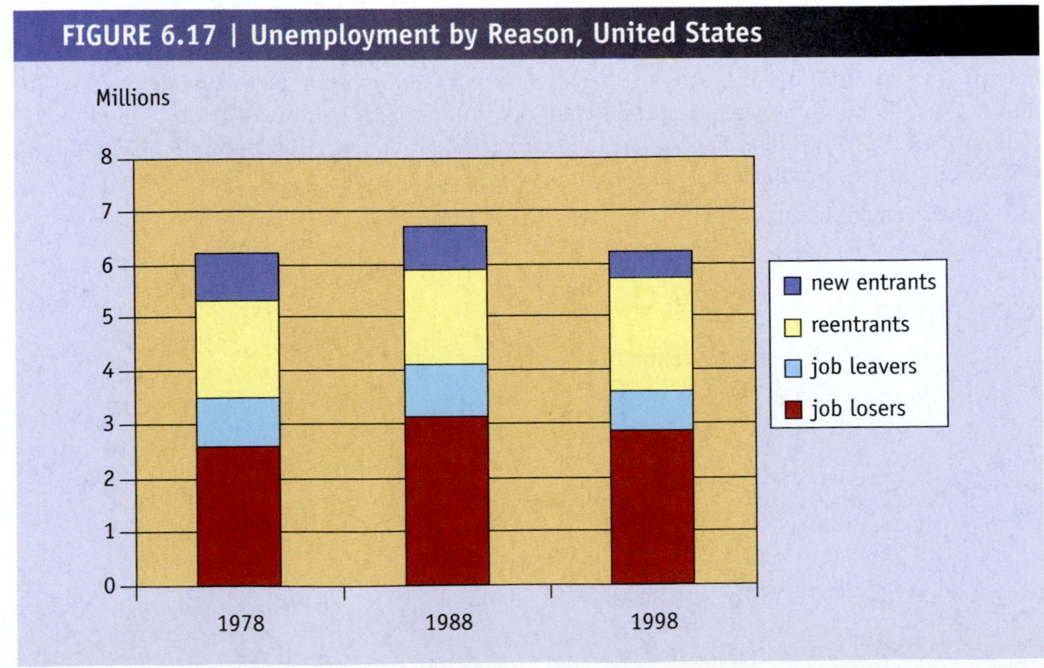

6.12 Pie Charts

We now turn to an all-time favorite of descriptive statisticians. It is a graph of a segmented circle that clearly portrays divisions of some aggregate (clearly, that is, *provided* there are not too many divisions). The aggregate in question might be an industry's annual sales and the divisions might be the sales of major firms in the industry so that the chart depicts their market shares. Or the aggregate might be the federal government's total annual expenditures, while the divisions list major government programs. The possibilities are endless.

DEFINITION 6.10 A portrayal of divisions of some aggregate by a segmented circle in such a way that the sector areas are proportional to the sizes of the divisions in question is called a **pie chart.**

To create a pie chart, we first draw a circle. Then we cut the resulting "pie" into slices in such a way that the central angles and, therefore, the circumference arcs and sector areas are proportional to the sizes of the divisions we wish to display. Let the aggregate in question equal the \$2.8 billion 1998 revenues of USA Networks, Inc., of which \$1.2 billion, or 42.9 percent, came from the company's Cable Networks and Studios division. The corresponding slice in the pie would be represented by a central angle of 0.429 (360 degrees) = 154.44 degrees, because a circle has a total of 360 degrees and 154.44 degrees equal 42.9 percent of that total. Similar calculations could be made for other portions of the aggregate. Luckily, we do not have to make such calculations nowadays. Computers do them for us.

EXCEL Example 6.12

In 1998, USA Networks, Inc., had revenues of \$2.8 billion. Of this total, \$1.2 billion came from the firm's Cable Networks and Studios division (including the USA Network, the Sci-Fi Channel, and more), \$1.1 billion came from the firm's Home Shopping Network, \$0.4 billion from the firm's Ticketmaster division, and \$0.1 billion from various Internet Services. Illustrate the information with the help of a *pie chart.*

SOLUTION

1. Enter the data into an EXCEL worksheet, as shown:

A	B
Cable Networks and Studios	1.2
Home Shopping Network	1.1
Ticketmaster	0.4
Internet Services	0.1

2. Select columns A and B. Click the **Chart Wizard** on the standard toolbar, then **Standard Types > Pie,** the first of the graphical choices, and **Next > Next.**
3. In the third dialog box, click the **Titles** tab; under *Chart title,* type the title shown below.
4. Click the **Legend** tab and eliminate all checkmarks.
5. Click the **Data labels** tab, choose *Show labels and percent,* and click **Next > Finish.**
6. In the fashion shown in previous examples, enlarge the graph and make it prettier.

Figure 6.18 is one possible result:

FIGURE 6.18 | Sources of USA Networks 1998 Revenues

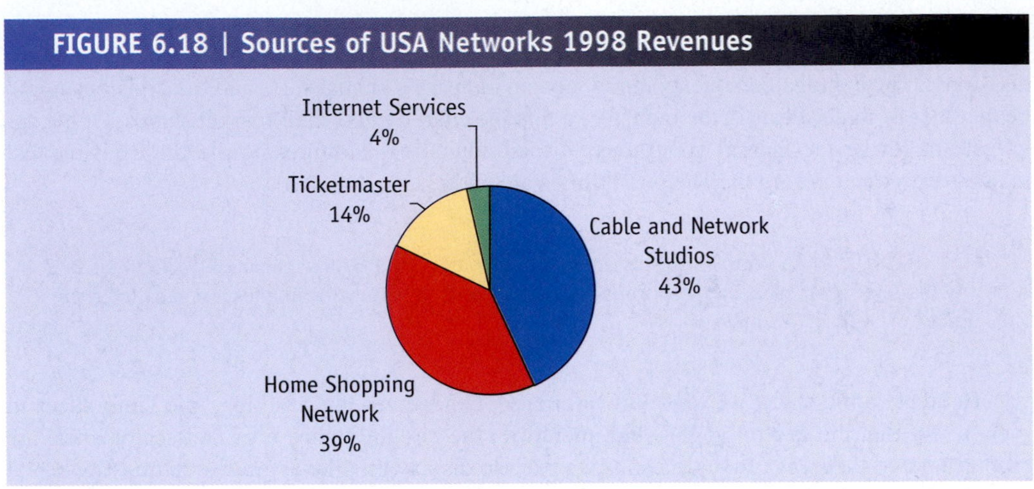

The story told by the pie chart speaks for itself. (The percentages, incidentally, except for rounding error, must always add to 100. Also note this: While the chart resides in EXCEL, you can point to any of the slices and activate a screen tip with additional information.)

6.13 Unusual Graphs

A number of specialty graphs, including *statistical maps, pictograms, stem-and-leaf diagrams,* and *box-and-whisker diagrams,* are probably less well known than bar and pie charts. Nevertheless, you are likely to run into them sooner or later—either in the popular press (with regard to the first two) or in the scientific literature (so far as the latter two are concerned).

STATISTICAL MAPS

As this chapter's Preview illustrates, quite a bit of useful information can be conveyed by a well-drawn geographic map to which statistical data are attached.

DEFINITION 6.11 A portrayal of data for areal units (such as world regions, nations, states, counties, or even census tracts) by differentiating these units in different ways on a geographic map is called a **statistical map.**

Although such maps can be very effective, many of them are hard to read. In addition, these graphs simply *assume* appropriate geographical knowledge on the part of the reader. Take another look at Figure 6.1 on page 166 and note that the 48 contiguous states are not named. Do you think it is realistic to believe that everyone could instantly extract the relevant statistic for Minnesota, New Hampshire, or Delaware? Even harder to read are three-dimensional maps that attempt, for example, to depict the extent of urban sprawl or air pollution by drawing pictures of buildings or billowing smokestacks on top of a geographic map. Almost always, such three-dimensional maps turn out to be little more than chart junk.

PICTOGRAMS

Sometimes writers use symbols to create pictorial charts. A set of symbols used to depict data is called a **pictogram.** Figure 6.19 is a case in point.

As you can imagine, creators of pictograms use all kinds of symbols, from stars to stacks of silver coins, from tanks to trees, from crosses to castles, from smiling faces to billowing smokestacks. Typically, each symbol represents a definite and uniform value, as is the case in Figure 6.19, but sometimes the size of the pictorial symbol is made proportional to the values that are to be portrayed. Making the size of the symbol proportional to values is tricky business, however, and can easily lead to confusion. How, for instance, does one double the size of a three-dimensional symbol, such as a box? By doubling length and width, one inevitably quadruples the areas portrayed, and one raises the volume eightfold. For an illustration of this problem, see Application 6.4, *How to Lie with Statistics*, on the next page.

FIGURE 6.19 | Employment at City Motors, 1980 versus 2000

A pictogram such as this might depict the employment increase at a firm from one year (1980 = 30,000) to another (2000 = 55,000).

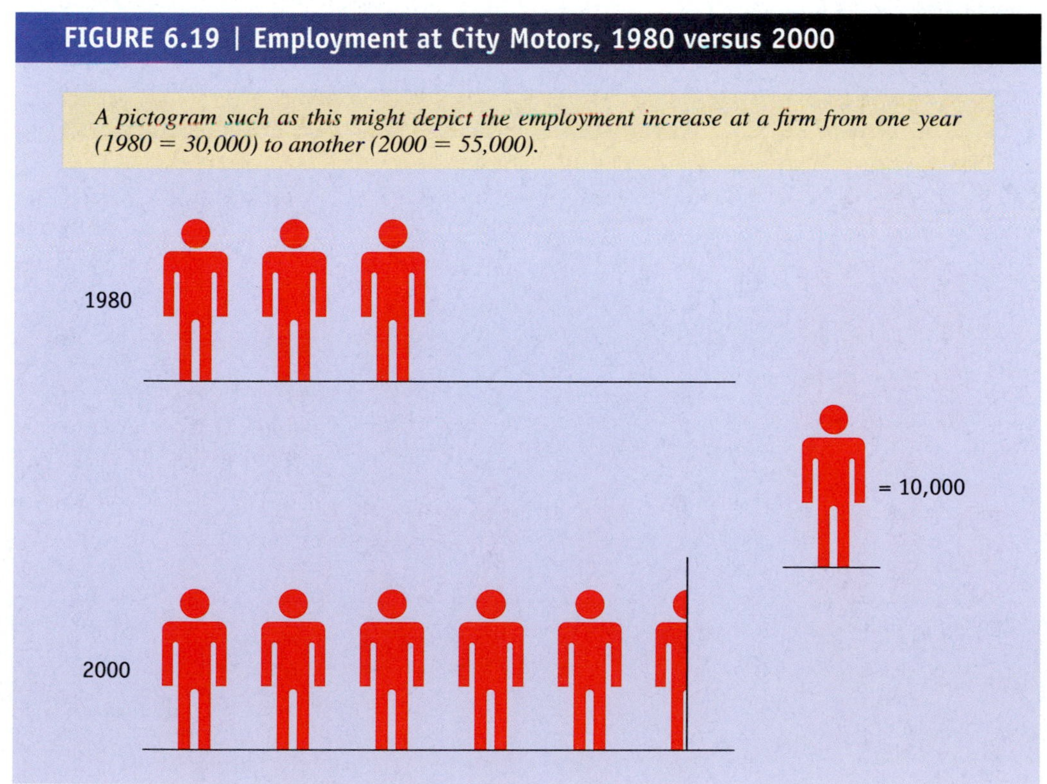

STEM-AND-LEAF DIAGRAMS

A **stem-and-leaf diagram** combines the features of an ordered array of numbers, such as Table 6.3 on page 168, and a frequency histogram, such as Figure 6.4 on page 186. The diagram is created by separating each numerical observation into a *stem,* consisting of one or more of the leftmost digits, and a *leaf,* consisting of the last digit, and then displaying the stems in ascending order in separate rows, followed by their leaves.

APPLICATION 6.4

How to Lie with Statistics

Benjamin Disraeli, British prime minister from 1874 to 1880, purportedly said: "There are three kinds of lies: ordinary lies, damned lies, and statistics." Regardless of whether Disraeli actually made this statement, it is a fact that one can lie with statistics. Such distortion may happen accidentally, out of ignorance; it may also happen deliberately, out of malice, in order to defraud the gullible. The ways of doing so are legion. Consider just two cases in point.

Figure 6.C, once again, pictures employment changes at City Motors. Panel (a) pictures a 3.5-fold increase in the number of the firm's employees with the help of two human figures, the second of which is 3.5 times as *tall* as the first. Note the false impression this type of pictogram is likely to give. Compare it with the alternative version given in panel (b).

Now consider the column charts of Figure 6.D on the next page. Panel (a) was used by savings bank C to convince potential customers that it paid substantially more interest than its competitors, A, B, D, and E.

But note: In panel (a), the vertical axis is broken between 0 and 6.5; this enables savings bank C to give the impression that it pays two or three times as much interest to its depositors as its competitors do. Yet, as panel (b) attests, the differences among the savings banks were quite negligible.

FIGURE 6.C

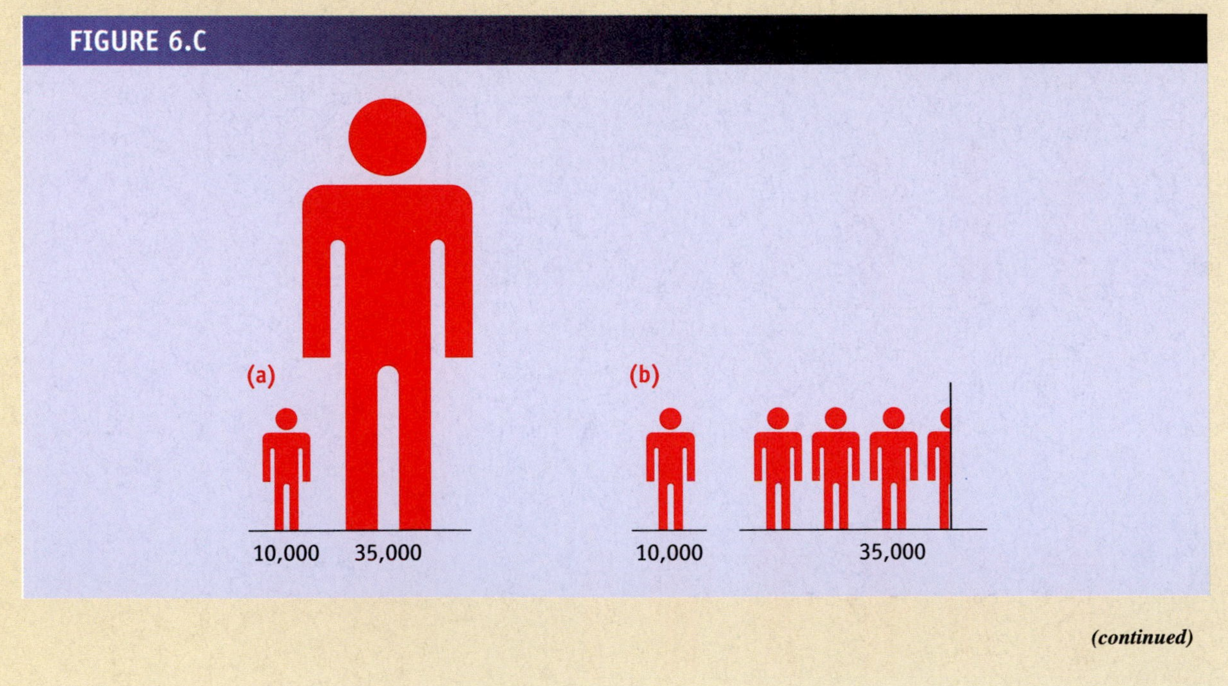

(continued)

To illustrate the concept of a stem-and-leaf diagram, consider yourself the marketing manager of an economic newsletter who has just selected a simple random sample of 80 persons from a complete list of subscribers. If you interviewed each customer, you might acquire a variety of information, including the data found in Table 6.9.

One way to display these data is the stem-and-leaf diagram of Figure 6.20 on page 210. The possible decade numbers are arranged in a column to the left of a vertical line. These first digits of the two-digit numbers are called the *stems*. (When large numbers are involved, the stems can consist of several digits.) Subsequently, each of the numbers in Table 6.9 is inspected and its

Application 6.4 (continued)

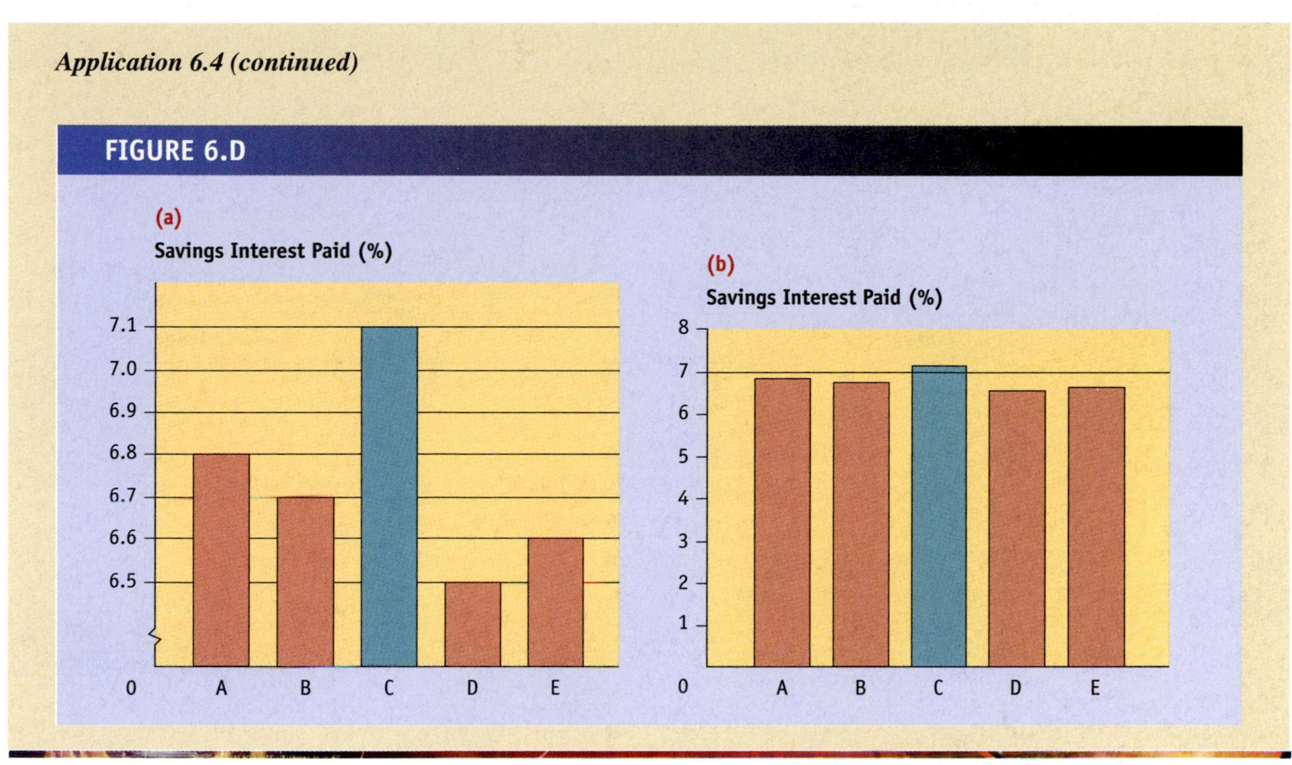

TABLE 6.9 | A Population of Ages

This table shows the ages of a simple random sample of 80 subscribers to an economic newsletter.

40	50	42	40	41	54	47	55	30	45
21	70	60	31	45	50	54	50	30	35
30	19	50	52	29	25	60	60	34	47
50	45	60	55	30	35	40	48	43	56
70	58	50	65	32	41	48	40	55	53
51	66	65	85	49	75	45	52	40	42
47	66	58	20	48	37	69	55	65	53
49	46	40	51	55	73	20	50	75	52

second digit only is recorded as a *leaf* to the right of the vertical line next to the appropriate stem. With some skill, the leaves belonging to a given stem can even be put in order at the same time, 0's being placed before 1's, 1's before 2's, and so on. The result is Figure 6.20, and its interpretation is easy: As row 1 shows, only one subscriber in the sample is a teenager and is 19 years old. Row 2 shows that there are five subscribers in their twenties; they are aged 20, 20, 21, 25, and 29, respectively. And so it goes.

FIGURE 6.20 | A Stem-and-Leaf Diagram

This unusual diagram involves no dots or lines and can be read simply as an ***ordered array*** *of the raw data given in Table 6.9. Yet when looked at from the side, the array serves the same function as a* ***histogram.*** *Suggestion: Rotate this page counterclockwise by 90 degrees so that the table's left side appears at the bottom. Then note its similarity to a graph such as Figure 6.4.*

Stem	Leaf	Frequency
1	9	1
2	0 0 1 5 9	5
3	0 0 0 0 1 2 4 5 5 7	10
4	0 0 0 0 0 0 1 1 2 2 3 5 5 5 5 6 7 7 7 8 8 8 9 9	24
5	0 0 0 0 0 0 0 1 1 2 2 2 3 3 4 4 5 5 5 5 5 6 8 8	24
6	0 0 0 0 5 5 5 6 6 9	10
7	0 0 3 5 5	5
8	5	1

As the caption indicates, the diagram can be viewed both as an ordered array of raw data and as a histogram. Can a computer create a diagram like this? It sure can, as the following example shows.

EXCEL Example 6.13

Retrieve the file HKMISC from the CD-ROM. Worksheet column A contains the data of Table 6.9. Illustrate them with a *stem-and-leaf diagram.*

SOLUTION EXCEL is not programmed to create such a diagram automatically, but you can create one nevertheless:

1. Select cell range A2:A81; click **Edit > Copy.**
2. Select cell B2; then click the **Paste** and **Sort Ascending** buttons on the standard toolbar. You have an ordered array of the original data.
3. Select cell C2; type **=B2-10** and Enter. You have extracted the second (leaf) digit from the C2 entry.
4. Select cell C3; type **=B3-20** and drag the entry with the lower right handle to C7. You have extracted the second (leaf) digit from all numbers in the 20s.
5. Select cell C8; type **=B8-30** and drag the entry with the lower right handle to C17. You have extracted the second (leaf) digit from all numbers in the 30s.
6. Select cell C18; type **=B18-40** and drag the entry with the lower right handle to C41. You have extracted the second (leaf) digit from all numbers in the 40s.
7. Select cell C42; type **=B42-50** and drag the entry with the lower right handle to C65. You have extracted the second (leaf) digit from all numbers in the 50s.

8. Select cell C66; type **=B66-60** and drag the entry with the lower right handle to C75. You have extracted the second (leaf) digit from all numbers in the 60s.
9. Select cell C76; type **=B76-70** and drag the entry with the lower right handle to C80. You have extracted the second (leaf) digit from all numbers in the 70s.
10. Enter a 5 in C81, which is the second (leaf) digit for the only number in the 80s.
11. In the range D1:D8, enter patterned data from 1 to 8, representing the *stems* of your data set. Center the numbers and make them bold.
12. Enter 9 in E1, the only leaf of stem 1.
13. Select C3:C7, which are all the leaves on stem 2. Click **Edit** > **Copy.** Select E2; click **Edit** > **Paste Special,** choose *Values* and *Transpose,* and click **OK.** The stem 2 leaves appear to the right of that stem.
14. Select C8:C17, which are all the leaves on stem 3. Click **Edit > Copy.** Select E3; click **Edit > Paste Special,** choose *Values* and *Transpose,* and click **OK.** The stem 3 leaves appear to the right of that stem.
15. Select C18:C41, which are all the leaves on stem 4. Click **Edit > Copy.** Select E4; click **Edit > Paste Special,** choose *Values* and *Transpose,* and click **OK.** The stem 4 leaves appear to the right of that stem.
16. Select C42:C65, which are all the leaves on stem 5. Click **Edit > Copy.** Select E5; click **Edit > Paste Special,** choose *Values* and *Transpose,* and click **OK.** The stem 5 leaves appear to the right of that stem.
17. Select C66:C75, which are all the leaves on stem 6. Click **Edit > Copy.** Select E6; click **Edit > Paste Special,** choose *Values* and *Transpose,* and click **OK.** The stem 6 leaves appear to the right of that stem.
18. Select C76:C80, which are all the leaves on stem 7. Click **Edit > Copy.** Select E7; click **Edit > Paste Special,** choose *Values* and *Transpose,* and click **OK.** The stem 7 leaves appear to the right of that stem.
19. Enter 5 in E8, the only leaf of stem 8.
20. Select the range E1:AB8. Click **Format > Column > AutoFit Selection.** The result looks very much like Figure 6.20 on the previous page.

1	9																							
2	0	0	1	5	9																			
3	0	0	0	0	1	2	4	5	5	7														
4	0	0	0	0	0	0	1	1	2	2	3	5	5	5	5	6	7	7	7	8	8	8	9	9
5	0	0	0	0	0	0	0	1	1	2	2	2	3	3	4	4	5	5	5	5	5	6	8	8
6	0	0	0	0	5	5	5	6	6	9														
7	0	0	3	5	5																			
8	5																							

BOX-AND-WHISKER DIAGRAMS

Almost at a glance, the stem-and-leaf diagram of Figure 6.20 reveals additional useful information, often referred to as a data set's *five-number summary.* The concepts involved are discussed in detail in the next chapter, but we can take a sneak preview here:

1. The highest value observed is 85.
2. The upper-quartile value (the value that separates the highest 25 percent of observed values from the lowest 75 percent) is 55. (Just count down 0.25 times 80 = 20 numbers from the highest number.)
3. The middle value (the value that separates the lowest half of observed values from the upper half) is 50. (Just count 0.50 times 80 = 40 numbers starting from the bottom or the top.)
4. The lower-quartile value (the value that separates the lowest 25 percent of observed values from the highest 75 percent) is 40. (Just count up 0.25 times 80 = 20 numbers from the lowest number.)
5. The lowest value observed is 19.

This summary information is sometimes plotted in a **box-and-whisker diagram,** a graphical device that highlights the highest and lowest values in a data set, along with a number of other key observations in an ordered array of the data, such as the upper quartile, the middle value, and the lower quartile. This type of diagram is particularly useful when compared with similar information gathered at another place or time.

Consider the left-hand side of Figure 6.21 first. The upper asterisk represents the highest value observed in the 1998 survey (85); the lower one represents the lowest value (19). The range between the two must contain all the observations, but half of them are found between the top and bottom of the box (between values of 55 and 40). The values within the box fall, in turn, with equal frequencies into each of its two parts (that meet at a value of 50). Someone familiar with this type of graph can thus determine at a glance that half the subscribers are younger and

FIGURE 6.21 | Box-and-Whisker Diagrams

Box-and-whisker diagrams highlight extreme values in a data set (here by the upper and lower asterisks), as well as a number of other key values (by the box). Note: Other types of such diagrams exist as well.

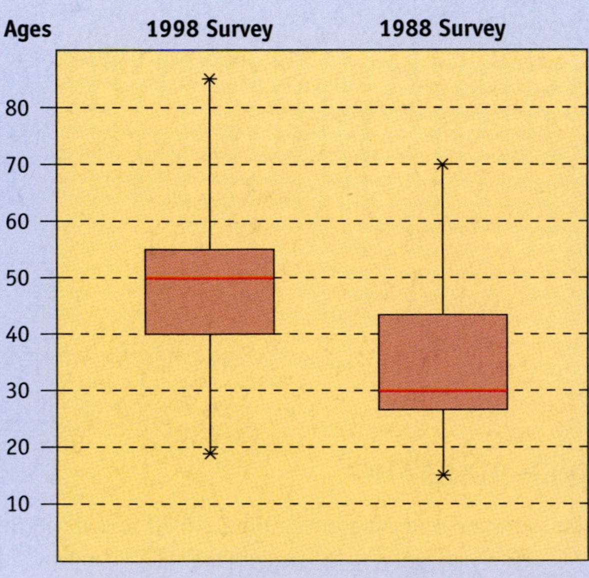

half are older than 50 years of age and that a quarter each fall in the 55–85 year range (the upper "whisker"), the 55–50 year range (the upper part of the box), the 50–40 year range (the lower part of the box), and the 40–19 year range (the lower "whisker").

All this becomes even more useful when compared, say, with another survey of 10 years earlier that is summarized in the right half of the graph. Apparently, subscribers have been getting older, the middle age having risen from 30 to 50, along with the ranges of the four quarters of observations. Clearly, this is important information that the producers of the newsletter must keep in mind if they wish to remain relevant to their audience.

How does a computer handle all this? The following example explains.

EXCEL Example 6.14

Retrieve the file HKMISC from the CD-ROM. Worksheet column A contains the data of Table 6.9. Illustrate them with a *box-and-whisker diagram.*

SOLUTION EXCEL is not programmed to create such a diagram automatically, but you can create a fairly similar diagram. Although Figure 6.22 on the next page contains neither a box nor any whiskers, it does provide the same information as a box-and-whisker diagram.

1. In cells B1:B5, respectively, type *Minimum, First Quartile, Median, Third Quartile,* and *Maximum.* Center the labels and make them bold.
2. In cell C1, type the formula **=Quartile(A2:A81,0)** and press **Enter.**
3. In cell C2, type the formula **=Quartile(A2:A81,1)** and press **Enter.**
4. In cell C3, type the formula **=Quartile(A2:A81,2)** and press **Enter.**
5. In cell C4, type the formula **=Quartile(A2:A81,3)** and press **Enter.**
6. In cell C5, type the formula **=Quartile(A2:A81,4)** and press **Enter.**

Your worksheet now contains the following additional data:

Minimum	19
First Quartile	40
Median	49.5
Third Quartile	55
Maximum	85

7. Select the five numbers. Click the **Chart Wizard > Standard Types > XY(Scatter);** then click the first graphical choice and **Next.**
8. In the second dialog box, click **Data Range,** choose *Series in Rows,* and click **Next.**
9. In the third dialog box, eliminate check marks under the **Gridlines** and **Legend** tabs.
10. Click **Data labels,** choose *Show value* and click **Next > Finish.**
11. Enlarge the graph by clicking on it and dragging its handles.
12. Right-click the horizontal axis labels, click **Format Axis > Scale,** and choose .9, 1.1, .1, and .1, respectively, in the first four boxes. Click **OK.**
13. Right-click the new horizontal axis labels, click **Clear.** You have Figure 6.22:

FIGURE 6.22 | Ages of Subscribers, 1998 Survey

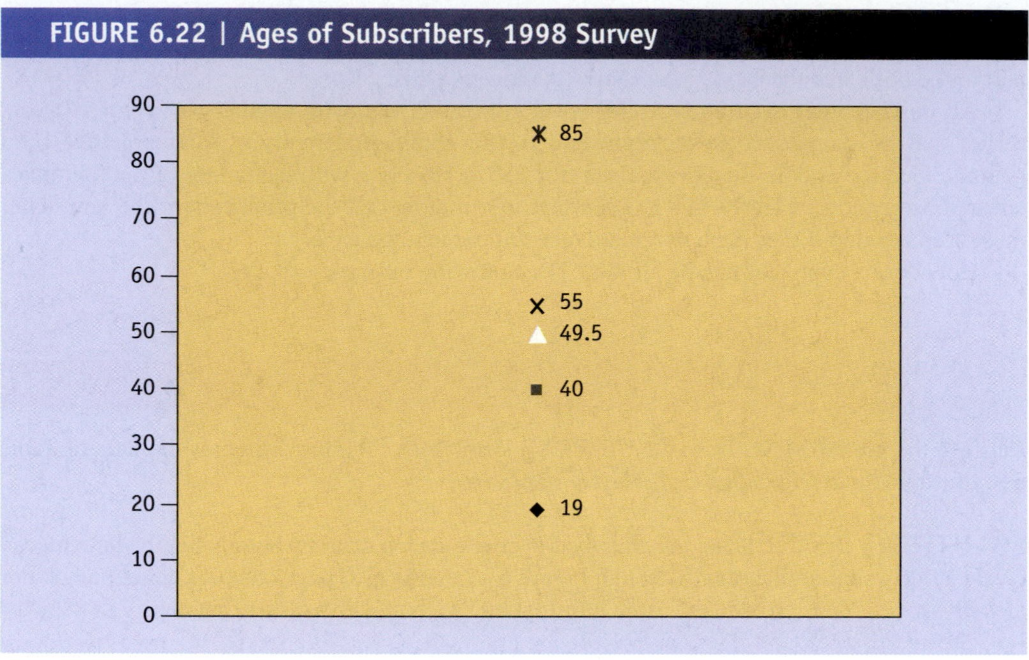

Note how Figure 6.22 provides the same information as the left-hand graph in Figure 6.21: The upper edge of the box in that earlier graph, also known as the *upper hinge,* represents the *third quartile* and corresponds to an age of 55. (Three quarters of all subscribers are younger than that.) The red middle line in the earlier graph represents the *second quartile* or *median* and corresponds to an age of 50, rendered more precisely as 49.5 in EXCEL. (Half of all subscribers are younger than that.) The lower edge of the box in the earlier graph, also known as the *lower hinge,* represents the *first quartile* and corresponds to an age of 40. (One quarter of all subscribers is younger than that.) The whiskers in the earlier graph extend to the highest and lowest observations (of 85 and 19). They are shown here as well.

Note: For a much more rapid solution, use *HKStat*, Sheet 3.

Summary

1. This chapter discusses the two most common procedures for making masses of data intelligible: the construction of tables and the drawing of graphs. Any considerable quantity of unorganized numerical data is likely to be confusing; even an *ordered array* is an improvement.
2. Greater clarity still is provided by dividing the range of available data into a relatively small number of collectively exhaustive and mutually exclusive classes, noting how many observations fall into each, and constructing a table on that basis. Such a table is known as an *absolute frequency distribution.*
3. If desired, an absolute frequency distribution can easily be converted into a *relative frequency distribution* that shows the proportions of all observations in the chosen classes (rather than the absolute number of observations).
4. In the case of quantitative data, further insight can be gained from the construction of (absolute or relative) *cumulative frequency distributions* (of the LE or ME type).
5. More sophisticated *cross tabulations* allow information about two variables to be presented in a single table at the same time.
6. Some of the most important devices for presenting absolute or relative frequency distributions of continuous quantitative data graphically include *frequency histograms, frequency polygons,* and *frequency curves.* Cumulative frequency distributions are, in turn, graphed as *ogives.*
7. Two variables can be graphed simultaneously as well. Favorite devices for doing that include the *scatter diagram* and *time-series line graphs.*

8. Many types of qualitative and quantitative data are most effectively presented in *bar charts* and *pie charts.*

9. Somewhat unusual data displays include *statistical maps, pictograms, stem-and-leaf diagrams,* and *box-and-whisker diagrams.*

Key Terms

absolute class frequency
absolute frequency distribution
bar chart
box-and-whisker diagram
classes
class mark
class width
collectively exhaustive classes
column chart
cross tabulations
cumulative class frequency
cumulative frequency distribution
dotplot
frequency curve
frequency density
frequency histogram
frequency polygon
mutually exclusive classes
ogive
open-ended classes
ordered array
pictogram
pie chart
relative class frequency
relative frequency distribution
scatter diagram
statistical map
stem-and-leaf diagram
Sturgess's rule
time-series line graph

Practice Problems

NOTES

1. Some problems assume that you are connected to the Internet. The addresses noted in these problems, and the solutions described on the accompanying CD-ROM, were current at the time of this writing. However, Web sites are forever evolving. If things have changed, you can still learn much by solving a slightly different problem in a slightly different way.

2. Some problems require the use of a statistical program, EXCEL or MINITAB. The program's major features are explained in text Chapter 2. Plenty of additional advice is available via the program's built-in Help feature.

SECTION 6.1 AN INTRODUCTION TO TABLE MAKING

1. Start EXCEL or MINITAB and retrieve the file HK100MN97 from the CD-ROM. Column E (in EXCEL) or column C5 (in MINITAB) contains the *net profit* figures of 100 multinational companies that were turned into the *ordered array* of Table 6.3. Create such an array in *descending* order. (*Hint:* EXCEL or MINITAB Example 6.1 can help.)

2. Start EXCEL or MINITAB and retrieve the file HK100MN97 from the CD-ROM. Column B (in EXCEL) or column C2 (in MINITAB) contains 1997 *foreign revenue* figures of the 100 multinational companies listed in Table 4.1. Create an ordered array and identify the maximum, minimum, and range of these data.

3. Start EXCEL or MINITAB and retrieve the file HK100MN97 from the CD-ROM. Column C (in EXCEL) or column C3 (in MINITAB) contains 1997 *total revenue* figures of the 100 multinational companies listed in Table 4.1. Create an ordered array and identify the maximum, minimum, and range of these data.

4. Start EXCEL or MINITAB and retrieve the file HK100MN97 from the CD-ROM. Column D (in EXCEL) or column C4 (in MINITAB) contains 1997 *net profits from foreign operations only* of the 100 multinational companies listed in Table 4.1. Create an ordered array and identify the maximum, minimum, and range of these data.

5. Start EXCEL or MINITAB and retrieve the file HK100MN97 from the CD-ROM. Column F (in EXCEL) or column C6 (in MINITAB) contains 1997 *foreign assets* figures of the 100 multinational companies listed in Table 4.1. Create an ordered array and identify the maximum, minimum, and range of these data.

SECTION 6.2 THE ABSOLUTE FREQUENCY DISTRIBUTION

6. Visit http://www.forbes.com/500s, a site maintained by *Forbes* magazine and devoted to information about the 500 largest U.S. corporations. Find out how many of the *Forbes 500* companies are located in each of the *New England* states (that is, in Connecticut, Massachusetts, Maine, New Hampshire, Rhode Island, and Vermont) and what these companies' employment levels are in each of these states. Set up an *absolute frequency distribution* to convey the information.

7. Visit http://www.forbes.com/500s, a site maintained by *Forbes* magazine and devoted to information about the 500 largest U.S. corporations. Find out which *airlines* are on the *Forbes 500* list and

record their employment levels and sales. Set up an *absolute frequency distribution* to convey the information.

8. Visit http://www.forbes.com/500s, a site maintained by *Forbes* magazine and devoted to information about the 500 largest U.S. corporations. Find out which *department stores* are on the *Forbes 500* list and record their employment levels and sales. Set up an *absolute frequency distribution* to convey the information.

9. Visit http://www.forbes.com/500s, a site maintained by *Forbes* magazine and devoted to information about the 500 largest U.S. corporations. Find out which *telecom-Internet* companies are on the *Forbes 500* list and record their employment levels and market values. Set up an *absolute frequency distribution* to convey the information.

10. The data of Table 6.10 were collected by a quality control engineer at a food processing plant. Present the data in an *absolute frequency distribution,* starting at 15.3 ounces and using
    a. classes of 0.1 ounce.
    b. classes of 0.8 ounce.

TABLE 6.10 | Actual Filling Weights of 80 Cans of Peas (ounces)

15.83	15.39	15.93	15.98	15.98	15.85	16.00	15.98	16.04	15.79
16.01	15.91	16.21	15.89	15.77	16.05	15.77	15.96	15.75	16.37
16.24	15.71	15.84	16.09	15.75	16.38	16.43	16.49	16.60	16.63
16.42	16.01	16.17	15.91	16.13	15.82	15.91	16.27	15.92	15.92
15.33	15.90	16.01	16.08	15.57	16.12	16.11	16.81	16.65	16.68
15.44	15.51	15.92	15.72	16.25	15.90	15.53	16.00	16.29	15.69
16.88	16.10	16.20	15.94	15.93	15.73	16.47	16.07	16.00	16.53
16.31	15.62	15.81	15.99	16.40	15.84	15.95	16.19	15.74	15.90

11. **a.** Review Practice Problem 10 and comment on the required task.
    b. Comment on the following two arrangements for dividing the net weights of vegetable cans into classes.

Arrangement 1	Arrangement 2
15.3 to under 15.5	15.3 to 15.5
15.6 to under 15.8	15.5 to 15.7
15.8 to under 16.0	15.7 to 15.9
and so forth	and so forth

    c. Redo Practice Problem 10 with Sturgess's Rule in mind.

12. Review Practice Problem 2, apply Sturgess's Rule, and present the data as an *absolute frequency distribution.*

13. Review Practice Problem 3, apply Sturgess's Rule, and present the data as an *absolute frequency distribution.*

SECTION 6.3 THE RELATIVE FREQUENCY DISTRIBUTION

14. At the beginning of fiscal year 2000, the U.S. government estimated the Table 6.11 breakdown of a projected $1,883 billion in federal receipts. Fill in the blanks.

TABLE 6.11 | Estimated U.S. Federal Receipts, Fiscal Year 2000

Receipt Category	Relative Frequency (proportions)	Absolute Frequency ($ billions)
Individual Income Taxes	0.478	
Social Security Taxes	0.338	
Corporate Income Taxes	0.101	
All others		
Totals		**$1,883.0**

15. At the beginning of fiscal year 2000, the U.S. government estimated the Table 6.12 breakdown of a projected $1,222.8 billion in state and local government receipts. Fill in the blanks.

TABLE 6.12 | Estimated State and Local Government Receipts, Fiscal Year 2000

Receipt Category	Relative Frequency (proportions)	Absolute Frequency ($ billions)
Sales Taxes	0.204	
Federal Aid	0.192	
Property Taxes	0.171	
Individual Income Taxes	0.120	
Corporate Income Taxes	0.026	
All others		
Totals	**1.000**	**$1,222.8**

16. Review Practice Problem 2, apply Sturgess's Rule, and present the data as a *relative frequency distribution.*

17. Review Practice Problem 3, apply Sturgess's Rule, and present the data as a *relative frequency distribution.*

SECTION 6.4 CUMULATIVE FREQUENCY DISTRIBUTIONS

18. Consider Table 6.13 on the next page concerning the households in a suburban development.

a. Fill in the missing values.

b. What percentage of these households has at least one TV set? Has at most three sets? Has three or four sets?

19. Use the Table 6.10 data to create the cumulative absolute frequency distribution and the cumulative relative frequency distribution, each of the less-than-or-equal type. (*Hint:* The answer to Practice Problem 11c can help.)

TABLE 6.13 | Household Survey

Class (number of TV sets per household) (1)	Absolute Class Frequency (number of households) (2)	Relative Class Frequency (proportion of all households in class) (3)	Cumulative Relative Class Frequency: "Less Than or Equal" (proportion of all households in class and lower ones) (4)	Cumulative Relative Class Frequency: "More Than or Equal" (proportion of all households in class and higher ones) (5)
0	60			
1		.28		
2			.72	
3				
4	24			
5				.04
Totals	**300**			

20. Use the Table 6.10 data to create the cumulative absolute frequency distrbution and the cumulative relative frequency distribution, each of the more-than-or-equal type. (*Hint:* The answer to Practice Problem 11c can help.)

Section 6.5 Cross Tabulations

21. Imagine you were working for a chemicals firm that is interested in expanding its fertilizer sales in California and Florida. You are supposed to provide information about current fertilizer usage, and you instantly think of *oranges.* Create a relevant *cross tabulation* for your next staff meeting. (*Hint:* You may find it helpful to visit http://www.fedstats.gov, a site maintained by the Interagency Council on Statistical Policy and introduced in Chapter 3 of this text. Click on *Regional Statistics* and look for *Agriculture.*)

22. Imagine you were working for a chemicals firm that is interested in expanding its fertilizer sales in California and Florida. You are supposed to provide information about current fertilizer usage, and you instantly think of *grapefruit.* Create a relevant *cross tabulation* for your next staff meeting. (*Hint:* You may find it helpful to visit http://www.fedstats.gov, a site maintained by the Interagency Council on Statistical Policy and introduced in Chapter 3 of this text. Click on *Regional Statistics* and look for *Agriculture.*)

23. Imagine you were working for a chemicals firm that is interested in expanding its herbicide and insecticide sales. You are supposed to make it happen and come up with relevant information about current usage. Somehow you think of growing *corn.* Create a relevant *cross tabulation* for your next staff meeting. (*Hint:* Visit http://www.fedstats.gov, a site maintained by the Interagency Council on Statistical Policy and introduced in Chapter 3 of this text. Click on *Regional Statistics* and look for *Agriculture.*)

24. Imagine you were working for a chemicals firm that is interested in expanding its sales of herbicides, insecticide, and similar chemicals. You are supposed to make it happen and come up with relevant information about current usage. Somehow you think of growing *apples.* Create a relevant *cross tabulation* for your next staff meeting. (*Hint:* Visit http://www.fedstats.gov, a site maintained by the Interagency Council on Statistical Policy and introduced in Chapter 3 of this text. Click on *Regional Statistics* and look for *Agriculture.*)

25. Imagine you were working for an insurance company that is interested in expanding its business into new geographic areas. You are supposed to make an economic survey of *Utah* and come up with relevant information about its industries, the number of firms in each, their sales, employment numbers, and more. Create a relevant *cross tabulation* for your next staff meeting. (*Hint:* Visit http://www.census.gov/statab, a site maintained by the U.S. Bureau of the Census. Click on *State and County Profiles* and pick *Utah* on the U.S. map.)

26. Imagine you were working for a veterinary supply company that is interested in launching a marketing campaign. You are supposed to find out the latest about the extent of pet ownership and the characteristics of owners, ranging from their income and pet expenditures to family size. Somehow you think of *cats and dogs.* Create a relevant *cross tabulation* for your next staff meeting. (*Hint:* Visit http://www.census.gov/statab, a site maintained by the U.S. Bureau of the Census. Click on *Frequently Requested Tables* and see what you can find.)

27. Review Practice Problem 26. Then imagine that your boss yelled at you about all that information you gathered concerning cats and dogs. She is interested in *pet birds and horses;* so do the work all over again.

28. Imagine you have just been hired by a mail-order house on the verge of a major ad campaign. You are to help direct the ads toward the highest-income states across the United States. Come up with a plan for your next staff meeting. A *cross tabulation* of per capita personal income by state over several years might be welcome. (*Hint:* Visit http://www.census.gov/statab, a site maintained by the U.S. Bureau of the Census. Click on *Frequently Requested Tables* and see what you can find.)

Section 6.6 An Introduction to Drawing Graphs

Note: Because EXCEL does not draw dotplots, the problems in this section apply only to MINITAB users.

29. Review the data noted in Practice Problem 2. Present them as a *dotplot.*

30. Review the data noted in Practice Problem 3. Present them as a *dotplot.*

31. Review the data noted in Practice Problem 4. Present them as a *dotplot.*

Section 6.7 Frequency Histograms

32. Review the data noted in Practice Problem 2. Present them as an *absolute frequency histogram.* (*Hint:* The answer to Practice Problem 12 may help.)

33. Review the data noted in Practice Problem 3. Present them as a *relative frequency histogram.* (*Hint:* The answer to Practice Problem 13 may help.)

34. Consider whether each of the following variables (measured on the horizontal axis) is likely to be described by a histogram approximating a frequency distribution that is normal (symmetrically bell-shaped), skewed to the right, skewed to the left, exponential, or rectangular:

a. family money incomes in the United States

b. random numbers

c. the dollar values of mail-order-house sales

d. the height of boats on the Mississippi

e. the ages of pinball machine players

f. the ages of people with false teeth or bald heads

g. the last digits of all New York City telephone numbers

h. the grades of all students at midterm

i. the ages of children in elementary school

j. the number of printing errors found on a book's pages

k. the number of minutes people have to wait at the bank, doctor's office, post office, supermarket checkout counter

l. the number of days people spend in a hospital

m. the size of errors made by a bank teller

n. the number of days it takes people to pay their credit card bills

o. response times of a fire or police department

p. the yields per acre of U.S. wheat farmers

q. the ages at which famous authors wrote their best books

r. the miles driven in a year by all cars registered in the United States

Section 6.8 Frequency Polygon and Frequency Curve

35. Start EXCEL or MINITAB and retrieve the file HK100MN97 from the CD-ROM. Column G (in EXCEL) or column C7 (in MINITAB) contains 1997 data on the *total assets* of the 100 largest U.S.-based multinationals. Depict the data with the help of a *frequency polygon.*

Section 6.9 Ogives

36. Review the answer to Practice Problem 19. Based on columns 1 and 2 of Table 6.23, create a less-than-or-equal *ogive.*

37. Review the answer to Practice Problem 19. Based on columns 1 and 3 of Table 6.23, create a more-than-or-equal *ogive.*

SECTION 6.10 GRAPHING TWO VARIABLES

38. Start EXCEL or MINITAB and retrieve the file HK100MN97 from the CD-ROM. Columns D and F (in EXCEL) or columns C4 and C6 (in MINITAB) contain 1997 data on the *net profits from foreign operations* and the *foreign assets* of the 100 largest U.S.-based multinationals. Create a *scatter diagram* of the data. (*Hint:* Follow the procedure laid out in EXCEL or MINITAB Example 6.5.)

39. Visit http://www.globalfindata.com, a site maintained by Global Financial Data. (Alternatively, look at recent print copies of the *Statistical Abstract of the United States.*) Create a semilogarithmic *time-series line graph* showing the movements since 1990 of two foreign stock market indices: (a) Tokyo's Nikkei 225 and (b) London's FTSE 100. (*Hint:* You may wish to follow the procedure laid out in EXCEL or MINITAB Examples 6.7 and 6.8.)

40. Visit http://www.census.gov, a site maintained by the U.S. Bureau of the Census. (Alternatively, look at the latest print copy of the *Statistical Abstract of the United States.*) Create a *time-series line graph* showing how the purchasing power of the dollar has changed since 1950. (*Hint:* You may wish to follow the procedure laid out in EXCEL or MINITAB Example 6.7.)

SECTION 6.11 BAR CHARTS

41. In 1998, the advertising revenues, in millions of dollars, of five well-known Web sites were $203.3 for Yahoo!, $154.1 for Excite, $49.4 for CNET, $17.7 for SportsLine USA, and $9.1 for iVillage. Using the procedure laid out in EXCEL or MINITAB Examples 6.9 and 6.10, present this information

a. in a *horizontal bar chart.*

b. in a *vertical bar chart.*

42. In the first quarter of 1999, the five best-performing diversified stock funds in the United States were VanWagoner Emerging Growth (+55.84%), Van Wagoner Micro-Cap (+33.36%), Van Wagoner Mid-Cap (+32.10%), Morgan Stanley Dean Witter's Mid-Cap Equity Trust B (+28.89%), and TCW Galileo I Aggressive Growth Equity (+28.49%). The five worst-performing funds were Munder K. Small Company Growth (−16.82%), Paine Webber A Small Cap (−17.22%), Preferred Small Cap (−18.87%), Seligman Frontier D (−19.08%), and Profunds Ultrashort OTC Investor (−29.91%). Present this information in a duo-directional *bar chart.* (*Hint:* EXCEL or MINITAB Example 6.9 may help.)

SECTION 6.12 PIE CHARTS

43. In 1998, with almost 16 million subscribers, America Online was the gateway to cyberspace for more Americans than the next 15 Internet service providers combined. The market shares were 42.6% for America Online and, in decreasing order, 6.4% for MSN, 5.0% for AT&T WorldNet, 4.3% for the Regional Bells, 4% for Compuserve, and the remaining 37.7% for all the rest, including Prodigy, Earthlink/Sprint Passport, IBM Global Network, GTE, Mindspring, and more. Present this information in a *pie chart.* (*Hint:* EXCEL or MINITAB Example 6.12 may help.)

44. In late 1998, the portion of the U.S. national debt that was *not* owed to federal government agencies (such as the Social Security trust fund) came to $3,301 billion. Of this total, $1,217.2 billion was owed to foreigners and the rest to Americans, including $469 billion to state and local governments, $352.3 billion to individuals, $260 billion to commercial banks, $188 billion to insurance companies, and 814.5 billion to all others, Illustrate this breakdown with a pie chart. (*Hint:* EXCEL or MINITAB Example 6.12 may help.)

SECTION 6.13 UNUSUAL GRAPHS

45. You are about to set up a new business and want to do so in a state with rapid population growth. Set up a *statistical map* showing population growth between the 1980 and 1990 censuses or between the 1990 and 2000 censuses. (If you are connected to the Internet, visit http://www.census.gov/statab, a site maintained by the U.S. Bureau of the Census. Otherwise look at the latest print copy of the *Statistical Abstract of the United States.*)

46. Find an example of how people lie with statistics. Comment on it.

47. Review the data noted in Practice Problem 3. Present them as a *stem-and-leaf diagram.* (*Hint:* EXCEL or MINITAB Example 6.13 may help.)

48. Review the data noted in Practice Problem 4. Present them as a *stem-and-leaf diagram.* (*Hint:* EXCEL or MINITAB Example 6.13 may help.)

49. Review the data noted in Practice Problem 3. Present them as a *box-and-whisker diagram.* (*Hint:* EXCEL or MINITAB Examples 6.14 may help.)

50. Review the data noted in Practice Problem 4. Present them as a *box-and-whisker diagram.* (*Hint:* EXCEL or MINITAB Examples 6.14 may help.)

Presenting Data: Summary Measures

LOOKING AHEAD

After reading this chapter, you will be able to condense masses of raw data into a large variety of succinct summary measures. Among other things, you will learn to compute and appreciate the meaning of:

1. measures of central tendency, including the arithmetic mean, the median, the mode, and more,
2. measures of dispersion, including the overall range, interfractile ranges (such as those between quartiles and deciles), the mean absolute deviation, the variance, and the standard deviation,
3. measures of shape, notably those of skewness and kurtosis, and
4. proportions, which are the most important summary measures of qualitative data.

AND HERE IS A TYPICAL PROBLEM YOU WILL BE ABLE TO SOLVE:

Your boss wants to acquire a major software company. You are to gather relevant information. Visit http://www.fortune.com, a site maintained by *Fortune* magazine. Identify the revenues, profits, and numbers of employees of each of the *Fortune 500* companies in the *computer software* industry. Using EXCEL or MINITAB, compute and print out descriptive summary statistics on the three types of data series just noted.

PREVIEW

Imagine you had two jobs. Job A paid you \$6 per hour, while job B brought you a much more respectable \$14 of hourly pay. Would your *average* hourly pay come to \$6 + \$14, divided by 2, or \$10? It would, provided you worked the same number of hours at both jobs. But suppose you did not, working 17 hours at the lower rate and 3 hours at the higher one. Then you would have to figure your average hourly pay by counting the \$6 number 17 times and the \$14 number 3 times. By this procedure, you would derive a *weighted* average hourly pay of (\$6 × 17) + (\$14 × 3) = \$144, divided by 20, which comes to a mere 7 dollars and 20 cents. Unlike the *unweighted* average of \$10 noted above, the lower \$7.20 would correctly summarize the average pay during your 20 hours of work. People continually use numbers such as these to summarize much more complex data sets. Unfortunately, they do not always compute their summary measures correctly. Consider two recent cases in point.

CASE 1 In the early 1990s, Congress reviewed federally funded welfare programs. Among them was the Aid to Families with Dependent Children (AFDC) program that provided cash grants to low-income people, mostly single mothers. Nearly all AFDC recipients also qualified for food stamps. The House Ways and Means Committee, therefore, estimated the *combined* monthly benefits that were available to low-income mothers and their children in the 50 states and the District of Columbia, as shown in Table 7.1.

It would have been easy to draw a statistical map, similar to Figure 6.1, to illustrate the Table 7.1 data and highlight the fact that monthly benefits were generally highest in the Far West and North, lowest in the South. Congress, however, wanted *numbers,* the kind of numerical summary measures that we discuss in this chapter. In fact, one Capitol Hill journalist who got hold of these data was, perhaps, a bit too eager to summarize them. He simply added all the numbers in our table ($703 + $748 + . . . + $1,077), divided the total by 51, and then reported the $666.40 *arithmetic average* as the typical monthly benefit provided to mothers and children across the land. A bit of reflection leads us to reject that approach. Just consider the fact that California's $850 benefit went to 1.833 million people, while Mississippi's $412 went to only 178,000 of them. Careful statisticians, including those working for Congress, computed a *weighted*

TABLE 7.1 | Combined Monthly AFDC and Food Stamps Benefits in 1991

New England		East North Central		West South Central	
ME	$703	OH	$624	AR	$496
NH	748	IN	580	LA	482
VT	857	IL	649	OK	625
MA	764	MI	729	TX	476
RI	812	WI	748	**Mountain**	
CT	862	**East South Central**		MT	$659
Mid-Atlantic		KY	$520	ID	607
NY	$806	TN	477	WY	638
NJ	691	AL	441	CO	636
PA	681	MS	412	NM	613
South Atlantic		**West North Central**		AZ	620
DE	$623	MN	$759	UT	668
MD	668	IA	685	NV	647
DC	673	MO	584	**Pacific**	
VA	634	ND	667	WA	$784
WV	541	SD	669	OR	744
NC	564	NE	641	CA	850
SC	502	KS	697	AK	1,184
GA	572			HI	1,077
FL	595				

national average benefit by multiplying each state's figure by the number of recipients (just as we multiplied, in the earlier example, each hourly wage by the number of hours worked), added the components, and divided the total by the 11.183 million recipients nationwide. By pure accident, their $671 result was remarkably close to the journalist's cruder estimate.

CASE 2 A similar example is inspired by *Fortune* magazine's 1999 release of financial data for the 500 largest U.S. corporations, ranked by 1998 total revenues. The data included each company's profit as a percentage of stockholders' equity. Another journalist, also eager to summarize the numbers, added the percentages: 221.8 percent for General Mills (the company with the highest return) + 94.3 percent for Ford + 21.0 percent for Wal-Mart Stores + 3.3 percent for Sprint . . . and, finally, −1,336.6 percent for Clark USA (the worst performer on the *Fortune 500* list). Dividing by 500 yielded an average return of 12.44 percent, but, surely, that figure was wrong. Not every one of these returns was earned on the same number of invested dollars, just as the hourly wages noted earlier were not earned for an equal number of hours. The stockholders of General Mills, for example, earned that spectacular return on a mere 190 million equity dollars, while the stockholders of Ford made those lower, but still remarkable, returns on 23,409 million equity dollars. Similarly, Sprint's low return was earned on 12,448 million equity dollars, while the worst performance noted above reflected a $29.7 million loss on an equity of just over 2 million dollars. What then was the true, weighted average return earned by all those *Fortune 500* companies? As the magazine noted, it was a solid 15.0 percent.

CONCLUSION This chapter introduces a variety of procedures for summarizing masses of data in meaningful ways, without making the kinds of errors just noted. Again, however, be forewarned: *Descriptive* statistics, even when done well, merely tells us how things are; we need *inferential* statistics to interpret such results. For example, you should not conclude from Table 7.1 that a poor welfare recipient would be almost three times better off by moving from Mississippi to Alaska, merely because $1,184 is almost three times as large as $412. Living costs in Alaska may be that much higher as well.

7.1 Major Types of Summary Measures

As Chapter 6 showed, properly constructed tables and graphs can make otherwise confusing masses of data intelligible and reveal secrets hidden in unorganized data. An even more radical approach to condensing data collections is to calculate *arithmetic summary measures*. These measures express the most important features of data sets compactly. Data about quantitative variables can be neatly summarized in three ways: by measures of central tendency, measures of dispersion, and measures of shape. For qualitative data, the only summary measure available is the proportion. We discuss all of these in turn.

MEASURES OF CENTRAL TENDENCY

Summary **measures of central tendency** (or **measures of location**) are values around which observations tend to cluster and that describe the location of what in some sense might be called the "center" of a data set. Consider the two frequency curves in panel (a) of Figure 7.1 on the next page. They describe two hypothetical data sets about the sizes of life-insurance policies taken out by women and men. You will notice immediately that men in general take out larger policies than women do, in spite of the fact that *some* women take out policies for as much as $100,000, while *some* men take out policies for as little as $50,000. If we wanted to identify a single "typical" measure of the size of policies, it would be $50,000 for women and $100,000 for men. Each of these numbers would be a *measure of central tendency* because it would locate the general center

FIGURE 7.1 | Summary Measures and Frequency Curves

Different summary measures describe different aspects of frequency curves, such as the curves shown here. Measures of ***central tendency*** *locate the center of a data set, as at 50 (women) or 100 (men) in panel (a). Measures of* ***dispersion*** *focus on the spread of data around their center, as on the ranges from 0 to 100 (women) or 50 to 150 (men) in panel (a) or from 9.7 to 10.3 (pounds of cookies) or 9.9 to 10.1 (pounds of sugar) in panel (b). Measures of* ***shape*** *describe how symmetrical frequency curves are—as are the curves in panels (a) and (b)—or how asymmetrical they are—as are the curves in panel (c). Measures of shape also describe how peaked (sugar) or how flat (cookies) frequency curves are.*

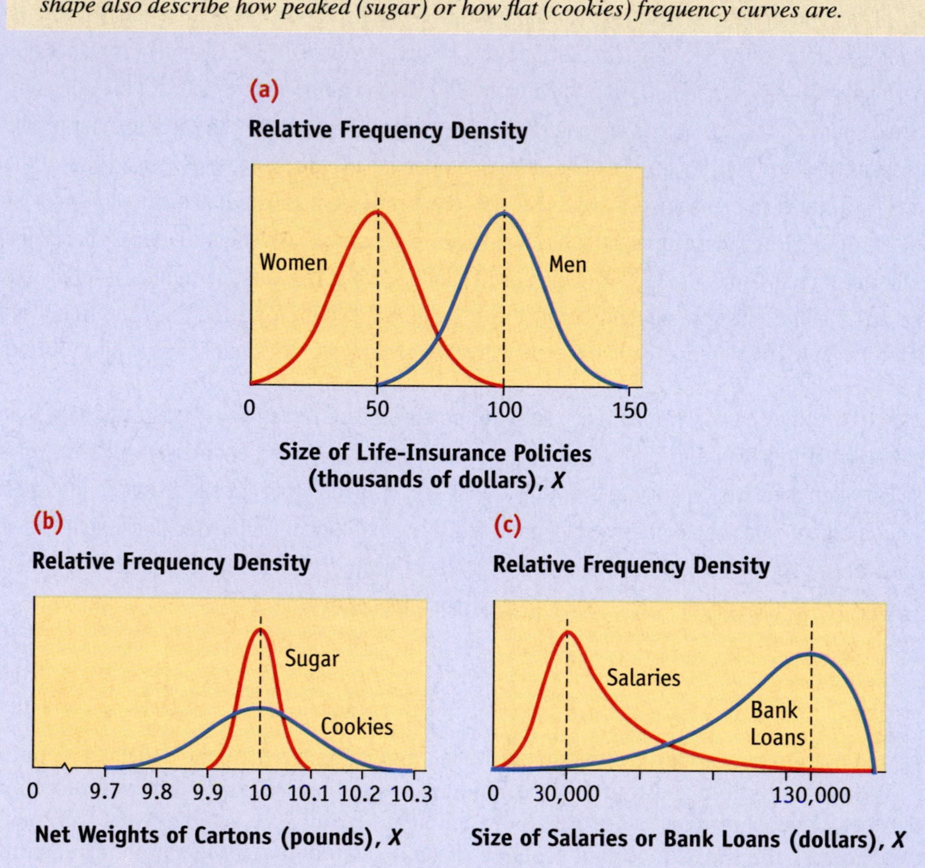

of the respective data sets (in this case, on the horizontal axis of our graph). But what would you say are the centers of the asymmetrical data sets in panel (c)? The answer is less obvious and depends very much on how the term *center* is defined. In later sections of this chapter, a number of alternatives are discussed. They include the *arithmetic mean,* the *median,* the *mode,* and more.

MEASURES OF DISPERSION

Summary **measures of dispersion** (or **measures of variability**) are numbers that indicate the spread or scatter of observations; they show the extent to which individual values in a data set differ from one another and, hence, differ from their central location. The two data sets on life-insurance policies that are visually summarized in panel (a) of Figure 7.1 do not differ from each other with respect to variability. Note how both women's and men's policies vary ±$50,000 from their respective centers. Women's policies cover a $100,000 range (from $0 to $100,000); men's policies also cover a $100,000 range (from $50,000 to $150,000).

But now consider the two frequency curves in panel (b), which describe two data sets on the actual net weights of supposedly 10-pound cartons of cookies and of sugar. Even though both data sets have the identical central tendency (of 10 pounds per carton), they differ significantly as far as data dispersion is concerned. The sugar-carton net weights are tightly packed around the center of the distribution. All these weights fall within the 0.2-pound range from 9.9 to 10.1 pounds, that is, within 1 percent of the stated weight. The net weights of cookie cartons, on the other hand, are more widely spread; they range over 0.6 pounds, that is, within ±3 percent of the desired weight. The cookie-carton weights may be more widely dispersed because their final weight must be determined by adding or subtracting an entire cookie rather than a few tiny grains of sugar. Clearly, the two net-weight data sets could quite nicely be described by some measure of central tendency, but we would also need appropriate *measures of dispersion* before we could visualize those data sets. In later sections of this chapter, a number of alternative measures of dispersion are discussed. They include the *range,* the *variance,* the *standard deviation,* and more.

MEASURES OF SHAPE

Summary **measures of shape** are numbers that indicate either the degree of asymmetry or the degree of peakedness in a frequency distribution. Note how the four distributions pictured in panels (a) and (b) of Figure 7.1 are symmetrical about the dashed vertical lines; the left and right halves of the distributions in each case are mirror images of each other. Such symmetry is not present in all distributions, however, as is indicated in panel (c). The salaries received by the employees in an industry might cluster near a dominant value of $30,000. Because no salaries fall below zero, the spread below $30,000 would be limited, while the spread above that number may be extreme. As a result, the frequency curve comes to look like the side view of a child's slide. Asymmetry may be found in the other direction as well: The sizes of loans made by a bank may be concentrated near $130,000, with none much larger because of the bank's lending limit. Yet there may be many scattered loans of much lower amount. Measures of shape try to capture this type of asymmetry, as well as the flatness or peakedness of frequency curves such as those depicted graphically in panel (b) of Figure 7.1. In later sections of this chapter, we discuss a number of alternative *measures of shape.* They include measures of *skewness* and *kurtosis.*

SUMMARIZING QUALITATIVE DATA

For qualitative data, the only summary measure available is the **proportion,** a number that describes the frequency of observations in a particular category as a fraction of all observations made. However, as the Chapter 6 discussion of pie charts indicates, proportions can be calculated for quantitative data as well.

PARAMETERS AND STATISTICS

In the remainder of this chapter, we will discuss each of the summary measures just noted, but before we do so, we should be aware of two things:

1. Any summary measure can be calculated for a population or for a sample. If the summary measure is based on population data, it is called a **parameter** and is designated by a Greek

letter. (Appendix Table B at the end of this text lists the Greek alphabet.) If the summary measure is based on sample data, it is referred to as a **statistic** and is designated by a letter from the ordinary Roman alphabet that we normally use. In Chapter 6, we noted that population data are often unavailable because it is costly and time-consuming to conduct censuses. Thus, most of the time, statisticians gather data by sampling and, therefore, end up computing *statistics* rather than *parameters.* As we will see, however, these statistics can also be used to *estimate* the values of corresponding unknown parameters.

2. It is well to note that parameters and statistics must be calculated with the help of different formulas, depending on whether the raw material in question involves original, raw, ungrouped data or secondhand, processed, grouped data, such as those found in a frequency distribution.

7.2 The Arithmetic Mean

The most often encountered and most widely known measure of central tendency is, no doubt, the *mean*—more precisely called the *arithmetic mean.* In casual conversation, however, people refer to it simply as *"the average."*

DEFINITION 7.1 The **arithmetic mean** is a measure of central tendency in a data set. It is computed by adding together all the individual observations and dividing the sum so obtained by the number of observations. As a result, the sum of deviations of all observations from this mean equals zero.

As is true of all summary measures, the arithmetic mean can be calculated with precision from any set of raw, unprocessed, ungrouped data. It can also be *approximated* from processed, grouped data, such as an absolute frequency distribution.

CALCULATION FROM UNGROUPED DATA

In millions of dollars, let the annual profits of five firms equal 2, 2, 4, 7, and 15. Their arithmetic mean equals

$$\frac{2 + 2 + 4 + 7 + 15}{5} = \frac{30}{5} = 6$$

The $6 million arithmetic mean just computed would be the *population mean* (and, thus, a parameter) if the frame of interest contained only five firms, such as all the makers of airplanes in the United States or all the makers of beer in Detroit. The number would be a *sample mean* (and, thus, a statistic) if it referred to five firms among a much larger group of interest, say, five among dozens of airplane manufacturers in the world or five among hundreds of breweries in the United States. The procedure just followed can also be expressed symbolically, as in Formula 7.A.

FORMULA 7.A | Arithmetic Mean from Ungrouped Data

For a population:

$$\mu = \frac{X_1 + X_2 + X_3 + \cdots + X_N}{N} = \frac{\Sigma X}{N}$$

For a sample:

$$\overline{X} = \frac{X_1 + X_2 + X_3 + \cdots + X_n}{n} = \frac{\Sigma X}{n}$$

where the X's are the observed population or sample values, N is the number of observations in the population, n is the number of observations in the sample, and Σ (pronounced *sigma*) is the capital Greek S that stands for *sum* and is commonly used as a shortcut *summation sign.* Here and throughout this text, the letter Σ symbolizes that *all* available data are to be added together.

SYMBOLIC EXPRESSION

By tradition, the small letter x or the capital letter X is used to represent an observed value. In this text, we use capital X. Different values are distinguished by subscripts 1, 2, 3, . . . and so on, yielding the series X_1, X_2, X_3, . . . and so on for a set of data. The symbol X_1 is pronounced "X sub one," and, in the example discussed before, $X_1 = 2$. Similarly, $X_2 = 2$, $X_3 = 4$, $X_4 = 7$, and $X_5 = 15$. Also by tradition, the total number of observations (here 5) is referred to as N in the case of a population and as n in the case of a sample. Finally, because *parameters* are always symbolized by Greek letters, the population mean is represented by μ, the lowercase Greek *m,* which is pronounced "mu" and stands for *mean.* Like all statistics, the sample mean, in turn, is represented by a Roman letter, in this case a capital $\overline{X}$ (pronounced "X bar"). Thus, the calculation of the arithmetic mean from ungrouped data is summarized by Formula 7.A.

Luckily, you will never have to apply Formula 7.A to any large data set. That chore is quickly taken care of by modern computer programs.

EXCEL Example 7.1

Start EXCEL and retrieve the file HK100MN97 from the CD-ROM. Column E contains the total profit figures of those 100 multinational companies first listed in Table 4.1 on page 110. What is the *arithmetic mean* of these profit data?

SOLUTION Instead of applying Formula 7.A manually to the 100 numbers found in Table 6.2 (as well as Table 6.3) on pages 167 and 168, you can let EXCEL do the number crunching. After selecting the column E data, you can use one of two approaches:

APPROACH A

1. Click **Tools** > **Data Analysis** > **Descriptive Statistics** > **OK.**
2. In the *Descriptive Statistics* dialog box, enter *Input Range* **E1:E101,** check *Labels in First Row,* check *Summary Statistics,* and click **OK.**

   The mean of **1,848.86** (million dollars) is listed along with many other data.

APPROACH B

1. On the standard toolbar, click the **Function Wizard (*fx*).**
2. In the *Paste Function* dialog box, under *Function category,* click **Statistical;** under *Function name,* click **AVERAGE** > **OK.**
3. In the box, enter **E2:E101** and click **OK.**

   The mean of **1,848.86** (million dollars) appears at the head of column E.

CALCULATION FROM GROUPED DATA

Sometimes raw data are unavailable and if we want to calculate the mean at all, we must use a frequency distribution to do so. At other times, raw data are available but are so massive in number that it is preferable to use grouped data rather than spend forever entering all the ungrouped data into a computer.

Unfortunately, we can calculate the mean from grouped data only by assuming, perhaps incorrectly, that the observations falling into a given class are equally spaced within it and are, therefore, on the average, equal to the midpoint of the class interval. (In the case of open-ended classes, the procedure must be abandoned or a wild estimate of the midpoint must be made.) Each midpoint is then multiplied by the absolute class frequency, and the sum of these products is divided by the population size, N, or the sample size, n. If each midpoint is represented by X, and the corresponding absolute class frequency by f, the procedure can be described by Formula 7.B.

FORMULA 7.B | Arithmetic Mean from Grouped Data

For a population:

$$\mu = \frac{\Sigma fX}{N}$$

For a sample:

$$\bar{X} = \frac{\Sigma fX}{n}$$

where ΣfX is the sum of all class-frequency (f) times class-midpoint (X) products, N is the number of observations in the population, and n is the number of observations in the sample. The letter Σ (pronounced *sigma*) is the capital Greek S that stands for *sum* and is commonly used as a shortcut *summation sign.* Here and throughout this text, the letter Σ symbolizes that *all* available data are to be added together.

Example Problem 7.1 illustrates the procedure of estimating an arithmetic mean from grouped data.

EXAMPLE PROBLEM 7.1

Review the absolute frequency distribution of Table 6.4 on page 171. In the absence of additional information, use Formula 7.B to *estimate* the arithmetic mean of the net profits data.

SOLUTION: See Table 7.2.

TABLE 7.2 | Approximation of the Arithmetic Mean from a Frequency Distribution

When the arithmetic mean is to be calculated from a frequency distribution, and (as is usually the case) the actual sums of values in each class are not known, an approximation can still be derived by weighting each class midpoint, X, by the corresponding class frequency, f, and dividing the sum of the weighted products, ΣfX, by the population size, N, or the sample size, n.

Class (net profit in millions of dollars)	Absolute Class Frequency (number of companies in class) f	Class Midpoint X	fX
−1,250 to under 0	6	−625	−3,750
0 to under 1,250	49	625	30,625
1,250 to under 2,500	18	1,875	33,750
2,500 to under 3,750	15	3,125	46,875
3,750 to under 5,000	3	4,375	13,125
5,000 to under 6,250	2	5,625	11,250
6,250 to under 7,500	4	6,875	27,500
7,500 to under 8,750	2	8,125	16,250
8,750 to under 10,000	1	9,375	9,375
	$\Sigma f = N = 100$		$\Sigma fX = 185{,}000$

Based on the ratio 185,000/100, we estimate the arithmetic mean as $1,850 million. Compared to the precise figure given in EXCEL or MINITAB Example 7.1, this is an excellent result, but such accuracy is never assured. Indeed, this example problem brings out an interesting point: When discussing the construction of absolute frequency distributions in Chapter 6, we noted how helpful it would be for subsequent users of such data if the maker of the distribution provided the sums of observations for each class. This assertion now becomes clear. If those sums were available, the data in the last column of Table 7.2 would be precise (rather than estimated) and the computed arithmetic mean would be precise as well.

THE NATURE OF THE MEAN

Knowing how to calculate the mean is one thing; knowing what it tells us is another. We can best view the mean as a point of balance in a data set, very much like the fulcrum of a seesaw. In the case of a seesaw, or teeterboard, the number of (equal-sized) weights on one side of the fulcrum, multiplied by their respective distances from it, must equal the number of such weights times their distances on the other side in order for the board to be balanced horizontally. Like the fulcrum, the arithmetic mean balances the number of observations on one side of the mean times their respective deviations from this mean with the number of observations times their deviations on the other side. This role of the mean is illustrated in Figure 7.2 on the next page.

FIGURE 7.2 | The Nature of the Arithmetic Mean

The mean of a data set can be compared to the fulcrum of a seesaw. The mean occupies a ***central position*** *in the sense that the sum of negative and positive deviations of individual observations from the mean equals zero. Thus, for the data set represented by the blocks in panel (a), the mean equals 6, and the sum of deviations equals* $-4 - 4 - 2 + 1 + 9 = 0$. *For the data set represented by the blocks in panel (b), the mean equals 8, and the sum of deviations equals* $-6 - 6 - 4 - 1 + 17 = 0$. *Note how the arithmetic mean responds to the change in any single observation (as when 15 becomes 25) and how it is quite possible for the vast majority of all observations to be on one side of the mean—as in panel (b).*

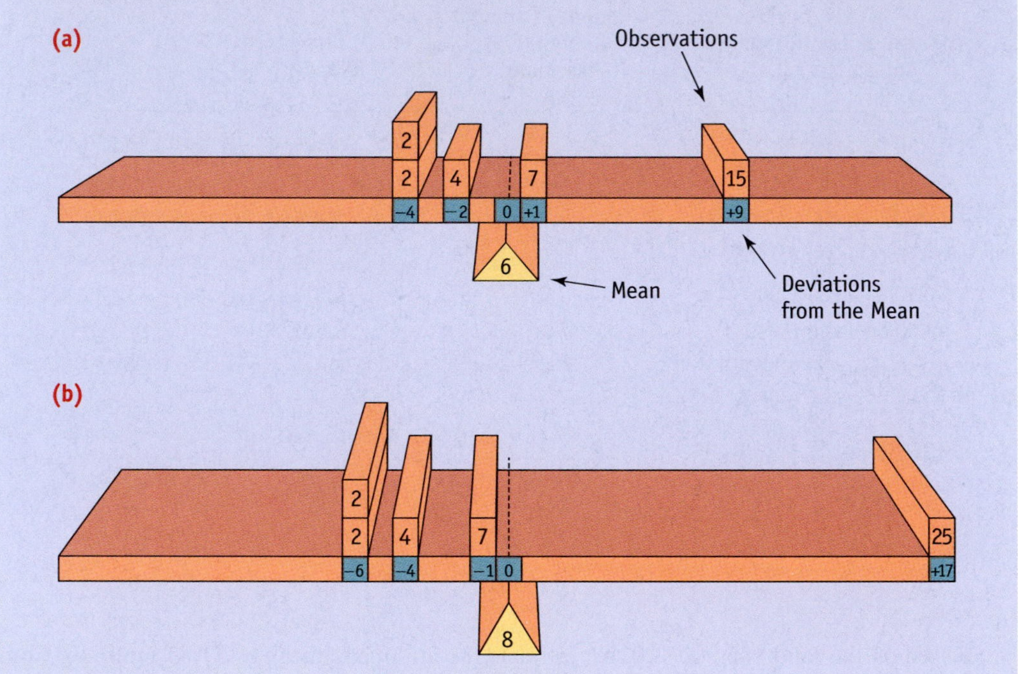

Panel (a) shows the relationship between the five hypothetical profit figures noted earlier and the mean calculated from them. The five original observations are represented by the numbered blocks on top of the teeterboard; the $6 million mean is represented by the numbered fulcrum. The deviations from the mean are shown on the side of the board. Note how one observation of $4 million lies $2 million below the mean, while two observations of $2 million lie $4 million below the mean; hence, the negative deviations add to −$2 million −$4 million −$4 million = −$10 million. They are perfectly matched by the positive deviations from the mean of the $7 million and $15 million profit figures, the deviations of which come to +$1 million + $9 million = +$10 million.

Panel (b) shows how the arithmetic mean instantly responds to a change in even a single observation, such as a change from $15 million to $25 million. Indeed, the mean is so sensitive to extreme values that it can easily lie above or below the vast majority of individual observations! Contrary to what most people think, it is, therefore, quite possible for *most* people to weigh more than the average, be less intelligent than the average, or even be shorter than the average. The mean always remains a *central* value, however, in the sense that the sum of deviations of all observations from the mean equals zero. Nevertheless, and quite understandably, many people are confused when confronted with situations, such as that in panel (b), in which the vast majority of observations are to one side of the average. This situation is not what *average* denotes to them; they prefer to use an entirely different concept of central tendency, a concept to which we turn in the next section.

7.3 The Median

Another important measure of central tendency, quite different from the mean, is the *median* or *middle value* in an ordered array. It, too, can be calculated precisely from ungrouped data, or it can be approximated from grouped data.

DEFINITION 7.2 The **median** is a measure of central tendency that divides an ordered array of data into halves. If the data are arranged in ascending order from smallest to largest, all the observations below the median are smaller than or equal to it, while all the observations above the median are equal to it or larger. If the total number of observations is odd, the median is the middle observation in the ordered array; if the total number of observations is even, the median is the average of the two middle values.

CALCULATION FROM UNGROUPED DATA

Once again, consider the annual profits of five firms, such as those depicted in panel (a) of Figure 7.2. For the profit figures (in millions of dollars) of 2, 2, 4, 7, and 15, the median equals 4 because that number is located at the center of the ordered array. Two values lie above it; two values lie below it; their sizes do not matter.

If the array had been 2, 2, 4, 7, and 25, as in panel (b) of Figure 7.2, the median would still have been 4; and so it would have been for the array of 4, 4, 4, 4, and 25. Finding the median is easy when the total number of observations is *odd,* because in that case the ordered array will always contain a middle value above and below which an equal number of observations can be found.

However, when the number of observations is *even,* as in the series 2, 2, 4, 7, 15, and 25, there would seem to be two central values (of 4 and 7, in this example). In such a case, the two central values are averaged, and that average, here $(4 + 7)/2$ or 5.5, is designated as the median. In our example, three firms would earn less and three firms would earn more than the median: The values of 2, 2, and 4 would lie below 5.5, and those of 7, 15, and 25 would lie above it.

SYMBOLIC EXPRESSION

FORMULA 7.C | Median from Ungrouped Data (in an ordered array arranged in ascending order)

For a population:

$$M = X_{\frac{N+1}{2}}$$

For a sample:

$$m = X_{\frac{n+1}{2}}$$

where X is a population (or sample) value, N is the number of observations in the population, n is the number of observations in the sample, and the subscript refers to the position of X in the ordered array.

Note: If the subscript in Formula 7.C is a whole number, X corresponds to an actually observed population or sample value. Otherwise, X is an interpolated hypothetical value that lies between two actual values.

Denoting the median by M (the Greek capital mu) for a population and by m for a sample, we can express the definition of median symbolically as Formula 7.C, which holds for *both* odd-numbered and even-numbered data sets. The median, these formulas tell us, always equals the value of the middle observation in an ordered array. In our above *odd-numbered* sample of five profit figures, the median equals the value of observation

$$X_{\frac{5+1}{2}} = X_3$$

and the value of that third observation was 4.

What if there had been an *even-numbered* sample of 100 multinational-company profit figures? Then the median would equal the value of observation

$$X_{\frac{100+1}{2}} = X_{50.5}$$

which means it would equal the average of the 50th and 51st observations in the data set. Have a quick look at the ordered array of Table 6.3 on page 168, and this average can be identified as the mean of 1,086 and 1,170, or as 1,128. Half of all the profit figures were smaller and half were larger than this amount. Once again, however, modern computer programs can do the work for us.

EXCEL Example 7.2

Start EXCEL and retrieve the file HK100MN97 from the CD-ROM. Column E contains the total profit figures of those 100 multinational companies first listed in Table 4.1 on page 110. What is the *median* of these profit data?

SOLUTION Instead of applying Formula 7.C manually to the 100 numbers found in Table 6.2 on page 167, you can let EXCEL do the number crunching: After selecting the column E data, you can use one of two approaches:

APPROACH A

1. Click **Tools** > **Data Analysis** > **Descriptive Statistics** > **OK.**
2. In the *Descriptive Statistics* dialog box, enter *Input Range* **E1:E101,** check *Labels in First Row,* check *Summary Statistics,* and click **OK.**

   The median of **1,128** (million dollars) is listed along with many other data.

APPROACH B

1. On the standard toolbar, click the **Function Wizard (*fx*).**
2. In the *Paste Function* dialog box, under *Function category,* click **Statistical;** under *Function name,* click **MEDIAN** > **OK.**
3. In the box, enter **E2:E101** and click **OK.**

   The median of **1,128** (million dollars) appears at the head of column E.

CALCULATION FROM GROUPED DATA

Just as we can approximate the arithmetic mean from grouped data, we can also approximate the median. Consider Table 7.2 again. We can easily find the class that contains the median and is, therefore, called the **median class.** Because we have 100 observations, the median is the average of the 50th and 51st observations in an ordered array of the data. Since the table shows 6 + 49 = 55 observations in the first two classes, the median cannot lie in the first class, but can be found among the next 49 observations in the second class. Indeed, the median must be the average of the 44th and 45th observations in this median class, which correspond to the 50th and 51st observations among all the data. If we imagined all 49 observations in the second (and median) class to be equally spaced within the $1,250 million width of that class, each observation would be 25.51 units apart from the next one. If we further assumed that the first observation within the class was one-half this distance above the lower class limit, while the last observation within the class was one-half this distance below the upper limit, the 44th and 45th observations would equal $1,109.685 and $1,135.195, respectively. This would make their arithmetic mean—*and our approximation of the median*—equal to M = $1,122.44 million.

Other interpolation procedures are possible, but note that our procedure estimated the median within 1 percent of the correct figure of $1,128 million, which was determined in EXCEL or MINITAB Example 7.2. Our procedure is summarized by Formula 7.D.

FORMULA 7.D | Median from Grouped Data

For a population:

$$M = L + \frac{(N/2) - F}{f} w$$

For a sample:

$$m = L + \frac{(n/2) - F}{f} w$$

where L is the lower limit of the median class, f is its absolute frequency, and w is its width, while F is the sum of frequencies up to (but not including) those of the median class, N is the number of observations in the population, and n is the number of observations in the sample.

If we apply Formula 7.D to the Table 7.2 data, it produces a median estimate identical to the one made above:

$$0 + \frac{(100/2) - 6}{49} 1{,}250 = \frac{44}{49} 1{,}250 = 1{,}122.44$$

MEDIAN VERSUS MEAN

Although many people refer to both median and mean as averages, they are such in very different senses of the term. The arithmetic mean is an average of the observed values; the median is whatever value happens to be found at the average of all the *positions* in an ordered array. It is, for example, the value found at position (1 + 100) ÷ 2 = 50.5 among 100 ordered numbers. As a result, the mean can be algebraically manipulated in many ways; the median cannot. For example, if we know the means and the sizes of two populations, we can calculate their combined mean; yet we cannot calculate the combined median, given a knowledge of the medians and sizes of two populations. Consider the two populations, A and B:

A:	10	**17**	39					Mean: 22
B:	6	20	31	**57**	82	97	99	Mean: 56

The arithmetic means are 22 and 56, respectively; the medians are the boldfaced 17 and 57. We can easily calculate the combined mean as $[(3 \times 22) + (7 \times 56)] / 10 = 45.8$, knowing only the sizes of the two populations and their means. Yet we *cannot* calculate the combined median by a similar procedure, such as $[(3 \times 17) + (7 \times 57)] / 10 = 45$. The combined median is, in fact, not 45, but the average of the 5th and 6th values in an ordered array of the combined populations, or $(31 + 39) / 2 = 35$.

In spite of this disadvantage, the median is a better measure of central tendency than the mean when the data set contains a few extreme values, high or low. Consider these annual income figures of the families living on a certain street:

$15,000 $17,000 $17,000 **$18,000** 19,000 $19,000 $301,000

The arithmetic mean of these incomes equals $58,000, which certainly does not look like a very good summary of neighborhood incomes. The boldfaced median of $18,000, on the other hand, is much more representative. Indeed, the median is often called "democratic" because it gives each value, regardless of its size, an equal "vote" in determining the central location. In the above example, the three values below $18,000 have one vote each, the three values above $18,000 have one vote each, so $18,000 is the "winner." Unlike in the case of the arithmetic mean, the *sizes* of the individual values below or above the median are irrelevant for determining the median. In the presence of extreme values in a data set, the median is less likely to mislead us.

We can visualize the issue by reviewing Figure 7.2 on page 230. Under the influence of one extreme observation, the mean changes from 6 in panel (a) to 8 in panel (b), and the mean of 8 hardly seems representative of the panel (b) data. Yet the median in both panels equals 4.

7.4 The Mode

A third measure of central tendency, the *mode,* is simply the most frequently occurring value in a set of data. In both panels (a) and (b) of Figure 7.2, for example, the mode equals 2. Just as the expression to be "à la mode" means to be in fashion, the mode is the most "fashionable" value in a data set. If you were a retailer selling books or shoes or anything else for that matter, you would certainly want to identify the mode in order to plan your ideal inventory. Yet there are also reasons for *not* using the mode:

1. As the examples of Figure 7.2 suggest, the mode can easily be found at either extreme of a data set and can then be quite atypical of the majority of observations. Indeed, the mode in the Table 6.3 profit figures on page 168 equals $302 million, hardly a central figure in an ordered array that stretches from –$1,045 million to +$9,163 million.
2. Oftentimes a data set contains no mode at all, because no single observation occurs more than once.
3. At other times, a data set contains two modes or even a multitude of modes. (Consider a data set of 500 numbers in which 37 values occur twice and no value occurs more than twice. A listing of 37 modes would be pretty confusing.)

DEFINITION 7.3 Another measure of central tendency is the **mode;** it is the most frequently occurring value in a data set.

CALCULATION FROM GROUPED DATA

In the case of grouped data, the class containing the mode is the **modal class** and is the class with the highest frequency density. Consider Table 7.2 on page 229. The modal class is the second one, but several alternative ways of approximating the mode exist. One possibility is simply to designate the midpoint of the modal class, here $625 million, as the mode. Another possibility proceeds from the assumption that the mode will be closer to the adjacent class that has the greater frequency density, here closer to the third class (with 18 companies per $1,250 million range) than to the first class (with only 6 companies per $1,250 million range). A favorite formula for finding the mode based on the second alternative just described is Formula 7.E.

FORMULA 7.E | Mode from Grouped Data

For a population or sample:

$$\text{Mode} = L + \frac{d_1}{d_1 + d_2} w$$

where L is the lower limit of the modal class, w is its width, d_1 is the difference between the modal class frequency density and the (lower) density of the preceding class, and d_2 is the difference between the modal class frequency density and the (lower) density of the following class.

EXAMPLE PROBLEM 7.2

Calculate the *mode* of the profit data given in Table 7.2 on page 229.

SOLUTION: Using Formula 7.E, the mode equals $726.4 million:

$$\text{Mode} = 0 + \frac{49 - 6}{(49 - 6) + (49 - 18)} 1{,}250 = \frac{43}{74} 1{,}250 = 726.4$$

Note: Formula 7.E assumes that the mode is found in the modal class but is also "attracted" to the two adjacent classes by forces that are proportional to the frequency densities of these classes. But such a mode is highly unstable. It is likely to change with every change in the grouping of data.

THE MODE AND THE FREQUENCY CURVE

The mode can also be found on a smooth frequency curve as the value lying underneath its highest point. However, if two or more different values in a data set occur with the highest frequency, or almost that, two or more modes exist, and the data set is said to have a **multimodal frequency distribution.** This distribution shows up as two or more peaks on a frequency curve. Such a situation usually arises because the population or sample in question contains two or more groups that are fairly similar internally but differ significantly from each other. For purposes of statistical analysis, it is often wiser to study such groups separately.

Consider Figure 7.3. Panels (a) and (b) give two examples of the **bimodal frequency distribution,** so called because it contains *two* modes. Panel (a) portrays the frequency distribution of the heights of all the production workers in a large firm. Two modes are visible, at 5′2″ and 5′11″, but they reflect nothing more mysterious than the fact that the firm has an equal number of female and male workers, and that women tend to be shorter. To illustrate why we should usually study such groupings separately, imagine that someone compared the mean heights of production workers now and 50 years ago, when almost all the workers were male.

FIGURE 7.3 | Multimodal Frequency Distributions

Multipeaked frequency curves illustrate the presence of two or more modes and strongly suggest the existence of some nonhomogeneous factor in the underlying data set. Under such circumstances, any single measure of central location is likely to be misleading; it is advisable to describe the two or more underlying data sets separately.

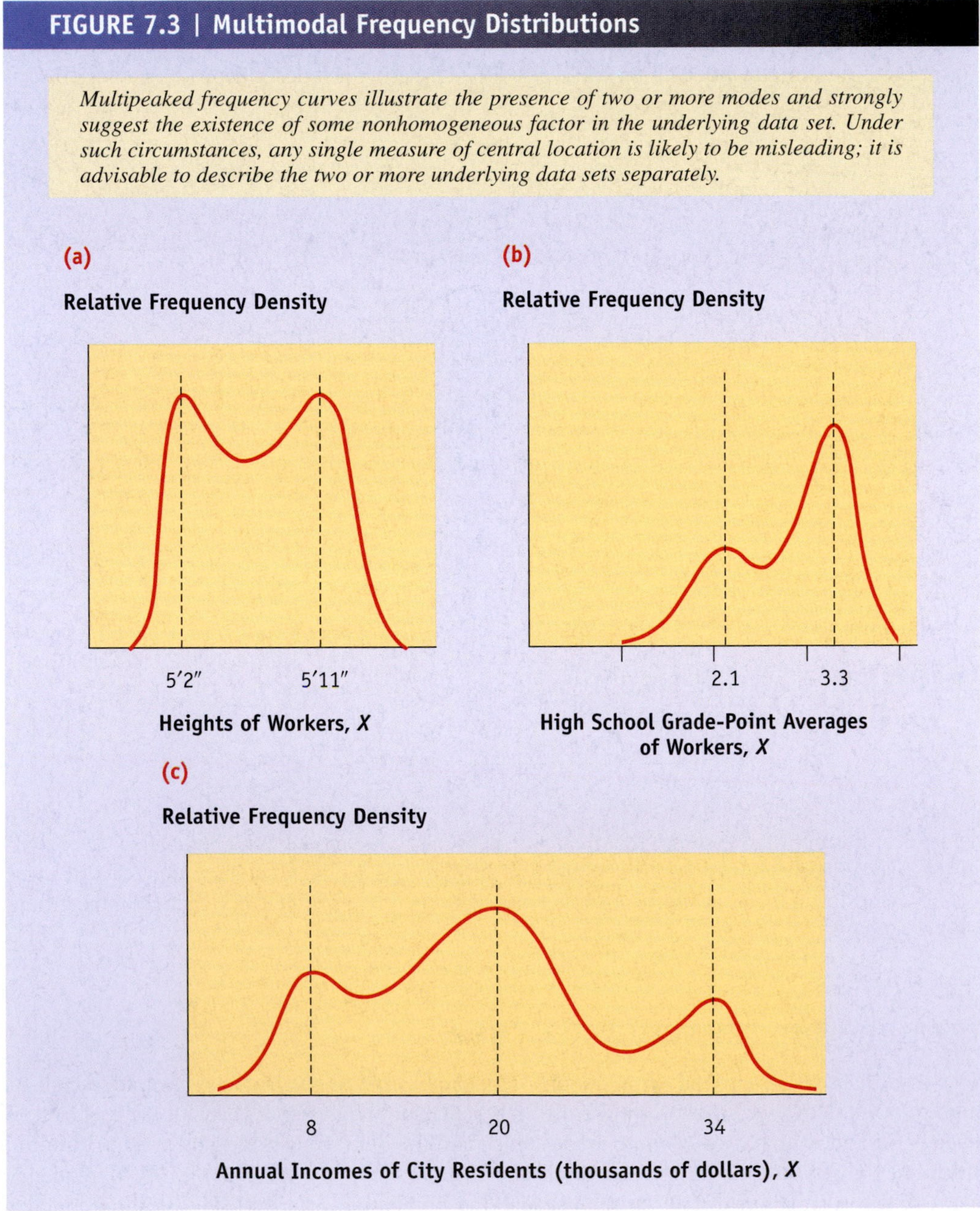

The apparent conclusion that workers had become shorter would be false, a fact that would become obvious if female workers of 50 years ago were compared with female workers now, while male workers then and now were also compared separately. The presence of more than one mode, therefore, is a warning signal to the investigator to exercise caution.

Panel (b) presents another example. It shows the frequency distribution of the high school grade-point averages of newly hired production workers. Humps in the distribution occur at 2.1 and 3.3. Although the frequency of the former is below that of the latter, which, strictly speaking, makes 3.3 the mode, we still refer to this distribution as bimodal. The reason might be that two groups of workers were hired: a large group of apparently highly qualified workers, a small group of seemingly unqualified workers. Yet the latter group may be given special training and be expected, eventually, to perform as well as the other on the production line. Once again, the presence of these heterogeneous groups suggests to an investigator, who might wish to compare early and later work performance, that these two groups should be studied separately. The mean performance at work of the entire group may hardly change over time; the mean performance at work of the small special-training group may improve dramatically over time.

Finally, panel (c) gives an example of an even more heterogeneous statistical population. The city's residents may, for example, fall into three distinct groups: the unemployed, unskilled laborers, and semiskilled workers. Their respective modal incomes of \$8,000, \$20,000, and \$34,000 per year may produce the three-peaked frequency curve shown when all of them are included in a single data set. Once again, such a graphical view of the data can help an investigator decide how to proceed with data analysis.

7.5 Other Measures of Central Tendency

Statisticians may well compute still other measures of central tendency, depending on what information their audiences need to have. Here we consider three that are commonly used: the *midrange,* the *trimmed mean,* and the *weighted mean.*

THE MIDRANGE

The **midrange** is the simplest possible summary of any data set. It equals the sum of a data set's minimum plus maximum values, divided by 2. In the case of our multinational-company profit data (summarized by the ordered array of Table 6.3 on page 168), the minimum value came to −\$1,045 million and the maximum to \$9,163 million. Therefore,

$$\text{midrange} = \frac{-\$1{,}045 \text{ million} + \$9{,}163 \text{ million}}{2} = \$4{,}059 \text{ million}$$

The midrange always lies precisely in the middle between a data set's minimum and maximum values, which implies one major disadvantage: the midrange is very sensitive to outliers. Add any unusually small or large value to a given data set and the midrange number will change drastically.

THE TRIMMED MEAN

The concept of the *trimmed mean* is specifically designed to eliminate the influence of outliers. The **trimmed mean** of a data set is its arithmetic mean after an equal percentage of smallest and largest observations have been deleted from its ordered array. Most computer programs calculate trimmed means; oftentimes, they produce a 5 percent trimmed mean after eliminating both the 5 percent smallest and 5 percent largest observations. In principle, however, one can compute many different types of trimmed means: 2 percent trimmed means, 10 percent trimmed means, and so on.

EXCEL Example 7.3

Start EXCEL and retrieve the file HK100MN97 from the CD-ROM. Column E contains the total profit figures of those 100 multinational companies first listed in Table 4.1 on page 110. What is the *5% trimmed mean* of these profit data?

SOLUTION

Instead of manually removing both the smallest and largest five numbers from the 100 numbers found in Table 6.3 on page 168, and then applying Formula 7.A to the remaining 90 numbers, you can let EXCEL do the number crunching:

1. After selecting the column E data, click the **Function Wizard (*fx*)** on the standard toolbar.
2. In the *Paste Function* dialog box, under *Function category,* click **Statistical;** under *Function name,* click **TRIMMEAN > OK.**
3. A dialog box requests two entries. Under *Array,* enter the range of values to be trimmed and averaged as **E2:E101.** Under *Percent,* enter the fraction of values to be *excluded* as **.1** and click **OK.** (You must enter a number between 0 and 1. Thus, if you enter .1, precisely 10% of all values in the ordered array will be excluded; 5% from the top and 5% from the bottom.)

The trimmed mean of **1,644.055556** (million dollars) appears at the head of column E.

THE WEIGHTED MEAN

The **weighted mean** is a measure of central tendency that gives unequal weights to different observations according to their unequal relative importance. As we learned in this chapter's Preview, the weighted mean is a special type of arithmetic mean, equal to the sum of the products of observed values and their respective weights, divided by the sum of weights. If a firm pays hourly wages of $5, $10, and $15 to different groups of workers, it would be unwise to conclude that its workers were earning, on the average, $10 per hour, unless equal numbers of workers were found in the three categories. If, however, there were 100 unskilled workers earning $5, 50 semiskilled workers earning $10, and 10 skilled workers earning $15, these numbers of workers should be used as weights to count $5 one hundred times, $10 fifty times, and $15 ten times.

In fact, the calculation of a weighted mean is a special case of the calculation of an arithmetic mean from grouped data. Therefore, Formula 7.B can be adapted for the purpose. The class frequencies, f, can be viewed as weights, while the total number of observations, N or n, can be used as the sum of these weights.

EXAMPLE PROBLEM 7.3

In a given firm, the hourly wage is $5 for 100 workers, $10 for 50 workers, and $15 for 10 workers. What is the average wage?

SOLUTION: The *weighted mean* equals

$$\frac{(100 \times \$5) + (50 \times \$10) + (10 \times \$15)}{100 + 50 + 10} = \frac{\$1{,}150}{160} = \$7.19$$

This result is a far cry from the unweighted arithmetic mean of $10 per hour.

7.6 Measures of Dispersion: An Overview

Knowing how data vary around their center of location is crucial in many situations. Consider someone about to decide which of two types of businesses to enter. Both types may promise the same median income, yet the incomes observed in one type of activity may be scattered widely about the median, while the incomes in the other type may fall within a relatively narrow range of the median. Depending on their attitudes toward risk (a matter we discuss at length in Chapter 23), different people will evaluate these two business prospects differently. Risk seekers will welcome a high variability of income: At the risk of getting a very low income, this high variability of income offers them a chance to get an exceptionally high income. Risk-averse people, on the other hand, will prefer the activity with a low variability of income. It offers them a middle-level income with near-certainty and offers them no chance for a very low or very high income. The importance of variability is reviewed in Figure 7.4 on the next page.

We can measure dispersion within a data set in two ways: as distances between selected observations or as average deviations of individual observations from a central value. Distance measures of dispersion include the *overall range* and all sorts of *interfractile ranges* in a data set that are defined with the help of *quartiles, deciles, percentiles,* and more. Average deviation measures include the *mean absolute deviation,* the *variance,* and the *standard deviation.* We consider all of these possibilities in turn.

7.7 The Range

The *overall range,* usually just called the **range,** equals the difference between the largest and smallest observation in a set of ungrouped data. For grouped data, it is the difference between the upper limit of the largest class and the lower limit of the smallest class and, therefore, cannot be determined at all if grouped data have open-ended classes. Thus, the range in our set of ungrouped profit figures listed in Table 6.3 on page 168 is

$$\$9{,}163 \text{ million} - (-\$1{,}045 \text{ million}) = \$10{,}208 \text{ million}$$

The 1997 net profits of the largest 100 U.S.-based multinationals, this number tells us, spread over a vast range, more than $10 billion wide. (Modern computer programs can quickly determine a data set's maximum and minimum values that allow you to compute the range.)

FIGURE 7.4 | The Importance of Variability

Even though two populations may have identical medians, the spread of observations around these central values may differ significantly. This spread of observations is likely to be a crucial factor in decision making. Thus, a risk-averse individual may prefer the Type A Business, which promises a less varied income, while a risk-seeking person may choose to enter the Type B Business just because it offers a chance of fairly large incomes, along with the danger of extremely low incomes.

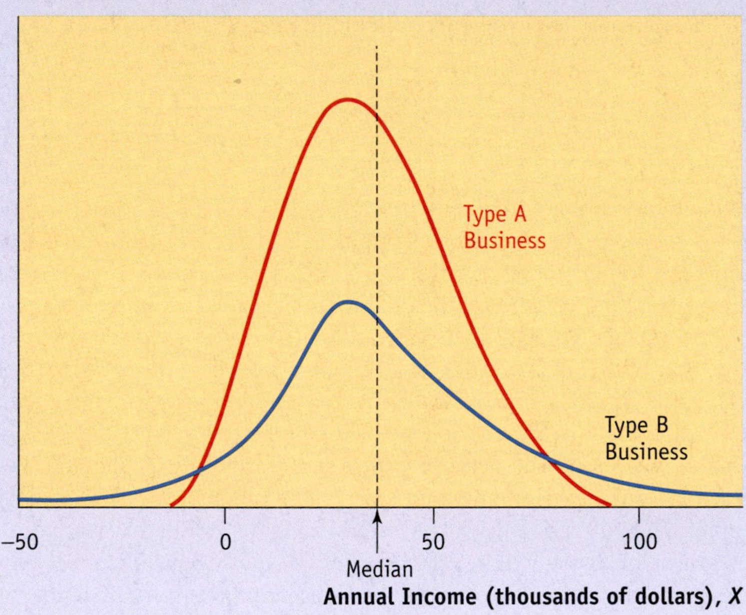

DISADVANTAGE The range measure of dispersion, however, has a major disadvantage: It ignores all the values except the two extremes. These extremes may be atypical not only among all the values in the data set, but even among the higher and lower values—which surely is the case here. As another look at Table 7.2 confirms (see page 229), 82 percent of all net profits are found in the much narrower \$3.75 billion-wide range between \$0 and \$3.75 billion. This problem becomes more serious still when the range is calculated from the corresponding grouped data, also found in Table 7.2. Here the range appears to be even larger, equaling \$10,000 million − (−\$1,250 million) = \$11,250 million.

7.8 Interfractile Ranges

Popular measures of dispersion within a data set other than the overall range include a variety of **interfractile ranges,** which measure differences between two values called *fractiles* or *percentiles.*

DEFINITION 7.4 Any value in a data set such that a specified *proportion* of all values is smaller than or at most equal to it is called a **fractile;** any value such that a specified *percentage* of all values is smaller than or at most equal to it is called a **percentile.**

INTERFRACTILE RANGES DEFINED BY QUARTILES

We have already met the most popular fractile (or percentile) when discussing the *median* earlier in this chapter. The median equals the 0.50 fractile (or the 50th percentile) because half (or 50 percent) of all values in a data set are smaller than or at most equal to it. After the median, the most common fractiles or percentiles used are the **quartiles,** which divide the array of all observations into four quarters, each of which contains 0.25 (or 25 percent) of the observed values. The 0.25 fractile (or 25th percentile) is called the **first quartile,** and a quarter (or 25 percent) of all values are smaller than or at most equal to it. As just noted, the median itself is the **second quartile.** Last but not least, the 0.75 fractile (or 75th percentile) is referred to as the **third quartile,** and three quarters (or 75 percent) of all values are smaller than or at most equal to it.

Most popular among interfractile ranges is the **interquartile range** (also known as the **H-spread** in the context of last chapter's box-and-whisker diagrams), which is the difference between the third and first quartiles and, hence, is the range containing the middle 50 percent of all values observed. Formula 7.F summarizes how the relevant quartile values are found. The subsequent examples illustrate how this formula is used.

FORMULA 7.F | Quartiles from Ungrouped Data (in an ordered array arranged in ascending order)

For a population:

$$Q_1 = X_{\frac{N+1}{4}} \quad \text{and} \quad Q_3 = X_{3\left(\frac{N+1}{4}\right)}$$

For a sample:

Replace population size, N, by sample size, n

where X is a population (or sample) value, N is the number of observations in the population, n is the number of observations in the sample, and the subscript refers to the position of X in the ordered array.

Note: If the subscript is a whole number, X corresponds to an actually observed population or sample value. Otherwise, X is an interpolated hypothetical value that lies between two actual values.

EXAMPLE PROBLEM 7.4

Review the 100 profit data of Table 6.3 on page 168. Determine (a) the first quartile, (b) the third quartile, and (c) the interquartile range.

SOLUTION:

a. According to Formula 7.F, the first quartile of the 100 ordered data equals

$$Q_1 = X_{\frac{100+1}{4}} = X_{25.25}$$

which is a value somewhere between the 25th and 26th observation in the array. Different computer programs handle this matter differently. Some merely round the subscript to the nearest integer, here 25, and call the 25th observation in the array, here $454 million, the *first quartile.* Others interpolate and designate a hypothetical value as first quartile, in this case, a value that lies above the 25th observation 0.25 times the distance between the 25th and 26th observations. (This would produce a first quartile of $455 million in this example.)

b. According to Formula 7.F, the third quartile of the 100 ordered data equals

$$Q_3 = X_{3\left(\frac{100+1}{4}\right)} = X_{75.75}$$

which is a value somewhere between the 75th and 76th observation in the array. Different computer programs handle this matter differently. Some merely round the subscript to the nearest integer, here 76, and call the 76th observation in the array, here $2,603 million, the *third quartile.* Others interpolate and designate a hypothetical value as third quartile, in this case, a value that lies above the 75th observation 0.75 times the distance between the 75th and 76th observations. (This would produce a third quartile of $2,598.75 million in this example, which might be rounded to the nearest integer.)

c. The *interquartile range* equals

$$Q_3 - Q_1 = \$2{,}603 \text{ million} - \$454 \text{ million} = \$2{,}149 \text{ million}$$

by the first of the two procedures noted. It equals

$$Q_3 - Q_1 = \$2{,}598.75 \text{ million} - \$455 \text{ million} = \$2{,}143.75 \text{ million}$$

by the second of the two procedures.

EXCEL Example 7.4

Start EXCEL and retrieve the file HK100MN97 from the CD-ROM. Column E contains the total profit figures of those 100 multinational companies first listed in Table 4.1 on page 110. Find the *three quartiles* of these profit data.

SOLUTION

1. After selecting the column E data, click the **Function Wizard (*fx*)** on the standard toolbar.
2. In the *Paste Function* dialog box, under *Function category,* click **Statistical;** under *Function name,* click **QUARTILE > OK.**
3. A dialog box requests two entries. Under *Array,* enter the range of values to be used as **E2:E101.** Under *Quart,* enter the quartile to be computed, such as **1,** and click **OK.** The first quartile of **457** (million dollars) appears at the head of column E.

4. Repeat the procedure for the second quartile or median by entering **2** in Step 3. The second quartile of **1,128** (million dollars) appears at the head of column E, just as in EXCEL Example 7.2.
5. Repeat the procedure for the third quartile by entering **3** in Step 3. The third quartile of **2,590.25** (million dollars) appears at the head of column E.

INTERFRACTILE RANGES DEFINED BY DECILES

Sometimes, statisticians decide to convey additional information by constructing interfractile ranges with the help of **deciles**—the values in a data set that divide the array of all observations into 10 parts rather than into 4 parts, as quartiles do, or into 100 parts, as percentiles do. Each part then contains 0.10 (or 10 percent) of the observed values. Thus, the range between the 1st and 9th deciles (or the 0.10 and 0.90 fractiles or the 10th and 90th percentiles) contains the middle 80 percent of all values observed. In the center of that range lies the 5th decile, which is yet another name for the median.

EXAMPLE PROBLEM 7.5

Review the 100 profit data of Table 6.3 on page 168. Determine (a) the first decile, (b) the ninth quartile, and (c) the 0.1 to 0.9 interfractile range.

SOLUTION:

a. In analogy to Formula 7.F, the first decile of the 100 ordered data equals

$$D_1 = X_{\frac{100+1}{10}} = X_{10.1}$$

which is a value somewhere between the 10th and 11th observation in the array. Different computer programs handle this matter differently. Some merely round the subscript to the nearest integer, here 10, and call the 10th observation in the array, here $114 million, the *first decile.*

b. In analogy to Formula 7.F, the ninth decile of the 100 ordered data equals

$$D_9 = X_{9\left(\frac{100+1}{10}\right)} = X_{90.9}$$

which is a value somewhere between the 90th and 91st observation in the array. Different computer programs handle this matter differently. Some merely round the subscript to the nearest integer, here 91, and call the 91st observation in the array, here $4,777 million, the *ninth decile.*

c. The *0.1 to 0.9 interfractile range* equals

$$D_9 - D_1 = \$4{,}777 \text{ million} - \$114 \text{ million} = \$4{,}663 \text{ million}$$

DISADVANTAGES OF DISTANCE MEASURES

All the distance measures of dispersion share a common disadvantage: They do not take all observations into account. Many values within or outside the specified range are totally ignored. In contrast, *average* deviation measures of dispersion do take all observations into account. The following sections explain.

7.9 The Mean Absolute Deviation

In order not to ignore a single observed value, we might be tempted to calculate how much each individual observation, X, deviates from some central value, such as μ or $\overline{X}$, and then to combine these deviations by averaging them. However, averaging deviations from the arithmetic mean necessarily produces a result of zero, as a review of Definition 7.1 or of Figure 7.2 (the seesaws) can quickly remind us. Consider the five numbers 2, 2, 4, 7, and 15. Their arithmetic mean equals 6. Subtracting this mean from each value yields deviations of -4, -4, -2, $+1$, and $+9$, as panel (a) of Figure 7.2 shows. These deviations sum to and, therefore, average to 0.

We can overcome this difficulty by realizing that the objective is merely to find the average distance of all the data from their center. For this purpose, it is irrelevant whether the individual data lie above or below the center. Hence, positive and negative deviations can be treated alike. We can ignore all those plus and minus signs, and we can average all the *absolute* values of the deviations of individual observations from the mean. We indicate such use of absolute values symbolically by placing vertical lines before and after each deviation value. In this example, this procedure yields

$$\frac{|2-6| + |2-6| + |4-6| + |7-6| + |15-6|}{5} = \frac{4+4+2+1+9}{5} = 4$$

which means that the five individual observations vary from their mean of 6 by an average distance of 4. This result has a special name: the *mean absolute deviation.*

DEFINITION 7.5 The **mean absolute deviation (MAD)** is an average measure of dispersion in a data set. It equals the arithmetic mean of all the absolute differences between each individual observation and the data set's mean (or, sometimes, median).

Formula 7.G provides a symbolic expression of this measure; the subsequent example shows how one can use a computer to put this formula to use.

FORMULA 7.G | Mean Absolute Deviation from Ungrouped Data

For a population:

$$\text{MAD} = \frac{\Sigma|X-\mu|}{N}$$

For a sample:

$$\text{MAD} = \frac{\Sigma|X-\overline{X}|}{n}$$

where the numerators are the sums of the absolute differences between each observed population (or sample) value, X, and the population mean, μ (or sample mean, $\overline{X}$), while N is the number of observations in the population, and n is the number of observations in the sample.

Note: For grouped data, denoting absolute class frequencies by f and class midpoints by X, substitute $\Sigma f|X - \mu|$ or $\Sigma f|X - \overline{X}|$ for the numerators given here. Occasionally, absolute deviations from the median rather than the mean are calculated, in which case μ is replaced by M and $\overline{X}$ is replaced by m.

EXCEL Example 7.5

Start EXCEL and retrieve the file HK100MN97 from the CD-ROM. Column E contains the total profit figures of those 100 multinational companies first listed in Table 4.1 on page 110. What is the *mean absolute deviation* of these profit data?

SOLUTION Instead of applying Formula 7.G formula manually to the 100 numbers found in Table 6.3 on page 168, you can let EXCEL do the number crunching:

1. After selecting the column E data, click the **Function Wizard (*fx*)** on the standard toolbar.
2. In the *Paste Function* dialog box, under *Function category,* click **Statistical;** under *Function name,* click **AVEDEV > OK.**
3. In the dialog box, enter the range of values to be used as **E2:E101** and click **OK.**

The MAD statistic of **1,533.1464** (million dollars) appears at the head of column E.

7.10 The Variance

A much more common measure of dispersion, which we calculate by averaging the *squares* of the individual deviations from the mean, is the *mean of squared deviations,* also called the *variance.*

When the variance is calculated from a statistical population, it is symbolized by σ^2 (the letter σ is the lowercase Greek *sigma,* and σ^2 is pronounced "sigma squared"). When the variance refers to sample data, it is denoted by s^2 instead, in line with the common procedure of labeling parameters by Greek letters and statistics by Roman letters.

DEFINITION 7.6 The **variance** is an average measure of dispersion in a data set. For a population, it is constructed by taking the difference between each observed value and the population mean, squaring each of these deviations, and then finding the arithmetic mean of the squared values. For a sample, a roughly analogous expression is constructed with the help of the sample mean.

CALCULATION FROM UNGROUPED DATA

Formula 7.H provides alternative symbolic expressions of this variance measure; they are mathematically equivalent. The subsequent examples show how we can put the formula to use. Note that Formula 7.H contains one surprise: The *sample* variance is obtained by dividing the sum of the squared deviations of individual sample values, X, from the sample mean, $\bar{X}$, by $n - 1$ rather than by the sample size, n. The reason, to be explained in Chapter 12, is that this procedure makes the sample variance, s^2, a more accurate estimator of the usually unknown population variance, σ^2.

FORMULA 7.H | Variance from Ungrouped Data

For a population:

$$\sigma^2 = \frac{\Sigma(X - \mu)^2}{N} = \frac{\Sigma X^2 - N\mu^2}{N}$$

For a sample:

$$s^2 = \frac{\Sigma(X - \bar{X})^2}{n - 1} = \frac{\Sigma X^2 - n\bar{X}^2}{n - 1}$$

where the numerators equal the sum of squared deviations between each population (or sample) value, X, and the population mean, μ (or sample mean, $\bar{X}$), with N being the number of observations in the population, and n being the number of observations in the sample.

EXAMPLE PROBLEM 7.6

Review the five population values appearing in panel (a) of Figure 7.2 on page 230. Calculate their *variance.*

SOLUTION: See Table 7.3.

Applying Formula 7.H, we find

$$\sigma^2 = \frac{\Sigma(X - \mu)^2}{N} = \frac{118}{5} = 23.6$$

Note how the process of squaring the deviations of each observed value from the population mean has two consequences: First, it eliminates negative values and thus produces a measure of

TABLE 7.3 | Calculating the Variance for a Population of $N = 5$ Values

Observed Values X	Population Mean $\mu = \frac{\Sigma X}{N}$	Deviations $X - \mu$	Squared Deviations $(X - \mu)^2$
2	6	−4	16
2	6	−4	16
4	6	−2	4
7	6	+1	1
15	6	+9	81
			$\Sigma(X - \mu)^2 = 118$

dispersion that focuses on the size of deviations from the mean rather than their direction. Second, it emphasizes large deviations more than small ones; for example, a 9 squared counts not 9 times, but 81 times as much as a 1 squared.

EXCEL Example 7.6

Start EXCEL and retrieve the file HK100MN97 from the CD-ROM. Column E contains the population of total profit figures for those 100 multinational companies first listed in Table 4.1 on page 110. What is the *population variance* of these profit data?

SOLUTION Instead of applying Formula 7.H manually to the 100 numbers found in Table 6.3 on page 168, you can let EXCEL do the number crunching:

1. After selecting the column E data, click the **Function Wizard (*fx*)** on the standard toolbar.
2. In the *Paste Function* dialog box, under *Function category,* click **Statistical;** under *Function name,* click **VARP > OK.**
3. In the dialog box, enter the range of values to be used as **E2:E101** and click **OK.**

The population variance of **4,208,014.8** (million squared dollars) appears at the head of column E.

CALCULATION FROM GROUPED DATA

The variance, too, can be estimated from grouped data by the now-familiar procedure of using class midpoints and class frequencies, as shown in Formula 7.I.

FORMULA 7.I | Variance from Grouped Data

For a population:

$$\sigma^2 = \frac{\Sigma f(X - \mu)^2}{N} = \frac{\Sigma f X^2 - N\mu^2}{N}$$

For a sample:

$$s^2 = \frac{\Sigma f(X - \overline{X})^2}{n - 1} = \frac{\Sigma f X^2 - n\overline{X}^2}{n - 1}$$

where absolute class frequencies are denoted by f, class midpoints of grouped population or sample values by X, the population mean by μ, the sample mean by $\overline{X}$, and the number of observations in the population (or sample) by N (or n).

TABLE 7.4 | Approximation of the Population Variance from Grouped Data

This table illustrates how closely one can approximate the true variance of ungrouped data (such as that computed in EXCEL or MINITAB Example 7.6) with the help of corresponding grouped data. Compare the approximation calculated on the next page with the precise calculation of 4,208,015 million squared dollars found earlier.

Class (net profit in millions of dollars)	Absolute Class Frequency (number of companies in class) f	Class Midpoint X	fX	X^2	fX^2
−1,250 to under 0	6	−625	−3,750	390,625	2,343,750
0 to under 1,250	49	625	30,625	390,625	19,140,625
1,250 to under 2,500	18	1,875	33,750	3,515,625	63,281,250
2,500 to under 3,750	15	3,125	46,875	9,765,625	146,484,375
3,750 to under 5,000	3	4,375	13,125	19,140,625	57,421,875
5,000 to under 6,250	2	5,625	11,250	31,640,625	63,281,250
6,250 to under 7,500	4	6,875	27,500	47,265,625	189,062,500
7,500 to under 8,750	2	8,125	16,250	66,015,625	132,031,250
−8,750 to under 10,000	1	9,375	9,375	87,890,625	87,890,625
	$N = 100$		$\Sigma fX = 185{,}000$		$\Sigma fX^2 = 760{,}937{,}500$

EXAMPLE PROBLEM 7.7

Review the absolute frequency distribution of Table 6.4 on page 171. In the absence of additional information, use Formula 7.I to *estimate* the population variance of the net profit data.

SOLUTION: See Table 7.4.

Based on the ratio 185,000/100, the *arithmetic mean*, μ, is estimated as \$1,850 million.

The variance is estimated as

$$\sigma^2 = \frac{760{,}937{,}500 - 100(1{,}850)^2}{100} = \frac{418{,}687{,}500}{100} = 4{,}186{,}875 \text{ million squared dollars}$$

However, as the next example shows, such awkward calculations can easily be left to the computer.

EXCEL Example 7.7

Rework the computations shown in Table 7.4 with the help of EXCEL.

SOLUTION

1. Fire up EXCEL and assume that the raw profit data are not available on the CD-ROM. Label B1:E1 with **f, X, fX,** and **fX^2.** Then enter the Table 7.4 frequencies in B2:B10 and the class midpoints in C2:C10.
2. In D2, enter **=B2*C2** and drag the entry to D10. This reproduces the **fX** column.
3. In E2, enter **=B2*C2^2** and drag the entry to E10. This reproduces the **fX**^{2} column.
4. Type **SUM** in A11; then enter the sums of columns B, D, and E in that row. (In each case, simply click on the column head and note the sum that is displayed in the last row of the EXCEL worksheet.)
5. Click G5 and type the population variance formula for grouped data into the formula bar: **=(SUM(E2:E10)−100*1850^2)/100** and press **Enter.**

The result appears in G5 as **4,186,875** (million squared dollars).

PRACTICAL PROBLEMS

Unfortunately, two practical problems arise with the use of the variance concept. First, the variance tends to be a large number compared to the original values whose spread it is meant to describe. When the original observations are equal to a few million units, their variance can easily equal trillions of units. Second and worse yet, the variance, being a squared number, is not expressed in the same units as the observed values themselves. Thus, the variance of our profit population is not expressed in *dollars,* but in *squared* dollars. In fact, as we have just seen, it equals 4.2 trillion squared dollars and who knows the meaning of that? But there is good news as well: Both of the conceptual difficulties just cited can be overcome in one fell swoop by working with the square root of the variance, a concept to which we now turn.

7.11 The Standard Deviation

The most important summary measure of dispersion is derived from the variance. Called the **standard deviation,** it equals the positive square root of the variance. By adapting Formulas 7.H and 7.I, the standard deviation, like the variance, can be calculated for ungrouped or grouped data. Thus, we compute

$$\text{population standard deviation, } \sigma = \sqrt{\sigma^2}$$

and

$$\text{sample standard deviation, } s = \sqrt{s^2}$$

Any standard deviation measure has one immediate advantage over the variance: It falls in the same range of magnitude as, and appears in the same units as, the observations themselves. Thus, the population standard deviation for EXCEL or MINITAB Example 7.6 equals

$$\sigma = \sqrt{4{,}208{,}015 \text{ million squared dollars}} = 2{,}051.34 \text{ million dollars}$$

which is a much more comprehensible number than the variance.

The special significance of the standard deviation is illustrated in the following sections by three of its manifold uses: describing the normal frequency distribution, applying Chebyshev's theorem, and comparing the degree of dispersion among different data sets.

DESCRIBING THE NORMAL FREQUENCY DISTRIBUTION

In Chapter 10 there is a detailed discussion of the **normal frequency distribution.** This distribution describes a special type of population whose relative frequency density is characterized by three features:

- It is single-peaked above the population's mean, median, and mode, which coincide.
- It is perfectly symmetric about this central value.
- It has tails extending indefinitely in both directions from the center, approaching, but never touching, the horizontal axis.

As a matter of fact, panel (a) of Figure 6.5 on page 187 described a somewhat similar case; that figure's perfectly symmetrical and peaked histogram is reproduced by the blocks in Figure 7.5

FIGURE 7.5 | The Normal Frequency Distribution

When population values are distributed according to the color normal curve shown here, certain conditions hold: (1) mean, median, and mode coincide at the center of the distribution and (2) predictable percentages of all population values lie within ±1, ±2, and ±3 standard deviations from the mean. These percentages equal roughly 68, 95, and 100; they can be applied even when the frequency curve is only roughly normal, a procedure known as the ***empirical rule.***

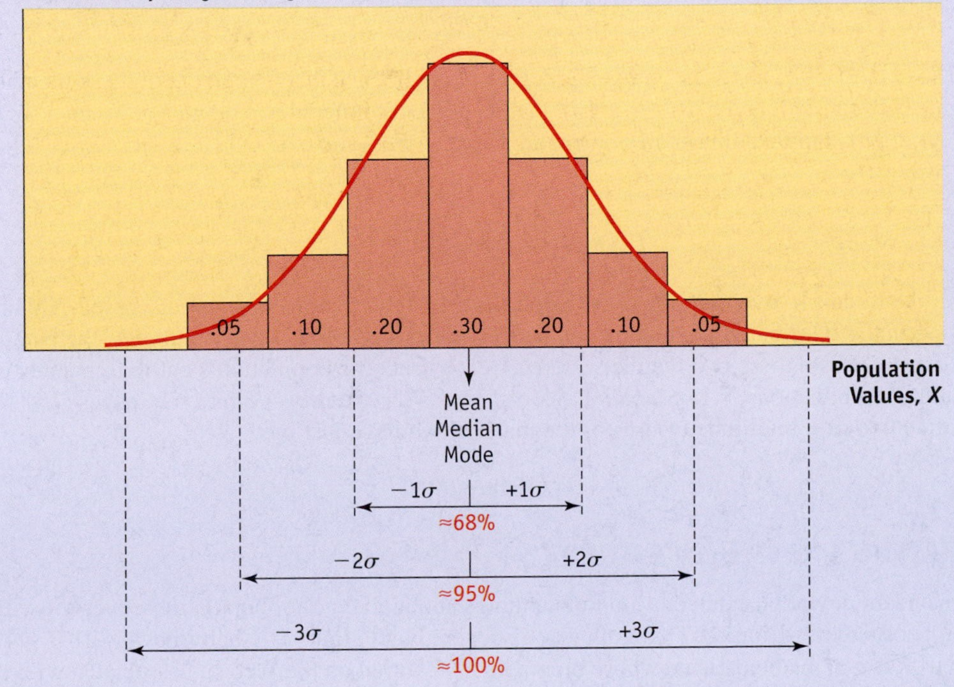

here. The histogram's shape is nicely approximated by the color frequency curve, also called a **normal curve,** because it has the three characteristics of the normal frequency distribution just defined. Note how the bell-shaped curve peaks above the mean, median, and mode, is perfectly symmetrical, and steadily approaches the horizontal axis as it moves away from the center. All this brings us to the main point: Whenever a population is correctly described by a normal curve, we can predict the precise percentages of population values that fall within any given number of standard deviations from the mean. Some 68.3 percent of all observations will then lie within the range of $\mu \pm 1\sigma$, that is, within one standard deviation of the mean. Similarly, some 95.4 percent of population values will lie within the range of $\mu \pm 2\sigma$, and 99.7 percent will lie within $\mu \pm 3\sigma$.

Even when population data are described by a slightly different frequency curve that does not precisely meet the strict requirements of the normal curve, one will not be far off in using its mean and standard deviation for making similar estimates, a condition known as the *empirical rule.*

DEFINITION 7.7 Whenever a statistical population can be described, at least roughly, by the perfectly symmetrical, bell-shaped normal curve, we can use the **empirical rule** to estimate the percentages of all population values that lie within specified numbers of standard deviations from the mean: Approximately 68 percent of all values lie within 1 standard deviation from the mean; about 95 percent lie within 2 standard deviations from the mean; and practically all values lie within 3 standard deviations from the mean.

EXAMPLE PROBLEM 7.8

The heights of male production workers in a large firm are roughly distributed like a *normal curve,* with a mean of $\mu = 5'8''$ and a standard deviation of $\sigma = 2''$. Apply the empirical rule.

SOLUTION: We can assert with a fair degree of confidence that 68 percent of these men have heights between 5′6″ and 5′10″ ($\mu \pm 1\sigma$), that 95 percent of them have heights between 5′4″ and 6′0″ ($\mu \pm 2\sigma$), and that almost all of them are between 5′2″ and 6′2″ tall ($\mu \pm 3\sigma$).

It is difficult to overemphasize the importance of the relationships just discussed. Think of it: A normally distributed population can be fully described by just two numbers—the parameters μ and σ. From these two numbers, we can reconstruct the population's entire frequency distribution! Applications 7.1, *Standard Scores,* and 7.2, *Control Charts,* on pages 254–256 illustrate two of a multitude of uses of the material we have just met.

APPLYING CHEBYSHEV'S THEOREM

The standard deviation can tell us important things about all types of populations, even those that are *not* normally distributed. This truth was discovered by Pafnuty L. Chebyshev (1821–1894), a famous Russian mathematician whose biography is featured on the Web site associated with this text and who stated an important theorem:

DEFINITION 7.8 According to **Chebyshev's theorem,** regardless of the shape of a population's frequency distribution, the proportion of observations falling within k standard deviations of the mean is at least

$$1 - \frac{1}{k^2}$$

given that k equals 1 or more.

The theorem implies consequences such as those shown in Table 7.5.

TABLE 7.5 | Implications of Chebyshev's Theorem

If the number of standard deviations, k, equals	then the proportion of all observations lying within the range of $\mu \pm k\sigma$ equals *at least*
1	$1 - (1/1^2) = 0$
2	$1 - (1/2^2) = 0.75$
3	$1 - (1/3^2) = 0.89$
4	$1 - (1/4^2) = 0.94$

Notice that Chebyshev's predictions are much more conservative than those of the empirical rule that are summarized in Figure 7.5 and Definition 7.7. The empirical rule substitutes "about 0.68" for Chebyshev's "at least 0" and "about 0.95" for "at least 0.75" and "about 1.00" for "at least 0.89."

EXAMPLE PROBLEM 7.9

Show that Chebyshev's theorem is vindicated by the net profit data of Table 6.3 on page 168. (The data's mean and standard deviation, respectively, were calculated as \$1,848.9 million and \$2,051.34 million earlier in this chapter.)

SOLUTION:

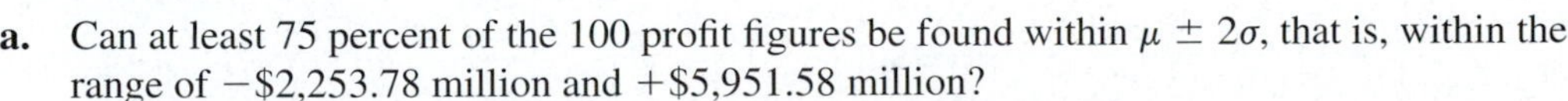

a. Can at least 75 percent of the 100 profit figures be found within $\mu \pm 2\sigma$, that is, within the range of $-\$2,253.78$ million and $+\$5,951.58$ million?

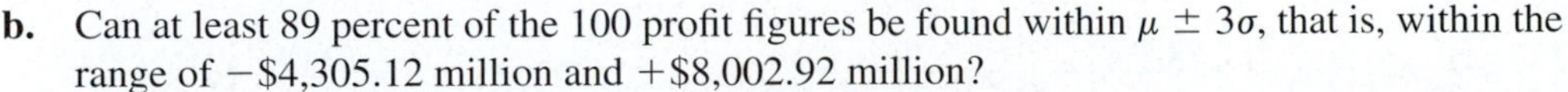

b. Can at least 89 percent of the 100 profit figures be found within $\mu \pm 3\sigma$, that is, within the range of $-\$4,305.12$ million and $+\$8,002.92$ million?

c. Can at least 94 percent of the 100 profit figures be found within $\mu \pm 4\sigma$, that is, within the range of $-\$6,356.46$ million and $+\$10,054.26$ million?

As a look at Table 6.3 attests, the answers are *yes* in all cases. In fact, the answers provided by Chebyshev's theorem are most conservative; the actual percentages of observations found within these ranges are 92, 97, and 100, respectively, in this example.

APPLICATION 7.1

STANDARD SCORES

As we have just noted, one of the significant features of the standard deviation is the fact that it can be used to describe the precise percentage of observations falling within various ranges from the mean, provided the frequency distribution fits the so-called *normal curve,* such as the one introduced in Figure 7.5. Now consider Figure 7.A.

This graph shows a hypothetical normal distribution of aptitude test scores, such as the familiar SAT scores, with a mean score of $\mu = 500$ and a standard deviation of $\sigma = 100$. As a result of the normal distribution of the population of scores, 68.3 percent of all scores lie between 400 and 600 (that is, within 1 standard deviation of the mean), 95.4 percent of all scores lie between 300 and 700 (within 2 standard deviations of the mean), and 99.7 percent of all scores lie between 200 and 800 (within 3 standard deviations of the mean). As we will discuss at length in Chapter 10, it is also true that 68.3 percent of the *area* under a normal curve lies within 1 standard deviation of the mean, while 95.4 and 99.7 percent of the area, respectively, lie within 2 and 3 standard deviations.

To enable easy comparisons among normal distributions of different types of populations—be they test scores, heights, weights, or wages—we must first convert any observed value into a **standard score.** That score measures the distance between any particular observation in a data set and the mean of all observations in terms of so many standard deviations. As is indicated underneath the graph in Figure 7.A, the standard score, z, equals the difference between an observed value, X, and the mean, μ, divided by the standard deviation, σ. Thus, a z-score always shows how many standard deviations *away from the mean* a corresponding X score is located.

$$\text{Standard Score:} \quad z = \frac{X - \mu}{\sigma}$$

In this example, with $\mu = 500$ and $\sigma = 100$, someone scoring $X = 300$ has a standard score of $z = -2$, because $(300 - 500) \div 100 = -2$. Such a score lies below 50 percent of all scores (the area under the right half of the bell-shaped curve) and also below an additional $(95.4/2) = 47.7$ percent of all scores (the area under the left side of the bell between the mean and $X = 300$). Thus, a score of $X = 300$ lies below 97.7 percent of all scores.

Can you see, similarly, why a score of 800 would correspond to a standard score of $+3$ and would lie above 99.85 percent of all scores? Why someone with standard scores of $+0.5$ on the weight distribution and -1 on the wage distribution would be heavier and less well paid than the average person whose weight and wages were plotted?

FIGURE 7.A

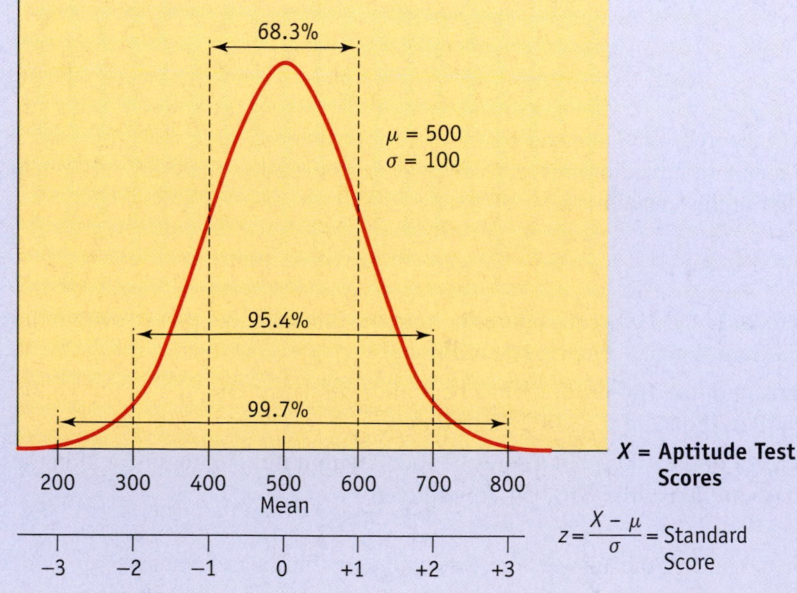

APPLICATION 7.2

CONTROL CHARTS

Business managers know that an inherent amount of variability exists in any data series, whether the series describes the sugar content of bottled drinks; the extent of clerical errors; the size of inventories, labor costs, or advertising expenses; or even the loss rate of old customers. Graphical devices, called **control charts,** such as those shown in Figure 7.B, highlight the average performance of data series and the dispersion around this average. They were introduced in 1924 by Walter A. Shewhart of the Bell Telephone Laboratories and are discussed at much greater length in Chapter 22, *Quality Control.*

In control charts, the average performance of the past is viewed as a standard by which to compare current performance, and the typical dispersion of the past is used to set allowable limits for current performance. When plotting new data, it becomes immediately obvious whether they fall within the expected range or whether there are undesirable trends that need the immediate attention of the manager.

Note how all the data series in Figure 7.B, except panels (c) and (e), proceed within normal limits of, say, ± 2 standard deviations from the average observed over some

FIGURE 7.B

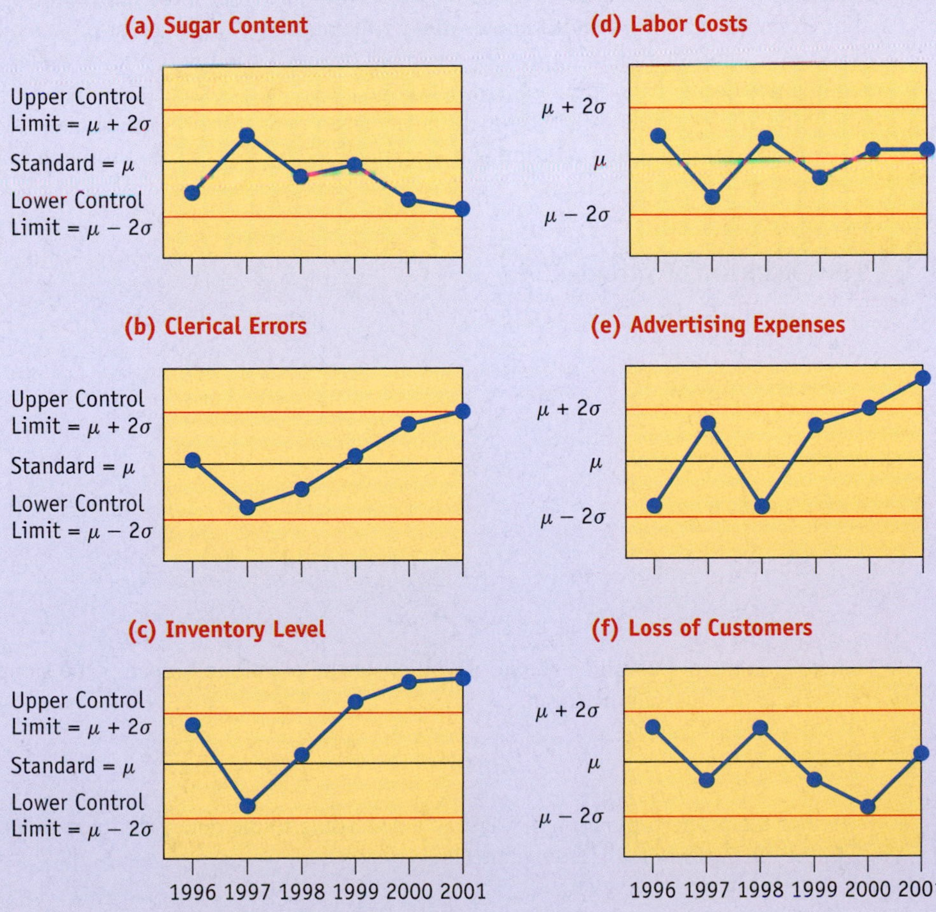

(continued)

Application 7.2 (continued)

past period. Managers would waste their time if they worried about the recent decrease observed in series (a) or the recent increase in series (f). Both these changes are still within the upper and lower control limits of $\mu \pm 2\sigma$. Managers would be well advised, however, to pay special attention to series (c) and (e), which have broken through the limits and are, thus, "out of control." Managers might even consider checking up on series (b), which seems to be exhibiting a lengthy undesirable trend.

Note, finally, that it is unimportant how the original data of the various series are measured—whether, for example, sugar content is measured in milligrams per bottle or milligrams per cubic inch and whether advertising expenses are expressed in dollars per million bottles sold or dollars per year. Control charts require only that the data of each series, however originally measured, be converted into "standard scores" defined by their own means and standard deviations.

COMPARING THE DEGREE OF DISPERSION OF DIFFERENT DATA SETS

Sometimes we may want to compare the variability of two or more data series with one another. For example, we may want to know whether the *domestic* revenues or profits of the 100 largest U.S.-based multinational companies are more or less varied than the revenues or profits these companies derive from their *foreign* operations. For such comparisons, we can use the ratio of the standard deviation to the arithmetic mean as an indicator of *relative* dispersion. This ratio is called the **coefficient of variation** and is symbolized by V (or v), as shown in Formula 7.J.

FORMULA 7.J | The Coefficient of Variation

For a population:

$$V = \frac{\sigma}{\mu}$$

For a sample:

$$v = \frac{s}{\bar{X}}$$

where σ is the population standard deviation, μ the population mean, s the sample standard deviation, and $\bar{X}$ the sample mean.

For the profit population of Table 6.3, according to the data just noted in Example Problem 7.9, the *coefficient of variation* comes to

$$V = \frac{\sigma}{\mu} = \frac{\$2{,}051.34 \text{ million}}{\$1{,}848.9 \text{ million}} = 1.1$$

Put differently, the standard deviation equals 110 percent of the mean. We can also make the computation by computer.

EXCEL Example 7.8

Start EXCEL and retrieve the file HK100MN97 from the CD-ROM. Column E contains the population of total profit figures for those 100 multinational companies first listed in Table 4.1 on page 110. What is the *coefficient of variation* of these profit data?

SOLUTION You can get the answer from EXCEL, despite the fact that EXCEL does not provide a *coefficient-of-variation* value directly.

1. Select an empty cell, such as I1.
2. Type the formula **=STDEVP(E2:E101)/AVERAGE(E2:E101)** and press **Enter.** The *coefficient-of-variation* value of **1.10951864** appears in the selected cell.

Note that the coefficient of variation, unlike all *absolute* dispersion measures, is a pure number, unencumbered by any units of measurement, such as dollars, inches, or pounds. As a result, the coefficient of variation can be used to compare the relative dispersion of two or more distributions that are expressed in different units. For example, if the employees of a firm have a mean height of 66 inches with a standard deviation of 4 inches, but a mean weight of 150 pounds with a standard deviation of 30 pounds, we can say that heights are less varied than weights because

$$\text{for heights, } V = \frac{4''}{66''} = 0.06$$

$$\text{but for weights, } V = \frac{30 \text{ lb}}{150 \text{ lb}} = 0.20$$

Application 7.3, *On the Accuracy of National Income Statistics,* on the next page shows another use of the concept.

7.12 Measures of Shape

The *shape* of a frequency distribution can be described by (1) its symmetry or lack of it *(skewness)* and (2) its peakedness *(kurtosis).* We turn to these concepts now.

SKEWNESS

The matter of **skewness,** or a frequency distribution's degree of distortion from horizontal symmetry, is illustrated in Figure 7.6 on page 259.

Panel (a) depicts the bell-shaped normal curve that possesses *zero* skewness because the frequency density tapers off equally in both directions from the mode. Panel (b) shows *positive skewness,* so called because the frequency density tapers off more slowly toward the right of the

APPLICATION 7.3

On the Accuracy of National Income Statistics

People pay almost religious attention to statistics on national income. Every quiver of a decimal point is reported and widely analyzed, but rarely are people aware of the large margins of error associated with the data. Simon Kuznets, the great pioneer in national income estimation, was quite aware of these error margins and once examined the errors pertaining to U.S. national income between 1919 and 1935. Table 7.A gives some of his results.

Kuznets found the *weighted* margin of error of national income to be 20 percent but thought this was exaggerated for a variety of reasons. Yet he did not hesitate to view a 10 percent error in national income data as rather likely!

Consider the implications. If the 1999 U.S. GDP data contained a similar 10 percent margin of error, this margin would amount to ±$925 billion, an amount roughly equal to *all* the durable-goods purchases of consumers, or *all* nonresidential private domestic investment, or *all* of exports or well over half of the spending of the entire government sector (federal, state, and local). Yet ordinary citizens and government officials alike seriously debate the meaning of changes of even 1/10 of 1 percent of the GDP and continually draw what can only be called totally unwarranted conclusions therefrom.

SOURCES: Adapted from Simon Kuznets, *National Income and Its Composition, 1919–1938,* vol. 2 (New York: National Bureau of Economic Research, 1941), pp. 512–513; and *Economic Report of the President,* February 2000, pp. 306–307.

TABLE 7.A

Sector Contributing to National Income	Mean Error, μ (in percent of stated figure)	Standard Deviation of Error, σ (percent)	Coefficient of Variation, σ / μ
Manufacturing	9.45	3.40	0.36
Agriculture	12.40	4.96	0.40
Mining	13.10	5.90	0.45
Trade	20.50	12.71	0.62
Government	17.66	3.18	0.18
Construction	26.91	3.23	0.12
Services	27.27	3.82	0.14

mode than toward the left, and the longer right tail of the frequency curve points in the *positive* direction along the horizontal axis—toward larger values of X. Panel (c), finally, illustrates *negative* skewness, so called because the frequency density tapers off more slowly toward the left of the mode than toward the right, and the longer left tail of the frequency curve points in the *negative* direction along the horizontal axis—toward smaller values of X.

The type of skewness has certain implications for the positions of the mean, median, and mode. In the case of zero skewness, as in panel (a), mean, median, and mode coincide. When the frequency distribution exhibits positive skewness, as in panel (b), a relatively few extremely large values raise the mean considerably above the mode; the median, which is less sensitive to extreme values, often ends up somewhere between the mean and the mode. When the frequency distribution shows negative skewness, as in panel (c), a relatively few unusually small values lower the mean considerably below the mode; the median, again, often ends up between the mean and mode. By tradition, statisticians prefer to use the median as the most meaningful measure of central tendency whenever the underlying distribution is skewed.

FIGURE 7.6 | The Shape of a Frequency Curve: Skewness

These graphs illustrate the three basic types of skewness. Note their implications for the positions of the mean, the median, and the mode. While these measures of central tendency coincide in the case of zero skewness, the mean is pulled toward the extreme values in the case of positive or negative skewness. Moving away from the tail, and just as in the alphabetical listing of a dictionary, the mean is followed by median and mode. Also as in the dictionary, the median is typically closer to the mean than to the mode. For moderately skewed distributions, the median lies about one-third of the way between mean and mode.

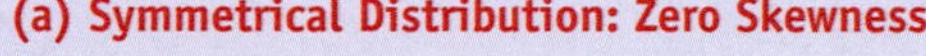

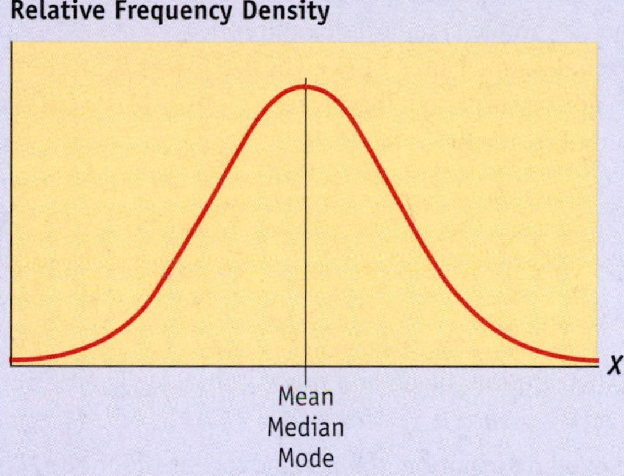

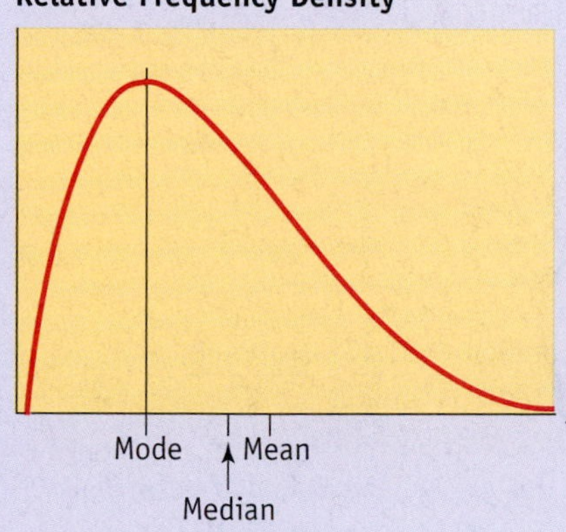

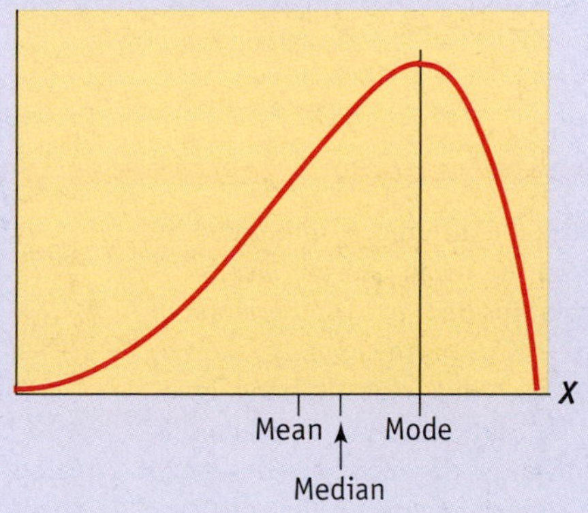

THE COEFFICIENT OF SKEWNESS

The positional differences among mean, median, and mode can be used to create arithmetic measures of skewness. Of the several such measures that exist, the most useful is **Pearson's coefficient of skewness, *Sk* or *sk*,** which is a measure of skewness that focuses on the difference between the mode and the mean and then relates it to the standard deviation, as in Formula 7.K on the next page. The coefficient is named after Karl Pearson (1895–1980), a British statistician whose biography appears on the Web site associated with this text.

FORMULA 7.K | Pearson's Coefficient of Skewness

For a population:

$$Sk = \frac{\mu - Mo}{\sigma}$$

For a sample:

$$sk = \frac{\overline{X} - mo}{s}$$

where μ or $\overline{X}$ is the population or sample mean, *Mo* or *mo* is the population or sample mode, and σ or s is the population or sample standard deviation.

Note: Several alternative measures of skewness exist and different computer programs pick different formulas. Do not be surprised, therefore, if your favorite software computes a value that differs from the Formula 7.K result.

By looking at the various panels of Figure 7.6, we can summarize the implications of Formula 7.K as follows:

- In a symmetrical distribution, mean and mode coincide. Therefore, Pearson's coefficient of skewness equals zero because $\mu - Mo = 0$.
- In a positively skewed distribution, the mean exceeds the mode. Therefore, Pearson's coefficient of skewness is positive because $\mu > Mo$.
- In a negatively skewed distribution, the mean lies below the mode. Therefore, Pearson's coefficient of skewness is negative because $\mu < Mo$.

CAUTION

Sometimes the difference, multiplied by 3, between the mean and the *median* is substituted for the two numerators in Formula 7.K. For moderately skewed distributions, this substitution gives roughly the same result as Formula 7.K because, as Figure 7.6 shows, the distance between mean and median then equals about one-third the distance between mean and mode. Thus, for the population of total profit figures in Table 6.3, the coefficient of skewness might be calculated as

$$Sk = \frac{3(\mu - M)}{\sigma}$$

$$= \frac{3(\$1{,}848.9 \text{ million} - \$1{,}128.0 \text{ million})}{\$2{,}051.34 \text{ million}} = 1.05$$

using the values for μ, M, and σ found earlier in this chapter.

The result indicates *positive* skewness. For a visual confirmation, have another look on page 186 at the Figure 6.4 histogram, which was based on the same data.

KURTOSIS

A frequency curve's degree of peakedness, or **kurtosis,** is illustrated in Figure 7.7. Kurtosis is measured by the **coefficient of kurtosis,** given in Formula 7.L.

FORMULA 7.L | Coefficient of Kurtosis

For a population:

$$K = \frac{\frac{\Sigma(X - \mu)^4}{N}}{\sigma^4}$$

For a sample:

$$k = \frac{\frac{\Sigma(X - \overline{X})^4}{n}}{s^4}$$

where the X's are observed population or sample values, μ or $\overline{X}$ is the population or sample mean, N or n is the population or sample size, and σ or s is the population or sample standard deviation.

Note: Several alternative measures of kurtosis exist and different computer programs pick different formulas. Do not be surprised, therefore, if your favorite software computes a value that differs from the Formula 7.L result.

FIGURE 7.7 | The Shape of a Frequency Curve: Kurtosis

This graph illustrates three basic types of kurtosis, ranging from flat to moderate to "leaping into the sky."

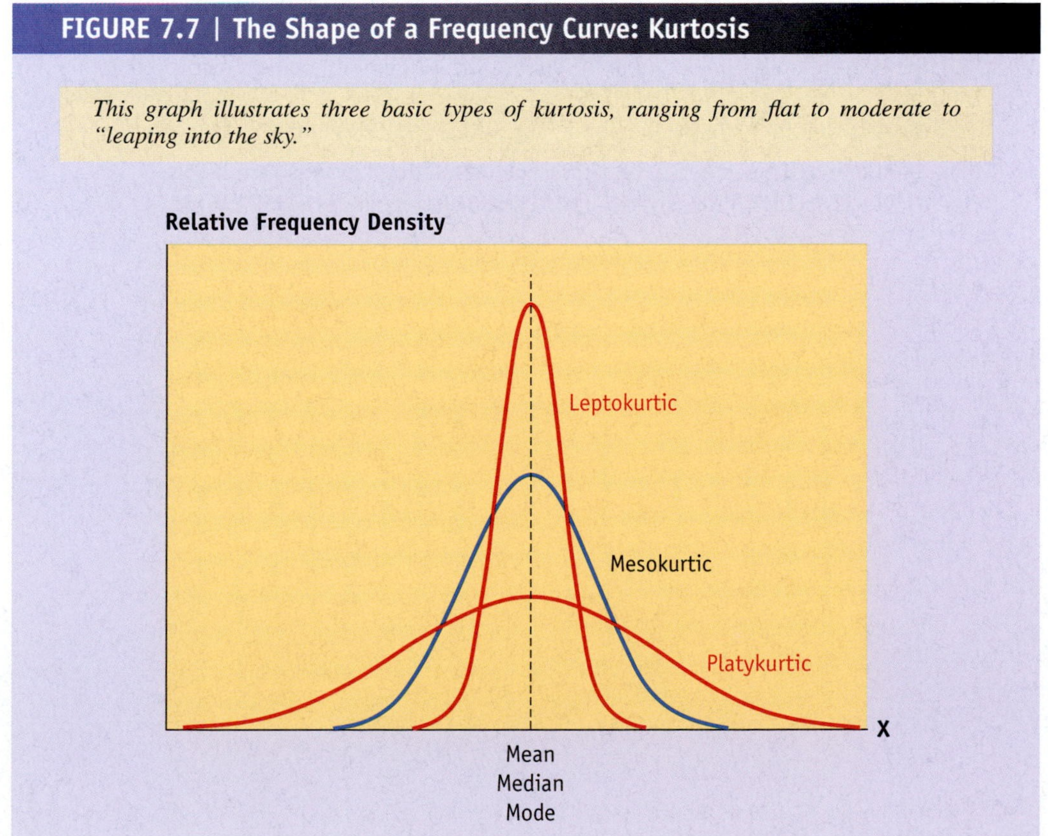

Clearly, the calculation of a coefficient of kurtosis is best left to a computer, as is shown below. In general, frequency curves with a kurtosis of 3 are called *mesokurtic;* those with larger values are more peaked and are called *leptokurtic;* those with smaller values are flatter and are called *platykurtic.* The coefficient of kurtosis for our profit data turns out to be above 5, suggesting a leptokurtic distribution, as the page 186 Figure 6.4 histogram confirms. Like the coefficient of variation and the coefficient of skewness, that of kurtosis is expressed as a pure number; hence, different distributions can easily be compared with respect to their degree of kurtosis.

EXCEL Example 7.9

Start EXCEL and retrieve the file HK100MN97 from the CD-ROM. Column E contains the population of total profit figures for those 100 multinational companies first listed in Table 4.1 on page 110. What is the *coefficient of kurtosis* of these profit data?

SOLUTION EXCEL's **Function Wizard (*fx*)** can lead us to a **KURT** function, but it employs an alternative formula, which differs from Formula 7.L. It also assumes that data are sample data rather than population data. Nevertheless, we can use EXCEL to make the computations required by *population* Formula 7.L:

1. Click the head of column E and note the sum of the 100 column values displayed at the bottom of the screen: 184,886. Thus, the mean profit is 1,848.86.
2. Activate an empty cell, such as I2, enter the formula **=(E2−1848.86)^4,** and drag the cell to E101.
3. Click the head of column I and note the sum of the 100 column values displayed at the bottom of the screen: 9.48619E+15. Thus, the mean of these values (and the numerator of our kurtosis formula) is that value divided by 100, or **9.48619E+13.**
4. Click an empty cell, such as K2, and enter the population kurtosis formula as **=9.48619E+13/(STDEVP(E2:E101))^4.** The result appears as **5.35719311.**

7.13 The Proportion

For *qualitative* data, most of the summary measures described so far cannot be used. Thus, if 138 of 200 firms sampled were single proprietorships, 18 were partnerships, and the rest were corporations, one could designate the first group as the modal type of firm, but one could hardly calculate the arithmetic mean, the median, or the standard deviation of firm types. It would be meaningful, however, to compute *proportions*.

DEFINITION 7.9 A number that describes the frequency of observations in a particular category as a fraction of all observations made is called a **proportion.** When referring to a population, the proportion is denoted by π (the lowercase Greek *p,* which is pronounced "pi" and here clearly stands for *proportion* and not the well-known geometric constant $\pi = 3.1416$, which equals the ratio of the circumference to the diameter of a circle). When referring to a sample, the proportion is represented by the capital Roman letter P.

In the example just cited, the proportion of single proprietorships and partnerships among all types of firms equals $(138 + 18)/200$, or 0.78. By the same token, corporations make up a proportion of 0.22. Naturally, these numbers, like all proportions, can instantly be converted to percentages, here of 78 and 22 percent.

Although proportions are, perhaps, the most simpleminded of all statistics, they can be powerful decision-making tools, as the following Applications show.

APPLICATION 7.4

THE SAFETY OF ANESTHETICS

As you can well imagine, pharmaceutical companies are always eager to find some kind of new best-seller. In 1958, one of them seemed to have hit the jackpot. Before long, many U.S. hospitals began using its new type of anesthetic, called *halothane.* Unlike other anesthetics traditionally used, it was not flammable, which reduced explosion hazards during surgery, and it was agreeable to patients, who recovered faster and suffered fewer aftereffects. By the time halothane was used in half the operations, a suspicion arose: Many hospitals reported strikingly unusual, but similar, deaths of patients after the use of halothane. Was halothane responsible for these unusual deaths?

A search of 850,000 records in 34 hospitals revealed 17,000 postoperative deaths within six weeks after surgery, a proportion of 0.02. Naturally, these deaths were attributable to all kinds of causes and not necessarily to the use of halothane. In fact, the proportions of postoperative deaths associated with but not necessarily *caused* by various anesthetics were found to be as shown in row 1 of Table 7.B on the next page.

Contrary to the aforementioned suspicion, was halothane *twice as safe* as cyclopropane and certainly no worse than any other anesthetic? The statistical investigators were hesitant to argue on the basis of row 1 alone. They realized that:

(continued)

Application 7.4 (continued)

- some anesthetics were used more often in difficult operations (cyclopropane) than in easy ones (pentothal)
- some types of operations had vastly different death rates than other types (the range went from 0.0025 to 0.14)
- the physical status of patients affected death rates (the range went from 0.005 for young patients to 0.26 for old ones)
- women patients had lower death rates than men
- different hospitals had different death rates as well

Conceivably, all the favorable factors, such as simple operations, young or female patients, and so forth, could have been associated with the use of halothane, and all the unfavorable factors could have been associated with the use of other anesthetics, thus *masking* the bad effect of the suspicious anesthetic in table row 1.

Accordingly, all the proportions were adjusted to account for these other factors. The result is given in row 2. The masking effect just referred to was present, but even after adjusting the data, halothane proved to be at least as safe as any of the other anesthetics. In fact, the suspicious deaths were also present with other anesthetics but had not been noticed because the traditional anesthetics had not been watched as closely as the new one.

SOURCE: Adapted from Lincoln E. Moses and Frederick Mosteller, "Safety of Anesthetics," in Judith M. Tanur et al., eds., *Statistics: A Guide to the Unknown* (San Francisco: Holden-Day, 1972), pp. 14–22. Data in Table 7.B

TABLE 7.B

Data	Halothane	Pentothal	Cyclopropane	Ether	Others
1. Raw	0.017	0.017	0.034	0.019	0.030
2. Adjusted	0.021	0.020	0.026	0.020	0.025

APPLICATION 7.5

Networks Battle Nielsen

One of the most important uses of the *proportion,* perhaps, is linked to the eternal battle for audience share among television networks. Since the birth of television, Nielsen Media Research, Inc., has been at the forefront of measuring audience response, publishing *ratings* and *share* statistics by which television producers live or die.

Ratings show the proportion of all homes owning televisions, whether or not sets are in use, that are tuned to a particular network show. Thus, during a recent prime time period, the rating was 0.091 for CBS, 0.089 for NBC, 0.083 for ABC, and 0.074 for Fox. These numbers are often converted into percentages, such as 9.1, 8.9, 8.3, and 7.4.

Shares show the proportion of all homes with televisions in use that are tuned to a particular network show. Thus, during the same recent prime time period, the share was 0.15 for CBS, 0.15 for NBC, 0.14 for ABC, and 0.12 for Fox. These numbers, too, are often converted into percentages, such as 15, 15, 14, and 12 in this case.

Networks receive advertising revenue based on such statistics, and they were hopping mad when Nielsen announced a 10 percent *drop* in the 18-to-34-year-old TV audience during the fall 1998 season. NBC, facing an immediate loss of $66 million in revenue, called Nielsen's measurements "seriously flawed" and "not plausible" and threatened to file suit for breach of contract. As NBC saw it, it had just spent $12 million to get *inaccurate* ratings and shares, and it was not averse to the idea of trying out a brand-new competitor, Statistical Research, Inc., which was promoting *Smart,* short for Systems for Measuring And Reporting Television.

SOURCES: Adapted from http://www.nielsenmedia.com; and Bill Carter, "Networks Battle Nielsen as Young Viewers Turn Up Missing," *The New York Times,* December 21, 1998, pp. C1 and 4.

Summary

1. This chapter discusses an approach to condensing collections of data that is even more radical than the construction of tables and graphs: the calculation of *arithmetic summary measures.* The most important summary measures are the measures of *central tendency,* of *dispersion,* and of *shape* for quantitative variables, and the *proportion* for qualitative ones.
2. *Measures of central tendency* or *location* are values around which observations tend to cluster and that describe the location of the "center" of a data set. They can be calculated with precision from ungrouped data and can be approximated from grouped data. The most commonly used measures of central tendency are the (arithmetic, unweighted) *mean,* the *median,* and the *mode.* Others discussed here include the *midrange,* the *trimmed mean,* and the *weighted mean.*
3. *Measures of dispersion* or *variability* are numbers that indicate the spread or scatter of observations. They show the extent to which individual values in a data set differ from one another and, hence, differ from their central location. Dispersion can be measured as distances between selected observations or as average deviations of individual observations from a central value.
4. The most important *distance* measures of dispersion include the (overall) *range* and a variety of *interfractile ranges,* usually defined by *quartiles, deciles,* or *percentiles.*
5. The most important *average* deviation measures of dispersion include the *mean absolute deviation,* the *variance,* and the *standard deviation.*
6. There are numerous important uses for the *standard deviation* (and its derivative *coefficient of variation*). These are illustrated by discussions of (a) the normal frequency distribution, standard scores, and control charts, (b) Chebyshev's theorem, and (c) comparisons of dispersion in different data sets, such as those found in national income statistics.
7. *Measures of shape* are numbers that indicate either the degree of asymmetry *(skewness)* or that of peakedness *(kurtosis)* in a frequency curve. The bell-shaped *normal curve* possesses zero skewness because the frequency density tapers off equally in both directions from the mode. This contrasts with positive (or negative) skewness when the frequency density tapers off more slowly toward the right (or left) of the mode. Depending on their peakedness, frequency curves are platykurtic, mesokurtic, or leptokurtic.
8. The only summary measure available for qualitative data is the *proportion,* a number that describes the frequency of observations in a particular category as a fraction of all observations made. Even this humble measure can lead to important insights that are hidden in raw data.

Key Terms

arithmetic mean (μ or $\bar{X}$)
bimodal frequency distribution
Chebyshev's theorem
coefficient of kurtosis (K or k)
coefficient of variation (V or v)
control charts
deciles
empirical rule
first quartile
fractile
H-spread
interfractile ranges
interquartile range
kurtosis
mean absolute deviation (MAD)
measures of central tendency (or of location)
measures of dispersion (or of variability)
measures of shape
median (M or m)
median class
midrange
modal class
mode (Mo or mo)
multimodal frequency distribution
normal curve
normal frequency distribution
parameter
Pearson's coefficient of skewness (Sk or sk)
percentile
proportion (π or P)
quartiles
range
second quartile
skewness
standard deviation (σ or s)
standard score (z)
statistic
third quartile
trimmed mean
variance (σ^2 or s^2)
weighted mean

Practice Problems

NOTES

1. Some problems assume that you are connected to the Internet. The addresses noted in these problems, and the solutions described on the accompanying CD-ROM, were current at the time of this writing. However, Web sites are forever evolving. If things have changed, you can still learn much by solving a slightly different problem in a slightly different way.

2. Some problems require the use of a statistical program, EXCEL or MINITAB. The programs' major features are explained in text Chapter 2. Plenty of additional advice is available via the programs' built-in Help feature.

SECTION 7.2 THE ARITHMETIC MEAN

1. Each year, *Fortune* magazine ranks U.S. corporations on the basis of total revenues taken in during the previous year. The 500 largest revenue-makers enter the *Fortune 500* list. Numerous data about companies on the 1999 list have been entered into the file HK99F500, which can be found on the CD-ROM that accompanies this text. Retrieve the file and compute the *arithmetic mean* of the *Fortune 500* companies' *1998 total revenues,* which are listed in column B (EXCEL) or column C2 (MINITAB). (*Hint:* EXCEL or MINITAB Example 7.1 can help.)

2. Each year, *Fortune* magazine ranks U.S. corporations on the basis of total revenues taken in during the previous year. The 500 largest revenue-makers enter the *Fortune 500* list. Numerous data about companies on the 1999 list have been entered into the file HK99F500, which can be found on the CD-ROM that accompanies this text. Retrieve the file, and compute the *arithmetic mean* of the *Fortune 500* companies' *1998 total profits,* which are listed in column C (EXCEL) or column C3 (MINITAB). (*Hint:* EXCEL or MINITAB Example 7.1 can help. In EXCEL, you may have to delete column C cells with asterisks that denote missing data. *Caution:* Copy column C to another place first; then sort the new column to get all the asterisks to line up at the end.)

3. Each year, *Fortune* magazine ranks U.S. corporations on the basis of total revenues taken in during the previous year. The 500 largest revenue-makers enter the *Fortune 500* list. Numerous data about companies on the 1999 list have been entered into the file HK99F500, which can be found on the CD-ROM that accompanies this text. Retrieve the file, and compute the *arithmetic mean* of the *Fortune 500* companies' *1998 total assets,* which are listed in column D (EXCEL) or column C4 (MINITAB). (*Hint:* EXCEL or MINITAB Example 7.1 can help.)

4. Each year, *Fortune* magazine ranks U.S. corporations on the basis of total revenues taken in during the previous year. The 500 largest revenue-makers enter the *Fortune 500* list. Numerous data about companies on the 1999 list have been entered into the file HK99F500, which can be found on the CD-ROM that accompanies this text. Retrieve the file, and compute the *arithmetic mean* of the *Fortune 500* companies' *1998 total equity data,* which are listed in column E (EXCEL) or column C5 (MINITAB). (*Hint:* EXCEL or MINITAB Example 7.1 can help.)

5. Each year, *Fortune* magazine ranks U.S. corporations on the basis of total revenues taken in during the previous year. The 500 largest revenue-makers enter the *Fortune 500* list. Numerous data about companies on the 1999 list have been entered into the file HK99F500, which can be found on the CD-ROM that accompanies this text. Retrieve the file, and compute the *arithmetic mean* of the *Fortune 500* companies' *March 15, 1999, market values,* which are listed in column F (EXCEL) or column C6 (MINITAB). (*Hint:* EXCEL or MINITAB Example 7.1 can help. In EXCEL, you may have to delete column F cells with asterisks that denote missing data. *Caution:* Copy column F to another place first; then sort the new column to get all the asterisks to line up at the end.)

SECTION 7.3 THE MEDIAN

6. Each year, *Fortune* magazine ranks U.S. corporations on the basis of total revenues taken in during the previous year. The 500 largest revenue-makers enter the *Fortune 500* list. Numerous data about companies on the 1999 list have been entered into the file HK99F500, which can be found on the CD-ROM that accompanies this text. Retrieve the file, and compute the *median* of the *Fortune 500* companies' *1998 total revenues,* which are listed in column B (EXCEL) or column C2 (MINITAB). (*Hint:* EXCEL or MINITAB Example 7.2 can help.)

7. Each year, *Fortune* magazine ranks U.S. corporations on the basis of total revenues taken in during the previous year. The 500 largest revenue-makers enter the *Fortune 500* list. Numerous data about companies on the 1999 list

have been entered into the file HK99F500, which can be found on the CD-ROM that accompanies this text. Retrieve the file, and compute the *median* of the *Fortune 500* companies' *1998 total profits,* which are listed in column C (EXCEL) or column C3 (MINITAB). (*Hint:* EXCEL or MINITAB Example 7.2 can help. In EXCEL, you may have to delete column C cells with asterisks that denote missing data. Caution: Copy column C to another place first; then sort the new column to get all the asterisks to line up at the end.)

8. Each year, *Fortune* magazine ranks U.S. corporations on the basis of total revenues taken in during the previous year. The 500 largest revenue-makers enter the *Fortune 500* list. Numerous data about companies on the 1999 list have been entered into the file HK99F500, which can be found on the CD-ROM that accompanies this text. Retrieve the file, and compute the *median* of the *Fortune 500* companies' *1998 total assets,* which are listed in column D (EXCEL) or column C4 (MINITAB). (*Hint:* EXCEL or MINITAB Example 7.2 can help.)

9. Each year, *Fortune* magazine ranks U.S. corporations on the basis of total revenues taken in during the previous year. The 500 largest revenue-makers enter the *Fortune 500* list. Numerous data about companies on the 1999 list have been entered into the file HK99F500, which can be found on the CD-ROM that accompanies this text. Retrieve the file, and compute the *median* of the *Fortune 500* companies' *1998 total equity data,* which are listed in column E (EXCEL) or column C5 (MINITAB). (*Hint:* EXCEL or MINITAB Example 7.2 can help.)

10. Each year, *Fortune* magazine ranks U.S. corporations on the basis of total revenues taken in during the previous year. The 500 largest revenue-makers enter the *Fortune 500* list. Numerous data about companies on the 1999 list have been entered into the file HK99F500, which can be found on the CD-ROM that accompanies this text. Retrieve the file, and compute the *median* of the *Fortune 500* companies' *March 15, 1999, market values,* which are listed in column F (EXCEL) or column C6 (MINITAB). (*Hint:* EXCEL or MINITAB Example 7.2 can help. In EXCEL, you may have to delete column F cells with asterisks that denote missing data. *Caution:* Copy column F to another place first; then sort the new column to get all the asterisks to line up at the end.)

SECTION 7.4 THE MODE

11. Create three lists of 5 numbers, one containing a single mode, one containing two modes, and one containing no mode at all.

12. From 1973 to 1998, Japan's civilian unemployment rate (in percent) was 1.3, 1.4, 1.9, 2.0, 2.0, 2.3, 2.1, 2.0, 2.2, 2.4, 2.7, 2.8, 2.6, 2.8, 2.9, 2.5, 2.3, 2.1, 2.1, 2.2, 2.5, 2.9, 3.2. 3.4, 3.4, and 4.1. Find the *mode.* Compare it with the (unweighted) *mean* and the *median.*

13. From 1960 to 1998, the annual percentage changes in the U.S. consumer price index were 1.7, 1.0, 1.0, 1.3, 1.3, 1.6, 2.9, 3.1, 4.2, 5.5, 5.7, 4.4, 3.2, 6.2, 11.0, 9.1, 5.8, 6.5, 7.6, 11.3, 13.5, 10.3, 6.2, 3.2, 4.3, 3.6, 1.9, 3.6, 4.1, 4.8, 5.4, 4.2, 3.0, 3.0, 2.6, 2.8, 3.0, 2.3, and 1.6. Find the *mode.* Compare it with the (unweighted) *mean* and the *median.*

SECTION 7.5 OTHER MEASURES OF CENTRAL TENDENCY

14. Review Practice Problem 10. Then compute the *midrange* and the *5% trimmed mean* of the *Fortune 500* companies' *March 15, 1999, market values,* which are listed in column F (EXCEL) or column C6 (MINITAB). (*Hint:* EXCEL or MINITAB Example 7.3 can help.)

15. Review Practice Problem 9. Then compute the *midrange* and the *5% trimmed mean* of the *Fortune 500* companies' *1998 total equity data,* which are listed in column E (EXCEL) or column C5 (MINITAB). (*Hint:* EXCEL or MINITAB Example 7.3 can help.)

16. Review the data in Practice Problem 12. Compute their *midrange* and *5% trimmed mean.* (*Hint:* EXCEL or MINITAB Example 7.3 can help.)

17. Review the data in Practice Problem 13. Compute their *midrange* and *5% trimmed mean.* (*Hint:* EXCEL or MINITAB Example 7.3 can help.)

18. In the United States in 1997, the civilian labor force included 114.7 million whites and 15.5 million blacks. Their respective unemployment rates were 4.2 and 10.0 percent. Compute the *weighted mean* unemployment rate.

19. Consider the data of Table 7.6. Compute the *weighted mean* unemployment rate for the nation as a whole. (*Hint:* The number sought equals the ratio of the number unemployed to the civilian labor force, times 100.)

TABLE 7.6 | Unemployment in the United States, 1996

Region	Number Unemployed (1,000s)	Unemployment Rate (% of civilian labor force)
Alabama	107	5.1
Alaska	25	7.8
Arizona	124	5.5
Arkansas	67	5.4
California	1,126	7.2
Colorado	89	4.2
Connecticut	99	5.7
Delaware	20	5.2
District of Columbia	23	8.5
Florida	352	5.1
Georgia	173	4.6
Hawaii	38	6.4
Idaho	32	5.2
Illinois	322	5.3
Indiana	127	4.1
Iowa	60	3.8
Kansas	60	4.5
Kentucky	105	5.6
Louisiana	135	6.7
Maine	34	5.1
Maryland	136	4.9
Massachusetts	137	4.3
Michigan	234	4.9

(continued)

TABLE 7.6 *(continued)*

Region	Number Unemployed (1,000s)	Unemployment Rate (% of civilian labor force)
Minnesota	104	4.0
Mississippi	77	6.1
Missouri	132	4.6
Montana	24	5.3
Nebraska	27	2.9
Nevada	46	5.4
New Hampshire	26	4.2
New Jersey	255	6.2
New Mexico	64	8.1
New York	540	6.2
North Carolina	165	4.3
North Dakota	11	3.1
Ohio	278	4.9
Oklahoma	64	4.1
Oregon	102	5.9
Pennsylvania	313	5.3
Rhode Island	25	5.1
South Carolina	111	6.0
South Dakota	13	3.2
Tennessee	142	5.2
Texas	549	5.6
Utah	35	3.5
Vermont	15	4.6
Virginia	149	4.4
Washington	188	6.5
West Virginia	61	7.5
Wisconsin	103	3.5
Wyoming	13	5.0

20. Consider the data of Table 7.7. Compute the *weighted mean* unemployment rate for the nation as a whole. (*Hint:* The number sought equals the ratio of the number unemployed to the civilian labor force, times 100.)

TABLE 7.7 | Selected U.S. Labor Force Data, December 1981

	Civilian Labor Force (millions)	Unemployment Rate (percent)
Both sexes, 16–19 years	8.62	21.5
Males, 20 years and over	57.51	7.9
Females, 20 years and over	42.91	7.4

SECTIONS 7.7–7.8 THE RANGE AND INTERFRACTILE RANGES

21. Review Practice Problem 1. For the *Fortune 500 total revenue* data in question, find (a) the *range,* (b) the *interquartile range,* and (c) the *midhinge,* which is another summary measure yet, equal to the sum of the first and third quartiles, divided by 2.

22. Review Practice Problem 2. For the *Fortune 500 total profit* data in question, find (a) the *range,* (b) the *interquartile range,* and (c) the *midhinge,* which is another summary measure yet, equal to the sum of the first and third quartiles, divided by 2.

23. Review Practice Problem 3. For the *Fortune 500 total asset* data in question, find (a) the 2nd decile, (b) the 8th decile, and (c) the 0.2 to 0.8 interfractile range.

24. Review Practice Problem 4. For the *Fortune 500 total equity* data in question, find (a) the 7th percentile, (b) the 50th percentile, (c) the 85th percentile, and d) the median.

25. Start EXCEL or MINITAB and retrieve the file HK100MN97 from the CD-ROM. Column E (EXCEL) and column C5 (MINITAB) contains the *total profit* figures of 100 U.S.-based multinational companies.

a. Compute the median and the first and third quartiles.

b. Review panel (a) of last chapter's Figure 6.8 on page 194. In that graph, illustrate the three statistics just computed.

SECTION 7.9 THE MEAN ABSOLUTE DEVIATION

26. Review Practice Problem 1. Compute the *mean absolute deviation* of the *Fortune 500* companies' *total revenues.* (*Hint:* EXCEL or MINITAB Example 7.5 can help.)

27. Review Practice Problem 2. Compute the *mean absolute deviation* of the *Fortune 500* companies' *total profits.* (*Hint:* EXCEL or MINITAB Example 7.5 can help.)

28. Review Practice Problem 3. Compute the *mean absolute deviation* of the *Fortune 500* companies' *total assets.* (*Hint:* EXCEL or MINITAB Example 7.5 can help.)

SECTIONS 7.10–7.11 THE VARIANCE AND THE STANDARD DEVIATION

29. The manager of a firm announced: "The lightbulbs produced by our firm have a mean lifetime of 1,500 hours, with a standard deviation of 150 hours; thus, it follows that almost all of our lightbulbs last between 1,200 and 1,800 hours." What was the manager assuming? What if the assumption did not hold?

30. The quality controller of a vegetable-canning firm is constructing a control chart. The production process fills cans of peas with an average of $\mu = 16.02763$ ounces, the standard deviation being $\sigma = 0.3168132$ ounce. Any can filled with $\mu \pm 2\,\sigma$ is considered acceptable. A sample reveals net weights of 15.33, 15.53, 15.77, 15.94, 16.05, 16.24, 16.43, 16.68, 16.88. Is the production process "out of control"?

31. An airline announces that the mean time loss to passengers from transfers between planes or flight delays equals 16.0 minutes per trip, with a standard deviation of 3.5 minutes. If the frequency distribution of time losses fit a normal curve, what range of time losses would fit 95.4 percent of all delays? What if the frequency distribution did not fit a normal curve? Finally, in light of the foregoing, how confident would you be in making a connecting flight that left you only 33 minutes for transferring between planes?

32. A computer firm offers a paid leave of absence to those of its engineers who wish to get an advanced degree. However, applicants are tested and their aptitude test scores must indicate a superb chance of success (as defined by z-scores of $+2$ or better). In one test, applicants A through F earned raw scores of 500, 631, 760, 438, 598, and 720. The mean score of all 200 applicants was 520, the standard deviation was 60. Who among the six will go back to school?

33. Consider the frequency curve in Figure 7.8. What is the minimum proportion of observations falling in the crosshatched area? In the dotted area?

34. In a recent year, the 33 public school districts of New York City reported the mathematics and reading scores given in Table 7.8. For which of the two subjects did these sample data reveal the greater variability?

FIGURE 7.8

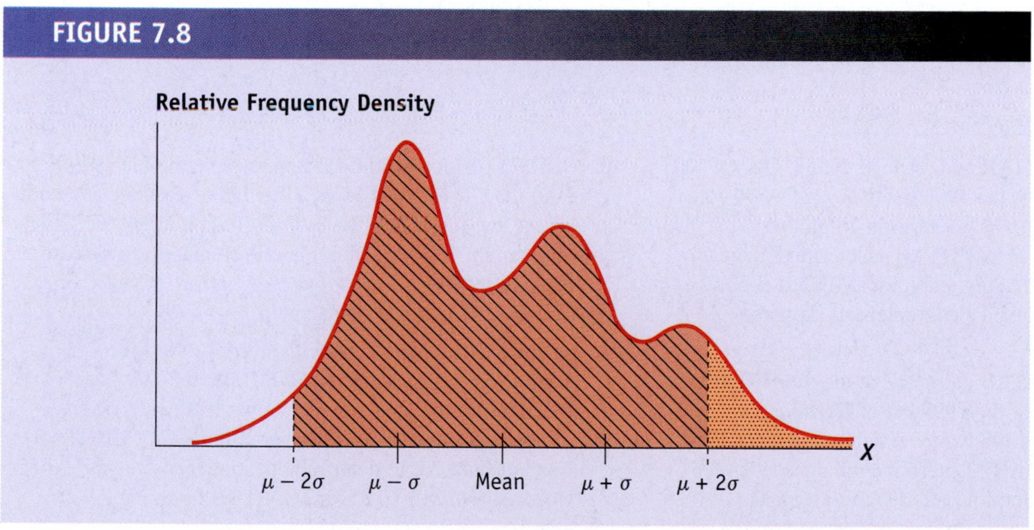

TABLE 7.8

Mathematics Scores				Reading Scores			
44.0	54.2	49.9	50.3	37.6	57.0	42.7	48.5
69.9	55.3	54.4	43.9	42.4	32.8	34.2	43.1
48.0	44.2	57.9	50.8	34.4	37.9	56.3	37.4
41.8	63.5	62.9	67.6	47.5	41.1	46.1	38.1
46.3	38.9	61.3	78.7	42.5	60.5	39.7	59.0
43.7	81.4	60.2	63.7	57.3	63.8	38.5	52.7
43.3	63.6	67.0	75.9	71.0	79.7	54.5	58.5
46.3	44.9	65.9	41.2	59.9	57.9	74.1	39.1
46.1				74.3			

TABLE 7.9

Stock A	$0.75	0.80	1.00	1.20	1.40	1.00	1.50	1.70	0.80	1.80
Stock B	$6.30	5.90	7.60	8.50	6.90	7.30	5.10	9.30	7.85	6.30

35. Over a recent 10-year period, the earnings per share for two stocks, A and B, were as shown in Table 7.9. For which of the two stocks do these sample data reveal the greater variability?

36. Start EXCEL or MINITAB and retrieve the file HK100MN97 from the CD-ROM. For the 100 largest U.S-based multinationals, the file shows 1997 *foreign revenues, total revenues, foreign net profits, total net profits, foreign assets,* and *total assets* (in columns B–G for EXCEL and columns C2–C7 for MINITAB). Compare the degrees of dispersion among these six data sets. (*Hint:* EXCEL or MINITAB Example 7.8 can help.)

37. Start EXCEL or MINITAB and retrieve the file HK99F500 from the CD-ROM. For the 1999 list of *Fortune 500* companies, the file shows 1998 *revenues, profits, assets, equity,* and *March 15, 1999, market value* (in columns B–F for EXCEL and columns C2–C6 for MINITAB). Compare the degrees of dispersion among these five data sets. (*Hint:* EXCEL or MINITAB Example 7.8 can help.)

Section 7.12 Measures of Shape

38. Start EXCEL or MINITAB and retrieve the file HK99F500 from the CD-ROM. For the 1999 list of *Fortune 500* companies, the file shows 1998 *revenues* in column B (EXCEL) or column C2 (MINITAB). Determine the data set's *skewness* by (a) making a dotplot (MINITAB only) and (b) computing Pearson's coefficient of skewness (EXCEL or MINITAB).

39. Start EXCEL or MINITAB and retrieve the file HK99F500 from the CD-ROM. For the 1999 list of *Fortune 500* companies, the file shows 1998 *assets* in column D (EXCEL) or column C4 (MINITAB). Determine the data set's *skewness* by (a) making a dotplot (MINITAB only) and (b) computing Pearson's coefficient of skewness (EXCEL or MINITAB).

40. Start EXCEL or MINITAB and retrieve the file HK99F500 from the CD-ROM. For the 1999 list of *Fortune 500* companies, the file shows 1998 *profits* in column C (EXCEL) or column C3 (MINITAB). Use Formula 7.L to determine the data set's *coefficient of kurtosis.* (*Hint:* EXCEL or MINITAB Example 7.9 can help.)

41. Start EXCEL or MINITAB and retrieve the file HK100MN97 from the CD-ROM. For the 100 largest U.S-based multinationals, the file shows 1997 *net foreign profits* in column D (EXCEL) or column C4 (MINITAB). Use Formula 7.L to determine the data set's *coefficient of kurtosis.* (*Hint:* EXCEL or MINITAB Example 7.9 can help.)

Section 7.13 The Proportion

42. An inspector of incoming materials is supposed to reject all shipments containing a sample proportion of defective items in excess of 0.04. Which of the shipments in Table 7.10 would be rejected?

TABLE 7.10

Shipment	Sample Size	Number Defective
A	500	5
B	1,000	37
C	200	3
D	750	31
E	900	47

43. Review Application 6.1, *Deciphering Secret Codes,* on page 175. Determine the proportion of vowels and consonants in 200 letters of a normal English-language text.

44. Visit http://www.nielsenmedia.com, a Web site maintained by Nielsen Media Research, the company that brings us TV ratings and such. Find out how Nielsen samples the TV habits of Americans and determine (a) how many TV stations and cable systems it monitors, (b) the proportion of all households with televisions that is included in its national sample, and (c) the proportion of black households in its national sample.

45. Visit http://www.fortune.com, a site maintained by *Fortune* magazine and featuring data about the *Fortune 500* companies and more.

a. Find the proportion of *Fortune 500* companies that are headquartered in this set of states: New York, California, Illinois, and Texas.

b. Find the proportion of 51 regions (50 states plus the District of Columbia) that contains no *Fortune 500* companies.

c. Use EXCEL or MINITAB to compute and print out descriptive summary statistics on the numbers of *Fortune 500* companies that are headquartered in each of the 50 states and the District of Columbia. Interpret the results.

Entire Chapter

46. Visit http://www.fortune.com, a site maintained by *Fortune* magazine and featuring data about the *Fortune 500* companies and more.

a. Identify the revenues, profits, and numbers of employees of each of the *Fortune 500* companies headquartered in Alabama.

b. Use EXCEL or MINITAB to compute and print out descriptive summary statistics on the three types of data noted in (a).

47. Visit http://www.fortune.com, a site maintained by *Fortune* magazine and featuring data about the *Fortune 500* companies and more.

a. Identify the revenues, profits, and numbers of employees of each of the *Fortune 500* companies headquartered in Colorado.

b. Use EXCEL or MINITAB to compute and print out descriptive summary statistics on the three types of data noted in (a).

48. Visit http://www.fortune.com, a site maintained by *Fortune* magazine and featuring data about the *Fortune 500* companies and more.

a. Identify the revenues, profits, and numbers of employees of each of the *Fortune 500* companies in the *advertising and marketing* industry.

b. Use EXCEL or MINITAB to compute and print out descriptive summary statistics on the three types of data noted in (a).

49. Visit http://www.fortune.com, a site maintained by *Fortune* magazine and featuring data about the *Fortune 500* companies and more.

a. Identify the revenues, profits, and numbers of employees of each of the *Fortune 500* companies in the *computer software* industry.

b. Use EXCEL or MINITAB to compute and print out descriptive summary statistics on the three types of data noted in (a).

50. Visit http://www.fortune.com, a site maintained by *Fortune* magazine and featuring data about the *Fortune 500* companies and more.

a. Identify the revenues, profits, and numbers of employees of each of the *Fortune 500* companies in the *securities* industry.

b. Use EXCEL or MINITAB to compute and print out descriptive summary statistics on the three types of data noted in (a).

PART IV

Probability Concepts: The Foundations of Inference

Chapter 8

The Theory of Probability

Chapter 9

Discrete Probability Distributions

Chapter 10

Continuous Probability Distributions

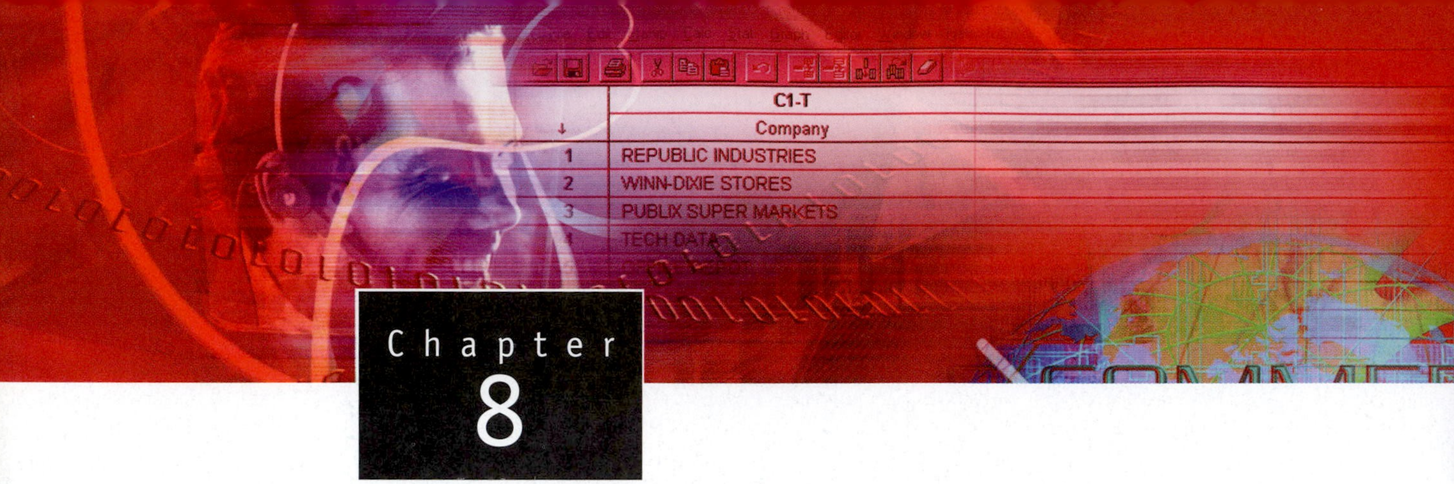

Chapter 8

THE THEORY OF PROBABILITY

LOOKING AHEAD

After reading this chapter, you will be able to employ basic probability concepts that are the very foundation of statistical inference—the set of techniques by which business executives and economists turn sample evidence into valid conclusions about statistical populations of interest. Among other things, you will learn about:

1. the nature of random events,
2. different types of relationships, such as unions or intersections, among such events,
3. objective versus subjective probability,
4. counting techniques involving factorials, permutations, and combinations,
5. addition and multiplication laws that apply to probability,
6. probability laws and tree diagrams, and
7. Bayesian probability.

AND HERE IS A TYPICAL PROBLEM YOU WILL BE ABLE TO SOLVE:

You are a wine producer. In the hope of increasing sales, you have designed a distinctive bottle. You view the probability of success as 50 percent but also order a survey of customers. You know that when consumers are enthusiastic and sales are about to rise, this type of survey will so indicate 90 percent of the time, but in 10 percent of the cases, the survey will say the opposite. Also, when consumers are unimpressed and sales prospects look dim, the survey will so indicate 60 percent of the time, but in 40 percent of the cases, it will say the opposite. The survey is taken and shows great consumer enthusiasm about the bottle. How do you now assess the probability of success?

PREVIEW

Newspapers love *coincidences,* those surprising circumstances when events that have no apparent causal connection nevertheless occur together. Consider the headlines in 1986 when a New Jersey woman won the state's lottery jackpot *twice* in four months. Picture the commotion in 1992 when someone apparently spent a single dollar and instantly won a prize exceeding $27 million in Virginia's state lottery. Yet such seeming coincidences may not be as unusual as they seem.

True enough, if a single person chooses a combination of numbers and, within the space of four months, chooses another combination, the chances may well be 1 in 17 trillion that lottery officials, at a different time and place, will make identical choices. Yet, if millions upon millions of people spend their *lifetimes* buying such tickets, a double winner within four months will almost surely arise somewhere and sometime, ascribable to "the luck of the draw."

The Virginia story, on the other hand, turned out to be trickier than it seemed. Buyers had to choose 6 numbers out of 44, which allowed for 7,059,052 possible combinations. Unbeknownst to anyone on February 15, 1992, when officials announced the winning numbers—they were 8, 11, 13, 15, 19, and 20—a group of Australian investors had come tantalizingly close to having fulfilled an age-old gambler's dream: waiting until the jackpot reaches an astronomical sum and then buying every possible number combination, thereby *guaranteeing* a win. At a cost of $1 per ticket, the group had been prepared to spend $7,059,052 to win the $27 million so far unclaimed. The logistics were incredible: Some 1.4 million slips, with five bets each, had to be filled out—by hand. The investors used 125 stores, each printing out tickets at a rate of 2,400 per hour. Yet, when the allotted time ran out, the group held only 5 million of the possible 7 million tickets. Still, they won and, luckily, they did not have to share the prize with anyone else, as they might well have had to do.

Statisticians spend much of their time analyzing events that seem to be related by coincidence. Sometimes, as in the New Jersey case, their explanation points to chance: It shows that *any* outrageous thing is likely to happen if we examine a large enough sample. At other times, as in the Virginia case, the coincidence might be explained by a hitherto hidden cause. Either way, the theory of probability provides the very foundation for statistical inference—the set of techniques by which business executives and economists turn the results of single random samples or single controlled experiments into important conclusions about the statistical populations that interest them.[1]

[1]Adapted from Gina Kolata, "1-in-a-Trillion Coincidence, You Say? Not Really, Experts Find," *The New York Times,* February 27, 1990, pp. C1 and 2; and "Group Invests $5 Million to Corner Lottery Market," *The New York Times,* February 25, 1992, pp. A1 and 18.

8.1 Introduction

Picture yourself running a national real estate company. Your clients—mostly top-ranked professionals and executives—want to know all there is to know about current prices of single-family homes, but you have neither the money nor the time to take a national census. So you take a lesson from Chapter 4 and collect relevant data with a multistage random sample. First, you identify high-income areas among all U.S. ZIP codes and randomly select $n = 25$ such areas. Second, you record the price paid at the latest home sale in each of the selected areas. The result, ordered by price, appears in Table 8.1 on the next page.

Using what you have learned about descriptive statistics in Chapters 6 and 7, you could easily summarize your data in a variety of ways. Possibly, your clients would be interested in the *range* of prices, going from $210,000 to $1,080,000. You could also provide them with the *arithmetic average* of $536,407 or with the *median* of $526,800.

But you might also be troubled by the knowledge that you merely took a single random sample—a procedure that is subject to *sampling error.* Surely, if you took another such sample, you would get different results! How then could you supply your clients with numbers that are representative of the *population* of home prices throughout the nation?

TABLE 8.1 | Elite Home Prices, Selected U.S. Areas, Summer 2000

ZIP Code	Area	Price
10546	Millwood, NY	$210,000
19085	Villanova, PA	347,500
20854	Potomac, MD	379,545
07945	Mendham, NJ	383,015
07046	Mountain Lakes, NJ	393,977
10510	Briarcliff Manor, NY	410,393
10506	Bedford, NY	416,944
07021	Essex Fells, NJ	447,500
22039	Fairfax, VA	448,159
60043	Kenilworth, IL	480,000
10514	Chappaqua, NY	481,441
90077	Los Angeles, CA	494,000
60022	Glencoe, IL	526,800
07417	Franklin Lakes, NJ	564,056
07078	Short Hills, NJ	580,793
60069	Lincolnshire, IL	585,100
06903	Stamford, CT	606,371
91108	San Marino, CA	610,444
07458	Saddle River, NJ	611,276
22066	Great Falls, VA	613,903
94025	Menlo Park, CA	668,233
60045	Lake Forest, IL	677,191
06883	Weston, CT	694,813
19035	Gladwyne, PA	698,718
07620	Alpine, NJ	1,080,000

This is the type of question that business executives and economists face every day. Can they accept the results of a single sample (or those of a single controlled experiment) as valid for the entire population of interest? Or must they reject such daring inference? The answer has a lot to do with *probability*. You will learn about the concept in this chapter. In later chapters, you will see how probability can be used as a yardstick for assessing the reasonableness of letting a particular sample (or experimental) result speak for the population as a whole.

In fact, without taking a census, you may never be able to tell your clients that the national average price of "elite homes" equals $536,407, but you may be able to pinpoint the average as lying somewhere between $480,000 and $580,000. And you may be able to add that your estimating procedure has a 95 percent *chance* of being right, that is, can be relied upon to give correct (census-like) results in 95 out of 100 investigations you conduct.

8.2 Basic Probability Concepts

Every day, we each make decisions about events that have uncertain outcomes, but we do not make them blindly. Figuring the *chances* of various possible outcomes helps us make the right choices. Without even knowing it, we rely on a special kind of calculus to make our choices—"the calculus of the likelihood of specific occurrences," as the **theory of probability** has been called. Consider how we cancel the planned picnic or move a graduation ceremony indoors when the chance of rain seems too high; how we proceed with a wedding or introduce a new product whenever success seems more likely than failure. Wherever we turn, we weigh the chances. How likely is it, we ask, that a price hike will reduce sales, that a new process will raise productivity, that a merger will raise profit, that an inspection will turn up defective parts, that a tax cut will end a recession? What are the chances, we ask, for life on other planets, for nuclear war in this century, for our candidate's election, for this horse to win, for this item to be on the quiz? The list goes on.

As we noted in Chapter 1, we can view the discipline of statistics as a guide to the unknown. Is it any wonder that all of inferential statistics derives from the theory of probability? As the Latin origin of the word suggests (*probabilis* means "likely" or "like truth"), probability theory helps us find the likely truth when we cannot know it with certainty. But we must be patient. Some parts of the current chapter may seem remote from business and economics applications. But this chapter will turn out to be the very foundation for the development, in later chapters, of a host of statistical techniques to routinely and successfully solve problems arising in these very fields. We begin by introducing two crucial concepts: the *random experiment* and the *sample space.*

THE RANDOM EXPERIMENT

Although you may never have heard the term, you are already familiar with random experiments:

> **DEFINITION 8.1** Any activity that results in one and only one of several clearly defined possible outcomes but that does not allow us to tell in advance which of these will prevail in any particular instance is called a **random experiment.**

Tossing a coin is a good example. Assuming that tosses with such unlikely outcomes as the coin landing on its edge or disappearing into a hole do not count, we know the *type* of outcome with certainty: Each toss must result in either *heads* or *tails.* Yet the *actual* outcome associated with a given toss will vary from one trial to the next. Therefore, we cannot predict the outcome of any single toss with certainty. Rolling a die is another such random experiment. So is drawing a card from a deck of cards or spinning a roulette wheel.

These examples come most easily to mind because probability was first studied some 300 years ago in connection with gambling. However, the concept of probability applies just as much to matters outside gambling situations. Pulling selected items from the production line for inspection or selecting invoices for an audit represent other examples of random experiments, with possible alternative outcomes like *defective* or *satisfactory* in the first case and *correct* or *erroneous* in the second. We can even view the investment of a billion dollars to develop a new type of car as a random experiment, which could lead to profit, loss, or even bankruptcy. So can we view inserting a coin into a vending machine, which could lead to the desired coffee, the money returned, an infuriating neither, or even quite unwelcome chicken soup.

THE SAMPLE SPACE

A random experiment may generate a few or many possible outcomes. When one result rules out all alternative outcomes, we call it a **basic outcome.** Our vending machine experiment had four such outcomes: coffee, money returned, neither, and chicken soup. The concept of basic outcomes helps us define another: that of sample space.

DEFINITION 8.2 A listing of all the basic outcomes of a random experiment is called its **sample space.** On occasion, other terms, such as **outcome space** or **probability space,** are used as well.

We can represent the basic outcomes that constitute a sample space symbolically, pictorially, and in other ways as well. Below we consider some of these possibilities.

TOSSING A SINGLE COIN ONCE The single toss of a single coin involves a sample space (S) of two basic outcomes only: heads (H) and tails (T). This sample space might be represented symbolically as

$$S = (H, T)$$

This sample space can also be shown pictorially, as in panel (a) of Figure 8.1. In any single toss, one (and only one) of the two outcomes shown must occur.

ROLLING A SINGLE DIE ONCE Rolling a single die one time involves a slightly larger sample space because six basic outcomes exist. Symbolically,

$$S = (1, 2, 3, 4, 5, 6)$$

This sample space is shown pictorially in panel (b) of Figure 8.1.

DRAWING A SINGLE CARD ONCE Larger still is the sample space that describes the possible consequences of randomly selecting a single card from a standard deck of 52 playing cards. Such a deck has four colored *suits*—namely, black clubs, red diamonds, red hearts, and black spades—and each suit has 13 *denominations,* from ace to 10 plus three face cards (jack, queen, and king). Symbolically,

$$S = (\text{ace of clubs, deuce of clubs, 3 of clubs}, \ldots, \text{king of spades})$$

Pictorially, we can represent this set of alternative outcomes as in panel (c) of Figure 8.1.

SPINNING A ROULETTE WHEEL ONCE The set of basic outcomes from spinning a roulette wheel is also large. The Monte Carlo wheel shown in panel (d) of Figure 8.1 has 37 numbers, ranging from 0 to 36. The zero is red; half of the remaining numbers are black, half red. Symbolically,

$$S = (\text{red } 0, \text{red } 1, \text{black } 2, \ldots, \text{red } 36)$$

Note: The Monte Carlo wheel shown here should not be confused with the American wheel, which adds a double zero or even a triple zero to the numbers shown (and one version of which appears in Practice Problem 1 at the end of this chapter).

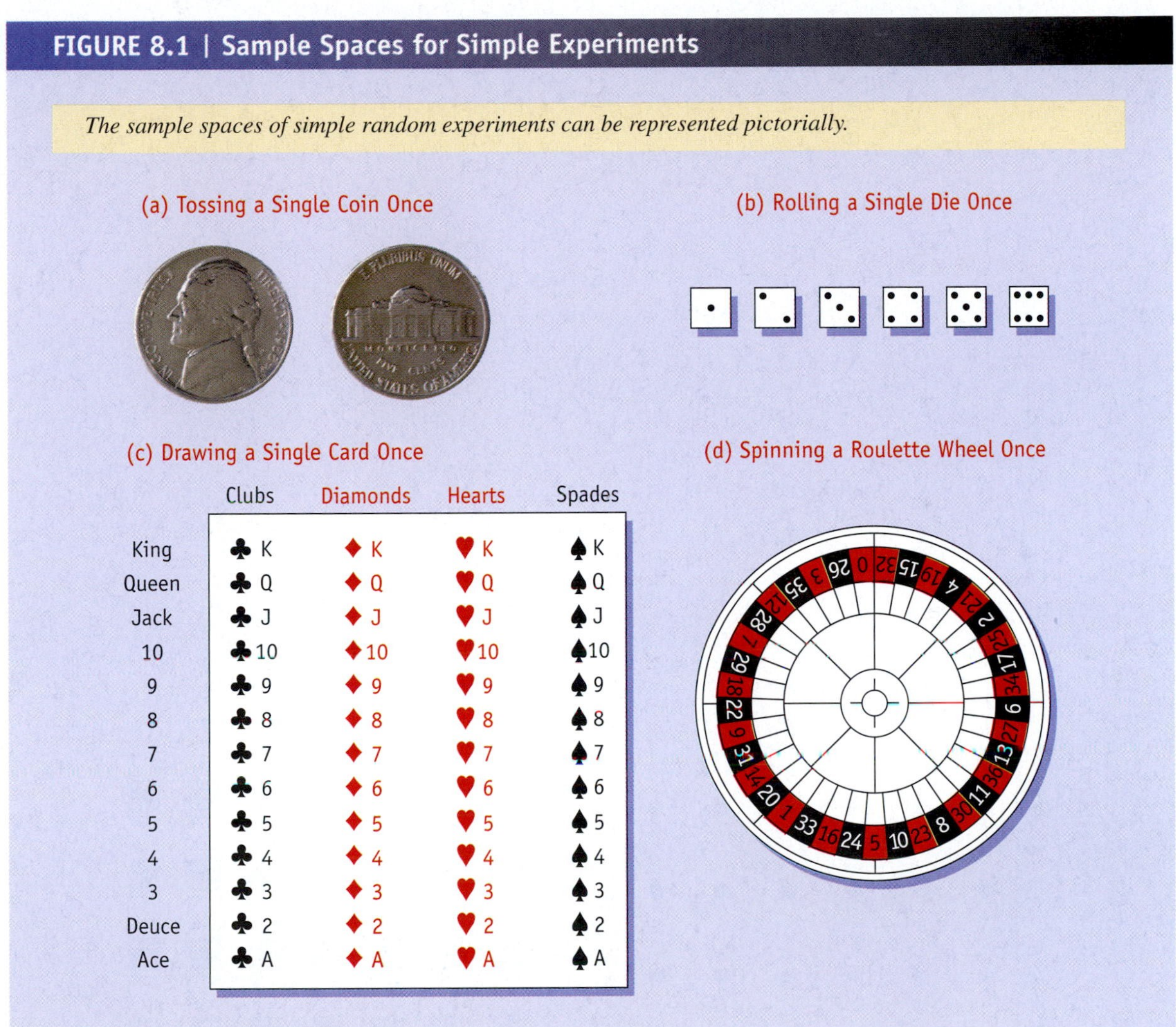

FIGURE 8.1 | Sample Spaces for Simple Experiments

TOSSING A SINGLE COIN TWICE Though we could similarly depict more complicated experiments, such as tossing a coin twice or tossing two coins at a time, various other ways to depict these sample spaces give clearer descriptions. Among the favorite devices for defining the sample space of random experiments involving multiple steps is the **tree diagram,** so called because it resembles the branches of a tree. Consider panel (a) of Figure 8.2. The tree diagram illustrates the two possible outcomes of the first toss of a coin: heads (H_1) or tails (T_1), where the subscripts denote the number of the toss. For either contingency, two further possibilities exist on the second toss: H_2 or T_2. Thus, we can follow the various paths along the branches from the starting position prior to the first toss and trace out the four basic outcomes of the entire two-stage experiment. These outcomes are conveniently summarized in the box to the right of the tree diagram.

Note how the identical panel diagram would identify the possible consequences of tossing two coins at once. You would only have to replace "First Toss" with "First Coin" and "Second Toss" with "Second Coin" to see the perfect analogy. Naturally, we could draw more complex trees, too, in order to find, say, the sample space associated with tossing a coin three times or even with tossing it more often than that.

FIGURE 8.2 | Sample Spaces for Multiple-Step Experiments

Sample spaces for multiple-step experiments are typically represented by the devices shown here. Panel (a) pictures a ***tree diagram*** *and its associated sample space. The diagrams in panels (b) and (c) are often said to depict* ***sample points.***

(a) Tossing a Coin Twice

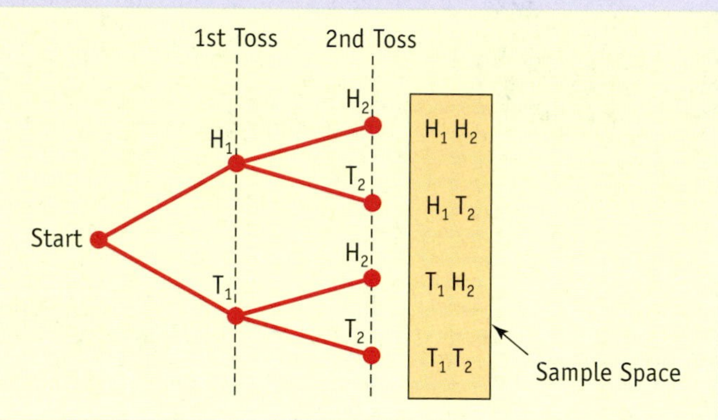

(b) Rolling Two Dice Once

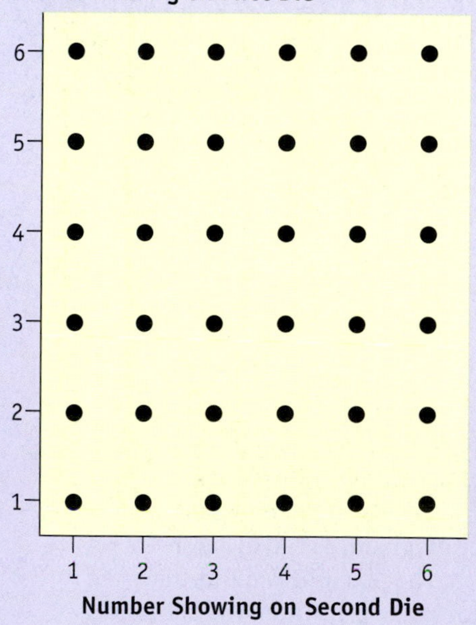

(c) Rolling Two Dice Once

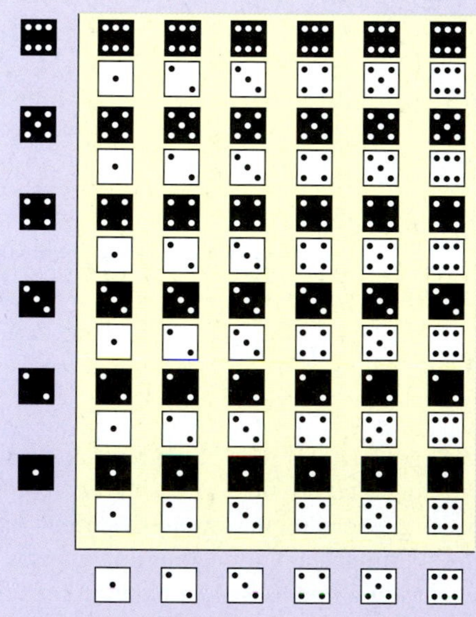

Rolling Two Dice at Once Finally, consider panels (b) and (c) of Figure 8.2. They depict still other ways to determine the sample space in multiple-step experiments. In this case, both panels show us immediately the 36 basic outcomes of an experiment that rolls two dice at once (or, for that matter, rolls a single die twice).

8.3 The Nature of Random Events

We have now seen that any random experiment will yield one of two or more possible outcomes and that these basic outcomes, as a group, make up the sample space. If you were to run the real estate firm noted in Section 8.1, for example, you might consider three possible outcomes this year: incurring a loss (outcome A), earning a profit in the $0 to $100 million range (outcome B), or earning a profit in excess of $100 million (outcome C). Sometimes, however, a portion of the sample space is of particular interest to a decision maker. You may wish to focus on the likelihood of outcome A only (because it can get you fired) or on the likelihood of outcome C only (because it will bring you a bonus). You may even be interested in the combined likelihood of outcomes A and C (because either one could trigger a hostile takeover of your firm). In short, you may wish to pay particular attention to a *portion* of the sample space for all kinds of reasons, which gives rise to another set of crucial concepts:

DEFINITION 8.3 Any subset of the sample space is called a **random event.** There are two types. Any single one of a random experiment's basic outcomes is a **simple event;** any combination of two or more basic outcomes is a **composite event.**

SIMPLE EVENTS

The sample space for random experiment (a) in Figure 8.1, for example, consists of two *simple events:* the appearance of a head and the appearance of a tail. The sample spaces for experiments (b) through (d) are, similarly, made up of 6, 52, and 37 simple events, respectively.

In Figure 8.2, we find four simple events in panel (a) and 36 simple events each in panels (b) and (c), although each of these events (unlike those in Figure 8.1) inextricably links together two elements, such as "head on the first toss" with "head on the second toss" or "6 on the black die" with "1 on the white die."

We can further distinguish basic outcomes or simple events that are *univariate,* such as those in Figure 8.1, where each outcome is defined by the appearance of a single element, from those that are *bivariate,* such as those in Figure 8.2, where each outcome is defined by the joint appearance of two elements. Basic outcomes may even be *multivariate* (not shown here).

Finally, note that some statisticians refer to a simple event as an **elementary event** or **sample point**—the latter name, perhaps, being suggested by the type of graphical representation of the sample space shown in panel (b) of Figure 8.2.

COMPOSITE EVENTS

We noted earlier why you might wish to assess the joint chances of incurring a loss *or* making a huge profit. More abstract examples are equally easy to find. Consider the event "getting an even number" when rolling a single die once. Consider the event "getting a face card" when drawing a single card from a deck. Consider, finally, "getting a sum of 10 or more" when rolling two dice. Such *composite events* appear as the shaded areas in Figure 8.3.

FIGURE 8.3 | Composite Events

The shaded subsets of the three boxed sample spaces shown here illustrate the nature of composite events. As the shaded portion of panel (a) shows, "getting an even number" when rolling a single die once is a composite event that consists of three basic outcomes or simple events (getting a 2, a 4, or *a 6). The shaded portion of panel (b) shows, similarly, that "getting a face card" when drawing a single card from a deck is a composite event that consists of 12 basic outcomes or simple events (getting a jack, a queen,* or *a king from any one of the four suits). Finally, panel (c) tells us that "getting a sum of 10 or more" on a single roll of two dice is a composite event that consists of six simple (but bivariate) events; namely, those depicted by the six combinations of two faces of dice in the shaded area.*

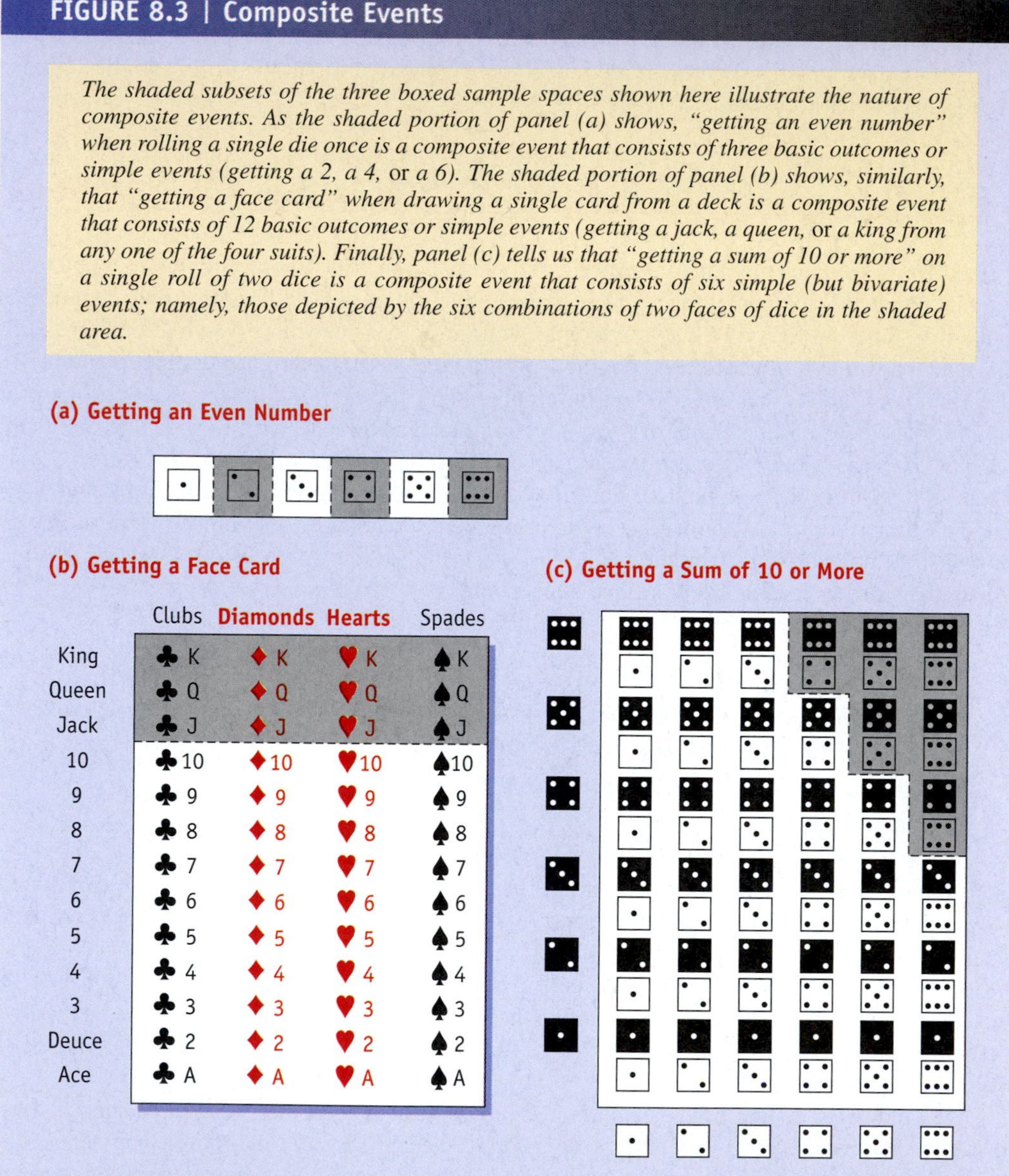

8.4 How Random Events Relate to Each Other

Before we can compute probabilities concerning the occurrence of various random events, we must learn to distinguish clearly among alternative event relationships. In particular, we must distinguish among:

- mutually exclusive events
- collectively exhaustive events
- complementary events

- unions of events
- intersections of events

MUTUALLY EXCLUSIVE EVENTS

Different random events that have no basic outcomes in common are called **mutually exclusive events** or **disjoint events** or **incompatible events.** Such events cannot occur at the same time; the occurrence of one event automatically precludes the occurrence of the other. As a business executive, you know that it is impossible to incur a loss while also earning a profit in excess of $100 million. As an economist, you know that we cannot have inflation in the 0 to 5 percent range while also suffering from inflation in excess of 13 percent. More abstract examples abound.

Consider "getting an even number" and "getting an odd number" when rolling a single die once. If one of these composite events occurs, the other one cannot possibly occur. The same random experiment can yield *simple* events that are mutually exclusive as well, such as "getting a 6" (when rolling a single die) and "getting a 4." Equally incompatible is "getting the king of hearts" and "getting the ace of hearts" when drawing a single card from a deck or "getting a defective part" and "getting a perfect part" when pulling a single item off the production line. In all these cases, it is one *or* the other.

Take another look at Figure 8.3 and note this: Mutually exclusive events always occupy entirely different parts of the sample space. In panel (a), the even numbers are found in some areas (shaded) and the odd numbers are found in other areas (unshaded). Equally distinct parts of the sample space are occupied by the six-face and the four-face in panel (a), or by the king of hearts and the ace of hearts in panel (b).

COLLECTIVELY EXHAUSTIVE EVENTS

Different random events that jointly contain all the basic outcomes in the sample space are called **collectively exhaustive events.** When the appropriate random experiment is conducted, one of these events is bound to occur. Again consider the experiment of running a firm for a year and then "incurring a loss," "earning a profit in the $0 to $100 million range," or "earning a profit in excess of $100 million." Jointly, these alternatives cover all logical possibilities.

More abstractly, consider "getting an even number" and "getting an odd number" when rolling a single die once. These two events are mutually exclusive, but they are collectively exhaustive as well. Although they cannot occur at the same time, one of them is bound to occur on each roll. This characteristic is shown in panel (a) of Figure 8.3 by the fact that the shaded areas (even numbers) and the unshaded areas (odd numbers) jointly cover the entire sample space represented by the box.

But not every set of mutually exclusive events is collectively exhaustive. In the same experiment, the events "getting a six" and "getting a four" are mutually exclusive, but they hardly exhaust the sample space. On the other hand, not every set of collectively exhaustive events need consist of mutually exclusive ones, either. Consider "getting a six," "getting an even number," and "getting an odd number." In our experiment, these events are surely collectively exhaustive; they cover the entire sample space in panel (a). Yet these events are not mutually exclusive because "getting a six" is a simple event that is already included in the composite event of "getting an even number."

COMPLEMENTARY EVENTS

Two random events such that precisely all those basic outcomes that are *not* contained in one event *are* contained in the other event are called **complementary events.** Such events, therefore, are both mutually exclusive and collectively exhaustive at the same time. If your firm this year gains a market share of 62 percent, we know that your competitors enjoy a share of 38 percent. Sometimes, such seemingly simple minded logical implications can be very helpful. Thus, you may be unable to gather information about one event, while it is easy to gather information about a complementary event. If you do the latter, you have the former.

Once more, Figure 8.3 on page 284 provides more abstract examples if we contrast, in each panel, the event pictured by the shaded area with that described by the unshaded area. Thus, in panel (a), one event is "getting an even number"; its complement of "not getting an even number" is equivalent to "getting an odd number." Together, these two mutually exclusive events exhaust the sample space.

Similarly, in panel (b), one event is "getting a face card" (shaded area); its complement is "not getting a face card" (unshaded area). Finally, in panel (c), one event is "getting a sum of 10 or more"; its complement is "not getting a sum of 10 or more" or "getting a sum of 9 or less." Again, the two mutually exclusive events precisely exhaust the sample space.

UNIONS AND INTERSECTIONS

Sometimes random events are **compatible events** in the sense that the occurrence of one does not rule out the occurrence of the other. The two events "getting a face card" and "getting a heart" provide an example. They are pictured in panels (a) and (b) of Figure 8.4. The shaded area in panel (a) depicts 12 simple events associated with the composite event of "getting a face card." The shaded area in panel (b) shows 13 simple events described by the composite event "getting a heart." Clearly, either event does not rule out the other. When compatible events occur, statisticians often want to identify one of two things:

- all the basic outcomes contained in *either one* of the events, or
- all the basic outcomes contained simultaneously in one *and* the other event.

These two possibilities give rise to two crucial concepts that are formally defined in the following Definition Box and pictured in Figure 8.4.

DEFINITION 8.4 All the basic outcomes contained in one *or* the other of two random events (or possibly in both) make up the **union of two events.** The union of events A and B is symbolized by $A \cup B$ or by A *or* B.

DEFINITION 8.5 All the basic outcomes contained in both one random event *and* another make up the **intersection of two events.** The intersection of events A and B is symbolized by $A \cap B$ or by A *and* B.

The shaded area of panel (c) in Figure 8.4 illustrates Definition 8.4 and, thus, the *union* of two events, namely, of "getting a face card" *or* "getting a heart." In contrast, the shaded area of panel (d) illustrates Definition 8.5 and, thus, the *intersection* of two events; namely, of "getting a face card" *and* "getting a heart" at the same time.

VENN DIAGRAMS

We can neatly summarize event relationships with the help of **Venn diagrams,** which are graphical devices, such as those in Figure 8.5 on page 288, that depict sample spaces and random events symbolically. The graphs are named after their originator, John Venn (1834–1888). In each panel, the box represents the sample space containing all the basic outcomes of a random experiment. Particular events are depicted by circles or sections within the sample space.

FIGURE 8.4 | Union and Intersection

Two composite events, such as those pictured by the shaded areas in panels (a) and (b), can be considered together either by focusing on their union—panel (c)—or on their intersection—panel (d). The union contains all the simple events found in either one *of the composite events—found, that is, in one of the composite events only* or *in the other only* or *in both at the same time. The key word describing such a situation is* or. *In contrast, the intersection contains only the simple events found in* both *of the composite events at the same time—found that is, in one of the composite events* and *also in the other. The key word for this situation is* and.

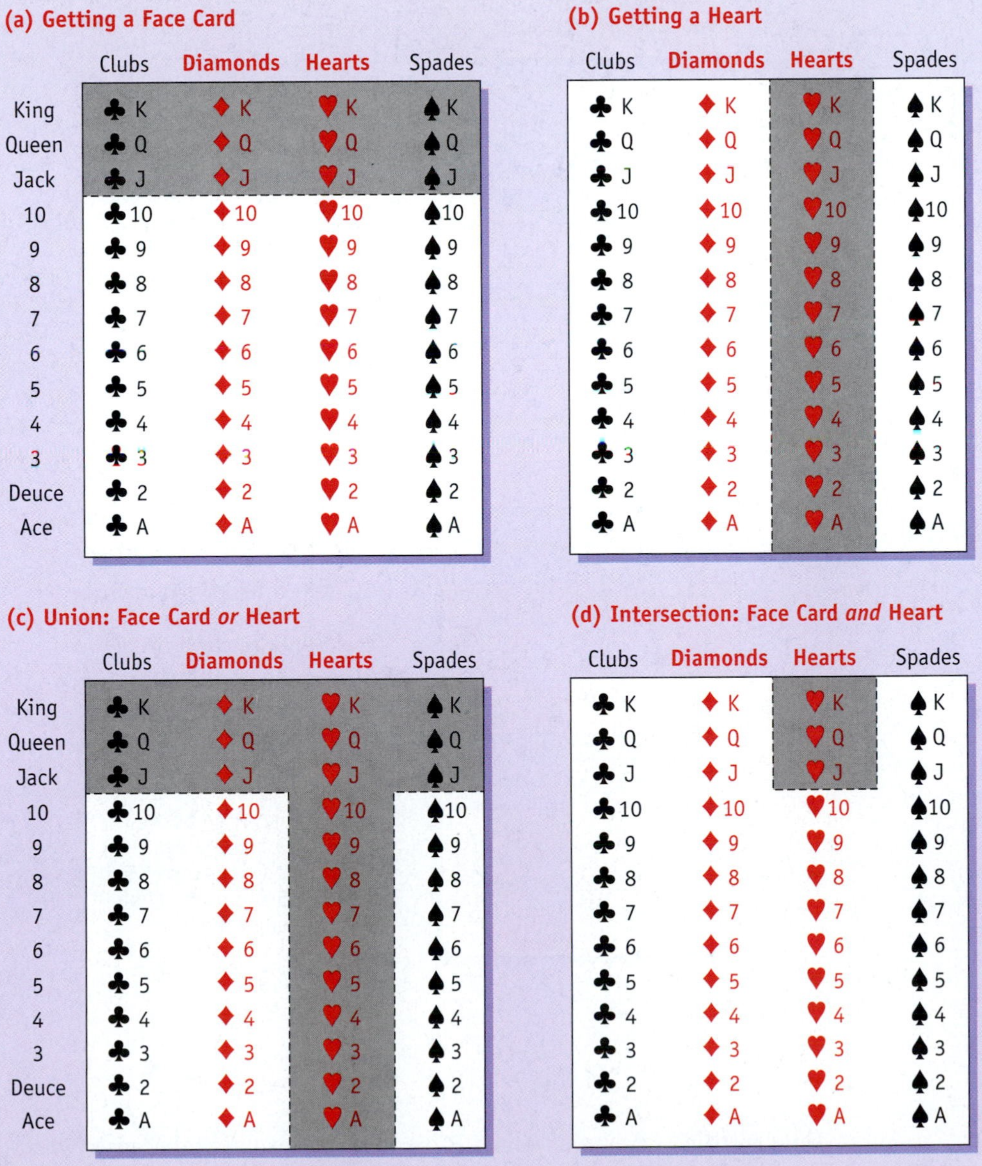

(a) Getting a Face Card

	Clubs	Diamonds	Hearts	Spades
King	♣K	♦K	♥K	♠K
Queen	♣Q	♦Q	♥Q	♠Q
Jack	♣J	♦J	♥J	♠J
10	♣10	♦10	♥10	♠10
9	♣9	♦9	♥9	♠9
8	♣8	♦8	♥8	♠8
7	♣7	♦7	♥7	♠7
6	♣6	♦6	♥6	♠6
5	♣5	♦5	♥5	♠5
4	♣4	♦4	♥4	♠4
3	♣3	♦3	♥3	♠3
Deuce	♣2	♦2	♥2	♠2
Ace	♣A	♦A	♥A	♠A

(b) Getting a Heart

Clubs	Diamonds	Hearts	Spades
♣K	♦K	♥K	♠K
♣Q	♦Q	♥Q	♠Q
♣J	♦J	♥J	♠J
♣10	♦10	♥10	♠10
♣9	♦9	♥9	♠9
♣8	♦8	♥8	♠8
♣7	♦7	♥7	♠7
♣6	♦6	♥6	♠6
♣5	♦5	♥5	♠5
♣4	♦4	♥4	♠4
♣3	♦3	♥3	♠3
♣2	♦2	♥2	♠2
♣A	♦A	♥A	♠A

(c) Union: Face Card *or* Heart

	Clubs	Diamonds	Hearts	Spades
King	♣K	♦K	♥K	♠K
Queen	♣Q	♦Q	♥Q	♠Q
Jack	♣J	♦J	♥J	♠J
10	♣10	♦10	♥10	♠10
9	♣9	♦9	♥9	♠9
8	♣8	♦8	♥8	♠8
7	♣7	♦7	♥7	♠7
6	♣6	♦6	♥6	♠6
5	♣5	♦5	♥5	♠5
4	♣4	♦4	♥4	♠4
3	♣3	♦3	♥3	♠3
Deuce	♣2	♦2	♥2	♠2
Ace	♣A	♦A	♥A	♠A

(d) Intersection: Face Card *and* Heart

Clubs	Diamonds	Hearts	Spades
♣K	♦K	♥K	♠K
♣Q	♦Q	♥Q	♠Q
♣J	♦J	♥J	♠J
♣10	♦10	♥10	♠10
♣9	♦9	♥9	♠9
♣8	♦8	♥8	♠8
♣7	♦7	♥7	♠7
♣6	♦6	♥6	♠6
♣5	♦5	♥5	♠5
♣4	♦4	♥4	♠4
♣3	♦3	♥3	♠3
♣2	♦2	♥2	♠2
♣A	♦A	♥A	♠A

FIGURE 8.5 | Venn Diagrams

Venn diagrams depict symbolically various relationships among random events.

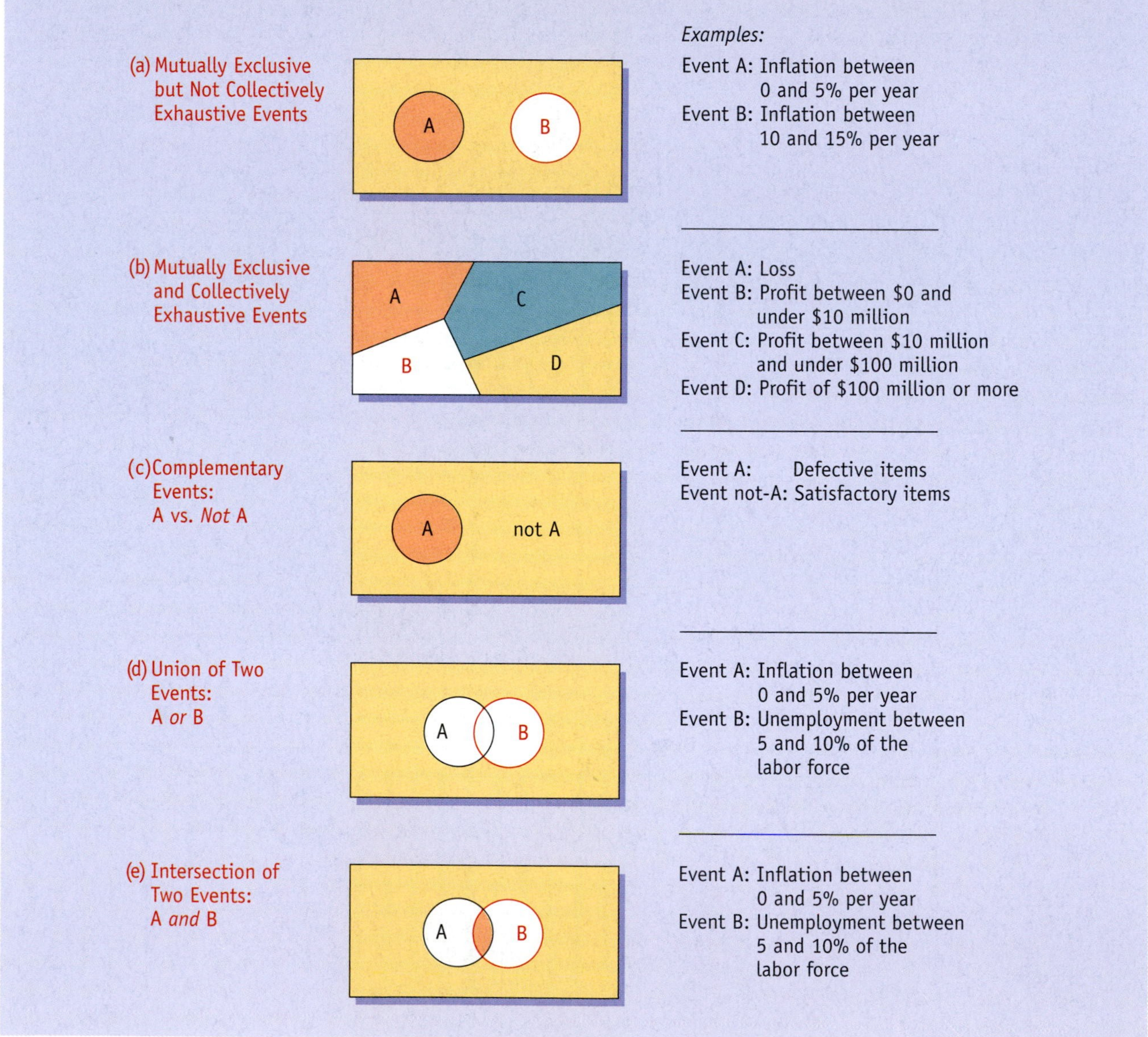

Thus, in panel (a), events A and B are mutually exclusive because, when performing the random experiment of "running the economy for a year," it is impossible to find inflation simultaneously at 0–5 percent and also at 10–15 percent. On the other hand, these two events are not collectively exhaustive; other outcomes, such as inflation above 5 but below 10 percent or inflation above 15 percent, are possible also.

Panel (b), on the other hand, depicts a complete *partition of* the sample space. When performing the random experiment of "running a firm for a year," one of the four noted events is bound to occur.

Panel (c) depicts the sample space for the random experiment of "checking the quality of items produced." Only two events are possible; they are complementary. Such events will be described symbolically as *A* vs. *not A,* or *A* vs. $\bar{A}$ in this text; another symbol often used for the complement of *A* is A'.

Panels (d) and (e) once more relate to the experiment of "running the economy for a year." Note that the two events cited do not exhaust all the possibilities; therefore, they do not cover all of the sample space. On the other hand, the two events may or may not happen simultaneously. To the extent that they do, the two circles overlap. Thus, in panel (d), any outcome that fits *either* event A *or* B (and, perhaps, even both) is found in the white area, and such a *union* of the two events is generally symbolized by $A \cup B$ or by A *or* B. (Think of $\cup$ as a symbol for "union.") Finally, the smaller number of outcomes that fit *both* event A *and* B is found in the smaller orange area of overlap in panel (e), and such an intersection of two events is always described by $A \cap B$ or by A *and* B.

In the remaining sections of this chapter, we put all of these new concepts to work in examining the meaning of the probability concept, counting techniques, the nature of probability laws, and more.

8.5 Alternative Probability Concepts

Two types of random experiments exist: those that can be repeated over and over again under (essentially) identical conditions and those that are unique and cannot be repeated because the conditions surrounding them are forever changing. The daily sampling of lightbulbs coming off your assembly line would be an example of the former. Setting up a brand new lightbulb factory in Russia right after the fall of Communism would illustrate the latter type of random experiment.

As a result, two different concepts of **probability** exist as well, although both are represented by similar-looking numbers that seek to measure the degree of likelihood that a particular event will occur. A numerical measure of chance that estimates the likelihood of a specific occurrence (event A) in a repeatable random experiment is called an **objective probability.** A corresponding value for a random experiment that can occur only once is called a **subjective probability.**

The following sections show how such probability values are determined. Objective probability values can be figured in one of two ways: theoretically, by conducting repeated *thought* experiments, or empirically, by conducting repeated *actual* experiments. Determining subjective probability values is considerably less exact.

OBJECTIVE PROBABILITY: THE THEORETICAL APPROACH

The theoretical approach to determining probability is also called the *classical approach.* The originators of probability theory, such as Pierre Simon de Laplace (1749–1827), whose biography appears on the Web site that accompanies the text, used this approach. They relied entirely on abstract reasoning. They did not resort to performing actual experiments because they deemed *logic* to be sufficient for providing all the answers. As Laplace saw it, if a hypothetical experiment could have *N* equally likely basic outcomes, and if *n* of these outcomes were favorable to event A, then the probability of this event, *p*(A), equaled the ratio of *n* to *N.* This definition of probability is summarized in Formula 8.A and put to work in Example Problems 8.1 and 8.2.

FORMULA 8.A | The Probability of Event A: Classical Approach

$$p(\text{A}) = \frac{n}{N}$$

where n is the number of equally likely basic outcomes that are favorable to the occurrence of event A, while N is the total number of equally likely basic outcomes that is possible.

EXAMPLE PROBLEM 8.1

You are about to roll a pair of dice, one black (B) and the other white (W). What is the probability of getting a total of 4 points on the two dice?

SOLUTION: Following Laplace's advice, you can first determine all possible basic outcomes; there are 36 of them:

B1, W1	B2, W1	B3, W1	B4, W1	B5, W1	B6, W1
B1, W2	B2, W2	B3, W2	B4, W2	B5, W2	B6, W2
B1, W3	B2, W3	B3, W3	B4, W3	B5, W3	B6, W3
B1, W4	B2, W4	B3, W4	B4, W4	B5, W4	B6, W4
B1, W5	B2, W5	B3, W5	B4, W5	B5, W5	B6, W5
B1, W6	B2, W6	B3, W6	B4, W6	B5, W6	B6, W6

If you throw your dice once, each one of these basic outcomes has an equal chance of occurring; hence, $N = 36$. However, you are only interested in event A, which is getting a total of 4 points. As a perusal of the above sample space shows, the favorable outcome you seek can only occur in three ways:

B1, W3 B2, W2 B3, W1

Therefore, the value of $n = 3$. Accordingly, the probability of getting a total of 4 points when rolling a pair of dice once is

$$p(4) = \frac{n}{N} = \frac{3}{36} = 0.0833$$

Put differently, you have an 8.33 percent chance of getting a sum of 4 when rolling two dice just once.

EXAMPLE PROBLEM 8.2

A woman is about to give birth; it is not going to be a multiple birth. What is the probability of her giving birth to a cat? To a girl? To a girl or a boy?

SOLUTION: Laplace's armchair reasoning identifies two possible outcomes (boy or girl), which he holds equally likely. Hence, $N = 2$. A cat is not part of the sample space; hence, $p(\text{cat}) = (0/2) = 0$. There is one girl in the sample space; hence, $p(\text{girl}) = (1/2) = 0.5$. Boy *or* girl appears twice in the sample space; hence, $p(\text{boy } or \text{ girl}) = (2/2) = 1$.

Note: Laplace's armchair reasoning about boys being *equally likely* as girls leads us, in fact, to a wrong conclusion. Experience shows that 104 boys are born for every 100 girls.

THE PROBABILITY NUMBER As in the two examples just cited, the application of Laplace's formula always produces a number between 0 and 1. Because negative basic outcomes of a random experiment are impossible, the lowest possible number of basic outcomes favorable to an event A is 0, and such an occurrence makes the probability of that event zero as well. [As a look at Formula 8.A can confirm, when $n = 0$ and N is positive, $p(A) = (n/N) = 0$.] On the other hand, the highest possible number of basic outcomes favorable to an event equals the total number of basic outcomes that are possible, and such an occurrence makes the probability of that event equal to 1. [When $n = N$, $p(A) = (n/N) = 1$. All this is summarized in Figure 8.6.]

FIGURE 8.6 | Measuring Probability

Probability as defined by Formula 8.A is inevitably measured on a scale from 0 to 1.

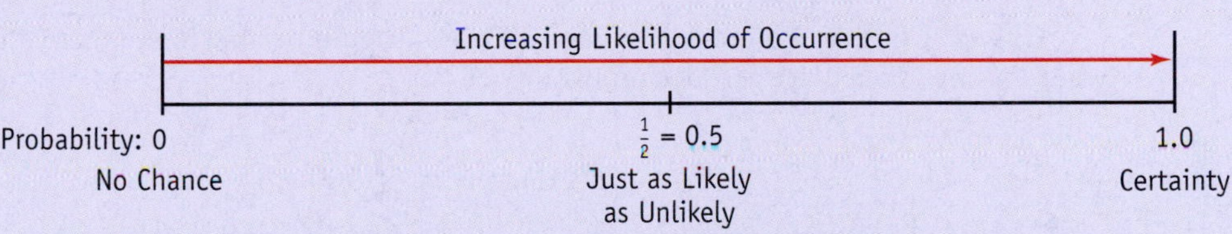

TECHNICAL DETAIL

Although probability will usually be measured by a number between 0 and 1 throughout this text, we can express it in alternative ways—for example, in terms of percentages, chances, or odds. Thus, a probability of event E equal to 7/10 or 0.7 might be expressed as a probability of 70 percent or as 70 chances in 100 or as odds of 70:30 *for E* or even as odds of 30:70 *against E.*

Symbolically, if $p(E)$ is the probability of event E, the odds *for* $E = \frac{p(E),}{1 - p(E)}$ provided $p(E) \neq 1$. Likewise, the odds *against* $E = \frac{1 - p(E)}{p(E)}$ provided $p(E) \neq 0$. Thus, if $p(E) = 0.7$, , the odds *for E* are 0.7/0.3 or 2.33 to 1; the odds *against E* are 0.3/0.7 or 0.43 to 1.

APPLICATIONS The classical formula for measuring probability applies easily to games of chance, such as those pictured earlier. Regardless of whether the event is a simple or composite one, the juxtaposition of the number of favorable basic outcomes to that of all possible basic outcomes immediately produces a probability value.

Case 1: Consider Figure 8.1 on page 281. The probability of getting a head when tossing a fair coin (one that doesn't have a lead weight attached on one side) is $p(\text{H}) = 1/2$; that of getting a 6 when rolling a balanced die is $p(6) = 1/6$; and that of getting the king of hearts when randomly drawing a card from a well-shuffled deck is $p(\text{king of hearts}) = 1/52$, always by reference to the Formula 8.A. Similarly, the probability of getting a 15 when drawing a card is

$$p(15) = \frac{0}{52} = 0$$

(because there is no such card), while that of getting a black card is

$$p(\text{black}) = \frac{26}{52} = \frac{1}{2} = 0.5000$$

In contrast, the probability of getting black when spinning the Monte Carlo wheel is somewhat less:

$$p(\text{black}) = \frac{18}{37} = 0.4865$$

Case 2: Consider Figure 8.2 on page 282. You should be able to see that getting two heads when tossing a coin twice carries a probability of

$$p(2\text{H}) = \frac{1}{4} = 0.2500$$

while that of getting two heads *or* two tails in the same game has a probability of

$$p(2\text{H } or \text{ 2T}) = \frac{2}{4} = 0.5000$$

and that of getting two fives when rolling two dice has a probability of

$$p(2 \text{ fives}) = \frac{1}{36} = 0.0278$$

Case 3: Consider Figure 8.3 on page 284. You should be able to confirm that getting an even number when rolling a die once carries a probability of

$$p(\text{even number}) = \frac{3}{6} = 0.5000$$

while that of getting a face card when drawing one card has a probability of

$$p(\text{ face card}) = \frac{12}{52} = 0.2308$$

and that of getting a sum of 10 or more when rolling two dice once has a probability of

$$p(\text{sum of 10 or more}) = \frac{6}{36} = 0.1667$$

Case 4: Consider Figure 8.4 on page 287. It should be evident that getting a face card *or* a heart carries a probability of

$$p(\text{face card or heart}) = \frac{22}{52} = 0.4231$$

while that of getting a face card *and* a heart has a probability of only

$$p(\text{face card and heart}) = \frac{3}{52} = 0.0577$$

How easy! The classical approach allows probability values to be determined by armchair reasoning alone, without ever *actually* tossing a coin, rolling a die, and the like.

OBJECTIONS TO THE CLASSICAL APPROACH Yet there are those who have trouble with the classical definition of probability: The definition seems circular, for by specifying *equally likely* basic outcomes it employs the notion of probability in order to define probability! In addition, for certain repeatable random experiments (such as tossing a biased coin, rolling a loaded die, or sampling the quality of items coming off the production line), no amount of armchair reasoning can ever discover probability values for the various possible outcomes. In such cases, numerical assignments require *experience*, which is the basis of the empirical approach.

OBJECTIVE PROBABILITY: THE EMPIRICAL APPROACH

In order to counter the criticisms of the classical approach, many prefer to think of probability values as derived from experience, the more of it the better. They suggest that the probability of an event be considered equal to the *relative frequency* with which it has actually been observed in the past over the course of a large number of random experiments.

FORMULA 8.B | The Probability of Event A: Empirical Approach

$$p(\text{A}) = \frac{k}{M}$$

where k is the number of times event A *did* occur in the past during a large number of random experiments, while M is the maximum number of times event A *could have* occurred during these experiments.

The probability value is still a ratio between 0 and 1, but it is now based on empirical data rather than on theoretical reasoning unrelated to actual experience. Thus, the probability of getting a head with a *biased* coin might be established by experiment as $p(\text{H}) = (9/10)$ and that of finding a defective item on the production line as $p(\text{D}) = (3/100)$. Both of these are values that could not be derived by abstract reasoning alone.

EXAMPLE PROBLEM 8.3

Centuries of experience show that 104 boys are born for every 100 girls. What is the probability of a woman giving birth to a boy? To a girl?

SOLUTION: Consider 204 births. The maximum number of times a boy could be born is $M = 204$. In fact, experience shows, $k = 104$ boys are born. Hence,

$$p(\text{boy}) = \frac{104}{204} = 0.5098$$

At the same time, $M = 204$ girls could be born, but only $k = 100$ girls are born. Hence,

$$p(\text{girl}) = \frac{100}{204} = 0.4902$$

Compare these results with Example Problem 8.2.

OBJECTIONS TO THE EMPIRICAL APPROACH The experience-based approach to measuring probability has elicited controversy as well: What is a "large number" of experiments? Do we need a thousand of them, or even a million, or must M (the maximum number of times an event could have occurred) approach infinity? The latter would certainly not be practical, but it is true that the probability of an event, calculated by empirical Formula 8.B, will vary with the number of experiments performed and will hardly be very meaningful if that number is small. To appreciate this fact, consider tossing a (presumably unbiased) coin to determine *empirically* the probability of getting a head.

At the time of this writing, the author performed such an experiment. Fifty tosses were made; some of the results are shown in Table 8.2, and all of them are graphed in Figure 8.7 on page 296. Note how the probability measure so determined varies with the number of experiments performed. What number of trials, therefore, reveals the "true" probability? This question is particularly acute in situations where the empirical approach is the only one available.

Contrary to popular belief among nonstatisticians, and contrary to what Figure 8.7 might suggest, we cannot be *certain* that the empirical probability value will cease to fluctuate after a "large enough" number of trials and will thus reveal a probability number that we can rely upon. Even if we continued the experiment for 20,000 tosses, the probability value might well rise again to the high of 0.67 observed after the ninth toss or it might even fall by an equivalent amount *below* the classical 0.5. However, as the **law of large numbers** suggests, the probability that an empirically determined probability value will deviate significantly from a theoretically determined value becomes smaller as we increase the number of repetitions of the random experiment in question.

In fact, in the 18th century, the French naturalist Georges Louis Leclere, known as the Comte de Buffon, tossed a coin 4,040 times, only to end up with 2,048 heads and, thus, $p(\text{H}) = 0.5069$. The Australian mathematician John Kerrich, while in a German POW camp during World War II, tossed a coin 10,000 times, getting 5,067 heads and $p(\text{H}) = 0.5067$. And the British statistician Karl Pearson, whose biography appears on the Web site associated with this text, even tossed a coin 24,000 times. He got 12,012 heads and $p(\text{H}) = 0.5005$.

SUBJECTIVE PROBABILITY

Even though objectively determined probability values are subject to debate, subjective probabilities are even more controversial. Such quantitative measures of uncertainty constitute purely personal degrees of belief in the likelihood of the occurrence of some event. Subjective probabilities thus reflect the hunches people have, their "feelings in the bone," and the associated numbers vary for any given person over time as well as from one person to the next at any given time.

TABLE 8.2 | Determining Probability Empirically: Tossing a Coin

When the probability of getting a head while tossing a coin is determined by actual experiment, the computed value (here shown in the last column) differs depending on the number of trials.

Toss Number	Result	Cumulative Number of Heads, k	Cumulative Number of Tosses, M	Probability of Head Implied by Past Experience, $p(H) = k / M$
1	T	0	1	0
2	T	0	2	0
3	H	1	3	0.3333
4	H	2	4	0.5000
5	H	3	5	0.6000
.	.	.	.	.
.	.	.	.	.
10	T	6	10	0.6000
.	.	.	.	.
.	.	.	.	.
20	T	10	20	0.5000
.	.	.	.	.
.	.	.	.	.
30	H	14	30	0.4667
.	.	.	.	.
.	.	.	.	.
40	T	20	40	0.5000
.	.	.	.	.
.	.	.	.	.
50	H	26	50	0.5200

Consider how people speculate about matters such as the following:

- the likelihood of a recession this year
- the likelihood of their merger offer being accepted
- the likelihood of General Motors being in the red next fall
- the likelihood of research finding a source of abundant energy
- the likelihood of oil being found at a given site

"There are 3 chances out of 10," they might say, yet the named random experiments have never been performed before and will never be repeated. Such a probability value of 0.3 is based neither on logical deduction nor on repeated observations of actual events—that is, historical experience. Many probability theorists, therefore, would say that such values are totally worthless.

FIGURE 8.7 | Determining Probability: The Empirical Approach

The classical approach to probability determines the probability of getting a head when tossing a fair coin by reasoning alone, and the value equals 0.5. The empirical approach, pictured here, requires actual experiments. Their measurement of probability varies with the number of trials. Using the empirical approach raises the question of what number of trials can be relied upon to reveal the "true" probability—a question that is particularly disturbing when the alternative, classical approach is unavailable.

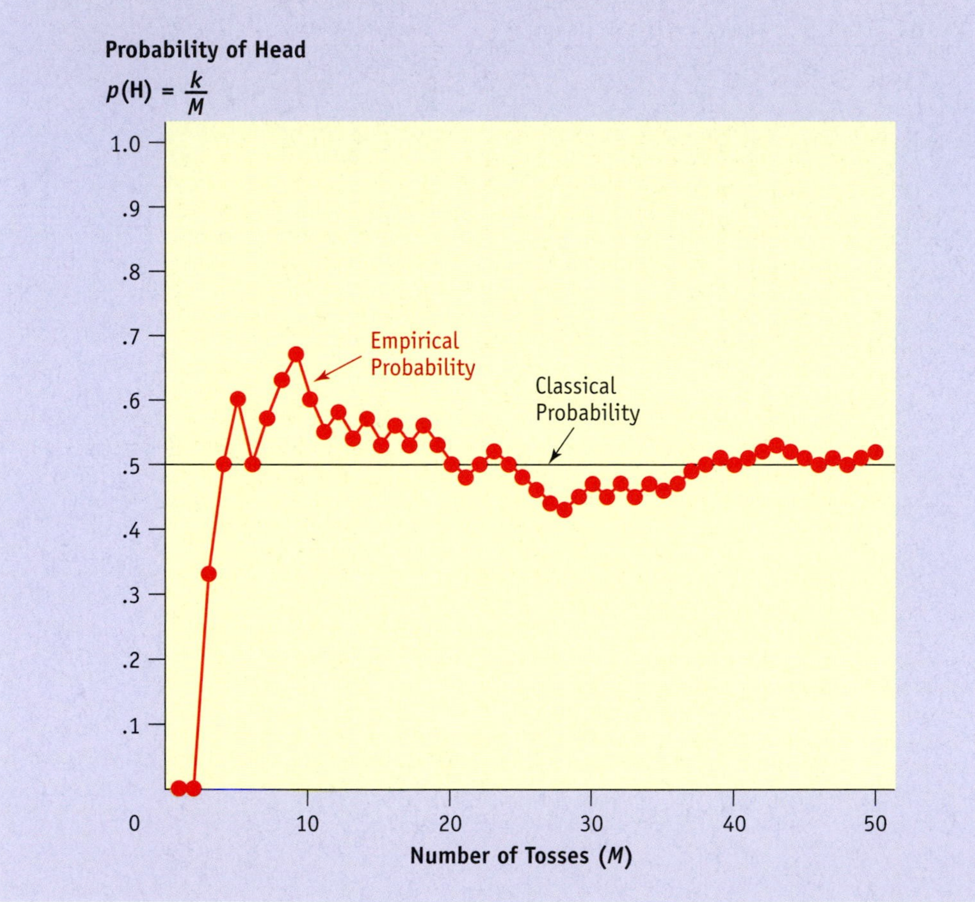

Yet such subjective estimates of the chances for various outcomes of unique random experiments still play an important role in millions of decisions every day. We will explore this fact further in Section 8.10, *Revising Probabilities: Bayes' Theorem,* and, at even greater length, in Chapter 23, *Decision Theory.* Application 8.1, *The Incredible Hole-in-One Record of 1989,* provides an immediate example of how subjective probability numbers are born.

8.6 Counting Techniques

All the random experiments discussed so far in this chapter have been easy ones in the sense that the numbers of favorable outcomes and the numbers of possible outcomes were invariably small, and counting them presented no real obstacle to calculating probabilities. But we cannot always

The Incredible Hole-in-One Record of 1989

People at the Oak Hill Country Club of Pittsford, New York, will never forget June 16, 1989. That was the day when four tournament golfers, using the same type of club, each had a hole-in-one at precisely the same spot. During 88 previous U.S. Opens, single golfers had achieved a hole-in-one only 17 times; now four of them had done so, all within two hours.

It all started when Doug Weaver waggled his 7-iron some 167 yards from the hole. His ball landed on the slope some 15 feet beyond the cup, but then spun back, rolling slowly into the cup. The grandstand roared with applause; the time was 8:15 A.M. At 9:25, Mark Wiebe placed his ball 3 feet behind the pin; it too rolled into the cup. By 9:50, Jerry Pate aced the same hole; so did Nick Price at 10:05. According to *Golf Digest Magazine,* the probability of such an event was

$$p = \frac{1}{332{,}000} = 0.000003$$

But what is the meaning of 332,000? Where would such a number originate? It is a splendid example of subjective probability.

SOURCE: Adapted from Dave Anderson, "Four! A Hole-in-One Record at Open," *The New York Times,* June 17, 1989, pp.1 and 45.

count on such simplicity. Some random experiments involve truly huge sample spaces; in such cases, we need special counting techniques to determine probabilities. In order to prepare for such occasions, we must learn a special way of counting and become familiar with the concepts of (1) factorials, (2) permutations, and (3) combinations.

FACTORIALS

Suppose we had to know the number of different ways n distinct items could be sequenced. If the number of such items were small enough and involved, say, only the three letters A, B, and C, we could do the counting rather quickly, perhaps with the help of the tree diagram in Figure 8.8 on the next page. If we started out with the three letters in our hands, we would have three alternative choices for placing a letter in the first position: A, B, and C. Having made that decision, only two choices would remain for the second position. If the first choice were A, for example, only B or C would be available for the second position. And having made the second choice, our hands would be tied; only one possibility would remain for the third position. If the first choice were A and the second B, for example, we would *have* to place C in the third place. By following the various branches of the tree diagram, we would discover the six possible sequences shown in the box and, thus, the answer to our question: 3 distinct items can be sequenced in 6 possible ways.

Our answer, however, can also be found by multiplying together the number of choices in the first, second, and third positions; that is, our 6 possible ways equal $3 \times 2 \times 1$. Such a product of a series of positive whole numbers that descends from a given number n down to 1 is called a **factorial product** or simply a **factorial.** A factorial always tells us in how many different ways n distinct items can be sequenced. In our example, where $n = 3$, the answer is written as 3! and pronounced "three factorial." The more general case is given in Formula 8.C.

FORMULA 8.C | The Factorial

$$n! = n \times (n-1) \times (n-2) \times \ldots\ldots . 3 \times 2 \times 1$$

where 0! and 1! are defined to equal 1.

FIGURE 8.8 | Alternative Sequences of Three Distinct Items

As this tree diagram indicates, three distinct items can be sequenced in six possible ways.

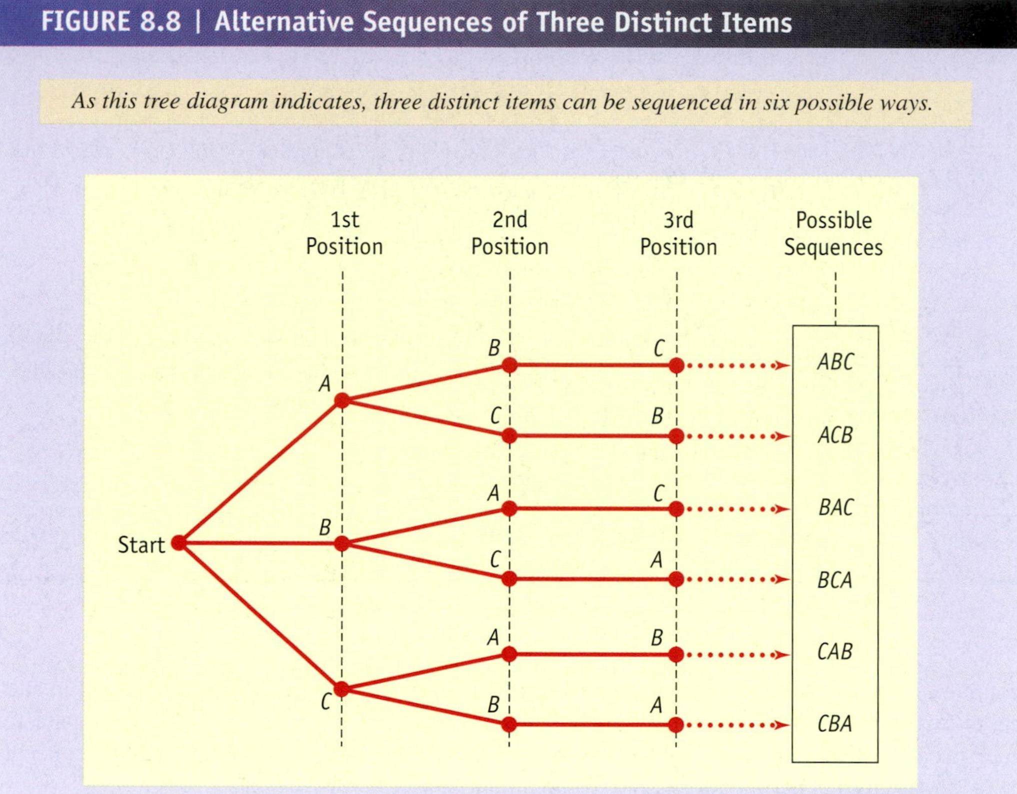

EXAMPLE PROBLEM 8.4

An advertising agency wants to place 6 different items in a sales brochure.

a. In how many different ways can those items be sequenced?

b. If a competitor soon brings out an identically sequenced brochure, would you be willing to attribute this event to pure chance?

SOLUTION:

a. The answer is $n!$, which in this case equals $6! = 6 \times 5 \times 4 \times 3 \times 2 \times 1 = 720$.

b. That's up to you, but unless there is some obvious logical reason for anybody to pick the sequence you have chosen, the probability of this happening by pure chance is a tiny 1/720.

As Example Problem 8.4 suggests, most of us would probably underestimate the number of different ways in which items can be sequenced. Even if there were only 10 items, the number would already be $10! = 3{,}628{,}800$; for 20 items, it would exceed 2.4 quintillion. (A *quintillion* is a 1 followed by 18 zeros.[2]) As these examples show, factorials of rather small numbers (such as 10!) can take the place of extremely large ordinary numbers (such as 3,628,800), which comes in handy as we compute probabilities. Can you imagine in how many different ways the thousands of items in the typical mail-order catalog could be sequenced? And why a lawyer, fighting a copyright infringement suit and armed with nothing but a factorial, would have an easy time convincing the court that a competitor's *identical* catalog couldn't possibly have been produced by pure chance? Application 8.2, *The Magic Number Seven,* on the next page provides an interesting example of a factorial that made headlines around the world.

PERMUTATIONS

The previous section in fact discussed special cases of **permutations,** which are distinguishable ordered arrangements of items all of which have been drawn from a given group of items. Thus, the box in Figure 8.8 contains 6 permutations of the letters *A, B, C* because (1) it shows 6 distinct alternative sequences of these letters and (2) all of these sequences have been created out of the same group of letters: *A, B,* and C. Nevertheless, the letter-sequencing example of Figure 8.8 constitutes a special case of permutations for two reasons: First, the example involves a selection of n items out of n, but one could select fewer than n. Second, in this example, selections are made out of a group of *clearly distinguishable* items, but all of the elements of some groups may not be this distinct from one another. Both of these matters are discussed in the remainder of this section.

SELECTING *x* OUT OF *n* DISTINCT ITEMS Our letter-sequencing example involved finding the permutations for all the items in existence—that is, it involved finding all the different ways of arranging n distinct items into groups of n. Oftentimes, however, we are interested in the possible number of ordered sequences of only x items out of n, where x is smaller than n. In how many different ways, we may ask, can we sequence $x = 3$ items taken out of $n = 10$ distinct items? The answer cannot be $n!$ because that number also includes the ways to sequence the other $(n - x) = 7$ items. Thus, we must eliminate the $(n - x)!$ portion of the expression $n!$ This can most easily be done by dividing $n!$ by $(n - x)!$ The resulting formula for the possible number of permutations, P, when x items at a time are taken out of n distinct items is Formula 8.D.

FORMULA 8.D | Permutations for x out of n Distinct Items (with no repetitions among the x items and $x \leq n$)

$$P_x^n = \frac{n!}{(n - x)!}$$

Note: We can apply this formula to the special case of $x = n$, but we must realize that $n - x$ then equals 0 and that $0! = 1$ *by definition.* Thus, if $x = n$, the entire formula collapses to $n!$, which returns us to Formula 8.C.

---

[2]If you have EXCEL, you can check it out by clicking the **Function Wizard** > **Math & Trig** > **FACT** > **OK** and entering 20 in the dialog box. MINITAB refuses to compute factorials that large, but you can find smaller factorials of n by entering $n + 1$ in the GAMMA function. To find 10!, click **Calc** > **Calculator**, in *Store result in variable,* enter **C1**, in *Expression,* enter **GAMMA (11)**, and click **OK**.

APPLICATION 8.2

THE MAGIC NUMBER SEVEN

As the remaining chapters of this book will show, many business and economics applications of statistical theory rely on probabilities calculated after taking a random sample from some sort of population. It is not always easy to ensure such randomness. This chapter, for example, frequently notes probability values that are valid after drawing cards from a *well-shuffled* deck, but how can one assure such initial randomness?

Consider Figure 8.A and note in row (1) how a suit of hearts is cut into two sequences: ace through six and seven through king. Row (2) shows the result of a first shuffle: the cards are no longer ordered, but the two sequences are still recognizable; they are merely interspersed.

How many shuffles would it take to achieve a true random sequence of cards? Two mathematicians, Dave Bayer and Persi Diaconis, recently tackled the issue by computer and concluded the following for a full deck of cards: Because any one of 52 cards might take the first spot in a random sequence, any one of the remaining 51 cards the second spot, any one of the remaining 50 cards the third spot, and so on, there exist $52! = 10^{63}$ possible random series. To achieve any one of these series (and, thus, ensure that any one card is equally likely to take any one of 52 possible positions), a single deck must be shuffled 7 times. Two decks must be shuffled 9 times and six decks 12 times. Yet, more often than not, this is *not* what happens. At the Trump Plaza in Atlantic City, blackjack dealers shuffle eight decks only twice at the beginning of each game, which means that the card series is far from random. People who know this can improve their odds at winning. By looking at the sequences of cards at the end of a prior hand, they can predict the distribution of cards during the next hand.

Using modern technology also helps. Take the case of Philip Preston Anderson, arrested at a Las Vegas blackjack table for "suspicious body movements." It turned out that he was wearing "computer shoes," tiny card-counting devices controlled by switches manipulated by his feet. By tapping his toes, he could tell the computer which cards had been played in what order. The computer calculated appropriate probabilities for other cards showing up. How was the information relayed? A wire from the computer delivered tiny electric shocks, which were coded signals.

SOURCES: Adapted from Ken Wells, "Philip Anderson Has a Feeling He Knows What's in the Cards," *The Wall Street Journal*, January 13, 1988, pp.1 and 12; and Gina Kolata, "In Shuffling Cards, 7 Is Winning Number," *The New York Times*, January 9, 1990, pp. C1 and C12.

FIGURE 8.A

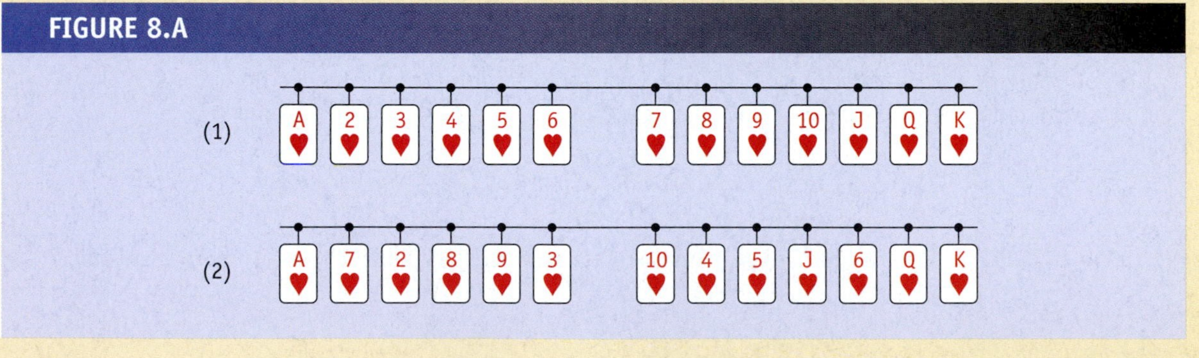

EXAMPLE PROBLEM 8.5

A firm wants to place new managers in 3 of its 10 plants. In how many different ways can it do so?

SOLUTION: Applying Formula 8.D to the selection of 3 items out of 10, we find the answer as

$$P_3^{10} = \frac{10!}{(10-3)!} = \frac{10!}{7!} = \frac{10 \times 9 \times 8 \times 7!}{7!} = 10 \times 9 \times 8 = 720$$

Out of a total of 10 items, one can create 720 different ordered sequences of 3 items.

Note: Can you see why permutations, just like factorials, have also found their way into the courts? In one discrimination suit, employees claimed that allegedly random work assignments couldn't possibly have been made by a random process, given that the assignments showed a repetitive pattern, while the number of possible assignment choices was huge.

EXAMPLE PROBLEM 8.6

A committee of two is to be created from three persons, *A, B,* and *C,* in such a way that the first person listed occupies the committee chair. How many possibilities exist? What are they?

SOLUTION: Applying Formula 8.D to the selection of $x = 2$ letters from $n = 3$ distinct letters (*A, B,* and *C*),

$$P_2^3 = \frac{3!}{(3-2)!} = \frac{3 \times 2 \times 1}{1} = 6$$

These six sequences are *AB, AC, BA, BC, CA,* and *CB.*

SELECTING *x* OUT OF *n* NONDISTINCT ITEMS In our letter-sequencing example of Figure 8.8, the elements contained in the given group of items (namely, the letters *A, B, C*) were *distinct* in the sense that every one of the $n = 3$ items in the group differed clearly from every other item in the group. Yet the elements contained in a given group of items can also be *nondistinct* in the sense that x_1 out of n items are of one kind, x_2 are of another kind, and so on for k different kinds, such that $x_1 + x_2 + \ldots + x_k = n$. Consider the group *A, A, A, B, B, C, C, C, C, C,* for example. In such a case, a sequence such as the one printed here cannot be distinguished from another in which only the first and second *A*'s have exchanged places. In how many *distinct* ways, we may ask, can one sequence the above 10 *nondistinct* items?

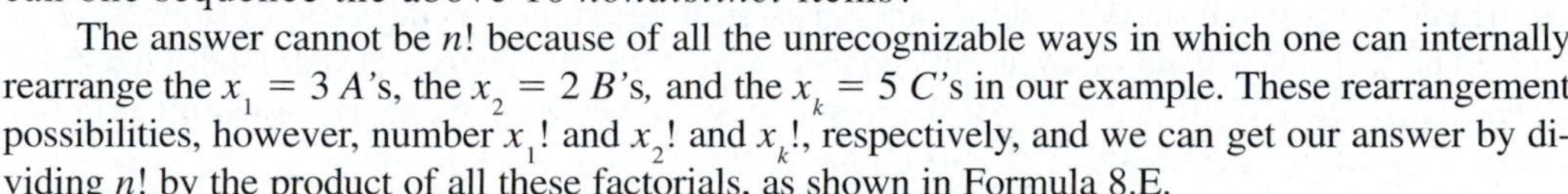

The answer cannot be $n!$ because of all the unrecognizable ways in which one can internally rearrange the $x_1 = 3$ *A*'s, the $x_2 = 2$ *B*'s, and the $x_k = 5$ *C*'s in our example. These rearrangement possibilities, however, number $x_1!$ and $x_2!$ and $x_k!$, respectively, and we can get our answer by dividing $n!$ by the product of all these factorials, as shown in Formula 8.E.

FORMULA 8.E | Permutations for x out of n Items, Given k Distinct Types of Items and $k < n$

$$P_{x_1 x_2 \ldots x_k}^{n} = \frac{n!}{x_1! x_2! \ldots\ldots x_k!}$$

where x_1 items are of one kind, x_2 items are of a second kind, and x_k items are of a kth kind and where $x_1 + x_2 + \ldots + x_k = n$.

When applying this formula, we discover that the above 10 nondistinct items can be put into 2,520 distinct sequences because

$$P^{10}_{3,2,5} = \frac{10!}{3!\,2!\,5!} = 2{,}520$$

EXAMPLE PROBLEM 8.7

How many distinct permutations can be formed from a group containing only two kinds of items, such as $x = 2$ A's and $(n - x) = 1$ B? Identify the possibilities as well.

SOLUTION: From this group of $n = 3$ (consisting of A, A, B), we can form only 3 distinct permutations:

$$P^{n}_{x,n-x} = \frac{n!}{x!\,(n-x)!} = \frac{3!}{2!\,(2-1)!} = 3$$

These permutations are *AAB, ABA,* and *BAA.*

COMBINATIONS

Sometimes we may not be interested in permutations, but rather in **combinations,** which are different selections of items such that possible alternative sequences among the components of any one such selection are viewed as identical. If you take a friend to a restaurant and order salad and dessert, while your friend orders dessert first and salad later, your orders represent different permutations of food items, but you are both consuming the same combination of them. Likewise, the boxed list in Figure 8.8 on page 298 shows six *permutations* but represents a single *combination* of the letters *A, B, C.* If we don't care about the order of the items, there is only one way to select three items out of three. Whereas the sequence of the elements in the selected group matters in the case of permutations (*ABC* is not considered the same as *ACB,* for example), sequence does not matter in the least for combinations (combination *ABC* is considered the same as combination *ACB* because each grouping contains the same elements). Sequence does not matter in the case of card hands or of committee members or of samples of all sorts. The fact that a hand of cards contains the king of hearts, the ace of diamonds, and the 2, 8, and 10 of clubs is all that matters. We would view the identical elements listed in a different order—say, ace of diamonds, 2 of clubs, king of hearts, 8 and 10 of clubs—as the same hand. They represent a different permutation but the same combination.

When we calculate probabilities, we are often interested in this question: In how many different ways can we select a given number of items (say, $x = 5$) from a group of distinct items (say, $n = 10$) without any concern whatsoever for the sequence in which the selected items appear? The answer cannot be $n!\,/\,(n - x)!$ precisely because this permutation formula counts separately all the different orderings of an identical group of x items, but order does not matter to us now. In order to count any given group of x items only once, we can divide $n!$ by $x!$ as well, because $x!$ shows all the different but now irrelevant ways in which x items can be sequenced, which yields Formula 8.F.

FORMULA 8.F | **Combinations for x at a Time out of n Distinct Items (with no repetitions among the x items | and $x \leq n$)**

$$C_x^n = \frac{n!}{x!(n-x)!}$$

Note: In the limiting case when $x = n$, this formula simplifies to 1:

$$C_n^n = \frac{n!}{n!\,(n-n)!} = \frac{n!}{n!\,0!} = \frac{n!}{n!\,1!} = 1$$

After all, when the order of selection is irrelevant, there exists only one way to select n items out of n items.

EXAMPLE PROBLEM 8.8

In how many ways could we select 5 cards from a deck of 52 if the order of selection did not matter?

SOLUTION: Formula 8.F gives us the answer almost instantly:

$$C_5^{52} = \frac{52!}{5!(52-5)!} = \frac{52!}{5!47!} = \frac{52 \times 51 \times 50 \times 49 \times 48 \times 47!}{5 \times 4 \times 3 \times 2 \times 1 \times 47!} = \frac{52 \times 51 \times 50 \times 49 \times 48}{5 \times 4 \times 3 \times 2 \times 1}$$

$$= \frac{311{,}875{,}200}{120} = 2{,}598{,}960$$

We could select 2,598,960 different hands of 5 cards from a deck of a mere 52 cards. Imagine how long it would take you to find this answer with the help of a tree diagram, such as the one in Figure 8.8.

Note: If you have EXCEL, you can check the result by clicking the **Function Wizard** > **Math & Trig** > **COMBIN** > **OK** and entering first 52 and then 5 in the dialog box.

EXAMPLE PROBLEM 8.9

What is the probability of picking the top 5 cards from a deck of 52 well-shuffled cards and ending up with a *straight,* an ordered denominational sequence of 5 cards in which the deuce counts as the lowest and the ace as the highest card acceptable?

SOLUTION: According to Formula 8.A, the probability sought equals the number of ways in which we could pick an ordered denominational sequence of 5 cards, divided by the total number of 5-card combinations we could possibly pick. Example Problem 8.8 already provides us with the denominator of this probability ratio; we must now find the numerator.

Although the lowest possible card in a 5-card straight can be a 2 (or deuce), it can belong to any one of the four different suits. The 2 can be clubs, diamonds, hearts, or spades, and the same possibilities exist for the next four cards (which would be 3, 4, 5, and 6). Thus, there can be 4 × 4 × 4 × 4 × 4 = 1,024 different straights starting with 2. Yet there are nine possible low cards—namely, all the numbers between 2 and 10. (A 5-card straight starting with 10 would reach to the end of the series, going 10, jack, queen, king, and ace.) Hence, there can be 9 × 1,024 = 9,216 such straights altogether. If we contrast this number with the entire sample space of 5-card sets, we find the (low) probability of a 5-card straight:

$$p(\text{5-card straight}) = \frac{9{,}216}{2{,}598{,}960} = 0.003546$$

Not all applications of the combinations formula are equally abstract. In one instance, a national restaurant chain was accused of false advertising because it claimed to offer "over 50,000 different dinner combinations." Yet its menu only featured 3 different salads, 5 different entrees, 4 different vegetables, 6 different drinks, and 7 different desserts. A dinner was defined as "2 of each." Do you think the firm was lying? It was not! Applications 8.3, *The ESP Mystery*, and 8.4, *Connecticut Lotto Chief Loses Job,* provide additional case studies in which our special counting techniques are applied.

Application 8.3
The ESP Mystery
http://www.harcourtcollege.com/business_stats/kohler/siteresources.html

APPLICATION 8.4

Connecticut Lotto Chief Loses Job

In 1989, Connecticut's lotto chief J. Blaine Lewis, Jr., lost his job. At a time when the state's lottery took in $513 million per year in revenues and kept $225 million for the state's general fund, the state's special revenue chief had ordered Mr. Lewis to go before the Connecticut Gaming Policy Board and recommend a change: replacing the current game in which jackpot winners had to pick correctly 6 out of 40 numbers with a new game in which 6 out of 44 numbers had to be picked. The negligible change, it was argued, would improve the state's lottery take.

Applying the combinations formula, Mr. Lewis disagreed. While C_6^{40} equals 3,838,380, implying a 1 in 3.8 million chance for a jackpot winner, C_6^{44} equals 7,059,052, reducing a winner's chance considerably to 1 in 7.1 million.

Mr. Lewis "did not care to deceive the public" and he was surely right on that account. But, from the point of view of his employer, he may have overlooked one consideration. It is conceivable that jackpots that are harder to win produce more rollovers of money not won and, thus, bigger jackpots. This prospect might increase sales and the state's net revenues.

SOURCE: Adapted from Dennis Hevesi, "Connecticut Lotto Chief Loses Job in Odds Battle," *The New York Times,* May 28, 1989, p. 36.

8.7 Laws of Probability: Addition

Deriving probability values for single events is one thing. Manipulating these values to determine the combined probability for the union or intersection of several events is another. Such manipulation is often useful because it can eliminate the need for repeated counting of favorable and possible basic outcomes once some probability values have been derived. A person who has separately counted the fingers on the left hand and on the right hand can determine the number of fingers on both hands by simply adding 5 + 5, rather than by looking at both hands simultaneously and counting again. Just so, a person who already has some probability values can often combine them to gain further knowledge. Two crucial laws govern such operations: (1) the addition law and (2) the multiplication law. Both were first stated by Abraham de Moivre (1667–1754), a biography of whom appears on the Web site that accompanies this text. In this section, we focus on the first of these laws.

The **addition law** is a law of probability theory that is used to compute the probability for the occurrence of a *union* of two or more events. Such an occurrence was first illustrated for the case of two events in panel (c) of Figure 8.4 (on page 287). For the time being, we will continue to focus on two events, but the law can easily be extended to a larger number of events. Regardless of the *number* of events, we can apply a *general* addition law to *all* types of events and a *special* (and simpler) law to *mutually exclusive* events.

THE GENERAL ADDITION LAW

The general addition law for two events is given in Formula 8.G, and it is easy to interpret. The law states that the probability of event A *or* B happening equals the probability of A alone plus the probability of B alone minus the probability of A *and* B happening at the same time.

FORMULA 8.G | General Addition Law for All Types of Events

$$p(\text{A } or \text{ B}) = p(\text{A}) + p(\text{B}) - p(\text{A } and \text{ B})$$

Note: Some statisticians prefer to use the symbol $p(\text{A} \cup \text{B})$ instead of $p(\text{A } or \text{ B})$ and to use the symbol $p(\text{A} \cap \text{B})$ instead of $p(\text{A } and \text{ B})$.

Consider panel (d) of Figure 8.5, which is reproduced here.

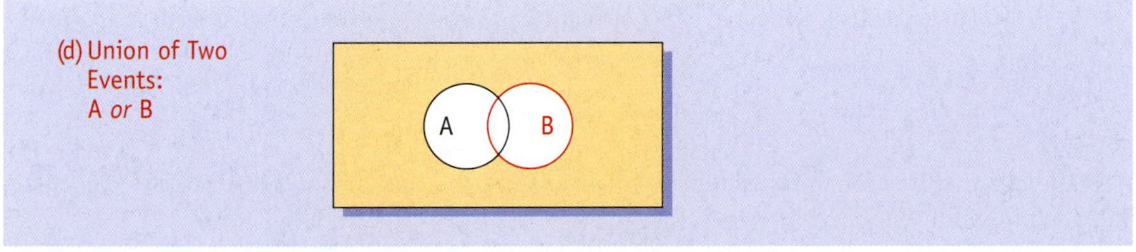

The probability of A alone, $p(\text{A})$, is the probability of getting the basic outcomes contained in the black circle, labeled A. The probability of B alone, $p(\text{B})$, is the probability of getting the basic outcomes contained in the red circle, labeled B. If we now determined the probability of either A *or* B happening by adding the separate probabilities of the two events, the probabilities of all the basic outcomes contained in the overlapping *intersection* of the two events would be counted twice: once as a part of circle A and again as a part of circle B. To eliminate the double counting, the probabilities of the basic outcomes found in this overlapping section are deducted once; hence, the *negative* term $p(\text{A } and \text{ B})$ in Formula 8.G. As a whole, the formula gives us precisely the probability of all the basic outcomes inside the white area of panel (d).

AN EXAMPLE Review Figure 8.4 on page 287. The probability of event A (getting a face card) equals

$$p(\text{A}) = \frac{12}{52}$$

This calculation requires nothing more difficult than applying the classical formula: counting the basic outcomes favorable to this event, of which there are 12 in the shaded area of panel (a), and relating the count to all the possible basic outcomes, of which there are 52 in the entire boxed sample space. Similarly, in panel (b), we can find the probability of event B (getting a heart) as

$$p(\text{B}) = \frac{13}{52}$$

What is the probability of the union of these events, of getting *either* a face card *or* a heart? Does it equal

$$\frac{12}{52} + \frac{13}{52} = \frac{25}{52}?$$

The answer is *no,* as a simple count of favorable *vs.* possible basic outcomes in panel (c) reveals. The probability of getting a face card *or* a heart, $p(\text{A} \cup \text{B})$, equals only 22/52, the number of panel (c) favorable basic outcomes (shaded) divided by the number of all possible basic outcomes (shaded plus unshaded). The difference of 3/52 between the incorrect result of 25/52 and the correct result of 22/52 is easily accounted for. It arises from the double counting of the jack, queen, and king of hearts when the probabilities implied by the shaded areas of panels (a) and (b) are thoughtlessly added together. We can eliminate the error by deducting the probability of getting a face card *and* a heart, $p(\text{A } and \text{ B})$, as the formula demands. That value equals 3/52, as panel (d) so vividly illustrates. The correct computation:

$$p(\text{A}) + p(\text{B}) - p(\text{A } \textit{and} \text{ B}) = p(\text{A } \textit{or} \text{ B})$$

$$p(\text{face card}) + p(\text{heart}) - p(\text{face card } \textit{and} \text{ heart}) = p(\text{face card } \textit{or} \text{ heart})$$

$$\frac{12}{52} + \frac{13}{52} - \frac{3}{52} = \frac{22}{52}$$

If we know the probabilities implied by panels (a), (b), and (d) in Figure 8.4, we can calculate the probability implied by panel (c).

TECHNICAL DETAIL

What if we wanted to figure the joint probability of three or more events? If there were three events, we would simply expand Formula 8.G to read

$$p(\text{A}) + p(\text{B}) + p(\text{C}) - p(\text{A } \textit{and} \text{ B}) - p(\text{A } \textit{and} \text{ C}) - p(\text{B } \textit{and} \text{ C}) + p(\text{A } \textit{and} \text{ B } \textit{and} \text{ C})$$

which equals $p(\text{A } or \text{ B } or \text{ C})$. Further expansion is carried out similarly.

THE SPECIAL ADDITION LAW

The general addition law can be used to calculate the probability for a union of all types of events, but it reduces to a simpler form for mutually exclusive events. Consider panel (a) of Figure 8.5, which is reproduced here:

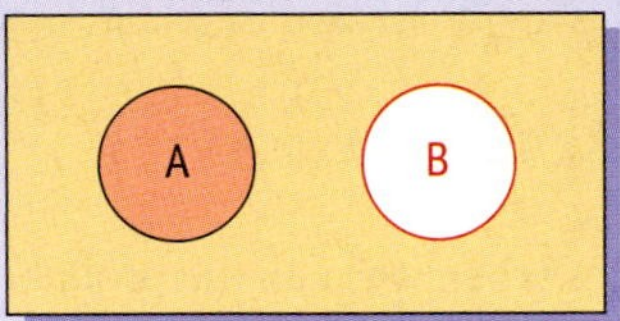

(a) Mutually Exclusive but Not Collectively Exhaustive Events

When we are dealing with such mutually exclusive events, there is no intersection, hence no double counting, hence no need for the negative term in our formula. We can still use Formula 8.G, but the expression $p(\text{A } and \text{ B})$ will equal zero; hence, we can just as well use the simpler Formula 8.H.

FORMULA 8.H | Special Addition Law for Mutually Exclusive Events

$$p(\text{A } or \text{ B}) = p(\text{A}) + p(\text{B})$$

Note: Some statisticians prefer to use the symbol $p(\text{A} \cup \text{B})$ instead of $p(\text{A } or \text{ B})$.

AN EXAMPLE Consider calculating the probability of getting a face card (event A) *or* getting an ace (event B) for the experiment of drawing one card at random from a well-shuffled deck. As a quick look at panel (a) of Figure 8.4 on page 287 confirms, the separate probabilities of these mutually exclusive events equal

$$p(\text{A}) = \frac{12}{52} \quad \text{and} \quad p(\text{B}) = \frac{4}{52}$$

and the probability of their union is

$$p(\text{A}) + p(\text{B}) = p(\text{A } or \text{ B})$$

$$p(\text{face card}) + p(\text{ace}) = p(\text{face card } or \text{ ace})$$

$$\frac{12}{52} + \frac{4}{52} = \frac{16}{52}$$

Naturally, the probability for any union of mutually exclusive events that are also collectively exhaustive must equal 1, and we can easily confirm this fact, too. Consider panel (c) of Figure 8.3 on page 284. In the experiment shown there, the probability of getting a sum of 10 or more (event A) or getting a sum of 9 or less (event B) exhausts the sample space. Accordingly, our special formula tells us that

$$p(\text{A}) + p(\text{B}) = p(\text{A } or \text{ B})$$

$$p(\text{sum of 10 or more}) + p(\text{sum of 9 or less}) = p(\text{sum of} \geq 10 \text{ } or \text{ sum of} \leq 9)$$

$$\frac{6}{36} + \frac{30}{36} = 1$$

Thus, the probability for a union of complementary events always equals 1. When event B is complementary to event A, we can write the above also as

$$p(\text{A}) + p(\overline{\text{A}}) = p(\text{A } or\ \overline{\text{A}}) = 1$$

Being aware of this truism often helps when we seek the probability of one event, say, A, but it is easier to calculate the probability of its complement, *not* A = $\overline{\text{A}}$. In that case, $p(\text{A})$ can simply be found as $1 - p(\overline{\text{A}})$. Similarly, $p(\overline{\text{A}})$ can always be found by computing $1 - p(\text{A})$.

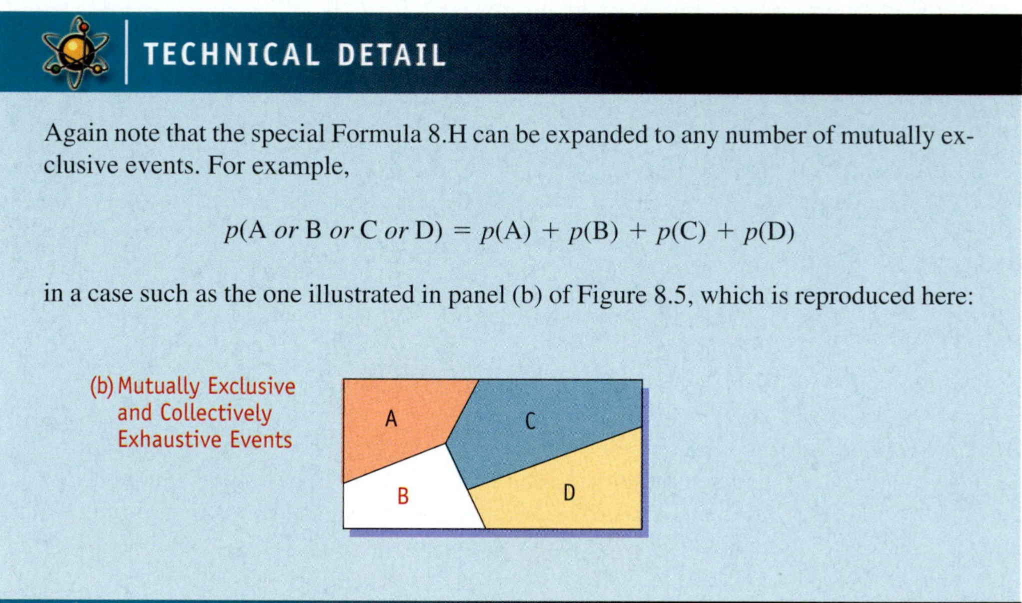

TECHNICAL DETAIL

Again note that the special Formula 8.H can be expanded to any number of mutually exclusive events. For example,

$$p(\text{A } or \text{ B } or \text{ C } or \text{ D}) = p(\text{A}) + p(\text{B}) + p(\text{C}) + p(\text{D})$$

in a case such as the one illustrated in panel (b) of Figure 8.5, which is reproduced here:

8.8 Laws of Probability: Multiplication

The **multiplication law** is a law of probability theory that is used to compute the probability for an *intersection* of two or more events. Such an occurrence was first illustrated for the case of two events in panel (d) of Figure 8.4 on page 287. We also met a symbolic expression in panel (e) of Figure 8.5, which is reproduced here:

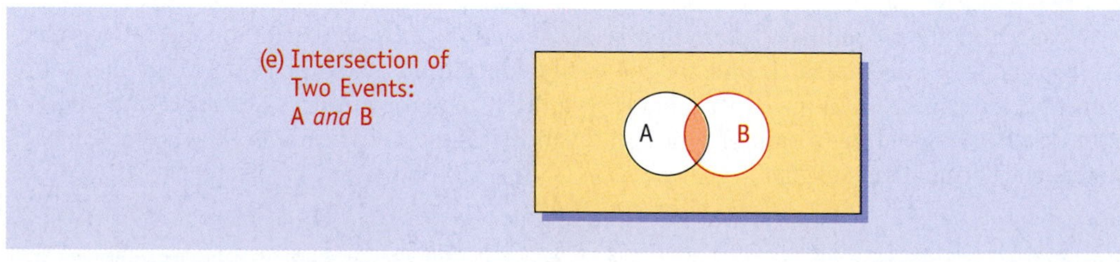

For the time being, we will once again focus on two events, but, as we will learn later, this law, too, can be extended to a larger number of events. As was true for the addition law, a *general* multiplication law can be formulated that applies to all types of events; a *special* and simpler law can be stated for a more restricted group of events. Before we can understand these laws, however, we must become familiar with a number of new concepts.

1. To understand the *general multiplication law,* we must first learn about:
   - unconditional probability
   - conditional probability
   - joint probability
2. To understand the *special multiplication law,* we must first learn about:
   - dependent events
   - independent events

UNCONDITIONAL PROBABILITY

Consider an appliance dealer who has been promoting a refrigerator with a major television advertising campaign. To evaluate the effectiveness of the campaign, let us suppose, all of the 600 customers who visit the dealership during a certain period are asked whether they remember the TV ad. Records are kept of customer answers as well as their possible purchase of the product in question. The results of this survey are given in Table 8.3.

Now consider the following four events:

- purchasing the refrigerator, P
- not purchasing the refrigerator, $\overline{\text{P}}$
- remembering the TV ad, R
- not remembering the TV ad, $\overline{\text{R}}$

Note how we can calculate regular empirical probability values for these four events by using the numbers in the shaded last column and shaded last row of Table 8.3:

$$p(\text{P}) = \frac{180}{600} = 0.30 \qquad p(\text{R}) = \frac{200}{600} = 0.33$$

$$p(\overline{\text{P}}) = \frac{420}{600} = 0.70 \qquad p(\overline{\text{R}}) = \frac{400}{600} = 0.67$$

TABLE 8.3 | Summary of Customer Survey

These hypothetical figures represent numbers of customers classified in two ways: whether they purchased a refrigerator and whether they remembered a TV ad promoting it.

	TV Ad:		
Refrigerator:	**Remembered, R**	**Not Remembered, $\overline{\text{R}}$**	**Total**
Purchased, P	120	60	180
Not Purchased, $\overline{\text{P}}$	80	340	420
Total	200	400	600

Experience thus reveals a probability of 0.30 that a customer buys the refrigerator, a probability of 0.70 that a customer doesn't, a probability of 0.33 that a customer remembers the ad, and a probability of 0.67 that a customer doesn't remember the ad. Because each of these values measures the likelihood that a particular event will occur, regardless of whether another event occurs, each of these values is called on *unconditional probability.* Thus, 0.30 equals the probability of purchase by a customer without regard to the question of whether that customer does or does not remember the ad. Similarly, the value of 0.67 equals the probability of not remembering by a customer without regard to the question of whether that customer does or does not purchase the refrigerator. Because these unconditional probabilities are calculated from the margins of our table, they are also referred to as *marginal probabilities.*

DEFINITION 8.6 A measure of the likelihood that a particular event will occur, regardless of whether another event occurs, is called an **unconditional probability.** Because relevant numbers are usually found in the margins of a table, such a measure is also called a **marginal probability.**

Note: In this context, our use of the term *marginal* has nothing to do with the economist's use of the term, as in *marginal cost* or *marginal propensity to consume*. In those other contexts, *marginal* stands for *change in* and is unrelated to the margins of a table.

CONDITIONAL PROBABILITY

It will come as no surprise that the concept of unconditional probability has a twin:

DEFINITION 8.7 A measure of the likelihood that a particular event will occur, given the fact that another event has already occurred or is certain to occur, is a **conditional probability.** For two events, A and B, such a probability is always denoted by $p(A|B)$ or $p(B|A)$, which is read as "the probability of A, given B" or as "the probability of B, given A" with the vertical line standing for "given."

EXAMPLE PROBLEM 8.10

From Table 8.3, we can calculate eight different conditional probability values. What are they?

SOLUTION: By focusing on the values in the first row only, then on those in the second row only, next on those in the first column only, and finally on those in the second column only, we can calculate the following conditional probabilities:

a. From the first row, we can calculate the probability of remembering, given the fact that a purchase has occurred, and also the probability of not remembering, given that a purchase has occurred:

$$p(R|P) = \frac{120}{180} = 0.67 \quad \text{and} \quad p(\overline{R}|P) = \frac{60}{180} = 0.33$$

b. From the second row, we can calculate the probability of remembering, given the fact that no purchase has occurred, and also the probability of not remembering, given that no purchase has occurred:

$$p(\text{R}|\overline{\text{P}}) = \frac{80}{420} = 0.19 \quad \text{and} \quad p(\overline{\text{R}}|\overline{\text{P}}) = \frac{340}{420} = 0.81$$

c. From the first column, we can calculate the probability of purchase, given the fact that the ad is remembered, and also the probability of no purchase, given that the ad is remembered:

$$p(\text{P}|\text{R}) = \frac{120}{200} = 0.60 \quad \text{and} \quad p(\overline{\text{P}}|\text{R}) = \frac{80}{200} = 0.40$$

d. From the second column, we can calculate the probability of purchase, given the fact that the ad is not remembered, and also the probability of no purchase, given that the ad is not remembered:

$$p(\text{P}|\overline{\text{R}}) = \frac{60}{400} = 0.15 \quad \text{and} \quad p(\overline{\text{P}}|\overline{\text{R}}) = \frac{340}{400} = 0.85$$

Note: It is no accident that each pair of these conditional probabilities sums to 1.00, just as the two pairs of unconditional probabilities given in the previous section do. The reason is that the events in question in each case are mutually exclusive and collectively exhaustive (either there was a purchase or there was no purchase, either the ad was remembered or it was not remembered), and the probabilities of such mutually exclusive and collectively exhaustive events always add to 1.

JOINT PROBABILITY

We must, finally, turn to a concept that measures the likelihood of the simultaneous occurrence of two or more events:

DEFINITION 8.8 A measure of the likelihood of the simultaneous occurrence of two or more events is called a **joint probability.** For events A and B, this probability is symbolized by $p(\text{A } and \text{ B})$ or $p(\text{A} \cap \text{B})$.

Four joint probability values can be calculated from Table 8.3 because the events P, $\overline{\text{P}}$, R, and $\overline{\text{R}}$ intersect in the four ways shown in the unshaded portion of our table. It is customary to present this information in a **joint probability table,** such as Table 8.4 on the next page, which shows the likelihood of the simultaneous occurrence of two or more events for all possible event combinations.

Note that each probability value in Table 8.4 simply equals the number of relevant observations given in Table 8.3, divided by the total number of observations, which is 600. The relative frequencies so computed are, thus, nothing else but probability numbers determined by the empirical approach (Formula 8.B). The numbers in the four shaded cells in Table 8.4 are the joint probabilities, and they are symbolized as follows:

$$p(\text{P } and \text{ R}) = 0.20 \qquad p(\text{P } and \text{ } \overline{\text{R}}) = 0.10$$

$$p(\overline{\text{P}} \text{ } and \text{ R}) = 0.13 \qquad p(\overline{\text{P}} \text{ } and \text{ } \overline{\text{R}}) = 0.57$$

Thus, we are told, the probability of finding a customer who purchases the refrigerator and also remembers the ad is 0.20, and the probability of finding a customer who does neither is 0.57.

TABLE 8.4 | A Joint Probability Table

The data in this table have been computed from those in Table 8.3. Joint probabilities for the designated events appear in the shaded cells; the remaining values are the marginal probabilities, which equal the respective sums of the joint probabilities in the various rows and columns.

Refrigerator:	TV Ad: Remembered, R	TV Ad: Not Remembered, $\bar{R}$	Total
Purchased, P	$\frac{120}{600} = 0.20$	$\frac{60}{600} = 0.10$	$\frac{180}{600} = 0.30$
Not Purchased, $\bar{P}$	$\frac{80}{600} = 0.13$	$\frac{340}{600} = 0.57$	$\frac{420}{600} = 0.70$
Total	$\frac{200}{600} = 0.33$	$\frac{400}{600} = 0.67$	$\frac{600}{600} = 1.00$

Again, it is no accident that the sum of the four joint probabilities of the four mutually exclusive and collectively exhaustive joint events equals 1. (The special addition law applies.)

Note two additional facts about Table 8.4: First, the margins of the joint probability table once again show the marginal or unconditional probabilities computed earlier. Second, by dividing any given joint probability by the marginal probability of its row (or column), the conditional probability for the given row (or column) event can be calculated. Thus,

$$\frac{0.20}{0.30} = 0.67, \text{ which means that } \frac{p(\text{P } \textit{and } \text{R})}{p(\text{P})} = p(\text{R}|\text{P})$$

The joint probability of purchase *and* remembering, this expression tells us, when divided by the unconditional probability of purchase, equals the conditional probability of remembering, given the fact of purchase.

Similarly, it is true that

$$\frac{0.20}{0.33} = 0.60, \text{ which means that } \frac{p(\text{P } \textit{and } \text{R})}{p(\text{R})} = p(\text{P}|\text{R})$$

By making similar calculations based on the other three joint probabilities in Table 8.4, you can confirm the remaining six conditional probability values computed in Example Problem 8.10.

THE GENERAL MULTIPLICATION LAW

The relationships just discovered between joint, unconditional, and conditional probabilities can be rewritten for any two events, A and B, as shown in Formula 8.I.

FORMULA 8.I | General Multiplication Law for All Types of Events

$$1.\ p(\text{A } \textit{and } \text{B}) = p(\text{A}) \times p(\text{B}|\text{A})$$

and also

$$2.\ p(\text{A } \textit{and} \text{ B}) = p(\text{B}) \times p(\text{A}|\text{B})$$

Note: Some statisticians prefer to use the symbol $p(\text{A} \cap \text{B})$ instead of $p(\text{A } \textit{and} \text{ B})$.

The law states that the joint probability of two events happening at the same time equals the unconditional probability of one event times the conditional probability of the other event, given that the first event has already occurred (or is certain to occur).

AN EXAMPLE Review Figure 8.4 on page 287. The unconditional probability of event A (getting a face card) is

$$p(\text{A}) = \frac{12}{52}$$

The conditional probability of event B, given event A (getting a heart, assuming a face card is being picked), is

$$p(\text{B}|\text{A}) = \frac{3}{12}$$

because there are 3 face cards with hearts among a total of 12 face cards. Version 1 of our formula tells us that the joint probability should be

$$p(\text{A } \textit{and} \text{ B}) = p(\text{A}) \times p(\text{B}|\text{A}) = \frac{12}{52} \times \frac{3}{12} = \frac{3}{52}$$

which is precisely what panel (d) of Figure 8.4 suggests (there are 3 basic outcomes in the shaded intersection and 52 basic outcomes in the entire sample-space box).

Note that the same result could have been reached by the use of Version 2 of the formula: The unconditional probability of event B (getting a heart) is

$$p(\text{B}) = \frac{13}{52}$$

The conditional probability of event A, given event B (getting a face card, assuming a heart is being picked), is

$$p(\text{A}|\text{B}) = \frac{3}{13}$$

because there are 3 face cards with hearts among a total of 13 cards with hearts. Thus, Version 2 of our formula tells us that

$$p(\text{A } \textit{and} \text{ B}) = p(\text{B}) \times p(\text{A}|\text{B}) = \frac{13}{52} \times \frac{3}{13} = \frac{3}{52}$$

Note also that the general multiplication law can be extended to more than two events such that (for three events)

$$p(\text{A } and \text{ B } and \text{ C}) = p(\text{A}) \times p(\text{B}|\text{A}) \times p(\text{C}|\text{A } and \text{ B})$$

For example, if the probability of a person seeing a TV ad is 0.3 (event A) and if the probability of such a person walking into the advertising dealership's showroom is 0.1 (event B, given A), and if the probability of such a visitor making a purchase is 0.5 (event C, given A *and* B), the joint probability of someone seeing the ad, visiting the showroom, and making a purchase (event A *and* B *and* C) is $0.3 \times 0.1 \times 0.5 = 0.015$. Obviously, this type of calculation gets more complicated as the number of events increases. For a fascinating demonstration of this statement, see Application 8.5, *The Miracle of the Matching Birthdays.*

APPLICATION 8.5

The Miracle of the Matching Birthdays

Imagine yourself in a group of people and consider the probability that the birthdays (day and month, but not year) of at least two people in the group are exactly the same. If you are at all typical, you will view such a match as a highly unlikely event, unless, of course, the group is extremely large and contains, perhaps, one person for every day of the year. Let us be less hasty and instead consider the chances by using the laws of probability. We will assume that all birthdays are equally likely, except February 29, which we will equate with March 1. It is easiest to attack the problem backwards, by finding the probability of the complementary event that there is *no* match of birthdays within a group of *n* persons. We imagine ourselves asking one person at a time to reveal the birthday and then to compare the date so stated with all those previously revealed. Clearly, the probability of no match for the first person is 1 because nobody else's birthday has yet been revealed that might be a match. More formally,

$$p(\overline{\text{M}}_1) = \frac{365}{365} = 1$$

Such certainty exists because there are 365 possible no-match dates when no previous date has been called (which accounts for the numerator), and there are 365 days in the year (which explains the denominator).

Yet the (conditional) probability for the second person's no-match, given the first person's no-match, is different because there are then only 364 possible no-match dates left (the date revealed by the first person might be a match). Thus,

$$p(\overline{\text{M}}_2|\overline{\text{M}}_1) = \frac{364}{365}$$

And so it goes, until, for the last and *n*th person in the group, the no-match probability equals

$$p(\overline{\text{M}}_n|\overline{\text{M}}_1 \; and \; \overline{\text{M}}_2 \; and \ldots\ldots \overline{\text{M}}_{n-1}) = \frac{365 - (n - 1)}{365}$$

Combining our results with the help of the general multiplication law, we have

$$p(\text{no matches}) = \frac{365}{365} \times \frac{364}{365} \times \frac{363}{365} \times \ldots\ldots \times \frac{365 - n + 1}{365}$$

At this point, we can also state the complement of this expression and, thus, get the probability we really care about:

$$p(\text{at least one match}) = 1 - p(\text{no match})$$

What size of group is needed to make the probability of at least one match exceed 0.5? Amazingly, the answer is 23, as one can figure out by plugging alternative values for *n* into the above expression. Some of these values are shown in Table 8.A.

Table 8.A shows that at least 23 persons are needed to achieve a probability of a *precise* match that is greater than 0.5. However, as is not shown here, only 14 people are needed to achieve a "match" within 1 day and only 7 people are needed for a "match" within 1 week of each other's birthdays.

(continued)

Application 8.5 (continued)

TABLE 8.A

Group Size, n	p (no matches)	p (at least one match)
5	0.973	0.027
10	0.883	0.117
15	0.747	0.253
20	0.589	0.411
23	0.493	0.507
30	0.294	0.706
40	0.109	0.891
50	0.030	0.970
60	0.006	0.994

As this example shows, the probability of at least one match is considerably higher than what most people think. In particular, that probability for a group of n is not $n/365$, as is often thought. Consider a group of $n = 5$. As the previous analysis suggests,

$$p(\text{at least one match in a group of 5}) = 1 - \left[\frac{365}{365} \times \frac{364}{365} \times \frac{363}{365} \times \frac{362}{365} \times \frac{361}{365}\right]$$

This expression can be rewritten as

$$p(\text{at least one match in a group of 5}) = 1 - \left[\frac{365!}{(365-5)!} \times \frac{1}{365^5}\right]$$

which shows the probability of no-match that is given in the brackets as equal to the set of all permutations of 365 days taken 5 days at a time, divided by the sample space of 365^5, which gives all the possible comparisons of each birthday with every other birthday. Symbolically, we have

$$p(\text{at least one match in a group of } n) = 1 - \left[\frac{365!}{(365-n)!365^n}\right]$$

which is a far cry from $n/365$.

EXCEL Example 8.1

The matching birthday problem can be neatly illustrated with the help of EXCEL. Simulate 12 sets of 23 birthdays and then determine how many of the 12 sets contain at least one matching birthday.

SOLUTION Assuming there are no leap years and all the days of the year are equally likely as birthdays, a list of integers from 1 to 365 might represent all possible birthdays in a year.

1. Enter integers from 1 to 365 into column A; then select the column.
2. Click **Tools > Data Analysis > Sampling > OK.**
3. Under *Input Range,* enter **A1:A365.**
4. Under *Sampling Method,* choose **Random** and enter **23.**
5. Under *Output Options,* choose **Output Range,** enter **B1:B23,** and click **OK.**
6. Click the **Sort Ascending** button on the standard toolbar.
7. Repeat Steps 2–6 for columns C–M, changing only the column letter in Step 5.

The result of such repeated sampling with replacement is something like the following:

B	C	D	E	F	G	H	I	J	K	L	M
3	1	16	1	3	24	45	33	49	2	17	27
21	3	16	10	43	50	66	34	54	18	37	41
41	80	49	62	60	72	70	43	60	42	54	46
44	94	71	80	65	74	81	47	75	49	91	50
44	98	74	82	70	90	110	54	76	78	117	79
79	106	85	96	94	118	112	54	94	84	131	83
81	117	124	109	114	122	142	59	106	100	138	106
85	144	134	130	139	151	155	71	111	108	139	106
85	144	136	189	140	156	201	72	147	116	150	124
101	156	137	191	144	163	208	78	156	118	165	168
109	163	139	197	152	166	233	84	167	129	172	184
137	166	157	197	184	169	246	94	196	132	180	201
142	173	159	214	214	173	248	110	200	143	193	253
165	197	218	216	229	187	253	120	204	145	196	266
202	231	219	243	231	187	257	149	207	169	202	270
207	231	231	268	257	212	274	154	233	214	214	270
220	242	240	269	264	212	276	226	269	236	221	272
283	250	261	278	274	235	290	234	294	275	223	287
286	253	280	297	282	274	314	236	302	306	280	299
287	259	311	299	290	326	316	246	305	323	291	321
300	291	337	324	305	338	327	301	325	343	309	330
310	309	347	325	345	350	358	352	336	355	329	346
354	337	348	334	359	358	362	361	349	357	354	362

Each column of simulated numbers might represent the birthdays of 23 people at a party. Note in column B that two persons share the same birthday, the 44th day of the year. The 85th day is another match. These matches have been highlighted in red. There are two similar matches in column C, involving the 144th and 231st days of the year. And so it goes. Overall, there is at least one match in 7 cases out of 12, which confirms the result noted in Table 8.A: The probability of at least one match exceeds 0.5 once group size reaches 23.

Caution: If you repeat the simulation, you will get different numbers, because a pseudorandom process is involved.

DEPENDENT VERSUS INDEPENDENT EVENTS

Working with the general multiplication law can get complicated. Fortunately, a special and simpler version of the law can be applied whenever the events in question are independent rather than dependent. Thus, we must learn about this crucial distinction.

DEFINITION 8.9 Two random events, A and B, are said to be **dependent events** when the probability of one event *is* affected by the occurrence of the other event. In this case, $p(\text{A}) \neq p(\text{A} \mid \text{B})$. In contrast, two random events are **independent events** when the probability of one event is *not* affected by the occurrence of the other event; hence, $p(\text{A}) = p(\text{A} \mid \text{B})$.

DEPENDENT EVENTS: SAMPLING WITHOUT REPLACEMENT A good example of dependent events is provided by an inspector who randomly picks selected items out of a warehouse in order to check quality and who sets each inspected item aside (which is the usual case) instead of returning it. During the process, the total number of items in the warehouse continually declines; therefore, the probability of finding a defective item continually changes. As a result, the events "checking a first item" and "checking a second item" and "checking a third item" are dependent events. We can see the issue most clearly, perhaps, by equating the inspection process with the drawing of more than one card from a deck *without replacing* the cards drawn. Prior to the first draw, the probability of getting the king of hearts is 1/52, and so is the probability of getting the ace of diamonds or the queen of spades. Now imagine drawing the king of hearts on the first try *and setting it aside.* Notice how all the probabilities will now differ because the deck is reduced to 51 cards, and the king of hearts is gone. The subsequent probabilities are zero for the king of hearts and 1/51 for all the other cards, and so it goes until, when only one card is left, the probability of drawing it equals 1, at which point the probability is zero for drawing any of the other cards already drawn.

INDEPENDENT EVENTS: SAMPLING WITH REPLACEMENT Consider, in contrast, the same random experiment, with any card drawn being immediately replaced. The probability of drawing any one card will then be unaffected by any of the preceding events; it will always equal 1/52. Even if the king of hearts were drawn on the first try, after replacing it and reshuffling the deck, the probability of drawing it on the second try would again be 1/52, just as for any other card. In this case, different drawings are independent events.

REPLACEMENT UNAVOIDABLE In some rare instances, replacement of a sampled item is inevitable. Consider tossing a coin. It is physically impossible to set aside a head (or tail) and then toss a coin again; hence, different tosses of a coin are *always* independent events. Nevertheless, many gamblers refuse to believe it. After observing a series of heads, they bet on a tail coming up next because, as they put it, "it is the tail's turn" or "the tail's chances are now mature." In fact, this is nonsense. The probability of getting a head (or a tail) remains 1/2 for any toss of a fair coin, even when 37 heads have just been tossed in a row. The coin has no conscience or memory and doesn't know or care whose turn is next.

REPLACEMENT UNLIKELY In many business applications, the replacement of sampled items does not occur because such replacement is awkward. While one can, if one wishes, return the king of hearts to the deck, reshuffle, and draw again, it would be extremely cumbersome to return each inspected item to a warehouse prior to the next random drawing. An inspector whose successive pickings are not replaced, therefore, must determine the probability of the existence of defective items with a formula applicable to *dependent* events.

TESTING FOR DEPENDENCE OR INDEPENDENCE It is easy to test for the dependence or independence of any two events, such as the remembering of an ad and the purchase of a product or the drawing of a king and a red card from a deck. Three simple steps are involved; all make use of Formula 8.B:

$$p(\text{A}) = \frac{k}{M}$$

1. **Determine the unconditional probability for one event in the pair.**
   You can figure the unconditional probability of remembering from Table 8.4 as

$$p(\text{R}) = \frac{200}{600} = 0.33$$

   And you can figure the unconditional probability of drawing a king from the deck shown in panel (c) of Figure 8.1 as

$$p(\text{king}) = \frac{4}{52} = 0.08$$

2. **Determine the conditional probability for the same event, given the occurrence of the other event in the pair.**
For example, note that the conditional probability of remembering, given purchase, is

$$p(\mathrm{R}|\mathrm{P}) = \frac{120}{180} = 0.67$$

And note that the conditional probability of drawing a king, given that a red card is drawn, equals

$$p(\text{king}|\text{red}) = \frac{2}{26} = 0.08$$

(there are 2 kings among 26 red cards).

3. **Compare the unconditional with the conditional probability.**
Here we rely on the facts that

- for dependent events, $p(\mathrm{A}) \neq p(\mathrm{A}|\mathrm{B})$
- for independent events, $p(\mathrm{A}) = p(\mathrm{A}|\mathrm{B})$

Thus, if our Step 1 and Step 2 values differ, the events are *statistically dependent;* if they do not differ, the events are *statistically independent.* In our case, $0.33 \neq 0.67$; remembering and purchase are dependent events. On the other hand, $(4/52) = (2/26)$; getting a king and getting a red card are independent events.

THE SPECIAL MULTIPLICATION LAW

The general multiplication law can be used to calculate the probability for an intersection of all types of events, but it reduces to an easier form for independent events. The reason: In the case of independent events, the unconditional and the conditional probabilities are identical; hence, the conditional probabilities, included in Formula 8.I, can be replaced by the unconditional probabilities, as shown in Formula 8.J.

FORMULA 8.J | Special Multiplication Law for Independent Events

$$p(\mathrm{A}\ \textit{and}\ \mathrm{B}) = p(\mathrm{A}) \times p(\mathrm{B})$$

Note: Some statisticians prefer to use the symbol $p(\mathrm{A} \cap \mathrm{B})$ instead of $p(\mathrm{A}\ \textit{and}\ \mathrm{B})$.

In the case of independent events, the joint probability of A *and* B, or of any number of such events, simply equals the product of the unconditional probabilities of these events.

EXAMPLE 1 As we noted above, drawing a king and drawing a red card from a deck are independent events. Hence, their joint probability is

$$p(\text{king } \textit{and} \text{ red card}) = \frac{4}{52} \times \frac{26}{52} = \frac{1}{26}$$

This probability is, indeed, obvious by looking at panel (c) of Figure 8.1 on page 281:There are 2 red kings in the deck of 52 cards.

EXAMPLE 2 Consider the quality inspector who selects 3 items from a group of 100. If the inspected item is replaced after each selection and the whole lot is remixed, what is the probability that the inspector will find 3 defective items if (unbeknownst to the inspector) there are only 10 defective items in the lot?

The answer: The unconditional probability of finding a defective item is $p(\text{D}) = (10/100) = 0.1$. Because replacement makes the events of finding a defective item on the first, second, and third try (D_1, D_2, D_3) independent ones, the special multiplication law applies:

$$p(\text{D}_1 \textit{ and } \text{D}_2 \textit{ and } \text{D}_3) = p(\text{D}_1) \times p(\text{D}_2) \times p(\text{D}_3) = 0.1 \times 0.1 \times 0.1 = 0.001$$

Application 8.6
Probability in Court
http://www.harcourtcollege.com/business_stats/kohler/siteresources.html

There is just one such chance in 1,000 tries.

Application 8.6, *Probability in Court,* reports on two famous cases in which the special multiplication law was applied when the general multiplication law should have been applied.

8.9 Probability Laws and Tree Diagrams

Both addition and multiplication laws can be illustrated with the help of tree diagrams, such as those in Figure 8.9. Both panels (a) and (b) illustrate the survey summarized in Table 8.3, but do so in slightly different ways.

PANEL (a) The first fork in panel (a) pictures the possibilities of a customer making or not making a purchase and lists the associated unconditional probabilities of these events along the two branches. Because a customer must do one or the other, the special addition law applies; the sum of 0.3 and 0.7 equals 1, implying certainty that one or the other of these events will occur. If a purchase is made, two mutually exclusive and collectively exhaustive possibilities exist once again at P: The customer does or does not remember seeing the ad. The conditional probabilities (*given* that a purchase has been made) equal 0.67 and 0.33 (as was noted in an earlier section) and, once more, add to 1. If no purchase is made, the same two possibilities exist at $\overline{\text{P}}$, but the conditional probabilities are 0.19 and 0.81; once more, they add to 1. If the numbers along any path to the ultimate outcome are multiplied, joint probabilities are found, just as the general multiplication law suggests. Note that the joint probabilities of the four possible outcomes again add to 1 and that each equals the value previously calculated (see Table 8.4).

PANEL (b) Panel (b) reaches the identical conclusion, but it does so in a different way, by employing the alternative version of the multiplication law. The choice between remembering and not remembering the ad is considered first; that between purchase and no purchase is considered second. The same joint probabilities result, but note that they are listed in a different order.

Dependent Events Note also how easy it is to recognize all the events in question as *dependent* events. The unconditional probability of purchase, given as 0.3 in panel (a), differs from the conditional probabilities of purchase, given remembering (or not remembering) shown as 0.6 (or 0.15) in panel (b). So purchase and remembering (or not remembering) are dependent events. Similarly, the unconditional probability of not remembering, given as 0.67 in panel (b), differs from the conditional probabilities of not remembering, given purchase (or no purchase) shown as 0.33 (or 0.81) in panel (a). Not remembering and purchase (or no purchase) are dependent events as well. Looking at numbers such as these, thus, is a way to establish whether an ad was memorable and therefore effective at increasing sales.

Panel (c) Panel (c) pictures the case of quality inspection *with replacement* in which 3 items are picked from a lot of 100, of which 10 percent are defective. Thus, the panel simultaneously illustrates a case of independent events and a case of more than two events. The fact of independence is visible in the tree diagram because the probabilities at every fork remain the same (0.1 for picking a defective item; 0.9 for picking a satisfactory item). Thus, $p(\text{A})$ symbolizes the unconditional probability of finding a defective or satisfactory item on the first trial; $p(\text{B})$ symbolizes the corresponding conditional probabilities on the second trial, given the result of the first trial, but these probabilities equal the unconditional ones. Similarly, $p(\text{C})$ symbolizes the conditional probabilities on the third trial, given the results of the first and second trials, but these probabilities, too, equal the unconditional ones, because the three trials

FIGURE 8.9 | Probability Laws and Tree Diagrams

The two equivalent versions of the general multiplication law that help us find the joint probability of two events by multiplying the unconditional probability of one event with the conditional probability of the other event, given the first event, are illustrated in panels (a) and (b). The special addition law is seen at work, too, although indirectly: The sum of probabilities at each fork and the sums of joint probabilities always equal 1, a requirement for mutually exclusive and collectively exhaustive events. Panel (c), finally, illustrates an application of the special multiplication law to the determination of joint probabilities for three independent events.

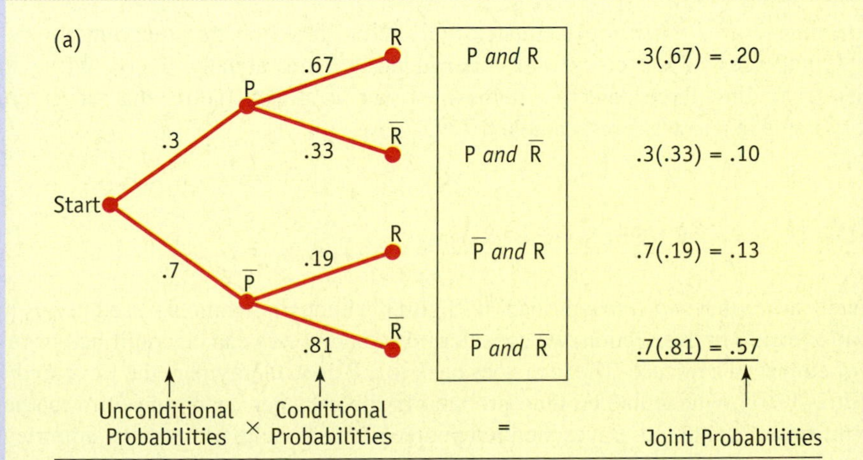

(continued)

FIGURE 8.9 | Probability Laws and Tree Diagrams *(continued)*

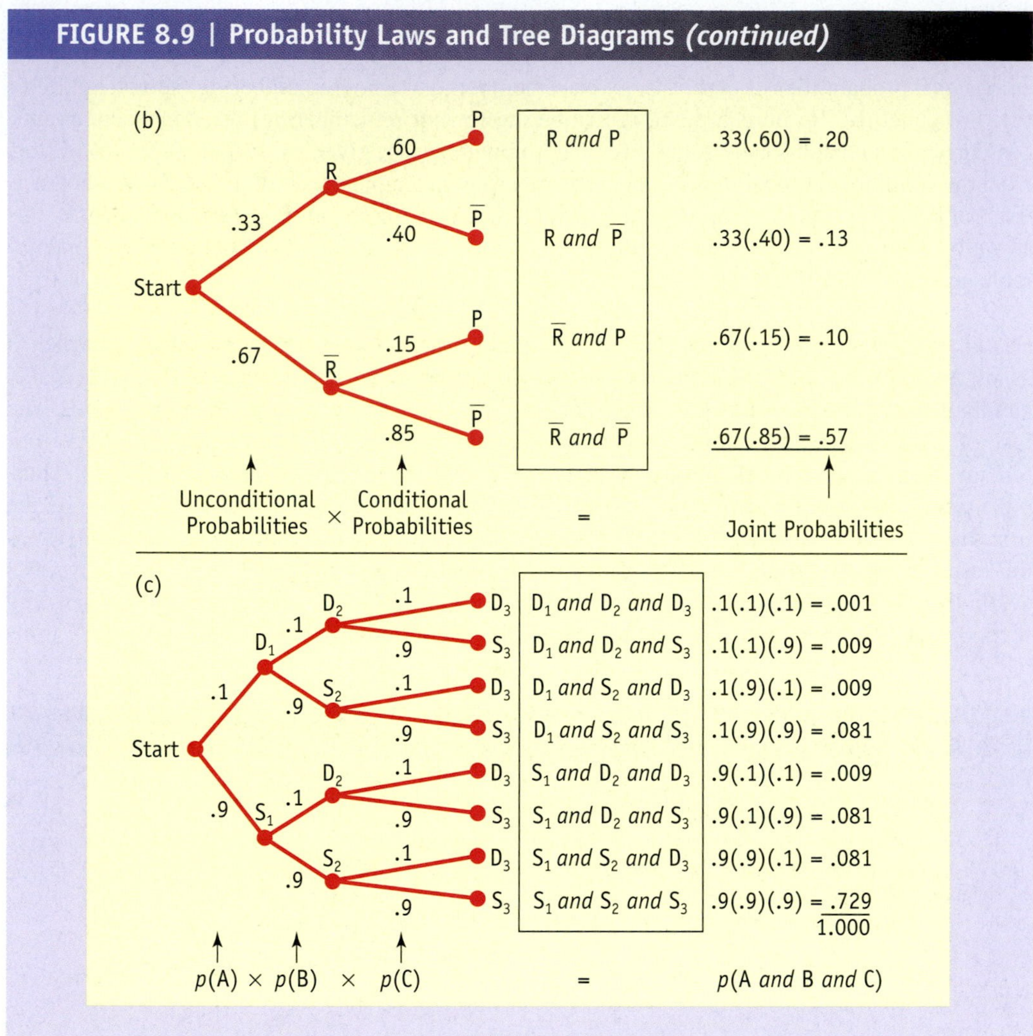

are independent events when replacement occurs. Note how the tree diagram shows clearly why the 8 outcomes of the completed experiments are not equally likely. While the joint probability of finding three defective items in a row is a tiny 0.001, that of finding three satisfactory items in a row is a respectable 0.729.

8.10 Revising Probabilities: Bayes' Theorem

It was noted earlier that *subjective* probability figures, although commonly used in business, are rather controversial. In this section, we consider how such values can be confirmed or revised in the light of empirical evidence. The idea goes back to a British clergyman, the Reverend Thomas Bayes (1702–1761), who stumbled onto probability theory when searching for a mathematical proof of the existence of God. Bayes pictured people as possessing, prior to any empirical investigation, an initial subjective estimate of the likelihood of an event; he called this value a **prior probability.** He then imagined an investigation to take place and to yield certain results. He developed what is now called **Bayes' theorem,** a formula for revising an initial subjective probability value on the basis of results obtained by an empirical investigation. The end result is a new probability value, which is a prior probability modified on the basis of new information and called a **posterior probability.** The sequence of probability revision can be summarized in the following sketch:

Prior Probability	+	New Information	+	Application of Bayes' Theorem	=	Posterior Probability

If we denote the probability of an event as $p(\text{E})$, the probability of its complement as $p(\overline{\text{E}})$, and the result of an investigation as R, Bayes suggested that the posterior probability of event E could be calculated by Formula 8.K.

FORMULA 8.K | Bayes' Theorem

$$p(\text{E}|\text{R}) = \frac{p(\text{E}) \times p(\text{R}|\text{E})}{p(\text{E}) \times p(\text{R}|\text{E}) + p(\overline{\text{E}}) \times p(\text{R}|\overline{\text{E}})}$$

Two things should be noted. First, the prior probability of the event, $p(\text{E})$, is an unconditional probability. The posterior probability, $p(\text{E}|\text{R})$, is a conditional probability, given the empirical result, R. Second, the entire formula can be rewritten to take the form of the expression given as Formula 8.L. As a quick glance at the general multiplication law (Formula 8.I) confirms, the numerator in Formula 8.K is nothing else but the joint probability of the given event and the empirical result, or $p(\text{E } \textit{and} \text{ R})$. The denominator, therefore, is the sum of two probabilities: the joint probability of the given event and the observed result, or $p(\text{E } \textit{and} \text{ R})$, and the joint probability of the given event's complement and the observed result, or $p(\overline{\text{E}} \textit{ and } \text{R})$. This sum, as Table 8.4 confirms, is nothing else but the unconditional probability of the result, or $p(\text{R})$. Thus, Bayes theorem can also be written as Formula 8.L.

FORMULA 8.L | Bayes' Theorem Rewritten

$$p(\text{E}|\text{R}) = \frac{p(\text{E } \textit{and} \text{ R})}{p(\text{R})}$$

The Bayesian posterior probability of an event, Formula 8.L tells us, is the ratio of the joint probability of this event and the empirical result to the unconditional probability of this result. The following examples illustrate the Bayesian approach.

EXAMPLE PROBLEM 8.11

Consider being faced with three dice, one of which is known to be crooked. The crooked die, let us suppose, contains a lead weight that makes a 6 appear on half the tosses; yet the dice all look alike. If you know all of the above and now select one of the dice, what is the probability that it is the crooked one?

SOLUTION: Bayes would have us follow the revision sequence sketched above.

Step 1. Prior Probabilities. Letting C stand for "crooked" and $\overline{C}$ for "not crooked," the prior probabilities that you subjectively and arbitrarily select (because you are considering one die out of three) are the following:

$$p(\text{C}) = 1/3 \quad \text{and} \quad p(\overline{\text{C}}) = 2/3$$

Step 2. New Information. Now comes the empirical investigation: You roll the die, and its face shows a 6. We have our result, and we can state the two conditional probabilities of this result, given each of the two possible events, easily enough:

$$p(6|\text{C}) = 1/2 \text{ (information given before)}$$

$$p(6|\overline{\text{C}}) = 1/6 \text{ (classical probability value)}$$

Step 3. Applying the Theorem. We now apply Bayes' theorem with Formula 8.K:

$$p(\text{C}|6) = \frac{p(\text{C}) \times p(6|\text{C})}{p(\text{C}) \times p(6|\text{C}) + p(\overline{\text{C}}) \times p(6|\overline{\text{C}})} = \frac{\frac{1}{3} \times \frac{1}{2}}{\left(\frac{1}{3} \times \frac{1}{2}\right) + \left(\frac{2}{3} \times \frac{1}{6}\right)} = \frac{3}{5}$$

Step 4. Posterior Probability. In light of the new information, the probability that the selected die is the crooked one is revised upward from the prior value of 1/3, when nothing was known about the particular die, to a posterior value of 3/5, when it was known that this die showed a 6 when rolled once. In light of the evidence, crookedness is more likely, but it is not certain. (The 6-face could have been rolled by any die.)

EXAMPLE PROBLEM 8.12

Consider an oil company about to drill for oil. The company geologists might state subjective probabilities for finding oil at the given site as follows:

$$p(\text{oil}) = 0.5$$

$$p(\text{no oil}) = 0.5$$

They drill for 500 feet, find no oil yet, but sample the soil. From past experience, they know the conditional probabilities of finding this type of soil, given oil or no oil:

$$p(\text{this type soil} \mid \text{oil}) = 0.2$$

$$p(\text{this type soil} \mid \text{no oil}) = 0.8$$

What is the posterior probability for finding oil, according to Bayes?

SOLUTION:

$$p(\text{oil} \mid \text{this type soil}) = \frac{0.5 \times 0.2}{(0.5 \times 0.2) + (0.5 \times 0.8)} = 0.2$$

The new information reduces the probability of an oil find from 0.5 to 0.2.

EXAMPLE PROBLEM 8.13

An employment agency administers a placement test to an equal number of men and women. Thus, the prior probability is 0.5 that any randomly selected test paper was written by a man. The tests are graded. Some 60 percent of the tests score a C, and 30 percent of the tests score a C *and* are written by a man.

Given this new information, what is the likelihood that a randomly selected paper with a score of C was written by a man?

SOLUTION: The alternative Formula 8.L version of Bayes' theorem might be applied:

$$p(\text{man} \mid \text{score C}) = \frac{p(\text{man } \textit{and} \text{ score C})}{p(\text{score C})} = \frac{0.3}{0.6} = 0.5$$

The posterior probability that a C paper was written by a man is 0.5, which equals the prior probability of 0.5 for any paper. There is no reason for revising the prior probability value.

Summary

1. The *theory of probability* helps us figure the likelihood of specific occurrences. Among the important concepts that the theory employs are those of the random experiment and the sample space. Any activity that will result in one and only one of several well-defined outcomes, but that does not allow us to tell in advance which of these will prevail in any particular instance, is called a *random experiment.* Any one of a random experiment's possible outcomes, the occurrence of which rules out the occurrence of all the alternative outcomes, is called a *basic outcome;* a listing of all basic outcomes constitutes the *sample space.*
2. Any subset of the sample space is a *random event,* it can be *simple* (containing one basic outcome) or *composite* (containing more than one). It is crucial to distinguish *mutually exclusive, collectively exhaustive,* and *complementary* events as well as to distinguish the *union* from the *intersection* of two events.
3. Two types of random experiments exist: those that can be repeated over and over again and those that are unique. Accordingly, there are two numerical measures of chance that estimate the likelihood that a particular event will occur. Such a measure for a repeatable random experiment is called an *objective* probability; a corresponding value for a unique random experiment is called a *subjective* probability.

   By conducting repeated thought experiments, an objective probability can be determined theoretically as the ratio of the number of equally likely basic outcomes favorable to an event A to the possible number of such outcomes. By conducting repeated actual experiments, an objective probability can also be determined empirically as the ratio of the number of times an event A did occur in the past to the maximum number of times event A could have occurred. In either case, the resultant ratio must lie between 0 and 1. The same value range applies to any subjective probability that is derived neither by logical deduction nor from repeated experiments but reflects solely a personal degree of belief in the likelihood of an occurrence.
4. When sample spaces are extremely large, special counting techniques are needed to determine the numbers of favorable and possible outcomes of random experiments (and, thus, probability values). Such counting techniques employ the concepts of *factorials, permutations,* and *combinations.*
5. Deriving probability values for single events is one thing; manipulating these values to determine the combined probability for the union or intersection of several events is another. The procedure for computing the probability for the occurrence of a *union* of two or more events is summarized by the *addition law.* A general version applies to all types of events; a special law applies to mutually exclusive events only. The procedure for computing the probability for the occurrence of an *intersection* of two or more events is summarized by the *multiplication law.* A general version applies to all types of events; a special law applies to independent events only.

   A full understanding of the general multiplication law requires an understanding of the concepts of unconditional, conditional, and joint probability. Any application of the special law presupposes an ability to distinguish dependent from independent events.

6. The laws of probability can be illustrated with the help of tree diagrams.
7. An important extension of the traditional calculus of probability is provided by *Bayes' theorem,* a formula for revising a subjective *prior* probability value on the basis of results obtained by an empirical investigation and for, thus, obtaining a *posterior* probability value.

Key Terms

addition law
basic outcome
Bayes' theorem
collectively exhaustive events
combinations
compatible events
complementary events
composite event
conditional probability
dependent events
disjoint events
elementary event
factorial
factorial product
incompatible events
independent events
intersection of two events
joint probability
joint probability table
law of large numbers
marginal probability
multiplication law
mutually exclusive events
objective probability
outcome space
permutations
posterior probability
prior probability
probability
probability space
random event
random experiment
sample point
sample space
simple event
subjective probability
theory of probability
tree diagram
unconditional probability
union of two events
Venn diagrams

Practice Problems

NOTES

1. Some problems assume that you are connected to the Internet. The addresses noted in these problems, and the solutions described on the accompanying CD-ROM, were current at the time of this writing. However, Web sites are forever evolving. If things have changed, you can still learn much by solving a slightly different problem in a slightly different way.
2. Some problems require the use of a statistical program, EXCEL or MINITAB. The program's major features are explained in text Chapter 2. Plenty of additional advice is available via the program's built-in Help feature.

SECTION 8.2 BASIC PROBABILITY CONCEPTS

1. a. Determine the number of basic outcomes on the *American-style* roulette wheel shown in Figure 8.10. Are they univariate?

FIGURE 8.10

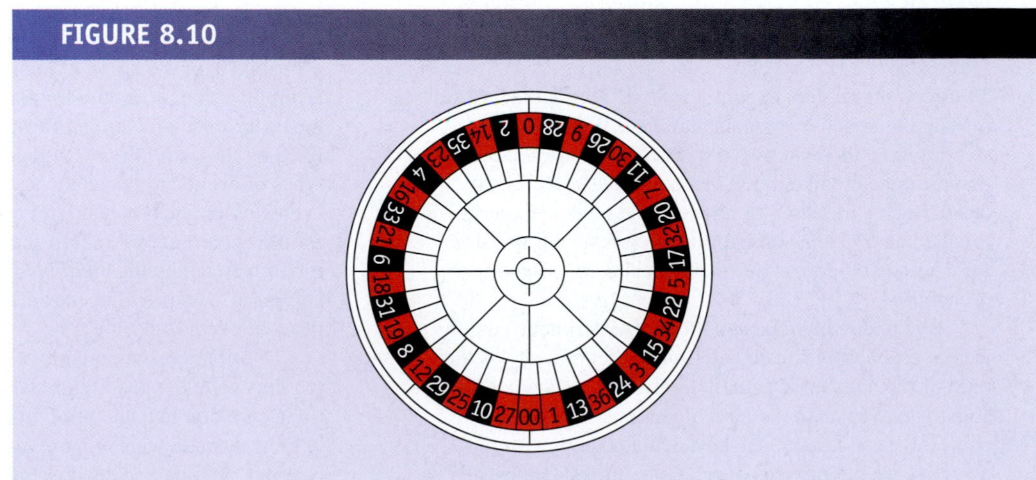

b. Determine the number of basic outcomes when tossing three coins at once. Are they univariate? Find your answer with the help of a tree diagram.

2. With the help of a tree diagram, determine the sample space for a random experiment that takes 3 balls from an urn containing 1 red ball, 1 green ball, and 1 white ball, and do so *with* replacement.

3. In the four sample spaces given in Figures 8.11 to 8.14, show the favorable outcomes for the events noted below by shading the appropriate subsets of the sample spaces.

a. Shade the subset of Figure 8.11 that corresponds to getting a sum of 5 or 6 when rolling two dice once.

b. Shade the subset of Figure 8.12 that corresponds to getting a sum of 2 when rolling two dice once.

c. Shade the subset of Figure 8.13 that corresponds to drawing a black king from a deck.

d. Shade the subset of Figure 8.14 that corresponds to drawing a black card or an ace from a deck.

4. Visit http:// www.fortune.com, a site maintained by *Fortune* magazine, and seek out the latest data about the *Fortune 500* companies. (If you prefer, look at the latest print issue of *Fortune* that features America's 500 largest corporations, ranked by total revenues.) Identify the sample space that sorts these 500 companies into the 50 states (and the District of Columbia) in which they maintain their headquarters.

5. Visit http:// www.fortune.com, a site maintained by *Fortune* magazine, and seek out the latest data about the *Fortune 1000* companies. (If you prefer, look at the latest print issue of *Fortune* that features America's 1,000 largest corporations, ranked by total revenue.) Identify the sample space that sorts these 1,000 companies into various industries.

FIGURE 8.11

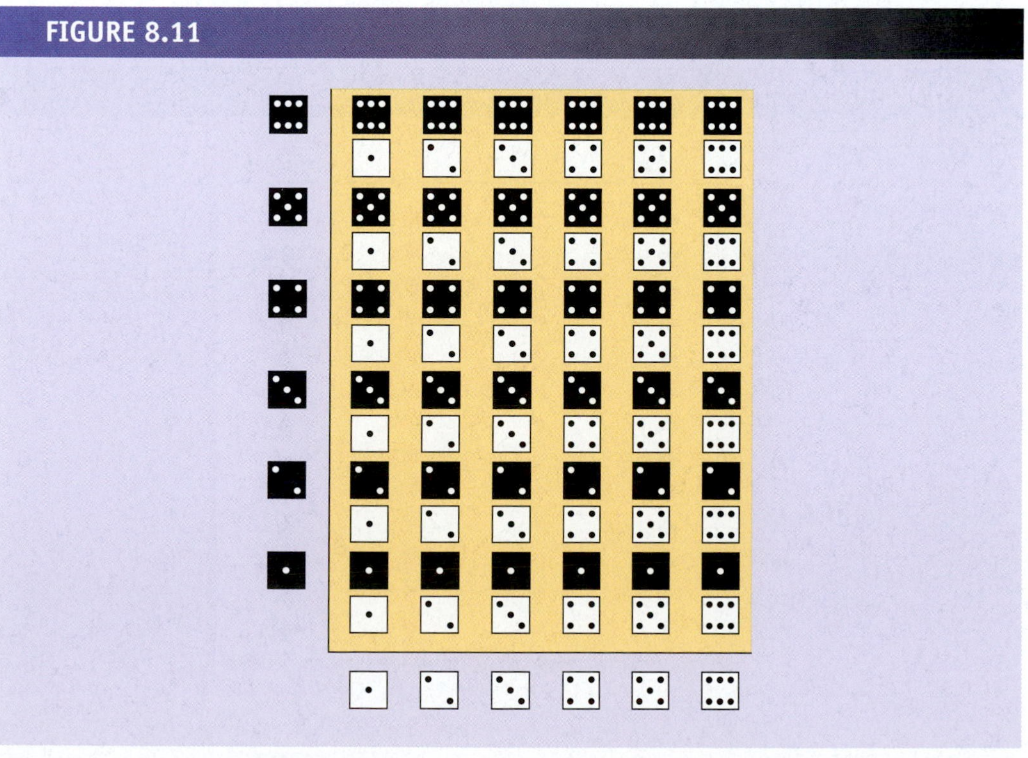

FIGURE 8.12

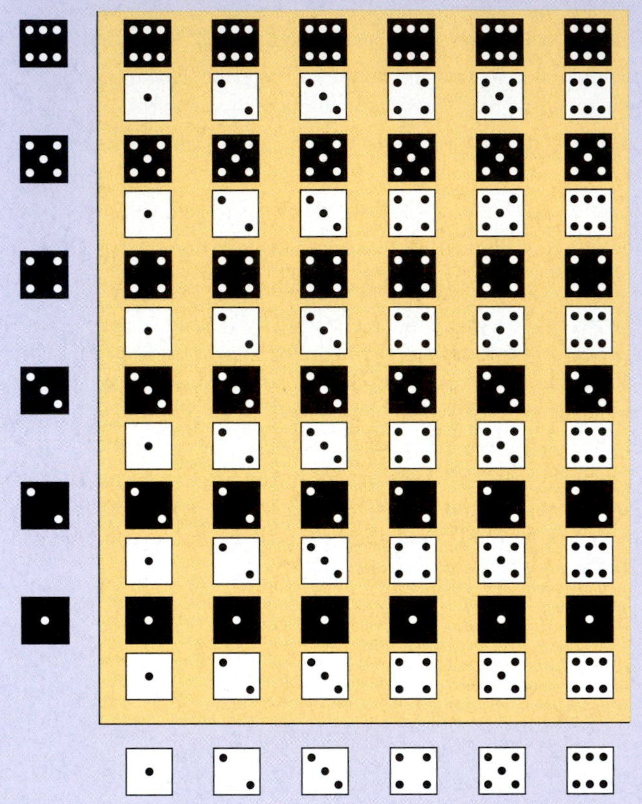

FIGURE 8.13

	Clubs	Diamonds	Hearts	Spades
King	♣ K	♦ K	♥ K	♠ K
Queen	♣ Q	♦ Q	♥ Q	♠ Q
Jack	♣ J	♦ J	♥ J	♠ J
10	♣ 10	♦ 10	♥ 10	♠ 10
9	♣ 9	♦ 9	♥ 9	♠ 9
8	♣ 8	♦ 8	♥ 8	♠ 8
7	♣ 7	♦ 7	♥ 7	♠ 7
6	♣ 6	♦ 6	♥ 6	♠ 6
5	♣ 5	♦ 5	♥ 5	♠ 5
4	♣ 4	♦ 4	♥ 4	♠ 4
3	♣ 3	♦ 3	♥ 3	♠ 3
Deuce	♣ 2	♦ 2	♥ 2	♠ 2
Ace	♣ A	♦ A	♥ A	♠ A

FIGURE 8.14

	Clubs	Diamonds	Hearts	Spades
King	♣K	♦K	♥K	♠K
Queen	♣Q	♦Q	♥Q	♠Q
Jack	♣J	♦J	♥J	♠J
10	♣10	♦10	♥10	♠10
9	♣9	♦9	♥9	♠9
8	♣8	♦8	♥8	♠8
7	♣7	♦7	♥7	♠7
6	♣6	♦6	♥6	♠6
5	♣5	♦5	♥5	♠5
4	♣4	♦4	♥4	♠4
3	♣3	♦3	♥3	♠3
Deuce	♣2	♦2	♥2	♠2
Ace	♣A	♦A	♥A	♠A

Section 8.3 The Nature of Random Events

6. Classify each of the following random events as simple or composite:
   a. Getting a 3 when rolling a single die once.
   b. Getting an odd number when rolling a single die once.
   c. Getting a sum of 5 or 6 when rolling two dice once.
   d. Getting a sum of 2 when rolling two dice once.
   e. Getting a 7 when drawing one card from a deck.

Section 8.4 How Random Events Relate to Each Other

7. Classify each of the following sets of events in two ways: first, as mutually exclusive or compatible and, second, as collectively exhaustive or not collectively exhaustive:
   a. Money supply growth of 5 percent per year; money supply growth of 9 percent per year.
   b. Sales under $5 million per year; sales between $5 million and under $10 million per year; sales of $10 million per year or more.
   c. Profits between $1 and $7 million per year; profit of $5 million per year.
   d. Defective parts below 7 percent of output; defective parts above 2 percent of output; defective parts equal to 5 percent of output.
   e. Real GDP growth of 3 percent per year; inflation of 7 percent per year; unemployment of 8 percent of the labor force.
8. Consider the sample space S = (1, 2, 3, 4, 5, 6, 7, 8, 9, 10), as well as these random events:

   A = (2, 4, 6, 8, 10) D = (3, 4, 5, 6, 7)

   B = (1, 2, 9, 10) E = (7, 8, 9)

   C = (1, 3, 5, 7, 9) F = (2, 3, 4, 5)

   Are the following sets of events mutually exclusive, collectively exhaustive, both, or neither?

   AB, AC, AD, AE, AF, BC, BD, BE, BF, CD, CE, CF, DE, DF, EF, ADF, BDE, CEF
9. State the *complements* of each of the following events:
   a. Finding defective items in a group of items.
   b. Inflation above 10 percent per year.
   c. Real GDP growth of 3 percent per year or more.
   d. Drawing an ace from a deck of cards.
   e. Finding no defective items in a group of items.

10. Review Figure 8.14 on page 329. Then identify the following:

a. Clubs ∪ Spades.

b. Diamonds ∪ Hearts.

c. Red Cards ∩ Ace.

d. Diamonds ∩ Face Cards.

11. Identify each of the following descriptions as either the *union* or the *intersection* of events:

a. Drawing the king of hearts from a deck of cards.

b. Selecting a New York–based telecommunications company from the *Fortune 500* list.

c. Drawing a black king from a deck of cards.

d. Drawing a black card or an ace from a deck of cards.

e. Selecting a New York–based company or an airline from the *Fortune 500* list.

f. Drawing an ace or a deuce from a deck of cards.

g. Selecting an insurance company or an airline, both from Pennsylvania, from the *Fortune 500* list.

h. Drawing a red face card from a deck of cards.

Section 8.5 Alternative Probability Concepts

12. Calculate the following (objective) probabilities:

a. Getting red when spinning the American roulette wheel (Figure 8.10) in Practice Problem 1a.

b. Getting two heads and one tail in the random experiment described in Practice Problem 1b.

c. Getting two (and not three) red balls in the random experiment described in Practice Problem 2.

d. For each of the four events described in Practice Problem 3.

e. For events a, c, d, f, and h in Practice Problem 11.

13. Review Practice Problem 5 and its answer on the CD-ROM. If you now selected one of those 1,000 companies at random, what is the probability of its industry being

a. advertising/marketing?

b. aerospace?

c. health care?

d. life and health insurance?

e. pipelines or railroads?

f. wholesale trade?

14. Review Practice Problem 4 and your answer to it. If you now selected one of those 500 companies at random, what is the probability of its headquarters being in

a. Alabama?

b. Connecticut?

c. Illinois?

d. Mississippi or Nebraska?

e. New Jersey or New York?

f. West Virginia?

15 Comment on the following bet someone suggests to you: "Let's toss two dimes at a time. Three outcomes are possible: 2 heads, 2 tails, or one of each. If two heads show or two tails, you win; if there is one tail and one head, I win. Because you have two chances out of three to win and I have only one, I will pay you 50 cents whenever you win, but you must pay me $1 whenever I win. In the long run, neither one of us will win or lose."

16. Comment on this reasoning by a sales clerk: "From past experience, I know that 1 customer out of 20 buys my product. I have just had 19 customers who didn't buy. The next one is certain to buy."

17. Review Table 6.5 on page 174 and Table 6.C on page 177 of the text.

a. If one of those multinational companies is selected at random, what is the probability of its net profit lying between $0 and under $1,250 million? Between $7,500 million and under $8,750 million?

b. If you select a single letter at random from the English alphabet, what is the probability of it being a vowel? What if you had selected this letter from the alphabet's first 10 letters? What is the probability of finding a vowel when selecting a single letter at random from an English-language book?

18. Review Table 6.19 and Table 6.20 on the CD-ROM.

a. If one of those cans of peas is selected at random, what is the probability of its net weight lying in the 15.3- to under 15.5-ounce range? In the 15.9- to under 16.3-ounce range?

b. If one of those multinational companies is selected at random, what is the probability of its total revenue lying between $5,000 million and under $27,000 million? Between $115,000 million and under $159,000 million?

19. Classify each of the following as an objective or subjective probability statement (and if the former, as a classical or empirical one):

a. There is one chance in two for a recession this fall.

b. There is 1 chance in 100 that we will meet a car coming up the other side of this hill.

c. The probability is 1/52 that one picks the king of spades when taking one card from a deck.

d. There is no chance for a meltdown of this nuclear plant.

e. The odds are 20 to 1 in favor of sales going up because of our product's new name.

f. Past experience indicates that the odds against engine-mount failure on this type of airplane are a million to one.

g. There is one chance in three that the next U.S. president will be a Democrat.

h. In 600 tosses of a die, you can expect to get a 3-face 100 times.

i. The probability is 0.0001 that radicals will get hold of nuclear weapons.

j. The probability of picking an even-denomination card from a deck equals 5/13.

20. Classify each of the following as an objective or subjective probability statement (and if the former, as a classical or empirical one):

a. There is one chance in three that the Dow Jones index will hit 12,000 in the next 6 months.

b. Our past experience indicates that there is one chance in 500 that this house will burn down this year.

c. Our past experience suggests that the probability of this audited voucher having an error is 0.002.

d. Our past experience suggests that the probability of this person having a *second* bankruptcy is 0.67.

e. Author: The probability of this book making the bestseller list is 0.8.

f. Publisher: Our past experience suggests that the probability of this book making the bestseller list is 0.01.

g. There is a 50 percent chance that this new product will capture half of the market in its first year.

h. The probability of randomly picking a Texas company from this *Fortune 500* list is 36/500.

i. The probability of randomly picking a California company from this *Fortune 500* list is 56/500.

j. The probability of randomly picking a furniture maker from this *Fortune 1000* list is 6/1,000.

SECTION 8.6 COUNTING TECHNIQUES

21. Compute *factorials* for the following numbers: 3, 11, 19, 25. (*Hint:* If you have EXCEL, you can click the **Function Wizard** > **Math & Trig** > **FACT** > **OK** and enter a number in the dialog box. To find $n!$ in MINITAB, enter $n + 1$ in the GAMMA function. To find 10!, click **Calc** > **Calculator**, in *Store result in variable,* enter **C1**, in *Expression,* enter **GAMMA (11)**, and click **OK**.)

22. For each of the following sets, compute the number of *permutations* of x at a time out of n distinct items, with no repetitions allowed.

n	x
2	1
6	4
15	2
25	7
25	32

23. A ship has five flags each of green, red, and yellow. How many different messages can it send if it uses all 15 flags for each message? What if it had ten flags, two of which were green and two red, while three each were blue and yellow?

24. For each of the sets on page 332, compute the number of *combinations* of x at a time out of n distinct items, with no repetitions allowed. (*Hint:* If you have EXCEL, you can click the **Function Wizard** > **Math & Trig** > **COMBIN** > **OK** and enter first n and then x in the dialog box.)

n	x
2	2
7	3
13	3
22	10
30	35

25. In the Massachusetts Megabuck Lottery, six numbers out of 1 to 36 must be picked (in any order, with no repetitions allowed). How many different tickets would one have to buy in order to be *certain* to win? Given the fact that the jackpot usually varies between $3 million and $10 million, and a ticket costs only $1, why doesn't anyone do it?

26. If a restaurant serves 3 salads, 5 entrees, 4 vegetables, 6 drinks, and 7 desserts, in how many different ways can one get 2 entrees, 2 vegetables, and 2 desserts? If a complete dinner includes two of everything, how many different dinner combinations are being offered?

27. How many different *combinations* of 3 cards can be taken from a deck of 52 cards? How many *permutations?* No repetitions allowed; show your calculations.

28. How many different committees of 3 males and 2 females can be formed from a group of 10 males and 10 females?

29. If each participant in a 10-player tournament must play every other participant, how many plays must be made?

30. If 13 cards are taken from a deck, what is the probability that they include the king of spades and the king of hearts?

31. If 5 cards are taken from a deck, what is the probability of getting a *royal* flush (a sequence from 10 to king plus ace of the same suit)? Of getting *any* straight flush (a sequence of 5 cards from the same suit, starting with any number between 2 and 10)?

32. In the United States, the 50 separate states design their own automobile license plates, usually using 6 spaces that contain numbers or letters.

a. If only numbers are used, starting with 000000, how many different plates are possible?

b. How many plates are possible if 2 letters and 4 numbers are used? What if the letters B, I, and O are excluded because they are too easily mixed up with 8, 1, and 0?

c. Would you expect the more populous states, such as California and New York, to use more or fewer letters? Explain.

Section 8.7 Laws of Probability: Addition

33. If you think it applies, use the general or special addition law to determine each of the following probabilities:

a. The probability of getting a sum of 5 or 6 when rolling two dice.

b. The probability of getting a black card or an ace from a deck of cards.

c. The probability of inflation or recession, if that of inflation is 0.8, that of recession is 0.2, and that of both at the same time is 0.1.

d. The probability for a city experiencing, before the end of this decade, a natural disaster such as an earthquake, a flood, or a tornado, if the separate probabilities are 0.1, 0.4, and 0.7, respectively.

34. A market survey shows that 60 percent of consumers like brand A, 40 percent like brand B, 15 percent like both. What is the probability of someone chosen at random liking A *or* B?

35. A market survey yields the results given in Table 8.5. What is the probability of someone chosen at random liking A *or* B *or* C?

TABLE 8.5 | Percent of Consumers Who Like Brand

A	20
B	10
C	5
A and B	8
A and C	2
B and C	7
All three	5

36. In the past, a bank has denied credit for four (mutually exclusive) reasons: (1) low income 15% of the time, (2) poor repayment history 40% of the time, (3) no collateral 25% of the time, and (4) excessive debts 20% of the time. What is the probability that its next credit denial will be due to reason 2 or 3?

SECTION 8.8 LAWS OF PROBABILITY: MULTIPLICATION

37. Consider Table 8.6. Use it to construct a joint probability table and clearly identify all the joint and marginal probabilities.

TABLE 8.6 | Number of Workers Whose . . .

Score on Hiring Test Was	First-Year Job Performance Was		
	Good, G	Bad, B	Total
High, H	240	60	300
Low, L	10	90	100
Total	250	150	400

38. Calculate all the conditional probabilities associated with Practice Problem 37. Do so in two ways: first, on the basis of Table 8.6 here; second, on the basis of Table 8.11 on the CD-ROM.

39. Consider Tables 8.7 through 8.10 on the next page. Calculate the following probabilities and identify them as conditional, joint, or marginal:

a. The probability of an inspector tagging a satisfactory item as unacceptable.

b. The probability of a female guest ordering dish A.

c. The probability of a random person being a nonsmoker with heart disease.

d. The probability of a person with heart disease being a nonsmoker.

e. The probability of a smoker being free of heart disease.

f. The probability of a loan being under $500 and also in excess of 30 days old.

g. The probability of a loan being above $500 in size.

TABLE 8.7 | Number of Items . . .

Inspected and . . .	Tagged As Acceptable, A	Tagged As Unacceptable, U	Total
In Fact Satisfactory, S	600	30	630
In Fact Defective, D	35	35	70
Total	635	65	700

TABLE 8.8 | Number of Restaurant Patrons Who . . .

	Ordered Dish A	Ordered Dish B	Total
Were Male, M	20	180	200
Were Female, F	90	10	100
Total	110	190	300

TABLE 8.9 | Number of Persons Who . . .

	Had Heart Disease, H	Were Free of Heart Disease, F	Total
Were Smokers, S	300	200	500
Were Nonsmokers, N	100	300	400
Total	400	500	900

TABLE 8.10 | Number of Loans . . .

	30 Days Old or Less, L	In Excess of 30 Days, E	Total
Up to $500, U	700	1,000	1,700
Above $500, A	1,400	2,000	3,400
Total	2,100	3,000	5,100

40. Still using Tables 8.7 to 8.10, calculate the following probabilities and identify them as conditional, joint, or marginal:

a. The probability of an item being defective.

b. The probability of a defective item being tagged acceptable.

c. The probability of a B order having come from a male.

d. The probability of a B order.

e. The probability of heart disease.

f. The probability of a loan being above $500 and also in excess of 30 days old.

g. The probability of a $12,000 loan being over a year old.

41. a. Apply the general multiplication law, according to which $p(\text{A } \textit{and} \text{ B}) = p(\text{A}) \times p(\text{B} \mid \text{A})$, to the intersection of the two events given in the first row and second column of each of Tables 8.6 to 8.10.

b. Confirm your results by direct calculation from the table data.

c. Are the events dependent or independent? Why?

42. a. Apply the general multiplication law, according to which $p(\text{A } \textit{and} \text{ B}) = p(\text{A}) \times p(\text{B} \mid \text{A})$, to the intersection of the two events given in the second row and first column of each of Tables 8.6 to 8.10.

b. Confirm your results by direct calculation from the table data.

c. Are the events dependent or independent? Why?

43. An analysis of a recent labor union vote on a new contract shows this: In the Northeast, 5,000 of 20,000 members voted yes; in the Southeast, 3,000 of 7,000 members voted no; in the Northwest, 4,000 of 10,000 members voted yes; and in the Southwest, 13,000 of 21,000 members voted yes. (There were no abstentions.) Calculate these probabilities:

a. that a randomly chosen member of this union was from the Northeast and voted no

b. that a randomly chosen no-voter was from the Southwest

c. that a randomly chosen member from the Northwest or Southwest voted yes

d. that a randomly chosen member voted yes

In each case, identify the nature of the probabilities involved.

44. If you discovered any joint probabilities among the four cases noted in Practice Problem 43, confirm your answer with the help of an appropriate law of probability.

SECTION 8.9 PROBABILITY LAWS AND TREE DIAGRAMS

45. On the basis of the data given in Table 8.7, draw two tree diagrams analogous to panels (a) and (b) of text Figure 8.9 (on pages 321–322).

46. On the basis of the data given in Table 8.10, draw two tree diagrams analogous to panels (a) and (b) of text Figure 8.9 (on pages 321–322).

47. In what important way do the two sets of illustrations produced in answering Practice Problems 45 and 46 differ from each other?

SECTION 8.10 REVISING PROBABILITIES: BAYES' THEOREM

48. A new movie is released. The producing company judges the probability of a smashing success at $p = 0.3$. It also knows that a certain reviewer has liked 75 percent of all movies that became greatly successful and has disliked 90 percent of all movies that later turned out to be ghastly failures. If the company followed the Bayesian approach, how would it revise its probability-of-success figure if it learned that the reviewer praised the movie? What if the reviewer criticized it severely?

49. A wine producer has designed a distinctive bottle in the hope of increasing sales. The manager views the probability of success as 0.5 but also orders a survey of customers. The manager knows that when consumers are enthusiastic and sales are about to rise, the type of survey about to be taken will so indicate 90 percent of the time, but in 10 percent of the cases, the survey will say the opposite. When consumers are unimpressed and sales prospects look dim, the survey will so indicate 60 percent of the time, but in 40 percent of the cases, it will say the opposite. The survey is taken and shows great consumer enthusiasm about the bottle. What is the manager's posterior probability of success?

50. A personnel manager knows that 50 percent of the workers who are hired without a screening test perform satisfactorily on the job. However, among workers who take the test and later do well on the job, 90 percent pass it, while among those who take the test and later do badly on the job, 90 percent fail it. What is the manager's posterior probability of satisfactory job performance if a randomly chosen applicant (a) passes the test and (b) fails the test?

Chapter 9

Discrete Probability Distributions

LOOKING AHEAD

After reading this chapter, you will be able to understand the nature of discrete random variables and their probability distributions. Among other things, you will discover useful applications based on:

1. the Bernoulli process and the binomial probability distribution family,
2. the Poisson process and the Poisson probability distribution family, and
3. the hypergeometric probability distribution.

AND HERE IS A TYPICAL PROBLEM YOU WILL BE ABLE TO SOLVE:

An automobile manufacturer has fitted all cars with identical pollution-control devices, designed to meet government standards, yet experience shows that 5 percent of cars tested perform below these pollution standards. Assume that 20 cars coming off the assembly line during a given month are selected at random. What is the probability that a government inspector who tests 20 cars a month in the above fashion will unjustly accuse the manufacturer of producing more than 5 percent of all cars below standard?

PREVIEW

In 1898, Ladislaus von Bortkiewicz published his research on accidental deaths of Prussian soldiers not caused directly by war. As he examined deaths from horse kicks that occurred in ten army corps over a 20-year period, he found the absolute frequency distribution given in the first two columns of Table 9.1.

Of the 200 annual observations, 109 showed zero deaths, 65 showed one death, and so on. No army corps ever recorded more than four such deaths—the numbers were always very small. Von Bortkiewicz then also computed the relative frequencies shown in our table and, thus, established the *empirical probabilities* for these deaths. For example, the probability that a randomly chosen army corps would experience three or four deaths from horse kicks in a given year equaled 0.015 and 0.005, respectively.

TABLE 9.1 | Prussian Army Study

Yearly Number of Deaths from Horse Kicks	Absolute Frequency	Relative Frequency = Empirical Probability	Poisson Probabilities
0	109	0.545	0.544
1	65	0.325	0.331
2	22	0.110	0.101
3	3	0.015	0.021
4	1	0.005	0.003
	200	**1.000**	**1.000**

SOURCE: Adapted from Ladislaus von Bortkiewicz, *Das Gesetz der kleinen Zahlen* (Leipzig: Teubner, 1898).

This brings us to a concept that is central to this chapter and the next: A systematic listing of each possible value of a random variable, such as our first-column horse-kick deaths, together with the associated likelihood of its occurrence, such as our third-column probability values, is called a *probability distribution*.

Several distinct types of probability distributions exist. Von Bortkiewicz, for example, made an interesting discovery about the probability distribution he found: It could be predicted almost perfectly by a *formula* first noted by Abraham de Moivre (1667–1754) and then rediscovered by and named after Siméon Poisson (1781–1840). Our table's last column shows the predicted Poisson probabilities.

A hundred years have passed, but Poisson's distribution and its many cousins have far from outlived their usefulness. Based on data similar to those in Table 9.1, modern airlines advertise their safety (and defend it in court), highlighting the probability that they conclude over 99 percent of their yearly flights *without* fatalities. Manufacturers of all sorts of products, ranging from anticancer drugs to lightbulbs and pollution control devices, make similar statements based on empirical probability values: that at least 50 percent of patients are helped by the drug, that the bulbs last a minimum of 1,000 hours, that at most 5 percent of pollutants get through. In turn, government and private agencies put such claims to the test and sometimes get sample results that contradict such claims: Only 10 percent of sampled patients were helped by the drug, the sampled lightbulbs burned out after only 600 hours, and 35 percent of pollutants failed to be caught by the sampled device. When they encounter such contradictory results, the agencies use probability distributions to assess the likelihood that the original claims were true.

As our study of probability distributions will show, such seeming contradictions are more common than people think. Have another look at Table 9.1. The Prussian army could truthfully claim that its cavalrymen, on average, encountered fewer than one death per year during years of peace. Yet it would not have been impossible for an investigator to observe three or four deaths in a particular year; there was a 2 percent chance for such an event—unlikely, but possible. In the same way, particular sample results obtained by the Food and Drug Administration, the Consumer Products Safety Commission, or Consumers' Union can contradict *truthful* claims made by manufacturers about their products. On the other hand, if the likelihood of a contradictory sample result is not 2 percent but merely 0.0002 percent, we might reasonably doubt the veracity of the original claim.

9.1 Basic Concepts

In Chapter 1, we defined *variables* as characteristics possessed by persons or objects, called elementary units, in which we are interested. Such variables, we noted, can be either *qualitative* or *quantitative.* Qualitative variables (such as sex or job title) differ in kind rather than in degree among elementary units and are normally not described numerically. Quantitative variables (such as salary or years of service), on the other hand, differ in degree rather than in kind among elementary units, and these variables *are* expressed numerically. This chapter and the next deal exclusively with such quantitative variables.

The present chapter, moreover, focuses on *discrete* quantitative variables (also discussed in Chapter 1) that can assume values only at specific points on a scale of values, with inevitable gaps between successive observations. When dealing with discrete quantitative variables, we can *count* all possible observations and, with some exceptions (such as the Poisson variable, which we discuss later in the chapter) that count leads to a finite result.

Before proceeding, we must become familiar with three important concepts:

- the random variable
- the probability distribution
- summary measures for probability distributions

THE RANDOM VARIABLE

More likely than not, you are already familiar with situations that involve random variables. The number of heads observed when tossing three coins is such a variable; chance determines whether the number is 0, 1, 2, or 3. The number of points showing on the top face of a die that you roll once is a random variable, too; so is the serial number of a lottery ticket about to be drawn from among 100,000 tickets in a bowl. Still other examples include von Bortkiewicz's horse-kick deaths, noted in the Preview above, the annual fatalities on U.S. airlines, the time it takes a stockbroker to execute an order, and the hourly number of arrivals at the hospital's emergency room.

DEFINITION 9.1 Any quantitative variable the numerical value of which is determined by a random experiment, and thus by chance, is a **random variable.** The variable's name (such as "heads "when tossing a coin) is designated by X; any one of its possible values (such as "2 heads in five tosses") is symbolized by x.

If the set of all possible values of a random variable is *countable,* as in 1, 2, 3, . . . and n, because the variable can assume values only at specific points on a scale of values, with inevitable gaps in between (3.62 heads can never be tossed), the variable is called a **discrete random variable.**

The concept of a *random variable* is applicable far beyond the world of games and gambling, however. Imagine us about to draw a random sample from among a list of employees of a firm. We may seek to determine, say, their mean salary or the proportion of women on the payroll without taking a time-consuming and expensive census. Before we take the sample, we can view the sample mean or proportion as a random variable because *chance* will determine which of many possible samples we will actually select and, therefore, which of many possible sample means or proportions we will actually observe. Innumerable other variables that interest business executives and economists are random variables, too. These range widely from the number of defective items found by a quality inspector among today's output, to tomorrow's closing price of a given stock, to the number of customers arriving at a supermarket checkout counter during the next 10 minutes, and to an investment's future rate of return.

THE PROBABILITY DISTRIBUTION

As we already saw in Table 9.1, each possible numerical value of a random variable occurs with a certain probability. Jointly listing all of a random variable's possible numerical values with those values' associated probabilities produces the variable's *probability distribution.*

DEFINITION 9.2 A table, graph, or formula that associates each possible value, x, of a random variable, X, with its probability of occurrence, $p(X = x)$, is said to illustrate the random variable's **probability distribution.**

If the variable is a discrete random variable, the distribution is called a **discrete probability distribution.**

TABULAR REPRESENTATION Table 9.2 on the next page provides an example of a discrete probability distribution. The random variable, X, is the hourly credit-verification requests received by a credit bureau. The first column lists possible numbers, x, of such requests during a given hour. It is clearly impossible for the bureau to receive fewer than zero calls per hour and we assume, for simplicity, that it never receives more than 11 requests per hour. The second column lists the probabilities associated with each value of x. For example, the probability of getting precisely 5 requests per hour, $p(X = 5)$, equals 0.09. The sum of the separate probabilities equals 1 because the 12 values of x are mutually exclusive and, we assumed, collectively exhaustive.

GRAPHICAL REPRESENTATION The information given in Table 9.2 can be presented in graphical form as well, as Figure 9.1 on page 341 demonstrates.

Panel (a) depicts the data of Table 9.2 directly. This regular probability distribution shows probabilities for all the individual values of our random variable. Panel (b), on the other hand, pictures the associated **cumulative probability distribution.** For each of our random variable's possible values, it shows the likelihood of the variable being less than or equal to that value. Nothing more complicated is involved than adding the probability of any given value of the random variable to the probabilities associated with all preceding values.

SYMBOLIC REPRESENTATION Sometimes we cannot express even a discrete probability distribution in a table or a graph because too many possible values of the random variable exist. For example, an actual credit bureau might well be flooded with 1,000 requests in an hour, but we conveniently assumed this possibility away when constructing Table 9.2. When a random variable has too many possible values to construct a table or graph of its probability distribution, we can only express the distribution symbolically. Take the case of drawing one item from among 100,000 items sitting in a warehouse or moving along a production line. It would be tedious and unnecessary to construct a table with 100,000 rows, stating that

$$p(X = \text{serial number 1}) = \frac{1}{100{,}000} \quad \text{and} \quad p(X = \text{serial number 2}) = \frac{1}{100{,}000}$$

and so on, until reaching $p(X = \text{serial number } 100{,}000) = \dfrac{1}{100{,}000}$

TABLE 9.2 | A Discrete Probability Distribution

A probability distribution provides a probability value, p, for each value, x, of a random variable, X. Thus, it is similar to a relative frequency distribution.

Random Variable X = Hourly Credit-Verification Requests

Possible Number of Requests x	Probability $p(X = x)$
0	0.05
1	0.10
2	0.15
3	0.17
4	0.19
5	0.09
6	0.08
7	0.06
8	0.06
9	0.02
10	0.02
11	0.01
	$\Sigma p = 1.00$

Instead, we simply designate the type of item by X and possible serial numbers by x and write

$$p(X = x) = \frac{1}{1000{,}000} \quad \text{where } x = 1, 2, \ldots 100{,}000$$

We will employ this notation throughout the text. In this case, it tells us succinctly that the probability equals 1/100,000 for the selected item, X, to have any specific serial number, x, where the latter can be any integer between 1 and 100,000.

SUMMARY MEASURES FOR THE PROBABILITY DISTRIBUTION

An investigator contemplating the information given in Table 9.1 might wonder about the *average* horse-kick fatality rate in the long run. The manager of our credit bureau contemplating the information given in Table 9.2 [graphed in panel (a) of Figure 9.1] might similarly wonder about the *average* hourly credit-verification requests over the long haul. For purposes such as these, we can calculate summary measures, just as we did in Chapter 7. A probability distribution can most easily be summarized and compared with other such distributions by using measures of location and spread. Let us consider calculating a random variable's arithmetic mean, variance, and standard deviation.

The Arithmetic Mean of a Random Variable The most important measure of location for a probability distribution is the (weighted) arithmetic mean of the random variable's

FIGURE 9.1 | Regular and Cumulative Probability Distributions of a Discrete Random Variable

A stick diagram, such as that in panel (a), is a graphical device that illustrates a discrete probability distribution, such as that of Table 9.2. As a comparison of panel (a) with (b) indicates, we can convert any regular probability distribution into a cumulative distribution by adding the probability of any given value of the random variable to that of all the preceding values. For example, while the probability of precisely 2 hourly credit-verification requests equals 0.15 (left-hand graph), that of 2 or fewer requests equals 0.05 + 0.10 + 0.15 = 0.30 (right-hand graph).

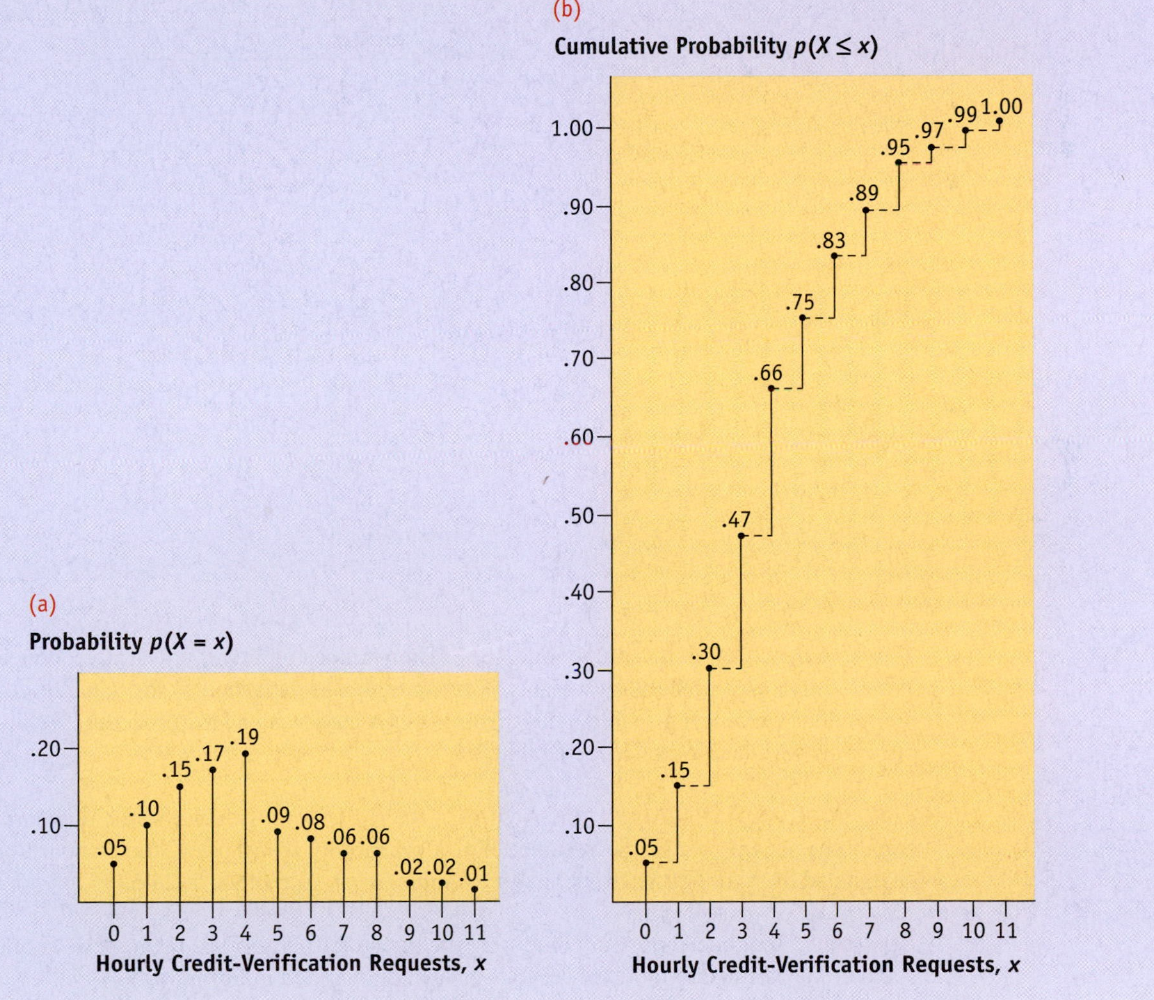

possible values. We compute it by weighting each of these possible values by its associated probability. This mean of the random variable X is symbolized by μ_x. It is also called the random variable's **expected value,** $E(X)$, because it is the value one can expect to find *on average* by numerous repetitions of the random experiment that generates the variable's actual values.

Using our Table 9.2 data, we can compute the weighted average number of credit-verification requests, for instance, as shown in Table 9.3 on the next page.

TABLE 9.3 | Weighted Arithmetic Mean or Expected Value of X = Number of Hourly Credit-Verification Requests

Given the data of Table 9.2, we can determine that the credit bureau receives an average of 3.99 requests per hour in the long run. The average can be computed as $\Sigma px/\Sigma p$, but Σp always equals 1 for a probability distribution, which makes $\mu_x = \Sigma px$.

Possible Number of Requests x	Probability $p(X = x)$	Weighted Value $p(X = x) \times x$
0	0.05	0
1	0.10	0.10
2	0.15	0.30
3	0.17	0.51
4	0.19	0.76
5	0.09	0.45
6	0.08	0.48
7	0.06	0.42
8	0.06	0.48
9	0.02	0.18
10	0.02	0.20
11	0.01	0.11
	$\Sigma p = 1.00$	$\Sigma px = 3.99$

THE VARIANCE OF A RANDOM VARIABLE The variance of a random variable, denoted by σ_x^2 or *VAR(X),* also uses probability weights. These weights are attached to the squared deviations of the random variable's possible values from its expected value. This procedure is illustrated for our credit-verification example in Table 9.4.

THE STANDARD DEVIATION OF A RANDOM VARIABLE As always, the standard deviation equals the square root of the variance. For a probability distribution, the standard deviation is designated by σ_x or *SD(X).* Thus, in our example, $\sigma_x = \sqrt{6.0898} = 2.4678$.

SUMMARY The procedures for computing the (weighted) arithmetic mean, the variance, and the standard deviation of a random variable, *X,* are summarized in Formulas 9.A–9.C.

FORMULAS 9.A–9.C | Summary Measures for the Probability Distribution of Random Variable *X*

9.A Arithmetic mean or expected value: $\mu_x = E(X) = \Sigma px$

9.B Variance: $\sigma_x^2 = VAR(X) = \Sigma p(x - \mu_x)^2$

9.C Standard deviation: $\sigma_x = SD(X) = \sqrt{\sigma_x^2}$

where p is the probability of random variable X being equal to x, while x is an observed value of that variable.

TABLE 9.4 | Variance of X = Number of Hourly Credit-Verification Requests

Given the data of Table 9.3, we can determine the variance of the hourly credit-verification requests as 6.0898. This value of the variance can be computed as $\Sigma p \times (x - \mu_x)^2/\Sigma p$, but Σp always equals 1 for a probability distribution, which makes $\sigma_x^2 = \Sigma p \times (x - \mu_x)^2$.

Possible Number of Requests x	Probability $p(X = x)$	Deviation $x - \mu_x$	Squared Deviation $(x - \mu_x)^2$	Weighted Value $p \times (x - \mu_x)^2$
0	0.05	−3.99	15.9201	0.7960
1	0.10	−2.99	8.9401	0.8940
2	0.15	−1.99	3.9601	0.5940
3	0.17	−0.99	0.9801	0.1666
4	0.19	0.01	0.0001	0.0000
5	0.09	1.01	1.0201	0.0918
6	0.08	2.01	4.0401	0.3232
7	0.06	3.01	9.0601	0.5436
8	0.06	4.01	16.0801	0.9648
9	0.02	5.01	25.1001	0.5020
10	0.02	6.01	36.1201	0.7224
11	0.01	9.01	49.1401	0.4914
	$\Sigma p = 1.00$			$\Sigma p \times (x - \mu_x)^2 =$ 6.0898

Note: Summary measures of shape, measuring skewness and kurtosis, are rarely used. When they are needed, we introduce them in the following sections when discussing particular types of discrete distributions.

9.2 The Binomial Probability Distribution

Different types of random experiments give rise to different types of probability distributions. When working with discrete random variables, we are most likely to make use of the **binomial probability distribution.** It shows the probabilities associated with possible values of a discrete random variable that are generated by a type of experiment called a *Bernoulli process.*

THE BERNOULLI PROCESS

The process discussed in this section is fairly common. It is named after a Swiss mathematician, James Bernoulli (1654–1705), a biography of whom is found on the Web site associated with this text.

DEFINITION 9.3 A **Bernoulli process** is a sequence of n identical trials of a random experiment such that each trial (1) produces one of two possible complementary outcomes that are conventionally called *success* and *failure* and (2) is independent of any other trial so that the probability of success or failure is constant from trial to trial.

The number of successes achieved in a Bernoulli process is the **binomial random variable.** A sequence of coin tosses provides a perfect example. Each toss necessarily produces one of two possible outcomes: heads or tails. Quite arbitrarily, one of these outcomes is called a "success," the other one a "failure"; it does not matter which is called which. No matter how many tosses are made, the probability of success (for example, of getting a head) is precisely 1/2; that of failure (for example, of getting a tail) remains a constant 1/2 as well. The same situation arises in a series of die tosses, provided the outcomes are classified as "odd" and "even" numbers of dots. Each toss must lead to one of these two outcomes, and each of these outcomes has an unchanging probability of 3/6.

CAUTION

The Bernoulli process requires that the success and failure probabilities be *constant* from one trial to the next; it does not require these two probabilities to be *equal* to each other, as happens to be the case in the examples just cited. A constant success probability of 0.1 and a constant failure probability of 0.9 satisfies the definition as well. Thus, if we wanted to examine an ongoing production process that continually generates 10 percent defective parts and 90 percent perfect parts, we would be dealing with a Bernoulli process (and would be justified employing the procedures we are about to meet).

Interestingly, the conditions defining the Bernoulli process are met by a multitude of random experiments, all of which lead to only one of two outcomes. Consider how a new baby must be male or female, how a new product must be liked or disliked, how a new drug must be effective or ineffective. Consider how a salesperson will sell or not sell, how a loan will be granted or denied, how a bid will be won or lost, how the quality of a product will be acceptable or unacceptable, how an account will be correct or in error, how an exam will be passed or failed, how a patient will be alive or dead, how an organ will be infected or not infected . . . the list goes on.

But note: Whenever the random experiment involves sampling from a finite population, successive elementary units must be selected *after replacement* of the units previously sampled in order to meet condition (2) and, thus, keep the probabilities of success and failure from changing as the sequence of trials proceeds. Consider the case of acceptance sampling just noted in the above Caution box. If, unbeknownst to us, there are 10 defective items in a lot of 100, and we take a sample of 20 items, the probability of finding a defective item is 10/100 for the first item sampled. If we then set aside the first item rather than return it to the lot, the corresponding probability is 10/99 or 9/99 for the second item sampled (depending on whether the first item taken was satisfactory or defective). And the probability continues to change for the next items selected until it might lie between 10/81 and 0/81 for the 20th item, depending on how many defectives we found in the meantime. Only by replacing each item after inspection and remixing the lot can we keep the probability unchanged and thus maintain the strict requirements of the Bernoulli process. For practical purposes, however, sampling without replacement can often be viewed as closely resembling a Bernoulli process, provided the sample is small relative to the population and constitutes, say, 5 percent or less of the population. In such a case, the probabilities involved do change from sampling one unit to the next, but the changes are negligible. If we took a sample of only 2 out of 100 or only 20 out of 1,000, and did so without replacement, the second item's probability of being defective could hardly be distinguished from that of the first item.

EXAMPLE PROBLEM 9.1

In order to confirm that the Bernoulli process requires constancy (rather than equality) of probabilities from trial to trial, consider a case of acceptance sampling in which items are checked for quality. Assume that 3 items are picked from a lot of 100 items of which 10 percent are known to be defective. Also assume that each sampled item is replaced before the next one is picked, which ensures that the strict conditions of the Bernoulli process are met. Graphically generate the binomial probability distribution, while defining the binomial random variable X as "finding a defective item."

SOLUTION: We can use a probability tree diagram to determine the possible outcomes of this experiment. In Figure 9.2, "finding a defective item" is designated as D and "finding a satisfactory item" as S. The subscripts 1, 2, and 3 refer to the first, second, and third item drawn, respectively.

As Figure 9.2 illustrates, the probability of "success" (finding a defective item) remains a constant 0.1 from one trial to the next, and the probability of "failure" (finding a satisfactory item) equals a constant 0.9. As the box tells us, 8 possible outcomes exist, containing different numbers of defectives. In the last column, the probability of each of these events is calculated by the special multiplication law (from Chapter 8), using the probabilities given along the branches of the tree diagram. Finally, because we are not interested in identifying particular defective items, but only in counting the total number of defectives, we can combine all the outcomes with the same total of defectives. For example, we can apply the special addition law to combine the

FIGURE 9.2 | Bernoulli Trials

This diagram illustrates the Bernoulli process with the sampling of 3 items to determine quality. At each fork of the tree, one of two outcomes must occur: The sampled item must be defective or satisfactory. Given the assumed replacement of sampled items, each trial is independent of all others, and the probabilities involved, although not equal to each other, are constant throughout the experiment.

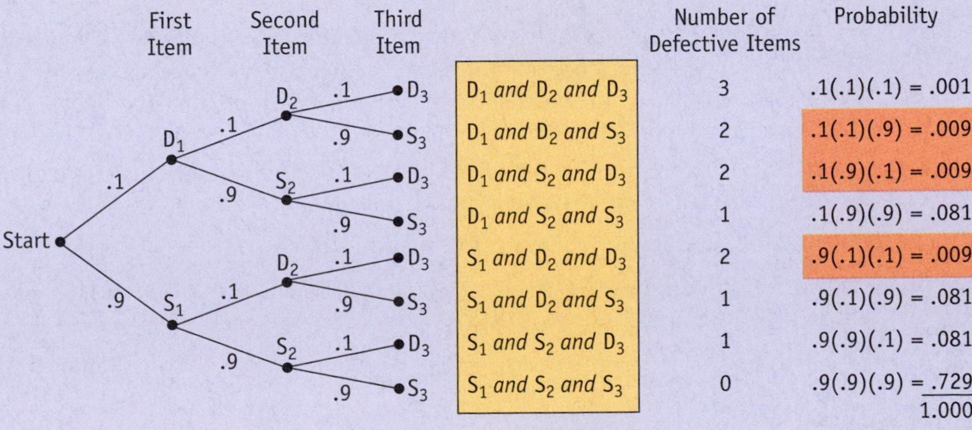

three shaded probabilities of 0.009 to find the probability of 2 defectives as 0.027. By this procedure, we derive the following binomial probability distribution:

$$p(X = 3 \text{ defectives}) = 0.001$$
$$p(X = 2 \text{ defectives}) = 0.027$$
$$p(X = 1 \text{ defective}) = 0.243$$
$$p(X = 0 \text{ defectives}) = \underline{0.729}$$
$$1.000$$

THE BINOMIAL FORMULA

Luckily, we need not always draw complicated tree diagrams to find probabilities like the ones just calculated. We can also determine them more directly with the help of the **binomial formula,** which gives us the probability of x successes in n trials of a random experiment that satisfies the conditions of a Bernoulli process.

FORMULA 9.D | The Binomial Formula

$$p(X = x|n,\pi) = c_x^n \times \pi^x \times (1 - \pi)^{n-x}$$

where $x = 0, 1, 2, \ldots n$ is the number of successes in n trials, π is the probability of success in any one trial, and $c_x^n = \dfrac{n!}{x!(n-x)!}$ is the binomial coefficient.

Note: $x \leq n$

TECHNICAL DETAIL

The binomial formula looks complicated, yet it is fairly easy to interpret:

1. The left-hand side of the equation symbolizes the probability of x successes, given the occurrence of n trials and given a probability of success of π in each of these trials. As the box indicates, x cannot exceed n: An experiment cannot succeed more often than it is conducted.
2. The first term on the right-hand side is called the **binomial coefficient.** It tells us how many permutations of x successes (and, therefore, $n - x$ failures) can be achieved in n trials. The answer is $c_x^n = \dfrac{n!}{x!(n-x)!}$. For example, how many sequences exist that contain $x = 2$ successes in $n = 3$ trials of a Bernoulli process? According to the coefficient, the answer is $c_2^3 = \dfrac{3!}{2!(3-2)!} = \dfrac{3 \times 2 \times 1}{2 \times 1(1)} = 3$, which is precisely what Figure 9.2 (page

(continued)

Technical Detail (continued)

345) confirms. Just look in the column labeled "Number of Defective Items." The kind of information given in these columns, (and laboriously derived in Figure 9.2), can thus be gained instantly by calculating the binomial coefficient. (Pascal's triangle, discussed in a later section of this chapter, is another device for generating binomial coefficients.)

3. The next term in the formula, π^x, represents the probability of success, π, in any one trial of the experiment, such as that of finding a defective item (0.1), raised to the xth power, where x is the number of successes. This term provides us with the joint probability of x successes, calculated by using the special multiplication law for independent events. In each of the three shaded rows in Figure 9.2, which correspond to the three outcomes with 2 successes, π^x appears as (0.1) (0.1), which is the same thing as $\pi^x = (0.1)^2$.

4. The last term in the formula, $(1 - \pi)^{n-x}$, represents the probability of failure, $1 - \pi$, in any one trial of the experiment, such as that of finding a satisfactory item (0.9), taken to the $(n - x)$th power, where $n - x$ is the number of failures. This term provides us with the joint probability of $n - x$ failures, once more calculated using the special multiplication law. In each of the three shaded rows in Figure 9.2, which correspond to the three outcomes with 2 successes and, therefore, 1 failure, the term $(1 - \pi)^{n-x}$ appears as $(0.9)^{3-2} = (0.9)^1 = 0.9$.

5. When the binomial formula *combines* the formula's last two terms and then calculates $\pi^x \times (1 - \pi)^{n-x}$, it is in fact calculating (once more by using the special multiplication law for independent events) the joint probability of x successes *and* $n - x$ failures in a specific sequence of experimental outcomes. Thus, in Figure 9.2, the joint probability of a sequence of 2 successes *and* 1 failure equals $(0.1)^2 (.9)^{3-2} = (0.1)(0.1)(0.9) = 0.009$, precisely as each one of the shaded rows indicates.

6. Because there exist $c_2^3 = 3$ different ways of getting the type of sequence just discussed (2 successes and 1 failure in 3 trials), and because these 3 outcomes are mutually exclusive events, the special addition law can be applied. It helps us calculate the overall probability of getting 2 successes in 3 trials of this experiment *somehow*—that is, regardless of whether this result occurs in the manner shown in row 2 or 3 or 5 of Figure 9.2. This overall probability equals 0.009 (first shaded row) + 0.009 (second shaded row) + 0.009 (third shaded row) = 0.027, which is the very result for the probability of 2 defective items that was calculated earlier. Instead of adding $\pi^x \times (1 - \pi)^{n-x} = 0.009$ three times, however, one could simply multiply the term by 3, which is precisely what the binomial coefficient in the binomial formula accomplishes.

EXAMPLE PROBLEM 9.2

We can test the accuracy of the binomial formula by pretending to seek with its help one of the answers already provided in Figure 9.2 on page 345: What is the probability of finding 0 defective items when sampling 3 items, provided the probability of finding a defective item in a single draw equals 0.1?

SOLUTION:

$$p(X = 0|n = 3, \pi = 0.1) = c_0^3 \times (0.1)^0 \times (1 - 0.1)^{3-0} = \frac{3!}{0!(3-0)!} \times 1 \times (0.9)^3$$
$$= 1 \times 1 \times 0.729 = 0.729$$

This result is confirmed by that found in the last line of Figure 9.2.

Note: While the binomial formula tells us directly the probability of x successes in n trials, it also tells us indirectly the probability of the complementary event. Thus, the probability of finding *some* defective items in our sample equals $1 - 0.729 = 0.271$.

EXAMPLE PROBLEM 9.3

To show how an entire binomial probability distribution can be determined by using the binomial formula without the tree diagrams seen in Figure 9.2, consider this: A manufacturer uses a production process that produces 20 percent defective items. A defect in any one item is, however, independent of possible defects in other items. (The problem is not a matter of some machine becoming occasionally maladjusted and turning out a whole series of defective items until a correction is made. If that were the case, the appearance of one defective item would significantly affect the probability of finding another such item, which would violate the conditions of the Bernoulli process.) If, under these conditions, 5 units are produced, what is the probability of 0, 1, 2, 3, 4, and 5 of them being defective?

SOLUTION: The answers are quickly found by a systematic application of the binomial formula, as Table 9.5 attests.

BINOMIAL SUMMARY MEASURES

We could compute a binomial probability distribution's major summary measures—mean, variance, and standard deviation—according to general Formulas 9.A–9.C. However, we can also derive them with the help of the simplified Formulas 9.E–9.G.

FORMULAS 9.E–9.G | Summary Measures: Probability Distribution of Binomial Random Variable *X*

9.E Arithmetic mean or expected value: $\mu_x = E(X) = n \times \pi$

9.F Variance: $\sigma_x^2 = VAR(X) = n \times \pi \times (1 - \pi)$

9.G Standard deviation: $\sigma^2 = SD(X) = \sqrt{\sigma_x^2}$

where n is the number of trials and π is the probability of success in any one trial.

Note: Skewness is zero for $\pi = 0.5$, positive for $\pi < 0.5$, and negative for $\pi > 0.5$.

EXAMPLE PROBLEM 9.4

Review the binomial probability distribution given in Table 9.5, which is defined by the parameters $n = 5$ and $\pi = 0.2$. Compute the distribution's arithmetic mean, variance, and standard deviation, and assess its skewness.

TABLE 9.5 | Determining a Binomial Probability Distribution for $n = 5$ and $\pi = 0.2$ by Using the Binomial Formula

The entries in the first column, together with those in the last column, represent a binomial probability distribution. Its mathematical determination, using the three terms in the binomial formula, is illustrated with the help of the three middle columns. The second row tells us, for example, that there exist 5 different ways of achieving 1 success (along with 4 failures) in the experiment in question and that the probability of each of these sequences equals (0.2) multiplied by (0.8)(0.8)(0.8)(0.8). Thus, the probability of getting any one of these 5 sequences is five times the product of the numbers just listed, or 0.4096.

Number of "Successes" (defective items found) x	$c_x^n = \frac{n!}{x!(n-x)!}$	π^x	$(1-\pi)^{n-x}$	$p(X = x\|n,\pi)$
0	$\frac{5!}{0!(5-0)!} = 1$	$(0.2)^0 = 1$	$(0.8)^{5-0} = 0.3277$	$1 \times 1 \times 0.3277 = 0.3277$
1	$\frac{5!}{1!(5-1)!} = 5$	$(0.2)^1 = 0.2$	$(0.8)^{5-1} = 0.4096$	$5 \times 0.2 \times 0.4096 = 0.4096$
2	$\frac{5!}{2!(5-2)!} = 10$	$(0.2)^2 = 0.04$	$(0.8)^{5-2} = 0.512$	$10 \times 0.04 \times 0.512 = 0.2048$
3	$\frac{5!}{3!(5-3)!} = 10$	$(0.2)^3 = 0.008$	$(0.8)^{5-3} = 0.64$	$10 \times 0.008 \times 0.64 = 0.0512$
4	$\frac{5!}{4!(5-4)!} = 5$	$(0.2)^4 = 0.0016$	$(0.8)^{5-4} = 0.8$	$5 \times 0.0016 \times 0.8 = 0.0064$
5	$\frac{5!}{5!(5-5)!} = 1$	$(0.2)^5 = 0.00032$	$(0.8)^{5-5} = 1$	$1 \times 0.00032 \times 1 = 0.00032$
				1.00000

SOLUTION:

Arithmetic mean: $\mu_x = n \times \pi = 5 \times 0.2 = 1$

Variance: $\sigma_x^2 = n \times \pi \times (1 - \pi) = 5 \times 0.2 \times 0.8 = 0.8$

Standard deviation: $\sigma_x = \sqrt{0.8} = 0.8944$

Skewness: Because π is less than 0.5, this distribution is positively skewed. An inspection of Table 9.5 confirms the skew to the right: Imagine depicting the distribution with a stick diagram, similar to panel (a) of Figure 9.1 on page 341. The heights of the sticks would vary from 0.33 for 0 successes to 0.41 for 1 success (the distribution's mean) to 0.20 for 2 successes, and so on, reaching 0.00032 for 5 successes at the end of a long right tail. [If you want to take a look now, this distribution is, in fact, graphed as panel (d) of Figure 9.3 in the next section.]

9.3 The Binomial Probability Distribution Family

A look at binomial Formula 9.D indicates that the probability for any given number of successes varies with two factors: the number of trials, n, and the probability of success in any one trial, π. Each different combination of n and π thus produces a different binomial probability distribution, even though we use the same formula to derive the distribution. It is customary to refer to any specific binomial probability distribution, such as that given in Table 9.5, as *a member of the binomial distribution family.* From this we automatically understand that other members can be found by varying the values of n or π. Figure 9.3 depicts nine members of this family, each of them determined by the procedure illustrated in Table 9.5. Indeed, the distribution calculated in Table 9.5 is graphed in panel (d).

MEETING THE FAMILY

Note three things in Figure 9.3.

First, given any number of trials, n, the probability of a high proportion of successes rises with the probability of achieving success in a given trial. Consider, for example, panels (a) through (c), all of which involve $n = 2$ trials of a random experiment. The probability of achieving two successes in two trials rises from .04 to .25 and to .64 as the probability of success in a single trial, π, rises from .2 to .5 and then to .8. Similar observations can be made for panels (d) through (f) and panels (g) through (i), respectively.

Second, any binomial probability distribution with a success probability of $\pi = .5$ is perfectly symmetrical regardless of the value of n, as panels (b), (e), and (h) indicate. On the other hand, any such distribution with $\pi < .5$ or $\pi > .5$ skews to the right or left, respectively. This is illustrated by panels (a), (d), and (g) for skewness to the right and by panels (c), (f), and (i) for skewness to the left. Although Figure 9.3 does not show it, the skewness gets more pronounced the closer π gets to 0 or 1, respectively.

Third, given any value of $\pi \neq .5$ and, therefore, the presence of skewness, the skewness becomes less pronounced as n rises. For high values of n, all such binomial probability distributions approach symmetry, as a progressive comparison of panel (a) with (d) and (g) or of panel (c) with (f) and (i) indicates. As will be noted in the next chapter, this tendency of the binomial probability distribution to take on a bell-shaped form as n increases allows one to approximate such distributions by a *normal probability distribution.*

BINOMIAL PROBABILITY TABLES

Undoubtedly, simply using the binomial formula for determining binomial probabilities is less cumbersome than drawing tree diagrams. However, even this mathematical approach can become awkward and can require much time and effort—especially when large factorials are involved and the formula requires us to raise numbers to large powers. Under such circumstances, it would be convenient to have the probabilities already computed for us and listed in tables similar to those of square roots and logarithms. Luckily, such **binomial probability tables** already exist. They list binomial probabilities for various combinations of possible values of n and π. Two types of binomial probability tables exist: one for individual values of x, such as Appendix Table C, and another for cumulative values of x, such as Appendix Table D.

Binomial Probabilities for Individual Values of x Probabilities for achieving x numbers of successes in a Bernoulli process, given various combinations of n and π, are listed in Appendix Table C. Each value in the body of the table was calculated by Formula 9.D. This particular table is set up for values of n ranging from 1 to 20 and for selected probabilities of success in any

FIGURE 9.3 | Nine Members of the Binomial Probability Distribution Family

In accordance with the binomial formula, each different combination of n (number of trials) and π (success probability in a given trial) gives birth to a different member of the binomial probability distribution family. Each of the nine distributions shown here has been calculated by the procedure illustrated in Table 9.5, with the results rounded to two decimals.

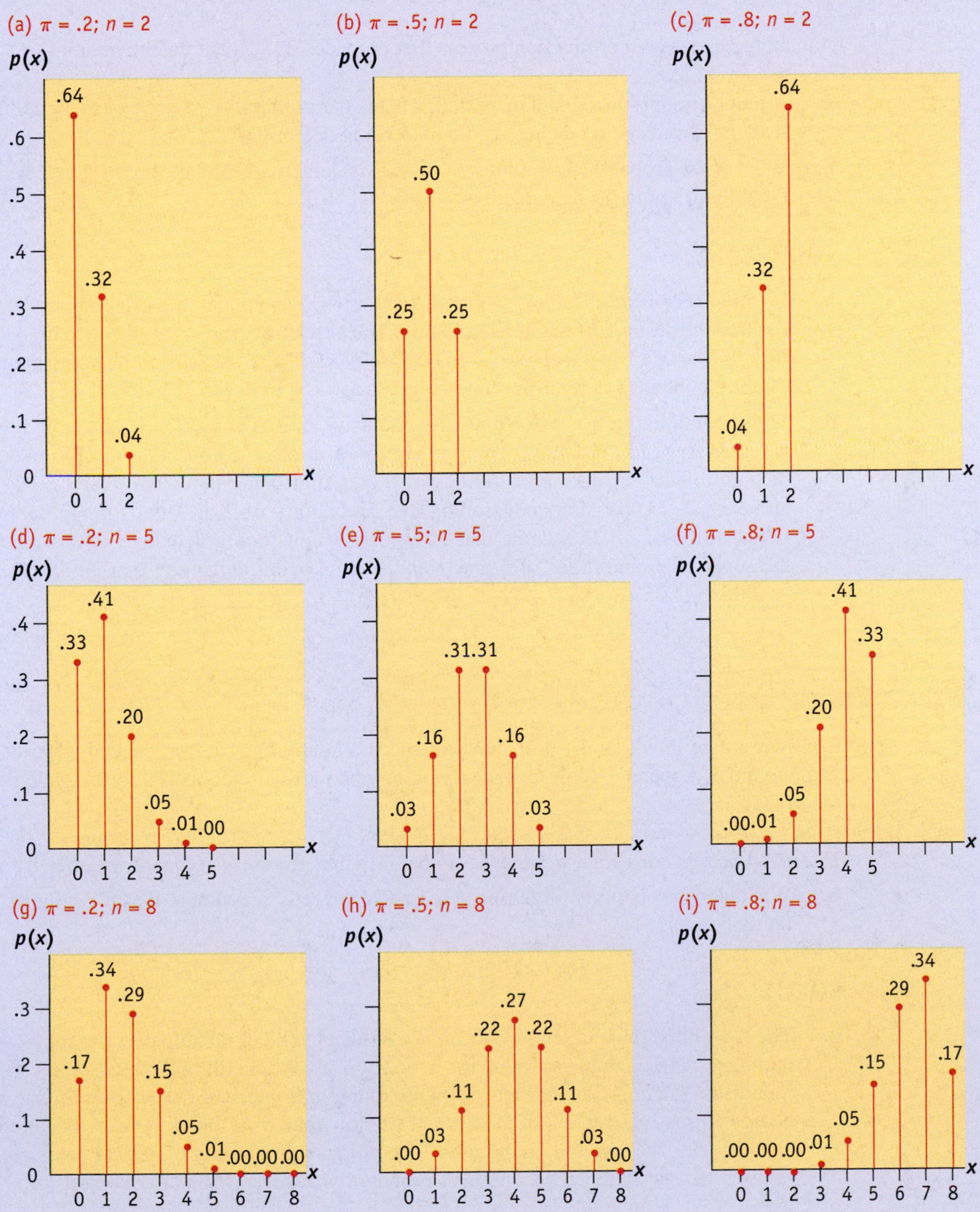

one trial, π, between .05 and .50. The table can, however, still be used to determine binomial probabilities for π in excess of .50, as we will learn below.

To become familiar with Appendix Table C consider the following experiments, always assuming that they meet the conditions of a Bernoulli process. (For a quick review, see Definition 9.3 on page 344.)

EXAMPLE PROBLEM 9.5

A manufacturer uses a production process that produces 20 percent defective items.

a. If 5 units are produced and inspected, what is the probability of none of them being defective? Of 3 units being defective? Of all 5 being defective?

b. What is the probability of at most 1 unit being defective? Of 2 or 3 units being defective? Of at least 3 units being defective?

SOLUTION:

a. Looking at Appendix Table C in the section for $n = 5$ and under the column for $\pi = .20$, you can find the desired probabilities instantly: The probability for $x = 0$ is seen to be .3277, that for $x = 3$ is .0512, and that for $x = 5$ is .0003. (*Note:* These answers correspond precisely to those calculated directly in the corresponding rows of Table 9.5.)

b. The special addition law for mutually exclusive events can be applied to the numbers given in Appendix Table C. The probability of at most 1 unit being defective equals the sum of the separate probabilities of 0 or 1 unit being defective; that is, .3277 + .4096 = .7373. By similar reasoning, the probability of 2 or 3 units being defective is .2048 + .0512 = .256, while that of at least 3 units being defective equals the sum of the separate probabilities of 3 and 4 and 5 units being defective; that is, .0512 + .0064 + .0003 = .0579.

EXAMPLE PROBLEM 9.6

Consider a case in which the probability of success in any one trial, π, exceeds .50, the highest value found in Appendix Table C. Take a worker who wires circuit boards correctly 95 percent of the time.

a. If 20 boards are wired, what is the probability that precisely 16 boards are wired correctly?

b. What is the probability of getting at least 4 incorrectly wired boards? Of getting at most 3 faulty boards?

SOLUTION:

a. The Appendix Table C section with $n = 20$ seems to be of no help because the row containing $x = 16$ contains no value for $\pi = .95$. Yet we can still find the desired answer by rephrasing the question in terms of failure rather than success. Our worker *fails* to wire boards correctly 5 percent of the time. If we now read π as the probability of failure on any one trial, we can find, in the $\pi = .05$ column, a probability of getting precisely 4 faulty boards as .0133. This implies a probability of getting 16 perfect boards of .0133 as well.

b. The answer again requires the addition of various probabilities. Getting at least 4 faulty boards involves adding the probabilities of 4 faulty boards, of 5 faulty boards, of 6 faulty boards, . . . , and, finally, of 20 faulty boards. As the .05 column in the $n = 20$ section of Appendix Table C tells us, this amounts to $.0133 + .0022 + .0003 = .0158$. Similarly, the probability of getting at most 3 faulty boards is found as the sum of the probabilities of getting 0, 1, 2, and 3 faulty boards, that is, $.3585 + .3774 + .1887 + .0596 = .9842$. It is no accident that our two answers sum to 1; the events described are complementary.

BINOMIAL PROBABILITIES FOR CUMULATIVE VALUES OF *X* Example Problem 9.6b illustrates why statisticians have found it desirable to construct tables of binomial probabilities for *cumulative* values of x as well as for individual values of x. Although it is easy enough to calculate cumulative probabilities when n is small (we had to sum only four separate probability values in Problem 9.6b), this process can become extremely tedious for large values of n. Appendix Table D presents binomial probabilities for cumulative values of x. It is set up for values of n ranging from 1 to 20, as well as for $n = 50$ and $n = 100$. Once again, selected probability-of-success values between .05 and .50 are given. Unlike in Appendix Table C, the values in the body of Appendix Table D now give the probabilities not of x successes, but of *x or fewer successes.*

EXAMPLE PROBLEM 9.7

Consider using Appendix Table D to answer questions about a population of consumers 30 percent of whom favor and 70 percent of whom dislike a new product. If we randomly sample 100 persons, rather than take a census, what are the probabilities of finding:

a. 8 or fewer consumers who favor the product?

b. precisely 40 consumers who favor the product?

c. fewer than 20 consumers who favor the product?

d. 26 or more consumers who favor the product?

e. more than 35 consumers who favor the product?

f. between 20 and 40 consumers, inclusive, who favor the product?

SOLUTION:

a. What is the probability of finding 8 or fewer consumers who favor the product? As a look at the $x = 8$ row and $\pi = .30$ column in the $n = 100$ section of Appendix Table D tells us, the probability is 0.

b. What is the probability of finding precisely 40 consumers who favor the product? The answer, in the $\pi = .30$ column and the $n = 100$ section of Appendix Table D, is the difference between the probabilities of finding 40 or fewer such consumers (.9875) and finding 39 or fewer such consumers (.9790), or .0085.

c. What is the probability of finding fewer than 20 consumers who favor the product? The answer is equivalent to finding 19 or fewer such consumers, or .0089.

d. What is the probability of finding 26 such consumers or more? The answer is equivalent to 1 minus the probability of finding 25 or fewer such consumers, or $1 - .1631 = .8369$.

e. What is the probability of finding more than 35 such consumers? The answer is equivalent to 1 minus the probability of finding 35 or fewer such consumers, or $1 - .8839 = .1161$.

f. What is the probability of finding between 20 and 40 such consumers, inclusive? The answer is equivalent to the probability of finding 40 or fewer such consumers (.9875) minus that of finding 19 or fewer of them (.0089), or .9786.

It should be noted that a *cumulative* probability table provides no information that you could not also gather from the equivalent section of an individual probability table. The only (though not inconsiderable) advantage of the cumulative table is that it frees the user from the need to add or subtract large numbers of probability values. Applications 9.1, *Budgeting Research and Development,* and 9.2, *Acceptance Sampling Plans,* provide two cases in point.

APPLICATION 9.1

BUDGETING RESEARCH AND DEVELOPMENT

Firms and governments throughout the world spend large sums of money on basic and applied research and on product development.[1] In the 1950s, the Rand Corporation developed a now-common approach called *parallel-path strategy* to help achieve research-and-development (R&D) goals at minimum cost. This strategy involves n teams working independently of one another trying to achieve the same goal, such as developing a new product. The teams are given annual budgets of, say, $10 million each. Despite this huge outlay, each team has a relatively low chance of succeeding—of, say, merely 5 percent. However, the more teams that are put to work, the greater is the chance of at least *one* of them succeeding, but the greater the overall budget must be. This is where probability theory comes in. It helps answer questions such as: How much money must a sponsoring firm or government agency spend if it wants to have a 90 percent chance of at least one success?

Because the activity in question involves a Bernoulli process (one of two outcomes, independent teams), the binomial probability distribution can be used to establish the probability of at least one success by n teams.

$$p(X \geq 1) = 1 - p(X = 0)$$
$$= 1 - c_0^n \times \pi^0 \times (1 - \pi)^{n-0} = 1 - (1 - \pi)^n$$

[1] *Basic research* is scientific inquiry not directed toward any specific "useful "discovery. (Biologists may simply want to know how cells proliferate.) *Applied research* is scientific inquiry aiming to apply the knowledge gained in basic research to a particular problem. (Biologists may conduct experiments to inhibit the growth of undesirable cells.) *Product development,* as the term suggests, turns research findings into new production processes and marketable products. (Think of the creation of an anti-cancer drug.)

TABLE 9.A

Desired Probability of at Least 1 Success	Number of R&D Teams Needed	Budget per Team ($ millions/year)	Total Required Budget ($ millions/year)
.50	14	10	140
.60	18	10	180
.70	24	10	240
.80	32	10	320
.90	45	10	450
.95	59	10	590
.99	90	10	900
1.00	∞	10	∞

(continued)

Application 9.1 (continued)

Given $\pi = .05$, we get $p(X \geq 1) = 1 - .95^n$.

If the agency were content with only a 90 percent chance of success, this expression would become

$$p(X \geq 1) = 1 - .95^n = .90, \quad \text{making } .95^n = .10$$

The value of n implied by this expression is about 45, implying (at $10 million per team) an annual budget of $450 million. Table 9.A shows the budgets required for other acceptable probabilities of achieving at least one success, given a .05 success probability for any one team.

Note how certainty of at least one success would require an infinite budget, but quite feasible budgets can produce near-certainty. Thus, in 1998, not counting $22.5 billion of federal government subsidies, American firms as a group spent $7.2 billion on basic research, $30.7 billion on applied research, and $102.9 billion on product development. Many individual firms had annual R&D budgets similar to those given in the last column of Table 9.A.

SOURCES: Adapted from Richard R. Nelson, "Uncertainty, Learning, and the Economics of Parallel Research and Development Efforts," *Review of Economics and Statistics,* November 1961, pp. 351–364; Moshe Ben Horim and Haim Levy, *Statistics* (New York: Random House, 1981), pp. 246–248; U.S. Census Bureau, *Statistical Abstract of the United States 1999* (Washington, D.C., 1999), p. 618.

APPLICATION 9.2

ACCEPTANCE SAMPLING PLANS

Chapter 22 of this text devotes itself entirely to matters of quality control, but we can anticipate some of its lessons here because they involve the use of binomial probability distributions. Most firms and government agencies regularly receive shipments of goods from outside suppliers, and they want to accept these shipments only if each contains a reasonably low percentage of defective items. Thus, they take random samples of each shipment to determine the percentage of defective items. To decide whether to accept or reject a shipment, however, they must have a *sampling plan;* that is, they must choose (1) the desirable sample size and (2) the maximum number of defective units they are willing to find, while still accepting the shipment. As long as the conditions of the Bernoulli process prevail (see Definition 9.3 on page 344), the binomial probability distribution can be extremely helpful here.

Consider the U.S. Air Force purchasing, say, electronic navigation equipment. If it sampled 5 such items in each shipment of 100 units and followed the self-imposed rule of accepting the entire shipment only if 0 defective units were found, what would it in fact be doing? The binomial formula provides a quick (and amazing) answer: With $n = 5$ and $x = 0$, the Air Force under this sampling plan would, nevertheless, be accepting shipments containing 5 percent defective items ($\pi = .05$) some 77 percent of the time! It would be accepting shipments containing 10 percent defective items 59 percent of the time, and it would even accept shipments with 30 percent defective items 17 percent of the time. These numbers can be confirmed quickly in Appendix Table C, section $n = 5$, $x = 0$, for π values of .05, .10, and .30.

If such a situation were deemed undesirable, matters could be improved by increasing the sample size to, say, $n = 20$. A sample plan of $n = 20$ and $x = 0$ would cause acceptance of lots with 5, 10, or 30 percent defectives only 36, 12, and 0 percent of the time.

Naturally, sampling plans need not be based on $x = 0$. We can decide to accept lots that contain $x = 3$ defective items or fewer of them. As Appendix Table D shows, shipments with 5 percent defective items ($\pi = .05$) will be accepted 98 percent of the time when samples of 20 are taken and findings of 3 or fewer defective items are deemed acceptable. On the other hand, shipments with 10 or 30 percent defective items will then be accepted only 87 or 11 percent of the time.

Can you show why someone who wanted to accept shipments with 10 percent defectives at most 3 percent of the time, but who was willing to accept all shipments where samples contained up to 1 defective item, would have to choose a sample size of $n = 50$? (*Hint:* Note in Appendix Table D how the cumulative probability numbers in the $x \leq 1$ row and the $\pi = .10$ column steadily decline as n increases.)

BINOMIAL PROBABILITIES AND COMPUTER PROGRAMS

Computer programs, such as EXCEL and MINITAB, provide another method yet of establishing entire binomial probability distributions or computing individual or cumulative probabilities for any given set of x, n, and π. The following examples illustrate this fact.

EXCEL Example 9.1

Use EXCEL to find the binomial probability distribution for $n = 5$ and $\pi = 0.2$.

SOLUTION

1. Fire up EXCEL and enter the labels **x** and **probability,** respectively, into cells A1 and B1.
2. Enter numbers 0–5 into cells A2–A7.
3. Place the pointer into cell B2; then click the **Function Wizard (*fx*)** > **Statistical** > **BINOMDIST** > **OK.** The BINOMDIST dialog box appears.
4. In the *Numbers* box, enter the cell containing the first value of x, or **A2**. Press TAB.
5. In the *Trials* box, enter the value of n, or **5**. Press TAB.
6. In the *Probability* box, enter the value of π, or **.2**. Press TAB.
7. In the *Cumulative* box, enter **FALSE** or **0** to indicate that you do *not* want cumulative probabilities.
8. Click **OK;** then drag the cell B2 entry by the handle in the lower right corner to B7. The resulting probabilities are identical to those found in Table 9.5 (and in Appendix Table C):

x	**probability**
0	0.32768
1	0.4096
2	0.2048
3	0.0512
4	0.0064
5	0.00032

EXCEL Example 9.2

Use EXCEL to find the binomial probability distribution for $n = 4$ and $\pi = 0.13$, which is a combination *not* found in Appendix Table C.

SOLUTION Using the same procedure as in EXCEL Example 9.1, you can derive this result:

x	probability
0	0.57289761
1	0.34242156
2	0.07674966
3	0.00764556
4	0.00028561

Note how the values found here lie in-between those given in the $\pi = .10$ and $\pi = .15$ columns of the $n = 4$ section in Appendix Table C.

EXCEL Example 9.3

Use EXCEL to find the *cumulative* binomial probability distribution for $n = 5$ and $\pi = 0.2$.

SOLUTION

1. Fire up EXCEL and enter the labels **x** and **cumulative probability,** respectively, into cells A1 and B1.
2. Enter numbers 0–5 into cells A2–A7.
3. Place the pointer into cell B2; then click the **Function Wizard (*fx*) > Statistical > BINOMDIST > OK.** The BINOMDIST dialog box appears.
4. In the *Numbers* box, enter the cell containing the first value of *x*, or **A2**. Press TAB.
5. In the *Trials* box, enter the value of *n*, or **5**. Press TAB.
6. In the *Probability* box, enter the value of π, or **.2**. Press TAB.
7. In the *Cumulative* box, enter **TRUE** or **1** to indicate that you *do* want cumulative probabilities.
8. Click **OK;** then drag the cell B2 entry by the handle in the lower right corner to B7. The resulting cumulative probabilities are identical to those found in Appendix Table D:

x	cumulative probability
0	0.32768
1	0.73728
2	0.94208
3	0.99328
4	0.99968
5	1

EXCEL Example 9.4

Use EXCEL to find the *cumulative* binomial probability distribution for $n = 4$ and $\pi = 0.13$, which is a combination *not* found in Appendix Table D.

SOLUTION Using the same procedure as in EXCEL Example 9.3, you can derive this result:

x	cumulative probability
0	0.57289761
1	0.91531917
2	0.99206883
3	0.99971439
4	1

Note how the values found here lie between those given in the $\pi = .10$ and $\pi = .15$ columns of the $n = 4$ section in Appendix Table D.

EXCEL Example 9.5

As an inspector for Consumers' Union, you have just bought a package of 4 outdoor floodlights. The manufacturer claims that 95 percent of these lights last a minimum of 1,000 hours. If the claim is true, what are the chances that

a. all four of your lights will last at least 1,000 hours?

b. at most three of your lights will last at least 1,000 hours, while one will fail earlier?

SOLUTION

1. Fire up EXCEL and enter the labels **x, probability,** and **cumulative probability** respectively, into cells A1–C1.
2. Enter numbers 0–4 into cells A2–A6.

PART (A)

3. Place the pointer into cell B2; then click the **Function Wizard (*fx*)** > **Statistical** > **BINOMDIST** > **OK.** The BINOMDIST dialog box appears.

4. In the *Numbers* box, enter the cell containing the first value of x, or **A2**. Press TAB.
5. In the *Trials* box, enter the value of n, or **4**. Press TAB.
6. In the *Probability* box, enter the value of π, or **.95**. Press TAB.
7. In the *Cumulative* box, enter **FALSE** or **0** to indicate that you do *not* want cumulative probabilities.
8. Click **OK** and drag the cell B2 entry to B6. The answer is highlighted in red in the probability column of the table below: **.8145**

PART (B)

9. Place the pointer into cell C2; then click the **Function Wizard (*fx*)** > **Statistical** > **BINOMDIST** > **OK.** The BINOMDIST dialog box appears.
10. In the *Numbers* box, enter the cell containing the first value of x, or **A2**. Press TAB.
11. In the *Trials* box, enter the value of n, or **4**. Press TAB.
12. In the *Probability* box, enter the value of π, or **.95**. Press TAB.
13. In the *Cumulative* box, enter **TRUE** or **1** to indicate that you *do* want cumulative probabilities.
14. Click **OK** and drag the cell C2 entry to C6. The answer is highlighted in red in the cumulative probability column of the table below: **.1855**

x	probability	cumulative probability
0	6.25E-06	6.25E-06
1	0.000475	0.00048125
2	0.0135375	0.01401875
3	0.171475	0.18549375
4	0.81450625	1

EXCEL Example 9.6

Review EXCEL Example 9.5. Then ask EXCEL to create, say, 50 random data that simulate the successes experienced in a Bernoulli process, with $n = 4$ and $\pi = .95$. What are percentages of a) four and b) three successes found in your experiment?

SOLUTION

1. Fire up EXCEL, place the pointer into cell A1; then click **Tools** > **Data Analysis** > **Random Number Generation** > **OK.** The *Random Number Generation* dialog box appears.
2. In the *Number of Random Numbers* box, enter **50**.
3. In the *Distribution* box, select **Binomial.**
4. Enter *p-Value* = **.95** and *Number of Trials* = **4**.

5. Click **OK.** Something like following output appears:

4	4	3	4	4
4	4	4	4	4
4	3	4	4	4
4	4	3	4	3
4	4	4	4	4
4	4	4	4	4
4	3	4	4	3
3	4	4	4	4
4	4	4	4	4
4	3	4	3	4

a. The probability of four successes in the simulation equals 41/50, or .82, compared to the theoretical probability of .8145 found in EXCEL Example 9.5.

b. The probability of three successes in the simulation equals 9/50, or .18, compared to the theoretical probability of .1855 found in EXCEL Example 9.5.

Caution: If you repeat this exercise, you will get a different answer because EXCEL will not create the same pseudo-random numbers again.

PASCAL'S TRIANGLE

Before the computer age, what did people do when they wanted to find binomial probabilities? A fascinating and simple method for finding binomial coefficients was popularized by Blaise Pascal (1623–1662), whose biography appears on the text Web site. His method involves the construction of what is now known as *Pascal's triangle* (although, contrary to Pascal's own claims in his *Traité du Triangle Arithmétique,* he was surely not its originator). The triangle represents an ancient system of quickly answering questions such as these:

In a family of 10 children, what is the likelihood that exactly 3 will be girls? When tossing a coin 10 times, what is the probability that exactly 3 heads will appear? When spinning the roulette wheel 10 times (and not counting the zero), what is the chance for getting red precisely 3 times?

The answers could be found with the help of a tree diagram that noted all the possible $2^{10} = 1{,}024$ outcomes and allowed the outcomes that met the specifications to be counted. Yet, less laboriously, one can create the triangle in question, as shown in Figure 9.4.

To begin with, note how the triangle is constructed, without trying to fathom its meaning. To construct it, one begins by writing down two 1's in the first row, side by side. Next, in the second

FIGURE 9.4 | Pascal's Triangle

```
                1   1
              1   2   1
            1   3   3   1
          1   4   6   4   1
        1   5  10  10   5   1
      1   6  15  20  15   6   1
    1   7  21  35  35  21   7   1
  1   8  28  56  70  56  28   8   1
1   9  36  84 126 126  84  36   9   1
1  10  45 120 210 252 210 120  45  10   1
```

Row Number = Number of Trials, n	Number of Possible Outcomes, 2^n
1	2
2	4
3	8
4	16
5	32
6	64
7	128
8	256
9	512
10	1,024

row below, to the right and the left of the first 1's, two more 1's are put, and the gap between them is filled in with the *sum* of the two numbers above the gap. Since the numbers in row 1 are 1's, a 2 is put in the gap in row 2. Next, 1's are placed at the extremes of the third row, and the two gaps are filled in with 3's (once more the *sum* of the numbers above each gap, which are 2 and 1). And so it goes. By the time the 10th line is reached, one would have constructed Pascal's triangle as printed here. But note: There is no limit to the number of rows one could construct. Can you see why an 11th row would contain entries of 1, 11 (the sum of 1 + 10), 55 (the sum of 10 + 45), 165, 330, 462, 462, 330, 165, 55, 11, and 1?

What does it all mean? First, as the accompanying box shows, the *number of each row* represents the number of trials of some experiment with two possible types of outcome per trial. Row 1 represents *one* trial, such as tossing a coin once. Row 2 represents two trials, such as tossing a coin twice. Row 10 represents *ten* trials, such as tossing a coin ten times.

Second, the *sum of the actual entries in each row* represents the number of possible outcomes. The numbers in row 1 sum to 2; there are 2 possible outcomes of one trial, such as heads or tails, if a coin is tossed once. The numbers in row 2 sum to 4; there are 4 possible outcomes of two trials, such as HH, HT, TH, and TT, if a coin is tossed twice. And the sum of entries in row 10 tells us that there are 1,024 possible outcomes in 10 trials, as when a coin is tossed ten times.

Third, *each individual number in a given row* represents the possible number of times some particular outcome, such as x heads, will occur. The first number in a given row tells us how often n particular outcomes, such as n heads, will occur in n trials. The second number tells us how often $n - 1$ particular outcomes, such as $n - 1$ heads, will occur in n trials, and so on. In row 1, for example, the first 1 might denote 1 possibility of getting $n = 1$ heads in 1 trial; the second 1 might denote 1 possibility of getting $n - 1 = 0$ heads in 1 trial. In row 2, similarly, the first 1 might denote 1 possibility of getting $n = 2$ heads in 2 trials; the 2 might denote 2 possibilities of getting $n - 1 = 1$ head in 2 trials; and the last 1 might denote 1 possibility of getting $n - 2 = 0$ heads in 2 trials. Given the 4 possible outcomes, these numbers imply probabilities of 1/4, 2/4, and 1/4, respectively. Now consider row 10. It helps us find the probabilities for a sequence of 10 children, 10 tosses of a coin, 10 spins of the wheel at roulette, or 10 of any series of equal chances. Note how the numbers in row 10 add to 1,024. These are all the *possible* outcomes. We can read the numbers in the row, from left to right. The first number is a 1. There is a probability of 1 in 1,024, it tells us, of having 10 girls out of 10 children (or 10 heads in 10 tosses or 10 reds in 10 spins of the wheel).

We turn to the second number, a 10. There is a probability of 10 in 1,024, it says, of having 9 girls out of 10 children (or 9 heads or 9 reds). And there is a probability of 45 in 1,024, the third number says, of having 8 girls out of 10 (or 8 heads or 8 reds). And so it goes until the final number in row 10 gives us the probability of 0 girls (or heads or reds) out of 10: It is 1 in 1,024.

Thus, we have our answer: There are 120 chances in 1,024 for each of the 3-in-10 events listed in the second paragraph.

Note: Can you see that row 2 tells us the same thing as the tree diagram in panel (a) of Figure 8.2 on page 282? There are four possibilities, it says, the sum of the numbers in line 2. There is 1 chance in 4 of getting 2 heads, there are 2 chances in 4 of getting 1 head, there is 1 chance in 4 of getting 0 heads. Pascal's triangle, it turns out, is another way of getting some of the results a tree diagram might provide.

9.4 The Poisson Probability Distribution

In the previous section of this chapter, we explored discrete probability distributions for binomial random variables. Such variables, we noted, are defined as *numbers of successes,* and these successes are reaped *within a fixed number of trials* of some random experiment. Early in the 19th century, Siméon Poisson (1781–1840) noted that many processes involve a type of random variable that differs from a binomial random variable in two important ways:

1. Poisson's random variable does not generate a binomial either/or outcome because only a single type of outcome or "event" is occurring.
2. Poisson's random variable is not confined to a fixed number of trials because its value can equal any discrete integer between zero and infinity, along a continuum of time or space.

Accordingly, Poisson defined what is now called a **Poisson random variable** as the number of occurrences of a specified event within a specified time or space. He also defined an alternative to the Bernoulli process, which underlies the binomial probability distribution.

THE POISSON PROCESS

The process that generates various values, x, for the Poisson random variable, X, is central to our discussion.

DEFINITION 9.4 A **Poisson process** is the occurrence of a series of events of a given type in a random pattern over time or space such that (1) the number of occurrences within a specified time or space can equal any integer between zero and infinity, (2) the number of occurrences within one unit of time or space is independent of that in any other such (nonoverlapping) unit, and (3) the probability of occurrences is the same in all such units.

The kinds of events Poisson had in mind are encountered in all areas of life, as the next two sections abundantly show.

Events Occurring Randomly over Time A large class of events satisfying the definition of the Poisson process involves arrivals of "customers" at a "service facility," the two terms in quotation marks being defined in the widest possible sense. Consider the arrival of people demanding service at the bank, the barbershop, or the bus stop; at the checkout counter of a supermarket, the doctor's office, or the elevator door; at the hospital emergency room, the post office, or the restaurant. Consider the arrival of cars at car washes, entrances to major roads, or gas stations; at parking lots, traffic lights, or toll stations. Think of the arrival of planes at airports, of ships at ports, of trucks at terminals. Consider the arrival of telephone calls at the switchboard requesting services from ambulances, firefighters, and police officers. Contemplate the arrival of claims at the insurance company, of parcels at the post office, of orders at the warehouse, of semifinished products at the next stage of production, of refund requests at the complaint department, of suicide victims at the morgue. In all these cases and a million more, the conditions of the Poisson process may well apply.

CAUTION

In order to qualify as examples for a Poisson process, the "customer" arrivals just discussed must be truly random. Thus, *private* planes arriving at an airport may qualify, while *scheduled* airliners may not. Note also that, within a given span of time and for any one of these types of events, we might count any number of occurrences, yet we can never count the number of complementary events or nonoccurrences. Unlike in the Bernoulli process, wherein we might count successes (heads) as well as failures (tails), in the Poisson process, we can count only one thing, such as the people arriving at the bank, but not its complement, such as the people *not* arriving at the bank.

Arrivals at service facilities, however, are not the only types of Poisson events that occur randomly over time. The Poisson process has been found to describe well a great variety of other events, including occurrences of accidents at manufacturing plants, breakdowns of equipment at hospitals, failures of components in satellites, and even vacancies on the U.S. Supreme Court.

EVENTS SPREAD RANDOMLY OVER SPACE Examples of Poisson events are just as abundant in the medium of space as in that of time, regardless of whether "space" is viewed as lines, areas, or volumes.

First, view space as a *line* and consider such events as the appearance of defects in a roll of coated wire, of leaks in a pipeline, of misspelled names in a telephone book, of potholes on a road, of typesetting errors in a book.

Second, view space as an *area* and contemplate the occurrence of births (or bomb bursts) in a city, of blisters on a painted wall, of bubbles in a plate-glass window. Think of crimes in a town, of defects in a carpet, of farmhouses in a county, of lightning-caused fires in a forest; of mines, meteorites, or weeds in a field. Consider stars in a photograph or schools of fish or submarines in the ocean.

Third, and finally, view space as *volume* and envision events such as finding bacteria in a gel, raisins in a loaf, or weed seeds in a packet of flower seeds.

CONCLUSIONS Possible examples of the Poisson process at work are truly infinite in number. In the areas of business and economics, major applications involve waiting-line or queuing problems, inventory policy, and quality control. A bank or restaurant, for example, must know something about the probability distribution of customer arrivals. During a given hour, might there be 2 customers or 20 or 299? Should there be 5 employees ready to serve them, or would 25 be a better bet? Clearly, a trade-off arises between possible idle time of employees (if there are too many of them) and possible waiting time of customers (if there are too many of *them*). Paying idle employees is costly, but losing angry customers who don't like to wait is costly, too.

Maintaining the right amount of inventory in the warehouse presents a similar problem. If inventories in, say, an automotive parts department are huge relative to requests for parts, all customers can always be satisfied without waiting, but inventory holding costs are high. Like the employees above, much of the inventory is "idle" much of the time. When inventories are extremely low, however, many angry customers who don't like waiting for products to arrive will be lost. Having an inventory that is too "busy" is costly as well.

In a sense, both of the examples just given can be viewed as involving quality control of various types of services. Quality control of physical products—be they carpets, heart-lung machines, plate-glass windows, or taxicabs—can, thus, be seen as an analogous issue. A manufacturer surely would not want to produce a heart-lung machine that fails during open-heart surgery, but a trade-off is again unavoidable: Building in a lot of redundant capability (akin to having mostly idle bank tellers or parts inventories) raises costs; not having enough capability and losing customers (akin to having people switch away from crowded banks and unreliable parts suppliers) is costly as well. Once more, knowing the relevant probability distribution can help us.

THE POISSON FORMULA

The probabilities associated with alternative values of the Poisson random variable can be determined with the help of Formula 9.H. This **Poisson formula** gives the probability, within a specified time or space, of x occurrences of a specified event that satisfy the conditions of a Poisson process.

FORMULA 9.H | The Poisson Formula

$$p(X = x|\mu) = \frac{e^{-\mu} \times \mu^x}{x!}$$

where x is the number of occurrences per unit of time or space, reaching from zero to infinity, μ is the mean number of such occurrences within the examined units of time or space, and $e \cong 2.71828$.

TECHNICAL DETAIL

The Poisson formula is less forbidding than appears to be the case at first sight:

1. The left-hand side of the equation symbolizes the probability of x occurrences of the event in question within a specified time or space under examination, given that the expected or mean number of such occurrences in this time or space equals μ.
2. The constant e equals approximately 2.71828; it is the base of the natural logarithms:

   The constant e is equal to $\left(1 + \frac{1}{n}\right)^n$ as n approaches infinity. Thus,

(continued)

Technical Detail (continued)

$$\left(1 + \frac{1}{1}\right)^1 = 2.00000$$

$$\left(1 + \frac{1}{2}\right)^2 = 2.25000$$

$$\left(1 + \frac{1}{3}\right)^3 = 2.37037$$

$$\left(1 + \frac{1}{4}\right)^4 = 2.44141$$

.

.

$$\text{and } \lim_{n \to \infty} = \left(1 + \frac{1}{n}\right)^n \cong 2.71828$$

In the Poisson formula, the constant e is raised to the power of $-\mu$, which makes the expression equal to

$$\frac{1}{e^{\mu}}$$

Appendix Table E, Exponential Functions, provides ready-made calculations of this expression for selected values of μ.

3. The expression μ can itself be viewed as the product of two magnitudes: namely, the **Poisson process rate,** or mean number of occurrences of the event in question *per unit* of time or space (symbolized by the lowercase Greek lambda, λ), and the total number of units of time or space examined, t. Thus, $\mu = \lambda \times t$. The expression λ might, for instance, measure the arrival of cars at a toll booth at a rate of 2 per minute or the making of typesetting errors at a rate of 1 per page. The expression t would then be defined analogously, in this case as the total number of minutes studied, say, 60, or the total number of pages examined, say, 100. Thus, $\mu = \lambda \times t$ would equal 120 cars per 60 minutes or 100 errors per 100 pages.

EXAMPLE PROBLEM 9.8

Consider a bank manager who must decide how many tellers should be available during the Friday afternoon rush when the customers arrive at a rate of 5 customers per minute but in a pattern described by the Poisson process. Such a manager might wish to know the probability distribution for the numbers of customer arrivals within a 30-second period. Derive it with the help of the Poisson formula.

SOLUTION: In this case, $\lambda = 5$ customers per minute; $t = .5$ minutes; hence, $\mu = 2.5$ customers per half-minute. Table 9.6 shows the derivation of the desired probability distribution.

TABLE 9.6 | Determining a Poisson Probability Distribution for $\lambda = 5$, $t = .5$ (hence, $\mu = 2.5$) Using the Poisson Formula

The entries in the first column, together with those in the last column, represent a ***Poisson probability distribution.*** *Its mathematical determination, using the three terms in the Poisson formula, is illustrated with the help of the three middle columns.*

Number of Occurrences of Specified Event (customer arrival) x	$e^{-\mu}$ (from Appendix Table E)	μ^x	$x!$	$p(X = x\|\mu)$
0		$2.5^0 = 1$	$0! = 1$	.0821
1		$2.5^1 = 2.5$	$1! = 1$	.2052
2		$2.5^2 = 6.25$	$2! = 2$	.2565
3		$2.5^3 = 15.625$	$3! = 6$	.2138
4		$2.5^4 = 39.0625$	$4! = 24$	.1336
5		$2.5^5 = 99.6563$	$5! = 120$	.0668
6	→ .082085	$2.5^6 = 244.1406$	$6! = 720$	.0278
7		$2.5^7 = 610.3516$	$7! = 5{,}040$	.0099
8		$2.5^8 = 1{,}525.8788$	$8! = 40{,}320$	.0031
9		$2.5^9 = 3{,}814.697$	$9! = 362{,}880$	.0009
10		$2.5^{10} = 9{,}536.7425$	$10! = 3{,}628{,}800$	.0002
11		$2.5^{11} = 23{,}841.856$	$11! = 39{,}916{,}800$	.0000
12		$2.5^{12} = 59{,}604.64$	$12! = 479{,}001{,}600$	.0000
				.9999

When examining the table, you should note two things:

First, the probabilities of 11 or 12 customer arrivals in a 30-second period are not zero, but tiny positive numbers rounded to zero. For example, $p(X = 12) = .00001021$. This fact reminds us that the Poisson process sets no upper limit to the number of possible occurrences in the specified time or space. In this example, there exists even a positive tiny probability for the arrival of 500 customers in a 30-second period!

Second, we must be careful not to assume that the value of X holds over an extended duration. The Poisson process rate frequently varies with the time of day, the day of the week, the season, and more. Customers surely arrive at the bank at a different rate during Friday afternoons than on Tuesday mornings. The same holds for the arrival of cars at toll booths and for all the other examples given earlier.

EXAMPLE PROBLEM 9.9

Consider a fishing company on the coast of New England. It operates a search plane to find schools of salmon that are randomly located in the North Atlantic. On average, 1 school of salmon appears per 100,000 square miles of sea. On a given day, the plane can fly 1,000 miles, effectively searching a lateral distance of 5 miles on either side of its path.

a. What is the probability of finding at least 1 school of salmon during 3 days of searching?

b. How many days of search are needed before the probability of finding at least 1 school reaches .95?

SOLUTION:

a. We realize that $\lambda = .00001$ school per square mile and that the plane can search a total area of $t = 1{,}000 \times 10 \times 3 = 30{,}000$ square miles in 3 days. Thus, the expected number of schools to be found in 3 days is $\mu = \lambda \times t = .3$.

We also note that the probability of finding at least 1 school equals 1 minus that of finding no school:

$$p(X \geq 1) = 1 - p(X = 0) = 1 - \frac{e^{-.3} \times .3^0}{0!} = 1 - e^{-.3} = 1 - .7408 = .2592$$

b. We note that $p(X \geq 1)$ is supposed to equal .95. Hence,

$$.95 = 1 - p(X = 0) = 1 - \frac{e^{-\mu} \times \mu^0}{0!} = 1 - e^{-\mu}$$

and

$$e^{-\mu} = 1 - .95 = .05$$

Appendix Table E shows this value of $e^{-\mu}$ to be associated with $\mu = 3$. Hence, we know that $\lambda \times t$ must equal 3. Given $\lambda = .00001$, t must equal $(3/.00001) = 300{,}000$. To achieve the desired result, 300,000 square miles of ocean must be searched, and at a rate of 10,000 square miles per day, this search would take 30 days.

POISSON SUMMARY MEASURES

We could compute a Poisson probability distribution's major summary measures—mean, variance, and standard deviation—according to general Formulas 9.A–9.C. However, we can also derive them with the help of the simplified Formulas 9.I–9.K.

FORMULAS 9.I–9.K | Summary Measures: Probability Distribution of Poisson Random Variable *X*

9.I Arithmetic mean or expected value: $\mu_x = E(X) = \lambda \times t$

9.J Variance: $\sigma_x^2 = VAR(X) = \lambda \times t$

9.K Standard deviation: $\sigma_x = SD(X) = \sqrt{\sigma_x^2}$

where λ is the Poisson process rate and t is the total number of units of time or space examined.

Note: Skewness always positive, but it approximates zero as μ_x approaches infinity.

EXAMPLE PROBLEM 9.10

Review the Poisson probability distribution given in Table 9.6, which is defined by the parameters $\lambda = 5$ and $t = .5$. Compute the distribution's arithmetic mean, variance, and standard deviation, and assess its skewness.

SOLUTION:

Arithmetic mean: $\mu_x = \lambda \times t = 5 \times .5 = 2.5$

Variance: $\sigma_x^2 = \lambda \times t = 5 \times .5 = 2.5$

Standard deviation: $\sigma_x = \sqrt{2.5} = 1.5811$

Skewness: Like all Poisson distributions, this distribution is positively skewed. An inspection of Table 9.6 confirms the skew to the right: Imagine depicting the distribution with a stick diagram, similar to panel (a) of Figure 9.1 on page 341. The heights of the sticks would vary from 0.08 for $x = 0$ to 0.21 for $x = 1$ to 0.26 for $x = 2$ . . . , eventually reaching 0.0002 for $x = 10$, and so on. Even larger values of x are associated with tiny positive probabilities. It is for this reason that the Poisson probability distribution has been called *the probability distribution of rare events:* The probabilities tend to be high for small numbers of occurrences, but still positive for very large numbers of events.

9.5 The Poisson Probability Distribution Family

As was shown to be true for the binomial distribution, a whole family of Poisson probability distributions exists. In this case, the members of the family are distinguished from one another by different values of μ (the mean number of occurrences).

POISSON PROBABILITY TABLES

Ready-made **Poisson probability tables** list probabilities of x occurrences in a Poisson process for various values of μ. Appendix Table F gives Poisson probabilities for *individual* values of x and for selected values of μ, ranging from 0.1 to 20. Appendix Table G gives Poisson probabilities for *cumulative* values of x and the same range of μ values.

To become familiar with these tables, consider the following examples of Poisson processes, using in each case first Appendix Table F and then Appendix Table G to solve the problem. These problems will show why in some cases a table for individual probabilities is preferable, while in other cases you can obtain the result more quickly from the table for cumulative probabilities.

EXAMPLE PROBLEM 9.11

Private (unscheduled) planes arrive at an airport at the rate of 2 per minute during a Friday evening.

a. What are the probabilities that 6, 9, or 20 planes arrive between 8:00 and 8:10 P.M.?

b. In the same situation, what is the probability of *at most* 18 planes arriving?

SOLUTION:

a. In this case, $\lambda = 2$, $t = 10$, and $\mu = 20$. (Planes arrive at a rate of 2 per minute, we are examining 10 minutes, and on average 20 planes arrive during a 10-minute interval.) Therefore, Appendix Table F shows the answers directly in the $\mu = 20$ column, and the $x = 6$, 9, and 20 rows, as .0002, .0029, and .0888, respectively.

Using Appendix Table G is awkward: It gives the answers only indirectly as .0003 − .0001 = .0002; .0050 −.0021 = .0029; and .5591 − .4703 = .0888. In each case, the probability of *one number or fewer ones* must be reduced by the probability of the *next lower number or fewer ones* in order to find the desired probability of the first-stated number of occurrences.

b. From Appendix Table F, we must sum the separate probabilities of 0, 1, 2, . . . , 18 planes arriving (still in the $\mu = 20$ column), and this sum is .0000 + .0000 + .0000 + . . . + .0844 = .3814.

Appendix Table G, on the other hand, gives the same result directly in the $x = 18$ row and $\mu = 20$ column.

EXAMPLE PROBLEM 9.12

In a pipeline, 2 leaks occur per 100 miles.

a. What is the probability of finding between 7 and 9 leaks in a 500-mile stretch?

b. Considering again the situation in (a), what is the probability of finding at least 20 leaks in that 500-mile stretch?

SOLUTION:

a. In this case, $\lambda = 2$, $t = 5$, $\mu = 10$. (Leaks occur at a rate of 2 per 100 miles, we are examining 5 such 100-mile units, and on average 10 leaks occur during a 500-mile stretch.) Therefore, Appendix Table F shows the answer in the $\mu = 10$ column as the sum of .0901 + .1126 + .1251 = .3278.

Appendix Table G shows the answer as the difference between the probabilities of 9 or fewer leaks (.4579) and 6 or fewer leaks (.1301), or as .3278 as well.

b. Appendix Table F suggests the answer as the sum of .0019 + .0009 + .0004 + .0002 + .0001 = .0035.

Appendix Table G gives the answer as the difference between 1.0000 and the probability of finding 19 or fewer leaks (.9965), or as .0035 as well.

Applications 9.3, *Probability Applied to Anti-Aircraft Fire,* and 9.4, *Supplying Spare Parts to Polaris Submarines*, provide yet other examples of the manifold uses of Poisson probabilities.

Application 9.3
Probability Applied to Anti-Aircraft Fire
http://www.harcourtcollege.com/business_stats/kohler/siteresources.html

POISSON PROBABILITIES AND COMPUTER PROGRAMS

Computer programs, such as EXCEL or MINITAB, provide another method yet of establishing entire Poisson probability distributions or computing individual or cumulative probabilities for any given values of x and μ. The computer examples on pages 370–374 illustrate this fact.

APPLICATION 9.4

SUPPLYING SPARE PARTS TO POLARIS SUBMARINES

Polaris submarines go on missions that last about 60 days; during this time they must rely on their own supply of spare parts. At the end of each mission, they are met by a supply ship that replenishes spare parts used up during the mission. Defense Department analysts who plan supply ship inventory have found the *Poisson probability distribution* extremely helpful. The minimum number of units of any given spare part that must be on hand when the two ships meet equals the number that failed during the mission, and the occurrence of failures is well described by a Poisson process.

According to a Defense Department study of the first 61 patrols of these submarines, the value of μ varied between 0 and 5, depending on the part. Thus, Appendix Table F quickly provides the implied probabilities: For a part with $\mu = 2$, the probability of 0 failures on a mission equals .1353, that of 1 failure equals .2707, and so on, while that of 7 or more failures is practically zero. The knowledge of this distribution has, thus, helped to promote an effective and yet economical inventory policy for submarine tenders.

SOURCES: Adapted from Sheldon E. Haber and Rosedith Sitgreaves, "An Optimal Inventory Model for the Intermediate Echelon When Repair Is Possible," *Management Science*, February 1975, pp. 638–648; and Edwin Mansfield, *Statistics for Business and Economics* (New York: W. W. Norton, 1980), pp.164–165.

EXCEL Example 9.7

Use EXCEL to find all the Poisson probabilities for individual values of x, given $\mu = 2.5$.

SOLUTION

1. Fire up EXCEL and enter the labels **x** and **probability,** respectively, into cells A1 and B1.
2. Enter numbers 0–12 into cells A2–A14.
3. Place the pointer into cell B2; then click the **Function Wizard (*fx*)** > **Statistical** > **POISSON** > **OK.** The POISSON dialog box appears.
4. In the *x* box, enter the cell containing the first value of *x*, or **A2**. Press TAB.
5. In the *Mean* box, enter the value of μ, or **2.5**. Press TAB.
6. In the *Cumulative* box, enter **FALSE** or **0** to indicate that you do *not* want cumulative probabilities.
7. Click **OK;** then drag the cell B2 entry by the handle in the lower right corner to B14. The resulting probabilities are identical to those found in Table 9.6 (and in Appendix Table F):

x	probability
0	0.082084999
1	0.205212497
2	0.256515621
3	0.213763017
4	0.133601886

5	0.066800943
6	0.027833726
7	0.009940617
8	0.003106443
9	0.000862901
10	0.000215725
11	4.90285E-05
12	1.02143E-05

EXCEL Example 9.8

Use EXCEL to find the Poisson probability distribution for $\mu = 0.15$, which is *not* found in Appendix Table F.

SOLUTION Using the same procedure as in EXCEL Example 9.7, you can derive this result:

x	probability
0	0.860707976
1	0.129106196
2	0.009682965
3	0.000484148
4	1.81556E-05

Note how the values found here lie in-between those given in the $\mu = 0.1$ and $\mu = 0.2$ column of Appendix Table F.

EXCEL Example 9.9

Use EXCEL to find the *cumulative* Poisson probability distribution for $\mu = 1.0$.

SOLUTION

1. Fire up EXCEL and enter the labels **x** and **cumulative probability,** respectively, into cells A1 and B1.
2. Enter numbers 0–7 into cells A2–A9.
3. Place the pointer into cell B2; then click the **Function Wizard (*fx*)** > **Statistical** > **POISSON** > **OK.** The POISSON dialog box appears.
4. In the *x* box, enter the cell containing the first value of *x*, or **A2**. Press TAB.
5. In the *Mean* box, enter the value of μ, or **1**. Press TAB.
6. In the *Cumulative* box, enter **TRUE** or **1** to indicate that you *do* want cumulative probabilities.
7. Click **OK;** then drag the cell B2 entry by the handle in the lower right corner to B9. The resulting cumulative probabilities are identical to those found in Appendix Table G:

x	cumulative probability
0	0.367879441
1	0.735758882
2	0.919698603
3	0.981011843
4	0.996340153
5	0.999405815
6	0.999916759
7	0.999989751

EXCEL Example 9.10

Use EXCEL to find the *cumulative* Poisson probability distribution for $\mu = 0.95$, which is a value *not* found in Appendix Table G.

SOLUTION Using the same procedure as in EXCEL Example 9.9, you can derive this result:

x	cumulative probability
0	0.386741023
1	0.754144996
2	0.928661883
3	0.983925563
4	0.997050688
5	0.999544461
6	0.999939309
7	0.999992895

Note how the values found here lie in-between those given in the $\mu = 0.9$ and $\mu = 1.0$ columns of Appendix Table G.

EXCEL Example 9.11

Between 8 and 10 A.M. on Saturdays, planes arrive at a runway at a rate of 60 per hour. The manager of the approach control position wants you to determine the probability distribution for up to 10 arrivals between 8:00 and 8:03 A.M.

SOLUTION Here $\lambda = 60$ per hour and we are interested in 3 minutes out of 60, or $t = .05$ hours. Thus, $\mu = 3$. Using the procedure introduced in EXCEL Example 9.7, the following is derived:

x	probability
0	0.04978707
1	0.14936121
2	0.22404181
3	0.22404181
4	0.16803136
5	0.10081881
6	0.05040941

(continued)

7	0.02160403
8	0.00810151
9	0.0027005
10	0.00081015
11	0.00022095
12	5.5238E-05
13	1.2747E-05

EXCEL Example 9.12

Review EXCEL Example 9.11. Then ask EXCEL to create, say, 50 random data that simulate a Poisson process with $\lambda = 3$ per 3-minute period. What are percentages of a) $x = 2$ and b) $x = 9$ found in your experiment?

SOLUTION

1. Fire up EXCEL, place the pointer into cell A1; then click **Tools** > **Data Analysis** > **Random Number Generation** > **OK.** The *Random Number Generation* dialog box appears.
2. In the *Number of Random Numbers* box, enter **50**.
3. In the *Distribution* box, select **Poisson**.
4. In the *Lambda* box, enter **3**.
5. Click **OK.** Something like following output appears in column A:

2	3	3	5	3
6	3	4	1	4
4	1	3	4	3
3	5	1	3	1
1	3	6	3	2
2	3	2	2	1
4	5	2	2	2
2	3	2	5	1
2	4	1	5	4
5	3	3	2	0

a. The probability of $x = 2$ in the simulation equals 12/50, or .24, compared to the theoretical probability of .2240 found in EXCEL Example 9.11.

b. The probability of $x = 9$ in the simulation equals 0/50, or 0, compared to the theoretical probability of .0027 found in EXCEL Example 9.11.

Caution: If you repeat this exercise, you will get a different answer because EXCEL will not create the same pseudo-random numbers again.

9.6 The Hypergeometric Probability Distribution

The binomial probability distribution, discussed earlier in this chapter, helps us find the probability of x successes in a Bernoulli process. As we noted, when the random experiment in question involves sampling, the binomial probability distribution provides a precise answer only if sampling occurs *with replacement* so that the probability of success in any one trial remains constant throughout the experiment. Ordinarily, however, sampling is performed *without* replacement, often as a matter of convenience: One unit is selected from a population and set aside; then another is selected, and another. This procedure is easier than inspecting each unit, making a record of its characteristics, returning it to the population, and remixing the population before the next unit is selected. In addition, in some circumstances, sampling without replacement is unavoidable. Consider cases wherein sampling destroys the unit in question, as in the testing of flashbulbs, for instance. In such circumstances, we could not return sampled items to the population, even if we wanted to. This brings us to this section's topic. The **hypergeometric probability distribution** discussed in this section provides probabilities associated with possible values of a discrete random variable precisely when these values are generated by sampling *without replacement* and the probability of success, therefore, changes from one trial to the next.

EXAMPLE PROBLEM 9.13

Consider a personnel manager who has on file the names of $N = 10$ job applicants, of whom $S = 6$ are female; hence, $N - S = 4$ are male. If the manager were to select at random $n = 4$ names from the file and were to do so without replacement (taking one name at a time and setting it aside), what kind of probability distribution would describe the random variable, $X =$ the number of females selected?

SOLUTION: A tree diagram can help us find the answer, and such a diagram appears as Figure 9.5 on the next page. Consider yourself at the starting point, the leftmost box in the diagram, representing the original content of the file, 6 female and 4 male applicants. The first selection made might be a female (F_1) or a male (M_1), and the respective probabilities of selection are 6/10 and 4/10, reflecting the makeup of the population. If a female is selected, we have moved along the color line in Figure 9.5 to a new box, containing the names of 5 females and 4 males. The conditional probabilities that the second selection will be a female (F_2) or a male (M_2), given F_1 (that a female was selected on the first try), are 5/9 and 4/9, respectively, as indicated once more along the forks of the tree. If now a male is selected on the second try, we move on farther, perhaps along the colored line to the one of the 16 possible outcomes that is shown, along with its probability, in the box outlined in red. Note, however, that we have three other ways (shaded) of selecting 3 females by this procedure; thus, the probability of selecting 3 females equals not 480/5,040, but four times this value, or 1,920/5,040. By similar reasoning, we can derive the entire hypergeometric probability distribution for selecting female applicants:

$$p(X = 4 \text{ females}) = 1 \times \frac{360}{5{,}040} = .0714$$

$$p(X = 3 \text{ females}) = 4 \times \frac{480}{5{,}040} = \frac{1{,}920}{5{,}040} = .3810$$

$$p(X = 2 \text{ females}) = 6 \times \frac{360}{5{,}040} = \frac{2{,}160}{5{,}040} = .4286$$

(continued on page 377)

FIGURE 9.5 | Tree Diagram for Sampling without Replacement

This tree diagram illustrates sampling of $n = 4$ persons without replacement from a group of $N = 10$, containing 6 females and 4 males. The probabilities of selecting a female or a male change from one trial to the next, depending on the prior selections made, as is indicated along the forks of the tree. If selecting a female is called a "success," the probabilities associated with achieving various degrees of success, that is, with selecting various numbers of them, can be determined from the information generated here.

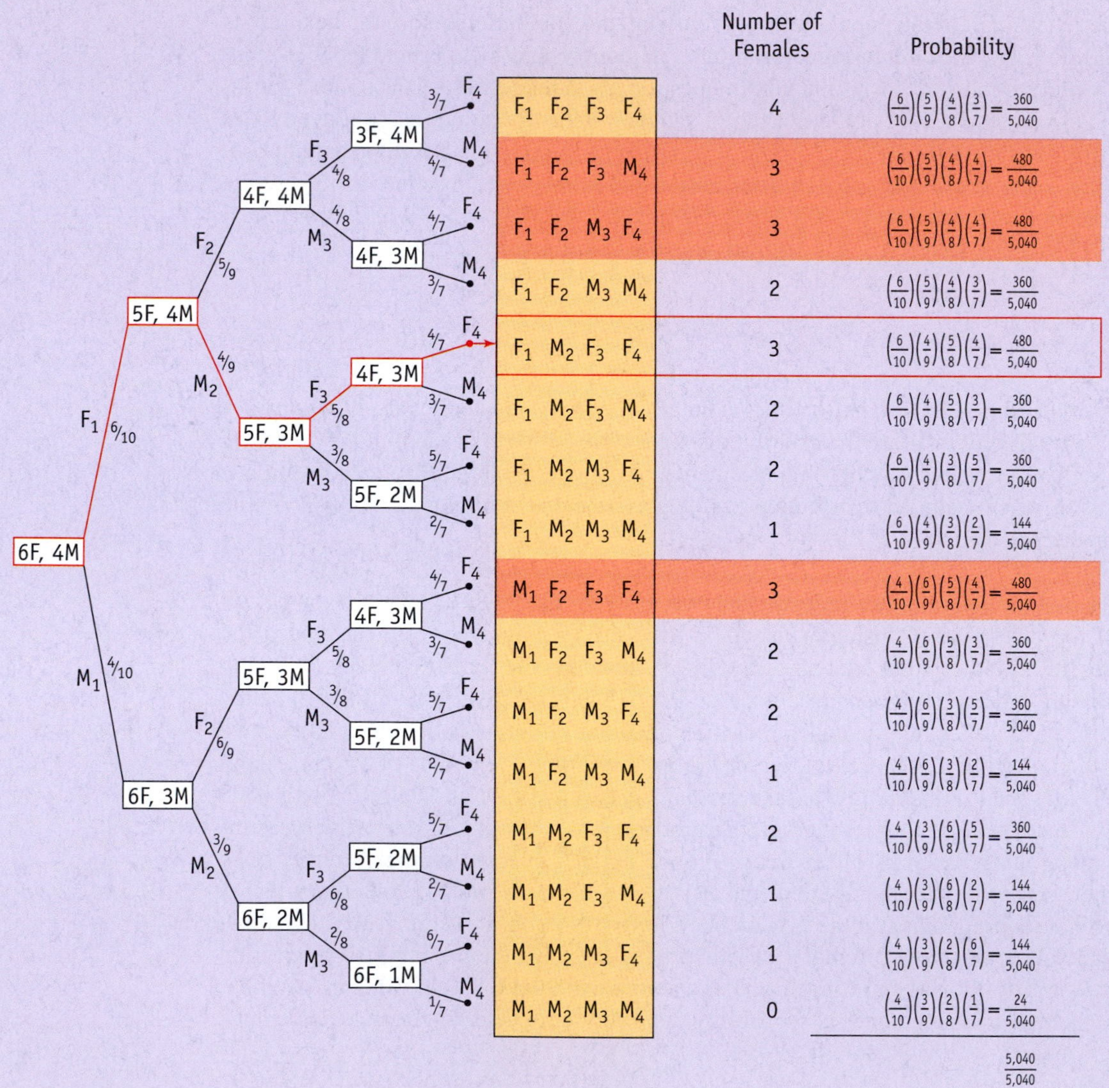

(continued from page 375)

$$p(X = 1 \text{ female}) = 4 \times \frac{144}{5{,}040} = \frac{576}{5{,}040} = .1143$$

$$p(X = 0 \text{ females}) = 1 \times \frac{24}{5{,}040} = .0048$$

$$\text{Total} = \frac{5{,}040}{5{,}040} = 1.0000$$

THE HYPERGEOMETRIC FORMULA

Fortunately, as was true of the binomial probability distribution, we have a less cumbersome way of determining a hypergeometric probability distribution. This approach uses Formula 9.L:

FORMULA 9.L | The Hypergeometric Formula

$$p(X = x|n,N,S) = \frac{c_x^S \times c_{n-x}^{N-S}}{c_n^N}$$

where x is the number of "successes" in a sample sized n, taken from a population sized N that contains S units with the "success" characteristic. Clearly, $x = 0, 1, 2, \ldots n$ or S (whichever is smaller); $n < N$; and $S < N$.

TECHNICAL DETAIL

Formula 9.L, complicated as it seems, is easy to interpret:

1. The left-hand side of the equation symbolizes the probability of x successes, given that a random sample of size n is drawn without replacement from a population sized N that contains S units with whatever characteristic has been labeled "success." As the note indicates, x cannot exceed n: We cannot succeed more often than we try. Nor can x exceed S: We cannot succeed more often than is possible, which depends on the number of units in the population, S, that have the success characteristic.
2. The term c_x^S represents the number of ways in which one can get x successes out of S possible successes, while c_{n-x}^{N-S} is the associated number of ways in which $n - x$ failures can be selected from among $N - S$ possible failures. Since each of the former can be combined with each of the latter, the product of the two terms gives the possible number of outcomes with exactly x successes and, therefore, $n - x$ failures.
3. The term c_n^N, finally, gives the total number of ways of selecting a sample of n (whether "successful" or not) from a population of N. Hence the numerator described above, divided by c_n^N, gives the probability of x successes.

The **hypergeometric formula** gives the probability of x successes when a random sample of n is drawn *without replacement* from a population of N within which S units have the characteristic that denotes success. The number of successes achieved under these circumstances is the **hypergeometric random variable.**

We can test the accuracy of the hypergeometric formula by pretending to seek with its help some of the answers already provided above.

EXAMPLE PROBLEM 9.14

Review Example Problem 9.13. Then use the hypergeometric formula to determine, for the sampling case discussed there,

a. the probability of selecting 4 females.

b. the probability of selecting 3 females.

SOLUTION:

a. $$p(X = 4|n = 4, N = 10, S = 6) = \frac{c_4^6 \times c_{4-4}^{10-6}}{c_4^{10}} = \frac{\frac{6!}{4!\,2!} \times \frac{4!}{0!\,4!}}{\frac{10!}{4!\,6!}} = \frac{6!}{4!\,2!} \times \frac{4!\,6!}{10!} = \frac{6 \times 5 \times 4 \times 3}{10 \times 9 \times 8 \times 7}$$

$$= \frac{360}{5{,}040} = .0714$$

The result is precisely the one given in the top row of Figure 9.5.

b. $$p(X = 3|n = 4, N = 10, S = 6) = \frac{c_3^6 \times c_{4-3}^{10-6}}{c_4^{10}} = \frac{\frac{6!}{3!\,3!} \times \frac{4!}{1!\,3!}}{\frac{10!}{4!\,6!}} = \frac{6!}{3!\,3!} \times \frac{4!}{1!\,3!} \times \frac{4!\,6!}{10!} = \frac{6 \times 5 \times 4 \times 4 \times 4}{10 \times 9 \times 8 \times 7}$$

$$= \frac{1{,}920}{5{,}040} = .3810$$

Once more, the result corresponds precisely to that calculated before.

EXAMPLE PROBLEM 9.15

To show how an entire hypergeometric probability distribution can be determined by using the hypergeometric formula, without resorting to the type of tree diagram seen in Figure 9.5, consider this situation: A committee of $n = 5$ members is to be formed randomly from among $N = 50$ members of a labor union local in which $S = 40$ workers are electricians. If, as is typical under such circumstances, we make the selection without replacement, what are the probabilities for $x = 0, 1, 2, 3, 4,$ and 5 committee members to be electricians?

SOLUTION: The answers are found by a systematic application of the hypergeometric formula, as Table 9.7 shows.

TABLE 9.7 | Determining a Hypergeometric Probability Distribution for $n = 5$, $N = 50$, and $S = 40$ Using the Hypergeometric Formula

The entries in the first column, together with those in the last column, represent a hypergeometric probability distribution. Its mathematical determination, using the hypergeometric formula, is illustrated with the help of the three middle columns. The last row tells us, for example, that there exist $\frac{40!}{5!\,35!}$ *different ways of getting 5 successes out of 40 possible ones, while there are* $\frac{10!}{0!\,10!}$ *associated ways of getting 0 failures from among 10 possible failures, as well as* $\frac{50!}{5!\,45!}$ *different ways of selecting a sample of 5 from a population of 50. The probability of getting a sequence of 5 successes and 0 failures under the specified conditions then equals the product of the first two expressions, divided by the third expression, or .3106.*

Number of "Successes" (electricians selected) x	$C_x^S = \frac{S!}{x!(S-x)!}$	$C_{n-x}^{N-S} = \frac{(N-S)!}{(n-x)![(N-S)-(n-x)]!}$	$C_n^N = \frac{N!}{n!(N-n)!}$	$p(X = x \mid n,N,S)$
0	$\frac{40!}{0!\,40!}$	$\frac{10!}{5!\,5!}$	$\frac{50!}{5!\,45!}$	$\frac{40!}{0!\,40!} \times \frac{10!}{5!\,5!} \times \frac{5!\,45!}{50!} = .0001$
1	$\frac{40!}{1!\,39!}$	$\frac{10!}{4!\,6!}$	$\frac{50!}{5!\,45!}$	$\frac{40!}{1!\,39!} \times \frac{10!}{4!\,6!} \times \frac{5!\,45!}{50!} = .0040$
2	$\frac{40!}{2!\,38!}$	$\frac{10!}{3!\,7!}$	$\frac{50!}{5!\,45!}$	$\frac{40!}{2!\,38!} \times \frac{10!}{3!\,7!} \times \frac{5!\,45!}{50!} = .0442$
3	$\frac{40!}{3!\,37!}$	$\frac{10!}{2!\,8!}$	$\frac{50!}{5!\,45!}$	$\frac{40!}{3!\,37!} \times \frac{10!}{2!\,8!} \times \frac{5!\,45!}{50!} = .2098$
4	$\frac{40!}{4!\,36!}$	$\frac{10!}{1!\,9!}$	$\frac{50!}{5!\,45!}$	$\frac{40!}{4!\,36!} \times \frac{10!}{1!\,9!} \times \frac{5!\,45!}{50!} = .4313$
5	$\frac{40!}{5!\,35!}$	$\frac{10!}{0!\,10!}$	$\frac{50!}{5!\,45!}$	$\frac{40!}{5!\,35!} \times \frac{10!}{0!\,10!} \times \frac{5!\,45!}{50!} = .3106$
				1.0000

EXCEL Example 9.13

Review the hypergeometric probability distribution derived in Table 9.7. Derive it with the help of EXCEL.

SOLUTION

1. Fire up EXCEL and enter the labels **x** and **probability,** respectively, into cells A1 and B1.
2. Enter numbers 0–5 into cells A2–A7.
3. Place the pointer into cell B2; then click the **Function Wizard (*fx*)** > **Statistical** > **HYPERGEOMDIST** > **OK.** The HYPERGEOMDIST dialog box appears.
4. In the *Sample_s* box, enter **A2**. Press TAB.
5. In the *Number_sample* box, enter the value of *n*, or **5**. Press TAB.

6. In the *Population_s* box, enter the value of S, or **40**. Press TAB.
7. In the *Number_pop* box, enter the value of N, or **50**.
8. Click **OK;** then drag the cell B2 entry by the handle in the lower right corner to B7. The resulting probabilities are identical to those found in Table 9.7:

x	probability
0	0.0001189
1	0.0039646
2	0.0441768
3	0.2098397
4	0.4313372
5	0.3105628

Application 9.5, *Evidence of Sexism?,* allows us to use the hypergeometric formula in a real-world setting.

APPLICATION 9.5

EVIDENCE OF SEXISM?

The Nation is a weekly magazine devoted to politics and the arts. The June 18, 1990, issue featured an angry exchange about a poetry contest. A reader from Hunter, New York, did not mince his words:

> Your poetry competition and its result were remarkable. Competitiveness is one of those traits of our present system I'd think you'd eschew. But what really irks me is your result: Four female poets win a competition cosponsored by a publication with a female poetry editor [Grace Schulman]. Yes, there were males on the judging panel just as the queens of old had eunuchs to attend them. Does *The Nation* mean to tell us that there were no entries by male poets that remotely approached the quality (however that's judged) of the winners? I can imagine the screams from the gallery if the results were as one-sided in the other direction—four male winners of a prize offered by a publication with a male poetry editor.
>
> If progressive principles include freedom from gender bias, you're as regressive as anyone, only you've exchanged Neanderthal attitudes for Amazonian. You're as helplessly carried about by the raging beast of gender prejudice as anyone you've ever criticized.

Ms. Schulman, the poetry editor, responded with reference to probability theory:

> The Discovery-Nation contest is nearly unique in that it is judged anonymously. Neither the judges nor I know the gender or the names of the poets who enter the competition. However, this information might enlighten [the angry writer]: According to the laws of probability, if an equal number of male and female poets submit entries, one out of sixteen times all the winners will be female, or male.

We can use hypergeometric Formula 9.L to judge her argument. Unfortunately, we were neither told how many contestants entered the poetry contest nor how many of them were male or female. Let us consider two possibilities:

CASE 1. Let there be $N = 10$ contestants. If half were women and half men and if we denote the selection of a woman as a "success," the value of $S = 5$. In fact, a sample of $n = 4$ winners was chosen; of these, there were $x = 4$ women. If we assume the selection was random and each entrant had an equal chance of being picked (not necessar-

(continued)

Application 9.5 (continued)

ily valid assumptions in this case), we can employ Formula 9.L and calculate the probability of 4 women being picked:

$$p(X = 4) = \frac{c_x^S \times c_{n-x}^{N-S}}{c_n^N} = \frac{c_4^5 \times c_{4-4}^{10-5}}{c_4^{10}} = \frac{\frac{5!}{4!\,0!} \times \frac{5!}{0!\,5!}}{\frac{10!}{4!\,6!}}$$

$$= \frac{5 \times 1}{210} = .0238$$

The probability of the event is considerably lower than the alleged 1/16, which is .0625.

CASE 2. Let there be $N = 100$ contestants. If again half were women and half men, $S = 50$; all other values are unchanged. The result:

$$p(X = 4) = \frac{c_x^S \times c_{n-x}^{N-S}}{c_n^N} = \frac{c_4^{50} \times c_{4-4}^{100-50}}{c_4^{100}}$$

$$= \frac{\frac{50!}{4!\,46!} \times \frac{50!}{0!\,50!}}{\frac{100!}{4!\,96!}} = \frac{230{,}300 \times 1}{3{,}921{,}225} = .0587$$

In this case, the probability of the event is much closer to the alleged .0625, although still lower.

CONCLUSION. It turns out that the actual probability gets ever closer to the alleged .0625 as the number of contestants rises—*provided* that half are male and half female. An inquiry indicates that there were in fact between 1,300 and 1,500 contestants, but no information is available about the division between the sexes. If the division was roughly half and half, the editor's answer is correct. If the division was very different, containing, say, 1,300 men and 200 women, the probability number would be much lower than alleged.

SOURCE: Michael Olinick, "Probabilistic Evidence of Sexism?" *NLA News* (Alfred P. Sloan Foundation, New Liberal Arts Program), October 1990, pp. 7–11. The exchange of letters is from p. 842 of the June 18, 1990, issue of *The Nation* magazine.

HYPERGEOMETRIC SUMMARY MEASURES

We could compute a hypergeometric probability distribution's major summary measures—mean, variance, and standard deviation—according to general Formulas 9.A–9.C. However, we can also derive them with the help of the simplified Formulas 9.M–9.O.

FORMULAS 9.M–9.O | Summary Measures for the Probability Distribution of Hypergeometric Random Variable X

9.M Arithmetic mean or expected value: $\mu_x = E(X) = n \times \pi = n \times \frac{S}{N}$

9.N Variance: $\sigma_x^2 = VAR(X) = n \times \pi \times (1 - \pi) \times \left(\frac{N - n}{N - 1}\right)$

9.O Standard deviation: $\sigma_x = SD(X) = \sqrt{\sigma_x^2}$

where n is sample size, N is population size, S is the number of population units with the "success "characteristic, and $\pi = \frac{S}{N}$ is the probability of success in the first trial.

EXAMPLE PROBLEM 9.16

Review the hypergeometric probability distribution given in Table 9.7, which is defined by $n = 5$, $N = 50$, and $S = 40$. Compute the distribution's arithmetic mean, variance, and standard deviation.

SOLUTION:

Arithmetic mean: $\mu_x = n \times \pi = 5 \times 0.8 = 4$

Variance: $\sigma_x^2 = VAR(X) = n \times \pi \times (1 - \pi) \times \left(\frac{N - n}{N - 1}\right)$

$$= 5 \times 0.8 \times 0.2 \times 0.9184 = 0.7347$$

Standard deviation: $\sigma_x = \sqrt{0.7347} = 0.8571$

Summary

1. Any quantitative variable whose numerical value is determined by a random experiment (and, thus, by chance) is called a *random variable.* A systematic listing of each possible value of a random variable, along with the associated likelihood of its occurrence, is called the random variable's *probability distribution.* Any probability distribution can be summarized by calculating the random variable's arithmetic mean or expected value, along with its variance and standard deviation. This chapter focuses on probability distributions of discrete random variables, which can assume values only at specific points on a scale of values, with inevitable gaps between values.
2. The *binomial probability distribution* is the most important probability distribution for discrete variables. It shows the probabilities associated with possible values of a random variable that are generated by a *Bernoulli process.* Such a process is a sequence of n identical trials of a random experiment such that each trial (a) produces one of two possible complementary outcomes that we conventionally call *success* and *failure* and (b) is independent of any other trial so that the probability of success or of failure is constant from trial to trial. The number of successes achieved in a Bernoulli process is called the *binomial random variable;* the probabilities for different values of it can be calculated with the help of the *binomial formula.* Simplified formulas exist for determining a binomial random variable's summary measures of location, spread, and skewness.
3. The binomial formula shows that the probability for any given number of successes varies with the number of trials, n, and with the probability of success in any one trial, π. A different binomial probability distribution can, therefore, be derived for each possible combination of n and π. Many such distributions have been tabulated in *binomial probability tables* for both individual and cumulative values of the binomial random variable. Alternative ways of deriving binomial probabilities are provided by computer software programs, such as EXCEL or MINITAB, and/or the use of Pascal's triangle.
4. The *Poisson probability distribution* describes another discrete random variable. This *Poisson random variable* is the number of occurrences of a specified event within a specified time or space. In a *Poisson process,* events of a given type occur in a random and, hence, unpredictable pattern over time or space such that (a) the Poisson random variable can equal any integer between zero and infinity, (b) the number of occurrences in one unit of time or space is independent of that in any other such (nonoverlapping) unit, and (c) the probability of occurrences is the same in all such units. The probabilities associated with alternative values of the Poisson random variable can be calculated with the help of the *Poisson formula.* Simplified formulas exist for determining a Poisson random variable's summary measures of location and spread.
5. The Poisson formula shows that the probability for any given event varies with the mean number of occurrences, μ, within the examined units of time or space. A different Poisson probability distribution can, therefore, be derived for each μ; many such distributions have been tabulated in *Poisson probability tables* for both individual and cumulative values of the Poisson random variable. Alternative ways of deriving Poisson probabilities are provided by computer software, such as EXCEL or MINITAB.
6. The *hypergeometric probability distribution* provides probabilities associated with possible values of a binomial random variable in situations in which these values are generated by sampling a finite population and in which such sampling is done without replacement. Thus the probability of success changes from one trial to the next. The number of successes achieved when a random sample of n is drawn *without replacement* from a population of N (within which S units exist with the characteris-

tic that denotes success) is the *hypergeometric random variable.* Probabilities for different values of it can be calculated with the help of the *hypergeometric formula.* Alternative ways of deriving hypergeometric probabilities are provided by computer software, such as EXCEL or MINITAB. Once again, various simplified formulas can be derived for calculating summary measures for the hypergeometric random variable.

Key Terms

Bernoulli process
binomial coefficient
binomial formula
binomial probability distribution
binomial probability tables
binomial random variable
cumulative probability distribution
discrete probability distribution
discrete random variable
expected value
hypergeometric formula
hypergeometric probability distribution
hypergeometric random variable
Poisson formula
Poisson probability tables
Poisson process
Poisson process rate
Poisson random variable
probability distribution
random variable

Practice Problems

NOTE

Some problems require the use of a statistical program, EXCEL or MINITAB. The program's major features are explained in text Chapter 2. Plenty of additional advice is available via the program's built-in Help feature.

Section 9.1 Basic Concepts

1. Could the following represent probability distributions? If so, write out the distribution and determine its major summary measures (mean, variance, standard deviation).

a. $p(x) = (x/10)$, where $x = 1, 2, 3,$ or 4.

b. $p(x) = 0.7x$, where $x = -1, 0, 1,$ or 2.

c. $p(x) = (x^2/14)$, where $x = 0, 1, 2,$ or 3.

d. $p(x) = (1/x)$, where $x = 1, 2,$ or 3.

e. $p(x) = [(10 - x)/50]$, where $x = -1, 0, 5,$ or 6.

f. $p(x) = [(10 - x)/40]$, where $x = 0, 1, 2, 3,$ or 4.

2. Consider the sample space in Figure 9.6 on the next page that is associated with simultaneously rolling two dice. Then write down the probability distribution of random variable X, where X is the *point spread* from rolling two dice. For example, if one die comes up with a 6 and the other one with a 1, the point spread is the difference between these two numbers, or 5.

3. Illustrate the probability distribution found in Practice Problem 2 with a stick diagram

a. for individual values of x.

b. for cumulative values of x.

4. Review Practice Problem 2. Compute the *expected value* of the point spread.

5. Review Practice Problems 2 and 4. Compute the *variance* of the point spread.

FIGURE 9.6 | Sample Space When Rolling Two Dice

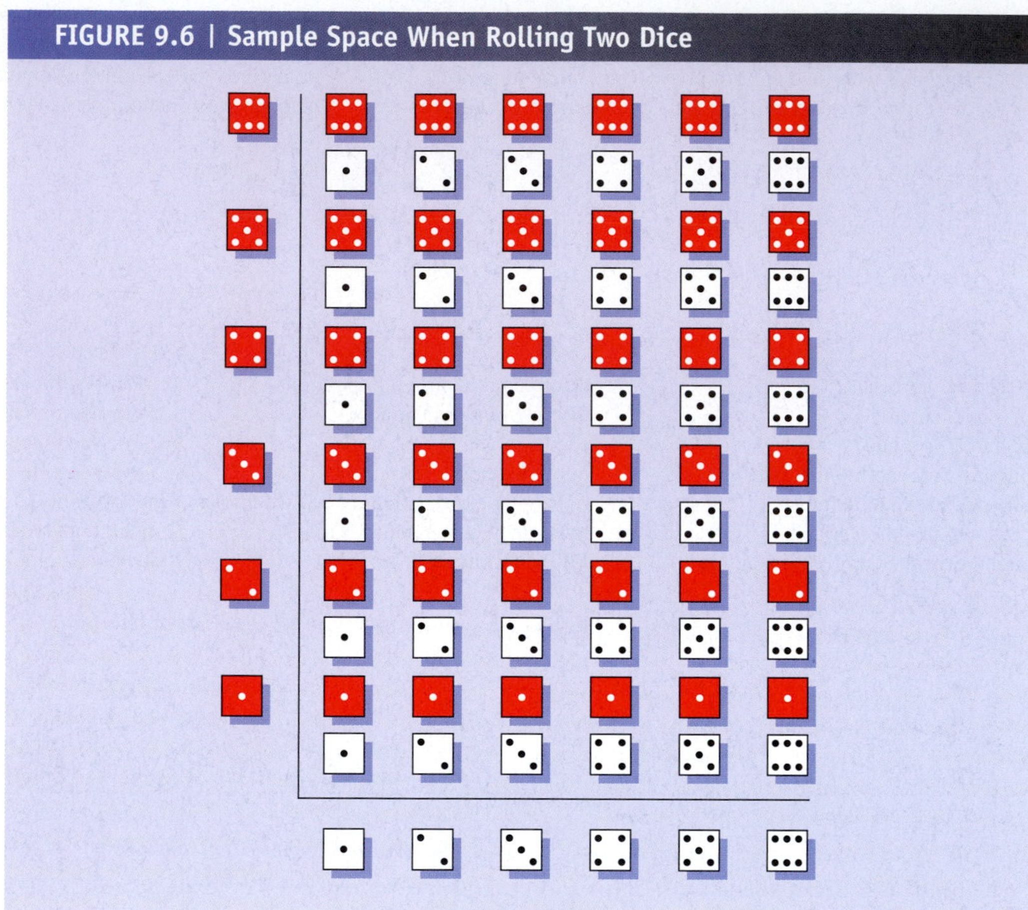

6. The Kentfield Hardware store is about to place an order for the *expected number* of lawn mowers demanded, based on the probability distribution in Table 9.8.

   a. How many will be ordered?

   b. What are the variance and standard deviation of the number demanded?

TABLE 9.8 | Probability Distribution of Lawn Mowers Demanded

Number Demanded	Probability
0	.05
1	.10
2	.20
3	.30
4	.20
5	.10
6	.05

7. A state auto inspection station collected the Table 9.9 data during the past year. If the observed pattern continued to hold, what would be the station's expected daily revenue if it instituted a $10 fee per car?

TABLE 9.9 | Frequency Distribution of Cars Coming for Inspection

Number of Cars	Absolute Frequency (days)
20	79
25	121
32	19
40	25
47	39
51	30

TABLE 9.10 | Requests for Servicing Broken-Down Copy Machines

Number of Requests	Absolute Frequency (days)
5	276
9	59
13	30
25	36
31	38
52	21

8. An office service company has collected the Table 9.10 data. The manager wants to know

a. the probability of fewer than 30 service calls on a given day.

b. the expected company revenue per day if the pattern observed in the past continues and all service requests are answered (at a $50 fee per call).

SECTION 9.2 THE BINOMIAL PROBABILITY DISTRIBUTION

9. With the help of a *tree diagram,* generate a binomial probability distribution by imagining a random experiment of tossing three coins, while defining the binomial random variable X as "the number of heads appearing."

10. An employer has noted a 10 percent annual quit rate among the firm's employees. Assume that three employees are sampled at random and that the conditions of a Bernoulli process are met. With the help of a *tree diagram,* determine the probability distribution for the numbers of employees in the sample who are likely to quit next year.

11. Review Practice Problem 9. Then use the *binomial formula* to compute the probability of getting three heads when tossing three coins once.

12. A test is administered ten times; the probability of getting the correct answer is .9. Assuming the conditions of a Bernoulli process are met, use an appropriate *formula* to figure the likelihood of getting precisely 9 correct tests.

13. A new computer is tested 8 times; the probability of its working satisfactorily is known to be $\pi = .8$. Use a relevant formula to determine the likelihood of the computer working satisfactorily precisely 7 times.

14. Review Practice Problem 9. Compute the random variable's mean, variance, and standard deviation.

15. Review Practice Problem 10. Compute the random variable's mean, variance, and standard deviation.

16. Determine whether each of the following statements about a binomial probability distribution is *true* or *false* and explain why:

a. If the mean is 4 and the variance is 0.8, the probability of success in any one trial must be 0.5.

b. If the mean is 3 and the probability of success in any one trial is 0.9, the variance must be 0.3.

c. If the mean is 10 and the standard deviation is 2, the probability of success in any one trial must be 0.2.

17. Determine whether each of the following statements about a binomial probability distribution is *true* or *false* and explain why:

a. If the mean is 6 and the probability of success in any one trial is 0.2, the number of trials must be 30.

b. If the number of trials is 50 and the probability of failure in any one trial is 0.8, the mean must be 10.

c. If the mean is 100 and the probability of success in any one trial is 0.7, the standard deviation must be 5.4772.

Section 9.3 The Binomial Probability Distribution Family

18. An automobile manufacturer has fitted all cars with identical pollution-control devices, designed to meet government standards, yet experience shows that 5 percent of cars tested perform below these pollution standards. Assume that 20 cars coming off the assembly line during a given month are selected at random and that the conditions of a Bernoulli process are met. Use appropriate *probability tables* to answer the following:

a. What is the probability distribution for the numbers, *x*, of below-standard cars found in the sample?

b. What is the probability that a government inspector who tests 20 cars a month in the above fashion will unjustly accuse the manufacturer of producing more than 5 percent of all cars below standard?

19. A car-rental firm rents only compact and medium-sized cars; experience shows that three persons out of four prefer compacts. Assuming that the conditions of a Bernoulli process apply, use appropriate *probability tables* to answer the following: Considering the next 15 requests, what is the probability distribution for the numbers of

a. medium-sized cars requested?

b. compact cars requested?

20. A manufacturer is sampling (with replacement) incoming shipments of 100 parts produced by other firms. Assuming that the conditions of a Bernoulli process apply, use appropriate *probability tables* to answer the following:

a. If (unbeknownst to the manufacturer) 5 percent of the parts are defective, what is the probability distribution for discovering defective units in a sample of 5 parts?

b. What is the probability distribution if in fact 40 percent of all units are defective and 5 of them are sampled?

c. What if 10 percent are defective and 3 units are sampled?

d. What if 60 percent are defective and 3 units are sampled?

21. Twenty radar transponders are sitting on the bench at an avionics repair shop; of these, nine are inoperative, but this is not obvious to a casual observer. A thief steals five transponders. Assuming that the conditions of a Bernoulli process apply, use appropriate *probability tables* to determine the probability that the thief got

a. five good transponders.

b. three bad transponders.

c. only bad transponders.

d. at least two good transponders.

22. A market survey shows that 30 percent of all families own a Polaroid camera. Assuming that the conditions of a Bernoulli process apply, use appropriate *probability tables* to answer the following concerning a random sample of 100 families:

a. What is the probability that 20 or fewer have such a camera?

b. What is the probability that precisely 31 have such a camera?

c. What is the probability that 47 or more have such a camera?

d. What are the distribution's summary measures?

23. A new disease affects 20 percent of the population (or a new "bug" affects 20 percent of all units produced by a production process). Assuming that the conditions of a Bernoulli process apply, use EXCEL or MINITAB to figure the likelihood that in a random sample of 5 units

a. all are affected.

b. none is affected.

c. at least 1 is affected.

d. at least 3 are affected.

e. precisely 2 are affected.

f. between 2 and 4, inclusive, are affected.

24. A new drug in nationwide use seems to be effective 40 percent of the time. Assuming that the conditions of a Bernoulli process apply, use EXCEL or MINITAB to figure the chances that a random sample of 100 patients using the drug will show success

a. in at most 20 patients.

b. in exactly 30 patients.

c. in at least 40 patients.

d. in fewer than 50 patients.

e. in more than 50 patients.

25. A polling organization randomly samples 100 consumers about the new design of a product. Assuming that the conditions of a Bernoulli process apply, use EXCEL or MINITAB to figure the following: If in fact 40 percent of all consumers favor the new design, what is the likelihood that among the sampled individuals the design will be favored by

a. 20 or fewer?

b. precisely 30?

c. fewer than 40?

d. more than 45?

e. 50 or more?

f. between 30 and 40, inclusive?

26. According to a well-known private firm, 90 percent of its parcels are delivered within 2 days. Assuming that the conditions of a Bernoulli process apply, use EXCEL or MINITAB to figure the following: If 14 parcels that were shipped at different times are sampled,

a. what is the probability that all 14 arrive within 2 days?

b. what is the probability that none arrives within 2 days?

c. what is the probability that precisely 8 arrive within 2 days?

d. what are the summary measures for the probability distribution of a random variable that denotes late deliveries?

27. According to a well-known stockbroker, 95 percent of all purchase orders are executed within 15 minutes of request. Assuming that the conditions of a Bernoulli process apply, use EXCEL or MINITAB to figure the following probabilities about a random sample of 7 orders:

a. that all are executed within 15 minutes.

b. that none is executed within 15 minutes.

c. that at least 5 are so executed.

d. that at most 6 are so executed.

28. What is the probability of having exactly 3 boys in a family of 10 children (assuming that boys and girls are equally likely and different births are independent events)? Find your answer with the help of *Pascal's triangle,* found on page 361. Then check your answer with the help of an appropriate table.

SECTION 9.4 THE POISSON PROBABILITY DISTRIBUTION

29. Between 9:00 and 12:00 A.M. on Saturdays, customers arrive at a supermarket checkout counter at a rate of 50 per hour, but on Monday mornings they arrive at a rate of 2 per hour. Assuming a Poisson process is occurring, determine the probability distribution for up to 11 arrivals between 9:00 and 9:06 A.M. on either day with the help of an appropriate *formula.*

30. A copy machine fails to print on every page. On average, 1 percent of the pages are blank. Assuming a Poisson process is occurring, use an appropriate *formula* to answer the following: If 100 copies are run off, what is the probability of

a. none of them being blank?

b. one being blank?

31. On the average, Amtrak repair crews have to replace three railroad ties per mile when they check the tracks. Assuming a Poisson process is occurring, use an appropriate *formula* to answer the following: In the next mile, what is the probability of

a. no needed replacements?

b. three or fewer needed replacements?

Furthermore, if each replacement costs $30,

c. what is the expected cost for the next 10 miles?

32. Accidents at a chemical plant occur at a rate of 1.9 per month. Assuming a Poisson process is occurring, use an appropriate *formula* to answer the following:

a. What is the expected number of accidents in a year?

b. What is the probability of no accident next month?

c. What is the probability of fewer than 3 accidents next month?

33. Small businesses are going bankrupt at a rate of 9.7 per month. Assuming a Poisson process is occurring, use an appropriate *formula* to determine the probability of

a. 5 businesses going bankrupt next month.

b. 24 businesses going bankrupt next month.

34. A firm is about to locate in a new town. Rumor has it that the area experiences power outages that can be described by a Poisson process with $\mu = 6$ per year. Using appropriate *formulas,* determine

a. the probability that there will be no outages next year.

b. the probability distribution's summary measures.

35. An airline claims that its accident rate equals 1.7 per year. When 5 accidents occur in one year, the government accuses it of lying. Assuming a Poisson process is occurring, use appropriate *formulas* to determine

a. the probability of 5 accidents in 1 year, if the airline's claim is true.

b. the probability distribution's summary measures.

36. A pipeline company claims that there are 100 leaks per 1,000 miles. Yet a government inspector finds 10 leaks in a single mile. Assuming a Poisson process is occurring, use appropriate *formulas* to determine

a. the probability of 10 leaks in a single mile, if the company's claim is true.

b. the probability distribution's summary measures.

SECTION 9.5 THE POISSON PROBABILITY DISTRIBUTION FAMILY

37. With the help of an appropriate *probability table,* draw a graph for individual values of x that depicts the member of the Poisson probability distribution family that is defined by $\mu = 0.1$.

38. With the help of an appropriate *probability table,* draw a graph for individual values of x that depicts the member of the Poisson probability distribution family that is defined by $\mu = 1.0$.

39. With the help of an appropriate *probability table,* draw a graph for individual values of x that depicts the member of the Poisson probability distribution family that is defined by $\mu = 10$.

40. With the help of an appropriate *probability table,* determine whether each of the following statements is *true* or *false* and explain why:

a. If potholes are found at the rate of 10 per 1,000 square yards in a stretch of road, the probability of finding at most 10 potholes in a 500-square-yard area equals .6160.

b. If a typesetter makes errors at a rate of .5 error per page, the probability of finding at least 10 errors in 40 pages equals .995.

c. If ships pass the Statue of Liberty at the rate of 2 per hour, a tourist watching for 30 minutes has at most a 50 percent chance of seeing 1 or 2 ships.

d. If crimes between 1:00 and 3:00 A.M. in a city occur at a rate of 2 per hour, the chances for more than two crimes in any 15-minute period are .0144.

e. If a taxicab company has on the average 4 cars laid up for repairs on a given day, it needs 6 spare cabs in order to keep the probability of having a driver without a car below 3 percent.

f. If people arrive at a restaurant at a rate of 15 groups per hour, the probability of more than 5 groups appearing in a 10-minute span equals .042.

g. If 4 bubbles are found per 1,000 square feet of plate glass, the chances that a 20-by-5-foot window contains no bubbles are 32.97 percent.

41. During the month of January, claims are arriving at an insurance company at a rate of 30 per hour. Determine the probability distribution for claim arrivals between 1:00 and 1:03 P.M. by using EXCEL or MINITAB.

42. Use EXCEL or MINITAB to determine the probability of more than 2 industrial accidents in a plant on a given day, if such accidents are generally occurring at a rate of two per (5-day) workweek.

43. During a given morning, defects at a rate of 120 per hour are appearing in a roll of wire that is being coated. Use EXCEL or MINITAB to determine the probability distribution for the appearance of defects between 9:10 and 9:13 A.M.

44. Between 8 and 10 A.M. on Saturdays, cars arrive at a toll station at a rate of 60 per hour. Use EXCEL or MINITAB to determine the probability distribution for arrivals between 8 and 8:03 A.M.

SECTION 9.6 THE HYPERGEOMETRIC PROBABILITY DISTRIBUTION

45. A medical laboratory received a shipment of 16 microscopes of which (unbeknownst to the lab) 4 were defective. If a random sample of 3 were taken without replacement, what would be the chances of finding 0, 1, 2, or 3 defective units? Determine the answer

a. with a tree diagram.

b. with the help of EXCEL or MINITAB.

46. Review Practice Problem 45.

a. Determine the answer by an appropriate formula.

b. Determine the summary measures of this probability distribution.

47. A garden center has 100 elm trees for sale. Although it is not obvious, 35 trees have Dutch elm disease. If you buy 10 trees, what is the probability that

a. all of them are infected?

b. half of them are infected?

c. all are healthy?

48. A city government is giving away wrappers for water heaters to cut people's fuel bills. The mayor "randomly" selects 50 lucky recipients from among 56 Eastside and 64 Westside applicants. Of the recipients, 47 come from the Eastside. Do you believe that the giveaway was "random"? Explain.

49. Four women and five men apply for three job openings. The manager finds them "equally qualified" and, therefore, "draws names randomly out of a hat." He hires three men; the women sue. A judge asks you to determine the probability of this hiring having truly occurred by random choice.

50. At Christmastime, a furniture manufacturer has 20 unsold chairs, but 10 of them are damaged. The chairs are offered to the employees as gifts; only 10 requests come in. The manager alleges that she picked the gift chairs at random, but 9 of them turn out to be damaged. What is the probability that the selection was truly random?

Chapter 10

CONTINUOUS PROBABILITY DISTRIBUTIONS

LOOKING AHEAD

After reading this chapter, you will understand the nature of continuous random variables and their probability distributions, now called probability density functions. Among other things, you will learn about useful applications based on:

1. the standard normal curve,
2. exponential probabilities, and
3. uniform probabilities.

AND HERE IS A TYPICAL PROBLEM YOU WILL BE ABLE TO SOLVE:

The miles-per-gallon (mpg) rating of all the registered cars in the nation is a normally distributed random variable with a mean of 25.9 and a standard deviation of 2.45. You work for an automobile manufacturer who wants to build a car with an mpg rating that improves upon 99 percent of existing cars. You are asked: "What must the new car's mpg rating be?"

PREVIEW

Not so long ago, a government agency investigated a manufacturer for fraud, claiming that the cans of cocoa marketed by the firm did *not* contain the 32 ounces advertised. Clearly, the government's case was not based on a census because it would be impossible to weigh the contents of every can of cocoa ever produced. The government had taken a random sample and based its conclusion on the concept of a *probability distribution,* a systematic listing of each possible value of a random variable, along with the associated likelihood of its occurrence. In the previous chapter, when this concept was first introduced, the random variables in question were *discrete:* Only selected values (such as 0, 1, 2 . . .) were possible, while others (such as 1.23 or 2.79 perhaps) did not exist. A discrete probability distribution, therefore, could be pictured in a stick diagram, such as Figure 10.1.

This chapter introduces *continuous* random variables, such as the ounces of cocoa in a can. Within a specified range, such variables can take on all conceivable values: not only 0, 1, 2, and so on, but also

FIGURE 10.1 | A Discrete Probability Distribution

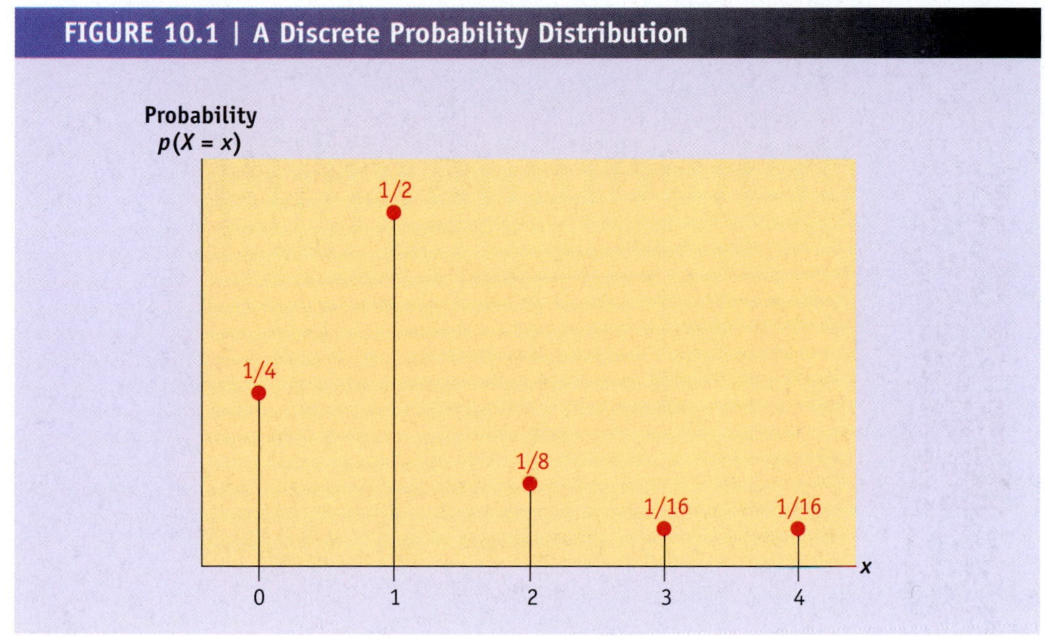

1.23 or 1.2352 or even 1.2352879. If we tried to plot such a distribution, we would get an infinite number of sticks, with an infinite number of color dots similar to those in Figure 10.1. These dots, one for each possible value of x, would join to form a solid line, such as the red line in Figure 10.2.

Furthermore, just as the sum of the probabilities associated with all permissible x values in Figure 10.1 necessarily equals 1, so must the sum of probabilities of the infinite number of x values in Figure 10.2. The infinite number of sticks for x values between 0 and 1 (which we could not possibly draw) would take up shaded area A and might represent a joint probability of .16. Likewise, area B might represent a joint probability of .29 for x values between 2 and 3.

FIGURE 10.2 | A Continuous Probability Distribution

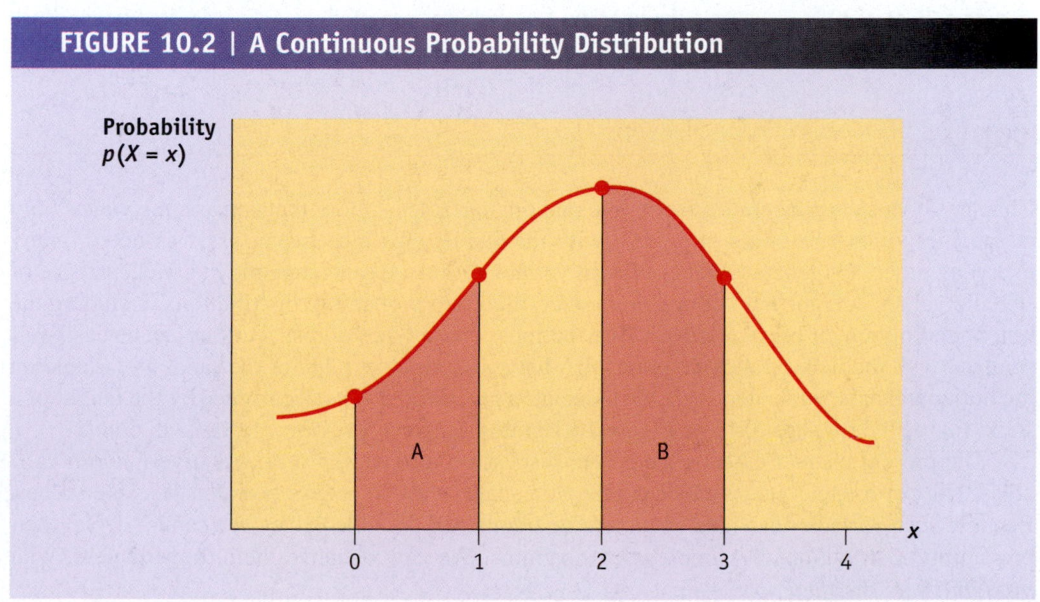

FIGURE 10.3 | A Normal Curve

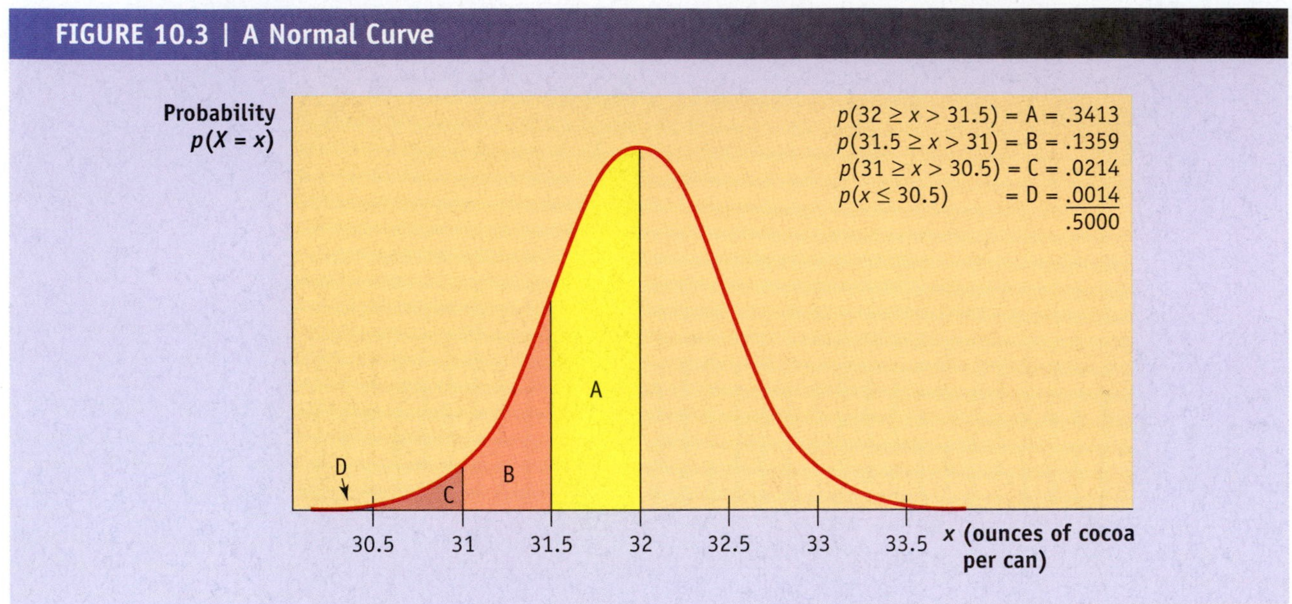

According to our cocoa manufacturer, the firm's filling machines were carefully calibrated to put an average of 32 ounces into each can, with a standard deviation of half an ounce. The government, therefore, postulated a continuous probability distribution of content weights that equaled a *normal curve,* first plotted as Figure 7.5 on page 251 and now as Figure 10.3.

For reasons noted in Figure 7.5 and to be explained in this chapter, if content weights are normally distributed and if it is true that $\mu = 32$ and $\sigma = .5$, we can expect A = 34.13 percent of all cans to contain between 31.5 and 32 ounces; B = 13.59 percent to contain between 31 and 31.5 ounces; C = 2.14 percent to contain between 30.5 and 31 ounces; and a mere D = .14 percent to contain less than 30.5 ounces. We can expect similar percentages *in excess* of the alleged 32-ounce mean (not shown). Yet the government's random sample of 200 cans produced 150 cans with less than 30.5 ounces of cocoa! Finding a 75 percent figure where a figure below 1 percent was expected strongly suggested fraud, which is the kind of issue that an understanding of continuous probability distributions can help address.

10.1 Basic Concepts

Chapter 9 focused on *discrete* quantitative random variables—those that can assume values only at specific points on a scale of values, with inevitable gaps in between. As was noted, many everyday processes generate values of such variables, and we can gauge the likely occurrence of specific values with the help of one or another of certain probability distributions, including the binomial, Poisson, or hypergeometric distributions. These types of distributions can be easily visualized with the help of stick diagrams that list each possible value of the random variable on the horizontal axis, while depicting the associated probability of its occurrence by the height of a stick. Figure 9.3 on page 351 and Figure 10.1 in this chapter's Preview are cases in point.

The present chapter extends the earlier discussion to *continuous* quantitative random variables that can assume values at all points on a scale, with no breaks between possible values. Because such variables can take on an infinite number of possible values, we cannot depict their probability distributions by simple stick diagrams. We can visualize them, nevertheless, with *probability density functions.*

CONTINUOUS RANDOM VARIABLES

Variables that can assume values at all points on a scale of values, with no breaks between possible values, are quite common. The possible observations about such variables are infinite in number. Consider characteristics measured in units of money, time, distance, or weight, to name just a few of the possibilities.

The *profit per dollar of sales* earned by a firm is an example of a continuous quantitative variable measured in units of money. It might be measured as −10 cents or +23 cents or even +41.37895 cents. The random experiment of operating a firm for a year can generate *any* value for this variable—negative, zero, or positive.

Now consider measuring the lifetime of new appliances, car batteries, lightbulbs, or tires, the flight time of a plane, the completion time of a task, the reaction time after a stimulus. Imagine recording distances, such as the drilling depths of oil wells, inches of rainfall, the length of steel rods or ears of corn, the thickness of tablets, the height of weather satellites. Or contemplate gathering data on the weight of apples harvested per tree, of cereal boxes filled, of ingots of metal produced. In all these cases and a million more, an infinite number of conceivable observations exists, and the variable in question is said to be a *continuous random variable.*

DEFINITION 10.1 Any quantitative variable, the numerical value of which is determined by a random experiment and, thus, by chance, is called a **random variable.** The variable's name is designated by X, and any one of its possible values by x. If the set of all possible values is *infinite,* because the variable can assume values at all points on a scale of values, the variable is said to be a **continuous random variable.**

THE PROBABILITY DENSITY FUNCTION

Clearly, we cannot *list* all the possible values of a continuous random variable; nor can we list the associated probabilities for each one of the infinite numbers of conceivable values. With continuous random variables, therefore, we commonly associate probabilities with *ranges* of values along the continuum of possible values that the random variable might take on. Figure 10.4 on the next page helps us see the point.

Panel (a) of Figure 10.4 represents one way of picturing the probability distribution of a continuous random variable. The graph is a *relative frequency histogram* of the type introduced in Chapter 6. (For a quick review, consider the discussion of relative frequency histograms on pages 185–191.) The continuous random variable in Figure 10.4 is the length of service, as of December 31 of a given year, of the 49,000 employees of a firm. For any one employee, this period could clearly be any positive number, such as 1 year, 5.2 years, or even as 7.13946 years. The possible values of this variable have been grouped on the horizontal axis in 5-year intervals.

The height of any column standing on top of any one of these equal-sized intervals represents the proportion of all service lengths that fall within the interval. (As long as all histogram class intervals have the same width, as is true throughout this text, comparisons of column *heights* and column *areas* convey the same information.) Thus, if 19,600 of the 49,000 employees have served between 5 and 10 years, the proportion of all employees within this range is (19,600/49,000) = .4, as the second column shows. Given equal-sized class intervals, therefore, column heights tell us simultaneously the proportion of all employees whose service length falls within the given range and the probability that any one employee, randomly chosen, will have a service length within that range. Naturally, the sum of these proportions and of these probabilities equals 1.

Thus, we can tell instantly the probability that a randomly chosen employee has been with the firm between 10 and 15 years: $p(X = 10 \text{ to } 15 \text{ years}) = .3$. Yet we cannot tell the probability of our

FIGURE 10.4 | A Continuous Probability Distribution

The probability distribution of a continuous random variable can be represented by a relative frequency histogram, as in panel (a). It can also be approximated by a smoothed frequency curve, such as the red line in panel (b), which is called a ***probability density function.***

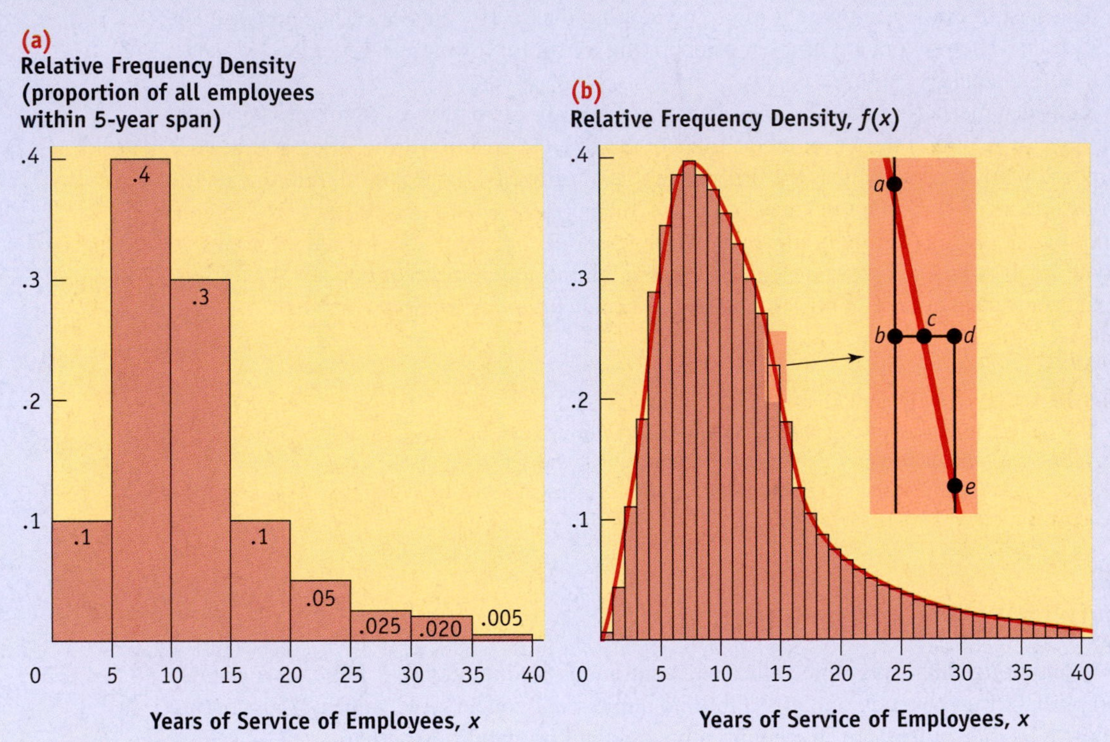

random variable lying in the range from 11 to 13 years because that interval is completely contained within the 10-to-15-year range in our histogram. We can imagine, however, constructing from our data a series of alternative histograms with ever-narrower years-of-service intervals. If we did, the columns would get ever more numerous and also narrower until a line along their tops would approach the smooth frequency curve given in panel (b). This curve has a special name: the probability density function.

DEFINITION 10.2 A smooth frequency curve that describes the probability distribution of a continuous random variable, X, is called a **probability density function.** It is denoted by $f(x)$, pronounced "function of x," where x represents all the possible values of the random variable.

Note that the total area under the probability density function, just as that under the relative frequency histogram, equals 1. As the inset in panel (b) indicates, the smooth frequency curve adds some areas, such as *abc,* to the total histogram area, but it cuts off equivalent areas, such as *cde.* Given the probability density function, the probability that a continuous random variable takes on values within any given range is, thus, represented by the area under the portion of this curve covering this range.

AN EXAMPLE Consider Figure 10.5, which shows probability density functions for the years of employee service in two firms, A and B. The total area underneath either function equals 1. One can instantly tell that the probability of finding an employee with 11 to 13 years of service equals whatever proportion the crosshatched area constitutes of the total area underneath the curve. This probability is clearly larger in Firm A than in Firm B. The total area equals 1 in both cases, but the crosshatched area is larger in panel (a). By the same token, although Figure 10.5 does not show it directly, we can see that the probability of finding an employee with 4 to 5 years of service is larger in Firm B than in Firm A.

Figure 10.5 pictures two rather differently shaped probability density functions. As you might expect, an infinite variety of such functions exists, each one describing the probabilities associated with different types of continuous random variables. However, you are likely to encounter three types of probability density functions more often than most. These are:

- the normal probability distribution
- the exponential probability distribution
- the uniform probability distribution

We turn to each of these in the remainder of this chapter.

FIGURE 10.5 | Two Probability Density Functions

The probability that a continuous random variable, such as years of employee service, takes on values within any given range of possible values, such as 11 to 13 years, is represented by the ratio of two areas: the area (here crosshatched) under the portion of the probability density function covering the range of interest and the entire area under the function, which is taken to equal 1. In this example, the probability that a randomly chosen employee has seen between 11 and 13 years of service is larger, therefore, in Firm A than in Firm B.

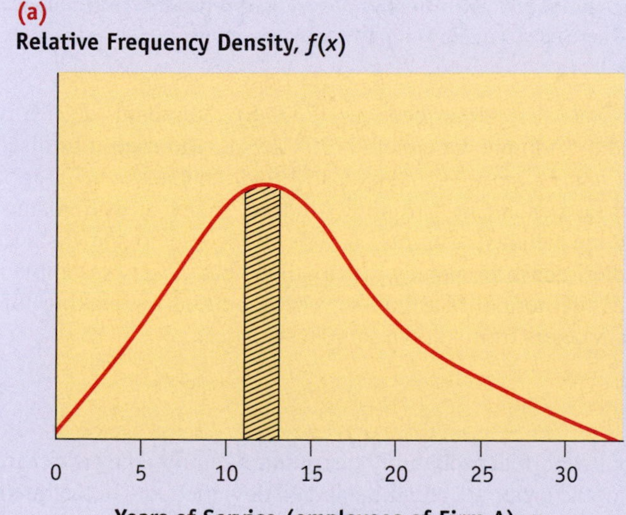

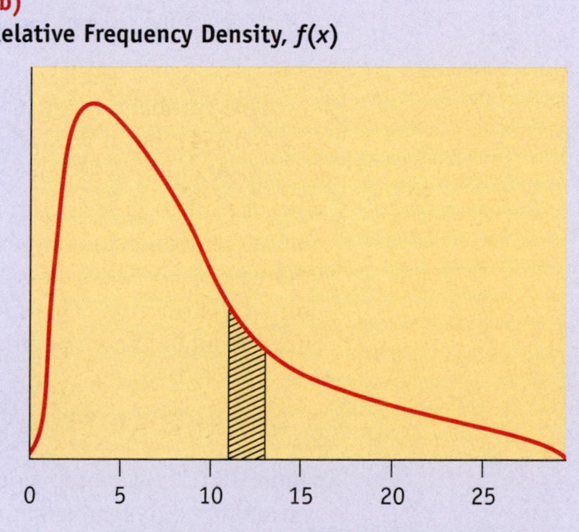

When we discussed table-making in Chapter 6, we noted the importance of making data classes mutually exclusive. It would be confusing to create one class for profits between \$0 and \$10 million, another class for profits between \$10 and \$20 million, and so on. Where would we place a firm earning exactly \$10 million, in the first class or in the second class? We solved the problem by being very precise and listing classes from \$0 to under \$10 million, \$10 million to under \$20 million, and so on. In the present context, however, when we are concerned with figuring the probability of encountering a certain range of values, the fine distinction between a range of values that reaches to \$10 million *inclusive* (≤ 10) and a range that reaches to *just under* \$10 million (<10) is of no importance.

In the case of continuous random variables, it is customary never to consider the probability of occurrence of a single value, such as precisely \$10 million of profit or precisely 11.92374 years of service, to be anything but zero. This probability would have to equal the area above a point on the horizontal axis up to the probability density function, and, given the fact that a point has no width, this area above the point equals zero. Indeed, given an infinite number of possible values, the probability of one specific value is practically nil. When calculating cumulative probabilities for continuous random variables, it is, therefore, unnecessary to make a distinction between the probability of the random variable being "smaller than x" and being "smaller than or equal to x":

$$p(X < x) = p(X \leq x) \text{ because } p(X = x) = 0$$

Similarly, no distinction is made between the probability of a continuous random variable being "larger than x" and being "larger than or equal to x":

$$p(X > x) = p(X \geq x) \text{ because } p(X = x) = 0$$

Don't be surprised, however, if some textbooks use one of these notations, while others use the alternative.

10.2 The Normal Probability Distribution

We have met the normal probability distribution once before, in Chapter 7; now we must look at it in much greater detail.

DEFINITION 10.3 A **normal probability distribution** is a probability density function that is (1) single-peaked above the random variable's mean, median, and mode, all of which are equal to one another; (2) perfectly symmetric about this peaked central value and, thus, said to be *bell-shaped;* and (3) characterized by tails extending indefinitely in both directions from the center, approaching (but never touching) the horizontal axis, which implies a positive probability for finding values of the random variable anywhere between minus infinity and plus infinity.

This probability distribution was first described in 1733 by Abraham de Moivre (1667–1754), but it was popularized by Adolphe Quetelet (1796–1874), who used it to discuss the concept of "the average man" (*l'homme moyen*), and by Carl Friedrich Gauss (1777–1855), who used it to describe errors of measurement in astronomy. Indeed, many measurements of natural phenomena—ranging from the heights, weights, or IQs of people to the distances, volumes, or speeds of heavenly bodies—have frequency distributions that closely resemble the normal distribution. This fact makes the normal distribution very important for making inferences about unknown population parameters from known sample statistics.

A GRAPHICAL EXPOSITION

Figure 10.6 shows three members of the normal probability distribution family. They differ from one another only by the magnitudes of the mean, μ_x, and the standard deviation, σ_x, of the random variable in question. (By definition, skewness is entirely absent and, as we will learn later in this

FIGURE 10.6 | Three Members of the Normal Probability Distribution Family

Members of the normal probability distribution family, called **normal curves** *for short, differ from one another only by the values of the distribution's mean* (μ_x) *and standard deviation* (σ_x)*. The value of* μ_x *positions the center of the distribution on the horizontal axis; that of* σ_x *determines its spread and, thus, its appearance as peaked (leptokurtic), when* σ_x *is small, or as flat (platykurtic), when* σ_x *is large. In every case, the normal probability density function has points of inflection precisely 1 standard deviation below and above the mean and then approaches, respectively, minus and plus infinity on the horizontal axis (which the graph can only suggest but not show). As a practical matter, the height of every normal curve is near 0 within 3 standard deviations of the mean, as all three curves here demonstrate.*

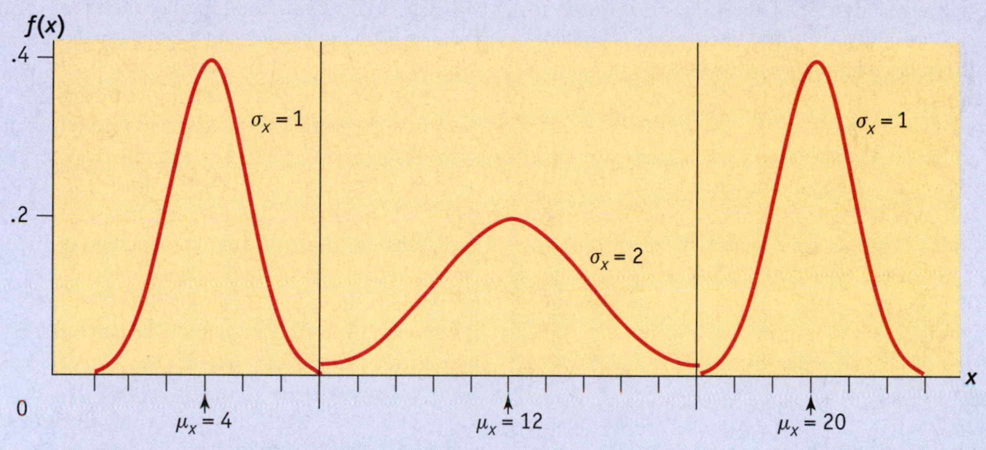

chapter, apparent differences in kurtosis can be eliminated by converting all normal distributions into an identical *standard* normal distribution.)

Note that every one of the three probability density functions shown in Figure 10.6 exhibits the three characteristics listed in Definition 10.3, although it is impractical in a graph to show how the tails of the functions extend indefinitely in both directions without ever touching the axes. Indeed, the graph has been divided into three segments by the two vertical lines and each of the three bell-shaped curves has been confined to one of these sections, although we know that the tails of each curve do not end where shown. In fact, the tails in both directions form asymptotes to the axes.

The graphical representation of the normal probability distribution was long called the *Gaussean curve,* and it is still known by that name in many countries today. In 1893, Karl Pearson (1857–1936) introduced the term *normal* curve, which is somewhat unfortunate because it creates the false impression that other-than-normal probability functions are somehow abnormal or rare.

Application 10.1, *Honest Weights and the Normal Curve of Error,* and Application 10.2, *The Great IQ Controversy,* provide fascinating illustrations of the use of the normal curve.

HONEST WEIGHTS AND THE NORMAL CURVE OF ERROR

Since time immemorial, merchants and their customers have argued over accurate measurement. Whether they were weighing bags of spices, live sheep, or flasks of olive oil, whether they were measuring off lengths of cloth or lengths of pastureland, they were soon aware that each trial of measurement could easily produce a different result. Even today, with infinitely more refined measurement techniques, repeated measurement of the same thing tends to produce different results each time. Each result is contaminated by a different *random error.* (See Chapters 4 and 5 for a more detailed discussion of this concept.) These errors are as likely to be positive as negative. They are also more likely to be small than large (that is, they are more likely to be close to zero than further away from it). In short, errors of careful measurement can be described by the normal curve. This fact was clearly stated in 1809 by Carl Friedrich Gauss (1777–1855) and, some eight decades later, led Francis Galton (1822–1911) to exclaim: "I know of scarce anything so apt to impress the imagination as the wonderful form of cosmic order expressed by the Law of Frequency of Error."

Consider, for example, how you can know that a pound of sugar you buy really *is* a pound. In 1875, a Treaty of the Meter was signed in Paris. Among other things, the signatories agreed to define a certain object as the International Prototype Kilogram and to determine all other weights in relation to it. The prototype kilogram is made of platinum-iridium and is held, under standard conditions of air pressure and temperature, at the International Bureau of Weights and Measures in Paris. Each signatory nation owns a copy of the original kilogram; that of the United States, number 20, is held at the National Bureau of Standards in Washington. With its help, similar weights are calibrated in each state, and these are used to check merchant scales periodically. In the end, the amount of sugar you buy is called 1 pound because its weight equals .4539237 of the original kilogram. (There are roughly 2.2 lbs in a kg.)

Yet even at the National Bureau of Standards, weighing the same object repeatedly may produce results such as these: 999.9231 grams, 999.9752 grams, 999.9603 grams, 1,000.0598 grams, 1,000.1003 grams, 999.9501 grams, 1,000.0001 grams, and so on. Slight variations in the position of weights or imperceptible amounts of play in the balance mechanism will yield ever-new results, but the probability distribution of these results may well fit a normal curve perfectly. If the distribution of results looks like Figure 10.A, the object may well be deemed to weigh 1 kilogram. If the distribution looks like Figure 10.B, the object may well be deemed to weigh less than 1 kilogram.

We can now see why the normal curve is also called the *normal curve of error.* If the mean result of many measurements is defined as the correct weight, the mean translates into an error of zero, while positive and negative

FIGURE 10.A

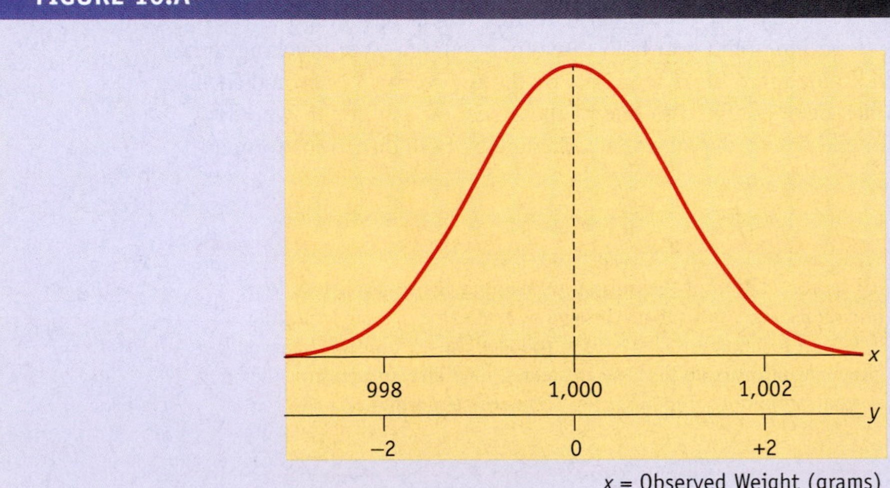

(continued)

Application 10.1 (continued)

errors, associated with results in excess of or below the mean, are normally distributed around the mean.

Note: Repeated comparisons of the U.S. kilogram (K20) with the Paris prototype suggest that the U.S. kilogram is 19 parts per billion lighter than the original.

SOURCES: Adapted from Francis Galton, *Natural Inheritance* (London: Macmillan, 1888); David Freedman, Robert Pisani, and Roger Purves, *Statistics* (New York: W. W. Norton, 1978), chapter 6; and Mort LaBrecque, "After 185 Years, Physicists Are Still Weighing the Kilogram," *Popular Science*, May 1984, pp. 96–99 and 170.

FIGURE 10.B

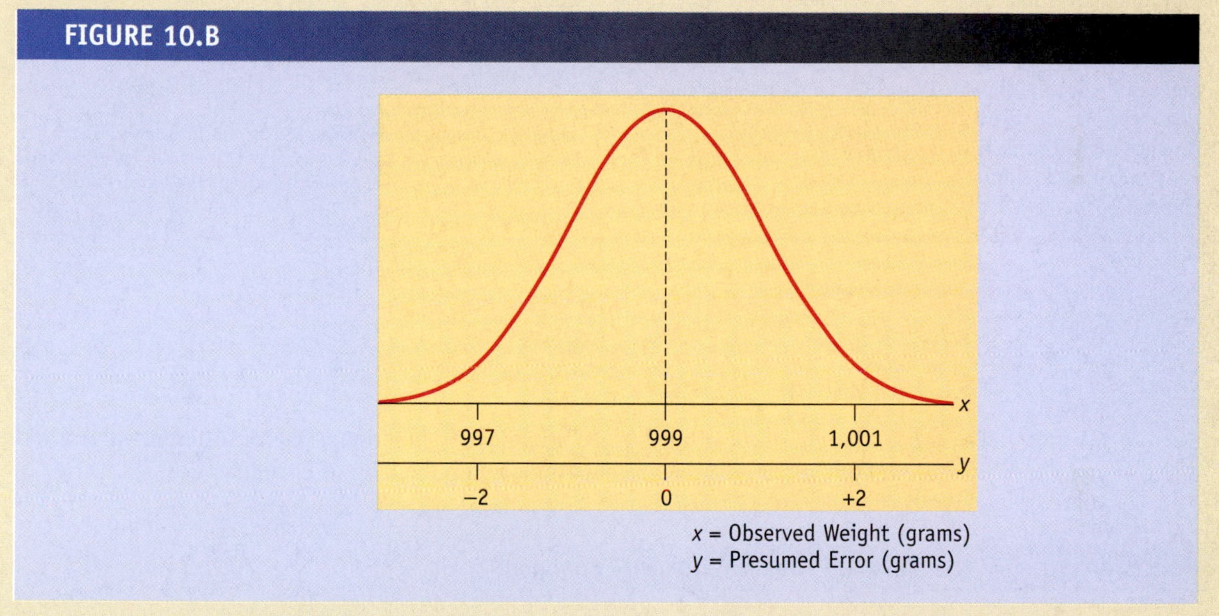

APPLICATION 10.2

THE GREAT IQ CONTROVERSY

In 1994, upon publication of *The Bell Curve: Intelligence and Class Structure in American Life,* the book's authors, Charles Murray and Richard Herrnstein, found themselves at the center of a huge and ugly controversy. They had argued that individuals differed substantially in their cognitive abilities, which the authors attributed largely to genetic inheritance. Thus, they rekindled a century-old controversy about *nature versus nurture:* Were people's characteristics mostly determined by their genes (i.e., nature) or by their upbringing (i.e., nurture)? The authors pictured the distribution of intelligence, allegedly determined by genes and traditionally measured by the intelligence quotient, IQ, along a *normal curve.* There were relatively few geniuses at the high end, with IQ scores of 150 or so. There was the mass of the populace in the middle of the curve, centered on an IQ of 100. And there were relatively few dullards at the bottom of the heap, with IQs of 50 or so. But the authors went further than that!

In their best-selling book, the authors used their alleged bell-shaped distribution of intelligence to "explain" some of the more unpalatable features of American life: (1) that the races do not perform equally in the IQ sweepstakes, with Asians doing better than average and African Americans worse than average; and (2) that the U.S. population is calcifying into veritable castes. Murray and Herrnstein asserted that high-IQ people are intermarrying, spawning bright offspring, and finding well-paid jobs, while low-IQ people lead lives centered on teenage pregnancy, welfare dependency, drugs, and crime.

(continued)

Application 10.2 (continued)

As you can well imagine, this kind of talk was equivalent to pouring gasoline on a smoldering fire. For over a century, people had debated the "nature versus nurture" issue of whether genetics or upbringing was more important in the formation of people's minds and psychological makeup. Eventually, a consensus emerged: Both factors played an equal role. But now that debate reemerged: The book's critics stressed the importance of environment over genetics in determining intelligence, reviewed the manifold flaws of IQ testing, and cited much evidence to the contrary. For example, on average, high-IQ parents often do *not* produce high-IQ children, nor do low-IQ parents automatically produce low-IQ children. (Indeed, as is shown in Chapter 16, one of the most important statistical techniques, *regression analysis,* was born as a result of and derived its very name from an investigation into this phenomenon.)

The point here, however, is not to discuss disputed evidence and questionable conclusions about intelligence. The point is to show how a simple concept, such as the normal curve, can have a huge impact on the ideas of our time.

SOURCES: Adapted from Charles Murray and Richard Herrnstein, *The Bell Curve: Intelligence and Class Structure in American Life* (New York: The Free Press, 1994); *The Economist,* December 24–January 6, 1995, pp. 69–71.

THE FORMULA

The precise height of the normal probability density function, $f(x)$, for different values, x, of the normal random variable, X, can be determined with the help of Formula 10.A.

FORMULA 10.A | The Normal Probability Density Function

$$f(x) = \frac{1}{\sigma_x \times \sqrt{2\pi}} \times e^{-\frac{1}{2}\left(\frac{x-\mu_x}{\sigma_x}\right)^2}$$

where $f(x)$ is a function of observed value x, while μ_x is the mean and σ_x is the standard deviation of the probability distribution of random variable X, and the remaining elements are well-known constants: $\pi \cong 3.14159$ and $e \cong 2.71828$.

This rather formidable expression is the equation for each of the curves seen in Figure 10.6 and for all other normal curves; it becomes less formidable upon closer inspection. The mean and standard deviation of the normal random variable's probability distribution appear as μ_x and σ_x and these values appear alongside two of the most famous constants in mathematics: π in this case is not the population proportion, but the ratio of the circumference to the diameter of the circle; it equals about 3.14159. The constant e, already noted in the Poisson formula on page 364, is the base of the natural logarithms and equals about 2.71828.

Thus, given μ_x and σ_x, we can calculate the height of the probability density function $f(x)$ for each x. By then integrating that function over a specified range of x, we can calculate the type of crosshatched area shown in Figure 10.5 and, thus, determine the probability of finding values of the random variable within that range of x. However, in order to facilitate the determination of such probabilities, statisticians have found a way of converting normal curves with differing shapes and positions into a single *standard* normal curve and of then finding probabilities in appropriately prepared tables.

10.3 The Standard Normal Curve

We are now ready to meet what are, perhaps, this chapter's most crucial concepts, the *standard normal curve* and the *standard normal deviate.*

DEFINITION 10.4 A normal probability density function with a mean of 0 and a standard deviation of 1 is called a **standard normal curve.** Any normal curve can be transformed into such a standard normal curve by changing each x value into z value, also known as a **standard normal deviate** (see Formula 10.B).

FORMULA 10.B | The Standard Normal Deviate

$$z = \frac{x - \mu_x}{\sigma_x}$$

where x is an observed value of random variable X, while μ_x is the mean and σ_x is the standard deviation of its probability distribution.

As Figure 10.7 on the next page illustrates, any normal curve—whatever the value of μ_x and σ_x—can quickly be transformed into a *standard* normal curve by plotting the value of μ_x as 0 and converting x values above and below this mean into standard normal deviates or z values.

According to Formula 10.B, we find z values by expressing the deviation, $x - \mu_x$, of any given x value from the normally distributed variable's mean in units of standard deviations, σ_x. (In education statistics, z is often referred to as the *standard* score, as was noted in Application 7.1 on page 254.)

Thus, if $\mu_x = 4$ and $\sigma_x = 1$, as in the upper left-hand graph of Figure 10.7, a value of $x = 2$ becomes $z = -2$ in the lower standard graph, indicating that this $x = 2$ value of the random variable lies 2 standard deviations below the mean. Similarly, when $\mu_x = 12$ and $\sigma_x = 2$, as in the upper central graph, a value of $x = 14$ becomes $z = +1$ in the lower standard graph, indicating that this $x = 14$ value lies 1 standard deviation *above* the mean. By the same procedure, any other x value can be turned into a z value by applying Formula 10.B.

EXAMPLE PROBLEM 10.1

Given a normal distribution with $\mu_x = 20$ and $\sigma_x = 1$, find z values for $x = 18$ and $x = 21$.

SOLUTION: Applying Formula 10.B,

$$\text{for } x = 18: \quad z = \frac{x - \mu_x}{\sigma_x} = \frac{18 - 20}{1} = -2$$

$$\text{for } x = 21: \quad z = \frac{x - \mu_x}{\sigma_x} = \frac{21 - 20}{1} = +1$$

FIGURE 10.7 | Constructing the Standard Normal Curve

The three different normal curves of Figure 10.6, reproduced here in the top panel, can be converted into an identical standard *normal curve, shown in the bottom panel. Each actual value,* x, *of the normal random variable is translated into a standardized value,* z, *by first calculating the deviation of* x *from the mean and then expressing this deviation in terms of standard deviation units. This procedure is equivalent to setting* μ *equal to 0 and treating the distance of 1σ as equal to 1.*

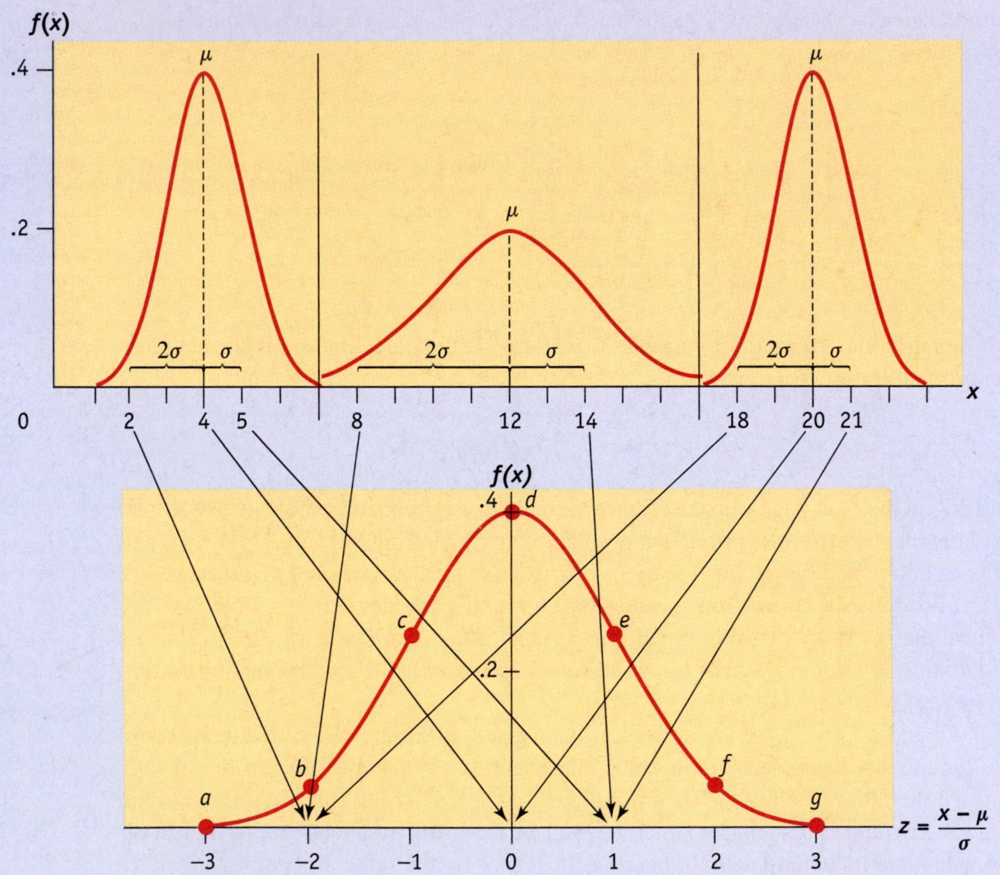

Note: Both of the Example Problem 10.1 answers can be confirmed by looking at the upper right-hand graph of Figure 10.7.

EXAMPLE PROBLEM 10.2

Given a normal distribution's x value of 22.5, find the corresponding z value if

a. $\mu_x = 20$ and $\sigma_x = 1$.

b. $\mu_x = 12$ and $\sigma_x = 2$.

SOLUTION: Applying Formula 10.B,

a. $z = \frac{x - \mu_x}{\sigma_x} = \frac{22.5 - 20}{1} = +2.5$

b. $z = \frac{x - \mu_x}{\sigma_x} = \frac{22.5 - 12}{2} = +5.25$

10.4 The Standard Normal Tables

When x values have been transformed into z values by setting $\mu_x = 0$ and $\sigma_x = 1$, Formula 10.A simplifies to Formula 10.C.

FORMULA 10.C | The Standard Normal Probability Density Function

$$f(x) = \frac{1}{\sqrt{2\pi}} \times e^{-\frac{1}{2}z^2}$$

where $\pi \cong 3.14159$, $e \cong 2.71828$, $z = \frac{x - \mu_x}{\sigma_x}$, and $-\infty \leq z \leq +\infty$.

Based on this simplified formula, two types of tables can be prepared. These are:

- *tables of ordinates* that show the height of the standard normal curve for any given value of z (which allows us to draw the curve with accuracy)
- *tables of cumulative relative frequencies* that show the area under the (properly drawn) standard normal curve for any given range of z values (which allows us to determine the probability of encountering that range of z values)

We will discuss the nature of these tables and will then show how helpful they can be in typical business and economics applications.[1]

TABLES OF ORDINATES

One set of these tables shows the *height* of the standard normal probability density function for different values of z. For example, the height of the curve corresponding to z values of 0, 1, 2, 3, and 4 is shown in Table 10.1 on the next page.

As was noted earlier, strictly speaking, the normal curve touches the horizontal axis only at minus and plus infinity, but for all practical purposes it can be considered to do so within 3 standard deviations of the mean (or when $z = \pm 3$).

[1]These tables were first prepared in 1799 by Chrétien Kramp, a French mathematician and physicist (who also invented the n! factorial notation that was discussed in Chapter 8). The most recent tables were issued in 1953 by the U.S. National Bureau of Standards, as noted in Appendix Table H.

TABLE 10.1 | Finding the Height of the Standard Normal Curve

The height of the standard normal curve at any given value of z can be found with the help of Formula 10.C. This information allows us to draw the curve with accuracy.

Absolute Value of z	Height of Curve	Corresponding Points in Figure 10.7
0	.39894	*d*
1	.24197	*c* and *e*
2	.05399	*b* and *f*
3	.00443	*a* and *g*
4	.00013	not shown

TABLES OF CUMULATIVE RELATIVE FREQUENCIES

A second set of tables shows the *area* under the standard normal probability density function, typically between $\mu = 0$ and alternative *positive* values of z. Because of the symmetry of the normal curve, these tables can also be interpreted to show the noted area between $\mu = 0$ and alternative *negative* values of z. This type of table, as we shall see presently, is of much greater importance than a table of ordinates, and it has been reproduced, for selected values of z, as Appendix Table H. An excerpt of this Appendix Table appears as Table 10.2 here:

TABLE 10.2 | Appendix Table H Excerpt: Standard Normal Curve Areas

Entries in this table give the area under the curve between the mean and z standard deviations above the mean.

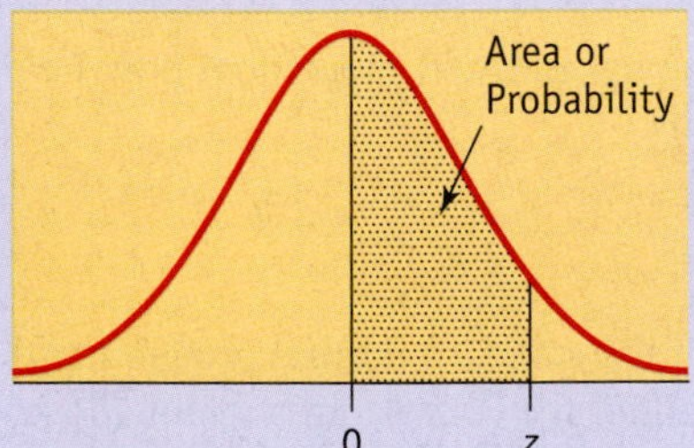

z	.00	.01	.02	.03	.04	.05	.06	.07	.08	.09
.0	.0000	.0040	.0080	.0120	.0160	.0199	.0239	.0279	.0319	.0359
.1	.0398	.0438	.0478	.0517	.0557	.0596	.0636	.0675	.0714	.0753
.2	.0793	.0832	.0871	0910	.0948	**.0987**	.1026	.1064	.1103	.1141
.3	.1179	.1217	.1255	.1293	.1331	.1368	.1406	.1443	.1480	.1517
.4	.1554	.1591	.1628	.1664	.1700	.1736	.1772	.1808	.1844	.1879

READING THE TABLE In Appendix Table H, the value of z is split in two. A first portion, including the first decimal, is shown in the leftmost column of that table, while a second decimal place of z is found in one of the 10 entries in the table's top row. By *adding together* any given row heading with any given column heading, we can reconstruct a z value with two decimal places.

Thus, a row heading of .2 and a column heading of .05, here shown in red, corresponds to a z value of .2 +.05 = .25. At the intersection of the .2 row and the .05 column, we find, accordingly, the area under the standard normal curve between the mean of 0 and a z value of .25, and this area value, also shown in red, equals .0987. This highlighted number gives us the probability that the value of a normally distributed random variable lies within one-quarter standard deviation above the mean. The curve's symmetry implies an equal probability of .0987 that such a value lies within one-quarter standard deviation *below* the mean. Thus, there exists a probability of .0987 + .0987 = .1974 that such a value lies somewhere between one-quarter standard deviation below to one-quarter standard deviation above the mean.

Moving along the z = .2 row to the columns headed .06, .07, .08, and .09, we can find, similarly, the probability of any value of the random variable lying z = .26, .27. .28, and .29 standard deviations above the mean. As our table shows, the probabilities involved equal .1026, .1064, .1103, and .1141, respectively. Hence, the probability of finding a value of a normally distributed random variable somewhere between .29 standard deviations below the mean and .29 standard deviations above it equals .1141 + .1141 = .2282.

A GRAPHICAL EXPOSITION We can highlight all this probability information graphically as well. Consider Figure 10.8 on the next page. The graph directly shows the likelihood of encountering values of a standard normal random variable within 1 or 2 standard deviations below or above the mean. The graph implies that the probability of finding a value of such a random variable that lies more than 2 standard deviations either below or above its mean equals a tiny 1 − .9544 = .0456. Yet the probability remains positive even for large values of z. (According to the calculations by the National Bureau of Standards, noted in Appendix Table H, the probability of finding a value that lies more than 3 standard deviations either below or above the mean equals 1 − .9972 = .0028; that for a value beyond 8 standard deviations above or below the mean equals a tiny .00000 00000 00001.)

The graphical exposition in Figure 10.8 also illustrates how we can answer more complicated questions. For example, the probability of finding a value of this normal random variable that lies between 2 standard deviations below the mean and 1 standard deviation above it can easily be found by combining panels (d) and (b) as .4772 + .3413 = .8185. Similarly, the probability of finding a value that lies more than 1 standard deviation below the mean *or* more than 2 standard deviations above it can be found by using panels (a) and (e) and combining the unshaded area in the *left* half of panel (a)—that is, .5000 − .3413 = .1587—with the unshaded area in the *right* half of panel (e)—that is, .5000 −.4772 = .0228. The result is .1815. (The area under half the normal curve always equals .5000.)

The following example problems provide illustrations of why we may want to know such normal-curve probabilities. So does Application 10.3, *The Decision to Seed Hurricanes,* that follows them on page 414.

FIGURE 10.8 | Finding Areas under the Standard Normal Curve

With the help of Appendix Table H, we can determine areas under the standard normal curve and, thus, the probability of finding values of a normally distributed random variable within specified numbers of standard deviations below or above the mean. Because the area under the standard normal curve between the mean and 1 standard deviation below it covers .3413 of the entire area under the curve, as represented by the shaded portion in panel (a), and because the same is true for the range of values between the mean and 1 standard deviation above it, as shown in panel (b), .3413 + .3413 = .6826 of the total area is found within the range of $\mu \pm 1\sigma$, as shown in panel (c). Thus, .6826 is the probability of finding a value of the random variable within that range. Similarly, the probability is .9544 of finding a value of the normal random variable within $\mu \pm 2\sigma$.

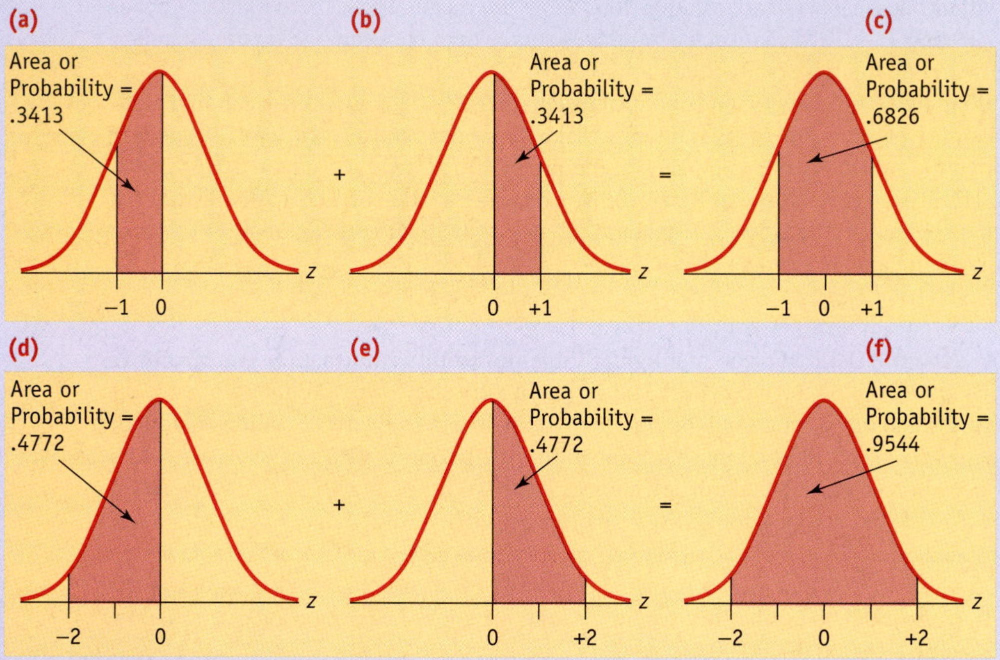

EXAMPLE PROBLEM 10.3

An aircraft engine manufacturer knows that engine lifetime is a normally distributed random variable with a mean of 2,000 hours and a standard deviation of 100 hours. For purposes of advertising and warranty offers, here are typical questions of interest to the manufacturer and to potential customers (along with their answers):

a. What is the probability that a randomly chosen engine has a lifetime between 2,000 and 2,075 hours?

SOLUTION: Symbolically, remembering the Caution Box on page 396, we can write

$$p(2{,}000 < x < 2{,}075) = ?$$

Thus, the problem amounts to finding an area under the normal curve between the mean and a value above it. It helps to sketch the problem, as in Figure 10.9, to convert x values into z values, and to find the answer in Appendix Table H. Because $\mu = 2{,}000$ hours and $\sigma = 100$

FIGURE 10.9

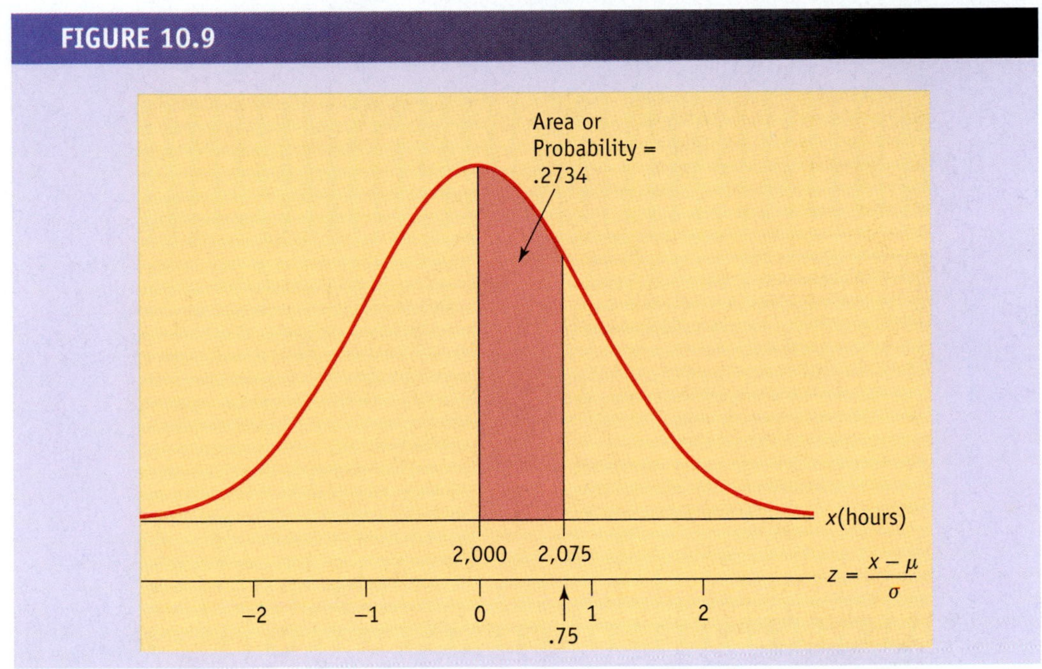

hours, the x value of 2,000 hours corresponds to a z value of 0, and the x value of 2,075 hours equals a z value of (2,075 − 2,000) divided by 100, or of .75. We can find the area between $z = 0$ and $z = .75$ (shaded in Figure 10.9) in Appendix Table H at the intersection of the .7 row and .05 column as .2734. This number is also the probability sought. Symbolically,

$$p(0 < z < .75) = .2734$$

There is a 27.34 percent chance that a randomly chosen engine will last between 2,000 and 2,075 hours.

b. What is the probability that a randomly chosen engine has a lifetime between 1,880 and 2,000 hours?

$$p(1{,}880 < x < 2{,}000) = ?$$

SOLUTION: The problem now amounts to finding an area under the normal curve between the mean and a value below it. We solve it by a procedure analogous to (a) above, as shown by Figure 10.10 on the next page.

Because $\mu = 2{,}000$ hours and $\sigma = 100$ hours, the x value of 1,880 equals a z value of -1.20 and the x value of 2,000 turns into $z = 0$. We can find the area between $z = 0$ and $z = -1.20$ (shaded in Figure 10.10) in Appendix Table H at the intersection of the 1.2 row and .00 column as .3849. This number is also the probability sought. Symbolically,

$$p(-1.20 < z < 0) = .3849$$

c. What is the probability that a randomly chosen engine has a lifetime between 1,950 and 2,150 hours?

$$p(1{,}950 < x < 2{,}150) = ?$$

FIGURE 10.10

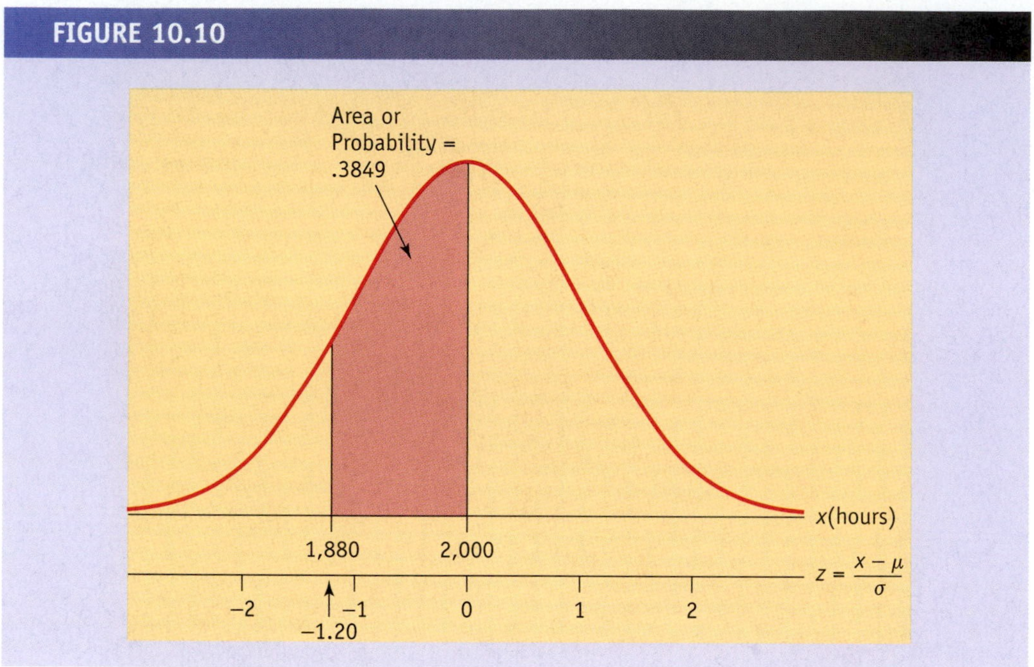

SOLUTION: The problem amounts to finding an area under the normal curve overlapping the mean, as shown in Figure 10.11.

Because $\mu = 2{,}000$ hours and $\sigma = 100$ hours, the x value of 1,950 hours (or 2,150 hours) equals a z value of $-.50$ (or $+1.50$). We can find the area between $z = 0$ and $z = -.50$ (crosshatched) and that between $z = 0$ and $z = +1.50$ (shaded) in Appendix Table H at the intersection of the .5 row and .00 column (and of the 1.5 row and .00 column) as .1915 (and .4332). Thus, the probability sought equals the sum of the crosshatched and shaded areas, or $.1915 + .4332 = .6247$. Symbolically,

$$p(-.50 < z < 1.50) = .6247$$

FIGURE 10.11

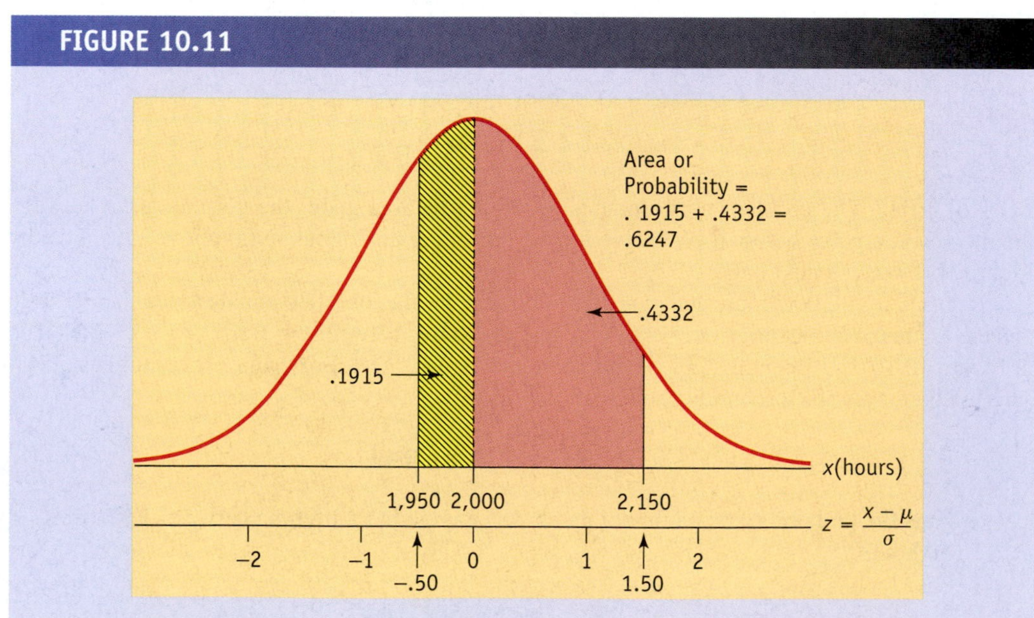

d. What is the probability that a randomly chosen engine has a lifetime above 2,170 hours?

$$p(x > 2{,}170) = ?$$

SOLUTION: The problem amounts to finding an area under the upper tail of the normal curve, as shown in Figure 10.12.

FIGURE 10.12

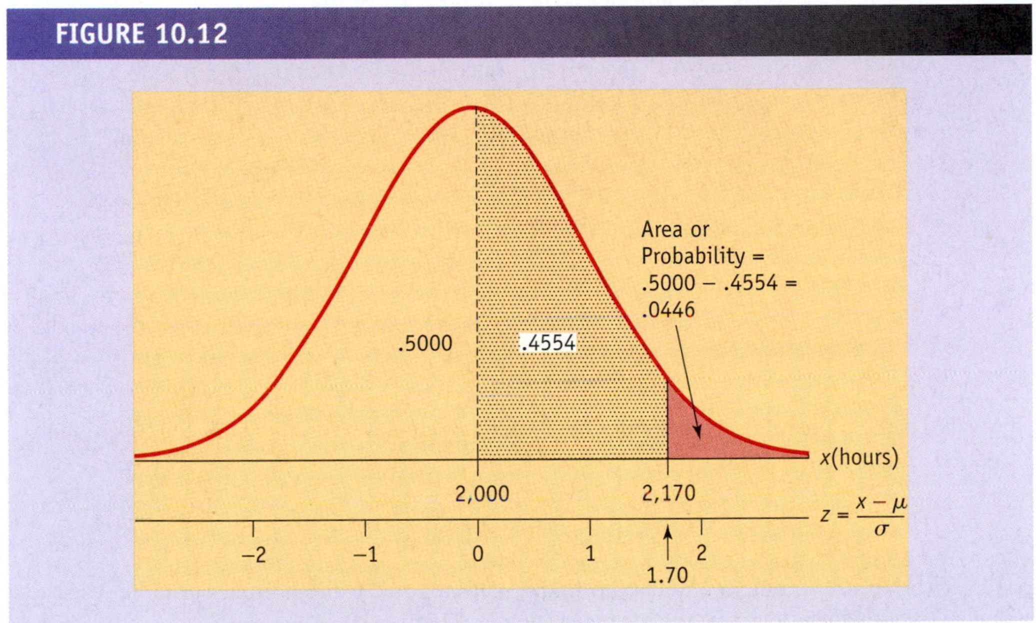

Because $\mu = 2{,}000$ hours and $\sigma = 100$ hours, the x value of 2,170 hours equals a z value of $+1.70$. The entire area to the right of μ (or $z = 0$) always equals .5; we can find that between $z = 0$ and $z = +1.70$ (dotted in Figure 10.12) in Appendix Table H at the intersection of the 1.7 row and .00 column as .4554. Thus, the probability sought (which corresponds to the shaded upper-tail area) equals $.5000 - .4554$, or .0446. Symbolically,

$$p(z > 1.70) = .0446$$

e. What is the probability that a randomly chosen engine has a lifetime below 1,840 hours?

$$p(x < 1{,}840) = ?$$

SOLUTION: The problem amounts to finding an area under the lower tail of the normal curve, as shown in Figure 10.13 on the next page.

Because $\mu = 2{,}000$ hours and $\sigma = 100$ hours, the x value of 1,840 hours equals a z value of -1.60. The entire area to the left of μ (or $z = 0$) always equals .5; we can find the area between $z = 0$ and $z = -1.60$ (dotted in Figure 10.13) in Appendix Table H at the intersection of the 1.6 row and .00 column as .4452. Thus, the probability sought (which corresponds to the shaded lower-tail area) equals $.5000 - .4452$, or .0548. Symbolically,

$$p(z < -1.60) = .0548$$

FIGURE 10.13

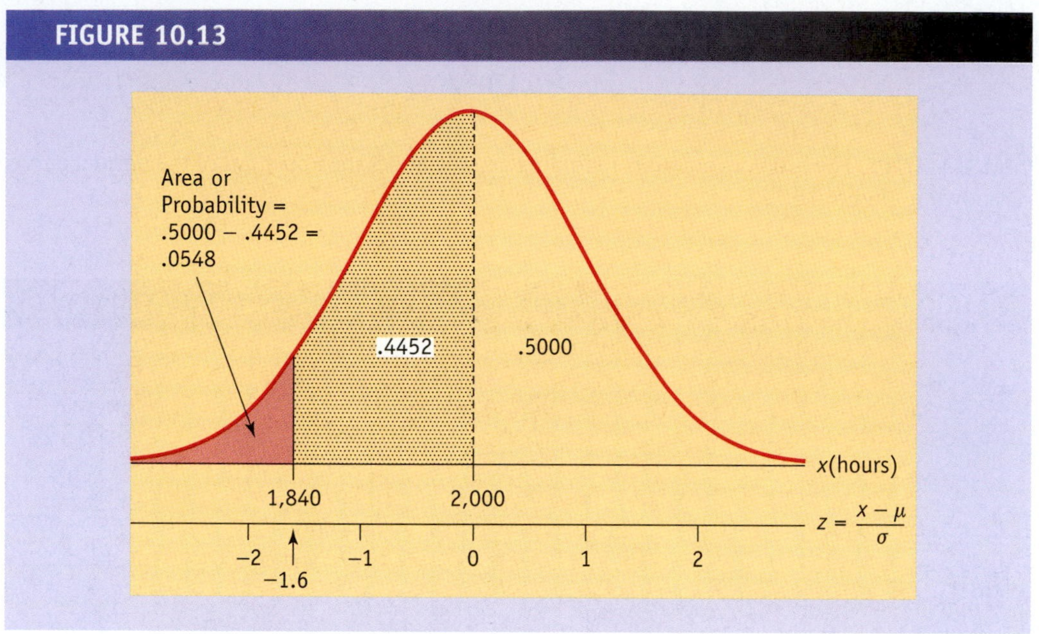

f. What is the probability that a randomly chosen engine has a lifetime between 2,071 and 2,103 hours?

$$p(2{,}071 < x < 2{,}103) = ?$$

SOLUTION: The problem amounts to finding an area under the normal curve between two values, *both* of which lie above the mean, as shown in Figure 10.14.

FIGURE 10.14

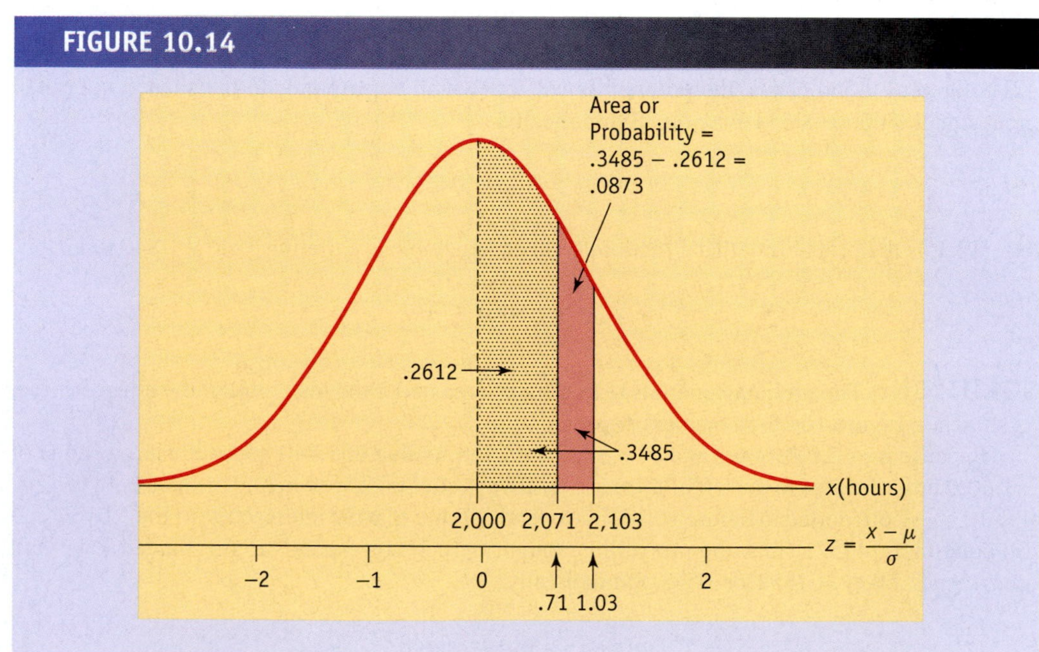

Because $\mu = 2{,}000$ hours and $\sigma = 100$ hours, the x values of 2,071 and 2,103 hours equal z values, respectively, of $+.71$ and $+1.03$. We can find the area between $z = 0$ and $z = +1.03$ (the dotted plus shaded areas in Figure 10.14) in Appendix Table H at the intersection of the 1.0 row and .03 column as .3485. Similarly, we can find the area between $z = 0$ and $z = +.71$ (the dotted area in Figure 10.14) at the intersection of the .7 row and .01 column as .2612. Thus, the probability sought, which corresponds to the shaded area only, equals $.3485 - .2612$, or .0873. Symbolically,

$$p(.71 < z < 1.03) = .0873$$

g. What is the probability that a randomly chosen engine has a lifetime between 1,849 and 1,923 hours?

$$p(1{,}849 < x < 1{,}923) = ?$$

SOLUTION: The problem amounts to finding an area under the normal curve between two values, *both* of which lie below the mean, as shown in Figure 10.15.

FIGURE 10.15

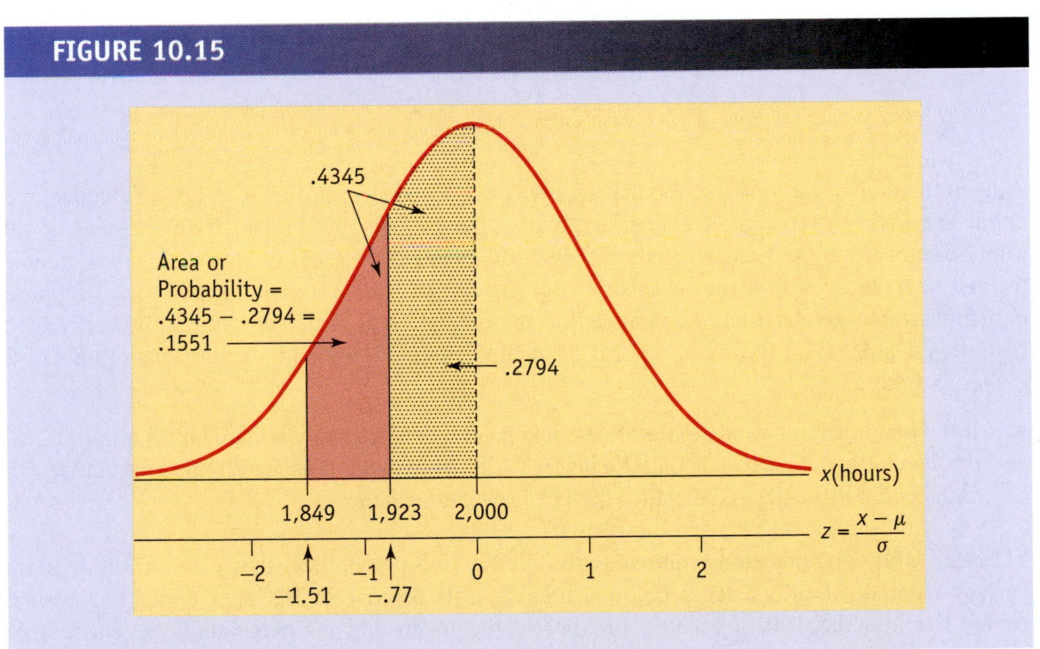

Because $\mu = 2{,}000$ hours and $\sigma = 100$ hours, the x values of 1,849 and 1,923 hours equal z values, respectively, of -1.51 and $-.77$. We can find the area between $z = 0$ and $z = -1.51$ (the dotted plus shaded areas in Figure 10.15) in Appendix Table H at the intersection of the 1.5 row and .01 column as .4345. Similarly, we can find the area between $z = 0$ and $z = -.77$ (the dotted area in Figure 10.15) at the intersection of the .7 row and .07 column as .2794. Thus, the probability sought (which corresponds to the shaded area only) equals $.4345 - .2794$, or .1551. Symbolically,

$$p(-1.51 < z < -.77) = .1551$$

h. What is the probability that a randomly chosen engine has a lifetime of less than 2,075 hours?

$$p(x < 2{,}075) = ?$$

SOLUTION: The problem amounts to finding an area under the normal curve to the left of a value that itself lies above the mean. Thus, the answer equals .5, for the area left of the mean, plus whatever probability is associated with values between the mean and the given value of 2,075 hours. In this case, as a look at Figure 10.9 on page 407 confirms, the answer equals .5000 + .2734, or .7734. Symbolically,

$$p(z < .75) = .7734$$

i. What is the probability that a randomly chosen engine has a lifetime of more than 1,880 hours?

$$p(x > 1{,}880) = ?$$

SOLUTION: The problem amounts to finding an area under the normal curve to the right of a value that itself lies below the mean. Thus, the answer equals .5, for the area right of the mean, plus whatever probability is associated with values between the mean and the given value of 1,880 hours. In this case, as a look at Figure 10.10 on page 408 confirms, the answer equals .3849 + .5000, or .8849. Symbolically,

$$p(z > -1.20) = .8849$$

EXAMPLE PROBLEM 10.4

A manufacturer of aircraft (or, for that matter, of any product) is likely to be very concerned about the ability of potential consumers to use the product with ease. If 60 percent of all pilots cannot reach the rudder pedals when seated in the pilot's seat or find themselves unable to tune navigation equipment because it is nicely out of reach, something is wrong. Suppose a manufacturer knows that the lengths of pilots' legs and arms are normally distributed random variables with means of 33 and 28 inches, respectively, and standard deviations of 2 inches in both cases.

a. If the manufacturer wants to design a cockpit such that precisely 90 percent of all pilots can reach the rudder pedals with their feet while seated and, thus, can fly this particular plane, what is the desired distance between seat and pedals?

SOLUTION: The question requires us to find the 10th percentile—that value of the random variable (length of pilots' legs) below which lies 10 percent of the area under the normal curve. Because the 10th percentile lies below the mean and 50 percent of the entire area under the normal curve lies below the mean, the 10th percentile corresponds to that negative value of z that places $50 - 10 = 40$ percent of the area between itself and the mean, as shown in Figure 10.16.

Accordingly, we can search the body of Appendix Table H for an entry of .4000, which is found between a z of -1.28 (area: .3997) and a z of -1.29 (area: .4015). Interpolation yields a z value of -1.2817 for the 10th percentile.[2]

[2]A change in the area from .3997 to .4015 (or of +.0018) is associated with an absolute change in the z value from 1.28 to 1.29 (or of +.01). Thus, our desired change in the area value from .3997 to .4000 (or of +.0003) is associated with an unknown absolute change, x, in the initial z value. We can write

$$\frac{+.0018}{+.01} = \frac{+.0003}{x} \quad \text{and} \quad x = \frac{.0003(.01)}{.0018} = .0017$$

Thus, the absolute value of z we seek is $1.28 + .0017 = 1.2817$, as noted.

FIGURE 10.16

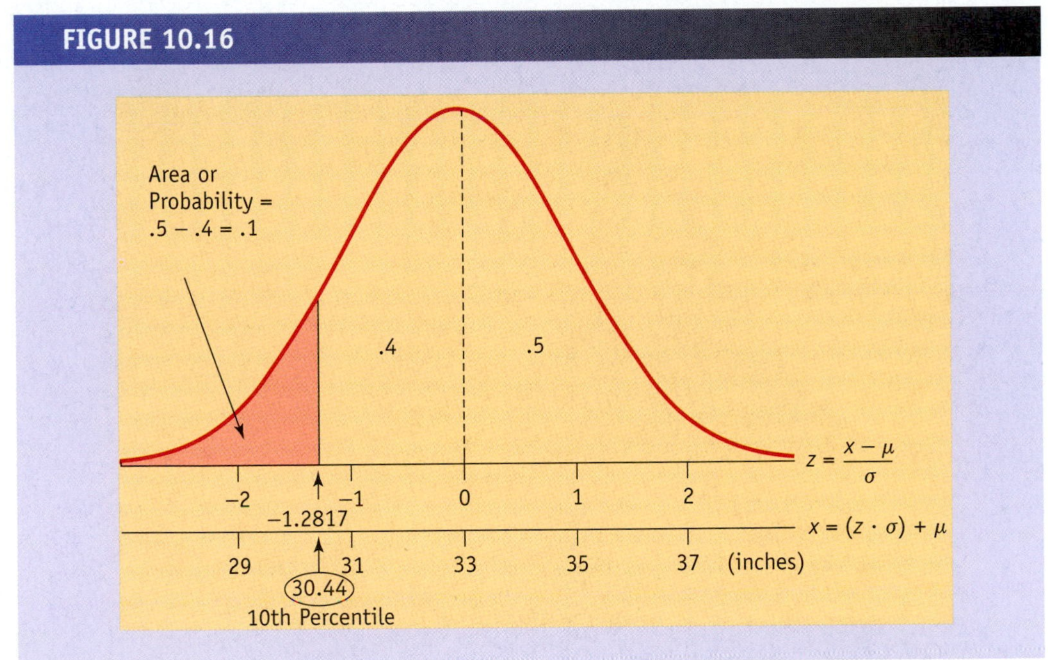

Just as x values can be converted into z values, so the reverse is also true. Given the assumed $\mu = 33$ inches and $\sigma = 2$ inches, a z of -1.2817 corresponds to 30.44 inches.[3]

This means that 10 percent of all pilots cannot reach as far as 30.44 inches—which is, therefore, the distance sought because it ensures that 90 percent of all pilots can easily reach the rudder pedals.

b. If it were true that precisely 60 percent of all pilots could *not* reach the navigation equipment when seated, what must have been the distance between the pilot's seat and the relevant knobs?

SOLUTION: The question requires us to find the 60th percentile—that value of the random variable (length of pilots' arms) below which 60 percent of the area under the normal curve lies. Because the 60th percentile lies above the mean, but 50 percent of the entire area under the normal curve lies below it, the 60th percentile corresponds to that positive value of z that places 10 percent of the area between itself and the mean, as shown in Figure 10.17 on the next page.

Accordingly, we can search the body of Appendix Table H for an entry of .1000, which is found between a z of .25 (area .0987) and a z of .26 (area .1026). Interpolation yields a z value of .2533 for the 60th percentile. Again, z values can be converted into x values; in this case, the 60th percentile corresponds to 28.51 inches. Such a distance would account for only 40 percent of all pilots being able to reach the navigation equipment knobs.

Note: The concerns noted in Example Problem 10.4 are not just academic exercises. In 1984, for example, the U.S. Navy issued flight-training standards that stipulated minimum values for a pilot's "sitting height" at 40.5 inches, "buttock-to-leg length" at 48 inches, and "functional reach" at 29 inches—all because of the design of new Navy fighter planes. The standards excluded 73 percent of all college-age women and 13 percent of all college-age men from naval flying. Since that time, the public has become increasingly concerned about such

[3]Rewriting Formula 10.B, we have $x = (z\sigma) + \mu$, which comes to $x = -1.2817(2) + 33 = 30.44$ inches in this example.

FIGURE 10.17

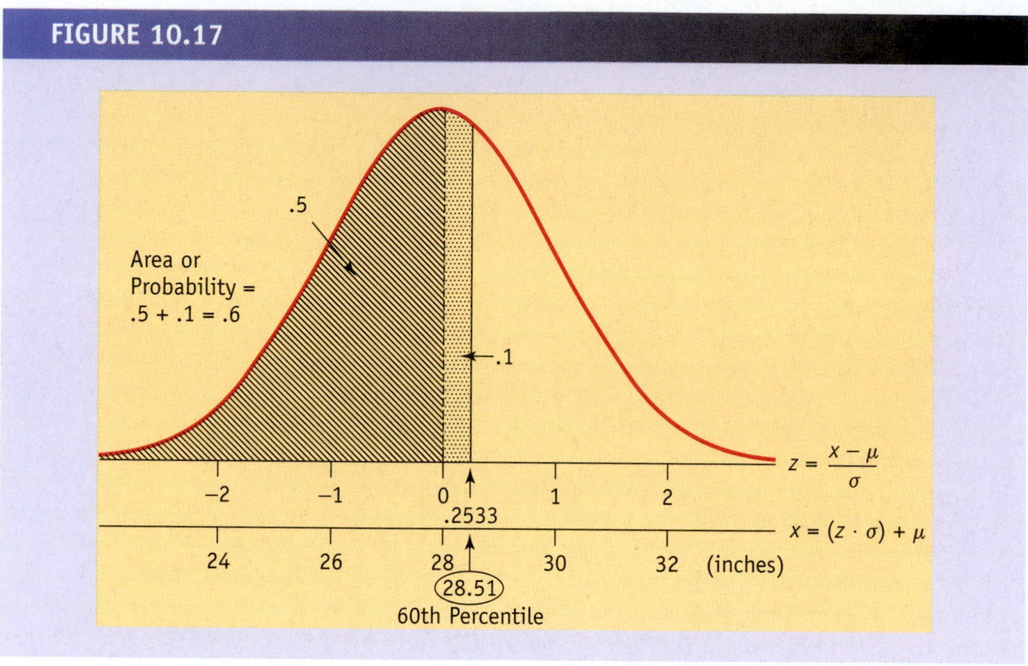

sexist implications of product design and so have the manufacturers of planes and all sorts of other products.[4]

[4]*The New York Times,* November 25, 1984, p. 49.

APPLICATION 10.3

The Decision to Seed Hurricanes

It comes as no surprise to you to learn that hurricanes are a deadly force of nature. Nevertheless, during the course of the 20th century, the human death toll from hurricanes in the United States declined steadily, from over 8,000 during 1901–1910 to fewer than 200 during the 1990s. This lucky trend resulted from better weather forecasts, which allowed timely evacuations. On the other hand, as a result of increasing economic development in the southeastern United States, which turned swamplands into beachfront malls, luxury hotels, and sprawling suburban subdivisions, property damage has climbed steadily. Measured in 1990 dollars, such damage amounted to less than $1 billion during the first decade of the last century, then climbed to almost $50 billion in the 1990s. Besides watching them, is there anything one can do about hurricanes? Interestingly, the answer may be *yes,* and it involves the normal curve.

Way back in 1961, scientists suggested that *seeding* hurricanes (that is, having airplanes spray them with silver iodide) would mitigate their destructive force. The extent of that force was evidenced when Hurricane Betsy in 1965 and Hurricane Camille in 1969 each caused $1.5 billion in property damage (in then-current dollars). Also in 1969, strong evidence for the effectiveness of the seeding procedure was obtained when Hurricane Debbie was seeded twice and reductions in peak wind speed of 31 and 15 percent, respectively, were observed as a result. The U.S. Department of Commerce subsequently sponsored a study of the behavior of hurricanes. The study found that in a "typical" 100-miles-per-hour hurricane the probability distribution of various percentage changes in maximum sustained surface winds within 12 hours before landfall could be described by a normal curve with a mean of 0 and a standard deviation of 15.6 percent. Such a curve is shown in Figure 10.C. Typical property damage totals (in then-current dollars) are also indicated.

Thus, according to the study, a hurricane in which a 100-mph sustained surface wind intensifies 32 percent within 12 hours prior to landfall could be expected to

(continued)

Application 10.3 (continued)

destroy property in excess of $335 million, but the damage would only be about $16 million if the winds decreased by 34 percent.

The probabilities for the two events can be determined by using the normal probabilities table. In this example, +32 percent equals a z-score of 32 − 0, divided by 15.6, or +2.05; −34 percent equals a z-score of −2.18. The associated probabilities, according to Appendix Table H, for $z >$ 2.05 or $z < -2.18$ equal .5 − .4798 = .0202 and .5 − .4854 = .0146, respectively.

Clearly, the kind of information embodied in the accompanying normal curve can become a crucial input in the decision to engage in or refrain from costly hurricane seeding.

Note: An update of this story can be found in the Preview of Chapter 23 (on pages 1111–1112) and in Application 23.1, *The Decision to Seed Hurricanes—A Second Look,* on pages 1127–1128.

SOURCE: Adapted from R. A. Howard, J. E. Matheson, D. W. North, "The Decision to Seed Hurricanes," *Science,* June 16, 1972, pp. 1191–1202.

FIGURE 10.C

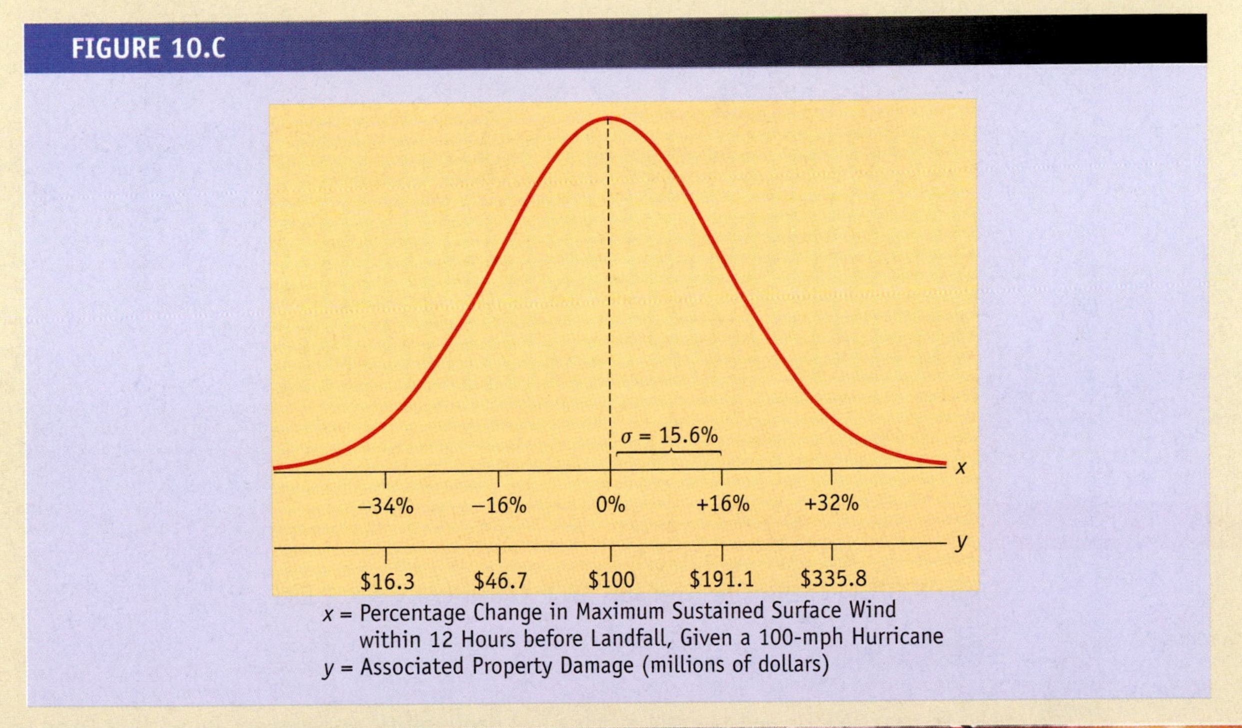

10.5 Normal Probabilities and Computer Programs

Computer programs such as EXCEL or MINITAB allow us to work all sorts of normal curve problems without the use of Appendix Table H. The following examples show how they can help us find:

- the height of the normal curve for specified values of x
- areas under the normal curve for specified ranges of x
- values of x corresponding to specified normal curve areas

Typically, all calculations are made for the standard normal curve defined by $\mu = 0$ and $\sigma = 1$.

EXCEL Example 10.1

You are about to draw a normal curve and want to do so with precision. Using EXCEL, confirm the heights of the normal curve for the selected z values given in Table 10.1 on p. 404.

SOLUTION

1. Fire up EXCEL and enter the labels **z** and **f(z),** respectively, into cells A1 and B1.
2. Enter numbers 0–4 into cells A2–A6.
3. Place the pointer into cell B2; then type the formula **=NORMDIST(A2,0,1,0)** and press Enter.
4. Drag cell B2 to B6 for this result:

z	f(z)
0	0.398942
1	0.241971
2	0.053991
3	0.004432
4	0.000134

EXCEL Example 10.2

Using EXCEL, confirm the Appendix Table H entries for $z = .3$ and $z = 2.25$.

SOLUTION

1. Fire up EXCEL and enter the labels **z** and **probability,** respectively, into cells A1 and B1.
2. Enter numbers .3 and 2.25 into cells A2–A3.
3. Place the pointer into cell B2; then click the **Function Wizard (*fx*)** > **Statistical** > **NORMSDIST** > **OK.** (The **S** indicates that you want to work with the normal *standard* distribution, having a mean of 0 and a standard deviation of 1. If you don't want that, you can use the alternative **NORMDIST** command and provide your own values of μ and σ.)
4. In the dialog box, type **.3** and click **OK.**
5. Place the pointer into cell B3; then click the **Function Wizard (*fx*)** > **Statistical** > **NORMSDIST > OK.**
6. In the dialog box, type **2.25** and click **OK.**

The following results show the areas under the standard normal curve between $-\infty$ and the chosen z values:

z	probability
0.3	0.61791136
2.25	0.98777557

The corresponding Appendix Table H entries show areas between the mean and z. Thus, .5 has to be deducted from each probability value to get the answers of .1179 and .4878.

(*Tip:* You can speed things up by entering A2 instead of .3 in Step 4, then dragging the B2 result down to B3.)

EXCEL Example 10.3

Using EXCEL, confirm the Appendix Table H claim that an area of .3413 is associated with a z value of 1.

SOLUTION While Appendix Table H provides areas under the standard normal curve between the mean and a specified z, EXCEL does so between $-\infty$ and z. Therefore, we must enter an area value of $.5000 + .3413 = .8413$ to find the proper z:

1. Fire up EXCEL and enter the labels **area** and **z,** respectively, into cells A1 and B1.
2. Enter .8413 into cell A2.
3. Place the pointer into cell B2; then click the **Function Wizard (*fx*)** > **Statistical** > **NORMSINV** > **OK.**
4. In the dialog box, type **.8413** and click **OK.** The result:

area	z
0.8413	0.999814

This value is rounded to 1 in Appendix Table H.

EXCEL Example 10.4

Using EXCEL, confirm the probabilities claimed in Figure 10.3 (on page 392).

SOLUTION For the x values shown in the graph, you must specify a normal curve with $\mu = 32$ and $\sigma = .5$. Before interpreting the output, remember that EXCEL always prints out area values from $-\infty$ to the specified x:

1. Fire up EXCEL and enter the labels **x** and **probability,** respectively, into cells A1 and B1.
2. Enter numbers 30.5, 31, 31.5, and 32 into cells A2–A5.
3. Place the pointer into cell B2; then click the **Function Wizard (*fx*)** > **Statistical** > **NORMDIST** > **OK.** (By using the alternative **NORMDIST** command, without the **S** in

the middle, you indicate that you want to provide your own values of μ and σ.)

4. In the NORMDIST dialog box, type **30.5** under *x* and press TAB.
5. Under *Mean,* type **32** and press TAB.
6. Under *Standard dev,* type **.5** and press TAB.
7. Under *Cumulative,* type **1** and click **OK** to get your first answer in cell B2.
8. Repeat Steps 3–7 for the other *x* values, making appropriate changes in Steps 3 and 4.

(*Tip:* To speed things up, you can also enter A2 instead of 30.5 in Step 4, then drag the cell B2 result to B5.)

The result is as follows:

x	probability
30.5	0.001349967
31	0.022750062
31.5	0.15865526
32	0.5

Before interpreting the output, remember that EXCEL always prints out area values from $-\infty$ to the specified *x*. Therefore, the first probability value of **.00134** corresponds to area D in the graph. The second value of .02275, however, equals D + C, making area C equal to **.0214.** The third value of .158655 equals D + C + B, making area B equal to **.1359.** The fourth value of .5 equals D + C + B + A, making area A equal to **.3413.**

10.6 Using the Normal Probability Distribution to Approximate Discrete Probability Distributions

Even though the normal probability distribution deals with continuous variables, under certain circumstances we can use it to *approximate* various discrete probability distributions. This use of the normal probability distribution is convenient whenever the calculation of precise discrete probabilities is particularly cumbersome—presumably because we do not have a computer at hand. As the following sections will show, the circumstances that make normal probabilities closely resemble probabilities of discrete random variables are these:

- in the case of binomial probabilities, n is large or π is close to .5
  [Rule of thumb: $n\,\pi \geq 5$ and also $n\,(1 - \pi) \geq 5$.]
- in the case of Poisson probabilities, $\mu > 20$
- in the case of hypergeometric probabilities, n is large or $\pi = (S/N)$ is close to .5
  [Rule of thumb: $n\,\pi \geq 5$ and also $n\,(1 - \pi) \geq 5$.]

APPROXIMATING BINOMIAL PROBABILITIES

Binomial probability tables typically do not extend to large values of n (numbers of trials of a random experiment), or they may not cover a given value of π (the probability of success in one trial). Appendix Table C, for example, contains no section for $n = 50$, nor does the more detailed table from which it is derived. Similarly, neither Appendix Table C, nor its source, contains a column for $\pi = .255$. To establish the probabilities for an experiment involving these numbers without a computer, you would have to go through the type of cumbersome calculations illustrated in Table 9.5 on page 349, using binomial Formula 9.D. Luckily, under some circumstances the normal probability distribution gives almost identical results. Such results can be obtained whenever the value of n is large or whenever that of π is close to .5. It is easy to see why this similarity in results occurs by having another look at Figure 9.3 on page 351: Regardless of the value of π, as n increases, a binomial probability distribution becomes less and less skewed and, thus, looks more and more like the symmetrical normal probability distribution. Furthermore, whenever $\pi = .5$, any binomial probability distribution is perfectly symmetrical regardless of the value of n. (Just look at the three graphs in the central column of Figure 9.3.)

THE RULE OF THUMB It is a matter of arbitrary judgment which combination of n and π makes a binomial probability distribution "sufficiently" symmetrical to justify the use of the normal curve as an approximation to it. According to one widely used rule of thumb, the normal-curve approximation can be used without undue loss of accuracy whenever

$$n\,\pi \geq 5 \quad \text{and also} \quad n\,(1 - \pi) \geq 5$$

Once you decide to substitute normal for binomial probabilities, you can discover the relevant probabilities quickly. Three simple steps are involved:

Step 1: Continuity Correction. Because the probability of a single x value, such as precisely 11 successes in so many trials, is theoretically zero for a continuous distribution (the area under the normal curve above a single point on the horizontal axis is mathematically zero), you must convert the discrete value of x into a small *range* of x by subtracting and adding half the distance between the discrete values to any one value of x. This so-called *continuity correction factor* turns a discrete 11 into a range of 10.5 to 11.5, for example. It also turns a discrete "11 or larger" into a range of "10.5 or more," while replacing a discrete "11 or fewer" with "11.5 or less." This correction having been made, you must transform the new continuous x value into a z value.

Step 2: Finding the z Value. You must apply Formula 10.B to find the standard normal deviate, while noting that the binomial $\mu = n\pi$ (Formula 9.E) and the binomial $\sigma = \sqrt{n\pi(1 - \pi)}$ (Formula 9.G). Hence,

$$z = \frac{x - \mu}{\sigma} = \frac{x - (n\pi)}{\sqrt{n\pi(1 - \pi)}}$$

Step 3: Finding the Probability. Given a z value, you can look up the associated probability in Appendix Table H.

EXAMPLE PROBLEM 10.5

Consider a company that has experienced 25.5 percent errors in its invoices. It takes a random sample (with replacement) of 50 invoices.

a. What is the probability that exactly 11 of the sample invoices are in error?

SOLUTION: You could calculate the precise probability with binomial Formula 9.D:

$$p(X = 11|50, .255) = \frac{50!}{11!(50 - 11)!} \times (.255)^{11} \times (.745)^{39} = .1144$$

You can also note that $\mu = n\pi = 50(.255) = 12.75$, while $\sigma = \sqrt{n\pi(1 - \pi)} = \sqrt{50(.255)(.745)} = \sqrt{9.49875} = 3.082$. Accordingly, you can picture the problem as shown in Figure 10.18.

The binomial value of 11 appears as the range from 10.5 to 11.5, and the corresponding z values equal $-.73$ and $-.41$. Accordingly, Appendix Table H gives the desired probability as the shaded area in Figure 10.18. It equals the dotted plus shaded areas corresponding to $z = -.73$ (or .2673) minus the dotted area corresponding to $z = -.41$ (or .1591), which comes to .1082. This value equals 94.6 percent of the correct value of .1144 and, thus, lies within 5.4 percent of it.

FIGURE 10.18

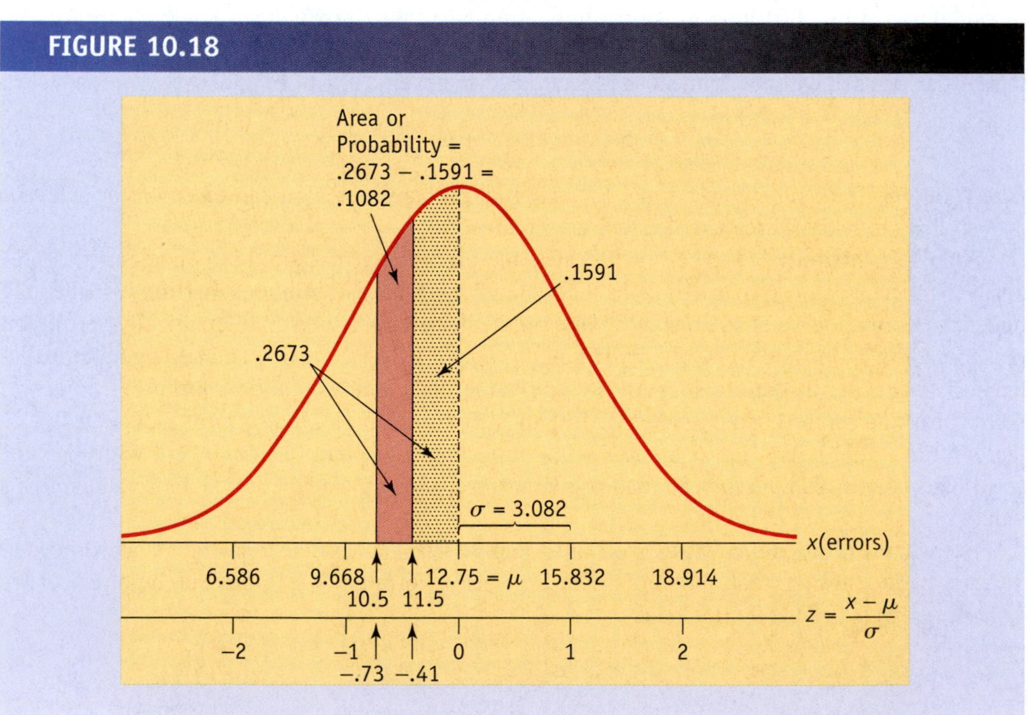

b. What is the probability of finding 13 or fewer errors?

SOLUTION: You can use the same procedure as in section (a), as shown in Figure 10.19.

The binomial value of 13 or fewer appears as "13.5 or less." The corresponding z value equals $+.24$. Accordingly, Appendix Table H gives the probability of the shaded area as .0948. The desired probability (crosshatched plus shaded areas), therefore, is approximated by .5948.

FIGURE 10.19

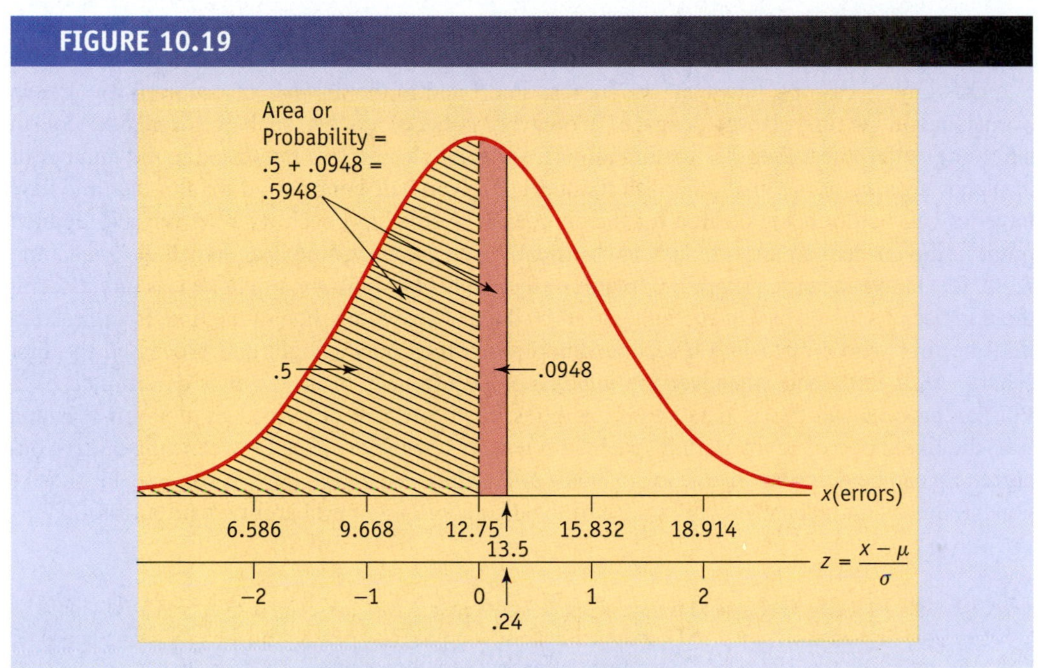

APPROXIMATING POISSON PROBABILITIES

As the value of μ in the Poisson probability distribution increases, the distribution becomes ever less skewed and approaches the shape of the normal distribution. Thus, for values of $\mu > 20$, which cannot be found in Appendix Table F, you can use the normal probability distribution to approximate Poisson probabilities. Just follow steps 1–3 noted in the previous section. Naturally, the appropriate summary measures of μ and σ must be calculated according to Poisson Formulas 9.I–9.K before z values are determined.

APPROXIMATING HYPERGEOMETRIC PROBABILITIES

Just as the normal probability distribution can be used to approximate the binomial, so it can also be used to approximate the hypergeometric. Approximations are best when n is large and $\pi = (S/N)$ is close to .5. Once more, just follow steps 1–3 noted above. When computing z values, make sure to use appropriate summary measures of μ and σ that have been determined with hypergeometric Formulas 9.M–9.O.

10.7 The Exponential Probability Distribution

Chapter 9 described how the Poisson probability distribution provides probabilities for x occurrences, in a segment of time or space, of a specified type of event. The applications, we noted, range widely: The Poisson formula and the tables derived from it give us the likelihood, for any specified period of *time,* of any specified number of people arriving at the bank, the hospital emergency room, or the airline ticket counter, or the likelihood of the arrival of specified numbers of cars at the car wash, of ships at the dock, of orders at the warehouse, of claims at the insurance company—the list goes on. The formula also gives us the likelihood of encountering, within any specified *space,* any specified number of events, be they defects on a role of wire, leaks in a pipeline, potholes in a road, or errors on a page.

On some occasions, however, we are less interested in the *number* of occurrences of such events than in the time elapsed or space encountered *between* any two such occurrences. Pilots in a holding pattern near their destination airport, for example, are less interested in the number of airplanes arriving at the final approach fix during a given half-hour period than in the time they have to wait before being cleared for the approach. (A final approach fix is a precisely defined point in the air near an airport, such as "vertically over an electronic beacon called *Romeo* and 1,700 feet above mean sea level.") Captains of fishing fleets, similarly, might be less interested in the number of schools of fish encountered in 10 days of searching than in the time it will take to find the first school or to find a second school once they have caught and processed the first school. As it turns out, whenever the *number* of occurrences of an event is determined by a Poisson process and the associated probabilities, therefore, are described by Poisson Formula 9.H, the likelihood of encountering specified *intervals* of time or space between consecutive occurrences can be described by the *exponential probability distribution.* So in some sense, the exponential is a continuous "mirror" image of the discrete Poisson probability distribution.

DEFINITION 10.5 The uncertain time or space between any two consecutive events in a Poisson process is called an **exponential random variable.** A probability density function for such intervals of time or space is called an **exponential probability distribution.** This distribution applies (1) only to positive values of x and (2) only to situations in which smaller values of x are more likely than larger values.

A GRAPHICAL EXPOSITION

Consider the three panels of Figure 10.20.

PANEL (a) The horizontal line in panel (a) pictures a continuum of time during which a Poisson process, such as the arrival of planes at a final approach fix, is occurring. The random arrival of planes is indicated by the placement of the red dots. The number of arrivals in each of four intervals of, say, 10 minutes can be determined by merely counting the dots within these intervals. Clearly, within the four time intervals shown, the mean number of plane arrivals is

$$\lambda = \frac{2 + 1 + 2 + 3}{4} = 2 \text{ planes per 10-minute interval}$$

Panel (a) also shows, however, the precise timing of the arrivals. Thus, the first plane that arrives within the 40-minute period between the first and last vertical line arrives at the end of the 6th minute, the second plane arrives at the end of the 8th minute, and so on, with the last plane arriving at the end of the 40th minute. The *interarrival times,* or the time gaps between the arrival times of the planes, have been indicated by the values of x_1, x_2, and so on. These values represent the exponential random variable, the uncertain time or space between any two successive events in a Poisson process.

For the 40-minute period just considered, the mean interarrival time equals $x_1 + x_2 + \ldots + x_8$, divided by 8, which comes to

$$\mu_x = \frac{6 + 2 + 7 + 12 + 2 + 2 + 4 + 5}{8} = \frac{40}{8} = 5 \text{ minutes between planes}$$

FIGURE 10.20 | Poisson Distribution versus Exponential Distribution

The Poisson probability distribution associates probabilities with numbers of occurrences of some event, shown by the red dots in panel (a), within specified intervals of time or space. The exponential distribution instead associates probabilities with the various gaps, shown by the values of x_1 to x_8 in panel (a), ***between*** *the Poisson events. The frequency of occurrence of different-sized gaps can be depicted by a histogram, as in panel (b) or by a smooth frequency curve, as in panel (c). Inevitably, the mean size of these gaps equals the reciprocal, 1/λ, of the Poisson process rate, λ. If, on the average, planes arrive at a rate of .38 per minute, as they might during a more extended period of observation than panel (a) indicates, the average gap between arriving planes is 1/.38 or 2.63 minutes.*

(a)

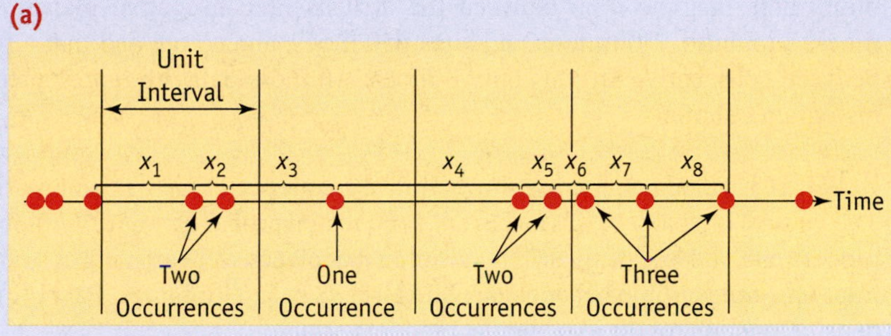

(b)

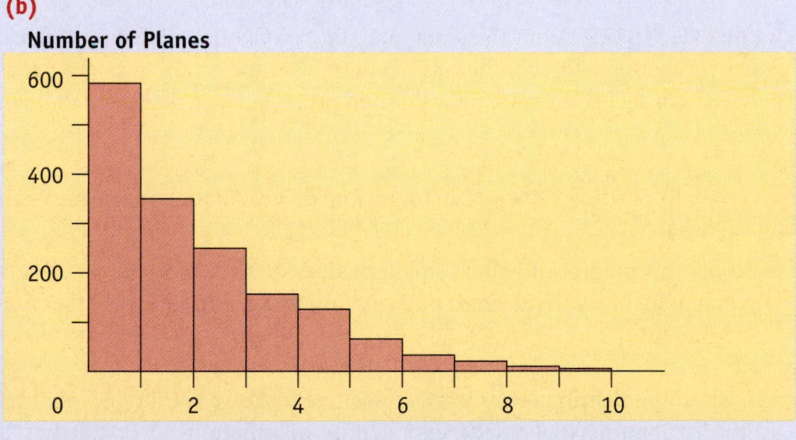

(c)

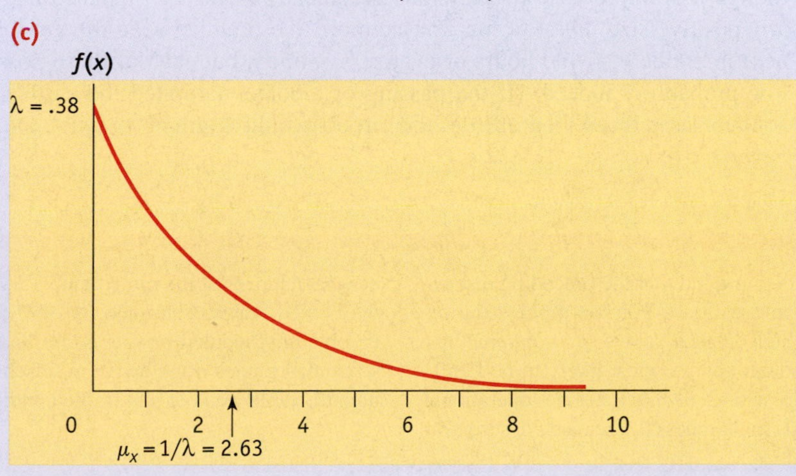

It is no accident that this number equals $1/\lambda$. If, on the average, $\lambda = 2$ planes arrive per 10-minute interval, then, on the average, 10 minutes elapse per 2 arriving planes, which is the same thing as 5 minutes per plane. Thus, the mean of the exponential random variable, μ_x, always equals $1/\lambda$, where λ is the Poisson process rate. (The standard deviation of the exponential random variable, σ_x, also equals $1/\lambda$, which differs from the case of the Poisson random variable, the *variance* of which equals its mean.)

PANEL (b) Panel (b) of Figure 10.20 pictures the type of histogram we can expect to find if the arrival of planes is a Poisson process and if we record the frequency of various interarrival times over an extended period. After studying the arrivals of 1,603 planes, for example, we might note that the time between the arrivals of consecutive planes equaled 1 minute 586 times, 2 minutes 350 times, 3 minutes 250 times, and so on, and that a full 10 minutes elapsed between consecutive arrivals only 3 times. All these data are represented by the heights of the histogram columns.

PANEL (c) Panel (c), finally, shows how a frequency curve can summarize the histogram data. The vertical intercept of this and every exponential probability density function equals the Poisson process rate, λ. Here it equals .38, meaning that planes were arriving at a rate of .38 per minute and implying a mean time between arrivals of 1/.38 or 2.63 minutes. Panel (c) shows the probability density function for the exponential random variable.

GENERAL NOTES As in this example, all exponential probability distributions are probability density functions for continuous random variables that measure intervals of time or space between consecutive events in a Poisson process. Note that the exponential distribution always applies:

- only to positive values of x (for example, we cannot have negative times between plane arrivals)
- only to situations in which smaller values of x are more likely than larger values (for example, interarrival times of 2 or 5 minutes are more likely then interarrival times of 2 or 5 months)

Thus, the distribution is always positively skewed. Like the right tail of the normal probability distribution, that of the exponential distribution never touches the horizontal axis (although it is impractical to show this graphically). This fact means that, theoretically, a gap of *any* positive size might occur. For example, the time between the arrival of one plane and the next might be $x = 400$ hours or even $x =$ infinity, but each of these possibilities carries a very low probability indeed. (If the passing of a comet saturated the earth's atmosphere with poisonous gases that killed all life, the airport would continue to exist, but the next plane would *never* arrive.)

Keep in mind that the preceding discussion assumes a Poisson process during which planes arrive at *random.* Although you are most likely to be familiar with *scheduled* airline operations, this randomness is a realistic description of what happens at the more than 7,000 landing facilities in the United States. The majority of U.S. airport operations involve unscheduled private and military planes, but even scheduled planes often arrive at unscheduled times due to unpredictable weather and traffic conditions.

THE FORMULAS

Depending only on the size of λ, the Poisson process rate, we can create many different members of the exponential probability distribution family. Each one looks similar to the probability density function given in panel (c) of Figure 10.20. The larger λ is, the smaller $\mu_x = \sigma_x$ is and the less spread out the distribution. In all cases, however, we will be interested in one of two things:

- the precise *height* of the exponential probability density function (which allows us to draw the curve with accuracy)
- the *area* under the (properly drawn) exponential curve for any given range of x values (which allows us to determine the probability of encountering that range of x values)

THE HEIGHT We can determine *height* of the exponential probability density function, $f(x)$, for different values, x, of the exponential random variable, X, with the help of Formula 10.D.

FORMULA 10.D | The Exponential Probability Density Function

$$f(x) = \lambda e^{-\lambda x}$$

where x is any value of the exponential random variable, λ is the Poisson process rate, $x > 0$ and $\lambda > 0$, and $e \cong 2.71828$.

Naturally, λ and x must refer to the same units. If λ is expressed per minute, x must be measured in minutes, not seconds or hours. If x is to be measured in units of 100,000 hours, the value of λ likewise must represent occurrences per 100,000 hours. Beyond that, as in the Poisson formula and in the normal probability density function, the constant e appears; it equals approximately 2.71828.

Because the mean interval between events, μ_x, equals $1/\lambda$, we can substitute $1/\mu_x$ for λ in all exponential formulas. Some texts do; the results are identical.

THE AREA As was true in the case of the normal curve, the total area under the exponential probability density function equals 1, and various probabilities can be found by focusing on areas under this curve for different ranges of the exponential random variable. The area under the exponential probability density function to the *right* of a given value, x, of the exponential random variable is given by Formula 10.E. On the other hand, the area to the *left* of a given value of the exponential random variable (that is, the area between zero and x) is represented by Formula 10.F. These two formulas imply that we can find the area *between* two positive values of this random variable, x_1 and x_2, by deducting from the total area (which equals 1) the area to the right of the upper limit of this range (the area to the right of x_2) as well as the area to the left of the lower limit of this range (the area to the left of x_1), as stated in Formula 10.G.

FORMULA 10.E | Greater-Than Cumulative Exponential Probabilities

$$p(X > x) = e^{-\lambda x} = e^{-\frac{x}{\mu_x}}$$

FORMULA 10.F | Less-Than Cumulative Exponential Probabilities

$$p(X < x) = 1 - e^{-\lambda x} = 1 - e^{-\frac{x}{\mu_x}}$$

FORMULA 10.G | Combination Formula for Exponential Probabilities

$$p(x_1 < X < x_2) = 1 - [e^{-\lambda x_2} + (1 - e^{-\lambda x_1})] = e^{-\lambda x_1} - e^{-\lambda x_2}$$

where x is any value of exponential random variable X, the mean of these values is μ_x, λ is the Poisson process rate, and $e \cong 2.71828$.

EXAMPLE PROBLEM 10.6

Consider a Poisson process in which $\lambda = 4$ planes per hour arrive at a fix. This makes $\mu_x = 1/4$, meaning that the average gap between consecutive arrivals equals 1/4 hour.

a. What is the probability for interarrival times in excess of 1/4 hour?

SOLUTION: Formula 10.E applies; hence,

$$p(X > 1/4) = e^{-4(1/4)} = e^{-1}$$

Appendix Table E, normally used in connection with the Poisson formula, can be used again by simply treating the column labeled μ as if it referred to our exponent, λx, while reading the column labeled $e^{-\mu}$ as if it read $e^{-\lambda x}$. We find, accordingly, that $e^{-1} = .367879$, which is the probability sought.

b. Picture the solution to (a) graphically.

SOLUTION: We can picture the part (a) result as shown in Figure 10.21.

We can use Formula 10.D to calculate the height of the exponential density function above various values of x, given $\lambda = 4$. Thus,

when $x = 0$: $f(x) = 4e^{-4(0)} = 4e^0 = 4$

when $x = .25$: $f(x) = 4e^{-4(.25)} = 4e^{-1} = \frac{4}{e^1} = \frac{4}{2.71828} = 1.47$

when $x = .50$: $f(x) = 4e^{-4(.50)} = 4e^{-2} = \frac{4}{e^2} = \frac{4}{7.38905} = .54$

when $x = .75$: $f(x) = 4e^{-4(.75)} = 4e^{-3} = \frac{4}{e^3} = \frac{4}{20.08550} = .20$

FIGURE 10.21

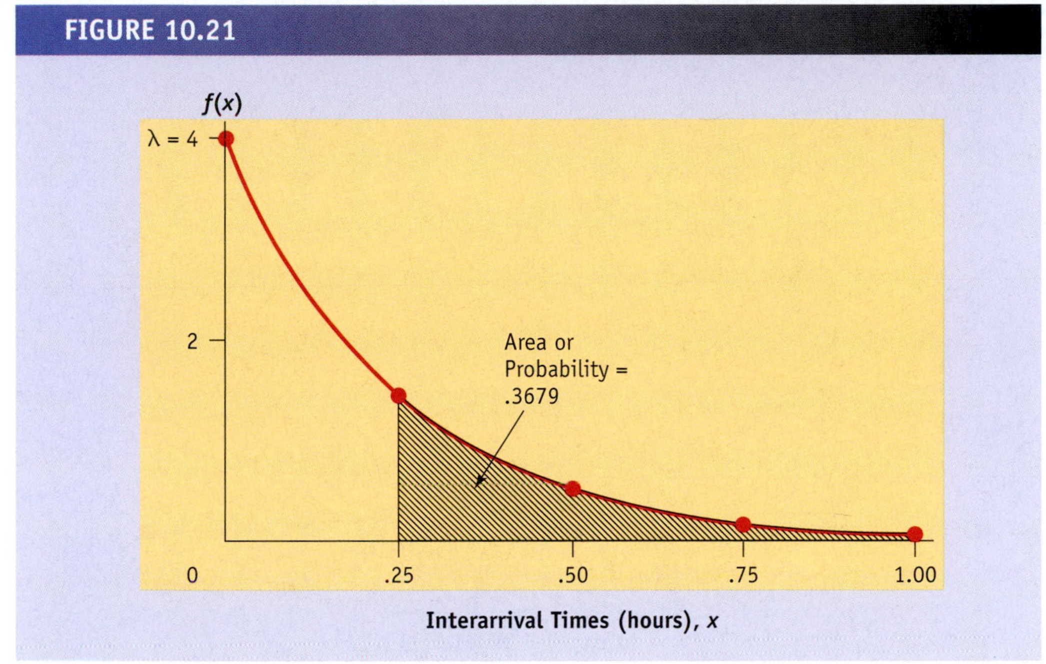

when $x = 1.00$: $\quad f(x) = 4e^{-4(1)} = 4e^{-4} = \dfrac{4}{e^4} = \dfrac{4}{54.59800} = .07$

These values are plotted as the five red dots in Figure 10.21. The probability calculated in part (a) above corresponds, in turn, to the crosshatched area of the graph.

c. What is the probability of interarrival times below 1/10 hour?

SOLUTION: Formula 10.F applies. With the help of Appendix Table E, we find

$$p(X < 1/10) = 1 - e^{-4(1/10)} = 1 - e^{-.4} = 1 - .670320 = .32968$$

We can find this solution graphically as well, as shown in Figure 10.22 on the next page. In this case, the probability sought (crosshatched area) equals the total area under the curve (1.0000) minus the yellow area (of .6703).

d. What is the probability for interarrival times between 1/10 hour and 1/4 hour (that is, between 6 and 15 minutes)?

SOLUTION: Formula 10.G applies. With the help of Appendix Table E, we find

$$p(1/10 < X < 1/4) = e^{-4(1/10)} - e^{-4(1/4)} = e^{-.4} - e^{-1} = .670320 - .367879 = .302441$$

This solution is shown graphically by the crosshatched area in Figure 10.23. Note that the desired probability equals the difference between the yellow area below the Figure 10.22 curve and the crosshatched area in Figure 10.21. It is no accident that the three crosshatched areas in Figures 10.21, 10.22, and 10.23 add precisely to 1.0000. It is inevitable that airplanes arrive in intervals of either more than .25 hour *or* less than .10 hour *or* something in between.

FIGURE 10.22

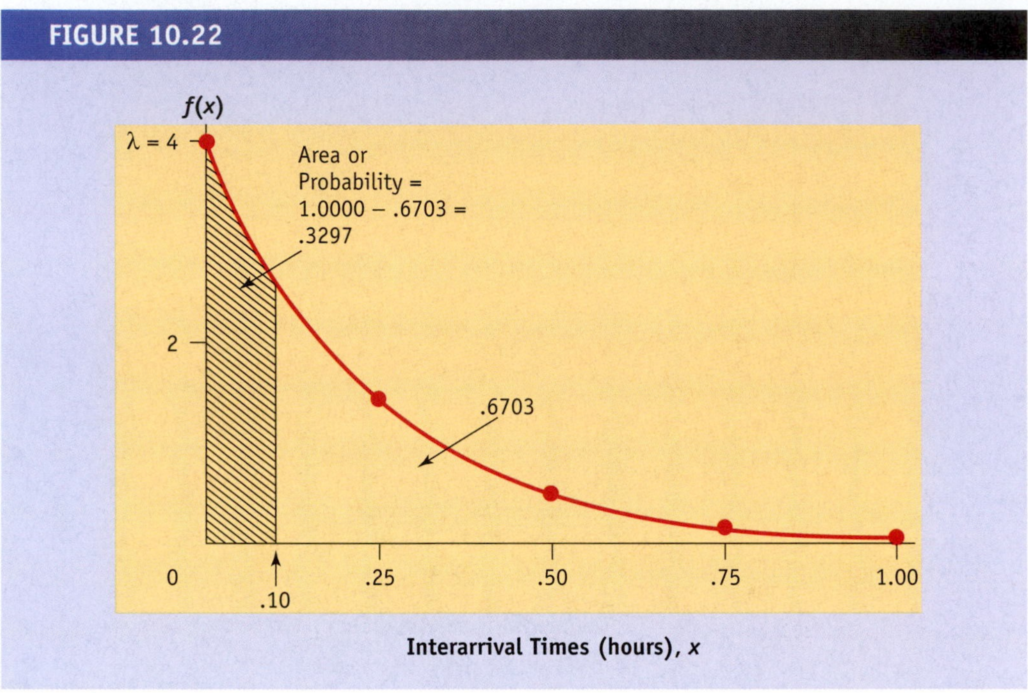

FIGURE 10.23

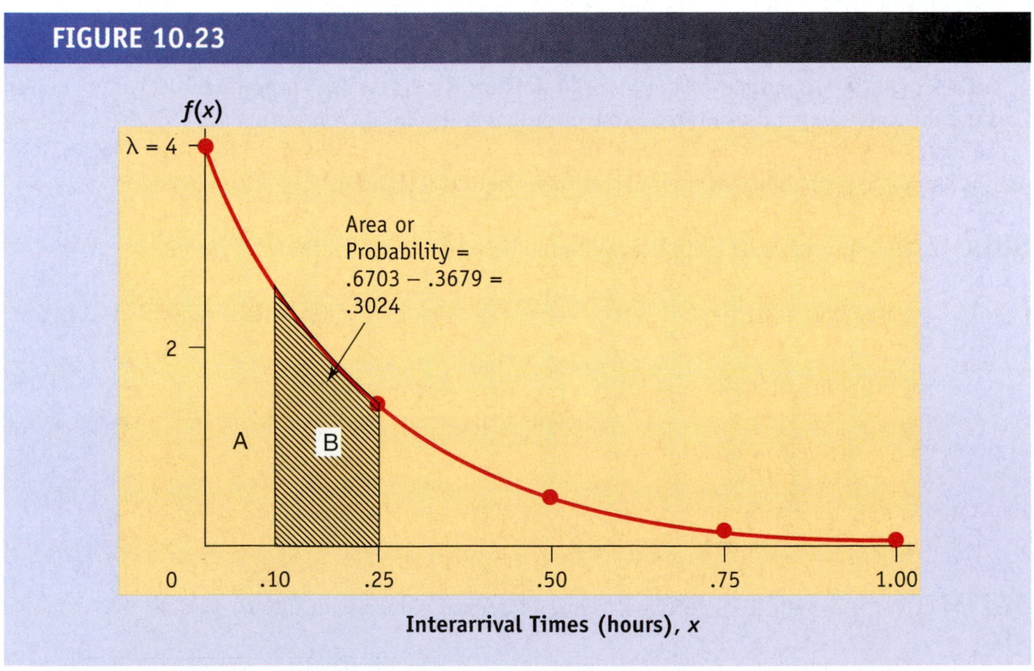

10.8 Exponential Probability Tables

As with most of the probability distributions discussed thus far, various types of exponential probability tables provide already computed values, making it unnecessary to apply any of the above formulas. Appendix Table I, an excerpt of which appears as Table 10.3 here, contains exponential probabilities for cumulative values of x, computed with the help of Formula 10.F.

In Appendix Table I, the value of λx is split in two. A first portion, including the first decimal, is shown in the leftmost column of that table, while a second decimal of λx is found in one of the 10 entries in the table's top row. By *adding together* any given row heading with any given column heading, we can reconstruct a λx value with two decimal places.

Thus, a row heading of .2 and a column heading of .03, here shown in red, corresponds to a λx value of $.2 + .03 = .23$. At the intersection of the .2 row and the .03 column, we find, accordingly, the area under the curve between 0 and x and this area value, also shown in red, equals .2055. This means there is a 20.55 percent chance that the value of the exponential random variable equals x or less.

EXAMPLE PROBLEM 10.7

Review Example Problem 10.6. Confirm the answers displayed in its three graphs with the help of Appendix Table I.

SOLUTION:

a. The probability of interarrival times in excess of 1/4 hour, depicted in Figure 10.21, equals 1 minus the probability (found in Appendix Table I) of interarrival times below 1/4 hour.

TABLE 10.3 | Appendix Table I Excerpt: Exponential Probabilities for Cumulative Values of x

Entries in this table give the area under the curve between zero and x.

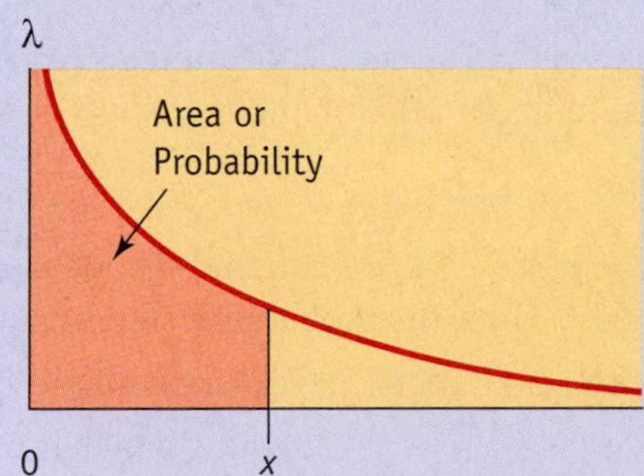

λx	.00	.01	.02	.03	.04	.05	.06	.07	.08	.09
0.0	0.0000	0.0100	0.0198	0.0296	0.0392	0.0488	0.0582	0.0676	0.0769	0.0861
0.1	0.0952	0.1042	0.1131	0.1219	0.1306	0.1393	0.1479	0.1563	0.1647	0.1730
0.2	0.1813	0.1894	0.1975	0.2055	0.2134	0.2212	0.2289	0.2366	0.2442	0.2517
0.3	0.2592	0.2666	0.2739	0.2811	0.2882	0.2953	0.3023	0.3093	0.3161	0.3229
0.4	0.3297	0.3363	0.3430	0.3495	0.3560	0.3624	0.3687	0.3750	0.3812	0.3874

Entering the table at the $\lambda x = 4(1/4) = 1.0$ row (and in the .00 column because the second decimal here is 0 as well), we find .6321. Deducting this value from 1, we get .3679, as in Figure 10.21.

b. The probability of interarrival times below 1/10 hour can be read directly from Appendix Table I (because it shows areas under the curve between 0 and some positive value of x). Entering the table at $\lambda x = 4(1/10) = .4$ (and again in the .00 column), we find .3297, as in Figure 10.22.

c. The probability of interarrival times between 1/10 and 1/4 hour must be read from Appendix Table I as the area between 0 and .25 *minus* the area between 0 and .10. In Figure 10.23, this difference comes to (A + B) minus A. Thus, we enter the table at $\lambda x = 4(.25) = 1$ (and find .6321) and again at $\lambda x = 4(.10) = .4$ (and find .3297). The difference, $.6321 - .3297$, equals .3024, as illustrated by crosshatched area B in Figure 10.23.

EXAMPLE PROBLEM 10.8

Manufacturers of all kinds of products—ranging from aircraft navigation equipment to automobile batteries, from simple lightbulbs to nuclear reactors, from home sound systems to satellite power cells—must be keenly interested in the mean length of time that elapses before their product fails, or in the average time between a first failure and another failure. Anybody about to offer a guarantee to customers, for example, will view this knowledge as crucial, indeed. Consider a manufacturer of aircraft distance-measuring equipment (DME). Experience might show that failures of DME units can be described by a Poisson process and that a unit fails on the average 4 times per 100,000 hours of use. The manufacturer may want to know:

a. the probability that a unit will operate without failure in excess of 50,000 hours.

b. the probability that a unit will operate without failure for up to 20,000 hours.

c. the required mean time between failures (often referred to as MTBF) before one can safely assume that 90 percent of all units will perform without failure in excess of 25,000 hours.

SOLUTION: The value of λ equals 4 failures per 100,000 hours. Thus, the failure times must be measured in units of 100,000 hours as well—that is, as .5 in (a), as .2 in (b), and as .25 in (c).

a. $p(X > .5) = 1 - p(X < .5)$. We can find the latter expression in Appendix Table I for $\lambda x = 4(.5) = 2$ as .8647. Thus, the probability sought equals $1 - .8647 = .1353$.

b. We can find $p(X < .2)$ directly in Appendix Table I for $\lambda x = 4(.2) = .8$ as .5507.

c. The answer requires that $p(X > .25) = .9$, which is equivalent (according to Formula 10.F) to $e^{-\lambda x} = .9$. From Appendix Table E, we can see that $e^{-\lambda x}$ equals .90 (rounded) when $\lambda x = .10$. Given $x = .25$, λ must equal .10/.25, or .4 failures per 100,000 hours. Since the MTBF equals $1/\lambda$, the answer is 1/.4, or 2.5 (units of 100,000 hours). Only when the mean time between failures has been raised from the current 25,000 hours (implied by 4 failures per 100,000 hours) to 250,000 hours can the manufacturer rely on 90 percent of all units performing without failure in excess of 25,000 hours.

We can check the answer to (c) with the help of Appendix Table I. If there were only .4 failures per 100,000 hours, we could find the probability of a time between failures in excess of 25,000 hours, as in answer (a) above, by consulting Appendix Table I for $\lambda x = .4\ (.25) = .1$ and subtracting the value found (.0952) from 1. The result is .9048. In this case, the probability would be slightly above .9 that no failures would occur prior to 25,000 hours of use.

EXAMPLE PROBLEM 10.9

An airport manager may justly worry about the possible loss of crucial approach, runway, and taxiway lighting as a result of a power blackout. The airport may have a standby generator, but it would also be subject to failure, having a mean time between failures (MTBF) of 100 hours. The manager may ask:

a. What is the probability of the standby generator failing during the next 12-hour blackout?

b. What is the probability of two such generators failing during such a blackout, assuming that the two generators operate independently of each other?

c. If the airport experienced 5 blackouts from its main power source in a year, what are the chances that a single standby generator would work through them all?

d. How would those chances look with a second backup or even a third?

SOLUTION: Since the MTBF of 100 hours equals $1/\lambda$, the value of $\lambda = .01$ (failure per hour).

a. The first question asks about $p(X \leq 12)$, which we can find directly in Appendix Table I for $\lambda x = .01(12) = .12$ as .1131.

b. We can use the answer derived in (a) and then apply the special multiplication law for independent events. (See Formula 8.J on page 319.) The probability of two such independent generators failing would equal $(.1131)^2 = .0128$.

c. We can use the answer derived in (a) and then pursue it further with binomial Formula 9.D (on page 346). Given $n = 5$ and a success probability of $\pi = 1 - .1131 = .8869$,

$$p(X = 5|n = 5, \pi = .8869) = \frac{5!}{5!0!} \times (.8869)^5 \times (.1131)^0 = .5487$$

The manager may not like this rather low probability.

d. We can use the answers derived in (a) and (b) and then pursue them further with binomial Formula 9.D (on page 346).

For 2 backups and a success probability of $\pi = 1 - .0128 = .9872$,

$$p(X = 5|n = 5, \pi = .9872) = \frac{5!}{5!0!} \times (.9872)^5 \times (.0128)^0 = .9376$$

For 3 backups, the probability of failure would be $(.1131)^3 = .0014$. Hence, the probability of at least one of them working through all 5 blackouts would be

$$p(X = 5|n = 5, \pi = .0014) = \frac{5!}{5!0!} \times (.9986)^5 \times (.0014)^0 = .9930$$

Note: The same type of reasoning is being applied to a multitude of similar situations that call for a high degree of reliability: the communications of air traffic control centers, power supplies to hospital surgical units or satellites, and more.

10.9 Exponential Probabilities and Computer Programs

Computer programs such as EXCEL or MINITAB allow us to work all sorts of exponential probability problems without the use of Appendix Tables E and I. The following examples show how they can help us find:

- the height of the exponential curve for specified values of x
- areas under the exponential curve for specified ranges of x

EXCEL Example 10.5

Using EXCEL, compute the height of the exponential probability density function pictured in Figure 10.21 (on page 427) for each of the five x values shown there.

SOLUTION

1. Fire up EXCEL and enter the labels **x** and **f(x),** respectively, into cells A1 and B1.
2. Enter numbers 0, .25, .50, .75, and 1 into cells A2–A6.
3. Place the pointer into cell B2; then click the **Function Wizard (*fx*)** > **Statistical** > **EXPONDIST** > **OK.**
4. In the dialog box, type **0** under x and press TAB.
5. Under *Lambda,* type **4** and press TAB.
6. Under *Cumulative,* type **0** and click **OK**.
7. Repeat Steps 3–6 for the other x values, making appropriate changes in Steps 3 and 4.

The result is as follows:

x	f(x)
0	4
0.25	1.471517765
0.5	0.541341133
0.75	0.199148273
1	0.073262556

EXCEL Example 10.6

According to Appendix Table I, the area under the exponential probability density function associated with $\lambda = 4$ and $x = .25$ and, thus, with $\lambda x = 1$ is equal to .6321. This is also the unshaded area in Figure 10.21 on page 427. Confirm with EXCEL.

SOLUTION

1. Fire up EXCEL and enter the labels **x** and **area,** respectively, into cells A1 and B1.
2. Enter **.25** into cell A2.
3. Place the pointer into cell B2; then click the **Function Wizard** (*fx*) > **Statistical** > **EXPONDIST** > **OK.**
4. In the dialog box, type **.25** under *x* and press TAB.
5. Under *Lambda,* type **4** and press TAB.
6. Under *Cumulative,* type **1** and click **OK.**

The result is as follows:

x	area
0.25	0.632121

(*Tip:* If you want area or probability values for several *x* values, you can speed things up by entering A2 instead of .25 in Step 4 and then dragging the cell B2 result down column B.)

10.10 The Uniform Probability Distribution

We now turn to a continuous random variable that is undoubtedly the simplest because it assumes any value within a specified range with equal likelihood:

DEFINITION 10.6 A **uniform random variable** has an equal chance of assuming any value within a specified range along a continuous scale. A probability density function for a random variable that is equally likely to take on any of the values within a given range is called a **uniform probability distribution.**

Consider the dial on a wheel of fortune that is equally likely to point to any one of various segments of the circle after being spun. Consider the arrival time of a bus, plane, or train that is equally likely to occur at any time in a 20-minute period. The same may be true about the ripening time of a crop, the random decimals generated by a computer, the daily sales of a wholesaler, the rate of inflation next year, next week's demand for electricity, or the time it takes to process a loan application. In all these cases and many more, the probability of any actual value may well be the same anywhere within a specified range.

A GRAPHICAL EXPOSITION

Figure 10.24 on the next page pictures two members of the uniform probability distribution family. For reasons noted in the caption, each of these distributions can also be called a **rectangular probability distribution.**

FIGURE 10.24 | Two Members of the Uniform Probability Distribution Family

A uniformly distributed random variable has an equal chance of assuming any value within a specified range, ab, along a continuous scale. When graphed, the probability density function is seen to be a rectangle; this probability distribution, therefore, is also called the ***rectangular probability distribution.***

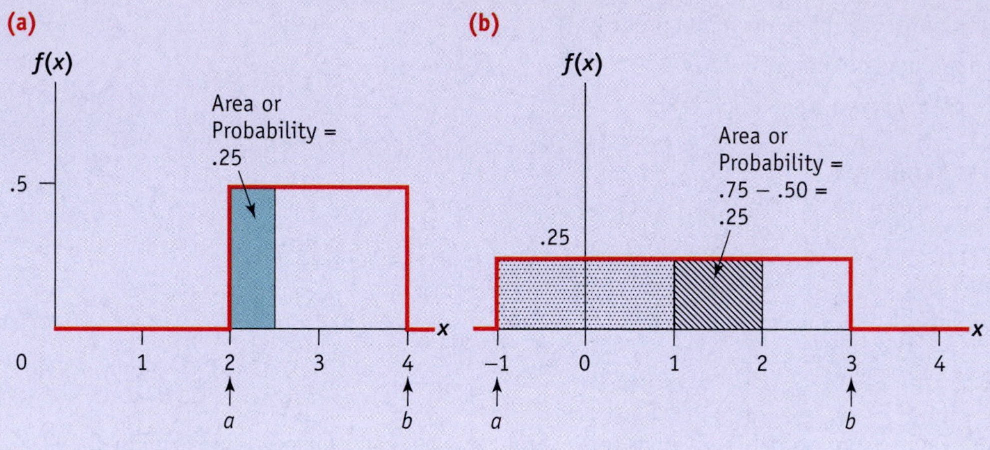

THE FORMULAS

Once again, we are interested in one of two things:

- the precise *height* of the uniform probability density function (which allows us to draw the function with accuracy)
- the *area* under the (properly drawn) uniform function for any given range of x values (which allows us to determine the probability of encountering that range of x values)

THE HEIGHT We can determine the precise *height* of the uniform probability density function with the help of Formula 10.H.

FORMULA 10.H | The Uniform Probability Density Function

$$f(x) = \frac{1}{b - a} \text{ if } a < x < b; \text{ otherwise, } f(x) = 0$$

where x is a value of the uniform random variable, while a is the lower and b is the upper limit of possible x values.

The uniform probability density function, this formula tells us, is a horizontal line segment of constant height, $1/(b - a)$, over the interval from a to b. Because values of the random variable below a and above b are impossible, $f(x) = 0$ outside the segment from a to b. In panel (a) of Figure 10.24, for example, the lowest possible value, x, of the random variable is $a = 2$, and the highest possible value is $b = 4$. According to Formula 10.H, the height of the probability density function within this range equals

$$f(x) = \frac{1}{b - a} = \frac{1}{4 - 2} = \frac{1}{2} = .5$$

We similarly calculate the height of the density function in panel (b), within the range of $a = -1$ and $b = 3$, as

$$f(x) = \frac{1}{b - a} = \frac{1}{3 - (-1)} = \frac{1}{4} = .25$$

Note how, in both cases, $f(x) = 0$ outside the range from a to b. Note also that the total area under the probability function once again equals 1: The rectangle's base times height equals $2 \times (.5) = 1$ in panel (a) and $4 \times (.25) = 1$ in panel (b).

AREAS Once again, we measure probability by the area above the interval of x values that is of interest. Cumulating x values from left to right, we derive Formula 10.I.

FORMULA 10.I | Less-Than Cumulative Uniform Probabilities

$$\text{if } a < x < b\text{:} \quad p(X < x) = \frac{x - a}{b - a}$$

$$\text{if } x < a\text{:} \quad p(X < x) = 0$$

$$\text{if } x > b\text{:} \quad p(X < x) = 1$$

where x is a value of the uniform random variable, while a is the lower and b is the upper limit of possible x values.

In panel (a) of Figure 10.24, for example, the probability of x lying between the lower limit of $a = 2$ and a value of 2.5 equals the area shaded in teal:

$$p(X < 2.5) = \frac{x - a}{b - a} = \frac{2.5 - 2}{4 - 2} = \frac{.5}{2} = .25$$

This probability implies a probability of $1 - .25 = .75$ for x between 2.5 and 4 (the light blue area underneath the red line in the graph).

In panel (b) of Figure 10.24, similarly, the probability of x lying between 1 and 2 equals the crosshatched area. This probability can be calculated as the dotted plus crosshatched area minus the dotted area. Hence:

$$p(1 < x < 2) = p(X < 2) - p(X < 1) = \frac{2 - (-1)}{3 - (-1)} - \frac{1 - (-1)}{3 - (-1)} = \frac{3}{4} - \frac{2}{4} = \frac{1}{4} = .25$$

This probability is visually obvious because the crosshatched area takes up one quarter of the entire rectangle under the density function.

SUMMARY MEASURES Because the uniform probability density function is so simple, summary measures can also be calculated in a simple fashion, as indicated by Formulas 10.J–10.L.

FORMULAS 10.J–10.L | Summary Measures: Probability Distribution of Uniform Random Variable *X*

10.J Arithmetic mean: $$\mu_x = \frac{a + b}{2}$$

10.K Variance: $$\sigma_x^2 = \frac{(b - a)^2}{12}$$

10.L Standard deviation: $$\sigma_x = \sqrt{\frac{(b - a)^2}{12}}$$

where x is a value of the uniform random variable, while a is the lower and b is the upper limit of possible x values.

Thus, in panel (a) of Figure 10.24, the mean or expected value of the random variable is

$$\mu_x = \frac{a + b}{2} = \frac{2 + 4}{2} = 3$$

which is visually quite obvious on page 434 above. The variance is

$$\sigma_x^2 = \frac{(b - a)^2}{12} = \frac{(4 - 2)^2}{12} = \frac{4}{12} = .3333$$

and the standard deviation is

$$\sigma_x = \sqrt{.3333} = .5774$$

EXAMPLE PROBLEM 10.10

Consider a flight scheduled to arrive at Keene, New Hampshire, at 1:30 P.M. but in fact equally likely to arrive at any time between 1:10 and 1:55 P.M. Someone may wish to know the probability of

a. the plane being on time or early.

b. being late for a connecting flight that leaves unless the arriving plane is on the ground by 1:45 P.M.

SOLUTION: We can sketch the problem as in Figure 10.25, denoting the scheduled arrival time of 1:30 P.M. as 0, denoting the earliest possible arrival time of 1:10 P.M. as $a = -20$ minutes, and denoting the latest possible arrival time of 1:55 P.M. as $b = +25$ minutes. As drawn and according to Formula 10.H, the height of the probability density function from a to b equals

FIGURE 10.25

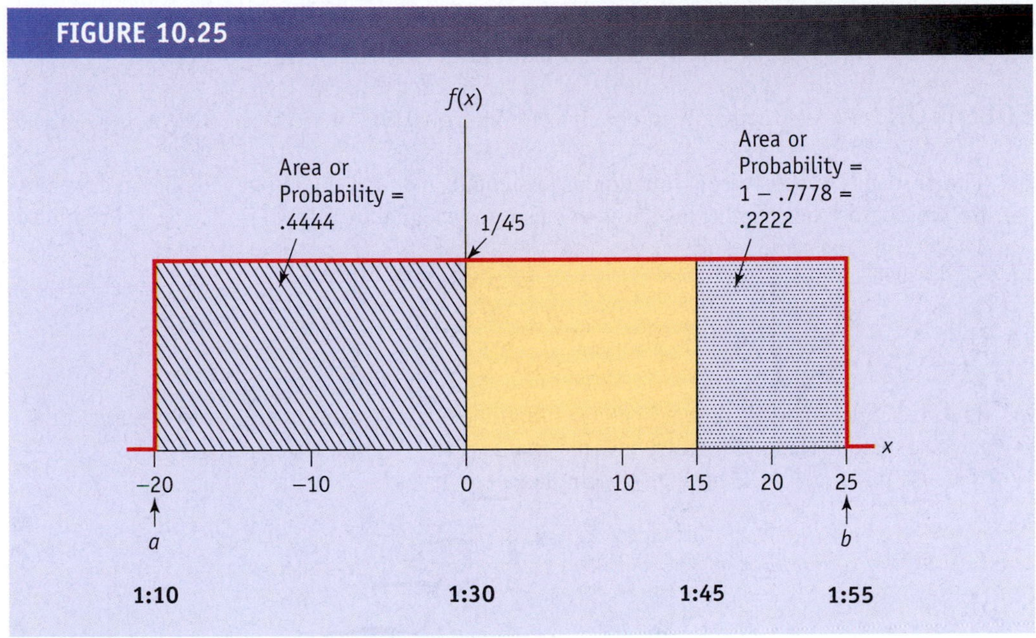

$$f(x) = \frac{1}{b-a} = \frac{1}{25-(-20)} = \frac{1}{45}$$

a. The probability of being on time or early, according to Formula 10.I, equals

$$p(X < 0) = \frac{x-a}{b-a} = \frac{0-(-20)}{25-(-20)} = \frac{20}{45} = .4444$$

and this probability is shown by the crossedhatched area.

b. The probability of being late for the connecting flight (because the first plane lands after 1:45 P.M.) is shown by the dotted area. It equals 1 minus the combined crosshatched and yellow areas under the density function:

$$p(X > 15) = 1 - p(X < 15) = 1 - \frac{15-(-20)}{25-(-20)} = 1 - \frac{35}{45} = \frac{10}{45} = .2222$$

Note: In both cases, we could also calculate the probability directly by multiplying the base of the relevant (crosshatched or dotted) rectangle (measuring 20 or 10, respectively) by its height (of 1/45).

EXAMPLE PROBLEM 10.11

Consider an "almost informationless state" in which economists know only that next year's inflation will not be below 5 percent nor above 15 percent. If all values between 5 and 15 percent are deemed equally likely,

a. what is the likelihood of inflation of 6 percent or less?

b. what is the likelihood of inflation of more than 8.3 percent?

c. what is the likelihood of inflation between 9.5 and 11.5 percent?

d. what is the random variable's mean and standard deviation?

SOLUTION: We can sketch the problem as in Figure 10.26.

a. The probability of 6 percent inflation or less equals the area shaded in teal. Geometry (multiplying base times height) instantly reveals it to be equal to 1(1/10) = .1. Using Formula 10.I, we get the same result:

$$p(X < 6) = \frac{x - a}{b - a} = \frac{6 - 5}{15 - 5} = \frac{1}{10} = .1$$

b. The probability of more than 8.3 percent inflation equals the sum of the two white areas plus the crosshatched area. Geometry says the result is (15 − 8.3)(1/10) = (6.7)(.1) = .67. Because $p(X > x) = 1 - p(X < x)$, Formula 10.I gives us

$$p(X > 8.3) = 1 - p(X < 8.3) = 1 - \frac{8.3 - 5}{15 - 5} = 1 - \frac{3.3}{10} = 1 - .33 = .67$$

c. The probability of 9.5 to 11.5 percent inflation equals the crosshatched area. Geometrically, this area equals 2(1/10) = .2. According to Formula 10.I,

$$p(9.5 < X < 11.5) = p(X < 11.5) - p(X < 9.5) = \frac{11.5 - 5}{15 - 5} - \frac{9.5 - 5}{15 - 5} = \frac{6.5}{10} - \frac{4.5}{10} = \frac{2}{10} = .2$$

d. According to Formulas 10.J and 10.L,

$$\mu_x = \frac{a + b}{2} = \frac{5 + 15}{2} = 10$$

$$\sigma_x = \sqrt{\frac{(b - a)^2}{12}} = \sqrt{\frac{(15 - 5)^2}{12}} = \sqrt{\frac{100}{12}} = \sqrt{8.3333} = 2.8868$$

FIGURE 10.26

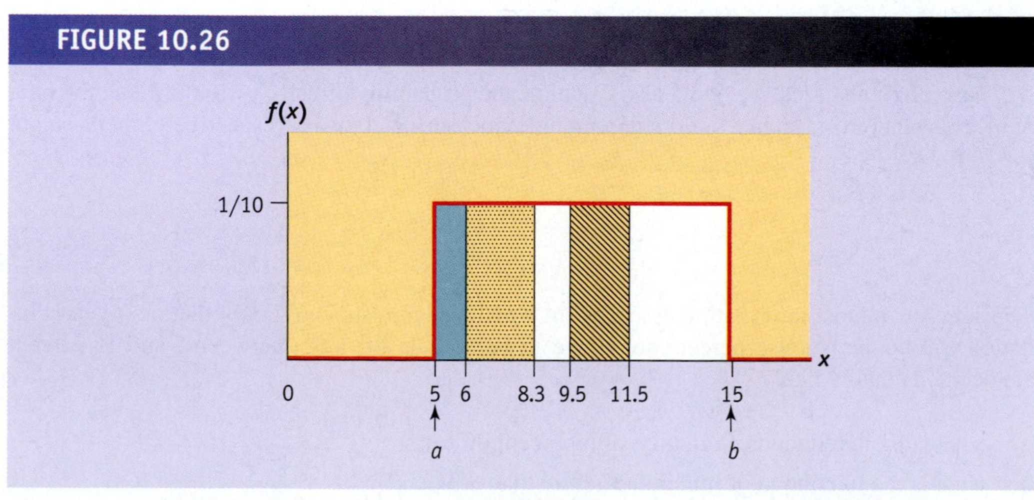

10.11 Uniform Probabilities and Computer Programs

Computer programs such as EXCEL or MINITAB allow us to work all sorts of uniform probability problems without the explicit use of formulas. The following examples show how they can help us find:

- the height of a uniform probability density function
- areas under the uniform probability density function for specified ranges of x
- values of x corresponding to specified uniform probability density function areas

EXCEL Example 10.7

Review panel (b) of Figure 10.24 on page 434. Using EXCEL, confirm

a. the function's height at $x = 2$

b. the area under the function between point $a = -1$ and $x = 2$

c. the x value associated with an area of .75.

SOLUTION Because of the utter simplicity of the uniform distribution, EXCEL does not have a special function to make calculations. After all, individual probability values are the same for all possible values of x and the cumulative probability is simply the area of a rectangle. Nevertheless, you can use EXCEL as follows:

1. Fire up EXCEL and enter the labels **x**, **f(x),** and **cumulative probability,** respectively, into cells A1–C1.
2. Enter x values of -1, 0, 1, 2, and 3 into cells A2–A6.
3. Enter $f(x)$ values of .25 into cells B2–B6. (To find the .25 height of the function, divide 1 by the range of values, which is $3 - (-1) = 4$ in this case.)
4. Enter cumulative probability values into cells C2–C6. (To find any given value, take the x value, deduct the minimum value of -1, and multiply by .25.)

The result:

x	f(x)	cumulative probability
−1	0.25	0
0	0.25	0.25
1	0.25	0.5
2	0.25	0.75
3	0.25	1

a. The value of $f(x)$ at $x = 2$ is **.25.**

b. The cumulative probability between x values of -1 and 2 is **.75.**

c. The x value associated with a cumulative probability of .75 is **2.**

Summary

1. This chapter focuses on probability distributions of *continuous* radom variables, which can assume values at all points on a scale of values. Because the number of such values is infinite, we cannot list all the conceivable values of such variables and then associate their infinite number with an equally infinite number of probabilities. Instead, we associate probabilities of continuous random variables with various *ranges* of their values. We measure these probabilities as appropriate areas under a smooth frequency curve that approximates a relative frequency histogram and is called a *probability density function.* An infinite variety of continuous probability distributions exists, although the normal, exponential, and uniform distributions are most frequently encountered.
2. A *normal probability distribution* is a probability density function that is (a) single-peaked above the random variable's mean, median, and mode, (b) perfectly symmetrical about this central value, and (c) characterized by tails extending indefinitely in both directions from the center, approaching but never touching the horizontal axis. The height of the normal probability density function for different values, x, of the normal random variable can be determined by Formula 10.A; probabilities for specified ranges of x values can be found by integrating that function over these ranges.
3. It is common practice to convert all members of the normal probability distribution family into a *standard normal curve* (with a mean of zero and a standard deviation of 1). Probabilities for ranges of x values associated with this curve are readily available in appropriately prepared tables, such as Appendix Table H. Another means of avoiding awkward computations, and quickly finding probabilities associated with the normal probability distribution, is provided by modern computer programs, such as EXCEL or MINITAB.
4. Under certain circumstances, the normal probability distribution can be used to *approximate* various discrete probability distributions, including the binomial, Poisson, and hypergeometric distributions.
5. Whenever the number of occurrences of an event is determined by a Poisson process, the likelihood of encountering specified intervals of time or space between consecutive occurrences can be described by the *exponential probability distribution.* The height of the exponential probability density function for different values, x, of the exponential random variable can be determined by Formula 10.D; probabilities for specified ranges of x values can be found by integrating that function over these ranges. The exponential functions of Appendix Table E are helpful in finding quick answers from the formula.
6. Other tables, such as Appendix Table I, provide ready-made probabilities for cumulative values of the exponential random variable. Computer programs, such as EXCEL or MINITAB, provide still another means of quickly finding probabilities associated with the exponential probability distribution.
7. The *uniform* or *rectangular probability distribution* is a probability density function for a random variable that is equally likely to take on any of the values within a given range. The (constant) height of the uniform probability density function can be determined by Formula 10.H. The formula is so simple, as is that for calculating areas under the density function (Formula 10.I), that there is no need to tabulate uniform probabilities. Summary measures are also easy to calculate (Formulas10.J–10.L), quite unlike those for other continuous random variables. Once again, computer programs, such as EXCEL or MINITAB, provide another means yet of finding probabilities associated with the uniform probability distribution.

Key Terms

continuous random variable
exponential probability distribution
exponential random variable
normal probability distribution
probability density function
random variable
rectangular probability distribution
standard normal curve
standard normal deviate
uniform probability distribution
uniform random variable

Practice Problems

NOTE

Some problems require the use of a statistical program, EXCEL or MINITAB. The program's major features are explained in text Chapter 2. Plenty of additional advice is available via the program's built-in Help feature.

SECTION 10.3 THE STANDARD NORMAL CURVE

1. Given a normal distribution with $\mu_x = 50$ and $\sigma_x = 10$, find z values for
   - a. $x = 18$.
   - b. $x = 48$.
   - c. $x = 68$.
2. Given a normal distribution's z value of 2.4, find the corresponding x value if
   - a. $\mu_x = 20$ and $\sigma_x = 3$.
   - b. $\mu_x = 12$ and $\sigma_x = 4$.
   - c. $\mu_x = 5$ and $\sigma_x = 1.3$.
3. Given a normal distribution's z value of 1.4, find the distribution's mean, μ_x, if
   - a. $x = 20$ and $\sigma_x = 3$.
   - b. $x = 12$ and $\sigma_x = 4$.
   - c. $x = 5$ and $\sigma_x = 1.3$.
4. Given a normal distribution's z value of -1.4, find the distribution's standard deviation, σ_x, if
   - a. $x = 2$ and $\mu_x = 3$.
   - b. $x = 12$ and $\mu_x = 4$.
   - c. $x = 50$ and $\mu_x = 63$.

SECTION 10.4 THE STANDARD NORMAL TABLES

5. The time required by a bank teller to cash a check is a normally distributed random variable with a mean of 30 seconds and a standard deviation of 10 seconds. Find the times representing
   - a. the 10th percentile.
   - b. the 75th percentile.
6. Assume that people's heights are a normally distributed random variable with a mean of 66 inches and a standard deviation of 4 inches. An architect wishes to design doors so that 95 percent of all people have at least a 1-inch clearance when passing through. How high must the doors be?
7. Assume that IQ test scores are a normally distributed random variable. If the Stanford-Binet IQ test has a mean of 100 and a standard deviation of 16, how likely is it that a randomly chosen person scores at least 140?
8. A multinational corporation has opened a new plant in Poland. The output of workers in the plant is a normally distributed random variable. The plant's manager suggests that workers switch from hourly pay ($5.16 per hour) to a piecework plan.
   - a. If workers on the average produce 30 pieces per hour and the standard deviation is 5 pieces, which pay per piece would assure workers of their current hourly pay at least 80 percent of the time?
   - b. If the workers were paid 25 cents per piece, what percentage of the time would they earn between $4.50 and $5.50 per hour?
9. A company administers a test to all of its employees. Test scores as well as finishing times are normally distributed random variables.
   - a. If the mean score is 500, the standard deviation is 100, and workers with the 25 percent highest scores are to be given special training, what is the lowest acceptable score for entrance into the training program?
   - b. If the average time required to finish the test equals 60 minutes, with a standard deviation of 12 minutes, when should the exam be terminated so that 95 percent of the workers have completed all parts of the test?
10. A firm uses 2,000 lightbulbs; their lifetime is a normally distributed random variable with a mean of 500 hours and a standard deviation of 50 hours. How often must the bulbs be replaced if all of them are to be replaced at once and at most 1 percent of them are to burn out between replacements?
11. The miles-per-gallon (mpg) rating of cars is a normally distributed random variable with a mean of 25.9 and a standard deviation of 2.45. If an automobile manufacturer wants to build a car with an mpg rating that improves upon 99 percent of existing cars, what must the new car's mpg rating be?
12. The shelf life of a battery is a normally distributed random variable with a mean of 525 days and a standard deviation of 50 days. If the battery has been on the shelf for 647 days, what is the probability of it being dead?

13. The time required to install a new aircraft engine is a normally distributed random variable with a mean of 20 hours and a standard deviation of 1 hour. What is the probability that the next installation takes

a. between 20 and 21.5 hours?

b. between 18 and 20 hours?

c. between 19 and 22 hours?

d. over 23 hours?

e. at most 16.1 hours?

f. between 21 and 22 hours?

g. between 17 and 18 hours?

h. at most 23.7 hours?

i. more than 18.3 hours?

14. A manufacturer has developed a new type of automobile tire. The marketing department believes that the mileage guarantee offered to customers will be the crucial factor in winning consumer acceptance. Naturally, management wants to know the probability distribution of the lifetimes of these tires. Accordingly, 400 tires are tested. Engineers report that lifetimes are normally distributed with a mean of 36,000 miles and a standard deviation of 4,800 miles.

a. How many of the tested tires had a lifetime between 31,200 and 40,800 miles?

b. How many lasted at most 45,600 miles?

c. How many lasted at least 26,400 miles?

d. How many lasted between 26,400 and 31,200 miles?

e. Within what limits were the lifetimes of the 20 percent worst tires?

f. What mileage guarantee should the firm offer if it wants to make no more than 10 percent of all tires eligible?

SECTION 10.5 NORMAL PROBABILITIES AND COMPUTER PROGRAMS

15. The weekly number of checks cleared by a bank is a normally distributed random variable with a mean of 122,000 checks cleared and a standard deviation of 10,000 checks. Use EXCEL or MINITAB to determine the proportion of weeks in which the bank will have to clear more than 140,000 checks.

16. The number of gallons of effluent processed at a sewage-treatment plant is a normally distributed random variable with a mean of 50,000 gallons per day and a standard deviation of 7,000 gallons per day. The chief engineer wants to know: In what proportion of days will the plant be called upon to process in excess of 60,000 gallons, the plant's designed capacity? Use EXCEL or MINITAB to find the answer.

17. A machine makes parts with lengths that are normally distributed with a mean of 3 inches and a standard deviation of .15 inch. The acceptable range of lengths is 2.87 to 3.10 inches. What proportion of output is *not* acceptable? Use EXCEL or MINITAB to find the answer.

18. A quality inspector tests the strength of aircraft control cables. Their breaking pressure is a normally distributed random variable with a mean of 500 lb. and a standard deviation of 50 lb. Some 100 cables ruptured under 475 lb. pressure or less. How many withstood pressure of 560 lb. or more? Use EXCEL or MINITAB to find the answer.

19. A quality inspector tests the strength of window panes. Their breaking pressure is a normally distributed random variable with a mean of 80 mph wind velocity and a standard deviation of 7 mph. Some 50 panes broke under simulated wind velocities of 73 mph and less. How many withstood the hurricane velocity of 100 mph or more? Use EXCEL or MINITAB to find the answer.

20. There are x gas stations in a state. Their net incomes are normally distributed with a mean of $29,000 per year and a standard deviation of $5,100 per year. Some 189 stations earn between $26,000 and $31,000 per year. How many gas stations are in the state? Use EXCEL or MINITAB to find the answer.

21. There are x psychiatrists in a city. Their net incomes are normally distributed with a mean of $89,000 per year and a standard deviation of $19,000 per year. Three psychiatrists earn more than $127,000 per year. How many psychiatrists are there in the entire city? Use EXCEL or MINITAB to find the answer.

22. An airline has 105 seats available per flight. If it sells 115 tickets, the actual arrivals are a normally distributed random variable with a mean of 100 and a standard deviation of 5. What is the probability that the number of passengers showing up exceeds the number of available seats? Use EXCEL or MINITAB to find the answer.

23. A cattle feedlot finds that the daily weight gain of animals is 1.5 lb. on the average with a standard deviation of .3 lb. If weight gain is a normally distributed random variable, what is the probability that a randomly chosen animal gains the following in a day? Use EXCEL or MINITAB to find the answers.

a. less than 1 lb.

b. less than 2 lb.

c. more than 1.4 lb.

d. between 1.6 and 1.7 lb.

24. The rents charged in a city are a normally distributed random variable with a mean of $551 per month and a standard deviation of $62. The mayor wants to know: What percentage of households would be eligible for rent subsidies if all households paying more than $600 were made eligible? Use EXCEL or MINITAB to find the answers.

25. A personnel manager has discovered that the hours of sick leave taken by employees during a year are a normally distributed random variable with a mean of 52 hours and a standard deviation of 10 hours. She considers the hours taken by A (63) and B (93) highly unusual. Do you agree? Use EXCEL or MINITAB to find the answers.

Section 10.6 Using the Normal Probability Distribution to Approximate Discrete Probability Distributions

26. A firm ships thermometers in boxes of 1,000. Typically 10 percent are broken upon arrival. *Using an approximation,* determine the probability that, in a randomly chosen box,

a. 100 to 130 thermometers are broken.

b. 75 thermometers are broken.

c. 200 thermometers are broken.

d. none is broken.

27. Consider the exact hypergeometric probability distribution derived in Example Problem 9.13 on pages 375 and 377. What probabilities would one find by using the *normal approximation?*

28. During the rush hour, cars pass over a bridge at a rate of 20 per minute. Using the *normal approximation* to an appropriate probability distribution, determine the probability of exactly 10 cars crossing the bridge during a given minute. Compare your result with the precise answer.

29. Experience shows that 25 percent of the people entering a store make a purchase. Without using binomial probability tables, determine

a. the probability distribution of purchases made for the next 20 customers.

b. the probability that at most 3 of the next 20 customers will make a purchase.

Section 10.7 The Exponential Probability Distribution

30. The time to service a car at a gas station is an exponential random variable with a mean of 2 minutes. Using formulas only, determine the probability that a newly arriving car will be serviced

a. within 1 minute.

b. within 4 minutes.

c. within 2 to 6 minutes.

d. only in 5 or more minutes.

Section 10.8 Exponential Probability Tables

31. The manager of an aircraft avionics repair station has found that the repair time on radar transponders is an exponential random variable with a mean of 66 minutes. Determine the probability that the next repair takes

a. at most 30 minutes.

b. at most 66 minutes.

c. at most 1.5 hours.

d. between 2 and 3 hours.

32. An automaker claims that only 5.82 percent of car radios have to be replaced under the firm's 5-year warranty. What must be the mean lifetime of the radio, assuming that the lifetime is an exponential random variable?

33. A washing machine manufacturer makes two claims:

a. that the lifetime of the firm's product is an exponential random variable

b. that only 4.88 percent of the firm's washing machines have to be replaced under the firm's generous 10-year unconditional warranty program

Do you believe the claims? Explain.

34. The arrival of claims at an insurance company can be described as a Poisson process occurring at a rate of 2 claims per day. Using an appropriate table, determine the probability that the next claim will be made

a. within 4 days.

b. after the passage of 2 days.

c. at some time between 3 and 5 days hence.

35. A hospital surgical unit cannot afford "ever" to be caught without electric power. Accordingly, the hospital administrator plans to purchase one or more standby generators to reduce the chances of such an occurrence to below 1 percent. The models available have a mean time between failures of 500 hours. Determine the probability of electric power loss in a surgical unit if

a. one standby generator is bought and the city has a 10-hour blackout.

b. two such generators are bought and the same event occurs.

What are the chances of avoiding any power loss if

c. one generator is bought, but there are 10 five-hour blackouts during a given year?

d. two such generators are bought, and there are 10 such blackouts?

36. The length of life of a computer component is an exponential random variable with a mean of 7 years.

a. If the warranty period is 5 years, what proportion of the components can the manufacturer expect to replace under the warranty?

b. What should the warranty period be if the manufacturer doesn't want to be bothered with having to replace more than 10 percent of the components?

37. The time people have to wait in line at a fast-food outlet is an exponential random variable with a mean of 2 minutes. Compute the probability that a customer must wait

a. more than 2 minutes.

b. more than 3 minutes.

c. less than 30 seconds.

d. between 2 and 3 minutes.

SECTION 10.9 EXPONENTIAL PROBABILITIES AND COMPUTER PROGRAMS

38. A hospital administrator has noted that treatments of patients in the emergency room take 45 minutes on the average. Assuming that treatment time is an exponential random variable, and using EXCEL or MINITAB whenever possible, determine

a. the median treatment time.

b. the probability that the next treatment exceeds 45 minutes.

c. the probability that the next treatment exceeds 2 hours.

d. the probability that the next treatment exceeds 45 minutes for each of the next 3 patients.

39. The shelf life of whole milk is an exponential random variable with a mean of 5 days. Using EXCEL or MINITAB, determine the percentage that is marketable

a. for 5 or fewer days.

b. for over 7 days.

c. for 5 to 7 days.

40. The relief time provided by the standard dose of a new drug averages 20 hours. Using EXCEL or MINITAB, determine the percentage of patients who experience relief

a. for at least 12 hours.

b. for more than 30 hours.

c. for 20 to 30 hours.

41. On average, a flight training aircraft is used 5.6 hours per day. Using EXCEL or MINITAB, determine

a. the median daily time of use.

b. the probability that the aircraft is used at least 7 hours per day.

42. A manufacturer of aircraft navigation equipment knows the lifetime of the company's glideslope indicators to be an exponential random variable with a mean of 10 years. Using EXCEL or MINITAB, determine

a. the median lifetime of this instrument.

b. the percentage of glideslope indicators that last at most 10 years.

c. the percentage of glideslope indicators that last more than 20 years.

43. A manufacturer of aircraft navigation equipment knows the lifetime of the company's directional gyros to be an exponential random variable with a mean of 3.7 years. Using EXCEL or MINITAB, determine

a. the median lifetime of this instrument.

b. the percentage of gyros that last at most 1 year.

c. the percentage of gyros that last more than 10 years.

SECTION 10.10 THE UNIFORM PROBABILITY DISTRIBUTION

44. A supervisor checks an employee's work every afternoon between 2:00 and 3:00 P.M., any arrival time within that range being equally likely.

a. Graph the probability density function and indicate the height of the function, its mean, and its standard deviation.

b. What is the probability that the supervisor arrives before 2:15 P.M.?

c. What is the probability that the supervisor arrives after 2:50 P.M.?

d. What is the probability that the supervisor arrives between 2:41 and 2:43 P.M.?

e. What is the probability that the supervisor arrives precisely at 2:31:10 P.M.?

45. A computer generates random decimal values such that any value between zero and one is equally likely to be picked. Determine the probability that the next value chosen is

a. less than .25.

b. less than .79.

c. greater than .79.

d. between .25 and .79.

46. The waiting time for an elevator is uniformly distributed between zero and 3 minutes.

a. Determine the probability of reaching the next floor in 1 minute or less if the trip itself takes 10 seconds.

b. Determine the distribution's summary measures.

47. The arrival of a bus is equally likely at any time during the next half hour. Determine

a. your expected waiting time.

b. the probability that you have to wait more than 25 minutes.

c. the probability that you have to wait fewer than 5 minutes.

d. the probability that you have to wait between 7 and 10 minutes.

48. If you wanted to draw the uniform probability distributions discussed in Practice Problems 45–47, what would the heights of the functions have to be? Prove that your answers are correct.

SECTION 10.11 UNIFORM PROBABILITIES AND COMPUTER PROGRAMS

49. A worker is painting the outside metal surface of a new aircraft with the help of a sprayer. It deposits a coat of paint the thickness of which is a uniformly distributed random variable, ranging from .4 to 1.4 millimeters. Use EXCEL or MINITAB to determine

a. the percentage of the area that is coated with .5 mm or less.

b. the percentage of the area that is coated with .9 mm or more.

50. A worker is filling sacks of birdseed with a machine. The quantity put in each sack is a uniformly distributed random variable that ranges from 20 to 25 lb. Use EXCEL or MINITAB to determine

a. the percentage of sacks filled with at most 21 lb.

b. the percentage of sacks filled with over 23 lb.

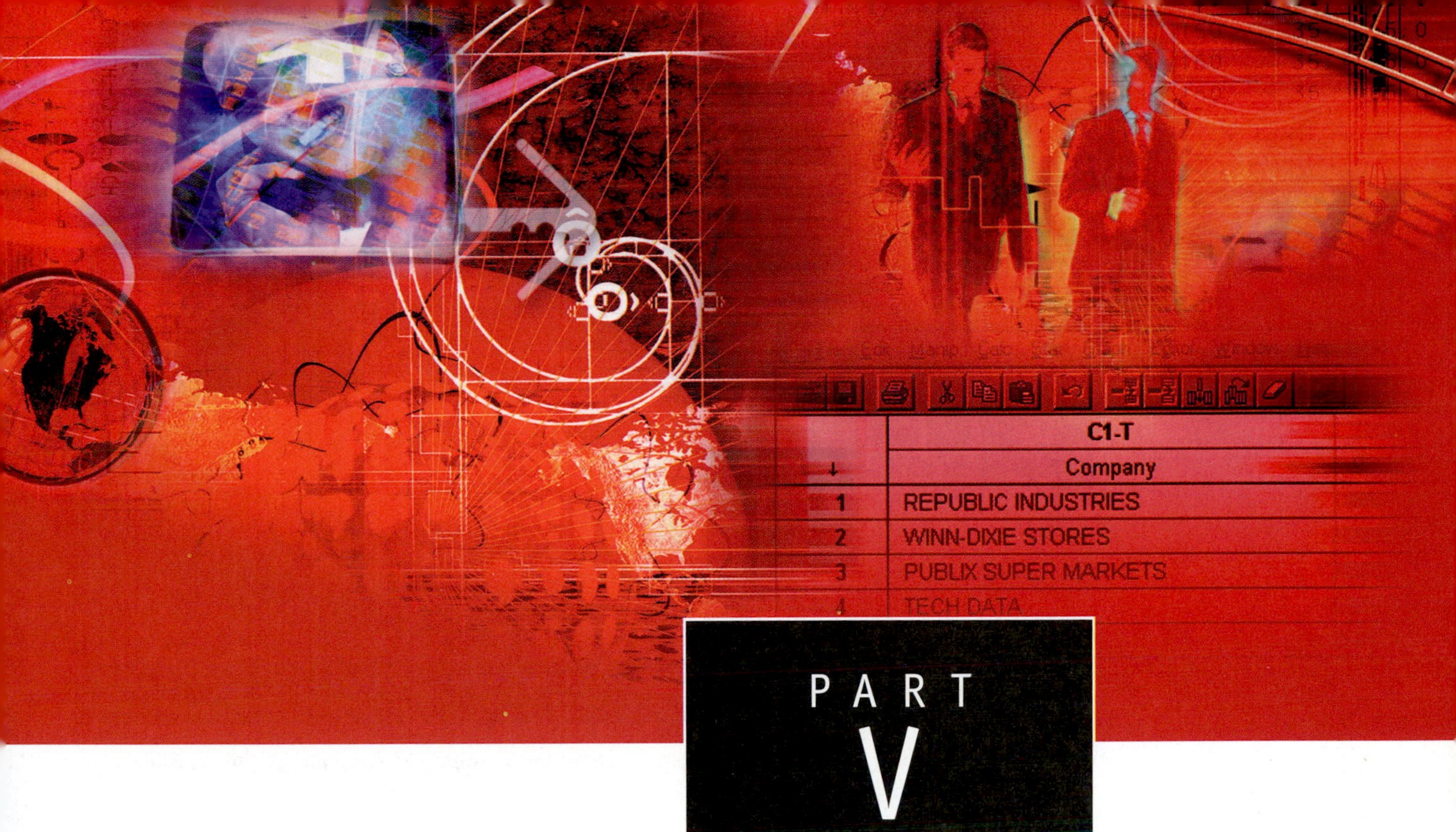

PART V

BASIC INFERENCE

SAMPLING DISTRIBUTIONS

LOOKING AHEAD

After reading this chapter, and reviewing such basic concepts as population, sample, parameter, and statistic, you will be able to:

1. apply the concept of the sampling distribution,
2. compute sampling distribution summary measures,
3. sketch the general shape of such distributions,
4. recognize the relationships among sampling distribution summary measures,
5. appreciate the importance of the central limit theorem, and
6. make computer simulations of sampling distributions.

AND HERE IS A TYPICAL PROBLEM YOU WILL BE ABLE TO SOLVE:

The manufacturer of batteries for aircraft emergency-locator transmitters claims that the lifetime of these batteries is normally distributed with a mean of 30 months and a standard deviation of 3 months. An aircraft manufacturer checks out 50 batteries and discovers a sample mean of only 29 months. What is the probability that the battery manufacturer's claim is true?

PREVIEW

To conduct an accurate blood test, doctors need not drain a person's entire blood supply; a few drops of blood will do nicely. Likewise, statisticians need not question 280 million Americans to gauge their opinions; a carefully chosen 1,000 citizens can speak for the nation. However, as we saw in Chapter 4, such random sampling is a delicate task. It can go wrong when subtle nuances invade the questions asked. Thus, during the Watergate scandal a few decades ago (when Republican Party employees were caught red-handed breaking into files at the Democratic Party headquarters), pollsters asked: "Should President Nixon be impeached and compelled to leave the presidency?" Only a third said yes. Yet fully two-thirds answered yes to this question: "Do you think there is enough evidence of possible wrongdoing in the case of President Nixon to bring him to trial before the Senate?" To the questioners, the second question *implied* the first. After all, if there were enough evidence, the president would be impeached and removed from office, they thought. Asking the "same thing" in different ways can elicit totally different answers.

TABLE 11.1 | Product Preferences of 20 Individuals

Prefer A over B	Prefer B over A		Indifferent
#1	#6	#11	#16
#2	#7	#12	#17
#3	#8	#13	#18
#4	#9	#14	#19
#5	#10	#15	#20

Businesses doing market research face the same problem every day. Yet even their most carefully wrought questions encounter an additional problem that cannot be escaped: *A given question can elicit many different answers, depending on the particular sample that the random process selects.* This chapter introduces that problem; a simple example can illustrate it here. Consider a population of 20 individuals, #1 to #20, who either prefer product A over B, prefer product B over A, or are indifferent between the two. The individual preferences are noted in Table 11.1.

Let a firm take a simple random sample of 3 from this population. Depending on the luck of the draw, it could select any one of $C_3^{20} = 1{,}140$ possible samples. (Recall Formula 8.F on page 303.) One of these samples would be #1, #2, and #3, which would give the impression that 100 percent of potential customers prefer A to B. Another such sample might be #16, #17, and #18, which would suggest universal indifference. A third sample might include #5, #11, and #15, suggesting a two-thirds majority in favor of B. Clearly, hundreds of possible answers exist. As we will see, a *sampling distribution* describes this range of possible answers for us. An understanding of such distributions, in turn, leads the way into the realm of *inferential* statistics and prepares us to make judgments about the likely truth whenever we cannot reasonably take a census and must instead rely upon random sampling.[1]

[1]Adapted from Michael R. Kagay and Janet Elder, "Numbers Are No Problem for Pollsters. Words Are." *The New York Times,* August 9, 1992, p. E5; and the Gallup Organization's Web site, http://www.gallup.com.

11.1 Reviewing Basic Concepts

As we begin our journey into the world of inferential statistics, we must first review a number of statistical concepts, including those of *population* and *sample* as well as *parameter* and *statistic.*

DEFINITION 11.1 The set of all possible observations about a specified characteristic of interest is called a statistical **population.** A summary measure calculated for such a population is called a **parameter** and is designated by Greek letters (such as μ for mean or π for proportion).

DEFINITION 11.2 A subset of a statistical population is called a **sample.** A summary measure based on sample data is called a **statistic** and is designated by Roman letters (such as $\overline{X}$ for mean or P for proportion).

For reasons noted in Chapter 4, decision makers frequently gain vital information about a statistical population by taking a relatively quick and inexpensive sample rather than conducting a full-fledged census. Consider a manufacturer who wants to know the average time that workers require to complete a given task, the average amount of fuel needed to ship a truckload a given distance, or the average age of those who use a given product. Consider questions about a product's market share, about the percentage of acceptable units in a shipment of parts, or about the proportion of people watching a TV show, favoring a tax hike, or opposing a labor contract. In all these cases and many more, statisticians are interested in learning something about a statistical population. In the absence of a census, the desired knowledge about such *parameters* as the population mean, μ, the population standard deviation, σ, or the population proportion, π, can be gained only by drawing a random sample from the population, calculating such *statistics* as the sample mean, $\bar{X}$, the sample standard deviation, s, or the sample proportion, P, and making inferences about the parameters from such statistics. The process of inferring the values of unknown population parameters from those of known sample statistics is called **estimation.** The entire *next* chapter is devoted to the technique of making meaningful estimates. Before we can do so, however, we must become familiar, in this chapter, with a new concept that is closely related to sampling.

11.2 The Concept of the Sampling Distribution

Before we meet the new concept of the *sampling distribution,* let us review that of the *simple random sample,* first noted in Chapter 4.

DEFINITION 11.3 A sample chosen in such a way that every possible subset of like size has an equal chance of being selected is called a **simple random sample.**

DEFINITION 11.4 When drawing all possible simple random samples of a given size from a population, many different values of a sample statistic might occur. A listing of all these possible values, along with the associated probabilities of their occurrence, is called the statistic's **sampling distribution.**

INFERRING PARAMETERS FROM STATISTICS

A sampling distribution provides an important link between the single sample that we typically take and the population about which we wish to make inferences. To illustrate the concept, let us consider the two statistical populations given in Table 11.2. For simplicity's sake, we imagine that there exist only $N = 5$ business executives in an industry. Their salaries and sexes are given in the table. With this complete information in hand, we can calculate such *population* summary measures (parameters) as the mean annual salary, μ, along with its variance, σ^2, and standard de-

TABLE 11.2 | Populations of Executive Salaries and Sexes

Executive	Annual Salary (thousands of dollars)	Sex
A	195	M
B	205	F
C	125	F
D	275	M
E	200	M

viation, σ, as well as the proportion of female executives, π_F. These computations appear in Example Problem 11.1.

EXAMPLE PROBLEM 11.1

Using appropriate formulas from Chapter 7, compute population summary measures from the data in Table 11.2.

SOLUTION:

Population Summary Measures

Salary	Sex
$\mu = \frac{\Sigma X}{N} = \frac{1{,}000}{5} = 200$	$\pi_F = \frac{2}{5} = .40$
$\sigma^2 = \frac{\Sigma(X-\mu)^2}{N} = \frac{11{,}300}{5} = 2{,}260$	
$\sigma = \sqrt{2{,}260} = 47.539$	

According to our population data, the mean annual salary equals \$200,000, with a standard deviation of \$47,539, and 40 percent of the executives are females. Suppose, however, that this census-type information were not available to us and couldn't easily be acquired. In reality, there might be 30,000 executives in the industry, and contacting them all might be too costly or time-consuming. Suppose we therefore decided to *estimate* the four population parameters computed in Example Problem 11.1 by taking a simple random sample of the executives. We might take a sample of size $n = 3$ and, following common practice, do so without replacement. If we picked a sample of executives B, D, and E, we could instantly calculate the appropriate *sample* summary measures (statistics), as shown in Example Problem 11.2.

EXAMPLE PROBLEM 11.2

Using appropriate formulas from Chapter 7, compute sample summary measures for a sample of executives B, D, and E in Table 11.2.

SOLUTION:

Sample Summary Measures (Executives B, D, and E)

Salary	Sex
$\overline{X} = \frac{\Sigma X}{n} = \frac{680}{3} = 226.667$	$P_F = \frac{1}{3} = .333$
$s^2 = \frac{\Sigma(X-\overline{X})^2}{n-1} = \frac{3{,}516.667}{2} = 1{,}758.333$	
$s = \sqrt{1{,}758.333} = 41.932$	

If we did not know the population parameters derived in Example Problem 11.1, we could now estimate them with the help of the sample statistics derived in Example Problem 11.2. Thus, we would *estimate* the population mean annual salary at $226,667, with a standard deviation of $41,932, and we would presume that 33.3 percent of the executives were female.

RANDOM ERROR REVISITED

Unfortunately, our hypothetical random sample of executives B, D, and E in the previous section was just one of many possible samples. And, as we learned in Chapter 4, the results derived from any *one* random sample are inevitably flawed by random error. Thus, we have reason to be bothered by a disturbing thought, which highlights the central issue of this chapter.

If the random-selection procedure had produced a different sample of n = 3, we would surely have calculated different summary measures for the sample and would, thus, have made different estimates of the corresponding population parameters.

Indeed, we can visualize the estimates made from different possible samples by looking at Table 11.3. The table lists all the possible simple random samples of size $n = 3$ that we might have taken, without replacement, from among our population of size $N = 5$. (This ability to list all the possible samples is a lucky circumstance due to the utter simplicity of our example; it would not be practical to do so if we had considered a population of, say, 30,000 executives, while taking a sample of, say, 1,500. In that case, the number of possible samples would have been too huge to list.) If we consider the order in which people enter a sample as irrelevant (so that a sample of B, D, E is treated as identical to a sample of E, D, B, and the like), we can apply combinatorial Formula 8.F and determine that the possible number of samples of $n = 3$ out of a population of $N = 5$ equals

$$C_3^5 = \frac{5!}{3!(5-3)!} = \frac{5!}{3!2!} = \frac{5 \times 4}{2 \times 1} = 10$$

These 10 samples are listed in Table 11.3. Four summary measures, calculated on the basis of the corresponding data in Table 11.2, are given for each of the samples. Note that the sample evaluated in Example Problem 11.2 now appears as sample number 9.

TABLE 11.3 | Possible Samples of $n = 3$ Taken without Replacement from a Population of $N = 5$, along with Sample Summary Measures

Sample Number	Executives in Sample	$\bar{X}$	s^2	s	P_F	Probability p
1	ABC	175.000	1,900.000	43.589	.667	.1
2	ABD	225.000	1,900.000	43.589	.333	.1
3	ABE	200.000	25.000	5.000	.333	.1
4	ACD	198.333	5,633.333	75.056	.333	.1
5	ACE	173.333	1,758.333	41.932	.333	.1
6	ADE	223.333	2,008.333	44.814	0	.1
7	BCD	201.667	5,633.333	75.056	.667	.1
8	BCE	176.667	2,008.333	44.814	.667	.1
9	BDE	226.667	1,758.333	41.932	.333	.1
10	CDE	200.000	5,625.000	75.000	.333	.1

Contemplating Table 11.3, we realize that every sample summary measure (such as $\overline{X}$, s^2, s, and P_F) is in fact a random variable prior to the selection of an actual sample. Before we picked sample number 9, the sample mean, $\overline{X}$, for instance, could have turned out to be any one of the values in the $\overline{X}$ column of Table 11.3, depending entirely on which elementary units happened to be included in our sample. Because we were about to engage in simple random sampling, each of the 10 possible samples given in Table 11.3 was equally likely to be picked; hence, each of the 10 sets of associated summary measures was equally likely to become the set of sample statistics that our procedure would ultimately reveal to us.

The probabilities for picking possible samples and then deriving the associated sample statistics appear in the last column of Table 11.3. For any given value that is listed only once in the $\overline{X}$ column (or s^2 column or s column or P_F column), there existed, prior to our sample selection, a probability of .1 that it would become the sample statistic, because there was a probability of .1 that any one of the listed samples would actually be drawn. Similarly, the probability equaled two times .1, or .2, for any value listed twice, and so on.

DERIVING SAMPLING DISTRIBUTIONS

The list of probabilities in the last column of Table 11.3 enables us to put together the *sampling distribution* for any one of that table's summary measures. For example, the data in the $\overline{X}$ column, along with those in the probability column, represent the sampling distribution of the sample mean. Similarly, the data in the s^2, the s, and the P_F columns, along with those in the probability column, represent the sampling distributions of the sample variance, the sample standard deviation, and the sample proportion, respectively.

To the extent that some values of the random variable occur more than once, we can simplify the presentation of the sampling distribution. For example, we can present the sampling distribution of the mean executive salary, or of the proportion of female executives, as shown in Table 11.4 on the next page.

One way to interpret Table 11.4 is this: If simple random samples of $n = 3$ were to be selected, say, 1,000 times from the population of $N = 5$ executives given in Table 11.2, we could expect to calculate a \$173,333 mean salary 100 times, a \$200,000 mean salary 200 times, and so on. In addition, we could expect to find a 0 proportion of females 100 times, a proportion of .333 some 600 times, and a proportion of .667 in the remaining 300 times. Thus, being aware of the very concept of sampling distributions helps us to be properly humble when using a sample statistic to estimate a population parameter. As we will learn in the next chapter, knowing about sampling distributions can also help us attach specified degrees of confidence to any one such estimate.

11.3 Sampling Distribution Summary Measures

In turn, we can describe any sampling distribution by summary measures of its own. Given the data of Table 11.4, for example, we can calculate the sampling distributions' means, variances, and standard deviations with the help of Formulas 9.A–9.C (on page 342). The results are shown in Table 11.5 on page 455.

Thus, $\mu_{\overline{X}}$ (pronounced "mu sub X bar") is the *arithmetic mean* of all the possible sample salary means or the *expected value* of the sampling distribution of the mean. Similarly, μ_P is the mean of all the possible sample proportions of female executives. The expressions $\sigma^2_{\overline{X}}$ (sigma squared sub X bar) and σ^2_P (sigma squared sub P) are the respective variances of the sampling distributions of the mean and of the proportion. Their square roots, $\sigma_{\overline{X}}$ (sigma sub X bar) and σ_P (sigma sub P), are the standard deviations of the two sampling distributions. They are also referred to as the *standard errors* of the respective sample statistics. Thus, $\sigma_{\overline{X}}$ is the **standard error of the sample mean,** and σ_P is called the **standard error of the sample proportion.** As

TABLE 11.4 | Sampling Distributions of the Mean and of the Proportion

These sampling distributions, culled from Table 11.3, show that, prior to sample selection, there exists a probability of .1 that the sample statistic of the mean salary will turn out to be $173,333. The probability also equals .1 that the sample mean will be calculated as $175,000, and so on. Similarly, the probability is .1 that the proportion of female executives will be found to be 0, but the probability is .6 that the proportion will be calculated as .333, and .3 that this sample statistic will equal .667.

Sampling Distribution of the Mean		Sampling Distribution of the Proportion	
Mean Salary (thousands of dollars) $\bar{X}$	Probability p	Proportion of Females P_F	Probability p
173.333	.1	0	.1
175.000	.1	.333	.6
176.667	.1	.667	.3
198.333	.1		1.0
200.000	.2		
201.667	.1		
223.333	.1		
225.000	.1		
226.667	.1		
	1.0		

we will see in Chapter 12, these terms are used because the standard deviation of all possible sample statistics plays a major role in the computation of possible errors associated with our estimation of population parameters.

Do not to confuse $\sigma_{\bar{X}}$ with s, nor with σ. This mistake is easy to make because all of these expressions are standard deviations. However, $\sigma_{\bar{X}}$ (the standard error of the sample mean) measures the variability of *possible* $\bar{X}$ values that might be obtained—a variability that a statistician is likely to contemplate while planning a sample survey. In contrast, s (the sample standard deviation) measures the variability of *actual* X values that were observed in a sample. This variability is calculated at the final stage of sampling, after one of the many possible samples has actually been selected and the actual sample mean, $\bar{X}$, has been computed. Finally, there is σ (the population standard deviation)—a value that measures the variability of all the X values in the population, which is unknown unless a census is taken.

As we will learn in a later section, when $n < .05\ N$, $\sigma_{\bar{X}} = \frac{\sigma}{\sqrt{n}}$, where n is sample size and N is population size.

11.4 The General Shape of Sampling Distributions

Before we can infer the values of unknown population parameters from known sample statistics with any degree of confidence, we must answer one question: What is the relationship between a sampling distribution and its parent population? We can answer the question in several ways.

TABLE 11.5 | Summary Measures of Two Sampling Distributions

With the help of Formulas 9.A–9.C, the two sampling distributions of Table 11.4 can be summarized as shown here.

Summary Measures of the Sampling Distribution of the Mean, $\bar{X}$	Summary Measures of the Sampling Distribution of the Proportion, P_F
$\mu_{\bar{x}} = 200$	$\mu_p = .40$
$\sigma^2_{\bar{x}} = 376.667$	$\sigma^2_p = .04$
$\sigma_{\bar{x}} = 19.408$	$\sigma_p = .20$

Here we focus on the general shape of the two frequency distributions of possible sample statistics on the one hand and of population values on the other.

THE SAMPLING DISTRIBUTION OF THE SAMPLE MEAN

Let us first consider the sampling distribution of the sample mean, $\bar{X}$, and how its shape relates to associated population values. Two of the most important theorems in the field of statistics describe this relationship. One is valid whenever population values are normally distributed, the other concerns situations in which population values are not normally distributed.

GIVEN A NORMALLY DISTRIBUTED POPULATION The following theorem summarizes the situation in which population values are normally distributed:

THEOREM 1 | Sampling Distribution of $\bar{X}$, Given Normal Population

If $\bar{X}$ is the mean of a simple random sample taken from a large population of X values and if the N population values are normally distributed, the sampling distribution of $\bar{X}$ is also normally distributed, regardless of sample size, n.

Given a population of X values that is normally distributed and given an associated sampling distribution of $\bar{X}$ that is, in accordance with Theorem 1, therefore also normally distributed, we can easily find the probability that the mean of any given simple random sample will lie within any given interval. All we need to do is transform the range of X values into corresponding z values (as we did in Chapter 10) and use Appendix Table H to establish the appropriate areas under the standard normal curve. An exercise will illustrate the point.

EXAMPLE PROBLEM 11.3

Given a normally distributed population of X values, a sampling distribution is summarized by $\mu_{\bar{X}} = 40$ and $\sigma_{\bar{X}} = 4.655$. Find the probability that a simple random sample will reveal a sample mean, $\bar{X}$, that lies

a. below 45.

b. between 37 and 41.5.

c. above 43.

SOLUTION:

a. Given Theorem 1, the sampling distribution will be normally distributed and can be sketched as in Figure 11.1.

FIGURE 11.1

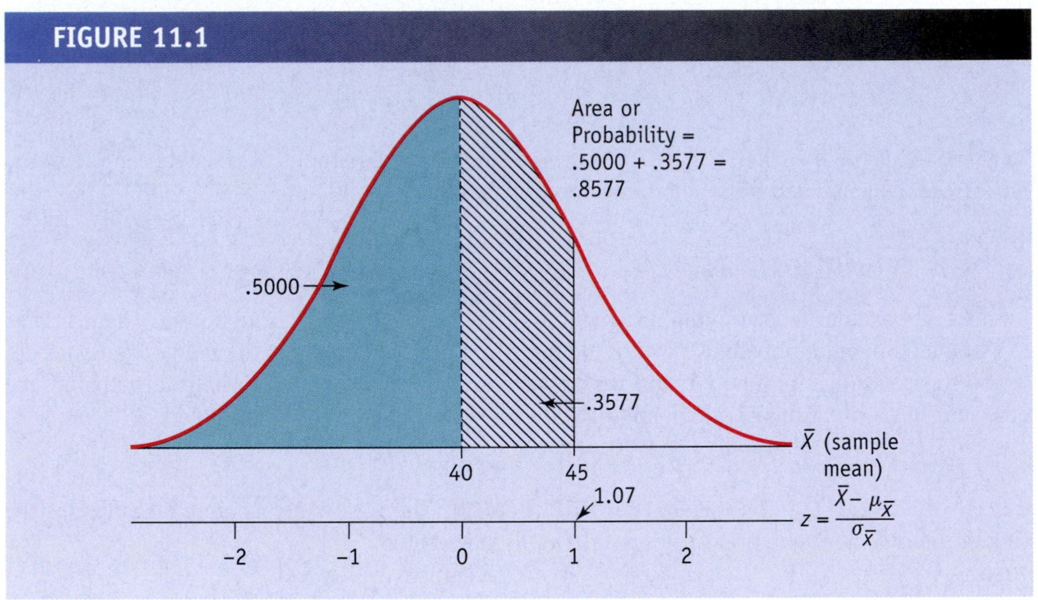

The center of the distribution corresponds to the mean of all sample means, or to $\mu_{\overline{X}} = 40$. Thus the value of $\overline{X} = 45$ lies to the right of this center. The corresponding z value is

$$z = \frac{\overline{X} - \mu_{\overline{X}}}{\sigma_{\overline{X}}} = \frac{45 - 40}{4.655} = 1.07$$

and the probability sought equals all of the area under the standard normal curve to the left of $z = 1.07$. That area equals .5 (shaded) plus .3577 (crosshatched), as Appendix Table H reveals. (Note the entry in the 1.0 row and the .07 column.) The probability in question is

$$p(\overline{X} < 45) = p(z < 1.07) = .8577$$

b. Given Theorem 1, the sampling distribution will be normally distributed and can be sketched as in Figure 11.2 on the following page.

The center of the distribution corresponds to the mean of all sample means, or to $\mu_{\overline{X}} = 40$. Thus the values of $\overline{X} = 37$ and $\overline{X} = 41.5$ lie to the left and right of this center, respectively. The corresponding z values are

$$z = \frac{\overline{X} - \mu_{\overline{X}}}{\sigma_{\overline{X}}} = \frac{37 - 40}{4.655} = -.64 \quad \text{and} \quad z = \frac{\overline{X} - \mu_{\overline{X}}}{\sigma_{\overline{X}}} = \frac{41.5 - 40}{4.655} = .32$$

FIGURE 11.2

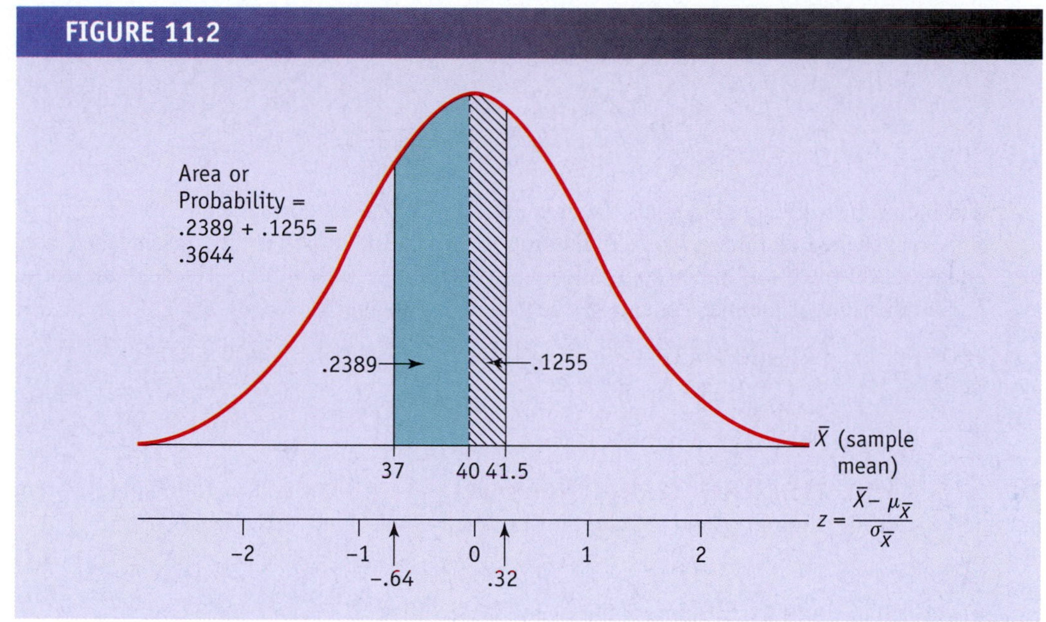

and the probability sought equals the area under the standard normal curve between $z = -.64$ and $z = .32$. According to Appendix Table H, this area equals .2389 (shaded) plus .1255 (crosshatched); thus, the probability in question is

$$p(37 < \overline{X} < 41.5) = p(-.64 < z < .32) = .2389 + .1255 = .3644$$

c. Given Theorem 1, the sampling distribution will be normally distributed and can be sketched as in Figure 11.3.

FIGURE 11.3

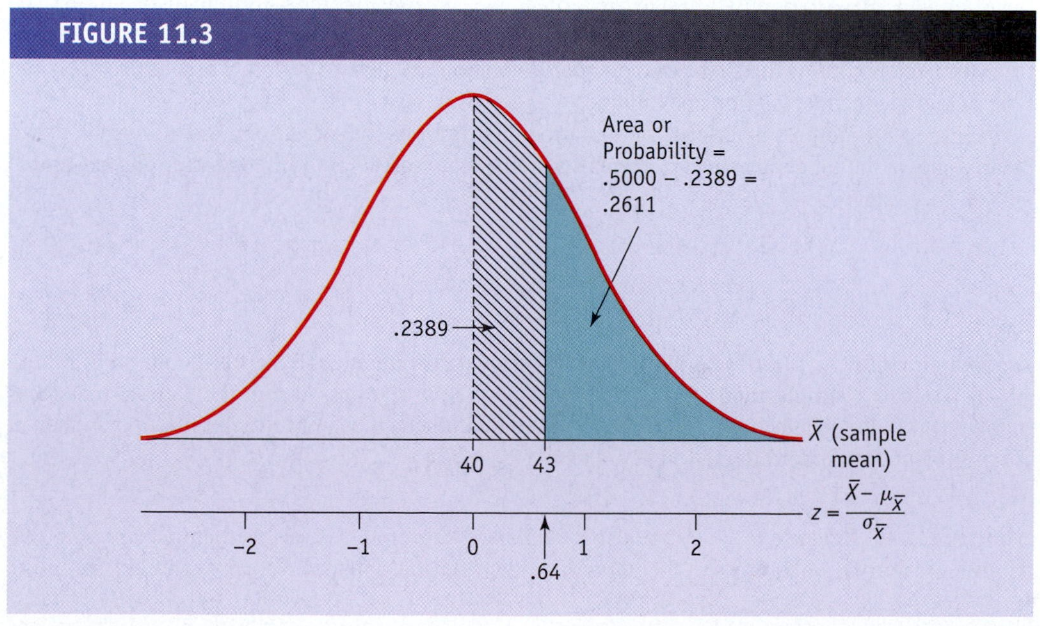

The center of the distribution corresponds to the mean of all sample means, or to $\mu_{\overline{X}} = 40$; thus the value of $\overline{X} = 43$ lies to the right of this center. The corresponding z value is

$$z = \frac{\overline{X} - \mu_{\overline{X}}}{\sigma_{\overline{X}}} = \frac{43 - 40}{4.655} = .64$$

and the probability sought equals the area under the standard normal curve to the right of $z = .64$ (shaded in Figure 11.3). According to Appendix Table H, the crosshatched area equals .2389 (note the intersection of the .6 row and the .04 column). Because the entire area to the right of the mean equals .5, the probability sought is

$$p(\overline{X} > 43) = p(z > .64) = .5000 - .2389 = .2611$$

GIVEN A POPULATION THAT IS NOT NORMALLY DISTRIBUTED The following theorem summarizes the situation in which population values are not normally distributed:

THEOREM 2 | Central Limit Theorem for Sample Mean

If $\overline{X}$ is the mean of a simple random sample taken from a large population of X values and if the N population values are *not* normally distributed, the sampling distribution of $\overline{X}$ nevertheless *approaches* a normal distribution as sample size, n, increases. (By convention, any sampling distribution of $\overline{X}$ is considered normal provided $n \geq 30$ and also $n < .05N$, because these values make the approximation of normality nearly perfect.)

Theorem 2 is called the **central limit theorem.** It is, perhaps, the most important theorem in the entire field of statistical inference. Consider what it says:

As long as we take random samples that are (1) sufficiently large absolutely ($n \geq 30$) and (2) fairly small relative to population size ($n < .05N$), we can consider the sampling distribution to be a normal curve and proceed to infer population parameters from sample statistics on that assumption. We need not know the shape of the underlying population distribution, which is precisely the type of knowledge that is often unavailable.

Figure 11.4 pictures a variety of population distributions that are anything but normal, and it clearly shows the tendency toward normality in the associated sampling distributions as sample size, n, increases.

EXAMPLE PROBLEM 11.4

A population of $N = 1{,}000$ is known to be uniformly distributed (as in the third column of Figure 11.4). We take a simple random sample of $n = 40$. How likely is it that the sample mean lies below 20 if independent information is available that places the sampling distribution's mean at $\mu_{\overline{X}} = 40$ and its standard deviation at $\sigma_{\overline{X}} = 15$?

SOLUTION: Because $n \geq 30$, but also $n < .05N$, Theorem 2 assures us that the *sampling* distribution is normal, regardless of the *population* distribution's shape. We can sketch the sampling

FIGURE 11.4 | Illustrations of the Central Limit Theorem

These graphs picture vividly the incredibly rapid tendency toward normality in sampling distributions as sample size increases, regardless of the shape of the associated population distributions—provided only that $n < .05N$. The vertical dotted lines coincide with the means of the various distributions.

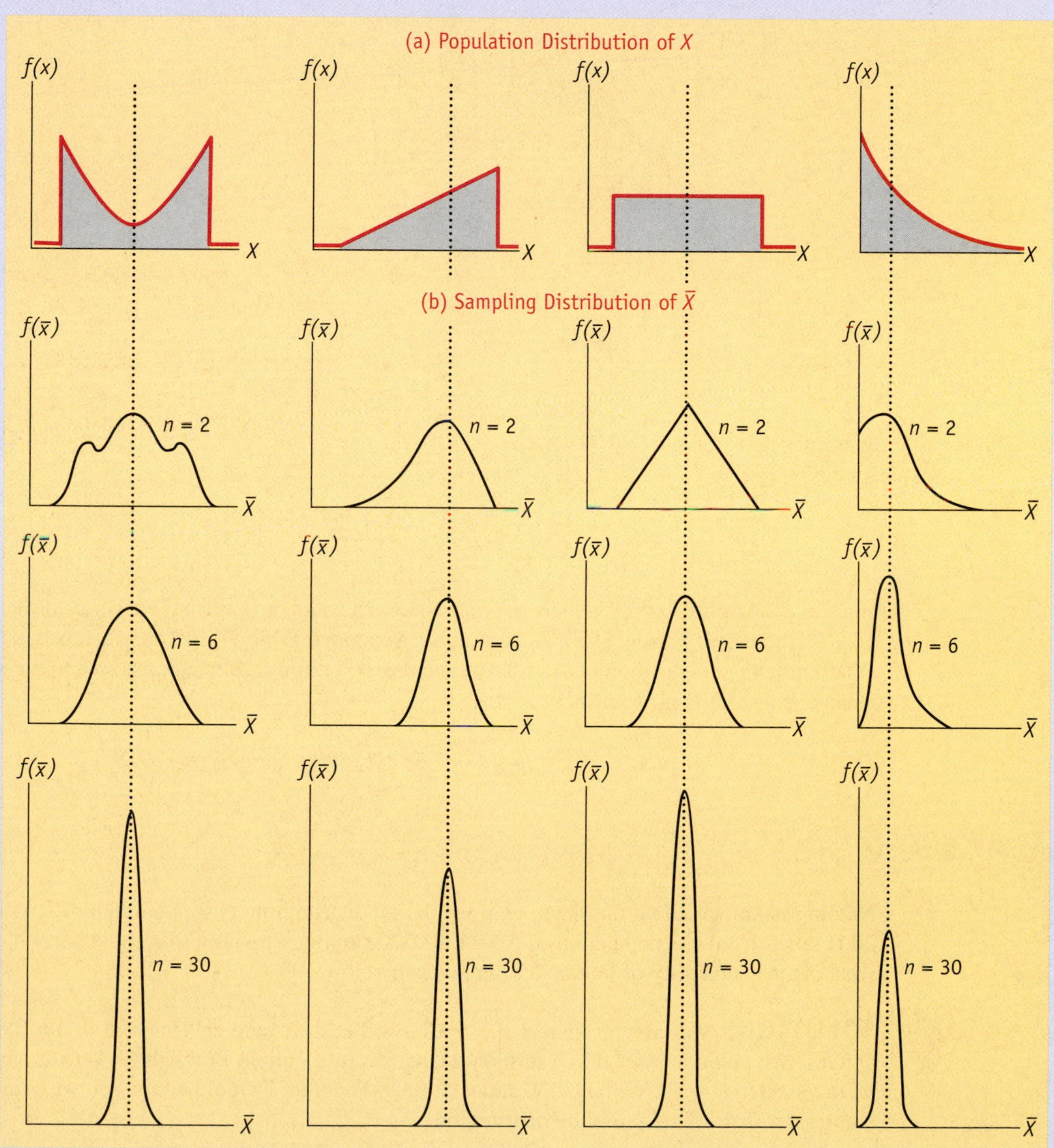

FIGURE 11.5

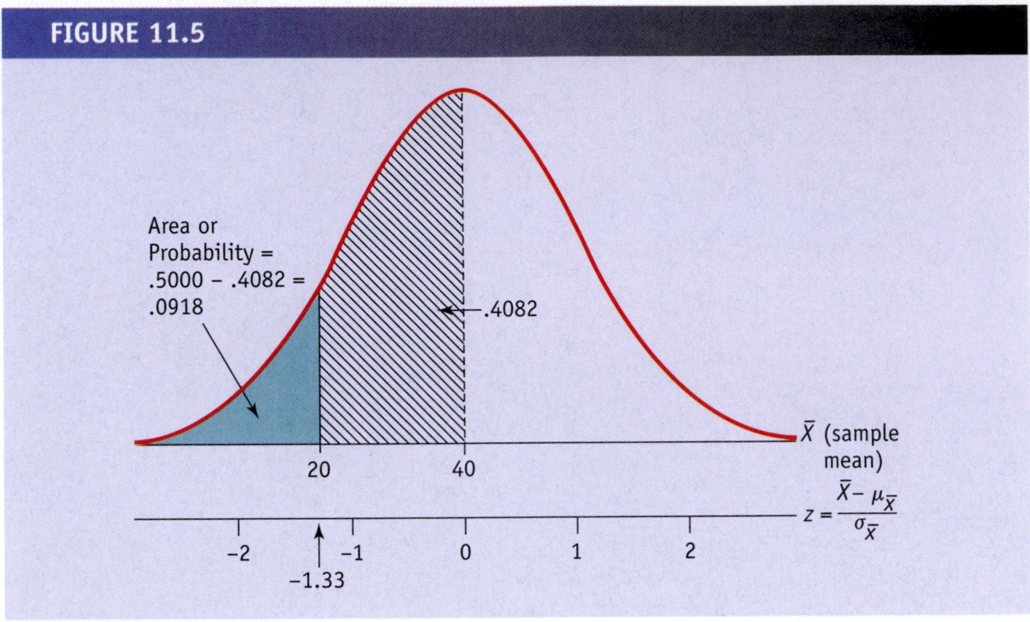

distribution as in Figure 11.5, with $\mu_{\overline{X}} = 40$ at the center and $\overline{X} = 20$ to the left of it. The corresponding z value is

$$z = \frac{\overline{X} - \mu_{\overline{X}}}{\sigma_{\overline{X}}} = \frac{20 - 40}{15} = -1.33$$

and the probability sought equals the area under the standard normal curve to the left of $z = -1.33$ (shaded in Figure 11.5). According to Appendix Table H, the crosshatched area equals .4082 (note the intersection of the 1.3 row and the .03 column). Because the area to the left of the mean equals .5, the probability sought is

$$p(\overline{X} < 20) = p(z < -1.33) = .5000 - .4082 = .0918$$

EXAMPLE PROBLEM 11.5

Nothing is known about the shape of a population distribution. A simple random sample of $n = 20$ is taken from the population of $N = 1{,}000$. Assuming we know that $\mu_{\overline{X}} = 50$ and $\sigma_{\overline{X}} = 10$, what is the probability of finding a sample mean below 40?

SOLUTION: We cannot answer the question, because neither Theorem 1 nor Theorem 2 applies. We could answer it in a fashion analogous to Example Problem 11.4 if the sample size were raised to $n = 30$. With $n = 30$ and $n < .05N$, Theorem 2 would apply, and we could assume a normally distributed sampling distribution.

THE SAMPLING DISTRIBUTION OF THE SAMPLE PROPORTION

Under specified circumstances, the sampling distribution of the sample proportion, P, can also be treated as if it were normally distributed. For example, review Figure 9.3 on page 351 and focus on the proportion of successes in a Bernoulli process. As sample size increases, this binomial random variable's probability distribution approaches normality. If we consider that a binomial sample proportion is really a sample mean of zeros and ones (*zero* for failure and *one* for success), it is not surprising that the central limit theorem applies here as well.

THEOREM 3 | Central Limit Theorem for Sample Proportion

If P is the proportion in a simple random sample of size n taken from a large population in which a certain characteristic occurs in proportion π, the sampling distribution of P *approaches* a normal distribution as sample size increases. (By convention, any sampling distribution of P is considered normal provided $n\pi \geq 5$ and also $n(1 - \pi) \geq 5$, because these values make the approximation nearly perfect.)

In fact, we already met the parenthetical rule of thumb just noted when we discussed the approximation of discrete probability distributions by the normal probability distribution in Section 10.6. For example, we saw how the binomial distribution comes to resemble the normal distribution whenever $n\pi \geq 5$ and $n(1 - \pi) \geq 5$ as well. Whenever this rule of thumb is satisfied, we can determine probabilities for various ranges of sample proportion values by using the standard-normal-curve table, calculating

$$z = \frac{P - \mu_P}{\sigma_P}$$

EXAMPLE PROBLEM 11.6

Suppose that 60 percent of all Americans approve of the way their president handles the economy; thus, $\pi = .6$. If you had independent information that the mean of the sampling distribution of the proportion so approving was $\mu_P = .6$, while the standard deviation was $\sigma_P = .049$, how likely would it be that a simple random sample of $n = 100$ Americans yielded an approval proportion in excess of .7?

SOLUTION: Because $n\pi = 100(.6) = 60$ and $n(1 - \pi) = 100(.4) = 40$, Theorem 3 applies. We can assume a normally distributed sampling distribution of the proportion. We can sketch it as in Figure 11.6 on the next page, with $\mu_P = .6$ at the center and $P = .7$ to the right of it.

The corresponding z value is

$$z = \frac{P - \mu_P}{\sigma_P} = \frac{.7 - .6}{.049} = 2.04$$

and the probability sought equals the area under the standard normal curve to the right of $z = 2.04$ (shaded in Figure 11.6). According to Appendix Table H, the crosshatched area equals .4793. Because the area to the right of the mean equals .5, the probability sought is

$$p(P > .7) = p(z > 2.04) = .5000 - .4793 = .0207$$

FIGURE 11.6

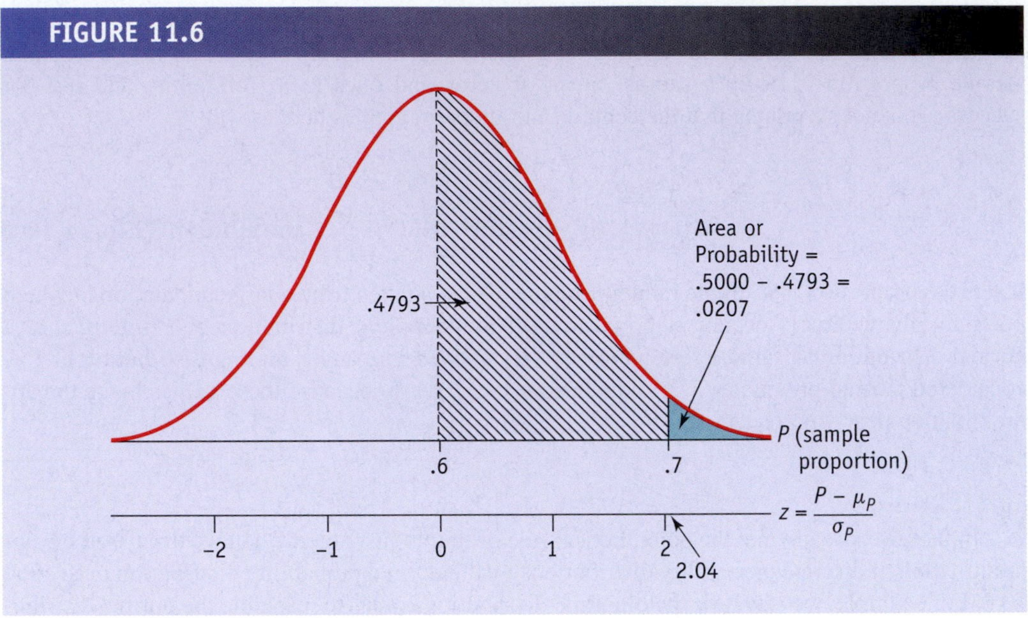

The answer has an interesting implication: Given the assumptions made (concerning the values of π, μ_P, σ_P, and n), if someone took such a sample of $n = 100$ and reported an approval rating of, say, .70 or even .95, that person would *almost certainly* be lying.

11.5 Mathematical Relationships among Summary Measures

The process of estimating the parameters of statistical populations with the help of sample statistics is aided considerably by this fact:

Summary measures of sampling distributions, such as their means, variances, and standard deviations, are uniquely related to the summary measures of corresponding population distributions. We will show these relationships for the sampling distribution of the mean as well as of the proportion.

THE SAMPLING DISTRIBUTION OF $\overline{X}$

Formulas 11.A–11.E indicate the ways in which the summary measures of the sampling distribution of the sample mean relate to those of the parent population.

COMPARING MEANS Note that the mean of all possible sample means, $\mu_{\overline{X}}$, always equals the population mean, μ. This fact is made evident by comparing Tables 11.5 and 11.2, which show $\mu_{\overline{X}} = \mu = 200$. This fact is also shown by the vertical dotted lines in Figure 11.4 that coincide with the means of the various distributions shown there.

COMPARING VARIANCES AND STANDARD DEVIATIONS The relationship between the variance of the sampling distribution, $\sigma^2_{\overline{X}}$, or the standard deviation, $\sigma_{\overline{X}}$, on the one hand, and the corresponding population measures, on the other hand, is somewhat more complicated. The relationship differs according to whether the selections of sample elements are statistically independent or dependent events. As we noted in Chapter 8, two events are *statistically independent*

FORMULAS 11.A–11.E | Summary Measures of the Sampling Distribution of $\overline{X}$

Formula 11.A $\mu_{\overline{X}} = \mu$

Large Population Case	*Small Population Case*
When selections of sample elements are *statistically independent events;* typically re ferred to as "the large population case," because $n < .05N$	When selections of sample elements are *statistically dependent events;* typically referred to as "the small population case," because $n \geq .05N$
Formula 11.B $\sigma^2_{\overline{X}} = \frac{\sigma^2}{n}$	**Formula 11.D** $\sigma^2_{\overline{X}} = \frac{\sigma^2}{n}\left(\frac{N-n}{N-1}\right)$
Formula 11.C $\sigma_{\overline{X}} = \frac{\sigma}{\sqrt{n}}$	**Formula 11.E** $\sigma_{\overline{X}} = \frac{\sigma}{\sqrt{n}}\sqrt{\frac{N-n}{N-1}}$

Note: $\mu_{\overline{X}}$ is the mean, $\sigma^2_{\overline{X}}$ is the variance, and $\sigma_{\overline{X}}$ is the standard deviation of the sampling distribution of the sample mean, $\overline{X}$. In turn, μ, σ^2, and σ are the population parameters—mean, variance, and standard deviation, respectively—while n or N is the sample or population size. The expression $\frac{N-n}{N-1}$ is the "finite population correction factor."

if the probability of the occurrence of one event is the same regardless of whether the other event does or does not occur. In contrast, two events are *statistically dependent* if the occurrence of one event does affect the probability of the occurrence of the other.

Now consider the event of selecting an element of the population for inclusion in a sample. Selecting one element does not in the least affect the probability of selecting any other element if the population is infinite in size or if sampling occurs with replacement. Even if sampling occurs without replacement, selecting one element does not affect the probability of selecting any other element *noticeably* as long as population size, N, is large relative to the sample size, n. (By tradition, a population is considered relatively large whenever $n < .05N$). Statistical independence in sample selection is, therefore, frequently referred to as "the large population case."

On the other hand, selecting an element of the population for inclusion in a sample *does* noticeably affect the probability of selecting any other element when sampling occurs without replacement *and* when the population is small relative to the sample (so that $n \geq .05N$). Statistical dependence in sample selection is, therefore, typically referred to as "the small population case." The formulas for the variance and standard deviation are then adjusted with the help of the expression $\frac{N-n}{N-1}$, which is called the **finite population correction factor.**

As Formulas 11.B–11.E attest, as long as $n > 1$, the variance or standard deviation of the sampling distribution of $\overline{X}$ is smaller than the corresponding population summary measure. Tables 11.5 and 11.2 once more provide examples:

While $\sigma^2_{\overline{X}} = 376.667$, the corresponding population parameter is larger: $\sigma^2 = 2{,}260$.

While $\sigma_{\overline{X}} = 19.408$, the corresponding population parameter is larger: $\sigma = 47.539$.

Note, in addition, that the larger the population variance or standard deviation is, given sample size, n, the larger is the variance or standard deviation of the sampling distribution of $\overline{X}$.

On the other hand, the larger the sample size, given the population variance or standard deviation, the smaller is the variance or standard deviation of the sampling distribution.

EXAMPLE PROBLEM 11.7

The summary data of the sampling distribution of $\overline{X}$ in Table 11.5 on page 455 were derived with the help of Formulas 9.A–9.C. Confirm these results with Formulas 11.A, 11.D, and 11.E, applied to the population summary data of Table 11.2.

SOLUTION:

$$\mu_{\overline{X}} = \mu = 200$$

$$\sigma^2_{\overline{X}} = \frac{\sigma^2}{n}\left(\frac{N-n}{N-1}\right) = \frac{2{,}260}{3}\left(\frac{5-3}{5-1}\right) = 753.333(.5) = 376.667$$

$$\sigma_{\overline{X}} = \frac{\sigma}{\sqrt{n}}\sqrt{\frac{N-n}{N-1}} = \frac{47.539}{\sqrt{3}}\sqrt{\frac{5-3}{5-1}} = 27.447(.707) = 19.405$$

Except for rounding error, the results are identical.

EXAMPLE PROBLEM 11.8

A production process creates tires with an average life span of $\mu = 40{,}000$ miles and a standard deviation of $\sigma = 5{,}000$ miles. A simple random sample of $n = 30$ tires is taken and their life span is determined.

a. Sketch the sampling distribution of $\overline{X}$.

b. Compute the probability that the simple random sample will discover a sample mean that lies within 500 miles of the population mean.

SOLUTION:

a. The ongoing production process provides us with an infinite population and, thus, "the large population case." According to Formulas 11.A and 11.C,

$$\mu_{\overline{X}} = \mu = 40{,}000$$

$$\sigma_{\overline{X}} = \frac{\sigma}{\sqrt{n}} = \frac{5{,}000}{\sqrt{30}} = 912.87$$

Figure 11.7 provides the relevant sketch.

b. We must compute the probability of $p(39{,}500 < \overline{X} < 40{,}500)$, which corresponds to

$$p\left(\frac{39{,}500 - 40{,}000}{912.87} < z < \frac{40{,}500 - 40{,}000}{912.87}\right) = p(-.55 < z < .55)$$

$$= .2088 + .2088$$

$$= .4176$$

as Appendix Table H can show. The relevant area is shaded in Figure 11.8.

FIGURE 11.7

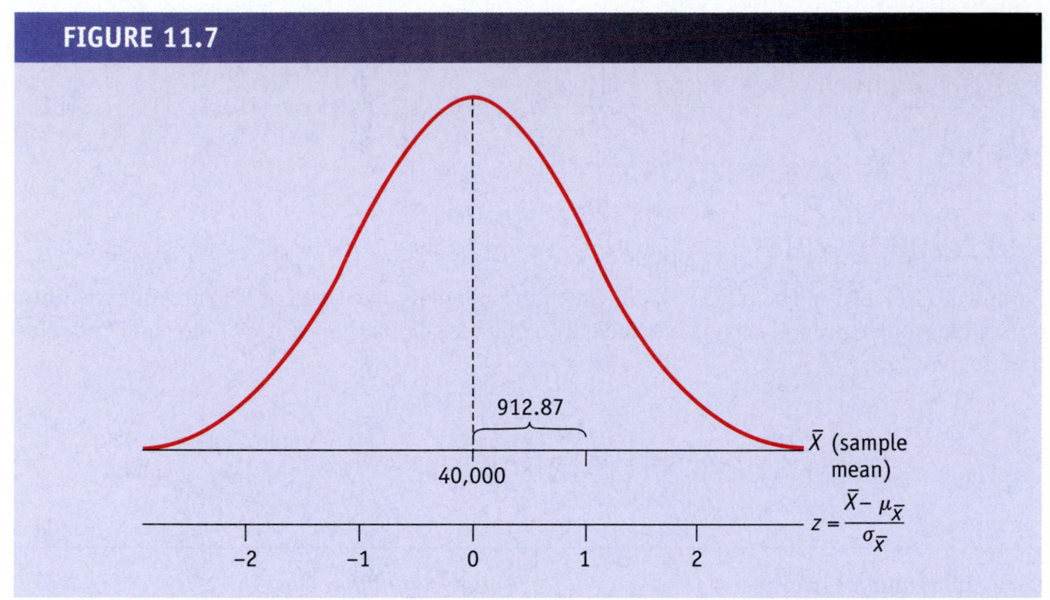

FIGURE 11.8

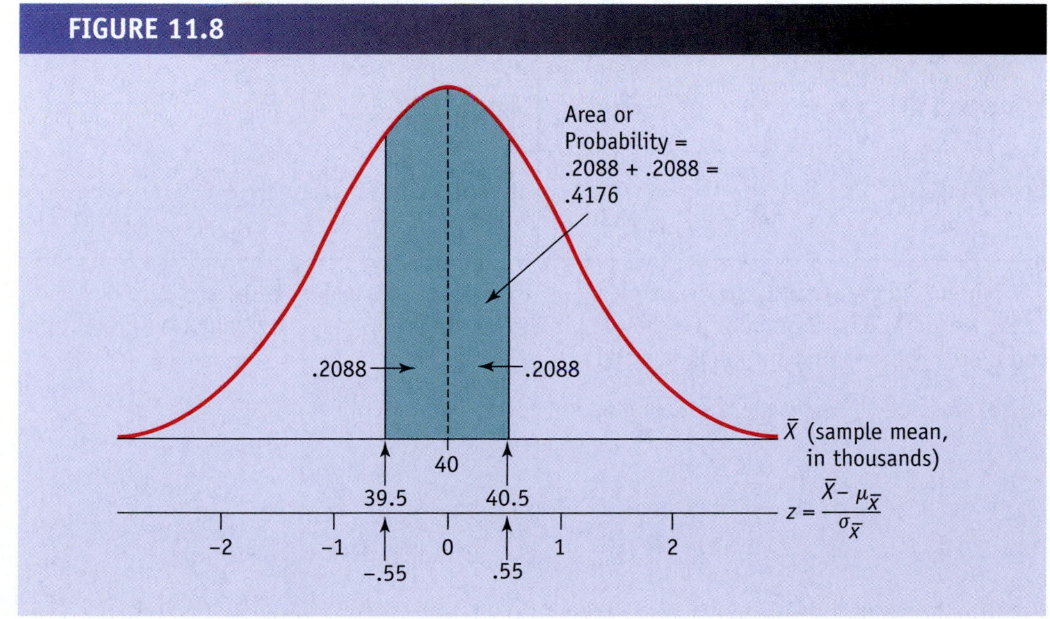

EXAMPLE PROBLEM 11.9

Would your answers to Example Problem 11.8 change if a sample of $n = 100$ instead of $n = 30$ were taken? Explain.

SOLUTION: First, the sampling distribution of $\overline{X}$ would have a smaller standard error:

$$\sigma_{\overline{X}} = \frac{\sigma}{\sqrt{n}} = \frac{5{,}000}{100} = 500$$

Second, the probability value would differ as well:

$$p\left(\frac{39{,}500 - 40{,}000}{500} < z < \frac{40{,}500 - 40{,}000}{500}\right) = p(-1 < z < 1) = .3413 + .3413 = .6826$$

THE SAMPLING DISTRIBUTION OF *P*

Formulas 11.F–11.J indicate the ways in which the summary measures of the sampling distribution of the sample proportion relate to the only available summary measure of the parent population (namely, π).

FORMULAS 11.F–11.J | Summary Measures of the Sampling Distribution of *P*

Formula 11.F $\mu_P = \pi$

Large Population Case	*Small Population Case*
When selections of sample elements are *statistically independent events;* typically referred to as "the large population case," because $n < .05N$	When selections of sample elements are *statistically dependent events;* typically referred to as "the small population case," because $n \geq .05N$
Formula 11.G $\sigma_P^2 = \dfrac{\pi(1-\pi)}{n}$	**Formula 11.I** $\sigma_P^2 = \dfrac{\pi(1-\pi)}{n}\left(\dfrac{N-n}{N-1}\right)$
Formula 11.H $\sigma_P = \sqrt{\dfrac{\pi(1-\pi)}{n}}$	**Formula 11.J** $\sigma_P = \sqrt{\dfrac{\pi(1-\pi)}{n}}\sqrt{\dfrac{N-n}{N-1}}$

Note: In these formulas μ_P is the mean, σ_P^2 is the variance, and σ_P is the standard deviation of the sampling distribution of the sample proportion, P, while π is the population proportion, and n or N is the sample or population size.

The expression $\dfrac{N-n}{N-1}$ is the "finite population correction factor."

EXAMPLE PROBLEM 11.10

Confirm the results of (the right half of) Table 11.5 on page 455 by now applying Formulas 11.F, 11.I, and 11.J to the only population summary value available (Table 11.2).

SOLUTION:

$$\mu_P = \pi = .40$$

$$\sigma_P^2 = \frac{\pi(1-\pi)}{n}\left(\frac{N-n}{N-1}\right) = \frac{.4(.6)}{3}\left(\frac{5-3}{5-1}\right) = .04$$

$$\sigma_P = \sqrt{\frac{\pi(1-\pi)}{n}}\sqrt{\frac{N-n}{N-1}} = \sqrt{\frac{.4(.6)}{3}}\sqrt{\frac{5-3}{5-1}} = .2828(.707) = .20$$

EXAMPLE PROBLEM 11.11

The manager of a mail-order house knows that 40 percent of all orders come from first-time customers. A simple random sample of 20 orders is taken.

a. Sketch the sampling distribution of P.

b. Compute the probability that the simple random sample taken here will discover a sample proportion of first-time customers that lies within .05 of the population proportion, $\pi = .40$.

SOLUTION:

a. Because $n\pi = 20(.4) = 8$ and $n(1 - \pi) = 20(.6) = 12$, Theorem 3 applies: The sampling distribution of P is normally distributed as in Figure 11.9.

FIGURE 11.9

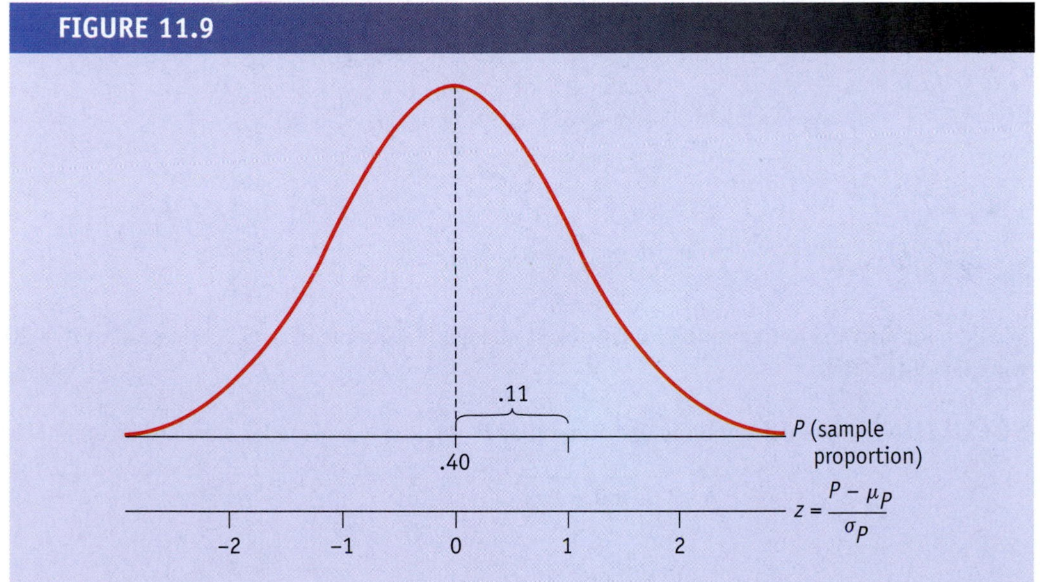

According to Formulas 11.F and 11.H,

$$\mu_P = \pi = .40$$

$$\sigma_P = \sqrt{\frac{\pi(1 - \pi)}{n}} = \sqrt{\frac{.4(.6)}{20}} = .11$$

b. We must compute the probability of $p(.35 < P < .45)$, which corresponds to

$$p\left(\frac{.35 - .40}{.11} < z < \frac{.45 - .40}{.11}\right) = p(-.45 < z < .45)$$

The relevant area is shaded in Figure 11.10 on the next page, and Appendix Table H provides the probability sought:

$$p(-.45 < z < .45) = .1736 + .1736 = .3472$$

FIGURE 11.10

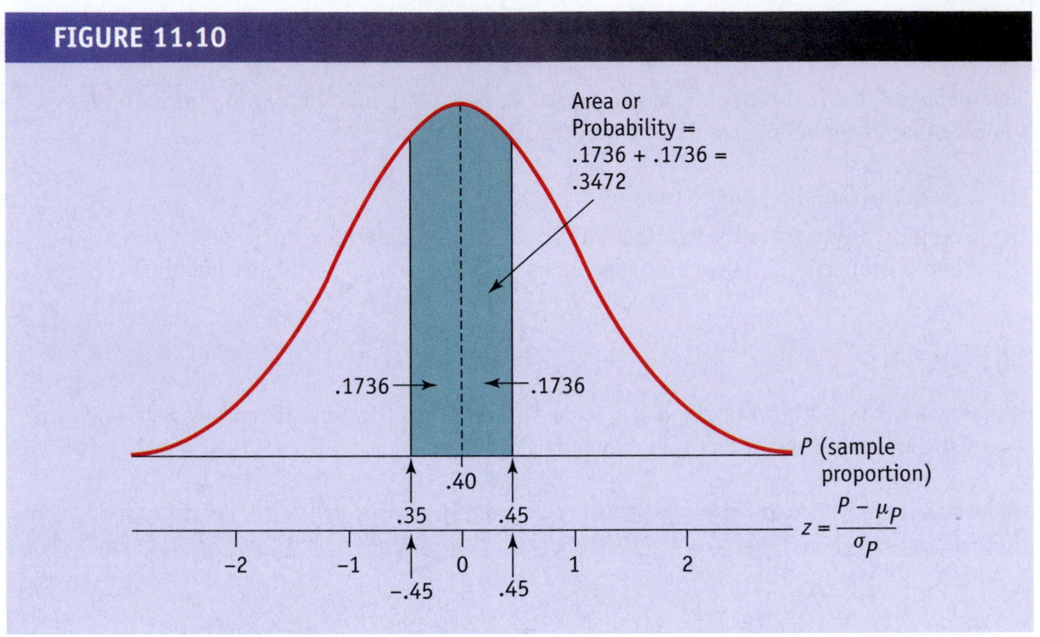

EXAMPLE PROBLEM 11.12

Would your answers to Example Problem 11.11 change if a sample of $n = 200$ instead of $n = 20$ were taken? Explain.

SOLUTION: First, the sampling distribution of P would have a smaller standard error:

$$\sigma_P = \sqrt{\frac{\pi(1 - \pi)}{n}} = \sqrt{\frac{.4(.6)}{200}} = .035$$

Second, the probability value would differ as well:

$$\begin{aligned} p(.35 < P < .45) &= p\left(\frac{.35 - .40}{.035} < z < \frac{.45 - .40}{.035}\right) \\ &= p(-1.43 < z < 1.43) = .4236 + .4236 = .8472 \end{aligned}$$

11.6 The Central Limit Theorem Reviewed

As many of this chapter's example problems have shown, when sampling distributions of the sample mean or the sample proportion are normally distributed, we can calculate many kinds of interesting probability values. Further, as later chapters will show, we can then estimate many kinds of population values and test all sorts of hypotheses. For this reason, we must have confidence in the normality of the sampling distribution. To be sure, for the sampling distribution of the mean, such normality is ensured, regardless of sample size, whenever the population that is being sampled is itself normally distributed (Theorem 1). Yet, more often than not, those who take simple random samples from some population have no knowledge about the shape of the underlying statistical population they are sampling. They may even know, to their chagrin, that the population is definitely *not* normally distributed. In such cases, the *central limit theorem* comes to their rescue (Theorems 2 and 3). Indeed, the central limit theorem is so important for the entire field of statistical inference that it is well worth reviewing here.

THE CENTRAL LIMIT THEOREM

a. Concerning the Sample Mean, $\overline{X}$

If $\overline{X}$ is the mean of a simple random sample of size n taken from a large* population of size N, which has a mean of μ and a standard deviation of σ, and if the population values are normally distributed, the sampling distribution of $\overline{X}$, regardless of sample size, is also normally distributed, with a mean of $\mu_{\overline{X}} = \mu$ and a standard deviation of $\sigma_{\overline{X}} = \frac{\sigma}{\sqrt{n}}$. If the N population values are *not* normally distributed, the sampling distribution of $\overline{X}$, nevertheless, *approaches* a normal distribution with $\mu_{\overline{X}} = \mu$ and $\sigma_{\overline{X}} = \frac{\sigma}{\sqrt{n}}$ as sample size n increases. [By convention, this approximation is considered nearly perfect whenever $n \geq 30$ and also $n < .05N$.]

b. Concerning the Sample Proportion, P

If P is the proportion in a simple random sample of size n taken from a large* population in which a certain characteristic occurs in proportion π, the sampling distribution of P *approaches* a normal distribution with a mean of $\mu_P = \pi$ and a standard deviation of $\sigma_P = \sqrt{\frac{\pi(1 - \pi)}{n}}$ as sample size n increases. [By convention, this approximation is considered nearly perfect whenever $n\pi \geq 5$ and also $n(1 - \pi) \geq 5$.]

*To qualify as *large,* strictly speaking, population size, N, must be infinite or sampling must occur with replacement. In practical applications, a sample size of $n < .05N$ is considered sufficient to meet the "large population" criterion.

Application 11.1, *Improvements in Sampling Techniques: Nielsen's People Meter,* and Application 11.2, *Poll on Abortion Finds Nation Sharply Divided,* provide illustrations of how this chapter's lessons are ultimately being put to work.

APPLICATION 11.1

IMPROVEMENTS IN SAMPLING TECHNIQUES: NIELSEN'S PEOPLE METER

The Chapter 4 Preview discussed the *Literary Digest* case that made us aware of the fact that incorrect sampling techniques (such as the selection of a *convenience* sample) and incorrect interpretations of sample results (such as the failure to identify all kinds of *bias*) can lead to disastrously misleading results. Those who engage in sampling, therefore, are well advised to scrutinize their methods again and again. Recent changes in the production of television's famous Nielsen ratings provide a case in point.

The A. C. Nielsen Company has been rating America's TV shows ever since 1950, and its announcements about the *proportion* of people watching particular shows or particular

(continued)

Application 11.1 (continued)

ads have been based on carefully selected *simple random samples* of American households. In recent years, the company's national ratings have been based on a sample of about 5,000 households containing more than 13,000 people who have agreed to participate. The same sample is observed repeatedly on a weekly basis, sometimes for years. For many years, participating households had to keep diaries, noting when the TV set was turned on and to what channel it was tuned. The information so gathered, however, failed to tell television companies and advertisers who precisely was watching what: the parents, the children, or the grandmother. This problem led to the introduction of personalized ID buttons that television viewers in the household sample were told to push whenever *they* watched. The results were questionable; children, in particular, were unlikely to comply. Worse yet, many critics questioned the Nielsen ratings on the grounds that TV sets tuned to Channel 3, with ID buttons on for persons A, B, and E, might still be watched by nobody at all. Especially during advertising breaks, person A may be chatting on the phone, person B may have fallen asleep, and person E may be microwaving a pizza.

All this has led to yet another improvement. Recently, Nielsen Media Research came up with the "passive people meter" and placed it in its sample households across the nation. The device measures people's TV viewing without their active participation. The new meter, an image recognition device, continually scans the television room. It recognizes all household members and measures, second by second, who is watching what, who enters or leaves the room—even who falls asleep or diverts the eyes to read a magazine. The new device has drastically changed ratings. Some shows, apparently, were watched mostly by the family dog!

All this sounds a bit like Big Brother in George Orwell's *1984,* but we can anticipate all kinds of other sampling applications. The new device may soon scan airports for known drug dealers or terrorists. It may scan supermarket aisles to see who buys what. It may aid blind people in object recognition.

SOURCES: Adapted from http://www.nielsenmedia.com; and Bill Carter, "TV Viewers Beware: Nielsen May Be Looking," *The New York Times,* June 1, 1989, pp. Al and D19.

APPLICATION 11.2

POLL ON ABORTION FINDS NATION SHARPLY DIVIDED

Polling Americans on the products they like, the politicians they favor, and the opinions they hold about hundreds of issues has become commonplace. Some of these polls are anything but scientific; we cannot possibly rely on such results to reflect the population as a whole.

Consider the case when viewers rush to their phones in response to a TV host's prompting and dial 800-numbers. The self-selected sample will produce results that are riddled with bias. Purely scientific samples, on the other hand, are another matter. They can take advantage of the *central limit theorem* to produce extremely reliable results from even tiny samples. In 1989, for instance, a sample of 1,412 Americans was contacted by pollsters working for *The New York Times* and *CBS News.* Given that there were about 250 million Americans, the sample of $n \geq 30$ was surely also a sample of $n < .05N$, satisfying the "large population" criterion.

Pollsters created the sample from a complete list of telephone exchanges in the country, making sure that each region of the country was represented in proportion to its population. A computer then selected telephone numbers for each chosen exchange, using a table of random numbers, such as that in Appendix Table A. This procedure permitted access to both listed and unlisted numbers. The numbers were then screened to limit calls to residences and to adults only. (Given that nearly everyone has a phone these days, the kind of bias problem noted in the Chapter 4 Preview is allegedly no longer a concern, but some experts disagree.)

The respondents were asked: "Please tell me whether or not you think it should be possible for a pregnant woman to obtain a legal abortion if [specified conditions hold]." The conditions specified included the following; proportions of *yes* answers are given in parentheses:

1. The woman's health is seriously endangered by the pregnancy. (.87)
2. There is a strong chance of serious defect in the baby. (.69)

(continued)

Application 11.2 (continued)

3. The family has a very low income and cannot afford any more children. (.43)
4. The woman is not married and does not want to marry the man. (.42)
5. The pregnancy interferes with work or education. (.26)

From the sampling error (σ_p), the pollsters determined a long-run probability of .95 that the proportions found in a national census would lie within .03 of the above results. For example, if the same sampling procedure were used again and again, a census on question 1 would confirm a population proportion between .84 and .90 in 95 out of 100 attempts, but 5 percent of the time, the pollsters would be proven wrong.

The pollsters also reported results for numerous subcategories, broken down by age, sex and marital status, education, race, religion, political philosophy, and exposure to previous abortions. Thus, while 9 percent of all respondents were against abortion under any and all circumstances (a proportion of .09), the proportions were .09 for women who had already had an abortion, .12 for persons aged 45–64, .13 for blacks, .13 for political conservatives, .14 for married women, .16 for people without a high-school education, and .22 for those Roman Catholics who considered religion very important.

Because the sampling error of the proportion equals $\sqrt{\frac{\pi(1-\pi)}{n}}$, a smaller sample size n (as for the various subgroups noted) produced a larger sampling error. Thus, it equaled ±.05 for married women and ±.07 for unmarried men.

Note: As many other polls do, this poll confirmed the importance (noted in Chapter 4) of not asking leading questions. When asked whether they favored a constitutional amendment prohibiting abortions, a majority said *no.* Yet when asked the identical question in a different way—whether they favored such an amendment to protect the lives of unborn children—a majority said *yes.*

SOURCE: Adapted from E. J. Dionne, Jr., "Poll on Abortion Finds the Nation Is Sharply Divided," *The New York Times,* April 26, 1989, pp. Al and 25.

11.7 Computer Simulations

Modern computer programs are ideally suited to explore the implications of the central limit theorem. EXCEL's Random Number Generation tool, for example, can fill a specified number of rows and columns with random values drawn from some specified probability distribution. Your choices include uniform, normal, Bernoulli, binomial, Poisson, patterned, and discrete distributions. More than that! The data so generated can be used to derive sample summary measures, which can then be compared with those of the underlying populations. In turn, one can generate histograms of the sampling distributions of means, proportions, and such for ever-increasing values of *n,* thereby providing a visual picture, akin to Figure 11.4 on page 459, of the tendency toward normality. The following two examples illustrate the possibilities.

EXCEL Example 11.1

a. Simulate 100 observations from a *normal distribution* with a mean of 50 and a standard deviation of 7 into each of 10 columns.

b. Considering each row as a separate sample, sized $n = 10$, compute the means of the 100 samples and derive a histogram of the sampling distribution of $\overline{X}$.

c. Finally, compare the simulated sampling distribution's basic statistics with those we would expect, given Formulas 11.A-11.E.

SOLUTION

Part (a)

1. Click **Tools** > **Data Analysis** > **Random Number Generation** > **OK** to activate the *Random Number Generation* dialog box.
2. In the *Number of Variables* box, type **10** and press TAB.
3. In the *Number of Random Numbers* box, type **100** and press TAB.
4. Under *Distribution,* select **Normal**.
5. Under *Parameters,* enter a *Mean* of **50** and a *Standard Deviation* of **7**.
6. Choose *New Worksheet Ply* and click **OK**.

The first 100 rows of worksheet columns A–J are filled with the requested numbers.

Part (b)

1. In order to compute the mean of the first sample given in row 1, select cell L1 and enter the formula **=AVERAGE(A1:J1)**.
2. Select L1 and drag the entry by the lower right handle to cell L100. Column L now contains 100 sample means.
3. Click **Tools** > **Data Analysis** > **Histogram** > **OK** to activate the *Histogram* dialog box.
4. Under *Input Range,* enter **L1:L100**.
5. Check *New Worksheet Ply* and *Chart Output* and click **OK**.
6. After appropriate editing, the result is something like this:

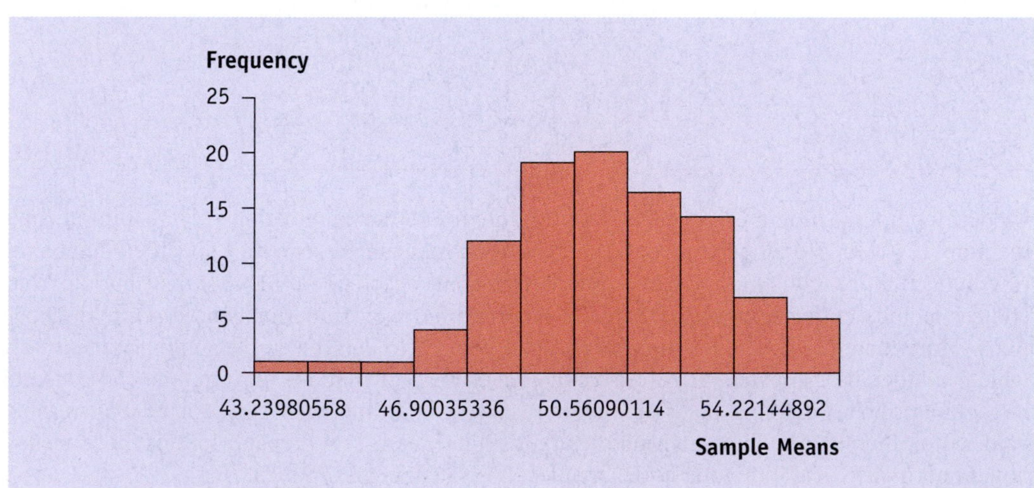

Part (c)

1. Click **Tools** > **Data Analysis** > **Descriptive Statistics** > **OK** to activate the *Descriptive Statistics* dialog box.
2. Under *Input Range,* enter **L1:L100**.
3. Check *Grouped by Columns, New Worksheet Ply,* and *Summary statistics* and click **OK**.

Among other things, the output includes a mean of **50.17545**, a median of **50.11898**, and a standard deviation of **2.401261**. Note how closely the mean in this simulation approaches the expected $\mu_{\bar{X}} = \mu = 50$. (In a precisely normal distribution, the median would, of course, equal the mean.) Similarly, the simulated standard deviation is fairly close to the expected $\sigma_{\bar{X}} = \frac{\sigma}{\sqrt{n}} = \frac{7}{\sqrt{10}} = 2.214$.

EXCEL Example 11.2

Simulate 100 observations from a *uniform distribution,* reaching from $a = -1$ to $b = 3$, into each of 30 columns. Considering each row as a separate sample, compute the means of 100 samples of size $n = 1$, $n = 10$, and $n = 30$, and show how the associated histograms approach the normal distribution as n rises (just as in the third column of Figure 11.4).

SOLUTION

1. Click **Tools** > **Data Analysis** > **Random Number Generation** > **OK** to activate the *Random Number Generation* dialog box.
2. In the *Number of Variables* box, type **30** and press TAB.
3. In the *Number of Random Numbers* box, type **100** and press TAB.
4. Under *Distribution,* select **Uniform**.
5. Enter *Parameters Between* **−1** *and* **3**.
6. Choose *New Worksheet Ply* and click **OK**.

The first 100 rows of worksheet columns A-AD are filled with the requested numbers.

Sample $n = 1$

1. Copy column A and paste it into column AF. You have the means of 100 samples of size $n = 1$.
2. Click **Tools** > **Data Analysis** > **Histogram** > **OK** to activate the *Histogram* dialog box.
3. Under *Input Range,* enter **AF1:AF100**.
4. Check *New Worksheet Ply* and *Chart Output* and click **OK**.

After appropriate editing, the result is something like this:

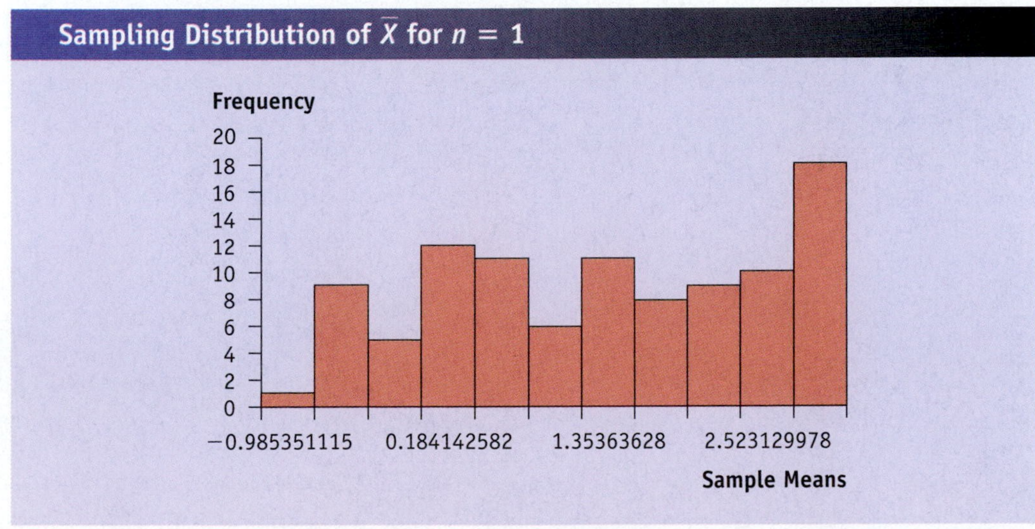

Sample $n = 10$

1. In order to compute the mean of the first sample of $n = 10$, select cell AH1 and enter the formula **=AVERAGE(A1:J1)**.
2. Select AH1 and drag the entry by the lower right handle to cell AH100. Column AH now contains 100 sample means for samples of $n = 10$.
3. Click **Tools** > **Data Analysis** > **Histogram** > **OK** to activate the *Histogram* dialog box.
4. Under *Input Range,* enter **AH1:AH100**.
5. Check *New Worksheet Ply* and *Chart Output* and click **OK**.

After appropriate editing, the result is something like this:

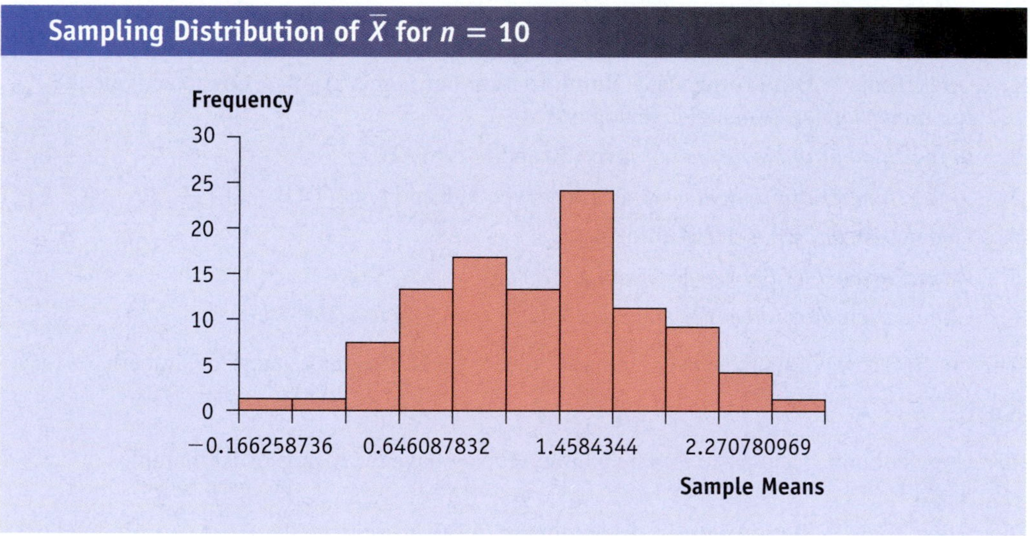

Sample $n = 30$

Repeat the process used for samples of $n = 10$, making changes as appropriate. The result is something like this:

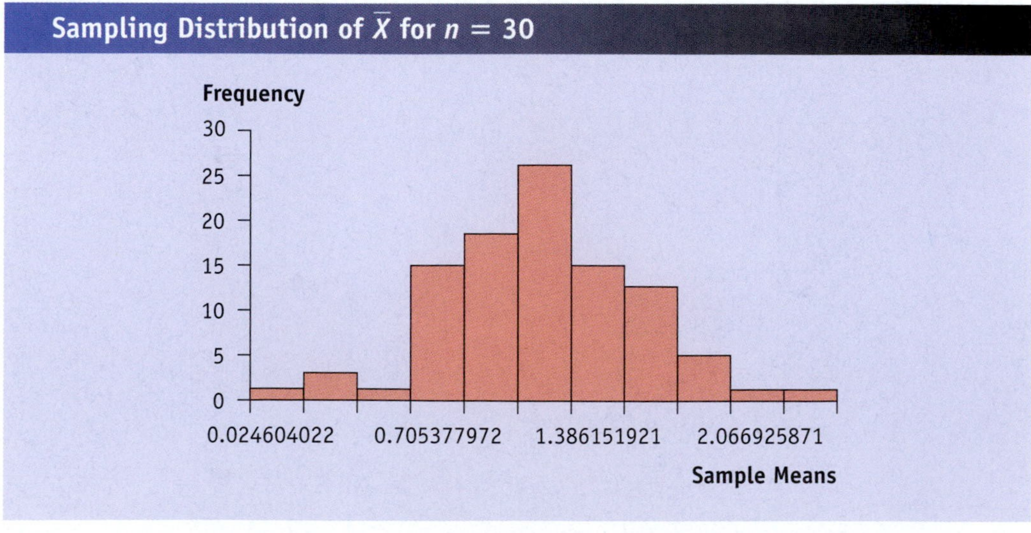

Summary

1. Because census taking is costly and time-consuming, decision makers frequently gain vital information about a statistical population by sampling. Subsequently, they can infer the values of unknown population *parameters* from known sample *statistics*—a process that is referred to as *estimation.*
2. The concept of the *sampling distribution* is crucial to understanding the nature of estimation. Every sample summary measure is in fact a random variable prior to the selection of an actual sample, and a sampling distribution is simply a probability distribution of a random variable that happens to be a summary measure based on sample data. A sampling distribution, thus, shows the likelihood of occurrence associated with all the possible values of a sample statistic, values that would be obtained when drawing all possible simple random samples of a given size from a population.
3. Any sampling distribution can, in turn, be described by summary measures of its own, such as mean, variance, and standard deviation. The standard deviation of a sampling distribution is also referred to as the *standard error* of the sample statistic in question.
4. The relationship between a sampling distribution and its parent population is of great importance. It can be described in a general way by focusing on the general shapes of the two frequency distributions or more precisely by focusing on mathematical relationships among their summary measures.
5. Two important theorems relate the general shape of the sampling distribution of the sample mean to the population distribution:
   - **a.** If $\overline{X}$ is the mean of a simple random sample taken from a large population of X values and if the N population values are normally distributed, the sampling distribution of $\overline{X}$ is also normally distributed, regardless of sample size, n.
   - **b.** If $\overline{X}$ is the mean of a simple random sample taken from a large population of X values and if the N population values are *not* normally distributed, the sampling distribution of $\overline{X}$ nevertheless *approaches* a normal distribution as sample size, n, increases. This is the *central limit theorem* as it relates to the sample mean. By convention, any sampling distribution of $\overline{X}$ is considered normal, provided $n \geq 30$, but also $n < .05N$.
6. The central limit theorem can also be applied to the sample proportion: If P is the proportion in a simple random sample of size n taken from a large population in which a certain characteristic occurs in proportion π, the sampling distribution of P *approaches* a normal distribution as sample size increases. By convention, any sampling distribution of P is considered normal provided $n\,\pi \geq 5$ and $n(1 - \pi) \geq 5$ as well.
7. Computer programs, such as EXCEL or MINITAB, are ideally suited to *simulate* sampling distributions from any type of statistical population and for any sample size, thereby illustrating the rapid tendency of these distributions to approach the normal distribution as n rises.

Key Terms

central limit theorem
estimation
finite population correction factor
parameter
population
sample
sampling distribution
simple random sample
standard error of the sample mean
standard error of the sample proportion
statistic

Practice Problems

NOTE

Some problems require the use of a statistical program such as EXCEL or MINITAB. The program's major features are explained in text Chapter 2. Plenty of additional advice is available via the program's built-in Help feature.

Section 11.2 The Concept of the Sampling Distribution

1. How many different simple random samples of size $n = 3$ can be drawn from a population of $N = 10$? $N = 20$?

2. How many different simple random samples of size $n = 4$ can be drawn from a population of $N = 20$? $N = 100$?

3. A company's $N = 6$ sales representatives have annual sales (in millions of dollars) as indicated in Table 11.6. Establish the sampling distribution for average sales, $\overline{X}$, for a simple random sample of $n = 2$.

TABLE 11.6 | Annual Sales

Representative	Millions of Dollars
A	50
B	31
C	79
D	45
E	27
F	63

4. Annual advertising expenditures by $N = 5$ competitors (in millions of dollars) are indicated in Table 11.7. Establish the sampling distribution for average expenditures, X, for a simple random sample of $n = 3$.

TABLE 11.7 | Annual Advertising Expenditures

Competitor	Millions of Dollars
A	100
B	35
C	18
D	7
E	59

5. Last month, a real estate agent sold five houses, three of which were priced below \$200,000 and two above \$200,000, as Table 11.8 shows. For a simple random sample of $n = 2$, establish the sampling distribution of P, the proportion of houses sold that were priced above \$200,000.

TABLE 11.8 | House Prices

House	Price
A	\$180,000
B	259,000
C	378,500
D	165,000
E	99,000

6. A consumer holds four credit cards with interest rates as given in Table 11.9. For a simple random sample of $n = 2$, establish the sampling distribution of P, the proportion of cards charging interest above 15 percent.

TABLE 11.9 | Credit Card Interest Rates

Credit Card	Percent per Year
A	9.9
B	12.7
C	18.9
D	17.9

SECTION 11.3 SAMPLING DISTRIBUTION SUMMARY MEASURES

7. Review Practice Problem 3. Compute the mean, variance, and standard deviation for the sampling distribution.
8. Review Practice Problem 4. Compute the mean, variance, and standard deviation for the sampling distribution.
9. Review Practice Problem 5. Compute the mean, variance, and standard deviation for the sampling distribution.
10. Review Practice Problem 6. Compute the mean, variance, and standard deviation for the sampling distribution.

SECTION 11.4 THE GENERAL SHAPE OF SAMPLING DISTRIBUTIONS

11. Review Example Problem 11.3 on pages 455–458. Using EXCEL or MINITAB, confirm the answers to parts (a)–(c).
12. Given a normally distributed population, a sampling distribution is summarized by $\mu_{\overline{X}} = 100$ and $\sigma_{\overline{X}} = 15$. Use Appendix Table H to determine the probability that a simple random sample will reveal a sample mean
    - **a.** below 120.
    - **b.** between 120 and 130.
    - **c.** between 90 and 125.
    - **d.** below 88.
    - **e.** between 88 and 95.
13. Given a normally distributed population, a sampling distribution is summarized by $\mu_{\overline{X}} = 50$ and $\sigma_{\overline{X}} = 15$. Use EXCEL or MINITAB to determine the probability that a simple random sample will reveal a sample mean
    - **a.** above 63.
    - **b.** between 53 and 63.
    - **c.** between 40 and 63.
    - **d.** below 30.
    - **e.** between 30 and 45.
14. A population of $N = 500$ is uniformly distributed.
    - **a.** A simple random sample of $n = 20$ is taken. How likely is it that the sample mean lies between 30 and 40 if independent information tells us that $\mu_{\overline{X}} = 30$ and $\sigma_{\overline{X}} = 5$?
    - **b.** What would your answer be for $n = 100$?
15. A population of $N = 5{,}000$ is uniformly distributed. A simple random sample of $n = 100$ is taken. How likely is it that the sample mean lies between 400 and 500 if independent information tells us that $\mu_{\overline{X}} = 600$ and $\sigma_{\overline{X}} = 75$?
16. On a certain street, cars are driving at an average speed of 27 mph. The standard deviation is 2.3 mph. For a simple random sample of $n = 12$ cars, compute the probability of discovering an average speed in excess of 30 mph.

SECTION 11.5 MATHEMATICAL RELATIONSHIPS AMONG SUMMARY MEASURES

17. Using Formulas 11.A–11.E as appropriate, compute the mean, variance, and standard deviation for the sampling distribution derived in
    - **a.** Practice Problem 3.
    - **b.** Practice Problem 4.
    - **c.** Practice Problem 5.
    - **d.** Practice Problem 6.

(*Hint:* the answers were derived independently in Practice Problems 7–10.)

18. Various samples are drawn from normally distributed (infinite) populations with means and variances as shown below. In each case, determine the mean and standard deviation of the sampling distribution of $\overline{X}$.

a. $n = 10; \mu = 30; \sigma^2 = 9$

b. $n = 15; \mu = 50; \sigma^2 = 4$

c. $n = 30; \mu = 100; \sigma^2 = 100$

d. $n = 100; \mu = 400; \sigma^2 = 64$

19. In a statistics class of 60 students, the exam mean is 80, the standard deviation is 14. Compute the mean of a sampling distribution for a simple random sample of 20 as well as the associated standard error.

20. Suppose that weights for women in their 20s average 125 lb., with a standard deviation of 14 lb. Describe the sampling distribution of the mean for a simple random sample of $n = 50$. How likely is it that the random sample will produce a mean

a. below 100 lb.?

b. above 140 lb.?

c. between 100 and 140 lb.?

21. International telephone calls average 11 minutes with a standard deviation of 3.1 minutes. Describe the sampling distribution of the mean for a simple random sample of $n = 35$. How likely is it that the random sample will produce a mean

a. between 13 and 13.4 minutes?

b. above 13.2 minutes?

22. Workers in an industry earn $17.35 per hour on the average; the standard deviation is $2.10 per hour. Describe the sampling distribution of the mean for a simple random sample of $n = 40$, given $N = 600{,}000$. How likely is it that the random sample will produce a mean

a. between $16.80 and $17.00?

b. between $17.00 and $17.50?

c. above $17.47?

23. A machine fills cans of soup with an average 15.9 ounces; the standard deviation is .1 ounce. Describe the sampling distribution of the mean for a simple random sample of $n = 80$. How likely is it that the random sample will produce a mean

a. below 15.8 ounces?

b. between 15.8 and 16.1 ounces?

c. above 15.95 ounces?

24. Assume that 28 percent of all people have a college degree. Describe the sampling distribution of the proportion of people with a college degree

a. for a simple random sample of $n = 50$.

b. for a simple random sample of $n = 200$.

25. Assuming a population of $N = 100$, with a mean of $\mu = 30$ and a standard deviation of $\sigma = 3$, compute the mean and standard deviation of the sampling distribution of $\overline{X}$ for a simple random sample of

a. $n = 4$.

b. $n = 50$.

26. Given a population of $N = 1{,}000$ and $\sigma = 50$, compute the standard deviation of the sampling distribution of $\overline{X}$ for simple random samples of 20, 80, 200, and 500.

27. The shape of a population distribution is unknown, but we know that $\mu = 200$ and $\sigma = 22$. If a simple random sample is taken and the population is infinite, for which of the following sample sizes can we assume a *normal* sampling distribution? Describe these normal distributions by computing $\mu_{\overline{X}}$ and $\sigma_{\overline{X}}$.

a. $n = 10$

b. $n = 25$

c. $n = 50$

d. $n = 100$

SECTION 11.6 THE CENTRAL LIMIT THEOREM REVIEWED

28. A production process creates aircraft engines with an average life span of $\mu = 2{,}500$ hours and a standard deviation of $\sigma = 400$ hours. A simple random sample of $n = 50$ engines is taken and their life span is determined.

a. Describe the sampling distribution of $\overline{X}$.

b. Compute the probability that the simple random sample will reveal a sample mean between 2,000 and 2,100 hours.

c. Compute the probability of finding a sample mean that lies within 50 hours of the population mean.

29. An IRS agent knows that 25 percent of all tax returns contain arithmetic errors. A simple random sample of 30 tax returns is taken.

a. Describe the sampling distribution of P.

b. Compute the probability that the simple random sample will reveal a sample proportion of errors that lies below .10.

30. A bank reports (accurately) that the population of its demand deposit balances is normally distributed with a mean of $1,200 and a standard deviation of $250. An auditor refuses to certify the bank's claim and takes a random sample of 36 account balances. The auditor will certify the bank's report only if the sample mean lies within $50 of the alleged population mean. What is the probability for such a finding?

31. A manufacturer of strapping tape claims that the lengths of tape on the firm's rolls have a mean of 90.10 feet and a standard deviation of .14 foot. If you take a random sample of $n = 49$ units of the firm's output,

a. what is the nature of the sampling distribution of the sample mean?

b. what are the chances that your sample mean will be 90 feet or less?

c. what do you conclude about the truthfulness of the manufacturer's claim if you do find a sample mean of 89.8 feet?

32. The speed of cars along the interstate averages 71 mph, with a standard deviation of 5 mph. The population of speeds is normally distributed.

a. Describe the sampling distribution of the mean for a simple random sample of 20 cars.

b. Compute the probability that this sample will reveal a mean speed of 56 mph or less. Of between 71 and 72 mph. Of 68 mph or more.

33. In a large city, an ambulance takes an average of 12 minutes to arrive after an emergency call; the standard deviation is 4 minutes.

a. Describe the sampling distribution of the mean response time for a simple random sample of 36 calls.

b. Compute the probability of finding a sample mean of more than 11 minutes. Of between 13 and 14 minutes. Of over 15 minutes.

c. What is the likelihood of finding a sample mean that lies within 30 seconds of the population mean?

34. Assume that 40 percent of all people respond when contacted in a telephone survey. What is the likelihood that at least 188 will respond when a simple random sample of 500 people is taken?

35. An ongoing production process produces 10 percent defective items. A quality inspector takes a simple random sample of 70 items and will reject the entire output if more than 5 percent of the sample is defective. What is the probability of rejection?

36. If half of all orders at McDonald's include a soft drink, what is the probability that between 40 and 55 percent of the next 36 orders will include a soft drink?

37. A bank's accounting firm finds that in the long run 60 percent of customers respond to verification requests. A simple random sample of 20 customers is taken. What is the probability that between 57 and 67 percent will respond?

38. If 28 percent of all Americans think there is too much violence on TV and a simple random sample of 20 viewers is taken, what is the likelihood that the sample percentage of those abhorring TV violence lies above 30 percent? Above 25 percent?

39. If 8 percent of a firm's employees are fired because of sexual harassment of co-workers and a simple random sample of 75 past workers is taken, what is the likelihood that more than 25 were fired for this reason? Between 5 and 20 were so fired?

40. If 72 percent of all managers have an MBA and a simple random sample of 20 managers is taken, what is the likelihood of finding

a. between 10 and 12 managers with MBAs?

b. more than 15 with MBAs?

c. fewer than 8 with MBAs?

41. If 43 percent of all consumers use Ivory soap and a random sample of 15 consumers is taken, what is the likelihood of finding

a. more than 5 Ivory users?

b. between 6 and 12 Ivory users?

c. fewer than 5 Ivory users?

42. If 83 percent of all drivers are willing to pump their own gas and a simple random sample of 30 drivers is taken, what is the likelihood of finding a sample proportion in excess of .85?

43. A pharmaceutical company knows that 5 percent of all users of a certain drug experience a serious side effect. If a simple random sample of 120 users is examined, what is the probability of finding

a. no side effects?

b. between 5 and 10 cases with side effects?

c. more than 20 cases with side effects?

44. New mortgages in the nation have an average interest rate of 10.79 percent; the standard deviation is .88 percent. For a simple random sample of 32 mortgages,

a. describe the sampling distribution of the mean interest rate.

b. compute the probability of finding a mean interest rate within 0.2 percentage points of the national average.

45. The average salary of the nation's elementary teachers equals $39,075 per year, with a standard deviation of $5,036. What is the probability that a simple random sample will reveal an average salary, $\overline{X}$, that lies within $400 of the national average

a. if $n = 30$?

b. if $n = 300$?

c. How large a sample would one have to take in order to assure that the probability equaled .9?

46. A proportion of .2 of all consumers has never heard a certain advertising slogan. If a simple random sample of 30 consumers is taken, what is the probability that 5 or more will never have heard the slogan?

47. Suppose you were told that 80 percent of all General Motors employees had contributed to a charity drive. You then took a simple random sample of 36 workers and found that only 5 had contributed.

a. What would you conclude? Explain.

b. What if you had found 25 contributors?

48. The manufacturer of batteries for aircraft emergency-locator transmitters claims that the lifetime of these batteries is normally distributed with a mean of 30 months and a standard deviation of 3 months. An aircraft manufacturer checks out 50 batteries and discovers a sample mean of only 29 months. What is the probability that the battery manufacturer's claim is true?

Section 11.7 Computer Simulations

49. Using EXCEL or MINITAB, simulate 100 observations from a *Poisson distribution* with a mean of 6 into each of 10 columns. Considering each row as a separate sample, compute the means of 100 samples of size $n = 1$, $n = 3$, and $n = 10$, and show how the associated histograms approach the normal distribution as n rises.

50. Using EXCEL, simulate 100 observations from a *uniform distribution,* reaching from $a = -10$ to $b = 7$, into each of 30 columns. (If using MINITAB, simulate 100 observations from an *exponential distribution* with a mean of .2 into each of 30 columns.) Considering each row as a separate sample, compute the means of 100 samples of size $n = 1$, $n = 5$, and $n = 30$, and show how the associated histograms approach the normal distribution as n rises.

ESTIMATION

LOOKING AHEAD

After reading this chapter, you will be able to:

1. appreciate that good estimators must be unbiased, efficient, and consistent,
2. make single-number *point estimates* of population means, population proportions, and differences between two population means or between two population proportions,
3. use data derived from large samples to construct *confidence intervals* that wrap margins of error around point estimates,
4. use *Student's t distribution* to construct confidence intervals based on small samples, and
5. determine the *optimal sample size* for interval estimation procedures so as to achieve any desired combination of margin of error and confidence level.

AND HERE IS A TYPICAL PROBLEM YOU WILL BE ABLE TO SOLVE:

A bank claims that no more than 2 percent of its monthly customer statements are in error. An auditor doesn't believe the claim, selects 100 accounts randomly from the bank's 15,233 accounts, and contacts the customers in question. Of these, 12 report and prove at least one error in their last month's statements. Construct a 98 percent confidence interval for the true proportion of erroneous bank statements that the bank mails out. What, precisely, is the *meaning* of this interval?

PREVIEW

Full-fledged censuses are often costly and time-consuming. Business managers and economists, therefore, routinely employ sample statistics in order to *estimate* the values of relevant parameters, such as population means and population proportions. Thus, an executive who seeks to do business in a new city, county, state, or even in a foreign country, may well want to know the mean income of the firm's potential customers there. Someone about to launch a product in a given market may wonder about the proportion of people who are already consuming a competing product. And an economist working to forecast next year's GDP may need to gauge current consumer attitudes about the economy and, thus, get an inkling of their spending plans.

Indeed, some businesses devote themselves entirely to gathering crucial data such as these for anyone willing to pay for them. A list of the better known sample survey firms in the United States includes the

Gallup Organization (found at http://www.gallup.com), Harris (see http://www.harrisInteractive.com), Nielsen (see http://www.acnielsen.com), and Roper Starch (see http://www.roper.com). Table 12.1 summarizes some of the surveys taken by these companies in 1999; sample proportions have been multiplied by 100 and thus turned into percentages.

In 1999, questions 1–4 were of great concern to the Microsoft Corporation, which had been embroiled in a highly publicized antitrust suit for over a year. Bill Gates, the founder and CEO of Microsoft, wanted to know whether the suit was hurting the company's image and ultimately its bottom line. The answer was clearly *no*. Although other industry leaders, along with the Justice Department, wanted to see the computer giant's power and dominance curtailed on the grounds that it was unfairly driving competitors out of business, the American public disagreed. (Nevertheless, the ultimate court decision in 2000 found Microsoft guilty of monopolistic practices.)

Another hot issue of 1999 was addressed by questions 5–7. Prosperous economic conditions led Congress and the President to anticipate huge budget surpluses in future years. Both political parties agreed to use much of that money to keep the Social Security program solvent, but they sharply disagreed on how

TABLE 12.1 | Selected Sample Survey Results, United States, 1999

Question	Result	
1. Thinking about Microsoft—the computer software company that produces Windows 95 and other products—do you have a favorable or unfavorable opinion of the Microsoft Corporation?	Favorable	58%
	Unfavorable	13%
	No opinion	29%
2. As you may know, a lawsuit by the Justice Department against Microsoft is currently being tried in court. Based on what you know about the case, do you side more with the Justice Department or the Microsoft Corporation?	Justice Department	26%
	Microsoft Corporation	42%
	No opinion	32%
3. Just your opinion, should the U.S. government force Microsoft to break up into several smaller companies or allow Microsoft to remain as it is?	Break up	21%
	Remain as is	69%
	No opinion	10%
4. Overall, do you think Microsoft has had more of a positive impact on the computer industry or more of a negative impact on the computer industry?	Positive	80%
	Negative	8%
	No opinion	12%
5. How would you rate economic conditions in this country today, excellent, good, only fair, or poor?	Excellent	18%
	Good	56%
	Only fair	21%
	Poor	5%
6. How important is Social Security for your next vote for Congress?	Extremely or very important	84%
	Somewhat important	12%
	Not important, no opinion, or don't plan to vote	4%
7. If you had to choose, which combination would you prefer—a smaller tax cut and larger increases in spending on Medicare or a larger tax cut and smaller increases in spending on Medicare?	Smaller tax cut and more Medicare spending	69%
	Larger tax cut and less Medicare spending	28%
	Other or no opinion	3%

to spend the rest. Republicans hoped for tax cuts; Democrats wanted to fund current and new Medicare programs. The polls showed that a majority of the public favored the latter approach.

All this crucial intelligence was provided by pollsters with the help of relatively small national random samples. The answer to question 2, for instance, came from a sample of 1,021 adults, aged 18 and over; that to question 7 was derived from a sample of 513 adults. But we learned in Chapter 11 that it is possible to take many different random samples of a given size from a given population. Surely, if the pollsters had asked *different* samples of 1,021 or 513 people, respectively, those Table 12.1 numbers would have differed as well. Why then should we ever trust estimates such as these?

Indeed, the data gatherers were quite aware of this problem and provided *confidence intervals* for each of the numbers in our table to account for sampling error, the fact that answers might have differed if a different sample had been picked. Thus, the answers to question 2 were said to be correct within a *margin of error* of ± 3 percentage points and those to question 7 within ± 5 percentage points of the stated figures. Furthermore, argued the poll takers, we could be *95 percent confident* in the interval estimates so defined: In 95 out of 100 similar surveys, the confidence-interval answer derived for any one question would definitely contain the population proportion that a full-fledged U.S. census would reveal—assuming that the very wording of questions and the practical difficulties of survey taking had not introduced systematic error or bias. Admittedly, in 5 out of 100 cases, including possibly any one of our Table 12.1 answers, the sought-after *population* proportion could lie outside the confidence interval. In that case, a census figure could differ from the stated sample result by more than the stated percentage points.

12.1 Basic Concepts

More often than not, it is impractical or impossible to conduct a census whenever we want to know the value of some *parameter,* such as a population mean, population standard deviation, or population proportion. So we take a random sample, use the sample data to compute a *statistic,* such as a sample mean, sample standard deviation, or sample proportion, and guess the value of the desired parameter from that of the corresponding statistic. This process of inferring the values of unknown population parameters from those of known sample statistics is called **estimation.** In this section, we meet three concepts related to estimation, namely,

- estimator
- point estimate
- interval estimate

The type of sample statistic used to make inferences about a given type of population parameter is called the **estimator** of that parameter. Thus, the sample mean $\bar{X}$ becomes the estimator of the population mean μ. The sample standard deviation s becomes the estimator of the population standard deviation σ. And the sample proportion P becomes the estimator of the population proportion π. Understandably, statisticians always seek estimators that are likely to take on numerical values close to parameters of interest. The very fact that they insist on *random* sampling, rather than convenience sampling or judgment sampling, helps control error because random sampling eliminates the *systematic error* or *bias* that arises in nonrandom sampling. In addition, although we cannot eliminate the *sampling error* inherent in random sampling entirely, we can always reduce it if it is deemed too large. This feat can be accomplished by taking larger and (unfortunately) costlier samples.

The process of *estimation* begins by sampling an already existing, *present* population. It must not be confused with *forecasting,* to be discussed in Chapter 19, which seeks to make statements about parameters of *future* populations—for example, about the median incomes of Americans in 2025, the proportion of consumers likely to favor a new product that is still on the drawing board, or the average daily demand for electric power five years hence.

This chapter discusses two types of estimates. When the estimate of a parameter is expressed as a single numerical value, it is referred to as a **point estimate.** Thus, the average time workers require to complete a given task may be estimated at 32 minutes. A product's market share may be estimated at 70 percent. Just like the numbers in Table 12.1, these are point estimates.

If we need to know the value of some parameter, having a point estimate is better than nothing. It is far from perfect, however. Recall the crucial concept of the *sampling distribution,* perhaps by reviewing Table 11.4 on page 454. The sample mean or sample proportion computed from any *one* random sample may well differ from that derived from any other (equal-sized) random sample that is taken from the same population. Which of the many possible sample means or sample proportions, therefore, can we rely upon to point to the population mean or population proportion in which we are ultimately interested? Users of point estimates, therefore, are always eager to know how far wrong any given estimate may be. That is why statisticians often provide a range of values within which the unknown but true population parameter presumably lies. Such a range is called an **interval estimate.** Depending on the size of the interval, we can attach varying degrees of confidence to it. Based on random sampling, we can state with (perhaps) 95 percent confidence that a product's market share equals 70% ± 6% (and, thus, lies between 64 and 76 percent) or with 80 percent confidence that the share equals 70% ± 3% (and, thus lies between 67 and 73 percent). Such interval statements call attention to the inevitability of sampling error. They wrap a margin of error around each point estimate and, by thus providing lower and upper bounds for any unknown parameter, put point estimates in perspective.

12.2 Defining a Good Estimator

The linkage between sampling distributions and statistical estimation becomes evident the moment we consider the question of what makes a good estimator. Three major criteria are commonly employed: unbiasedness, efficiency, and consistency.

UNBIASEDNESS

A sample statistic that, on the average, across many samples, takes on a value equal to the population parameter that the statistic seeks to estimate is said to be *unbiased.* Whenever the sampled population is normally distributed or whenever the conditions of the central limit theorem are fulfilled, the sample mean, $\bar{X}$, for example, is an unbiased estimator of the population mean, μ. This is true because the mean of the sampling distribution of the sample mean, $\mu_{\bar{X}}$, then equals μ. (Review Formula 11.A on page 463). Under the same conditions, the sample proportion, P, is an unbiased estimator of the population proportion, π, because the mean of the sampling distribution of the sample proportion, μ_p, then equals π. (Review Formula 11.F on page 466.)

DEFINITION 12.1 A sample statistic is an **unbiased estimator** of the corresponding population parameter if the mean of all possible values of that statistic equals the parameter the statistic seeks to estimate. On the other hand, a sample statistic is a **biased estimator** of the corresponding population parameter if the mean of all possible values of that statistic differs from the parameter the statistic seeks to estimate.

Panel (a) of Figure 12.1 on the next page illustrates the difference just noted. The upper graph shows the sampling distribution of an unbiased estimator, E. Its mean, μ_E, equals the true value, T, of the corresponding population parameter. The lower graph, in contrast, shows the sampling distribution of a biased estimator. Its mean, μ_E, does *not* equal the true value, T, of the corresponding population parameter. In this case, the estimator exhibits an upward bias, but bias can also go in the other direction. The extent of bias is always measured as $\mu_E - T$. (For an alternative discussion of the subject, see Figure 4.1 on page 123.)

TECHNICAL DETAIL

At this point, we can also solve a riddle first noted on page 246 in Chapter 7, where the formula for the sample variance was introduced. Recall that the *population* variance had been defined as the mean of the squared deviations of all population values from their mean, or as

$$\sigma^2 = \frac{\Sigma(X - \mu)^2}{N} \tag{1}$$

Yet, the analogous *sample* variance was *not* defined as the mean of the squared deviations of all sample values from *their* mean, which would make

$$s^2 = \frac{\Sigma(X - \overline{X})^2}{n} \tag{2}$$

Rather, the divisor was changed from the expected n to a surprising $n - 1$, leading to the Formula 7.H entry of

$$s^2 = \frac{\Sigma(X - \overline{X})^2}{n - 1} \tag{3}$$

The reason for this change in the divisor can now be understood: The mean of the squared deviations of all sample values from the sample mean, shown as (2) here, is a *biased* estimator of the population variance, σ^2. It produces an underestimate of σ^2. This underestimate is intuitively reasonable because a part cannot be more varied than the whole from which it comes, but it can easily be less diverse. Therefore, in order to estimate the population variance, σ^2, correctly from sample data, statisticians inflate the expression for the sample variance, s^2, by using the $n - 1$ divisor. This counteracts the σ^2 underestimate that would otherwise result. It turns out that s^2, defined as in (3) above, is an unbiased estimator of σ^2, *provided* that selections of sample elements are statistically independent events. In the small-population case, however, s^2, even with the divisor of $n - 1$, remains a biased estimator of σ^2. Finally, the sample standard deviation, s, is a biased estimator of the population standard deviation, σ, regardless of whether sampling involves the large- or small-population case.

FIGURE 12.1 | Criteria Employed in the Choice of Estimators

This set of graphs employs a variety of sampling distributions to illustrate three major criteria commonly used to define good estimators of unknown population parameters. Panel (a) shows an estimator to be ***unbiased*** *if its expected value, μ_E, equals the true value, T, of the corresponding population parameter. Panel (b) identifies an estimator as* ***efficient*** *if it has the smallest variance among several unbiased estimators. Panel (c) shows an estimator to be* ***consistent*** *if it homes in on its parameter target as sample size increases. In that case, bias and variance approach zero as sample size approaches infinity.*

(a) Unbiased vs. Biased Estimator

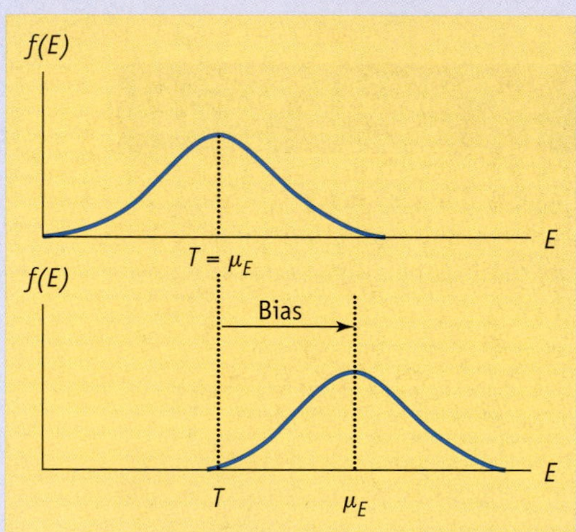

(b) Efficient vs. Inefficient Estimator

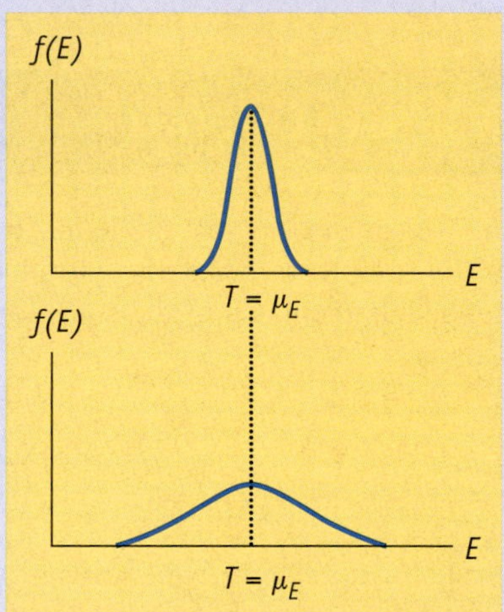

(c) Consistent Estimator

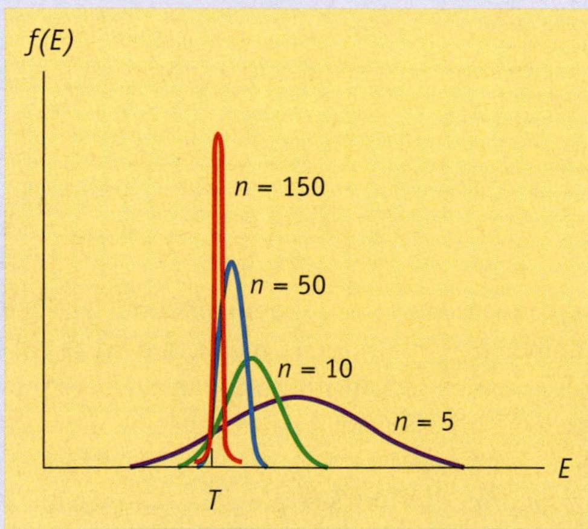

EXAMPLE PROBLEM 12.1

Table 11.2 on page 450 lists a population of $N = 5$ executives, along with their salaries and sexes. Table 11.3, in turn, shows all possible samples of $n = 3$ that can be taken from this population of executives, along with associated sample statistics for salary mean, variance, and standard deviation, and the proportion of female executives. Review the relevant data on pages 450–455 and confirm that in this *small-population case:*

a. $\bar{X}$ and P_F, respectively, are *unbiased* estimators of μ and π.

b. s^2 and s, respectively, even with the $n - 1$ divisor, are *biased* estimators of σ and σ^2.

SOLUTION:

a. The population mean salary is $\mu = 200$ (thousand dollars), while the population proportion of female executives is $\pi_F = .40$. As Table 11.5 shows, $\mu_{\bar{X}} = 200$ as well, while $\mu_P = .40$ as well. We conclude:

Any given $\bar{X}$ is an *unbiased* estimator of μ because $\mu_{\bar{X}} = \mu$.

Any given P is an *unbiased* estimator of π because $\mu_P = \pi$.

b. The population variance is 2,260 (thousand squared dollars), while the population standard deviation is 47.539 (thousand dollars). Using the Table 11.3 data, we can compute the mean of all possible sample variances and the mean of all possible sample standard deviations, respectively, as

$$\mu_{s^2} = \frac{\Sigma s^2}{n} = \frac{28{,}250}{10} = 2{,}825 \quad \text{and} \quad \mu_s = \frac{490.782}{10} = 49.0782$$

Neither one of these values equals the corresponding population parameter. In the small population case, we conclude:

Any given s^2 is a *biased* estimator of σ^2 because $\mu_{s^2} \neq \sigma^2$.

Any given s is a *biased* estimator of σ because $\mu_s \neq \sigma$.

EFFICIENCY

As a look at the upper graph in panel (a) of Figure 12.1 confirms, even though an estimator, E, may be right on target *on the average,* it can, nevertheless, be off—even way off—on any specific occasion. We are looking, after all, at a bell-shaped curve. Not all values of E fall in the center of the distribution; many of them lie on either side of the center. That is why statisticians consider another criterion when assessing an estimator's merit: All else being equal, if more than one unbiased estimator is available, they prefer to use the estimator with the smallest variance; that is, one with a sampling distribution that is highly concentrated near the mean. Because such an estimator provides relatively more estimates close to the targeted parameter than an alternative estimator with a larger variance, it is said to be relatively *efficient.*

DEFINITION 12.2 Among all the available unbiased estimators of a given parameter, the sample statistic that has the smallest variance for a given sample size is the relatively **efficient estimator.**

The efficiency criterion is illustrated in panel (b) of Figure 12.1. Note that both panel (b) estimators have a sampling distribution with a mean that precisely equals the true parameter. Yet the estimator with the sampling distribution shown in the upper graph of panel (b) is the efficient statistic because of its lower variability around the mean. A famous case in point (which we will not prove here) is provided by the attempt to estimate the population mean with the help of sample data taken from a normally distributed population. The sample median and the sample mean are then both unbiased estimators of such a population mean, but the variance of the sample median is 57 percent larger than that of the sample mean. This makes it less likely that any one sample median, rather than sample mean, will correctly estimate the population mean. Put differently, the variance of the sample mean is only 64 percent as large as that of the sample median (100/157 equals .637). This difference makes $\bar{X}$ the more efficient estimator of the population mean.

CONSISTENCY

Because an estimator is undesirable if its sampling distribution has a large variance, anything that can reduce this variance improves our chances for making good estimates. This feat can sometimes be accomplished quite easily. Take the case of $\bar{X}$: According to Formula 11.B on page 463, we can lower the variance of its sampling distribution, repeatedly if we so choose, merely by increasing sample size. In the large-population case, for instance, given the population variance, σ^2, any increase in n reduces $\sigma_{\bar{X}}^2$ because the latter equals $\frac{\sigma^2}{n}$. Whenever larger sample size brings an estimator closer to the parameter that is being estimated, the statistic in question is said to be *consistent.* Both sample mean and sample proportion are such consistent estimators of the corresponding population parameters. Panel (c) of Figure 12.1 illustrates the case of a consistent estimator. Note how its sampling distribution increasingly concentrates on its target as sample size increases.

DEFINITION 12.3 A sample statistic is a **consistent estimator** if its value gets ever closer to the parameter being estimated as sample size increases.

A COMPROMISE: MEAN SQUARED ERROR

More often than not, the search for a good estimator yields several prospects, none of which is perfect. One estimator may be unbiased but have a huge variance (and thus a low efficiency rating). Another may have a tiny variance but a huge bias. A third one may combine a bit of both faults. This problem of choosing among imperfect estimators is illustrated in Figure 12.2.

This graph pictures the sampling distributions of three estimators, *A, B,* and *C.* The population parameter's true and unknown value is *T.* We can visualize the extent of *bias* by noting the degree to which the centers of the sampling distributions diverge from *T.* Thus, bias is zero for *A,* small for *B,* and huge for *C.* We can visualize the *variance* (and, thus, the relative efficiency of the three estimators) by focusing on the spread of data around the center of any one distribution. The spread is largest for *A,* smaller for *B,* and smallest for *C* (which makes the curves increasingly peaked as well).

The estimator with distribution *A* has a mean right on target and wins with respect to unbiasedness, but it has the largest variance and is the least efficient. The estimator with distribution *C,* which is centered way to the right of *T,* has the worst bias, but its low variance makes it the most efficient of the three. The estimator with distribution *B* stands in the middle with respect to both criteria. Surely, it would be foolish in this case to insist on no bias and to choose estimator *A.* It would be equally foolish to insist on the highest efficiency rating and choose estimator *C.* Note how a trade-off could be made by switching from *A* to *B,* accepting some bias, but vastly reducing variability. Or consider how a switch from *C* to *B* would increase variability (lower efficiency), but vastly reduce bias.

FIGURE 12.2 | Choosing among Estimators

When all available estimators are imperfect, it is wise to choose an estimator with a combination of small bias and small variance (such as the one with distribution B).

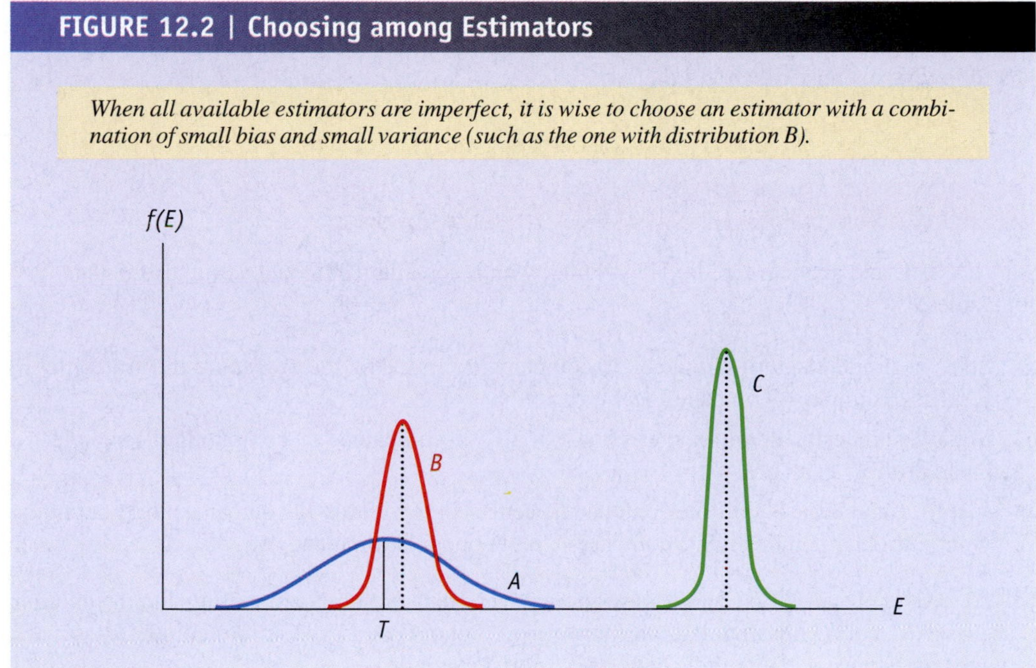

Statisticians do, in fact, choose the best estimator under such circumstances by compromising in the fashion just shown: For each of several possible estimators, they calculate the **mean squared error** (MSE), which is the sum of an estimator's squared bias plus its variance, or

$$\text{MSE} = (\mu_E - T)^2 + \sigma_E^2$$

Then they choose the estimator with the lowest of these values. In the case of Figure 12.2, this procedure picks the statistic with sampling distribution *B* as the best estimator.

12.3 Making Point Estimates

Under many circumstances, the sample mean and the sample proportion are unbiased, efficient, and consistent estimators of the corresponding population parameters. Therefore, the sample mean, $\overline{X}$, has become the favorite estimator of the population mean, μ, when a single sample is taken, and the difference between two sample means, $\overline{X}_1 - \overline{X}_2$, is routinely used to estimate the difference between two population means, $\mu_1 - \mu_2$, when independent samples of two populations are taken. Likewise, just as the sample proportion, P, has become the favorite estimator of the population proportion, π, when a single sample is taken, so the difference between two sample proportions, $P_1 - P_2$, is routinely used to estimate the difference between two population proportions, $\pi_1 - \pi_2$, when two populations are independently sampled.

ESTIMATING A SINGLE POPULATION MEAN

Imagine you wanted to estimate the mean profit of all *Fortune 500* companies in 1998. Having neither the time nor the money to contact all of them, you could take a simple random sample of

$n = 30$ company names from the *Fortune 500* list, contact only the selected companies, record their profits, and compute the sample mean, $\overline{X}$, as your best estimate of the population mean, μ. The following exercise illustrates the procedure.

EXCEL Example 12.1

Start EXCEL and activate the file HK99F500, which contains 1998 data about all *Fortune 500* companies.

a. Select a simple random sample of 30 company profits, using the procedure illustrated in EXCEL Example 4.3 on page 115.

b. Make a point estimate of the mean profit of all 500 companies by computing the sample mean profit.

c. Just for fun, because your file contains the census data for all 500 companies, find out how your particular point estimate compares with the population mean.

SOLUTION Because EXCEL despises nonnumeric data, you must first eliminate the column C asterisks (denoting missing data). Simply copy column C and paste it into column P, sort the data in P, and then delete the three cells with asterisks.

Part (a)

1. Click **Tools** > **Data Analysis** > **Sampling** > **OK** to activate the *Sampling* dialog box.
2. Under *Input Range,* enter **P2:P498**.
3. Under *Sampling Method,* choose **Random** and under *Number of Samples* enter **30**.
4. Under *Output Options,* choose **Output Range** and enter **R2** as the first cell to receive the output.
5. Click **OK**. The sample appears in cell range R2–R31.

Part (b)

You can compute the **sample mean** as follows:

1. Click any empty cell and then the **Function Wizard (*fx*)** > **Statistical** > **AVERAGE** > **OK**.
2. In the dialog box, next to *Number 1,* enter **R2:R31** and click **OK**.

The sample mean appears in your chosen cell; in this particular case, equal to **812.00** (million dollars). The point estimate equals this sample mean. (Note: You would get a different answer because yours would be a different sample.)

Part (c)

You can compute the **population mean** as follows:

1. Click any empty cell and then the **Function Wizard (*fx*)** > **Statistical** > **AVERAGE** > **OK**.
2. In the dialog box, next to *Number 1,* enter **P2:P498** and click **OK**.

The population mean appears in your chosen cell, equal to **672.71** (million dollars). You would get the same answer.

ESTIMATING A SINGLE POPULATION PROPORTION

Imagine you wanted to estimate the proportion of *Fortune 500* companies that had California headquarters in 1998. Being pressed for a quick answer, you could forgo looking at the entire *Fortune 500* list, instead take a simple random sample of $n = 30$ company names, and count the number of California addresses in your sample. Then you could use the sample proportion, P, as your best estimate of the population proportion, π.

EXCEL Example 12.2

Start EXCEL and activate the file HK99F500, which contains 1998 data about all *Fortune 500* companies.

a. Select a simple random sample of 30 state headquarters, using the procedure illustrated in the Caution Box on page 116.

b. Make a point estimate of the California headquarters proportion of all 500 companies by computing the sample proportion of California headquarters.

c. Just for fun, because your file contains the census data for all 500 companies, find out how your particular point estimate compares with the population proportion.

SOLUTION

Part (a)

1. Enter company code numbers 2–501 into P2–P501.
2. Copy column L and paste it into column Q. (The company codes and associated state names should now reside side-by-side in range P2:Q501.)
3. Type **=RAND( )** in cell R2, select the number appearing in R2, and drag to R501.
4. Select the R2:R501 range, click **Edit** > **Copy** and **Edit** > **Paste Special**.
5. In the *Paste Special* dialog box, select *Values* and *None* (which replaces the formulas in the R column with the values they create), and click **OK**.
6. With the R range selected, click **Data** > **Sort**. (If the *Sort Warning* box appears, expand the selection to sort.)
7. In the *Sort* dialog box, select *Sort by Column R Ascending* and *Header row* and click **OK**.

The (linked) column P and Q data now appear in random order, without duplication. You can use the first 30 company codes and associated states as your sample.

Part (b)

You can compute the **sample proportion** as follows:

1. Select the range Q2:Q31, copy it, and paste it into S2:S31.
2. Select column S and click **Sort Ascending**.
3. Count the number of CA headquarters and divide by sample size, $n = 30$. Your answer will differ, but in this particular exercise, the resulting point estimate was 1/30, or **.033**. Thus, it was estimated that 3.3 percent of *Fortune 500* companies were headquartered in California.

Part (c)

You can compute the **population proportion** as follows:

1. Select column Q and click **Sort Ascending**.
2. Count the number of CA headquarters and divide by population size, $N = 500$. The answer is 56/500, or **.112**. Thus, we find that 11.2 percent of *Fortune 500* companies were in fact headquartered in California. The above point estimate was far off the truth.

ESTIMATING THE DIFFERENCE BETWEEN TWO PARAMETERS

It is easy to see how we can make point estimates of the difference between two population means, or of the difference between two population proportions, by taking two independent samples and then contrasting two sample statistics. Thus, an investigator who wanted to compare the *Fortune 500* companies' mean profits in 1998 and 2001 might sample $n = 30$ companies from the 1999 list (which contains 1998 data) and compute their mean profit as, say, $\overline{X}_1 = \$812$ million, while sampling another $n = 30$ companies from the 2002 list (which contains 2001 data) and computing *their* mean profit as $\overline{X}_2 = \$1{,}289$ million. The difference between the two population means, $\mu_1 - \mu_2$, would then be *estimated* as

$$\overline{X}_1 - \overline{X}_2 = \$812 \text{ million} - \$1{,}289 \text{ million} = -\$477 \text{ million}$$

We would interpret this result to mean that the *Fortune 500* companies' mean profit in 1998 was $477 million less than in 2001, and, thus, had risen by that amount during those 3 years.

EXAMPLE PROBLEM 12.2

Visit one of the Web sites noted in this chapter's Preview and find real-world examples of estimating the difference between two population proportions.

SOLUTION: Answers can vary. In 1999, Roper Starch undertook a major study for clients who wanted to enter the world of e-commerce. The firm sampled 1,000 consumers in each of 30 countries to determine the extent to which one might find customers on the Internet. In all age groups, use of the Internet for commerce was considerably higher in the United States than in the other countries studied. Table 12.2 shows selected results.

TABLE 12.2 | 1999 Proportions of Internet Shoppers

Age Group	U.S. Sample Proportions	Sample Proportions in 29 Other Countries	Estimated Differences between Population Proportions
13–19	.41	.14	.41 − .14 = .27
20–29	.31	.14	.31 − .14 = .17
30–39	.33	.11	.33 − .11 = .22
40–49	.30	.10	.30 − .10 = .20
50 and over	.22	.05	.22 − .05 = .17

12.4 The Nature of Interval Estimates

Even though an unbiased point estimator will, on the average, take on a value equal to the parameter being estimated, any one estimate is unlikely to be exactly on target. Yet, typically, only one estimate is made because only one sample is taken; hence the typical point estimate is almost certain to lie above or below the true value of the parameter of interest. Consider how, in the previous section, a population mean was estimated at $812 million when its true value was $672.7

million, while a population proportion was estimated as .067 when its true value was .112. (Unlike the readers of this textbook, a practicing statistician who was sampling a population would, of course, have no idea of the true parameter value.)

THE MARGIN OF ERROR

We can make the inevitable uncertainty attached to any point estimate explicit by presenting an *interval estimate* and reporting the point estimate as lying between a lower and upper interval limit.

interval estimate: lower limit $\leq$ point estimate $\leq$ upper limit

Statisticians routinely construct such intervals by making their point estimate the interval center and creating a range of other possible values, known as the **margin of error,** below and above the center. The margin of error, thus, is a half-width of an interval estimate, equal to the difference between the point estimate on the one hand and either the lower or upper limit of the interval on the other hand. We presume that the unknown parameter lies somewhere within the interval, at least most of the time, but not necessarily at its center. We control the extent to which we can trust the unknown parameter to lie within the limits of the interval by making the margin of error small or large and, thus, making the interval narrow or wide.

CONSTRUCTING CONFIDENCE INTERVALS

The range of values among which an unknown population parameter can presumably be found is called a **confidence interval.** This name reflects the fact that the width of an interval estimate has important implications for the degree of confidence with which we can assert that the true value of the population parameter lies within the two interval limits. For this reason, the limits of an interval estimate are also called **confidence limits.** But how do statisticians figure the degree of confidence we can place in such an interval? One common approach involves two steps:

- Statisticians make sure that the sampling distribution of the estimator is *normal.*
- Statisticians express the margin of error as a fraction or multiple of the estimator's *standard error* (a concept we met in Chapter 11).

NORMAL DISTRIBUTION Recall that a sampling distribution (such as that of a sample mean) is a *normal* distribution (1) whenever the underlying population values themselves are normally distributed and (2) even when the population is not normal, provided only that the central limit theorem applies. The latter is assured whenever the sample size is sufficiently large absolutely ($n \geq 30$) and sufficiently small relative to the population ($n < .05N$). By choosing a proper sample size, a statistician, therefore, can *ensure* an approximately normal sampling distribution of the chosen estimator.

MARGIN OF ERROR Statisticians construct the margin of error with the help of the standard deviation of the estimator's sampling distribution, which, as we learned in Chapter 11, is also called the estimator's *standard error.* Thus, they write

$$\text{limits of interval estimate} = \text{point estimate} \pm (\text{margin of error})$$

or

$$\text{limits of interval estimate} = \text{point estimate} \pm (z \times \text{standard error of estimator})$$

where z is the familiar standard normal deviate that can equal any desired (fractional or whole) positive number.

Depending on the parameter of interest, this general expression can be made more specific. When estimating a population mean, for example, we can write

$$\text{limits of interval estimate of } \mu = \bar{X} \pm (z \times \sigma_{\bar{X}})$$

80 PERCENT CONFIDENCE INTERVALS

Now consider a normally distributed sampling distribution of $\bar{X}$ such as that found in Figure 12.3. For purposes of illustration, we assume $\mu_{\bar{X}} = 40$ and $\sigma_{\bar{X}} = 4.68$, but a statistician seeking to estimate μ would not have that numerical information. Under the conditions specified earlier, that statistician would only know that the sampling distribution was a bell-shaped normal curve, centered on an unknown $\mu_{\bar{X}} = \mu$. As we will show later, the statistician may be able to *estimate* $\sigma_{\bar{X}}$, and the statistician would certainly be free to choose the value of z as any (fractional or whole) positive number, such as .5, 1.0, 2.0, or even 2.575. This choice would, in turn, influence the size of the margin of error (here equal to $z \times \sigma_{\bar{X}}$) and, thus, the width of the entire interval. If the choice fell on $z = 1.2817$, the margin of error would equal 1.2817 times the standard error of the sample mean (in our case, $1.2817 \times 4.68 = 6$) and, after being placed below and above the point estimate, the interval itself would be twice that size (in our case equal to 12). We can envision the width of the implied interval in our example by looking at the horizontal axis in Figure 12.3, where an example interval (the double arrow) has been centered on $\mu_{\bar{X}} = \mu$, reaching from $\mu - 1.2817\sigma_{\bar{X}} = 34$ to $\mu + 1.2817\sigma_{\bar{X}} = 46$. (The value of z is rounded in the graph.)

The choice of $z = 1.2817$ has an interesting implication. According to Appendix Table H, a z value of 1.2817 places 40 percent of the normal curve area between itself and the (lower) mean; hence 80 percent of the area under our curve (shaded in our graph) is found above our example interval, between -1.2817 and $+1.2817$ standard deviations from the mean. This implies, in turn, that a statistician who took all possible samples of the chosen size from the population in question would discover sample means within this range (and, thus, between 34 and 46 in our case) 80 percent of the time. Corresponding to the lower and upper (unshaded) tails of the sampling distribution, another 10 percent of all sample means would lie below 34, and a final 10 percent above 46.

The heavy dots in the lower part of Figure 12.3 identify the sample means associated with 10 possible samples our statistician might take. Eight of the dots are black; they represent the 80 percent of all sample means, such as $\bar{X} = 35$ for sample (1) and $\bar{X} = 45$ for sample (2), that fall within the limits of our example interval, now highlighted by the two dashed vertical lines. Two of the dots are red; they represent the 20 percent of all sample means, such as $\bar{X} = 31$ for sample (5) and $\bar{X} = 49$ for sample (9), that will fall outside the $\mu - 1.28\sigma_{\bar{X}}$ and $\mu + 1.28\sigma_{\bar{X}}$ limits, respectively.

Now imagine what would happen if our statistician, as is typical, took a single sample from among thousands of possible samples. If it turned out to be sample (1), the statistician would compute $\bar{X} = 35$, which would be the *point estimate* of μ. As is also typical, the statistician would then determine the value of $\sigma_{\bar{X}}$ by computing either $\frac{\sigma}{\sqrt{n}}$ (if the population's standard deviation, σ, was known from prior experience) or $\frac{s}{\sqrt{n}}$ (where s is the standard deviation of the sample just taken). If the value of $\sigma_{\bar{X}}$ was 4.68, as in our graph, the statistician would compute the sample (1) *interval estimate* shown in Figure 12.3:

$$\mu = \bar{X} \pm (z \times \sigma_{\bar{X}})$$

$$\mu = 35 \pm (1.2817 \times 4.68)$$

FIGURE 12.3 | 80 Percent Confidence Intervals

An interval estimate of a population mean, μ, can be constructed around a sample mean, $\overline{X}$, as $\overline{X} \pm z\sigma_{\overline{X}}$. Depending on the value of z, we can place different degrees of confidence in the method of estimation. In this example, $z = 1.28$, which implies that 80 percent of the $\overline{X}$ values (heavy dots) that might be found by repeated sampling from the same population lie within the range of $\mu_{\overline{X}} \pm 1.28\sigma_{\overline{X}}$. Because $\mu = \mu_{\overline{X}}$, this procedure also implies that 80 percent of the intervals that might be constructed will contain μ. Any interval constructed by this method is, therefore, called an ***80 percent confidence interval.*** *By choosing smaller or larger z values, we can, however, construct narrower or wider intervals with smaller or higher confidence levels. What is illustrated here for a population mean and sample mean holds equally for other parameters and other estimators.*

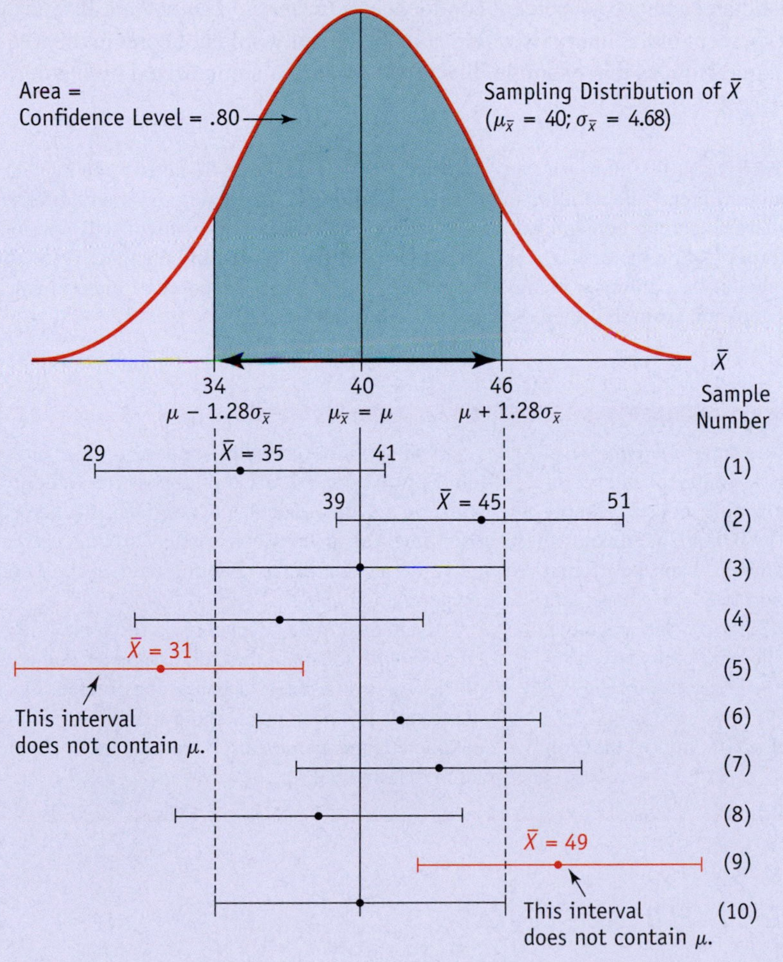

$$\mu = 35 \pm 6$$

$$29 \leq \mu \leq 41$$

We can see (but the statistician could not) that the point estimate of 35 is wrong: μ actually equals 40; hence, a sampling error of -5 was made. We can also see (and, again, the statistician would not know) that the interval estimate of 29 to 41 does contain the true value of μ. Notice how the solid vertical line below the $\mu = 40$ center of our sampling distribution intersects the interval estimate just made.

But what if the statistician had selected sample (2)? Then the sample mean would have been computed as $\overline{X} = 45$ (also, unbeknownst to the statistician, a wrong point estimate of μ). The interval estimate would then have ranged from 39 to 51 (again, unbeknownst to the statistician, containing the true value of $\mu = 40$). A few of many other possible sample results are indicated by the other heavy dots in Figure 12.3, along with the confidence intervals our statistician would calculate. Notice that fully 8 of the 10 interval estimates, being intersected by that solid vertical line, would contain the true value of μ—the two exceptions here being the intervals constructed after taking samples (5) and (9). And that is why any confidence interval constructed with a z value of 1.2817 is termed an *80 percent confidence interval.* Given the choice of that z value, any one confidence interval will be either dead right or dead wrong (i.e., will or will not contain μ) but the statistician can have 80 percent confidence *in the method employed.* If repeated sampling occurred, 80 percent of the intervals would and 20 percent would not contain the true value of the parameter in question, as this example illustrates. All this is summarized by Definition 12.4.

DEFINITION 12.4 If simple random samples of size n are repeatedly taken from a given population, many different values of a given sample statistic will be found, and many different confidence intervals can be constructed. Some of them will and some of them will not contain the unknown population parameter. The percentage of intervals that can be expected to contain the actual value of the parameter being estimated, when the same procedure of interval construction is used again and again, is called the interval's **confidence level.**

CAUTION

We must use the term *confidence level* with great care. A confidence level of 80 percent, for example, does *not* imply a probability of .80 that the unknown population parameter can be found within the limits of any *one* 80 percent confidence interval. As Figure 12.3 shows, the unknown parameter either does or does not lie within any given interval, *and, without a census, we will never know which is true.*

The stated confidence level *does* imply the following:

If all possible samples of a given size are selected from a given population and if all possible values of a given estimator are then calculated and if an 80 percent confidence interval is then constructed around each of these values, 80 percent of the resulting intervals will contain the true population value.

A stated confidence level gives the probability *prior to actual sample selection* that the parameter being estimated will lie within the interval being constructed. Once a specific sample has been taken and a specific interval has been constructed, the parameter is certain to lie or not to lie within that interval.

FAVORITE CONFIDENCE LEVELS

As we have just seen, anyone who wishes to make a parameter estimate with 80 percent confidence must choose a z value corresponding to $(.80/2) = .4000$ in Appendix Table H, or $z = 1.2817$. Any given point estimate, however, can be wrapped up in a variety of confidence intervals, narrow or wide, depending on the chosen value of z. The degree of confidence attached to the estimate varies accordingly. Statisticians have a number of favorite confidence levels, such as 80, 90, 95, and 99 percent. Appendix Table J, "Critical Normal Deviate Values for Statistical Estimation," contains z values for the most commonly used confidence levels. Others can be derived from Appendix Table H.

EXAMPLE PROBLEM 12.3

Sample (5) in Figure 12.3 yielded a sample mean of $\overline{X} = 31$ and an 80 percent confidence interval for μ stretching from 25 to 37. Create alternative interval estimates for confidence levels of:

a. 90 percent.

b. 95 percent.

c. 99 percent.

SOLUTION: In all cases, $\mu = \overline{X} \pm (z \times \sigma_{\overline{X}})$. The appropriate z value can be computed from Appendix Table H or, more easily, found directly in Appendix Table J. Relevant computations appear on the next page.

FIGURE 12.4 | Confidence Level and Interval Width

Given sample size, the level of confidence attached to an interval estimate varies directly with the value of z and, thus, with interval width. A smaller z value produces a narrower interval and a more precise estimate, but also implies a smaller degree of confidence in the estimate. A larger z value means a wider interval and less precision, but implies a greater degree of confidence.

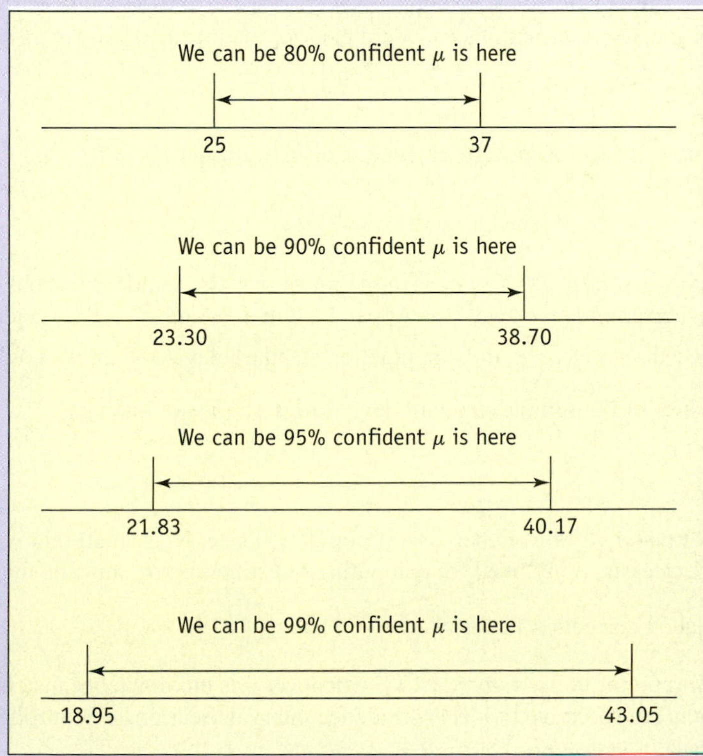

a. *For a 90 percent confidence level,*

$\mu = 31 \pm (1.645 \times 4.68)$

$\mu = 31 \pm 7.70$

$23.30 \leq \mu \leq 38.70$. This interval does not contain μ.

b. *For a 95 percent confidence level,*

$\mu = 31 \pm (1.96 \times 4.68)$

$\mu = 31 \pm 9.17$

$21.83 \leq \mu \leq 40.17$. This interval does contain μ.

c. *For a 99 percent confidence level,*

$\mu = 31 \pm (2.575 \times 4.68)$

$\mu = 31 \pm 12.05$

$18.95 \leq \mu \leq 43.05$. This interval does contain μ.

Figure 12.4 on the previous page summarizes the lesson implied by Example Problem 12.3.

12.5 Large-Sample Interval Estimates of a Population Mean

In this section, we learn to construct a confidence interval for a population mean when taking a large sample ($n \geq 30$) from a large population ($n < .05N$). Under these circumstances, regardless of whether the population values are normally distributed or not, we can consider the sampling distribution of the sample mean to be normally distributed (see *The Central Limit Theorem for Sample Mean* on page 458.) As Formula 12.A shows, the chosen value of z determines the confidence level and, together with the standard error of the mean, $\sigma_{\overline{X}}$, the margin of error, $z\sigma_{\overline{X}}$.

FORMULA 12.A | Confidence Interval for a Population Mean, Large Sample ($n \geq 30$)

$$\mu = \overline{X} \pm z\sigma_{\overline{X}}$$

where μ is the population mean, $\overline{X}$ is the sample mean, z is the standard normal deviate associated with the desired confidence level (see Appendix Table J), and $\sigma_{\overline{X}}$ is the standard error of the mean (*precisely* computed as $\frac{\sigma}{\sqrt{n}}$ if the population standard deviation, σ, is known, or *estimated* as $\frac{s}{\sqrt{n}}$ with the help of the sample standard deviation, s, if σ is not known).

Notes:

1. It is assumed that $n < .05N$. Otherwise, if population size, N, is small relative to sample size, n, the expression employed for computing or estimating $\sigma_{\overline{X}}$ must be multiplied by the finite population correction factor of $\sqrt{\frac{N-n}{N-1}}$.
2. Some analysts prefer to use Formula 12.F whenever σ is unknown because that procedure creates a more conservative (wider) confidence interval. Section 12.9 introduces the alternative formula.

EXAMPLE PROBLEM 12.4

The editor of a business magazine is about to write an article on the cost of staying in downtown hotels this summer. The editor takes a simple random sample of $n = 32$ from a list of 1,000 downtown hotels across the country, then records the dollar prices of single rooms for one-night stays as follows:

191	227	228	146	165	158	278	147	153	187	153
146	170	169	162	125	130	165	286	260	225	298
167	187	193	123	251	188	199	239	234	259	

The editor estimates the population standard deviation as \$61, based on similar studies undertaken in prior years.

a. Using Formula 12.A, compute a 95 percent confidence interval for the mean hotel room price this summer.

b. Interpret the result.

c. Explain why no one asks you to illustrate your 95 percent confidence interval in a graph, similar to the graphs drawn in other chapters.

SOLUTION:

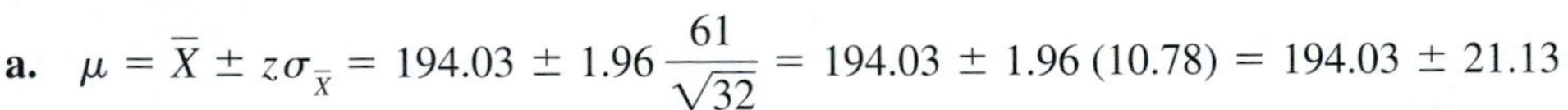

a. $\mu = \overline{X} \pm z\sigma_{\overline{X}} = 194.03 \pm 1.96\frac{61}{\sqrt{32}} = 194.03 \pm 1.96\,(10.78) = 194.03 \pm 21.13$

The 95 percent confidence interval: $172.90 < \mu < 215.16$

b. With 95 percent confidence, the population mean room rental is estimated to lie between \$172.90 and \$215.16. Nevertheless, the true population mean could lie outside these limits. We only know that the *procedure* used here will give us the correct result 95 percent of the time. It will fail us 5 percent of the time.

c. You are not being asked to do so because it cannot be done. True enough, $n \geq 30$ and the central limit theorem about the mean applies. Thus, you can assume the existence of a normally distributed sampling distribution of $\overline{X}$, similar to Figure 12.3. Given $n < .05N$ and knowing the value of σ, you can even compute with precision the value of $\sigma_{\overline{X}} = \frac{\sigma}{\sqrt{n}}$ as in (a) above. But you have no idea of the value of $\mu_{\overline{X}} = \mu$, which is the center of that bell-shaped curve. Worst of all, as another look at Figure 12.3 can remind you, you do not know which of many possible samples you picked. Was it sample 1, sample 7, or sample 3,456? And does the interval you created on the basis of your sample even contain the population parameter, μ? As answer (b) noted, you only know that the *procedure* used here will give you the correct result 95 percent of the time. It will fail you 5 percent of the time. Where then would you place your particular confidence interval in relation to the sampling distribution if you *could* sketch it (as you cannot)?

EXCEL Example 12.3

Check the answer to Example Problem 12.4 with the help of EXCEL.

SOLUTION

1. Enter the Example Problem 12.4 data into cells A2–A33 of a new worksheet. (You can achieve the same result by copying and pasting column B of the file HKMISC.)
2. Enter labels *Sample mean=Point estimate, Sample size, Critical z, Population standard deviation, Standard error of sample mean, Half-width of confidence interval, Lower limit of confidence interval,* and *Upper limit of confidence interval* into cells C1–C8, respectively.
3. Enter corresponding formulas or known values into adjacent cells in column D; namely **=AVERAGE(A2:A33)** into D1.

   =COUNT(A2:A33) into D2.

   =NORMSINV(95/100/2+.5) into D3. (In this formula, the specified confidence level of 95% is converted from percentage to decimal form by dividing by 100, is then changed to the two-tailed value by dividing by 2, and to a value on the right side of the distribution by adding .5.)

   61 (the known population standard deviation) into D4. [If the population standard deviation were not known, you would estimate this value from the sample standard deviation as **=STDEV(A2:A33)**.]

   =D4/SQRT(D2) into D5.

   =D3*D5 into D6.

   =D1–D6 into D7.

   =D1+D6 into D8.

The result confirms the Example Problem 12.4 computations:

Sample mean=Point estimate	194.0313
Sample size	32
Critical z	1.959961
Population standard deviation	61
Standard error of sample mean	10.78338
Half-width of confidence interval	21.135
Lower limit of confidence interval	172.8962
Upper limit of confidence interval	215.1663

Note: This type of problem can also be solved much more rapidly by using HKStat, Sheet 4.

12.6 Large-Sample Interval Estimates of a Population Proportion

In this section, we learn to construct a confidence interval for a population proportion when taking a large sample [$n\pi \geq 5$ and $n(1-\pi) \geq 5$]. Under the circumstances, we can consider the sampling distribution of the sample proportion to be normally distributed (see *The Central Limit Theorem for Sample Proportion* on page 461.) As Formula 12.B shows, the chosen value of z determines the confidence level and, together with the standard error of the proportion, σ_p, the margin of error, $z\sigma_p$.

FORMULA 12.B | Confidence Interval for a Population Proportion, Large Sample [$n\pi \geq 5$ and $n(1-\pi) \geq 5$]

$$\pi = P \pm z\sigma_P$$

where π is the population proportion, P is the sample proportion (equal to the number of successes, x, found in the sample, divided by sample size, n), z is the standard normal deviate associated with the desired confidence level (see Appendix Table J), and σ_P is the standard error of the proportion (*precisely* computed as $\sqrt{\frac{\pi(1-\pi)}{n}}$ or *estimated* as $\sqrt{\frac{P(1-P)}{n}}$).

Note: It is assumed that $n < .05N$. Otherwise, if population size, N, is small relative to sample size, n, the expression employed for computing or estimating σ_P must be multiplied by the finite population correction factor of $\sqrt{\frac{N-n}{N-1}}$.

EXAMPLE PROBLEM 12.5

As the new manager of a bank's credit card department, you have been asked to persuade the 1.5 million cardholders to spend an extra $10 a month on credit card insurance. The insurance would make monthly payments to the bank when the cardholder is unable to do so because of sickness or unemployment. Because it mainly protects the bank, you have your doubts about people's willingness to buy the new "product." You take a simple random sample of $n = 300$ cardholders. A mere 33 say they would buy the insurance.

a. Using Formula 12.B, compute a 98 percent confidence interval for the proportion of all cardholders who would buy the insurance.

b. Interpret the result.

SOLUTION

a. $\pi = P \pm z\sigma_P \cong \frac{33}{300} \pm 2.3267\sqrt{\frac{.11(1-.11)}{300}} = .11 \pm 2.3267(.0181) = .11 \pm .04$

The 98 percent confidence interval: $.07 < \pi < .15$

b. With 98 percent confidence, the population proportion of those who might buy the insurance is estimated to lie between .07 and .15. Nevertheless, the true population proportion *could* lie outside these limits. We only know that the *procedure* used here will give us the correct result 98 percent of the time. It will fail us 2 percent of the time.

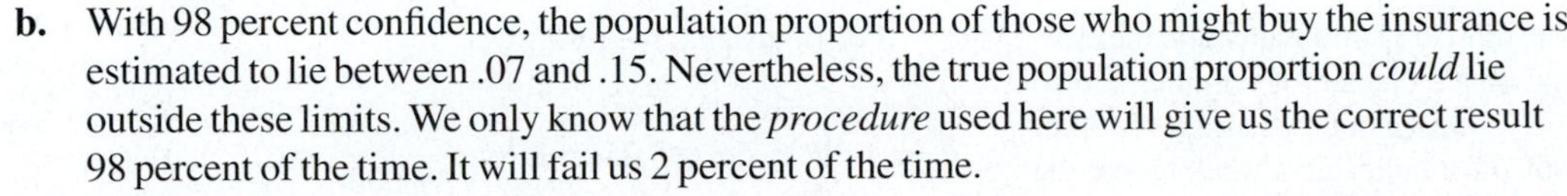

EXCEL Example 12.4

Check the answer to Example Problem 12.5 with the help of EXCEL.

SOLUTION

1. Open a new EXCEL worksheet.
2. Enter labels *Sample size, Number of successes in sample, Sample proportion = Point estimate, Critical z, Standard error of sample proportion, Half-width of confidence interval, Lower limit of confidence interval,* and *Upper limit of confidence interval* into cells A1–A8, respectively.

3. Enter corresponding formulas or known values into adjacent cells in column B; namely
300 into B1.
33 into B2.
=B2/B1 into B3.
=NORMSINV(98/100/2+.5) into B4. (In this formula, the specified confidence level of 98% is converted from percentage to decimal form by dividing by 100, is then changed to the two-tailed value by dividing by 2, and to a value on the right side of the distribution by adding .5.)
=SQRT(B3*(1−B3)/B1) into B5.
=B4*B5 into B6.
=IF(B3−B6<0,0,B3−B6) into B7. (The IF function is used because the lower confidence limit for a proportion cannot be less than 0.)
=IF(B3+B6>1,1,B3+B6) into B8. (The IF function is used because the upper confidence limit for a proportion cannot be greater than 1.)

The result confirms the Example Problem 12.5 computations:

Sample size	300
Number of successes in sample	33
Sample proportion=Point estimate	0.11
Critical z	2.32634
Standard error of sample proportion	0.018065
Half-width of confidence interval	0.042025
Lower limit of confidence interval	0.067975
Upper limit of confidence interval	0.152025

Note: This type of problem can also be solved much more rapidly by using HKStat, Sheet 11.

Application 12.1, *Election Advice,* provides another example of this procedure.

APPLICATION 12.1

ELECTION ADVICE

Advisers to presidential candidates continually poll the electorate to assess the candidate's chance of winning and to decide where to place the greatest campaign effort. A poll of 1,000 voters in California once indicated a week before the election that 450 voters favored the Republican, while an identical poll in Louisiana showed only 250 voters similarly inclined. Should the Republican have conceded both states to the Democrat and shifted the campaign elsewhere?

The point estimates of $P_C = .45$ and $P_L = .25$ might so indicate, but in each state, a 95 percent confidence interval for the true proportion was constructed just to make sure.

For California, the result was

$$\pi_C = P \pm z\sigma_P \cong .45 \pm 1.96\sqrt{\frac{.45(.55)}{1{,}000}} = .45 \pm .03$$

For Louisiana, the result was

$$\pi_L = P \pm z\sigma_P \cong .25 \pm 1.96\sqrt{\frac{.25(.75)}{1{,}000}} = .25 \pm .03$$

Clearly, the Republican candidate had practically no chance of winning Louisiana because, under the best of circumstances, a population proportion of .28 would have had to be increased to slightly over .50 in a mere week. Yet moving a population proportion that was possibly as high as .48 up to .50 was not equally inconceivable. The candidate was advised to campaign heavily in California.

12.7 Large-Sample Interval Estimates of the Difference between Two Population Means

Often decision makers seek an estimate not of a single population mean, but of the *difference* between two population means. Two production methods may be available; on the average, which one requires the greater amount of labor time? Two drugs may be effective in reducing high blood pressure; which one, on the average, is more effective? Two types of raw material may be usable; which one, on the average, has the greater tensile strength? Which of two work rules is more conducive to raising average labor productivity? Which of two types of tires has the longer average life? To answer questions such as these, statisticians take samples from two populations, A and B, with means μ_A and μ_B and estimate the difference, $\mu_A - \mu_B$. The existence of two populations, however, offers a choice: whether to take independent or matched-pairs samples. We will consider both possibilities.

LARGE AND INDEPENDENT SAMPLES

We first imagine taking two completely independent samples of sizes n_A and n_B from the two populations. These samples need not be of equal size. They will yield sample means $\bar{X}_A$ and $\bar{X}_B$; their difference, $d = \bar{X}_A - \bar{X}_B$, is an unbiased point estimator of $\mu_A - \mu_B$.

We could take such samples again and again, each time getting a different d. If we take large and independent samples of $n_A \geq 30$ and $n_B \geq 30$ (as we assume in this section), the sampling distribution of d will be normally distributed when $n < .05N$, because the central limit theorem then holds, and even when $n \geq .05N$, provided the underlying populations are normally distributed. This normally distributed sampling distribution will have a mean of $\mu_A - \mu_B$ and a standard deviation of $\sigma_d = \sqrt{\frac{\sigma_A^2}{n_A} + \frac{\sigma_B^2}{n_B}}$, where σ_A^2 and σ_B^2 are the two population variances. Formula 12.C tells us how to proceed.

FORMULA 12.C | Confidence Interval for the Difference between Two Population Means, Large Independent Samples ($n_A \geq 30$ and $n_B \geq 30$)

$$\mu_A - \mu_B = d \pm z\sigma_d = (\bar{X}_A - \bar{X}_B) \pm z\sqrt{\frac{\sigma_A^2}{n_A} + \frac{\sigma_B^2}{n_B}}$$

where $\mu_A - \mu_B$ is the difference between the means of populations A and B; d is the difference, $\bar{X}_A - \bar{X}_B$, between the means of samples A and B, sized n_A and n_B; z is the standard normal deviate associated with the desired confidence level (see Appendix Table J), and σ_d is the standard error of the sample mean differences (*precisely* computed as $\sqrt{\frac{\sigma_A^2}{n_A} + \frac{\sigma_B^2}{n_B}}$ if the population variances, σ_A^2 and σ_B^2, are known, or *estimated* as $\sqrt{\frac{s_A^2}{n_A} + \frac{s_B^2}{n_B}}$ with the help of the sample variances, s_A^2 and s_B^2, if the population variances are not known).

Notes:

1. It is assumed that $n < .05N$ for both populations.
2. Some analysts prefer to use Formula 12.G whenever the two σ's are unknown because that procedure creates a more conservative (wider) confidence interval. Section 12.10 introduces the alternative formula.

EXAMPLE PROBLEM 12.6

Consider a tire manufacturer who wishes to estimate, with 99 percent confidence, the difference between the mean lives of two types of tires, A and B, as a prelude to a major advertising campaign. A sample of 100 tires is taken from each production process, making $n_A = n_B = 100$. (As noted earlier, this equality of the two sample sizes is not a necessity.) The sample mean lifetimes turn out to be $\overline{X}_A = 30{,}100$ miles and $\overline{X}_B = 25{,}200$ miles; the sample variances are $s_A^2 = 1{,}500{,}000$ miles squared and $s_B^2 = 2{,}400{,}000$ miles squared.

SOLUTION: Using Formula 12.C,

$$\mu_A - \mu_B \cong (\overline{X}_A - \overline{X}_B) \pm z\sqrt{\frac{s_A^2}{n_A} + \frac{s_B^2}{n_B}}$$

$$= (30{,}100 - 25{,}200) \pm 2.575\sqrt{\frac{1{,}500{,}000}{100} + \frac{2{,}400{,}000}{100}}$$

$$= 4{,}900 \pm [2.575(197.48)] = 4{,}900 \pm 508.51$$

We can estimate the 99 percent confidence interval with the help of the sample variances as ranging from 4,391.49 miles to 5,408.51 miles. The tire from population A lasts that much longer. Thus, it is clearly superior and could safely be advertised as such.

Application 12.2, *The Danger of Being Left-Handed,* provides another illustration of the use of this procedure.

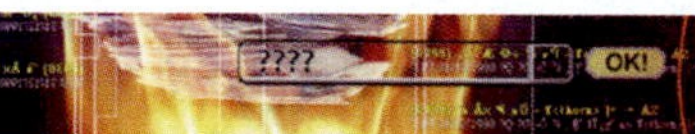

APPLICATION 12.2

THE DANGER OF BEING LEFT-HANDED

For many years, anecdotal evidence has accumulated suggesting that being left-handed may be dangerous to life. Left-handed people seemed to have a higher rate of accidental injuries than right-handers, and the life spans of left-handed baseball players were 9 months shorter than those of right-handed players. All of these stories prompted two medical researchers, Doctors Diane Halpern and Stanley Coren, to take a sample of 1,000 Californians and test the matter scientifically. In 1991, the *New England Journal of Medicine* reported their results.

While right-handers lived an average of 75 years, left-handers averaged 66 years. A 95 percent confidence interval of the difference between these means confirmed the significance of these results. The differences were equally pronounced for the two sexes taken separately. On average, right-handed women lived 5 years longer and right-handed men 10 years longer than their left-handed counterparts. Possible explanations included a world dominated by appliances designed for the right-handed as well as underlying neurological and immune system problems that only left-handers face.

But the last word on the subject has, perhaps, not yet been spoken. A six-year study undertaken by Harvard researchers and the National Institute of Aging focused on 3,800 East Boston residents, all aged 65 and older. No difference in the mean life spans of left-handers and right-handers was detected.

SOURCES: "Being Left-Handed May Be Dangerous to Life, Study Says," *The New York Times,* April 4, 1991, p. A21; *Journal of the American Public Health Association,* February 1993.

LARGE MATCHED-PAIRS SAMPLE

We could take an alternative approach to making interval estimates of the difference between two population means. Consider matching each elementary unit in population A with a "twin" from population B so that any sample observation about a unit in population A automatically yields an associated observation about a unit in population B. This procedure, known as **matched-pairs sampling,** is designed to control for extraneous factors that might influence the characteristic being measured in addition to the variable under study. For example, when testing the effectiveness of a new drug compared to a traditional one, each patient in an *experimental group* might be matched with a partner in a *control group* of the same age, weight, height, sex, occupation, medical history, lifestyle, and so on. The individual differences in response to the experimental stimulus between each pair are then used to estimate population differences.

The procedure can be summarized as follows: Let the sample observation for the ith pair equal X_{Ai} and X_{Bi}, depending on whether it refers to the partner from population A or B. Then the matched-pair difference equals $D_i = X_{Ai} - X_{Bi}$. From all such matched-pair differences involving n pairs, a mean and standard deviation can be calculated in the usual fashion as $\bar{D}$ and s_D. Now we can treat $\bar{D}$ and s_D like $\bar{X}$ and s in Formula 12.A. Given our large sample ($n \geq 30$) and large population ($n < .05N$), we can assume that $\bar{D}$ is normally distributed with a mean of $\mu_A - \mu_B$ and a standard deviation of $\sigma_{\bar{D}}$. Accordingly, we can establish the desired confidence interval as indicated in Formula 12.D.

FORMULA 12.D | Confidence Interval for the Difference between Two Population Means, Large Matched-Pairs Sample ($n \geq 30$)

$$\mu_A - \mu_B = \bar{D} \pm z\sigma_{\bar{D}} = \bar{D} \pm z\frac{\sigma_D}{\sqrt{n}}$$

where $\mu_A - \mu_B$ is the difference between the means of populations A and B; $\bar{D}$ is the sample mean of individual matched-pair differences, $X_{Ai} - X_{Bi}$; z is the standard normal deviate associated with the desired confidence level (see Appendix Table J); and $\sigma_{\bar{D}}$ is the standard error of the matched-pair sample differences (*precisely* computed as $\frac{\sigma_D}{\sqrt{n}}$ if the population standard deviation, σ_D, is known, or *estimated* as $\frac{s_D}{\sqrt{n}}$ with the help of the sample standard deviation, s_D, if σ_D is not known).

Notes:

1. It is assumed that $n < .05N$.
2. Some analysts prefer to use Formula 12.H whenever σ_D is unknown because that procedure creates a more conservative (wider) confidence interval. Section 12.10 introduces the alternative formula.

EXCEL Example 12.5

Before the Food and Drug Administration will permit the sale of a new drug for treating high blood pressure, its manufacturer must compare the drug's performance with that of another drug that has been traditionally used. Accordingly, 60 people are combined into 30 pairs of "near-twins." In each pair, one person receives the new drug (A), and the other person receives the old drug (B). The individual percentage reductions in blood pressure are recorded as follows:

New Drug									
22	21	26	23	21	23	24	30	25	24
27	23	27	26	23	25	21	23	25	28
28	30	29	28	21	30	24	30	25	22
Old Drug									
18	22	19	22	22	23	19	18	23	22
23	19	22	17	25	17	19	23	15	25
16	18	16	20	20	18	25	20	15	25

a. Compute a 95 percent confidence interval for the difference in population means.

b. Interpret your result.

SOLUTION

Part (a)

1. In a new worksheet, label cells A1 and B1 *New drug* and *Old drug,* respectively; then enter the above data into the two columns just below the labels. (You can achieve the same result by copying and pasting columns C and D of the file HKMISC.)
2. Label cell C1 *Difference* and enter the formula **=A2−B2** into cell C2. Select the result and drag it to cell C31 to create a column of differences.
3. Enter labels *Sample mean=Point estimate, Sample size, Critical z, Standard error of sample mean, Half-width of confidence interval, Lower limit of confidence interval,* and *Upper limit of confidence interval* into cells D1–D7, respectively.
4. Enter corresponding formulas into adjacent cells in column E; namely

   =AVERAGE(C2:C31) into E1.

   =COUNT(C2:C31) into E2.

   =NORMSINV(95/100/2+.5) into E3. (In this formula, the specified confidence level of 95% is converted from percentage to decimal form by dividing by 100, is then changed to the two-tailed value by dividing by 2, and to a value on the right side of the distribution by adding .5.)

   =STDEV(C2:C31)/SQRT(E2) into E4.

   =E3*E4 into D5.

   =E1−E5 into D6.

   =E1+E5 into D7.

The result:

Sample mean=Point estimate	4.933333
Sample size	30
Critical z	1.95996
Standard error of sample mean	0.90329
Half-width of confidence interval	1.77042
Lower limit of confidence interval	3.16291
Upper limit of confidence interval	6.70375

Part (b)

The 95 percent confidence interval ranges from 3.16291 percent to 6.70375 percent. We can say with 95 percent confidence that drug A reduces blood pressure between 3.2 and 6.7 percentage points more than drug B. Caution is advised: While the procedure used is correct 95 percent of the time, it will be wrong 5 percent of the time.

Note: This type of problem can also be solved much more rapidly by using HKStat, Sheet 8.

12.8 Large-Sample Interval Estimates of the Difference between Two Population Proportions

Frequently, decision makers seek an estimate not of a single population proportion, but of the difference between the proportions of two populations. Two production methods may be available; which one is associated with a smaller percentage of defective units? Of two types of new machines capable of performing a given task, which type requires fewer repairs within three years of purchase? An airline can use airport A or B; which choice is likely to yield a greater percentage of filled seats? A massive ad campaign was designed to raise the occupancy rate in a chain of hotels; does the percentage of rented rooms differ before and after the campaign? To answer questions such as these, statisticians take samples from two populations, A and B, with proportions π_A and π_B and estimate the difference, $\pi_A - \pi_B$. The samples need not be of equal size. They will yield sample proportions P_A and P_B; their difference, $d = P_A - P_B$, is an unbiased point estimator of $\pi_A - \pi_B$. We could take such samples again and again, each time getting a different d. If we take large and independent samples so that $n\pi \geq 5$ and $n(1 - \pi) \geq 5$ for both samples (as we assume in this section), the sampling distribution of d will be normally distributed, because the central limit theorem then holds. This normally distributed sampling distribution will have a mean of $\pi_A - \pi_B$ and a standard deviation of $\sigma_d = \sqrt{\dfrac{\pi_A(1 - \pi_A)}{n_A} + \dfrac{\pi_B(1 - \pi_B)}{n_B}}$. Accordingly, we can establish a confidence interval for the difference between two population proportions with the help of Formula 12.E on the next page. We apply the formula presently:

EXAMPLE PROBLEM 12.7

An executive of a tax preparation firm wants to compare the quality of work done at different offices around the country. A simple random sample of $n_A = 300$ returns filed last April is collected at office A. The returns are checked by company supervisors and 33 returns are found in error. Another such sample of $n_B = 400$ returns is collected at office B. Of these returns, 37 contain errors. A 97 percent confidence interval of the difference in the proportions of erroneous returns is sought.

FORMULA 12.E | **Confidence Interval for a Difference between Two Population Proportions, Large Independent Samples [$n_A\pi_A \geq 5$ and $n_A(1 - \pi_A) \geq 5$ and $n_B\pi_B \geq 5$ and $n_B(1 - \pi_B) \geq 5$]**

$$\pi_A - \pi_B = d \pm z\sigma_d = (P_A - P_B) \pm z\sqrt{\frac{\pi_A(1 - \pi_A)}{n_A} + \frac{\pi_B(1 - \pi_B)}{n_B}}$$

where $\pi_A - \pi_B$ is the difference between the proportions of populations A and B; d is the difference, $P_A - P_B$, between the proportions of samples A and B, sized n_A and n_B; z is the standard normal deviate associated with the desired confidence level (see Appendix Table J); and σ_d is the standard error of the sample proportion differences (*precisely* computed as $\sqrt{\frac{\pi_A(1 - \pi_A)}{n_A} + \frac{\pi_B(1 - \pi_B)}{n_B}}$ or *estimated* as $\sqrt{\frac{P_A(1 - P_A)}{n_A} + \frac{P_B(1 - P_B)}{n_B}}$).

SOLUTION The sample proportions of erroneous returns are $P_A = (33/300) = .11$ and $P_B = (37/400) = .0925$. According to Formula 12.E,

$$\pi_A - \pi_B = d \pm z\sigma_d \cong (P_A - P_B) \pm z\sqrt{\frac{P_A(1 - P_A)}{n_A} + \frac{P_B(1 - P_B)}{n_B}}$$

$$= (.11 - .0925) \pm 2.17\sqrt{\frac{.11(.89)}{300} + \frac{.0925(.9075)}{400}} = .0175 \pm 2.17\,(.0232)$$

$$= .0175 \pm .0503$$

Thus, $-.0328 \leq (\pi_A - \pi_B) \leq .0678$. Because the interval estimate straddles a proportion difference of zero, there is no reason to believe that the quality of work differs in the two sampled offices.

EXCEL Example 12.6

Use EXCEL to confirm the Example Problem 12.7 result and interpret the outcome.

SOLUTION

1. Open a new EXCEL worksheet.
2. Enter labels *Sample A, Size, Number of successes, Sample B, Size, Number of successes, Sample proportions =Point estimates, Sample A, Sample B, Difference A-B, Critical z, Standard error of difference, Half-width of confidence interval, Lower limit of confidence interval,* and *Upper limit of confidence interval* into cells A1-A15, respectively.
3. Enter corresponding formulas or known values into adjacent cells in column B; namely

   300 into B2.
   33 into B3.
   400 into B5.
   37 into B6.
   =B3/B2 into B8.

=B6/B5 into B9.
=B8−B9 into B10.
=NORMSINV(97/100/2+.5) into B11. (In this formula, the specified confidence level of 97% is converted from percentage to decimal form by dividing by 100, is then changed to the two-tailed value by dividing by 2, and to a value on the right side of the distribution by adding .5.)
=SQRT((B8*(1−B8)/B2)+(B9*(1−B9)/B5)) into B12.
=B11*B12 into B13.
=B10−B13 into B14.
=B10+B13 into B15.

The result confirms the Example Problem 12.7 computations:

Sample A	
Size	300
Number of successes	33
Sample B	
Size	400
Number of successes	37
Sample proportions=Point estimates	
Sample A	0.11
Sample B	0.0925
Difference A-B	0.0175
Critical z	2.170091
Standard error of difference	0.023156
Half-width of confidence interval	0.05025
Lower limit of confidence interval	−0.03275
Upper limit of confidence interval	0.06775

The 97 percent confidence interval for the difference in the proportion of erroneous returns found in the two offices ranges from −.03275 to .06775. This suggests that the first office may have anywhere from 3.3 percent fewer to 6.8 percent more erroneous returns; thus, there may well be no difference at all. Also note: The *procedure* employed produces confidence intervals containing the true difference in population proportions 97 percent of the time, but fails to do so 3 percent of the time.

Note: This type of problem can also be solved much more rapidly by using HKStat, Sheet 12.

12.9 Small-Sample Interval Estimates of a Population Mean

Consider the estimation of means from small samples of $n < 30$. Such cases are quite common for a variety of reasons, including the high cost of sampling, the desire to get faster results, and the rarity of some phenomena. Unfortunately, when $n < 30$, the central limit theorem about the mean does not apply. Yet it is still possible for the sampling distribution to be normal, provided only that the underlying population values are normally distributed. If such is known to be the case, and if the population standard deviation is also known, we can again estimate a confidence interval for a population mean with the help of z values, using Formula 12.A. (Indeed, even if we knew that the underlying population values were *not* normally distributed, as long as we knew the population standard deviation, we could still estimate a confidence interval with the help of

Chebyshev's theorem, noted on pages 252–253. But it would probably be easier just to raise sample size to $n \geq 30$.)

This section, however, focuses on a different type of small-sample case that is much more common: *the presence of a normally distributed population but the absence of any information about the population standard deviation.* In this situation, the standard error of the mean, $\sigma_{\bar{X}}$, is only poorly estimated with the help of the sample standard deviation, s. Therefore, we need an entirely different approach for constructing a confidence interval for a population mean.

STUDENT'S T DISTRIBUTION

As William S. Gosset (1876–1937), a British beer brewer who wrote under the name "Student," first showed, under the circumstances highlighted above, better interval estimates can be derived by using a probability density function somewhat different from the normal curve. Gosset, whose biography appears on the text's Web site, described a sampling distribution for a random variable, t, derived from a normally distributed population and defined in analogy to the standard normal deviate, z:

$$t = \frac{\bar{X} - \mu}{\frac{s}{\sqrt{n}}} \qquad \text{whereas} \qquad z = \frac{X - \mu}{\sigma}$$

Like the standard normal curve, Gosset's probability density function, now called **Student's *t* distribution,** is (1) single-peaked above the random variable's mean, median, and mode of zero, (2) perfectly symmetrical about this central value, and (3) characterized by tails extending indefinitely in both directions from the center, approaching, but never touching, the horizontal axis. The only difference is that the random variable is t rather than z. As a result, the distribution's variance does not equal 1 (as is true of the z distribution) but equals $\frac{n-1}{(n-1)-2}$. This variance of t implies that a different t distribution exists for each sample size, n, and also that the t distribution approaches the z distribution as sample size increases. The t distribution for $n = \infty$ has a variance of 1 and is indistinguishable from the standard normal curve. All these characteristics of the t distribution are illustrated in Figure 12.5.

As Figure 12.5 shows, members of the t-distribution family are labeled not on the basis of sample size, n, but on the basis of **degrees of freedom,** $n - 1$, which equal the number of independent pieces of information that enter the computation of a given statistic and, in this sense, can be "freely chosen." Consider the number of *independent* deviations, $X - \bar{X}$, of sample observations from the sample mean that enter the computation of the sample standard deviation, $s = \sqrt{\frac{\Sigma(X - \bar{X})^2}{n - 1}}$. For a sample of size n, we have n pieces of information; namely, $X_1 - \bar{X}$, $X_2 - \bar{X}$, $X_3 - \bar{X}$, . . . , and, finally, $X_n - \bar{X}$. But for any data set, the sum of all deviations of individual observations from their mean always equals zero: $\Sigma(X - \bar{X}) = 0$. (Recall our discussion in Figure 7.2, "The Nature of the Arithmetic Mean," on page 230.) Therefore, only $n - 1$ of our n pieces of information are independent: Once we know or have "freely chosen" $n - 1$ of these deviation values, the remaining deviation value is determined for us because the sum of all deviations necessarily equals 0. Thus, we have $n - 1$ degrees of freedom.

EXAMPLE PROBLEM 12.8

Consider a sample mean of $\bar{X} = 23$. How many degrees of freedom are involved in its computation if sample size $n = 3$?

FIGURE 12.5 | Student's t Distributions

Different bell-shaped t distributions exist for different degrees of freedom, d.f., defined as sample size minus one, n − 1. Unless the degrees of freedom are infinite (which makes the t distribution equal to the red standard normal curve shown here), the t distribution is flatter than the standard normal curve, and more of its area is found in the tails. Strictly speaking, each t distribution is a sampling distribution of the t statistic derived by taking a small sample from a normally distributed population. Nevertheless, in practice, statisticians use the t distribution to make small-sample inferences about all types of populations, provided only that these populations are not highly skewed.

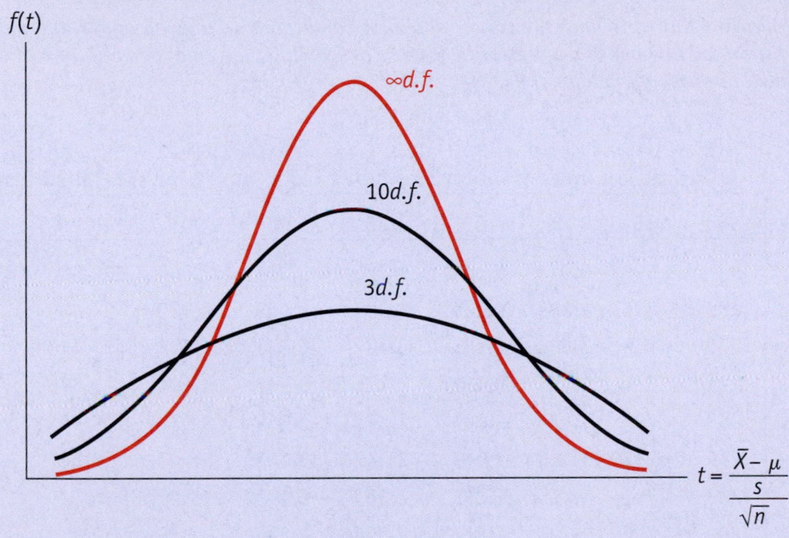

SOLUTION: There are 2 degrees of freedom. You can freely choose any two sample observations, such as $X_1 = 39$ and $X_2 = 41$; thereafter your hands are tied. Given your two choices, the value of X_3 *must* equal -11, because $(X_1 - \bar{X}) + (X_2 - \bar{X}) + (X_3 - \bar{X}) = 0$. Thus $(39 - 23) + (41 - 23) + (X_3 - 23) = 0$ and $16 + 18 + X_3 - 23 = 0$ and $X_3 = 23 - 16 - 18 = -11$.

THE t DISTRIBUTION TABLE

Just as areas under the standard normal curve have been tabulated to make it easy for us to gauge various probabilities, so there exist tables for areas under various t distributions. Appendix Table K, "Student's t Distributions," is a case in point. An excerpt appears as Table 12.3 on the next page.

By tradition, the table shows the area under a specified curve, defined by a given number of degrees of freedom, that lies *to the right* of a specified value of t. As is pictured in Appendix Table K, this upper-tail area is called α (the lowercase Greek letter alpha), and this t value is designated as t_α. Frequently, the applicable degrees of freedom (*d.f.*) are added to the α subscript, either in parentheses or following a comma: $t_{\alpha(d.f.)}$ or $t_{\alpha,d.f.}$. As a look at Appendix Table K will confirm, for an upper-tail area of $\alpha = .05$ and 9 degrees of freedom, $t_{.05(9)} = 1.833$. In other words, .05 of the area under the t curve appropriate for a sample of $n = 10$ (and, therefore, 9 degrees of freedom) is associated with $t > 1.833$.

TABLE 12.3 | Excerpt from Appendix Table K, Student's *t* Distributions

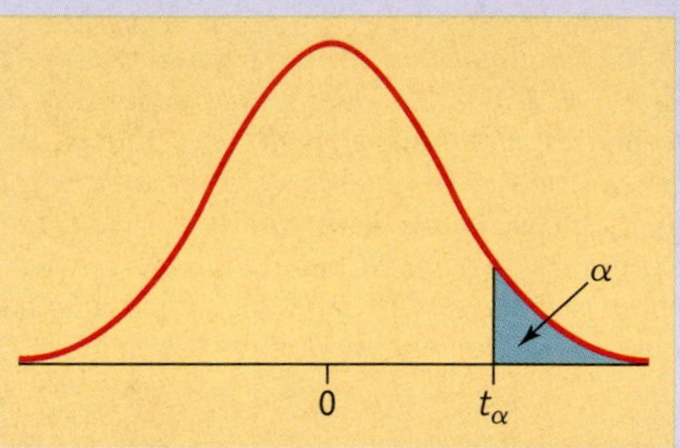

The following table provides the values of t_α that correspond to a given upper-tail area α and a specified number of degrees of freedom. For example, for an upper-tail area of α = .05 and 9 degrees of freedom, the critical value of t_α = 1.833.

Degrees of Freedom	Critical Tail Areas (= α for one-tailed tests, = α/2 for two-tailed tests)								
	.4	.25	.1	.05	.025	.01	.005	.0025	.001
1	.325	1.000	3.078	6.314	12.706	31.821	63.657	127.32	318.31
2	.289	.816	1.886	2.920	4.303	6.965	9.925	14.089	22.327
3	.277	.765	1.638	2.353	3.182	4.541	5.841	7.453	10.214
4	.271	.741	1.533	2.132	2.776	3.747	4.604	5.598	7.173
5	.267	.727	1.476	2.015	2.571	3.365	4.032	4.773	5.893
6	.265	.718	1.440	1.943	2.447	3.143	3.707	4.317	5.208
7	.263	.711	1.415	1.895	2.365	2.998	3.499	4.029	4.785
8	.262	.706	1.397	1.860	2.306	2.896	3.355	3.833	4.501
9	.261	.703	1.383	**1.833**	2.262	2.821	3.250	3.690	4.297
10	.260	.700	1.372	1.812	2.228	2.764	3.169	3.581	4.144

Because of the curve's symmetry, .05 of the area under this curve is also associated with $t < -1.833$. Consequently, .9 of the area under this curve is associated with t values between -1.833 and $+1.833$; the probability for such t values equals .9. To construct an interval estimate with a confidence level of .9, or 90 percent, we must use $t = 1.833$. Formula 12.F tells us how to construct our confidence interval.

FORMULA 12.F | Confidence Interval for a Population Mean, Small Sample ($n < 30$)

$$\mu = \bar{X} \pm \left(t\frac{s}{\sqrt{n}}\right)$$

where μ is the population mean, $\bar{X}$ is the sample mean, t is the value of the t distribution appropriate for the desired confidence level and the given sample size (see Appendix Table K), s is the sample standard deviation, and n is the sample size.

Notes:

1. The population distribution is assumed to be normal.
2. It is assumed that $n < .05N$. Otherwise, if population size, N, is small relative to sample size, n, the expression $\frac{s}{\sqrt{n}}$ must be multiplied by the finite population correction factor of $\sqrt{\frac{N-n}{N-1}}$.

EXAMPLE PROBLEM 12.9

Consider a manufacturing plant. On many occasions during the course of a year, the firm loses labor hours because machinery breaks down. The manager, who knows from previous experience that the time-lost population is normally distributed, decides to keep track of the time lost during a randomly chosen week and calculates the mean time lost during 10 breakdowns as 820 hours, with a standard deviation of 510 hours. Construct a 98 percent confidence interval for the mean time lost during all of the year's breakdowns.

SOLUTION For sample size $n = 10$, there are 9 degrees of freedom, while the 98 percent confidence level corresponds to an upper-tail area of $\alpha = .01$. From Appendix Table K, we find $t_{.01(9)} = 2.821$. Accordingly, $\mu = \bar{X} \pm \left(t\frac{s}{\sqrt{n}}\right) = 820 \pm \left(2.821\frac{510}{\sqrt{10}}\right) = 820 \pm 455$.

The 98 percent confidence interval is disconcertingly wide; it goes from 365 hours to 1,275 hours.

EXCEL Example 12.7

According to the Internal Revenue Service, the average American small business in 1999 needed 10 hours and 18 minutes to file Schedule C. Allegedly, this time was sufficient for keeping records, learning about the law and the form, preparing the form, and copying, assembling, and sending the form to the IRS. The manager of an accounting firm doubted the claim, took a simple random sample of 10 clients, and came up with these times: 183, 201, 245, 101, 34, 178, 233, 6, 289, and 196 hours.

Prepare a 95 percent confidence interval for the mean time burden of filing Schedule C.

SOLUTION Assuming the population of times is normally distributed, and after entering the data into cells A1–A10 of an EXCEL worksheet, proceed as follows:

1. Enter labels *Sample mean = Point estimate, Sample standard deviation, Sample size, Degrees of freedom, Critical t, Standard error of sample mean, Half-width of confidence*

interval, Lower limit of confidence interval, and *Upper limit of confidence interval* into cells B1–B9, respectively.

2. Enter corresponding formulas into adjacent cells in column C; namely

   =AVERAGE(A1:A10) into C1.

   =STDEV(A1:A10) into C2.

   =COUNT(A1:A10) into C3.

   =C3−1 into C4.

   =TINV(1−95/100,C4) into C5. (The TINV function returns a two-tailed value. However, the confidence level must be converted from percent to decimal form by dividing by 100; this value must be subtracted from 1 to obtain the probability in the tail of the distribution, given the specified degrees of freedom.)

   =C2/SQRT(C3) into C6.

   =C5*C6 into C7.

   =C1−C7 into C8.

   =C1+C7 into C9.

   The result:

Sample mean = Point estimate	166.6
Sample standard deviation	91.68933
Sample size	10
Degrees of freedom	9
Critical t	2.262159
Standard error of sample mean	28.99471
Half-width of confidence interval	65.59065
Lower limit of confidence interval	101.0094
Upper limit of confidence interval	232.1906

The 95 percent confidence interval ranges from 101.0 to 232.2 hours, a far cry from the IRS claim of 10.3 hours.

Note: This type of problem can also be solved much more rapidly by using HKStat, Sheet 5.

12.10 Small-Sample Interval Estimates of the Difference between Two Population Means

We now consider constructing small-sample interval estimates of the difference between two population means. We assume two populations that are normally distributed, while a precise knowledge of their variances is missing. As in the large-samples case, the task can be tackled in one of two ways: by taking two small independent samples or by taking a small matched-pairs sample.

SMALL AND INDEPENDENT SAMPLES

Formula 12.G spells out the procedure when two small and independent samples of sizes $n_A < 30$ and $n_B < 30$ are taken from two normal populations. Essentially, the procedure equals that for large samples, except that t_α replaces z.

The examples on the following two pages illustrate how easy it is to apply Formula 12.G—with the help of a computer or even by hand.

FORMULA 12.G | Confidence Interval for the Difference between Two Population Means, Small Independent Samples ($n_A < 30$ and $n_B < 30$)

$$\mu_A - \mu_B = d \pm t\sigma_d = (\bar{X}_A - \bar{X}_B) \pm t\sqrt{\frac{s_A^2}{n_A} + \frac{s_B^2}{n_B}}$$

where $\mu_A - \mu_B$ is the difference between the means of populations A and B; d is the difference, $\bar{X}_A - \bar{X}_B$, between the means of samples A and B, sized n_A and n_B; σ_d is the standard error of the sample mean differences; t is the value of the t distribution appropriate for the desired confidence level and $(n_A - 1) + (n_B - 1)$ degrees of freedom (see Appendix Table K); while s_A^2 and s_B^2 are the two sample variances.

Notes:

1. It is assumed that the two populations are normally distributed and that $n < .05N$ for both populations.
2. If nothing is known about the population variances, the standard error of the sample mean differences is *estimated* as $\sigma_d = \sqrt{\frac{s_A^2}{n_A} + \frac{s_B^2}{n_B}}$. If one is certain that the two population variances (although unknown) are equal, the sample variances are pooled to estimate the common population variance as $\sigma_E^2 = \frac{(n_A - 1)s_A^2 + (n_B - 1)s_B^2}{n_A + n_B - 2}$ and σ_E^2 is substituted for both s_A^2 and s_B^2.

EXCEL Example 12.8

Chemical company executives are eager to market a newly developed pesticide. In advance of an advertising blitz, they set up an agricultural experiment in which the effectiveness of the new pesticide is compared to a competitor's product by measuring cotton production on 30 acres of identical land. Of the 30 1-acre plots, 15 use the new pesticide (A); another 15 use the competitor's pesticide (B). In pounds per acre, the cotton harvests on the experimental plots are as follows:

A-plots:	1,575	1,678	1,345	1,233	1,699	1,790	1,544	1,890	1,111
	1,022	1,459	1,389	1,700	999	1,003			
B-plots:	1,475	1,768	1,100	1,333	1,423	1,899	1,390	2,000	978
	1,222	1,344	1,399	1,500	1,698	876			

Develop a 99 percent confidence interval for the difference in pesticide effectiveness.

SOLUTION

Assuming the two output populations are normally distributed and nothing is known about the population variances, proceed as follows:

1. In a new worksheet, label cells A1 and B1 *A-plots* and *B-plots*, respectively; then enter the above data into the two columns just below the labels. (You can achieve the same result by copying and pasting columns E and F of the file HKMISC.)
2. Enter labels *Sample A, Mean, Variance, Size, Sample B, Mean, Variance, Size, Difference of means =Point estimate, Degrees of freedom, Critical t, Standard error of difference, Half-width of confidence interval, Lower limit of confidence interval,* and *Upper limit of confidence interval* into cells C1–C15, respectively.
3. Enter corresponding formulas or known values into adjacent cells in column D; namely
   =**AVERAGE(A2:A16)** into D2.

   =**VAR(A2:A16)** into D3.

   =**COUNT(A2:A16)** into D4.

   =**AVERAGE(B2:B16)** into D6.

   =**VAR(B2:B16)** into D7.

   =**COUNT(B2:B16)** into D8.

   =**D2−D6** into D9.

   =**D4+D8−2** into D10.

   =**TINV(1−99/100,D10)** into D11. (The TINV function returns a two-tailed value. However, the confidence level must be converted from percent to decimal form by dividing by 100; this value must be subtracted from 1 to obtain the probability in the tail of the distribution, given the specified degrees of freedom.)

   =**SQRT((D3/D4)+(D7/D8))** into D12.

   =**D11*D12** into D13.

   =**D9–D13** into D14.

   =**D9+D13** into D15.

   The result:

Sample A	
Mean	1429.13333
Variance	90488.981
Size	15
Sample B	
Mean	1427
Variance	101465.571
Size	15
Difference of means=Point estimate	2.13333333
Degrees of freedom	28
Critical t	2.76326318
Standard error of difference	113.123694
Half-width of confidence interval	312.590539
Lower limit of confidence interval	−310.457206
Upper limit of confidence interval	314.723872

The 99 percent confidence interval ranges from −310 to +315 pounds per acre, leaving open the possibility that the new pesticide is worse *or* better, which is hardly conclusive evidence in its favor.

Note: This type of problem can also be solved much more rapidly by using HKStat, Sheet 9.

EXAMPLE PROBLEM 12.10

Having spent millions of dollars to develop their new pesticide, the executives noted in the previous example hire you to redo the analysis by hand. They believe the computer program must have been wrong.

SOLUTION: You can use Formula 12.G, along with the above-noted sample means and standard deviations (which *are* correct). Consult Appendix Table K in the column for an upper tail $\alpha = .005$ and the row for 28 degrees of freedom, finding $t_{.005(28)} = 2.763$. Thus,

$$\mu_A - \mu_B = (\bar{X}_A - \bar{X}_B) \pm t\sqrt{\frac{s_A^2}{n_A} + \frac{s_B^2}{n_B}} = (1{,}429 - 1{,}427) \pm 2.763\sqrt{\frac{301^2}{15} + \frac{319^2}{15}}$$

$$= 2 \pm 2.763(113.244) = 2 \pm 312.893$$

Accordingly, the 99 percent confidence interval ranges from −310.89 to +314.89 pounds per acre, just as the computer said (except for rounding).

SMALL MATCHED-PAIRS SAMPLE

Formula 12.H spells out the procedure when a small matched-pairs sample of size $n < 30$ is taken from two normal populations. Essentially, the procedure equals that for large samples, except that t_α with $n - 1$ degrees of freedom replaces z.

FORMULA 12.H | Confidence Interval for the Difference between Two Population Means, Small Matched-Pairs Sample ($n < 30$)

$$\mu_A - \mu_B = \bar{D} \pm t\sigma_{\bar{D}} = \bar{D} \pm t\frac{\sigma_D}{\sqrt{n}}$$

where $\mu_A - \mu_B$ is the difference between the means of populations A and B; $\bar{D}$ is the mean of all individual matched-pair differences, $X_{Ai} - X_{Bi}$; t is the value of the t distribution appropriate for the desired confidence level and $n - 1$ degrees of freedom (see Appendix Table K); and $\sigma_{\bar{D}}$ is the standard error of the matched-pair differences. The value of $\sigma_{\bar{D}}$ is computed as $\frac{\sigma_D}{\sqrt{n}}$ if the population standard deviation, σ_D, is known, or *estimated* as $\frac{s_D}{\sqrt{n}}$ with the help of the sample standard deviation, s_D, if σ_D is not known.

Note: It is assumed that the population of matched-pair differences is normally distributed and that $n < .05N$.

EXAMPLE PROBLEM 12.11

An auto manufacturer, annoyed by a rival's advertising claims, wishes to estimate the difference between the mean miles per gallon of two car models, A and B. The firm's statistician is to construct a 98 percent confidence interval for the *difference* between the mean miles per gallon. Ten pairs of drivers, matched according to driving skill, are observed. The mean and standard deviation of the differences between miles per gallon achieved by model A and miles per gallon achieved by model B are found to be $\bar{D} = 5$ miles per gallon, and $s_D = 2$ miles per gallon.

SOLUTION: We can use Formula 12.H, along with $t_{.01(9)} = 2.821$ from Appendix Table K.

$$\mu_A - \mu_B = \bar{D} \pm t\sigma_{\bar{D}} \cong \bar{D} \pm t\frac{s_D}{\sqrt{n}} = 5 \pm 2.821\frac{2}{\sqrt{10}} = 5 \pm 1.784$$

The 98 percent confidence interval for the mileage difference reaches from 3.216 to 6.784 miles per gallon, which suggests that model A is indeed superior as far as gasoline mileage is concerned. Model A achieves at least 3.2 *extra* miles per gallon and perhaps as many as 6.8 *extra* miles per gallon when compared to Model B. However, the procedure used here (while being correct 98 percent of the time) leads to incorrect results 2 percent of the time.

Application 12.3, *Matched-Pairs Sampling in the Chemical Industry,* provides another example of this procedure.

APPLICATION 12.3

MATCHED-PAIRS SAMPLING IN THE CHEMICAL INDUSTRY

Imperial Chemical Industries, a British firm, wanted to test the effect of a chlorinating agent on the abrasion resistance of a certain type of rubber. Ten pieces of rubber were cut in half. One of the two halves in each pair was chosen by the toss of a coin to be treated with the agent, and the other one was not treated. Subsequently, the abrasion resistance of all the pieces was tested by a machine, and the difference for each pair of halves was recorded, as indicated in Table 12.A.

TABLE 12.A | Abrasion Resistance

Pair	Difference in Resistance of Treated Minus Untreated Piece, *D*
1	2.6
2	3.1
3	−.2
4	1.7
5	.6
6	1.2
7	2.2
8	1.1
9	−.2
10	.6

The mean and standard deviation for the sample differences were computed as $\bar{D} = 1.27$ and $s_D = 1.1265$. The firm's statisticians then calculated a 98 percent confidence interval for the mean difference (using $t_{.01}$ for 9 degrees of freedom):

$$\mu_A - \mu_B = \bar{D} \pm t\sigma_{\bar{D}} \cong \bar{D} \pm t\frac{s_D}{\sqrt{n}}$$

$$= 1.27 \pm 2.821\frac{1.1265}{\sqrt{10}} = 1.27 \pm 1.005$$

Thus, the mean difference in abrasion resistance of treated and untreated (otherwise identical) rubber pieces was an increase between .265 and 2.275, suggesting, with 98 percent confidence, a positive effect of such treatment.

SOURCE: Adapted from Owen L. Davies, ed., *The Design and Analysis of Industrial Experiments* (London: Oliver and Boyd, 1960), p. 13. Table 12.A data reprinted with permission of the Longman Group U.K., Ltd.

12.11 The Optimal Sample Size

One question inevitably arises whenever we employ sampling to estimate population parameters: How can we minimize the total cost of sampling? Figure 12.6 brings together the major elements that must be considered.

We imagine a population of size $N = 1{,}000$ for which the cost of making each observation equals \$40. Thus, the total cost of collecting data equals \$40 for a sample of 1, \$400 for a sample of 10, and so on, finally amounting to \$40,000 for a census. For alternative sample sizes, these costs of collection are shown by the upward-sloping line C_C. To reduce these sample-collection costs, we clearly want to keep sample size, n, as small as possible.

Another consideration, however, mitigates against this desire. As a look at this chapter's formulas can confirm, given a specified confidence level, and, hence, a specified value of z or t, any decrease in sample size, n, raises the standard error of the estimator and, thus, the margin of error attached to a parameter estimate. Table 12.4 on the next page can help us understand this relationship.

Consider a large-sample confidence interval estimate of a population mean. Given a known or estimated population standard deviation of, say, 100, the choice of a 95 percent confidence level and, thus, $z = 1.96$, produces a margin of error of $e = z\sigma_{\bar{X}} = 1.96 \frac{100}{\sqrt{n}}$. If $n = 100$, $e =$

FIGURE 12.6 | The Costs of Sampling

The optimal sample size (here n = 460) minimizes the total cost of sampling, C_T (here at d = \$29,000) and maximizes the savings (here \$11,000) that can be achieved by sampling rather than by taking a census. The total cost of sampling equals the sum of the costs of collection, C_C, and of errors, C_E. Note how, at the optimal sample size, C_C = \$18,400 (distance ac) plus C_E = \$10,600 (distance ab = cd) equals C_T = \$29,000.

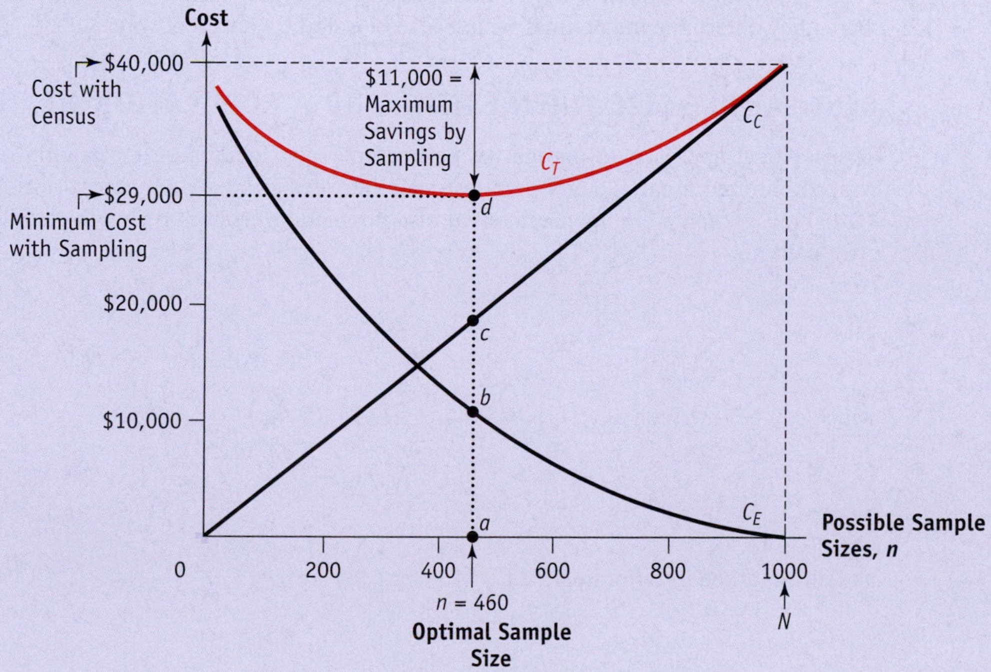

TABLE 12.4 | Interval Estimation Procedures and Margins of Error

Large-Sample Confidence Interval Estimation Procedure	Margin of Error, e	Precise Value of Standard Error of Estimator	Approximate Value of Standard Error of Estimator
For a Population Mean (see Formula 12.A)	$z\sigma_{\bar{X}}$	$\sigma_{\bar{X}} = \frac{\sigma}{\sqrt{n}}$	$\sigma_{\bar{X}} \cong \frac{s}{\sqrt{n}}$
For a Population Proportion (see Formula 12.B)	$z\sigma_P$	$\sigma_P = \sqrt{\frac{\pi(1-\pi)}{n}}$	$\sigma_P \cong \sqrt{\frac{P(1-P)}{n}}$

19.60 and the confidence interval equals the point estimate ± 19.60. If sample size is cut to $n = 50$, $e = 27.72$ and the confidence interval equals the point estimate ± 27.72. A similar prediction can be made for the population proportion and all the other parameters discussed in this chapter: All else being equal, every decrease in sample size, n, raises the margin of error, e, and thus raises the width and reduces the precision of the associated interval estimate.

Unfortunately, any such widening of a confidence interval represents an increase in the sampling error, and sampling error is costly, too. Decisions made on the basis of erroneous figures can reduce the profits of a firm just as easily as spending a fortune on large samples. Line C_E in Figure 12.6 represents a hypothetical estimate of the costs of sampling errors, which are zero for a census but get increasingly larger as the sample size falls.

We can now add these two types of sampling costs for each possible sample size and determine the total cost of sampling, C_T. Note how this total cost reaches a minimum at point d, implying an optimal sample size of $n = 460$. Unfortunately, the theoretical ideal illustrated by Figure 12.6 eludes practical decision makers. Being unable to draw the types of curves shown there, they determine the optimal sample size in a slightly different way.

BEST SAMPLE SIZE WHEN ESTIMATING A POPULATION MEAN

The practical approach to finding the best sample size focuses on the margin of error that is wrapped around a parameter's point estimate in order to create an interval estimate. As Table 12.4 shows, when a confidence interval of a population mean is being created, that margin of error equals

$$e = z\sigma_{\bar{X}} = z\frac{\sigma}{\sqrt{n}}$$

which can be rewritten as

$$e^2 = z^2\frac{\sigma^2}{n}$$

and, thus, turned into Formula 12.I.

FORMULA 12.I | Sample Size Required for Specified Confidence Level and Margin of Error When Estimating a Population Mean

$$n = \left(\frac{z\sigma}{e}\right)^2$$

where n is the sample size required to achieve two conditions (both specified prior to sampling):

1. a desired confidence level (which, in turn, implies a particular value of the standard normal deviate, z).
2. a desired margin of error, e.

Note: The value of σ, the standard deviation of the population about to be sampled, is commonly estimated in one of three ways:

1. as equal to the sample standard deviation, s, computed from a prior sample of the same population.
2. as equal to the sample standard deviation, s, computed from a pilot study of the same population.
3. by estimating the smallest and largest datum in the population about to be sampled, computing the range of the population data as the estimated maximum value minus the estimated minimum value, and assuming that σ equals a quarter of that range.

EXAMPLE PROBLEM 12.12

Example Problem 12.4 on page 499 featured a study of hotel room rentals. Based on a sample of $n = 32$, and a \$61 estimate of the population standard deviation, an investigator produced a \$194.03 point estimate and a 95 percent confidence interval of $\$172.90 \leq \mu \leq \$215.16$. You are asked to design another survey that reduces the sampling error from $\pm\$21.13$ to a more tolerable $\pm\$10$, while keeping the confidence level unchanged.

SOLUTION: With the help of Formula 12.I, you can achieve the desired goal by raising sample size to $n = 143$.

$$n = \left(\frac{z\sigma}{e}\right)^2 = \left(\frac{1.96(61)}{10}\right)^2 = 142.95$$

Presumably, the user of the estimate can decide whether such increased precision is worth the added cost of data collection. If it is not, the desire for increased precision provides an incentive for finding alternative and cheaper ways of collecting information.

Application 12.4, *Reducing Sample-Collection Costs by Work Sampling,* shows how imaginative sampling procedures can sometimes reduce the cost of collecting sample data.

APPLICATION 12.4

Reducing Sample-Collection Costs by Work Sampling

Frequently, several ways of collecting sample data exist, and they are unlikely to be equally costly. The management of one firm wanted to know the mean time its workers required to spray-paint a household appliance. One manager assigned 30 individuals to keep a continuous watch over a 30-member random sample of the firm's 1,000-member workforce. During a 40-hour period, every move the sampled workers made was duly recorded and measured. The observed workers, of course, disliked being watched, and critics feared that the very presence of observers changed the behavior of the observed so as to bias the results obtained. Nevertheless, at a cost of $200 per observed worker (and a lot of griping), the mean time the sampled workers needed to complete the task was established at 46 minutes, with a standard deviation of 12 minutes. The firm's statisticians then computed the limits of a 95 percent confidence interval for the mean painting time by *all* workers as

$$\mu = \bar{X} \pm z\frac{s}{\sqrt{n}}$$

$$= 46 \pm 1.96\frac{12}{\sqrt{30}} = 46 \pm 4.29 \text{ minutes}$$

This knowledge cost the firm 30($200) = $6,000.

An Alternative. In the meantime, another executive took a different approach. Two observers were hired for a week at $200 each. Without anyone's knowledge, these observers watched another sample of 30 workers, but each worker was observed only at randomly scattered *moments.* With the help of a random-numbers table, it was determined, for example, that worker A would be observed on Monday at 9:05, 9:47, 11:12, and 13:32, on Tuesday at 9:31, 10:11, and so on. Only the type of activity undertaken at these moments was then recorded. Thus, in 100 observations, worker A might have been found 81 times painting the appliance, 3 times being absent from the workbench, twice drinking coffee, twice chatting, and so on. It was then assumed that the proportion of *time* spent by a worker in the pursuit of a given activity during the entire week was identical to the relative frequency of momentary observations showing this worker engaged in this activity. Thus, having found worker A painting at 81 out of 100 *moments,* it would have been concluded that worker A also spent 81/100 of the entire 40-hour week actually painting the appliance. If worker A also painted 36 appliances, which would be easy enough to check, that particular worker's mean completion time could be figured as 54 minutes. (81/100 of 40 hours comes to 32.4 hours = 1,944 minutes and 1,944 minutes divided by 36 equals 54 minutes.) The mean painting time of all workers in the second sample turned out to be 47 minutes, with a standard deviation of 10 minutes—almost identical to the results noted above. Thus, the second method of collecting sample data, which is referred to as **work sampling,** was found to be a considerably cheaper way of getting identical information (costing, in our example, a mere $400 and completely avoiding the alienating effect of the overseer's presence).

Widespread Use. Firms are applying work sampling widely to set reasonable work standards and to improve labor productivity. The method allows auto manufacturers to know precisely how much time must be planned for installing a bumper or a steering wheel. It allows restaurants and hospitals to plan personnel assignments for clearing tables, pouring coffee, and figuring bills or charting fevers, dispensing pills, and nursing patients, respectively. Indeed, the method has been used outside the workplace, as by city governments intent on charting traffic flows. By observing anybody or anything often enough, for a second at a time, we can figure out quite easily the proportion of total time that is being spent on various activities.

BEST SAMPLE SIZE WHEN ESTIMATING A POPULATION PROPORTION

The determination of the best sample size for estimating a population proportion, rather than a population mean, follows an analogous route. As Table 12.4 shows, when a confidence interval of a population proportion is being created, the margin of error equals

$$e = z\sigma_p = z\sqrt{\frac{\pi(1-\pi)}{n}}$$

which can be rewritten as

$$e^2 = z^2 \frac{\pi(1 - \pi)}{n}$$

and, thus, as Formula 12.J.

FORMULA 12.J | Sample Size Required for Specified Confidence Level and Margin of Error When Estimating a Population Proportion

$$n = \frac{z^2\pi(1 - \pi)}{e^2}$$

where n is the sample size required to achieve two conditions, both specified prior to sampling:

1. a desired confidence level (which, in turn, implies a particular value of the standard normal deviate, z).
2. a desired margin of error, e.

Note: The value of π, the population proportion of interest, is commonly estimated in one of four ways:

1. as equal to the sample proportion, P, computed from a prior sample of the same population.
2. as equal to the sample proportion, P, computed from a pilot study of the population.
3. on the basis of the investigator's best guess.
4. as equal to .5, because this choice is most cautious in that it maximizes the expression $\pi(1 - \pi)$ at .25 and thereby produces the largest sample size recommendation, compared to all alternative estimates of π.

EXAMPLE PROBLEM 12.13

Example Problem 12.5 on page 501 featured a study of the proportion of credit card holders who might be persuaded to buy credit card insurance. Based on a sample of $n = 300$, an investigator produced a point estimate of .11 and a 98 percent confidence interval of reaching from .07 to .15. You are asked to design another survey that reduces the sampling error from ±.04 to a more tolerable ±.01, while keeping the confidence level unchanged.

SOLUTION: Given the prior sample, you might estimate π as .11. With the help of Formula 12.J, you can show that the desired goal can be reached, but only by raising sample size to $n =$ 5,300.

$$n = \frac{z^2\pi(1 - \pi)}{e^2} = \frac{(2.3267)^2(.11)(.89)}{(.01)^2} = 5{,}299.85$$

Presumably, the user of the estimate could decide whether such increased precision was worth the added cost of data collection.

12.12 A Note on Bayesian Estimation

The estimation techniques discussed so far in this chapter regard the parameter to be estimated as a constant, while the estimator is viewed as a random variable. **Bayesian estimation** differs from this approach in that it views the parameter itself as a random variable as well. This may be reasonable whenever statisticians (as a result of prior experience or *a priori* reasoning) hold strong opinions about what the value of the unknown parameter is likely to be. These opinions about likely values of population mean or proportion, for example, may be represented by a prior (subjective) probability distribution. Unlike standard techniques, Bayesian estimation techniques take into account prior probabilities. (For an earlier discussion of prior probabilities, see Section 8.10, *Revising Probabilities: Bayes' Theorem,* on pages 322–325.)

If a statistician's prior subjective probability distribution of the population mean is normal, the Bayesian estimate of the population mean, for example, is given by

$$\mu = \left(\frac{n\sigma_*^2}{n\sigma_*^2 + \sigma^2}\right)\overline{X} + \left(\frac{\sigma^2}{n\sigma_*^2 + \sigma^2}\right)\mu_*$$

where n is the sample size, $\overline{X}$ is the sample mean, and σ^2 is the population variance (as usual); while σ_*^2 and μ_*, respectively, are the variance and the mean of the prior subjective probability distribution of the population mean.

Thus, the Bayesian estimate of the population mean is a weighted average of the sample mean, $\overline{X}$, and the mean of the prior subjective probability distribution of the population mean, μ_*. It is, in short, a weighted average of what the sample actually finds ($\overline{X}$) and what the statistician believes to be true about the population (μ_*). Note that the formula gives more weight to $\overline{X}$, and less to μ_*, the larger is the sample (the greater is n) and the greater is the statistician's uncertainty about the population mean (the greater is σ_*^2).

The opposite is true for a small n and a small σ_*^2 because then $\overline{X}$ is less trustworthy, but the low variance makes μ_* more believable. This approach is eminently sensible.

EXAMPLE PROBLEM 12.14

As an illustration of Bayesian estimation, reconsider the page 490 point estimate of μ = \$812 million of the mean 1998 profit of all *Fortune 500* companies. Suppose the investigator had held a strong prior opinion about the population mean and that the mean and standard deviation of the investigator's prior probability distribution had been, respectively, $\mu_* = 500$ and $\sigma_* = 1{,}000$. What would a Bayesian estimate have been?

SOLUTION: If the sample variance of $s^2 = (1{,}070)^2$ is used as an estimate of the missing population variance, σ, the Bayesian point estimate is

$$\mu = \left(\frac{30(1{,}000)^2}{30(1{,}000)^2 + (1{,}070)^2}\right)812 + \left(\frac{(1{,}070)^2}{30(1{,}000)^2 + (1{,}070)^2}\right)500$$

$$= .9632\,(812) + .0368\,(500) = 800.52$$

The result, clearly, is a compromise between what the sample discovered and what the investigator believed all along. Also, in this particular instance, the result is practically the same as that obtained by the non-Bayesian technique earlier in this chapter because the large variance of the investigator's prior probability distribution causes little weight to be attached to the associated prior mean.

Summary

1. The process of inferring values of unknown population parameters from known sample statistics is referred to as *estimation.* The type of sample statistic that serves the purpose of making inferences about a given type of population parameter is called the *estimator* of that parameter.
2. Ideally, an estimator should be unbiased, efficient, and consistent. A sample statistic is an *unbiased estimator* of the corresponding population parameter if the mean of all possible values of that statistic equals the parameter the statistic seeks to estimate. A sample statistic is an *efficient estimator* if, for a given sample size, it has the smallest variance among all the available unbiased estimators of a given parameter. A sample statistic is a *consistent estimator* if its value gets ever closer to the parameter being estimated as sample size increases. Whenever several possible estimators exist, but none of them is perfect by the above criteria, statisticians choose the best estimator by calculating (and then minimizing) *mean squared error* (MSE), the sum of an estimator's squared bias plus its variance.
3. The estimate of a population parameter can be expressed as a single numerical value, called a *point estimate.* Because the sample mean and sample proportion are unbiased, efficient, and consistent estimators of the corresponding population parameters, $\overline{X}$ has become the favorite point estimator of μ, and P has become the favorite point estimator of π. Differences between sample means or sample proportions, similarly, are used to make point estimates of differences between population means or differences between population proportions.
4. The typical point estimate, even if the estimator is unbiased, is almost certain to lie below or above the true value of the parameter being estimated. Statisticians, therefore, construct *interval estimates* centered on the point estimate and ranging below and above this value by a *margin of error* equal to x standard errors of the estimator, where x can equal any (fractional or whole) positive value. The width of the interval has important implications for the degree of confidence with which we can state that the population parameter lies within the lower and upper limits of the interval, generally known as a *confidence interval.*
5. This chapter discusses the construction of numerous types of confidence intervals:
   - **a.** large-sample confidence intervals of a population mean (Formula 12.A on page 498).
   - **b.** large-sample confidence intervals of a population proportion (Formula 12.B on page 501).
   - **c.** large-sample confidence intervals of the difference between two population means, using large and independent samples (Formula 12.C on page 503) or a large matched-pairs sample (Formula 12.D on page 505).
   - **d.** large-sample confidence intervals of the difference between two population proportions (Formula 12.E on page 508).
   - **e.** small-sample confidence intervals of a population mean (Formula 12.F on page 513).
   - **f.** small-sample confidence intervals of the difference between two population means, using small and independent samples (Formula 12.G on page 515) or a small matched-pairs sample (Formula 12.H on page 517).
6. The small-sample estimation procedures make use of special types of probability distributions, known as Student's t distributions. Tabular presentations of t values facilitate the use of these special types of sampling distributions.
7. Anyone engaged in estimation is inevitably concerned about finding the optimal sample size that minimizes the total cost of sampling, or the sum of data-collection and sampling-error costs. Special procedures exist that allow investigators to determine a best sample size, prior to sampling, that simultaneously endows their interval estimate with a confidence level they desire and a margin of error they can tolerate.
8. While regular estimation procedures view the parameter being estimated as a constant, *Bayesian estimation* views it, just like the estimator itself, as a random variable. This approach may be reasonable whenever a statistician, as a result of prior experience or *a priori* reasoning, holds a strong opinion about the likely value of an unknown parameter. The Bayesian estimate of the population mean, for example, is a weighted average of what the sample actually finds and what the statistician believed to be true even before the population was sampled. Bayesian estimation, thus, makes use of *all* available information, not only that which is revealed by sampling.

Key Terms

Bayesian estimation
biased estimator
confidence interval
confidence level
confidence limits
consistent estimator
degrees of freedom
efficient estimator
estimation
estimator
interval estimate
margin of error
matched-pairs sampling
mean squared error
point estimate
Student's *t* distribution
unbiased estimator
work sampling

Practice Problems

NOTE

Some problems require the use of a statistical program, Excel or MINITAB. The program's major features are explained in text Chapter 2. Plenty of additional advice is available via the program's built-in Help feature.

Section 12.2 Defining a Good Estimator

1. *Fortune* magazine's 1999 list of the *Global 500* included six entertainment companies. Selected data about them are provided in Table 12.5.

a. Establish a sampling distribution of mean revenues for a sample of $n = 4$.

b. Show that the sample mean, $\overline{X}$, is an *unbiased* estimator of the population mean, μ.

TABLE 12.5 | *Global 500* Entertainment Companies in 1999

Company	1998 Revenue (millions)	Country
A = Walt Disney	$22,976	United States
B = Time Warner	14,582	United States
C = News Corporation	12,995	Australia
D = Viacom	12,096	United States
E = Seagram	10,734	Canada
F = CBS	9,061	United States

2. Consider the revenue population of Table 12.5.

a. Establish the sampling distribution of the standard deviation for a sample of $n = 4$.

b. Show that the sample standard deviation, s, is a *biased* estimator of the population standard deviation, σ.

3. Consider the country designations in Table 12.5.

a. Establish the sampling distribution of the proportion of U.S. companies for a sample of $n = 3$.

b. Show that the sample proportion, P, is an *unbiased* estimator of the population proportion, π.

Section 12.3 Making Point Estimates

4. Start EXCEL or MINITAB and activate the file HK99F500, which contains 1998 data about all *Fortune 500* companies.

a. With the help of a simple random sample of 30 company revenues, make a point estimate of the mean revenue of all 500 companies.

b. Because you are actually in possession of census data, compare your point estimate with the population mean (which an investigator would not ordinarily know).

5. Start EXCEL or MINITAB and activate the file HK99F500, which contains 1998 data about all *Fortune 500* companies.

a. With the help of a simple random sample of 30 companies, make a point estimate of the proportion of all 500 companies that are headquartered in Texas.

b. Because you are actually in possession of census data, compare your point estimate with the population proportion (which an investigator would not ordinarily know).

6. Construct point estimates in the following situations:

a. A labor union is negotiating a new contract. The bargaining committee randomly samples the opinions of 100 workers of whom 61 favor the contract. Estimate the proportion of all workers in favor.

b. After taking a random sample of 50 students, an economics professor discovers that 30 of them have no idea of the meaning of the term *c.i.f.* Estimate the proportion of all the students equally ignorant.

c. A rental-car company takes a simple random sample of three of its cars, finding annual repair costs of $510, $98, and $121. Estimate the annual repair cost per car for all the firm's cars.

d. At an automobile assembly plant, a simple random sample of 40 workers is taken. Of these, 21 are found to have been vaccinated against tetanus. Estimate the proportion of all the workers who are so vaccinated.

e. The state fisheries department caught 1,000 fish in a lake, marked them, and returned them to the lake. A week later, it caught another 1,000 fish and found 200 of them marked. Estimate the proportion of all the fish in the lake so marked and, hence, the size of the lake's fish population.

7. A simple random sample of $n = 4$ discount stores selects Dayton Hudson, Dollar General, Kmart, and Wal-Mart and discovers their latest and 1-year-ago monthly sales:

Last month:	2,220	272.7	2,498	11,311 (million dollars)
1 year ago:	2,054	217.3	2,357	9,726 (million dollars)

Make a point estimate of the difference over this time period in mean monthly sales of all such discount stores.

8. Construct point estimates of the difference in proportions in the following situations:

a. The governor wants to finance a new prison by raising the state's sales tax from 3 percent to 4 percent. Of 900 male voters randomly sampled, 810 oppose the idea. Of 500 female voters, 200 are opposed. Estimate the difference in the proportion of male and female voters so opposed.

b. A soap maker wants to replace unscented white soap with scented pink soap. Of 500 male consumers randomly sampled, 176 favor the idea. Of 500 female consumers, 432 favor it. Estimate the difference in the proportion of male and female consumers in favor.

Section 12.4 The Nature of Interval Estimates

9. Review Figure 12.3 on page 495 and focus on the two 80 percent confidence intervals, based on sample (5) $\overline{X} = 31$ and sample (9) $\overline{X} = 49$, that do *not* include the true value of $\mu = 40$.

Show what would happen if you created:

a. a 90 percent confidence interval for sample (5).

b. a 90 percent confidence interval for sample (9).

c. a 95 percent confidence interval for sample (5).

d. a 95 percent confidence interval for sample (9).

10. Appendix Table J provides z values for a variety of confidence levels. What would the confidence levels be for nicely rounded z values of .5, 1.0, 1.5, 2.0, 2.5, and 3.0?

11. Review Figure 12.4 on page 497 and note that higher confidence levels produce ever-wider confidence intervals, given sample size. What happens to confidence intervals if sample size is raised, given a chosen confidence level? Create three examples.

Section 12.5 Large-Sample Interval Estimates of a Population Mean

12. A credit card company has been billing its millions of customers on the last day of each month, receiving payment an average 13 days later. It decides to experiment with the billing date, hoping to accelerate payments. A simple random sample of 500 customers is switched to a billing date in the middle of the month. The average length of time between billing and payment in the sample comes to 18.9 days, with a standard deviation of 5.3 days. Prepare a 98 percent confidence interval for the mean period between billing and payment for all customers if all of them were given the midmonth billing date.

13. A would-be new telephone company is aware that the population of telephone-call durations in its potential market is normally distributed with a standard deviation of 4 minutes. In order to project their revenues, the firm's executives need to know the average duration of calls originating in the area. A sample of 50 calls yields a mean duration of 9.1 minutes. Construct a 95 percent confidence interval for the mean duration of all calls.

14. The executives of a company are about to offer their employees a new retirement plan. First, though, they want to know the employees' current investments in stock. The normally distributed population of stock investments by the 75 employees of the firm is known to have a standard deviation of \$99. A random sample of 36 employees shows a mean investment of \$736. Construct a 99.8 percent confidence interval for the mean investment of all the employees.

15. The Internal Revenue Service is auditing the operators of some 13,000 private airports by taking a random sample of 100 of them. The IRS discovers an average error in reported taxable income of \$14,750, with a sample standard deviation of \$3,600. Determine a 95 percent confidence interval for the average error made by all the existing airports.

16. There are 200 gas stations in a city; an economist takes a random sample of 50 of them. Their average gasoline price is \$1.339 per gallon, with a sample standard deviation of 23.10 cents per gallon. Determine an 80 percent confidence interval for the average price citywide, while assuming that the population distribution of gas prices is normal.

Section 12.6 Large-Sample Interval Estimates of a Population Proportion

17. In a random sample of 100 households, 59 are found to prefer brand X. Construct a 98 percent confidence interval for the proportion of all households so inclined.

18. A lumber company ships 1 million pine boards. A random sample of 50 boards shows 17 being excessively warped. Construct a 95 percent confidence interval for the proportion of all boards so warped.

19. A random sample of 300 floppy disks taken from an ongoing production process shows 12 to be defective. Construct a 95 percent confidence interval for the proportion of defective disks in the firm's entire output.

20. A personnel manager is investigating why 1,900 employees quit last year. In a random sample of 500 former employees, 225 answer "boredom." Determine a 68.76 percent confidence interval for the proportion of all former employees who left the firm because of boredom. What would a 95 percent confidence interval be?

21. A bank claims that no more than 2 percent of its monthly customer statements are in error. An auditor doesn't believe the claim, selects 100 accounts randomly from the bank's 15,233 accounts, and contacts the customers in question. Of these, 12 report and prove at least one error in their last month's statements. Construct a 98 percent confidence interval for the true proportion of erroneous bank statements that the bank mails out. What, precisely, is the *meaning* of this interval?

Section 12.7 Large-Sample Interval Estimates of the Difference between Two Population Means

22. The credit card company noted in Practice Problem 12 takes a second random sample of 500 customers and switches their billing date to the 24th of the month. The average period between billing and payment in that sample comes to 7.5 days, with a standard deviation of 2.1 days. Construct a 99 percent confidence interval for the difference between the mean days until payment if all customers are switched to a billing date of the 15th or the 24th.

23. A flight insurance specialist who is studying aircraft accidents wants to determine the difference between mean thunderstorm intensities (measured by peak gust velocities) for two regions of the country. The following data for a five-year period are obtained and used as a sample:

Region A: 290 occurrences; sample mean, 59 miles per hour; sample standard deviation, 20 miles per hour.

Region B: 333 occurrences; sample mean, 71 miles per hour; sample standard deviation, 30 miles per hour.

Construct a 99 percent confidence interval for the difference between the mean intensities.

24. The manager of a chain of retail stores wants to determine, with 95 percent confidence, whether an advertising campaign has had any effect. A sample of 50 days prior to the campaign shows mean sales per store of $3,952 (with a standard deviation of $296). A sample of 40 days after the campaign shows corresponding numbers of $4,102 and $306. Make the determination.

25. On a given day, the average price per share is $59.05 for 42 randomly selected stocks traded on the New York Stock Exchange (and the standard deviation is $7.92), while it is $70.08 for 32 stocks on the American Stock Exchange (and the standard deviation for that sample is $25.39). Construct a 90 percent confidence interval for the difference between the mean prices per share.

26. United Parcel Service wants to determine the gasoline savings if all of its trucks were switched from regular to radial tires. Some 150 trucks are given new tires; half of them get regular tires, the others radial tires. One truck in each group is further matched with one in the other group by make, age, region of the world, and more. After three months, the mileage on trucks with radial tires is found, on average, to be 5 miles per gallon higher than on trucks with regular tires. The sample standard deviation of the differences is 3 mpg. Construct a 98 percent confidence interval for the potential mileage gain if a similar switchover were made on all of the firm's trucks worldwide.

27. In preparation for marketing its "revolutionary" plant food, a firm creates 45 identical twin plots of tomato plants. On each plot, half the plants are treated with the new food; the other half are not. At the end of the season, the treated plants yield, on average, 7.3 pounds more tomatoes. The sample standard deviation of the differences is 5.4 pounds. Construct a 99 percent confidence interval for the crop gain that can be expected by using the new plant food.

28. The Home Shopping Network claims that it can increase retail sales of selected products once households are connected to its cable TV outlet, featuring 24 hours of commercials each day, along with 800 numbers. An investigator takes a simple random sample of 100 households in a metropolitan area, then records their expenditures on the products in question during 4 weeks before and again during 4 weeks after the TV hookup. On average, expenditures rise by $56.78 per week; the standard deviation of the sample differences is $43.28. Construct a 95 percent confidence interval for the weekly expenditure increase that can be expected among all area households.

29. A weight control firm wants to test the effectiveness of its "revolutionary" liquid diet against a competitor's product. A simple random sample of 100 persons is taken; each is given the competitor's product for a month, or the new liquid diet for a month. The order of application is assigned by the flip of a fair coin. On average, the monthly weight loss with the liquid diet exceeds the weight loss with the competitive product by 5.9 pounds. The standard deviation of the sample differences is 4.3 pounds. Construct a 90 percent confidence interval for the additional monthly weight loss that can be expected among all consumers who use the liquid diet.

Section 12.8 Large-Sample Interval Estimates of the Difference between Two Population Proportions

30. A polling organization wants to estimate the difference between the proportion of urban and rural residents favoring agricultural price-support programs. It draws a simple random sample of 500 urban residents (250 favor the programs) and of 500 rural residents (400 favor the programs). Construct a 95 percent confidence interval for the difference between the proportions of those favoring the program.

31. An airline wants to estimate the difference between the proportion of passengers who carry only hand luggage on its New York-to-Chicago versus its New York-to-Miami flights. Two random samples of 50 passengers each show

34 versus 11 such passengers. Construct a 98 percent confidence interval for the difference between the proportions of hand-luggage-only passengers.

32. A firm producing batteries has introduced two different quality-control systems, each on a different assembly line. One day, 400 batteries are randomly selected from the 10,000-unit output of line 1, and an equal number are pulled from the identical output of line 2. The proportions of defective items are, respectively, .06 and .04. Construct a 99 percent confidence interval for the difference in the proportion of defective items produced under the two quality-control systems.

33. In a recent month, the proportions of the unemployed among workers in durable and nondurable goods manufacturing industries were estimated as .116 and .092, respectively. These point estimates were made on the basis of simple random samples of 4,900 and 3,900 households. Find a 98 percent confidence interval for the difference between the population unemployment rates in durable goods manufacturing and nondurable goods manufacturing.

Section 12.9 Small-Sample Interval Estimates of a Population Mean

34. A manufacturer is aware that the lifetimes of batteries the firm produces are normally distributed. A random sample of 10 batteries shows a mean lifetime of 6 hours with a standard deviation of 1 hour. Construct a 99 percent confidence interval for the mean lifetime of all batteries produced by the same process.

35. The daily gasoline consumption of a fleet of 500 taxis is known to be normally distributed. One day, a random sample of 10 taxis is taken, and their mean gasoline consumption is found to have been 20.8 gallons, with a standard deviation of 3.7 gallons. Construct a 95 percent confidence interval for the day's mean gasoline consumption by all the taxis.

36. An insurance company wants to estimate the average claim on its automobile collision policies. It believes the sizes of such claims are normally distributed. It uses the last 21 claims as a sample and finds their average to equal $657, with a standard deviation of $310. Construct a 95 percent confidence interval for the average claim on all policies.

37. A pharmaceutical company deliberately infects 20 volunteers and then tests a new drug on them, finding a mean recovery time of 8 days, with a standard deviation of 2.5 days. Construct a 95 percent confidence interval for the mean recovery time of all potential users of this drug on the assumption that recovery times are:

a. normally distributed.

b. definitely *not* normally distributed, but the population standard deviation equals 3 days.

38. A quality engineer is checking out the machinery that is supposed to put 20 oz. of liquid detergent into a container. A sample of 12 containers shows the mean amount dispensed to be 18.9 oz., the standard deviation being 3.1 oz. Construct a 90 percent confidence interval for the mean amount dispensed by the machine, assuming that the amounts dispensed are normally distributed.

39. A defense contractor is supposed to build the fastest submarine in the world. The firm's analysts believe that the top speeds of the 5,000 enemy submarines are normally distributed around an unknown mean. They do, however, have information on a random sample of five submarines. Their average top speed is 52 nautical miles per hour, the standard deviation is 2.3 knots. Construct a 99 percent confidence interval for the average top speed of all enemy submarines.

40. An accountant believes that the value of telephone services stolen by the theft of telephone-company credit cards is a normally distributed random variable, but knows nothing else about the population in question. However, a random sample of 15 thefts shows the mean amount stolen to be $532, with a standard deviation of $17.63. Construct a 98 percent confidence interval for the mean amount stolen by all such thefts.

Section 12.10 Small-Sample Interval Estimates of the Difference between Two Population Means

41. A space agency wants to compare the magnification achieved by two types of cameras delivered by a defense contractor. Camera A is placed on one satellite, camera B on another satellite. Subsequently, each satellite camera takes 15 photographs of identical areas at almost identical moments, using identical films and exposure settings. Afterward, the number of houses in each picture are counted; the sample means and standard deviations are as follows: $\bar{X}_A = 139$; $s_A = 21$; $\bar{X}_B = 115$; $s_B = 52$. The relevant population distributions are normal; the populations have equal variances. Construct a 95 percent confidence interval for the difference between mean house counts for the two types of cameras.

42. An executive of a construction company is contacted by a glass manufacturer who claims that a revolutionary new shipping container can reduce the breakage of window panes dramatically and who graciously offers to replace the construction company's current supplier. At the same price, more usable panes will be received. The construction company executive is intrigued but decides to test the claim. A dozen cases of 100 panes are ordered from the new would-be supplier, and the number of unbroken panes is counted; a similar count is made on the latest shipment of 18 cases received from the old supplier. The results of this sampling are shown in Table 12.6. Construct a 95 percent confidence interval for the difference between the mean numbers of unbroken panes in the populations of all possible cases delivered by the new and the old supplier, using:

a. an appropriate formula.

b. EXCEL or MINITAB.

TABLE 12.6 | Numbers of Unbroken Panes in Cases . . .

From New Supplier		From Old Supplier		
88	92	85	82	84
91	89	81	81	86
91	93	85	85	81
95	91	87	87	80
86	88	88	88	84
87	94	90	92	83

43. A restaurant owner wishes to estimate the difference between the mean daily sales of two restaurants on Main Street. A 98 percent confidence interval is desired. The two restaurants are matched up for 14 days, their sales being compared on Monday, then on Tuesday, and so on. The mean and standard deviation of the differences between A's daily sales and B's daily sales are found to be $\overline{D}$ = \$133 and s_D = \$41. Make the estimate, assuming a normal population distribution.

44. An economist wants to estimate the difference, if any, between downtown and suburban motel room charges. From among hundreds of motels in a large metropolitan area, a sample of 6 is selected from each location and one motel from each sample is matched with another motel from the other sample. Various relevant characteristics are considered in the matching process so as to create 6 near-twins. For each "twin," the room charge difference is recorded. On average, the downtown charge is \$37.10 higher; the sample standard deviation is \$9.39. Determine a 99 percent confidence interval for the mean room charge difference between all of the area's downtown and suburban motels.

Section 12.11 The Optimal Sample Size

45. In each of the following situations, determine the required sample size.

a. A firm is split into several divisions; each of these uses a central computer. Management is interested in the amount of time the computer is used by division A on the average day. Given that the population standard deviation of computer use times is known to equal .5 hour, the desired margin of error equals 1 hour, and the desired confidence level is 95 percent, what is the sample size needed to establish the mean daily computer time used by division A?

b. A new product is to be marketed. Management wants to know the proportion of people who will like it enough to buy it. How big a sample must be interviewed to ensure a 98 percent confidence level and a .05 margin of error if preliminary estimates make a population proportion of .25 likely? What if no such preliminary estimate exists?

46. In each of the following situations, determine the required sample size.

a. The population of starting salaries of engineers is known to have a standard deviation of \$2,800. How big a sample is needed to estimate the mean starting salary with 95 percent confidence and a margin of error of $100? Of $200? Of $400?

b. A pharmaceutical company wants to know the mean number of milligrams a machine puts into capsules. The population standard deviation is known to equal 2 milligrams, and the desired confidence level is 95 percent. What must the sample size be for a margin of error of .05 milligram? Of .1 milligram? Of .5 milligram?

47. In each of the following situations, determine the required sample size.

a. A bill concerning business is about to be brought before the state senate. An executive wants to know, with 95 percent confidence and a margin of error of .01, the proportion of voters favoring the bill.

b. A bank auditor believes that 12 percent of a bank's 15,233 monthly customer statements are in error. A 98 percent confidence level is desired, along with a margin of error of .0757.

48. In each of the following situations, determine the required sample size.

a. The Environmental Protection Agency wants to determine the mean daily sulfur emissions from an industrial complex. How many air samples must be taken if the population standard deviation of pollution measurements is known to equal 2 parts per million (ppm), the desired margin of error is 1 ppm, and a 95 percent confidence level is desired?

b. An auto importer wants to estimate the average age of all registered cars in the northeastern United States. The population standard deviation of ages is known as 3 years, the desired confidence level is 99.9 percent, and the desired margin of error is .1 year.

c. The population of sick leaves at a large corporation is known to have a standard deviation of 3.1 days. An executive seeks to estimate the mean number of employee sick days with 90 percent confidence and a margin of error of .51 day.

SECTION 12.12 A NOTE ON BAYESIAN ESTIMATION

49. Review Example Problem 12.14. What would the outcome have been if the statistician's prior standard deviation had been 50 instead of 1,000?

50. The manager of a cattle feedlot is about to ship 800 head of cattle by train and must estimate the mean weight per animal. A simple random sample of 30 animals comes up with a sample mean of 1,301 lb., but the manager hesitates to use this number as the point estimate of the population mean. A Bayesian estimate is to be prepared, using the sample standard deviation of 290 lb. as an estimate of the population standard deviation and making use of the manager's prior probability distribution of weights, with $\mu_* = 1{,}500$ lb. and $\sigma_* = 150$ lb.

Chapter 13

HYPOTHESIS TESTING: THE CLASSICAL TECHNIQUE

LOOKING AHEAD

After reading this chapter, you will be able to:

1. formulate two appropriate opposing hypotheses about the value of an unknown population parameter,
2. select a suitable test statistic for conducting a hypothesis test about that parameter,
3. derive a decision rule for assessing the test result,
4. use sample data to compute the test statistic and confront it with the decision rule, and
5. conduct and evaluate hypothesis tests about a single population mean, a single population proportion, and differences between two population means or two population proportions.

AND HERE IS A TYPICAL PROBLEM YOU WILL BE ABLE TO SOLVE:

The manufacturer of Lycoming aircraft engines knows from long experience that up to 10 percent of these engines develop problems by the time they reach 2,000 flight hours. The manufacturer believes, however, that a new series of these engines will do no worse and possibly better. Accordingly, a random sample of 225 of the new engines is selected from owners who have flown 2,000 hours or more. Of the sampled owners, 12 have had problems before the 2,000-hour mark. A hypothesis test at the $\alpha = .05$ level of significance is desired to determine whether the manufacturer's faith in the new engine series is justified.

PREVIEW

In 1999, with hog manure fouling streams in the rolling countryside of northern Missouri, the giant pork producer Premium Standard Farms agreed to pay \$25 million to settle a lawsuit accusing it of violating the state's Clean Water Act. At the time, corporate hog farmers stood accused of having degraded some 35,000 miles of rivers in 22 states, and the agreement with the company, which processed 2 million pigs a year, was the largest environmental settlement so far. As a harbinger of things to come, the case alerted business executives throughout the industry. To avoid similar threats to their bottom line, they quickly moved to line their waste pits with plastic to keep manure out of the groundwater.

Not all pollution problems, however, are that straightforward. Take sunglasses manufacturer Foster Grant. At its Leominster, Massachusetts, plant, the company had dumped PVC chemicals into the air, into a river, and onto the soil for decades. Then, a major U.S. television network reported the remarkable results of two samples. A sample of 600 families in Leominster had uncovered 43 cases of *autism*, a serious disorder that affects children from birth or within the first 30 months of life. Affected individuals cannot develop normal human relationships with anybody, even their parents. Autistic children have difficulty with feeding and toilet training and do not give smiling recognition to others. Speech, facial expressions, and other forms of communication are absent or unintelligible. If autistic people speak at all, they may repeat words interminably, for no apparent reason. Afflicted persons make no distinction among people, other living things, and inanimate objects and treat them all in the same way. They cannot evaluate situations and, therefore, react inappropriately to them. For example, an autistic individual may become fiercely agitated when the furniture is rearranged or may run across a dangerously busy highway without any sign of concern. Moving unpredictably from violence to sitting completely still for hours on end, such a person may give the (mistaken) impression of being intellectually subnormal or deaf.

Yet, while 43 such cases arose among the 600 neighbors of the Leominster plant, a second sample of 10,000 families elsewhere in the nation uncovered only 15 cases of the disease. Thus, the proportion of autistic children was $(43/600) = .0717$ in Leominster and $(15/10{,}000) = .0015$ elsewhere, and the difference was quickly blamed on Foster Grant. In fact, within a week of the television report, an additional 30 persons reported incidences of autism in their families—all of them lived far away from Massachusetts, but they had parents who had lived in Leominster!

If you were running Foster Grant, or any other company accused of misconduct, you would surely welcome a *scientific* approach to testing whether the differences in the proportions just noted are attributable to the alleged misconduct or, perhaps, to something else entirely, including bias in the survey data or plain sampling error. You would surely wish your company to be considered innocent until proven guilty beyond a reasonable doubt. This chapter's *hypothesis testing* techniques do precisely this: They allow us to establish the verity of evidence beyond a reasonable doubt.[1]

[1]Adapted from Dirk Johnson, "Pork Producer Settles Suit as Pollution Rules Tighten," *The New York Times*, August 16, 1999, p. A12; ABC, *20/20*, March 1992; The American Medical Association, *Family Medical Guide* (New York: Random House, 1987), p. 688.

13.1 Introduction

When people make decisions, they inevitably do so based on their beliefs about the true state of the world. They carry in their minds certain images of reality; they hold some things to be true, and others to be false, and they act accordingly. Thus, one government agency may ban cigarette ads because its officials have come to believe that smoking causes heart and lung disease; another one may refuse to license a new anticancer drug because no credible case has been made for its alleged effectiveness. Business executives, similarly, make crucial decisions every day because they hold certain beliefs: that a given type of filling machine puts at least one pound of detergent into a box, that a certain steel cable has a breaking strength of 5,000 pounds or more, that the average lifetime of a battery equals 100 hours, that a certain process yields capsules that contain precisely 100 milligrams of a drug, that shipping company A has faster delivery times than company B, that the output of the east-coast plant contains fewer defective units than that of the west-coast plant. . . .

In all these cases and a million more, people act on the basis of some belief about reality, a belief that may have first come into the world as a mere conjecture, as little more than an informed guess, a proposition tentatively advanced as possibly true, and therefore, called a **hypothesis.** Sooner or later, however, every hypothesis must confront evidence that either substantiates or refutes it. In this way, people's image of reality moves from much uncertainty to less. This chapter and the next consider how we can test people's beliefs in a systematic way.

Do not confuse this chapter's *hypothesis testing* with last chapter's *estimation.* The two types of procedures are, however, similar in the sense that they both seek to enlighten us about the value of an unknown parameter, such as the mean of a statistical population. The estimation procedure does so by using sample data to develop a *point estimate* and an *interval estimate.* These parameter estimates might claim, for example, that the mean profit of *all* companies on the year 2000 *Fortune 500* list equals $820 million (the point estimate) and can be found, with 95 percent confidence, somewhere between $800 million and $840 million (the interval estimate). As we learned, the latter statement means that the estimation procedure, in the long run, produces correct intervals 95 percent of the time and incorrect ones 5 percent of the time.

The hypothesis testing procedure, in contrast, first formulates *two alternative hypotheses* about the parameter of interest. The hypotheses might claim, respectively, that the *population* mean profit (a) equals $820 million and (b) does *not* equal $820 million. For the first of these hypotheses, the procedure then develops ranges of values, called *acceptance region* and *rejection region,* to which sample data can be compared. At 95 percent confidence, the acceptance region might be "$800 million to $840 million," while the rejection region might be "less than $800 million or more than $840 million." If sample data then indicate a *sample* mean profit of, say, $812 million (which lies in the acceptance region), we accept the first hypothesis (about the *population* mean equaling $820 million).

Interestingly, as long as we choose the same confidence level, the *acceptance region* of the hypothesis test equals the *interval estimate* of the estimation procedure. In our example, both stretch from $800 million to $840 million.

DEFINITION 13.1 A systematic approach to assessing tentative beliefs about reality is called **hypothesis testing.** It involves confronting those beliefs with evidence and deciding, in light of this evidence, whether the beliefs can be maintained as reasonable or must be discarded as untenable.

In the following sections, we consider the testing of hypotheses about a single population mean, about a single population proportion, and about the difference between two such means or two such proportions. In every case, hypothesis testing involves four major steps:

1. Formulating two opposing hypotheses
2. Selecting a test statistic
3. Deriving a decision rule
4. Using sample data to compute the test statistic and confronting it with the decision rule

13.2 Step 1: Formulating Two Opposing Hypotheses

The first step in hypothesis testing is always the formulation of two hypotheses that are mutually exclusive and also collectively exhaustive of all possible states of reality. Each of these complementary hypotheses is a proposition about a population parameter such that the truth of one hypothesis implies the falsity of the other. The first hypothesis in the set, symbolized by H_0, is called the *null hypothesis.* The second hypothesis, symbolized by H_A, is the *alternative hypothesis.*

DEFINITION 13.2 The **null hypothesis,** H_0, is the first of two opposing hypotheses in a hypothesis test. It is a description of the status quo, of conventional wisdom, of a "state of innocence," of what people have long believed to be true. If H_0 is corroborated in a hypothesis test, no action need be taken by anyone.

DEFINITION 13.3 The **alternative hypothesis,** H_A, is the second of two opposing hypotheses in a hypothesis test. It is a vehicle for making startling new claims that contradict the conventional wisdom, that assert "guilt without a reasonable doubt." If H_0 cannot be corroborated in a hypothesis test, H_A is tentatively embraced, which calls for action. Thus, we can think of H_A as the *action* hypothesis.

The above procedure of formulating two opposing hypotheses is similar to the procedure in a criminal trial in which the defendant is given the benefit of the doubt and assumed to be innocent until proven guilty. Being free of guilt is the conventional wisdom—what has traditionally been believed to be true. Hence, a *null* hypothesis of *zero* guilt is made, which also helps explain the hypothesis name. However, contrary evidence can reverse the tentative zero-guilt judgment. Then we can substitute an alternative hypothesis of guilt—provided that we have evidence *beyond a reasonable doubt.* Such doubt causes the null hypothesis to be rejected or *nullified,* which gives us yet another way to account for its name. Accepting the alternative hypothesis then leads to *action:* The defendant is sentenced to pay a fine or go to jail.

HYPOTHESES ABOUT A POPULATION MEAN

The opposing hypotheses about the value of a population mean are typically stated in one of three forms by reference to a specified value of the mean, μ_0.

Form 1: Exact vs. Inexact	Form 2: At Least vs. Less Than	Form 3: At Most vs. More Than
H_0: $\mu = \mu_0$	H_0: $\mu \geq \mu_0$	H_0: $\mu \leq \mu_0$
H_A: $\mu \neq \mu_0$	H_A: $\mu < \mu_0$	H_A: $\mu > \mu_0$

FORM 1 The null hypothesis is stated as an **exact hypothesis;** it specifies a single value for the unknown parameter. The alternative hypothesis, on the other hand, is stated as an **inexact hypothesis;** it specifies a range of values for the unknown parameter. As examples, consider the null hypothesis that an industrial process yields metal parts with an average length of 5 inches, drills holes with an average diameter of 1.2 inches, or makes windshields with an average length of 33 inches. The alternative hypothesis in each case suggests that the average is larger *or* smaller than μ_0. Whenever an alternative hypothesis in this way holds for deviations from the null hypothesis in either direction, it is called a **two-sided hypothesis.**

We usually set up our two hypotheses as Form 1 indicates when precision is very important and when deviations in either direction are equally unacceptable. An aircraft windshield, for example, might have to be precisely 33 inches long; if it were shorter *or* longer, it would be equally useless for the workers who must fit it into the designed space.

FORM 2 The null hypothesis claims that the parameter is greater than or equal to a specified value, while the alternative hypothesis claims it to be smaller than that value. It is a matter of *at least versus less than.* As examples, consider the null hypothesis that the average quantity of detergent put into a box by a filling machine is *at least* 1 pound, that the average breaking strength of a certain type of cable is *at least* 5,000 pounds, or that the average lifetime of a certain type of battery is *at least* 100 hours. The alternative hypothesis in each case suggests that the average is *less than* the specified value of μ_0. Whenever an alternative hypothesis holds for deviations from the null hypothesis in one direction only, it is called a **one-sided hypothesis.**

We usually set up our two hypotheses as Form 2 indicates when something can safely be greater than a certain value, while smaller values are unacceptable. If an aircraft battery, for example, is guaranteed to last 100 hours, no one would worry if it lasted longer; the alternative of it lasting less, however, might be serious and call for quick remedial action.

FORM 3 The null hypothesis claims that the parameter is less than or equal to a specified value, while the alternative hypothesis claims it is larger than that value. It is a matter of *at most versus more than.* As examples, consider the null hypothesis that a shipping company's average delivery time is *at most* 3 days, that the average drying time of a paint is *at most* 4 hours, or that an engine's exhaust emissions average *at most* 17 parts per million. The one-sided alternative hypothesis in each case suggests that the average is *more than* the specified value of μ_0.

We usually set up our two hypotheses as Form 3 indicates when something can safely be smaller than a certain value, while larger values are unacceptable. If a delivery time, for example, is guaranteed to be 3 days, no one will complain if it is less; the alternative of it being longer, however, would be cause for alarm.

EXAMPLE PROBLEM 13.1

Set up the two opposing hypotheses for each of the following situations:

a. An aircraft manufacturer wants to test whether the thickness of aluminum sheets averages .03 inch, no more and no less, as required.

b. An aircraft manufacturer wants to test whether specialty steel rods have an average tensile strength of at least 5,000 pounds.

c. A computer manufacturer wants to test a supervisor's claim that a single computer assembly averages at most 40 minutes.

SOLUTION:

a. $H_0: \mu = .03$ $\quad$ $H_A: \mu \neq .03$

b. $H_0: \mu \geq 5{,}000$ $\quad$ $H_A: \mu < 5{,}000$

c. $H_0: \mu \leq 40$ $\quad$ $H_A: \mu > 40$

HYPOTHESES ABOUT THE DIFFERENCE BETWEEN TWO POPULATION MEANS

The opposing hypotheses about the difference between two population means, μ_A and μ_B, similarly appear in one of three forms:

Form I: Exact vs. Inexact	Form II: At Least vs. Less Than	Form III: At Most vs. More Than
$H_0: \mu_A = \mu_B$	$H_0: \mu_A \geq \mu_B$	$H_0: \mu_A \leq \mu_B$
$H_A: \mu_A \neq \mu_B$	$H_A: \mu_A < \mu_B$	$H_A: \mu_A > \mu_B$

Thus, the null hypothesis may claim (Form I) that two population means are the same; for example, that the average lifetimes of two tire brands are identical. Or it may claim (Form II) that one population mean equals or exceeds another; for example, that average construction-industry wages in New York are at least equal to, but possibly larger than, those in Chicago. Or it may claim (Form III) that one population mean equals or falls short of another; for example, that the average yield on acres using one type of fertilizer is at most equal to, but possibly less than, that on acres using a different type of fertilizer. In each case, the alternative hypothesis suggests the opposite.

CAUTION

Sometimes, hypotheses about the difference between two population means are stated in slightly different ways that are mathematically equivalent to Forms I–III.

Here, the null hypothesis claims that the difference between the mean of population A and population B is precisely zero (Form A), is zero or positive (Form B), or is zero or negative (Form C). The alternative hypothesis sees this difference, respectively, as positive or negative (Form A), as negative (Form B), or as positive (Form C).

Form A: Exact vs. Inexact	Form B: At Least vs. Less Than	Form C: At Most vs. More Than
H_0: $\mu_A - \mu_B = 0$	H_0: $\mu_A - \mu_B \geq 0$	H_0: $\mu_A - \mu_B \leq 0$
H_A: $\mu_A - \mu_B \neq 0$	H_A: $\mu_A - \mu_B < 0$	H_A: $\mu_A - \mu_B > 0$

HYPOTHESES ABOUT A POPULATION PROPORTION (OR THE DIFFERENCE BETWEEN TWO SUCH PROPORTIONS)

We formulate hypotheses about a population proportion, π, such as the proportion of defective units put out by a production process, in a manner precisely analogous to those about a population mean. We simply substitute π for μ in Forms 1 to 3 on page 536, leaving all else unchanged, including subscripts.

Again, we formulate hypotheses about the difference between two population proportions, π_A and π_B, such as the proportions of cancer victims among smokers on the one hand and nonsmokers on the other, similarly to those about the difference between population means. We simply substitute π for μ in Forms I to III on page 537 (or in the equivalent Forms A to C), again leaving all else unchanged, subscripts included.

EXAMPLE PROBLEM 13.2

Imagine yourself working for Foster Grant, the sunglasses manufacturer noted in this chapter's Preview. Formulate the opposing hypotheses for a test of autism proportions in Leominster (A) and elsewhere (B).

SOLUTION: The burden of proof has to be placed on the unusual claim that the proportion of autism cases in Leominster exceeds that proportion elsewhere. Thus, a statement equivalent to Form III or C above is in order:

$H_0: \pi_A \leq \pi_B$ $\qquad$ $H_0: \pi_A - \pi_B \leq 0$

$H_A: \pi_A > \pi_B$ $\qquad$ $H_A: \pi_A - \pi_B > 0$

13.3 Step 2: Selecting a Test Statistic

The second step in hypothesis testing is the selection of a *test statistic:*

DEFINITION 13.4 A **test statistic** is a statistic computed from a simple random sample taken from the population of interest in a hypothesis test and then used for establishing the probable truth or falsity of the null hypothesis.

Obvious candidates for test statistic are:

- the sample mean, $\overline{X}$, when the hypothesis test involves the population mean
- the difference between two sample means, $\overline{X}_A - \overline{X}_B$, when the test involves the difference between two population means
- the sample proportion, P, when the test is about the population proportion
- the difference between two sample proportions, $P_A - P_B$, when the test is about the difference between two population proportions

USING *z* or *t* Values Remember that every sample statistic has a sampling distribution of its own. Such a distribution can often be approximated by the normal distribution for large

TECHNICAL DETAIL

Additional test statistics commonly employed in hypothesis testing can be found:

- for a large-sample test of a population proportion in Example Problem 13.8 on page 558.
- for a large, independent samples test of the difference between two population means in Example Problem 13.10 on page 561.
- for a large, matched-pairs sample test of the difference between two population means in Example Problem 13.12 on page 564.
- for a large, independent samples test of the difference between two population proportions in Example Problem 13.14 on page 567.
- for a small, independent samples test of the difference between two population means in Example Problem 13.19 on page 578.
- for a small, matched-pairs sample test of the difference between two population means in Example Problem 13.21 on page 584.

In all cases, it is assumed that $n < .05N$; otherwise, as is demonstrated in Example Problem 13.7 on page 553, the standard deviation employed in the denominator of the test statistic must be multiplied by the finite population correction factor of $\sqrt{\frac{N-n}{N-1}}$.

samples [when $n \geq 30$ but $n < .05N$ or when $n\pi \geq 5$ and $n(1 - \pi) \geq 5$ as well] or by a Student t distribution for small samples (when the underlying population values are normally distributed). When we can thus approximate a sample statistic's sampling distribution, we can convert each of the four sample statistics noted above into a corresponding z value or t value *by dividing the difference between the sample statistic and the value of the population parameter postulated in the null hypothesis by the standard error of the sample statistic.* In tests about the population mean, for example, instead of using $\bar{X}$ directly as the test statistic, it is common practice to use $z = \dfrac{\bar{X} - \mu_0}{\sigma_{\bar{X}}}$ in the large-sample case and $t = \dfrac{\bar{X} - \mu_0}{s_{\bar{X}}}$ in the small-sample case. The use of these and similar z or t values as test statistics is demonstrated in numerous Example Problems later in this chapter. The Technical Detail box on the preceding page is a guide to these commonly used test statistics.

13.4 Step 3: Deriving a Decision Rule

Having formulated two opposing hypotheses and selected the type of statistic with which to test them, the next step in hypothesis testing is the derivation of a decision rule:

DEFINITION 13.5 A **decision rule** is a hypothesis-testing rule that specifies in advance, for all possible values of a test statistic that might be computed from a sample, whether the null hypothesis should continue to be accepted or whether it should be rejected in favor of the alternative hypothesis. Numerical values of the test statistic for which H_0 is accepted are said to lie in the **acceptance region** and are each viewed as a **not statistically significant result.** Numerical values of the test statistic for which H_0 is rejected are said to lie in the **rejection region** and are each viewed as a **statistically significant result.** The latter values counsel the substitution of the alternative hypothesis for the (then discredited) null hypothesis and, thus, call for some kind of action.

At first thought, the selection of a decision rule may seem superfluous. Isn't it bound to be obvious whether the computed value of the test statistic agrees with the null hypothesis or contradicts it? On reflection it becomes clear, however, that the matter is more complicated than it appears to be at first sight.

A DILEMMA

While surely anyone can tell instantly whether the computed value of the test statistic does or does not agree with the null hypothesis, it is not so obvious that a given divergence between the observed value and the hypothetical value automatically proves the null hypothesis to be false. What such divergence does prove is questionable because any sample statistic is a *random variable:* Its value depends very much on the particular sample that happens to be selected from the population in question. Consider, for example, the population of metal parts produced by an industrial process. The average length of these parts may in fact be $\mu = 5$ inches, as required by the users of these parts. A quality inspector who does not know that the average length is okay may set out to test these hypotheses:

$$H_0: \mu = 5$$
$$H_A: \mu \neq 5$$

FIGURE 13.1 | A Sampling Distribution of the Sample Mean

This graph shows the sampling distribution of the sample mean, $\overline{X}$, for a large simple random sample taken from a population of metal parts with a mean length of $\mu = 5$ inches. The sampling distribution is approximately normal, with a mean, $\mu_{\overline{X}}$, equal to the population mean of 5 and a standard deviation, $\sigma_{\overline{X}}$, of .1 inch. Thus, even though a null hypothesis of H_0: $\mu = 5$ is true, half of all possible sample statistics show $\overline{X} < 5$, and half of them show $\overline{X} > 5$. Thus, a finding of $\overline{X} \neq 5$ does not prove that the alternative hypothesis of H_A: $\mu \neq 5$ is correct.

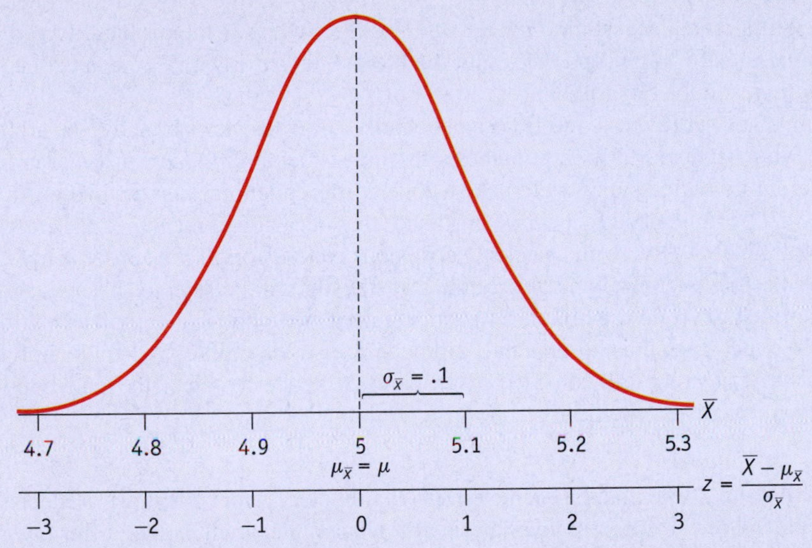

Now suppose the inspector takes a large sample of $n \geq 30$ from this infinite population. Even though *we* know H_0 to be true, the chance factor operating in the sampling process can, nevertheless, provide the inspector with many possible sample means, as shown in Figure 13.1 (which is centered on the true *population* mean, $\mu = 5$). All kinds of *sample* means might be found: $\overline{X} = 5$, $\overline{X} = 4.9$, $\overline{X} = 5.2$, and even $\overline{X} = 5.32$. Yet all these results, many of which apparently contradict the null hypothesis, are consistent with the null hypothesis being true! So what is our quality inspector to do?

THE DILEMMA SOLVED

We escape the dilemma by recognizing this: Even though we might discover all kinds of $\overline{X}$ values when we take a simple random sample from a population for which the null hypothesis is true, not all of these values are equally probable. In Figure 13.1, for example, finding a sample mean between 5 and 5.1 is more likely than finding a sample mean between 5.1 and 5.2, and that is more likely still than finding a sample mean between 5.2 and 5.3. Given that H_0: $\mu = 5$ is true, finding a sample mean of 5.5 or larger, even though possible, would be a *highly unusual result.* Thus, we can follow this general rule for assessing our sample results:

GENERAL RULE FOR ASSESSING SAMPLE RESULTS If a seemingly contradictory sample result has a high probability of occurring when H_0 is true, and, thus, is not at all surprising, we ascribe any divergence between the observed and hypothesized values to chance factors operating during the sampling process, and we accept the null hypothesis as true. If, on the other hand, a particular sample result is very unlikely to occur when H_0 is true, and, thus, is very surprising, we ascribe the divergence between the observed and hypothesized values to nonchance factors, such as the fact that H_A is true, and we reject the null hypothesis as false.

THE LEVEL OF SIGNIFICANCE

The foregoing discussion of surprising and nonsurprising results makes a lot of sense but still leaves us with a crucial question: Given that H_0 is true, when is the probability of observing a given sample statistic "high" and the result, therefore, "not surprising"? When is that probability "low" and the result "very surprising"?

No single answer to these questions exists. Indeed, the answer is bound to be arbitrary in the sense that whoever undertakes a hypothesis test must make a *subjective* decision here, and a dozen different individuals may well make a dozen different choices on the matter. In each case, the choice will be influenced by the circumstances that occasioned the hypothesis test and by the person's willingness to live with a possibly erroneous conclusion. If the consequences of making an error are deemed serious, one value of the test statistic will be selected as critical. If the consequences of being wrong are minor, a statistician may well choose a completely different critical value. In either case, the chosen value will be viewed as so unlikely when the null hypothesis is true that its appearance is considered sufficient evidence to reject the null hypothesis and embrace the alternative hypothesis.

AN EXAMPLE In the situation depicted in Figure 13.1, for example, a decision maker might decide to reject the null hypothesis for all sample results that differ by more than $2\sigma_{\bar{X}}$ from the mean of the sampling distribution, $\mu_{\bar{X}}$, and, therefore, from the population mean, μ, when the null hypothesis is true. Thus, values of $\bar{X}$ below 4.8 and above 5.2, two ranges that correspond to all the values beyond $\pm 2z$, would be regarded as occurring with a sufficiently low probability (if H_0: $\mu = 5$ were true) to call H_0 false. As we can see in Appendix Table H, the combined area under the normal curve beyond $\pm 2z$ equals $1 - [2(.4772)] = .0456$. Thus, the decision rule just stated treats all sample results that differ from the null hypothesis—and that could occur by chance at most 4.56 percent of the time if H_0 were true—as sufficiently strong evidence to reject H_0. Any such sample result that leads to the rejection of H_0 is said to be *statistically significant.*

On the other hand, the above decision rule treats all sample results that differ from the null hypothesis—but that could occur by chance more than 4.56 percent of the time if H_0 were true—as evidence too weak to reject H_0. Any such sample result that leads to the continued acceptance of H_0 is said to be *not statistically significant.* Such a result does not prove H_0 to be true, but it doesn't disprove it either. It does, however, make H_0 somewhat more credible than it was before the sample was taken.

CONCLUSION Indeed, among all the sample results that are possible when the null hypothesis is true, the (arbitrary) maximum proportion of these results that is considered sufficiently unusual to reject the null hypothesis is called the **significance level** of a hypothesis test, and it is symbolized by α (the lowercase Greek letter *alpha*). In the above example, α equals .0456; more commonly used values are .10, .05, .025, and even lower values than that. Thus, when the significance level, α, is set at .05, or 5 percent, only statistics that occur with a probability of .05 or less when H_0 is true are sufficient evidence to *reject* H_0.

THREE ILLUSTRATIONS

Figure 13.2 on the next page illustrates how a decision rule can be derived once we have specified the desired significance level of a hypothesis test. The three examples focus (1) on hypothesis tests about a population mean, stated in each of the three forms noted above, and (2) on the large-sample case of $n \geq 30$ but $n < .05N$ (so that the sampling distribution is represented by the normal curve). Decision rules for other types of hypothesis tests, or for sampling distributions that are more accurately described by t distributions, can be derived analogously.

A TWO-TAILED HYPOTHESIS TEST Panel (a) pictures the case in which the opposing hypotheses take Form 1. The null hypothesis claims, for example, that the lengths of metal parts produced average 5 inches; the alternative hypothesis denies it. The alternative hypothesis, thus, is two-sided. We are concerned about departures from the 5-inch norm in *both* directions. We would view very low as well as very high values of the test statistic ($\bar{X}$ or z) as evidence against H_0. If the desired significance level is set at $\alpha = .05$, then values of the test statistic that are so far below the hypothesized mean as to occur with a probability of at most $(\alpha/2) = .025$ when H_0 is true become evidence against H_0. The same is true for values so far above the hypothesized mean as to occur with the same low probability. Jointly, the statistically significant values of the test statistic, thus, have a probability of $\alpha = .05$ of occurring when H_0 is true. By consulting Appendix Table H, we can determine the lower value of the test statistic (here of $-z_{\alpha/2}$ or $-z_{.025}$) and the upper value of the test statistic (here $+z_{\alpha/2}$ or $+z_{.025}$) that marks the border between two regions of values—namely, those that would signal the acceptance of H_0, and, thus, lie in the *acceptance region,* and those that would signal the rejection of H_0, and, thus, lie in the *rejection region.* The value of z below (or above) which .025 of the area under the standard normal curve lies is also the value that places $.500 - .025 = .475$ of that area between itself and the mean. Therefore, as Appendix Table H shows, $-z_{.025} = -1.96$, while $+z_{.025} = +1.96$. If we assume that $\sigma_{\bar{X}} = .1$, the corresponding values of $\bar{X}$ equal $5 - [1.96(.1)] = 4.804$ and $5 + [1.96(.1)] = 5.196$.

The value of a test statistic that in this way divides all possible values into an acceptance region and a rejection region is called the **critical value.** As panel (a) of Figure 13.2 indicates, the decision rule emerging in this example is:

> "Accept H_0 for any sample mean between 4.804 and 5.196 inches (or for any corresponding z value between -1.96 and $+1.96$). Reject H_0, and accept H_A, for values of the test statistic outside these limits."

A LOWER-TAILED HYPOTHESIS TEST Panel (b) of Figure 13.2 pictures the case in which the opposing hypotheses take Form 2. The null hypothesis claims, for example, that the lifetime of a battery is at least 100 hours; the alternative hypothesis posits that the battery lasts fewer than 100 hours. The alternative hypothesis is one-sided, because we are only concerned about departures from the 100-hour norm in the lower direction (nobody will complain if the batteries last longer than 100 hours). Only very low values of the test statistic count as evidence against H_0. If the desired significance level is again set at $\alpha = .05$, values of the test statistic that fall so far below the hypothesized mean as to occur with a maximum probability of $\alpha = .05$ when H_0 is true become evidence against H_0. According to Appendix Table H, the critical z value of $-z_\alpha$ or $-z_{.05}$ equals -1.64 because this value places $.50 - .05 = .45$ of the area under the standard normal curve between itself and the mean above it and, thus, leaves .05 of that area in the lower tail of the sampling distribution. If we assume that $\sigma_{\bar{X}} = 10$ hours, the corresponding critical value of $\bar{X}$ equals 83.6 hours. Thus, the decision rule is:

> "Accept H_0 for any sample mean of 83.6 hours or more (or for corresponding z values of -1.64 and above). Reject H_0, and accept H_A, for all lower values of the test statistic."

FIGURE 13.2 | Two-Tailed versus One-Tailed Hypothesis Tests

This set of graphs pictures sampling distributions of sample means (and their corresponding standard normal deviates) on the assumption that the stated null hypotheses are true. When the alternative hypothesis is two-sided, as in panel (a), any hypothesis test is said to be a ***two-tailed test*** *because the null hypothesis is then rejected for values of the test statistic located in either tail of that statistic's sampling distribution. The rejection region is then split between the two tails of that distribution. When, on the other hand, the alternative hypothesis is one-sided, as in panels (b) and (c), any hypothesis test is said to be a* ***one-tailed test*** *because the null hypothesis is then rejected only for very low (or only for very high) values of the test statistic located entirely in one tail of the sampling distribution. The entire rejection region is then found in either the lower tail, making for a* ***lower-tailed test,*** *as in panel (b), or in the upper tail, making for an* ***upper-tailed test,*** *as in panel (c). Note the encircled critical test statistic values.*

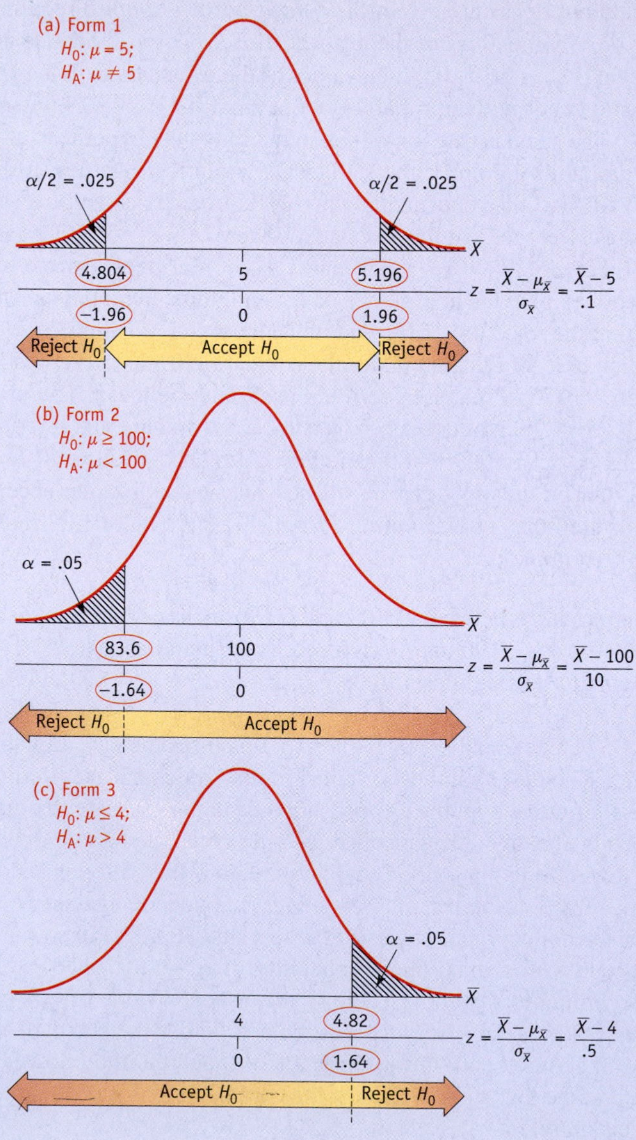

AN UPPER-TAILED HYPOTHESIS TEST Panel (c) of Figure 13.2 pictures the case in which the opposing hypotheses take Form 3. The null hypothesis claims, for example, that the drying time of a type of paint is at most 4 hours; the alternative hypothesis claims that the paint takes more than 4 hours to dry. The alternative hypothesis is again one-sided, but this time the story differs from that in panel (b). Now we are concerned about departures from the 4-hour norm only in the upper direction (nobody will complain if the paint in fact dries faster than claimed). Only very *high* values of the test statistic count as evidence against H_0. If the desired significance level is again set at $\alpha = .05$, values of the test statistic so far above the hypothesized mean as to occur with a maximum probability of $\alpha = .05$ when H_0 is true become evidence against H_0. This time, the critical z value equals $+1.64$; if we assume that $\sigma_{\bar{X}} = .5$ hour, the corresponding critical value of $\bar{X}$ equals 4.82 hours. Thus, the decision rule is:

> "Accept H_0 for any sample mean of 4.82 hours or less (or for corresponding z values of 1.64 and below). Reject H_0 and accept H_A, for all higher values of the test statistic."

DECISION RULES SUMMARIZED Formula 13.A summarizes the decision rules for large-sample hypothesis tests about a mean. However, we can easily extend these rules to the small-sample case, provided that underlying population values are normally distributed. In that case, we simply substitute Student t values for z in the Formula 13.A expressions. Similarly, we can derive analogous decision rules for hypothesis tests about a proportion, by substituting π for μ and P for $\bar{X}$, and about the difference between two means or between two proportions, by substituting differences where now individual values appear.

FORMULA 13.A | **Decision Rules for Large-Sample Hypothesis Tests about a Mean ($n \geq 30$ and $n < .05N$ or population normal)**

1. Two-tailed test, $H_A: \mu \neq \mu_0$

$$\text{Accept } H_0 \text{ if } \mu_0 - (z_{\alpha/2} \times \sigma_{\bar{X}}) \leq \bar{X} \leq \mu_0 + (z_{\alpha/2} \times \sigma_{\bar{X}})$$

or

$$-z_{\alpha/2} \leq z \leq +z_{\alpha/2}$$

2. Lower-tailed test, $H_A: \mu < \mu_0$

$$\text{Accept } H_0 \text{ if } \bar{X} \geq \mu_0 - (z_\alpha \times \sigma_{\bar{X}})$$

or

$$z \geq -z_\alpha$$

3. Upper-tailed test, $H_A: \mu > \mu_0$

$$\text{Accept } H_0 \text{ if } \bar{X} \leq \mu_0 + (z_\alpha \times \sigma_{\bar{X}})$$

or

$$z \leq +z_\alpha$$

Note: Appendix Table L provides critical z values for two-tailed and one-tailed hypothesis tests and for the most commonly used significance levels.

13.5 Step 4: Using Sample Data to Compute the Test Statistic and Confronting It with the Decision Rule

The final step in hypothesis testing involves:

- the selection of a random sample from the population of interest
- the computation, with the help of the sample data, of the test statistic selected in Step 2
- the confrontation of the actual value of the test statistic with the critical value embodied in the decision rule derived in Step 3

If, for example, a sample of metal parts proved to have an average length of $\mu = 5.1$ inches ($z = 1.00$), the null hypothesis stated in panel (a) of Figure 13.2 would be upheld. Similarly, if a sample of batteries turned out to last an average of $\mu = 90$ hours ($z = -1.00$), the null hypothesis stated in panel (b) of Figure 13.2 would be upheld. If, however, a sample of paint canisters showed an average drying time of $\mu = 4.9$ hours ($z = 1.80$), the null hypothesis given in panel (c) of Figure 13.2 would be rejected.

But note an important point: Given $\alpha = .05$, the latter conclusion (that the paint's average drying time exceeded the mere 4 hours claimed for it) would be incorrect in 5 out of 100 times in which this type of statistical procedure was employed. After all, the unusual sample result cited does occur with a 5 percent probability when the panel (c) null hypothesis is true!

13.6 The Possibility of Error

The hypothesis-testing procedure outlined in this chapter so far can lead to one of four results, which we summarize in Table 13.1.

TABLE 13.1 | Four Possible Outcomes of a Hypothesis Test

*Depending on the true state of the world, the result reached in a hypothesis test can be correct, as in cells A and D, or erroneous, as in cells B and C. The probabilities associated with these outcomes are shown as well. Note the terminology involved: The cell A probability of correctly accepting a true null hypothesis equals $1 - \alpha$ and is called the **confidence level** of the hypothesis test. The cell B probability of making the **type I error** of incorrectly rejecting a true null hypothesis equals α and is called the test's **significance level** or **α risk.** The cell C probability of making the **type II error** of incorrectly accepting a false null hypothesis equals β and is called the **β risk.** The cell D probability of correctly rejecting a false null hypothesis equals $1 - \beta$ and is called the **power** of the hypothesis test.*

True but Unknown State of the World:	Test Result: Null Hypothesis Accepted	Test Result: Null Hypothesis Rejected
Null Hypothesis Is True	A) Correct Result $p = 1 - \alpha$ = confidence level of test	B) Type I Error $p = \alpha$ = significance level or α risk of test
Null Hypothesis Is False	C) Type II Error $p = \beta$ = β risk of test	D) Correct Result $p = 1 - \beta$ = power of test

WHEN THE NULL HYPOTHESIS IS TRUE

When the null hypothesis is in fact true (and remember that those who engage in hypothesis testing do not know this, or they would have no reason to undertake the test), two possible consequences can flow from a hypothesis test: The null hypothesis may be accepted (a correct result), or it may be rejected (an erroneous outcome). The latter possibility—the erroneous rejection of a null hypothesis that is in fact true—is referred to as a **type I error,** or as the **error of rejection.** Such an error can be costly indeed. It may lead to the interruption of the production process in order to adjust machinery that needs no adjusting. It may lead a firm to switch to a new supplier of raw materials although the performance of the old one was satisfactory. It may lead a government agency to condemn a firm for ignoring pollution standards even though it has done no such thing. In a medical setting, committing a type I error is equivalent to producing "false positives," such as telling people who don't have AIDS that they do. In the legal realm, it amounts to condemning an innocent defendant in a criminal trial.

But note: The logic of hypothesis testing *guarantees* that this type of error occurs sometimes. Picture in your mind a sampling distribution, as any one of the Figure 13.2 panels, which shows all the possible values of a test statistic, given that the null hypothesis is true. Then recall what happens when we select a significance level for a hypothesis test. We arbitrarily place some of these possible values in the rejection region and we thus interpret the occurrence of those values that have a low probability of occurring when H_0 is true as evidence that H_0 is false. Hence, in the long run, as we use a given procedure again and again, we are bound to reject a true null hypothesis the proportion of times we have set as the significance level. In short, the probability of making the type I error—of erroneously rejecting a null hypothesis that is in fact true — is equal to α, the significance level of the hypothesis test, which is why the significance level is also referred to as the **α risk.** (Some students find it helpful to link the type *one* error with α because that is letter number *one* in the Greek alphabet.)

It follows that the complementary probability of *avoiding* the type I error (and coming to the correct decision) equals $1 - \alpha$, a value that is also called the **confidence level** of the hypothesis test.

EXAMPLE PROBLEM 13.3

A company statistician is about to test whether specialty steel rods still have a tensile strength of at least 5,000 pounds, as they used to. If the significance level of the hypothesis test is set at $\alpha =$ .08, what are the implications with respect to making or not making a type I error?

SOLUTION: Given the hypotheses of H_0: $\mu \geq 5{,}000$ and H_A: $\mu < 5{,}000$, the procedure assures the following: Even if the rods have *in fact* an average tensile strength of 5,000 pounds or more, in 8 percent of all tests the conclusion will be to the contrary. Nevertheless, 92 percent of such tests avoid this type of error, which indicates the *confidence level* of the test.

WHEN THE NULL HYPOTHESIS IS FALSE

When the null hypothesis is in fact false, a hypothesis test once again leads to one of two possible consequences: The null hypothesis may be accepted (an erroneous outcome), or it may be rejected (a correct result). The former possibility—the erroneous acceptance of a null hypothesis that is in fact false—is referred to as a **type II error,** or as the **error of acceptance.** Such an error, too, has its costs. It may lead to uninterrupted production at a time when the machinery badly needs to be adjusted. It may lead a firm to continue using a supplier whose performance is unsatisfactory, or it may lead a government agency to do nothing about a firm's violation of pollution standards—in each case, because the truth is not recognized. In a medical setting, committing a type II error is equivalent to producing "false negatives," such as telling people who do have AIDS that they don't. In the legal realm, it amounts to acquitting a guilty defendant in a criminal trial. And just as it is deemed less serious in the field of criminal justice to let a guilty person go than to convict an innocent one, it is common practice to regard a type II error as less serious than a type I error.

The probability of committing a type II error is symbolized by β and is referred to as the **β risk.** (Some students find it helpful to link the type *two* error with β because that is letter number *two* in the Greek alphabet.)

In turn, the complementary probability of *avoiding* the type II error (and coming to the correct decision) equals $1 - \beta$, which is also called the **power** of the hypothesis test.

EXAMPLE PROBLEM 13.4

A company statistician is about to test whether computer assembly still takes at most 40 minutes, as used to be true. If the test's α risk equals .2, what are the implications with respect to making or not making a type II error?

SOLUTION: Given the hypotheses of H_0: $\mu \leq 40$ and H_A: $\beta > 40$, the procedure ensures the following: Even if the assembly time *in fact* averages more than 40 minutes, in 20 percent of all tests, the conclusion will be to the contrary. Nevertheless, in 80 percent of such tests, this type of error is avoided, which indicates the *power* of the test.

THE TRADE-OFF BETWEEN A TYPE I ERROR AND A TYPE II ERROR

Statisticians who conduct hypothesis tests can never know, neither before sampling nor afterward, whether they have made a type I error or type II error. It is possible, however, to control the probability of having a given error occur. Unfortunately, given sample size, n, anything that reduces α automatically raises β; the reverse is also true, as can be seen with the help of Figure 13.3.

Panel (a) of Figure 13.3 is a copy of panel (c) of Figure 13.2. It shows the sampling distribution of the mean drying time of paint when the null hypothesis ("average drying time equals at most 4 hours") is in fact true. If we select a significance level of $\alpha = .05$ and if, as in the earlier example, $\sigma_{\bar{X}} = .5$, the critical values are $\bar{X} = 4.82$ hours and $z = 1.64$, respectively. The probability of making a type I error, thus, appears as the crosshatched area in panel (a). It equals the area under the upper tail of the sampling distribution prevailing if H_0 is true.

Panel (b) of Figure 13.3 shows the sampling distribution when the null hypothesis is in fact false and the average drying time equals 5.8 hours. The critical value of $\bar{X} = 4.82$, which was established on the basis of assuming H_0 to be true, now is shown to be lower than the mean of the true panel (b) sampling distribution. A corresponding z value is -1.96. To the left of this value (and thus in the acceptance region) we find .025 of the area under the standard normal curve. This crosshatched area in panel (b) gives us the probability of making a type II error. For any given sample, the selection of α, which leads to the decision rule, thus, ultimately determines β.

FIGURE 13.3 | The Trade-Off between α and β

Someone about to test a null hypothesis does not know whether it is true or false and whether, therefore, the sampling distribution looks like that shown in panel (a) or like that in panel (b). By assuming the former and selecting a value for α, the tester derives a decision rule; this decision rule automatically determines the value of β if H_0 is in fact false. Given sample size, any decrease in α raises β (as the dashed vertical line moves right). The opposite is also true; any increase in α lowers β (as that line moves left). This result is analogous to our experience with the criminal justice system: Anything that lowers the probability, α, of convicting an innocent person (such as a rule against self-incrimination) also raises the probability, β, of acquitting a guilty person. Anything that lowers the probability, β, of acquitting a guilty person (such as a rule that allows split juries to convict) thereby raises the probability, α, of convicting an innocent person.

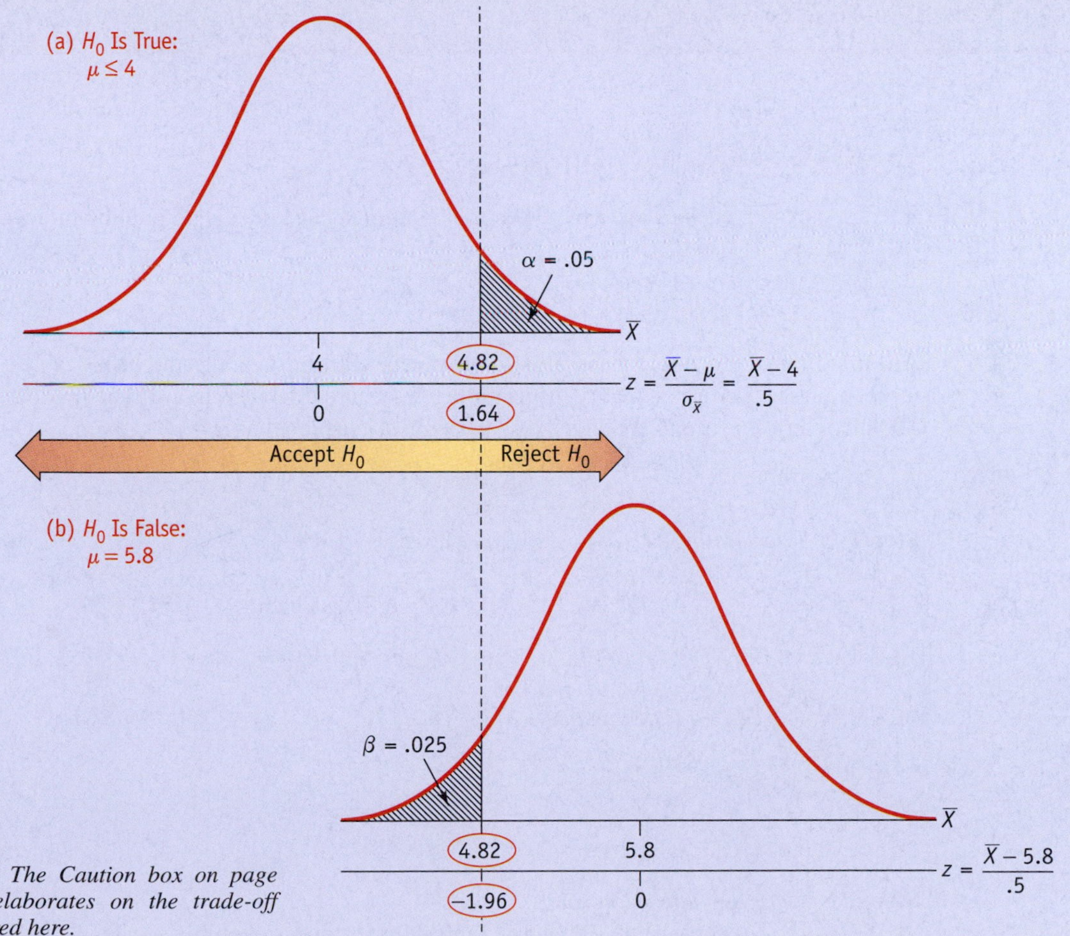

Note: *The Caution box on page 550 elaborates on the trade-off pictured here.*

13.7 Large-Sample Hypothesis Tests

We now apply the four-stage hypothesis-testing procedure to typical testing situations. In this section, we assume samples to be large: $n \geq 30$ but $n < .05N$ for tests involving one or two means; $n\pi \geq 5$ and $n(1 - \pi) \geq 5$ for tests involving one or two proportions. Therefore, we can assume that any test statistic's sampling distribution is approximated by the normal curve.

Carefully note two facts about type I and type II errors:

1. A lower α, which would move the dashed borderline between the acceptance and rejection region to the right, would raise β. A higher α, which would move that borderline left, would lower β. As more advanced texts show, only a larger sample size can reduce α and β at the same time or can reduce one of the two without raising the other.
2. Unscrupulous investigators could manipulate the size of α, and, thus, the position of the borderline between the acceptance and rejection regions, so as to accommodate *any* observed value of a test statistic. Someone eager to have a null hypothesis accepted could make α extremely small, at the cost of having β very large. Someone eager to have a null hypothesis rejected could make α extremely large, which would make β very small. Obviously, such behavior would make a mockery of scientific inquiry. The only way to avoid it is for the investigator to select α *before* seeing the sample data. Step 3 must be performed before Step 4.

TESTS OF A POPULATION MEAN

We first consider each of the three types of hypothesis tests of a single population mean.

EXAMPLE PROBLEM 13.5

An aircraft manufacturer needs aluminum sheets with an average thickness of .01 inch—no more, no less. The firm's quality inspector is to measure thickness in a simple random sample of 100 incoming sheets and conduct a test at a significance level of $\alpha = .05$.

SOLUTION:

Step 1: *Formulating two opposing hypotheses.*

$$H_0: \mu = .01 \text{ inch}$$
$$H_A: \mu \neq .01 \text{ inch}$$

Step 2: *Selecting a test statistic.*

$$z = \frac{\bar{X} - \mu_0}{\sigma_{\bar{X}}}$$

Step 3: *Deriving a decision rule.*

According to Appendix Table L, the chosen significance level implies critical values of $\pm z_{\alpha/2} = \pm 1.96$ (this being a two-tailed test). Thus, the decision rule must be:

"Accept H_0 if $-1.96 \leq z \leq +1.96$."

The critical values are encircled in Figure 13.4.

Step 4: *Using sample data to compute the test statistic and confronting it with the decision rule.*

After taking a sample of $n = 100$, the inspector finds a sample mean thickness of $\bar{X} = .009$ and a sample standard deviation of $s = .01$. Given an infinite population (the

FIGURE 13.4 | Testing the Thickness of Aluminum Sheets

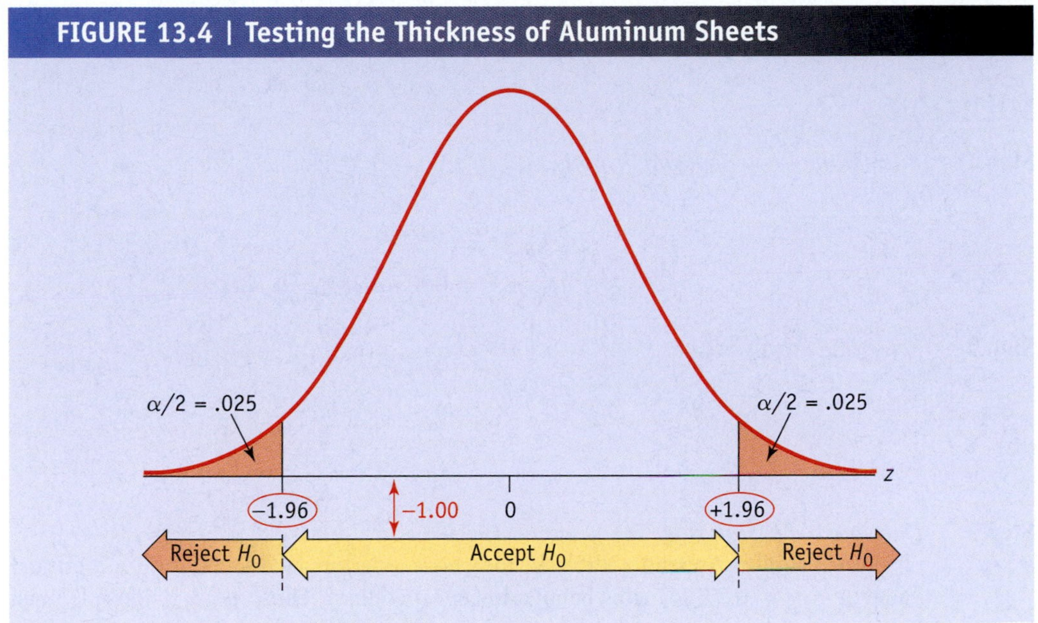

sheets come from an ongoing production process), the large-population case applies; hence the inspector *estimates* $\sigma_{\bar{X}}$ as

$$\sigma_{\bar{X}} \cong \frac{s}{\sqrt{n}} = \frac{.01}{\sqrt{100}} = .001$$

Accordingly, the computed value of the test statistic equals

$$z = \frac{\bar{X} - \mu_0}{\sigma_{\bar{X}}} = \frac{.009 - .01}{.001} = -1.00$$

This value corresponds to the red arrow in Figure 13.4; it suggests that the null hypothesis should be *accepted.* At the 5 percent significance level, the sample result is not statistically significant. The observed divergence from the desired average .01-inch standard of thickness is more likely due to chance factors at work during the sampling process than to a faulty production process that systematically puts out sheets with an average thickness other than .01 inch.

EXAMPLE PROBLEM 13.6

For purposes of mounting engines on aircraft, a manufacturer needs specialty steel rods with an average tensile strength of at least 5,000 pounds. At a significance level of $\alpha = .01$, the firm's quality inspector is to test incoming supplies by figuring the tensile strength evidenced in a simple random sample of 64 rods. (This test is performed by noting the force at which the rods become distorted.)

SOLUTION:

Step 1: *Formulating two opposing hypotheses.*

$$H_0\text{: } \mu \geq 5{,}000 \text{ lb.}$$
$$H_A\text{: } \mu < 5{,}000 \text{ lb.}$$

Step 2: *Selecting a test statistic.*

$$z = \frac{\bar{X} - \mu_0}{\sigma_{\bar{X}}}$$

Step 3: *Deriving a decision rule.*

According to Appendix Table L, the chosen significance level implies a critical value of $-z_\alpha = -2.3267$ (this being a lower-tailed test). Thus, the decision rule must be:

"Accept H_0 if $z \geq -2.3267$."

The (rounded) critical value is encircled in Figure 13.5.

Step 4: *Using sample data to compute the test statistic and confronting it with the decision rule.*

After taking a sample of $n = 64$, the inspector finds that the rods become distorted by a mean strength of $\bar{X} = 4{,}700$ lb., the sample standard deviation being $s = 800$ lb.

FIGURE 13.5 | Testing the Tensile Strength of Steel Rods

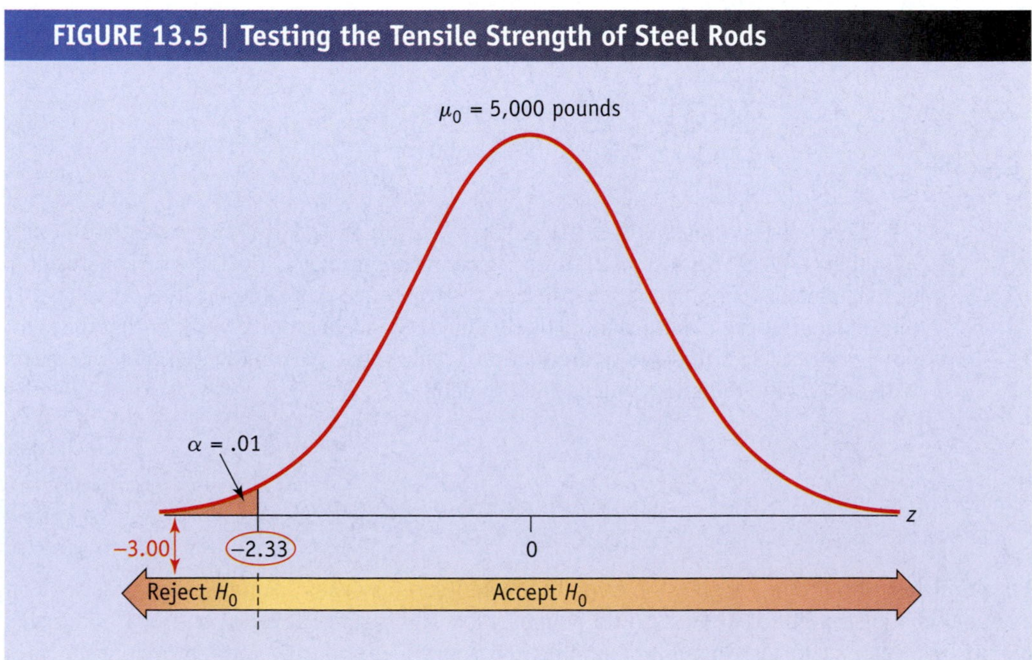

Given an infinite population (the rods come from an ongoing production process), the large-population case applies; hence the inspector *estimates* $\sigma_{\bar{X}}$ as

$$\sigma_{\bar{X}} \cong \frac{s}{\sqrt{n}} = \frac{800}{\sqrt{64}} = 100$$

Accordingly, the computed value of the test statistic equals

$$z = \frac{\bar{X} - \mu_0}{\sigma_{\bar{X}}} = \frac{4{,}700 - 5{,}000}{100} = -3.00$$

This value corresponds to the red arrow in Figure 13.5; it suggests that the null hypothesis should be *rejected.* At the 1 percent significance level, the sample result is statistically significant. The observed divergence from the 5,000-pound standard is unlikely to result from chance factors operating during sampling; it is more likely to be the result of a production process that puts out low-quality and, therefore, unusable rods.

EXAMPLE PROBLEM 13.7

An airline executive wants to test a manufacturer's claim that one ounce of additive per gallon will significantly increase the performance of aviation fuel. The airline's records show that the fuel without the additive has traditionally delivered an average of at most 6 minutes of flight time per gallon. The next 100 flights are to be flown with the additive. At a significance level of $\alpha = .10$, a random sample of 36 flights is to be evaluated by the airline's statistician, who has reason to assume that the minutes-per-gallon population will be normally distributed.

Note: In case you wonder why airlines don't evaluate fuel performance in *miles* per gallon, as car owners would, consider the effect of the wind. An airplane in flight can be pushed ahead by tailwinds, held back by headwinds, and drifted sideways by crosswinds, none of which is known by the engine. Thus, a given amount of fuel that feeds the engine for 60 minutes might deliver 300 miles of travel over the ground on one day and 600 miles on another day, depending on the winds aloft.

SOLUTION:

Step 1: *Formulating two opposing hypotheses.*

$$H_0: \mu \leq 6 \text{ minutes per gallon}$$
$$H_A: \mu > 6 \text{ minutes per gallon}$$

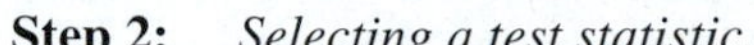

Step 2: *Selecting a test statistic.*

The statistician selects the sample mean minutes per gallon, $\bar{X}$ (which gives us a chance to see what happens when the test statistic is not a z value).

Step 3: *Deriving a decision rule.*

According to Appendix Table L, the chosen significance level implies a critical value of $+z_\alpha = +1.2817$ (this being an upper-tailed test). Thus, the decision rule must be:

"Accept H_0 if $\bar{X} \leq \mu_0 + 1.2817\sigma_{\bar{X}}$."

Assuming the population standard deviation, σ, is unknown, the precise magnitude of $\sigma_{\bar{X}} = \frac{\sigma}{\sqrt{n}}\sqrt{\frac{N-n}{N-1}}$ cannot be determined. However, the critical

FIGURE 13.6 | Testing Additive in Aviation Fuel

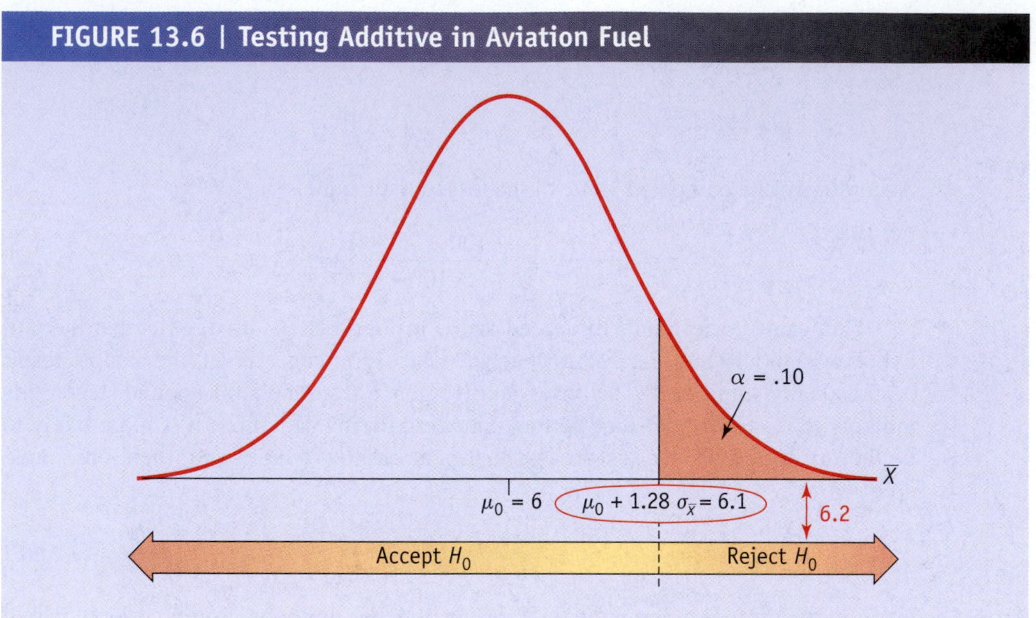

$\overline{X}$ can be established after the sample has been taken, at which point the statistician can *estimate* $\sigma_{\overline{X}}$ from the sample standard deviation. The critical value of $\overline{X} = 6.1$ given in Figure 13.6, therefore, is in this case found in Step 4.

Step 4: *Using sample data to compute the test statistic and confronting it with the decision rule.*

After 100 flights have been flown with the additive, the statistician takes a sample of $n = 36$ flight records and finds the mean minutes per gallon to be $\overline{X} = 6.2$, with a sample standard deviation of $s = .6$ minute. Because the small-population case applies ($n > .05N$), the statistician *estimates*

$$\sigma_{\overline{X}} \cong \frac{s}{\sqrt{n}}\sqrt{\frac{N-n}{N-1}} = \frac{.6}{\sqrt{36}}\sqrt{\frac{100-36}{100-1}} = .0804$$

Accordingly, the critical value of $\overline{X}$ equals $6 + [1.2817(.0804)] = 6.1$ minutes per gallon.

This result suggests that the null hypothesis should be *rejected.* At the 10 percent significance level, the sample result is statistically significant. The additive does stretch the flight time squeezed out of a gallon.

This is a good place to observe that *statistical* significance is not necessarily the same thing as *practical* significance. The statistical significance of this test simply tells us that the divergence of the sample result (an average 6.2 minutes of flight time per gallon) from the previous experience (an average 6 minutes per gallon) is probably not merely the result of sampling error, but is quite likely attributable to the additive. Yet the practical significance of all this may be nil: It may be cheaper, for example, to buy the added 3.3 percent of flight time by paying for extra fuel than by paying for a possibly expensive additive.

EXCEL Example 13.1

Create a hypothetical sample of $n = 100$ measurements of the thickness of aluminum sheets. Let the sample contain 50 values of .01 inches, 35 values of .009 inches, and 15 values of .011 inches. Assuming the population standard deviation equals .001 inches, conduct a hypothesis test of H_0: $\mu = .01$ inches and do so at a significance level of $\alpha = .05$.

SOLUTION:

1. Enter **.01** into cell A1, select the cell, and use the lower right handle to drag the entry to A50. In like manner, enter **.009** into cells A51–A85 and **.011** into cells A86–A100.
2. To perform the (two-tailed) hypothesis test, enter the labels *Hypothesized mean, Significance level, Critical z, Sample mean=Point estimate, Population standard deviation, Sample size, Standard error of sample mean,* and *Test statistic* into cells B1–B8.
3. Enter corresponding formulas or known values into adjacent cells in column C; namely

   .01 into C1

   .05 into C2

   =−1*NORMSINV(C2/2) into C3. (This determines the critical value of z for a two-tailed test. The function must be multiplied by −1 to obtain a positive value. The resulting value of 1.96 indicates that the acceptance region stretches from −1.96 to +1.96.)

   =AVERAGE(A1:A100) into C4

   .001 into C5. [If the population standard deviation were not known, one would compute the sample standard deviation as **=STDEV(A1:A100)**.]

   =COUNT(A1:A100) into C6

   =C5/SQRT(C6) into C7

   =(C4−C1)/C7 into C8

   The result:

Hypothesized mean	0.01
Significance level	0.05
Critical z	1.95996108
Sample mean=Point estimate	0.0098
Population standard deviation	0.001
Sample size	100
Standard error of sample mean	0.0001
Test statistic	−2

INTERPRETATION The test statistic is computed as $z = \frac{\bar{X} - \mu_0}{\sigma/\sqrt{n}} = \frac{.0098 - .01}{.001/\sqrt{100}} = -2.00$ (shown in red). At a significance level of $\alpha = .05$, Appendix Table L tells us, the acceptance region stretches from −1.96 to +1.96 (just as in Figure 13.4). Therefore, H_0: $\mu = .01$ must be *rejected.* According to the sample, the sheets are thinner on average.

Note: This type of problem can also be solved much more rapidly by using HKStat, Sheet 13.

EXCEL Example 13.2

Create a hypothetical sample of $n = 64$ measurements of the tensile strength of steel rods. Let the sample contain 32 values of 5,000 lb., 16 values of 5,200 lb., and 16 values of 4,900 lb. Assuming the population standard deviation equals 100 lb., conduct a hypothesis test of H_0: $\mu \geq 5{,}000$ lb. and do so at a significance level of $\alpha = .01$.

SOLUTION:

1. Enter **5000** into cell A1, select the cell, and use the lower right handle to drag the entry to A32. In like manner, enter **5200** into cells A32–A48 and **4900** into cells A49–A64.
2. To perform the (lower-tailed) hypothesis test, enter the labels *Hypothesized mean, Significance level, Critical z, Sample mean=Point estimate, Population standard deviation, Sample size, Standard error of sample mean,* and *Test statistic* into cells B1-B8.
3. Enter corresponding formulas or known values into adjacent cells in column C; namely

   5000 into C1

   .01 into C2

   =NORMSINV(C2) into C3. (This determines the critical value of z for a lower-tailed test. The resulting value of –2.3263 indicates that the acceptance region stretches from –2.3263 to $+ \infty$.)

   =AVERAGE(A1:A64) into C4

   100 into C5. [If the population standard deviation were not known, one would compute the sample standard deviation as **=STDEV(A1:A64)**.]

   =COUNT(A1:A64) into C6

   =C5/SQRT(C6) into C7

   =(C4−C1)/C7 into C8

   The result:

Hypothesized mean	5000
Significance level	0.01
Critical z	−2.32634193
Sample mean=Point estimate	5025
Population standard deviation	100
Sample size	64
Standard error of sample mean	12.5
Test statistic	2

INTERPRETATION The test statistic is computed as $z = \dfrac{\overline{X} - \mu_0}{\sigma/\sqrt{n}} = \dfrac{5025 - 5000}{100/\sqrt{64}} = 2.00$ (shown in red). At a significance level of $\alpha = .01$, Appendix Table L tells us, the acceptance region for a lower-tailed test lies above -2.3267 (just as in Figure 13.5). Therefore, H_0: $\mu \geq$ 5,000 can be *accepted.* According to the sample, the tensile strength is at least 5,000 lb.

Note: This type of problem can also be solved much more rapidly by using HKStat, Sheet 14.

EXCEL Example 13.3

Create a hypothetical sample of $n = 36$ measurements of minutes of flight time per gallon achieved by putting an additive into aviation fuel. Let the sample contain 18 values of 6 minutes, 9 values of 8 minutes, and 9 values of 5 minutes. Assuming the population standard deviation equals 1 minute, conduct a hypothesis test of H_0: $\mu \leq 6$ minutes and do so at a significance level of $\alpha = .10$.

SOLUTION:

1. Enter **6** into cell A1, select the cell, and use the lower right handle to drag the entry to A18. In like manner, enter **8** into cells A19–A27 and **5** into cells A28–A36.
2. To perform the (upper-tailed) hypothesis test, enter the labels *Hypothesized mean, Significance level, Critical z, Sample mean=Point estimate, Population standard deviation, Sample size, Standard error of sample mean,* and *Test statistic* into cells B1–B8.
3 Enter corresponding formulas or known values into adjacent cells in column C; namely

6 into C1

.10 into C2

=−1*NORMSINV(C2) into C3. (This determines the critical value of z for an upper-tailed test. Thc resulting value of 1.28155 indicates that the acceptance region stretches from $-\infty$ to $+1.28155$.)

=AVERAGE(A1:A36) into C4

1 into C5. [If the population standard deviation were not known, one would compute the sample standard deviation as **=STDEV(A1:A36)**.]

=COUNT(A1:A36) into C6

=C5/SQRT(C6) into C7

=(C4−C1)/C7 into C8

The result:

Hypothesized mean	6
Significance level	0.1
Critical z	1.28155079
Sample mean=Point estimate	6.25
Population standard deviation	1
Sample size	36
Standard error of sample mean	0.16666667
Test statistic	1.5

INTERPRETATION The test statistic is computed as $z = \frac{\overline{X} - \mu_0}{\sigma/\sqrt{n}} = \frac{6.25 - 6}{1/\sqrt{36}} = 1.50$ (shown in red). At a significance level of $\alpha = .10$, Appendix Table L tells us, the acceptance region for an upper-tailed test lies below $+1.2817$. Therefore, H_0: $\mu \leq 6$ must be *rejected.* According to the sample, the flight time with the additive exceeds 6 minutes per gallon.

Note: This type of problem can also be solved much more rapidly by using HKStat, Sheet 15.

TESTS OF A POPULATION PROPORTION

Hypothesis tests concerning a single population proportion are conducted analogously to those about a mean, as the following examples show.

EXAMPLE PROBLEM 13.8

A hospital administrator needs to know whether it is still true that 90 percent of the drug dosages prepared by a machine weigh precisely 100 milligrams. Neither a lower nor a higher percentage is acceptable. A random sample of 200 dosages from among thousands prepared during a week is to be taken to evaluate the claim at a significance level of $\alpha = .05$.

SOLUTION:

Step 1: *Formulating two opposing hypotheses.*

$$H_0: \pi = .9$$
$$H_A: \pi \neq .9$$

Step 2: *Selecting a test statistic.*

$$z = \frac{P - \pi_0}{\sigma_P}$$

Step 3: *Deriving a decision rule.*

According to Appendix Table L, the chosen significance level implies critical values of $\pm z_{\alpha/2} = \pm 1.96$ (this being a two-tailed test). Thus, the decision rule must be:

"Accept H_0 if $-1.96 \leq z \leq +1.96$."

The critical values are encircled in Figure 13.7.

Step 4: *Using sample data to compute the test statistic and confronting it with the decision rule.*

A sample of $n = 200$ indicates that the sample proportion of precise 100-milligram dosages is $P = .85$. Given the large-population case, the value of σ_P is estimated, with the help of the hypothesized value of $\pi_0 = .9$, as

$$\sigma_P = \sqrt{\frac{\pi_0(1 - \pi_0)}{n}} = \sqrt{\frac{.9(.1)}{200}} = .02$$

Accordingly, the computed value of the test statistic equals

$$z = \frac{P - \pi_0}{\sigma_P} = \frac{.85 - .9}{.02} = -2.5$$

This value corresponds to the red arrow in Figure 13.7; it suggests that the null hypothesis should be *rejected.* At the 5 percent significance level, the sample result is statistically significant. The observed divergence between the hypothesized population proportion and the sample proportion is unlikely to be the result of pure chance. Fewer than 90 percent of the dosages are precise. The machine needs to be recalibrated.

FIGURE 13.7 | Testing Drug Dosages

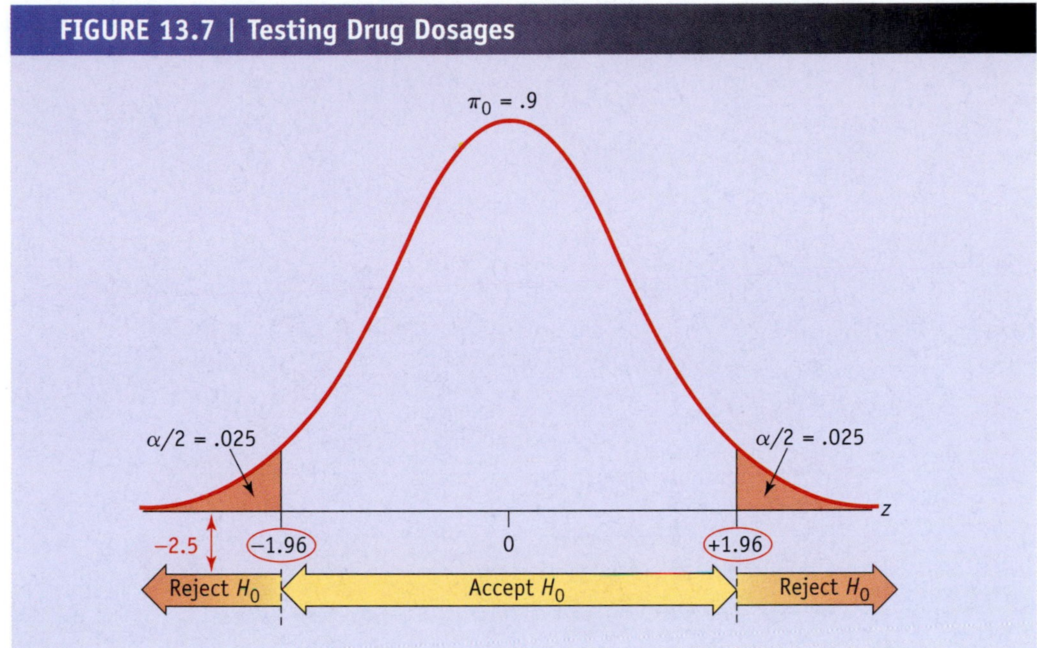

EXAMPLE PROBLEM 13.9

An executive believes that at least 50 percent of shoppers entering a department store recognize the company's brand name, as was true in the past. A random sample of 25 shoppers is to test the claim at a significance level of $\alpha = .005$.

SOLUTION:

Step 1: *Formulating two opposing hypotheses.*

$$H_0: \pi \geq .5$$
$$H_A: \pi < .5$$

Step 2: *Selecting a test statistic.*

The firm's statistician selects the sample proportion, P (which gives us a chance to see what happens when the test statistic is not a z value).

Step 3: *Deriving a decision rule.*

According to Appendix Table L, the chosen significance level implies a critical value of $-z_\alpha = -2.575$ (this being a lower-tailed test). Thus, the decision rule must be:

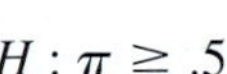

"Accept H_0 if $P \geq \pi_0 - 2.575\sigma_P$."

The value of σ_P is estimated, with the help of the hypothesized value of $\pi_0 = .5$, as

$$\sigma_P = \sqrt{\frac{\pi_0(1 - \pi_0)}{n}} = \sqrt{\frac{.5(.5)}{25}} = .1$$

The implied critical value (rounded) is encircled in Figure 13.8 on the next page.

FIGURE 13.8 | Testing Brand Recognition

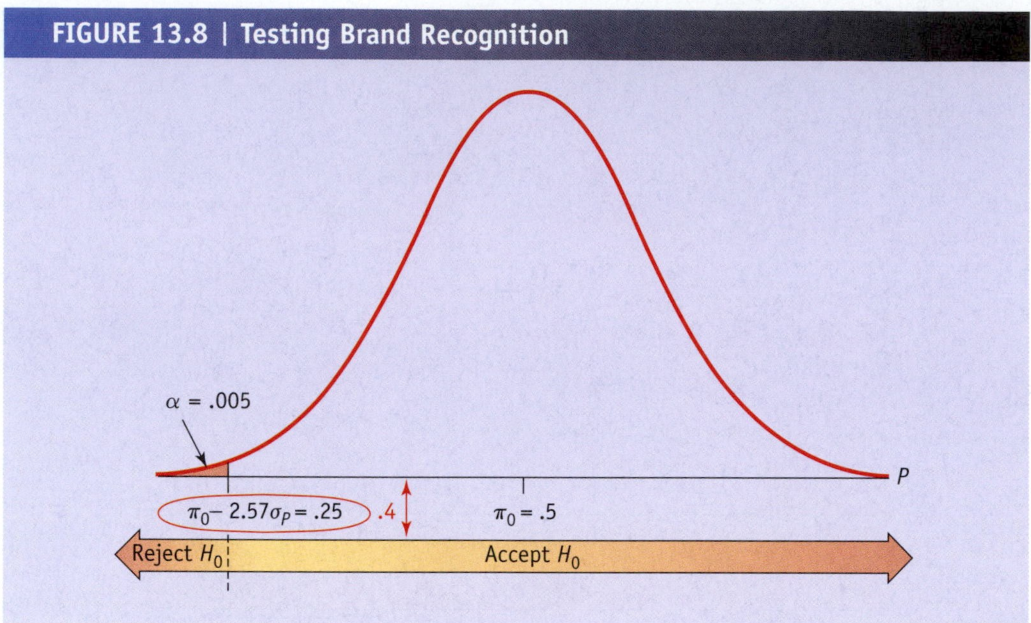

Step 4: *Using sample data to compute the test statistic and confronting it with the decision rule.*

After taking a sample of $n = 25$, it is found that 10 of the 25 shoppers recognize the brand name; thus, $P = .4$. This result suggests that the null hypothesis should be *accepted.* At the .5 percent significance level, the sample result is not statistically significant. It is quite consistent with at least 50 percent of *all* shoppers recognizing the brand name.

EXCEL Example 13.4

Review Example Problem 13.8; confirm its solution with the help of EXCEL.

SOLUTION:

1. To perform the (two-tailed) hypothesis test, enter the labels *Hypothesized proportion, Significance level, Critical z, Sample size, Number of successes in sample, Sample proportion=Point estimate, Standard error of sample proportion,* and *Test statistic* into cells B1–B8.
2. Enter corresponding formulas or known values into adjacent cells in column C; namely

   .90 into C1

   .05 into C2

   = −1*NORMSINV(C2/2) into C3. (This determines the critical value of z for a two-tailed test. The function must be multiplied by -1 to obtain a positive value. The resulting value of 1.96 indicates that the acceptance region stretches from -1.96 to $+1.96$.)

   200 into C4

   170 into C5

   =C5/C4 into C6.

   =SQRT(C1*(1−C1)/C4) into C7

   =(C6−C1)/C7 into C8

The result:

Hypothesized proportion	0.9
Significance level	0.05
Critical z	1.96
Sample size	200
Number of successes in sample	170
Sample proportion=Point estimate	0.85
Standard error of sample proportion	0.0212
Test statistic	−2.357

Notice the z value of -2.357. It differs from the Example Problem 13.8 result of $z = -2.5$ only as a result of rounding. (The precise value of σ_p, used by EXCEL, is actually .0212132 rather than the .02 used earlier.) Thus EXCEL confirms the conclusion reached in Example Problem 13.8.

Note: This type of problem can also be solved much more rapidly by using HKStat, Sheet 19.

TESTS OF THE DIFFERENCE BETWEEN TWO POPULATION MEANS: INDEPENDENT SAMPLES

We first consider hypothesis tests of the difference between means, while employing two *independent samples* such that the elements making up the sample taken from population A are chosen independently of the elements making up the sample taken from population B.

EXAMPLE PROBLEM 13.10

An airline executive wants to test a supplier's claim that the mean lifetimes of two types of aircraft radios are identical. The airline installs 800 radios of each type in its current fleet and later selects two simple random samples of 36 radios of each type. The company statistician is to make the comparison test at the $\alpha = .10$ significance level.

SOLUTION:

Step 1: *Formulating two opposing hypotheses.*

$$H_0: \mu_A - \mu_B = 0$$
$$H_A: \mu_A - \mu_B \neq 0$$

Step 2: *Selecting a test statistic.*

$$z = \frac{d}{\sigma_d} = \frac{\bar{X}_A - \bar{X}_B}{\sigma_{\bar{X}_A - \bar{X}_B}}$$

Step 3: *Deriving a decision rule.*

According to Appendix Table L, the chosen significance level implies critical values of $\pm z_{\alpha/2} = \pm 1.645$ (this being a two-tailed test because we are equally interested

FIGURE 13.9 | Testing Lifetimes of Aircraft Radios

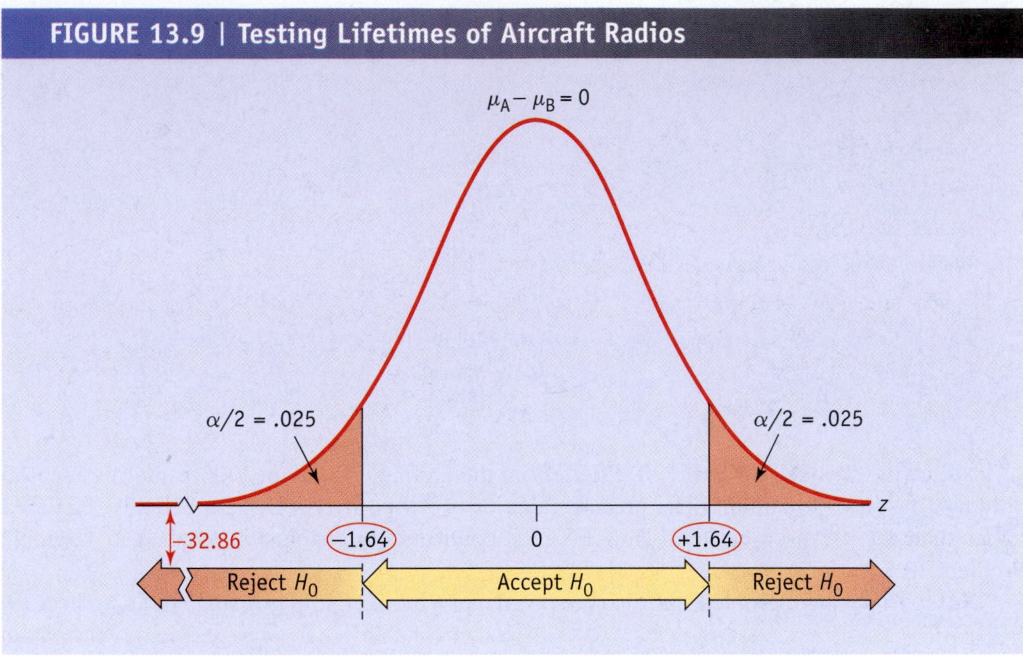

to learn whether the lifetime of one radio type is shorter or longer than that of the other). Thus, the decision rule must be:

$$\text{“Accept } H_0 \text{ if } -1.645 \leq z \leq +1.645.\text{”}$$

The critical values (rounded) are encircled in Figure 13.9 above.

Step 4: *Using sample data to compute the test statistic and confronting it with the decision rule.*

After taking two samples of $n = 36$ each, the statistician finds mean lifetimes and sample standard deviations of $\bar{X}_A = 4{,}120$ hours, $s_A = 80$ hours and $\bar{X}_B = 4{,}910$ hours, $s_B = 120$ hours. The large-population case applies ($n \leq .05N$); σ_d is *estimated* as

$$\sigma_d \cong \sqrt{\frac{s_A^2}{n_A} + \frac{s_B^2}{n_B}} = \sqrt{\frac{80^2}{36} + \frac{120^2}{36}} = 24.04$$

Accordingly, the computed value of the test statistic equals

$$z = \frac{d}{\sigma_d} = \frac{4{,}120 - 4{,}910}{24.04} = -32.86$$

This value corresponds to the red arrow in Figure 13.9; it suggests that the null hypothesis should be *rejected.* At the 10 percent significance level, the sample result is statistically significant. It is very likely that radio B lasts longer than radio A.

EXAMPLE PROBLEM 13.11

An orchardist wants to test a chemical company's claim that the mean yield of fruit trees that are sprayed with gypsy-moth parasites (A), is at most equal to that of fruit trees sprayed with traditional pesticides (B). Some 250 trees are sampled in each of two large orchards that were given one treatment or the other. A test at a significance level of $\alpha = .005$ is desired.

SOLUTION:

Step 1: *Formulating two opposing hypotheses.*

$$H_0: \mu_A - \mu_B \leq 0$$
$$H_A: \mu_A - \mu_B > 0$$

Step 2: *Selecting a test statistic.*

$$z = \frac{d}{\sigma_d} = \frac{\bar{X}_A - \bar{X}_B}{\sigma_{\bar{X}_A - \bar{X}_B}}$$

Step 3: *Deriving a decision rule.*

According to Appendix Table L, the chosen significance level implies a critical value of $+z_\alpha = +2.575$ (this being an upper-tailed test). Thus, the decision rule must be:

"Accept H_0 if $z \leq +2.575$."

The critical value (rounded) is encircled in Figure 13.10.

Step 4: *Using sample data to compute the test statistic and confronting it with the decision rule.*

After taking two samples of $n = 250$ each, the orchardist finds mean fruit yields and sample standard deviations of $\bar{X}_A = 10.5$ bushels, $s_A = 8$ bushels and $\bar{X}_B = 8.9$ bushels, $s_A = 3$ bushels. The large-population case applies ($n \leq .05N$); σ_d is *estimated* as

$$\sigma_d \cong \sqrt{\frac{s_A^2}{n_A} + \frac{s_B^2}{n_B}} = \sqrt{\frac{8^2}{250} + \frac{3^2}{250}} = .54$$

FIGURE 13.10 | Testing Fruit Tree Sprays

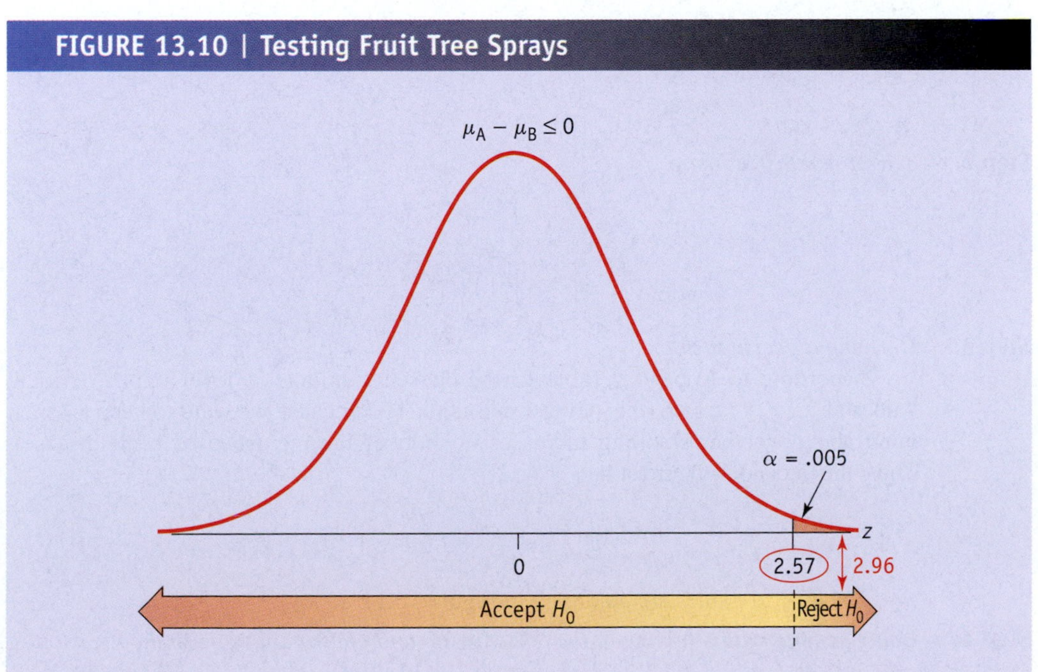

Accordingly, the computed value of the test statistic equals

$$z = \frac{d}{\sigma_d} = \frac{10.5 - 8.9}{.54} = 2.96$$

This value corresponds to the red arrow in Figure 13.10; it suggests that the null hypothesis should be *rejected.* At the .5 percent significance level, the sample result is statistically significant. Parasites are *more* effective than pesticides.

TESTS OF THE DIFFERENCE BETWEEN TWO POPULATION MEANS: MATCHED-PAIRS SAMPLES

We now turn to hypothesis tests of the difference between means, while employing *matched-pairs samples,* taken after each elementary unit in population A has been matched with a "twin" from population B.

EXAMPLE PROBLEM 13.12

The Food and Drug Administration wants to test a tobacco company's claim that there is no connection between smoking and heart disease because the mean age at which heart disease is first detected is the same for smokers (A) and nonsmokers (B). Some 100 smokers are matched with 100 nonsmokers according to age, lifestyle, medical history, occupation, sex, and so on. A two-tailed test at the $\alpha = .05$ significance level is desired.

SOLUTION:

Step 1: *Formulating two opposing hypotheses.*

$$H_0: \mu_A - \mu_B = 0$$
$$H_A: \mu_A - \mu_B \neq 0$$

Step 2: *Selecting a test statistic.*

$$z = \frac{\overline{D}}{s_D/\sqrt{n}}$$

Step 3: *Deriving a decision rule.*

According to Appendix Table L, the chosen significance level implies critical values of $\pm z_{\alpha/2} = \pm 1.96$ (this being a two-tailed test because we want to keep an open mind about whether smoking increases or reduces the incidence of heart disease). Thus, the decision rule must be:

"Accept H_0 if $-1.96 \leq z \leq +1.96$."

The critical values are encircled in Figure 13.11.

Step 4: *Using sample data to compute the test statistic and confronting it with the decision rule.*

FIGURE 13.11 | Testing Smoking and Heart Disease

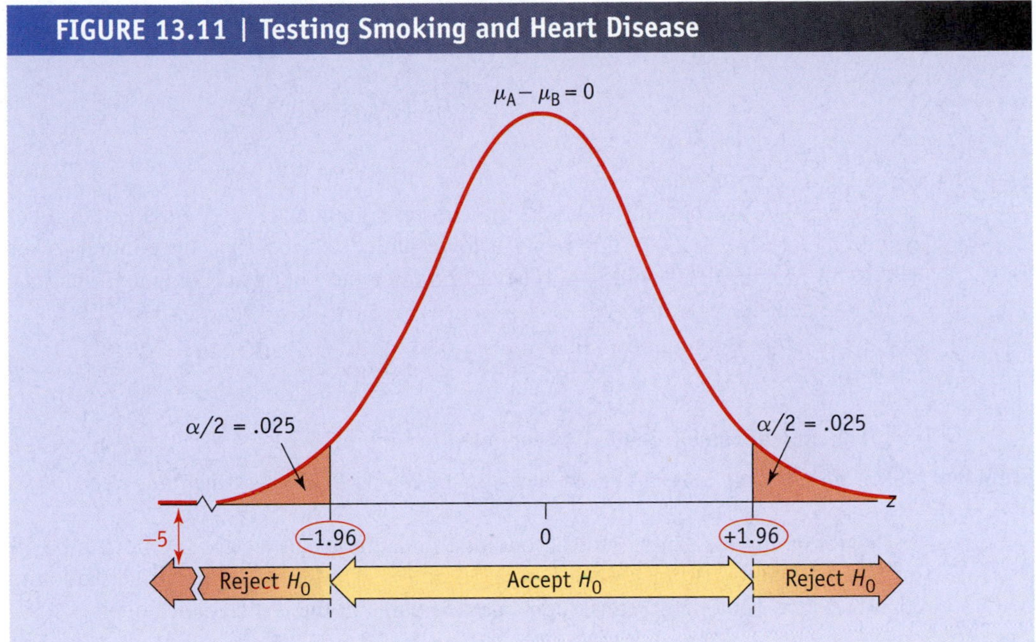

After taking the sample, the researcher finds the mean age of the onset of heart disease to be 6 years earlier for smokers than for their "twin" nonsmokers; thus, $\overline{D} = -6$ years. The sample standard deviation is found as $s_D = 12$ years. Thus, the computed value of the test statistic equals

$$z = \frac{\overline{D}}{s_D/\sqrt{n}} = \frac{-6}{12/\sqrt{100}} = -5$$

This value corresponds to the red arrow in Figure 13.11; it suggests that the null hypothesis should be *rejected.* At the 5 percent significance level, the sample result is statistically significant. Because the test statistic is negative, we conclude, furthermore, that smoking *hastens* the onset of heart disease. (If z had been in the right-hand rejection region, it would have indicated that smoking *delays* the onset of heart disease.)

EXAMPLE PROBLEM 13.13

An agronomist who has matched adjacent plots of land is growing strawberries on 49 such pairs, always using nitrate-based fertilizer (A) on one "twin" and phosphate-based fertilizer (B) on the other. The agronomist wants to determine whether yields on the nitrate plots, as claimed in a chemical company's advertising, exceed yields on the phosphate plots. A test at the $\alpha = .1$ level of significance is desired.

SOLUTION:

Step 1: *Formulating two opposing hypotheses.*

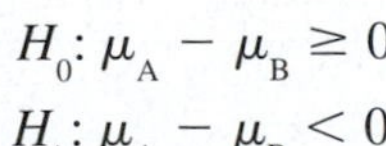

$$H_0: \mu_A - \mu_B \geq 0$$
$$H_A: \mu_A - \mu_B < 0$$

Step 2: *Selecting a test statistic.*

$$z = \frac{\overline{D}}{s_D / \sqrt{n}}$$

Step 3: *Deriving a decision rule.*

According to Appendix Table L, the chosen significance level implies a critical value of $-z_\alpha = -1.2817$ (this being a lower-tailed test because only much lower yields on nitrate plots would seriously contradict the chemical company's claim). Thus, the decision rule must be:

"Accept H_0 if $z \geq -1.2817$."

The critical value (rounded) is encircled in Figure 13.12.

Step 4: *Using sample data to compute the test statistic and confronting it with the decision rule.*

After taking the sample, the agronomist finds the mean yield on A plots to be 50 quarts less than on B plots; thus, $\overline{D} = -50$ quarts. The sample standard deviation is found as $s_D = 140$ quarts. Thus, the computed value of the test statistic equals

$$z = \frac{\overline{D}}{s_D / \sqrt{n}} = \frac{-50}{140/\sqrt{49}} = -2.5$$

This value corresponds to the red arrow in Figure 13.12. It suggests that the null hypothesis should be *rejected.* At the 10 percent significance level, the sample result is statistically significant. Phosphates, not nitrates, produce a greater strawberry yield.

FIGURE 13.12 | Testing Nitrates versus Phosphates

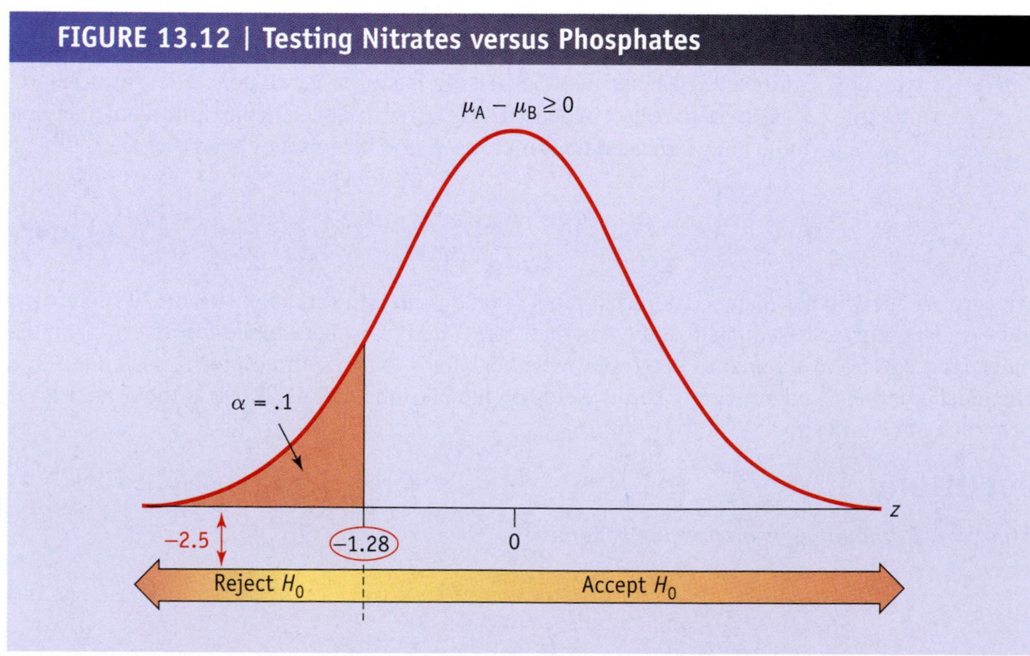

TESTS OF THE DIFFERENCE BETWEEN TWO POPULATION PROPORTIONS

Finally, we consider large-sample hypothesis tests of the difference between two population proportions.

EXAMPLE PROBLEM 13.14

The manager of a television station wants to know whether there is any difference in the proportion of men (A) or women (B) who favor a given program over another during a certain time slot. Two simple random samples of 100 each are to be taken from among the city's adult population. A test at the $\alpha = .05$ significance level is desired.

SOLUTION:

Step 1: *Formulating two opposing hypotheses.*

$$H_0: \pi_A - \pi_B = 0$$
$$H_A: \pi_A - \pi_B \neq 0$$

Step 2: *Selecting a test statistic.*

$$z = \frac{d}{\sigma_d} = \frac{P_A - P_B}{\sigma_{P_A - P_B}}$$

Step 3: *Deriving a decision rule.*

According to Appendix Table L, the chosen significance level implies critical values of $\pm z_{\alpha/2} = \pm 1.96$ (this being a two-tailed test because the manager has no initial reason to believe that the difference is positive or negative). Thus, the decision rule must be:

"Accept H_0 if $-1.96 \leq z \leq +1.96$."

The critical values are encircled in Figure 13.13 on the next page.

Step 4: *Using sample data to compute the test statistic and confronting it with the decision rule.*

After taking two samples of $n = 100$ each, the statistician finds $P_A = .6$ and $P_B = .7$ and then calculates a **pooled estimator of the population proportion** as

$$P_P = \frac{n_A P_A + n_B P_B}{n_A + n_B} = \frac{100(.6) + 100(.7)}{200} = .65$$

Accordingly, σ_d is *estimated* as

$$\sigma_d \cong \sqrt{P_P(1 - P_P)\left(\frac{1}{n_A} + \frac{1}{n_B}\right)} = \sqrt{.65(.35)\left(\frac{1}{100} + \frac{1}{100}\right)} = .0675$$

and the value of the test statistic equals

$$z = \frac{d}{\sigma_d} = \frac{.6 - .7}{.0675} = -1.48$$

FIGURE 13.13 | Testing Sex and TV Preferences

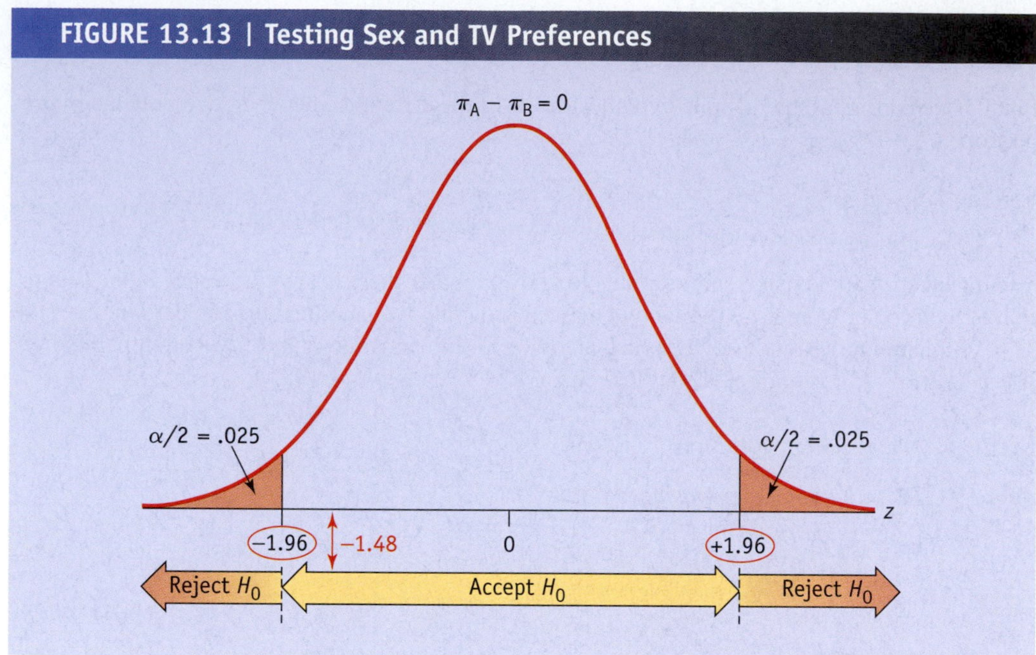

This value corresponds to the red arrow in Figure 13.13. It suggests that the null hypothesis should be *accepted.* At the 5 percent significance level, the sample result is not statistically significant. It is quite likely that the relevant proportions of men and women are the same.

EXCEL Example 13.5

Review Example Problem 13.14; confirm its solution with the help of EXCEL.

SOLUTION:

1. To perform the (two-tailed) hypothesis test, enter the labels *Hypothesized proportion difference, Significance level, Critical z, Sample A, Size, Number of successes, Proportion, Sample B, Size, Number of successes, Proportion, Sample proportion difference=Point estimate, Combined samples proportion, Pooled standard error of sample proportion difference,* and *Test statistic* into cells B1–B15.
2. Enter corresponding formulas or known values into adjacent cells in column C; namely

   0 into C1

   .05 into C2

   = −1*NORMSINV(C2/2) into C3. (This determines the critical value of z for a two-tailed test. The function must be multiplied by −1 to obtain a positive value. The resulting value of 1.96 indicates that the acceptance region stretches from −1.96 to +1.96.)

   100 into C5

   60 into C6

   =C6/C5 into C7

   100 into C9

   70 into C10

   =C10/C9 into C11

=C7−C11 into C12

=(C6+C10)/(C5+C9) into C13

=SQRT(C13*(1−C13)*(1/C5+1/C9)) into C14

=(C12−C1)/C14 into C15

The result:

Hypothesized proportion difference	0
Significance level	0.05
Critical z	1.95996
Sample A	
Size	100
Number of successes	60
Proportion	0.6
Sample B	
Size	100
Number of successes	70
Proportion	0.7
Sample proportion difference=Point estimate	−0.1
Combined samples proportion	0.65
Pooled standard error of sample proportion difference	0.06745
Test statistic	−1.4825

Notice the z value of −1.48. It corresponds to the Example Problem 13.14 result. Thus EXCEL confirms the conclusion reached.

Note: This type of problem can also be solved much more rapidly by using HKStat, Sheet 31.

APPLICATION 13.1

ANTITRUST PORK BARREL

Here is a story that provides an interesting application of hypothesis tests about differences in proportions. Many critics have long asserted that federal regulatory agencies are significantly impaired in their tasks by their dependence on Congress. This impairment is said to occur because each member of Congress inevitably seeks to further the provincial interests of citizens in the home district, whose welfare may depend disproportionately on a few key industries. When those industries are threatened in any way by regulatory agencies, members of Congress who have power over these agencies will naturally deflect the agencies' actions. A group of researchers decided to test whether the case-bringing activity of the Federal Trade Commission (FTC) during the 1961–1979 period was biased in favor of firms that operated in the districts of members of those congressional committees (three in the Senate and five in the House) that had important budgetary and oversight powers with respect to the FTC.

Although the FTC can initiate antitrust investigations on its own, almost 90 percent of its investigations are begun as a result of cases brought to it by the public. Ultimately, these investigations lead to a consent decree (by which the accused party promises to reform) or to a formal complaint. The latter, in turn, leads to dismissal for insufficient evidence of a violation or to a cease-and-desist order. The investigators formulated the null hypothesis that there was a zero difference between (1) the proportion of dismissals to cases brought affecting districts with representatives on FTC-relevant committees (π_A) and (2) this proportion in districts without such representatives (π_B). Accordingly, the alternative hypothesis supported the pork-barrel thesis:

$$H_0: \pi_A - \pi_B = 0$$

$$H_A: \pi_A - \pi_B \neq 0$$

(continued)

Application 13.1 (continued)

Using

$$z = \frac{d}{\sigma_d} = \frac{P_A - P_B}{\sigma_{P_A - P_B}}$$

as a test statistic and choosing the 10 percent significance level, the critical values for accepting H_0 were $\pm z_{\alpha/2} = \pm z_{.05} = \pm 1.645$. Selected sample results and computed values of z are shown in Table 13.A.

There was no reason to reject the null hypothesis in cases 1 and 2, but plenty of reason to do so for cases 3–5 because of statistically significant z values.

After reviewing similar data for the 1970–1979 period (as well as for the ratio of dismissals to *formal complaints*), the investigators concluded that there was considerable support for the thesis that members of certain congressional committees that have important oversight and budgetary powers with respect to the FTC do deflect commission decisions in favor of firms in their home districts.

SOURCE: Adapted from Roger L. Faith, Donald R. Leavens, Robert D. Tollison, "Antitrust Pork Barrel," *Journal of Law and Economics*, October 1982, pp. 329–342. Table copyright © 1982 by the University of Chicago. All rights reserved. Reprinted by permission of the University of Chicago Press.

TABLE 13.A | Ratio of Dismissals to Cases Brought (1961–1969)

Congressional Committee	Within Committee Members' Districts P_A	Outside Committee Members' Districts P_B	z value
1. Senate Committee on Interior and Insular Affairs	$\frac{17}{285} = .0596$	$\frac{148}{2{,}190} = .0675$	−.50
2. Senate Committee on Commerce, Science, and Transportation	$\frac{32}{570} = .0561$	$\frac{133}{1{,}905} = .0698$	−1.14
3. Senate Subcommittee on Antitrust and Monopoly of the Senate Judiciary Committee	$\frac{60}{638} = .0940$	$\frac{105}{1{,}837} = .0572$	3.22
4. House Subcommittee on Independent Offices of the House Appropriations Committee	$\frac{14}{87} = .1609$	$\frac{151}{2{,}388} = .0632$	3.59
5. All Five Relevant House Subcommittees as a Group	$\frac{84}{1{,}104} = .0761$	$\frac{81}{1{,}371} = .0591$	1.69

13.8 Using *p* Values: A Famous Controversy

Although certain ideas about hypothesis testing have a long history, the construction of formal hypothesis tests is a 20th-century innovation. It comes to us from three famous statisticians: Ronald A. Fisher (1890–1962), Jerzy Neyman (1894–1981), and Egon S. Pearson (1895–1980). While Neyman and Pearson developed and advocated the careful four-step procedure outlined in the previous sections, Fisher had other ideas, and the three carried on a bitter lifelong controversy over the matter.

Fisher introduced the concept of *p values,* which are nowadays routinely computed by most statistical software programs and enable us to make an alternative assessment of hypothesis test results. We introduce the concept here and explain it in the remainder of this section.

DEFINITION 13.6 In hypothesis testing, a ***p* value** or **observed significance level** is the probability that a test statistic as contradictory to the null hypothesis as that computed from the sample data, or an even more contradictory value, could have occurred by chance if the hypothesized parameter value was true. Therefore, given a test's actual significance level, α, which measures the arbitrarily chosen maximum proportion of all possible sample results that is considered sufficiently unusual to reject the null hypothesis,

p value $> \alpha$ means accepting H_0
p value $\leq \alpha$ means rejecting H_0

NEYMAN/PEARSON VERSUS FISHER

Neyman and Pearson viewed hypothesis testing as a procedure by which a *decision maker,* such as a business manager operating under uncertainty, could *make a clear choice* between two alternatives. Fisher viewed hypothesis testing as a procedure by which a *researcher,* such as a university professor, could *form an opinion* about some population parameter. Rejecting the practice of setting up a decision rule ahead of time, Fisher suggested five hypothesis-testing steps:

1. Hypothesizing the value of some parameter (*not* setting up two alternative hypotheses)
2. Selecting a test statistic (such as z or t) the distribution of which was completely known if the hypothesized parameter value was true (by selecting a sufficiently large sample, for example, researchers would know that the sampling distribution was normally distributed; they would also know that it was centered on the hypothesized parameter when the latter was in fact true)
3. Taking a random sample from the population of interest and computing the value of the test statistic
4. Calculating the probability, also called the *p value* or the *observed significance level,* that a test statistic as extreme as, or even more extreme than, the computed value could have occurred by chance if the hypothesized parameter was true
5. Reporting the p value and letting readers make up their own minds about the truth or falsity of the hypothesized parameter value

CALCULATING *p* VALUES

The computation of p values, as defined in Definition 13.6, is fairly straightforward when the test statistic involves a normal curve. Two steps are involved:

- We express the test statistic as a z value.
- We find the p value as the area under the normal curve between the value of z computed from the sample and either (a) the lower tail for a lower-tailed test, (b) the upper tail for an upper-tailed test, or (c) the nearest tail, multiplied by 2, for a two-tailed test.

***p* VALUE IN LOWER-TAILED TEST** Figure 13.14 on the next page illustrates the computation of a p value for a lower-tailed test that was conducted at a significance level of $\alpha = .05$ and produced a test statistic of $z = -.82$. The red normal curve represents the sampling distribution of the test statistic, z, on the assumption that the null hypothesis is true (and the value specified in the null hypothesis is represented by the center of this distribution). The crosshatched area is relevant for the Neyman/Pearson approach. It represents the (arbitrarily chosen) maximum probability, α, of making the type I error of erroneously rejecting a null hypothesis that is true. The combined crosshatched plus shaded area is relevant for the Fisher approach; it represents the p value. Given that the area between the mean and a z value of $-.82$ covers .2939 of the area under the normal curve, the p value equals $.5 - .2939 = .2061$. It indicates a 20.61 percent chance of

FIGURE 13.14 | p Value and Lower-Tailed Test (H_0: $z \geq 0$)

The Neyman/Pearson approach focuses on the significance level, α, and the associated rejection and acceptance regions. The Fisher approach ignores all of these and simply looks at the p value. On the assumption that the null hypothesis is true, this p value measures the probability, here equal to .2061, of getting a test statistic as contradictory to the null hypothesis as, or even more contradictory than, the statistic actually computed from the sample data. For a believer in H_0, a large p value signals "no surprise" and acceptance of H_0. However, the smaller the p value, the greater the surprise and the more the sample data point to the rejection of H_0 and the acceptance of H_A.

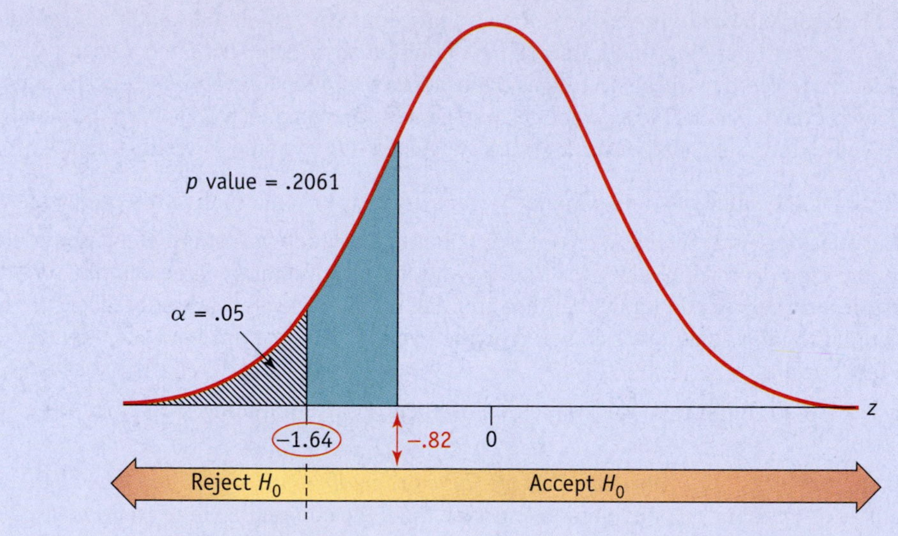

computing a test statistic as contradictory to the null hypothesis as ours, or of computing an even more contradictory one, when the null hypothesis is true. For a believer in H_0, such a large p value signals "no surprise" and acceptance of H_0.

***p* VALUE IN TWO-TAILED TEST** Figure 13.15 illustrates the computation of a p value for a two-tailed test that was conducted at a significance level of $\alpha = .05$ and produced a test statistic of $z = -.92$. In this example, $\alpha = .05$ is split between the two tails. Similarly, the p value is split. Thus, if the observed test statistic is $z = -.92$, the crosshatched plus shaded areas on the left (equal to $.5 - .3212 = .1788$) represent only half the p value. Combined with a similar area on the right, the p value equals .3576. Thus, it indicates a 35.76 percent chance of computing a test statistic as contradictory to the null hypothesis as ours, or of computing an even more contradictory one, when the null hypothesis is true. Once again, such a large p value is almost certain to cause an observer to accept the null hypothesis.

EXAMPLE PROBLEM 13.15

Review Example Problems 13.5 to 13.7, then compute Fisher's p value for each.

SOLUTION:

Example Problem 13.5

Given a test statistic of $z = -1.00$, we can use Appendix Table H and figure the area under the normal curve to the left of $z = -1.00$ as $.5000 - .3413 = .1587$. Because this is a two-tailed test,

FIGURE 13.15 | p Value and Two-Tailed Test (H_0: $z = 0$)

The Neyman/Pearson approach focuses on the significance level, α, and the associated rejection and acceptance regions. The Fisher approach ignores all of these and simply looks at the p value. In a two-tailed test, the p value is found as the area under the normal curve between the value of z computed from the sample and the nearest tail of the test statistic's sampling distribution, multiplied by 2. Thus, it equals .3576 in this example.

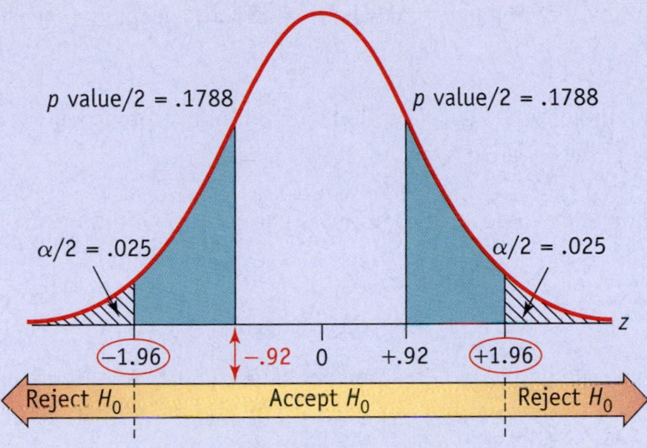

this number is doubled for a similar area to the right of $z = +1.00$; hence, the p value is 2(.1587) = .3174.

Example Problem 13.6

Given a test statistic of $z = -3.00$, we can use Appendix Table H and figure the area under the normal curve to the left of $z = -3.00$ as .5000 − .4986 = .0014. Because this is a lower-tailed test, this is the p value.

Example Problem 13.7

We must turn the test statistic of $\overline{X} = 6.2$ into a z value:

$$z = \frac{\overline{X} - \mu_0}{\sigma_{\overline{X}}} = \frac{6.2 - 6}{.0804} = 2.49$$

Then we can use Appendix Table H and figure the area under the normal curve to the right of $z = 2.49$ as .5000 − .4936 = .0064. Because this is an upper-tailed test, this is the p value.

FORMING AN OPINION

Although Fisher strongly resisted the formulation of a decision rule prior to sampling, he did *suggest* the following arbitrary cutoff points when judging the plausibility of a hypothesized parameter value on the basis of p values:

a. If a p value was $<.01$, a person would render a strong judgment against the hypothesized parameter value.

b. If $.01 \leq p$ value $\leq .05$, a person would render a weak judgment against the hypothesized parameter value.

c. If a p value was $>.05$, the person would judge in favor of the hypothesized parameter value.

EXAMPLE PROBLEM 13.16

In light of the p values computed in Example Problem 13.15, how would Fisher conclude the three hypothesis tests?

SOLUTION:

Example Problem 13.5

The hypothesized parameter value (μ = .01 inch) would be accepted as reasonable.

Example Problem 13.6

The hypothesized parameter value (μ = 5,000 lb.) would be strongly rejected.

Example Problem 13.7

The hypothesized parameter value (μ = 6 minutes per gallon) would be strongly rejected.

RECONCILING THE NEYMAN/PEARSON AND FISHER APPROACHES

You will notice that anyone who chooses a personal significance level, α, such as .05 or .01, will come to the same conclusion, regardless of whether the Neyman/Pearson or Fisher approach is used. Any test statistic that falls in the acceptance region, such as $z = -1$ in Example Problem 13.5, will also have a p value (greater than α) that leads to the acceptance of H_0 if Fisher's guidelines are used. On the other hand, any test statistic that falls in the rejection region, such as $z = -3.00$ in Example Problem 13.6, will have a p value (smaller than α) that leads to a rejection of H_0 if Fisher's guidelines are used.

$$p \text{ value} > \alpha \text{ means accepting } H_0$$

$$p \text{ value} \leq \alpha \text{ means rejecting } H_0$$

Neyman and Pearson, nevertheless, rejected the Fisher approach because they feared that unscrupulous researchers who did *not* set up a clear decision rule prior to sampling would be tempted afterward to choose an α level that would cater to their personal preferences. If their sample led to a p value of .09, for example, and they had a personal interest in maintaining the null hypothesis, they might simply set α at .05 and claim confirmation of H_0. Given the same sample result of p value = .09, if they had a personal interest in defeating the null hypothesis, they might then choose α = .10 and claim that H_0 had been shown to be untenable. Still, modern computer programs pretty much ignore the controversy and routinely calculate p values, along with their test statistics.

13.9 Small-Sample Hypothesis Tests

We now turn to cases where samples are small ($n < 30$), but the test statistic's sampling distribution can be approximated by a t distribution. Such approximation is possible when the underlying population values are normally distributed, and, when two populations are involved, their standard deviations, though unknown, are known to be equal. The following examples omit the graphical illustrations because graphs would be analogous to those given in the large-sample section above, except that t distributions for specified degrees of freedom would replace the normal curves.

TESTS OF A POPULATION MEAN

We first consider two tests concerning a single population mean.

EXAMPLE PROBLEM 13.17

An executive of a new telephone company wants to know whether the average length of evening long-distance telephone calls in a metropolitan area still equals 18.1 minutes, as it did in the past. A simple random sample of 25 evening calls is to be used to find the answer at a significance level of $\alpha = .05$.

SOLUTION:

Step 1: *Formulating two opposing hypotheses.*

$$H_0: \mu = 18.1 \text{ minutes}$$
$$H_A: \mu \neq 18.1 \text{ minutes}$$

Step 2: *Selecting a test statistic.*

Assuming that the population of telephone-call durations is normally distributed and that the large-population case applies ($n < .05N$) because of the large number of calls made, the company statistician selects

$$t = \frac{\bar{X} - \mu_0}{\sigma_{\bar{X}}} \cong \frac{\bar{X} - \mu_0}{s/\sqrt{n}}$$

Step 3: *Deriving a decision rule.*

According to Appendix Table K, the chosen significance level implies critical values of $\pm t_{\alpha/2} = \pm t_{.025(24)} = \pm 2.064$ (this being a two-tailed test and there being $n - 1 = 24$ degrees of freedom). Thus, the decision rule must be:

"Accept H_0 if $-2.064 \leq t \leq +2.064$."

Step 4: *Using sample data to compute the test statistic and confronting it with the decision rule.*

After taking a sample of $n = 25$, the statistician finds a sample mean duration of calls of $\bar{X} = 17.2$ minutes and a sample standard deviation of $s = 4$ minutes.

Accordingly, the computed value of the test statistic equals

$$t \cong \frac{\bar{X} - \mu_0}{s/\sqrt{n}} = \frac{17.2 - 18.1}{4/\sqrt{25}} = -1.125$$

This value suggests that the null hypothesis should be *accepted.* At the 5 percent significance level, the sample result (a somewhat shorter duration of calls than noted in the past) is not statistically significant. The observed divergence is likely due to chance factors at work during the sampling process.

EXAMPLE PROBLEM 13.18

A government agency has received a consumer complaint that boxes allegedly containing 15 ounces of raisins actually contain less. A simple random sample of 10 such boxes is to be selected from various stores to clarify the issue at a significance level of $\alpha = .01$.

SOLUTION:

Step 1: *Formulating two opposing hypotheses.*

$$H_0: \mu \geq 15 \text{ ounces}$$
$$H_A: \mu < 15 \text{ ounces}$$

Step 2: *Selecting a test statistic.*

Assuming that the population of net weights is normally distributed and that the large-population case applies ($n < .05N$) because of the large number of boxes being marketed, the government statistician selects

$$t = \frac{\bar{X} - \mu_0}{\sigma_{\bar{X}}} \cong \frac{\bar{X} - \mu_0}{s/\sqrt{n}}$$

Step 3: *Deriving a decision rule.*

According to Appendix Table K, the chosen significance level implies critical values of $-t_\alpha = -t_{.01(9)} = -2.821$ (this being a lower-tailed test and there being $n - 1 = 9$ degrees of freedom). Thus, the decision rule must be:

"Accept H_0 if $t \geq -2.821$."

Step 4: *Using sample data to compute the test statistic and confronting it with the decision rule.*

After taking a sample of $n = 10$, the statistician finds a sample mean net weight of $\bar{X} = 13.5$ ounces and a sample standard deviation of $s = 1$ ounce.

Accordingly, the computed value of the test statistic equals

$$t \cong \frac{\bar{X} - \mu_0}{s/\sqrt{n}} = \frac{13.5 - 15}{1/\sqrt{10}} = -4.74$$

This value suggests that the null hypothesis should be *rejected.* At the 1 percent significance level, the sample result is statistically significant. The observed divergence of the mean sample net weight from the advertised weight is unlikely to be the result of chance factors operating in the sampling process. It is more likely due to the fact that the population of raisin boxes being marketed has a mean net weight below 15 ounces, as the alternative hypothesis claims.

EXCEL Example 13.6

The Automobile Manufacturers Association is advertising that consumer satisfaction with new cars is at an all-time high, with an average customer satisfaction index at 91 out of a possible

100. A government economist doubts the claim and collects the following index scores after interviewing a simple random sample of customers:

86, 86, 86, 85, 83, 83, 82, 82, 81, 81, 80, 80, 79, 79, 78, 77, 77, 76, 76, 75, 68, 98, 95, 99

Using EXCEL, conduct an appropriate hypothesis test at a significance level of $\alpha = .01$.

SOLUTION:

1. Enter the data into cells A2–A25 of a new worksheet (or copy column G of the file HKMISC and paste it into a new column A).
2. To perform the (lower-tailed) hypothesis test, enter the labels *Hypothesized mean, Significance level, Sample mean=Point estimate, Sample standard deviation, Sample size, Degrees of freedom, Critical t, Standard error of sample mean,* and *Test statistic* into cells B1–B9.
3. Enter corresponding formulas or known values into adjacent cells in column C; namely

   91 into C1

   .01 into C2

   =AVERAGE(A2:A25) into C3

   =STDEV(A2:A25) into C4

   =COUNT(A2:A25) into C5

   =C5−1 into C6

   = −1*TINV(2*C2,C6) into C7.

   =C4/SQRT(C5) into C8

   =(C3−C1)/C8 into C9

   The result:

Hypothesized mean	91
Significance level	0.01
Sample mean=Point estimate	82.167
Sample standard deviation	7.1728
Sample size	24
Degrees of freedom	23
Critical t	−2.4999
Standard error of sample mean	1.4641
Test statistic	−6.0331

INTERPRETATION The test statistic is computed as $t = \frac{\bar{X} - \mu_0}{s/\sqrt{n}} = \frac{82.17 - 91}{7.17/\sqrt{24}} = -6.03$ (shown in red). At a significance level of $\alpha = .01$, and with 23 degrees of freedom, Appendix Table K tells us, the acceptance region for a lower-tailed test lies above −2.5. Therefore, H_0: $\mu \geq 91$ must be *rejected.* According to the sample, the satisfaction score is lower.

Note: This type of problem can also be solved much more rapidly by using HKStat, Sheet 17.

TESTS OF THE DIFFERENCE BETWEEN TWO POPULATION MEANS: INDEPENDENT SAMPLES

We now consider small-sample hypothesis tests concerning two means that involve independent samples.

EXAMPLE PROBLEM 13.19

The American Dental Association wants to determine whether there is a difference in the cavity-fighting ability of two toothpastes, A and B. A simple random sample of 21 users of each type is taken, and the mean number of cavities over a decade is counted. A test at the $\alpha = .01$ significance level is desired.

SOLUTION:

Step 1: *Formulating two opposing hypotheses.*

$$H_0\colon \mu_A - \mu_B = 0$$
$$H_A\colon \mu_A - \mu_B \neq 0$$

Step 2: *Selecting a test statistic.*

Assuming that the two populations of cavity numbers are normally distributed and that the two population variances are equal, the statistician selects

$$t = \frac{d}{\sigma_d} = \frac{\bar{X}_A - \bar{X}_B}{\sigma_{\bar{X}_A - \bar{X}_B}} \cong \frac{\bar{X}_A - \bar{X}_B}{\sqrt{s_p^2\left(\frac{1}{n_A} + \frac{1}{n_B}\right)}}$$

where

$$s_p^2 = \frac{(n_A - 1)s_A^2 + (n_B - 1)s_B^2}{n_A + n_B - 2}$$

which is the best available estimate of the identical but unknown population variances. As we can see, this **pooled variance** is a weighted average of the two sample variances, where the weights equal the degrees of freedom associated with each sample.

Step 3: *Deriving a decision rule.*

According to Appendix Table K, the chosen significance level implies critical values of $\pm t_{\alpha/2} = \pm t_{.005(40)} = \pm 2.704$ (this being a two-tailed test) and there being $n_A + n_B - 2 = 40$ degrees of freedom. Thus, the decision rule must be:

"Accept H_0 if $-2.704 \leq t \leq +2.704$."

Step 4: *Using sample data to compute the test statistic and confronting it with the decision rule.*

After taking two samples of $n = 21$ each, the statistician finds sample mean numbers of cavities (and associated sample standard deviations) of $\bar{X}_A = 27$, $s_A = 6$ and $\bar{X}_B = 23$, $s_B = 2$. Thus, the pooled variance is

$$s_p^2 = \frac{(n_A - 1)s_A^2 + (n_B - 1)s_B^2}{n_A + n_B - 2} = \frac{20(6)^2 + 20(2)^2}{40} = 20$$

while the value of the test statistic is computed as

$$t \cong \frac{\bar{X}_A - \bar{X}_B}{\sqrt{s_p^2\left(\frac{1}{n_A} + \frac{1}{n_B}\right)}} = \frac{27 - 23}{\sqrt{20\left(\frac{1}{21} + \frac{1}{21}\right)}} = 2.90$$

Accordingly, the null hypothesis should be *rejected.* At the 1 percent significance level, the sample result (fewer cavities with toothpaste B) is statistically significant. The observed divergence of the sample difference from the hypothesized zero population difference is unlikely to be due to chance. Toothpaste B does a better job.

Note: Application 13.2, *The Never-Ending Search for New and Better Drugs,* at the end of this section provides another instance of the use of this procedure.

EXAMPLE PROBLEM 13.20

A property manager of thousands of apartments wants to test the difference in net annual income between two types of leasing arrangements. In arrangement A, a lower rent is charged, but tenants are required to make repairs. In arrangement B, a higher rent is charged, and the landlord makes repairs. Two simple random samples of $n_A = 15$ and $n_B = 12$ leases are to be used to test the claim that A, on average, produces a lower or at best the same mean net annual income as B. A significance level of $\alpha = .025$ is desired.

SOLUTION:

Step 1: *Formulating two opposing hypotheses.*

$$H_0\colon \mu_A - \mu_B \leq 0$$
$$H_A\colon \mu_A - \mu_B > 0$$

Step 2: *Selecting a test statistic.*

$$t = \frac{d}{\sigma_d} = \frac{\bar{X}_A - \bar{X}_B}{\sigma_{\bar{X}_A - \bar{X}_B}} \cong \frac{\bar{X}_A - \bar{X}_B}{\sqrt{s_p^2\left(\frac{1}{n_A} + \frac{1}{n_B}\right)}}$$

Step 3: *Deriving a decision rule.*

According to Appendix Table K, the chosen significance level implies a critical value of $t_\alpha = t_{.025(25)} = +2.060$ (this being an upper-tailed test and there being $n_A + n_B - 2 = 25$ degrees of freedom). Thus, the decision rule must be:

"Accept H_0 if $t \leq +2.060$."

Step 4: *Using sample data to compute the test statistic and confronting it with the decision rule.*

After taking two samples, the manager finds sample mean net annual incomes (and associated sample standard deviations) of $\overline{X}_A = \$1{,}532.50$, $s_A = \$400$ and $\overline{X}_B = \$1{,}489.20$, $s_B = \$100$. Thus, the pooled variance is

$$s_p^2 = \frac{(n_A - 1)s_A^2 + (n_B - 1)s_B^2}{n_A + n_B - 2} = \frac{14(400)^2 + 11(100)^2}{25} = 94{,}000$$

while the value of the test statistic is computed as

$$t \cong \frac{\overline{X}_A - \overline{X}_B}{\sqrt{s_p^2\left(\frac{1}{n_A} + \frac{1}{n_B}\right)}} = \frac{1{,}532.50 - 1{,}489.20}{\sqrt{94{,}000\left(\frac{1}{15} + \frac{1}{12}\right)}} = 3.65$$

Accordingly, the null hypothesis should be *accepted.* At the 2.5 percent significance level, the sample result (more income from plan A) is not statistically significant. The manager is justified in the continuing belief that plan B is at least as good as plan A in creating net income for landlords.

Note: Application 13.3, *Do Nursing Homes Discriminate against the Poor?,* at the end of this section provides another instance of the use of this procedure.

EXCEL Example 13.7

The maker of Kenmore household appliances claims to have sampled its own customers as well as those of its competitors (Maytag, Whirlpool, General Electric, and others) and to have found a vastly higher degree of customer satisfaction with respect to its own products. A government economist doubts the claim and collects the following index scores out of a possible 100 after interviewing two simple random samples of customers:

Kenmore: 86, 86, 85, 83, 83, 82, 97, 89, 90, 80, 79, 79, 78, 77, 76, 76, 75, 68, 98, 95, 99

Others: 69, 45, 99, 86, 89, 77, 99, 100, 34, 45, 66, 76, 81

Using EXCEL, conduct an appropriate hypothesis test at a significance level of $\alpha = .05$.

SOLUTION:

1. In a new worksheet, label cells A1 and B1 *Kenmore* and *Others,* respectively; then enter the above data into the two columns just below the labels. (You can achieve the same result by copying and pasting columns H and I of the file HKMISC.)
2. Let us assume you have reason to believe that the two population variances are equal. In that case, click **Tools** > **Data Analysis** > **t-test: Two Sample Assuming Equal Variances** > **OK**. [For the opposite assumption, you would click the *Unequal Variances* choice.]
3. In the dialog box, under *Variable 1 Range,* enter **A2:A22** and under *Variable 2 Range,* enter **B2:B14**.
4. Enter a *Hypothesized Mean Difference* of **0** and an *Alpha* of **.05**.
5. Choose *Output Range,* enter an upper left cell of **D1,** and click **OK**.

The following output appears:

t-Test: Two-Sample Assuming Equal Variances

	Variable 1	Variable 2
Mean	83.85714	74.30769
Variance	70.12857	477.2308
Observations	21	13
Pooled Variance	222.7919	
Hypothesized Mean Difference	0	
df	32	
t Stat	1.812886	
P(T<=t) one-tail	0.03962	
t Critical one-tail	1.693888	
P(T<=t) two-tail	0.07924	
t Critical two-tail	2.036932	

INTERPRETATION To test H_0: $\mu_A - \mu_B \geq 0$, focus on the two highlighted values. The test statistic is 1.81. The acceptance region for this lower-tailed test is defined by the *negative* t Critical one-tail of -1.69, reaching from -1.69 to $+\infty$. Thus, the null hypothesis can be accepted. Kenmore is not lying.

Note: The test statistic is computed as $t = \dfrac{\bar{X}_A - \bar{X}_B}{\sqrt{s_p^2\left(\dfrac{1}{n_A} + \dfrac{1}{n_B}\right)}} = \dfrac{83.86 - 74.3}{\sqrt{222.79\left(\dfrac{1}{21} + \dfrac{1}{13}\right)}} = 1.81$ (shown in red). At a significance level of $\alpha = .05$, and with 32 degrees of freedom, Appendix Table K tells us, the acceptance region for a lower-tailed test lies above -1.694. Therefore, H_0: $\mu_A - \mu_B \geq 0$ can be accepted.

APPLICATION 13.2

THE NEVER-ENDING SEARCH FOR NEW AND BETTER DRUGS

Pharmaceutical companies are engaged in a never-ending search for better drugs. There exists a virtually infinite supply of substances—some of them coming from such unlikely sources as Arctic lichens, rainforest molds, and plain old swamp water—that might possibly be effective against one disease or another. In the United States, perhaps as many as 175,000 compounds are evaluated in research labs each year; only 20 of these eventually make it to the drugstore. In the year 2000 alone, total research and development costs exceeded $20 billion. Sometimes success comes fairly soon: The remarkable antibiotic Aureomycin was found after screening "merely" 4,000 soil samples. At other times, success eludes researchers for decades. The search for an anticancer drug is a case in point. In all cases, however, the hypothesis-testing procedures introduced in this chapter are put to work.

In one actual case, researchers implanted cancer cells in 9 mice, then treated 3 mice with a new chemical compound to test whether it would retard the growth of cancer tumors. After a certain period, all the tumors were removed and weighed. The researchers expected that the compound, if effective, would have caused the tumor weights of the

(continued)

Application 13.2 (continued)

treated mice (experimental group) to be less than those of the untreated mice (control group). The results are shown in Table 13.B.

Was the .53-gram reduction in the average tumor weight of the experimental group significant enough to warrant further tests with the compound? A two-sided hypothesis test employing a known standard error of the difference between the two population means of $\sigma_d = .35$ gram and a significance level of $\alpha = .001$ concluded in the negative:

Step 1: *Formulating two opposing hypotheses.*

$$H_0: \mu_A - \mu_B = 0$$

$$H_A: \mu_A - \mu_B \neq 0$$

Step 2: *Selecting a test statistic.*

$$t = \frac{d}{\sigma_d} = \frac{\bar{X}_A - \bar{X}_B}{\sqrt{\sigma_d^2\left(\frac{1}{n_A} + \frac{1}{n_B}\right)}}$$

TABLE 13.B | Tumor Weights (grams)

Experimental Group	Control Group
.96	1.29
1.59	1.60
1.14	2.27
	1.31
	1.88
	2.21
$\bar{X}_A = 1.23$	$\bar{X}_B = 1.76$

Step 3: *Deriving a decision rule.*

According to Appendix Table K, the chosen significance level implies critical values of $\pm t_{\alpha/2} = \pm t_{.0005(7)} = \pm 5.408$ (this being a two-tailed test) and there being $n_A + n_B - 2 = 7$ degrees of freedom. Thus, the decision rule must be:

"Accept H_0 if $-5.408 \leq t \leq +5.408$."

Step 4: *Using sample data to compute the test statistic and confronting it with the decision rule.*

$$t = \frac{\bar{X}_A - \bar{X}_B}{\sqrt{\sigma_d^2\left(\frac{1}{n_A} + \frac{1}{n_B}\right)}} = \frac{1.23 - 1.76}{\sqrt{.35^2\left(\frac{1}{3} + \frac{1}{6}\right)}} = -2.14$$

Thus, the null hypothesis of no difference was upheld.

Note: An interesting update: In the 1990s, pharmaceutical companies were growing tired of the old-fashioned trial-and-error system of finding new drugs. Increasingly, they designed drugs on computer screens, which obviated the need to mix up random samples of, say, soil and swamp water. On computers, drugs can be designed atom by atom, with specific biological targets in mind. Currently, such "rational drug design" may well account for half the research dollars spent by pharmaceutical companies.

SOURCES: Adapted from Charles W. Dunnett, "Drug Screening: The Never-Ending Search for New and Better Drugs," in Judith M. Tanur et al., eds., *Statistics: A Guide to the Unknown* (San Francisco: Holden-Day, 1972), pp. 23–33; Julie Pitta, "Designer Drugs," *Forbes,* February 4, 1991, pp. 124–125; and Sheryl Gay Stolberg and Jeff Gerth, "In a Drug's Journey to Market, Discovery Is Just the First of Many Steps," *The New York Times,* July 23, 2000, p. 13.

APPLICATION 13.3

Do Nursing Homes Discriminate against the Poor?

For-profit nursing homes set their own fees for private patients but must accept lower fees, called *reimbursements,* for patients supported by government agencies. Provided that the cost of care is the same for both types of patients, it seems reasonable to assume that such nursing homes will give preference in admissions to private patients who bring in the greatest revenue and will discriminate in admissions against other patients (such as the poor, who are supported by Medicaid) who bring in less revenue. A group of researchers investigated the practices of 18 southern Califor-

(continued)

Application 13.3 (continued)

nia nursing homes to test this proposition. Of these, $n_A = 11$ facilities (group A) claimed not to discriminate in admissions, the other $n_B = 7$ facilities (group B) clearly preferred non-Medicaid patients. The mean percentage of Medicaid-supported patient days (and the standard deviations) were found to be $\bar{X}_A = 75.4$, $s_A = 16.3$ and $\bar{X}_B = 40.4$, $s_B = 30.8$. A hypothesis test at the $\alpha = .05$ significance level was performed as follows:

Step 1: *Formulating two opposing hypotheses.*

$$H_0: \mu_A - \mu_B \leq 0$$
$$H_A: \mu_A - \mu_B > 0$$

Step 2: *Selecting a test statistic.*

$$t \cong \frac{\bar{X}_A - \bar{X}_B}{\sqrt{s_p^2\left(\frac{1}{n_A} + \frac{1}{n_B}\right)}}$$

Step 3: *Deriving a decision rule.*

According to Appendix Table K, the chosen significance level implies a critical value of $t_\alpha = t_{.05(16)} = +1.746$ (this being an upper-tailed test and there being $n_A + n_B - 2 = 16$ degrees of freedom). Thus, the decision rule was:

"Accept H_0 if $t \leq +1.746$."

Step 4: *Using sample data to compute the test statistic and confronting it with the decision rule.*

$$s_p^2 = \frac{(n_A - 1)s_A^2 + (n_B - 1)s_B^2}{n_A + n_B - 2}$$

$$= \frac{10(16.3)^2 + 6(30.8)^2}{16} = 521.8$$

$$t \cong \frac{\bar{X}_A - \bar{X}_B}{\sqrt{s_p^2\left(\frac{1}{n_A} + \frac{1}{n_B}\right)}} = \frac{75.4 - 40.4}{\sqrt{521.8\left(\frac{1}{11} + \frac{1}{7}\right)}} = 3.17$$

Accordingly, the null hypothesis was *rejected.* At the 5 percent significance level, the alternative hypothesis (that allegedly group A facilities, on the average, had more Medicaid-supported patient days than group B) was accepted.

SOURCE: Adapted from John S. Greenlees, John M. Marshall, Donald E. Yett, "Nursing Home Admission Policies under Reimbursement," *The Bell Journal of Economics,* Spring 1982, pp. 93–106.

TESTS OF THE DIFFERENCE BETWEEN TWO POPULATION MEANS: MATCHED-PAIRS SAMPLES

We now consider a hypothesis test concerning two means that uses matched-pairs sampling.

EXAMPLE PROBLEM 13.21

A manufacturer markets two models of a product, A and B. The manufacturer has suggested to retailers nationwide that the retail prices of the two models be kept the same. By sampling 10 retail outlets, all of which sell both models, the manufacturer wishes to test whether this suggestion is being followed. A test at the $\alpha = .05$ significance level is desired.

SOLUTION:

Step 1: *Formulating two opposing hypotheses.*

$$H_0: \mu_A - \mu_B = 0$$
$$H_A: \mu_A - \mu_B \neq 0$$

Step 2: *Selecting a test statistic.*

Given that each retail outlet in the sample provides two price observations (and, thus, the desired difference) and assuming that the national population of price differences is normally distributed, the statistician selects

$$t = \frac{\bar{D}}{s_D/\sqrt{n}}$$

Step 3: *Deriving a decision rule.*

According to Appendix Table K, the chosen significance level implies critical values of $\pm t_{\alpha/2} = \pm t_{.025(9)} = \pm 2.262$ (this being a two-tailed test and there being $n - 1 = 9$ degrees of freedom). Thus, the decision rule must be:

"Accept H_0 if $-2.262 \leq t \leq +2.262$."

Step 4: *Using sample data to compute the test statistic and confronting it with the decision rule.*

After taking the sample, the company statistician finds an average difference in model A versus B prices of $\bar{D} = \$18.23$, along with a standard deviation of $s_D = \$1.25$. Thus, the computed value of the test statistic is

$$t = \frac{\bar{D}}{s_D/\sqrt{n}} = \frac{18.23}{1.25/\sqrt{10}} = 46.12$$

Accordingly, the null hypothesis should be *rejected.* At the 5 percent significance level, the sample result (a large price difference is being maintained) is statistically significant. Model A is being sold for considerably more than model B; the observed sample difference is not a fluke inherent in the sampling process.

EXCEL Example 13.8

Ten years ago, an advertising agency took a random sample of 20 personal computer owners who used brands such as Dell, Gateway, Hewlett-Packard, IBM, Apple, Compaq, and others. At the time, the agency recorded a satisfaction score, with a maximum of 100 possible points. Now the same people are contacted and scored again. A hypothesis test is to be conducted to determine whether and how the satisfaction index has changed over time. These are the scores:

Past: 60, 68, 76, 78, 73, 66, 71, 89, 78, 82, 66, 69, 72, 89, 90, 93, 85, 77, 88, 70
Now: 80, 90, 88, 78, 88, 79, 74, 99, 88, 77, 78, 60, 72, 80, 90, 97, 66, 86, 88, 87

Using EXCEL, conduct an appropriate hypothesis test at a significance level of $\alpha = .05$.

SOLUTION:

1. In a new worksheet, label cells A1 and B1 *Past* and *Now,* respectively; then enter the above data into the two columns just below the labels. (You can achieve the same result by copying and pasting columns J and K of the file HKMISC.)
2. Click **Tools** > **Data Analysis** > **t-test: Paired Two Sample for Means** > **OK**.

3. In the dialog box, under *Variable 1 Range,* enter **A2:A21** and under *Variable 2 Range,* enter **B2:B21**.
4. Enter a *Hypothesized Mean Difference* of **0** and an *Alpha* of **.05**.
5. Choose *Output Range,* enter an upper left cell of **D1,** and click **OK**.

The following output appears:

t-Test: Paired Two Sample for Means

	Variable 1	*Variable 2*
Mean	77	82.25
Variance	90.94737	94.934211
Observations	20	20
Pearson Correlation	0.389132	
Hypothesized Mean Difference	0	
df	19	
t Stat	−2.20318	
P(T<=t) one-tail	0.020061	
t Critical one-tail	1.729131	
P (T<=t) two-tail	0.040123	
t Critical two-tail	2.093025	

INTERPRETATION To test H_0: $\mu_A - \mu_B = 0$, focus on the two highlighted values. The test statistic is −2.20. The acceptance region for this two-tailed test is defined by the t Critical two-tail of 2.093, reaching from −2.093 to +2.093. Thus the null hypothesis must be *rejected.* Over time, the scores have risen.

Note: The test statistic is computed as $t = \dfrac{\overline{D}}{s_D/\sqrt{n}} = \dfrac{-5.25}{10.66/\sqrt{20}} = -2.20$ (shown in red).

At a significance level of $\alpha = .05$, and with 19 degrees of freedom, Appendix Table K tells us, the acceptance region for a two-tailed test lies between critical values of $\pm t_{\alpha/2} = \pm t_{.025(19)} = \pm 2.093$.

13.10 *p* Values in Small-Sample Tests

Section 13.8 introduced the concept of *p* values and illustrated their calculation for a number of large-sample tests. Unless a computer program is used, the precise calculation of *p* values is sometimes difficult in the case of small-sample tests that use the *t* distribution. Readily available *t* distribution tables, such as Appendix Table K, contain values for only selected critical tail areas and selected degrees of freedom. Unless the computed value of the *t* statistic just happens to be listed in the table, a precise value of *p* cannot be determined. As a result, hand calculations often can come up only with a rough estimate of the *p* value, such as $p < .005$ or $.025 < p < .05$. The following Example Problem illustrates the procedure.

EXAMPLE PROBLEM 13.22

Review Example Problems 13.17 and 13.18. In each case, compute and interpret the p value without the aid of a computer.

SOLUTION:

Example Problem 13.17

The problem involves 24 degrees of freedom and a computed $t = -1.125$. In the 24 d.f. row of Appendix Table K, the value of $t = 1.125$ lies between .685 (with $\alpha/2$ of .25 in this two-tailed test) and 1.318 (with $\alpha/2$ of .1). Thus, t lies between $\alpha = .5$ and $\alpha = .2$, and we conclude: If H_0 is true, the probability of finding a t value such as the one found in this test (or of finding one even more extreme) is $.2 < p < .5$ and, by Fisher's own criteria, H_0 is accepted.

Example Problem 13.18

The problem involves 9 degrees of freedom and a computed $t = -4.74$. In the 9 d.f. row of Appendix Table K, the value of $t = 4.74$ lies between 4.297 (with $\alpha = .001$ in this one-tailed test) and 4.781 (with $\alpha = .0005$). Accordingly, if H_0 is true, the probability of finding the t value actually found in this test (or of finding one even more extreme) is $.0005 < p < .001$ and, by Fisher's own criteria, H_0 is strongly rejected.

Note: Modern computer programs routinely calculate precise p values, along with their test statistics. For example, if you enter the Example Problem 13.17 and 13.18 data into Sheet 6 and 7, respectively, of the EXCEL add-in, HKStat, you discover p values of .27 and .000527, respectively.

13.11 Criticisms of Hypothesis Testing

The testing procedures discussed in this chapter are widely used, yet there is considerable controversy about their usefulness. Without trying to present an exhaustive list, we shall consider three of the criticisms that are commonly encountered.

SERIOUS VIOLATIONS OF ASSUMPTIONS

Some critics charge that many people perform hypothesis tests even though the assumptions that would validate the procedure used are not met. There might be a difference, for example, between the statistical target population about which inferences are to be made and the population that is actually being sampled. This difference is likely because a perfect frame is usually unavailable for any nontrivial population. In addition, an intended simple random sample can in fact turn out to be a nonprobability sample. This result is likely because many surveys suffer from high nonresponse rates. Or, perhaps, the sampled populations may not be normally distributed, or they may not have equal variances—requirements for using the t statistic in two-sample tests. In situations such as these, the testing procedure will grind out irrelevant and invalid results.

RIGID INTERPRETATION OF THE "ACCEPTANCE" CRITERION

While it is meaningful to reject a null hypothesis as a result of uncovering contrary evidence that cannot reasonably be attributed to chance, it is not meaningful, critics claim, to accept a null hypothesis in the absence of such contrary evidence. Yet these words are commonly used (as they are in this text). It would be much wiser, critics urge, to talk of "failure to reject" rather than "acceptance of" a null hypothesis. Ultimately, all the things we know are things that haven't yet been proven false and are, therefore, most appropriately, regarded with a wait-and-see attitude. All that we know is at best tentatively accepted. Critics conclude that we must avoid any rigid interpretation of the acceptance criterion, as if it assured us of the truth with certainty.

However, this criticism is semantic and can be met by agreeing to interpret "acceptance" loosely, as a token word for "failure to reject," except, perhaps, in cases where the probability β of a type II error is known to be extremely small. Admittedly, it is often difficult to know this probability.

NONPUBLICATION OF NONSIGNIFICANT RESULTS

Results of hypothesis tests that are statistically not significant and, thus, nonsurprising are unlikely to be published. This situation has serious consequences, critics note. Consider a null hypothesis that is in fact true (unbeknownst to researchers) and that is tested independently by many, always at the $\alpha = .05$ level of significance. Each of these investigators has only 5 chances out of 100 of (incorrectly) finding statistical significance (and falsely rejecting H_0). Yet the chance that at least one among the many will reach such a result is much higher. If there are 10 such investigators, the probability that at least one will falsely reject H_0 equals $1 - (.95)^{10} = .401$—and that person's (wrong) results will be published!

Summary

1. When people make decisions, they inevitably do so on the basis of beliefs they hold concerning the true state of the world. Every one of these beliefs originates as a *hypothesis,* a proposition tentatively advanced as possibly true. *Hypothesis testing* is a systematic approach to assessing beliefs about reality; it involves confronting a belief with evidence and deciding whether that belief can be maintained as reasonable or must be discarded as untenable. Four major steps are involved.
2. Step 1 is the formulation of two opposing hypotheses, called the *null hypothesis* (H_0) and the *alternative hypothesis* (H_A). These hypotheses are mutually exclusive and also collectively exhaustive of the possible states of reality. They can be stated in various forms. While the null hypothesis may be stated either as an exact (=) or inexact (≤ or ≥) hypothesis, the alternative hypothesis is always inexact, either two-sided (≠) or one-sided (< or >).
3. Step 2 is the selection of a *test statistic*—the statistic to be computed from a simple random sample taken from the population of interest and to be used for establishing the probable truth or falsity of the null hypothesis. Most common test statistics are z values or t values, derived by dividing the difference between the computed sample statistic and the value of the population parameter postulated in the null hypothesis by the standard error of the sample statistic.
4. In Step 3, a *decision rule* is derived that specifies in advance, for all possible values of a test statistic that might be computed from a sample, whether the null hypothesis should be accepted or whether it should be rejected in favor of the alternative hypothesis. Such a rule is needed because the test statistic is a random variable; therefore, simply as a result of sampling error, it can take on all kinds of values apparently contradicting the null hypothesis even when H_0 is true. We escape the dilemma by accepting the null hypothesis for all sample results (even seemingly contradictory ones) that are highly likely and nonsurprising when H_0 is true and by rejecting it for results that are highly unusual and surprising when H_0 is true. The cutoff point between values of the test statistic that are "surprising" (that have a low probability of occurring when H_0 is true) and those that are "not surprising" (that have a high probability of occurring when H_0 is true) must necessarily be arbitrary. "Surprising" results that lead to the rejection of the null hypothesis are said to be *statistically significant.* "Nonsurprising" results that lead to the acceptance of the null hypothesis are *not statistically significant.* Among all the sample results that are possible when the null hypothesis is true, the (arbitrary) maximum proportion, α, that is considered sufficiently unusual to reject the null hypothesis is called the *significance level* of the test.
5. In Step 4, a simple random sample is selected, the actual value of the test statistic is computed, and it is confronted with the decision rule. The null hypothesis, accordingly, is accepted or rejected. In a two-tailed test, the alternative hypothesis is two-sided; hence the null hypothesis can be rejected for values of the test statistic located in either tail of that statistic's sampling distribution. In a one-tailed test, the alternative hypothesis is one-sided and the rejection region is confined entirely to the lower or upper tail of the sampling distribution; accordingly, the null hypothesis is rejected only for very low (or very high) values of the test statistic.
6. We must note, however, that either outcome in a hypothesis test can be a correct or an erroneous interpretation of the true state of reality. The erroneous rejection of a null hypothesis that is in fact true is called a *type I error;* it occurs with a probability of α. The erroneous acceptance of a null hypothesis that is in fact false is called a *type II error;* it occurs with a probability of β. Given sample size, n, anything that reduces α automatically raises β. The two

complementary probabilities, $1 - \alpha$ (with respect to α) and $1 - \beta$ (with respect to β) are, respectively, referred to as the *confidence level* and the *power* of the hypothesis test.

7. A somewhat different approach to hypothesis testing is attributable to Ronald A. Fisher. It involves the computation of p values. They indicate the probability that a test statistic at least as contradictory to a postulated parameter as the statistic actually observed could have occurred by chance if the hypothesized value of a parameter were true.

8. Modern hypothesis-testing procedures are still subject to considerable controversy. Critics are concerned about serious violations of assumptions, a rigid interpretation of the "acceptance" criterion, the nonpublication of nonsignificant results, and other problems.

Key Terms

α risk
acceptance region
alternative hypothesis
β risk
confidence level
critical value
decision rule
error of acceptance
error of rejection
exact hypothesis
hypothesis
hypothesis testing
inexact hypothesis
lower-tailed test
not statistically significant result
null hypothesis
observed significance level
one-sided hypothesis
one-tailed test
pooled estimator of the population proportion
pooled variance
power
p value
rejection region
significance level
statistically significant result
test statistic
two-sided hypothesis
two-tailed test
type I error
type II error
upper-tailed test

Practice Problems

NOTE

Some problems require the use of a statistical program, EXCEL or MINITAB. The program's major features are explained in text Chapter 2. Plenty of additional advice is available via the program's built-in Help feature.

Section 13.4 Deriving a Decision Rule

1. Determine the significance levels of the following two-tailed hypothesis tests:
   a. $z_{\alpha/2} = 1.96$
   b. $z_{\alpha/2} = .85$
   c. $z_{\alpha/2} = .15$

2. Expand Appendix Table L to include entries for two-tailed tests and:
   a. $\alpha = .08$
   b. $\alpha = .06$
   c. $\alpha = .02$

3. Determine the significance levels of the following one-tailed hypothesis tests:
   a. $z = 1.96$
   b. $z = 1.25$
   c. $z = .15$

4. Expand Appendix Table L to include entries for one-tailed tests and:
   a. $\alpha = .09$
   b. $\alpha = .08$
   c. $\alpha = .02$

Section 13.6 The Possibility of Error

5. If you were the manager of a firm making a hypothesis test and the rejection of H_0 would mean that the firm would have to be liquidated, would you favor a large or a small value for α? Explain.

6. Given "H_0: Tire A is better than tire B," consider the following four situations. In each case, indicate whether the decision is correct or false and, if it is false, what type of error is being made.
   a. Tire A is in fact better and A is used.
   b. Tire A is in fact better, but B is used.
   c. Tire B is in fact better and B is used.
   d. Tire B is better, but A is used.

SECTION 13.7 LARGE-SAMPLE HYPOTHESIS TESTS

7. Given the sample data of Table 13.2, perform the indicated hypothesis tests, assuming each N is infinite and the desired $\alpha = .10$.

TABLE 13.2 | Sample Data

Case	$\bar{X}$	s	n	H_0
a	19.2	2.0	52	$\mu = 21$
b	301.0	7.2	96	$\mu = 327$
c	57.6	3.1	40	$\mu \geq 58$
d	19.1	2.6	250	$\mu \leq 17$

8. Given the sample data of Table 13.3, perform the indicated hypothesis tests, assuming each N is infinite and the desired $\alpha = .05$.

TABLE 13.3 | Sample Data

Case	$\bar{X}$	s	n	H_0
a	13.7	2	39	$\mu = 14$
b	207	7.1	150	$\mu = 210$
c	93	10	42	$\mu \geq 95$
d	13	3	300	$\mu \geq 18$

9. The buyer of shirts for a department store wants to test whether shirts with sleeve labels of "33 inches" really meet that specification on average. A random sample of $n = 100$ from 10,000 incoming shirts is to be taken; the desired significance level is $\alpha = .025$. The sample shows a mean length of $\bar{X} = 34$ inches, with a standard deviation of $s = 2$ inches. Make the test.

10. An economist wants to test whether the average salary of aircraft mechanics really is $600 per week as has been alleged. A random sample of $n = 100$ from the nation's 29,952 mechanics is taken; the desired significance level is $\alpha = .05$. The sample shows a mean salary of $\bar{X} = \$657$, with a standard deviation of $s = \$22$. Make the test.

11. In order to rule on a potential federal grant, the size of which varies with household income, a government official must confirm a local government's claim that the average family income in an Illinois county is $12,357. A random sample of $n = 36$ families is taken; the desired significance level is $\alpha = .001$. The sample shows a mean income of $13,950, with a standard deviation of $3,972. To prove the validity of the claim, make the test.

12. The manager of a firm wants to test a competitor's advertising claim: "There are 15 chunks of beef in every can of Eric's Homemade Stew." A random sample of 50 cans of Eric's stew is acquired; a hypothesis test at the $\alpha = .025$ level of significance is to be performed. The sample shows a mean of 11 chunks of beef per can, with a standard deviation of 2 chunks. Make the test.

13. The manager of an airport has the distinct impression that the monthly maintenance cost of planes used in agricultural work does not equal the projected average of $500 per plane, but is higher or lower. A sample of 32 planes is taken; a hypothesis test at the $\alpha = .02$ level of significance is to be performed on the assumption that the population of cost figures is normally distributed. The sample shows costs of $592 per plane, with a standard deviation of $101. Make the test.

14. The manager of a retail business suspects that people other than customers are using the store's parking lot. She wants to test, at a significance level of $\alpha = .05$, whether cars in the lot are typically parked for less than an hour, as those of customers would be. A random sample of 50 cars shows a mean parking time of 101 minutes, with a standard deviation of 21 minutes. Make the test.

15. The Environmental Protection Agency is allowing a plant to dump its effluent into a river—as long as the effluent averages no more than 4 parts per million (ppm) of a certain toxic substance. During the course of one week, the EPA randomly samples the effluent and finds, in $n = 64$ samples, an average of $\overline{X} = 4.2$ ppm of toxic substance, with a standard deviation of $s = 1$ ppm. Is the plant in violation? Conduct an appropriate hypothesis test at $\alpha = .025$.

16. The Federal Aviation Administration believes that the mean number of takeoffs and landings at some 7,000 U.S. airports last year was at most 50 per day. Make an appropriate hypothesis test of this belief at the $\alpha = .001$ level of significance, while using these sample data: $n = 100, \overline{X} = 71, s = 30$.

17. The buyer of tomatoes for a ketchup producer wants to test whether it is true that at least 80 percent of the tomatoes being received deserve the label "superior." A random sample of $n = 100$ from 5,000 incoming tomatoes is to be taken; the desired significance level is $\alpha = .05$. The sample shows 72 "superior" tomatoes.

a. Make the test using appropriate formulas.

b. Confirm your result with EXCEL or MINITAB.

18. An advertiser wants to test a magazine publisher's claim that at least 25 percent of the magazine's readers are college students. A random sample of $n = 200$ from 2.1 million subscribers finds 38 college students. The desired significance level is $\alpha = .01$.

a. Make the test using appropriate formulas.

b. Confirm your result with EXCEL or MINITAB.

19. The manager of a firm wants to test the accountant's claim that the firm's cash-flow problem is due to the fact that at least 80 percent of accounts receivable are more than three months old. A random sample of $n = 50$ from 10,000 accounts is to be taken; the desired significance level is $\alpha = .001$. The sample shows 30 such delinquent accounts.

a. Make the test using appropriate formulas.

b. Confirm your result with EXCEL or MINITAB.

20. An aircraft manufacturer knows that up to 12 percent of engine crankcases shrink too much when cooling down after being cast. A new process is proposed and tried: of 250 castings, some 27 are equally bad. At the $\alpha = .05$ level of significance, a hypothesis test is to be conducted to find out whether the new process produces crankcases that are no worse (and possibly better) than those produced by the old process.

a. Make the test using appropriate formulas.

b. Confirm your result with EXCEL or MINITAB.

21. The manufacturer of Lycoming aircraft engines knows from long experience that up to 10 percent of these engines develop problems by the time they reach 2,000 flight hours. The manufacturer believes, however, that a new series of these engines will do no worse and possibly better. Accordingly, a random sample of 225 of the new engines is selected from owners who have flown 2,000 hours or more. Of the sampled owners, 12 have had problems before the 2,000-hour mark. A hypothesis test at the $\alpha = .05$ level of significance is desired to determine whether the manufacturer's faith in the new engine series is justified.

a. Make the test using appropriate formulas.

b. Confirm your result with EXCEL or MINITAB.

22. Review Example Problem 12.6 on page 504, in which a tire manufacturer wishes to estimate the difference between the mean lives of two types of tires. A 99 percent confidence interval of the difference in tire A and tire B lifetimes was computed as 4,900 miles ± 508.51 (as reaching, that is, from 4,391.49 miles to 5,408.51 miles). Perform a hypothesis test on the same example and discover the relationship between estimation and hypothesis testing.

23. An economist wants to test the claim that the wages of construction workers in New York (A) are different from those in Chicago (B). Random samples of workers, $n_A = 100$ and $n_B = 80$, are to be taken; the desired significance level is $\alpha = .025$. The samples show average weekly wages of $\overline{X}_A =$ \$500 and $\overline{X}_B =$ \$410, with sample standard deviations of $s_A =$ \$200 and $s_B =$ \$100. Make the test, assuming normally distributed populations.

24. A government administrator wants to know whether there is any difference in the quality of training given to new air traffic controllers at two different training centers. Exams are administered to two random samples of recent trainees. At center A, the sample is $n_A = 36$, the mean score is $\overline{X}_A = 93$, the standard deviation is $s_A = 8$. At center B, the corresponding data are $n_B = 49$, $\overline{X}_B = 87$, $s_B = 3$. Conduct a hypothesis test at the $\alpha = .005$ level of significance, assuming normally distributed populations.

25. A firm's manager wants to know whether the delivery time of raw materials is still longer with one shipping company (A) than another (B), as has been true in the past. Random samples of $n_A = 50$ and $n_B = 30$ shipments from among the thousands received in a month are to be taken; the desired significance level is .10. The samples show mean delivery times of $\overline{X}_A = 14$ days and $\overline{X}_B = 12$ days, with sample standard deviations of $s_A = 1$ day and $s_B = .4$ day. Make the test.

26. The owner of a sawmill is about to purchase one of two tree lots, but wonders whether lot A still has the larger trees, as used to be true. Two random samples of $n_A = n_B = 100$ are taken. The average diameter of trees in lot A is $\overline{X}_A = 48.25$ inches with a standard deviation of $s_A = 18.2$ inches. The corresponding data for the sampled trees in lot B are $\overline{X}_B = 39.95$ inches and $s_B = 3.2$ inches. Conduct a hypothesis test to find out whether lot A trees are still larger than lot B trees, using a significance level of $\alpha = .05$.

27. A company psychologist wants to test whether age influences IQ. A random sample of 50 middle-aged workers whose IQ score at age 20 is available is to be taken; the desired significance level is $\alpha = .001$. The sample shows a mean difference between the current and earlier score of +12 points, with a sample standard deviation of 8 points. Make the test.

28. The IRS commissioner wants to test whether the quality of work done in two regional offices is the same. Random samples of $n_A = 300$ and $n_B = 200$ tax returns are taken from each office and checked for accuracy; the desired significance level is $\alpha = .01$. The samples show 39 errors in office A, 20 in office B.

a. Make the test using appropriate formulas.

b. Confirm your result with EXCEL or MINITAB.

29. The study described in Application 13.1, *Antitrust Pork Barrel,* also showed the following for the House Subcommittee on Monopolies and Commercial Law of the House Judiciary Committee: During the 1970–1979 period, 18 of 25 formal complaints brought by the FTC were dismissed when a committee member's district was affected; 46 of 171 such complaints were dismissed when no committee member's district was involved.

a. Using appropriate formulas, test the null hypothesis of "no difference" in these proportions at the $\alpha = .10$ level of significance.

b. Confirm your result with EXCEL or MINITAB.

30. A quality inspector wants to test the claim that the proportion of acceptable electronics components delivered by a foreign supplier (A) is at best equal to that coming from a domestic supplier (B). Random samples of $n_A = 100$ and $n_B = 150$ are to be taken from incoming shipments; the desired significance level is $\alpha = .005$. The samples show 90 good components coming from A and 105 from B.

a. Make the test using appropriate formulas.

b. Confirm your result with EXCEL or MINITAB.

31. Review this chapter's Preview and the formulation, in Example Problem 13.2 on pages 538–539, of a possible hypothesis test about the Foster Grant liability in the Leominster autism cases. Suppose the samples had truly been random samples and someone hired you to conduct such a hypothesis test at the $\alpha = .05$ level of significance.

a. Make the test using appropriate formulas.

b. Confirm your result with EXCEL or MINITAB.

32. An executive of Pizza Hut is testing the proposition, based on experience, that more of the phone orders received during the day (A) than during the night (B) are in fact being picked up. In a three-month test, 250 each of day and night phone orders are sampled; the desired significance level is $\alpha = .05$. It turns out that 240 of the day orders but only 220 of the night orders are picked up.

a. Make the test using appropriate formulas.

b. Confirm your result with EXCEL or MINITAB.

33. An economist is testing the proposition that the percentage of firms in industry A that are making advertising expenditures in excess of 5 percent of sales revenue is larger than in industry B. A test at the $\alpha = .01$ significance level is desired. A random sample of 200 firms from each industry reveals *percentages* of 18 and 19, respectively.

a. Make the test using appropriate formulas.

b. Confirm your result with EXCEL or MINITAB.

34. An advertising agency wishes to test the claim that, as in years past, a larger percentage of adult women watches *As the World Turns* than *The Guiding Light* on daytime TV. A test at the $\alpha = .10$ significance level is desired. One random sample of 150 women shows 102 watching *As the World Turns,* another random sample of 250 women shows 182 watching *The Guiding Light.*

a. Make the test using appropriate formulas.

b. Confirm your result with EXCEL or MINITAB.

Section 13.8 Using *p* Values: A Famous Controversy

35. Many statisticians like to report a p value for each hypothesis test. On the assumption that the null hypothesis is true, this p value measures the probability of getting a test statistic as contradictory to the null hypothesis as, or even more contradictory than, the statistic actually computed from the sample data. Compute the p value for:

a. Example Problem 13.9.

b. Example Problem 13.13.

36. To test your understanding of p values,

a. draw a graph similar to Figure 13.14, depicting the difference between α and p value for an upper-tailed hypothesis test.

b. compute similar p values for Practice Problems 21 and 31.

37. Compute the p value for:

a. Example Problem 13.12.

b. Example Problem 13.14.

Section 13.9 Small-Sample Hypothesis Tests

38. A manufacturer has been receiving complaints from customers about their orders arriving fully 12 days after being shipped. The manufacturer selects 20 of the following week's orders at random and ships them differently. A statistician is to test whether the new procedure is better or worse and to do so at a significance level of $\alpha = .05$. The mean delivery time in the sample turns out to be $\overline{X} = 9$ days, with a sample standard deviation of $s = 3$ days. Make the test.

39. The process of producing steel is designed to use an average 6 quarts of hydrochloric acid per ton of steel, no more or less. Yet a random sample of 9 different tons of steel shows a mean usage of 9 quarts per ton, with a standard deviation of 1 quart. At a significance level of $\alpha = .05$, conduct an appropriate hypothesis test to determine whether the production process needs recalibration.

40. The mean operating temperature of an aircraft engine during level cruise is supposed to be 190°F, no more or less. An airline tested one particular engine at randomly selected times. The mean temperature on these 25 tests was 193°F, with a standard deviation of 3°F. Should the pilot worry about the engine running hot? Conduct an appropriate hypothesis test at a significance level of $\alpha = .05$.

41. A manager wishes to test the tensile strength of yarn that is to be used in the firm's new machines and that must be at least 25 lb. A random sample of 16 spools is taken from a number of incoming shipments. The average tensile strength is 23 lb., with a standard deviation of .2 lb. Conduct an appropriate hypothesis test at a significance level of $\alpha = .10$ and tell the manager whether the yarn is suitable.

42. An advertising agency wants to test whether beer drinkers rate alike two brands that are presented in unmarked cans. Two independent samples of 16 each are used; the desired significance level is $\alpha = .05$. Scoring on a scale from 0 to 100, the two sample mean scores are 65 and 79, with sample standard deviations of 20 and 3. Make the test assuming that the two populations in question are normally distributed and have equal variances.

43. The manager noted in Practice Problem 41 now wishes to test whether the tensile strength of yarn is alike for two suppliers. In addition to the sample noted earlier ($n_A = 16$, $\overline{X}_A = 23$ lb., $s_A = .2$ lb.), a second sample of yarns coming from another firm is taken and the results are $n_B = 26$, $\overline{X}_B = 24$ lb., $s_B = 2.3$ lb. Conduct an appropriate hypothesis test at the $\alpha = .10$ level of significance, while assuming that the two populations of tensile strengths are normally distributed and have equal variances.

44. A government official wants to determine whether it remains true that the average motorcycle-accident fatality rate (average ratio of fatal accidents to all accidents) is lower in states requiring motorcyclists to wear helmets. The record is reviewed: The official finds that 5 states had helmet laws (A) during the entire past decade, while 6 states were without such laws (B) throughout the period. A test at the $\alpha = .05$ significance level is to be conducted, using the observed mean fatality rates of $\overline{X}_A = .1021$ and $\overline{X}_B = .2133$, along with standard deviations of $s_A = .0918$ and $s_B = .0547$. Make the test, assuming that the underlying populations are normally distributed and have equal variances.

45. A pharmaceutical company researcher wants to check out a rumor according to which occasional coffee drinkers (A), when given a cup of coffee just before bedtime, will take longer to fall asleep than habitual coffee drinkers (B) under the same circumstances. A test is to be conducted on $n_A = 9$ occasional and $n_B = 16$ habitual coffee drinkers; a significance level of $\alpha = .10$ is desired. The average times needed to fall asleep turn out to be $\overline{X}_A = 56$ minutes and $\overline{X}_B = 29$ minutes, with sample standard deviations of $s_A = 25$ minutes and $s_B = 22$ minutes. Make the test, assuming that the underlying populations of times are normally distributed and have equal variances.

46. A production engineer wants to test the assertion that workers using method A will on average complete a job in the same time as they would by using method B. Six workers are selected at random, and each is made to do a given job first in one way and then in the other way (although half use A first and the other half use B first). A significance level of $\alpha = .01$ is desired. The results of the experiment are shown in Table 13.4. Make the test with the help of EXCEL or MINITAB, assuming that the underlying population of differences is normally distributed.

TABLE 13.4 | Work Completion Times (minutes)

Worker	Method A	Method B
1	10.0	9.8
2	11.1	11.0
3	9.8	8.2
4	10.0	9.5
5	10.3	10.6
6	10.5	10.2

Section 13.10 *p* Values in Small-Sample Tests

47. Review Example Problem 13.19. Compute and interpret the p value.

48. Review Example Problem 13.20. Compute and interpret the p value.

49. Review Example Problem 13.21. Compute and interpret the p value.

50. Review EXCEL or MINITAB Examples 13.6, 13.7, and 13.8.

a. In each case, use the computer to find the p value.

b. Apply Fisher's criteria to interpret the p value.

Chapter 14

HYPOTHESIS TESTING: THE CHI-SQUARE TECHNIQUE

LOOKING AHEAD

After reading this chapter, you will be able to use the chi-square technique to:

1. test the alleged independence of two qualitative variables in a population of data,
2. make inferences about the relative sizes of more than two population proportions,
3. make inferences about the likely value of a population variance, and
4. conduct goodness-of-fit tests to determine whether sample data came from a larger data set that conforms to a specified population distribution (such as a binomial, Poisson, normal, uniform, or other type still).

AND HERE IS A TYPICAL PROBLEM YOU WILL BE ABLE TO SOLVE:

Consider the process of assembling television sets. Management is interested in testing the hypothesis that the proportion of defective units produced (which has been .05 in the past) would be the same for each of 6 possible assembly-line speeds. The company statistician is asked to take 6 samples of 100 TV sets each while different assembly-line speeds are being maintained, and then perform a test at the 1 percent significance level.

PREVIEW

In 1992, the Federal Reserve released detailed data from its massive study of the U.S. mortgage market, including regional summaries, such as that given in Table 14.1.

This kind of table is called a *contingency table* because it illustrates the nature of one qualitative variable, such as the disposition of mortgage applications, contingent upon the nature of another such variable, such as the race of mortgage applicants. People often use such tables to make a point, namely, that one variable "obviously" influences the other. In this case, they might argue for the existence of racial discrimination on the grounds that so many more white applicants (71,950) than black applicants (3,117) were approved. Yet such a hasty conclusion hardly seems warranted. For one thing, many more white applicants than black applicants were also denied: Compare 12,997 to 979. At a minimum, we would surely wish to relate the numbers of approvals and denials to the total numbers of applications and restate

TABLE 14.1 | Number of Mortgage Applications by Race of Applicant and Subsequent Disposition; Los Angeles, 1990

Race of Applicant	Approved	Denied	Total
Black	3,117	979	**4,096**
White	71,950	12,997	**84,947**
Total	**75,067**	**13,976**	**89,043**

the Table 14.1 data in percentage terms. Then we would note that 3,117 of 4,096 black applicants, or 76.1 percent, were approved, while 71,950 of 84,947 white applicants, or 84.7 percent, were approved. By implication, the rejection rate for blacks was 23.9 percent, but it was only 15.3 percent for whites. Yet an important issue would remain even then: Were black and white applicants equal with respect to relevant factors, such as their income and ability to pay back their loans? And if they were equally qualified for mortgages, how massive and persistent must such sample evidence be before we can say, beyond a reasonable doubt, that racial discrimination pervades this market?

What would you say if another sample, taken in another year, showed rejection rates of 20.0 percent for blacks as well as whites? What if another sample showed 20.8 percent for blacks and 19.2 percent for whites? Or 22 percent for blacks and 18 percent for whites? How could you distinguish between a random fluctuation (a mere sampling error) and a real underlying cause (a true bias)? The *chi-square* statistical technique, developed in this chapter, helps provide answers to important questions such as these. And just as juries are ready to convict the presumably innocent only when evidence to the contrary is simply too overwhelming, so the chi-square technique helps us sort out mere suspicion from certainty beyond a reasonable doubt.

14.1 Introduction

Earlier chapters have demonstrated the importance of the normal probability distribution (or z distribution) and of the Student t distribution for making estimates of unknown population parameters or testing hypotheses about them. There are occasions, however, when these techniques cannot be used—consider cases in which the assumptions underlying them are not fulfilled. As this chapter will show, statisticians often use a different statistical method, known as the **chi-square technique,** in such circumstances. It has four major applications:

1. testing the alleged independence of two qualitative variables, such as the race of mortgage applicants versus the disposition of their applications, noted in this chapter's Preview.
2. making inferences about the relative sizes of more than two population proportions, such as the market shares of different firms.
3. making inferences about the likely value of a population variance, such as that of pill dosages prepared by a pharmaceutical firm.
4. conducting goodness-of-fit tests to assess the plausibility that sample data come from a population that conforms to a particular type of probability distribution, such as the binomial, Poisson, normal, or uniform distribution, to name a few.

The following sections illustrate each of these chi-square applications.

14.2 Testing the Alleged Independence of Two Qualitative Variables

As we noted in Chapter 1, qualitative variables are characteristics that are usually not expressed numerically because they differ in kind rather than in degree among the elementary units of a statistical population. Consider the race of mortgage applicants (white, black) or the disposition of mortgage applications (approved, denied). On many occasions, we will be interested to know whether the joint appearance of two qualitative variables, such as *white* and *approved* (or *black* and *denied*), is a mere fluke or has some deeper significance, denoting a cause-and-effect relationship. The issue crops up in all areas of life: Is there a causal linkage, people ask, between heart attacks and lifestyle, between the occurrence of disease and having been vaccinated, between equipment failure and prior years of service, between the percentage of defective units produced and the time of day of their production, between the causes of airplane accidents and the extent of pilot qualification, between the educational level, age, sex, or geographic location of consumers and their brand preferences, between the severity of auto accidents and the location of their occurrence, between people's major in college and their type of employment later on, between attitudes toward a piece of legislation and people's political affiliation, between sex and type of job held?

INDEPENDENT VERSUS DEPENDENT EVENTS

In order to answer the types of questions asked in the last paragraph, we must first review the distinction, introduced in Chapter 8, between statistically independent and dependent events.

DEFINITION 14.1 Two random events, A and B, are **independent events** if the probability of one event is *not* affected by the occurrence of the other event. Hence the unconditional probability of the occurrence of event A is exactly the same as the conditional probability of event A, given the occurrence of event B:

$$p(\text{A}) = p(\text{A}|\text{B})$$

DEFINITION 14.2 Two random events, A and B, are **dependent events** if the probability of one event *is* affected by the occurrence of the other event. Hence the unconditional probability of the occurrence of event A differs from the conditional probability of event A, given the occurrence of event B:

$$p(\text{A}) \neq p(\text{A}|\text{B})$$

EXAMPLE PROBLEM 14.1

In a certain city, 75,067 out of 89,043 mortgage applications are approved. Thus, the unconditional probability of approval is $p(\text{A}) = (75{,}067/89{,}043) = .843$. Now determine whether the conditional probability of approval, if the applicant is black, is an independent or a dependent event, given

a. that 3,453 out of 4,096 black applicants gain approval.

b. that 3,117 out of 4,096 black applicants gain approval.

SOLUTION:

a. $p(\text{A}|\text{B}) = \dfrac{3{,}453}{4{,}096} = .843$, which equals $p(\text{A}) = .843$. The events are *independent.* Race is unrelated to mortgage approval because the approval rate for blacks, $p(\text{A}|\text{B})$, is the same as that for all applicants, $p(\text{A})$.

b. $p(\text{A}|\text{B}) = \dfrac{3{,}117}{4{,}096} = .761$, which does not equal $p(\text{A}) = .843$. The events are *dependent.* Race is related to mortgage approval because the approval rate for blacks, $p(\text{A}|\text{B})$, is not the same as that for all applicants, $p(\text{A})$. *Caution:* Even though race and mortgage approval are dependent here, this fact alone does not prove a thing about racial discrimination. It is possible that other factors, not noted here, ultimately explain the dependence of the two variables.

CONTINGENCY TABLES

When seeking to test whether two qualitative variables are independent or dependent, it helps to employ a special tool, called a *contingency table.*

DEFINITION 14.3 A **contingency table** classifies data with respect to two qualitative variables that are each divided into two or more categories. Numbers in such a table show the frequency of occurrence of all possible combinations of categories, or of all possible *contingencies,* which accounts for the table's name.

A contingency table is ideally suited to bring together two pieces of information for all possible combinations of qualitative categories: (a) actually *observed* sample data and (b) hypothetically *expected* sample data, which are the kind of data we would expect to find if the two qualitative variables of interest were in fact statistically independent of one another. We can best illustrate the nature of such a table by example.

A CASE STUDY In the remainder of this section, we consider a prestigious law firm that specializes in aviation accident cases. The lawyers seek to determine whether officially reported causes of airplane accidents are statistically linked to the extent of pilot qualification. Accordingly, they gather relevant information from the last 300 aviation accident reports issued by the National Transportation Safety Board, and prepare a contingency table in three easy steps.

OBSERVED FREQUENCIES A first version of the table classifies actually observed frequencies by official accident cause and type of pilot's license held, as in Table 14.2 on the next page. Variable (A), the official accident cause, comes in six categories, while variable (B), the type of license held by the pilot-in-command, has been divided into two categories, namely, lower-level licenses issued to student pilots and private pilots, on the one hand, and upper-level licenses issued to commercial pilots and airline-transport pilots, on the other hand.

EXPECTED FREQUENCIES A second version of the table replaces observed frequencies with the frequencies we would expect if the two variables in question were statistically independent of one another. When such independence exists, the proportion of units having one attribute (such as the thunderstorm cause) is the same overall as in any subcategory defined by the other attribute (such as student/private pilots or commercial/airline-transport pilots). Thus, if thunderstorm-caused accidents are independent of pilot licensure and if 70 of all 300 accidents are caused by

TABLE 14.2 | Number of Civilian Aviation Accidents, Classified by Cause (A) and Type of Pilot's License (B): Observed Frequencies

This contingency table shows observed frequencies (typically symbolized by f_o) for various combinations of aviation-accident causes (A) and pilot's license types (B). Setting up such a table is the first step in testing for independence between the two variables, A and B.

(A) Official Accident Cause	(B) License Held by Pilot-in-Command: Student or Private	Commercial or Airline-Transport	Total
(1) Thunderstorm	50	20	**70**
(2) Icing	40	10	**50**
(3) Equipment Failure	25	6	**31**
(4) Controller Error	25	5	**30**
(5) Pilot Error	80	6	**86**
(6) Other	30	3	**33**
Total	**250**	**50**	**300**

thunderstorms (a proportion of .2333), we would expect thunderstorms also to have caused .2333 of the 250 accidents involving student and private pilots (a total of 58.33) as well as .2333 of the 50 accidents involving commercial and airline-transport pilots (a total of 11.67). These and similar numbers are shown in Table 14.3.

As the detail in Table 14.3 shows, we can find the expected frequency for any particular pair of attributes most rapidly by multiplying the known total frequencies for the two individual attributes and dividing the product by the total number of units observed. Thus,

$$\text{expected frequency, } f_e = \frac{\textit{row total} \times \textit{column total}}{\textit{sample size}}$$

A COMBINED TABLE To conduct a test of independence, we can conveniently show both the observed and expected frequencies in the same table, which we do in Table 14.4 on page 600.

In each of the twelve cells that are formed by the six numbered rows and the two numbered columns, the observed frequency (f_o) is shown in the upper-left portion, while the expected frequency (f_e) is shown in the lower-right portion. By comparing the actual with the expected in each cell, we can quickly get a general impression of how the variables relate to one another. Consider row 1. If accident cause and type of license held by the pilot were independent of one another, we would expect, given the boldfaced totals, about 58 student or private pilots and about 12 commercial or airline-transport pilots to have experienced thunderstorm accidents. Yet, in fact, pilots in the former group experienced fewer thunderstorm accidents than expected, while pilots in the latter group experienced more than expected. Could it be that student or private pilots know their limitations and stay on the ground when thunderstorms are about, while commercial or airline-transport pilots are induced by published schedules and presumably better training and equipment to take more risks? We shouldn't jump to that or any other conclusion quite that quickly. Our observed data, after all, are sample data and a different sample might tell a different story. In the following sections, we develop a more careful approach to assessing our Table 14.4 results.

TABLE 14.3 | Number of Civilian Aviation Accidents, Classified by Cause (A) and Type of Pilot's License (B): Expected Frequencies, Given Known Totals and Assuming Independence between A and B

This contingency table shows expected frequencies (typically symbolized by f_e) for various combinations of aviation-accident causes (A) and pilot's license types (B) under the assumption of independence. Setting up such a table is the second step in testing for independence between the two variables, A and B.

(A) Official Accident Cause	(B) License Held by Pilot-in-Command: Student or Private	(B) License Held by Pilot-in-Command: Commercial or Airline-Transport	Total
(1) Thunderstorm	[70(250)/300] = 58.33	[70(50)/300] = 11.67	**70**
(2) Icing	[50(250)/300] = 41.67	[50(50)/300] = 8.33	**50**
(3) Equipment Failure	[31(250)/300] = 25.83	[31(50)/300] = 5.17	**31**
(4) Controller Error	[30(250)/300] = 25.00	[30(50)/300] = 5.00	**30**
(5) Pilot Error	[86(250)/300] = 71.67	[86(50)/300] = 14.33	**86**
(6) Other	[33(250)/300] = 27.50	[33(50)/300] = 5.50	**33**
Total	**250**	**50**	**300**

TECHNICAL DETAIL

You may be wondering why expected frequencies can be computed rapidly as

$$\text{expected frequency, } f_e = \frac{\textit{row total} \times \textit{column total}}{\textit{sample size}}$$

The shortcut, in fact, employs the *special multiplication law for independent events* that we summarized as Formula 8.J on page 319. Under the assumption of independence,

$$p(\text{A } \textit{and} \text{ B}) = p(\text{A}) \times p(\text{B})$$

To take an example from Table 14.3,

$$p(\text{thunderstorm } \textit{and} \text{ student/private}) = p(\text{thunderstorm}) \times p(\text{student/private})$$

$$\frac{58.33}{300} = \frac{70}{300} \times \frac{250}{300}$$

Therefore, we can find the expected frequency of 58.33 as

$$58.33 = \left(\frac{70}{300} \times \frac{250}{300}\right)300 = \frac{70 \times 250}{300}$$

just as the shortcut formula demands.

TABLE 14.4 | Number of Civilian Aviation Accidents, Classified by Cause (A) and Type of Pilot's License (B): Observed Frequencies versus Expected Frequencies, Assuming Independence between A and B

This contingency table combines the information contained in Tables 14.2 and 14.3. Frequencies actually observed are shown in the upper-left portion of each cell; frequencies expected on the assumption of independence between variables A and B are shown in the lower-right portion.

(A) Official Accident Cause	(B) License Held by Pilot-in-Command				Total
	(1) Student or Private		(2) Commercial or Airline-Transport		
	f_o	f_e	f_o	f_e	
(1) Thunderstorm	50	58.33	20	11.67	**70**
(2) Icing	40	41.67	10	8.33	**50**
(3) Equipment Failure	25	25.83	6	5.17	**31**
(4) Controller Error	25	25.00	5	5.00	**30**
(5) Pilot Error	80	71.67	6	14.33	**86**
(6) Other	30	27.50	3	5.50	**33**
Total	**250**		**50**		**300**

COMPUTING THE CHI-SQUARE STATISTIC

Answers to questions such as that posed in last section can be found by calculating and interpreting a special kind of statistic that was introduced a century ago by Karl Pearson (1857–1936). The **chi-square statistic,** χ^2, is the sum of all the ratios that can be constructed by taking the difference between each cell's observed and expected frequency in a contingency table, squaring the difference, and then dividing this squared deviation by the expected frequency. Formula 14.A explains.

FORMULA 14.A | Chi-Square Statistic Used to Test the Alleged Independence of Two Qualitative Variables

$$\chi^2 = \sum \frac{(f_o - f_e)^2}{f_e}$$

where Σ stands for "sum of," f_o is an observed frequency, and f_e is the associated expected frequency.

Notes:

1. Contrary to the common practice of denoting population parameters by Greek letters and sample statistics by Roman letters, this statistic is denoted by the lowercase Greek letter χ, which is pronounced "ki" as in *kite*.
2. Each f_e value must equal 5 or more. If necessary, two or more rows or columns must be combined to achieve this result.

Table 14.5 illustrates the calculation of χ^2 with the help of our Table 14.4 data. The subsequent section explains the procedure.

TABLE 14.5 | The Calculation of Chi Square

This table shows the calculation of the chi-square statistic from the data embodied in Table 14.4. Because the χ^2 formula calls for the squaring of deviations between the observed and expected, χ^2 can never be negative but can take on values only of zero or above, as is the case here.

Row, Column	Observed Frequency, f_o	Expected Frequency (assuming independence) f_e	Deviation $f_o - f_e$	Squared Deviation $(f_o - f_e)^2$	Standardized Squared Deviation $\frac{(f_o - f_e)^2}{f_e}$
A1, B1	50	58.33	−8.33	69.39	1.19
A1, B2	20	11.67	8.33	69.39	5.95
A2, B1	40	41.67	−1.67	2.79	.07
A2, B2	10	8.33	1.67	2.79	.33
A3, B1	25	25.83	−.83	.69	.03
A3, B2	6	5.17	.83	.69	.13
A4, B1	25	25.00	0	0	0
A4, B2	5	5.00	0	0	0
A5, B1	80	71.67	8.33	69.39	.97
A5, B2	6	14.33	−8.33	69.39	4.84
A6, B1	30	27.50	2.50	6.25	.23
A6, B2	3	5.50	−2.50	6.25	1.14
Total	**300**	**300**	**0**		χ^2 **= 14.88**

INTERPRETING THE CHI-SQUARE STATISTIC

Formula 14.A certainly makes *intuitive* sense: We are interested in assessing differences between (1) values we have observed and (2) values we would expect if our two qualitative variables were independent of one another. Thus, it is reasonable for us to compute the difference between the observed frequency, f_o, and the expected frequency, f_e, for each cell of the contingency table.

Yet we cannot reach an *overall* assessment by simply summing these differences, because such a sum necessarily equals zero, as Table 14.5 confirms. For this reason, we square the deviations. That procedure has the added advantage of magnifying large deviations (which are probably the result of some kind of dependence between the variables studied) relative to small deviations (which are more likely the result of sampling error). Consider, in Table 14.5, the deviation of 8.33 relative to that of .83, a tenfold difference in magnitude. When squared, the numbers become 69.39 and .69, a 100-fold difference in magnitude. Large squared numbers are like a red flag, indicating likely *dependence* between our two qualitative variables.

Why, finally, does the formula divide each squared difference by the expected frequency? This division converts absolute into relative squared deviations and thereby puts all the cells on an equal footing. Consider the first two rows of Table 14.5. The absolute value of the deviation, and, therefore, of its squared value, is the same in each case, but a deviation of 8.33 from an expected value of 58.33 is surely less indicative of a dependent relationship than an identical deviation of 8.33 from an expected value of 11.67. This fact is evidenced by the different entries in the last column: 1.19 versus 5.95.

Yet all the intuitive sense that is embodied in our formula cannot rescue us from one problem: Our computational result ($\chi^2 = 14.88$) depends entirely on the particular sample that we selected. In a different sample, all the observed frequencies would have been different, and we would have computed a different value of χ^2 as well. Thus, we need to learn something about the sampling distribution of this statistic. That knowledge, in turn, will finally enable us to test the hypothesis of independence between any two qualitative variables and to do so while specifying a maximum acceptable α risk of erroneously rejecting a hypothesis of independence when it is true. Given sample size, that α value, in turn, implies a specific β risk of erroneously accepting a hypothesis of independence when it is false.

SAMPLING DISTRIBUTIONS OF CHI SQUARE

The nature of the sampling distribution of chi square depends on the number of *degrees of freedom* associated with the problem under investigation. We calculate degrees of freedom by counting the number of expected-frequency values we are free to set before the constraints of the problem dictate the remaining values. Consider Table 14.4. Given the column and row totals, which are the constraints of that problem, we are free to set any 5 of the 12 expected-frequency values. Once we have calculated, say, the first five f_e values in column B1—once we have calculated, that is, 58.33, 41.67, 25.83, 25.00, and 71.67—all of the remaining f_e values in both columns are automatically determined by the constraints. Because the first column sums to 250, the last f_e value of column B1 must equal 27.50. Then, given the six column B1 f_e values and the row totals, the remaining f_e values (in column B2) must necessarily be precisely what the table shows them to be. Thus, the problem involves only 5 degrees of freedom. In any contingency-table test, this number can most easily be found with the help of Formula 14.B. In our example, the formula confirms the degrees of freedom as $(6 - 1) \times (2 - 1) = 5$.

FORMULA 14.B | Number of Degrees of Freedom in a Contingency Table Test

$$d.f. = (\text{number of rows} - 1) \times (\text{number of columns} - 1)$$

Note: The table must have a minimum of 2 rows and 2 columns.

Not surprisingly, a probability distribution of the χ^2 random variable is called a **chi-square distribution,** and a different chi-square distribution exists for each possible number of degrees of freedom. This fact is illustrated in Figure 14.1 and discussed further in the Technical Detail box on page 604.

FIGURE 14.1 | Four Members of the Chi-Square Distribution Family

A different chi-square distribution exists for each possible number of degrees of freedom, d.f. Because the χ^2 random variable is a sum of squared deviations, negative values are impossible. All values, therefore, range between zero and positive infinity. Even though all chi-square distributions are, thus, skewed to the right, the extent of skewness decreases with increasing numbers of degrees of freedom. Chi-square distributions with 30 degrees of freedom or more very closely approach the normal distribution, a fact that is already evident by comparing panels (a) through (d).

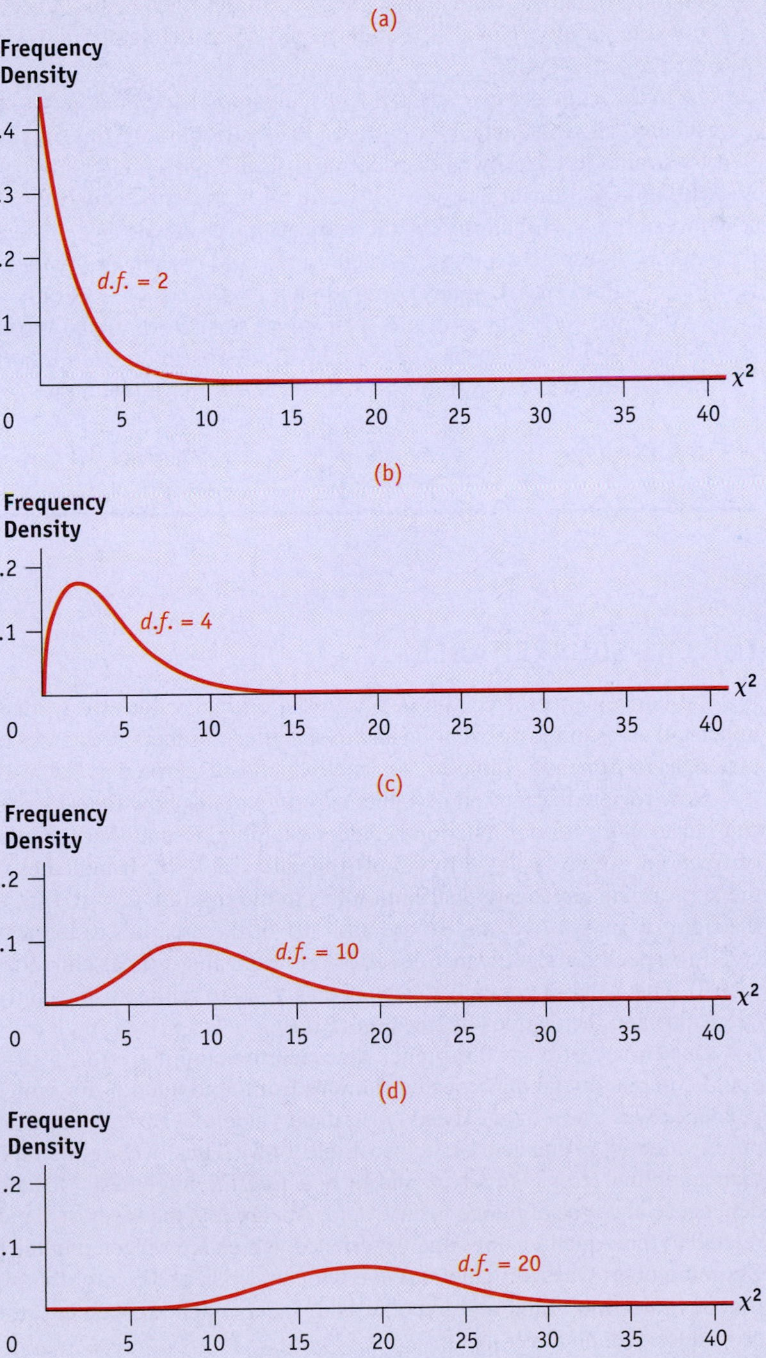

TECHNICAL DETAIL

The nature of a chi-square distribution is fairly complex. To understand it, consider a population of values, X, that are normally distributed. The corresponding standard normal deviates, $z = \frac{X - \mu}{\sigma}$, would be normally distributed as well. Yet the *squares* of these deviates, z^2, would *not* be normally distributed. Their distribution would be continuous, unimodal, and strongly skewed to the right, with values ranging from zero to positive infinity. This distribution would equal the sampling distribution of χ^2 with 1 degree of freedom.

Now consider two independent standard normal random variables, z_a, and z_b. If we squared each and added the squares, the distribution of this expression, $z_a^2 + z_b^2$, would be similar to the skewed distribution just discussed and would equal the sampling distribution of χ^2 with 2 degrees of freedom. In the same way, we can imagine finding the probability distributions for the sum of 4, 10, 20, or any other number of squared z values. In each case, these distributions would correspond to the sampling distribution of χ^2 with 4, 10, 20, or any other number of degrees of freedom.

Figure 14.1 shows several such chi-square distributions. What the caption does not tell you is this: The mean of every chi-square distribution equals the number of degrees of freedom, while its variance equals precisely twice that number. Thus,

$$\text{mean, } \mu_{\chi^2} = d.f. \quad \text{variance, } \sigma^2_{\chi^2} = 2\, d.f. \quad \text{standard deviation, } \sigma_{\chi^2} = \sqrt{2\, d.f.}$$

THE CHI-SQUARE TABLE

For the convenience of conducting χ^2 tests, critical values of χ^2 that correspond to specified upper-tail areas of the distribution and to specified numbers of degrees of freedom have been tabulated, as in Appendix Table M, a part of which is excerpted as Table 14.6.

Now review the caption of Table 14.6. It explains how to use Appendix Table M, which we can put to work for our aviation accident example. Recall that the example involves 5 degrees of freedom, so we focus on row 5 of Appendix Table M. It indicates that .95 of the area under the appropriate chi-square distribution lies to the right of $\chi^2 = 1.145$, that .90 of the area lies to the right of $\chi^2 = 1.610$, and so on, until .01 of the area lies to the right of $\chi^2 = 15.086$. If we cared to specify a significance level of $\alpha = .05$, the critical chi-square value would be $\chi^2 = 11.070$. This value is typically designated as $\chi^2_{.05(5)}$ to remind us instantly of the significance level ($\alpha = .05$) and the degrees of freedom (5 *d.f.*).

Our choice of $\alpha = .05$ implies that, due to sampling error, 5 percent of the χ^2 values we could compute by taking repeated samples from a population for which the hypothesis of independence was true would exceed our critical value of 11.07. In our example, however, the computed value of χ^2 equaled 14.88 (see Table 14.5). Thus, we are justified in suspecting that more than sampling error is involved and in *rejecting* the hypothesis of independence between accident cause and type of pilot's license held. Apparently, the types of accidents pilots encounter *are* related to their qualifications and experience, which are reflected in the type of license they hold. But remember: Our willingness to live with an α risk of .05 implies a willingness to make an erroneous rejection of the null hypothesis of independence 5 percent of the time when using this procedure over and over again.

TABLE 14.6 | Appendix Table M Excerpt: Chi-Square Distributions

This table provides values of χ^2_α that correspond to a given upper-tail area, α, and a specified number of degrees of freedom. For example, for an upper-tail area of .05 and 5 degrees of freedom, the critical value of $\chi^2_{.05(5)}$ equals 11.070.

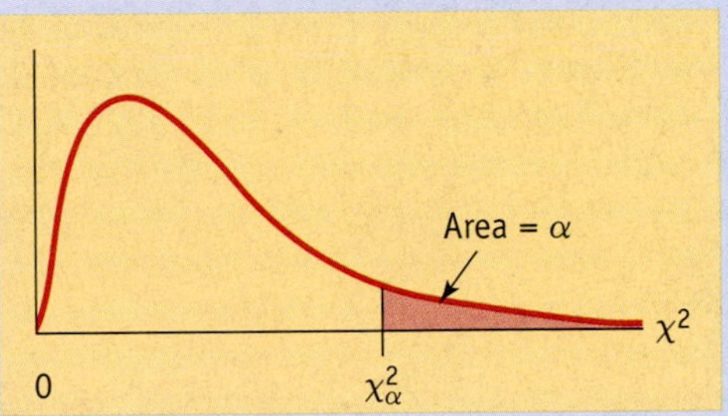

	Critical Values for Upper-Tail Area, α								
d.f.	.95	.90	.80	.50	.20	.10	.05	.02	.01
1	.00393	.0158	.0642	.455	1.642	2.706	3.841	5.412	6.635
2	.103	.211	.446	1.386	3.219	4.605	5.991	7.824	9.210
3	.352	.584	1.005	2.366	4.642	6.251	7.815	9.837	11.345
4	.711	1.064	1.649	3.357	5.989	7.779	9.488	11.668	13.277
5	1.145	1.610	2.343	4.351	7.289	9.236	**11.070**	13.388	15.086

SUMMARY OF PROCEDURE

We can summarize the procedure just introduced by showing how it relates to the hypothesis-testing steps introduced in Chapter 13.

Step 1: *Formulating two opposing hypotheses.*

H_0: The two variables (accident cause and type of pilot's license) are independent.

H_A: The two variables are dependent.

Step 2: *Selecting a test statistic.*

$$\chi^2 = \sum \frac{(f_o - f_e)^2}{f_e}$$

Step 3: *Deriving a decision rule.*

We set a significance level of $\alpha = .05$; hence, for 5 degrees of freedom, the critical value is $\chi^2_{.05(5)} = 11.070$ (Appendix Table M). Thus, the decision rule must be:

"Accept H_0 if $\chi^2 < 11.070$."

The decision rule is illustrated in Figure 14.2 on the next page; the critical value is encircled.

Step 4: *Using sample data to compute the test statistic and confronting it with the decision rule.*

After taking the sample, as noted in Table 14.2, an actual $\chi^2 = 14.88$ is calculated (Table 14.5). This value corresponds to the red arrow in Figure 14.2; it suggests that the null hypothesis should be *rejected.* At the 5 percent significance level, it appears that the accident cause and the type of pilot's license are statistically *dependent* variables.

FIGURE 14.2 | Testing the Alleged Independence of Two Qualitative Variables

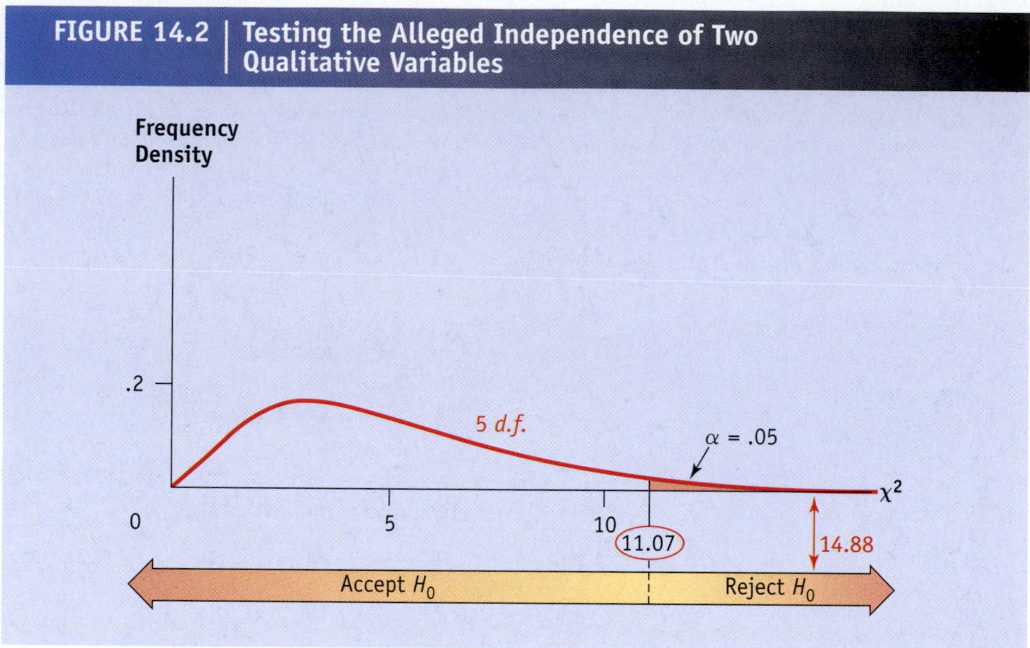

Note: χ^2 tests of independence (unlike χ^2 tests about variances discussed later in this chapter) are always upper-tailed because a perfect fit between f_o and f_e makes $\chi^2 = 0$. Because deviations between f_o and f_e are being squared, the greater the deviations are (positive or negative), the greater the computed value of χ^2 becomes.

EXCEL Example 14.1

Perform a chi-square test of independence with the sample data of Table 14.2 and thereby confirm the results of the preceding sections. Once again, use a significance level of .05.

SOLUTION:

1. Enter the data from the two center columns of Table 14.2, excluding the totals, into a new worksheet, using cells A1–A6 and B1–B6, respectively.
2. To compute expected frequencies for the column A data, enter the following formulas:
   =SUM(A1:A6)*SUM(A1:B1)/SUM(A1:B6) into D1
   =SUM(A1:A6)*SUM(A2:B2)/SUM(A1:B6) into D2
   =SUM(A1:A6)*SUM(A3:B3)/SUM(A1:B6) into D3
   =SUM(A1:A6)*SUM(A4:B4)/SUM(A1:B6) into D4
   =SUM(A1:A6)*SUM(A5:B5)/SUM(A1:B6) into D5
   =SUM(A1:A6)*SUM(A6:B6)/SUM(A1:B6) into D6
3. To compute expected frequencies for the column B data, enter the following formulas:
   =SUM(B1:B6)*SUM(A1:B1)/SUM(A1:B6) into E1
   =SUM(B1:B6)*SUM(A2:B2)/SUM(A1:B6) into E2
   =SUM(B1:B6)*SUM(A3:B3)/SUM(A1:B6) into E3
   =SUM(B1:B6)*SUM(A4:B4)/SUM(A1:B6) into E4
   =SUM(B1:B6)*SUM(A5:B5)/SUM(A1:B6) into E5
   =SUM(B1:B6)*SUM(A6:B6)/SUM(A1:B6) into E6

The result so far:

A	B	C	D	E
50	20		58.33333	11.66667
40	10		41.66667	8.333333
25	6		25.83333	5.166667
25	5		25	5
80	6		71.66667	14.33333
30	3		27.5	5.5

4. Enter labels *Number of row categories, Number of column categories, Significance level, Degrees of freedom, Critical chi-square, p-Value, and Chi-square test statistic,* respectively, into cells G1–G7.
5. Enter the following formulas or known values into adjacent column H cells:

   6 into H1

   2 into H2

   .05 into H3

   =(H1−1)*(H2-1) into H4

   =CHIINV(H3,H4) into H5
6. To find the p value, select H6. Click the **Function Wizard (*fx*)** > **Statistical** > **CHITEST** > **OK** to activate a dialog box. Under *Actual range,* enter **A1:B6**. Under *Expected range,* enter **D1:E6**. Click **OK**.
7. To find the chi-square test statistic, select H7. Click the **Function Wizard (*fx*)** > **Statistical** > **CHIINV** > **OK** to activate a dialog box. Under *Probability,* enter **H6**. Under *Deg freedom,* enter **H4**. Click **OK**.

   The result:

Number of row categories	6
Number of column categories	2
Significance level	0.05
Degrees of freedom	5
Critical chi-square	11.0705
p-Value	0.01088
Chi-square test statistic	14.8817

INTERPRETATION EXCEL confirms the earlier computations of expected frequencies (Tables 14.3 and 14.4) as well as the χ^2 value (shown in red) of Table 14.5. It also presents a p value of .011: If the hypothesis of independence is true, there exists a mere 1.1 percent chance of finding the χ^2 value obtained here. Given the larger $\alpha = .05$, the hypothesis of independence is *rejected.* Depending on the type of license they hold (and, presumably, the type of training and experience they have had), pilots have different types of accidents.

Note: This type of problem can also be solved much more rapidly by using HKStat, Sheet 34.

Application 14.1, *Racial Bias in Mortgage Lending?,* provides another example of the use of this technique.

APPLICATION 14.1

Racial Bias in Mortgage Lending?

Under the provisions of the Home Mortgage Disclosure Act of 1989, the Federal Reserve collected some 6.6 million mortgage applications from nearly 10,000 banks and other lenders in 1990. Table 14.A shows information supplied by the largest lender; Table 14.B relates similar data for one of the smallest.

TABLE 14.A | Number of Mortgage Applications by Race of Applicant and Subsequent Disposition; Security Pacific Housing Services of California, 1990

Race of Applicant	Approved	Denied	Total
Black	2,662	4,837	**7,499**
White	38,555	43,651	**82,206**
Total	**41,217**	**48,488**	**89,705**

TABLE 14.B | Number of Mortgage Applications by Race of Applicant and Subsequent Disposition; Wachovia Bank of North Carolina, 1990

Race of Applicant	Approved	Denied	Total
Black	275	785	**1,060**
White	3,008	766	**3,774**
Total	**3,283**	**1,551**	**4,834**

Let us consider the expected frequencies for the Table 14.A case. Overall, 41,217 of 89,705 applications were approved, or 45.9 percent. Identical percentages for blacks and whites would have produced entries of 3,442 and 37,733 in the Approved column. By implication, the numbers in the Denied column would have been 4,057 and 44,473, reflecting the overall denial rate of 54.1 percent.

We can similarly figure the expected frequencies for Table 14.B. Overall, 3,283 of 4,834 applications were approved, or 67.9 percent. Identical percentages for blacks and whites would have produced entries of 720 and 2,563 in the Approved column. By implication, the numbers in the Denied column would have been 340 and 1,211, reflecting the overall denial rate of 32.1 percent.

We can quickly perform a χ^2 test:

Step 1: H_0: Race and mortgage disposition are independent.
H_A: Race and mortgage disposition are dependent.

Step 2: We select the test statistic of Formula 14.A.

Step 3: If we set a significance level of $\alpha = .001$, and given 1 degree of freedom (Formula 14.B), the critical value of $\chi^2_{.001(1)} = 10.827$ (Appendix Table M). The decision rule is: "Accept H_0 if $\chi^2 \leq 10.827$." Thus, there is only 1 chance in 1,000 that χ^2 is equal to this value or a larger one if H_0 is true.

Step 4: A computer calculation produces χ^2 values of 359.754 for Table 14.A and of 1,097.609 for Table 14.B. In both cases, the p value is .000. Accordingly, H_0 is *rejected.* Race and mortgage disposition are *dependent* variables.

Caution, however, is advised: The preceding analysis is only a first step in *proving* racial bias. So far, the analysis has completely ignored other crucial factors, such as applicants' income levels, debt levels, and credit histories.

SOURCE: Data from Federal Reserve System.

14.3 Making Inferences about More Than Two Population Proportions

As the previous examples have shown, when we calculate expected frequencies for the various cells of a contingency table, we effectively assume that certain *proportions* (such as those of approved mortgage applicants) are identical for all the categories of some variable, such as black applicants and white applicants. It is not surprising, therefore, that the same technique that allows us to test for the independence of two qualitative population variables can also be used to test whether a number of population proportions equal each other or are equal to any predetermined set of values. The following sections provide illustrations.

EXAMPLE PROBLEM 14.2

Consider the process of assembling television sets. Management is interested in testing the hypothesis that the proportion of defective units produced (which has been .05 in the past) would be the same for each of 6 possible assembly-line speeds. The company statistician is asked to take 6 samples of 100 TV sets each while different assembly-line speeds are being maintained, and then perform a test at the 1 percent significance level.

SOLUTION:

Step 1: *Formulating two opposing hypotheses.*

H_0: The population proportion of defectives is the same for each of 6 assembly-line speeds; that is, $\pi_1 = \pi_2 = \pi_3 = \pi_4 = \pi_5 = \pi_6 = .05$.

H_A: The population proportion of defectives is not the same for each of 6 assembly-line speeds; that is, at least one of the equalities in H_0 does not hold.

Step 2: *Selecting a test statistic.*

$$\chi^2 = \sum \frac{(f_o - f_e)^2}{f_e}$$

Step 3: *Deriving a decision rule.*

Given $\alpha = .01$ and 5 degrees of freedom (2 possible product qualities and 6 possible assembly-line speeds make for 1×5 *d.f.*), the critical $\chi^2_{.01(5)} = 15.086$ (Appendix Table M). The decision rule is: "Accept H_0 if $\chi^2 \leq 15.086$."

Step 4: *Using sample data to compute the test statistic and confronting it with the decision rule.*

The sample, we assume, reveals the data of Table 14.7 on the next page. The calculation of the test statistic is illustrated in Table 14.8.

Given the computed test statistic, H_0 should be *accepted* at the 1 percent level of significance. The population proportion of defectives is the same for each assembly-line speed tested.

TABLE 14.7 | Sample Results

Product Quality	Assembly-Line Speeds (units per hour)						Total
	A = 60	B = 70	C = 80	D = 90	E = 100	F = 110	
(1) Defective	6	4	5	5	6	4	**30**
(2) Acceptable	94	96	95	95	94	96	**570**
Total	**100**	**100**	**100**	**100**	**100**	**100**	**600**

TABLE 14.8 | Computing χ^2 (Assembly-Line Speeds)

Row, Column	Observed Frequency f_o	Expected Frequency (assuming independence) f_e	Deviation $f_o - f_e$	Squared Deviation $(f_o - f_e)^2$	Standardized Squared Deviation $\frac{(f_o - f_e)^2}{f_e}$
1,A	6	5	1	1	.20
1,B	4	5	−1	1	.20
1,C	5	5	0	0	0
1,D	5	5	0	0	0
1,E	6	5	1	1	.20
1,F	4	5	−1	1	.20
2,A	94	95	−1	1	.01
2,B	96	95	1	1	.01
2,C	95	95	0	0	0
2,D	95	95	0	0	0
2,E	94	95	−1	1	.01
2,F	96	95	1	1	.01
Total	**600**	**600**	**0**		χ^2 = **.84**

EXCEL Example 14.2

Use EXCEL to confirm the Example Problem 14.2 result.

SOLUTION:

1. Enter the row (1) and (2) data of Table 14.7, excluding the totals, into a new worksheet, using cells A1–F1 and A2–F2, respectively.
2. To compute expected frequencies for the row (1) data, enter the following formulas:
   =SUM(A1:A2)*SUM(A1:F1)/SUM(A1:F2) into A4
   =SUM(B1:B2)*SUM(A1:F1)/SUM(A1:F2) into B4
   =SUM(C1:C2)*SUM(A1:F1)/SUM(A1:F2) into C4
   =SUM(D1:D2)*SUM(A1:F1)/SUM(A1:F2) into D4

=SUM(E1:E2)*SUM(A1:F1)/SUM(A1:F2) into E4

=SUM(F1:F2)*SUM(A1:F1)/SUM(A1:F2) into F4

3. To compute expected frequencies for the row (2) data, enter the following formulas:

   =SUM(A1:A2)*SUM(A2:F2)/SUM(A1:F2) into A5

   =SUM(B1:B2)*SUM(A2:F2)/SUM(A1:F2) into B5

   =SUM(C1:C2)*SUM(A2:F2)/SUM(A1:F2) into C5

   =SUM(D1:D2)*SUM(A2:F2)/SUM(A1:F2) into D5

   =SUM(E1:E2)*SUM(A2:F2)/SUM(A1:F2) into E5

   =SUM(F1:F2)*SUM(A2:F2)/SUM(A1:F2) into F5

   The result so far:

A	B	C	D	E	F
6	4	5	5	6	4
94	96	95	95	94	96
5	5	5	5	5	5
95	95	95	95	95	95

4. Enter labels *Number of row categories, Number of column categories, Significance level, Degrees of freedom, Critical chi-square, p-Value,* and *Chi-square test statistic,* respectively, into cells G1–G7.
5. Enter the following formulas or known values into adjacent column H cells:

   2 into H1

   6 into H2

   .01 into H3

   =(H1−1)*(H2−1) into H4

   =CHIINV(H3,H4) into H5
6. To find the p value, select H6. Click the **Function Wizard (*fx*)** > **Statistical** > **CHITEST** > **OK** to activate a dialog box. Under *Actual range,* enter **A1:F2**. Under *Expected range,* enter **A4:F5**. Click **OK**.
7. To find the chi-square test statistic, select H7. Click the **Function Wizard (*fx*)** > **Statistical** > **CHIINV** > **OK** to activate a dialog box. Under *Probability,* enter **H6**. Under *Deg freedom,* enter **H4**. Click **OK**.

   The result:

Number of row categories	2
Number of column categories	6
Significance level	0.01
Degrees of freedom	5
Critical chi-square	15.0863
p-Value	0.97427
Chi-square test statistic	0.8421

INTERPRETATION EXCEL confirms the earlier computations of expected frequencies (Table 14.8) and the χ^2 value (shown in red). It also presents a *p* value of .97427: If the null hypothesis is true, there exists a 97.4 percent chance of finding the χ^2 value obtained here. Given the smaller $\alpha = .01$, the null hypothesis is *accepted.*

Note: This type of problem can also be solved much more rapidly by using HKStat, Sheet 34.

EXAMPLE PROBLEM 14.3

The population proportions being tested need not all be the same size. Consider three firms, A, B, and C, holding current market shares of 10, 40, and 50 percent for a particular product. The smallest firm (A) wants to change its product design and wonders whether the subsequent market shares will be the same as before. A statistical test is to be conducted at the 5 percent significance level after asking a random sample of 300 consumers to indicate preferences among the newly designed product of firm A and the traditional products of firms B and C.

SOLUTION:

Step 1: *Formulating two opposing hypotheses.*

H_0: The population proportions (market shares) will be the same as in the past; that is, $\pi_A = .10$, $\pi_B = .40$, and $\pi_C = .50$.

H_A: The population proportions will not be the same as in the past; that is, they will differ from those given in H_0.

Step 2: *Selecting a test statistic.*

$$\chi^2 = \sum \frac{(f_o - f_e)^2}{f_e}$$

Step 3: *Deriving a decision rule.*

Given $\alpha = .05$ and 2 degrees of freedom, the critical $\chi^2_{.05(2)} = 5.991$ (Appendix Table M). The decision rule is: "Accept H_0 if $\chi^2 \leq 5.991$."

TABLE 14.9 | Computing χ^2 (Market Shares)

Product	Number Preferring Product: Observed Frequency f_o	Number Preferring Product: Expected Frequency (if H_0 is true) f_e	Deviation $f_o - f_e$	Squared Deviation $(f_o - f_e)^2$	Standardized Squared Deviation $\frac{(f_o - f_e)^2}{f_e}$
New A	90	300(.10) = 30	60	3,600	120.0
Old B	90	300(.40) = 120	−30	900	7.5
Old C	120	300(.50) = 150	−30	900	6.0
Total	**300**	**300**	**0**		$\chi^2 = 133.5$

Step 4: *Using sample data to compute the test statistic and confronting it with the decision rule.*

The sample, we assume, reveals the observed frequencies in Table 14.9. The expected frequencies have been calculated on the assumption that the null hypothesis is true. Given the computed test statistic, H_0 should be *rejected.* Future market shares are unlikely to be the same as in the past.

Another example of this procedure is provided by Application 14.2, *Were Mendel's Data Fudged?*

APPLICATION 14.2

WERE MENDEL'S DATA FUDGED?

In the 1860s, the Austrian monk Gregor Mendel (1822–1884) wrote an important paper about inheritance. He postulated the existence of entities, now called *genes,* that determine how one generation passes various characteristics on to the next. For example, according to one of his theories, now known as Mendel's Second Law of Inheritance, the cross-fertilization of two pure strains of pea plants—one producing only round yellow seeds, the other one only wrinkled green seeds—would produce a first generation of hybrids with nothing but round yellow seeds. Yet a mating of these hybrids with one another would yield plants with round yellow, round green, wrinkled yellow, as well as wrinkled green seeds, and would produce these in definite proportions of 9 : 3 : 3 : 1. Mendel performed numerous experiments to back up his theories. One experiment involved the just-mentioned law and yielded the data for the second-generation hybrids given in Table 14.C.

We can easily perform a χ^2 test of the null hypothesis that this sample of 556 observations has come from a population obeying Mendel's Second Law. The theoretical proportions of 9 : 3 : 3 : 1 translate into the expected frequencies given in Table 14.D, which also shows the calculation of $\chi^2 = .47$.

TABLE 14.C | Mendel's Experiment

Pea Type	Observed Frequency f_o
Round yellow	315
Round green	108
Wrinkled yellow	101
Wrinkled green	32
Total	**556**

If we were to perform a χ^2 test at the 5 percent level of significance (there being 3 degrees of freedom), the critical value would be $\chi^2_{.05(3)} = 7.815$. Thus, the null hypothesis of experimental data confirming Mendel's Second Law would be *accepted.* But note the tiny value of χ^2 calculated in Table 14.D. The fit between expected and observed frequencies is almost perfect. The great statistician Ronald A. Fisher (1890–1962) thought this fit was too good to be true, especially after noting that such unusually close agreement between the observed and the expected could be found in *all* of Mendel's experiments! Fisher, therefore, made an experiment of his own. For each of Mendel's experiments, he computed the χ^2 value. Then he pooled the results by adding all the χ^2 values and also adding *all* the numbers of degrees of freedom. (This is a legitimate procedure as long as all the experiments are independent of one another. Thus, if one experiment yields $\chi^2 = .47$ and has 3 degrees of freedom, while another experiment yields $\chi^2 = .61$ and has 5 degrees of freedom, the two have a pooled χ^2 of $.47 + .61 = 1.08$ with $3 + 5 = 8$ degrees of freedom.) For all of Mendel's data, Fisher found a pooled χ^2 value of 41.6 with 84 degrees of freedom. More importantly, such a low pooled χ^2 value, or a lower value, would occur, Fisher found, only 7 times in 100,000 experiments. That is, if 100,000 scientists each repeated Mendel's experiments, only 7 of them would manage to match Mendel's own low χ^2; 99,993 would get results with a larger χ^2. Thus, Mendel was either very, very lucky indeed or his data were fudged. It is hard to escape the latter conclusion.

Postscript: Fisher believed that Mendel's gardening assistant, who was overly eager to please his master, was to blame. We should note, however, that Mendel helped *invent* modern science; his standards were not ours. Anticipating

(continued)

Application 14.2 (continued)

stiff criticism, he may have used mathematical sleight of hand to persuade recalcitrant colleagues of the correctness of his insight. Indeed, other giants of science have also been accused of fabricating data in order to support what were then "outrageous" theories. The accused include Johannes Kepler (1571–1630), who claimed that planets moved around the sun in elliptical orbits, and Isaac Newton (1642–1727), who formulated the law of gravitation.

SOURCES: Adapted from J. H. Bennett, ed., *Experiments in Plant Hybridisation* (Edinburgh: Oliver and Boyd, 1965), especially pp. 23 and 78; and William J. Broad, "After 400 Years, a Challenge to Kepler: He Fabricated His Data, Scholar Says," *The New York Times,* January 23, 1990, pp. C1 and C6.

TABLE 14.D | Computing χ^2 (Mendel's Experiment)

Pea Type	Observed Frequency f_o	Expected Frequency (if H_0 is true) f_e	Deviation $f_o - f_e$	Squared Deviation $(f_o - f_e)^2$	Standardized Squared Deviation $\frac{(f_o - f_e)^2}{f_e}$
Round yellow	315	312.75	2.25	5.0625	.016
Round green	108	104.25	3.75	14.0625	.135
Wrinkled yellow	101	104.25	−3.25	10.5625	.101
Wrinkled green	32	34.75	−2.75	7.5625	.218
Total	**556**	**556**	**0**		χ^2 **= .47**

14.4 Making Inferences about a Population Variance

The sample variance, s^2, is an unbiased estimator of the population variance, σ^2, provided the selections of sample elements are statistically independent events. Prior to the selection of an actual sample, however, the sample variance, like every sample summary measure, is a random variable. As it turns out, probabilities concerning the sample variance can be established with the help of χ^2 distributions because the sample variance can be converted into a chi-square random variable with $n - 1$ degrees of freedom, by a procedure indicated in Formula14.C.

FORMULA 14.C | Chi-Square Statistic for Variance Tests

$$\chi^2 = \frac{s^2(n-1)}{\sigma^2}$$

where s^2 is the sample variance, n is sample size, and σ^2 is the population variance.

PROBABILITY INTERVALS FOR THE SAMPLE VARIANCE

Given Formula 14.C, we can quickly establish probability intervals for s^2 with the help of Appendix Table M.

EXAMPLE PROBLEM 14.4

After years of careful record keeping, the executives of a pharmaceutical firm claim that the weights of the company's best-selling tablets are normally distributed with a population standard deviation of $\sigma = 2$ milligrams. The population variance, therefore, is $\sigma^2 = 4$.

a. If we took a simple random sample of 25 tablets from this population, what would be the probability of finding a sample variance between 3 and 5?

b. Below which limit would we find the 5 percent lowest sample variances?

c. Above which limit would we find the 5 percent highest sample variances?

d. Why would anyone ever want to know answers to questions such as the above?

SOLUTION:

a. *For the lower limit* of $s^2 = 3$, we get a lower χ^2 value of

$$\chi_L^2 = \frac{s^2(n-1)}{\sigma^2} = \frac{3(24)}{4} = 18$$

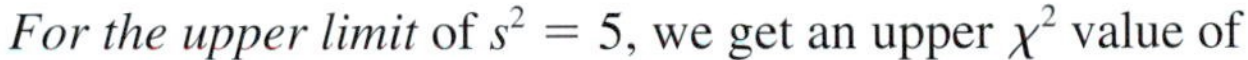

For the upper limit of $s^2 = 5$, we get an upper χ^2 value of

$$\chi_U^2 = \frac{s^2(n-1)}{\sigma^2} = \frac{5(24)}{4} = 30$$

The probability sought, accordingly, equals the probability of finding χ^2 values within the range of 18 to 30. An inspection of the appropriate row of Appendix Table M (for 24 degrees of freedom) reveals that an upper-tail area of slightly more than .8 lies to the right of $\chi^2 = 18$, while an upper-tail area of slightly less than .2 lies to the right of $\chi^2 = 30$. Thus, an area of about $.8 - .2 = .6$ lies between these values; this value of about .6 is also the probability of finding a sample variance between 3 and 5 in our example.

b. We can rewrite Formula 14.C to define the *lower* variance limit sought as

$$s_L^2 = \frac{\sigma^2 \times \chi_L^2}{n-1}$$

wherein 95 percent of the area under the χ^2 distribution with 24 degrees of freedom lies to the right and 5 percent to the left of the *lower* chi-square value of $\chi^2_{.95(24)} = 13.848$. Accordingly,

$$s_L^2 = \frac{\sigma^2 \times \chi_L^2}{n-1} = \frac{4(13.848)}{24} = 2.308$$

c. We can rewrite the Box 14.C formula to define the *upper* variance limit sought as

$$s_U^2 = \frac{\sigma^2 \times \chi_U^2}{n-1}$$

wherein 5 percent of the area under the χ^2 distribution with 24 degrees of freedom lies to the right and 95 percent to the left of the *upper* chi-square value of $\chi^2_{.05(24)} = 36.415$. Accordingly,

$$s^2_U = \frac{\sigma^2 \times \chi^2_U}{n-1} = \frac{4(36.415)}{24} = 6.069$$

Thus, 5 percent of all s^2 values lie below 2.308, another 5 percent lie above 6.069, and 90 percent lie between these values.

d. Imagine you were a statistician who was asked to help defend the company in a lawsuit. If repeated samples were to validate the values derived in (a) − (c), the court might believe the original claim.

CONFIDENCE INTERVALS FOR THE POPULATION VARIANCE

Unlike in the example just employed, the population variance, σ^2, is typically unknown and the problem is to make an estimate of it. In that case, the procedure used above can be adjusted to yield a *confidence-interval estimate* of σ^2. By appropriately rewriting the expressions used in part (a) of Example Problem 14.4, we can derive Formula 14.D.

FORMULA 14.D | Confidence Interval for the Population Variance, σ^2

$$\frac{s^2(n-1)}{\chi^2_U} \leq \sigma^2 \leq \frac{s^2(n-1)}{\chi^2_L}$$

where s^2 is the sample variance, n is sample size, χ^2_U is the value of the chi-square variable with $n - 1$ degrees of freedom such that larger values have a probability of $\alpha/2$, while χ^2_L is the value of the chi-square variable with $n - 1$ degrees of freedom such that smaller values have a probability of $\alpha/2$, and the confidence level is $1 - \alpha$.

EXAMPLE PROBLEM 14.5

Consider a pharmaceutical firm that wants to estimate the variance in a population of tablet weights. A sample of 30 tablets yields a sample variance of $s^2 = 3$. What would a 90 percent confidence interval of the population variance be?

SOLUTION: Given 29 degrees of freedom, and $\alpha = .10$, Appendix Table M yields $\chi^2_U = \chi^2_{.05(29)} = 42.557$ and $\chi^2_L = \chi^2_{.95(29)} = 17.708$. Accordingly, the interval sought is

$$\frac{3(29)}{42.557} \leq \sigma^2 \leq \frac{3(29)}{17.708}$$

or

$$2.04 \leq \sigma^2 \leq 4.91$$

With 90 percent confidence, the population variance can be said to lie between 2.04 and 4.91 milligrams squared. Hence, the population standard deviation is between 1.43 and 2.22 milligrams, the square roots of these values.

TESTING HYPOTHESES ABOUT THE POPULATION VARIANCE

We can easily adapt the foregoing technique further in order to test various hypotheses about the population variance. These hypotheses can be one-sided or two-sided and, in the former case, lower-tailed or upper-tailed, just as noted in Chapter 13 with respect to other population parameters. Three examples illustrate the possibilities.

EXAMPLE PROBLEM 14.6

The manager of a bank is thinking of introducing a "single-line" policy that directs all customers to a single waiting line in the order of their arrival. That line, in turn, "feeds" customers to different tellers as they become available. Although such a policy does not change the average time customers must wait, the manager prefers it because it decreases waiting-time variability. The manager's critics, however, claim that this variability will be *at least* as great as under the bank's traditional multiple-independent-lines policy. According to the bank's records, waiting times in multiple independent lines in the past had a standard deviation of $\sigma \geq 8$ minutes per customer (and, thus, a variance of 64 or more). A hypothesis test at the 2 percent significance level is to settle the issue, based on the experience of a random sample of 30 customers subjected to the new policy.

SOLUTION:

Step 1: *Formulating two opposing hypotheses.*

$$H_0: \sigma_0^2 \geq 64$$
$$H_A: \sigma_0^2 < 64$$

Step 2: *Selecting a test statistic.*

$$\chi^2 = \frac{s^2(n-1)}{\sigma_0^2}$$

Step 3: *Deriving a decision rule.*

Given a desired significance level of $\alpha = .02$ and 29 degrees of freedom, Appendix Table M suggests a critical value of $\chi^2_{.98(29)} = 15.574$, this being a lower-tailed test. (The startling new claim is that variability is less, not the same or larger, as critics say.) Thus, the decision rule must be: "Accept H_0 if $\chi^2 > 15.574$." The critical value is encircled in Figure 14.3.

Step 4: *Using sample data to compute the test statistic and confronting it with the decision rule.*

After taking a sample of 30 customers, the statistician finds the sample single-line waiting times to have a standard deviation of $s = 3$ minutes per customer. Accordingly, the computed value of the test statistic equals

$$\chi^2 = \frac{s^2(n-1)}{\sigma_0^2} = \frac{3^2(30-1)}{64} = 4.08$$

FIGURE 14.3 | Testing the Waiting Line Policy

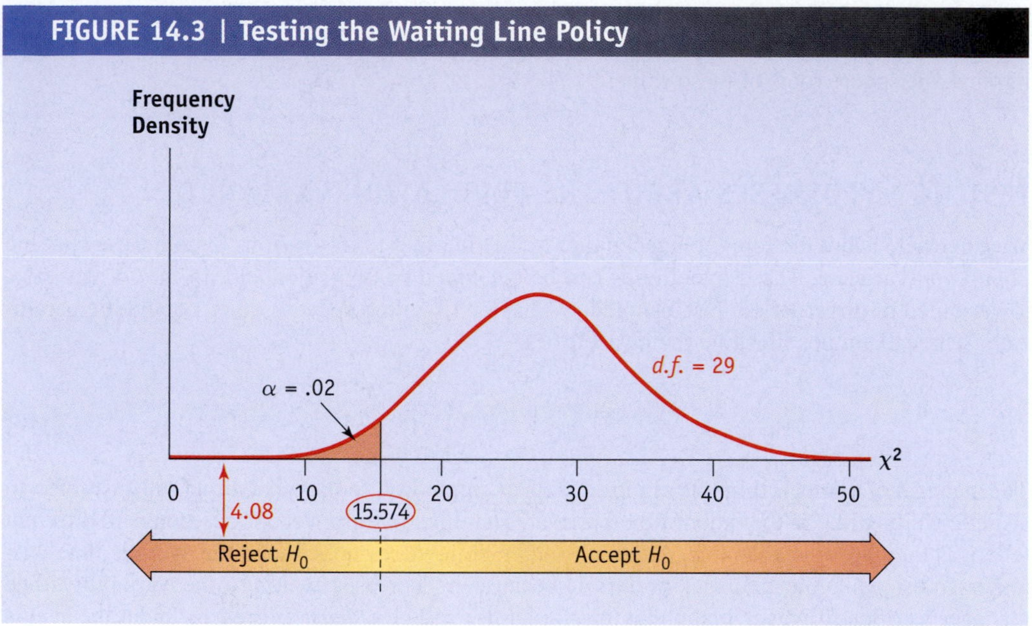

This value corresponds to the red arrow in Figure 14.3; it suggests that the null hypothesis should be *rejected.* At the 2 percent significance level, the sample result is statistically significant. The observed divergence from the hypothesized value of $\sigma_0 = 8$ minutes is unlikely to be the result of chance factors operating during sampling. It is more likely to be the result of the manager being right: A single line feeding to many tellers does reduce waiting-time variability.

EXAMPLE PROBLEM 14.7

A manufacturer of precision instruments is bringing out a "new and better" model of a radar altimeter, an instrument that measures aircraft height above the ever-changing ground rather than above mean sea level (as traditional altimeters measure altitude). The standard deviation of altitude readouts on the old model was *at most* $\sigma = 5$ feet, making the variance 25 or less. A hypothesis test at the 5 percent significance level is to be conducted concerning a pilot's claim that the readout variability on the new model actually exceeds that on the old model. The test involves getting 20 readings from a known height above the ground.

SOLUTION:

Step 1: *Formulating two opposing hypotheses.*

$$H_0: \sigma_0^2 \leq 25$$
$$H_A: \sigma_0^2 > 25$$

Step 2: *Selecting a test statistic.*

$$\chi^2 = \frac{s^2(n-1)}{\sigma_0^2}$$

FIGURE 14.4 | Testing Radar Altimeters

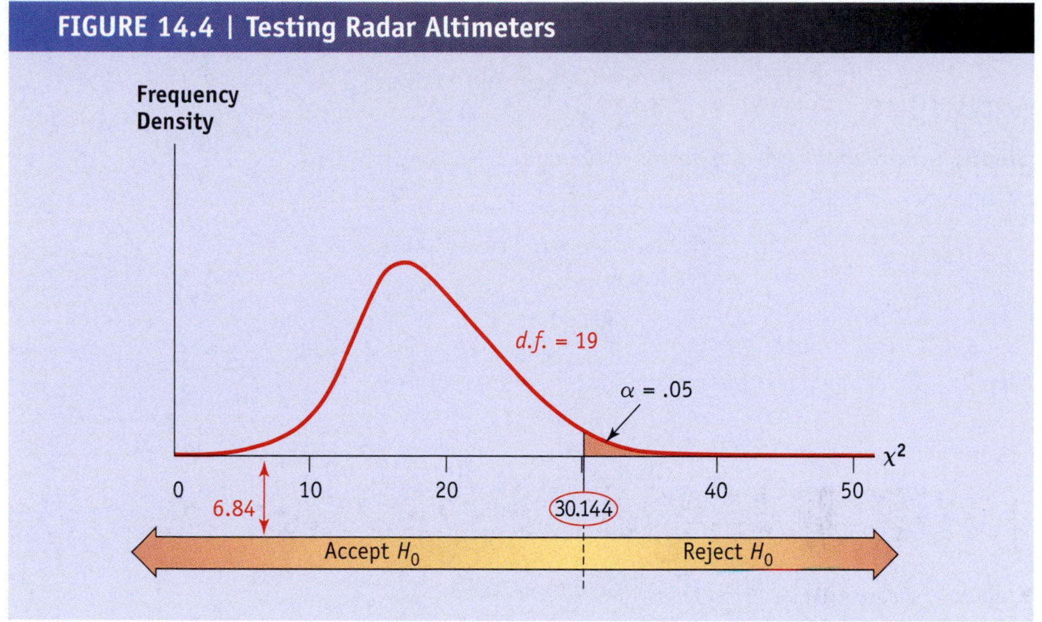

Step 3: *Deriving a decision rule.*

Given a desired significance level of $\alpha = .05$ and 19 degrees of freedom, Appendix Table M suggests a critical value of $\chi^2_{.05(19)} = 30.144$, this being an upper-tailed test. (The startling new claim is that variability is greater, not the same or less, as the manufacturer says.) Thus, the decision rule must be: "Accept H_0 if $\chi^2 \leq 30.144$." The critical value is encircled in Figure 14.4.

Step 4: *Using sample data to compute the test statistic and confronting it with the decision rule.*

After taking the 20 readings, an engineer finds them to have a standard deviation of $s = 3$ feet. Accordingly, the computed value of the test statistic equals

$$\chi^2 = \frac{s^2(n-1)}{\sigma_0^2} = \frac{3^2(20-1)}{25} = 6.84$$

This value corresponds to the red arrow in Figure 14.4; it suggests that the null hypothesis should be *accepted.* At the 5 percent significance level, the sample result is not statistically significant. The new model is equal to or better than the old one, as claimed by the manufacturer.

EXAMPLE PROBLEM 14.8

An aircraft manufacturer is concerned about variability in the diameters of lids used to seal fuel tanks located inside aircraft wings. Only a narrow range of diameters is acceptable. Lids that fit too tightly prevent air from entering the tanks as the fuel is being used, creating a vacuum and, ultimately, causing the wing structure to collapse. Lids that fit too loosely can allow fuel to be sucked out of the tank during flight, which is equally undesirable from the point of view of flight safety. A test at the 2 percent significance level is to be conducted with a random sample of 20 fuel-tank lids to see whether the population variance of lid diameters equals .0001 inch squared, as specified by engineers.

SOLUTION:

Step 1: *Formulating two opposing hypotheses.*

$$H_0: \sigma_0^2 = .0001$$
$$H_A: \sigma_0^2 \neq .0001$$

Step 2: *Selecting a test statistic.*

$$\chi^2 = \frac{s^2(n - 1)}{\sigma_0^2}$$

Step 3: *Deriving a decision rule.*

Given a desired significance level of $\alpha = .02$ and a two-tailed test, a lower and upper critical χ^2 value must be established so that .01 of the area under the χ^2 distribution lies, respectively, below or above these values. According to Appendix Table M (and for 19 degrees of freedom) these values are $\chi^2_{.99(19)} = 7.633$ and $\chi^2_{.01(19)} = 36.191$. Thus, the decision rule must be: "Accept H_0 if $7.633 \leq \chi^2 \leq 36.191$." The critical values are encircled in Figure 14.5.

FIGURE 14.5 | Testing Fuel Tank Lids

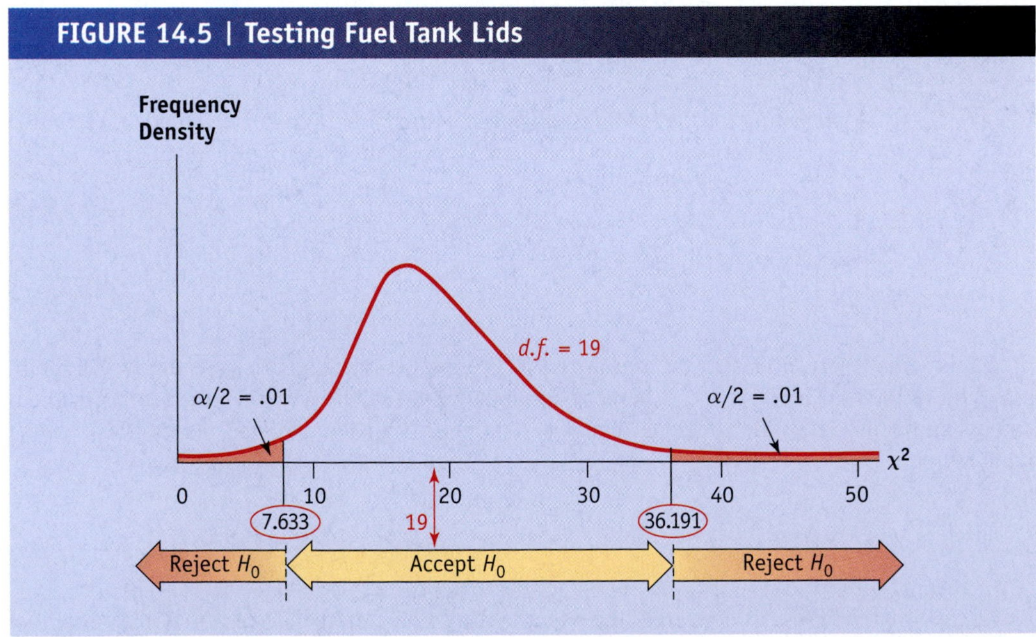

Step 4: *Using sample data to compute the test statistic and confronting it with the decision rule.*

After measuring the 20 diameters, an engineer finds them to have a standard deviation of $s = .01$ inch. Accordingly, the computed value of the test statistic equals

$$\chi^2 = \frac{s^2(n-1)}{\sigma_0^2} = \frac{(.01)^2(20-1)}{.0001} = 19$$

This value corresponds to the red arrow in Figure 14.5; it suggests that the null hypothesis should be *accepted.* At the 2 percent significance level, the sample result is not statistically significant. The lids do meet specifications.

14.5 Conducting Goodness-of-Fit Tests

Many statistical procedures make crucial assumptions about the type of population from which sample data are generated. Unless these assumptions are fulfilled, the procedures generate invalid results. (Consider, for example, last chapter's independent small-samples test of the difference between two population means. It assumes that the two sampled populations are normally distributed *and* have equal variances.) Our need to know things about the populations we sample explains the popularity of yet another kind of χ^2 test:

DEFINITION 14.4 A statistical test that determines the likelihood that sample data have been generated from a population that conforms to a specified type of probability distribution is a **goodness-of-fit test.**

Any goodness-of-fit test compares the entire shapes of two (discrete or continuous) probability distributions: one describing known sample data and the other one describing hypothetical population data. The aim of the test might be limited to identifying only the family to which the underlying distribution belongs, or it might go further, seeking even to identify a particular member of that family. Accordingly, the null hypothesis to be tested might be rather general, such as "The sample data come from a population that is normally distributed." It can also be more specific: "The sample data come from a normally distributed population with a mean of 100 and a standard deviation of 10." In every case, the alternative hypothesis claims that "the sample data come from some other kind of population."

In this type of test, a null hypothesis can be false in many different ways. In the example just cited, sample data might come from all sorts of populations that are *not* normally distributed, or even from one that is normally distributed but which has population parameters that differ from those specified. As a result, it is difficult to calculate the β risk (of erroneously accepting a null hypothesis that is false) for a goodness-of-fit test, unless we first specify in what particular way the null hypothesis is false. As a matter of fact, as more advanced texts show, the best approach to protecting against a type II error lies in taking a fairly large sample.

The following sections provide examples of how observed frequency distributions based on sample data can help us make inferences about the distribution of the underlying population data. Given a single sample, a perfect match between the two is highly unlikely, but on the average, across many samples, we expect that the sample data will reveal to us the nature of the population distribution.

DEGREES OF FREEDOM As Formula 14.E illustrates, in any goodness-of-fit test, the number of degrees of freedom equals the number of classes for which observed and expected frequencies are to be compared minus 1 minus the number of population parameters that are being estimated from the sample data. The negative 1 in the expression reflects a now-familiar fact: Once all but one of the expected frequencies have been calculated, the last of these frequencies is predetermined because the sum of expected frequencies must equal sample size (that is, the sum of observed frequencies). The further reduction of the number of degrees of freedom by 1 for each estimated parameter provides more precise results, as more advanced texts show.

FORMULA 14.E | Degrees of Freedom in a Goodness-of-Fit Test

$$d.f. = \text{number of classes (adjusted)} - 1 - \text{number of parameters estimated from sample}$$

Note: Each expected frequency must equal 5 or more. If necessary, the number of classes must be *adjusted* by combining adjacent classes until this result is achieved.

TESTING A FIT TO THE BINOMIAL DISTRIBUTION

The following example introduces the goodness-of-fit procedure by testing whether sample data come from a binomially distributed population.

EXAMPLE PROBLEM 14.9

A city inspector investigates the compliance of landlords with six housing code conditions. A simple random sample of 200 apartments reveals the data in the first two columns of Table 14.10. The inspector wants to conduct a hypothesis test at the 5 percent significance level to determine whether the sample comes from a population in which the number of actual violations per apartment (out of six possible violations) is a binomially distributed random variable.

SOLUTION:

Step 1: *Formulating two opposing hypotheses.*

H_0: The number of violations per apartment in the population of all city apartments is binomially distributed with a probability of success in any one trial of $\pi = .3$.

H_A: The number of violations per apartment in the population of all city apartments is not correctly described by H_0.

TABLE 14.10 | Computing χ^2 (Housing Code Violations)

Number of Possible Violations	Observed Frequency f_o	Binomial Probability, p for $n = 6$ and $\pi = .3$	Expected Frequency (if H_0 is true) $f_e = 200p$	$\frac{(f_o - f_e)^2}{f_e}$
0	31	.1176	23.52	2.3788
1	51	.3025	60.50	1.4917
2	70	.3241	64.82	.4140
3	32	.1852	37.04	.6858
4	9 } 16	.0595	11.90 } 14.08	
5	5 }	.0102	2.04 }	.2618
6	2 }	.0007	.14 }	
Total	**200**		**200***	$\chi^2 = \mathbf{5.2321}$

*allowing for rounding

Note: The inspector, we assume, has estimated the parameter π by noting that the mean of a binomial random variable is $n\,\pi$, which must equal the mean number of violations per apartment in the sample if H_0 is true. Thus,

$$n\,\pi = \frac{0(31) + 1(51) + 2(70) + 3(32) + 4(9) + 5(5) + 6(2)}{200} = 1.8$$

There being $n = 6$ possible violations, π is estimated as 1.8/6, or as .3.

Step 2: *Selecting a test statistic.*

$$\chi^2 = \sum \frac{(f_o - f_e)^2}{f_e}$$

Step 3: *Deriving a decision rule.*

The inspector first establishes in Table 14.10 the expected frequencies for the various numbers of possible violations per apartment, assuming H_0 is true. This process involves finding the binomial probabilities for $n = 6$ and $\pi = .3$ from Appendix Table C and multiplying each by the total number of observations, which is 200. Subsequently, if expected frequencies in any class are less than 5, which is true for 5 and 6 violations per apartment in this example, adjacent classes are combined as needed to yield minimum expected frequencies of 5 in every class.

The number of degrees of freedom must be established next, using Formula 14.E. In our example, 5 classes remain after 3 of 7 classes are combined (note the brackets in Table 14.10), while 1 parameter (π) was estimated. Hence, there are $5 - 1 - 1 = 3$ degrees of freedom. Given $\alpha = .05$ and 3 degrees of freedom, the critical $\chi^2_{.05(3)} = 7.815$ (Appendix Table M). The decision rule is: "Accept H_0 if $\chi^2 \leq 7.815$."

Step 4: *Using sample data to compute the test statistic and confronting it with the decision rule.*

The computation of the test statistic is shown in the last column of Table 14.10. In view of the computed χ^2 value, the null hypothesis should be *accepted.* Any discrepancy between the observed set of frequencies and the set of frequencies expected from a binomially distributed population is most likely the result of sampling error.

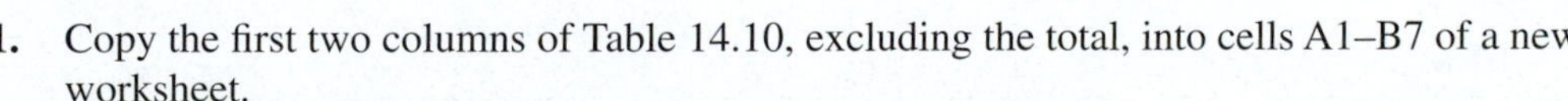

EXCEL Example 14.3

Review Example Problem 14.9. Using EXCEL,

a. confirm the computation of the χ^2 value.

b. compute and interpret the p value.

SOLUTION:
Part (a)

1. Copy the first two columns of Table 14.10, excluding the total, into cells A1–B7 of a new worksheet.
2. To compute expected frequencies, select C1 and click the **Function Wizard (*fx*)** > **Statistical** > **BINOMDIST** > **OK**.
3. In the BINOMDIST dialog box, enter **A1**, **6**, **.3**, and **FALSE**, respectively, into the four fields, click **OK**, and drag the C1 entry to C7.

4. Enter **=200*C1** into D1, select D1 and drag to D7.

The result so far looks just like Table 14.10:

A	B	C	D
0	31	0.117649	23.5298
1	51	0.302526	60.5052
2	70	0.324135	64.827
3	32	0.18522	37.044
4	9	0.059535	11.907
5	5	0.010206	2.0412
6	2	0.000729	0.1458

5. To eliminate expected frequencies lower than 5, combine the last three entries of columns B and D by entering **=SUM(B5:B7)** into B8 and **=SUM(D5:D7)** into D8. Jot down the values involved, delete B5–B7 and D5–D7, and enter the sums into B5 and D5.
6. To compute chi-square, enter **=(B1−D1)^2/D1** into E1, select E1 and drag to E5, and enter **=SUM(E1:E5)** into E7. (*Tip:* You can also save the last step and click on the column E header. The sum appears near the bottom of the screen.)

   Except for rounding, the resultant values look just like those in the last column of Table 14.10, summing to a $\chi^2 = 5.2222$.

Part (b)

1. Select an empty cell. Click the **Function Wizard (*fx*)** > **Statistical** > **CHIDIST** > **OK**.
2. In the dialog box, under *X,* enter **5.2222** (or simply **E7**); under *Deg freedom,* enter **3**.

A p-value of .1562 appears.

INTERPRETATION The computed χ^2 value of 5.2222, when confronted with a critical $\chi^2_{.05(3)} = 7.815$, calls for the *acceptance* of the null hypothesis. The p value of .1562 calls for such acceptance as well, because it exceeds $\alpha = .05$. When the null hypothesis is true, there is a 15.6 percent chance of finding the kind of χ^2 and p values found here, or of finding even more contradictory values. Therefore, the null hypothesis is considered true.

(You can find the critical $\chi^2_{.05(3)}$ in EXCEL by selecting any empty cell, clicking the **Function Wizard (*fx*)** > **Statistical** > **CHIINV** > **OK**, entering **.05** and **3** in the dialog box, and clicking **OK**.)

Note: This type of problem can also be solved much more rapidly by using HKStat, Sheet 35.

TESTING A FIT TO THE POISSON DISTRIBUTION

The following example applies the goodness-of-fit procedure to testing whether sample data come from a Poisson-distributed population.

EXAMPLE PROBLEM 14.10

To construct employee work schedules, a hospital administrator wants to determine whether the number of hourly arrivals in the outpatient department can be described by a Poisson distribution with a mean of $\mu = 3.8$ (which is a number known from prior experience). A test at the 1 percent level of significance is to be conducted; a simple random sample of 50 hours reveals the data in the first two columns of Table 14.11.

SOLUTION:

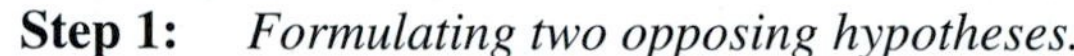

Step 1: *Formulating two opposing hypotheses.*

H_0: The number of hourly arrivals at the hospital's outpatient department is Poisson-distributed with a mean of $\mu = 3.8$ arrivals.

H_A: The number of hourly arrivals at the hospital's outpatient department is not correctly described by H_0.

Step 2: *Selecting a test statistic.*

$$\chi^2 = \sum \frac{(f_o - f_e)^2}{f_e}$$

Step 3: *Deriving a decision rule.*

The administrator first establishes in Table 14.11 the expected frequencies for the various numbers of hourly arrivals, assuming H_0 is true. This process involves finding the Poisson probabilities for $\mu = 3.8$ from Appendix Table F and multiplying each by the total number of observations, which is 50. Subsequently, if expected frequencies in any class are less than 5, which is true for 0, 1, 6, 7, and 8 or more arrivals in this example, adjacent classes are combined as needed to yield minimum expected frequencies of 5 in every class.

TABLE 14.11 | Computing χ^2 (Outpatient Arrivals)

Number of Arrivals per Hour	Observed Frequency f_o	Poisson Probability, p for $\mu = 3.8$	Expected Frequency (if H_0 is true) $f_e = 50p$	$\frac{(f_o - f_e)^2}{f_e}$
0	0 } 1	.0224	1.12 } 5.37	3.5562
1	1	.0850	4.25	
2	5	.1615	8.075	1.1710
3	8	.2046	10.23	.4861
4	15	.1944	9.72	2.8681
5	9	.1477	7.385	.3532
6	7	.0936	4.68	
7	3 } 12	.0508	2.54 } 9.22	.8382
8 or more	2	.0400	2.00	
Total	**50**	**1.0000**	**50**	**$\chi^2 = 9.2729$**

We must establish the number of degrees of freedom next. In our example, 6 classes remain after several classes are combined (note the brackets in Table 14.11), while no parameter was estimated. Hence, there are 6 − 1 − 0 = 5 degrees of freedom (see Formula 14.E). Given α = .01 and 5 degrees of freedom, the critical $\chi^2_{.01(5)}$ = 15.086 (Appendix Table M). The decision rule is: "Accept H_0 if $\chi^2 \leq 15.086$."

Step 4: *Using sample data to compute the test statistic and confronting it with the decision rule.*

The computation of the test statistic is shown in the last column of Table 14.11. In view of the computed χ^2 value, the null hypothesis should be *accepted.* Any discrepancy between the observed set of frequencies and the set of frequencies expected from a Poisson-distributed population is most likely the result of sampling error.

EXCEL Example 14.4

Review Example Problem 14.10. Using EXCEL,

a. confirm the computation of the χ^2 value.

b. compute and interpret the p value.

SOLUTION:
Part (a)

1. Copy the first two columns of Table 14.11, excluding the total, into cells A1–B9 of a new worksheet.
2. To compute expected frequencies, select C1 and click the **Function Wizard (*fx*)** > **Statistical** > **POISSON** > **OK**.
3. In the POISSON dialog box, enter **A1**, **3.8**, and **FALSE**, respectively, into the three fields, click **OK,** and drag the C1 entry to C8. Select C9 and enter **=1−SUM(C1:C8)**.
4. Enter **=50*C1** into D1, select D1 and drag to D9.

The result so far looks just like Table 14.11:

A	B	C	D
0	0	0.0224	1.1185
1	1	0.085	4.2504
2	5	0.1615	8.0758
3	8	0.2046	10.229
4	15	0.1944	9.7179
5	9	0.1477	7.3856
6	7	0.0936	4.6776
7	3	0.0508	2.5393
8 or more	2	0.0401	2.0054

5. To eliminate expected frequencies lower than 5, combine entries just as in Table 14.11, creating adjusted columns E and F of observed and expected frequencies.

6. To compute chi-square, enter **=(E1−F1)^2/F1** into G1, select G1 and drag to G6, and enter **=SUM(G1:G6)** into G8. (*Tip:* You can also save the last step and click on the column G header. The sum appears near the bottom of the screen.)

Except for rounding, the resultant values look just like those in the last column of Table 14.11, summing to a $\chi^2 = 9.2731$.

Part (b)

1. Select an empty cell. Click the **Function Wizard (*fx*)** > **Statistical** > **CHIDIST** > **OK**.
2. In the dialog box, under *X,* enter **9.2731** (or simply **G8**); under *Deg freedom,* enter **5**.

A p-value of .0987 appears.

INTERPRETATION The computed χ^2 value of 9.2731, when confronted with a critical $\chi^2_{.01(5)} = 15.086$, calls for the *acceptance* of the null hypothesis. The p value of .0987 calls for such acceptance as well, because it exceeds $\alpha = .01$. When the null hypothesis is true, there is a 9.9 percent chance of finding the kind of χ^2 and p values found here, or of finding even more contradictory values. Therefore, the null hypothesis is considered true.

(You can find the critical $\chi^2_{.01(5)}$ in EXCEL by selecting any empty cell, clicking the **Function Wizard (*fx*)** > **Statistical** > **CHIINV** > **OK**, entering **.01** and **5** in the dialog box, and clicking **OK**.)

Note: This type of problem can also be solved much more rapidly by using HKStat, Sheet 36.

TESTING A FIT TO THE NORMAL DISTRIBUTION

The following example applies the goodness-of-fit procedure to testing whether sample data come from a normally distributed population.

EXAMPLE PROBLEM 14.11

A financial analyst wishes to determine whether the daily volume of futures contracts traded at U.S. commodities exchanges is still normally distributed, with a mean of 50 million contracts and a standard deviation of 10 million contracts, as indicated by a study conducted a decade ago. A test at the 2 percent level of significance is desired. During the next 90 business days, the analyst collects the data given in the first two columns of Table 14.12 on the next page.

SOLUTION:

Step 1: *Formulating two opposing hypotheses.*

H_0: The daily volume of futures contracts traded is normally distributed with a mean of 50 million contracts and a standard deviation of 10 million contracts.

H_A: The daily volume of futures contracts traded is not correctly described by H_0.

Step 2: *Selecting a test statistic.*

$$\chi^2 = \sum \frac{(f_o - f_e)^2}{f_e}$$

TABLE 14.12 | Computing χ^2 (Futures Contracts)

Millions of Contracts Traded per Day	Observed Frequency f_o		Expected Frequency (if H_0 is true) f_e	$\frac{(f_o - f_e)^2}{f_e}$
Under 10	5			
10 to under 20	9	52	14.283	99.5990
20 to under 30	15			
30 to under 40	23			
40 to under 50	20		30.717	3.7391
50 to under 60	8		30.717	16.8005
60 to under 70	6			
70 to under 80	3	10	14.283	1.2843
80 and above	1			
Total	**90**		**90**	χ^2 **= 121.4229**

TABLE 14.13 | Computing Expected Frequencies (Futures Contracts)

Millions of Futures Contracts Traded per Day: Upper Class Limit, x	Normal Deviate $z = \frac{x - \mu}{\sigma} = \frac{x - 50}{10}$	Area under Standard Normal Curve Left of x	Area of Class Interval p	Expected Frequency (if H_0 is true) $f_e = 90p$	
10	−4	.0000	.0000	0	
20	−3	.0014	.0014	.126	14.283
30	−2	.0228	.0214	1.926	
40	−1	.1587	.1359	12.231	
50	0	.5000	.3413	30.717	
60	1	.8413	.3413	30.717	
70	2	.9772	.1359	12.231	
80	3	.9986	.0214	1.926	14.283
∞	∞	1.0000	.0014	.126	
Total			**1.0000**	**90**	

Step 3: *Deriving a decision rule.*

The analyst first establishes in Table 14.13 the expected frequencies for the various classes of daily volumes, assuming H_0 is true. This process involves finding areas under the normal curve for the various classes in Table 14.12 with the help of Appendix Table H and then multiplying each of these probabilities by the total number of observations, bines several classes, as shown, leaving 4 classes for the χ^2 test. No parameters having been estimated, there are $4 - 1 - 0 = 3$ degrees of freedom (see Formula 14.E). Given $\alpha = .02$ and 3 degrees of freedom, the critical $\chi^2_{.02(3)} = 9.837$ (Appendix Table M). The decision rule is: "Accept H_0 if $\chi^2 \leq 9.837$."

Step 4: *Using sample data to compute the test statistic and confronting it with the decision rule.*

The computation of the test statistic is shown in the last column of Table 14.12. In view of the computed χ^2 value, the null hypothesis should be *rejected.* This decision does not necessarily mean, however, that the daily numbers of futures contracts traded are not *normally* distributed, but it does mean (at the 2 percent level of significance) that the distribution, if it is normal, does not conform to the historical $\mu = 50$ and $\sigma = 10$.

EXCEL Example 14.5

Review Example Problem 14.11. Using EXCEL,

a. confirm the computation of the χ^2 value.

b. compute and interpret the p value.

SOLUTION:

Part (a)

1. Enter the four adjusted observed and expected frequencies from Table 14.12 into the first four rows of worksheet columns A and B.
2. To compute chi-square, enter **=(A1−B1)^2/B1** into C1, select C1 and drag to C4, and enter **=SUM(C1:C4)** into C6. (*Tip:* You can also save the last step and click on the column C header. The sum appears near the bottom of the screen.)

Except for rounding, the resultant values look just like those in the last column of Table 14.12, summing to a $\chi^2 = 121.4229$.

Part (b)

1. Select an empty cell. Click the **Function Wizard (*fx*)** > **Statistical** > **CHIDIST** > **OK.**
2. In the dialog box, under *X,* enter **121.4229** (or simply **C6**); under *Deg freedom,* enter **3**.

A p value of 3.81E-26 appears, which is 0.

INTERPRETATION The computed χ^2 value of 121.4229, when confronted with a $\chi^2_{.02(3)} = 9.837$, calls for the *rejection* of the null hypothesis. The p value of 0 calls for such rejection as well, because it falls short of $\alpha = .02$. When the null hypothesis is true, there is a 0 percent chance of finding the kind of χ^2 and p values found here, or of finding even more contradictory values. Therefore, the null hypothesis is considered false.

(You can find the critical $\chi^2_{.02(3)}$ in EXCEL by selecting any empty cell, clicking the **Function Wizard (*fx*)** > **Statistical** > **CHIINV** > **OK**, entering **.02** and **3** in the dialog box, and clicking **OK.**)

Note: This type of problem can also be solved much more rapidly by using HKStat, Sheet 37.

TESTING A FIT TO THE UNIFORM DISTRIBUTION

The simplest of all the goodness-of-fit tests involves the hypothesis that sample data come from a uniformly distributed population because in that case, as the next example shows, the expected frequencies in all categories are the same.

EXAMPLE PROBLEM 14.12

The manager of a dry-cleaning establishment wants to know whether requests for service are spread evenly over the six business days of the week. Employee work schedules are to be set accordingly. A test at the 5 percent significance level is desired; records for the past three months reveal the data in the first two columns of Table 14.14.

TABLE 14.14 | Computing χ^2 (Dry Cleaner)

Day of Service Request	Observed Frequency f_o	Expected Frequency (for uniform distribution) f_e	$\frac{(f_o - f_e)^2}{f_e}$
Monday	1,251	1,836	186.3971
Tuesday	1,830	1,836	.0196
Wednesday	1,675	1,836	14.1182
Thursday	1,450	1,836	81.1525
Friday	1,905	1,836	2.5931
Saturday	2,905	1,836	622.4188
Total	**11,016**	**11,016**	χ^2 **= 906.6993**

SOLUTION:

Step 1: *Formulating two opposing hypotheses.*

H_0: The numbers of service requests are uniformly distributed over the six business days of the week.

H_A: The numbers of service requests are not uniformly distributed over the six business days of the week.

Step 2: *Selecting a test statistic.*

$$\chi^2 = \sum \frac{(f_o - f_e)^2}{f_e}$$

Step 3: *Deriving a decision rule.*

Under the null hypothesis, the manager expects the total of 11,016 service requests to be equally distributed among the six business days; this expectation is reflected in the third column of Table 14.14. There being six classes with expected frequencies of at least 5, and because no parameters are being estimated, the degrees of freedom equal $6 - 1 - 0 = 5$ (see Formula 14.E). Given $\alpha = .05$ and 5 degrees of freedom, the critical $\chi^2_{.05(5)} = 11.070$ (Appendix Table M). The decision rule is: "Accept H_0 if $\chi^2 \leq 11.070$."

Step 4: *Using sample data to compute the test statistic and confronting it with the decision rule.*

The computation of the test statistic is shown in the last column of Table 14.14. In view of the computed χ^2 value, the null hypothesis should be *rejected.* The numbers of service requests are not uniformly distributed over the six business days of the week.

EXCEL Example 14.6

Review Example Problem 14.12. Using EXCEL,

a. confirm the computation of the χ^2 value.

b. compute and interpret the p value.

SOLUTION:

Part (a)

1. Enter the observed and expected frequencies from Table 14.14 into the first six rows of worksheet columns A and B.
2. To compute chi-square, enter **=(A1−B1)^2/B1** into C1, select C1 and drag to C6, and enter **=SUM(C1:C6)** into C8. (*Tip:* You can also save the last step and click on the column C header. The sum appears near the bottom of the screen.)

Except for rounding, the resultant values look just like those in the last column of Table 14.14, summing to a $\chi^2 = 906.6993$.

Part (b)

1. Select an empty cell. Click the **Function Wizard (*fx*)** > **Statistical** > **CHIDIST** > **OK**.
2. In the dialog box, under *X,* enter **906.6993** (or simply **C8**); under *Deg freedom,* enter **5**.

A p value of 9.44E-194 appears, which is 0.

INTERPRETATION The computed χ^2 value of 906.6993, when confronted with a critical $\chi^2_{.05(5)} = 11.070$, calls for the *rejection* of the null hypothesis. The p value of 0 calls for such rejection as well, because it falls short of $\alpha = .05$. When the null hypothesis is true, there is a 0 percent chance of finding the kind of χ^2 and p values found here, or of finding even more contradictory values. Therefore, the null hypothesis is considered false.

(You can find the critical $\chi^2_{.05(5)}$ in EXCEL by selecting any empty cell, clicking the **Function Wizard (*fx*)** > **Statistical** > **CHIINV** > **OK**, entering **.05** and **5** in the dialog box, and clicking **OK**.)

Note: This type of problem can also be solved much more rapidly by using HKStat, Sheet 38.

Application 14.3, *Testing Random Digits for Randomness,* provides another illustration of this type of situation.

APPLICATION 14.3

Testing Random Digits for Randomness

The Rand Corporation's famous table of a million random digits (from which we have excerpted Appendix Table A) has been subjected to a great variety of χ^2 tests to determine whether the table is free from serious bias. (It is.)

In one of these tests, a researcher divided the million digits into 20 blocks of 50,000 digits each and then noted how often each possible digit between 0 and 9 appeared within each block. For block number 1, the observed frequencies—along with the expected frequencies, given perfect randomness—are shown in Table 14.E. The calculation of the χ^2 statistic is also shown. Given 9 degrees of freedom and a significance level of 1 percent, the critical $\chi^2_{.01(9)} = 21.666$. Therefore, the null hypothesis of perfect randomness is quite acceptable.

TABLE 14.E | Computing χ^2 (Random Digits)

Digit	Observed Frequency f_o	Expected Frequency (for uniform distribution) f_e	$\frac{(f_o - f_e)^2}{f_e}$
0	4,923	5,000	1.1858
1	5,013	5,000	.0338
2	4,916	5,000	1.4112
3	4,951	5,000	.4802
4	5,109	5,000	2.3762
5	4,993	5,000	.0098
6	5,055	5,000	.6050
7	5,080	5,000	1.2800
8	4,986	5,000	.0392
9	4,974	5,000	.1352
Total	**50,000**	**50,000**	$\chi^2 = \mathbf{7.5564}$

SOURCE: Adapted from The Rand Corporation, *A Million Random Digits with 100,000 Normal Deviates* (Glencoe, Ill.: The Free Press, 1955), p. xiii.

TESTING A FIT TO ANY SPECIFIED DISTRIBUTION

Goodness-of-fit tests can be performed with respect to any distribution we care to specify, not just with respect to members of some well-known distribution family. This fact is illustrated by the following final example comparing the television-viewing habits of people in 1950 and 2000.

EXAMPLE PROBLEM 14.13

A TV station needs to update information about its viewers in order to sell advertising time to various sponsors. A simple random sample of 100 viewers reveals current viewing habits shown

TABLE 14.15 | Computing χ^2 (TV Viewing Habits)

Hours of TV Watched per Week	Year 2000 Sample Data: Observed Frequency f_o	1950 Census Data = Year 2000 Expected Frequency (if H_0 is true) f_e	$\frac{(f_o - f_e)^2}{f_e}$
0 to under 5	12	7	3.5714
5 to under 7	9	10	.1000
7 to under 15	21	20	.0500
15 to under 25	44	45	.0222
25 or more	14	18	.8889
Total	**100**	**100**	χ^2 = **4.6325**

in the first two columns of Table 14.15. Data from a 1950 census, showing the percentage of all viewers in each category in that earlier year and, therefore, year 2000 *expected* frequencies if viewing habits are unchanged, are shown in the next column. The station manager wants to test, at the 5 percent level of significance, whether the year 2000 viewing habits of the population at large differ from those of 1950.

SOLUTION:

Step 1: *Formulating two opposing hypotheses.*

H_0: Year 2000 viewing habits equal those of 1950.

H_A: Year 2000 viewing habits differ from those of 1950.

Step 2: *Selecting a test statistic.*

$$\chi^2 = \sum \frac{(f_o - f_e)^2}{f_e}$$

Step 3: *Deriving a decision rule.*

Under the null hypothesis, the manager expects the frequencies of 1950 to prevail in 2000. There being five classes with expected frequencies of at least 5, and because no parameters are being estimated, the degrees of freedom equal $5 - 1 - 0 = 4$ (see Formula 14.E). Given $\alpha = .05$ and 4 degrees of freedom, the critical $\chi^2_{.05(4)} = 9.488$ (Appendix Table M). The decision rule is: "Accept H_0 if $\chi^2 \leq 9.488$."

Step 4: *Using sample data to compute the test statistic and confronting it with the decision rule.*

The computation of the test statistic is shown in the last column of Table 14.15. In view of the computed χ^2 value, the null hypothesis should be *accepted.* Viewing habits have not changed.

EXCEL Example 14.7

Review Example Problem 14.13. Using EXCEL,

a. confirm the computation of the χ^2 value.

b. compute and interpret the p value.

SOLUTION:

Part (a)

1. Enter the observed and expected frequencies from Table 14.15 into the first five rows of worksheet columns A and B.
2. To compute chi-square, enter **=(A1−B1)^2/B1** into C1, select C1 and drag to C5, and enter **=SUM(C1:C5)** into C7. (*Tip:* You can also save the last step and click on the column C header. The sum appears near the bottom of the screen.)

Except for rounding, the resultant values look just like those in the last column of Table 14.15, summing to a $\chi^2 = 4.6325$.

Part (b)

1. Select an empty cell. Click the **Function Wizard (*fx*)** > **Statistical** > **CHIDIST** > **OK**.
2. In the dialog box, under *X,* enter **4.6325** (or simply **C7**); under *Deg freedom,* enter **4**.

A p value of .32712 appears.

INTERPRETATION The computed χ^2 value of 4.6325, when confronted with a critical $\chi^2_{.05(4)} = 9.488$, calls for the *acceptance* of the null hypothesis. The p value of .32712 calls for such acceptance as well, because it exceeds $\alpha = .05$. When the null hypothesis is true, there is a 32.7 percent chance of finding the kind of χ^2 and p values found here, or of finding even more contradictory values. Therefore, the null hypothesis is considered true.

(You can find the critical $\chi^2_{.05(4)}$ in EXCEL by selecting any empty cell, clicking the **Function Wizard (*fx*)** > **Statistical** > **CHIINV** > **OK**, entering **.05** and **4** in the dialog box, and clicking **OK**.)

Note: This type of problem can also be solved much more rapidly by using HKStat, Sheet 39.

Summary

1. The *chi-square technique* can often be employed for purposes of estimation or hypothesis testing when use of the normal or *t* distributions is inadmissible. The first major application of the technique involves tests of the alleged statistical independence of two qualitative variables each of which, in turn, is divided into two or more categories. Typically, when a census cannot be conducted, sample data are collected to assess the issue. A *chi-square statistic* is constructed on the basis of observed frequencies, on the one hand, and expected frequencies computed on the assumption of statistical independence, on the other hand. Different sampling distributions of the chi-square statistic exist for different numbers of degrees of freedom. Critical values of χ^2 that correspond to specified upper-tail areas of such distributions have been tabulated in the chi-square table (Appendix Table M). This table greatly facilitates the comparison of computed and critical χ^2 values and, thus, the assessment of the statistical independence issue.
2. A second major application of the χ^2 technique is in the making of inferences about more than two population proportions. This technique can be used to test the equality or inequality of three or more proportions.

3. Third, the χ^2 technique allows us to make inferences about a population variance. Confidence intervals for a population variance (and also probability intervals for a sample variance) can be established with the help of an appropriate χ^2 distribution. Hypotheses about a population variance can be tested with the help of the χ^2 statistic as well.

4. Fourth, the χ^2 technique allows us to conduct goodness-of-fit tests to assess the plausibility that sample data come from a population whose elements conform to a specified type of probability distribution. This technique can be used to test the goodness of fit of sample data to the binomial distribution, the Poisson distribution, the normal distribution, the uniform distribution, and more.

Key Terms

chi-square distribution
chi-square statistic
chi-square technique
contingency table
dependent events
goodness-of-fit test
independent events

Practice Problems

NOTE

Some problems require the use of a statistical program, EXCEL or MINITAB. The program's major features are explained in text Chapter 2. Plenty of additional advice is available via the program's built-in Help feature.

Section 14.2 Testing the Alleged Independence of Two Qualitative Variables

1. Consider Table 14.16. Without conducting a full-fledged χ^2 test, assess the issue of statistical dependence or independence between sex and type of pilot's license held on the assumption that the frequencies are

   a. census data.

   b. sample data.

TABLE 14.16 | Numbers of Pilots, Classified by Sex and Type of License

	(B) Type of License				
(A) Sex	Student	Private	Commercial	Airline-Transport	Total
Male	1,050	4,200	3,150	2,100	**10,500**
Female	850	1,500	50	100	**2,500**
Total	**1,900**	**5,700**	**3,200**	**2,200**	**13,000**

2. Consider Table 14.17. Without conducting a full-fledged χ^2 test, assess the issue of statistical dependence or independence between the loan officer's sex and type of decision made on the assumption that the frequencies are

a. census data.

b. sample data.

TABLE 14.17 | Numbers of Loan Applications, Classified by Loan Officer's Sex and Type of Decision

(A) Sex	(B) Type of Decision		Total
	Approved	Denied	
Male	1,050	4,200	**5,250**
Female	850	1,500	**2,350**
Total	**1,900**	**5,700**	**7,600**

3. In each of the following situations, determine whether a null hypothesis of independence between the stated variables should be accepted on the basis of a χ^2 test.

a. The variables are sex of viewers and their most preferred among ten TV shows. Desired $\alpha = .001$; a sample yields $\chi^2 = 41.72$.

b. The variables are marital status (single, married) and type of car owned (foreign, domestic). Desired $\alpha = .01$; a sample yields $\chi^2 = 2.39$.

c. The variables are type of soap used (4 choices) and most preferred TV show (10 choices). Desired $\alpha = .02$; a sample yields $\chi^2 = 137.02$.

d. The variables are college major (12 choices) and later type of employment (3 choices). Desired $\alpha = .05$; a sample yields $\chi^2 = 55.19$.

4. In each of the following situations, determine whether a null hypothesis of independence between the stated variables should be accepted on the basis of a χ^2 test.

a. The variables are income level (5 levels) and political affiliation (3 choices). Desired $\alpha = .10$; a sample yields $\chi^2 = 105.00$.

b. The variables are social class (3 classes) and newspaper read (5 choices). Desired $\alpha = .01$; a sample yields $\chi^2 = 3.52$.

c. The variables are sex and age at heart attack (3 classes). Desired $\alpha = .001$; a sample yields $\chi^2 = 1$.

d. The variables are women's preferred clothing stores (3 choices) and women's ages (3 classes). Desired $\alpha = .05$; a sample yields $\chi^2 = 7.78$.

5. Review Table 14.1 in this chapter's Preview. Conduct an appropriate hypothesis test of independence between the two stated variables (race of applicant and application result) and do so at the 5 percent level of significance.

6. An advertising agency wants to know whether the sex of consumers is independent of their preferences for three brands of coffee. The answer will determine whether different ads must be created for men's and women's magazines. A test at the 5 percent significance level is desired; a simple random sample of 100 persons yields Table 14.18.

TABLE 14.18 | Preferences Indicated by Coffee Drinkers

	(B) Brand Preference			
(A) Sex	A	B	C	Total
Male	18	25	17	**60**
Female	32	5	3	**40**
Total	**50**	**30**	**20**	**100**

7. An insurance company collected the sample data of Table 14.19 for 100 accidents. Conduct an appropriate hypothesis test of independence between the two stated variables (A and B) and do so at the 2 percent level of significance.

TABLE 14.19 | Auto Accident Data

	(B) Accident Location			
(A) Severity of Accident	Freeway	Rural Road	City Road	Total
Property damage	10	20	20	**50**
Injury	10	10	5	**25**
Fatality	10	10	5	**25**
Total	**30**	**40**	**30**	**100**

8. An insurance company collected the sample data of Table 14.20 for 100 heart attacks. Conduct an appropriate hypothesis test of independence between the two stated variables (A and B) and do so at the 10 percent level of significance.

TABLE 14.20 | Heart Attack Data

	(B) Sex of Victim		
(A) Age of Victim	Male	Female	Total
<30	6	4	**10**
30–60	38	42	**80**
>60	6	4	**10**
Total	**50**	**50**	**100**

9. A plant manager wants to determine the relative merits of different raw material suppliers and collects the sample data of Table 14.21 for 600 shipments. Conduct an appropriate hypothesis test of independence between the two stated variables and do so at the 1 percent level of significance.

TABLE 14.21 | Raw Material Quality Data

(A) Supplier	(B) Type of Defect						Total
	A	B	C	D	E	F	
Green	5	0	3	12	50	30	**100**
Jones	18	32	42	68	0	40	**200**
Smith	27	38	35	70	20	110	**300**
Total	**50**	**70**	**80**	**150**	**70**	**180**	**600**

10. An economist is studying the relationship between unemployment and inflation. Using the sample data of Table 14.22 for 100 months studied, conduct an appropriate hypothesis test of independence between the two stated variables and do so at the 5 percent level of significance.

TABLE 14.22 | Economic Performance Data

(A) Unemployment	(B) Inflation			Total
	Abated	Unchanged	Accelerated	
Lower	5	5	10	**20**
Unchanged	5	35	20	**60**
Higher	20	0	0	**20**
Total	**30**	**40**	**30**	**100**

11. An economist is studying the relationship between stock prices and dividends. Using the sample data of Table 14.23 for 240 stocks, conduct an appropriate hypothesis test of independence between the two stated variables and do so at the 2 percent level of significance.

TABLE 14.23 | American Stock Exchange Data

(A) Price per Share of Stock	(B) Dividend Yield			Total
	Under 3%	3 to under 10%	10% and more	
$0 to 25	27	52	12	**91**
$25.01 to 75.00	38	46	3	**87**
$75.01 and more	19	3	40	**62**
Total	**84**	**101**	**55**	**240**

12. An insurance company has collected the sample data of Table 14.24 for 312 claims. Conduct an appropriate hypothesis test of independence between the two stated variables and do so at the 2 percent level of significance.

TABLE 14.24 | Medical Insurance Claims Data

(A) Maternity Benefits Provided by Insurance	(B) Days New Mothers Stayed in Maternity Ward				Total
	0–2	3–4	5–6	7 and more	
Poor	34	20	6	1	**61**
Fair	52	37	18	6	**113**
Excellent	12	38	59	29	**138**
Total	**98**	**95**	**83**	**36**	**312**

13. A manufacturer of aviation oxygen systems has collected the sample data of Table 14.25 from 700 magazine subscribers. Conduct an appropriate hypothesis test of independence between the two stated variables and do so at the 5 percent level of significance.

TABLE 14.25 | Advertising Effectiveness Data

(A) Awareness of Scott Oxygen Systems Ad	(B) Subscribers to			Total
	The Pilot	*Flying*	*Aviation Consumer*	
Don't remember	100	125	132	**357**
Remember vaguely	52	65	32	**149**
Remember well	15	43	136	**194**
Total	**167**	**233**	**300**	**700**

14. The owners of a shopping mall have collected the sample data of Table 14.26 from 554 households. Conduct an appropriate hypothesis test of independence between the two stated variables and do so at the 0.1 percent level of significance.

TABLE 14.26 | Shopping Preferences Data

(A) Distance from Residence	(B) Preferred Shopping Center				Total
	A	B	C	D	
0 to 5 miles	40	55	27	18	**140**
5 to under 15 miles	128	72	12	3	**215**
15 miles and more	178	12	6	3	**199**
Total	**346**	**139**	**45**	**24**	**554**

15. An executive of Perdue has collected the sample data of Table 14.27 from 1,500 households. Conduct an appropriate hypothesis test of independence between the two stated variables and do so at the 10 percent level of significance.

TABLE 14.27 | Advertising Effectiveness Data

(A) Type of Chicken Consumed	(B) Regularly Watch *20/20*		
	Yes	No	Total
Perdue brand	255	127	**382**
Regular unbranded	301	609	**910**
None	62	146	**208**
Total	**618**	**882**	**1,500**

16. An insurance company has collected the sample data of Table 14.28 for 1,321 of its clients. Conduct an appropriate hypothesis test of independence between the two stated variables and do so at the 5 percent level of significance.

TABLE 14.28 | Auto Insurance Claims Data

	(B) Age of Insured				
(A) Action	Under 25	25–35	36–55	Over 55	Total
Filed claim	86	92	121	67	**366**
None	92	121	603	139	**955**
Total	**178**	**213**	**724**	**206**	**1,321**

17. A marketing manager has collected the sample data of Table 14.29 for recent sales pitches. Conduct an appropriate hypothesis test of independence between the two stated variables and do so at the 10 percent level of significance.

TABLE 14.29 | Sales Data

(A) Type of Sales Letter Used	(B) Response		
	Sale	No Sale	Total
A	17	83	**100**
B	33	67	**100**
C	51	49	**100**
D	23	77	**100**
Total	**124**	**276**	**400**

18. A marketing manager has collected the sample data of Table 14.30 for 709 recent insurance policy sales. Conduct an appropriate hypothesis test of independence between the two stated variables and do so at the 1 percent level of significance.

TABLE 14.30 | Insurance Policy Sales Data

	(B) Region of Sale				
(A) Type of Contract	**Northeast**	**Midwest**	**South**	**West**	**Total**
Whole life	69	72	23	56	**220**
Level term	23	29	38	77	**167**
Decreasing term	105	93	105	19	**322**
Total	**197**	**194**	**166**	**152**	**709**

19. For Practice Problems 15 and 16, calculate the mean, variance, and standard deviation of the χ^2 random variable.

20. For Practice Problems 17 and 18, calculate the mean, variance, and standard deviation of the χ^2 random variable.

Section 14.3 Making Inferences about More Than Two Population Proportions

21. A bakery manager wants to determine whether the proportion of defective pie crusts is the same for each of four oven temperatures as it is overall. A sample of 200 crusts reveals the frequencies listed in Table 14.31. Make the test at the 10 percent significance level.

TABLE 14.31 | Pie Crust Baking Test Data

	Oven Temperature				
Product Quality	**A = 300°**	**B = 350°**	**C = 400°**	**D = 450°**	**Total**
Defective	10	0	20	40	**70**
Perfect	40	50	30	10	**130**
Total	**50**	**50**	**50**	**50**	**200**

22. The manager of a travel bureau wants to know whether the proportion of potential customers who prefer the Massachusetts historical tour to the Bay State nature tour is the same for four ethnic groups as it is overall. A sample reveals the frequencies listed in Table 14.32. Make the test at the 5 percent significance level.

TABLE 14.32 | Sightseeing Preferences Data

	Ethnic Group				
Tour Offered	**A = English**	**B = French**	**C = German**	**D = Spanish**	**Total**
Mass. historical	57	33	29	76	**195**
Bay State nature	103	105	132	77	**417**
Total	**160**	**138**	**161**	**153**	**612**

23. A sales manager wants to determine whether the proportion of people who own the Polaroid SX-70 camera is the same in all parts of the country. A sample shows that the camera is owned by 10 of 30 Northerners, by 20 of 50 Easterners, by 30 of 60 Southerners, and by 30 of 90 Westerners. Make the test at the 10 percent level of significance.

24. An engineer wants to determine whether the proportion of defective pieces produced is the same for two machines. A sample shows that machine A produces 24 defectives out of 400, and machine B produces 42 defectives out of 600. Make the test at the 1 percent level of significance.

25. A car dealer wants to determine whether the proportion of people under 30 who own cars is the same for 3 makes of cars. A sample shows that 27 of 120 car A owners, 56 of 203 car B owners, and 13 of 31 car C owners are under 30 years old. Make the test at the 2 percent level of significance.

26. An insurance industry analyst wants to determine whether the proportion of people who renew their policies only during the last week of the grace period is the same for 4 companies. A sample shows that 17 out of 52 customers of company A fall into this category. The corresponding numbers for company B are 12 out of 19; for company C, 30 out of 51; and for company D, 22 out of 25. Make the test at the 0.1 percent level of significance.

27. An economist wants to test whether the proportion of firms planning to increase investment spending next year is the same in each of four industries as it is overall. A sample of 200 firms reveals the frequencies listed in Table 14.33. Make the test at the 2 percent significance level.

TABLE 14.33 | Business Confidence Data

Investment Spending Plans	Industry				Total
	A	B	C	D	
Higher	10	20	30	40	**100**
Same or lower	40	30	20	10	**100**
Total	**50**	**50**	**50**	**50**	**200**

28. A personnel manager wants to determine whether the taking of sick days by workers is explained by the workers' ages. The last 100 sick days taken are viewed as a random sample; they were distributed as in row 1 of Table 14.34. The percentage of the firm's labor force in the various age groups is given in row 2. A test at the 5 percent level of significance is desired, but the computer just broke. Make the test, nevertheless, showing your calculations.

TABLE 14.34 | Personnel Data

Distribution of	Age Groups				Total
	Under 25	25–35	36–50	51 and over	
(1) 100 sick days (number)	50	15	15	20	**100**
(2) Firm's labor force (%)	20	30	30	20	**100**

29. A lawyer wants to know whether the educational level of jurors chosen at the county court reflects the makeup of the county population that is eligible for jury duty. The last 100 jurors chosen are viewed as a random sample; their makeup is given in row 1 of Table 14.35. Row 2 shows countywide percentages. A test at the 10 percent level of significance is desired, but the computer just broke. Make the test, nevertheless, showing your calculations. (What if a 1 percent level of significance had been chosen?)

TABLE 14.35 | Jury Data

	Highest Educational Level				
Distribution of	**Elementary School (A)**	**High School (B)**	**Some College (C)**	**College Degree (D)**	**Total**
(1) 100 jurors (number)	12	64	12	12	**100**
(2) County population eligible for jury duty (%)	20	50	10	20	**100**

30. A lawyer wants to know whether the available professional and managerial jobs are distributed among the races in accordance with the racial makeup of the population (which is 80 percent white, 15 percent black, 5 percent other). A random sample of 1,000 professional/managerial jobs shows whites hold 792 jobs, blacks 98, others the rest. A test at the 5 percent level of significance is desired, but the computer just broke. Make the test, nevertheless, showing your calculations.

31. Review Practice Problems 28–30. In each case, use a computer program to

a. confirm your computed χ^2 value.

b. find the associated p value.

SECTION 14.4 MAKING INFERENCES ABOUT A POPULATION VARIANCE

32. A pharmaceutical firm is bringing out a new sleeping pill; it is tested on a random sample of 20 people. The sample standard deviation of the time to sleep turns out to be 11 minutes. An 80 percent confidence interval is desired for the population variance of the time to sleep. Construct it.

33. The manager of a chain of muffler-repair shops takes a random sample of 30 days from last year's sales records. The sample shows mean sales of 51.7 mufflers per day, with a standard deviation of 11.3 mufflers. Construct a 96 percent confidence interval for the population variance of daily muffler sales.

34. A product's diameter must have a maximum variance of .006 squared inch. The production manager takes a random sample of 25 units from the week's output. The sample shows a standard deviation of diameters of .07 inch. Construct a 90 percent confidence interval for the population variance of diameters and, thus, determine whether the production process turns out a product meeting specifications.

35. An aircraft altimeter must have readouts with a maximum variance of 25 squared feet. An inspector takes a random sample of 10 new altimeters; the sample variance is 26 squared feet. Construct a 98 percent confidence interval for the population variance of readouts and, thus, determine whether the altimeters meet specifications.

36. A machine that fills cereal boxes is supposed to do so with a maximum standard deviation of .01 ounce. An inspector takes a random sample of 15 boxes that were filled during the day; the sample standard deviation is .013 ounce. Construct a 96 percent confidence interval for the population standard deviation and, thus, determine whether the machine meets specifications.

37. In each of the following cases, indicate whether the hypothesis concerning the population variance is lower-tailed, upper-tailed, or two-sided. Then determine the critical and actual χ^2 values and show whether the null hypothesis should be accepted or rejected.

a. H_0: $\sigma^2 \geq 64$; $n = 26$; $\alpha = .01$; $s^2 = 10$

b. H_0: $\sigma^2 \geq .64$; $n = 15$; $\alpha = .02$; $s^2 = .1$

c. H_0: $\sigma^2 \leq 100$; $n = 5$; $\alpha = .001$; $s^2 = 110$

38. For many years, the Federal Aviation Administration has been giving a pilot's exam with a mean score of 85 and a variance of 64. It is introducing a completely new exam and wants to know whether the population of exam scores for the new exam has the same variance. A hypothesis test at the 2 percent significance level is desired. When a sample of 15 persons takes the exam, the sample variance equals 36. Make the test.

39. The manager of a firm has found the variance in the firm's daily net cash flow to be very important for proper cash management. In the past, this figure was $\sigma^2 = 100{,}000$ dollars squared. The manager has reason to suspect, however, that this figure might have changed drastically. A hypothesis test at the 4 percent level of significance is to settle this issue. In thousands of dollars, the daily net-cash-flow figures over a recent two-week period were: −17, +22, +5, 0, +8, −3, +13, +20, +25, −41, 0, −4, +8, and +13. Use these data to make the test.

40. A manufacturer claims that the light emitted by a cathode ray tube used in computer terminals is so uniform that the light intensity variance is .0001 squared unit per pixel. A user takes a random sample of 14 pixels (dots on the screen) and measures the light intensity, finding a sample standard deviation of .0094 unit per pixel. Can the manufacturer's claim be accepted? Make a test at the 4 percent level of significance.

41. A builder claims that the compressive strength of his concrete has a variance of at least 80 squared-pounds per square inch. A skeptic takes a random sample of 25 batches of concrete; the sample standard deviation is 8 psi. Make a hypothesis test at the 5 percent level of significance.

SECTION 14.5 CONDUCTING GOODNESS-OF-FIT TESTS

42. A Boeing company test pilot knows the probability to be $\pi = .5$ that an engine on a four-engine plane requires additional oil after a 7-hour flight. The experience of the last 200 flights is summarized in Table 14.36. The pilot wonders whether these sample data are consistent with an underlying binomial distribution of population data. A test at the 2 percent significance level is desired. Make the test.

TABLE 14.36 | Engine Oil Data

Numbers of Engines Requiring Oil after 7-Hour Flight	Observed Frequency f_o
0	15
1	44
2	75
3	56
4	10
Total	**200**

43. A quality inspector wishes to test the null hypothesis that the number of defective items found in a box of 3 is a binomially distributed random variable with a probability of success in any one trial of $\pi = .2$. A test at the 10 percent level of significance is desired; a simple random sample of 200 boxes yields the results given in Table 14.37. Make the test.

TABLE 14.37 | Quality Control Data

Numbers of Defectives Found in a Box of 3	Observed Frequency f_o
0	46
1	60
2	58
3	36
Total	**200**

44. The director of a corporate computer network wonders whether the hourly number of computer access requests can be described by a Poisson distribution. Using the data of Table 14.38, make the appropriate test and do so at the 5 percent level of significance.

TABLE 14.38 | Computer Access Requests

Number of Access Requests per Hour	Number of Hours Observed f_o
0	55
1	61
2	50
3	32
4	18
5	9
6	5
7	2
8	1
9 or more	0
Total	**233**

45. A hotel manager wonders whether the number of daily cancellations can be described by a Poisson distribution. Using the data of Table 14.39, make the appropriate test and do so at the 2 percent level of significance.

TABLE 14.39 | Hotel Cancellations

Number of Cancellations per Day	Number of Days Observed f_o
0	22
1	30
2	22
3	10
4	5
5	2
6	0
7	1
8	1
9	0
10 or more	3
Total	**96**

46. An economist wants to determine whether the annual incomes of a nation's lawyers can be described by a normal curve with $\mu = \$45{,}000$ and $\sigma = \$10{,}000$. A simple random sample of 100 lawyers yields the results given in Table 14.40. Make the test at the 5 percent level of significance.

TABLE 14.40 | Lawyers' Incomes

Annual Incomes of Lawyers (thousands of dollars)	Observed Frequency f_o
Under 20	2
20 to under 30	5
30 to under 40	10
40 to under 50	60
50 to under 60	10
60 to under 70	5
70 to under 80	3
80 to under 90	0
90 and over	5
Total	**100**

47. An advertising agency asks a random sample of 500 people to taste 5 brands of coffee and records the brand most preferred. It wishes to test, at the 10 percent level of significance, whether the preferences of coffee drinkers in general are uniformly distributed among the brands. The sample results are listed in Table 14.41. Make the test.

TABLE 14.41 | Consumer Survey

Most Preferred Brand	Observed Frequency f_o
A	91
B	109
C	85
D	100
E	115
Total	**500**

48. Review Application 14.3 on page 632. Use a computer program to

a. confirm the computed χ^2 value.

b. find the associated p value.

49. A polling organization recorded the opinions given in Table 14.42 at the two indicated times. It wishes to test, at the 2 percent significance level, whether public opinion at the more recent date equals that at the earlier date. Make the test.

TABLE 14.42 | President's Performance

Opinion of President's Performance	Observed Frequency f_o	
	1 Year after Inauguration	3 Years after Inauguration
Does superb job	50	68
Does good job	25	33
Does fair job	15	22
Does lousy job	10	27
Total	**100**	**150**

50. A medical doctor checks the record of 200 patients who have taken a certain drug and makes the observations given in Table 14.43. A test at the 0.1 percent level of significance is to be conducted to see whether these data could possibly come from a larger population that conforms with the manufacturer's claim that 50 percent of users improve, 30 percent show no change, 15 percent show minor deterioration, and 5 percent show major deterioration. Make the test.

TABLE 14.43 | Drug Tests

Effect of Drug on Patients	Observed Frequency f_o
Improvement	90
No change	40
Minor deterioration	30
Major deterioration	40
Total	**200**

PART
VI

ADVANCED INFERENCE

Chapter 15

Analysis of Variance

LOOKING AHEAD

After reading this chapter, you will be able to use the analysis of variance, usually referred to as ANOVA, to test whether the means of more than two quantitative populations are equal. Possible approaches include:

1. one-way ANOVA, performed with data derived from experiments based on the randomized group design, in which only one factor (the type of treatment that is deliberately introduced) is believed to affect the variable of interest,
2. two-way ANOVA without interaction, performed with data derived from experiments based on the randomized block design, in which two factors (the type of treatment deliberately introduced and a single extraneous factor that does not interact with the treatment variable) are believed to affect the variable of interest,
3. two-way ANOVA with interaction, performed with data derived from experiments based on the randomized block design, in which two factors (the type of treatment deliberately introduced and a single extraneous factor that does interact with the treatment variable) are believed to affect the variable of interest,
4. three-way ANOVA, performed with data derived from experiments based on the Latin square design, in which three factors (the type of treatment deliberately introduced and two types of extraneous variables) are believed to affect the variable of interest,
5. establishing confidence intervals for individual population means or differences between them, and
6. applying Tukey's *HSD* test to ferret out *honestly significant differences* between paired sample means.

AND HERE IS A TYPICAL PROBLEM YOU WILL BE ABLE TO SOLVE:

The manager of a collection agency wants to know whether the mean amount of delinquent debt repaid is the same for four types of collection methods (friendly letter, nasty letter, telephone call, personal visit) and three categories of overdue debt (under \$500, over \$1,000, and in between). Given appropriate sample data, you are to conduct the test at the 5 percent significance level.

PREVIEW

Business executives and economists can facilitate their decision making by gathering crucial *new* data in one of two ways. They can conduct observational surveys (recall our discussion of census taking and sampling in Chapter 4) or they can perform controlled experiments (discussed in Chapter 5). An interesting example of the latter approach came to light in 1999 when the U.S. federal government took "the biggest enforcement action in the nation's history" and sued seven giant electric companies for their continued defiance of antipollution regulations. The suit focused on 32 coal-fired plants in ten midwestern and southern states, many of which had been conducting the experiments in question.

It all started in 1991, a year in which American power companies burned 900 million tons of American coal. Because the coal contained sulfur, the process generated huge emissions of sulfur dioxide (SO_2) and, ultimately, serious environmental damage through acid rain. Amendments to the federal Clean Air Act prodded some companies into conducting experiments designed to discover a cost-effective method of reducing SO_2 emissions. Major alternatives included the following:

1. Installing smokestack scrubbers to remove SO_2 from the exhaust
2. Cleaning high-sulfur American coal chemically before burning it
3. Changing high-sulfur American coal into a low-sulfur liquid fuel
4. Changing high-sulfur American coal into a low-sulfur gaseous fuel
5. Using low-sulfur fuel imported from abroad[1]

Now picture this hypothetical test: The Florida Power and Light Company conducts 20 weeks of experiments, devoting 4 weeks each to the five methods on our list. Each day, company statisticians record the percentage reduction of SO_2 emissions relative to a similar day prior to the experiments. Ultimately, they compute *average* percentage reductions (per million megawatts) of $\bar{X}_1 = 30.6$ for method 1, of $\bar{X}_2 = 27.9$ for method 2, and of $\bar{X}_3 = 32.8$, $\bar{X}_4 = 41.3$, and $\bar{X}_5 = 36.5$, respectively, for the other methods. Can we conclude that method 4 is best and method 2 worst? Having learned about random error and systematic error in experiments (review Figure 5.4 on page 154), we may well wonder: Are the differences in these $\bar{X}$ values indicative of true differences in the sulfur-reducing capabilities of the five methods on our list, or are they attributable to one or both of the errors noted above?

One tempting answer to this vexing question is provided by what we learned in Chapters 12 and 13. We might compute numerous confidence intervals or conduct hypothesis tests for differences between two means at a time, comparing $\bar{X}_1$ with $\bar{X}_2$, then $\bar{X}_1$ with $\bar{X}_3$, and so on, but such an approach would be seriously flawed.

First, the procedure of comparing two means at a time is terribly inefficient. Even our simple example, which contains a mere five means, would require us to compare

$$C_2^5 = \frac{5!}{2!\,3!} = \frac{5 \times 4}{2 \times 1} = 10$$

combinations of two means at a time.

[1]Venezuela markets *Orimulsion,* a low-sulfur liquid coal created by forcing heated salt water into its extra-heavy crude oil and bitumen deposits. An Indonesian mining company offers *enviro-coal* that contains 80 percent less sulfur than the cleanest American coal, apparently because Borneo deposits lie close to the surface and have been drenched with heavy rains for millions of years.

Second, and much more important, the procedure would involve an unacceptable error probability. Consider selecting a confidence level of 95 percent. Then the long-run probability of reaching the correct conclusion in a test that compares two means is .95, and the probability of making a type I error (and of incorrectly rejecting a null hypothesis of equal means) is .05. Yet the corresponding probability of reaching the correct conclusion in all ten comparisons of means then equals $.95^{10}$, or .5987. This implies a long-run probability of $1 - .5987 = .4013$ of getting at least one wrong set of test results with the pair-wise comparison procedure.

This chapter introduces an alternative approach to testing differences among more than two means, which avoids the problems just noted. The procedure, called the *analysis of variance,* does not require numerous pair-wise comparisons and involves only a single test. Its only problem, perhaps, is its name. It may seem farfetched to use *variances* to test differences among *means,* but we have good reasons for doing so: The variance is the square of the standard deviation, and the standard deviation is the standard measure of dispersion about the *mean.*[2]

---

[2]Adapted from James Brooke, "Venezuela Pushing 'Liquid Coal,'" *The New York Times,* October 16, 1990, pp. D1 and 2; Matthew L. Wald, "Help for Cleaner Air from a Mystery Coal," *The New York Times,* August 10, 1992, pp. D1 and 3; and David Stout, "7 Utilities Sued by U.S. on Charges of Polluting Air," *The New York Times,* November 4, 1999, pp. A1 and 22.

15.1 Introduction

We learned in Chapter 13 that independent random samples taken from two appropriate quantitative populations can help us answer questions such as these: Are the mean lifetimes of two types of aircraft radios the same? Is the mean yield of fruit trees sprayed with gypsy-moth parasites larger than that of trees sprayed with traditional pesticides? Is the mean number of cavities associated with the use of toothpaste 1 smaller than that associated with the use of toothpaste 2? We also learned that the normal probability distribution (in the case of large samples) and Student's t distribution (in the case of small samples) are ideally suited to help us perform any desired hypothesis test about the comparative magnitudes of two population means. In this chapter, we take this type of analysis one step further. We compare the means not merely of two, but of more than two quantitative populations.

The need to compare the means of more than two statistical populations arises quite often. Consider the manager of a farm who wants to know whether there is any difference in the average crop yield associated with the use of five types of fertilizer, or with five alternative quantities of a given type of fertilizer that might be applied, or even with five alternative times at which a given quantity of a given type might be applied. Consider the industrial manager who wants to know whether the average lifetime or delivery time of components is the same regardless of which one of seven outside contractors supplies them, or the manager who wants to test whether the average number of units assembled in a day differs among seven possible production methods or workers or machines that may be employed. Consider a sales manager who wonders whether average sales vary among six alternative window displays, TV ads, types of packaging, or price levels. In all these cases and a million more, sample evidence can help us make inferences about the population means of interest. Yet tempting as it may be, stringing together the results of several two-sample tests is not wise, as this chapter's Preview already pointed out. This chapter, therefore, explains an alternative procedure, the *analysis of variance,* abbreviated as *ANOVA,* that avoids compounding the probability of a type I error when comparing many means.

DEFINITION 15.1 The **analysis of variance,** generally known by the acronym **ANOVA,** is a statistical technique designed to test whether the means of more than two quantitative populations are equal. The technique can be applied to data derived from controlled experiments or from observational surveys.

15.2 The Nature of ANOVA

The ANOVA technique is typically used to test the equality of more than two means, but we should note that it could also be used to test the equality of only two means. In the latter case, the ANOVA test yields the same result as the normal-distribution or *t*-distribution tests of Chapter 13. To perform ANOVA, we first take an independent simple random sample from each of several populations of interest and then analyze the data. We must recognize, however, that the validity of our test rests on two important assumptions.

CRUCIAL ASSUMPTIONS

Like the *t* test, the ANOVA test assumes that the sampled populations are normally distributed *and* have identical variances. (The latter assumption is often referred to as **homoscedasticity,** an awkward word created by the Greek *homo* = "same" and *skedastikos* = "scatter.") It turns out that the analysis-of-variance test is quite *robust* with respect to violations of the normality assumption but quite fragile with respect to violations of the equal-variances assumption. Given that **robustness** describes a statistical test's sensitivity to any breach of basic assumptions, we can state: Even moderate departures from the assumption that all populations are normally distributed do not affect the test results much, but any violation of the assumption that all populations have equal variances seriously undermines the validity of the test.

COMPARING TWO VARIANCES

The sensitivity of the test to unequal population variances is not surprising because the basis of the entire test is to develop, from the sample data, two independent estimates of the assumed *common* variance, σ^2, of the populations of interest. The first of these independent estimates of σ^2 is based on the variation *among the sample means.* This estimate, denoted by s_A^2, is an unbiased estimate of σ^2 only if the population means really are equal. The second independent estimate of σ^2 is based on the weighted average of the variations of *individual sample observations within each sample.* This weighted average of individual sample variances, denoted by s_W^2, *always* provides an unbiased estimate of σ^2. ANOVA then compares these estimates as a ratio, s_A^2/s_W^2, which will be close to 1 if, and only if, the population means are equal to each other. On the other hand, the more the value of this ratio diverges from 1 (and, in principle, this ratio of squares can take on any value between zero and positive infinity), the greater is the probability that the population means are *not* equal to each other. Thus, an analysis of *variances* helps us test hypotheses about the equality of *means,* which accounts for the seemingly inappropriate name of the test.

A GRAPHICAL EXPOSITION

Figure 15.1 presents the idea of comparing two variances graphically. In each panel, the density functions shown refer to three populations, consisting, say, of the numbers of cavities observed, *X*, among all the users of toothpastes 1, 2, and 3, respectively. The populations are normally distributed and have identical variances, σ^2. The positions of the density functions, however, differ

FIGURE 15.1 | The Nature of ANOVA

*Whenever the estimate, s_A^2, of the common population variance that is derived from the dispersion **among** sample means is considerably larger than such an estimate, s_W^2, that is based on the dispersion **within** samples, the populations have unequal means, as panels (a) and (b) show. Whenever the two estimates are about the same, as in panel (c), the populations have equal means.*

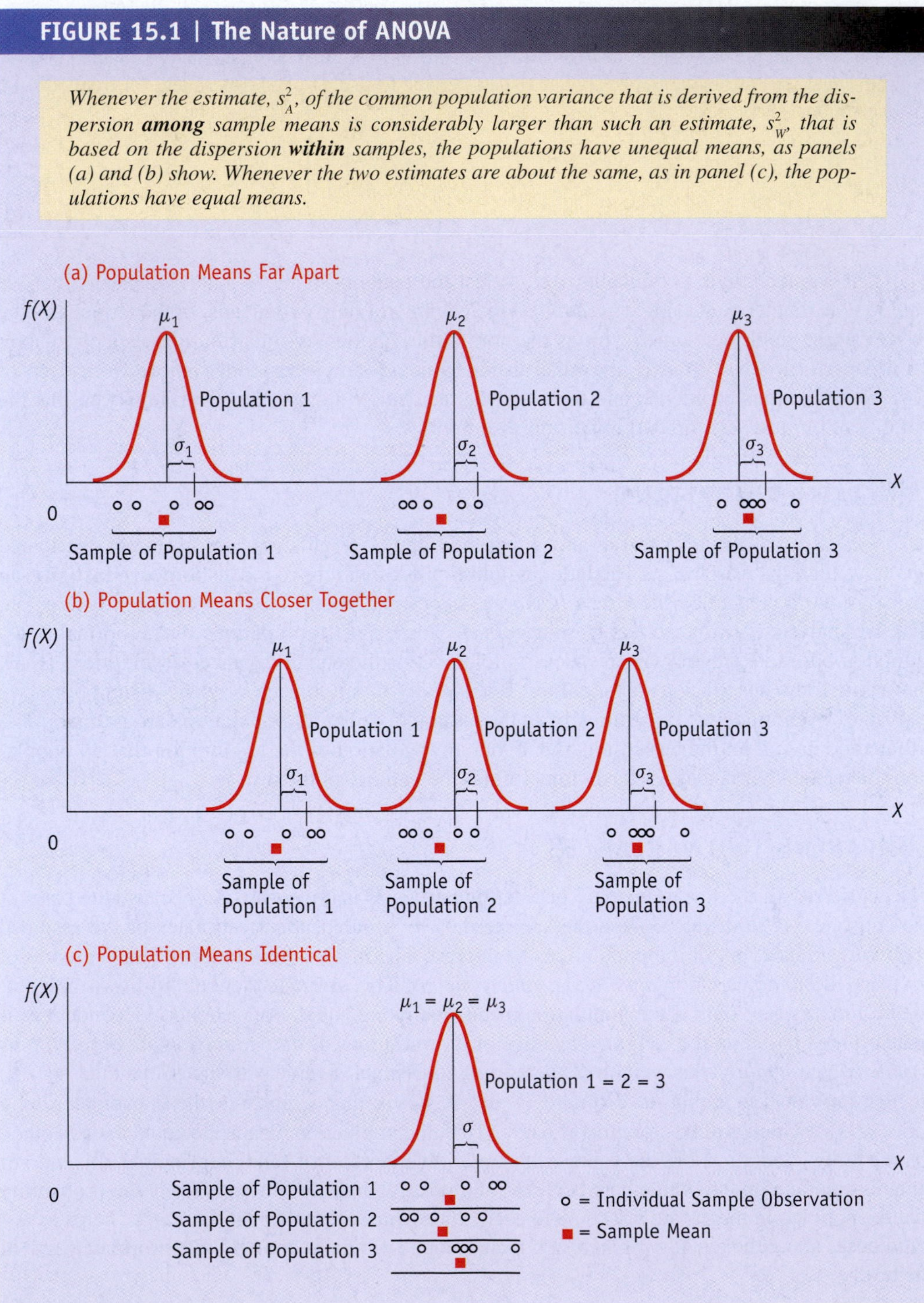

in the three panels. In panel (a) the population means (μ_1, μ_2, and μ_3) are wide apart. In panel (b), they are closer together. In panel (c), they are identical; hence, the three density functions have merged into one. If a sample of $n = 5$ were taken from each of these populations, the individual sample observations might have values corresponding to the positions of the small circles underneath each graph. The corresponding sample *means* are given by the red squares. It is immediately clear that the common population variance ($\sigma^2 = \sigma^2_1 = \sigma^2_2 = \sigma^2_3$) would be estimated well in panel (c) by the dispersion among the five individual observations (small circles) within each sample as well as by the average of these sample variances, s^2_W. It is also clear that this common population variance would not be estimated well (but instead would be vastly exaggerated) by the dispersion among the three sample means (red squares) in panel (a) and, to only a slightly lesser extent, in panel (b). Only in panel (c), wherein the red squares are not any more dispersed than any one set of small circles, could we derive, from the dispersion among the sample means, an unbiased estimate, s^2_A, of σ^2. We conclude:

Whenever the estimate, s^2_A, of the common population variance that is derived from the dispersion *among* sample means is considerably larger than such an estimate, s^2_W, that is based on the dispersion *within* samples, the populations have unequal means, as panels (a) and (b) show. Whenever the two estimates are about the same, as in panel (c), the populations have equal means.

15.3 Alternative Versions of ANOVA

All types of situations that compare means are experiments in the sense that we are interested in the effects of different "treatments" (such as different types of toothpaste) on different experimental units (such as people), while somehow controlling extraneous factors. Yet it is all too easy to mix up or confound the effects of treatments (such as types of toothpaste used) with the effects of other factors that are also operating (such as the users' ethnic backgrounds and, hence, dietary habits, or the users' age and, hence, general state of health). Depending on how we control extraneous factors, several versions of ANOVA exist, including:

- one-way ANOVA
- two-way ANOVA
- three-way ANOVA

When we control extraneous factors by using the randomized group design (which you may wish to review in Chapter 5), the subsequent data analysis is called **one-way ANOVA** or **one-factor ANOVA.** In a toothpaste experiment, for instance, a pharmaceutical firm might create one treatment group for each treatment, such as toothpastes 1, 2, and 3, and then randomly assign each experimental unit to one of these groups. As a result, a randomly chosen third of all participants ends up using toothpaste 1, another such third uses toothpaste 2, and the last third uses toothpaste 3. In the end, only *one* factor, the treatment, is considered to be responsible for any variations in the variable of interest, such as the number of cavities observed. Randomly assigning human subjects to each of the three treatment groups is believed to neutralize the effects of any other, extraneous influences.

When we control extraneous factors by using the randomized block design (which you may wish to review in Chapter 5), the subsequent data analysis is called **two-way ANOVA** or **two-factor ANOVA.** In a toothpaste experiment, for instance, we might create two blocks of experimental units, such as sweets-loving Germans on the one hand and spice-loving Italians on the other hand. Having divided the available experimental units into distinctly different, but internally homogeneous blocks, we can then randomly match each treatment (toothpastes 1, 2, and 3) with one or more units within each block. Ultimately, we can observe differences attributable to *two* factors, treatments and blocks. For example, within any one block (as among persons of Italian background) we might observe differential impacts of toothpastes 1, 2, and 3 on the number of cavities. In addition, we might also observe potential differences among blocks given the same treatment. For example, sweets-loving Germans using toothpaste 1 may have more cavities than Italians using toothpaste 1.

Finally, we will consider **three-way ANOVA** or **three-factor ANOVA,** which is based on the Latin square experimental design (which you may wish to review in Chapter 5). Here we recognize *three* factors that might influence the variable of interest. In a toothpaste experiment, the number of cavities observed might vary not only with the type of toothpaste used and with the users' ethnic backgrounds (and dietary habits), but also with the users' ages (and, thus, the initial conditions of their teeth). We can take all three factors explicitly into account in this analysis.

15.4 One-Way ANOVA

It is easiest to introduce one-way ANOVA by example. Consider a 10-year study in which someone has observed a sample of 15 people using either toothpaste 1, 2, or 3, respectively. Let us assume that a third of the participants has been randomly assigned to each of the three treatments and that the study has provided the data given in Table 15.1.

A statistician about to analyze these data would formulate opposing hypotheses:

H_0: The mean number of cavities for all possible users of toothpaste 1 is the same as that for all possible users of toothpaste 2 or 3; that is, $\mu_1 = \mu_2 = \mu_3$.

H_A: At least one of these population means differs from the others. (At least one of the equalities in H_0 doesn't hold.)

The analyst would proceed by studying the variation in the sample data listed in the $r = 5$ observation rows and $c = 3$ treatment columns of our table. This variation has two components:

- variation among columns, which is explained by treatments
- variation within columns, which is attributed to (experimental or sampling) error

TABLE 15.1 | The Randomized Group Design: Numbers of Cavities Observed during 10-Year Period

	Treatment, *j*		
Observation, *i*	**Toothpaste 1**	**Toothpaste 2**	**Toothpaste 3**
1	19	20	18
2	15	25	12
3	22	22	16
4	17	19	17
5	19	23	15
Total	**92**	**109**	**78**
Sample Means	$\bar{X}_1 = \frac{92}{5} = 18.4$	$\bar{X}_2 = \frac{109}{5} = 21.8$	$\bar{X}_3 = \frac{78}{5} = 15.6$
Grand Mean	$\bar{\bar{X}} = \frac{18.4 + 21.8 + 15.6}{3} = 18.6$		

VARIATION AMONG COLUMNS: EXPLAINED BY TREATMENTS

The variation among the $c = 3$ sample means ($\overline{X}_1$, $\overline{X}_2$, and $\overline{X}_3$), which summarize the data associated with each of the treatments, is referred to as **explained variation** or **treatments variation,** because it is attributable not to chance, but to inherent differences among the treatment populations. As noted above, the measurement of this variation constitutes a first estimate, s_A^2, of the population variance, σ^2. This estimate is based on a complex series of considerations, which we consider in 8 small steps:

MEASURING EXPLAINED VARIATION

1. Given the assumed normality of the sampled populations, the sampling distribution of each sample mean, $\overline{X}_j$, will be normally distributed. (In our case, as noted in Table 15.1, the subscript j represents treatments and can equal 1, 2, or 3.)
2. The sampling distribution of each sample mean will itself have a variance of

$$\sigma_{\overline{X}_j}^2 = \frac{\sigma_j^2}{n_j}$$

as a quick review of Formula 11.B on page 463 can confirm.

3. Given the assumed equality of population variances ($\sigma_1^2 = \sigma_2^2 = \sigma_3^2$) and equal sample sizes ($n_1 = n_2 = n_3$), the value of σ_j^2 is the same for each j. Hence, we can drop the j subscripts in the preceding equation. Furthermore, the number of observations in each sample (which equals $n = 5$ in our case) also equals r, the number of observation rows in Table 15.1. Hence, we can extract the common population variance from the preceding equation as

$$\sigma^2 = n\sigma_{\overline{X}}^2 = r\sigma_{\overline{X}}^2$$

4. The variance, $\sigma_{\overline{X}}^2$, of the sampling distribution of $\overline{X}$ can itself be estimated by the variance of the individual sample means, $\overline{X}_j$, about *their* mean, which is called the **grand mean,** $\overline{\overline{X}}$ (pronounced "X double bar"). As Table 15.1 shows, we compute the grand mean as the arithmetic mean of the sample means. Then, in accordance with the sample variance formula, we can estimate the variance of the sampling distribution of $\overline{X}$ as

$$\sigma_{\overline{X}}^2 \cong s_{\overline{X}}^2 = \frac{\Sigma(\overline{X}_j - \overline{\overline{X}})^2}{c - 1}$$

Note: The individual sample observations here are themselves sample means; their deviations from the grand mean are being squared. In addition, the number of individual observations, normally called n, is now equal to c, the number of treatment columns, each of which provides us with one sample mean.

5. Steps 3 and 4 imply that

$$\sigma^2 = r\sigma_{\overline{X}}^2 \cong \frac{r\Sigma(\overline{X}_j - \overline{\overline{X}})^2}{c - 1}$$

6. The numerator of the step 5 ratio (the sum of the squared deviations between each treatment sample mean and the grand mean, multiplied by the number of observations made for each treatment) is referred to as the **treatments sum of squares,** or ***TSS.*** For our example, we can derive

$$TSS = r\Sigma(\bar{X}_j - \bar{\bar{X}})^2 = 5[(18.4 - 18.6)^2 + (21.8 - 18.6)^2 + (15.6 - 18.6)^2] = 96.4$$

7. The denominator of the step 5 ratio equals the degrees of freedom associated with the estimation of σ^2 with the help of the variation among sample means. In our case,

$$d.f. = c - 1 = 3 - 1 = 2$$

   This number of degrees of freedom indicates that two of the three sample means are free to vary, given the grand mean.

8. The step 5 ratio as a whole, finally, is the measure of explained variation we seek. It is also called the **treatments mean square *(TMS)*** or **explained variance.** It is identical to the population variance estimate symbolized by s_A^2, where the subscript A reminds us that this estimate of σ^2 is based on the observed variation *among* samples. Thus,

$$\sigma^2 \cong \frac{r\Sigma(\bar{X}_j - \bar{\bar{X}})^2}{c - 1} = TMS = s_A^2$$

   In our case,

$$TMS = s_A^2 = \frac{96.4}{2} = 48.2$$

VARIATION WITHIN COLUMNS: DUE TO ERROR

The variation of the sample data *within* each of the $c = 3$ columns (or samples) about the respective sample means is generally referred to as **unexplained variation** or **residual variation** or simply as **error,** attributable to chance. As noted above, the measurement of this variation constitutes a second estimate, s_W^2, of the population variance, σ^2. This estimate, in turn, is based on a number of additional considerations:

MEASURING UNEXPLAINED VARIATION

9. From each of the j samples in Table 15.1, we can derive a (probably different) sample variance by using the familiar formula, such that the variance of sample j equals

$$s_j^2 = \frac{\Sigma(X_{ij} - \bar{X}_j)^2}{n_j - 1}$$

   where X_{ij} is the sample observation in row i and column j, while $\bar{X}_j$ is the mean of sample j, and n_j is the number of observations in sample j (which also equals r, the number of rows in Table 15.1).

10. To get a single estimate of σ^2, we can take the weighted average of the j sample variances. In our case, with samples of equal size, taking this weighted average requires only that we

TABLE 15.2 | Calculating the Error Sum of Squares *(ESS)*

Observation, *i*	Sample 1 $(X_{i1} - \bar{X}_1)^2$	Sample 2 $(X_{i2} - \bar{X}_2)^2$	Sample 3 $(X_{i3} - \bar{X}_3)^2$
1	$(19 - 18.4)^2 = .36$	$(20 - 21.8)^2 = 3.24$	$(18 - 15.6)^2 = 5.76$
2	$(15 - 18.4)^2 = 11.56$	$(25 - 21.8)^2 = 10.24$	$(12 - 15.6)^2 = 12.96$
3	$(22 - 18.4)^2 = 12.96$	$(22 - 21.8)^2 = .04$	$(16 - 15.6)^2 = .16$
4	$(17 - 18.4)^2 = 1.96$	$(19 - 21.8)^2 = 7.84$	$(17 - 15.6)^2 = 1.96$
5	$(19 - 18.4)^2 = .36$	$(23 - 21.8)^2 = 1.44$	$(15 - 15.6)^2 = .36$
Total	**27.20**	**22.80**	**21.20**
	$ESS = \Sigma\Sigma(X_{ij} - \bar{X}_j)^2 = 27.20 + 22.80 + 21.20 = 71.20$		

sum the $c = 3$ sample variances and divide by c. Thus, we derive the second estimate of the population variance as

$$\sigma^2 \cong \frac{\Sigma\Sigma(X_{ij} - \bar{X}_j)^2}{(r - 1)c}$$

11. The numerator of the step 10 ratio (the sum of each sample's sum of squared deviations of individual observations from the sample's mean) is generally referred to as the **error sum of squares** or ***ESS***. Its calculation for our example is illustrated in Table 15.2.

12. The denominator of the step 10 ratio equals the degrees of freedom associated with estimating σ^2 with the help of the variation within the samples. In our case,

$$d.f. = (r - 1)c = (5 - 1)3 = 12$$

This number of degrees of freedom indicates that, given a sample mean, $\bar{X}_j$, only $r - 1 = 4$ of the 5 observations in the sample can vary freely. There being $c = 3$ samples, however, the total number of values free to vary is 4(3) = 12.

13. The step 10 ratio as a whole, finally, is the measure of unexplained variation we seek. It is also called the **error mean square *(EMS)*** or **unexplained variance.** It is identical to the population variance estimate symbolized by s_W^2, where the subscript W reminds us that this estimate of σ^2 is based on the observed variation *within* the treatments samples. Thus,

$$\sigma^2 \cong \frac{\Sigma\Sigma(X_{ij} - \bar{X}_j)^2}{(r - 1)c} = EMS = s_W^2$$

In our case,

$$EMS = s_W^2 = \frac{71.2}{12} = 5.93$$

THE ONE-WAY ANOVA TABLE

Our computations so far are conveniently summarized in Table 15.3 on the next page, a kind of table that is typically produced by computer. Among other things, this **ANOVA table** shows, for

TABLE 15.3 | The One-Way ANOVA Table

Source of Variation	Sum of Squares (1)	Degrees of Freedom (2)	Mean Square (3) = (1) ÷ (2)	Test Statistic (4)
Treatments	$TSS = 96.4$	$c - 1 = 2$	$TMS = \frac{96.4}{2} = 48.2$	$F = \frac{TMS}{EMS} = \frac{48.2}{5.93} = 8.13$
Error	$ESS = 71.2$	$(r - 1)c = 12$	$EMS = \frac{71.2}{12} = 5.93$	
Total	$Total\ SS = 167.6$	$rc - 1 = 14$		

each source of variation, the sum of squares, the associated degrees of freedom, and the ratio of the sum of squares to the degrees of freedom. This ratio is called the **mean square** and is the desired estimate of the population variance, as steps 8 and 13 have just shown.

The last row of the ANOVA table introduces two types of totals:

- the total sum of squares
- the total degrees of freedom

We can find the **total sum of squares** or ***Total SS*** by adding the preceding column entries, but we can also calculate it independently by summing the squared deviations of each individual sample observation (regardless of the sample to which it belongs) from the mean of all observations, $\bar{\bar{X}}$. Thus, we can use the data of Table 15.1 to calculate:

$$Total\ SS = (19 - 18.6)^2 + (15 - 18.6)^2 + (22 - 18.6)^2 + \ldots + (15 - 18.6)^2 = 167.6$$

In one-way ANOVA, this *Total SS* value always equals the sum of the treatments sum of squares and the error sum of squares:

$$Total\ SS = TSS + ESS = 96.4 + 71.2 = 167.6$$

Thus, if we know any two of these values, we can instantly compute the third.

Table 15.3 also shows that the **total degrees of freedom** equal the sum of the separate degrees of freedom associated with each source of variation. In the one-way ANOVA case,

$$\text{total degrees of freedom} = (c - 1) + (r - 1)c = c - 1 + rc - c = rc - 1$$

This sum is $5(3) - 1 = 14$ in our example, which equals the total number of observations (15) minus 1. This *d.f.* reflects the fact that, given the grand mean, all but one of the $rc = 15$ values in Table 15.1 are free to vary.

The next section, finally, discusses the meaning of the last column of our ANOVA table and reveals the results of our hypothesis test.

THE *F* DISTRIBUTION

Earlier in this chapter, we noted that the ratio of the two independent estimates of the common population variance (then denoted by s_A^2/s_W^2 and now found to equal *TMS/EMS*) would be close to

1 whenever the null hypothesis of equal population means was true. Indeed, this ratio is used as the ANOVA test statistic. It is known as the ***F* statistic** (and denoted by F), in honor of Ronald A. Fisher (1890–1962), who developed its probability distribution.

FORMULA 15.A | The *F* Statistic

$$F = \frac{s_A^2}{s_W^2} = \frac{\text{explained variance}}{\text{unexplained variance}} = \frac{TMS}{EMS}$$

where s_A^2 is the variation *among* sample means, s_W^2 is the variation of individual sample observations *within* samples, TMS is the treatments mean square, and EMS is the error mean square.

Note: The explained variance equals TMS in one-way ANOVA, but it can equal other expressions in other types of ANOVA. As later sections explain, depending on the hypothesis being tested, the explained variance can equal TMS or BMS in two-way ANOVA without interaction; TMS, BMS, or IMS in two-way ANOVA with interaction; and TMS, $CBMS$, or $RBMS$ in three-way ANOVA.

The probability distribution of F helps us decide whether any given divergence of a computed F statistic from 1 (such as $F = 8.13$ in Table 15.3) is significant enough to warrant the rejection of the null hypothesis of equal population means. The rule is this:

Whenever the computed F statistic exceeds a chosen critical value of F, the null hypothesis of equal population means should be rejected.

READY-MADE TABLES For our convenience, critical values of F have been tabulated in a series of tables. Appendix Table N, an excerpt of which appears as Table 15.4 on the next page, provides critical values of F for significance levels of $\alpha = .10, .05, .025$, and $.01$.

Note that the F statistic, unlike the t and χ^2 statistics, is not associated with a single number of degrees of freedom, but with a pair of them. This is so because F is a ratio of two variances. One of the two *d.f.* numbers (equal to $c - 1 = 2$ in our example) goes with the numerator of the ratio; the other one [equal to $(r - 1)c = 12$ in our example] goes with the denominator.

GRAPHICAL ILLUSTRATIONS Different members of the continuous probability distribution family of the F statistic, distinguished from one another by different numerator and denominator degrees of freedom, can also be shown graphically. Figure 15.2 on page 663 shows a number of such ***F* distributions** for selected pairs of degrees of freedom. In each case, the first *d.f.* number within the parentheses refers to the numerator; the second number refers to the denominator of the F ratio.

TABLE 15.4 | Excerpt of Appendix Table N: *F* Distributions

Entries in this table give F_α values, where α is the area or probability in the upper tail of the F distribution. For example, with 12 numerator degrees of freedom, 4 denominator degrees of freedom, and an $\alpha = .10$ area in the upper tail, $F_{.10} = 3.90$.

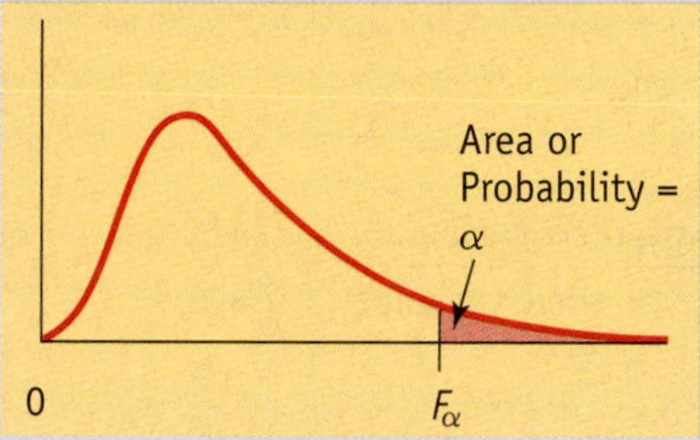

$F_{.10}$ Values

Denominator Degrees of Freedom	Numerator Degrees of Freedom 1	2	4	6	8	10	12	15	20	30
1	39.86	49.50	55.83	58.20	59.44	60.19	60.71	61.22	61.74	62.26
2	8.53	9.00	9.24	9.33	9.37	9.39	9.41	9.42	9.44	9.46
3	5.54	5.46	5.34	5.28	5.25	5.23	5.22	5.20	5.18	5.17
4	4.54	4.32	4.11	4.01	3.95	3.92	3.90	3.87	3.84	3.82
5	4.06	3.78	3.52	3.40	3.34	3.30	3.27	3.24	3.21	3.17
6	3.78	3.46	3.18	3.05	2.98	2.94	2.90	2.87	2.84	2.80
7	3.59	3.26	2.96	2.83	2.75	2.70	2.67	2.63	2.59	2.56

CAUTION

Be careful: An *F* distribution with 1 numerator degree of freedom and 6 denominator degrees of freedom *must not* be confused with one that has 6 numerator degrees of freedom and 1 denominator degree of freedom. The shapes of these distributions are entirely different. This fact becomes evident when inspecting Appendix Table N. Note how the critical value of $F_{.10}$ equals 3.78 for a numerator/denominator degrees of freedom pair of 1, 6 but equals 58.20 for a pair of 6, 1.

EXAMPLE PROBLEM 15.1

Review the discussion of the toothpaste study from the beginning of Section 15.4 on page 656. Use the tools introduced above to analyze the data.

a. Select a significance level of $\alpha = .05$, then reach a conclusion about these hypotheses:

H_0: The mean number of cavities for all possible users of toothpaste 1 is the same as that for all possible users of toothpaste 2 or 3; that is, $\mu_1 = \mu_2 = \mu_3$.

H_A: At least one of the population means differs from the others. (At least one of the equalities in H_0 doesn't hold.)

b. Would your conclusions differ for alternative significance levels of $\alpha = .10$, $\alpha = .025$, and $\alpha = .01$?

FIGURE 15.2 | *F* Distributions

A different F distribution curve can be drawn for each possible pair of numerator and denominator degrees of freedom that is associated with the two variance estimates making up the F ratio. All members of this continuous probability distribution family are positively skewed between values of zero and positive infinity, but F distributions tend toward normality as both numerator and denominator of degrees of freedom become large. Indeed, as more advanced texts show, the normal, t, and χ^2 distributions are special cases of the F distribution family.

Note: *The numerator degrees of freedom and the denominator degrees of freedom happen to be equal to one another in each of the curves pictured here. There is no logical necessity for this, as Table 15.3 and numerous other examples in this chapter illustrate.*

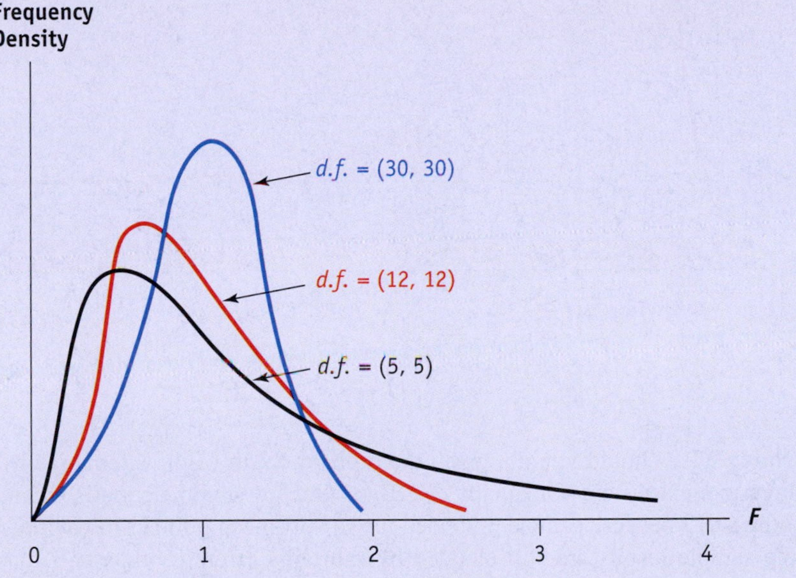

SOLUTION:

a. As Appendix Table N shows, with 2 numerator degrees of freedom and 12 denominator degrees of freedom, the critical value of $F_{.05}$ is 3.89. This means there is only a 5 percent chance that a computed value of F will exceed the indicated magnitude when the null hypothesis is true. Because the actual value of $F = 8.13$ in our example exceeds the critical value, we must *reject* H_0.

Figure 15.3 on the next page illustrates this example graphically. The critical value of $F_{.05(2,12)} = 3.89$ is encircled. Thus, if an experiment of this type were to be repeated over and over again, while the null hypothesis of equal population means was true, the computed value of F, shown by the red arrow, would exceed 3.89 in only 5 percent of these experiments. This result leads us to *reject* the null hypothesis and to conclude that the three toothpastes do have different effects.

b. The alternative critical values are $F_{.10} = 2.81$, $F_{.025} = 5.10$, and $F_{.01} = 6.93$. This means there is only a 10 percent, 2.5 percent, or 1 percent chance, respectively, that a computed value of F will exceed the indicated magnitudes when the null hypothesis is true. Thus, regardless of which of these other significance levels we select, the actual value of $F = 8.13$ in our example exceeds the critical value, and we must *reject* H_0.

FIGURE 15.3 | Toothpaste Study: One-Way ANOVA

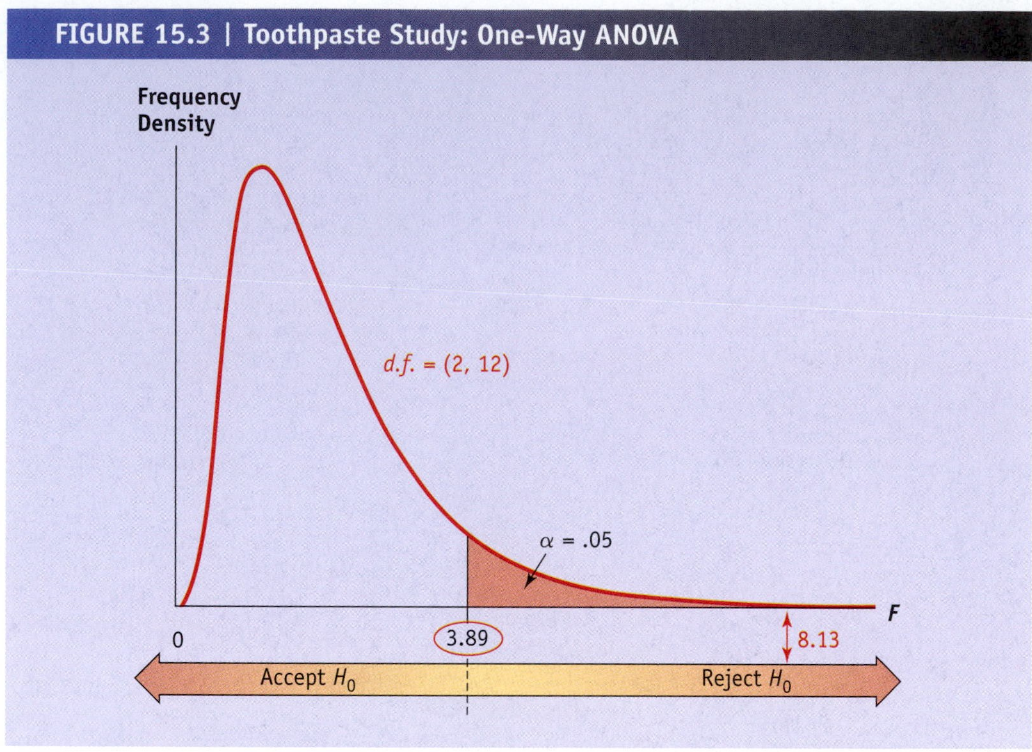

Note: What should you do, given the probable truth of the alternative hypothesis that the three toothpastes are *not* equally effective? One possible reaction is recommending use of toothpaste 3 because sample 3 yielded the lowest mean number of cavities (Table 15.1). Yet the sample results are still clouded by sampling error. Toothpaste 1 may actually be better than 3 but an unfortunate sample may have been drawn from population 1 and a lucky one from population 3. Thus, further analysis is in order. We will examine possible methods in the last section of this chapter.

EXCEL Example 15.1

Perform a one-way analysis of variance with the data of Table 15.1 and, thus, confirm the results noted in Table 15.3 and illustrated in Figure 15.3. Once again, choose $\alpha = .05$.

SOLUTION:

1. Enter the data from the three treatment columns of Table 15.1, exclusive of column heads and totals, into columns A–C of a new worksheet.
2. Click **Tools** > **Data Analysis** > **Anova: Single Factor** > **OK**.
3. In the dialog box, under *Input Range,* enter **A1:C5**
4. Choose *Grouped By Columns* and leave *Labels in First Row* blank.
5. Under *Alpha,* enter **.05**
6. Choose *New Worksheet Ply* and click **OK** to get the following output:

Anova: Single Factor

SUMMARY

Groups	*Count*	*Sum*	*Average*	*Variance*
Column 1	5	92	18.4	6.8
Column 2	5	109	21.8	5.7
Column 3	5	78	15.6	5.3

ANOVA

Source of Variation	*SS*	*df*	*MS*	*F*	*P-value*	*F crit*
Between Groups	96.4	2	48.2	8.123596	0.005878	3.88529
Within Groups	71.2	12	5.933333			
Total	167.6	14				

The output contains all of the information given in Table 15.3, along with a p value and the critical $F_{.05\,(2,12)} = 3.89$ noted in Figure 15.3. The p value indicates a 0.6 percent chance of encountering this F value when H_0 is true.

15.5 Two-Way ANOVA: No Interaction

Sometimes we may wish to consider the effects of two factors on the variable of interest. If we have reason to believe, for example, that dietary habits associated with ethnic background affect the number of cavities *independently of* and *in addition to* the type of toothpaste used, we can use this additional factor to explain some of the previously unexplained variation *within* the samples taken from the different toothpaste-user populations. We can correspondingly reduce the error sum of squares and can ultimately derive a more discriminating F statistic.

Two basic types of two-way ANOVA exist, depending on whether the two factors under consideration (such as type of toothpaste used and ethnic background) do or do not *interact* with one another. In this section, we assume that such interaction does *not* occur. Thus, if use of toothpaste 1 instead of 2 has a significant cavity-reducing effect among people in general, we assume this to be equally true for all ethnic groups, regardless of their (possibly differing) initial rate of cavity formation. Similarly, if being German (and therefore sweets-loving) has a significant cavity-increasing effect in general, we assume this to be equally true regardless of the type of toothpaste used. As a result, the joint effect of the two factors on the number of cavities simply equals the sum of the factors' separate effects. When interaction is absent, the factor effects are *additive:* If using toothpaste 1 instead of 2 lowers cavities by 5 a year (regardless of ethnic group), while eating sweets raises them by 8 a year (regardless of toothpaste type), doing both will raise them by 3 a year ($-5 + 8 = 3$).

THE TOOTHPASTE STUDY REVISITED

The toothpaste study discussed in the previous section was based on the *randomized group design,* which supposedly controls for extraneous factors. Yet someone who was convinced that dietary habits, formed by ethnic background, strongly influence the number of cavities observed might well feel uncomfortable about that experimental design. What if the random process that assigns experimental units to treatments just happened to assign lots of sweets-loving Germans to toothpaste 2 and lots of sweets-disdaining Britishers to toothpaste 3? Then it could well appear that toothpaste 3 was more effective than 2, as the data in Table 15.1 possibly suggest. Yet this result might well arise not from differences in the toothpastes used, but from the dietary habits of their users. To avoid such a possible pitfall, we can employ the *randomized block design,* which was also introduced in Chapter 5. We can first split the experimental units into homogeneous blocks such that the different blocks reflect the second factor (ethnic grouping in our case) that is believed to influence the results. Having created blocks, we would then assign units within each block randomly to each of the treatments. As a result, each block would be represented equally in each treatment. The possible results of such a study appear in Table 15.5.

The analysis of the data proceeds in perfect analogy to that of the previous section, the only difference being that we can simultaneously assess the effects of *two* factors (type of toothpaste used and ethnic group). However, the major hypothesis test remains the same as in the one-way ANOVA test:

MAJOR HYPOTHESIS TEST

H_0: The mean number of cavities for all possible users of toothpaste 1 is the same as that for all possible users of toothpaste 2 or 3; that is, $\mu_1 = \mu_2 = \mu_3$.

H_A: At least one of these population means differs from the others. (At least one of the equalities in H_0 doesn't hold.)

TABLE 15.5 | The Randomized Block Design with No Interaction: Number of Cavities Observed during 10-Year Period

Block, *i* (ethnic group)	Treatment, *j* (type of toothpaste used)			Row Totals	Row Means
	1	2	3		
(A) British	15	12	16	43	$\bar{X}_A = (43/3) = 14.33$
(B) French	19	19	19	57	$\bar{X}_B = (57/3) = 19.00$
(C) German	25	23	22	70	$\bar{X}_C = (70/3) = 23.33$
(D) Italian	22	20	18	60	$\bar{X}_D = (60/3) = 20.00$
(E) Spanish	17	15	17	49	$\bar{X}_E = (49/3) = 16.33$
Column Totals	98	89	92		
Column Means	$\bar{X}_1 = \frac{98}{5} = 19.6$	$\bar{X}_2 = \frac{89}{5} = 17.8$	$\bar{X}_3 = \frac{92}{5} = 18.4$		
Grand Mean	$\bar{\bar{X}} = \frac{19.6 + 17.8 + 18.4}{3} = 18.6$ or $\bar{\bar{X}} = \frac{14.33 + 19.00 + 23.33 + 20.00 + 16.33}{5} = 18.6$				

SECOND HYPOTHESIS TEST

H_0: The mean number of cavities for all the members of ethnic group A is the same as that for all the members of ethnic group B, C, D, and E; that is, $\mu_A = \mu_B = \mu_C = \mu_D = \mu_E$.

H_A: At least one of these population means differs from the others. (At least one of the equalities in H_0 doesn't hold.)

Ordinarily, this second hypothesis about blocks is of lesser interest because the only purpose of blocking is to allow us to produce a more reliable test concerning treatments. However, the existence of blocks has another implication. While the total variation in the data is again broken into explained variation and unexplained variation (or error), the explained variation now has two components: treatments variation and blocks variation. Thus, we calculate three types of variation in two-way ANOVA without interaction:

- variation among columns, which is explained by treatments
- variation among rows, which is explained by blocks
- variation due to (experimental or sampling) error

VARIATION AMONG COLUMNS: EXPLAINED BY TREATMENTS

We compute treatments variation precisely as we did in the previous section (as the ratio of the treatments sum of squares to associated degrees of freedom, which is the treatments mean square). The treatments sum of squares is the number of rows multiplied by the sum of the squared deviations of the column means from the grand mean. Thus,

$$TSS = r\Sigma(\overline{X}_j - \overline{\overline{X}})^2 = 5[(19.6 - 18.6)^2 + (17.8 - 18.6)^2 + (18.4 - 18.6)^2] = 8.4$$

Also as before, the applicable degrees of freedom equal $c - 1 = 2$. Thus, the treatments mean square is $TMS = (8.4/2) = 4.2$.

VARIATION AMONG ROWS: EXPLAINED BY BLOCKS

The variation among the $r = 5$ block means ($\overline{X}_A$, $\overline{X}_B$, $\overline{X}_C$, $\overline{X}_D$, and $\overline{X}_E$) that summarize the data associated with each of the blocks (ethnic groups in our example) is referred to as **blocks variation.** In perfect analogy to treatments variation, blocks variation is attributed to inherent differences among the blocks of experimental units rather than to chance. Blocks variation, too, is measured by a ratio, called the **blocks mean square *(BMS)*,** which equals the blocks sum of squares divided by associated degrees of freedom. We compute the **blocks sum of squares *(BSS)*** as the number of columns multiplied by the sum of the squared deviations of the *row* means from the grand mean. In our example,

$$\begin{aligned} BSS &= c\Sigma(\overline{X}_i - \overline{\overline{X}})^2 \\ &= 3[(14.33 - 18.6)^2 + (19 - 18.6)^2 + (23.33 - 18.6)^2 + (20 - 18.6)^2 + (16.33 - 18.6)^2] = 143.6 \end{aligned}$$

The applicable degrees of freedom are $r - 1 = 4$. Thus, the blocks mean square is $BMS = (143.6/4) = 35.9$.

VARIATION DUE TO ERROR

In the two-way ANOVA problem, we calculate the unexplained variation due to error as the difference between the total sum of squares on the one hand and the sum of the treatments sum of squares and the blocks sum of squares on the other hand. Thus,

$$ESS = Total\ SS - (TSS + BSS) = Total\ SS - TSS - BSS$$

Using our Table 15.5 data, we can derive the total sum of squares as

$$Total\ SS = (15 - 18.6)^2 + (19 - 18.6)^2 + \ldots + (17 - 18.6)^2 = 167.6$$

Thus, $ESS = 167.6 - 8.4 - 143.6 = 15.6$.

Similarly, the degrees of freedom applicable to the error sum of squares equal those of the total sum of squares minus those associated with the treatments and blocks sums of squares:

$$d.f._{ESS} = d.f._{Total\ SS} - d.f._{TSS} - d.f._{BSS}$$
$$d.f._{ESS} = [(rc) - 1] - (c - 1) - (r - 1) = (r - 1)(c - 1)$$

In our case, $(r - 1)(c - 1) = 4(2) = 8$. Hence, the error mean square is $EMS = (15.6/8) = 1.95$.

THE TWO-WAY ANOVA TABLE WITHOUT INTERACTION

Table 15.6 summarizes the results of this two-way ANOVA test without interaction. Compare it to Table 15.3. Note that the total sum of squares is unchanged (a logical necessity), while its breakdown is more detailed in the more powerful two-way ANOVA test.

TABLE 15.6 | A Two-Way ANOVA Table without Interaction

Source of Variation	Sum of Squares (1)	Degrees of Freedom (2)	Mean Square (3) = (1) ÷ (2)	Test Statistic (4)
Treatments	$TSS = 8.4$	$c - 1 = 2$	$TMS = \frac{8.4}{2} = 4.2$	$F_T = \frac{TMS}{EMS} = \frac{4.2}{1.95} = 2.15$
Blocks	$BSS = 143.6$	$r - 1 = 4$	$BMS = \frac{143.6}{4} = 35.9$	$F_B = \frac{BMS}{EMS} = \frac{35.9}{1.95} = 18.41$
Error	$ESS = 15.6$	$(r - 1)(c - 1) = 8$	$EMS = \frac{15.6}{8} = 1.95$	
Total	$Total\ SS = 167.6$	$rc - 1 = 14$		

EXAMPLE PROBLEM 15.2

Review the discussion of the toothpaste study from the beginning of Section 15.5 on page 665. At a significance level of $\alpha = .05$, reach a conclusion about the two null hypotheses:

H_0: The mean number of cavities for all possible users of toothpaste 1 is the same as that for all possible users of toothpaste 2 or 3; that is, $\mu_1 = \mu_2 = \mu_3$.

H_0: The mean number of cavities for all the members of ethnic group A is the same as that for all the members of ethnic group B, C, D, and E; that is, $\mu_A = \mu_B = \mu_C = \mu_D = \mu_E$.

SOLUTION: The critical values for $F_{.05}$ from Appendix Table N are $F_{.05\,(2,8)} = 4.46$ for treatments and $F_{.05\,(4,8)} = 3.84$ for blocks. The critical F value for treatments exceeds the computed value of $F_T = 2.15$. The critical F value for blocks falls short of the computed value of $F_B = 18.41$. Thus, we should *accept* the null hypothesis about treatments but *reject* the null hypothesis about blocks. The mean number of cavities is the same for the three toothpastes but differs among ethnic groups. The critical values are encircled in Figure 15.4; the computed values are designated by the red arrows.

FIGURE 15.4 | Toothpaste Study: Two-Way ANOVA

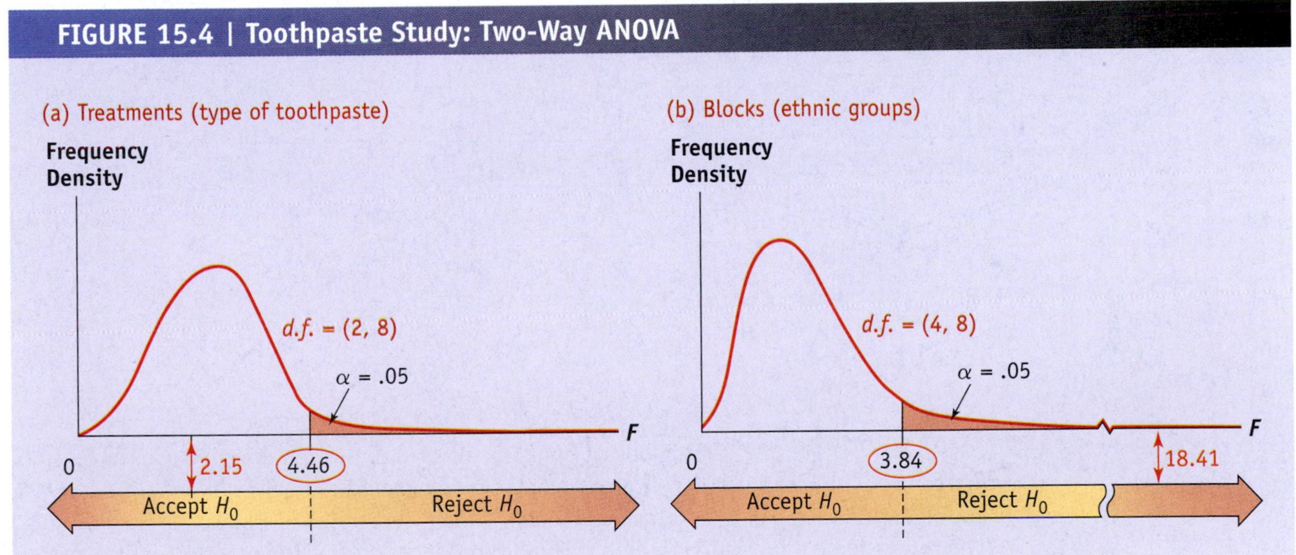

EXCEL Example 15.2

Perform a two-way analysis of variance with the data of Table 15.5 and, thus, confirm the results noted in Table 15.6 and illustrated in Figure 15.4. Once again, choose $\alpha = .05$.

SOLUTION:

1. Enter the data from the three treatment columns of Table 15.5, exclusive of column heads and totals, into columns A–C of a new worksheet.
2. Click **Tools** > **Data Analysis** > **Anova: Two-Factor Without Replication** > **OK**.
3. In the dialog box, under *Input Range,* enter **A1:C5**
4. Leave *Labels* blank.
5. Under *Alpha,* enter **.05**
6. Choose *New Worksheet Ply* and click **OK** to get the following output:

Anova: Two-Factor Without Replication

SUMMARY	Count	Sum	Average	Variance
Row 1	3	43	14.33333	4.333333
Row 2	3	57	19	0
Row 3	3	70	23.33333	2.333333
Row 4	3	60	20	4
Row 5	3	49	16.33333	1.333333
Column 1	5	98	19.6	15.8
Column 2	5	89	17.8	18.7
Column 3	5	92	18.4	5.3

ANOVA

Source of Variation	SS	df	MS	F	P-value	F crit
Rows	143.6	4	35.9	18.41026	0.000425	3.837854
Columns	8.4	2	4.2	2.153846	0.178506	4.458968
Error	15.6	8	1.95			
Total	167.6	14				

INTERPRETATION: EXCEL's output contains all of the information given in Table 15.6, but in a somewhat different order. It also includes p values and critical F values (of $F_{.05\ (4,8)} = 3.84$ for blocks and $F_{.05\ (2,8)} = 4.46$ for treatments), which were noted in Figure 15.4.

The rows source of variation (ethnic grouping) produces an F value of 18.41 and an associated p value of .000. We have a near 0 percent chance of getting this kind of F statistic if the null hypothesis about ethnic groups is true. Thus, these groups *do,* on average, have different numbers of cavities.

On the other hand, the columns source of variation (different toothpastes) produces an F value of 2.15 and an associated p value of .179. We have a 17.9 percent chance of getting this kind of F statistic if the null hypothesis about toothpaste types is true. Thus, we consider it to be true, which may be bad news for the toothpaste manufacturer: the apparently different numbers of cavities associated with different toothpastes may well be caused by dietary differences among ethnic groups.

15.6 Two-Way ANOVA: With Interaction

In this section, we will show that two factors can also interact with each other, and when that happens, their joint effect *does not* equal the sum of their separate individual effects. Such would be the case, for example, if the use of toothpaste 2 instead of 1 had a cavity-increasing effect when considered by itself, if eating lots of sweets had the same bad effect when considered by itself, but doing both together miraculously *reduced* cavities. As we shall see, this type of situation (unlikely to occur in the toothpaste-diet example, but not unusual in other circumstances) calls for a more complex type of analysis.

Consider the manager who wants to test whether 3 machines really produce the same average output. He suspects that the answer may depend on which of 4 crews operates the machines. There may even be interaction such that crew A is more productive than crew B with one machine, while crew A is less productive than crew B with another machine (rather than crew A being consistently better or worse than crew B, regardless of the type of machine). Such a situation calls for an experiment with the randomized block design. But to test interaction, we need at least two observations for each combination of treatments (machines) and blocks (crews). An appropriate experiment, in which precisely two observations are made for each of these combinations, may yield the results given in Table 15.7.

TABLE 15.7 | The Randomized Block Design with Interaction: Number of Units Produced during Six Monthly Experiments

Block, *i* (crews)	Treatment, *j* (type of machine) 1	2	3	Block Totals	Block Means
A	50 48 Total = 98 Mean, $\bar{X}_{A1} = 49$	42 46 Total = 88 Mean, $\bar{X}_{A2} = 44$	43 45 Total = 88 Mean, $\bar{X}_{A3} = 44$	274	$\bar{X}_A = \frac{274}{6} = 45.67$
B	56 58 Total = 114 Mean, $\bar{X}_{B1} = 57$	38 32 Total = 70 Mean, $\bar{X}_{B2} = 35$	40 38 Total = 78 Mean, $\bar{X}_{B3} = 39$	262	$\bar{X}_B = \frac{262}{6} = 43.67$
C	51 55 Total = 106 Mean, $\bar{X}_{C1} = 53$	39 33 Total = 72 Mean, $\bar{X}_{C2} = 36$	42 40 Total = 82 Mean, $\bar{X}_{C3} = 41$	260	$\bar{X}_C = \frac{260}{6} = 43.33$
D	40 38 Total = 78 Mean $\bar{X}_{D1} = 39$	47 51 Total = 98 Mean, $\bar{X}_{D2} = 49$	45 39 Total = 84 Mean, $\bar{X}_{D3} = 42$	260	$\bar{X}_D = \frac{260}{6} = 43.33$
Column Totals	396	328	332		
Column Means	$\bar{X}_1 = \frac{396}{8} = 49.5$	$\bar{X}_2 = \frac{328}{8} = 41$	$\bar{X}_3 = \frac{332}{8} = 41.5$		

Grand Mean

$$\bar{\bar{X}} = \frac{49.5 + 41 + 41.5}{3} = 44 \quad \text{or}$$

$$\bar{\bar{X}} = \frac{45.67 + 43.67 + 43.33 + 43.33}{4} = 44 \quad \text{or}$$

$$\bar{\bar{X}} = \frac{(49 + 44 + 44) + (57 + 35 + 39) + (53 + 36 + 41) + (39 + 49 + 42)}{12} = 44$$

This design allows us to test *three* null hypotheses simultaneously as shown:

MAJOR HYPOTHESIS TEST Testing this first hypothesis may help the manager decide which type of machine to buy in the future:

H_0: The average number of units produced is the same with each type of machine; that is, $\mu_1 = \mu_2 = \mu_3$.

H_A: At least one of these population means differs from the others. (At least one equality in H_0 doesn't hold.)

SECOND HYPOTHESIS TEST Testing this second hypothesis may help the manager decide on wages, promotions, or firings:

H_0: The average number of units produced is the same with each crew; that is, $\mu_A = \mu_B = \mu_C = \mu_D$.

H_A: At least one of these population means differs from the others. (At least one equality in H_0 doesn't hold.)

THIRD HYPOTHESIS TEST Testing this third hypothesis may help the manager decide on the best assignment of particular crews to various machines:

H_0: Machines and crews *do not* interact with respect to the average number produced.

H_A: There *is* interaction between machines and crews.

Once again, we break the total variation in the data down into explained and unexplained categories, but this time the explained variation has *three* components: treatments variation, blocks variation, and interaction variation. Thus, we calculate four types of variation in two-way ANOVA with interaction:

- variation among columns, which is explained by treatments
- variation among rows, which is explained by blocks
- variation that is explained by interaction
- variation due to (experimental or sampling) error

VARIATION AMONG COLUMNS: EXPLAINED BY TREATMENTS

We calculate treatments variation almost precisely as earlier in this chapter, the only difference being that we must multiply the above *TSS* formula by *k*, the number of observations per cell. Thus, the treatments sum of squares now equals *k* times the number of *rows* (or blocks) multiplied by the sum of the squared deviations of the *column* (or treatment) means from the grand mean:

$$TSS = k\, r\Sigma(\overline{X}_j - \overline{\overline{X}})^2 = 2(4)[(49.5 - 44)^2 + (41 - 44)^2 + (41.5 - 44)^2] = 364$$

The applicable degrees of freedom equal the number of treatments columns minus 1, as before: $c - 1 = 2$. Thus, the treatments mean square is $TMS = (364/2) = 182$.

VARIATION AMONG ROWS: EXPLAINED BY BLOCKS

We calculate blocks variation, too, in analogy to the way we calculated it above. The blocks sum of squares now equals *k* times the number of *columns* (or treatments) multiplied by the sum of the squared deviations of the *row* (or block) means from the grand mean. Thus,

$$BSS = k\,c\Sigma(\overline{X}_i - \overline{\overline{X}})^2$$
$$= 2(3)[(45.67 - 44)^2 + (43.67 - 44)^2 + (43.33 - 44)^2 + (43.33 - 44)^2] = 22.67$$

The applicable degrees of freedom equal the number of block rows minus 1, as before: $r - 1 = 3$. Thus, the blocks mean square is $BMS = (22.67/3) = 7.56$.

VARIATION EXPLAINED BY INTERACTION

Interaction is measured by the difference between two expressions, A and B, which we will define shortly. Interaction is said to be present whenever A and B are *not* equal to each other; it is said to be absent when they are equal. If we symbolize interaction by I, we can say that

- interaction is present whenever $I = \text{A} - \text{B} \neq 0$
- interaction is absent whenever $I = \text{A} - \text{B} = 0$

What are the expressions symbolized by A and B?

Expression A is the deviation of the mean observation for a given treatment/block combination (such as $\overline{X}_{A1} = 49$ in the first cell of Table 15.7) from the grand mean (such as $\overline{\overline{X}} = 44$).

Expression B, in turn, equals the *combined* deviations of the corresponding block mean from the grand mean (such as $\overline{X}_A - \overline{\overline{X}} = 45.67 - 44 = 1.67$) and the corresponding treatment mean from the grand mean (such as $\overline{X}_1 - \overline{\overline{X}} = 49.5 - 44 = 5.5$).

In short, we measure interaction as

$$I = (\overline{X}_{ij} - \overline{\overline{X}}) - [(\overline{X}_i - \overline{\overline{X}}) + (\overline{X}_j - \overline{\overline{X}})]$$

This expression can be simplified to

$$I = \overline{X}_{ij} - \overline{X}_i - \overline{X}_j + \overline{\overline{X}}$$

The **interactions sum of squares *(ISS)*** equals the number of observations per cell, k, times the sum of the squared interactions:

$$ISS = k\Sigma(\overline{X}_{ij} - \overline{X}_i - \overline{X}_j + \overline{\overline{X}})^2$$

In our example, we can figure the value of ISS as

$$\begin{aligned} ISS = 2[&(49 - 45.67 - 49.5 + 44)^2 + (44 - 45.67 - 41 + 44)^2 + (44 - 45.67 - 41.5 + 44)^2 \\ &+ (57 - 43.67 - 49.5 + 44)^2 + (35 - 43.67 - 41 + 44)^2 + (39 - 43.67 - 41.5 + 44)^2 \\ &+ (53 - 43.33 - 49.5 + 44)^2 + (36 - 43.33 - 41 + 44)^2 + (41 - 43.33 - 41.5 + 44)^2 \\ &+ (39 - 43.33 - 49.5 + 44)^2 + (49 - 43.33 - 41 + 44)^2 + (42 - 43.33 - 41.5 + 44)^2] \\ = 629.33& \end{aligned}$$

The applicable degrees of freedom equal $(c - 1)(r - 1)$, where c is the number of treatment columns and r is the number of block rows. Thus, $(c - 1)(r - 1) = 2(3) = 6$ and the associated **interactions mean square,** or ***IMS,*** is $(629.33/6) = 104.89$.

VARIATION DUE TO ERROR

In two-way ANOVA with interaction, we compute the unexplained variation once again as the ratio of error sum of squares to associated degrees of freedom. However, the value of *ESS* now is the difference between the total sum of squares on the one hand and the sum of the treatments sum of squares, the blocks sum of squares, and the interactions sum of squares on the other hand:

$$ESS = Total\ SS - (TSS + BSS + ISS) = Total\ SS - TSS - BSS - ISS$$

Using our Table 15.7 data, we can calculate the total sum of squares as

$$Total\ SS = (50 - 44)^2 + (48 - 44)^2 + \ldots + (39 - 44)^2 = 1{,}106$$

Thus, $ESS = 1{,}106 - 364 - 22.67 - 629.33 = 90$.

Similarly, the degrees of freedom applicable to the error sum of squares equal those of the total sum of squares [now equal to $(rck) - 1$] minus those associated with the treatments, blocks, and interactions sums of squares:

$$d.f._{ESS} = d.f._{Total\ SS} - d.f._{TSS} - d.f._{BSS} - d.f._{ISS}$$
$$d.f._{ESS} = [(rck) - 1] - (c - 1) - (r - 1) - [(c - 1)(r - 1)] = rc\,(k - 1)$$

In our case, $rc\,(k - 1) = 4(3)(2 - 1) = 12$. Hence, the error mean square is $EMS = (90/12) = 7.5$.

THE TWO-WAY ANOVA TABLE WITH INTERACTION

Table 15.8 summarizes our two-way ANOVA test with interaction.

TABLE 15.8 | A Two-Way ANOVA Table with Interaction

Source of Variation	Sum of Squares (1)	Degrees of Freedom (2)	Mean Square (3) = (1) ÷ (2)	Test Statistic (4)
Treatments	$TSS = 364$	$c - 1 = 2$	$TMS = \frac{364}{2} = 182$	$F_T = \frac{TMS}{EMS} = \frac{182}{7.5} = 24.27$
Blocks	$BSS = 22.67$	$r - 1 = 3$	$BMS = \frac{22.67}{3} = 7.56$	$F_B = \frac{BMS}{EMS} = \frac{7.56}{7.5} = 1.01$
Interactions	$ISS = 629.33$	$(c - 1)(r - 1) = 6$	$IMS = \frac{629.33}{6} = 104.89$	$F_I = \frac{IMS}{EMS} = \frac{104.89}{7.5} = 13.99$
Error	$ESS = 90$	$rc(k - 1) = 12$	$EMS = \frac{90}{12} = 7.5$	
Total	$Total\ SS = 1{,}106$	$(rck) - 1 = 23$		

EXAMPLE PROBLEM 15.3

Review the discussion concerning the effect of machines, crews, and machine/crew interaction on output from the beginning of Section 15.6 on page 670. At a significance level of $\alpha = .01$, reach a conclusion about the three null hypotheses:

H_0: The average number of units produced is the same with each type of machine; that is, $\mu_1 = \mu_2 = \mu_3$.

H_0: The average number of units produced is the same with each crew; that is, $\mu_A = \mu_B = \mu_C = \mu_D$.

H_0: Machines and crews do not interact with respect to the average number produced.

SOLUTION: The critical values for $F_{.01}$ from Appendix Table N are $F_{.01(2,12)} = 6.93$ for treatments, $F_{.01(3,12)} = 5.95$ for blocks, and $F_{.01(6,12)} = 4.82$ for interactions. Given the corresponding computed values of F_T, F_B, and F_I, in column 4 of Table 15.8, you should (1) reject H_0 with respect to treatments, (2) accept H_0 with respect to blocks, and (3) reject H_0 with respect to interactions. You should conclude that

a. the average number of units produced is *not* the same with each type of machine,

b. the average number of units produced *is* the same with each crew, and

c. there *is* interaction between machine types and crews.

Can you show that a test at the 5 percent level of significance would have reached the same conclusions?

EXCEL Example 15.3

Perform a two-way analysis of variance with the data of Table 15.7 and, thus, confirm the results noted in Table 15.8. Once again, choose $\alpha = .01$.

SOLUTION:

1. Enter relevant data from Table 15.7 into columns A–D of a new worksheet as follows:

A	B	C	D
	Machine 1	Machine 2	Machine 3
Crew A	50	42	43
Crew A	48	46	45
Crew B	56	38	40
Crew B	58	32	38
Crew C	51	39	42
Crew C	55	33	40
Crew D	40	47	45
Crew D	38	51	39

(*Caution:* Unlike in its other ANOVA programs, EXCEL's analysis of variance *with* interaction requires row and column labels or the program will not work properly.)

2. Click **Tools** > **Data Analysis** > **Anova: Two-Factor With Replication** > **OK**.
3. In the dialog box, under *Input Range,* enter **A1:D9**
4. Under *Rows per sample,* enter **2**

5. Under *Alpha,* enter **.01**
6. Choose *New Worksheet Ply* and click **OK** to get the following output:

Anova: Two-Factor With Replication

SUMMARY	Machine 1	Machine 2	Machine 3	Total
Crew A				
Count	2	2	2	6
Sum	98	88	88	274
Average	49	44	44	45.66667
Variance	2	8	2	9.066667
Crew B				
Count	2	2	2	6
Sum	114	70	78	262
Average	57	35	39	43.66667
Variance	2	18	2	114.2667
Crew C				
Count	2	2	2	6
Sum	106	72	82	260
Average	53	36	41	43.33333
Variance	8	18	2	66.66667
Crew D				
Count	2	2	2	6
Sum	78	98	84	260
Average	39	49	42	43.33333
Variance	2	8	18	26.66667
Total				
Count	8	8	8	
Sum	396	328	332	
Average	49.5	41	41.5	
Variance	53.14286	45.71429	7.142857	

ANOVA

Source of Variation	*SS*	*df*	*MS*	*F*	*P-value*	*F crit*
Sample	22.66667	3	7.555556	1.007407	0.423177	5.952529
Columns	364	2	182	24.26667	6.07E-05	6.926598
Interaction	629.3333	6	104.8889	13.98519	8.56E-05	4.820549
Within	90	12	7.5			
Total	1106	23				

INTERPRETATION

EXCEL's ANOVA table confirms the results of text Tables 15.7 and 15.8, although in a somewhat different order. The Sample source of variation (crew types) produces an F value of 1.01 and an associated p value of .423. We have a 42.3 percent chance of getting this kind of F statistic if the null hypothesis about crews is true. Thus, different crews *do,* on average, produce the same output.

On the other hand, the Columns source of variation (different machines) produces an F value of 24.27 and an associated p value of .000. We have a 0 percent chance of getting this kind of F statistic if the null hypothesis about machine types is true. Different machines produce different output quantities.

Finally, EXCEL discovers interaction between crews and machines. The F value of 13.99, along with a p value of .000, tells us that we have a 0 percent chance of getting this kind of F statistic if the null hypothesis about machine/crew interaction is true. So we conclude that it is false.

15.7 Three-Way ANOVA

We can illustrate the usefulness of three-way ANOVA by expanding our toothpaste study to include the possible effect of age on cavity formation. Thus, the three factors under consideration are the treatment variable (type of toothpaste used) and *two* blocking variables (the ethnic grouping *and* the age level of the experimental units). We imagine that a 10-year study of a mere 9 people has provided the data in Table 15.9 on the next page.

Note the clever way in which the two possible extraneous factors have been controlled: Each treatment (toothpaste 1, 2, and 3) has been applied precisely once under each category of each blocking variable. While these categories (ethnic groups A, B, and C and age levels Y, M, and O) are indicated in the row and column heads, respectively, the type of toothpaste applied to any of these combinations is indicated by the boldfaced numbers in the upper-left corners of the nine central table cells. (The upper leftmost cell indicates, for example, that a young member of ethnic group A used toothpaste 1 and had 20 cavities, while the lower rightmost cell shows that an old member of ethnic group C used toothpaste 2 and had 16 cavities.) Thus, toothpaste 1 has been used once by each ethnic group and once by each age level; the same is true of toothpastes 2 and 3.

The *Latin square* experimental design embodied in Table 15.9 was introduced in Chapter 5. Although it is typically used only to test the effectiveness of the treatment variable (here the effect of toothpaste type on cavity development), it can be used to test three sets of hypotheses simultaneously, as we will see presently.

TABLE 15.9 | The Latin Square Design: Number of Cavities Observed during 10-Year Period while Using Toothpastes 1, 2, or 3

Row Blocking Factor, i (ethnic group)	Column Blocking Factor, k (age level): Y = young	M = middle-aged	O = old	Row Totals	Sample Means for Rows
A	**1** 20	**2** 15	**3** 23	58	$\bar{X}_A = \frac{58}{3} = 19.33$
B	**2** 14	**3** 22	**1** 19	55	$\bar{X}_B = \frac{55}{3} = 18.33$
C	**3** 25	**1** 18	**2** 16	59	$\bar{X}_C = \frac{59}{3} = 19.67$
Column Totals	59	55	58		
Sample Means for Columns	$\bar{X}_Y = \frac{59}{3} = 19.67$	$\bar{X}_M = \frac{55}{3} = 18.33$	$\bar{X}_O \frac{58}{3} = 19.33$		
	Treatments, j: #1	**#2**	**#3**		
Treatment Totals	20 + 18 + 19 = 57	14 + 15 + 16 = 45	25 + 22 + 23 = 70		
Sample Means for Treatments	$\bar{X}_1 = \frac{57}{3} = 19$	$\bar{X}_2 = \frac{45}{3} = 15$	$\bar{X}_2 = \frac{70}{3} = 23.33$		

Grand Mean

$$\bar{\bar{X}} = \frac{19.33 + 18.33 + 19.67}{3} = 19.11 \quad \text{or}$$

$$\bar{\bar{X}} = \frac{19.67 + 18.33 + 19.33}{3} = 19.11 \quad \text{or}$$

$$\bar{\bar{X}} = \frac{19 + 15 + 23.33}{3} = 19.11$$

Major Hypothesis Test Concerning Treatments

H_0: The mean number of cavities for all users of toothpaste 1 is the same as that for all users of toothpaste 2 and 3; that is, $\mu_1 = \mu_2 = \mu_3$.

H_A: At least one of these population means differs from the others. (At least one equality in H_0 doesn't hold.)

Second Hypothesis Test Concerning the Column-Blocking Factor

H_0: The mean number of cavities for all three age groups is the same; that is, $\mu_Y = \mu_M = \mu_O$.

H_A: At least one of these population means differs from the others. (At least one equality in H_0 doesn't hold.)

Third Hypothesis Test Concerning the Row-Blocking Factor

H_0: The mean number of cavities for all three ethnic groups is the same; that is, $\mu_A = \mu_B = \mu_C$.

H_A: At least one of these population means differs from the others. (At least one equality in H_0 doesn't hold.)

We test these hypotheses once again by examining the variation in the sample data and breaking it down into an explained and unexplained portion. The former now has *three* components: treatments variation, column-blocks variation, and row-blocks variation.

Thus, we calculate four types of variation in three-way ANOVA:

- variation explained by treatments
- variation explained by column blocks
- variation explained by row blocks
- variation due to (experimental or sampling) error

VARIATION EXPLAINED BY TREATMENTS

To compute treatments variation we must once again establish the now-familiar ratio. Its numerator is the treatments sum of squares, computed as the number of rows (or columns—the two are equal in this design) multiplied by the sum of the squared deviations of the treatment sample means from the grand mean. Thus,

$$TSS = r\Sigma(\overline{X}_j - \overline{\overline{X}})^2 = 3[(19 - 19.11)^2 + (15 - 19.11)^2 + (23.33 - 19.11)^2] = 104.14$$

The applicable degrees of freedom provide the denominator; they equal $r - 1 = 2$. Thus, treatments variation is measured by the treatments mean square of $TMS = (104.14/2) = 52.07$.

VARIATION EXPLAINED BY COLUMN BLOCKS

We compute column-blocks variation as a similar ratio. Its numerator is the **column-blocks sum of squares *(CBSS)*,** which equals the number of rows (*or* columns) multiplied by the sum of the squared deviations of the column-block sample means from the grand mean. Thus,

$$CBSS = r\Sigma(\overline{X}_k - \overline{\overline{X}})^2 = 3\,[(19.67 - 19.11)^2 + (18.33 - 19.11)^2 + (19.33 - 19.11)^2] = 2.91$$

The applicable degrees of freedom provide the denominator; they equal $r - 1 = 2$. Thus, column-blocks variation is measured by the **column-blocks mean square *(CBMS)*** of $(2.91/2) = 1.46$.

VARIATION EXPLAINED BY ROW BLOCKS

We compute row-blocks variation analogously. The numerator of the ratio is the **row-blocks sum of squares *(RBSS)*,** which equals the number of columns (*or* rows) multiplied by the sum of the squared deviations of the row-block sample means from the grand mean. Thus,

$$RBSS = c\Sigma(\overline{X}_i - \overline{\overline{X}})^2 = 3\,[(19.33 - 19.11)^2 + (18.33 - 19.11)^2 + (19.67 - 19.11)^2] = 2.91$$

The applicable degrees of freedom provide the denominator; they equal $r - 1 = 2$. Thus, row-blocks variation is measured by the **row-blocks mean square *(RBMS)*** of $(2.91/2) = 1.46$.

VARIATION DUE TO ERROR

In the three-way ANOVA problem, we compute the unexplained variation due to error as the difference between the total sum of squares on the one hand and the sum of the treatments sum of squares, the column-blocks sum of squares, and the row-blocks sum of squares on the other hand:

$$ESS = Total\ SS - (TSS + CBSS + RBSS) = Total\ SS - TSS - CBSS - RBSS$$

In our example, we can compute the total sum of squares from Table 15.9 as

$$Total\ SS = (20 - 19.11)^2 + (15 - 19.11)^2 + \ldots + (16 - 19.11)^2 = 112.89$$

Thus, $ESS = 112.89 - 104.14 - 2.91 - 2.91 = 2.93$.

Similarly, the degrees of freedom applicable to the total sum of squares ($rc - 1$, or, in this type of test, $r^2 - 1$) minus those associated with the treatments, column-blocks, and row-blocks sums of squares equal those associated with the error sum of squares.

$$d.f._{ESS} = d.f._{Total\ SS} - d.f._{TSS} - d.f._{CBSS} - d.f._{RBSS}$$
$$d.f._{ESS} = (r^2 - 1) - (r - 1) - (r - 1) - (r - 1) = (r - 1)(r - 2)$$

In our case, $(r - 1)(r - 2) = 2$.

Thus, the unexplained variation is measured by the error mean square of $EMS = (2.93/2) = 1.47$.

THE THREE-WAY ANOVA TABLE

Table 15.10 summarizes our three-way ANOVA test.

TABLE 15.10 | Three-Way ANOVA Table

Source of Variation	Sum of Squares (1)	Degrees of Freedom (2)	Mean Square (3) = (1) ÷ (2)	Test Statistic (4)
Treatments	$TSS = 104.14$	$r - 1 = 2$	$TMS = \frac{104.14}{2} = 52.07$	$F_T = \frac{TMS}{EMS} = \frac{52.07}{1.47} = 35.42$
Column Blocks	$CBSS = 2.91$	$r - 1 = 2$	$CBMS = \frac{2.91}{2} = 1.46$	$F_{CB} = \frac{CBMS}{EMS} = \frac{1.46}{1.47} = .99$
Row Blocks	$RBSS = 2.91$	$r - 1 = 2$	$RBMS = \frac{2.91}{2} = 1.46$	$F_{RB} = \frac{RBMS}{EMS} = \frac{1.46}{1.47} = .99$
Error	$ESS = 2.93$	$(r - 1)(r - 2) = 2$	$EMS = \frac{2.93}{2} = 1.47$	
Total	$Total\ SS = 112.89$	$r^2 - 1 = 8$		

EXAMPLE PROBLEM 15.4

Review the discussion concerning the effect of toothpaste type, age, and ethnicity on cavity formation from the beginning of Section 15.7 on page 677. At a significance level of $\alpha = .05$, reach a conclusion about the three null hypotheses:

H_0: The mean number of cavities for all users of toothpaste 1 is the same as that for all users of toothpaste 2 and 3; that is, $\mu_1 = \mu_2 = \mu_3$.

H_0: The mean number of cavities for all three age groups is the same; that is, $\mu_Y = \mu_M = \mu_O$.

H_0: The mean number of cavities for all three ethnic groups is the same; that is, $\mu_A = \mu_B = \mu_C$.

SOLUTION: The critical Appendix Table N value for $F_{.05(2,2)}$—this F value applies in all three cases here—equals 19.00. Thus, we should reject the first of our null hypotheses (concerning treatments) but accept the other two. The type of toothpaste *does* make a difference in the number of cavities; ethnic group and age make no difference.

Note: The kind of test described here could be performed using two-way ANOVA; namely, by creating nine (row) blocks for each possible ethnic-group/age combination. Yet given 3 treatment columns, this type of ANOVA test would require a minimum of $9(3) = 27$ experimental units. The great advantage of the Latin-square design is that it reduces the required number of these units (and, thus, the cost of the experiment). The design, however, has disadvantages, too. To name just one, it can be used only when the number of categories of interest is precisely the same for treatments and both blocking variables. (In our example, there were *three* types of toothpaste, *three* ethnic groups, and *three* age levels.)

EXCEL Example 15.4

Perform a three-way analysis of variance with the data of Table 15.9 and, thus, confirm the results summarized in Table 15.10 and Example Problem 15.4. Use $\alpha = .05$.

SOLUTION: EXCEL is not equipped to perform a three-way analysis directly, but we can do so indirectly in two steps.

STEP 1 First, we can perform three separate one-way analyses after entering relevant data from Table 15.9 into a new worksheet as follows:

A	B	C	D	E	F	G	H	I
	Toothpastes			Age Groups			Ethnic Groups	
#1	#2	#3	Y	M	O	A	B	C
20	15	23	20	15	23	20	14	25
18	14	22	14	22	19	15	22	18
19	16	25	25	18	16	23	19	16

Toothpastes

1. Click **Tools > Data Analysis > Anova: Single Factor > OK**.
2. In the dialog box, under *Input Range,* enter **A3:C5**

3. Choose *Grouped By Columns* and leave *Labels in First Row* blank.
4. Under *Alpha,* enter **.05**
5. Choose *New Worksheet Ply* and click **OK** to get the following output:

SUMMARY

Groups	*Count*	*Sum*	*Average*	*Variance*
Column 1	3	57	19	1
Column 2	3	45	15	1
Column 3	3	70	23.33333	2.333333

ANOVA

Source of Variation	*SS*	*df*	*MS*	*F*	*P-value*	*F crit*
Between Groups	104.2222	2	52.11111	36.07692	0.000452	5.143249
Within Groups	8.666667	6	1.444444			
Total	112.8889	8				

The paste treatment F value of 36.08 is associated with a p value of 0, which indicates a 0 percent chance, when the null hypothesis is true, of deriving an F statistic as contradictory to H_0 as the value found here or even more contradictory to it than that. Thus, there is good reason to *reject* H_0 with respect to types of paste, given the chosen significance level of $\alpha = .05$.

Age Groups

1. Click **Tools** > **Data Analysis** > **Anova: Single Factor** > **OK.**
2. In the dialog box, under *Input Range,* enter **D3:F5**
3. Choose *Grouped By Columns* and leave *Labels in First Row* blank.
4. Under *Alpha,* enter **.05**
5. Choose *New Worksheet Ply* and click **OK** to get the following output:

SUMMARY

Groups	*Count*	*Sum*	*Average*	*Variance*
Column 1	3	59	19.66667	30.33333
Column 2	3	55	18.33333	12.33333
Column 3	3	58	19.33333	12.33333

ANOVA						
Source of Variation	*SS*	*df*	*MS*	*F*	*P-value*	*F crit*
Between Groups	2.888889	2	1.444444	0.078788	0.925176	5.143249
Within Groups	110	6	18.33333			
Total	112.8889	8				

The age variable F value of .08 is associated with a p value of .925, which indicates a 92.5 percent chance, when the null hypothesis is true, of deriving an F statistic as contradictory to H_0 as the value found here or even more contradictory to it than that.

Thus, there is good reason to *accept* H_0 with respect to age, given the chosen significance level of $\alpha = .05$.

Ethnic Groups

1. Click **Tools** > **Data Analysis** > **Anova: Single Factor** > **OK**.
2. In the dialog box, under *Input Range,* enter **G3:I5**
3. Choose *Grouped By Columns* and leave *Labels in First Row* blank.
4. Under *Alpha,* enter **.05**
5. Choose *New Worksheet Ply* and click **OK** to get the following output:

SUMMARY				
Groups	*Count*	*Sum*	*Average*	*Variance*
Column 1	3	58	19.33333	16.33333
Column 2	3	55	18.33333	16.33333
Column 3	3	59	19.66667	22.33333

ANOVA						
Source of Variation	*SS*	*df*	*MS*	*F*	*P-value*	*F crit*
Between Groups	2.888889	2	1.444444	0.078788	0.925176	5.143249
Within Groups	110	6	18.33333			
Total	112.8889	8				

The ethnic variable F value of .08 is associated with a p value of .925, which indicates a 92.5 percent chance, when the null hypothesis is true, of deriving an F statistic as contradictory to H_0 as the value found here or even more contradictory to it than that.Thus, there is good reason to *accept* H_0 with respect to ethnic groups, given the chosen significance level of $\alpha = .05$.

STEP 2 It is easy to convert the results achieved here to those of a genuine three-way analysis, which are found in Table 15.10. Note the entries here highlighted in red. Except for rounding, they correspond to eleven of the values found in that earlier table. More than that! The missing six values are implied by those we have. (Just compute the three values in the Error row; then find those in column 4.) The conclusions, stated in Example Problem 15.4 follow.

15.8 Discriminating among Different Population Means

Whenever the analysis of variance leads to the rejection of the null hypothesis of multiple equal population means, and, thus, suggests that there *are* significant differences among them, the analyst inevitably asks *which* of the means differs from which other mean. Consider the *one-way* ANOVA problem concerning the effectiveness of three different brands of toothpaste. It concluded that they differed, but we would surely want to know whether $\mu_1 = \mu_2$, while μ_3 is different, or whether $\mu_1 = \mu_3$, while μ_2 is different, or whether, perhaps, $\mu_2 = \mu_3$, while μ_1 is different. Yet, given sampling error, we would hesitate to make that determination solely on the basis of the known sample means. In this final section of the chapter, we discuss three different approaches to discriminating among three or more population means, some of which are known to be different from the others.

ESTABLISHING CONFIDENCE INTERVALS FOR INDIVIDUAL POPULATION MEANS

The first approach uses the technique, introduced in Chapter 12, of estimating an individual mean. As noted in Formula 12.F on page 513, we can estimate the limits of a confidence interval for a population mean from a small sample with the help of Student's t distribution:

$$\mu = \overline{X} \pm \left(t \frac{s}{\sqrt{n}}\right)$$

We can rewrite this expression by changing $\frac{s}{\sqrt{n}}$ to $\sqrt{\frac{s^2}{n}}$, wherein s^2 can serve as an estimate of the unknown population variance, σ^2. However, in the ANOVA situation, in which we take several samples from different populations that are assumed to have identical variances, we can obtain a better estimate of σ^2. We can do so by pooling the sample results and using the unexplained variance (or error mean square, *EMS*) in place of the single sample variance, s^2. If we let n equal sample size (the number of observations made about any treatment, j, and used to calculate any one sample mean), we derive the expression given in Formula 15.B.

FORMULA 15.B | Confidence Interval Limits for the Population Mean of Treatment *j*

$$\mu_j = \overline{X}_j \pm \left(t\sqrt{\frac{EMS}{n}}\right)$$

where μ_j is the population mean and $\overline{X}_j$ is the sample mean for the jth treatment, *EMS* is the error mean square, and n is sample size (equal to the number of observations made about treatment j), while t is the Student t distribution critical value (Appendix Table K) that is associated with the chosen confidence level and the degrees of freedom of *EMS*.

EXAMPLE PROBLEM 15.5

Review the sample means of Table 15.1 and the subsequent one-way ANOVA test summarized in Table 15.3. (See pages 656 and 660, respectively.) Compute 95 percent confidence intervals for the three population means.

SOLUTION: Given sample means of 18.4, 21.8, and 15.6, $n = 5$ observations per treatment, an $EMS = 5.93$, and $t_{.025(12)} = 2.179$, we can establish the following 95 percent confidence interval limits:

For $\boldsymbol{\mu_1}$

$$\mu_1 = 18.4 \pm \left(2.179\sqrt{\frac{5.93}{5}}\right) = 18.4 \pm 2.37$$

Therefore, the interval is $16.03 \leq \mu_1 \leq 20.77$.

For $\boldsymbol{\mu_2}$

$$\mu_2 = 21.8 \pm \left(2.179\sqrt{\frac{5.93}{5}}\right) = 21.8 \pm 2.37$$

Therefore, the interval is $19.43 \leq \mu_2 \leq 24.17$.

For $\boldsymbol{\mu_3}$

$$\mu_3 = 15.6 \pm \left(2.179\sqrt{\frac{5.93}{5}}\right) = 15.6 \pm 2.37$$

Therefore, the interval is $13.23 \leq \mu_3 \leq 17.97$.

This analysis suggests that μ_1 and μ_2 and also μ_1 and μ_3 may well be the same (their confidence intervals overlap), while μ_2 and μ_3 clearly differ (their confidence intervals do *not* overlap).

ESTABLISHING CONFIDENCE INTERVALS FOR THE DIFFERENCE BETWEEN TWO POPULATION MEANS

A second approach to discriminating among three or more means also uses Chapter 12 material but focuses not on one mean at a time, but on the difference between two means. For this purpose, we refer to Formula 12.G on page 515, according to which we can estimate the limits of a confidence interval for the difference between two population means from small and independent samples as

$$\mu_1 - \mu_2 \cong (\bar{X}_1 - \bar{X}_2) \pm \left(t\sqrt{\frac{s_1^2}{n_1} + \frac{s_2^2}{n_2}}\right)$$

The square root can be replaced by $\sqrt{2EMS/n}$ because the common population variance is estimated by the error mean square and because variability is additive for the two samples. The result is Formula 15.C.

FORMULA 15.C | Confidence Interval Limits for the Difference between Two Population Means

$$\mu_1 - \mu_2 \cong (\bar{X}_1 - \bar{X}_2) \pm \left(t\sqrt{\frac{2EMS}{n}}\right)$$

where the μ's are the population means, the $\bar{X}$'s are the sample means, *EMS* is the error mean square, and n is sample size, while t is the Student t distribution critical value (Appendix Table K) that is associated with the chosen confidence level and the degrees of freedom of *EMS*.

EXAMPLE PROBLEM 15.6

Review the sample means of Table 15.1 and the subsequent one-way ANOVA test summarized in Table 15.3. (See pages 656 and 660, respectively.) Compute 95 percent confidence intervals for the differences between any two of the three population means.

SOLUTION: Given sample means of 18.4, 21.8, and 15.6, $n = 5$ observations per treatment, an $EMS = 5.93$, and $t_{.025\,(12)} = 2.179$, we can establish the following 95 percent confidence interval limits:

For $\boldsymbol{\mu_1 - \mu_2}$

$$\mu_1 - \mu_2 \cong (18.4 - 21.8) \pm \left(2.179\sqrt{\frac{2(5.93)}{5}}\right) = -3.4 \pm 3.36$$

Therefore, the interval is $-6.76 \le (\mu_1 - \mu_2) \le -.04$. The fact that the interval does not overlap zero and lies entirely below it suggests that a null hypothesis H_0: $\mu_1 = \mu_2$ should be rejected at the 5 percent significance level and that toothpaste 1 produces *fewer* cavities than toothpaste 2.

For $\boldsymbol{\mu_1 - \mu_3}$

$$\mu_1 - \mu_3 \cong (18.4 - 15.6) \pm \left(2.179\sqrt{\frac{2(5.93)}{5}}\right) = 2.8 \pm 3.36$$

Therefore, the interval is $-.56 \le (\mu_1 - \mu_3) \le +6.16$. Because this interval does overlap zero, the null hypothesis H_0: $\mu_1 = \mu_3$ can be accepted at the 5 percent significance level. Given the fact that the difference between the two population means can be negative or positive, we conclude that the two toothpastes probably are associated with the same numbers of cavities.

For $\boldsymbol{\mu_2 - \mu_3}$

$$\mu_2 - \mu_3 \cong (21.8 - 15.6) \pm \left(2.179\sqrt{\frac{2(5.93)}{5}}\right) = 6.2 \pm 3.36$$

Therefore, the interval is $2.84 \le (\mu_2 - \mu_3) \le 9.56$. The fact that this interval does not overlap zero and lies entirely above it suggests that the null hypothesis H_0: $\mu_2 = \mu_3$ should be rejected at the 5 percent significance level and that toothpaste 2 produces *more* cavities than toothpaste 3.

The stated confidence level of 95 percent applies to each test individually, but not to the series of all three. We cannot state with a 95 percent degree of confidence that toothpaste 1 is better than toothpaste 2, which is worse than toothpaste 3, which is as good as toothpaste 1. The chance of making at least one erroneous rejection in the *series* of null hypotheses exceeds 5 percent (for reasons indicated in this chapter's Preview).

TUKEY'S *HSD* TEST

Yet another approach to discriminating among three or more means comes to us from John Tukey (1915–2000), one of the 20th century's great statisticians. (Incidentally, Tukey also enlivened our language by inventing the word *software* some three decades before the founding of Microsoft and by coining the term *bit* as an abbreviation of "binary digit" that describes the 1's and 0's that are the basis of our computer programs. A biography of Tukey appears on the text's Web site.) **Tukey's *HSD* test,** frequently employed as a follow-up to ANOVA, seeks out "honestly significant differences" between paired sample means.

Imagine that an analysis of variance has rejected equality among all the population means of interest, as in our one-way Example Problem 15.1 on page 662. Let us call k the number of such means to be compared (such as the $k = 3$ treatment means in our earlier example). Then the number of pair-wise comparisons equals

$$\frac{k(k-1)}{2}$$

which, as we have already noted, also equals 3 in our case. According to Tukey, *the difference between any two population means is statistically significant at level* α *if the absolute difference between the corresponding sample means equals or exceeds the honestly significant difference, HSD.*

The value of *HSD* is calculated according to Formula 15.D.

FORMULA 15.D | Tukey's Honestly Significant Difference, *HSD*

$$HSD = q_\alpha \sqrt{\frac{EMS}{n}}$$

where *EMS* is the error mean square, n is sample size, and q_α (found in Appendix Table O) is a number that varies with the number, k, of means to be compared, with the error degrees of freedom, and with the desired significance level, α.

Appendix Table O provides values of q_α for different values of k, various error degrees of freedom, and α levels of .05 and .01. Every ANOVA test itself provides the value of the error mean square, *EMS,* which also appears in the formula, while n equals the number of observations used to calculate the sample mean (which corresponds to r, the number of rows, in Table 15.1).

EXAMPLE PROBLEM 15.7

Apply Tukey's *HSD* test to Example Problem 15.1 on page 662. Evaluate the differences between each of the three population means at a significance level of $\alpha = .05$.

SOLUTION: Given $k = 3$ means, error degrees of freedom = 12, and $\alpha = .05$, Appendix Table O yields $q_{.05} = 3.77$. Given $r = 5$ observations per sample and $EMS = 5.93$,

$$HSD = q_{\alpha}\sqrt{\frac{EMS}{n}} = 3.77\sqrt{\frac{5.93}{5}} = 4.11$$

Now consider the (absolute) differences between our Table 15.1 sample means:

$$\bar{X}_1 - \bar{X}_2 = 18.4 - 21.8 = |3.4|$$
$$\bar{X}_1 - \bar{X}_3 = 18.4 - 15.6 = |2.8|$$
$$\bar{X}_2 - \bar{X}_3 = 21.8 - 15.6 = |6.2|$$

Only the last number equals or exceeds $HSD = 4.11$. The test, therefore, concludes that only population means μ_2 and μ_3 are different.

EXCEL Example 15.5

Review EXCEL Example 15.1 on page 664. Redo the work, while including Tukey's *HSD* test and thereby confirm the results of Example Problem 15.7.

SOLUTION: EXCEL does not directly conduct the *HSD* test, but we can do so indirectly.

1. EXCEL Example 15.1 provided the following output:

Anova: Single Factor

SUMMARY

Groups	*Count*	*Sum*	*Average*	*Variance*
Column 1	5	92	18.4	6.8
Column 2	5	109	21.8	5.7
Column 3	5	78	15.6	5.3

ANOVA

Source of Variation	*SS*	*df*	*MS*	*F*	*P-value*	*F crit*
Between Groups	96.4	2	48.2	8.123596	0.005878	3.88529
Within Groups	71.2	12	5.933333			
Total	167.6	14				

2. The three sample means and the error mean square are highlighted here; enter these values into column A of a new worksheet.
3. Enter the labels *Xbar1−Xbar2, Xbar1−Xbar3, Xbar2−Xbar3,* and *HSD* into cells B1–B4.
4. Enter relevant formulas into adjacent cells in column C:

   =**A1−A2** into C1

   =**A1−A3** into C2

   =**A2−A3** into C3

   =**3.77*SQRT(A4/5)** into C4. (Given $k = 3$ means, 12 error degrees of freedom found in the ANOVA table, and a significance level of $\alpha = .05$, we can find Tukey's value of $q = 3.77$ in Appendix Table O. We also know sample size as $n = 5$.)

   The result:

Xbar1−Xbar2	−3.4
Xbar1−Xbar3	2.8
Xbar2−Xbar3	6.2
HSD	4.10682

Comparing the *HSD* value with the *absolute* differences between the sample means, we note that only the third difference equals or exceeds *HSD*. Thus, only population means 2 and 3 are deemed to differ from one another.

Summary

1. The *analysis of variance,* frequently referred to by the acronym *ANOVA,* is a statistical technique specially designed to test whether the means of more than two quantitative populations are equal. Relevant data can be derived with the help of observational surveys or controlled experiments.
2. In order to perform ANOVA, an independent simple random sample is taken from each of several populations that are assumed to be normally distributed and to have identical variances. From the sample data, in turn, two independent estimates of σ^2, the assumed common variance of the populations of interest, are derived. A first estimate, s_A^2, is based on the variation *among* the sample means; it is an unbiased estimate of σ^2 only if the population means happen to be equal. A second estimate, s_W^2, is based on the variation of individual sample observations *within* each sample; this weighted average of individual sample variances is always an unbiased estimate of σ^2. Therefore, the ratio of s_A^2/s_W^2 is close to 1 if the population means are equal to each other; the more it diverges from 1, the greater is the probability that the population means are not equal to each other. Thus, an analysis of *variance* helps us test hypotheses about *means.*
3. Alternative versions of ANOVA reflect alternative experimental designs. *One-way ANOVA* is performed with data derived from experiments based on the randomized group design that controls extraneous factors by creating one treatment group for each treatment and assigning each experimental unit to one of these groups by a random process. This random assignment is believed to cause each treatment group to be equally affected by extraneous variables so that only one factor (the treatment) remains responsible for observed variations in the variable of interest. *Two-way ANOVA* is performed with data derived from experiments based on the randomized block design that controls extraneous factors by (1) dividing the available experimental units into distinctly different, but internally homogeneous blocks and (2) randomly matching each treatment with one or more units within any given block. Thus, two factors (treatments and blocks) are considered as possibly affecting the variable of interest. *Three-way ANOVA,* based on the Latin square experimental design, recognizes three factors—one deliberately introduced and two extraneous ones—as possible influences on the variable of interest.
4. The *ANOVA table* summarizes the analysis of variance and contains the ANOVA test statistic, *F*. Because *F* equals the ratio of s_A^2/s_W^2, the probability distribution of *F* (first developed by Ronald A. Fisher) helps us decide whether any given divergence of *F* from 1 is significant enough to warrant rejection of a null hypothesis of equal population means. The ANOVA table gets increasingly complex as one moves from one-way to two-way and three-way analy-

sis of variance. In addition, two-way ANOVA procedures differ depending on whether the two factors of interest are acting independently of one another or are interacting.

5. Whenever the analysis of variance leads to the rejection of the null hypothesis of equal population means, further analysis can be conducted to determine how these means differ. This further analysis can involve the establishment of confidence intervals for individual population means or for the difference between them. It can also involve the application of *Tukey's HSD test.*

Key Terms

analysis of variance (ANOVA)
ANOVA table
blocks mean square *(BMS)*
blocks sum of squares *(BSS)*
blocks variation
column-blocks mean square *(CBMS)*
column-blocks sum of squares *(CBSS)*
error
error mean square *(EMS)*
error sum of squares *(ESS)*
explained variance
explained variation
F distributions
F statistic
grand mean
homoscedasticity
interactions mean square *(IMS)*)
interactions sum of squares *(ISS)*
mean square
one-factor ANOVA
one-way ANOVA
residual variation
robustness
row-blocks mean square *(RBMS)*
row-blocks sum of squares *(RBSS)*
three-factor ANOVA
three-way ANOVA
total degrees of freedom
total sum of squares *(Total SS)*
treatments mean square *(TMS)*
treatments sum of squares *(TSS)*
treatments variation
Tukey's *HSD* test
two-factor ANOVA
two-way ANOVA
unexplained variance
unexplained variation

Practice Problems

NOTE

Some problems require the use of a statistical program, EXCEL or MINITAB. The program's major features are explained in text Chapter 2. Plenty of additional advice is available via the program's built-in Help feature.

Section 15.4 One-Way ANOVA

1. A manager wants to test, at the 2.5 percent level of significance, whether the mean delivery time of components supplied by five outside contractors is the same. Given the sample data of Table 15.11, perform the desired test by
   a. creating an ANOVA table and interpreting its *F* statistic.
   b. finding and interpreting the associated *p* value.

TABLE 15.11 | Delivery Times of 5 Contractors (days)

Sample Observation	Contractor				
	1	2	3	4	5
1	3	4	2	7	2
2	3	1	4	1	3
3	2	3	3	1	4
4	5	5	1	2	5
5	3	2	2	3	4

2. A government agency wants to test, at the 1 percent level of significance, whether the average cost of a given market basket of goods is the same in three cities. A random sample of 8 stores in each of the cities reveals the data given in Table 15.12. Perform the desired test by

   a. creating an ANOVA table and interpreting its *F* statistic.

   b. finding and interpreting the associated *p* value.

TABLE 15.12 | The Average Cost of a Given Market Basket

Store	Boston	Chicago	Los Angeles
1	$73.64	$67.05	$72.20
2	69.27	77.50	53.20
3	63.88	75.30	52.22
4	77.50	68.15	55.55
5	74.11	73.11	56.80
6	67.82	69.72	54.72
7	68.28	76.00	68.39
8	70.03	71.85	51.20

3. An economist wants to test, at the 2.5 percent level of significance, whether mean housing prices are the same regardless of which of 3 air-pollution levels typically prevails. A random sample of house purchases in 3 areas yields the price data given in Table 15.13. Perform the desired test by

   a. creating an ANOVA table and interpreting its *F* statistic.

   b. finding and interpreting the associated *p* value.

TABLE 15.13 | Mean Housing Prices (thousands of dollars)

	Air-Pollution Level		
Observation	Low	Moderate	High
1	240	122	80
2	136	118	110
3	80	220	146
4	190	150	90
5	166	160	128

4. An advertising manager wants to test, at the 5 percent level of significance, whether average sales are the same regardless of which of four available displays is used to advertise a product. Independent random samples of stores using displays A–D, respectively, show the following daily sales (in dollars):

A: 102, 113, 98, 123, 141, 152, 173, 129

B: 53, 66, 88, 79, 41, 52, 71, 50

C: 172, 189, 193, 205, 252, 98, 87, 79

D: 130, 131, 133, 141, 129, 118, 106, 100

Perform the desired test by

a. creating an ANOVA table and interpreting its *F* statistic.

b. finding and interpreting the associated *p* value.

c. identifying the assumptions you are you making.

5. An office manager wants to test, at the 2.5 percent level of significance, whether output per worker is the same regardless of which of three degrees of office crowding prevails. Independent random samples from three offices show the following data (in typed pages per day):

Office A (no crowding): 56, 63, 71, 46, 61, 66
Office B (some crowding): 32, 41, 43, 46, 38, 49
Office C (severe crowding): 28, 32, 30, 26, 25, 31

Perform the desired test by

a. creating an ANOVA table and interpreting its *F* statistic.

b. finding and interpreting the associated *p* value.

c. identifying the assumptions you are you making.

6. A corporate executive wants to test, at the 1 percent level of significance, whether the average total cost of producing lawnmowers is the same in four parts of the country. Independent random samples of seven plants in each of four regions show the following data (in dollars per mower):

Region A: 88, 92, 85, 80, 78, 81, 80
Region B: 92, 96, 98, 91, 88, 97, 106
Region C: 57, 88, 102, 99, 62, 49, 59
Region D: 76, 79, 80, 81, 88, 59, 93

Perform the desired test by

a. creating an ANOVA table and interpreting its *F* statistic.

b. finding and interpreting the associated *p* value.

c. identifying the assumptions you are you making.

7. A manufacturer of dog food wants to test, at the 1 percent level of significance, whether dogs, on average, like three new foods equally well. Each of the new foods is fed to six different dogs at their regular mealtime; their consumption is recorded as follows (in ounces):

Food A: 16, 18, 22, 10, 19, 23
Food B: 3, 6, 18, 29, 36, 48
Food C: 12, 22, 32, 28, 10, 6

Perform the desired test by

a. creating an ANOVA table and interpreting its *F* statistic.

b. finding and interpreting the associated *p* value.

c. identifying the assumptions you are you making.

8. An airline executive wants to test, at the 5 percent level of significance, whether airplanes, on average, get the same minutes of flight time with three different brands of gas. An appropriate experiment yields the following data (in minutes per 10 gallons):

A: 100 octane, low-lead: 50, 59, 51, 48, 43, 63
B: 130 octane, low-lead: 59, 63, 66, 71, 65, 73
C: 180 octane, no-lead: 63, 76, 81, 79, 80, 85

Perform the desired test by

a. creating an ANOVA table and interpreting its *F* statistic.
b. finding and interpreting the associated *p* value.
c. identifying the assumptions you are you making.

9. An economist wants to test, at the 5 percent level of significance, whether the debt-to-equity ratio is, on average, the same for firms in four industries. Independent random samples of six firms in each industry show the following results:

Industry A: .1, .2, .3, 0, .1, .2
Industry B: .3, .2, .4, .5, .3, .1
Industry C: .1, .2, .3, .1, 0, 0
Industry D: .9, .8, .1, 1.2, 1.3, .4

Perform the desired test by

a. creating an ANOVA table and interpreting its *F* statistic.
b. finding and interpreting the associated *p* value.
c. identifying the assumptions you are you making.

10. An analyst wants to test, at the 2.5 percent level of significance, whether the price per share, on average, differs among the New York Stock Exchange, the American Stock Exchange, and the over-the-counter market. Independent random samples of eight stocks from each market yield the following (in dollars per share):

A: NYSE: 45, 56, 82, 49, 53, 61, 48, 51
B: ASE: 17, 19, 27, 22, 31, 41, 15, 16
C: OTC: 30, 19, 82, 49, 31, 19, 16, 51

Perform the desired test by

a. creating an ANOVA table and interpreting its *F* statistic.
b. finding and interpreting the associated *p* value.
c. identifying the assumptions you are you making.

SECTION 15.5 TWO-WAY ANOVA: NO INTERACTION

11. An agricultural researcher wants to test, at the 2.5 percent level of significance, whether the mean yield of strawberry patches associated with 5 types of fertilizer and 3 types of soil is the same. No interaction is assumed. An experiment (using a randomized block design) reveals the data in Table 15.14. Perform the desired test by

a. creating an ANOVA table and interpreting its *F* statistics.

b. finding and interpreting the associated *p* values.

TABLE 15.14 | Strawberry Yields (pints per season per unit of land)

Soil Quality, *i*	Fertnilizer, *j*				
	1	2	3	4	5
A	15	13	8	17	9
B	10	12	15	15	11
C	14	9	6	14	12

12. A manager wants to test, at the 5 percent level of significance, whether the mean amount of delinquent debt repaid is the same for 4 types of collection methods and 3 categories of amount overdue. No interaction is assumed. Given the sample data of Table 15.15, perform the desired test by

a. creating an ANOVA table and interpreting its *F* statistics.

b. finding and interpreting the associated *p* values.

TABLE 15.15 | Dollars Paid per Overdue Account

	Collection Method, *j*			
Amount Overdue, *i*	Friendly Letter F	Nasty Letter N	Telephone Call T	Personal Visit P
A. Under $500	$10	$30	$10	$200
B. $500 to under $1,000	100	300	50	500
C. $1,000 and more	500	1,000	100	1,200

13. A manager wants to test, at the 2.5 percent level of significance, whether the average quality of a paint job is the same for 5 types of paint and 5 different surface types to which it is applied. No interaction is assumed. Given the sample data of Table 15.16, perform the desired test by

a. creating an ANOVA table and interpreting its *F* statistics.

b. finding and interpreting the associated *p* values.

14. The manager of a fast-food chain wants to test, at the 1 percent level of significance, whether average monthly sales are the same for 5 types of outlet and 6 months of the year. No interaction is assumed. Given the sample data of Table 15.17, perform the desired test by

a. creating an ANOVA table and interpreting its *F* statistics.

b. finding and interpreting the associated *p* values.

TABLE 15.16 | Assessment of Paint Jobs (quality scores)

Surface, i	Paint Type, j				
	1	2	3	4	5
A. Pine	80	86	89	93	100
B. Oak	90	94	95	97	100
C. Cedar	73	69	88	92	96
D. Plastic	60	73	72	79	86
E. Metal	100	85	73	84	61

TABLE 15.17 | Monthly Sales (thousands of dollars)

Month, i	Outlet, j				
	1	2	3	4	5
A. July	15.1	8.9	22.3	5.9	9.2
B. August	20.7	23.6	56.6	25.0	19.2
C. September	13.2	13.2	27.8	25.0	19.2
D. October	12.8	10.9	25.8	16.7	10.3
E. November	8.7	9.9	25.9	10.2	9.3
F. December	5.2	9.6	13.0	2.1	5.0

15. An engineer wants to test, at the 5 percent level of significance, whether the tensile strength of steel rods is, on average, the same for 4 production temperatures and 3 production pressures. No interaction is assumed. Given the sample data of Table 15.18, perform the desired test by

a. creating an ANOVA table and interpreting its F statistics.

b. finding and interpreting the associated p values.

TABLE 15.18 | Tensile Strength of Steel Rods (pounds per square inch)

Pressure during Production, i	Production Temperatures, j			
	Low 1	Medium 2	High 3	Extreme 4
A. Low	600	700	800	900
B. Medium	700	800	900	1,000
C. High	800	900	1,000	500

16. An economist wants to test, at the 1 percent level of significance, whether the price of advertising is, on average, the same for 4 geographic areas and 3 sizes of radio stations. No interaction is assumed. Given the sample data of Table 15.19 on the next page, perform the desired test by

a. creating an ANOVA table and interpreting its F statistics.

b. finding and interpreting the associated p values.

TABLE 15.19 | Price of Radio Ads (dollars per minute)

Size of Radio Station, i	Geographic Area, j			
	North	East	South	West
A. 1,000 watts	100	150	90	150
B. 5,000 watts	200	250	120	290
C. 10,000 watts	500	600	220	850

17. A mayor wants to test, at the 5 percent level of significance, whether property-tax assessments are, on average, the same for 4 assessors and 5 types of property. No interaction is assumed. Given the sample data of Table 15.20, perform the desired test by

a. creating an ANOVA table and interpreting its F statistics.

b. finding and interpreting the associated p values.

TABLE 15.20 | Property Tax Assessments (thousands of dollars)

Property Type, i	Assessor, j			
	1	2	3	4
A	20.5	19.8	21.0	22.5
B	30.7	39.8	43.0	29.9
C	89.0	92.0	87.0	73.5
D	100.7	110.8	120.0	105.6
E	23.2	37.9	120.0	67.3

18. The Environmental Protection Agency wants to test, at the 2.5 percent level of significance, whether, on average, sulfur dioxide levels in the air over Massachusetts are found to be the same by 3 alternative detection methods and 4 laboratories that analyze air samples. No interaction is assumed. Given the sample data of Table 15.21, perform the desired test by

a. creating an ANOVA table and interpreting its F statistics.

b. finding and interpreting the associated p values.

TABLE 15.21 | Sulfur Dioxide Reported in Massachusetts Air (ppm)

Laboratory, i	Detection Method, j		
	1	2	3
A	3.1	5.6	11.7
B	3.1	6.5	7.1
C	5.9	11.6	23.0
D	1.0	6.7	2.3

19. An economist wants to test, at the 2.5 percent level of significance, whether the amount of taxes figured by 3 tax preparers for 5 types of returns is, on average, the same. No interaction is assumed. Given the sample data of Table 15.22, perform the desired test by

a. creating an ANOVA table and interpreting its F statistics.

b. finding and interpreting the associated p values.

TABLE 15.22 | Taxes Due Figured by Tax Preparers

Type of Return, i	Preparer, j		
	1	2	3
A	$250.97	$147.31	$0
B	1,900.00	1,782.57	1,300.28
C	2,878.00	2,878.00	1,300.99
D	9,822.87	9,822.87	7,929.25
E	22,357.00	39,852.00	18,999.53

20. An economist wants to test, at the 5 percent level of significance, whether the mean annual income of workers in 4 occupations is the same regardless of whether their education levels are low, medium, or high. No interaction is assumed. Given the sample data of Table 15.23, perform the desired test by

a. creating an ANOVA table and interpreting its F statistics.

b. finding and interpreting the associated p values.

TABLE 15.23 | Workers' Annual Earnings (thousands of dollars)

Education Level, i	Occupation, j			
	A	B	C	D
Low	20	60	11	30
Medium	50	70	20	50
High	80	80	50	70

Section 15.6 Two-Way ANOVA: With Interaction

21. An economist wants to test, at the 1 percent level of significance, whether average annual price increases associated with 3 levels of industry concentration and 3 firm sizes are the same. Interaction between the two factors is suspected. Given the sample data of Table 15.24 on the next page, perform the desired test by

a. creating an ANOVA table and interpreting its F statistics.

b. finding and interpreting the associated p values.

TABLE 15.24 | Annual Price Increases (percent)

Size of Firm, i	Industry Concentration Level, j		
	Low (1)	Medium (2)	High (3)
Small	12	5	2
	10	6	5
	9	9	7
	9	7	4
Medium	8	6	5
	8	9	9
	9	11	7
	10	8	8
Large	3	8	12
	5	10	15
	6	12	20
	4	11	16

22. An engineer wants to test, at the 5 percent level of significance, whether the average tensile strength of plastic sheets is the same for 3 temperatures and 3 pressures applied during production. Interaction between the two factors is suspected. Given the sample data of Table 15.25, perform the desired test by

a. creating an ANOVA table and interpreting its F statistics.

b. finding and interpreting the associated p values.

TABLE 15.25 | Strength of Plastic Sheets (pounds per square inch)

Pressure, i	Temperature, j					
	(1) Low		(2) Medium		(3) High	
Low	18	23	18	23	27	39
	19	16	19	17	29	40
	21	20	21	22	35	39
Medium	27	39	39	42	18	15
	29	40	40	42	19	14
	35	42	41	42	20	17
High	35	48	18	12	9	6
	38	50	17	13	7	5
	42	56	14	10	8	4

23. An engineer wants to test, at the 2.5 percent level of significance, whether the average strength of plywood boards is the same for 3 types of glue and 4 types of wood. Interaction between the two factors is suspected. Given the sample data of Table 15.26, perform the desired test by

a. creating an ANOVA table and interpreting its *F* statistics.

b. finding and interpreting the associated *p* values.

TABLE 15.26 | Strength of Plywood (pounds per square inch)

Type of Wood, *i*	Type of Glue, *j*: 1		2		3	
Birch	30	33	40	43	50	56
	36	35	46	45	75	63
Fir	40	48	56	61	71	79
	45	47	63	70	82	87
Larch	41	49	69	79	22	29
	47	56	75	86	36	31
Pine	72	75	50	49	22	31
	80	86	51	47	36	27

24. The captain of a fishing fleet wants to test, at the 1 percent level of significance, whether the average weight of fish caught is the same for 5 species and 3 fishing areas. Interaction between the two factors is suspected. Given the sample data of Table 15.27, perform the desired test by

a. creating an ANOVA table and interpreting its *F* statistics.

b. finding and interpreting the associated *p* values.

TABLE 15.27 | Weight of Fish (pounds)

Fishing Area, *i*	Species, *j*: Cod		Flounder		Haddock		Perch		Whiting	
Casco Bay	.9	.3	2.6	2.9	8.9	9.3	5.4	4.0	5.4	6.6
	1.1	2.0	3.1	5.0	10.5	5.1	2.9	3.6	4.3	3.3
Georges Bank	2.0	2.3	6.9	5.1	10.5	11.2	1.7	1.9	3.3	6.9
	6.1	6.0	7.0	4.9	9.3	7.5	7.7	5.0	9.0	10.3
Long Island Sound	.9	.3	1.2	3.1	6.1	2.3	1.2	3.6	3.0	2.1
	1.1	1.2	3.7	6.1	1.7	1.9	2.1	7.0	2.6	.9

25. The manager of a new radio station wants to test, at the 5 percent level of significance, whether the average approval score for a station theme song is the same for 3 alternative songs and the 2 sexes. Interaction between the two factors is suspected. Given the sample data of Table 15.28, perform the desired test by

a. creating an ANOVA table and interpreting its F statistics.

b. finding and interpreting the associated p values.

TABLE 15.28 | Approval Scores

Sex of Listener, i	Theme Song, j								
	1			2			3		
Male	50	60	63	75	75	81	99	100	100
Female	99	100	100	75	75	81	50	50	0

26. A company psychologist wants to test, at the 2.5 percent level of significance, whether the average job satisfaction score is the same for 3 types of work and 4 types of employment experience. Interaction between the two factors is suspected. Given the sample data of Table 15.29, perform the desired test by

a. creating an ANOVA table and interpreting its F statistics.

b. finding and interpreting the associated p values.

TABLE 15.29 | Job Satisfaction Scores

Job Experience i	Nature of Work, j					
	No Structure		Some Structure		Highly Structured	
A. Less than 5 years	50	60	60	70	70	60
B. 5 to under 10 years	70	80	70	80	80	80
C. 10 years and more	89	92	92	88	100	92

27. An economist wants to test, at the 1 percent level of significance, whether the price of soap is the same for 3 brands and 5 supermarkets. Interaction between the two factors is suspected. Given the sample data of Table 15.30, perform the desired test by

a. creating an ANOVA table and interpreting its F statistics.

b. finding and interpreting the associated p values.

28. A personnel director wants to test, at the 5 percent level of significance, whether the average productivity score is the same for 3 types of work and the two sexes. Interaction between the two factors is suspected. Given the sample data of Table 15.31, perform the desired test by

a. creating an ANOVA table and interpreting its F statistics.

b. finding and interpreting the associated p values.

TABLE 15.30 | Soap Prices (dollars per pound)

Supermarket, i	Brand, j 1		2		3	
A	5.60	7.20	10.25	11.50	2.20	1.70
B	5.90	8.33	7.90	12.00	2.90	3.10
C	6.71	7.90	14.00	17.00	2.90	3.10
D	8.50	8.50	10.00	11.00	1.70	1.29
E	9.10	5.90	11.75	12.01	1.56	6.00

TABLE 15.31 | Productivity Scores

Employee Sex, i	Nature of Work, j Relaxed			Some Stress			Extreme Stress		
Male	88	92	61	66	76	85	66	76	88
Female	90	99	100	85	76	60	75	89	93

29. An economist wants to test, at the 2.5 percent level of significance, whether the average charge per minute of telephone conversation originating in Berlin, Germany, is the same for 3 telephone companies and 5 destination cities in the United States. Interaction between the two factors is suspected. Given the sample data of Table 15.32, perform the desired test by

a. creating an ANOVA table and interpreting its F statistics.

b. finding and interpreting the associated p values.

TABLE 15.32 | Telephone Charges (dollars per minute)

Cities Called, i	Phone Company, j AT&T		GTE		Sprint	
Atlanta	.29	.35	.15	.12	.10	.09
Dallas	.40	.32	.23	.23	.19	.21
Fresno	.40	.40	.53	.61	.59	.61
Lincoln	.18	.19	.60	.42	.33	.29
Roanoke	.18	.20	.33	.39	.46	.58

30. A farm manager wants to test, at the 1 percent level of significance, whether the average yield per acre of wheat is the same for 3 degrees of fertilization and 3 types of wheat. Interaction between the two factors is suspected. Given the sample data of Table 15.33 on the next page, perform the desired test by

a. creating an ANOVA table and interpreting its F statistics.

b. finding and interpreting the associated p values.

TABLE 15.33 | Wheat Yields (bushels per acre)

Type of Wheat, i	Fertilizer Amount, j								
	Low			Medium			High		
A	24	29	31	66	70	71	87	85	81
B	36	39	43	29	23	24	15	12	10
C	40	43	45	77	87	80	39	29	33

31. A shopper wants to test, at the 1 percent level of significance, whether the average price of electric dryers is the same in 4 department stores and for 3 brands. Interaction between the two factors is suspected. Given the sample data of Table 15.34, perform the desired test by

a. creating an ANOVA table and interpreting its F statistics.

b. finding and interpreting the associated p values.

TABLE 15.34 | Prices of Electric Dryers (dollars)

Brand, i	Department Store, j								
	1			2			3		
A	129	150	135	150	150	150	200	150	100
B	220	220	220	200	200	200	300	310	315
C	150	160	175	250	250	250	150	250	170

Section 15.7 Three-Way ANOVA

32. A farmer wishes to conduct an ANOVA test, at the 1 percent level of significance, concerning the hypothesis that 4 different pesticides (a–d) produce identical average yields per acre. The crop data of

TABLE 15.35 | Crop Yields (bushels per acre)

Type of Fertilizer Used	Precipitation Level			
	1	2	3	4
A	c 510	b 490	a 502	d 380
B	b 480	a 450	d 470	c 450
C	a 680	d 706	c 690	b 710
D	d 290	c 300	b 310	a 450

Table 15.35 are available to the farmer from an experiment based on the Latin-square design. Perform the desired test by

a. creating an ANOVA table and interpreting its F statistics.

b. finding and interpreting the associated p values.

33. An experiment about the effect of factors X, Y, and Z on a variable of interest was based on a 6 by 6 Latin-square design and yielded the following: *TSS* (factor X) = 853, *CBSS* (factor Y) = 159, *RBSS* (factor Z) = 702, total *SS* = 2,005. On this basis, a statistician was to construct an ANOVA table, compute F values for each factor, and test at $\alpha = .025$ whether the population means for the 6 levels of each of these factors were the same or different. Replicate the statistician's work.

Section 15.8 Discriminating among Different Population Means

34. Reconsider Practice Problem 2. Calculate a 99 percent confidence interval for each of the three population means.

35. Reconsider Practice Problem 4. Calculate a 95 percent confidence interval for each of the four population means.

36. Reconsider Practice Problem 6. Calculate a 99 percent confidence interval for each of the four population means.

37. Reconsider Practice Problem 15. Calculate a 95 percent confidence interval for each of the four treatment and three block population means.

38. Reconsider Practice Problem 12. Calculate a 99 percent confidence interval for each of the three treatment and three block population means.

39. Reconsider Practice Problem 21. Calculate a 99 percent confidence interval for the difference between each of the three pairs of treatment population means and between each of the three pairs of block population means.

40. Reconsider Practice Problem 22. Calculate a 95 percent confidence interval for the difference between each of the three pairs of treatment population means and between each of the three pairs of block population means.

41. Reconsider Practice Problem 24. Calculate a 99 percent confidence interval for the difference between each of the three pairs of block population means.

42. Reconsider Practice Problem 25. Calculate a 95 percent confidence interval for the difference between each of the three pairs of treatment population means and between the two block population means.

43. Reconsider Practice Problem 27. Calculate a 99 percent confidence interval for the difference between each of the three pairs of treatment population means.

44. Reconsider Practice Problem 28. Calculate a 95 percent confidence interval for the difference between each of the three pairs of treatment population means and between the two block population means.

45. Review Example Problem 15.3 on pages 674–675. Using Tukey's *HSD* test and $\alpha = .01$, discriminate among the reportedly different treatment means. Then make a decision about machine purchases.

46. Review Example Problem 15.3 on pages 674–675. Note that the F test rejected the null hypothesis of equal interactions means. Apply Tukey's *HSD* test at $\alpha = .01$ to discriminate among these means.

47. Reconsider Practice Problem 2, but this time employ Tukey's *HSD* test at $\alpha = .05$ to assess the difference between each of the three pairs of treatment population means.

48. Reconsider Practice Problem 8, but this time employ Tukey's *HSD* test at $\alpha = .05$ to assess the difference between each of the three pairs of treatment population means.

49. Reconsider Practice Problem 30, but this time employ Tukey's *HSD* test at $\alpha = .01$ to assess the difference between each of the three pairs of treatment population means and each of the three pairs of block population means.

50. Reconsider Practice Problem 31, but this time employ Tukey's *HSD* test at $\alpha = .01$ to assess the difference between each of the three pairs of treatment population means and each of the three pairs of block population means.

Chapter 16

SIMPLE REGRESSION AND CORRELATION

LOOKING AHEAD

After reading this chapter, you will be able to employ simple regression and correlation techniques to test whether and how the value of one variable, X, affects the value of another variable, Y. Among other things, you will learn to:

1. construct *scatter diagrams* that picture the relationship between two variables visually,
2. compute linear *least-squares regression equations* that summarize the relationship between two variables mathematically,
3. distinguish between estimated regression equations based on sample data and true regression equations based on census data,
4. perform regression diagnostics to determine whether you can use an estimated regression equation to make valid inferences about the underlying true regression,
5. estimate the average value of Y that is associated with any given value of X in the population of interest,
6. estimate the next value of Y likely to be encountered by sampling the population of interest, given any value of X,
7. develop confidence intervals and conduct hypothesis tests about the coefficients of true regression equations,
8. compute *correlation coefficients* and similar indexes that summarize the strength of association between X and Y in a single number, and
9. transform observed X or Y values so that you can use straight-line regression equations to describe curvilinear relationships.

AND HERE IS A TYPICAL PROBLEM YOU WILL BE ABLE TO SOLVE:

The following has been hypothesized about U.S. presidential elections: The percentage of the popular vote, Y, that goes to the candidate put up by the party of the incumbent president depends on the change in the unemployment rate during the election year, X, in such a way that any increase in unemployment detracts from, and any decrease in unemployment adds to, the vote for the incumbent-party candidate. Given relevant data since 1892, test the relationship between Y and X with the help of regression analysis.

PREVIEW

People with higher levels of schooling have always been financially rewarded in the labor market, but in recent years, this effect has become more pronounced than in earlier times. When Congress was debating the Higher Education Bill of 1992, advocates noted that the earnings of college-educated workers (adjusted for inflation) had risen during the 1980s not only absolutely, but also relative to workers with only high school or less education. Economists readily explained this fact: The demand for skilled workers had risen more than that for unskilled workers, and the supplies of such workers had not changed correspondingly. These trends continue to hold today.

The single most important factor on the demand side has been skill-biased technological change. Rapid workplace computerization provides one example. The introduction of, say, computerized office phone mail *reduces* the demand for unskilled receptionists who answer phones and stuff message boxes, while it *creates* demand for skilled computer specialists who can set up and maintain the system. On the production line, where computer-driven robots replace old-style assembly-line workers, similar substitutions occur. Fewer unskilled workers are needed; more skilled workers are required.

A second force with similar consequences has been the rapid expansion of international trade. Compared to the rest of the world, the United States has a relatively educated labor force. As a result, as the theory of comparative advantage predicts, goods made with skilled labor are relatively cheaper here, but goods made with unskilled labor are relatively cheaper abroad. As free trade opens up between, say, the United States and Mexico, the United States starts to export more goods made with skilled labor, and the demand for skilled labor rises here. On the other hand, the United States starts to import more goods made with unskilled labor, and the demand for unskilled labor in U.S. import-competing industries falls.

In the early 1990s, the Federal Reserve Bank of Cleveland analyzed Bureau of the Census data for employed Americans, aged 25 to 34. The data, which are summarized in Figure 16.1 on the next page, supported the arguments made in the congressional debate. Both in 1980 and in 1987, more years of education had been associated with higher real income. In addition, the real income of more educated workers (relative to less educated ones) had risen over time. For example, the *ratio* of the last 1980 column to the first 1980 column in our graph is 2.6, indicating that workers with 17 or more years of education in 1980 earned 2.6 times as much as workers with fewer than 8 years of education. Yet by 1987, the more educated workers earned 3.2 times as much as the less educated ones, as the corresponding ratio of the last 1987 column to the first 1987 column indicates.

On many occasions, however, we may wish to present masses of statistical data even more succinctly than in Figure 16.1. Sometimes data such as these can be summarized by an *equation* that allows us to predict the value of one variable, such as real income, R, by the value of another variable, such as years of education, E. This chapter's *regression analysis* produces equations such as these:

for 1980: $R = 30.86 + 1{,}239.79E$

for 1987: $R = -4{,}617.57 + 1{,}618.64E$

FIGURE 16.1 | Median Annual Real Income by Educational Level, U.S. Employed Workers, Aged 25–34

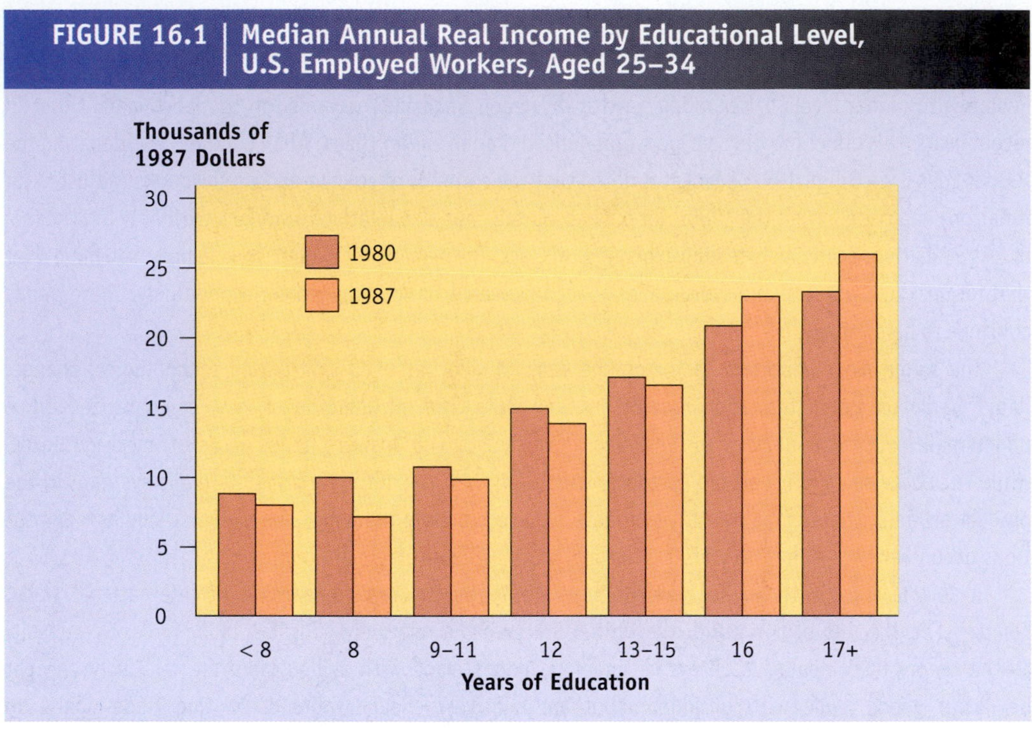

Using the 1980 equation, we can predict the real income associated with, say, 16 years of education as $R = 30.86 + 1{,}239.79(16) = 19{,}867.50$ dollars of 1987 purchasing power. Using the 1987 equation, we can similarly predict the real income associated with 16 years of education as $R = -4{,}617.57 + 1{,}618.64(16) = 21{,}280.67$ dollars of 1987 purchasing power.

On other occasions, we may wish to summarize data, such as those in Figure 16.1, by a *single number* that somehow measures the strength of association between two variables (such as real income and education here). This chapter's *correlation analysis* produces coefficients, r, that lie between 0 and 1 such as these:

for 1980: $r = .98$
for 1987: $r = .97$

In this example, a correlation coefficient of 0 would indicate that educational level and real income were totally unrelated. A coefficient of 1 would indicate that variations in real income were perfectly explained by educational attainment.[1]

[1]Adapted from Erica L. Groshen and Colin Drozdowski, "The Recent Rise in the Value of Education: Market Forces at Work," The Federal Reserve Bank of Cleveland, *Economic Commentary,* August 15, 1992.

16.1 Introduction

Business executives, economists, and practitioners of almost any other field of human endeavor are often interested in how the value of one variable relates to the value of another variable in some systematic way. Consider how:

- the quantity demanded (or supplied) varies with price
- output varies with input
- cost varies with output
- saving varies with income
- income varies with education
- interest rates vary with money supply
- investment varies with interest rates
- unemployment varies with inflation

Consider the link between the frequency of repairs and the age of equipment, between advertising expenditures and sales, R&D spending and corporate profits, corporate profits and stock prices, entry barriers and economic concentration, grade-point averages of graduates and their starting salaries, pre-employment test scores and subsequent job performance, assembly-line speeds and defective units produced, the unemployment rate at election time and the percentage of votes captured by an incumbent president. The list goes on, but one thing instantly becomes clear: An awareness of such linkages is highly useful to researchers and decision makers because it enables them to predict the value of one variable from that of the other variable. Regression and correlation analysis aids such an endeavor by establishing (1) what types of linkages between variables exist and (2) how strong these linkages are.

CAUTION

The techniques introduced in this chapter and the next are designed to determine the existence and strength of associations between variables, but they cannot prove anything about possible *cause-and-effect relationships.* If high R&D spending, for example, were shown to be related to high corporate profit, this relationship would not prove that high R&D spending was *causing* high corporate profit. In fact, the opposite might be true (high profit might give rise to high R&D spending) or neither variable might be causally related to the other, despite the association we see. Nevertheless, our awareness of such an association would be helpful in that it would allow us to estimate, say, an unknown R&D spending figure from a known value of corporate profit. The knowledge of such an association could also constitute a first step in a broader investigation of cause-and-effect relations. Indeed, the discovery of a systematic association between two variables frequently provides the initial impetus to further studies about causation.

16.2 The Origin of Simple Regression Analysis

Any statistical method that seeks to establish an *equation* that allows the unknown value of one variable to be estimated from the known value of one or more other variables is called **regression analysis.** This chapter focuses on simple regression, in which we use a *single* variable to predict the value of another variable and which, in this sense, is *simple* compared to the multiple-variables case taken up in the next chapter.

DEFINITION 16.1 A statistical technique that establishes an equation that allows the unknown value of one variable to be estimated from the known value of *one* other variable (rather than from known values of several other variables) is **simple regression analysis.**

The origin of simple regression analysis is closely linked with the British geneticist and statistician Francis Galton (1822–1911). Galton experimented with sweet peas to determine the law of inheritance of size. He selected 7 groups of different sizes, persuaded friends in different parts of England to plant 10 seeds from each group, and eventually compared the sizes of parental seeds with those of their offspring. When he plotted the results, as in Figure 16.2, he made an unexpected discovery. Instead of each offspring being just like its parent, which would put his pair-wise data plots precisely on the 45° line in our graph, dwarf peas produced larger offspring, while giant peas produced smaller offspring. Note how the actual data plots diverge from the 45° line. Galton called this phenomenon "reversion" toward some average ancestral type; later he called it "regression toward mediocrity." Thus, Galton argued, for purposes of predicting the transmission of natural characteristics from one generation to the next,

FIGURE 16.2 | Galton's Experiment

In 1875, when Francis Galton experimented with sweet peas, he expected the sizes of parent seeds to predict perfectly the sizes of their offspring. If true, this would produce data plots on this graph's 45° line. To Galton's surprise, the actual data plots diverged considerably from the 45° line and were summarized more accurately by the red regression line shown here.

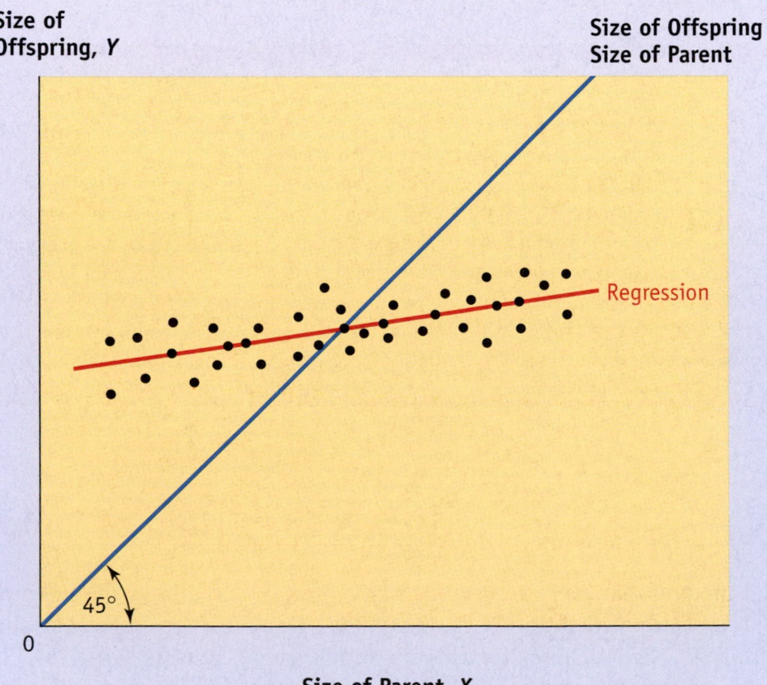

the 45° line in Figure 16.2 was inferior to another line going through the scatter of dots, which he called the *regression* line. Nowadays, this tendency of population members who are in an extreme position with respect to some characteristic at one time (below or above the population mean) to be in a less extreme position at a later time (either personally or via their offspring) is called the **regression effect.** It applies widely and not only to the sizes of sweet peas from one generation to the next.

Thus, as Galton also discovered, on average, extremely short fathers tend to have somewhat taller sons; extremely tall fathers tend to have somewhat shorter sons. The subset of all students with extremely poor grades on exam 1 tends to have better grades (closer to the average of all students) on exam 2, while the subset of all students with extremely good grades on exam 1 tends to have worse grades (again closer to the average of all students) on exam 2. And firms with the worst profit picture in year 1, on average, are not among the worst in year 2, while those with the highest profit in year 1, on average, are not in the top group in year 2.

CAUTION

It is one thing merely to observe the regression effect; it is quite another to succumb to the **regression fallacy** and incorrectly attribute the regression effect, as Galton did, to the operation of some important unseen factor, such as his "tendency toward mediocrity." The real explanation for Galton's observed phenomenon is that extreme values—whether of size, grades, or profit—often occur by pure chance; the odds are that such extremes do not occur twice in a row.

16.3 Basic Concepts of Regression Analysis

Crucial concepts employed in both simple and multivariable regression analysis include (1) independent and dependent variables, (2) deterministic and stochastic relationships, and (3) direct and inverse relationships.

INDEPENDENT VERSUS DEPENDENT VARIABLES

In simple regression analysis, we assume that we know the value of one variable. Such was the case with years of education in this chapter's Preview or with the size of parent seeds in Galton's experiment. This known value is used to predict the value of the other variable, such as real income or the size of offspring seeds.

DEFINITION 16.2 In (all types of) regression analysis, a variable whose value is known (and is being used to explain or predict the value of another variable) is referred to as an **independent variable.** It is symbolized by X. Alternative names for *independent variable* are **explanatory variable, predictor variable,** and **regressor.**

Having named one of the two variables encountered in simple regression analysis, the definition of the second variable follows easily:

DEFINITION 16.3 In (all types of) regression analysis, the variable whose value is unknown (and is being explained or predicted with the help of another variable) is called the **dependent variable.** It is symbolized by Y. Alternative names for *dependent variable* are **explained variable, predicted variable, regressand,** and **response variable.**

DETERMINISTIC VERSUS STOCHASTIC RELATIONSHIPS

The relationship between any two variables, Y and X, can be one of two types. It can be precise, exact, or *deterministic* in the sense that the value of Y is uniquely determined by that of X. This type of relationship abounds in the physical sciences. In contrast, the relationship can also be imprecise, inexact, or *stochastic* in the sense that many possible values of Y can be associated with any one value of X. This type of situation is common in the social sciences. Let us consider each of these relationships in turn.

DEFINITION 16.4 A **deterministic relationship** between any two variables, Y and X, is characterized by the fact that the value of Y is uniquely determined whenever the value of X is specified. Only one Y exists for each X.

Panel (a) of Figure 16.3 illustrates a deterministic relationship that is described by the equation $Y = a + bX$. In this particular example, Y equals degrees Fahrenheit and X equals degrees Celsius, while a and b are constants that represent, respectively, the vertical intercept and the slope of the straight line. Note that for any given value of X only one possible value of Y exists. Thus, 0° Celsius corresponds to 32° Fahrenheit, 50°C corresponds to 122°F, and 100°C corre-

FIGURE 16.3 | Deterministic versus Stochastic Relationship

In a ***deterministic relationship,*** *shown in panel (a), the value of Y is uniquely determined whenever the value of X is specified. The equation of the straight line, $Y = 32 + 1.8X$, predicts Y precisely for any given X. In a* ***stochastic relationship,*** *shown in panel (b), many possible values of Y can be associated with any one value of X. The equation of the straight line, $\hat{Y}_X = 100 + .05X$, therefore, predicts Y only roughly for any given X. This line in panel (b) is a* ***regression line.***

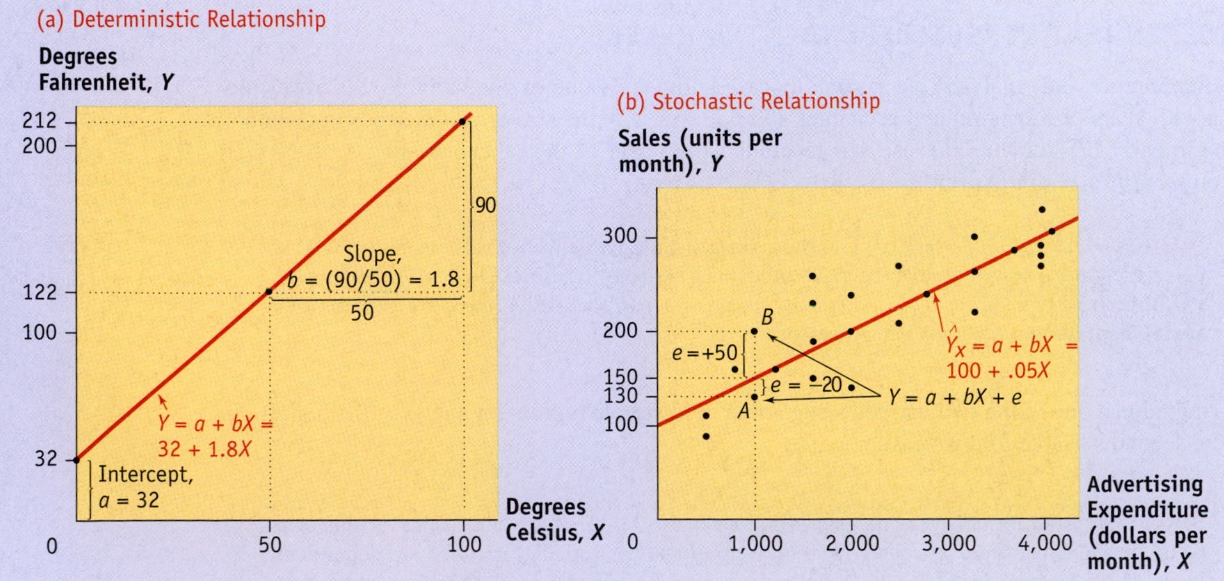

sponds to 212°F. Just like the three black dots shown in the graph, every other conceivable pair of Y and X values lies precisely on the straight line that represents the equation $Y = 32 + 1.8X$.

DEFINITION 16.5 A **stochastic relationship** between any two variables, Y and X, is imprecise in the sense that many possible values of Y can be associated with any one value of X. However, a **regression line** can provide a graphical summary of such a stochastic relationship. Ideally, such a line minimizes the errors made when its equation is used to estimate Y from X.

Panel (b) of Figure 16.3 illustrates a stochastic relationship that is described by the equation $\hat{Y}_X = a + bX$. In this particular example, $\hat{Y}_X$ (pronounced "Y hat sub X") equals the value of Y (sales) that we can predict from a knowledge of X (advertising expenditures), while a and b represent, respectively, the vertical intercept and the slope of the straight line. This time, however, we can observe several values of Y for any given X. Points A and B, for example, represent those two pairs of observations, among the 25 pairs plotted in the graph, that involve advertising expenditures of $X = \$1{,}000$ per month. Yet sales were not the same in these two instances: Sales equaled 130 units in one case (point A) and 200 units in the other (point B). Thus, anyone who would use the equation of the straight line in panel (b) to estimate the volume of sales associated with \$1,000 of advertising expenditures would get an imprecise answer of $\hat{Y}_X = 100 + .05(1{,}000) = 150$, which equals the height of the straight line at $X = 1{,}000$. Neither one of the actual observations of Y at $X = 1{,}000$, however, equals $\hat{Y}_X$. Instead, we can express both actual values of Y as

$$Y = \hat{Y}_X + e = a + bX + e$$

where e is an error term that can take on negative, zero, or positive values. This error term reflects the net effect on Y of numerous other variables besides X that are excluded from the analysis. Observation A, for example, might refer to the experience of one firm, while observation B refers to that of another firm that finds itself in different circumstances even though it also spends \$1,000 on advertising. For observation A, the value of $e = -20$; for observation B, $e = +50$. As we will show below, regression analysis seeks to establish a line such as the red *regression line* in panel (b), which somehow summarizes the stochastic relationship between X and Y in a trustworthy way.

DIRECT VERSUS INVERSE RELATIONSHIPS

We can classify the relationship between any two variables, Y and X, in still another way. If the values of the dependent variable, Y, increase with larger values of the independent variable, X, the variables are said to have a **direct relationship**—in which case, b, the slope of the regression line, is *positive*. If instead the values of the dependent variable, Y, decrease with larger values of the independent variable, X, the variables are said to have an **inverse relationship**—in which case the value of b is *negative*. Panels (a) and (b) of Figure 16.4 on the next page graphically illustrate the difference between direct and inverse relationships.

The straight lines of panels (a) and (b) might summarize, respectively, observations about the familiar macroeconomic consumption function or the equally familiar microeconomic demand line. Yet relationships between our two variables need not necessarily be *linear*.

As the remaining panels of Figure 16.4 indicate, the association between two variables is often better described as *curvilinear*. Yet, because it is easier to explain, and also because this simpler analysis can be extended to the curvilinear case (as this chapter's last section will show), the bulk of this chapter will focus on the analysis of linear relationships.

FIGURE 16.4 | Alternative Relationships between Y and X

Each dot in these graphs represents a hypothetical pair of observations about a dependent variable, Y, and an independent variable, X. The red lines summarize the nature of their relationship. It can be linear, as in panels (a) and (b), or curvilinear, as in panels (c) through (h). In addition, the relationship can be direct, as in panels (a), (e), and (g); it can be inverse, as in panels (b) and (f); or it can be a combination of both, as in panels (c), (d), and (h). Naturally, the values of the constants, such as a, b, and c, differ from one equation to the next.

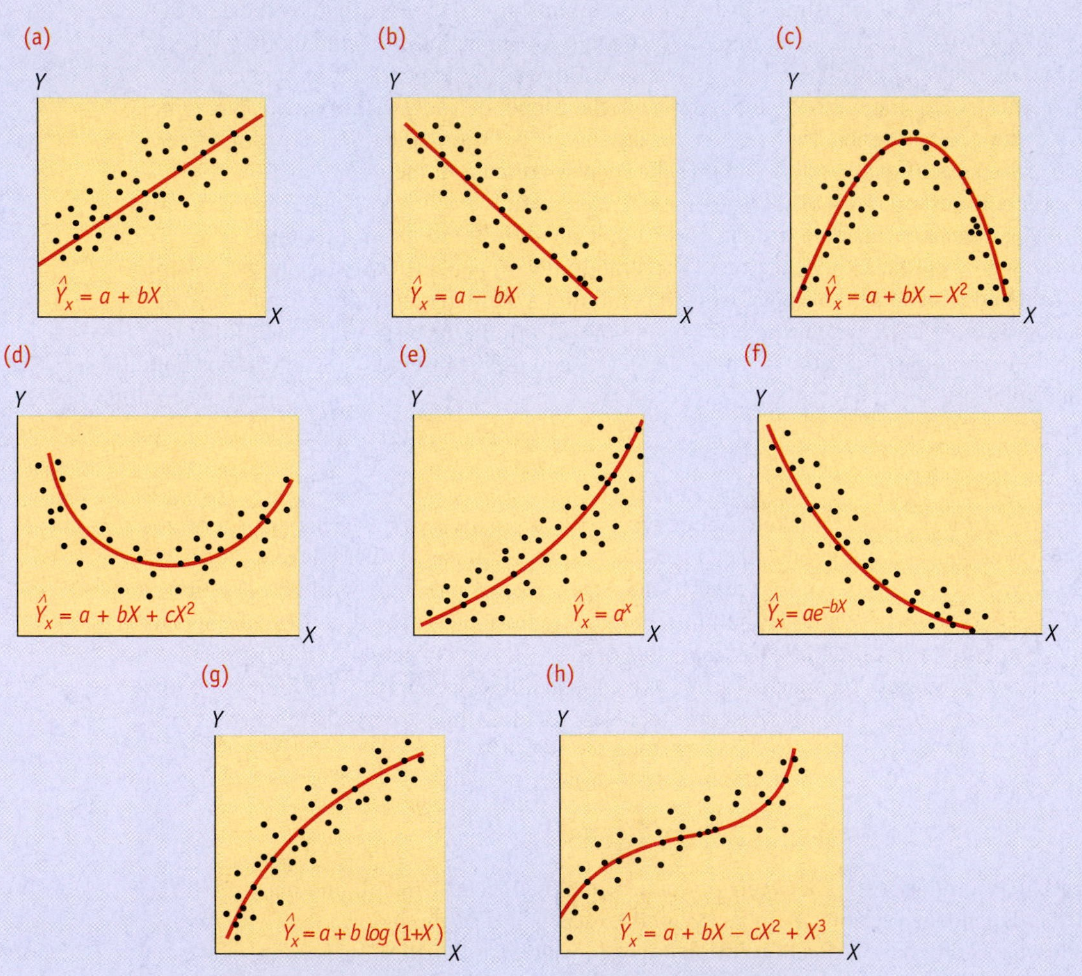

16.4 The Scatter Diagram

Regression analysis is hard to grasp in the abstract. The technique is more easily understood with the help of examples. Our first example introduces the scatter diagram.

DEFINTION 16.6 A **scatter diagram** is a graphical display used in regression analysis. It consists of a scatter of dots such that each dot represents one value of the independent variable (measured along the horizontal axis) and an associated value of the dependent variable (measured along the vertical axis).

EXAMPLE PROBLEM 16.1

Suppose we wanted to investigate a possible association between the annual incomes earned by the residents of a country and the extent of their formal education. Because it would be too cumbersome to gather relevant data for every adult member of society through a census, we might take a simple random sample. To minimize our burden of calculation, we assume that only 20 individuals are included in the sample. The result is Table 16.1.

a. In order to make a preliminary judgment about the type of regression line that might appropriately summarize the tabular data—and the panels of Figure 16.4 indicate just some of the many possibilities—plot the sample data as a scatter diagram.

b. Interpret the result.

SOLUTION:

a. The data pairs of Table 16.1 appear as the 20 fat dots of Figure 16.5 on the next page. Note how the information provided by individual R (an annual income of $22,050 and 16 years of education) has been highlighted in the graph.

TABLE 16.1 | Sample Data on Income and Education

Individual	Income ($ per year), *Y*	Education (years), *X*
A	5,012	2
B	9,680	4
C	28,432	8
D	8,774	8
E	21,008	8
F	26,565	10
G	25,428	12
H	23,113	12
I	22,500	12
J	19,456	12
K	21,690	12
L	24,750	13
M	30,100	14
N	24,798	14
O	28,532	15
P	26,000	15
Q	38,908	16
R	22,050	16
S	33,060	17
T	48,276	21

FIGURE 16.5 | The Scatter Diagram

The 20 fat dots found in this scatter diagram represent the data pairs of Table 16.1 and help us visualize the relationship of interest to us. The diagram suggests the existence of a ***direct relationship*** *between Y and X; that is, higher income seems to be associated with more education. This fact may well be summarized best by a positively sloping straight line (not shown).*

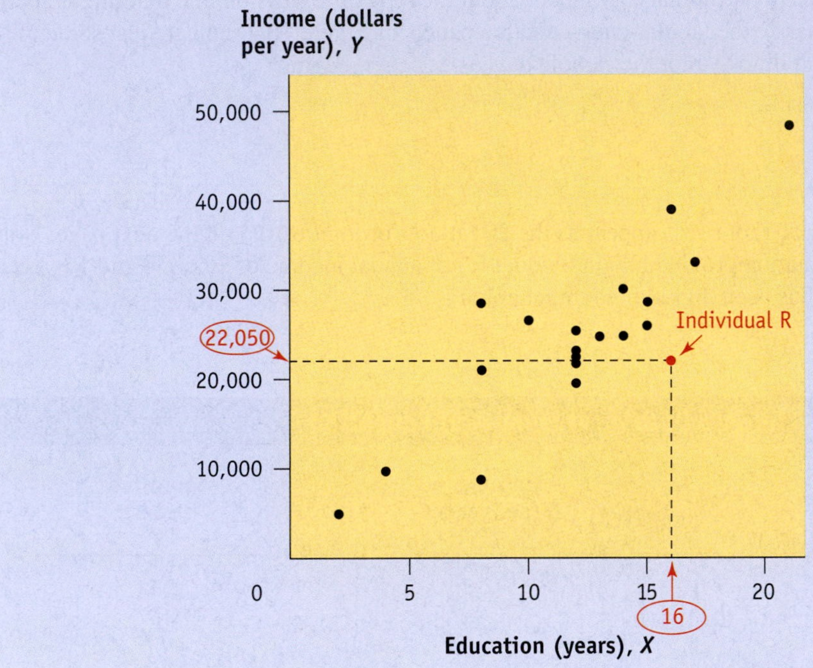

b. The scatter of dots provides an important clue: A *direct* relationship between income (Y) and education (X) seems to exist; this association may well be summarized best by a positively sloping straight line of the type found in panel (a) of Figure 16.4. Therefore, we can reasonably pursue linear regression analysis.

EXCEL Example 16.1

Rework Example Problem 16.1 with the help of a computer.

SOLUTION:

1. Enter the Table 16.1 education and income data, inclusive of column heads, into worksheet columns A and B, respectively. (You can copy and paste the data from columns L and M of the file HKMISC, but note that you must enter the X variable into the first column and the Y variable into the second.)
2. Click the **Chart Wizard**.
3. In the first dialog box, click **Standard Types** > **XY(Scatter)** > **Next**.

4. In the second dialog box, under *Data Range,* enter **A2:B21**, choose *Series in Columns,* and click **Next**.
5. Edit the graph in the fashion explained in EXCEL Example 2.10 on pages 59–62 to get a result such as this:

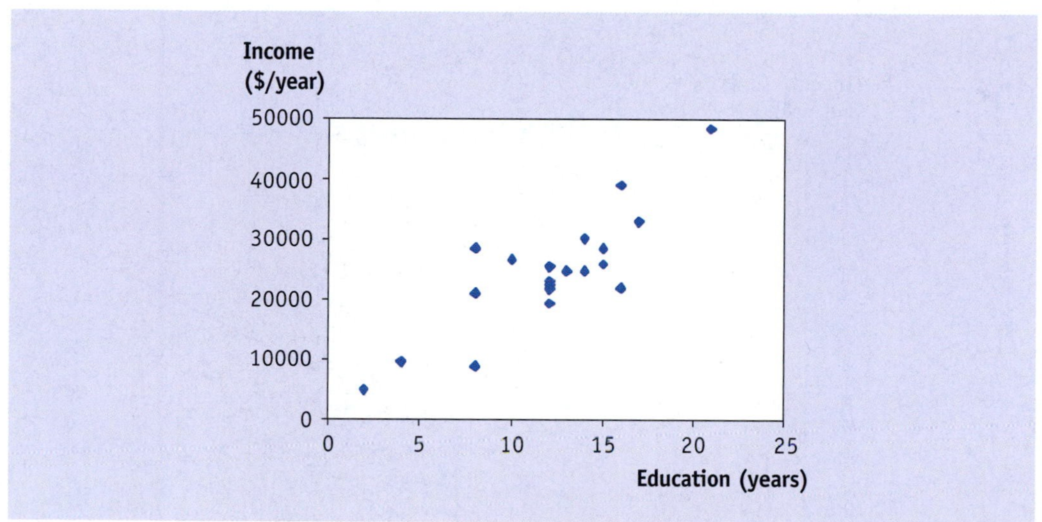

16.5 Drawing a Regression Line: The Eyeball Approach

One conceivable approach to drawing a regression line, with the help of which we might then predict the value of Y for any given value of X, is simple, indeed. The approach is often encountered in the popular press, which is why we take a look at it here. It involves nothing more complicated than using one's eyesight, a ruler, and a pen to draw a line in the scatter diagram that seems to "fit" the scattered dots. The procedure has been applied in Figure 16.6 on the next page, and, having drawn the line, we can proceed to determine its equation by carefully examining the graph. In this case, the vertical intercept of the line is seen to equal $a = \$10{,}000$, while its slope can be determined by placing a triangle underneath the line and calculating the ratio of its vertical side to its horizontal side, which comes to $b = \$1{,}333.33$ in this case.

This regression line, therefore, suggests that we can estimate a person's annual income as \$10,000 plus an additional \$1,333.33 for each year of education. Note that this estimate only holds on average, not for any particular individual. Thus, the income of individual R, which we know to be \$22,050, would be *overestimated* from a knowledge of this person's 16-year education and this regression line as

$$\hat{Y}_{16} = 10{,}000 + 1{,}333.33(16) = 31{,}333.33$$

Similarly, the income of individual T, which Table 16.1 shows to be \$48,276, would be *underestimated* from a knowledge of this person's 21-year education as

$$\hat{Y}_{21} = 10{,}000 + 1{,}333.33(21) = 38{,}000$$

Given the nature of the task—our desire to summarize a set of scattered dots by a straight line—such overestimation or underestimation is inevitable. Yet another problem that arises with

FIGURE 16.6 | A Regression Line Drawn by Sight

The regression line shown here has been drawn by sight with a view toward making it somehow "fit" the scatter of dots we first saw in Figure 16.5. Given this line, we would estimate a person's annual income as \$10,000 plus an additional \$1,333.33 for each year of education.

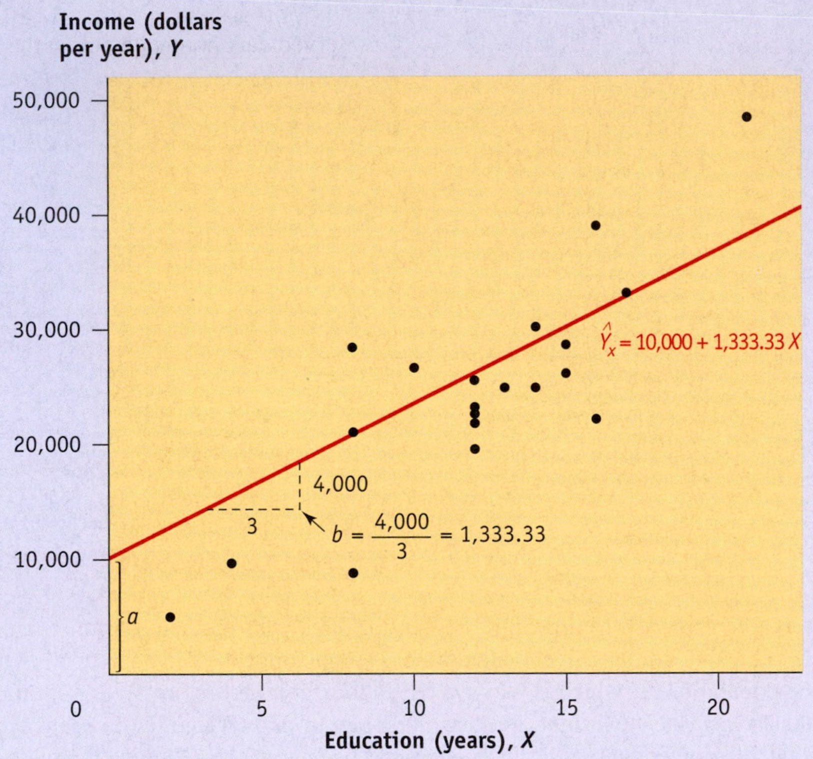

the above procedure—and the reason why statisticians reject regression lines drawn by sight alone as unacceptably crude—is that we cannot duplicate such a procedure, except by sheer accident. Different people, faced with an identical scatter of dots, such as that in Figure 16.6, would undoubtedly use different judgment and draw regression lines with different intercepts and slopes. Which of these different lines could we trust to be the best summary of the data plots? On what basis, furthermore, could we establish confidence intervals for the estimates we would make with the help of such a regression line? Because satisfactory answers to these questions do not exist, statisticians establish regression lines (and their associated equations) in a different way than mere eyesight and a ruler can provide. Their method, about to be discussed in the next section, produces results that different people can easily replicate.

16.6 Drawing the Best Regression Line: Least Squares

The best approach to fitting a line to sample data displayed in a scatter diagram is the **method of least squares.** A least-squares regression line minimizes the sum of the squares of the vertical deviations between the line and the individual data plots. As we noted above, these vertical deviations represent the errors associated with using the regression line to predict Y with the help of X when the two variables have a stochastic relationship. Figure 16.7 illustrates the nature of the squares whose sum is being minimized.

Why do statisticians use this particular method to establish a regression line? We can understand their desire to minimize errors easily enough, but why minimize the *squares* of the errors? One reason is that a summation of unsquared deviations always yields a number equal to zero and, thus, gives the impression of low error, even when the line exhibits many large errors relative to data points. Positive errors, arising when observed data points lie above the least-squares regression line, and negative errors, arising when observed data points lie below the line, cancel each other. Another reason, to be discussed later in this chapter, involves the fact that the coefficients of a least-squares regression line computed from sample data (that is, the values of the line's intercept and slope) turn out to be unbiased, efficient, and consistent estimators of corresponding coefficients that census data would produce.

FIGURE 16.7 | The Method of Least Squares

This scatter diagram displays eight data plots, only two of which lie precisely on the regression line drawn. The six remaining plots diverge from the line by varying distances, depicted by solid vertical line segments, such as AB. The ***method of least squares*** *establishes the only regression line, among all such conceivable lines, that minimizes the sum of the squares of such vertical deviations or errors. These squares are represented by the boxes in the graph. The line minimizes their combined area, called the error sum of squares and equal to* $ESS = \Sigma(Y - \hat{Y}_X)^2$. *In this expression,* Y *is an observed value, such as A, of the dependent variable, given a specific value of the independent variable.* $\hat{Y}_X$ *is the corresponding estimated value of the dependent variable, such as B, that the regression line suggests.*

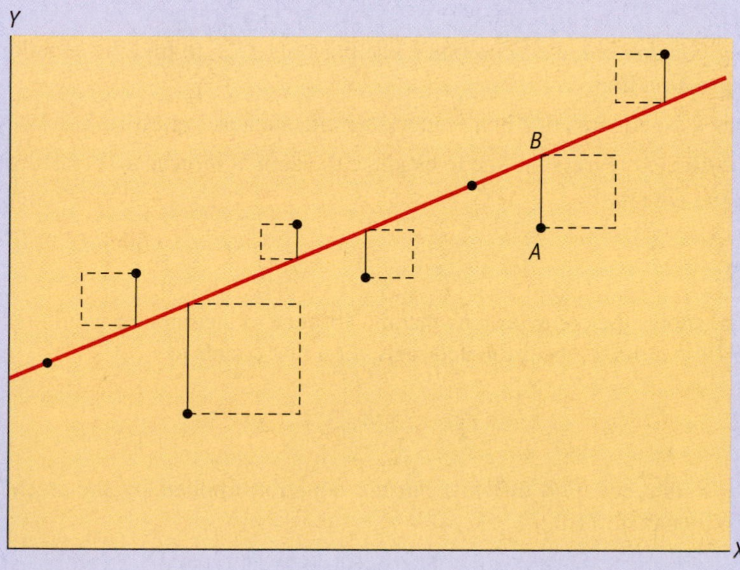

DEFINITION 16.7 A regression line calculated from sample data by the method of least squares is called an **estimated regression line** or **sample regression line.** In its equation, $\hat{Y}_X = a + bX$, the values of a and b are the **estimated regression coefficients.**

By minimizing the error sum of squares, $ESS = \Sigma(Y - \hat{Y}_X)^2 = (Y - a - bX)^2$, the estimated regression coefficients can be shown to equal the expressions given in Formula 16.A.

FORMULA 16.A | The Estimated Least-Squares Regression Line

$$\hat{Y}_X = a + bX$$

where $\hat{Y}_X$ is the estimated value of the dependent variable Y, given a specified value of the independent variable, X, while a is the intercept and b is the slope of the estimated regression line.

$$a = \overline{Y} - b\overline{X} \qquad b = \frac{\Sigma XY - n\overline{X}\,\overline{Y}}{\Sigma X^2 - n\overline{X}^2}$$

where X's are observed individual values of the independent variable ($\overline{X}$ being their mean), Y's are associated observed individual values of the dependent variable ($\overline{Y}$ being *their* mean), and n is sample size.

EXAMPLE PROBLEM 16.2

Review the data of Table 16.1 on page 713. Then accomplish the following:

a. Assuming you do *not* have a computer, use Formula 16.A to find the equation of the estimated regression line.

b. Graph this least-squares line in a scatter diagram, such as Figure 16.5.

c. Use the estimated regression line to estimate the annual income associated with 5 years or 20 years of education.

SOLUTION:

a. Table 16.2 shows the computations that the absence of a computer would require of you. Because $\hat{Y}_X = a + bX$, the estimated regression line comes to

$$\hat{Y}_X = 2{,}144.23 + 1{,}847.50X$$

Notice how this equation differs from the equation implied by the freehand drawing in Figure 16.6 on page 716.

b. See Figure 16.8 on page 720.

TABLE 16.2 | Calculating a Least-Squares Estimated Regression Line

Individual	X	Y	XY	X^2	$\hat{Y}_X$	$Y - \hat{Y}_X$
A	2	5,012	10,024	4	5,839.23	−827.23
B	4	9,680	38,720	16	9,534.23	145.77
C	8	28,432	227,456	64	16,924.23	11,507.77
D	8	8,774	70,192	64	16,924.23	−8,150.23
E	8	21,008	168,064	64	16,924.23	4,083.77
F	10	26,565	265,650	100	20,619.23	5,945.77
G	12	25,428	305,136	144	24,314.23	1,113.77
H	12	23,113	277,356	144	24,314.23	−1,201.23
I	12	22,500	270,000	144	24,314.23	−1,814.23
J	12	19,456	233,472	144	24,314.23	−4,858.23
K	12	21,690	260,280	144	24,314.23	−2,624.23
L	13	24,750	321,750	169	26,161.73	−1,411.73
M	14	30,100	421,400	196	28,009.23	2,090.77
N	14	24,798	347,172	196	28,009.23	−3,211.23
O	15	28,532	427,980	225	29,856.73	−1,324.73
P	15	26,000	390,000	225	29,856.73	−3,856.73
Q	16	38,908	622,528	256	31,704.23	7,203.77
R	16	22,050	352,800	256	31,704.23	−9,654.23
S	17	33,060	562,020	289	33,551.73	−491.73
T	21	48,276	1,013,796	441	40,941.73	7,334.27
	241	488,132	6,585,796	3,285		0
	ΣX	ΣY	ΣXY	ΣX^2		$\Sigma(Y - \hat{Y}_X)$

$$\bar{X} = \frac{\Sigma X}{n} = \frac{241}{20} = 12.05 \qquad \bar{Y} = \frac{\Sigma Y}{n} = \frac{488{,}132}{20} = 24{,}406.60$$

$$b = \frac{\Sigma XY - n\bar{X}\bar{Y}}{\Sigma X^2 - n\bar{X}^2} = \frac{6{,}585{,}796 - 20(12.05)(24{,}406.60)}{3{,}285 - 20(12.05)^2} = 1{,}847.50$$

$$a = \bar{Y} - b\bar{X} = 24{,}406.60 - 1{,}847.50(12.05) = 2{,}144.23$$

c. With the help of the equation found in (a) or the Figure 16.8 regression line found in (b), we can estimate the annual income of someone with 5 years or 20 years of education (and no such persons were included in the original sample) as

$$\hat{Y}_5 = 2{,}144.23 + 1{,}847.50(5) = 11{,}381.73$$
$$\hat{Y}_{20} = 2{,}144.23 + 1{,}847.50(20) = 39{,}094.23$$

In the graph, these numbers represent the height of the red line above X values of 5 and 20, respectively.

FIGURE 16.8 | A Regression Line Derived by the Method of Least Squares

The regression line shown here has been fitted by the method of least squares to the scatter of dots first seen in Figure 16.5. Given this line, we estimate a person's annual income as \$2,144.23 plus an additional \$1,847.50 for each year of education. Note two features of this—and every—least-squares regression line: First, the line goes through point $\overline{X}\overline{Y}$ (the respective means of the X and Y observations in the sample, here equal to 12.05 and 24,406.60.) Second, the sum of the vertical deviations of Y's from the regression line is zero: $\Sigma(Y - \hat{Y}_X) = \Sigma[Y - (a + bX)] = 0$, a fact that is illustrated in the last column of Table 16.2 and serves as an excellent check on the accuracy of calculations. In these two senses, the line can be said to "go through the center" of the scatter diagram.

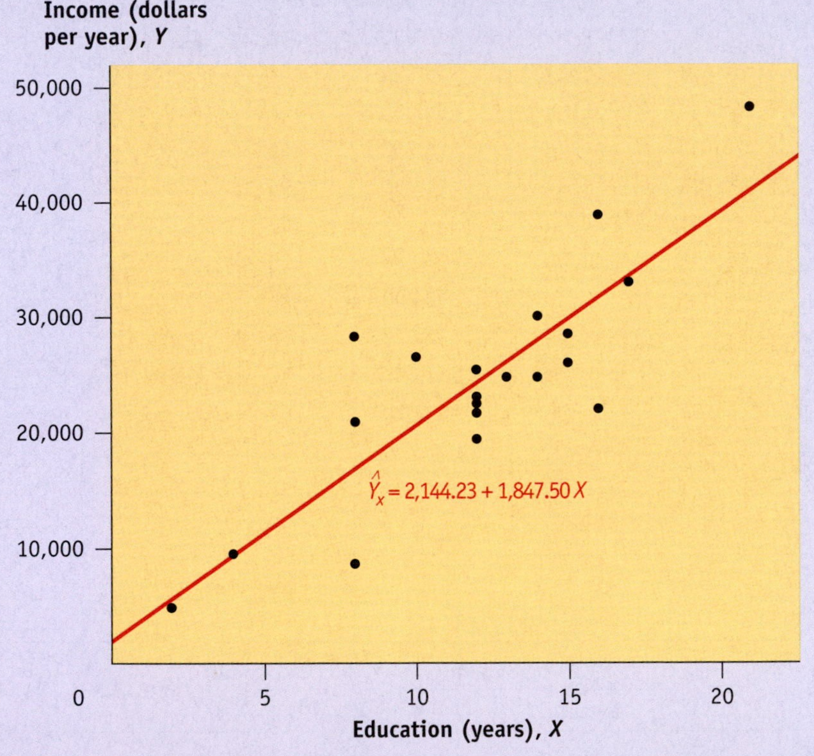

Most people recognize that it would be unwise to generalize the relationship summarized in our regression line to completely different times and places. What is true for 1999 may not be true for 2029; what is true for the United States may not be true for France. Fewer people realize, however, that it is equally unwise to use a regression line to make estimates of Y for values of X that lie outside the data range (here below 2 or above 21 years of education) from which the estimated regression line has been derived. Such extrapolation can easily lead to absurd results; for example, the association of certain low incomes with negative years of education or of certain high levels of education with near-infinite incomes. Such nonsensical results could be obtained because the apparently linear relationship that we see in our scatter diagram may fail to hold for smaller or larger values of X. Even if it does hold, additional data would probably lead us to estimate a much flatter or steeper regression line with quite a different intercept.

EXCEL Example 16.2

Review the data of Table 16.1 on page 713. Then confirm some of the results of Example Problem 16.2 by using your computer to

a. find the equation of the estimated regression line

b. graph this least-squares line in a scatter diagram.

SOLUTION: Enter the Table 16.1 education and income data, inclusive of column heads, into worksheet columns A and B, respectively. (You can copy and paste the data from columns L and M of the file HKMISC.) *Tip:* Although it does not apply in this case, it is wise to inspect the data and remove—across all columns—any row that contains nonnumeric data. Such data might be asterisks denoting missing values. EXCEL will refuse to perform all sorts of operations as long as such data exist. You can accomplish the task most quickly by pressing Ctrl while successively clicking the numbered heads of rows containing nonnumeric data in any column. Then click **Edit** > **Delete**.

Part (a)

1. Click **Tools** > **Data Analysis** > **Regression** > **OK**.
2. In the *Input Y Range* box, enter **B1:B21**
3. In the *Input X Range* box, enter **A1:A21**
4. Check *Labels* (because the first cell of each input column is a text label) and *New Worksheet Ply,* then click **OK**.

Along with all kinds of other things that you need not understand right now, the coefficients column of the output provides information to construct the following *regression equation:*

$$\text{Income (\$/year)} = 2{,}144.2163 + 1{,}847.50072\ \text{Education (years)}$$

EXCEL suggests that annual income can be best estimated as \$2,144.22 plus \$1,847.50 times the income recipient's years of education.

Part (b)

1. Repeat the steps noted in Part (a), but also check *Line Fit Plots* prior to the last **OK**.
2. EXCEL produces one of its really ugly graphs. It can be edited, in a fashion noted in EXCEL Example 2.10 (pages 59–62), to look something like this:

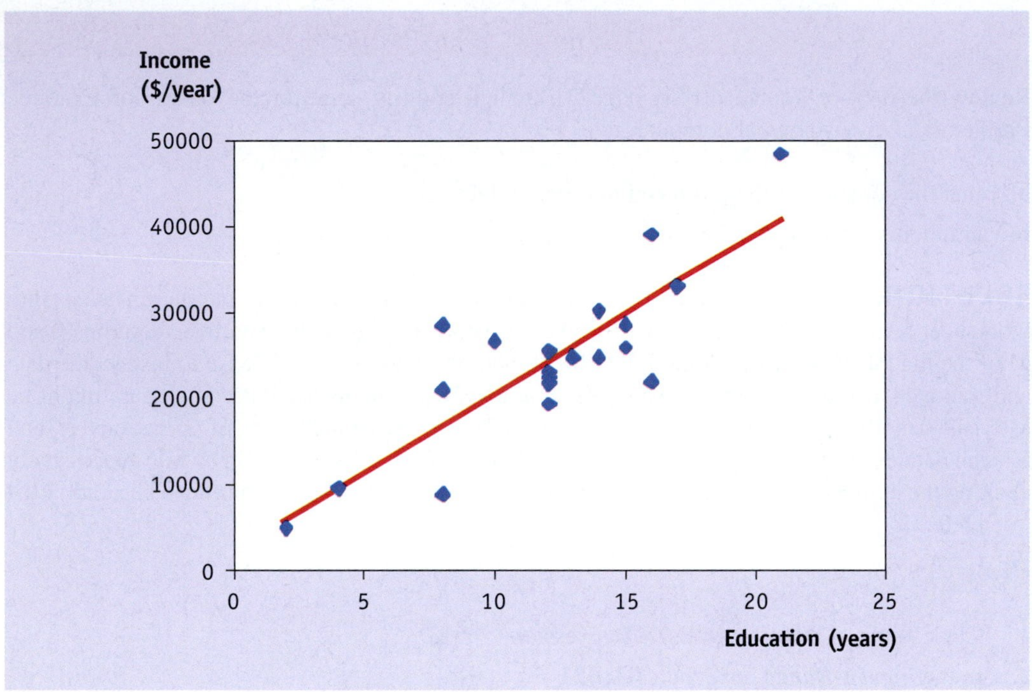

Note: Originally, EXCEL produces individual color dots, called *markers,* rather than a straight line, to indicate the predicted income at any given level of education. To turn the separate dots into the line shown here,

1. Click on one of the color dots, which selects the entire series.
2. Click **Format** > **Selected Data Series** > **Patterns**.
3. Under *Line,* choose *Automatic*.
4. Under *Marker,* choose *None* and click **OK**.

Tip: Here is an alternative way to work EXCEL Example 16.2:

1. Repeat the procedure illustrated in EXCEL Example 16.1.
2. In the finished scatter diagram, click on any point to select all points.
3. Click **Chart** > **Add Trendline**.
4. In the dialog box, click on the straight-line type, click **Options**, choose *Display equation on chart,* and click **OK**.

The following result appears:

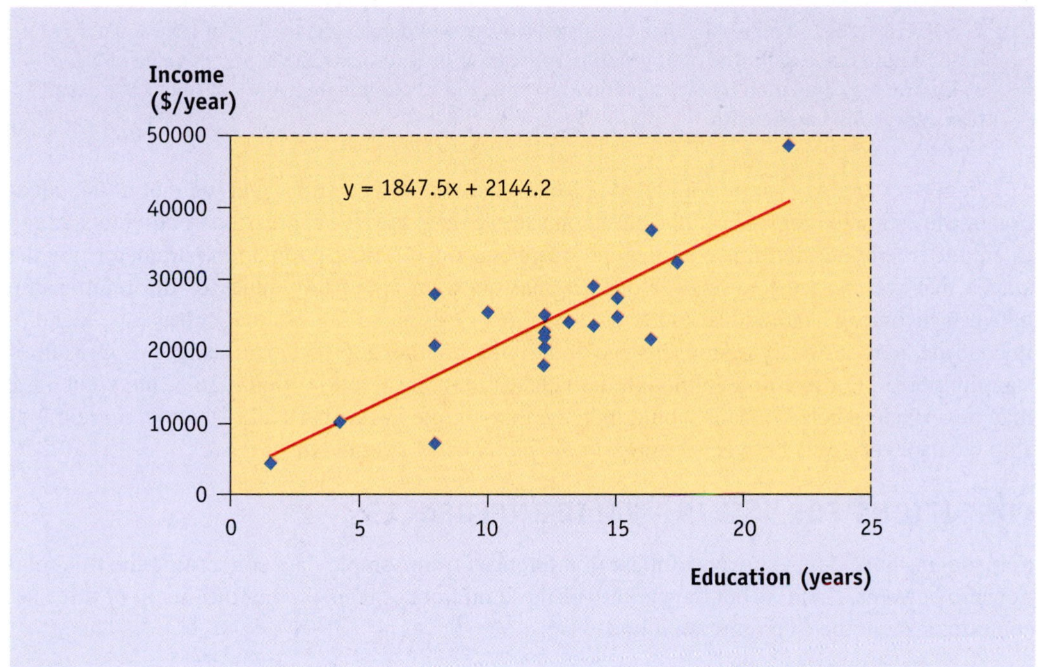

16.7 Estimated versus True Regression Line

Earlier in this chapter, we set out to discover the nature of a possible association between the years of formal education attained by the residents of a country and their annual incomes. Does the estimated regression line of Figure 16.8 answer our original quest? It certainly appears to do just that. It establishes the existence of a *direct* relationship between the two variables. It also specifies, by means of the equation of the estimated regression line, the mathematical details of that relationship. But now consider this sobering thought: The regression line of Figure 16.8 was fitted to data, first given in Table 16.1, that were obtained not by taking a full-fledged census of all the adult residents of the country, but by taking a *tiny* simple random sample of them. What if we were to take another such sample from the same population? Surely, we would acquire a different set of data, would end up with a different scatter diagram, and would derive a different estimated regression line! We could repeat the process, and for every new sample, we would estimate yet another regression line. Which one of these could be trusted to reveal the true relationship (if there is a relationship) between X and Y in the population as a whole? In fact, we could only find that true regression line if we took a census of the entire population of adult individuals, recorded data on education and income for every one of them, and derived a least-squares regression line on that basis.

THE TRUE REGRESSION LINE

Imagine a scatter diagram for the entire adult population of our country. For each and every value of X (not just for some of them), it would record not merely a few values of Y, as in Figure 16.8, but a great multitude of them. The least-squares regression line that we might derive from such census data contains the information that we really seek.

DEFINITION 16.8 A regression line calculated from census data by the method of least squares is called a **true regression line** or **population regression line.** It relates the expected value of Y for every X in the population by the equation $E(Y) = \alpha + \beta X$, wherein the values of α and β are the **true regression coefficients.**

In perfect analogy to the estimated regression coefficients a and b that we met in the equation of the estimated regression line based on sample data, the true regression coefficients, α and β, are the true regression line's vertical intercept and slope. These population parameters are the values that we can trust to answer our original question about the nature of the relationship between income, Y, and education, X. The sample or estimated regression coefficients, a and b, in contrast, may seriously distort the true underlying relationship between Y and X as a result of sampling error. For example, although the value of $b = 1{,}847.50$ in Figure 16.8, the value of β may nevertheless be zero. This would indicate that, unlike in this particular sample, no relationship whatsoever exists between Y and X *in the population as a whole.*

CONDITIONS FOR MAKING VALID INFERENCES

Statisticians have devised ways of making inferences from sample data concerning the true relationship between Y and X, but the validity of these inferences rests on the fulfillment of three assumptions about the true regression line.

ASSUMPTION 1 It is assumed that every population of Y values, a different one of which is associated with every possible value of X, is normally distributed.

Because each of these normal curves of Y values is associated with a specific value of X, each curve is referred to as a **conditional probability distribution of Y.** Each curve is said to have a **conditional mean of Y,** denoted by $\mu_{Y \cdot X}$, and a **conditional standard deviation of Y,** denoted by $\sigma_{Y \cdot X}$. This assumption is most easily understood with the help of Figure 16.9 on the next page. The graph is three-dimensional, containing the now familiar Y versus X plane, but also measuring, vertically above this plane, the probability density of Y values.

Imagine plotting, for specified values of $X = 5$, $X = 10$, and $X = 15$, all the associated values of Y found in the entire population. Given $X = 5$, the conditional mean of Y values might equal distance $0b$; it is designated as $\mu_{Y \cdot 5}$ (and pronounced "the conditional mean of Y, given X = 5"). Given $X = 10$, the conditional mean of Y values might equal distance $0c$; it is designated as $\mu_{Y \cdot 10}$. Finally, given $X = 15$, the conditional mean of Y values might equal distance $0d$; it is designated as $\mu_{Y \cdot 15}$. In each case, many individual Y values would be smaller or larger than this mean, of course, but the first assumption of linear regression analysis asserts that the frequency curve of Y values for any given X is a normal curve centered on $\mu_{Y \cdot X}$, such as each of the three solid red lines in Figure 16.9.

ASSUMPTION 2 It is assumed that all conditional probability distributions of Y, a different one of which is associated with every possible value of X, have the same conditional standard deviation of Y.

As we saw earlier, the conditional standard deviation of Y is denoted by $\sigma_{Y \cdot X}$. It is also referred to as the **population standard error of the estimate of Y, given X.** This second assumption, thus, assumes *homoscedasticity.* It postulates that the scatter of observed Y values above and below each conditional mean is the same. Notice how the normal curves shown in Figure 16.9 look alike even though they are centered on different means.

ASSUMPTION 3 It is assumed that the different sample observations about Y that are associated with any given X are statistically independent of each other.

FIGURE 16.9 | Three Conditional Probability Distributions of *Y* and the True Regression Line

The solid red lines shown here represent the three conditional probability distributions of Y that are associated with X values of 5, 10, and 15, respectively. Each of these frequency curves rises above the Y versus X plane into the third dimension; each is also a normal curve clustering around a central value, $\mu_{Y \cdot X}$. Hence, the probability of finding Y values declines progressively and equally the farther we move, either above or below any one of the three means, along the dashed lines that parallel the Y axis. The dashed red line that connects all the conditional means in the Y versus X plane is the true regression line.

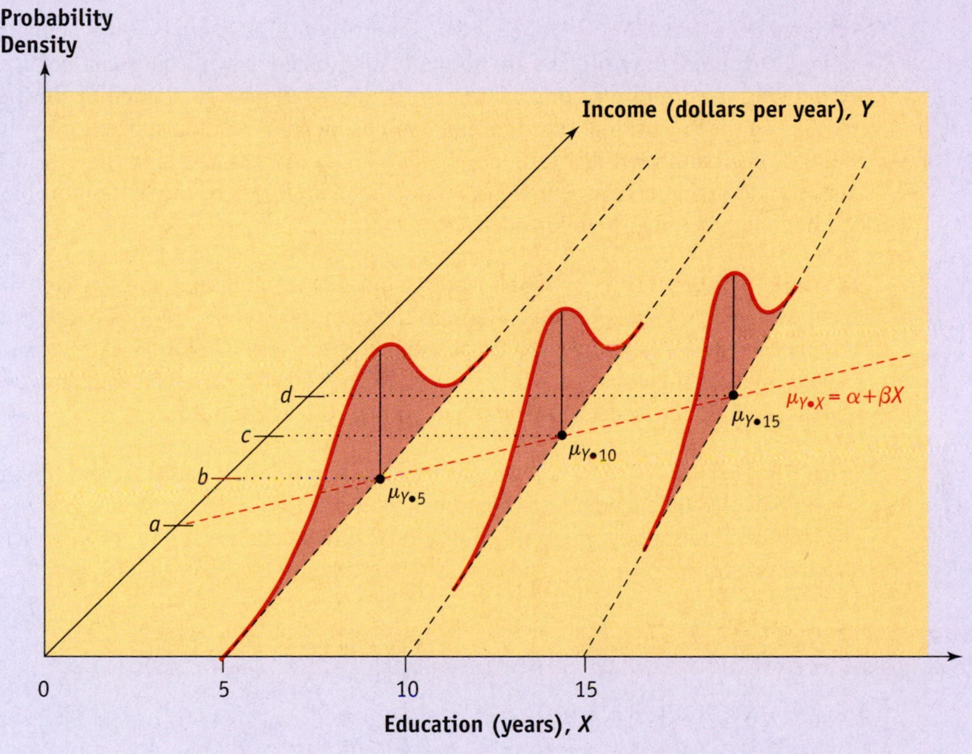

The fact that an observed value of Y is low, for example, is no reason for another Y observation to be low as well.

CONCLUSION The linear simple regression model pictures all conditional means, $\mu_{Y \cdot X}$, as lying on a straight line that is the *true regression line* and is described by the equation

$$E(Y) = \mu_{Y \cdot X} = \alpha + \beta X$$

The dashed red line in the Y versus X plane of Figure 16.9 is such a line. Its Y-intercept, α, equals distance $0a$ and its slope equals β.

16.8 Regression Diagnostics

Given the availability of sample data only, how can we ever know whether we can safely use an estimated regression line to make valid inferences about the true regression line? Statisticians have devised a series of steps, jointly known as the **analysis of residuals,** which help us decide whether the crucial assumptions noted in the previous section are fulfilled. When they are, we can safely make such inferences.

A review of Table 16.2 on page 719 can help us see what is involved. Every value, X, of the independent variable in our sample is associated with a particular observed value, Y, of the dependent variable. Once we have found the estimated regression line, every X value is also associated with a particular predicted or fitted Y value, $\hat{Y}_X$, suggested by the estimated regression line. The difference, at any given X, between the observed and fitted Y values is the estimation error, $e = Y - \hat{Y}_X$, and is generally called a **residual.** The last column of Table 16.2 contains a complete set of such residuals for our education versus income example. (For a graphical view of estimation errors, see Part (b) of Figure 16.3 on page 710.) A look at such residuals can help us determine whether the crucial assumptions noted in Section 16.7 are fulfilled. Here we consider three cases in point.

TESTING ASSUMPTION 1 When Assumption 1 is fulfilled and Y values at any given X are normally distributed, the residuals are normally distributed as well. This can be tested in two ways, by drawing a normal plot or a histogram of the residuals. In a **normal plot,** each residual is graphed against its normal score (residual minus mean of residuals, divided by their standard deviation). If Assumption 1 is fulfilled, the plot approximates a straight line. A histogram, in turn, can provide visual confirmation. If Assumption 1 is fulfilled, the histogram looks symmetrical and bell-shaped rather than lopsided.

TESTING ASSUMPTION 2 When Assumption 2 is fulfilled and all conditional probability distributions of Y have the same conditional standard deviation, a plot of each residual against the associated fitted $\hat{Y}$ value *or* the associated X value indicates a similar variation of residuals throughout the range of these $\hat{Y}$ or X values. A marked pattern of ever-widening or ever-narrowing scatter, on the other hand, points to a violation of the assumption.

TESTING ASSUMPTION 3 When Assumption 3 is fulfilled and different observations about Y are statistically independent of each other, sequentially collected Y data, as well as equally sequenced residuals, show no trend. A plot of residuals against the order in which data were collected then shows lots of ups and downs rather than long runs of values with the same sign.

EXCEL Example 16.3

Review EXCEL Example 16.2.

a. Once again find the estimated regression line, but this time also gather information about fitted values (predicted income), residuals (actual income minus predicted income), and standardized residuals (residual minus mean of residuals, divided by the standard deviation of residuals).

b. Perform regression diagnostics with your data.

SOLUTION: Repeat the steps noted in Part (a) of EXCEL Example 16.2, but also check *Residuals, Standardized Residuals, Residual Plots,* and *Normal Probability Plots* prior to the last **OK**.

Part (a) Along with the coefficients of the regression equation and more, the tabular output at the top of the next page appears.

Part (b)

1. To test **Assumption 1** about normality, we can create a scatter plot of each residual against its standardized self (or normal score) and see whether the plot approximates a straight line. Using relevant data gathered in Part (a), and following the procedure illustrated in EXCEL Example 16.1, we derive the graphical output on the next page.

RESIDUAL OUTPUT				PROBABILITY OUTPUT	
Observation	*Predicted Income*	*Residuals*	*Standard Residuals*	*Percentile*	*Income*
1	5839.217745	−827.21775	−0.158048353	2.5	5012
2	9534.219189	145.78081	0.027852905	7.5	8774
3	16924.22208	11507.778	2.198677867	12.5	9680
4	16924.22208	−8150.2221	−1.557182717	17.5	19456
5	16924.22208	4083.7779	0.780247255	22.5	21008
6	20619.22352	5945.7765	1.136000993	27.5	21690
7	24314.22496	1113.775	0.212798034	32.5	22050
8	24314.22496	−1201.225	−0.229506231	37.5	22500
9	24314.22496	−1814.225	−0.346626108	42.5	23113
10	24314.22496	−4858.225	−0.928213229	47.5	24750
11	24314.22496	−2624.225	−0.501384836	52.5	24798
12	26161.72569	−1411.7257	−0.269724532	57.5	25428
13	28009.22641	2090.7736	0.399463533	62.5	26000
14	28009.22641	−3211.2264	−0.613537424	67.5	26565
15	29856.72713	−1324.7271	−0.253102575	72.5	28432
16	29856.72713	−3856.7271	−0.736866894	77.5	28532
17	31704.22785	7203.7721	1.376353844	82.5	30100
18	31704.22785	−9654.2279	−1.844538298	87.5	33060
19	33551.72857	−491.72857	−0.093949739	92.5	38908
20	40941.73146	7334.2685	1.401286505	97.5	48276

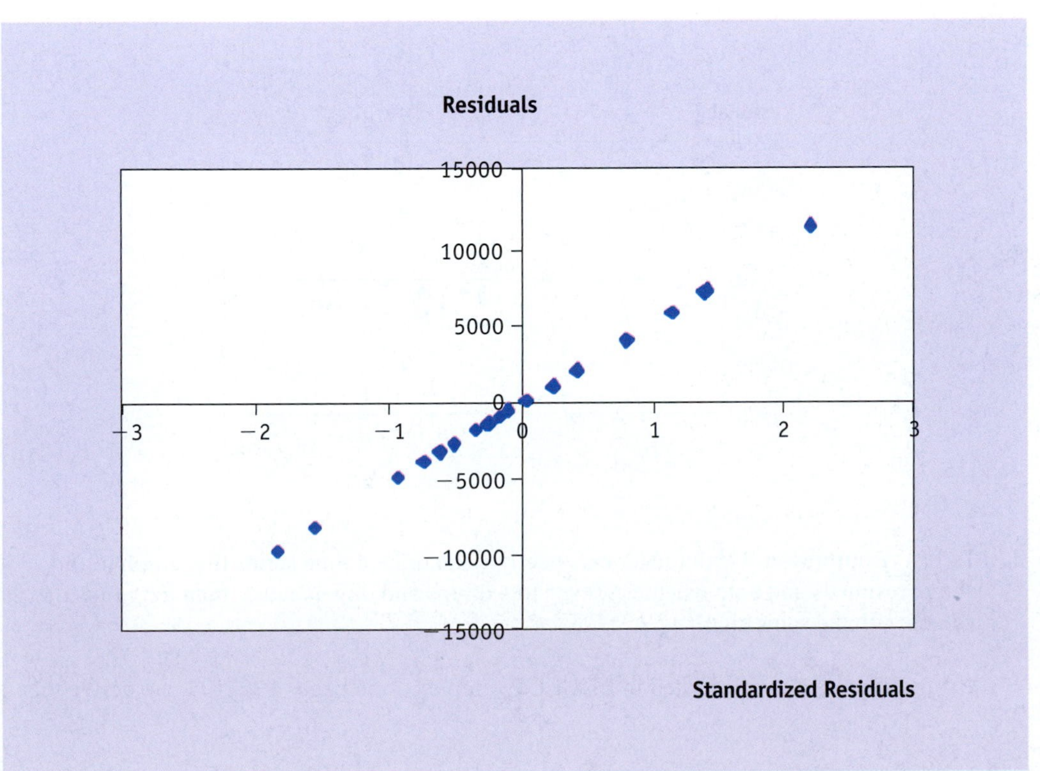

Note: We can also study EXCEL's own version of a normal probability plot:

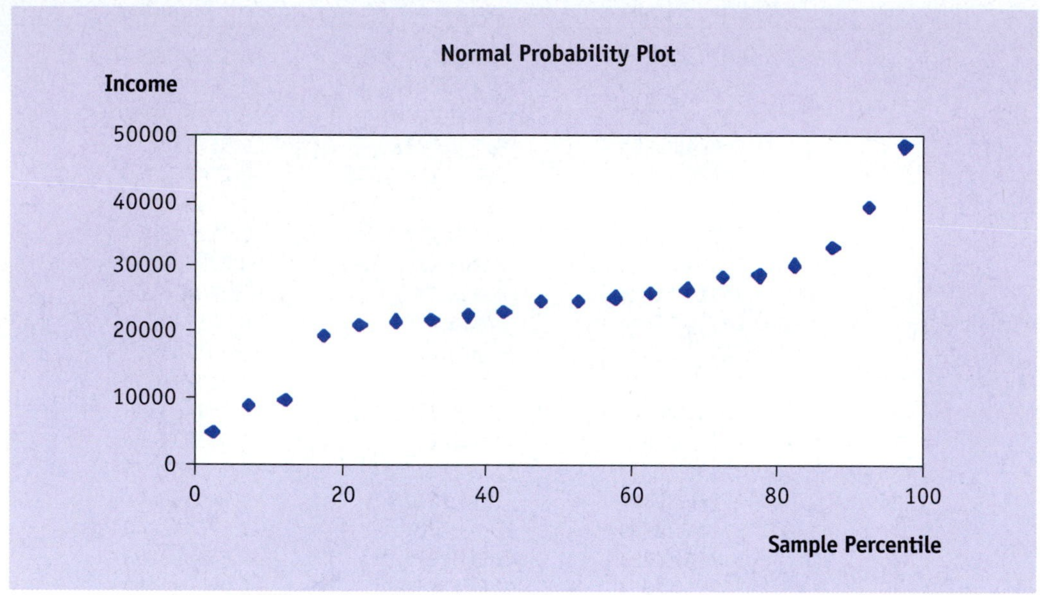

2. To test **Assumption 2** about homoscedasticity, we can plot each residual against the associated X value and note whether a similar variation of residuals exists throughout the range of X values. EXCEL has already done the plotting for us:

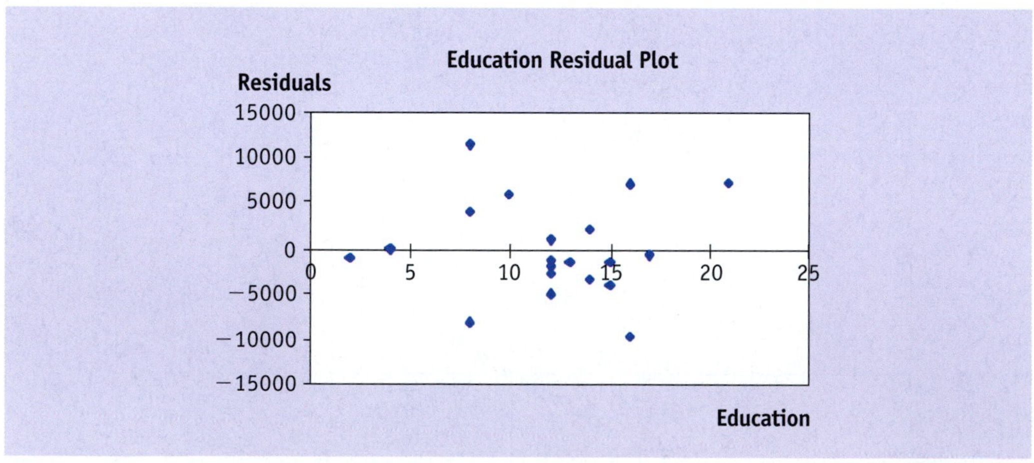

3. To test **Assumption 3** about independence, we can draw a time series line graph of the above residuals and note whether we see lots of ups and downs rather than long runs of values with the same sign.

Using the procedure illustrated in EXCEL Example 6.6 on pages 196–197, we derive this:

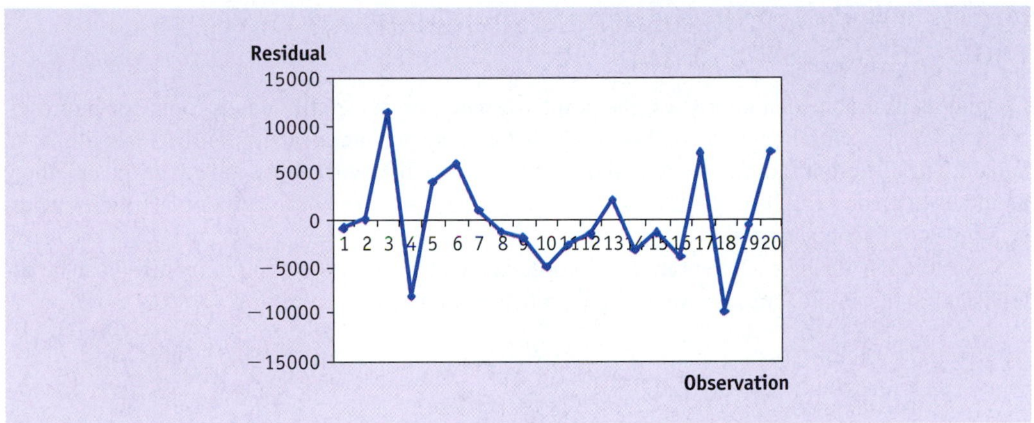

INTERPRETATION The first two graphs suggest that the normality assumption (1) is roughly satisfied. The second graph suggests the same about the homoscedasticity assumption (2); so does the third graph about the independence assumption (3).

16.9 Estimating the Average Value of *Y*, Given *X*

Once we are satisfied that the basic assumptions underlying regression analysis hold, we can use our sample regression line to make all sorts of valid inferences about the population of interest. For example, we can estimate the average value of *Y* in the population as a whole for any given *X*. And just as we did in Chapter 12, *Estimation,* we can make a simple *point estimate* or construct a *confidence interval* at any specified level of confidence.

MAKING A POINT ESTIMATE OF $\mu_{Y \cdot X}$

Suppose we wanted to estimate $\mu_{Y \cdot 10}$, the mean income of all members of a population with 10 years of education. Assuming that Table 16.1 shows sample data from that population, we can use the sample regression line derived from these data (see Example Problem 16.2 on page 718) to estimate

$$\hat{Y}_{10} = 2{,}144.23 + 1{,}847.50(10) = 20{,}619.23$$

And just as we routinely use the sample mean, $\overline{X}$, to estimate the population mean, μ, so we can now use $\hat{Y}_{10}$ (a point on the *sample* regression line) as a point estimate of $\mu_{Y \cdot 10}$ (a point on the *population* regression line).

DESIRABLE CHARACTERISTICS In fact, $\hat{Y}_{10}$ is the best possible point estimate of $\mu_{Y \cdot 10}$, because the method of least squares produces estimated regression coefficients, a and b, that are unbiased, efficient, and consistent estimators of the corresponding true regression coefficients, α and β. The characteristics of unbiasedness, efficiency, and consistency (which we first met in Chapter 12) tell us this:

If all possible random samples of a given size were taken from the population of interest and if a least-squares regression equation were calculated for each of these, the average value of the estimated coefficient a would equal the true coefficient α, while the average value of b would equal β (unbiasedness). In addition, the coefficients estimated by the method of least squares have the smallest variance for a given sample size among all available unbiased estimators (efficiency), and they get progressively closer to α and β as sample size is increased (consistency).

ESTABLISHING A CONFIDENCE INTERVAL FOR $\mu_{Y \cdot X}$ FROM A SMALL SAMPLE ($n < 30$)

Despite its desirable characteristics, the point estimate just made still leaves room for improvement. It ignores sampling error, and we may wish to take account of it explicitly. After all, if we had drawn a different sample, we would have estimated a different regression equation and, thus, would have made a different point estimate of $\mu_{Y \cdot 10}$. We can make our uncertainty explicit by presenting a confidence interval.

As noted in Chapter 12, the limits of a confidence interval for the population mean can be established in the small-sample case, using the t distribution, as

$$\mu = \overline{X} \pm (t\sigma_{\overline{X}})$$

In regression analysis, we seek to estimate the variable Y rather than X. Hence, an expression analogous to the previous one is

$$\mu_{Y \cdot X} = \hat{Y}_X \pm (t\sigma_{\hat{Y}_X})$$

In this expression, $\sigma_{\hat{Y}_X}$ is the standard error of $\hat{Y}_X$. It measures the variability, caused by the selection of different samples, of all possible $\hat{Y}_X$ values at the X value for which we wish to establish a confidence interval of the conditional mean.

THE VARIABILITY OF $\hat{Y}_X$ The variability of $\hat{Y}_X$ has two components. One of these, the variability in the mean of observed Y values, depends on the conditional standard deviation, $\sigma_{Y \cdot X}$, of the relevant population of Y's, as well as on sample size, n. In terms of Figure 16.9 on page 725, this variability in the mean of observed Y values depends on the shape of the frequency curve at the relevant X and on the number of sample observations made.

A second source of variability in $\hat{Y}_X$ is the distance of the specified X from $\overline{X}$ as illustrated in Figure 16.10. The graph features, in red, the (unknown) true regression line and, in black, estimated regression lines fitted to four different samples drawn from the same population. Note how these lines diverge increasingly as the specified value of X lies farther from $\overline{X}$. As a result, the estimated values of $\hat{Y}_X$ become more varied, too.

ESTIMATING $\sigma_{\hat{Y}_X}$ The value of $\sigma_{\hat{Y}_X}$ cannot be calculated directly because all possible values of $\hat{Y}_X$ are never determined. In practice, the standard error of $\hat{Y}_X$ is *estimated* as

$$\sigma_{\hat{Y}_X} \cong s_{Y \cdot X}\sqrt{\frac{1}{n} + \frac{(X - \overline{X})^2}{\Sigma X^2 - n\overline{X}^2}}$$

This complicated expression reflects both components of $\hat{Y}_X$ variability that we just noted. In this expression, $s_{Y \cdot X}$ is the **sample standard error of the estimate of Y, given X.** This standard error measures the dispersion of the observed Y values around the least-squares sample regression line and equals

$$s_{Y \cdot X} = \sqrt{\frac{\Sigma(Y - \hat{Y})^2}{n - 2}} = \sqrt{\frac{\Sigma Y^2 - a\Sigma Y - b\Sigma XY}{n - 2}}$$

FIGURE 16.10 | One Source of Variability in $\hat{Y}_X$

This graph features a true regression line (in red) with the equation $\mu_{Y \cdot X} = \alpha + \beta X$. It also shows estimated regression lines (in black) that might have been fitted to four different samples and are described by the equation $\hat{Y}_X = a + bX$ (where a and b, of course, differ from one sample regression line to the next.) Note how the computed values of $\hat{Y}_{10}$ (the four fat dots above X = 10) are closer together than the computed values of $\hat{Y}_{21}$ (the four fat dots above X = 21) even though they are derived from identical samples. This illustrates one source in the variability of $\hat{Y}_X$: the distance of the specified X from $\overline{X}$.

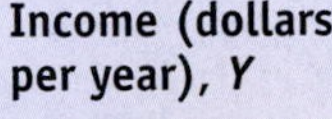

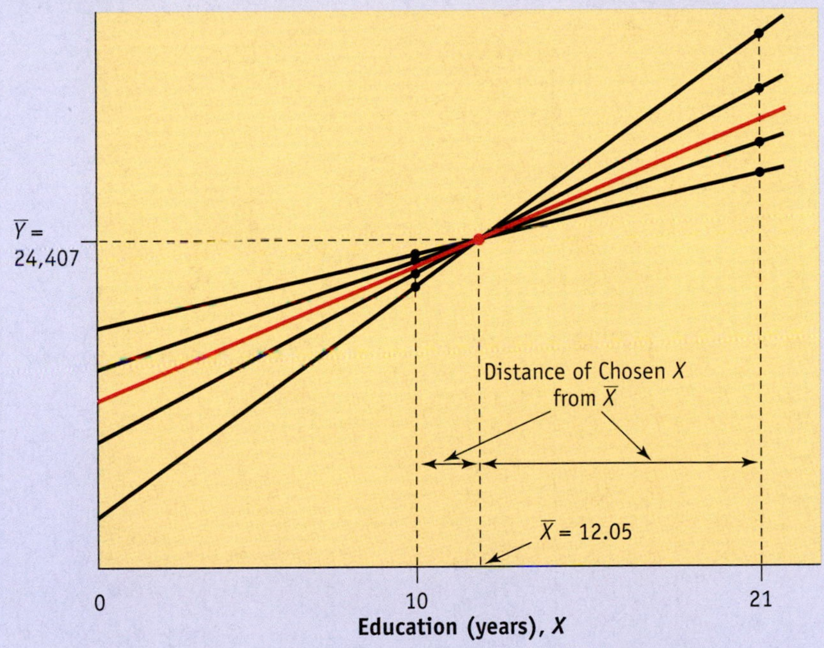

The divisor, $n - 2$, is used in the formula because it makes $s^2_{Y \cdot X}$ an unbiased estimator of the variance of Y values around the *true* regression line. The reduction of n by 2 indicates the loss of 2 degrees of freedom because the coefficients a and b (that allow the calculation of $\hat{Y}_X$) are being calculated from the same data as $s_{Y \cdot X}$. Figure 16.11 on the next page illustrates the nature of this dispersion measure.

CONCLUSION Formula 16.B on page 733 puts together the various strands of our discussion and becomes the basis for calculating confidence intervals for the conditional mean.

FIGURE 16.11 | The Sample Standard Error of the Estimate of Y, Given X

This graph reproduces the scatter diagram and the estimated regression line of Figure 16.8. It also illustrates, on the right-hand side, the kind of dispersion that the sample standard error of the estimate of Y, given X, measures. Note how the dashed arrows that parallel the red estimated regression line project points A and C, the two extreme deviations of observed Y values above and below the regression line, onto the vertical line at points B and D. All other observed Y values clearly diverge from the regression line to a lesser extent and would project to various points on the vertical line lying between B and D. The sample standard error of the estimate of Y, given X, which is symbolized by $s_{Y \cdot X}$*, measures this type of dispersion of observed Y values around the estimated regression line. But caution is advised: Do not confuse this sample standard error of the estimate of Y, given X, with the sample standard deviation of observed Y values,* s_Y*, that measures the dispersion of these values around their sample mean, as shown on the left-hand side of this graph.*

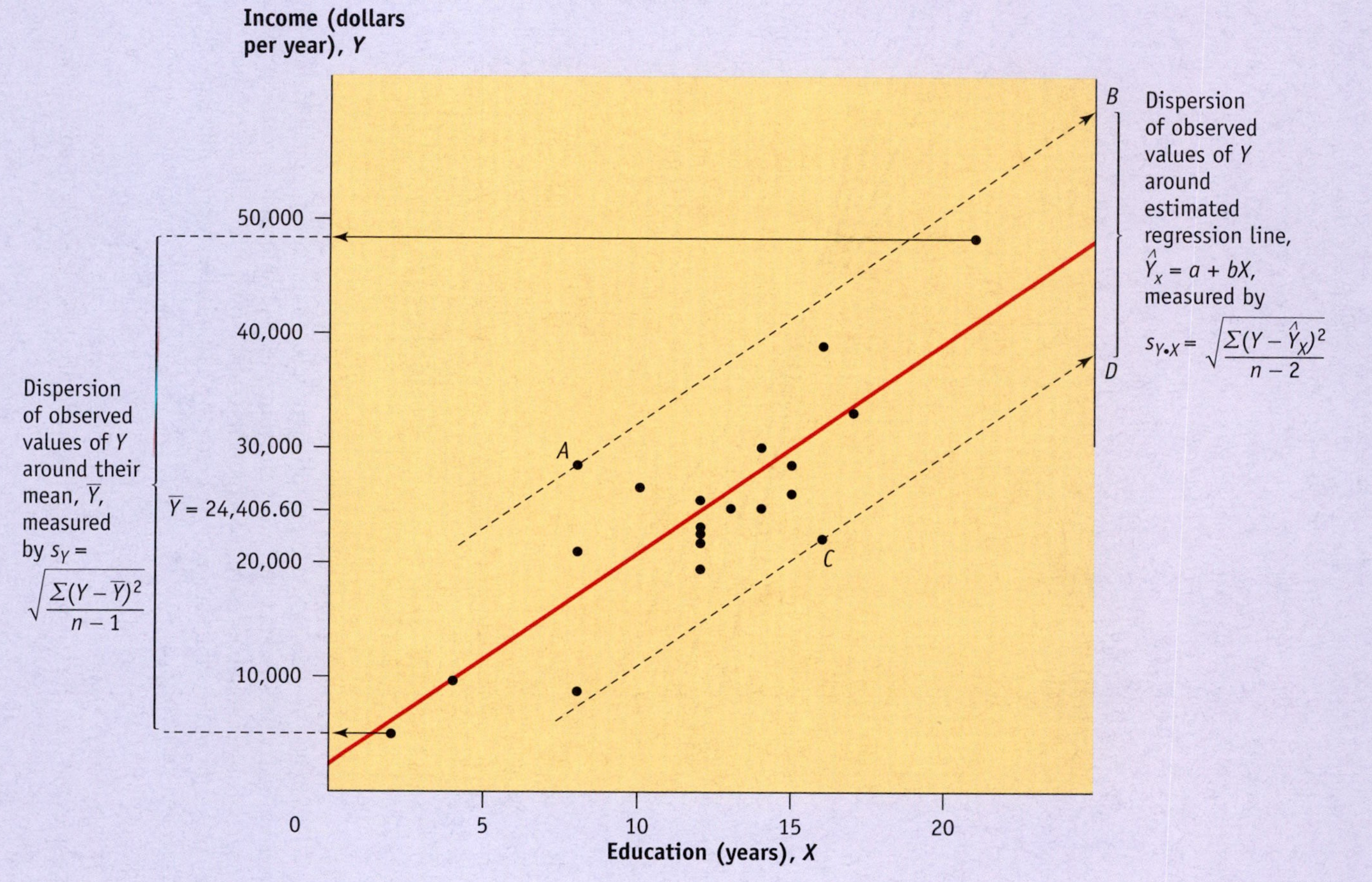

FORMULA 16.B | Confidence-Interval Limits for the Average Value of Y, Given X (small-sample case, $n < 30$)

$$\mu_{Y \cdot X} = \hat{Y}_X \pm \left(t_{\alpha/2} \times s_{Y \cdot X}\sqrt{\frac{1}{n} + \frac{(X - \bar{X})^2}{\Sigma X^2 - n\bar{X}^2}}\right)$$

where $\hat{Y}_X$ is the estimated value of dependent variable Y, the t statistic is found in Appendix Table K for $n - 2$ degrees of freedom, and $s_{Y \cdot X}$ is the sample standard error of the estimate of Y, given X, while n is sample size, and X's are observed individual values of the independent variable ($\bar{X}$ being their mean).

$$s_{Y \cdot X} = \sqrt{\frac{\Sigma(Y - \hat{Y})^2}{n - 2}} = \sqrt{\frac{\Sigma Y^2 - a\Sigma Y - b\Sigma XY}{n - 2}}$$

EXAMPLE PROBLEM 16.3

Review Example Problem 16.2. Then, assuming you do *not* have a computer, compute a 95 percent confidence interval for the conditional mean, $\mu_{Y \cdot 10}$, with the help of Formula 16.B.

SOLUTION: The point estimate is $\hat{Y}_{10} = 2{,}144.23 + 1{,}847.50(10) = 20{,}619.23$.

To calculate the 95 percent confidence interval for this conditional mean, we must now find the appropriate value of $t_{.025}$ from Appendix Table K. Table 16.2 shows $n = 20$; hence, we have $n - 2 = 18$ degrees of freedom and $t_{.025(18)} = 2.101$.

Still using Table 16.2, we can compute

$$s_{Y \cdot X} = \sqrt{\frac{\Sigma(Y - \hat{Y})^2}{n - 2}} = \sqrt{\frac{520{,}491{,}134}{18}} = 5{,}377.38$$

and

$$\mu_{Y \cdot X} = \hat{Y}_X \pm \left(t_{\alpha/2} \times s_{Y \cdot X}\sqrt{\frac{1}{n} + \frac{(X - \bar{X})^2}{\Sigma X^2 - n\bar{X}^2}}\right)$$

$$= 20{,}619.23 \pm \left(2.101(5{,}377.38)\sqrt{\frac{1}{20} + \frac{(10 - 12.05)^2}{3{,}285 - 20(12.05)^2}}\right) = 20{,}619.23 \pm 2{,}791.09$$

Thus, our 95 percent confidence interval is $17{,}828.14 \leq \mu_{Y \cdot 10} \leq 23{,}410.32$.

We can conclude with 95 percent confidence that the average income of all the people within our population who have 10 years of education lies between \$17,828.14 and \$23,410.32.

The true conditional mean could lie outside the confidence limits just computed. If we follow the above procedure of sampling and computation again and again, however, it will yield ever new, but similar, intervals, and they will contain the true conditional mean 95 percent of the time. For a quick review of the nature of confidence intervals, see Figure 12.3 and the accompanying Caution box on pages 495–496.

EXCEL Example 16.4

Review Example Problem 16.3. Then confirm its solution by using your computer.

SOLUTION:

MAKING THE POINT ESTIMATE OF $\mu_{Y \cdot 10}$

1. Enter the Table 16.1 education and income data, inclusive of column heads, into worksheet columns A and B, respectively. (You can also copy and paste the data from columns L and M of the file HKMISC.)
2. Select any empty cell; then click the **Function Wizard (*fx*)** > **Statistical** > **TREND** > **OK**.
3. In the *Known y's* box, enter **B2:B21** and press TAB.
4. In the *Known x's* box, enter **A2:A21** and press TAB.
5. In the *New x's* box, enter **10** and press TAB.
6. In the *Const* box, enter **1** (or **TRUE** or nothing at all) and click **OK**. (As a result, a regular regression line will be computed to determine the point estimate sought. If you enter 0 or FALSE, a regression line with a zero intercept will be computed.)

The result of **20619.22** appears in the selected cell.

CREATING A 95% CONFIDENCE INTERVAL FOR $\mu_{Y \cdot 10}$

1. Enter the labels *Point estimate, Sample size, Degrees of freedom, X-bar, Standard error of estimate, Critical t, Half-width of confidence interval, Lower limit of confidence interval,* and *Upper limit of confidence interval* into cells G1–G9 of your worksheet.
2. Enter corresponding formulas or known values into adjacent column H cells:

   20619.22 into H1

   20 into H2

   =H2−2 into H3

   =AVERAGE (A2:A21) into H4

   =STEYX(B2:B21,A2:A21) into H5

   =TINV(1−95/100,H3) into H6

   =H6*H5*SQRT(1/20+(10−H4)^2/(SUMSQ(A2:A21)−20*H4^2)) into H7

   =H1−H7 into H8

   =H1+H7 into H9

The result includes the desired 95% confidence interval (highlighted in red):

Point estimate	20619.22
Sample size	20
Degrees of freedom	18
X-bar	12.05
Standard error of the estimate	5377.376

Critical t	2.100924
Half-width of confidence interval	2790.989
Lower limit of confidence interval	17828.23
Upper limit of confidence interval	23410.21

Note: This type of problem can also be solved much more rapidly by using HKStat, Sheet 40.

ESTABLISHING A CONFIDENCE BAND FOR $\mu_{Y \cdot X}$

The segment reaching from *A* to *C* in Figure 16.12 shows graphically the confidence interval for the average *Y*, given $X = 10$, that was computed and confirmed in the previous section. The graph also shows that if we calculated and graphed similar 95 percent confidence intervals for all

FIGURE 16.12 | A 95 Percent Confidence Band for the Conditional Mean

*The red line in this graph is the least-squares estimated regression line of $\hat{Y}_X = 2{,}144.23 + 1{,}847.50X$ that was fitted to the sample data of Table 16.1 and first shown in Figure 16.8. Segment AC represents the 95 percent confidence interval for $\mu_{Y \cdot X}$ that reaches from \$17,828.14 (point A) past the point estimate of \$20,619.23 (point B) to \$23,410.32 (point C). We can easily calculate similar intervals for other values of X. For example, the interval reaches from \$6,582.21 to \$16,181.25 for $X = 5$, from \$21,880.33 to \$26,932.89 for $X = \bar{X} = 12.05$, and from \$33,844.59 to \$44,343.87 for $X = 20$. Thus, we can envelope the entire estimated regression line in a 95 percent (nonlinear) confidence band. And we can be confident—in the long run, as we use this procedure again and again—that 95 percent of conditional means **will** lie within the confidence-band limits that we compute.*

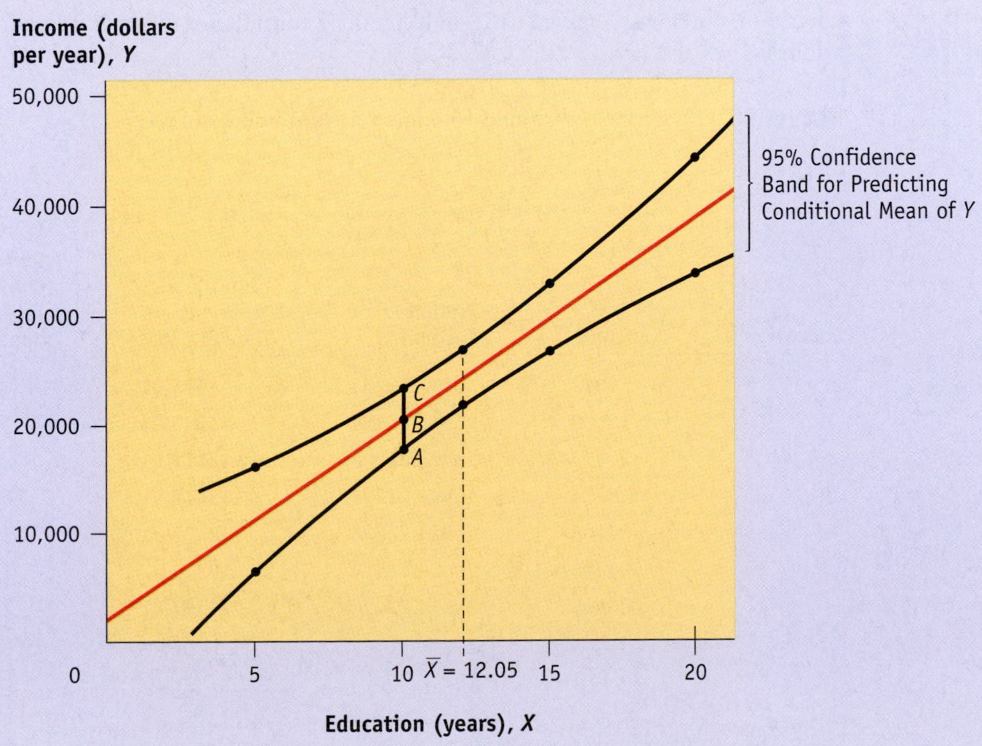

other values of X and connected the lower and upper limits of these intervals by solid lines, we could envelope the entire estimated regression line in a 95 percent **confidence band,** the width of which would be narrowest for $X = \bar{X}$ and would become increasingly wider the more X values diverged from their mean.

EXCEL Example 16.5

Review Figure 16.12, which is based on the Table 16.1 data. Create a similar graph by using your computer.

SOLUTION:

1. Enter the Table 16.1 education and income data, inclusive of column heads, into worksheet columns A and B, respectively. (You can also copy and paste the data from columns L and M of the file HKMISC.)
2. Enter labels *Predicted Income, 95% Confidence Interval Lower Limit,* and *95% Confidence Interval Upper Limit* into cells C1–E1.
3. Follow the procedure outlined in EXCEL Example 16.3 to generate a column of Predicted Income; then copy and paste that column into column C of your new worksheet.
4. Enter the lower and upper confidence limits for the average income of all persons with 10 years' education, which were generated in EXCEL Example 16.4, into cells D7 and E7, respectively, adjacent to the point estimate.
5. Following the procedure illustrated in EXCEL Example 16.4, fill in the remainder of columns D and E. (*Tip:* To find the confidence interval limits for any given level of predicted income, you need only change the value of the point estimate in H1 and the level of education, previously entered as 10 in the cell H7 formula for the confidence interval half-width.)

The result, with EXCEL Example 16.4 answers highlighted in red:

A Education	B Income	C Predicted Income	D 95% Confidence Interval Lower Limit	E 95% Confidence Interval Upper Limit
2	5012	5839.217745	-502.81	12181.24
4	9680	9534.219189	4233.95	14834.49
8	28432	16924.22208	13477.91	20370.54
8	8774	16924.22208	13477.91	20370.54
8	21008	16924.22208	13477.91	20370.54
10	26565	20619.22352	17828.23	23410.21
12	25428	24314.22496	21787.87	26840.58

(continued)

12	23113	24314.22496	21787.87	26840.58
12	22500	24314.22496	21787.87	26840.58
12	19456	24314.22496	21787.87	26840.58
12	21690	24314.22496	21787.87	26840.58
13	24750	26161.72569	23576.38	28747.07
14	30100	28009.22641	25242.35	30776.1
14	24798	28009.22641	25242.35	30776.1
15	28532	29856.72713	26807.58	32905.87
15	26000	29856.72713	26807.58	32905.87
16	38908	31704.22785	28297.02	35111.43
16	22050	31704.22785	28297.02	35111.43
17	33060	33551.72857	29731.93	37371.53
21	48276	40941.73146	35178.14	46705.32

6. Eliminate the above column B as well as all rows with duplicate education levels, retaining only 11 rows of data in 4 columns, which are the data to be graphed:

A Education	B Predicted Income	C 95% Confidence Interval Lower Limit	D 95% Confidence Interval Upper Limit
2	5839.217745	-502.81	12181.24
4	9534.219189	4233.95	14834.49
8	16924.22208	13477.91	20370.54
10	20619.22352	17828.23	23410.21
12	24314.22496	21787.87	26840.58
13	26161.72569	23576.38	28747.07
14	28009.22641	25242.35	30776.1
15	29856.72713	26807.58	32905.87
16	31704.22785	28297.02	35111.43
17	33551.72857	29731.93	37371.53
21	40941.73146	35178.14	46705.32

7. Select the new Range A1:D12, click the **Chart Wizard** > **Standard Types** > **XY (Scatter)**, click on the third chart subtype, and click **Next** > **Next** to reach the third *Chart Wizard* dialog box.
8. Under *Value (X) axis,* type *Education (years)* and press TAB.
9. Under *Value (Y) axis,* type *Income ($/year)* and click **Next** > **Finish**.
10. Enlarge and edit the graph with a result similar to Figure 16.12 as shown on the next page.

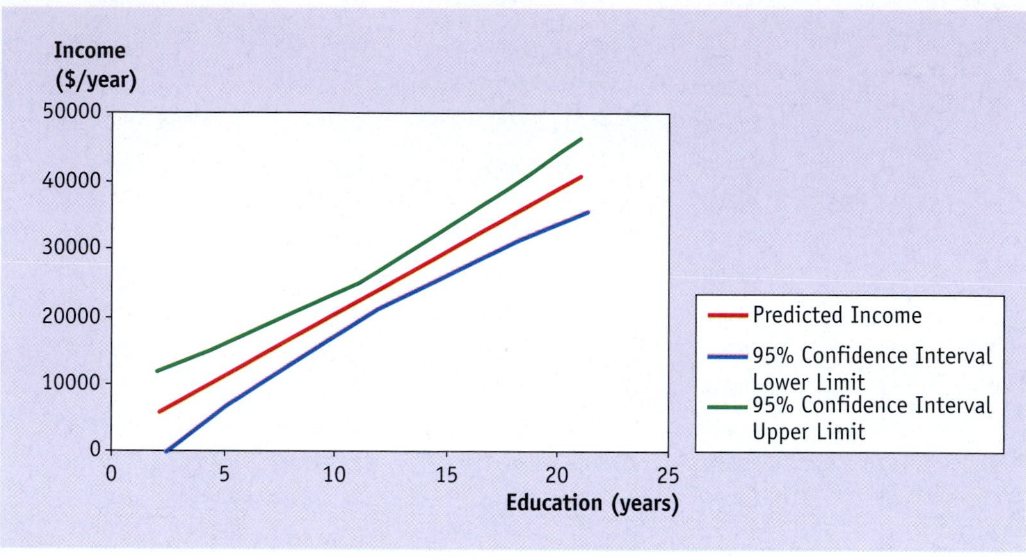

ESTABLISHING A CONFIDENCE INTERVAL FOR $\mu_{Y \cdot X}$ FROM A LARGE SAMPLE ($n \geq 30$)

In Chapter 12, using the normal distribution, we established the limits of a confidence interval for the population mean in the large sample case as

$$\mu = \overline{X} \pm (z\sigma_{\overline{X}}) \cong \overline{X} \pm z\frac{s}{\sqrt{n}}$$

In regression analysis, the analogous expression is

$$\mu_{Y \cdot X} = \hat{Y}_X \pm (z\sigma_{\hat{Y}_X}) \cong \hat{Y}_X \pm z\frac{s_{Y \cdot X}}{\sqrt{n}}$$

The result is Formula 16.C.

FORMULA 16.C | **Confidence-Interval Limits for the Average Value of *Y*, Given *X* (large-sample case, $n \geq 30$)**

$$\mu_{Y \cdot X} = \hat{Y}_X \pm \left(z_{\alpha/2}\frac{s_{Y \cdot X}}{\sqrt{n}}\right)$$

where $\hat{Y}_X$ is the estimated value of dependent variable Y, the z statistic is the standard normal deviate from Appendix Table J, and $s_{Y \cdot X}$ is the sample standard error of the estimate of Y, given X, while n is sample size.

$$s_{Y \cdot X} = \sqrt{\frac{\Sigma(Y - \hat{Y})^2}{n - 2}} = \sqrt{\frac{\Sigma Y^2 - a\Sigma Y - b\Sigma XY}{n - 2}}$$

EXAMPLE PROBLEM 16.4

A sample of 100 acres has revealed the association between bushels of wheat output per acre (Y) and pounds of fertilizer input per acre (X) that is summarized by the estimated regression line: $\hat{Y}_X = 100 + .1X$. Assume $s_{Y \cdot X} = 10$ bushels and derive a 95 percent confidence interval for the conditional mean of Y, given $X = 100$ pounds.

SOLUTION: The point estimate is $\mu_{Y \cdot 100} = 100 + .1(100) = 110$ bushels per acre. The appropriate z value can be found in Appendix Table J as 1.96. Thus, the interval limits are

$$\mu_{Y \cdot X} = \hat{Y}_X \pm \left(z_{\alpha/2} \frac{s_{Y \cdot X}}{\sqrt{n}}\right) = 110 \pm \left(1.96 \frac{10}{\sqrt{100}}\right) = 110 \pm 1.96$$

and the interval is $108.04 \leq \mu_{Y \cdot 100} \leq 111.96$ bushels of wheat.

16.10 Predicting an Individual Value of *Y*, Given *X*

Suppose now that we wished to predict, at a given X, not the average value of Y, or $\mu_{Y \cdot X}$, but an individual value, $I_{Y \cdot X}$, such as the next Y value we are likely to encounter in the process of sampling our population. Returning to our education versus income example, we may wish to predict the income of the next member of our population who has an education of, say, 10 years.

The point estimate for such an individual Y is the same as for the average Y; in our case it equals $\hat{Y}_{10} = 2{,}144.23 + 1{,}847.50(10) = 20{,}619.23$. The confidence interval for an individual value of Y encountered in sampling is once again determined differently for small and large samples, as the following sections will show. However, in order to differentiate the confidence interval for an individual value of Y from the confidence interval for the average value of Y, the former is now called a **prediction interval.** Likewise, the confidence band linking Y interval limits for all possible values of X is now called a **prediction band.**

ESTABLISHING A PREDICTION INTERVAL FOR $I_{Y \cdot X}$ FROM A SMALL SAMPLE ($n < 30$)

Formula 16.B has to be amended only slightly, as shown in Formula 16.D. The only difference is the "+ 1" appearing in the square root. Its presence acknowledges the existence of a third component yet in the variability of $\hat{Y}_X$; namely, the dispersion, illustrated in Figure 16.11, of individual Y values around the estimated regression line.

FORMULA 16.D | Prediction-Interval Limits for an Individual Value of *Y*, Given *X* (small-sample case, $n < 30$)

$$I_{Y \cdot X} = \hat{Y}_X \pm \left(t_{\alpha/2} \times s_{Y \cdot X}\sqrt{\frac{1}{n} + \frac{(X - \bar{X})^2}{\Sigma X^2 - n\bar{X}^2} + 1}\right)$$

where $\hat{Y}_X$ is the estimated value of dependent variable Y, the t statistic is found in Appendix Table K for $n - 2$ degrees of freedom, and $s_{Y \cdot X}$ is the sample standard error of the estimate of Y, given X, while n is sample size, and X's are observed individual values of the independent variable ($\bar{X}$ being their mean).

$$s_{Y \cdot X} = \sqrt{\frac{\Sigma(Y - \hat{Y})^2}{n - 2}} = \sqrt{\frac{\Sigma Y^2 - a\Sigma Y - b\Sigma XY}{n - 2}}$$

EXAMPLE PROBLEM 16.5

Review Example Problem 16.3. Then, assuming you do *not* have a computer, use Formula 16.D to compute a 95 percent prediction interval for $I_{Y\cdot 10}$, the income of the next individual encountered in sampling who has 10 years of education.

SOLUTION:

$$I_{Y\cdot 10} = 20{,}619.23 \pm 2.101(5{,}377.37)\sqrt{\frac{1}{20} + \frac{(10 - 12.05)^2}{3{,}285 - 20(12.05)^2} + 1}$$

$$= 20{,}619.23 \pm 11{,}637.51$$

Thus, our 95 percent prediction interval is $8{,}981.72 \leq I_{Y\cdot 10} \leq 32{,}256.74$. We can be 95 percent confident that the next person encountered in sampling who has 10 years of education will have an income that lies within this range.

EXCEL Example 16.6

Review Example Problem 16.5. Then confirm its solution by using your computer.

SOLUTION:

1. Enter the Table 16.1 education and income data, inclusive of column heads, into worksheet columns A and B, respectively. (You can also copy and paste the data from columns L and M of the file HKMISC.)
2. Make a *point estimate* just as in EXCEL Example 16.4, with the identical result.
3. Establish the *prediction interval* by using the confidence-interval procedure of EXCEL Example 16.4, with a single change: The formula to be entered into H7 now is

=H6*H5*SQRT(1/20+(10−H4)^2/(SUMSQ(A2:A21)−20*H4^2)+1)

The result includes the desired 95% prediction interval (highlighted in red):

Point estimate	20619.22
Sample size	20
Degrees of freedom	18
X-bar	12.05
Standard error of the estimate	5377.376
Critical t	2.100924
Half-width of prediction interval	11637.1
Lower limit of prediction interval	8982.116
Upper limit of prediction interval	32256.32

Note: This type of problem can also be solved much more rapidly by using HKStat, Sheet 40.

ESTABLISHING A PREDICTION BAND FOR $I_{Y \cdot X}$

Note that the above prediction interval for $I_{Y \cdot 10}$ is considerably wider than the confidence interval for $\mu_{Y \cdot 10}$ calculated earlier. Indeed, as Figure 16.13 shows, the entire prediction band for individual values of Y, given X, lies outside the confidence band for average values of Y.

FIGURE 16.13 | A 95 Percent Prediction Band for an Individual Y, Given X

The red line in this graph is the least-squares estimated regression line of $\hat{Y}_X = 2{,}144.23 + 1{,}847.50X$ that was fitted to the sample data of Table 16.1 and first shown in Figure 16.8. Segment AC represents the 95 percent prediction interval for $I_{Y \cdot 10}$ that reaches from \$8,981.72 (point A) past the point estimate of \$20,619.23 (point B) to \$32,256.74 (point C). We can easily calculate similar intervals for individual Y values for other specified values of X; in all cases, they are wider than those for $\mu_{Y \cdot X}$. Note how the solid prediction band for predicting individual values of Y lies beyond the dashed confidence band, copied from Figure 16.12, for average values of Y.

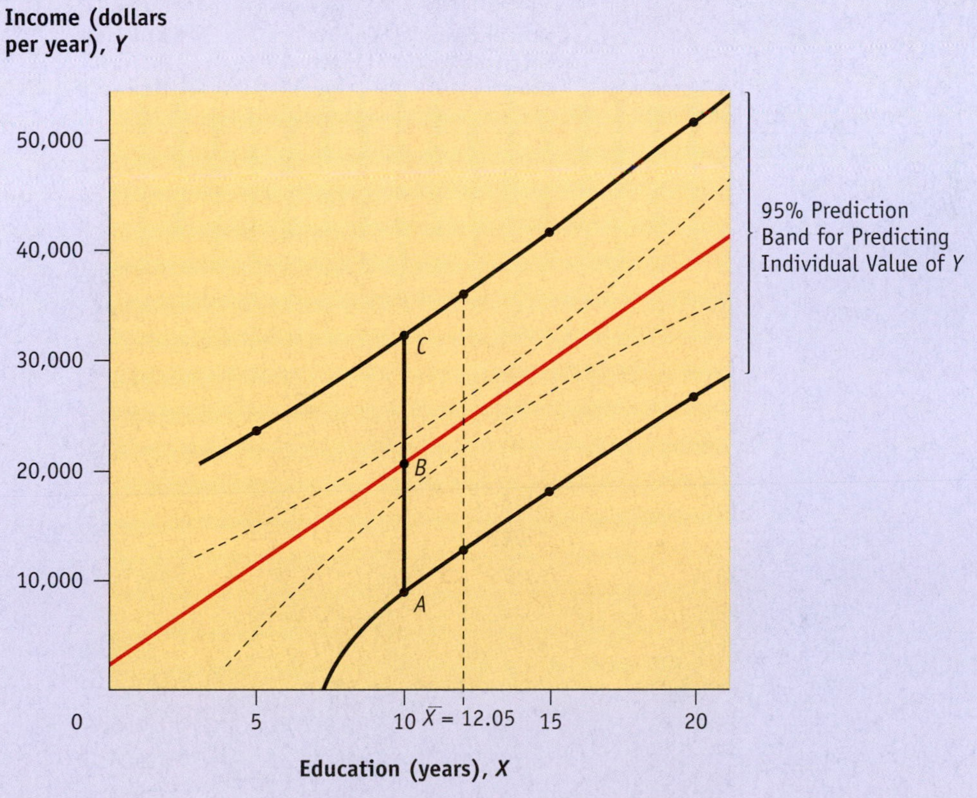

EXCEL Example 16.7

Review Figure 16.13, which is based on the Table 16.1 data. Create a similar graph by using your computer.

SOLUTION:

1. Copy the Education, Income, Predicted income, 95% Confidence Interval Lower Limit, and 95% Confidence Interval Upper Limit columns, inclusive of column heads, from EXCEL Example 16.5 into columns A–E of a new worksheet. (You can also find these data in columns L–P of the file HKMISC.)
2. Enter labels *95% Prediction Interval Lower Limit* and *95% Prediction Interval Upper Limit* into cells F1 and G1.
3. Enter the lower and upper prediction limits for the income of the next person encountered in sampling who has 10 years' education, which were generated in EXCEL Example 16.6, into cells F7 and G7, respectively.
4. Following the procedure illustrated in EXCEL Example 16.4 and 16.6, fill in the remainder of columns F and G, leading to this result:

A Education	B Income	C Predicted Income	D 95% Confidence Interval Lower Limit	E 95% Confidence Interval Upper Limit	F 95% Prediction Interval Lower Limit	G 95% Prediction Interval Upper Limit
2	5012	5839.218	-502.81	12181.24	-7116.62	18795.06
4	9680	9534.219	4233.95	14834.49	-2944.78	22013.22
8	28432	16924.22	13477.91	20370.54	5112.8	28735.64
8	8774	16924.22	13477.91	20370.54	5112.8	28735.64
8	21008	16924.22	13477.91	20370.54	5112.8	28735.64
10	26565	20619.22	17828.23	23410.21	8982.12	32256.32
12	25428	24314.22	21787.87	26840.58	12737.74	35890.71
12	23113	24314.22	21787.87	26840.58	12737.74	35890.71
12	22500	24314.22	21787.87	26840.58	12737.74	35890.71
12	19456	24314.22	21787.87	26840.58	12737.74	35890.71
12	21690	24314.22	21787.87	26840.58	12737.74	35890.71
13	24750	26161.73	23576.38	28747.07	14572.22	37751.23
14	30100	28009.23	25242.35	30776.1	16377.88	39640.57
14	24798	28009.23	25242.35	30776.1	16377.88	39640.57
15	28532	29856.73	26807.58	32905.87	18155.02	41558.43
15	26000	29856.73	26807.58	32905.87	18155.02	41558.43
16	38908	31704.23	28297.02	35111.43	19904.16	43504.3
16	22050	31704.23	28297.02	35111.43	19904.16	43504.3
17	33060	33551.73	29731.93	37371.53	21625.98	45477.48
21	48276	40941.73	35178.14	46705.32	28259.01	53624.46

5. Eliminate the above column B as well as all rows with duplicate education levels, retaining only 11 rows of data in 6 columns, which are the data to be graphed:

A	B	C	D	E	F
Education	Predicted Income	95% Confidence Interval Lower Limit	95% Confidence Interval Upper Limit	95% Prediction Interval Lower Limit	95% Prediction Interval Upper Limit
2	5839.218	−502.81	12181.24	−7116.62	18795.06
4	9534.219	4233.95	14834.49	−2944.78	22013.22
8	16924.22	13477.91	20370.54	5112.8	28735.64
10	20619.22	17828.23	23410.21	8982.12	32256.32
12	24314.22	21787.87	26840.58	12737.74	35890.71
13	26161.73	23576.38	28747.07	14572.22	37751.23
14	28009.23	25242.35	30776.1	16377.88	39640.57
15	29856.73	26807.58	32905.87	18155.02	41558.43
16	31704.23	28297.02	35111.43	19904.16	43504.3
17	33551.73	29731.93	37371.53	21625.98	45477.48
21	40941.73	35178.14	46705.32	28259.01	53624.46

6. Select the new Range A1:F12, click the **Chart Wizard** > **Standard Types** > **XY (Scatter)**, click on the third chart subtype, and click **Next** > **Next** to reach the third *Chart Wizard* dialog box.
7. Under *Value (X) axis,* type *Education (years)* and press TAB.
8. Under *Value (Y) axis,* type *Income ($/year)* and click **Next** > **Finish**.
9. Enlarge and edit the graph with a result similar to Figure 16.13:

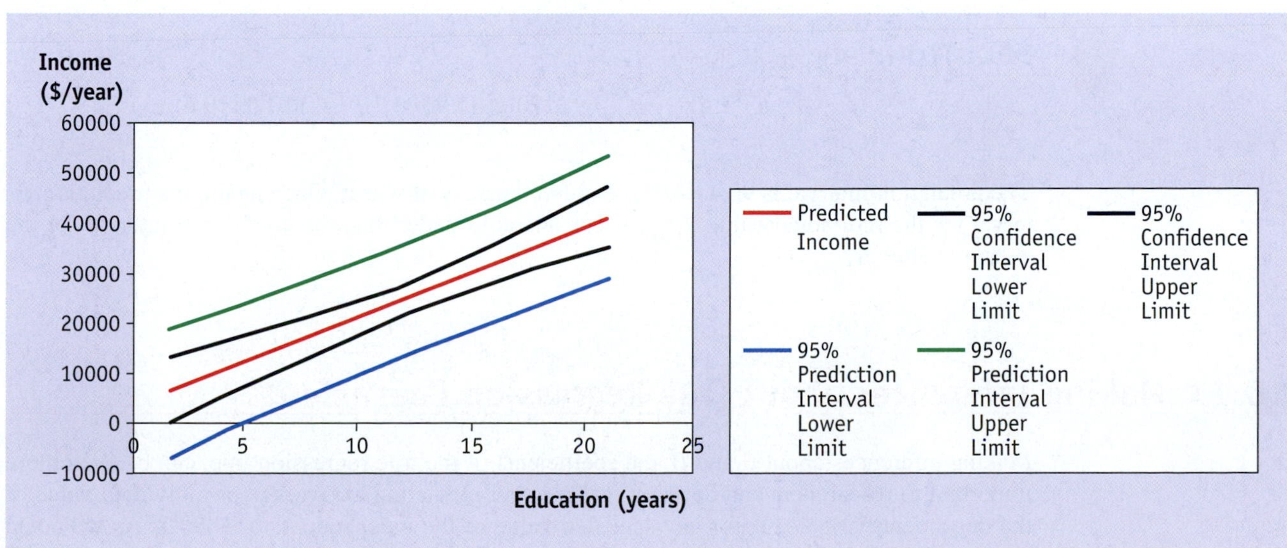

ESTABLISHING A PREDICTION INTERVAL FOR $I_{Y \cdot X}$ FROM A LARGE SAMPLE ($n \geq 30$)

In the large-sample case, Formula 16.C has to be amended only slightly, as shown in Formula 16.E.

FORMULA 16.E | Prediction-Interval Limits for an Individual Value of *Y*, Given *X* (large-sample case, $n \geq 30$)

$$I_{Y \cdot X} = \hat{Y}_X \pm (z_{\alpha/2} \cdot s_{Y \cdot X})$$

where $\hat{Y}_X$ is the estimated value of dependent variable *Y*, the *z* statistic is the standard normal deviate from Appendix Table J, and $s_{Y \cdot X}$ is the sample standard error of the estimate of *Y*, given *X*.

$$s_{Y \cdot X} = \sqrt{\frac{\Sigma(Y - \hat{Y})^2}{n - 2}} = \sqrt{\frac{\Sigma Y^2 - a\Sigma Y - b\Sigma XY}{n - 2}}$$

EXAMPLE PROBLEM 16.6

Review Example Problem 16.4. Then apply Formula 16.E to the earlier wheat-and-fertilizer study, the goal now being to predict, with 95 percent confidence, the output of the next acre, rather than the average output of many acres, on which $X = 100$ pounds of fertilizer is applied.

SOLUTION:

$$I_{Y \cdot 100} = \hat{Y}_X \pm (z_{\alpha/2} \cdot s_{Y \cdot X}) = 110 \pm (1.96 \times 10) = 110 \pm 19.6$$

The prediction interval is $90.4 \leq I_{Y \cdot 100} \leq 129.6$ bushels of wheat. Once again, the prediction interval for the individual value, $I_{Y \cdot 100}$, is considerably wider than the confidence interval for the average value, $\mu_{Y \cdot 100}$.

16.11 Making Inferences about True Regression Coefficients

Making inferences about α and β, the coefficients of the true regression line, can be even more important to researchers and decision makers than predicting an average or individual value of the dependent variable, *Y*, for any specified value of the independent variable, *X*. As we noted earlier, when the method of least squares is employed, the estimated regression coefficients, *a* and *b*, are unbiased, efficient, and consistent estimators of α and β. Yet, here, too, we may well wish to establish confidence intervals. Such is particularly common with respect to β, the slope of the true regression line. After all, there is always the danger that a positive or negative b is a fluke resulting from the selection of a highly improbable sample and that β is in fact zero, meaning there is no association whatsoever between Y and X in the population as a whole.

ESTABLISHING A CONFIDENCE INTERVAL FOR β

In any small-sample case, the limits of a confidence interval for β can be established using the t distribution as

$$\beta = b \pm t \cdot \sigma_b$$

where σ_b is the standard error of slope b and equals

$$\sigma_b = \frac{\sigma_{Y \cdot X}}{\sqrt{\Sigma X^2 - n\bar{X}^2}}$$

typically estimated by

$$s_b = \frac{s_{Y \cdot X}}{\sqrt{\Sigma X^2 - n\bar{X}^2}}$$

FORMULA 16.F | **Confidence-Interval Limits for β, the Slope of the True Regression Line (small sample case, $n < 30$)**

$$\beta \cong b \pm \left(t_{\alpha/2} \frac{s_{Y \cdot X}}{\sqrt{\Sigma X^2 - n\bar{X}^2}} \right)$$

where b is the slope of the estimated regression line, the t statistic is found in Appendix Table K for $n - 2$ degrees of freedom, $s_{Y \cdot X}$ is the sample standard error of the estimate of dependent variable Y, the X's are observed individual values of the independent variable ($\bar{X}$ being their mean), while n *is* sample size.

Note: For large samples, the normal deviate $z_{\alpha/2}$ replaces $t_{\alpha/2}$.

EXAMPLE PROBLEM 16.7

After reviewing prior example problems as needed, use Formula 16.F to establish a 95 percent confidence interval for β in the education versus income case. Interpret your result.

SOLUTION:

$$\beta \cong b \pm \left(t_{\alpha/2} \frac{s_{Y \cdot X}}{\sqrt{\Sigma X^2 - n\bar{X}^2}} \right) = 1{,}847.50 \pm \left(2.101 \frac{5{,}377.37}{\sqrt{3{,}285 - 20(12.05)^2}} \right)$$

$$= 1{,}847.50 \pm 578.84$$

Thus, the confidence interval is \$1,268.66 $\leq \beta \leq$ \$2,426.34. We can be 95 percent confident that, for the country's population as a whole, each additional year of education yields between \$1,269 and \$2,426 of additional annual income.

The confidence interval just calculated is distressingly imprecise, but nothing can increase the degree of precision except increasing sample size. (In that case, the t distribution approaches the normal distribution, and the normal deviate, z, can replace t in Formula 16.F.) You should also note that the true value of β could even lie outside the wide range calculated here. However, if we follow the above procedure of sampling and computation a large number of times, it will yield ever new but similar intervals, and they will miss the true value of β only 5 percent of the time.

EXCEL Example 16.8

Confirm the result of Example Problem 16.7 by computer.

SOLUTION:

1. Enter the Table 16.1 education and income data, inclusive of column heads, into columns A and B, respectively, of a new worksheet. (You can also copy and paste the data from columns L and M of the file HKMISC.)
2. Click **Tools** > **Data Analysis** > **Regression** > **OK**.
3. In the *Input Y Range* box, enter **B1:B21**
4. In the *Input X Range* box, enter **A1:A21**
5. Check *Labels* (because the first cell of each input column is a text label) and *New Worksheet Ply,* then click **OK**.

Along with all kinds of other things, the following output appears:

	Coefficients	*Standard Error*	*t Stat*	*P-value*	*Lower 95%*	*Upper 95%*
Intercept	2144.2163	3530.930065	0.607267	0.551258	−5273.99823	9562.4308
Education	1847.50072	275.5094036	6.705763	2.74E−06	1268.6765	2426.3249

The values of β and its 95% confidence interval limits are highlighted here.

ESTABLISHING A CONFIDENCE INTERVAL FOR α

In our small-sample case, the limits of a confidence interval for α can be established in a similar fashion as that for β.

$$\alpha = a \pm t \cdot \sigma_a$$

where σ_a is the standard error of intercept a and can be estimated by s_a as

$$\sigma_a \cong s_a = s_b \sqrt{\frac{\Sigma X^2}{n}}$$

FORMULA 16.G | **Confidence-Interval Limits for α, the Intercept of the True Regression Line (small sample case, $n < 30$)**

$$\alpha \cong a \pm \left(t_{\alpha/2} \frac{s_{Y \cdot X}}{\sqrt{\Sigma X^2 - n\overline{X}^2}} \sqrt{\frac{\Sigma X^2}{n}} \right)$$

where a is the intercept of the estimated regression line, the t statistic is found in Appendix Table K for $n - 2$ degrees of freedom, $s_{Y \cdot X}$ is the sample standard error of the estimate of dependent variable Y, the X's are observed individual values of the independent variable ($\overline{X}$ being their mean), while n *is* sample size.

Note: For large samples, the normal deviate $z_{\alpha/2}$ replaces $t_{\alpha/2}$.

EXAMPLE PROBLEM 16.8

After reviewing prior example problems as needed, use Formula 16.G to establish a 95 percent confidence interval for α in the education versus income case.

SOLUTION:

$$\alpha \cong a \pm \left(t_{\alpha/2} \frac{s_{Y \cdot X}}{\sqrt{\Sigma X^2 - n\overline{X}^2}} \sqrt{\frac{\Sigma X^2}{n}} \right)$$

$$= 2{,}144.23 \pm \left(2.101 \frac{5{,}377.37}{\sqrt{3{,}285 - 20(12.05)^2}} \sqrt{\frac{3{,}285}{20}} \right) = 2{,}144.23 \pm 7{,}418.48$$

Thus, the confidence interval is $-\$5{,}274.25 \leq \alpha \leq \$9{,}562.71$. We can be 95 percent confident that the vertical intercept of the true regression line between education and income lies within this income range.

TESTING HYPOTHESES ABOUT β

A commonly used alternative to establishing a confidence interval for β is testing a hypothesis about it. Sometimes the key question is not the precise value of β, but merely whether the value is zero. If it is zero—no matter what the value of X—the value of $\mu_{Y \cdot X}$ equals α, the true regression line is parallel to the X axis, and regression analysis is of no use in making predictions of Y from X. The usual four steps of hypothesis testing are involved.

EXAMPLE PROBLEM 16.9

Review this chapter's previous example problems on the income versus education case. Make a two-tailed hypothesis test about β, using a confidence level of 95 percent.

SOLUTION:

Step 1: H_0: $\beta = 0$ (because Y is *not* associated with X in the population)

H_A: $\beta \neq 0$ (because Y *is* associated with X in the population)

Step 2: For any small-sample case, such as our limited Table 16.1 data set, the Student t statistic is used as the test statistic. Given Formula 16.F above, and setting β equal to zero,

$$t = \frac{b}{\dfrac{s_{Y \cdot X}}{\sqrt{\Sigma X^2 - n\overline{X}^2}}}$$

Step 3: Given a desired confidence level of 95 percent (and, thus, a significance level of α = .05, where α clearly does *not* equal the vertical intercept of the true regression line), Appendix Table K implies, for $n - 2 = 18$ degrees of freedom, critical values of $\pm t_{\alpha/2} = \pm t_{.025(18)} = \pm 2.101$. Thus, the decision rule must be:

"Accept H_0 if $-2.101 \leq t \leq +2.101$."

Step 4: In our example, the actual value of t is

$$t = \frac{b}{\dfrac{s_{Y \cdot X}}{\sqrt{\Sigma X^2 - n\overline{X}^2}}} = \frac{1{,}847.50}{\dfrac{5{,}377.37}{\sqrt{3{,}285 - 20(12.05)^2}}} = 6.71$$

Accordingly, the null hypothesis should be *rejected.* At the 5 percent level of significance, the sample result (a positive slope b) is statistically significant. The observed divergence of b from the zero value of β hypothesized in the null hypothesis is unlikely to be caused merely by chance factors operating during sampling. There is good reason to embrace the alternative hypothesis: In the population as a whole, more education does mean more income.

Note: This conclusion is also evident by the nature of the 95 percent confidence interval for β calculated in Example Problem 16.7. That interval does not contain β = 0 as it would have to if H_0: $\beta = 0$ were true.

APPLICATION 16.1

EVALUATING A NEW FOOD PRODUCT

Americans are said to be eager for on-the-run meals, but only if quick meals are tasty and nutritious. The General Foods Corporation decided to bring out such a product, called H. In order to test the tastiness and nutritive quality of H, the company arranged for a 28-day rat-feeding experiment (because rats are said to have metabolic processes similar to people). Researchers then used regression techniques to evaluate the experimental data to draw conclusions about marketing such a product.

In order to provide randomization, 30 rats were divided into 10 blocks of 3 rats each such that the rats within any one block had about the same initial weight. One member of each trio was then assigned, at random, to a diet of either liquid H or solid H or to a control diet of casein. (Casein is a white, tasteless, odorless protein precipitated from milk. It is the basis of cheese, but is also used to make plastics, adhesive, paint, and various foods.) Each of the three diets contained about 9 percent protein, and the rats could eat all they wanted. Ultimately, researchers compared the rats' final and initial weights.

Panel (a) of Figure 16.A shows a scatter diagram of the results. Panel (b) shows the regression lines for the 3 dietary groups, relating 28-day weight gain, Y, to protein intake, X.

The equations of the panel (b) regression lines were as follows:

for liquid H:	$\hat{Y}_X = -4.124 + 3.72X$
for solid H:	$\hat{Y}_X = -8.478 + 3.66X$
for casein control:	$\hat{Y}_X = -3.644 + 2.91X$

The company statisticians concluded (1) from the position of the H lines to the right of the casein line that rats ate

(continued)

FIGURE 16.A

(a)

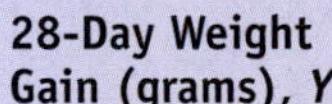

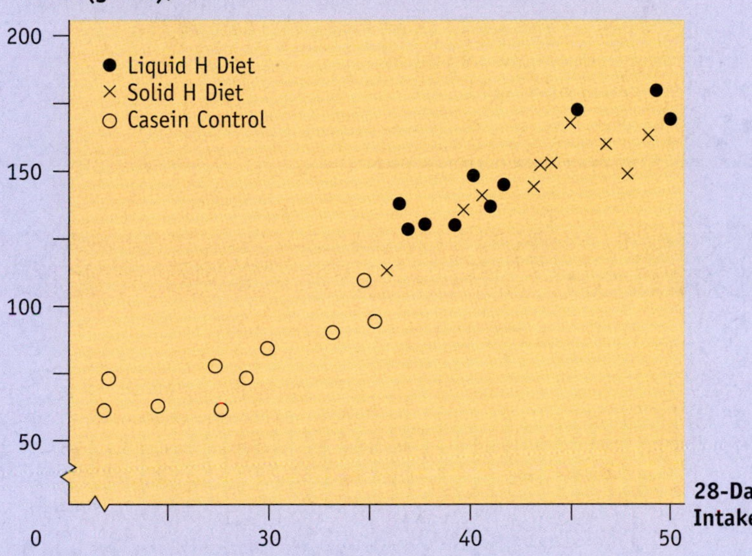

(b)

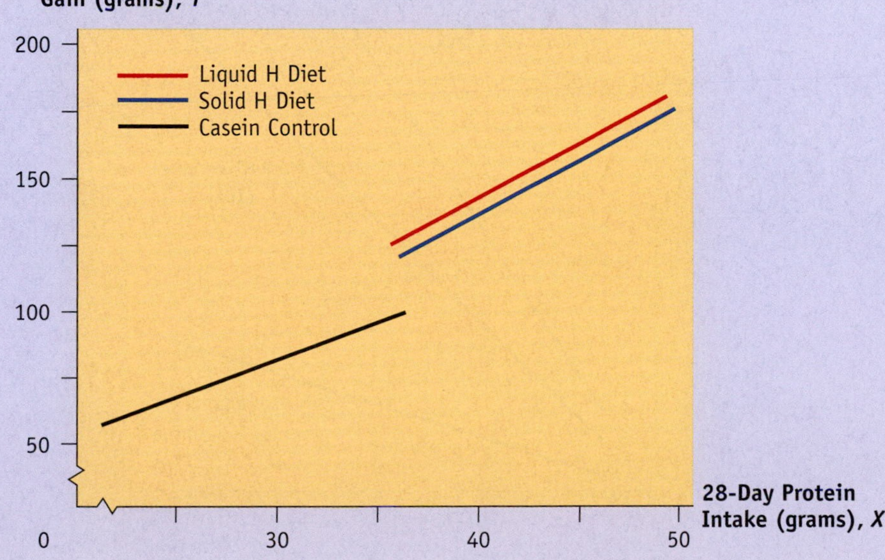

(continued)

Application 16.1 (continued)

more H than casein because H was more palatable (at least to rats) and (2) from the higher slope of the H lines that the protein efficiency of H was superior to that of the control diet (protein contained in H resulted in greater weight gain). The difference between the slopes of the H lines (3.72 versus 3.66) was not statistically significant; the difference between the H-line slopes and the slope of the casein line (2.91), however, was.

SOURCE: Adapted from Elisabeth Street and Mavis B. Carroll, "Preliminary Evaluation of a New Food Product," in Judith M. Tanur et al., eds., *Statistics: A Guide to the Unknown* (San Francisco: Holden-Day, 1972), pp. 220–228.

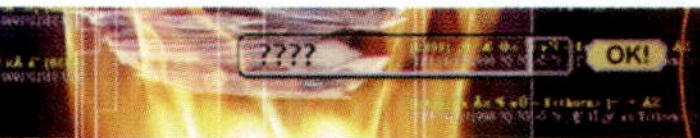

APPLICATION 16.2

Of Bulls, Bears, and Beauty

Stock market analysts sometimes characterize the riskiness of a particular stock, such as TWA, IBM, or Procter & Gamble in the 1980s, with the help of a sample regression line that relates the stock's rate of return to the average rate of return on all stocks, as in Figure 16.B.

Depending on whether the slope, β, of the true regression line is believed to exceed, equal, or fall short of 1, the stock is referred to as *aggressive, marketlike,* or *defensive.* In a bull market, when the average rate of return on all stocks is rising, an aggressive stock gains more than the

FIGURE 16.B

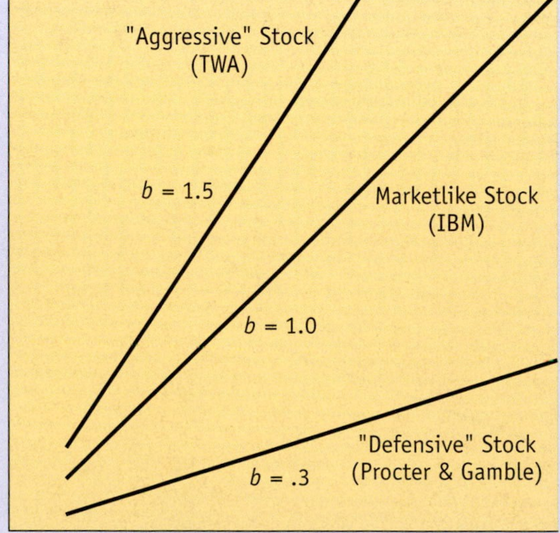

(continued)

Application 16.2 (continued)

FIGURE 16.C

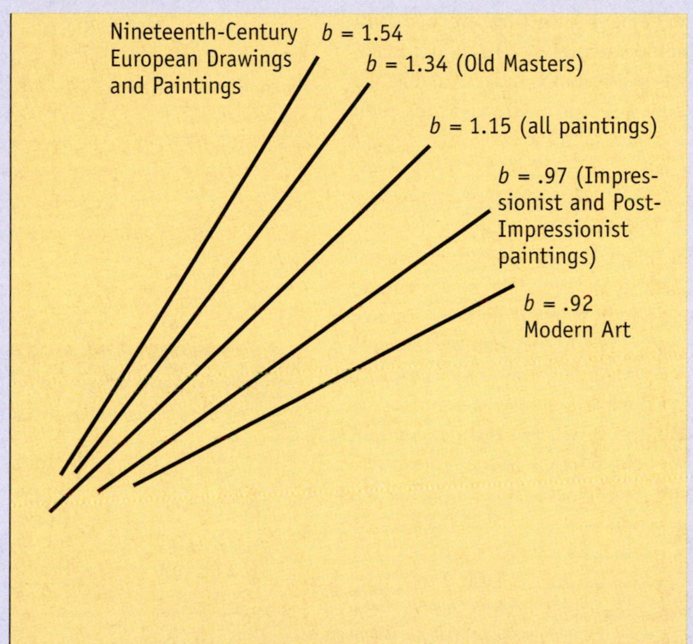

average; a defensive stock gains less. In a bear market, when the average rate of return on all stocks is falling, an aggressive stock loses more than the average; a defensive stock loses less. Clearly, an investor is well advised to own aggressive stocks in a bull market, but defensive stocks in a bear market. Thus, stock market analysts are always engaging in "beta analysis."

Note: Figure 16.B refers to stock behavior noted in the 1980s, which need not hold today. Indeed, TWA has since disappeared from the scene.

Figure 16.C tells a similar story. An economist derived 1971–1984 rates of return on particular types of paintings from components of the well-known art-market price index produced by Sotheby's London auction house and compared these returns on particular assets with the average rate of return on a market portfolio of bonds, real estate, and stocks. Differences in riskiness similar to those connected with particular stocks emerged.

SOURCES: Adapted from Charles L. Olson and Mario J. Picconi, *Statistics for Business Decision Making* (Glenview, Ill.: Scott, Foresman and Company, 1983), p. 496; and Michael F Bryan, "Beauty and the Bulls: The Investment Characteristics of Paintings," *Federal Reserve Bank of Cleveland Economic Review,* 1, 1985, pp. 2–10.

APPLICATION 16.3

THE ECONOMY AND THE BALLOT BOX

During the 1992 presidential campaign, the president, George Bush, had a problem. Voters clearly thought that he had concentrated too much on foreign policy, while being uninterested in domestic, pocketbook issues. This perception probably cost him the election, because the economy had entered a recession in the summer of 1990 and was terribly slow in climbing out of its slump. Indeed, as historic evidence shows, the popular vote for incumbent presidents has long been closely associated with the economic climate in the election year. Whenever real output has been rising rapidly or unemployment has been falling, incumbent parties have enjoyed the credit and received more votes. Whenever output has been stagnating or unemployment has been rising, incumbent parties have taken the blame and received fewer votes. Consider how prior declines in real output growth swept opposition-party candidates into office: Hayes in 1876, Cleveland in 1884, McKinley in 1896, Harding in 1920, Roosevelt in 1932, Kennedy in 1960, Reagan in 1980, Clinton in 1992. Consider, in contrast, how falling election-year unemployment rates were associated with incumbent-party candidates capturing the White House: Truman in 1948, Johnson in 1964, Nixon in 1972, Reagan in 1984, Bush in 1988.

Simple regression analysis is ideally suited to model the type of voter behavior described here. Consider the presidential election years between 1948 and 1996. Table 16.A presents data on popular vote percentages captured by the incumbent-party candidates, along with the election-year growth rates of real gross domestic product (GDP). A computer establishes the following regression equation based on these data:

$$\text{Vote} = 41.9 + 2.14\ \text{Growth}$$

This equation indicates that during 1948–1996, the party of the incumbent president could expect to capture 41.9 percent of the popular vote plus another 2.14 percentage points for every 1 percent of real GDP growth during the election year. Thus, 0 percent real GDP growth would produce 41.9 percent of the popular vote for the incumbent-party candidate and, quite probably, an associated loss in the Electoral College. On the other hand, a vigorous 5 percent real GDP growth would give the incumbent 41.9 + 2.14(5) = 52.6 percent of the popular vote and a likely win.

Caution is advised, however. The point of this application is to illustrate the possible uses of simple regression analysis. No claim is made that the model of voting behavior presented here is the best possible one or even a good one. For other discussions of similar models, see David E. Rosenbaum, "Recession and Reelection Don't Mix," *The New York Times,* October 9, 1991, pp. D1 and 5; Ray C. Fair, "The Effect of Economic Events on Votes for President," *The Review of Economics and Statistics,* May 1978, pp. 159–173; Peter Passell, "Sideshows Aside, Economy Is Still Key to Elections," *The New York Times,* January 2, 1996, p. C3.

TABLE 16.A | U.S. Presidential Election Data

Election Year	Percentage of Popular Vote Captured by Incumbent President, *Y*	Election-Year Growth Rate (percent), *X*
1948	49.6	3.8
1952	44.4	4.3
1956	57.4	2.0
1960	49.5	2.4
1964	61.1	5.8
1968	42.7	4.7
1972	60.7	5.5
1976	48.0	5.4
1980	41.0	−0.3
1984	58.8	7.0
1988	53.4	3.8
1992	37.4	2.7
1996	49.2	3.4

16.12 Simple Correlation Analysis

While simple regression analysis establishes a precise equation that links two variables, *simple correlation analysis* seeks to establish a general index about their strength of association. Depending on the size of this quantitative measure, we can tell how closely two variables move together and, therefore, how reliably we can estimate one variable with the help of the other. But note: As Chapter 5 has shown, just because two variables are associated with one another does not necessarily mean that there is a causal link between them.

DEFINITION 16.9 A statistical technique that establishes an index that provides, in a single number, a measure of the strength of association between two variables is **simple correlation analysis.**

Consider the three panels of Figure 16.14. When all the points in a scatter diagram lie precisely on the estimated regression line, as in panel (a), the index we discuss in this section will show the variables to be *perfectly correlated.* In that case, we can always predict Y with precision from a knowledge of the regression line and any value of X. When, on the other hand, the points in a scatter diagram are so widely scattered as to make X completely worthless as a predictor of Y, as in panel (b), the index will show the variables to be *completely uncorrelated.* When, finally, many scattered points diverge from the regression line, but still suggest some definite association between the variables, such as the direct association in panel (c), the index will show the variables to be *imperfectly correlated.*

FIGURE 16.14 | Different Degrees of Correlation

The three panels of this graph illustrate different degrees of correlation. Depending on whether the scatter of data points around a regression line is nonexistent, considerable, or moderate, correlation between the variables is said to be (a) perfect, (b) zero, or (c) weak.

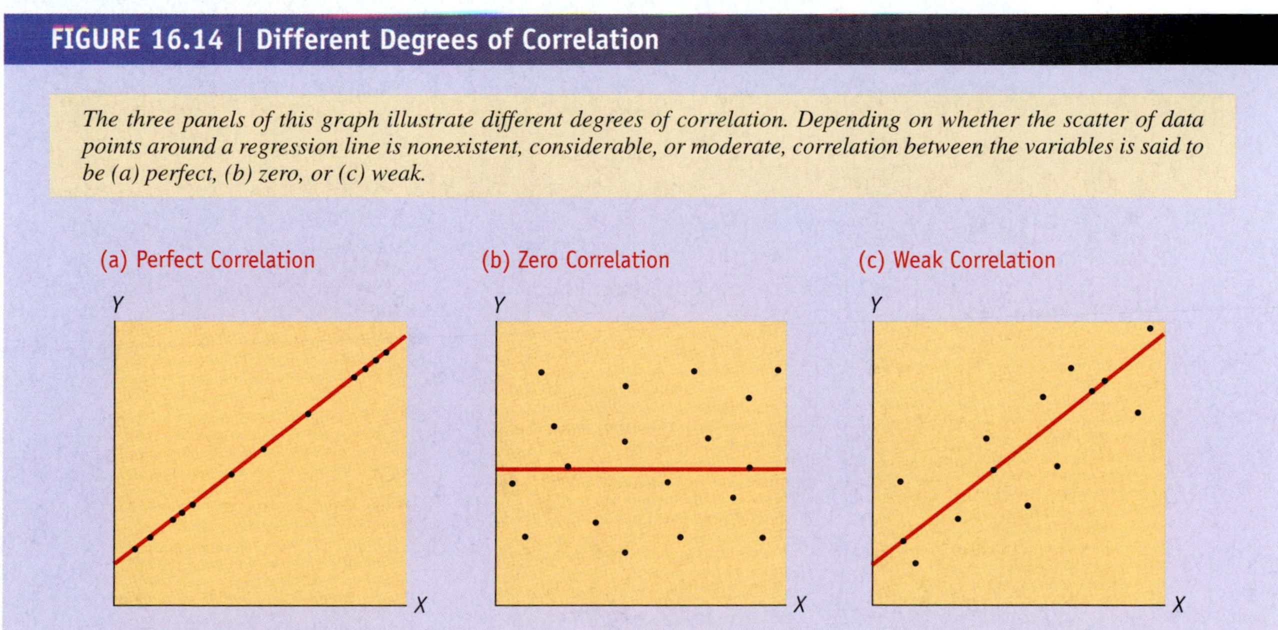

Statisticians use several indexes of association between quantitative variables, including:

- the coefficient of determination
- the coefficient of correlation
- the coefficient of nondetermination
- the coefficient of alienation

As the following sections will show, each of these indexes tells the same story in a different way (just as a glass half filled with water might be described as half full *or* half empty) and the use of one or the other is a matter of personal preference. (In Chapter 21, we will meet another such index yet: *Spearman's rank-correlation coefficient,* which is the most important measure of the degree of association between *qualitative* data, although we can use it with quantitative data as well.)

THE COEFFICIENT OF DETERMINATION

The most popular measure of how well an estimated regression line fits the sample data on which it is based is the **sample coefficient of determination.** It equals the proportion of the total variation in the values of the dependent variable, Y, that can be explained by the association of Y with X as measured by the estimated regression line. Figure 16.15 can help us see what is involved.

Imagine Figure 16.15 as a scatter diagram with all the dots removed except point A, which corresponds to the data pair of $X = 20$, $Y = 30$. Assume that the red line represents the estimated regression line calculated from the complete data set and that the average value of Y is $\overline{Y} = 15$, as illustrated by the horizontal line. The difference between any particular observation of the dependent variable, such as $Y = 30$ when $X = 20$ (point A) and the mean of all such observations, such as $\overline{Y} = 15$ (point C), is the **total deviation of** Y (distance AC).

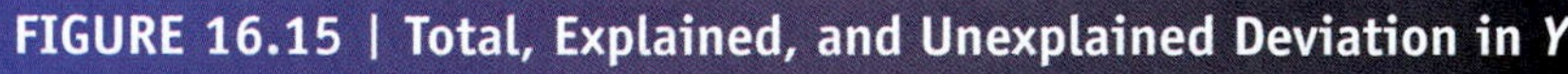

FIGURE 16.15 | Total, Explained, and Unexplained Deviation in *Y*

The total deviation (here AC) of any observed value of Y from the mean of all such observations ($\overline{Y}$) always equals the sum of the explained deviation (here BC) and the unexplained deviation (here AB).

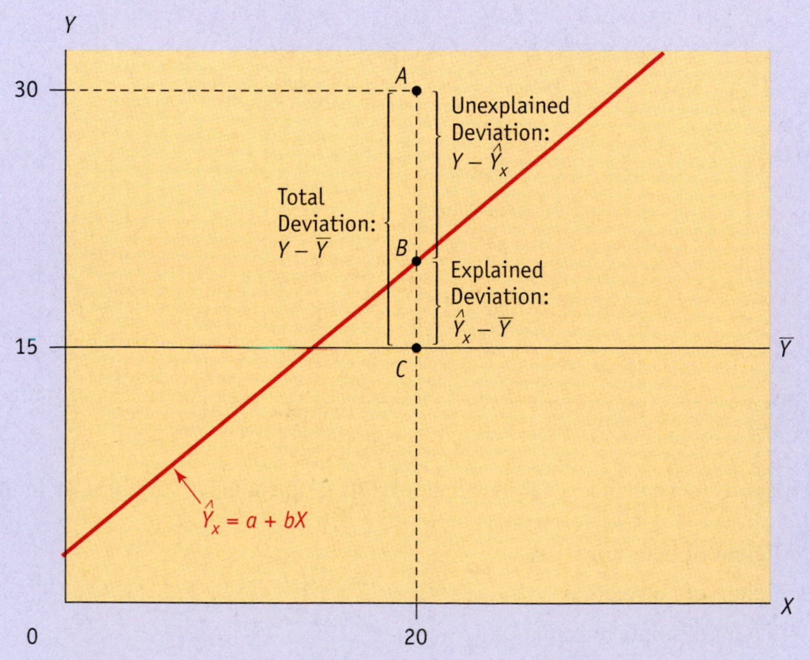

Of course, we see many such deviations in a scatter diagram, one between each individual observation of Y (of which only one, point A, is shown here) and the common mean of all these Y's. Now imagine squaring all these total deviations and summing them. The resulting sum of squares of total deviations, $\Sigma(Y - \overline{Y})^2$, is called the **total variation of *Y*,** or the **total sum of squares *(Total SS).***

Next, focus on the difference between the regression estimate of our observed Y, or $\hat{Y}_{20}$ (point B), and the average Y (point C). This difference is the **explained deviation of $\overline{Y}$** (distance BC). We can see where this name originates: The *positive* deviation, BC, of $\hat{Y}_X$ from $\overline{Y}$ is explained by the fact that Y rises with X and the value of $X = 20$ is above average. If we had chosen $X = 5$ for our example, we would explain a similar *negative* deviation in an analogous fashion—namely, by $X = 5$ being below average. Now imagine squaring all these explained deviations in the scatter diagram and summing them. The resulting sum of squares of the explained deviations, $\Sigma(\hat{Y}_X - \overline{Y})^2$, is called the **explained variation of *Y*,** or the **regression sum of squares *(RSS).***

Finally, focus on the difference between our particular observation of Y when $X = 20$ (point A) and the corresponding regression estimate, $\hat{Y}_{20}$ (point B). This difference is the **unexplained deviation of *Y*** (distance AB). Again, we can see the reason for this name: The fact that Y rises with X as shown by the regression line explains why our observed Y (point A) lies above $\overline{Y}$ to the extent of BC, but it does not explain the additional deviation of AB. Now imagine squaring all these unexplained deviations in the scatter diagram and summing them. The resulting sum of squares of unexplained deviations, $\Sigma(Y - \hat{Y}_X)^2$, is called the **unexplained variation of *Y*,** or the **error sum of squares *(ESS).*** The method of least squares guarantees that we minimize this error component.

Just as the total deviation is the sum of explained deviation and unexplained deviation (see Figure 16.15), so the total variation is the sum of explained variation and unexplained variation. Formula 16.H summarizes this result.

FORMULA 16.H | The Components of Total Variation

total variation = explained variation + unexplained variation

or

total sum of squares (*Total SS*)	=	regression sum of squares (*RSS*)	+	error sum of squares (*ESS*)

or

$$\Sigma(Y - \overline{Y})^2 = \Sigma(\hat{Y}_X - \overline{Y})^2 + \Sigma(Y - \hat{Y}_X)^2$$

where Y's are observed individual values of the dependent variable ($\overline{Y}$ being their mean) and $\hat{Y}_X$ is the estimated value of Y, given a value of independent variable X.

Given the relationships in Formula 16.H, the meaning of the sample coefficient of determination, usually symbolized by r^2, is quite clear—as shown in Formula 16.I on the next page.

FORMULA 16.I | The Sample Coefficient of Determination

$$r^2 = \frac{\text{explained variation}}{\text{total variation}} = \frac{RSS}{Total\ SS} = \frac{\Sigma(\hat{Y}_X - \overline{Y})^2}{\Sigma(Y - \overline{Y})^2}$$

or

$$r^2 = \frac{Total\ SS - ESS}{Total\ SS} = 1 - \frac{ESS}{Total\ SS} = 1 - \frac{\Sigma(Y - \hat{Y}_X)^2}{\Sigma(Y - \overline{Y})^2}$$

where Y's are observed individual values of the dependent variable ($\overline{Y}$ being their mean) and $\hat{Y}_X$ is the estimated value of Y, given a value of independent variable X.

Note: The following formula, which makes use of the estimated regression coefficients, a and b, is mathematically equivalent to the above:

$$r^2 = \frac{a\Sigma Y + b\Sigma XY - n\overline{Y}^2}{\Sigma Y^2 - n\overline{Y}^2}$$

When X and Y are perfectly correlated, as in panel (a) of Figure 16.14, every $Y = \hat{Y}_X$; hence, $\Sigma(Y - \hat{Y}_X)^2 = 0$, and $r^2 = 1$. When instead X and Y are completely uncorrelated, the regression line has a slope of zero, as in panel (b) of Figure 16.14. Then $\hat{Y}_X = \overline{Y}$, and $r^2 = 0$. Thus, the value of r^2 always lies between 1 (perfect correlation) and 0 (no correlation).

EXAMPLE PROBLEM 16.10

Review the previous example problems dealing with the education versus income case. Use Formula 16.I to compute the sample coefficient of determination, r^2 and interpret it.

SOLUTION:

$$r^2 = \frac{a\Sigma Y + b\Sigma XY - n\overline{Y}^2}{\Sigma Y^2 - n\overline{Y}^2}$$

$$= \frac{2{,}144.23(488{,}132) + 1{,}847.5(6{,}585{,}796) - 20(24{,}406.6)^2}{13{,}734{,}414{,}590 - 20(24{,}406.6)^2} = .71$$

This coefficient indicates that 71 percent of the total variation of Y observed in Figure 16.8 can be explained by the association of Y (income) with X (education) as estimated by the regression line shown there. Naturally, statisticians are always pleased with a high r^2 because it indicates that they have explained a large proportion of the variation in the variable of interest. However, the sample coefficient of determination varies from sample to sample; r^2 is only an estimate of the underlying **population coefficient of determination,** denoted by ρ^2 (the lowercase Greek rho, squared). The latter measures how well the *true* regression line fits the population data and equals the proportion of the total variation in the values of the dependent variable, Y, that can be explained by the association of Y with X as measured by the true regression line.

THE COEFFICIENT OF CORRELATION

The square root of the sample coefficient of determination is a common alternative index of the degree of association between two quantitative variables. This is the **sample coefficient of correlation (r)** and is a point estimator of the underlying **population coefficient of correlation (ρ).**

Just like r^2, the coefficient r takes on absolute values between 0 and 1. But note that the square root of any number can be positive or negative. Taking advantage of this fact, statisticians commonly place a plus sign or a minus sign in front of r to denote, respectively, a direct relationship or an inverse relationship between X and Y. Thus, $r = 0$ denotes no correlation, while $r = +1$ or $r = -1$ denotes perfect correlation between directly or inversely related variables, respectively. In our example, therefore, in which income *rises* with education, the $r^2 = .71$ translates into a *positive* number, denoting a direct relationship: $r = \sqrt{.71} = +.84$.

EXCEL Example 16.9

Confirm the computation of the correlation coefficient of $r = +.84$ in the income versus education case with the help of a computer.

SOLUTION:

1. Enter the Table 16.1 education and income data, inclusive of column heads, into columns A and B, respectively, of a new worksheet. (You can also copy and paste the data from columns L and M of the file HKMISC.)
2. Click on an empty cell; then click the **Function Wizard (*fx*)** > **Statistical** > **CORREL** > **OK**.
3. In the *Correlation* dialog box, under *Array 1,* enter **A1:A21** and press TAB.
4. Under *Array 2,* enter **B1:B21** and click **OK**.

The following result appears in the selected cell: **.845066**.

APPLICATION 16.4

THE UNEVEN BURDEN OF INTERNATIONAL TRADE RESTRAINTS

Many U.S. industries request governmental protection from international competition. When granted, such protection helps those who supply resources to the industries involved, such as factory owners and workers, but it harms consumers who must pay higher prices. In one year studied by the Federal Reserve, American consumers spent at least $16 billion more just because of the protective measures designed to help the domestic automobile, clothing, sugar, and steel industries. However, this burden was not shared equally. The higher prices caused by protection were equivalent to a 23 percent income-tax surcharge for families earning less than $10,000 a year, but equivalent to only a 3 percent income-tax surcharge for families earning over $60,000 a year. The correlation between harm so measured and size of family income was strong and negative: −.83.

SOURCE: Based on Susan Hickok, "The Consumer Cost of U.S. Trade Restraints," *Federal Reserve Bank of New York Quarterly Review,* Summer 1985, pp. 1–12.

The nature of correlation is often misunderstood—in at least three ways.

First, the correlation coefficient discussed in this section can only detect *linear* associations between variables. Our formula might quite possibly calculate $r = 0$ from a set of data such as that underlying panel (c) of Figure 16.4 on page 712—thus, falsely suggesting no association between X and Y—when, in fact, there is no *linear* association, but quite a pronounced curvilinear one.

Second, many statisticians prefer to use r^2 rather than r as a measure of association because fairly high absolute values of r (such as .70) can give the false impression of a strong association between Y and X (but in this case, $r^2 = .49$; thus, the association of Y with X explains less than half of the variation of Y). Only at the extremes, when $r = \pm 1$ or when $r = 0$ (and, therefore, $r = r^2$), does the value of r directly convey what proportion of the variation of Y is explained by X.

Third, we must reemphasize that the correlation coefficient measures only the strength of a statistical relationship between two variables, but the discovery of a strong statistical relationship between Y and X need not imply a causal one. Perhaps X does cause Y; perhaps Y is causing X, perhaps each is part cause, part effect of the other. Quite possibly, the two variables move together by pure chance. Indeed, the existence of a high positive or negative correlation between two variables that have no logical connection with one another at all is common and is called **nonsense correlation** or **spurious correlation.** By pure chance we might discover, for example, a correlation coefficient of $r = +.98$ between the numbers of ministers and of abortions in the 50 states or a correlation coefficient of $r = -.89$ between the numbers of whales caught in the world's oceans and congressional expenditures on stationery. Oftentimes, such statistical associations mean nothing at all. Sometimes, they reflect the operation of some third factor, such as population differences, that affects both of the variables, simultaneously producing, say, more ministers and also more abortions in states where population is larger. Application 16.5, *Snowfall and Unemployment,* provides a vivid illustration of the spurious correlation problem. The stories told by Applications 16.6, *Jukebox Economics,* and 16.7, *Small Is Beautiful: The Relationship between Height and Longevity,* may well fall in the same category.

APPLICATION 16.5

SNOWFALL AND UNEMPLOYMENT

A splendid example of spurious correlation is provided by the data in Table 16.B.

A scatter diagram reveals a strong positive association between the two variables; their relationship can be summarized by the least-squares regression line:

$$\hat{Y}_X = .3764 + .0955X$$

which is also shown in Figure 16.D on the next page. The coefficient of determination is $r^2 = .967$, implying that 96.7 percent of the variation in U.S. unemployment between 1973 and 1982 can be explained by variations in snowfall at Amherst, Massachusetts. Yet this association is totally unreasonable. Nobody would be prepared to argue that the strong association between U.S. unemployment and the extent of snowfall in a small New England town is anything but pure coincidence.

TABLE 16.B

Year	U.S. Unemployment Rate (percent), Y	Snowfall at Amherst, Mass. (inches per year), X
1973	4.9	45
1974	5.6	59
1975	8.5	82
1976	7.7	80
1977	7.1	71
1978	6.1	60
1979	5.8	55
1980	7.1	69
1981	7.6	79
1982	9.7	95

SOURCES: *Economic Report of the President* (Washington, D.C.: U.S. Government Printing Office, 1983), p. 199; and data collected by the author.

(continued)

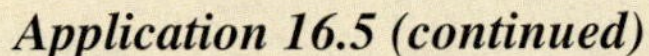

Application 16.5 (continued)

FIGURE 16.D

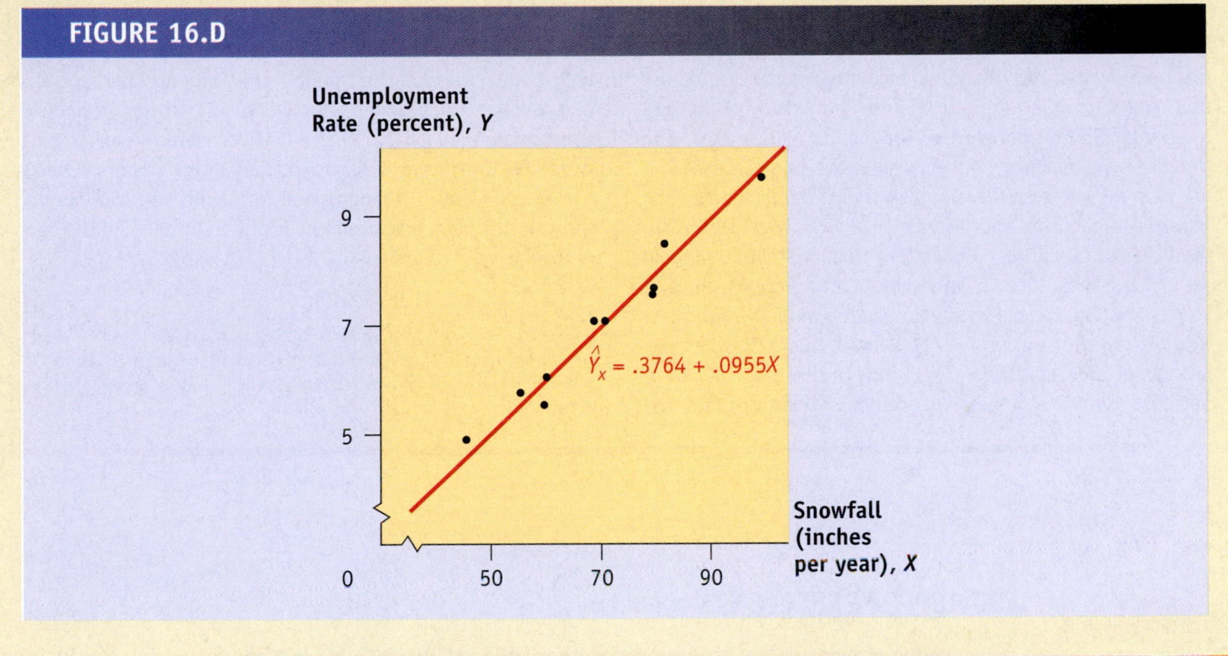

APPLICATION 16.6

JUKEBOX ECONOMICS

Economists are forever looking for a reliable forecaster of the business cycle, the ever-present tendency for national output and employment to rise and fall in alternating periods of time, along with similar variations in the overall price level. Recently, Harold Zullow, a research fellow in social psychiatry, came up with an unusual new device. He studied 40 years' worth of popular songs, from "Love Is a Many-Splendored Thing" (1955) to "Puff the Magic Dragon" (1963) and the more recent "Nothing Compares 2 U" (1990). From the lyrics of 1,344 songs, he learned much about consumer confidence, he says, and he noted a strong correlation between consumer confidence so measured and the timing of recessions.

For the seven major recessions since World War II (1958, 1960–1961, 1970, 1974–1975, 1980, 1981–1982, and 1990–1992) he found this: Pessimistic songs were issued a year before the economy turned sour, and optimistic songs appeared a year before things started to get better.

SOURCE: Adapted from James Barron, "Jukebox Economics," *The New York Times,* January 27, 1992, pp. B1 and 4.

Small Is Beautiful: The Relationship between Height and Longevity

For many years, anecdotal evidence has been accumulating that suggests a strong correlation between height and longevity: Shorter people live longer than taller ones. The longest-lived Japanese, for example, are Okinawans, who are also the shortest. The longest-living Pakistanis are the Hunzas—again, the shortest. Or take U.S. presidents who died of natural causes: Those less than 5′8″ tall averaged 80.2 years; those over 6′ tall averaged 68.5 years. Similar stories abound. Recent medical research pursuing the question of why women, on average, live longer than men has noted a greater incidence of all kinds of diseases, including varicose veins, pulmonary tuberculosis, heart disease, and breast cancer, among tall people than among short people of either sex. One economist, Dennis D. Miller, collected appropriate data on 1,679 deaths from natural causes that were investigated in 1985 by the Cuyahoga County (Ohio) Coroner's Office. A regression of death age on height showed that each additional inch of height reduced the age of death by 1.2 years.

SOURCE: Adapted from Dennis D. Miller, "Economies of Scale," *Challenge,* May–June 1990, pp. 58–61. For more on the subject, see Thomas T. Samaras, *The Truth about Your Height* (San Diego, Calif.: Tecolote Publications, 1994).

OTHER COEFFICIENTS

On occasion, we are apt to meet two other indexes of association, but they are merely mirror images of the two just discussed. The **sample coefficient of nondetermination (k^2)** equals the proportion of total variation in the values of the dependent variable, Y, that *cannot* be explained by the association of Y with X as measured by the estimated regression line. The square root of this measure, the **sample coefficient of alienation (k),** is used even less frequently. It is a measure of the lack of correlation. Formula 16.J explains.

FORMULA 16.J | The Sample Coefficient of Nondetermination

$$k^2 = 1 - r^2 = \frac{\text{unexplained variation}}{\text{total variation}} = \frac{ESS}{Total\ SS} = \frac{\Sigma(Y - \hat{Y}_X)^2}{\Sigma(Y - \overline{Y})^2}$$

where r^2 is the sample coefficient of determination, Y's are observed individual values of the dependent variable ($\overline{Y}$ being their mean), and $\hat{Y}_X$ is the estimated value of Y, given a value of independent variable X.

Note: The square root of the above measure, $\sqrt{k^2} = k$, known as the *sample coefficient of alienation,* serves as a measure of the lack of correlation.

EXAMPLE PROBLEM 16.11

Review Example Problem 16.10. Then use Formula 16.J to calculate

a. the sample coefficient of nondetermination.

b. the sample coefficient of alienation.

SOLUTION:

a. Given the result of Example Problem 16.10, the value of $k^2 = 1 - .71 = .29$, indicating that 29 percent of the total variation in Y observed in Figure 16.8 remains unexplained by the association of Y (income) with X (education) as estimated by the regression line shown there.

b. Given $k^2 = .29$, $k = \sqrt{k^2} = \sqrt{.29} = .54$. The closer this number is to 1, the weaker is the correlation between X and Y.

16.13 Testing β with Analysis of Variance

Example Problem 16.11 tested the hypothesis that $\beta = 0$. The analysis of variance, introduced in Chapter 15, provides an alternative way of testing this hypothesis. The ANOVA procedure yields the same result as the t test employed above, but with one major advantage: It can be applied to multiple regression problems as well (as the next chapter will show). The ANOVA test makes use of the three sums of squares defined in Formula 16.H, the regression sum of squares, the error sum of squares, and the total sum of squares.

EXAMPLE PROBLEM 16.12

Review the previous example problems dealing with the education versus income case. Then, without using a computer, make an ANOVA test of the hypothesis H_0: $\beta = 0$, and do so at a 5 percent level of significance.

SOLUTION: We can compute the sums of squares from the data of Table 16.2 and Formula 16. H, but we can also derive them from mathematically equivalent expressions:

$$RSS = \Sigma(\hat{Y}_X - \bar{Y})^2 = a\Sigma Y + b\Sigma XY - n\bar{Y}^2$$
$$= 2{,}144.23(488{,}132) + 1{,}847.5(6{,}585{,}796) - 20(24{,}406.6)^2 = 1{,}300{,}282{,}917.16$$
$$ESS = \Sigma(Y - \hat{Y}_X)^2 = \Sigma Y^2 - a\Sigma Y - b\Sigma XY$$
$$= 13{,}734{,}414{,}590 - 2{,}144.23(488{,}132) - 1{,}847.5(6{,}585{,}796) = 520{,}489{,}201.64$$
$$Total\ SS = \Sigma(Y - \bar{Y})^2 = \Sigma Y^2 - n\bar{Y}^2$$
$$= 13{,}734{,}414{,}590 - 20(24{,}406.6)^2 = 1{,}820{,}772{,}118.80$$

These sums of squares have been entered in column 1 of Table 16.3. The appropriate degrees of freedom appear in column 2. They equal the number of independent variables, m, for the regression sum of squares. They equal sample size n, minus 2 for the error sum of squares (there are n errors and 2 constraints—namely, the estimated regression coefficients, a and b). They equal $n - 1$ for the total sum of squares, because there are n deviations subject to the constraint that $\Sigma(Y - \bar{Y}) = 0$.

From this information, we can derive the regression and error mean squares of column 3. These mean squares are sample variances that we can use to calculate F, as shown in column 4.

We are ready to test H_0: $\beta = 0$ at the 5 percent level of significance. We can find the critical value of F in Appendix Table N for 1 numerator *d.f.* and 18 denominator *d.f.* as $F_{.05(1,18)} = 4.41$. Thus, there is only a 5 percent chance that the computed value of F exceeds 4.41 if H_0 is true. Accordingly, as in our t test in Example Problem 16.7, we *reject* H_0. We conclude that $\beta \neq 0$ and that X (education) does help explain the variation in Y (income) in the population as a whole.

TABLE 16.3 | The ANOVA Table

Source of Variation	Sum of Squares (1)	Degrees of Freedom (2)	Mean Square (3) = (1) ÷ (2)	Test Statistic (4)
Regression (variation explained by X)	RSS = 1,300,282,917.16	$m = 1$	RMS = 1,300,282,917.6	$F = \frac{RMS}{EMS} = 44.97$
Error (unexplained variation)	ESS = 520,489,201.64	$n - 2 = 18$	EMS = 28,916,066.76	
Total	$Total\ SS$ = 1,820,772,118.80	$n - 1 = 19$		

EXCEL Example 16.10

Review Example Problem 16.12. Confirm its result by computer.

SOLUTION:

1. Enter the Table 16.1 education and income data, inclusive of column heads, into columns A and B, respectively, of a new worksheet. (You can also copy and paste the data from columns L and M of the file HKMISC.)
2. Click **Tools** > **Data Analysis** > **Regression** > **OK**.
3. In the *Input Y Range* box, enter **B1:B21**
4. In the *Input X Range* box, enter **A1:A21**
5. Check *Labels* (because the first cell of each input column is a text label) and *New Worksheet Ply,* then click **OK**.

Along with all kinds of other things, the following output appears:

ANOVA

	df	*SS*	*MS*	*F*	*Significance F*
Regression	1	1300280985	1300280985	44.9673	2.74455E−06
Residual	18	520491134.2	28916174.12		
Total	19	1820772119			

COMMENT Except for rounding, the computer-produced ANOVA table corresponds to Table 16.3; the (highlighted) F statistic, and, therefore, the conclusion is identical to the one in Example Problem 16.12.

16.14 An Extension: Curvilinear Regression

So far, we have focused entirely on linear regression, but we can also adapt the technique to analyze data that clearly reveal a curvilinear association between two variables.

APPROXIMATING CURVILINEAR BY LINEAR REGRESSION LINES

One approach, illustrated in Figure 16.16, involves fitting piecewise linear regression lines to the data, with each of these lines being restricted to specified intervals of X values. This approach is particularly good when no simple curve can be found that summarizes the data very well.

FIGURE 16.16 | Approximating Curvilinear by Linear Regression

A curvilinear association between two variables can sometimes be approximated well by fitting several linear regression lines to the data and restricting the use of each line to specified ranges of X values. In the example given here, one linear regression line estimates the values of Y for X values between a and b, a second linear regression line estimates Y for X values between b and c, and a third linear regression line estimates Y for X values between c and d.

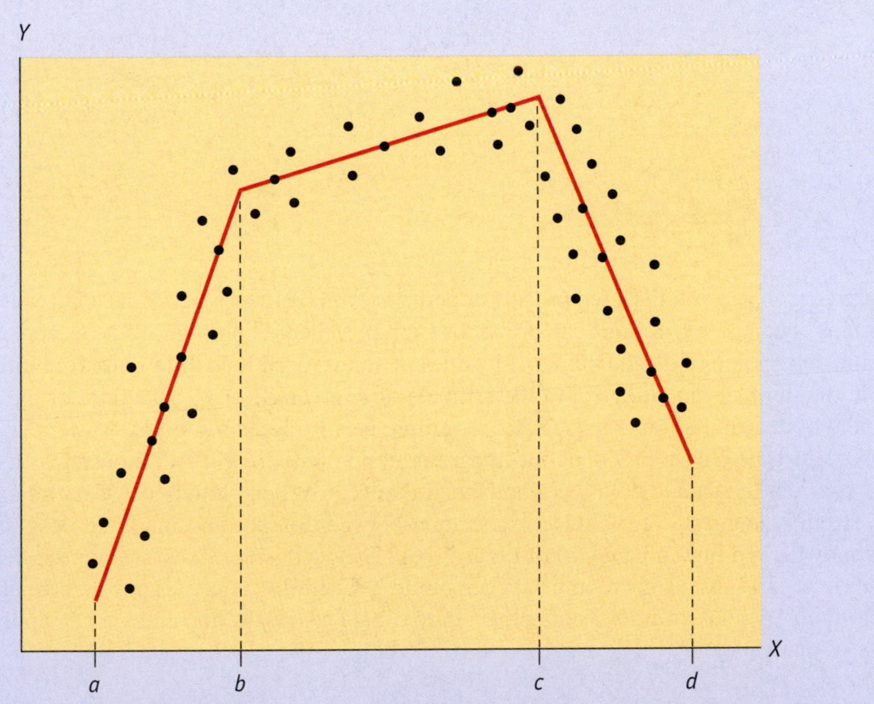

DATA TRANSFORMATION

A second approach to applying linear regression analysis to curvilinear data involves transforming (prior to analysis) the original values of one or both of the variables and then using the transformed values to compute the regression equation. For example, all the values of Y might be

TABLE 16.4 | Sample Data on Output and Marginal Cost

Output (thousands per year), X (1)	Marginal Cost ($/unit), Y (2)	Marginal Cost (logarithms), log Y (3)	X log Y (4)	X^2 (5)	$(\log Y)^2$ (6)
5	20	1.3010	6.5050	25	1.6926
7	60	1.7782	12.4474	49	3.1620
9	60	1.7782	16.0038	81	3.1620
9	100	2.0000	18.0000	81	4.0000
11	120	2.0792	22.8712	121	4.3231
12	120	2.0792	24.9504	144	4.3231
12	180	2.2553	27.0636	144	5.0864
14	240	2.3802	33.3228	196	5.6654
16	280	2.4472	39.1552	256	5.9888
16	360	2.5563	40.9008	256	6.5347
18	360	2.5563	46.0134	324	6.5347
18	480	2.6812	48.2616	324	7.1888
19	520	2.7160	51.6040	361	7.3767
19	640	2.8062	53.3178	361	7.8748
20	700	2.8451	56.9020	400	8.0946
20	1,000	3.0000	60.0000	400	9.0000
$\Sigma X =$ 225		$\Sigma \log Y =$ 37.2596	$\Sigma(X \log Y) =$ 557.319	$\Sigma X^2 =$ 3,523	$\Sigma(\log Y)^2 =$ 90.0077

squared or replaced by their reciprocals or perhaps even by their logarithms. (The statement says "perhaps" because exceptions can arise; for example, there is no logarithm for zero.) Such systematic conversion of all the numerical values of some variable is **data transformation.** If, as a result, the sample standard error of the estimate of Y, given X (or $s_{Y \cdot X}$) declines or the sample coefficient of determination (r^2) rises, the procedure is considered a success.

To illustrate a case in which our linear regression tools might still be used with curvilinear data, consider the data in columns 1 and 2 of Table 16.4. When plotted in a scatter diagram, these data strongly suggest a curvilinear association between output and marginal cost, such as that shown by the red line in panel (a) of Figure 16.17. Now consider transforming the marginal cost values to logarithms, as in column 3. When plotted on semilog paper, as in panel (b) of our graph, the column 1 versus column 3 data plots approximate a straight line and we can apply linear regression analysis.

EXAMPLE PROBLEM 16.13

Given the *linear* relationship between log Y and X shown in panel (b) of Figure 16.17, and employing the data from Table 16.4,

a. use Formula 16.A to find the equation of an estimated regression line between the logarithm of marginal cost, log Y, and output, X.

FIGURE 16.17 | The Effect of Data Transformation

A curvilinear relationship between two variables on an arithmetic scale, as in panel (a), may be transformed into a (roughly) linear relationship on a semilog scale, as in panel (b).

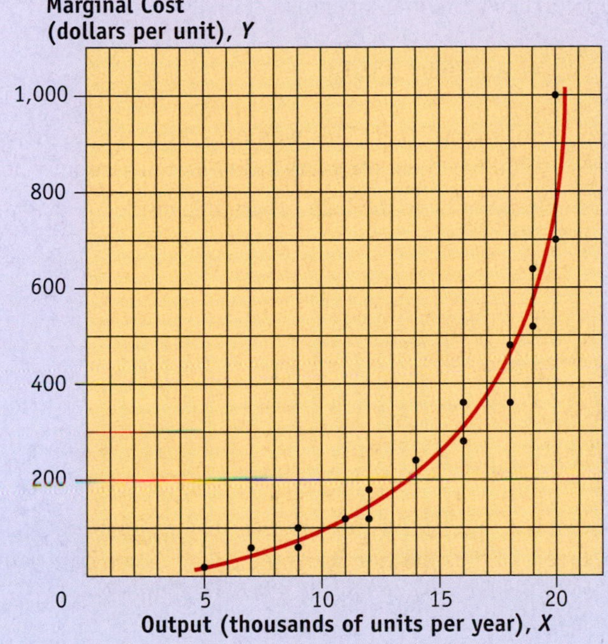

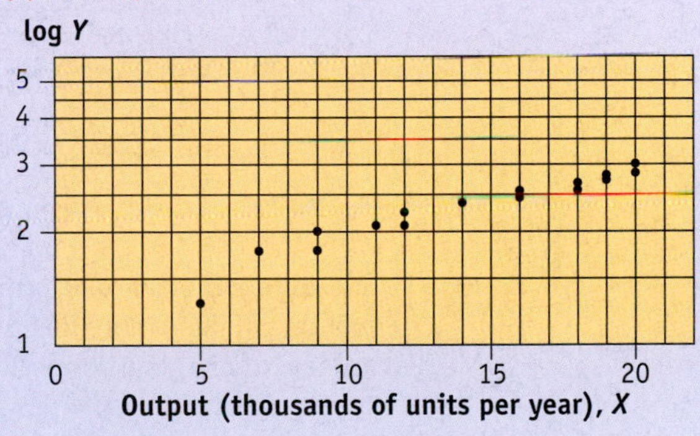

b. use the equation derived in (a) to estimate the marginal cost for output levels of 10 and 20 thousand units.

c. write the equation derived in (a) in antilog form and interpret it.

d. compute the coefficient of determination and interpret it.

SOLUTION:

a. Using columns 4–6 of Table 16.4, and appropriately adjusting Formula 16.A to our transformed data, we derive

$$\overline{X} = \frac{\Sigma X}{n} = \frac{225}{16} = 14.0625$$

$$\overline{\log Y} = \frac{\Sigma \log Y}{n} = \frac{37.2596}{16} = 2.3287$$

$$\log b = \frac{\Sigma(X \log Y) - n\overline{X}\,\overline{\log Y}}{\Sigma X^2 - n\overline{X}^2} = \frac{557.319 - 16(14.0625)(2.3287)}{3{,}523 - 16(14.0625)^2} = .0929$$

$$\log a = \overline{\log Y} - \log b\,\overline{X} = 2.3287 - .0929(14.0625) = 1.0223$$

Therefore, the estimated regression equation is

$$\log \hat{Y}_X = \log a + \log b\, X = 1.0223 + .0929\, X$$

b. $\log \hat{Y}_{10} = 1.0223 + .0929(10) = 1.9513$ and $\hat{Y}_{10} = anti\log(1.9513) = 89.4$
$\log \hat{Y}_{20} = 1.0223 + .0929(20) = 2.8803$ and $\hat{Y}_{20} = anti\log(2.8803) = 759.17$

All four of these results make sense with respect to the relevant panels in Figure 16.17.

c. The regression equation derived in (a) can be written in antilog form as

$$\hat{Y}_X = 10.5268(1.2386)^X$$

a general form suggested in panel (e) of Figure 16.4. This way of writing the relationship also tells us that marginal cost rises by 23.86 percent for every 1,000-unit increase in output.

d. We can calculate the coefficient of correlation with the help of our transformed data and an appropriately adjusted Formula 16.I:

$$r = \sqrt{\frac{\log a \Sigma \log Y + \log b \Sigma X \log Y - n\, \overline{\log Y}^2}{\Sigma \log Y^2 - n\, \overline{\log Y}^2}}$$

$$= \sqrt{\frac{1.0223\,(37.2596) + .0929\,(557.319) - 16(2.3287)^2}{90.0077 - 16(2.3287)^2}} = .9778$$

Thus, the coefficient of determination is $r^2 = .9561$, which suggests that the above regression equation explains more than 95 percent of the variation in Y by the association of Y with X. The level of marginal cost is almost perfectly explained by the level of output.

EXCEL Example 16.11

Review Example Problem 16.13. Confirm its parts (a) and (d) results by computer.

SOLUTION:

1. Enter the Table 16.4 output and marginal cost data, inclusive of column heads, into columns A and B, respectively, of a new worksheet. (You can also copy and paste the data from columns S and T of the file HKMISC.)
2. In cell C1, enter the label **LOGMC**
3. In cell C2, enter the formula **=LOG10(B2)**, select the result, and drag to C17.
4. Click **Tools** > **Data Analysis** > **Regression** > **OK**.
5. In the *Input Y Range* box, enter **C1:C17**
6. In the *Input X Range* box, enter **A1:A17**
7. Check *Labels* (because the first cell of each input column is a text label) and *New Worksheet Ply*, then click **OK**.

The following output appears; the desired values are highlighted:

SUMMARY OUTPUT

Regression Statistics	
Multiple R	0.9781079
R Square	0.956695
Adjusted R Square	0.9536018
Standard Error	0.1001122
Observations	16

ANOVA

	df	*SS*	*MS*	*F*	*Significance F*
Regression	1	3.099832031	3.099832	309.2886	6.09934E−11
Residual	14	0.140314423	0.010022		
Total	15	3.240146454			

	Coefficients	*Standard Error*	*t Stat*	*P-value*	*Lower 95%*	*Upper 95%*
Intercept	1.0218772	0.078410469	13.03241	3.22E−09	0.853703303	1.190051064
Output	0.0929308	0.005284181	17.5866	6.1E−11	0.081597345	0.10426425

Summary

1. In many situations that interest business executives and economists, the value of one variable is associated with the value of another variable in some systematic way. Regression and correlation analysis is concerned with such linkages. The central focus of *regression analysis* is to derive an equation that allows us to estimate the unknown value of one variable from the known value of one or more other variables. (A single variable is used to do the estimating in *simple* regression analysis.) The central focus of *simple correlation analysis* is to establish an index that provides, in a single number, an instant picture of the strength of association between two variables.
2. The performance of regression analysis requires a prior understanding of the basic concepts of *independent versus dependent variables, deterministic versus stochastic relationships,* and *direct versus inverse relationships.*
3. This chapter focuses on simple regression analysis for two variables that are related in *linear* fashion. The analysis begins by plotting sample data about the dependent variable, Y, and the independent variable, X, in a *scatter diagram* to confirm the linear relationship.
4. In principle, a straight *regression line* that summarizes the relationship between the variables can be fitted to the scatter of sample data by eyesight. The *method of least squares,* however, is preferred, because it alone is reliably reproducible and usable for making a variety of inferences about the population of interest.
5. The association between two variables, Y and X, present in a sample is summarized by the *estimated regression line,* but investigators are ultimately interested in the nature of the *true regression line,* which reveals the association of Y with X in the population as a whole.
6. Certain basic conditions must be met before we can make valid inferences about the true regression line with the help of an estimated regression line. The fulfillment of these conditions can be tested with an *analysis of residuals,* which are the differences between the observed values of the dependent variable and the associated fitted values that are computed with the estimated regression line.
7. Inferences are typically made concerning the average value of Y in a population, given X; concerning an individual value of Y in a population, given X; and concerning the

true regression coefficients (using confidence intervals or hypothesis tests).

8. Simple correlation analysis provides a variety of general indexes measuring the strength of linear association between two variables. These indexes include (a) the *sample coefficient of determination,* r^2, which equals the proportion of the *total variation* in the values of Y that can be explained by the association of Y with X as measured by the estimated regression line; (b) the *sample coefficient of correlation,* r; and (c) others that are employed less frequently.
9. An analysis of variance can play a role in regression analysis as well, notably in testing hypotheses concerning β, the slope of the true regression line.
10. Curvilinear regression analysis can be accomplished by using several linear regression lines to model a curvilinear relationship and by *transforming data.*

Key Terms

analysis of residuals
conditional mean of Y ($\mu_{Y \cdot X}$)
conditional probability distribution of Y
conditional standard deviation of Y ($\sigma_{Y \cdot X}$)
confidence band
data transformation
dependent variable
deterministic relationship
direct relationship
error sum of squares *(ESS)*
estimated regression coefficients
estimated regression line
explained deviation of Y
explained variable
explained variation of Y
explanatory variable
independent variable
inverse relationship
method of least squares
nonsense correlation
normal plot
population coefficient of correlation (ρ)
population coefficient of determination (ρ^2)
population regression line
population standard error of the estimate of Y, given X ($\sigma_{Y \cdot X}$)
predicted variable
prediction band
prediction interval
predictor variable
regressand
regression analysis
regression effect
regression fallacy
regression line
regression sum of squares *(RSS)*
regressor
residual
response variable
sample coefficient of alienation (k)
sample coefficient of correlation (r)
sample coefficient of determination (r^2)
sample coefficient of nondetermination (k^2)
sample regression line
sample standard error of the estimate of Y, given X ($s_{Y \cdot X}$)
scatter diagram
simple correlation analysis
simple regression analysis
spurious correlation
stochastic relationship
total deviation of Y
total sum of squares *(Total SS)*
total variation of Y
true regression coefficients
true regression line
unexplained deviation of Y
unexplained variation of Y

Practice Problems

NOTE

Some problems require the use of a statistical program, EXCEL or MINITAB. The program's major features are explained in text Chapter 2; plenty of additional advice is available via the program's built-in Help feature.

Section 16.4 The Scatter Diagram

Section 16.6 Drawing the Best Regression Line: Least Squares

1. Start EXCEL or MINITAB and activate the file HK99F500, which contains 1998 data about all *Fortune 500* companies. Then investigate the claim that the 500 firms' revenues are directly related to and easily predictable from their assets. Do so by
   a. finding the equation of the estimated regression line.
   b. drawing that regression line in a scatter diagram.
2. Start EXCEL or MINITAB and activate the file HK99F500, which contains 1998 data about all *Fortune 500* companies. Then investigate the claim that the 500 firms' profits are directly related to and easily predictable from their equity. Do so by

a. finding the equation of the estimated regression line.

b. drawing that regression line in a scatter diagram.

3. Start EXCEL or MINITAB and activate the file HK99F500, which contains 1998 data about all *Fortune 500* companies. Then investigate the claim that the 500 firms' market values are directly related to and easily predictable from their profits. Do so by

   a. finding the equation of the estimated regression line.

   b. drawing that regression line in a scatter diagram.

4. Start EXCEL or MINITAB and activate the file HK100MN97, which contains 1997 data about the 100 largest U.S.-based multinational companies. Then investigate the claim that the 100 firms' profits from foreign operations are directly related to and easily predictable from their foreign assets. Do so by

   a. finding the equation of the estimated regression line.

   b. drawing that regression line in a scatter diagram.

5. Start EXCEL or MINITAB and activate the file HK100MN97, which contains 1997 data about the 100 largest U.S.-based multinational companies. Then investigate the claim that the 100 firms' foreign revenues are directly related to and easily predictable from their foreign assets. Do so by

   a. finding the equation of the estimated regression line.

   b. drawing that regression line in a scatter diagram.

6. Start EXCEL or MINITAB and activate the file HK100MN97, which contains 1997 data about the 100 largest U.S.-based multinational companies. Then investigate the claim that the 100 firms' foreign profits are directly related to and easily predictable from their total profits. Do so by

   a. finding the equation of the estimated regression line.

   b. drawing that regression line in a scatter diagram.

7. An avionics manufacturer wants to establish the relationship between the monthly sales of long-range navigation units, Y, and the number of ads placed in monthly magazines, X. Given the data of Table 16.5,

   a. determine the estimated regression equation.

   b. draw the regression line in a scatter diagram.

TABLE 16.5

Loran Units Sold, Y	Number of Ads, X	Loran Units Sold, Y	Number of Ads, X
7	20	18	187
4	36	9	70
8	36	11	81
7	50	12	111
18	200	16	200
19	195	16	180
9	140	14	167
9	126	11	172
13	195	12	160
17	158	6	50
7	77	9	96
7	100	12	122
16	155	15	130
10	98	11	40

8. A realty firm wants to establish the relationship between the number of weeks homes are on the market prior to sale, Y, and the asking price, X. Given the data of Table 16.6,

a. determine the estimated regression equation.

b. draw the regression line in a scatter diagram.

TABLE 16.6

Weeks to Sale, Y	Asking Price ($1,000), X	Weeks to Sale, Y	Asking Price ($1,000), X
6.5	20	8.6	99
6.8	80	10.6	99
7.0	100	15.0	125
8.6	99	15.0	130
12.1	125	19.0	180
9.0	140	12.5	120
9.5	110	27.0	200

9. A marketing manager wants to establish the relationship between the number of cereal boxes sold, Y, and the shelf space devoted to them, X. Given the data of Table 16.7 on the next page,

a. determine the estimated regression equation.

b. draw the regression line in a scatter diagram.

TABLE 16.7

Number of Boxes Sold, Y	Feet of Shelf Space, X	Number of Boxes Sold, Y	Feet of Shelf Space, X
145	3	125	7
151	6	190	5
235	9	210	10
120	5	118	8
272	13	100	7
300	15	390	12
110	2	210	6

10. An economist wants to establish the relationship between the unemployment rate, Y, and the Treasury bill rate, X. Given the data of Table 16.8,

a. determine the estimated regression equation.

b. draw the regression line in a scatter diagram.

TABLE 16.8

Unemployment Rate (percent of labor force), Y	Treasury Bill Rate (percent per year), X
6.7	9.7
7.3	9.8
8.9	7.6
9.1	6.1
7.2	10.2
5.2	12.7
6.9	14.3
6.9	7.9
7.1	8.9

11. A marketing manager wants to establish the relationship between the second-year sales of sales representatives, Y, and their first-year sales, X. Given the data of Table 16.9 on the next page,

a. determine the estimated regression equation.

b. draw the regression line in a scatter diagram.

12. A marketing manager wants to establish the relationship between sales, Y, and the price of a similar product produced by a competitor, X. Given the data of Table 16.10 on the next page,

a. determine the estimated regression equation.

b. draw the regression line in a scatter diagram.

TABLE 16.9

Year-2 Units Sold, Y	Year-1 Units Sold, X
69	170
75	133
86	86
111	161
129	112
133	133
134	136
136	82
140	60
152	152
161	83
170	97

TABLE 16.10

Sales (units), Y	Competitor's Price ($/unit), X
520	13
550	13
600	15
610	15
620	16
724	21
680	21
300	14
962	40
270	12

13. An economist wants to establish the relationship between U.S. personal consumption expenditures, Y, and gross domestic product, X. Given the 1959–1998 data of Table 16.11,

a. determine the estimated regression equation.

b. draw the regression line in a scatter diagram.

TABLE 16.11

Personal Consumption Expenditures (billions of 1992 dollars), Y	Gross Domestic Product (billions of 1992 dollars), X	Personal Consumption Expenditures (billions of 1992 dollars), Y	Gross Domestic Product (billions of 1992 dollars), X
1,394.6	2,210.2	3,020.2	4,630.6
1,432.6	2,262.9	3,009.8	4,615.0
1,461.5	2,314.3	3,046.4	4,720.7
1,553.8	2,454.8	3,081.5	4,620.3
1,596.6	2,559.4	3,240.6	4,803.7
1,692.3	2,708.4	3,407.6	5,140.1
1,799.1	2,881.4	3,566.5	5,323.5
1,902.0	3,069.2	3,708.7	5,487.7
1,958.6	3,147.2	3,822.3	5,649.5
2,070.2	3,293.9	3,972.7	5,865.2
2,147.5	3,393.6	4,064.6	6,062.0
2,197.8	3,397.6	4,132.2	6,136.3
2,279.5	3,510.0	4,105.8	6,079.4
2,415.9	3,702.3	4,219.8	6,244.4
2,532.6	3,916.3	4,343.6	6,389.6
2,514.7	3,891.2	4,486.0	6,610.7
2,570.0	3,873.9	4,605.6	6,761.7
2,714.3	4,082.9	4,752.4	6,994.8
2,829.8	4,273.6	4,913.5	7,269.8
2,951.6	4,503.0	5,181.8	7,566.5

14. The following has been hypothesized about U.S. presidential elections: The percentage of the popular vote, Y, that goes to the candidate put up by the party of the incumbent president depends on the change in the unemployment rate during the election year, X, in such a way that any increase in unemployment detracts from, and any decrease in unemployment adds to, the vote for the incumbent-party candidate. Given data of Table 16.12 on the next page,

a. determine the estimated regression equation.

b. draw the regression line in a scatter diagram.

TABLE 16.12

Election Year	Party of Incumbent President (Democrats = 0 Republicans = 1)	Percentage of Popular Vote Captured by Party of Incumbent President, *Y*	Change in Election-Year Unemployment Rate, *X*
1892	1	48.3	−2.4
1896	0	47.8	+0.7
1900	1	53.2	−1.5
1904	1	60.0	+1.5
1908	1	54.5	+5.2
1912	1	54.7	−2.1
1916	0	51.7	−3.4
1920	0	36.1	+3.8
1924	1	54.3	+2.6
1928	1	58.8	+0.9
1932	1	40.9	+7.7
1936	0	62.5	−3.2
1940	0	55.0	−2.6
1944	0	53.8	−0.9
1948	0	49.6	−0.1
1952	0	44.4	−0.3
1956	1	57.4	−0.3
1960	1	49.5	0.0
1964	0	61.1	−0.5
1968	0	42.7	−0.2
1972	1	60.7	−0.3
1976	1	48.0	−0.8
1980	0	41.0	+1.3
1984	1	58.8	−2.1
1988	1	53.4	−0.7
1992	1	37.4	+0.7
1996	0	49.2	−0.2

15. Review Application 16.7, *Small Is Beautiful: The Relationship between Height and Longevity.* Then make a test of whether age at death depends on height. Given the data of Table 16.13,

a. determine the estimated regression equation.

b. draw the regression line in a scatter diagram.

TABLE 16.13

President	Age at Time of Death, Y	Height (inches), X
Madison	85	64
Van Buren	79	66
B. Harrison	67	66
J. Adams	90	67
J. Q. Adams	80	67
Jackson	78	73
Washington	67	74
Arthur	56	74
F. Roosevelt	63	74
L. Johnson	64	74
Jefferson	83	74.5

SOURCE: Thomas T. Samaras, "That Some Put Down Short People, But . . .," *Science Digest,* July 1978.

SECTION 16.8 REGRESSION DIAGNOSTICS

16. The scatter diagram found in the Practice Problem 2 answer reveals a direct relationship between profits and equity, which suggests that further analysis may be worthwhile. Now subject the data to a set of regression diagnostics concerning

a. the normality assumption.

b. the homoscedasticity assumption.

17. The scatter diagram found in the Practice Problem 6 answer reveals a direct relationship between foreign profits and total profits, which suggests that further analysis may be worthwhile. Now subject the data to a set of regression diagnostics concerning

a. the normality assumption.

b. the homoscedasticity assumption.

18. The scatter diagram found in the Practice Problem 9 answer reveals a direct relationship between boxes sold and shelf space, which suggests that further analysis may be worthwhile. Now subject the data to a set of regression diagnostics concerning

a. the normality assumption.

b. the homoscedasticity assumption.

19. The scatter diagram found in the Practice Problem 13 answer reveals a direct relationship between consumption and GDP, which suggests that further analysis may be worthwhile. Now subject the data to a set of regression diagnostics concerning

a. the normality assumption.

b. the homoscedasticity assumption.

20. The scatter diagram found in the Practice Problem 14 answer reveals a direct relationship between voting percentage and change in the unemployment rate, which suggests that further analysis may be worthwhile. Now subject the data to a set of regression diagnostics concerning

a. the normality assumption.

b. the homoscedasticity assumption.

SECTION 16.9 ESTIMATING THE AVERAGE VALUE OF *Y*, Given *X*

SECTION 16.10 ESTIMATING AN INDIVIDUAL VALUE OF *Y*, Given *X*

21. Review Practice Problem 7, featuring avionics sales and advertisements promoting them. Then

a. make a *point estimate* of Y_{150}; that is, monthly sales if there are 150 ads.

b. compute a *95 percent confidence interval* for $\mu_{Y \cdot 150}$; that is, average monthly sales in all months with 150 ads.

c. compute a *95 percent prediction interval* for $I_{Y \cdot 150}$; that is, sales during the next month that happens to be associated with 150 ads.

22. Review Practice Problem 8, featuring the relationship between weeks-to-sale and asking price for real estate. Then

a. make a *point estimate* of Y_{138}; that is, the weeks it takes for a sale to occur if the asking price is $138,000.

b. compute a *95 percent confidence interval* for $\mu_{Y \cdot 138}$; that is, average weeks-to-sale time on all the occasions when the asking price is $138,000.

c. compute a *95 percent prediction interval* for $I_{Y \cdot 138}$; that is, weeks-to-sale time for the next home on sale that happens to have a $138,000 price.

23. Review Practice Problem 9, featuring the relationship between cereal boxes sold and shelf space devoted to their display. Then

a. make a *point estimate* of Y_{11}; that is, the number of boxes sold, if there are 11 feet of shelf space.

b. compute a *98 percent confidence interval* for $\mu_{Y \cdot 11}$; that is, average number of boxes sold during all the periods when there are 11 feet of shelf space.

c. compute a *98 percent prediction interval* for $I_{Y \cdot 11}$; that is, the number of boxes sold during the next period when there happen to be 11 feet of shelf space.

24. Review Practice Problem 10, featuring the relationship between unemployment and the Treasury bill rate. Then

a. make a *point estimate* of Y_{14}; that is, the unemployment rate when the Treasury bill rate is 14 percent.

b. compute a *99.9 percent confidence interval* for $\mu_{Y \cdot 14}$; that is, the average unemployment rate during all the periods with a Treasury bill rate of 14 percent.

c. compute a *99.9 percent prediction interval* for $I_{Y \cdot 14}$; that is, the unemployment rate during the next period when the Treasury bill rate happens to be 14 percent.

d. comment on this entire investigation.

25. Review Practice Problem 11, featuring the relationship between second-year and first-year sales of sales representatives. Then

a. make a *point estimate* of Y_{100}; that is, second-year sales when first-year sales are 100 units.

b. compute a *98 percent confidence interval* for $\mu_{Y \cdot 100}$; that is, average second-year sales during all periods when first-year sales were 100 units.

c. compute a *98 percent prediction interval* for $I_{Y \cdot 100}$; that is, second-year sales during the next period when first-year sales happen to be 100 units.

26. Review Practice Problem 12, featuring the relationship between units sold and a competitor's price. Then

a. make a *point estimate* of Y_{25}; that is, units sold when the competitor's price is $25 per unit.

b. compute a *97 percent confidence interval* for $\mu_{Y \cdot 25}$; that is, average units sold during all the periods when the competitor's price was $25 per unit.

c. compute a *97 percent prediction interval* for $I_{Y \cdot 25}$; that is, units sold during the next period in which the competitor's price happens to be $25 per unit.

27. Review Practice Problem 13, featuring the relationship between consumption and the GDP. Then

a. make a *point estimate* of $Y_{7,000}$; that is, consumption at a GDP level of 7,000.

b. compute a *95 percent confidence interval* for $\mu_{Y \cdot 7,000}$; that is, the average consumption level in all years with a GDP of 7,000.

c. compute a *95 percent prediction interval* for $I_{Y \cdot 7,000}$; that is, the consumption level during the next year in which the GDP happens to be 7,000.

28. Review Practice Problem 14, featuring the relationship between the percentage of the popular vote captured by presidential candidates of the incumbent party and the election-year change in the unemployment rate. Then

a. make a *point estimate* of Y_{+5}; that is, the percentage of the vote captured by such candidates when the election-year unemployment rate rises by 5 points.

b. compute a *98 percent confidence interval* for $\mu_{Y \cdot +5}$; that is, the percentage of the vote captured by such candidates, on average, during all the election years in which the unemployment rate rises by 5 points.

c. compute a *98 percent prediction interval* for $I_{Y \cdot +5}$; that is, the percentage of the vote captured by the next such candidate who finds the unemployment rate rising by 5 points during the election year.

29. The manager of a life insurance company wants to establish the relationship between the amount of life insurance bought by insured persons, *Y*, and their incomes, *X*. Given the sample data of Table 16.14,

a. make a *point estimate* of Y_{250}; that is, the life insurance in force for someone with a $250,000 income.

b. compute a *95 percent confidence interval* for $\mu_{Y \cdot 250}$; that is, the average life insurance in force for all the insured who have a $250,000 income.

c. compute a *95 percent prediction interval* for $I_{Y \cdot 250}$; that is, the life insurance in force for the next person sampled who happens to have a $250,000 income.

TABLE 16.14

Life Insurance in Force (thousands of dollars), *Y*	Annual Income (thousands of dollars), *X*
50	10
80	29
100	30
130	31
150	36
150	40
200	40
300	29
300	50
350	90
400	90
400	120
500	127
500	150
500	188
800	213
800	540

30. An executive of a food corporation wants to establish the relationship between corn yield, Y, and the average July temperature, X, in Iowa, where the firm's acres are located. Given the sample data of Table 16.15,

a. make a *point estimate* of Y_{95}; that is, the corn yield when the average July temperature is 95 degrees Fahrenheit.

b. compute a *99 percent confidence interval* for $\mu_{Y \cdot 95}$; that is, the average corn yield in all the seasons in which the average July temperature is 95 degrees Fahrenheit.

c. compute a *99 percent prediction interval* for $I_{Y \cdot 95}$; that is, the corn yield in the next season in which the average July temperature happens to be 95 degrees Fahrenheit.

TABLE 16.15

Corn Yield (bushels per acre), Y	Average July Temperature (degrees Fahrenheit), X
115	91
119	95
126	101
91	88
107	92
89	89
111	95
90	87
68	79
34	71
99	90

Section 16.11 Making Inferences about True Regression Coefficients

31. Review Practice Problem 7, featuring avionics sales and advertisements promoting them. Then

a. establish a 95 percent *confidence interval for* β, the slope of the true regression line.

b. establish a 95 percent *confidence interval for* α, the true regression line's intercept.

c. make a *two-tailed hypothesis test* of H_0: $\beta = 0$, using a confidence level of 95 percent.

32. Review Practice Problem 8, featuring the relationship between the number of weeks homes are on the market prior to sale and their asking price. Then

a. establish a 95 percent *confidence interval for* β, the slope of the true regression line.

b. establish a 95 percent *confidence interval for* α, the true regression line's intercept.

c. make a *two-tailed hypothesis test* of H_0: $\beta = 0$, using a confidence level of 95 percent.

33. Review Practice Problem 9, featuring the relationship between the number of cereal boxes sold and the feet of shelf space devoted to their display. Then

a. establish a 95 percent *confidence interval for* β, the slope of the true regression line.

b. establish a 95 percent *confidence interval for* α, the true regression line's intercept.

c. make a *two-tailed hypothesis test* of H_0: $\beta = 0$, using a confidence level of 95 percent.

34. Review Practice Problem 11, featuring the relationship between second-year sales and first-year sales. Then

a. establish a 95 percent *confidence interval for* β, the slope of the true regression line.

b. establish a 95 percent *confidence interval for* α, the true regression line's intercept.

c. make a *two-tailed hypothesis test* of H_0: $\beta = 0$, using a confidence level of 95 percent.

35. Review Practice Problem 12, featuring the relationship between sales and a competitor's price. Then

a. establish a 95 percent *confidence interval for* β, the slope of the true regression line.

b. establish a 95 percent *confidence interval for* α, the true regression line's intercept.

c. make a *two-tailed hypothesis test* of H_0: $\beta = 0$, using a confidence level of 95 percent.

36. Review Practice Problem 13, featuring the relationship between consumption and the GDP. Then

a. establish a 95 percent *confidence interval for* β, the slope of the true regression line.

b. establish a 95 percent *confidence interval for* α, the true regression line's intercept.

c. make a *two-tailed hypothesis test* of H_0: $\beta = 0$, using a confidence level of 95 percent.

37. Review Practice Problem 14, featuring the relationship between percentage of the popular vote that goes to the candidate put up by the party of the incumbent president and the change in the unemployment rate during the election year. Then

a. establish a 95 percent *confidence interval for* β, the slope of the true regression line.

b. establish a 95 percent *confidence interval for* α, the true regression line's intercept.

c. make a *two-tailed hypothesis test* of H_0: $\beta = 0$, using a confidence level of 95 percent.

38. Review Practice Problem 29, featuring the relationship between life insurance in force and annual income. Then

a. establish a 95 percent *confidence interval for* β, the slope of the true regression line.

b. establish a 95 percent *confidence interval for* α, the true regression line's intercept.

c. make a *two-tailed hypothesis test* of H_0: $\beta = 0$, using a confidence level of 95 percent.

39. Review Practice Problem 30, featuring the relationship between corn yield and temperature. Then

a. establish a 95 percent *confidence interval for* β, the slope of the true regression line.

b. establish a 95 percent *confidence interval for* α, the true regression line's intercept.

c. make a *two-tailed hypothesis test* of H_0: $\beta = 0$, using a confidence level of 95 percent.

40. A railroad executive wants to establish the relationship between fuel costs, Y, and the number of cars on a freight train, X. Given the sample data of Table 16.16 on the next page,

a. establish a 95 percent *confidence interval for* β, the slope of the true regression line.

b. establish a 95 percent *confidence interval for* α, the true regression line's intercept.

c. make a *two-tailed hypothesis test* of H_0: $\beta = 0$, using a confidence level of 95 percent.

SECTION 16.12 SIMPLE CORRELATION ANALYSIS

SECTION 16.13 TESTING β WITH ANALYSIS OF VARIANCE

41. Review Practice Problem 40 concerning the relationship between fuel costs and cars on a train. Then

a. compute the sample coefficient of determination and explain its meaning.

b. perform an ANOVA test of the hypothesis H_0: $\beta = 0$, using a 5 percent level of significance.

42. An economist wants to examine the relationship between gross private domestic investment, Y, and Moody's Aaa corporate bond yields, X. Given the sample data of Table 16.17 on the next page,

a. compute the sample coefficient of determination and explain its meaning.

b. perform an ANOVA test of the hypothesis H_0: $\beta = 0$, using a 5 percent level of significance.

TABLE 16.16

Fuel Costs (cents per ton-mile), *Y*	Cars on Train (number), *X*
16.3	20
15.0	30
14.3	36
13.0	40
15.1	49
12.0	51
12.0	60
12.1	63
14.7	70
15.2	70
12.1	81
11.0	97
9.2	100
10.1	120
6.2	152
4.8	156

TABLE 16.17

Gross Private Domestic Investment (billions of dollars) per year), *Y*	Moody's Aaa Corporate Bond Yields (percent per year), *X*	Gross Private Domestic Investment (billions of dollars) per year), *Y*	Moody's Aaa Corporate Bond Yields (percent per year), *X*
75.9	4.41	195.0	7.21
74.8	4.35	229.8	7.44
85.4	4.33	228.7	8.57
90.9	4.26	206.1	8.83
97.4	4.40	257.9	8.43
113.5	4.49	324.1	8.02
125.7	5.13	386.6	8.73
122.8	5.51	423.0	9.63
133.3	6.18	401.9	11.94
149.3	7.03	474.9	14.17
144.2	8.04	414.5	13.79
166.4	7.39	471.3	12.04

43. An economist wants to examine the relationship between the demand for electricity, Y, and the price of natural gas, X. Given the sample data of Table 16.18,

a. compute the sample coefficient of determination and explain its meaning.

b. perform an ANOVA test of the hypothesis H_0: $\beta = 0$, using a 5 percent level of significance.

TABLE 16.18

Demand for Electricity (megawatts per day), Y	Price of Natural Gas (dollars per unit), X
173	33
161	36
142	22
193	41
211	38
219	42
260	50
250	51
181	30
129	25
333	78
279	54
199	40

44. An advertising executive wants to examine the relationship between a firm's market share, Y, and its annual spending on television ads, X. Given the sample data of Table 16.19,

a. compute the sample coefficient of determination and explain its meaning.

b. perform an ANOVA test of the hypothesis H_0: $\beta = 0$, using a 5 percent level of significance.

TABLE 16.19

Market Share (percent), Y	TV Ad Spending (million dollars per year), X
8.8	23
12.7	33
13.8	36
15.0	39
17.2	42
28.6	69
30.8	88
41.2	127
53.0	130
45.0	122
38.9	100
34.8	88
29.0	51

45. An insurance company executive wants to examine the relationship between fire damage, Y, and the distance of the victims' property from the nearest fire station, X. Given the sample data of Table 16.20,

a. compute the sample coefficient of determination and explain its meaning.

b. perform an ANOVA test of the hypothesis H_0: $\beta = 0$, using a 5 percent level of significance.

TABLE 16.20

Fire Damage (thousands of dollars), Y	Distance to Fire Station (miles), X
12.6	1.1
18.9	.9
33.0	2.0
4.1	.7
150.0	1.2
77.0	.8
6.1	3.1
9.2	3.2
10.2	7.0
300.0	1.3
78.9	12.3

46. An auto industry executive wants to examine the relationship between new car sales, Y, and the existing stock of old cars, X. Given the sample data of Table 16.21,

a. compute the sample coefficient of determination and explain its meaning.

b. perform an ANOVA test of the hypothesis H_0: $\beta = 0$, using a 5 percent level of significance.

TABLE 16.21

New Car Sales (millions per year), Y	Old Car Stock (millions at mid-year), X
9.3	68.9
8.4	80.4
8.6	95.2
10.7	104.7
9.0	104.6
8.5	105.8
8.0	106.9
11.9	100.5
15.6	98.1

47. A personnel manager wants to examine the relationship between the number of grievances filed by workers, Y, and the humidity index, X. Given the sample data of Table 16.22,

a. compute the sample coefficient of determination and explain its meaning.

b. perform an ANOVA test of the hypothesis $H_0: \beta = 0$, using a 5 percent level of significance.

TABLE 16.22

Grievances Filed (number per week), Y	Humidity Index (weekly average), X
11	.7
9	1.4
11	2.1
13	2.7
22	3.7
18	4.2
22	5.0
41	5.6
62	6.9
50	7.3
88	7.7
68	7.8
109	8.1
125	8.4
142	8.5
96	8.6
112	8.8
132	9.0

48. A small-aircraft manufacturer wants to examine the relationship between the number of airplanes sold, Y, and their price, X. Given the sample data of Table 16.23,

a. compute the sample coefficient of determination and explain its meaning.

b. perform an ANOVA test of the hypothesis $H_0: \beta = 0$, using a 5 percent level of significance.

TABLE 16.23

Airplanes Sold (number per year), Y	Price per Plane (thousands of dollars), X
451	49
437	63
411	89
389	111
359	141
350	150
345	155
331	169
267	233
207	293
87	413
98	415

49. Consider Figure 16.18. Then

a. determine which line (A, B, C, or D) is the least-squares regression line for the four red dots.

b. compute the sample coefficient of determination and explain its meaning.

c. perform an ANOVA test of the hypothesis H_0: $\beta = 0$, using a 5 percent level of significance.

FIGURE 16.18

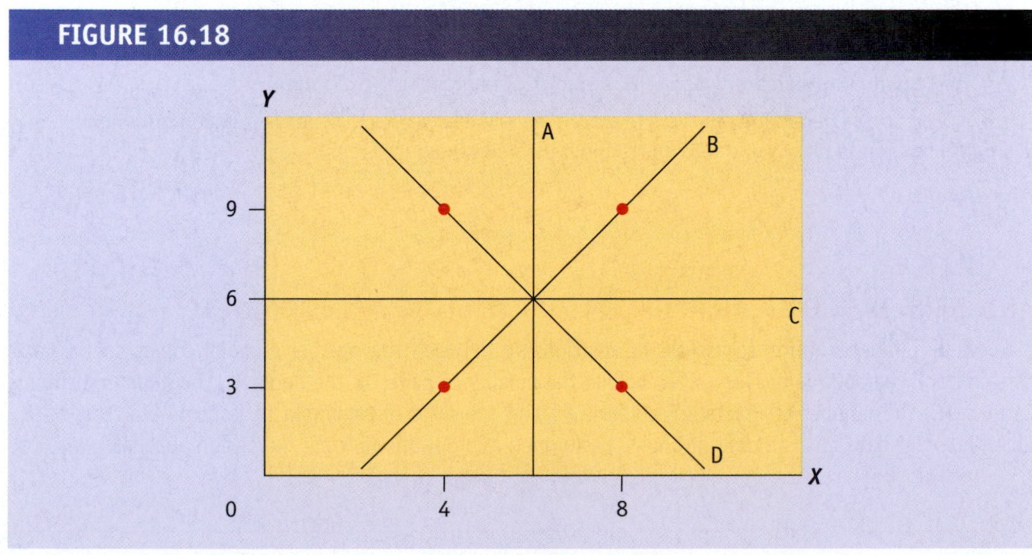

SECTION 16.14 AN EXTENSION: CURVILINEAR REGRESSION

50. Once again, consider Practice Problem 47. Suppose the personnel manager's boss believes that the personnel manager (a) should have drawn a scatter diagram, and (b) should have taken a hint from that diagram and produced a regression of Y versus X^2 "for a much better fit." Check the boss's claims.

Chapter 17

MULTIPLE REGRESSION AND CORRELATION

LOOKING AHEAD

After reading this chapter, you will be able to employ multiple regression and correlation techniques to test whether and how the value of one variable, Y, is affected by the values of two or more other variables, X_1, X_2, X_3, and so on. Among other things, you will learn to:

1. construct *least-squares multiple regression equations* that summarize the relationship among the variables mathematically,
2. estimate the average value of Y in the population of interest that is associated with any given set of X values,
3. estimate the next value of Y likely to be encountered by sampling the population of interest, given any set of X values,
4. develop confidence intervals and conduct hypothesis tests about the coefficients of true regression equations,
5. compute *coefficients of multiple determination* and similar indexes that summarize the strength of association among the variables of interest in a single number, and
6. perform regression diagnostics to determine whether you can use an estimated regression equation to make valid inferences about the underlying true regression.

AND HERE IS A TYPICAL PROBLEM YOU WILL BE ABLE TO SOLVE:

A textbook publisher wants to assess the relationship between the number of book copies sold, Y, and certain book characteristics. The latter include the number of pages in the book, X_1, the number of Applications, X_2, the number of Practice Problems, X_3, and the ratio of favorable to unfavorable reviews, X_4. Given relevant data for a number of books, perform an appropriate multiple regression analysis.

PREVIEW

A few years ago, pharmaceutical companies that had long promoted daily vitamins with iron to millions of Americans as "the way to a healthier and longer life" suddenly faced a serious problem. A major scientific journal, *Circulation,* published by the American Heart Association, reported the findings of a long-term study conducted by a Finnish doctor, Jukka T. Salonen. The study of 1,931 apparently healthy men, aged 42 to 60, had been initiated in 1984 and concluded that high levels of iron constituted a strong risk factor for heart attacks. Each 1 percent increase in ferritin (a protein that binds iron in the blood) increased the risk of heart attack by 4 percent. This made iron at least as dangerous as other long-known risk factors, including cigarette smoking, high blood pressure, lack of exercise, and high levels of LDL, a low-density lipoprotein generally known as bad cholesterol.

According to the study, iron hastens the formation of plaque that hardens artery walls and blocks the flow of blood, causing heart attacks. Furthermore, iron contributes to a chemical chain reaction that injures and kills heart muscle cells during heart attacks. If anything, therefore, people would want to have less rather than more iron in their bodies. Indeed, the study shed light on a number of interesting phenomena, including these: In the past, *bloodletting* was a common medical practice, although nobody knew why periodically bleeding people apparently made them healthier. The Finnish study suggested that losing blood would remove excess iron from the body and prevent heart disease because iron would be drawn away from typical storage places in the bone marrow, liver, and spleen. Medical practitioners had long wondered why premenopausal women had so few heart attacks; apparently, they lose not only blood but also dangerous iron each month. Likewise, taking aspirin seems to protect against heart attack precisely because the drug causes internal bleeding. Finally, regular blood donors have fewer heart attacks; they seem to be performing a service to themselves as well as to others.

As you can well imagine, pharmaceutical companies marketing products with iron supplements are keenly interested in proving the truth or falsity of this kind of story. If it were true, the iron supplement market would collapse, but the companies might then develop and market drugs that *remove* iron from the body. However, the truth or falsity of the iron effect on human health cannot easily be established with the help of controlled experiments. A few years ago, the American Heart Association listed 246 possible risk factors for heart attacks. It would be very difficult to hold all but one of these constant in a laboratory so as to observe the effect of a single factor, X, such as iron levels, on another factor, Y, such as the incidence of heart attacks. Yet, even though such *experimental control* is difficult to achieve, statisticians have developed a method of exercising *statistical control*. Such is the goal of this chapter's *multiple* regression analysis. It involves the establishment of an equation like

$$\hat{Y} = a + b_1X_1 + b_2X_2 + b_3X_3 + \cdots + b_nX_n$$

which allows us to determine the influence of any *one* independent variable, X_1, on the dependent variable Y, given specified values of other independent variables, X_2, X_3, and so on, that might affect Y as well. Thus, Y might be the incidence of heart attacks, X_1 the level of smoking, X_2 the iron content of the blood, X_3 the level of LDL, and so on. In business and economics texts, an "other things being equal" or *ceteris paribus* clause is frequently inserted in sentences to warn the reader that a given relationship was found while exercising such statistical control and might not be evident when other variables fail to remain constant.[1]

[1]Adapted from Lawrence K. Altman, "High Level of Iron Tied to Heart Risk," *The New York Times*, September 8, 1992, pp. A1 and C3; and David Stipp, "Base Metal: Heart-Attack Study Adds to the Cautions about Iron in the Diet," *The Wall Street Journal*, September 8, 1992, pp. A1 and 9.

17.1 Introduction

Simple regression analysis, we learned in Chapter 16, helps us predict the value of one variable from the known value of another variable, while simple correlation analysis helps us measure the overall strength of association between two such variables. This chapter's subject matter is analogously defined.

DEFINITION 17.1 **Multiple regression analysis** is a technique in which several independent variables are used to estimate the value of an unknown dependent variable. Hence, each of these predictor variables explains part of the total variation of the dependent variable. In addition, **multiple correlation analysis** measures the overall strength of association among more than two variables.

There are plenty of good reasons for utilizing the more complex techniques to be discussed in this chapter. Foremost among these is the fact that the world is a complicated network of interdependencies, which is rarely captured very well by models involving two variables only. Typically, the value of any one variable is influenced not only by one other variable, but by two, three, or even a multitude of other variables. People's income may, indeed, depend on their education (as noted in Chapter 16) but it can also depend on their job experience, perhaps on their age, and, in the presence of discriminatory practices, even on their sex or race. The demand for a good may well depend on the good's price, but, in addition, may vary with consumer incomes and tastes, the prices of substitutes or complements, and a host of other factors. A firm's sales may, indeed, vary with advertising expenditures but also with the number of competitors it has, with the size of the community in which it is located, and even with the local unemployment rate. A farmer's output per acre may be a function of fertilizer input, but will surely also vary with the quantity of labor used, with the amounts of pesticide used, and even with the extent of rainfall.

We could list examples such as these without end, but the message is already clear: Simple regression and correlation analysis is rarely adequate for exploring relationships, even between two variables of interest. Such simple analysis always leaves open the possibility of finding a fuller explanation of the dependent variable by considering more than one independent variable. A substantial amount of the variation in Y = income that is not explained by X_1 = education may, for example, be explained by X_2 = job experience, X_3 = age, or even X_4 = sex. In addition, the precise effect of a particular independent variable, such as education, on a dependent variable of interest, such as income, may be seriously distorted by the results of simple regression and correlation analysis because it has ignored the influence of other independent variables, such as job experience, age, or sex. The sample results noted in Table 16.1 on page 713, for example, are ambiguous if high or low income can also be caused by high or low job experience and not only by high or low education levels. If the sampled high-income individuals just happened to have above-average job experience, while the low-income individuals had below-average job experience, a simple regression that ignored job experience but used these data would mislead us. It would exaggerate both the income-raising effect of high education and the income-depressing effect of low education. In other words, if only a single independent variable is used in a regression equation, but several such variables operate in the real-life situation that this equation attempts to describe, the influence of all the ignored independent variables is absorbed into the coefficient attached to that single variable—which makes the coefficient misleading. The problem noted here is once again that of controlling for extraneous factors, a subject discussed in detail in Chapter 5.

17.2 Linear Multiple Regression with Two Explanatory Variables

Multiple regression techniques simply extend those of simple regression. Consider the case in which one dependent variable, Y, is related, in linear fashion, to two independent variables, X_1 and X_2. (Y might be income, X_1 might be education, and X_2 might be job experience.) A first goal of the analysis of such a case is to establish an *estimated multiple regression equation,* such as

$$\hat{Y} = a + b_1X_1 + b_2X_2$$

This equation gives us the estimated value, $\hat{Y}$, of the dependent variable for any specified pair of values of the independent variables. In contrast to Chapter 16, we now have three estimated regression coefficients, a, b_1, and b_2. Their meaning is easy to comprehend:

- a is the estimated value of Y when $X_1 = X_2 = 0$
- b_1 equals the change in estimated Y (also referred to as the *partial* change or *net* change in Y) that is associated with a unit change in X_1, when X_2 is held constant
- b_2 equals the change in estimated Y that is associated with a unit change in X_2 when X_1 is held constant

The values of b_1 and b_2 are **estimated partial-regression coefficients.** Each gives us the change in Y for a unit change in the associated independent variable, while holding all other independent variables constant.

Note: The partial regression coefficients noted here are, in fact, the partial derivatives of Y with respect to either X_1 or X_2. Thus,

$$b_1 = (\delta Y/\delta X_1) \qquad \text{and} \qquad b_2 = (\delta Y/\delta X_2)$$

where δ, the lowercase Greek delta, stands for "the change in."

THE REGRESSION PLANE

Unlike the two-variable simple regression equation of Chapter 16 (that related Y to X), our three-variable multiple regression equation (that relates Y to X_1 and X_2) does not correspond to a *line* in a two-dimensional scatter diagram; it corresponds to a *plane* in three-dimensional space. In our three-variable case, we make three observations for each sample unit: one for the value of Y, one for X_1, and one for X_2. To depict these observations in a scatter diagram, we must make it three-dimensional, like Figure 17.1 on the next page.

In Figure 17.1, the value of Y associated with any sample unit is measured vertically from the origin, 0; the value of X_1 is measured toward the right, and the value of X_2 is measured toward the left. Thus, a sample observation of Y = distance $0A$, of X_1 = distance $0B$, and of X_2 = distance $0C$ appears as the red sample point, labeled P.

Now imagine lots of sample observations, such as all the red dots suspended in the three-dimensional space of Figure 17.2 on page 791. The three-variable multiple regression technique establishes an estimated multiple regression equation in such a way that all the estimates derived from it fall on a surface, such as shaded area $ABCD$ in our graph, that is called the **regression plane.** The plane is positioned among the sample points in such a way as to minimize the sum of the squared vertical deviations between these sample points and their associated estimates, all of which lie on this plane. In Figure 17.2, the observed sample points, or the actual values of Y

FIGURE 17.1 | Sample Point in Three-Dimensional Scatter Diagram

When three observations are associated with each sample unit (such as Y = distance 0A, plus X_1 = distance 0B, plus X_2 = distance 0C), any set of these observations can be depicted like sample point P, as a dot suspended in three-dimensional space.

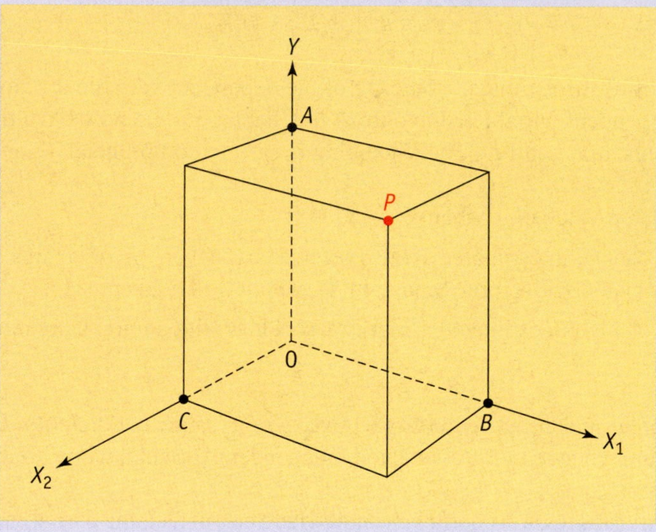

for any given combination of X_1 and X_2, are represented by the red dots; the associated estimates, $\hat{Y}$, are represented by the black crosses lying on the shaded plane. These crosses are positioned immediately below or above the red dots, depending on whether the latter are suspended above or below the regression plane.

We can also note the values of the regression coefficients in Figure 17.2. The value of a estimates Y for $X_1 = X_2 = 0$; hence, it is still the Y-intercept, equal to distance $0A$ in our graph. The value of b_1 is the slope of the regression plane when holding X_2 constant, at any desired level. Imagine cutting the regression plane parallel to the X_1 axis at $X_2 = 0$. The cut would trace line AB in the YX_1 plane and show the value of Y rising from $0A$ at $X_1 = 0$ to EB at $X_1 = 0E$. The slope of line AB, relative to $0E$, equals b_1. Imagine instead cutting the regression plane parallel to the X_1 axis at $X_2 = 0F$. The cut would trace line DC and show the value of Y rising from FD at $X_1 = 0$ to GC at $X_1 = 0E$. The slope of line DC, relative to FG, also equals b_1. Thus, b_1 always indicates how estimated Y changes with X_1, while *not* changing X_2.

Similarly, b_2 is the slope of the regression plane when holding X_1 constant at any particular level. Imagine cutting the regression plane parallel to the X_2 axis at $X_1 = 0$. That cut would trace line AD in the YX_2 plane and show the value of Y rising from $0A$ at $X_2 = 0$ to FD at $X_2 = 0F$. The slope of line AD, relative to $0F$, equals b_2. Imagine instead cutting the regression plane parallel to the X_2 axis at $X_1 = 0E$. The cut would trace line BC and show the value of Y rising from EB at $X_2 = 0$ to GC at $X_2 = 0F$. The slope of line BC, relative to EG, also equals b_2. Thus, b_2 always indicates how estimated Y changes with X_2, while not changing X_1.

What if X_1 and X_2 change at the same time? Then our regression equation would estimate the value of Y as changing from one point on the regression plane (such as, perhaps, the cross above Q) to another such point (such as, perhaps, the cross below P).

FIGURE 17.2 | The Regression Plane

Three-variable linear multiple regression analysis estimates an equation, $\hat{Y} = a + b_1X_1 + b_2X_2$, in such a way that all estimates of Y made with its help (and depicted by crosses in this graph) fall on a surface, such as ABCD, that is called the ***regression plane*** *and that is positioned among the red sample points in such a way as to minimize the sum of the squared vertical deviations between these sample points and their associated estimates. Note how point P from Figure 17.1 reappears here at a position above the regression plane and is projected by a vertical line to the cross lying on the plane directly below it. Similarly, a point such as Q is suspended below the plane and is projected by a vertical line to the cross lying on the plane directly above it.*

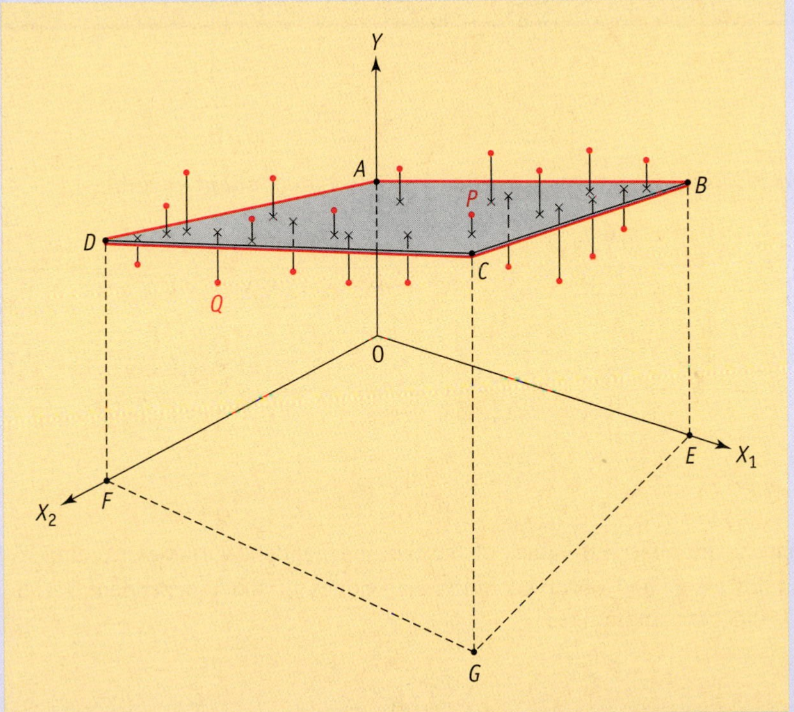

TECHNICAL DETAIL

The regression plane is positioned so as to minimize the sum of squared errors, or $\Sigma(Y - \hat{Y})^2$. In Figure 17.2, the heights of the red sample points above the X_1X_2 plane represent the values of Y, the heights of the crosses on the regression plane immediately below or above the red dots represent the associated values of $\hat{Y}$ that are estimated from the regression equation. The vertical differences, $Y - \hat{Y}$, are the errors, deviations, or residuals; the sum of their squares is to be minimized. Ronald A. Fisher (1890–1962), George Snedecor (1882–1974), and others have shown that the sum of the squared errors is minimized when three so-called *normal equations* are satisfied.

(continued)

Technical Detail (continued)

The normal equations are:

$$\Sigma Y = na + b_1\Sigma X_1 + b_2\Sigma X_2$$
$$\Sigma X_1 Y = a\Sigma X_1 + b_1\Sigma X_1^2 + b_2\Sigma X_1 X_2$$
$$\Sigma X_2 Y = a\Sigma X_2 + b_1\Sigma X_1 X_2 + b_2\Sigma X_2^2$$

From these equations one can, in turn, derive the expressions given in Formula 17.A. Clearly, we can be grateful for computer programs that eliminate the need to make such calculations by hand.

FORMULA 17.A | Estimated Multiple-Regression Coefficients (two independent variables)

$$b_1 = \frac{[\Sigma X_2^2 - n\overline{X}_2^2][\Sigma X_1 Y - n\overline{X}_1\overline{Y}] - [(\Sigma X_1 X_2 - n\overline{X}_1\overline{X}_2)(\Sigma X_2 Y - n\overline{X}_2\overline{Y})]}{[\Sigma X_1^2 - n\overline{X}_1^2][\Sigma X_2^2 - n\overline{X}_2^2] - [\Sigma X_1 X_2 - n\overline{X}_1\overline{X}_2]^2}$$

$$b_2 = \frac{[\Sigma X_1^2 - n\overline{X}_1^2][\Sigma X_2 Y - n\overline{X}_2\overline{Y}] - [(\Sigma X_1 X_2 - n\overline{X}_1\overline{X}_2)(\Sigma X_1 Y - n\overline{X}_1\overline{Y})]}{[\Sigma X_1^2 - n\overline{X}_1^2][\Sigma X_2^2 - n\overline{X}_2^2] - [\Sigma X_1 X_2 - n\overline{X}_1\overline{X}_2]^2}$$

$$a = \overline{Y} - b_1\overline{X}_1 - b_2\overline{X}_2$$

where X_1 and X_2 are observed values of the two independent variables ($\overline{X}_1$ and $\overline{X}_2$ being their means), Y's are associated observed individual values of the independent variable ($\overline{Y}$ being *their* mean), and n is sample size.

LEAST SQUARES REVISITED

Once more consider the hypothetical study of the link between income and education, first introduced in Example Problem 16.1 (on page 713). But now suppose that income is believed to be linked not only to education but to years of job experience as well. Conceivable sample data, based on Table 16.1, appear in Table 17.1.

EXCEL Example 17.1

Using the data of Table 17.1,

a. compute the estimated multiple regression equation

b. interpret each of the partial-regression coefficients

TABLE 17.1 | Sample Data on Income, Education, and Job Experience

Individual	Income (thousands of dollars per year), Y	Education (years), X_1	Job Experience (years), X_2
A	5,012	2	9
B	9,680	4	18
C	28,432	8	21
D	8,774	8	12
E	21,008	8	14
F	26,565	10	16
G	25,428	12	16
H	23,113	12	9
I	22,500	12	18
J	19,456	12	5
K	21,690	12	7
L	24,750	13	9
M	30,100	14	12
N	24,798	14	17
O	28,532	15	19
P	26,000	15	6
Q	38,908	16	17
R	22,050	16	1
S	33,060	17	10
T	48,276	21	17

c. make point estimates of income earned, given 11 years of education and 20 years of job experience and also given 8 years of education and 12 years of job experience

SOLUTION:

Part (a)

1. Enter the Table 17.1 income, education, and job experience data, inclusive of column headings, into columns A–C, respectively, of a new worksheet. (You can also copy and paste the data from columns U–W of the file HKMISC.)
2. Click **Tools** > **Data Analysis** > **Regression** > **OK** to open the *Regression* dialog box.
3. Under *Input Y Range,* enter **A1:A21**
4. Under *Input X Range,* enter **B1:C21**
5. Check *Labels* and *New Worksheet Ply,* and click **OK**.

Along with other things, the output includes the following:

	Coefficients
Intercept	−7125.62334
Education	1932.459565
Job Experience	651.8644734

Thus, the estimated multiple regression equation is

$$\text{Income} = -7{,}125.62 + 1{,}932.46 \text{ Education} + 651.86 \text{ Job Experience}$$

Part (b)

The value of $b_1 = 1{,}932.46$ implies that an estimated income increase of $1,932.46 is associated with each additional year in education, if job experience is held constant at any level.

The value of $b_2 = 651.86$ implies that an estimated income increase of $651.86 is associated with each additional year of job experience, if education is similarly held constant.

Not much should be made of $a = -7{,}125.62$, and the apparent implication that a person's income would be *negative* $7,125.62 with zero education and zero job experience. As noted in Chapter 16, such extrapolation beyond the range of sample data is not appropriate. Yet the equation can be used to predict the income of someone whose education and job experience does fall within the observed ranges of these variables—between 2 and 21 years of education and between 1 and 21 years of job experience.

Part (c)

We can predict the income of someone with 11 years of education and 20 years of job experience as

$$\hat{Y}_{11,20} = -7{,}125.62 + 1{,}932.46(11) + 651.86(20) = \$27{,}168.64$$

Similarly, we can predict the income of someone with 8 years of education and 12 years of job experience as

$$\hat{Y}_{8,12} = -7{,}125.62 + 1{,}932.46(8) + 651.86(12) = \$16{,}156.38$$

(In fact, such a person—individual D—is included in our sample, but is earning $8,774 per year.)

EXCEL can make both computations at once:

1. In addition to the data entered in step 1 of Part (a) above, enter the range of *X* values to be used for predicting. For example, enter the labels *X1, X2*, and *Predicted Y* into cells F1–H1. Then enter 11 and 20 into F2–G2 and 8 and 12 into F3–G3.
2. Select a range of cells to receive the predicted *Y* values, such as H2–H3.
3. Click the **Function Wizard (*fx*)** > **Statistical** > **TREND** > **OK** to activate a dialog box.
4. Under *Known y's,* enter **A2:A21** and press TAB.
5. Under *Known x's,* enter **B2:C21** and press TAB.

6. Under *New x's,* enter **F2:G3** and press TAB.
7. Under *Const,* enter **1** or **TRUE** or nothing at all (to indicate that the regression constant is not to be forced to a value of zero); then click **OK**.
8. The first prediction appears in cell H2. With H2:H3 still selected, press the F2 key. The word EDIT appears in the status bar below the worksheet.
9. Hold Ctrl + Shift and press Enter to get all remaining predictions:

X1	X2	Predicted Y
11	20	27168.7213
8	12	16156.4269

17.3 The Sample Standard Error of the Estimate of *Y*

As in Chapter 16, we can evaluate the quality of our estimated regression equation by computing the *sample standard error of the estimate of Y,* which in this case measures the dispersion of observed *Y* values about the regression *plane.* Once again, modern computer programs make the computations for us.

TECHNICAL DETAIL

Because two independent variables are being used to estimate *Y,* the standard error is not designated as $s_{Y \cdot X}$ (as in Chapter 16), but as $s_{Y \cdot X_1 X_2}$ or, more simply, as $s_{Y \cdot 12}$ (both pronounced "sample standard error of the estimate of *Y,* given X_1 and X_2"). In addition, because we lose 3 degrees of freedom when estimating the 3 regression coefficients, the divisor in the formula is adjusted accordingly from $n - 2$ (noted in Chapter 16) to $n - 3$, which makes $s^2_{Y \cdot 12}$ an unbiased estimator of the variance of *Y* about the regression plane. The two alternatives in Formula 17.B, accordingly, are adaptations of those found in Formula 16.B on page 733.

FORMULA 17.B | The Sample Standard Error of the Estimate of *Y* (two independent variables)

$$s_{Y \cdot 12} = \sqrt{\frac{\Sigma(Y - \hat{Y})^2}{n - 3}} = \sqrt{\frac{\Sigma Y^2 - a\Sigma Y - b_1 \Sigma X_1 Y - b_2 \Sigma X_2 Y}{n - 3}}$$

where *Y* is an observed individual value of the dependent variable; $\hat{Y}$ is its estimated value, given values of independent variables X_1 and X_2; a, b_1, and b_2 are the estimated regression coefficients; and n is sample size.

EXCEL Example 17.2

Using the data of Table 17.1, compute the *standard error of the estimate of Y* for

a. a simple regression of income versus education

b. a multiple regression of income versus education and job experience (and comment on the difference between the two results)

SOLUTION:

Part (a)

1. Enter the Table 17.1 income, education, and job experience data, inclusive of column headings, into columns A–C, respectively, of a new worksheet. (You can also copy and paste the data from columns U–W of the file HKMISC.)
2. Select an empty cell and click the **Function Wizard (*fx*)** > **Statistical** > **STEYX** > **OK**.
3. Under *Known y's,* enter **A2:A21** and press TAB.
4. Under *Known x's,* enter **B2:B21** and click **OK**.

The result appears in the chosen cell as 5377.38.

Part (b)

Repeat the five steps of Part (a) of EXCEL Example 17.1. Among other things, the output includes the desired standard error (here highlighted in red):

Regression Statistics	
Multiple R	0.91916
R Square	0.84485
Adjusted R Square	0.82659
Standard Error	4076.46
Observations	20

The standard error of the estimate of Y in (b) is smaller than in (a). Thus, the multiple regression provides a better explanation of the data. Much less of the variation in Y is left unexplained here. Therefore, predictions of Y with the help of the multiple regression equation are better than those made with the help of the simple regression equation.

17.4 Making Inferences

Provided that certain conditions hold, we can use estimated multiple-regression equations to make a variety of inferences about the populations from which samples were drawn. The necessary assumptions are analogous to those described in Chapter 16; we review them here, along with one addition.

CRUCIAL ASSUMPTIONS

ASSUMPTION 1 It is assumed that every population of Y values (a different one of which is associated with every possible X_1X_2 combination) is normally distributed, with a conditional mean of $\mu_{Y \cdot X_1X_2}$ (also denoted as $\mu_{Y \cdot 12}$) and a conditional standard deviation of $\sigma_{Y \cdot X_1X_2}$ (also denoted as $\sigma_{Y \cdot 12}$).

ASSUMPTION 2 It is assumed that all conditional probability distributions of Y (a different one of which is associated with every possible X_1X_2 combination) have the same conditional standard deviation, $\sigma_{Y \cdot 12}$ (homoscedasticity exists).

ASSUMPTION 3 It is assumed that the values of X_1 and X_2 are known without error and that the different sample observations about Y that are associated with any X_1X_2 combination are statistically independent of each other.

ASSUMPTION 4 It is assumed that all the conditional means, $\mu_{Y \cdot 12}$, lie on a surface, similar to *ABCD* in Figure 17.2, that is the *true regression plane* and is described by the equation

$$E(Y) = \mu_{Y \cdot 12} = \alpha + \beta_1 X_1 + \beta_2 X_2$$

The estimated regression coefficients a, b_1, and b_2 are, in turn, estimators of α, β_1, and β_2. As in the simple regression case, this assumption is still referred to as the assumption of linearity, even though the line has become a plane.

ASSUMPTION 5 It is assumed that no exact linear relationship exists between different independent variables. If different X's are perfectly linearly correlated, we cannot calculate the parameter estimates because two or more of the normal equations are then not independent. If different X's are imperfectly but highly correlated, we can calculate the regression coefficients, but cannot isolate the individual effects of each of these highly linearly correlated variables on Y.

ESTIMATING THE AVERAGE VALUE OF Y, Given X_1 AND X_2

Suppose we wanted to estimate the value of a conditional mean, $\mu_{Y \cdot X_1X_2}$, such as $\mu_{Y \cdot 11,20}$ (the average income of all members of our population who have 11 years of education and 20 years of job experience). The best *point estimate,* computed earlier in this chapter, equals \$27,166. For a small sample, such as ours, we can compute a confidence interval by using Formula 17.C, which involves matrix notation in the expression $\sqrt{M}$. Matrix algebra, however, is too complex for the intended level of this text. We rely on a computer program to find the answer.

FORMULA 17.C | Confidence-Interval Limits for the Average Value of Y, Given X_1 and X_2 (small-sample case, $n < 30$)

$$\mu_{Y \cdot 12} = \hat{Y} \pm \left(t_{\alpha/2} \cdot s_{Y \cdot 12} \cdot \sqrt{M}\right)$$

where $\hat{Y}$ is the estimated value of dependent variable Y; the value of $t_{\alpha/2}$ is found in Appendix Table K for $n - m - 1$ degrees of freedom (given n sample observations and m independent variables); $s_{Y \cdot 12}$ is the sample standard error of the estimate of Y; and M is the product of three matrices (as more advanced texts explain).

(continued on page 798)

Notes:

1. The parenthetical expression in Formula 17.C can be *approximated* by $t_{\alpha/2} \cdot \frac{s_{Y\cdot 12}}{\sqrt{n}}$. To pursue the precise solution with matrix algebra, see Thomas H. Wonnacott and Ronald J. Wonnacott, *Regression: A Second Course in Statistics* (New York: John Wiley & Sons, 1981, pp. 442–446).
2. In the large-sample case ($n \geq 30$), the normal deviate, z, replaces t.

EXCEL Example 17.3

Using the sample data of Table 17.1, construct a 95 percent confidence interval for the average income associated with 11 years of education and 20 years of job experience.

SOLUTION: EXCEL is not equipped to create the $\mu_{Y\cdot 11,20}$ confidence interval directly, but we can compute an *approximation*, using Formula 17.C as follows:

1. Enter the Table 17.1 income, education, and job experience data, inclusive of column headings, into columns A–C, respectively, of a new worksheet. (You can also copy and paste the data from columns U–W of the file HKMISC.)
2. Enter the labels *Point estimate, Sample size, Degrees of freedom, Standard error of estimate, Critical t, Half-width of confidence interval, Lower limit of confidence interval,* and *Upper limit of confidence interval* into cells E1–E8 of your worksheet.
3. Enter corresponding formulas or known values into adjacent column F cells:

   27168.7213 (from EXCEL Example 17.1) into F1

   20 into F2

   17 into F3

   4076.46 (from EXCEL Example 17.2) into F4

   =TINV(1−95/100,F3) into F5

   =F5*F4/SQRT(F2) into F6

   =F1−F6 into F7

   =F1+F6 into F8

The result includes the *approximation* of the desired 95 percent confidence interval (highlighted in red):

Point estimate	27168.7213
Sample size	20
Degrees of freedom	17
Standard error of estimate	4076.46
Critical *t*	2.10981852
Half-width of confidence interval	1923.15057
Lower limit of confidence interval	25245.5707
Upper limit of confidence interval	29091.8719

INTERPRETATION We can be 95 percent confident that the height of the regression plane at $X_1 = 11$ and $X_2 = 20$ lies within the stated limits. On average, people with 11 years of education and 20 years of job experience have annual incomes between \$25,245.57 and \$29,091.87.

Notes:

1. You can derive the preceding approximations more quickly by using HKStat, Sheet 42.
2. A precise calculation with matrix algebra yields an interval reaching from \$23,885 to \$30,453.

PREDICTING AN INDIVIDUAL VALUE OF Y, GIVEN X_1 AND X_2

Suppose we wanted to predict some $I_{Y \cdot X_1 X_2}$, such as $I_{Y \cdot 11,20}$ (the particular income of the next member of our population encountered in sampling who falls into the 11 years' education and 20 years' job experience category). The best *point estimate,* computed earlier in this chapter, equals \$27,166. We can compute a small-sample prediction interval with Formula 17.D, which once again employs matrix algebra.

FORMULA 17.D | Confidence-Interval Limits for an Individual Value of Y, Given X_1 and X_2 (small-sample case, $n < 30$)

$$I_{Y \cdot 12} = \hat{Y} \pm \left(t_{\alpha/2} \cdot s_{Y \cdot 12} \cdot \sqrt{1 + M}\right)$$

where $\hat{Y}$ is the estimated value of dependent variable Y; the value of $t_{\alpha/2}$ is found in Appendix Table K for $n - m - 1$ degrees of freedom (given n sample observations and m independent variables); $s_{Y \cdot 12}$ is the sample standard error of the estimate of Y; and M is the product of three matrices (as more advanced texts explain).

Notes:

1. The parenthetical expression can be *approximated* by $t_{\alpha/2} \cdot s_{Y \cdot 12}\sqrt{\frac{n+1}{n}}$. To pursue the precise solution with matrix algebra, see Thomas H. Wonnacott and Ronald J. Wonnacott, *Regression: A Second Course in Statistics* (New York: John Wiley & Sons, 1981, pp. 442–446).
2. In the large-sample case ($n \geq 30$), the normal deviate, z, replaces t.

EXCEL Example 17.4

Using the sample data of Table 17.1, construct a 95 percent prediction interval for the income of the next member of the population encountered in sampling who has 11 years of education and 20 years of job experience.

SOLUTION: EXCEL is not equipped to create the $I_{Y \cdot 11,20}$ prediction interval directly, but we can compute an *approximation,* using Formula 17.D as follows:

1. Enter the Table 17.1 income, education, and job experience data, inclusive of column headings, into columns A–C, respectively, of a new worksheet. (You can also copy and paste the data from columns U–W of the file HKMISC.)
2. Enter the labels *Point estimate, Sample size, Degrees of freedom, Standard error of estimate, Critical t, Half-width of prediction interval, Lower limit of prediction interval,* and *Upper limit of prediction interval* into cells E1–E8 of your worksheet.

3. Enter corresponding formulas or known values into adjacent column F cells:

27168.7213 (from EXCEL Example 17.1) into F1

20 into F2

17 into F3

4076.46 (from EXCEL Example 17.2) into F4

=TINV(1−95/100,F3) into F5

=F5*F4*SQRT((F2+1)/F2) into F6

=F1−F6 into F7

=F1+F6 into F8

The result includes the *approximation* of the desired 95 percent prediction interval (highlighted in red):

Point estimate	27168.7213
Sample size	20
Degrees of freedom	17
Standard error of estimate	4076.46
Critical t	2.10981852
Half-width of prediction interval	8812.98307
Lower limit of prediction interval	18355.7382
Upper limit of prediction interval	35981.7044

INTERPRETATION We can be 95 percent confident that the next person encountered in sampling with the characteristics of $X_1 = 11$ and $X_2 = 20$ has an annual income between \$18,355.74 and \$35,981.70.

Notes:

1. You can derive the preceding approximations more quickly by using HKStat, Sheet 42.
2. A precise calculation with matrix algebra yields an interval reaching from \$17,963 to \$36,375.

ESTABLISHING CONFIDENCE INTERVALS FOR β_1 AND β_2

In multiple regression, no less than in simple regression, we must determine whether a nonzero value of any sample coefficient, b, which estimates the corresponding population coefficient, β, is statistically significant or merely the result of a sampling error. In the latter case, the positive or negative value of b could be quite consistent with a β value of zero!

In the small-sample case, we can establish confidence intervals for β values by using the t distribution, in a fashion analogous to that noted in Chapter 16. Computer programs employ the formulas noted here (or compute key values used therein).

FORMULA 17.E | Confidence-Interval Limits for β_1 and β_2 (small-sample case, $n < 30$)

$$\beta_1 = b_1 \pm t_{\alpha/2} \cdot \sigma_{b_1} \cong b_1 \pm (t_{\alpha/2} \cdot s_{b_1})$$

$$= b_1 \pm \left(t_{\alpha/2} \cdot s_{Y \cdot 12} \sqrt{\frac{\Sigma X_2^2 - n\bar{X}_2^2}{(\Sigma X_1^2 - n\bar{X}_1^2)(\Sigma X_2^2 - n\bar{X}_2^2) - (\Sigma X_1 X_2 - n\bar{X}_1\bar{X}_2)^2}} \right)$$

$$\beta_2 = b_2 \pm t_{\alpha/2} \cdot \sigma_{b_2} \cong b_2 \pm (t_{\alpha/2} \cdot s_{b_2})$$

$$= b_2 \pm \left(t_{\alpha/2} \cdot s_{Y \cdot 12} \sqrt{\frac{\Sigma X_1^2 - n\bar{X}_1^2}{(\Sigma X_1^2 - n\bar{X}_1^2)(\Sigma X_2^2 - n\bar{X}_2^2) - (\Sigma X_1 X_2 - n\bar{X}_1\bar{X}_2)^2}} \right)$$

where b_1 and b_2 are estimated partial-regression coefficients (and s_{b_1} and s_{b_2} are their standard errors); the value of $t_{\alpha/2}$ is found in Appendix Table K for $n - m - 1$ degrees of freedom (given n sample observations and m independent variables); $s_{Y \cdot 12}$ is the sample standard error of the estimate of Y; and the X's are observed individual values of the independent variables (the $\bar{X}$'s being their means).

EXCEL Example 17.5

Using the sample data of Table 17.1, construct 95 percent confidence intervals for the true regression coefficients, β_1 and β_2.

SOLUTION:

1. Enter the Table 17.1 income, education, and job experience data, inclusive of column headings, into columns A–C, respectively, of a new worksheet. (You can also copy and paste the data from columns U–W of the file HKMISC.)
2. Click **Tools** > **Data Analysis** > **Regression** > **OK** to open the *Regression* dialog box.
3. Under *Input Y Range,* enter **A1:A21**
4. Under *Input X Range,* enter **B1:C21**
5. Check *Labels* and *New Worksheet Ply,* and click **OK**

Along with other things, the output includes the following:

	Coefficients	*Standard Error*	*t Stat*	*P-value*	*Lower 95%*	*Upper 95%*
Intercept	−7125.6233	3628.326093	−1.96389	0.066111	−14780.73	529.48626
Education	1932.45956	210.0602721	9.199548	5.18E−08	1489.2705	2375.6486
Job Experience	651.864473	172.2498255	3.784413	0.00148	288.4486	1015.2803

Thus, we can be 95 percent confident that the values of β_1 and β_2 are not zero, but lie within these intervals:

$$1{,}489.2705 \le \beta_1 \le 2{,}375.6486$$

$$288.4486 \le \beta_2 \le 1{,}015.2803$$

In the population as a whole, each extra year of education yields between $1,489 and $2,376 of extra annual income. In the population as a whole, each extra year of job experience yields between $288 and $1,015 of extra annual income.

USING *t* VALUES

Frequently, statisticians establish the significance of an estimated regression coefficient with the help of a ***t* value,** or ***t* ratio,** which is the ratio of an estimated partial-regression coefficient to its standard error. For example,

$$t_{b_1} = \frac{b_1}{s_{b_1}} \quad \text{and} \quad t_{b_2} = \frac{b_2}{s_{b_2}}$$

All modern computer regression programs provide such computed t values (although some of them designate them as capital T). We can easily compare these values with a critical t value, such as the $t_{.025(17)} = 2.11$ employed in our income versus education and job experience example (that involved a 95 percent confidence level and $n - m - 1 = 20 - 2 - 1 = 17$ degrees of freedom). Whenever the computed t value exceeds the critical t value, we conclude that the estimated partial-regression coefficient is statistically significant at the chosen level of confidence. Indeed, to facilitate this comparison, absolute magnitudes of computed t values are often printed in parentheses underneath the coefficients of the regression equation:

$$\begin{aligned} \text{Income} = \underset{(1.96)}{-7{,}126} + \underset{(9.20)}{1{,}932.5}\ \text{Educ.} + \underset{(3.78)}{651.9}\ \text{JobExp.} \end{aligned}$$

And here is an interesting fact: As the appropriate column of Appendix Table K shows, critical t values for 95 percent confidence levels (the favorite choice of many statisticians) are always roughly equal to 2. (The critical t equals 2.228 for $n = 10$ and 1.96 for $n = \infty$.) This convenient fact leads to the following rule of thumb:

FORMULA 17.F | Rule of Thumb for Assessing Computed *t* Values

Whenever the absolute magnitude of a computed t value exceeds 2 (we can ignore possible minus signs), we can instantly treat the associated estimate as statistically significant at the 95 percent level of confidence.

Note: Obviously, if we are not interested in this particular confidence level but prefer another, this rule of thumb is not for us. Then we check whether the computed t value exceeds the critical t value for our preferred confidence level and, when that is the case, conclude that the estimated partial-regression coefficient is statistically significant at that other level of confidence.

EXCEL Example 17.6

Using the sample data of Table 17.1, construct a multiple regression equation and make a t test of its coefficients.

SOLUTION:

1. Enter the Table 17.1 income, education, and job experience data, inclusive of column headings, into columns A–C, respectively, of a new worksheet. (You can also copy and paste the data from columns U–W of the file HKMISC.)
2. Click **Tools** > **Data Analysis** > **Regression** > **OK** to open the *Regression* dialog box.
3. Under *Input Y Range,* enter **A1:A21**
4. Under *Input X Range,* enter **B1:C21**
5. Check *Labels* and *New Worksheet Ply,* and click **OK**.

Along with other things, the output includes the following:

	Coefficients	*Standard Error*	*t Stat*	*P-value*	*Lower 95%*	*Upper 95%*
Intercept	−7125.6233	3628.326093	−1.96389	0.066111	−14780.73	529.48626
Education	1932.45956	210.0602721	9.199548	5.18E−08	1489.2705	2375.6486
Job Experience	651.864473	172.2498255	3.784413	0.00148	288.4486	1015.2803

COMMENT Given a 95 percent confidence level and $n - m - 1 = 20 - 2 - 1 = 17$ degrees of freedom, according to Appendix Table K, the critical $t_{.025(17)} = 2.11$. The computed t value for b_1 is 9.20, that for b_2 is 3.78. Both numbers exceed the critical value (and also satisfy the Formula 17.F rule of thumb). Therefore, we can be 95 percent confident that the corresponding population coefficients, β_1 and β_2, just as b_1 and b_2, are positive numbers rather than equal to zero. In the population as a whole, just as in our sample, more education as well as more job experience, translates into more income.

USING *p* VALUES

We have yet a third alternative for testing the degree of significance of an estimated regression coefficient computed from sample data. On the basis of the estimated coefficient's t value, we can calculate a ***p* value** that gives the probability of H_0 being true, given the claim H_0: The true regression coefficient equals 0. Once again, modern computer regression programs provide such p values.

EXCEL Example 17.7

Using the sample data of Table 17.1, construct a multiple regression equation and make a test the significance of its coefficients with the help of p values.

SOLUTION:

1. Enter the Table 17.1 income, education, and job experience data, inclusive of column headings, into columns A–C, respectively, of a new worksheet. (You can also copy and paste the data from columns U–W of the file HKMISC.)

2. Click **Tools** > **Data Analysis** > **Regression** > **OK** to open the *Regression* dialog box.
3. Under *Input Y Range,* enter **A1:A21**
4. Under *Input X Range,* enter **B1:C21**
5. Check *Labels* and *New Worksheet Ply,* and click **OK**.

Along with other things, the output includes the following:

	Coefficients	*Standard Error*	*t Stat*	*P-value*	*Lower 95%*	*Upper 95%*
Intercept	−7125.6233	3628.326093	−1.96389	0.066111	−14780.73	529.48626
Education	1932.45956	210.0602721	9.199548	5.18E−08	1489.2705	2375.6486
Job Experience	651.864473	172.2498255	3.784413	0.00148	288.4486	1015.2803

COMMENT Given the sample data, there is a 6.6 percent chance of α being zero, but a 0 percent chance for β_1 or β_2 being zero. In the population as a whole, just as in our sample, more education as well as more job experience, translates into more income.

17.5 ANOVA Revisited: Testing the Overall Significance of a Regression

A test of the overall significance of a regression, rather than a test of the significance of individual coefficients, amounts to testing the hypothesis that *all* of the true regression coefficients are zero and that, therefore, *none* of the independent variables helps explain the variation of the dependent variable. The procedure is most easily explained by example.

EXAMPLE PROBLEM 17.1

Review the data of Table 17.1 on page 793. At the 5 percent level of significance, perform an ANOVA test of the overall significance of the regression summarized by the equation

$$\text{Income} = -7{,}126 + 1{,}932.5 \text{ Educ.} + 651.9 \text{ JobExp.}$$

SOLUTION: Given two independent variables (education and job experience), the opposing hypotheses are the following:

$$H_0\text{: both } \beta_1 = 0 \text{ and } \beta_2 = 0$$

$$H_A\text{: either } \beta_1 \neq 0 \text{ or } \beta_2 \neq 0$$

We perform the test by constructing an ANOVA table, such as Table 17.2.

COLUMN 1 We can compute the various sums of squares in column 1 from the data of Table 17.1 and Formula 16.H (on page 755), but we can also derive them from mathematically equivalent expressions:

$$RSS = \Sigma(\hat{Y} - \overline{Y})^2 = a\Sigma Y + b_1\Sigma X_1 Y + b_2\,\Sigma X_2 Y - n\overline{Y}^2 = 1{,}538{,}273{,}843$$

$$ESS = \Sigma(Y - \hat{Y})^2 = \Sigma Y^2 - a\Sigma Y - b_1\,\Sigma X_1 Y - b_2\Sigma X_2 Y = 282{,}498{,}276$$

$$\textit{Total SS} = \Sigma(Y - \overline{Y})^2 = \Sigma Y^2 - n\overline{Y}^2 = 1{,}820{,}772{,}119$$

COLUMN 2 As usual, column 2 lists the appropriate degrees of freedom. They equal the number of independent variables, m, for the regression sum of squares. They equal sample size n, minus m minus 1 (here $n - 3$) for the error sum of squares. (In this example, there are $n = 20$ errors and 3 constraints—namely, the estimated regression coefficients, a, b_1, and b_2.) Finally, the degrees of freedom equal $n - 1$ for the total sum of squares. (In this example, we have $n = 20$ deviations subject to the single constraint that $\Sigma(Y - \overline{Y}) = 0$.)

COLUMN 3 We use the preceding information to compute the regression mean square and the error mean square in column 3. (The square root of the latter expression, or $\sqrt{EMS} = \sqrt{16{,}617{,}546} = 4{,}076$, equals $s_{Y \cdot 12}$, the standard error of the estimate of Y, which we computed earlier in this chapter.)

COLUMN 4 The two mean squares are the sample variances that we use to calculate $F = 46.28$, as shown in column 4. For a test of H_0 at the 5 percent level of significance, Appendix Table N provides the critical F for 2 numerator and 17 denominator degrees of freedom as $F_{.05(2,17)} = 3.59$. Thus, there is only a 5 percent chance that the computed value of F exceeds 3.59 if H_0 is true. Accordingly, we *reject* H_0. Far from being of no help, our regression is highly significant, indeed; a knowledge of X_1 and X_2 (years of education and job experience) does explain almost all of the variation of Y (income) in the population from which we drew our sample.

TABLE 17.2 | The ANOVA Table

Source of Variation	Sum of Squares (1)	Degrees of Freedom (2)	Mean Square (3) = (1) ÷ (2)	Test Statistic (4)
Regression (variation explained by X's)	$RSS =$ 1,538,273,843	$m = 2$	$RMS =$ 769,136,921	$F = \frac{RMS}{EMS} = 46.28$
Error (unexplained variation)	$ESS =$ 282,498,276	$n - m - 1 = n - 3 = 17$	$EMS =$ 16,617,546	
Total	*Total SS* = 1,820,772,119	$n - 1 = 19$		

EXCEL Example 17.8

Review Example Problem 17.1. Confirm its result with a computer ANOVA program.

SOLUTION:

1. Enter the Table 17.1 income, education, and job experience data, inclusive of column headings, into columns A–C, respectively, of a new worksheet. (You can also copy and paste the data from columns U–W of the file HKMISC.)

2. Click **Tools** > **Data Analysis** > **Regression** > **OK** to open the *Regression* dialog box.
3. Under *Input Y Range,* enter **A1:A21**
4. Under *Input X Range,* enter **B1:C21**
5. Check *Labels* and *New Worksheet Ply,* and click **OK**.

Along with other things, the output includes the following:

ANOVA

	df	*SS*	*MS*	*F*	*Significance F*
Regression	2	1538273843	7.69E+08	46.28463	1.3227E−07
Residual	17	282498276.2	16617546		
Total	19	1820772119			

COMMENT The computer-produced ANOVA table corresponds to Table 17.2. The *F* statistic, and, therefore, the conclusion, is identical to Example Problem 17.1. The printout also contains a *p* value, called *Significance F,* giving the zero probability of computing this kind of *F* statistic if the null hypothesis is true.

17.6 Multiple Correlation Analysis

The concept of correlation can be extended from an analysis dealing with one independent variable to one dealing with several of them. The aim is once again to calculate a single value that, in this case, describes the overall strength of association between a dependent variable and two or more independent variables. To distinguish between the coefficients of simple and multiple correlation, capital letters are often used to designate the coefficients of multiple correlation.

THE COEFFICIENT OF MULTIPLE DETERMINATION

The **sample coefficient of multiple determination** is denoted by R^2 and equals the proportion of the total variation in the values of the dependent variable, Y, that is explained by the multiple regression of Y on X_1, X_2, and possibly additional independent variables (X_3, X_4, and so on). In the case of two independent variables, this coefficient describes, therefore, how well the regression *plane* fits the data; its definition is given in Formula 17.G.

FORMULA 17.G | Sample Coefficient of Multiple Determination

$$R^2 = \frac{\text{explained variation}}{\text{total variation}} = \frac{RSS}{Total\ SS} = \frac{\Sigma(\hat{Y} - \overline{Y})^2}{\Sigma(Y - \overline{Y})^2}$$

When there are two independent variables only, this expression equals

$$R^2 = \frac{a\Sigma Y + b_1\Sigma X_1 Y + b_2\Sigma X_2 Y - n\overline{Y}^2}{\Sigma Y^2 - n\overline{Y}^2}$$

where Y's are observed individual values of the dependent variable ($\overline{Y}$ being their mean), $\hat{Y}$'s are estimated values of Y's, the X's are observed individual values of the independent variables, a's and b's are estimated partial-regression coefficients, and n is sample size.

As in the case of simple regression, R^2 can take on values between 0 and 1. The closer R^2 is to 0, the worse is the fit of the regression plane to the data; the closer it is to 1, the better the fit. (Computer programs often express R^2 in percentage terms by multiplying its value by 100.)

THE COEFFICIENT OF MULTIPLE CORRELATION

The **sample coefficient of multiple correlation** is an alternative index of the degree of linear association among more than two variables. Denoted by R, it equals the square root of R^2. Its sign is always considered positive.

THE ADJUSTED COEFFICIENT OF MULTIPLE DETERMINATION

In Chapter 12, we noted how important it is for sample statistics to be unbiased estimators of corresponding population parameters. (For a quick review, see pages 484–487.) Unfortunately, the value of R^2 that is computed according to Formula 17.G is anything but unbiased. It has a tendency to be "too large" in the sense that it overestimates the coefficient of multiple determination that one would compute with *census* data. This **true coefficient of multiple determination,** also known as the **population coefficient of multiple determination,** is designated by ρ^2 (the lowercase Greek rho squared). The R^2 bias just noted can be removed by computing an **adjusted sample coefficient of multiple determination,** R^2(adj.). While

$$R^2 = \frac{\text{explained variation}}{\text{total variation}} = \frac{RSS}{Total\ SS} = 1 - \frac{ESS}{Total\ SS}$$

the expression for R^2(adj.) makes an adjustment for degrees of freedom, as Formula 17.H shows.

FORMULA 17.H | Adjusted Sample Coefficient of Multiple Determination

$$R^2\,(\text{adj.}) = 1 - \frac{\dfrac{ESS}{error\ d.f.}}{\dfrac{Total\ SS}{total\ d.f.}} = 1 - \frac{\dfrac{ESS}{n-m-1}}{\dfrac{Total\ SS}{n-1}} = 1 - \frac{EMS}{TMS} = \frac{s_Y^2 - s_{Y\cdot 1,2,\ldots m}^2}{s_Y^2}$$

where ESS is the error sum of squares (with $n - m - 1$ error degrees of freedom), $Total\ SS$ is the total sum of squares (with $n - 1$ total degrees of freedom), n is sample size, m is the number of independent variables in the regression, EMS is the error mean square, TMS is the total mean square, s_Y^2 is the sample variance of the dependent variable, Y, around its mean, and $s_{Y\cdot 1,2,\ldots m}^2$ is the variance of Y around the estimated regression.

Note: The formula can also be employed to compute an adjusted sample coefficient of *simple* determination; in that case, $m = 1$; hence the error degrees of freedom equal $n - 2$.

EXCEL Example 17.9

Review the data of Table 17.1 on page 793. Then use a computer program to compute

a. the (unadjusted and adjusted) sample coefficient of determination between income and education only,

b. the (unadjusted and adjusted) sample coefficient of multiple determination for income versus education *and* job experience and comment on the difference between answers (a) and (b),

c. the (unadjusted and adjusted) sample coefficient of correlation between income and education only,

d. the (unadjusted and adjusted) sample coefficient of multiple correlation for income versus education *and* job experience.

SOLUTION: Enter the Table 17.1 income, education, and job experience data, inclusive of column headings, into columns A–C, respectively, of a new worksheet. (You can also copy and paste the data from columns U–W of the file HKMISC.)

Part (a)

1. Click **Tools** > **Data Analysis** > **Regression** > **OK** to open the *Regression* dialog box.
2. Under *Input Y Range,* enter **A1:A21**
3. Under *Input X Range,* enter **B1:B21**
4. Check *Labels* and *New Worksheet Ply,* and click **OK**.

Along with other things, the output includes the following:

Regression Statistics	
Multiple R	0.84507
R Square	0.71414
Adjusted R Square	0.69826
Standard Error	5377.38
Observations	20

COMMENT The value of $r^2 = .71414$, suggesting that 71.4 percent of the variation in income is explained by the regression of income on education. However, a less biased estimate of the population coefficient ρ^2 is $r^2(\text{adj.}) = .69826$, suggesting a somewhat lower value of 69.8 percent.

Part (b)

1. Click **Tools** > **Data Analysis** > **Regression** > **OK** to open the *Regression* dialog box.
2. Under *Input Y Range,* enter **A1:A21**
3. Under *Input X Range,* enter **B1:C21**
4. Check *Labels* and *New Worksheet Ply,* and click **OK**.

Along with other things, the output includes the following:

Regression Statistics	
Multiple R	0.9192
R Square	0.8448
Adjusted R Square	0.8266
Standard Error	4076.5
Observations	20

COMMENT The value of $R^2 = .8448$, suggesting that 84.5 percent of the variation in income is explained by the regression of income on education and job experience. However, a less biased estimate of the population coefficient ρ^2 is R^2(adj.) = .8266, suggesting a somewhat lower percentage of 82.7 percent. In either case, the multiple regression improves on the simple regression used in (a). More of the income variation is explained.

Part (c)

We merely take the square roots of the Part (a) answers:

$$r = \sqrt{.71414} = .845 \quad \text{and} \quad r(adj.) = \sqrt{.69826} = .836$$

Part (d)

We merely take the square roots of the Part (b) answers:

$$R = \sqrt{.8448} = .919 \quad \text{and} \quad R(adj.) = \sqrt{.8266} = .909$$

Note: Two of these values can also be found in the first rows of the above printouts.

CAUTION

An unadjusted coefficient of determination always increases when a relevant and previously ignored independent variable is added to a regression model (note the increase in our example from $r^2 = .714$ to $R^2 = .845$). In contrast, the value of R^2(adj.) can actually decrease and will do so when the addition of a new independent variable does not reduce the error sum of squares (*ESS*) enough to offset the loss of one degree of freedom that is occasioned by the increase in *m*. In that case, in an ANOVA table such as Table 17.2 on page 805, a lower *ESS* can nevertheless raise *EMS* and lower *F*. If that happens, the addition of the new independent variable did not improve the explanatory power of the regression.

PARTIAL CORRELATION

As we just recalled, our simple regression of income (Y) on education (X_1) in Chapter 16 produced an unadjusted simple coefficient of determination of $r^2 = .714$. The addition to our model, in this chapter, of job experience (X_2) as a second explanatory variable yielded a regression equation with considerably greater predictive power and produced an unadjusted multiple coefficient of determination of $R^2 = .845$. It is common practice to *quantify* the improvement achieved by such higher-dimensional regression analysis (that uses additional explanatory variables). The result is an index of association between the dependent variable and just *one* of the independent variables, given a prior accounting of the effects of other independent variables. The index is calculated as the proportional decrease in the previously unexplained variation (or increase in the previously explained variation) resulting from the higher-dimensional regression. Formula 17.I defines the new measure, called the **sample coefficient of partial determination,** for the case in which a regression with one independent variable is replaced by a regression with two such variables.

It is easy to see why statisticians often use the sample coefficient of partial determination, or its square root, the **sample coefficient of partial correlation,** to evaluate the merit of potentially adding an explanatory variable to a regression analysis. In our case, as Example Problem 17.2 shows, the addition of X_2 is worthwhile because that addition quite effectively sharpens the analysis.

FORMULA 17.I | Sample Coefficient of Partial Determination

$$r^2_{Y2\cdot 1} = \frac{\text{reduction in previously unexplained variation in } Y}{\text{previously unexplained variation in } Y} = \frac{R^2_{Y\cdot 12} - r^2_{Y\cdot 1}}{1 - r^2_{Y\cdot 1}}$$

where $R^2_{Y\cdot 12}$ is the sample coefficient of multiple determination, calculated for a regression of Y on X_1 *and* X_2, while $r^2_{Y\cdot 1}$ is the sample coefficient of simple determination, calculated for a regression of Y on X_1 only (that ignores other independent variables, such as X_2).

Note: The coefficient is defined analogously for additional moves to ever higher-dimensional regressions. For example, going from two to three independent variables produces $r^2_{Y3\cdot 12} = \dfrac{R^2_{Y\cdot 123} - R^2_{Y\cdot 12}}{1 - R^2_{Y\cdot 12}}$.

EXAMPLE PROBLEM 17.2

Using the data of Table 17.1 on page 793,

a. compute the sample coefficient of partial determination for a move from a simple regression of income (Y) against education (X_1) only to a multiple regression of income (Y) against education (X_1) *and* job experience (X_2).

b. interpret the result.

SOLUTION:

a. Applying Formula 17.I to coefficients previously calculated,

$$r^2_{Y2\cdot 1} = \frac{R^2_{Y\cdot 12} - r^2_{Y\cdot 1}}{1 - r^2_{Y\cdot 1}} = \frac{.845 - .714}{1 - .714} = .458$$

b. This result implies that 45.8 percent of the variation in Y (income) that was left unexplained by the simple regression of income on education has been explained by the addition of job experience as an explanatory variable. Indeed, we can confirm this result independently by comparing the error sums of squares found in the respective ANOVA tables. The value of *ESS* changed from 520,489,202 in Table 16.3 (page 762) to 282,498,276 in Table 17.2 (page 805), which is a 45.8 percent reduction.

17.7 Linear Multiple Regression Analysis with Three or More Explanatory Variables

When linear regressions involve three or more independent variables, the principles of analysis remain the same. In the case of three independent variables, the computer finds an estimated least-squares regression equation of the form

$$\hat{Y} = a + b_1X_1 + b_2X_2 + b_3X_3$$

and this procedure can be extended without end when we include additional predictor variables in the analysis (by adding b_4X_4, b_5X_5, and so on to the equation). The moment the analysis involves four variables, one dependent and three independent, we can no longer picture the data in a scatter diagram. The human mind can envision two dimensions (note Figure 16.5 on page 714) and even three dimensions (note Figure 17.2 on page 791), but it balks at four dimensions and more. As mathematicians put it, estimating a least-squares regression equation with three or more independent variables is analogous to fitting a **regression hyperplane** to the sample data. Such a plane exists in four or higher-dimensional space, but no one has ever seen it!

Higher-dimensional regression analysis still includes the calculation of the standard error of the estimate of *Y*, which is now symbolized by $s_{Y\cdot 123}$, $s_{Y\cdot 1234}$, and so on, depending on how many independent variables are included. The calculation of these standard errors is again a straightforward extension of our earlier methods. While

$$s_{Y\cdot 12} = \frac{\Sigma Y^2 - a\Sigma Y - b_1\Sigma X_1Y - b_2\Sigma X_2Y}{n - 3}$$

the calculation of $s_{Y\cdot 123}$ adds $-b_3\Sigma X_3Y$ to the numerator and changes the denominator to $n - 4$. And so it goes.

We can calculate prediction intervals, too, as noted earlier, except that the degrees of freedom for $t_{\alpha/2}$ change as they do for the standard error, from $n - 3$ to $n - 4$, and so on (always being equal to $n - m - 1$, where n is sample size and m is the number of independent variables). Modern computer programs routinely make the computations involved and print out an estimated regression equation, sample regression coefficients (a, b_1, b_2, etc.), along with their standard errors (s_a, s_{b_1}, s_{b_2}, etc.), t values (which are the ratios of each estimated regression coefficient to its standard error), and p values. Most of them also provide the standard error of the estimate of *Y*, the sample coefficient of determination, an ANOVA table, and more.

EXCEL Example 17.10

Review Table 17.1 on page 793. Then imagine to have gathered the following data on the ages (measured in years) of individuals A through T:

29, 50, 41, 55, 34, 36, 61, 29, 64, 30, 28, 29, 35, 59, 65, 30, 40, 23, 58, 44

Conduct a complete regression analysis of the relationship between income (Y), on the one hand, and three independent variables—education (X_1), job experience (X_2), and age (X_3)— on the other hand.

SOLUTION

1. Enter the Table 17.1 income, education, and job experience data, inclusive of column headings, into columns A–C, respectively, of a new worksheet. Label column D *Age* and enter the additional data from above in that column. (You can also copy and paste the data from columns U–X of the file HKMISC.)
2. Click **Tools** > **Data Analysis** > **Regression** > **OK** to open the *Regression* dialog box.
3. Under *Input Y Range,* enter **A1:A21**
4. Under *Input X Range,* enter **B1:D21**
5. Check *Labels* and *New Worksheet Ply,* and click **OK**.

The following output appears:

SUMMARY OUTPUT

Regression Statistics	
Multiple R	0.97198752
R Square	0.94475974
Adjusted R Square	0.93440219
Standard Error	2507.23855
Observations	20

ANOVA

	df	*SS*	*MS*	*F*	*Significance F*	
Regression	3	1720192197	5.73E+08	91.21461	2.82266E−10	
Residual	16	100579922.1	6286245			
Total	19	1820772119				
	Coefficients	***Standard Error***	***t Stat***	***P-value***	***Lower 95%***	***Upper 95%***
Intercept	−3010.054	2359.106445	−1.27593	0.220193	−8011.13508	1991.02717
Education	2098.55855	132.8363356	15.79808	3.5E−11	1816.958161	2380.15894
Job Experience	1200.17644	147.0128239	8.163753	4.26E−07	888.5232488	1511.82964
Age	−310.79068	57.77306172	−5.37951	6.14E−05	−433.2640722	−188.31729

INTERPRETING COMPUTER PRINTOUT

We can use the computer printout just derived in numerous ways:

THE REGRESSION EQUATION In research reports, it is customary to print the estimated regression equation, with t values underneath each coefficient, as follows:

$$\begin{array}{l}\text{Income} = -3010 + 2099\ \text{Educ.} + 1200\ \text{JobExp.} - 311\ \text{Age} \\ \qquad\qquad (-1.28) \quad (15.80) \qquad\quad (8.16) \qquad\qquad (-5.38)\end{array}$$

The interpretation is straightforward. Each year of education raises estimated annual income by \$2,099, if we hold job experience and age constant. Each year of job experience raises estimated annual income by \$1,200, if we hold education and age constant. Each year of age *lowers* estimated annual income by \$311, if we hold education and job experience constant.

In addition, the t values for the three independent variables, having absolute magnitudes in excess of 2, easily pass the rule-of-thumb test noted in Formula 17.F. Therefore, the estimated partial-regression coefficients can be treated as statistically significant at the 95 percent level of confidence. As noted previously on page 794, and for the reasons noted, we need not concern ourselves with the intercept of −3,010, nor with its t value of −1.28, which does not pass the 95 percent significance test. Mathematically, the intercept estimates the income of a person with zero years of education, zero years of job experience, and zero age, which has no practical meaning. Yet, the intercept is needed to make the best possible estimates for those (positive) values of the independent variables that lie within the ranges encountered in our sample.

The p values, finally, provide another way of assessing the significance of the estimated regression coefficients. Given the null hypothesis of H_0: The true regression coefficient equals 0, each p value gives the probability of H_0 being true, based on the t value computed from the sample data. Except for the intercept, all p values equal zero.

CAUTION

Take care when studying the results of other people's regression analyses: Instead of t values, some publications print standard errors or even p values underneath the estimated coefficients. You must read the fine print, lest utter confusion prevail.

THE STANDARD ERROR OF THE ESTIMATE OF *Y* The standard error of the estimate of Y equals $s_{Y \cdot 123}$ = \$2,507. Compare this standard error with $s_{Y \cdot 12}$ = \$4,076 (in the regression of income versus education and job experience only) or with $s_{Y \cdot X}$ = \$5,377 (in the regression of income versus education only), both noted earlier in this chapter. Clearly, we have further improved our regression's predictive ability by adding the age variable.

CONFIDENCE INTERVALS FOR THE TRUE REGRESSION COEFFICIENTS Using Formula 17.E, we can also produce confidence intervals for the true regression coefficients from our computer printout. Choosing 95 percent intervals and, thus, $t_{.025(16)} = 2.12$, the limits are

$$\alpha \cong a \pm (t_{\alpha/2} \cdot s_a) = -3010 \pm [2.12(2359)] = -3010 \pm 5001.08$$
$$\beta_1 \cong b_1 \pm (t_{\alpha/2} \cdot s_{b_1}) = 2098.6 \pm [2.12(132.8)] = 2098.6 \pm 281.536$$
$$\beta_2 \cong b_2 \pm (t_{\alpha/2} \cdot s_{b_2}) = 1200.2 \pm [2.12(147.0)] = 1200.2 \pm 311.64$$
$$\beta_3 \cong b_3 \pm (t_{\alpha/2} \cdot s_{b_3}) = -310.79 \pm [2.12(57.77)] = -310.79 \pm 122.4724$$

Thus, we conclude:

$$-\$8{,}011.08 \leq \alpha \leq +\$1{,}991.08$$
$$\$1{,}817.06 \leq \beta_1 \leq \$2{,}380.14$$
$$\$888.56 \leq \beta_2 \leq \$1{,}511.84$$
$$-\$433.26 \leq \beta_3 \leq -\$188.32$$

Only the true intercept, α, might conceivably be zero. We know this because the 95 percent confidence interval for α reaches from a negative value to a positive value and thus includes zero. The value of α, however, concerns us little—for the same reason that we dismissed as meaningless the value of $a = -\$3{,}010$ in the estimated regression equation noted earlier. The 95 percent confidence intervals for β_1 and β_2, on the other hand, lie entirely above zero and, thus, suggest positive true coefficients. The 95 percent confidence interval for β_3, finally, lies entirely below zero, which suggests a true coefficient that is negative.

Testing the Overall Significance of the Regression Our computer printout provides all the information needed to create ANOVA Table 17.3. The likelihood of having gotten such a large F by pure chance is zero. Given a critical $F_{.05(3,16)} = 3.24$, we resoundingly *reject* H_0: $\beta_1 = \beta_2 = \beta_3 = 0$. Education, job experience, and age do explain almost all of the income variation in the population from which our sample data were drawn.

TABLE 17.3 | The ANOVA Table

Source of Variation	Sum of Squares (1)	Degrees of Freedom (2)	Mean Square (3) = (1) ÷ (2)	Test Statistic (4)
Regression (variation explained by X's)	$RSS =$ 1,720,192,197	$m = 3$	$RMS =$ 573,397,399	$F = \frac{RMS}{EMS} = 91.21$
Error (unexplained variation)	$ESS =$ 100,579,922	$n - m - 1 = n - 4 = 16$	$EMS =$ 6,286,245	
Total	$Total\ SS =$ 1,820,772,119	$n - 1 = 19$		

The Sample Coefficient of Multiple Determination The values are $R^2 = .945$ and $R^2(\text{adj.}) = .934$. Thus, the regression of income on education, job experience, and age explains well over 90 percent of the income variation.

The Price of Heroin and the Incidence of Crime

Lawmakers have often claimed an important relationship between drug abuse and all kinds of crimes. Some time ago, this theory was tested with the help of data from New York City. A number of multiple regression equations were estimated, relating the incidence of various crimes (Y) to several independent variables, such as the per-gram retail price of heroin (X_1), the average temperature (X_2), and a time trend (X_3). Table 17.A summarizes selected results (t values appear in parentheses).

Partial Interpretation. We can use the data in each row to formulate a regression equation, such as for murder.

$$\hat{Y} = 51.66 + 1.45X_1 + .04X_2 + .05X_3$$

Focusing on the b_1 column, we invariably find higher heroin prices associated with higher numbers of crimes. All else being equal, a $1-per-gram increase in the retail price of heroin, for instance, was associated with 1 additional murder, 59 additional robberies, and 46 additional auto thefts per month.

SOURCE: Adapted from George F. Brown, Jr., and Lester P. Silverman, "The Retail Price of Heroin: Estimation and Applications," *Journal of the American Statistical Association*, September 1974, pp. 595–606. Table 17.A data Copyright © 1974 by Journal of the American Statistical Association. Reprinted by permission.

TABLE 17.A | Regression Results of Crime Study

	Coeffecients for				
Crime	Intercept, a	Heroin Price, b_1	Temperature, b_2	Time Trend, b_3	R^2
Murder	51.66	1.45 (2.89)	.04 (.22)	.05 (.07)	.523
Rape	113.26	.07 (.10)	.81 (3.03)	3.84 (4.11)	.670
Robbery	6,351.3	58.67 (2.24)	−14.18 (−1.40)	−87.84 (−2.48)	.314
Assault	1,188.3	9.88 (1.73)	19.74 (8.94)	9.52 (1.23)	.813
Burglary	13,251.0	61.19 (1.68)	25.11 (1.79)	−213.05 (−4.33)	.605
Larceny > $50	9,220.7	15.13 (.51)	49.83 (4.33)	−202.09 (−5.02)	.806
Auto Theft	6,235.3	46.07 (2.38)	26.58 (3.55)	−157.92 (−6.04)	.771
Total	36,412.0	192.48 (1.83)	107.93 (2.66)	−647.50 (−4.56)	.655

APPLICATION 17.2

HOUSING PRICES AND PROPOSITION 13

On June 7, 1978, California voters approved a statewide property-tax-limitation initiative known as Proposition 13. This initiative led to a substantial *and differential* reduction in property taxes among localities, and we would expect corresponding impacts on housing prices. A multiple regression equation was estimated from data on the San Francisco Bay area, relating the change in post–Proposition 13 mean house prices, *Y*, to a number of independent variables (*t* values appear in parentheses):

$$\hat{Y} = \underset{(3.21)}{-.171} + \underset{(2.97)}{7.275X_1} + \underset{(2.32)}{.5468X_2} + \underset{(1.34)}{.00073X_3}$$

$$+ \underset{(3.26)}{.0638X_4} - \underset{(2.24)}{.0043X_5} + \underset{(1.80)}{.857X_6}$$

R^2(adj.) = .89

The independent variables in the equation were defined as follows:

X_1 = post–Proposition 13 decrease in property-tax bill on mean house

X_2 = mean square footage of house

X_3 = median income

X_4 = mean age of house

X_5 = transportation time to San Francisco

X_6 = housing-quality index

PARTIAL INTERPRETATION. As the coefficient of X_1 indicates, each $1 decrease in relative property taxes increased relative property values by about $7. Thus, as stated by one analyst, "the results of this regression provide strong confirmation that the differential interjurisdictional tax reductions of Proposition 13 were partially capitalized in the year following the effective date of the statewide initiative. The capitalization rate implied by this equation is about 7, which is precisely the magnitude that one would expect given an interest rate of about 12–15 percent."

This conclusion makes sense because anyone who expects an eternal annual return of $1 (for example, as a result of a $1 property-tax reduction) will find that a one-time receipt of $7 is precisely equivalent to this future flow of returns, provided the applicable interest rate is (1/7)100, or 14.29 percent. This is so because $7, when invested at this rate, will generate a $1 return annually, forever.

SOURCE: Adapted from Kenneth T. Rosen, "The Impact of Proposition 13 on House Prices in Northern California: A Test of the Interjurisdictional Capitalization Hypothesis," *Journal of Political Economy,* February 1982, pp. 191–200.

APPLICATION 17.3

AN ECONOMIC INTERPRETATION OF CONGRESSIONAL VOTING

Many analysts have suggested a variety of explanations for the alleged fact that members of Congress often do *not* vote for the interests of the majority of their constituents. Others, on the contrary, believe that profound changes in congressional voting patterns during the 20th century can be traced precisely to corresponding changes in the economic interests of constituents. Some time ago, the controversy was subjected to an empirical test.

MODEL 1. One multiple regression equation regressed *SPEND/TAX* (the ratio of federal government expenditures in a state to the federal tax burden on the state—the best available proxy for the state's net benefit from federal programs) against *HHINC* (median household income in a state), *MFG* (the percentage of a state's nonagricultural labor force in manufacturing), and *URB* (the percentage of a state's population in urban areas). The result (with *t* values in parentheses):

$$SPEND/TAX = \underset{(-5.5)}{-11.8\ HHINC} - \underset{(-3.8)}{1.22\ MFG} + \underset{(.8)}{20\ URB}$$

R^2 = .58

Conclusion: The federal budget has tended to redistribute benefits away from states with high incomes and large manufacturing sectors.

(continued)

Model 2. A second multiple regression equation described voting patterns in the Senate. It regressed *ADA* (the senators' ratings by the pro-spending Americans for Democratic Action) against *HHINC, MFG, URB, METRO* (the percentage of state population in standard metropolitan statistical areas), and *DEMS* (the number of Democratic senators from the state divided by two). The result (with *t* values in parentheses):

$$ADA = \underset{(3.4)}{.65\,HHINC} + \underset{(2.4)}{.88\,MFG} + \underset{(.1)}{.03\,URB} - \underset{(-.5)}{.13\,METRO} + \underset{(3.9)}{29.5\,DEMS}$$

$R^2 = .51$

Conclusion: The characteristics that were *negatively* correlated with net spending benefits (income and manufacturing) have been *positively* correlated with voting for larger federal spending. This implies a perverse connection between the interests of constituents and the votes of their senators.

Additional analysis suggests a fascinating trend. As the South has become relatively better off economically and the North relatively worse off, the "price" of liberal votes (hurting constituents at home through the redistribution effect noted earlier) has risen in the South, but fallen in the North. This explains ever fewer liberal votes from Southern and ever more liberal votes from Northern members of Congress and, ultimately, the gain in "market share" by Republicans in the South and Democrats in the North.

SOURCE: Adapted from Sam Peltzman, "An Economic Interpretation of the History of Congressional Voting in the Twentieth Century," *The American Economic Review,* September 1985, pp. 656–675.

APPLICATION 17.4

Determinants of the Natural Unemployment Rate in Canada

Macroeconomists define a *natural unemployment rate* that differs from the actual unemployment rate. The natural rate measures the percentage of the civilian labor force that we can normally expect to be unemployed for reasons *other than* cyclical fluctuations of the nation's output. Such natural unemployment is believed to be an inevitable implication of free markets for labor and goods. When people are allowed to switch employers at will, move about geographically, and buy good A rather than B, a certain small percentage of the labor force will always be unemployed at any given time when statistics are gathered, even in a world in which recessions and depressions never occur. Beginning in 1970, however, this "natural" rate of unemployment seemed to grow in Canada, from roughly 5 percent early in the decade to about 9 percent by the late 1980s. One researcher employed multiple regression analysis to find the determinants of the natural rate between 1971 and 1988. The following equation was established (with *t* values in parentheses):

$$\hat{Y} = a + \underset{(2.7)}{.007X_1} + \underset{(2.1)}{.034X_2} + \underset{(3.8)}{.289X_3} + \underset{(4.1)}{.627X_4}$$

where

Y is the natural unemployment rate

a is a constant

X_1 = the maximum unemployment insurance replacement rate

X_2 = the minimum wage relative to the average market wage

X_3 = the percentage of the labor force unionized

X_4 = the average payroll tax on employers

Partial Interpretation. As the positive and statistically significant coefficient of X_1 indicates, all else being equal, the natural unemployment rate is increased by a more generous unemployment insurance system that raises the percentage of former wages that unemployed workers receive in the form of unemployment benefits. Thus, if people buy bicycles rather than cars, unemployed auto workers who receive, say, 90 percent of former wages from the government, rather than 45 percent, may well wait for their old job in the auto industry and take their time before finding and accepting a new job in the bicycle industry. So, naturally, recorded unemployment data are higher.

SOURCE: Adapted from David T. Coe, "Structural Determinants of Natural Unemployment in Canada," *IMF Staff Papers,* March 1990, pp. 94–115.

Application 17.5 *Bankers Assess Credit Card Risk*
http://www.harcourtcollege.com/business_stats/kohler/siteresources.html

Application 17.6 *The Geography of Medicare*
http://www.harcourtcollege.com/business_stats/kohler/siteresources.html

PREDICTING THE AVERAGE OR INDIVIDUAL VALUE OF Y

Computer programs are equally adept at helping us make point estimates or create confidence and prediction intervals.

EXCEL Example 17.11

Review Table 17.1 on page 793. Then imagine to have gathered the following data on the ages (measured in years) of individuals A through T:

29, 50, 41, 55, 34, 36, 61, 29, 64, 30, 28, 29, 35, 59, 65, 30, 40, 23, 58, 44

For $X_1 = 11$ years of education, $X_2 = 20$ years of job experience, $X_3 = 45$ years of age,

a. make a point estimate of annual income.

b. create a 95 percent confidence interval for the annual income of the average person with these characteristics.

c. create a 95 percent prediction interval for the annual income of the next person with these characteristics who is encountered in sampling.

SOLUTION: Enter the Table 17.1 income, education, and job experience data, inclusive of column headings, into columns A–C, respectively, of a new worksheet. Label column D *Age* and enter the additional data from above in that column. (You can also copy and paste the data from columns U–X of the file HKMISC.)

Part (a)

1. You must enter the range of X values to be used for predicting. For example, enter the labels *X1, X2, X3,* and *Predicted Y* into cells F1–I1. Then enter 11, 20, and 45 into F2–H2 and select I2.
2. Click the **Function Wizard (*fx*) > Statistical > TREND > OK** to activate a dialog box.
3. Under *Known y's,* enter **A2:A21** and press TAB.
4. Under *Known x's,* enter **B2:D21** and press TAB.
5. Under *New x's,* enter **F2:H2** and press TAB.
6. Under *Const,* enter **1** or **TRUE** or nothing at all (to indicate that the regression constant is not to be forced to a value of zero); then click **OK.**

The following output appears:

X1	*X2*	*X3*	*Predicted Y*
11	20	45	30092.03834

Part (b) EXCEL is not equipped to create the $\mu_{Y \cdot 11,20,45}$ confidence interval directly, but we can compute an *approximation,* using Formula 17.C as follows:

1. Given the column A-D data from Part (a), enter the labels *Point estimate, Sample size, Degrees of freedom, Standard error of estimate, Critical t, Half-width of confidence interval, Lower limit of confidence interval,* and *Upper limit of confidence interval* into cells E1–E8 of your worksheet.
2. Enter corresponding formulas or known values into adjacent column F cells:

30092.04 (from Part (a)) into F1

20 into F2

16 into F3

2507.239 (from EXCEL Example 17.10) into F4

=TINV(1−95/100,F3) into F5

=F5*F4/SQRT(F2) into F6

=F1=F6 into F7

=F1+F6 into F8

The result includes the *approximation* of the desired 95 percent confidence interval (highlighted in red):

Point estimate	30092.04
Sample size	20
Degrees of freedom	16
Standard error of estimate	2507.239
Critical *t*	2.119905
Half-width of confidence interval	1188.494
Lower limit of confidence interval	28903.54
Upper limit of confidence interval	31280.53

The 95 percent confidence interval is *approximated* by $\$28,904 \le \mu_{Y \cdot 123} \le \$31,281$.
Note: The precise interval, computed by MINITAB, is $\$27,758 \le \mu_{Y \cdot 123} \le \$32,426$.

Part (c) EXCEL is not equipped to create the $I_{Y \cdot 11,20,45}$ prediction interval directly, but we can compute an *approximation,* using Formula 17.D as follows:

1. Given the column A-D data from Part (a), enter the labels *Point estimate, Sample size, Degrees of freedom, Standard error of estimate, Critical t, Half-width of prediction interval, Lower limit of prediction interval,* and *Upper limit of prediction interval* into cells E1–E8 of your worksheet.
2. Enter corresponding formulas or known values into adjacent column F cells:

30092.04 (from Part (a)) into F1

20 into F2

16 into F3

2507.239 (from EXCEL Example 17.10) into F4

=TINV(1−95/100,F3) into F5

=F5*F4*SQRT((F2+1)/F2) into F6

=F1−F6 into F7

=F1+F6 into F8

The result includes the *approximation* of the desired 95 percent prediction interval (highlighted in red):

Point estimate	30092.04
Sample size	20
Degrees of freedom	16
Standard error of estimate	2507.239
Critical *t*	2.119905
Half-width of prediction interval	5446.364
Lower limit of prediction interval	24645.67
Upper limit of prediction interval	35538.4

The 95 percent prediction interval is *approximated* by $\$24,646 \leq I_{Y \cdot 123} \leq \$35,538$.
Note: The precise interval, computed by MINITAB, is $\$24,287 \leq I_{Y \cdot 123} \leq \$35,897$.

17.8 Discovering Possible Violations of Assumptions

This final section of the chapter elaborates upon Section 17.4 by considering how we might *check* on the fulfillment of those crucial assumptions that underlie all of regression analysis. Such a check is of importance because serious violations of the assumptions can call into question all the conclusions drawn from a regression analysis.

NORMALITY

The first assumption—concerning normality—can again be tested by an **analysis of residuals,** a careful study of the differences between actual observations concerning the dependent variable, Y, and their associated estimates, $\hat{Y}$, made by the regression equation. These differences, also known as *residuals* or *errors,* $e = Y - \hat{Y}$, are often plotted against their associated regression estimates to test the normality assumption.

The idea behind this type of graph is simple enough: Regression analysis assumes the existence of a normally distributed Y population for each possible combination of independent variables, such as X_1, X_2, and X_3. If this assumption of normality holds, a large number of actual Y observations (that would be associated with any given combination of, say, X_1, X_2, and X_3 and, therefore, with a single regression estimate, $\hat{Y}$, of the dependent variable) would be associated with an equally large number of *normally distributed* residuals or errors. If we graphed e against $\hat{Y}$, as in Figure 17.3 on the next page, we would find a vertical array of many dots at *each* value

FIGURE 17.3 | Testing for Normality

If we had large numbers of sample data used in a multiple regression, plotted residuals, e, against associated regression estimates, $\hat{Y}$, and observed the kind of pattern shown in this graph, we could be satisfied that the normality assumption underlying regression analysis was fulfilled.

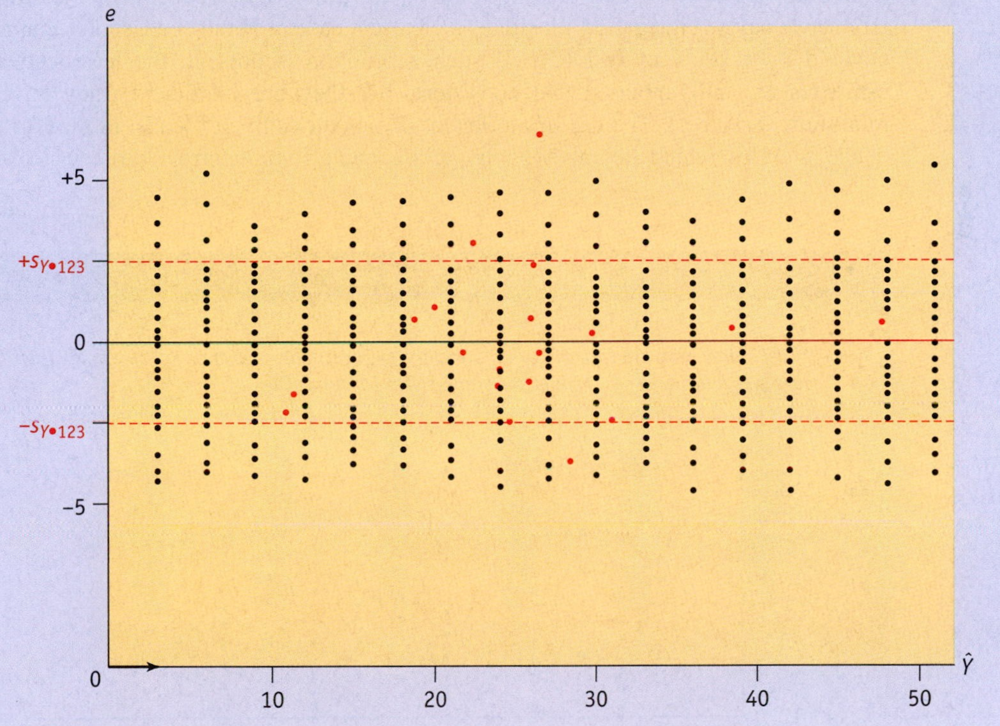

of $\hat{Y}$. Some actual Y observations for a given X_1, X_2, and X_3 (and, therefore, $\hat{Y}$) would equal $\hat{Y}$. The corresponding errors would be zero; the dots representing the e versus $\hat{Y}$ combination would lie on the solid horizontal line in the center of the graph. Half of the remaining Y observations at a given $\hat{Y}$ would exceed $\hat{Y}$; such positive errors would show up as dots *above* the horizontal centerline. The other half of the remaining Y observations at a given $\hat{Y}$ would fall short of $\hat{Y}$; such negative errors would show up as dots *below* the horizontal centerline. Indeed, we know more than that! If the assumption of normality holds, roughly 68 percent of the dots at a given $\hat{Y}$ would lie within plus or minus one standard error (shown by the red dashed horizontal lines in Figure 17.3) of the zero mean error, while roughly 95 percent of these dots would lie within plus or minus two such standard errors. [Recall from Appendix Table H that 2(.3413) = .6826 of the area under the standard normal curve falls within $\pm 1z$ of the mean, while 2(.4772) = .9544 of the area falls within $\pm 2z$ of the mean.]

In our income versus education, job experience, and age example, we do not have enough observations to make this test. The red dots in Figure 17.3 represent the data we do have. Together with the remaining dots, they illustrate the kind of pattern we expect to see if the normality assumption holds.

HOMOSCEDASTICITY

The second assumption—concerning equal variances of all the Y populations—can be tested by a residuals plot as well. We note whether the spread of the dots around the $e = 0$ centerline is about the same at all levels of $\hat{Y}$. If not, the homoscedasticity assumption is probably violated and our different Y populations (each defined by different value combinations of the independent variables) are likely to have different variances. Put differently, our analysis is then said to suffer from **heteroscedasticity,** the presence of unequal variances associated with the different Y populations we study. Figure 17.4 illustrates a clear-cut case of heteroscedasticity that might be discovered by a study of residuals. If such a problem is present, the least-squares parameter estimates are still unbiased and consistent, but they are inefficient (they have larger than minimum variances). The use of inefficient parameter estimates leads, in turn, to biased confidence intervals, which are unjustifiably precise, and also to incorrect hypothesis tests.

FIGURE 17.4 | The Heteroscedastic Fan

A residuals plot such as this one strongly suggests the presence of heteroscedasticity. In this particular case, variances increase with larger values of $\hat{Y}$.

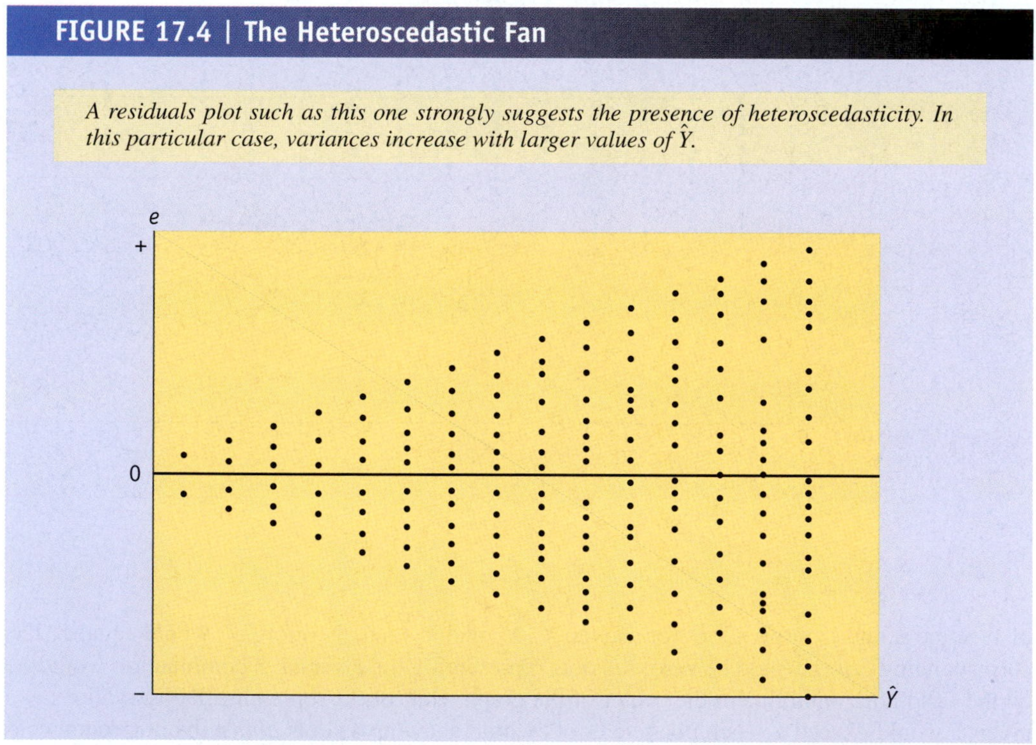

STATISTICAL INDEPENDENCE

The third assumption—concerning the statistical independence of different sample observations about the dependent variable, Y—if fulfilled, has this implication: The associated residuals will be statistically independent as well. In many business and economic applications, however, regression analysis involves **time-series data,** numerical values pertaining to a *given* population that has been observed repeatedly at different points in time (in the case of a stock variable) or during different periods of time (in the case of a flow variable). More often than not, such time-series data exhibit **autocorrelation** or **serial correlation,** which is said to exist whenever the value of Y (and the associated error term, $e = Y - \hat{Y}_X$) that is observed at one time, t, is correlated with that observed at an earlier time, such as $t - 1$ or $t - 2$. If e_t is correlated with e_{t-1}, we speak of **first-order serial correlation;** if e_t is correlated with e_{t-2}, we speak of **second-order serial correlation;** and so on for higher-order types of such correlation. In addition, if one large value (Y above its mean and $e > 0$) follows another, or if one small value (Y below its mean and $e < 0$) follows another, we speak of **positive serial correlation.** In contrast, if a small value follows a large value, or if a large value follows a small value, we speak of **negative serial correlation.**

An example of positive serial correlation might be the behavior of the Dow Jones index of stock prices. If stock prices are high by historical standards today, it is quite likely that they will be high tomorrow as well, and this pattern may continue for weeks. After a sudden break, the opposite may occur: Average prices that are low by historical standards may be followed by average prices that are low as well. Such positive serial correlation is illustrated in panel (a) of Figure 17.5.

Panel (b) illustrates the opposite case of negative serial correlation, which might depict the behavior of hog prices in accordance with the famous cobweb cycle discussed in economics texts: Low prices discourage hog breeding, lead to a shortage and, therefore, higher prices; these higher prices encourage breeding, lead to a surplus and, thus, lower prices. The cycle continues indefinitely.

THE PROBLEM WITH SERIAL CORRELATION Why is serial correlation a problem? In its presence, the least-squares method will still produce estimated regression coefficients (a, b_1, b_2, etc.) that are unbiased estimators of the true regression coefficients (α, β_1, β_2, etc.). However, the standard errors of these estimators (s_a, s_{b_1}, s_{b_2}, etc.) will be seriously underestimated. As a result, all kinds of inferences will be totally wrong: Confidence intervals will be more precise than is warranted; t values, the coefficient of determination, and the F statistic will all be vastly exaggerated; hypothesis tests will report statistical significance of parameters where there is none. Nor is this a complete list of serial-correlation problems!

FIGURE 17.5 | Serial Correlation

Serial correlation between residuals (that are depicted by the red dots) may be positive, as in panel (a), or negative, as in panel (b). In the first case, one large residual typically follows another, or one small residual follows another. In the second case, large and small residuals continually alternate over time.

(a) Positive Serial Correlation

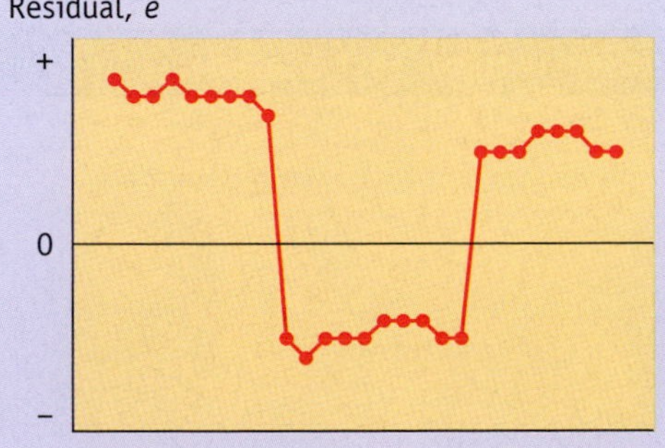

(b) Negative Serial Correlation

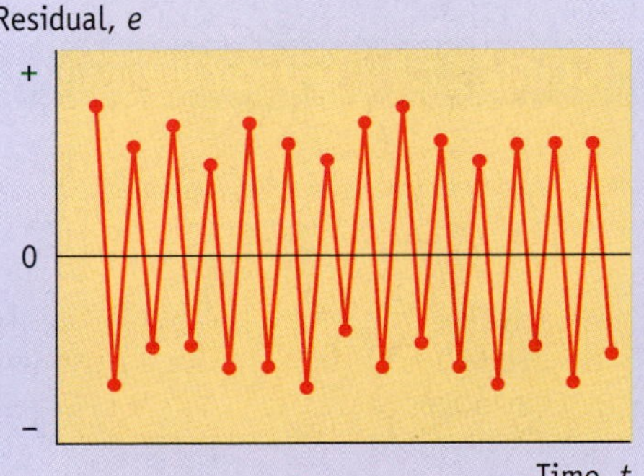

Here is one case in point: Earlier in this chapter, we subjected our income versus education, job experience, and age data to an ANOVA test. (See Table 17.3 on page 814.) Contrasting a critical $F_{.05(3,16)} = 3.24$ with our computed $F = 91.21$, we resoundingly *rejected* H_0: $\beta_1 = \beta_2 = \beta_3 = 0$. Education, job experience, and age, we concluded, do explain almost all of the income variation in the population from which our sample data were drawn. Yet if our sample data had been tainted by serial correlation, our computed F statistic would have been exaggerated and our conclusion could have been totally wrong.

THE DURBIN-WATSON TEST Several techniques for detecting the presence of serial correlation exist. These include the use of Chapter 21's *number-of-runs test* (to count runs of positive or negative *errors*) and the calculation of a special *serial-correlation coefficient.* Most common, however, is the use of the **Durbin-Watson test,** which is based on the type of statistic given in Formula 17.J.

FORMULA 17.J | The Durbin-Watson Test (for first-order serial correlation)

$$d = \frac{\sum_{t-2}^{n} (e_t - e_{t-1})^2}{\sum_{t-1}^{n} e_t^2}$$

where e_t is the residual or error, $Y - \hat{Y}$, at time t, and time stretches from period 1 to n.

The inventors of this test (after whom it is named) have provided tables, such as Appendix Table P, that show lower and upper limits of d (denoted by d_L *and* d_U, respectively) for specified significance levels (α), sample sizes (n), and numbers of independent variables in a regression (m). With the help of these d values, we can test the null hypothesis, "H_0: No serial correlation exists." As Figure 17.6 shows, values of d can range from 0 to 4; serial correlation is absent for values near 2.

Three types of Durbin-Watson tests can be made, depending on how the alternative hypothesis is formulated. Table 17.4 summarizes the rules.

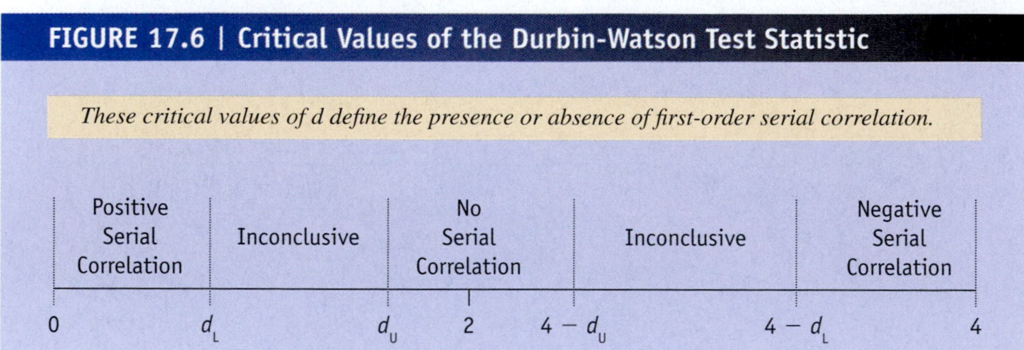

FIGURE 17.6 | Critical Values of the Durbin-Watson Test Statistic

These critical values of d define the presence or absence of first-order serial correlation.

TABLE 17.4 | Alternative Formulations of the Durbin-Watson Test

H_0: No Serial Correlation Exists

1. H_A: Positive serial correlation exists (e_t is directly related to e_{t-1})

if $d < d_L$, reject H_0
if $d > d_U$, accept H_0
if $d_L \leq d \leq d_U$, cannot decide

2. H_A: Negative serial correlation exists (e_t is inversely related to e_{t-1})

if $d > 4 - d_L$, reject H_0
if $d < 4 - d_U$, accept H_0
if $4 - d_U \leq d \leq 4 - d_L$, cannot decide

3. H_A: Positive or negative serial correlation exists

if $d < d_L$ or $d > 4 - d_L$, reject H_0
if $d_U < d < 4 - d_U$, accept H_0
if $d_L \leq d \leq d_U$ or $4 - d_U \leq d \leq 4 - d_L$, cannot decide

Note: In this two-tailed test, the significance levels in Appendix Table P double. If $\alpha = .05$ is desired, consult the $\alpha = .025$ section.

LINEARITY

The fourth assumption—concerning linearity—can also be tested with the help of a residuals plot, such as Figure 17.3. If the linearity assumption holds, we expect the dots to lie in a broad band around the horizontal $e = 0$ line. Anything else is highly suspicious and suggests possible curvilinear relationships among the variables. That, in turn, counsels fitting the data to a nonlinear equation or transforming the data in a fashion suggested in Section 16.14.

UNCORRELATED INDEPENDENT VARIABLES

The fifth assumption—concerning a lack of strong correlation between any two independent variables—can be tested in a variety of ways. Sometimes, the test occurs automatically: When two or more independent variables in a regression model are *perfectly* correlated, we simply cannot calculate the parameter estimates, because no unique solution of the normal equations exists. However, when independent variables are *imperfectly but highly* correlated, the underlying problem is less obvious. Regression coefficients can then be calculated, but they do not correctly isolate the individual effects of different independent variables on the dependent variable. This problem of high correlation between or among independent variables is the problem of **multicollinearity.** The following are symptoms of its presence:

1. The value of R^2 is large, yet the estimated regression coefficients have huge standard errors and are statistically insignificant. Multicollinearity causes the estimated coefficients to vary substantially from sample to sample; this fact raises their standard errors; hence, the ratio $(b/s_b) = t$ is unlikely to be greater than 2, or statistically significant.
2. The estimated regression coefficients change greatly in value as independent variables are dropped from or added to the regression equation.
3. The magnitudes of the estimated regression coefficients are unreasonable. They are unexpectedly large or small.

4. The signs of the estimated regression coefficients are nonsensical. They are negative when common sense suggests positive signs and vice versa.

A GRAPHIC TEST One way to check for multicollinearity involves drawing and inspecting scatter diagrams between the values of any two independent variables. As Figure 17.7 indicates, for example, there certainly exists no perfect linear correlation (nor any imperfect but strong correlation) between the two independent variables in our income versus education and job experience example.

FIGURE 17.7 | The Relation of X_1 to X_2

This scatter diagram illustrates the fulfillment of Assumption 5 for a multiple regression with two independent variables: There exists no perfect linear correlation between the values of the two independent variables listed in Table 17.1. In fact, the simple correlation coefficient between X_1 and X_2 equals −.11.

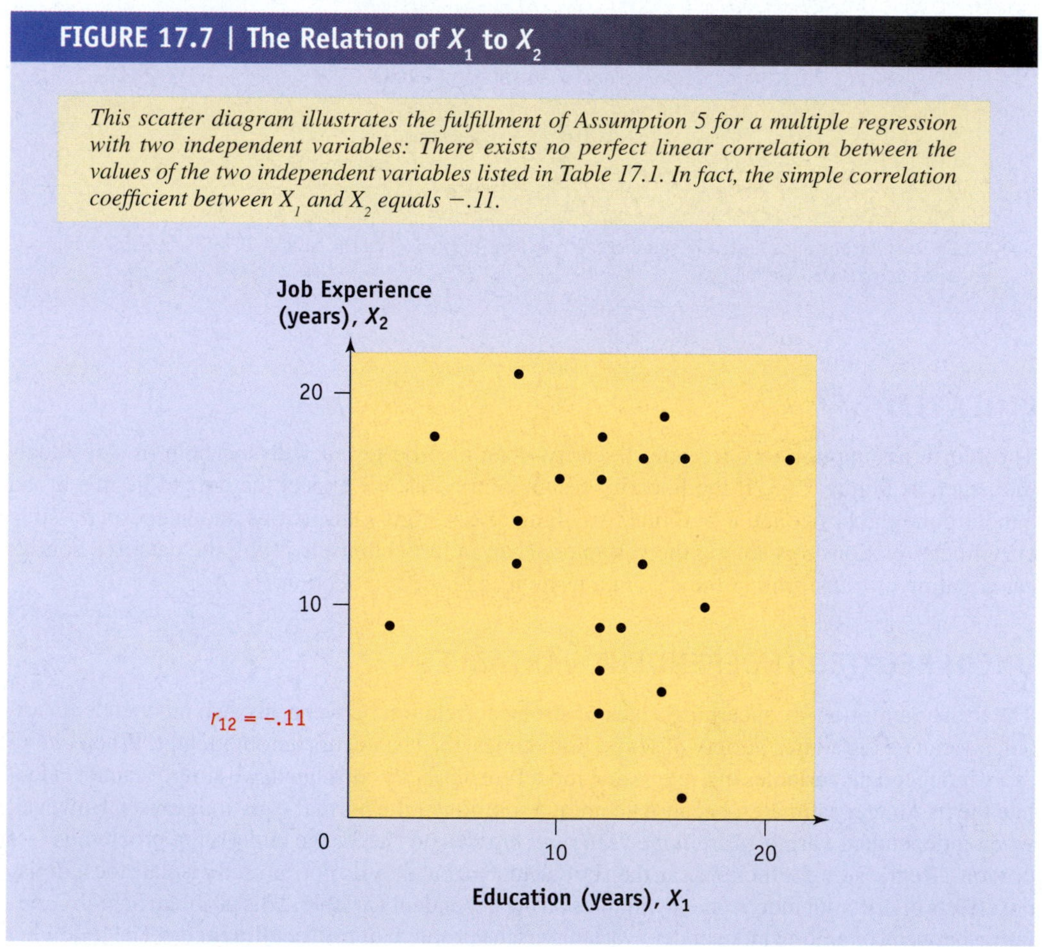

AN ARITHMETIC TEST A purely numerical test of multicollinearity involves the construction of a **correlation matrix,** a table showing simple correlation coefficients between each possible pair of variables included in a regression model. Table 17.5 contains such data for our income versus education, job experience, and age regression.

Naturally, each variable is correlated perfectly with itself; hence, we find four entries equal to 1.00 in the main diagonal of Table 17.5. In any case, it is the red entries that are of crucial interest here. A coefficient of .80 or larger between any pair of independent variables is considered suggestive of multicollinearity, which is not the case here.

TABLE 17.5 | A Simple Correlation Matrix

Variables	Income, Y	Education, X_1	Job Experience, X_2	Age, X_3
Income, Y	$r_{Y \cdot Y} = 1.00$	$r_{Y \cdot 1} = .845$	$r_{Y \cdot 2} = .269$	$r_{Y \cdot 3} = .106$
Education, X_1	—	$r_{1 \cdot 1} = 1.00$	$r_{1 \cdot 2} = -.107$	$r_{1 \cdot 3} = .098$
Job Exp., X_2	—	—	$r_{2 \cdot 2} = 1.00$	$r_{2 \cdot 3} = .676$
Age, X_3	—	—	—	$r_{3 \cdot 3} = 1.00$

EXCEL Example 17.12

Using relevant data provided earlier in this chapter, confirm the Table 17.5 entries by computer.

SOLUTION:

1. Enter the income, education, job experience, and age data, inclusive of column headings, into columns A–D, respectively, of a new worksheet. (You can also copy and paste the data from columns U–X of the file HKMISC.)
2. Click **Tools** > **Data Analysis** > **Correlation** > **OK** to activate the *Correlation* dialog box.
3. Under *Input Range,* enter **A1:D21**
4. Choose *Columns, Labels in First Row, New Worksheet Ply*, and click **OK**.

The following result appears, containing the same information as Table 17.5:

A	B	C	D	E
	Income	*Education*	*Job Experience*	*Age*
Income	1			
Education	0.845066	1		
Job Experience	0.269153	−0.106873	1	
Age	0.105759	0.0982121	0.6755143	1

REGRESSIONS A simple correlation matrix by itself, however, is not sufficient to rule out multicollinearity, because this matrix fails to take into account the possible correlation between any one independent variable with *all* the others as a group. Therefore, it is customary to regress each of the independent variables against all the others and to note whether any of the resultant R^2 values is close to 1. If that is the case, high multicollinearity is present. If we follow this procedure, using again this chapter's income versus education, job experience, and age data, we find the following:

$$\text{Education} = 11.109 - .261\text{ Job Exp.} + .1011\text{ Age} \qquad R^2_{1\cdot 23} = .065$$

$$\text{Job Exp.} = 3.777 - .2133\text{ Education} + .2725\text{ Age} \qquad R^2_{2\cdot 13} = .487$$

$$\text{Age} = 13.242 + .5344\text{ Education} + 1.7642\text{ Job Exp.} \qquad R^2_{3\cdot 21} = .486$$

Given the relatively low R^2 values, we do not have a multicollinearity problem.

VARIANCE INFLATION FACTORS Another way yet to identify the presence of multicollinearity involves the computation of a **variance inflation factor, VIF,** for each of the estimated regression coefficients. The concept measures how much the variance of an estimated regression coefficient increases if there is a strong linear correlation between one predictor variable and all others. Given k predictors, the VIF of the kth predictor equals $1/(1 - R^2)$, where R^2 refers to the regression of the kth predictor on the remaining $k - 1$ predictors. Given the R^2 values calculated in the previous section,

$$\text{VIF for education} = \frac{1}{1 - .065} = 1.07$$

$$\text{VIF for job experience} = \frac{1}{1 - .487} = 1.95$$

$$\text{VIF for age} = \frac{1}{1 - .486} = 1.95$$

VIF values above 10 are considered to be strong evidence that multicollinearity is present, which certainly is not the case in our example.

EXCEL Example 17.13

Using relevant data provided earlier in this chapter, confirm by computer the VIF values just listed.

SOLUTION: Enter the income, education, job experience, and age data, inclusive of column headings, into columns A–D, respectively, of a new worksheet. (You can also copy and paste the data from columns U–X of the file HKMISC.)

Regressing Education Versus Job Experience and Age

1. Click **Tools** > **Data Analysis** > **Regression** > **OK** to open the *Regression* dialog box.
2. Under *Input Y Range,* enter **B1:B21**.
3. Under *Input X Range,* enter **C1:D21**.
4. Check *Labels* and *New Worksheet Ply,* and click **OK**.

Among the output, note the R^2 value of .0648.

Regressing Job Experience Versus Education and Age

1. Copy and paste column B to column E so that the independent variables are next to one another, as required by EXCEL.

2. Click **Tools** > **Data Analysis** > **Regression** > **OK** to open the *Regression* dialog box.
3. Under *Input Y Range,* enter **C1:C21**
4. Under *Input X Range,* enter **D1:E21**
5. Check *Labels* and *New Worksheet Ply,* and click **OK**.

Among the output, note the R^2 value of .4866.

Regressing Age Versus Education and Job Experience

1. Copy and paste column C to column F so that the independent variables are next to one another, as required by EXCEL.
2. Click **Tools** > **Data Analysis** > **Regression** > **OK** to open the *Regression* dialog box.
3. Under *Input Y Range,* enter **D1:D21**
4. Under *Input X Range,* enter **E1:F21**
5. Check *Labels* and *New Worksheet Ply,* and click **OK**.

Among the output, note the R^2 value of .4857

Computing VIF values

1. Enter the label *R-squared* into cell A1 of a new worksheet; then enter the highlighted R^2 values into cells A2–A4, respectively.
2. Enter labels *VIF for education, VIF for job experience,* and *VIF for age* into cells C2–C4, respectively.
3. In adjacent column D cells, enter these formulas:

=1/(1−A2) into D2

=1/(1−A3) into D3

=1/(1−A4) into D4

The result confirms the VIF values noted earlier in the text:

R-squared		
0.0648	VIF for education	1.0693
0.4866	VIF for job experience	1.9478
0.4857	VIF for age	1.9444

Summary

1. *Multiple regression analysis* is a technique that uses several independent variables (rather than a single such variable) to estimate the value of a dependent variable; *multiple correlation analysis* measures the strength of association among all of these variables. Unlike simple regression analysis, multiple regression analysis allows us to exercise statistical control over extraneous factors and to determine the influence of any X on Y for specified constant values of other variables that might affect Y.

2. The techniques of multiple regression are straightforward extensions of those of simple regression. In the presence of two explanatory variables, they yield an estimated multiple regression equation of the form $\hat{Y} = a + b_1X_1 +$

b_2X_2. The b's are *estimated partial-regression coefficients;* they give the partial change in Y that is associated with a unit change in one of the independent variables when the other such variable is held constant. The above three-variable multiple regression (involving Y, X_1, and X_2) can be pictured as a *regression plane* in a three-dimensional scatter diagram.

3. In a manner analogous to that for simple regression, a *sample standard error of the estimate of Y* can be calculated; it measures the dispersion of observed Y values about the regression plane.

4. Provided certain conditions hold, estimated multiple regression equations can be used to make a variety of inferences about the populations from which samples were dawn. Such inferences include the interval estimation of an average (or individual) value of Y for a given X_1 and X_2 and the establishment of confidence intervals for the β's. The significance of estimated regression coefficients can be assessed with the help of t values or p values, and the overall significance of a multiple regression can also be tested by means of an analysis of variance.

5. Multiple correlation analysis, in turn, establishes single-number measures of the overall strength of association among the variables. The *sample coefficient of multiple determination,* R^2, is the most important of these measures. It equals the proportion of the total variation in the values of the dependent variable, Y, that is explained by the multiple regression of Y on X_1, X_2, and possibly on additional independent variables (X_3, X_4, and so on). The square root of R^2 is sometimes used as an alternative; it is the *sample coefficient of multiple correlation.* Because R^2 overestimates ρ^2, the corresponding population coefficient, an *adjusted sample coefficient of multiple determination,* R^2(adj.)—which is not so biased—is often calculated. Yet another important measure is the *sample coefficient of partial determination,* which is an index of association between the dependent variable and just *one* of the independent variables, given a prior accounting of the effects of any other independent variables.

6. While the principles remain the same, the calculations involved in multiple regression analysis become extremely burdensome once the analysis encompasses more than two explanatory variables. Luckily, the computer comes to the rescue.

7. Regression analysis must not be applied blindly. It is important to consider whether the assumptions underlying that analysis—assumptions about normality, homoscedasticity, statistical independence, and more—are at least roughly valid, lest the inferences made by means of regression analysis become invalid. One common problem, for example, is the presence of *serial correlation,* a situation in which the value of Y (and the associated error term, e) that is observed at one time, t, is correlated with that observed at an earlier time, such as $t - 1$ or $t - 2$. When such is the case, the standard errors of the estimated regression coefficients are being seriously underestimated, which, in turn, falsifies all kinds of inferences. The most common technique of detection is the *Durbin-Watson test.* Another common problem is *multicollinearity,* a high correlation between or among independent variables. This problem can be detected by inspecting scatter diagrams or by studying a variety of *correlation coefficients* and derivative *variance inflation factors.*

Key Terms

adjusted sample coefficient of multiple determination [R^2(adj.)]
analysis of residuals
autocorrelation
correlation matrix
Durbin-Watson test
estimated partial-regression coefficient
first-order serial correlation
heteroscedasticity
multicollinearity
multiple correlation analysis
multiple regression analysis
negative serial correlation
population coefficient of multiple determination (ρ^2)
positive serial correlation
p value
regression hyperplane
regression plane
sample coefficient of multiple correlation (R)
sample coefficient of multiple determination (R^2)
sample coefficient of partial correlation
sample coefficient of partial determination
second-order serial correlation
serial correlation
t ratio
t value
time-series data
true coefficient of multiple determination (ρ^2)
variance inflation factor (VIF)

Practice Problems

NOTE

Some problems require the use of a statistical program, EXCEL or MINITAB. The program's major features are explained in text Chapter 2; plenty of additional advice is available via the program's built-in Help feature.

SECTION 17.2 LINEAR MULTIPLE REGRESSION WITH TWO EXPLANATORY VARIABLES

SECTION 17.3 THE SAMPLE STANDARD ERROR OF THE ESTIMATE OF Y

1. Start EXCEL or MINITAB and activate the file HK99F500, which contains 1998 data about all *Fortune 500* companies. Then investigate the claim that the 500 firms' market values are directly related to and easily predictable from their profit *and* equity. As a first step, find
   a. the equation of the estimated regression line.
   b. the standard error of the estimate of Y.
2. Start EXCEL or MINITAB and activate the file HK99F500, which contains 1998 data about all *Fortune 500* companies. Then investigate the claim that the 500 firms' market values are directly related to and easily predictable from their revenue *and* assets. As a first step, find
   a. the equation of the estimated regression line.
   b. the standard error of the estimate of Y.
3. Start EXCEL or MINITAB and activate the file HK100MN97, which contains 1997 data about the 100 largest U.S.-based multinational companies. Then investigate the claim that the 100 firms' profits from foreign operations are directly related to and easily predictable from their foreign revenues *and* foreign assets. As a first step, find
   a. the equation of the estimated regression line.
   b. the standard error of the estimate of Y.
4. Start EXCEL or MINITAB and activate the file HK100MN97, which contains 1997 data about the 100 largest U.S.-based multinational companies. Then investigate the claim that the 100 firms' profits from foreign operations are directly related to and easily predictable from their total profits *and* foreign assets. As a first step, find
   a. the equation of the estimated regression line.
   b. the standard error of the estimate of Y.
5. Consider the loran-units-sold versus number-of-ads data of Table 16.5 on page 770, along with those on the interest rate charged credit customers, X_2, given here:

   X_2 (percent per year): 17, 18, 17, 17, 14, 14, 17, 17, 16, 16, 19, 19, 14, 15, 13, 16, 16, 16, 14, 14, 14, 15, 15, 18, 18, 17, 16, 17

   As a first step in a multiple regression analysis, find
   a. the equation of the estimated regression line.
   b. the standard error of the estimate of Y.
6. Consider the insurance versus income data of Table 16.14 on page 777, along with those on age, X_2, given here:

   X_2 (years): 60, 33, 49, 42, 43, 39, 48, 29, 27, 30, 45, 46, 35, 32, 58, 40, 60

   As a first step in a multiple regression analysis, find
   a. the equation of the estimated regression line.
   b. the standard error of the estimate of Y.
7. Consider the cereal-boxes-sold versus shelf-space data of Table 16.7 on page 771, along with those on the price of cereal, X_2, given here:

   X_2 (dollars per box): 2.20, 2.22, 1.50, 2.20, 1.60, 1.40, 3.00, 3.00, 1.70, 1.70, 2.90, 2.90, 1.70, 2.30

   As a first step in a multiple regression analysis, find
   a. the equation of the estimated regression line.
   b. the standard error of the estimate of Y.
8. Consider the yield versus temperature data of Table 16.15 on page 778, along with those on fertilizer input, X_2, given here:

   X_2 (pounds of fertilizer per acre): 200, 200, 220, 180, 190, 180, 190, 180, 150, 80, 150

   As a first step in a multiple regression analysis, find
   a. the equation of the estimated regression line.
   b. the standard error of the estimate of Y.
9. Consider the electricity-demand versus natural-gas-price data of Table 16.18 on page 781, along with those on the price of electricity, X_2, given here:

   X_2 (cents per kilowatt hour): 2.1, 2.3, 2.5, 2.6, 2.8, 2.9, 2.9, 4.6, 5.3, 7.9, 2.0, 2.5, 3.7

   As a first step in a multiple regression analysis, find
   a. the equation of the estimated regression line.
   b. the standard error of the estimate of Y.

10. Consider the units-sold versus competitor's-price data of Table 16.10 on page 772, along with those on the price of a complementary good, X_2, given here:

X_2 (dollars per unit): 50, 45, 40, 39, 38, 25, 31, 70, 20, 70

As a first step in a multiple regression analysis, find

a. the equation of the estimated regression line.

b. the standard error of the estimate of Y.

Section 17.4 Making Inferences

11. Review Practice Problem 1; then carry the analysis further by

a. establishing a 95 percent confidence interval for $\mu_{Y \cdot 12}$, given $X_1 = 5{,}000$ and $X_2 = 20{,}000$.

b. establishing a 95 percent prediction interval for $I_{Y \cdot 12}$, given $X_1 = 5{,}000$ and $X_2 = 20{,}000$.

c. establishing 95 percent confidence intervals for β_1 and β_2.

d. testing the significance of the regression coefficients with t values.

e. testing the significance of the regression coefficients with p values.

12. Review Practice Problem 2; then carry the analysis further by

a. establishing a 95 percent confidence interval for $\mu_{Y \cdot 12}$, given $X_1 = 50{,}000$ and $X_2 = 500{,}000$.

b. establishing a 95 percent prediction interval for $I_{Y \cdot 12}$, given $X_1 = 50{,}000$ and $X_2 = 500{,}000$.

c. establishing 95 percent confidence intervals for β_1 and β_2.

d. testing the significance of the regression coefficients with t values.

e. testing the significance of the regression coefficients with p values.

13. Review Practice Problem 3; then carry the analysis further by

a. establishing a 95 percent confidence interval for $\mu_{Y \cdot 12}$, given $X_1 = 30{,}000$ and $X_2 = 30{,}000$.

b. establishing a 95 percent prediction interval for $I_{Y \cdot 12}$, given $X_1 = 30{,}000$ and $X_2 = 30{,}000$.

c. establishing 95 percent confidence intervals for β_1 and β_2.

d. testing the significance of the regression coefficients with t values.

e. testing the significance of the regression coefficients with p values.

14. Review Practice Problem 4; then carry the analysis further by

a. establishing a 95 percent confidence interval for $\mu_{Y \cdot 12}$, given $X_1 = 2{,}000$ and $X_2 = 30{,}000$.

b. establishing a 95 percent prediction interval for $I_{Y \cdot 12}$, given $X_1 = 2{,}000$ and $X_2 = 30{,}000$.

c. establishing 95 percent confidence intervals for β_1 and β_2.

d. testing the significance of the regression coefficients with t values.

e. testing the significance of the regression coefficients with p values.

15. Review Practice Problem 5; then carry the analysis further by

a. establishing a 95 percent confidence interval for $\mu_{Y \cdot 12}$, given $X_1 = 100$ and $X_2 = 15$.

b. establishing a 95 percent prediction interval for $I_{Y \cdot 12}$, given $X_1 = 100$ and $X_2 = 15$.

c. establishing 95 percent confidence intervals for β_1 and β_2.

d. testing the significance of the regression coefficients with t values.

e. testing the significance of the regression coefficients with p values.

16. Review Practice Problem 6; then carry the analysis further by

a. establishing a 95 percent confidence interval for $\mu_{Y \cdot 12}$, given $X_1 = 250$ and $X_2 = 50$.

b. establishing a 95 percent prediction interval for $I_{Y \cdot 12}$, given $X_1 = 250$ and $X_2 = 50$.

c. establishing 95 percent confidence intervals for β_1 and β_2.

d. testing the significance of the regression coefficients with t values.

e. testing the significance of the regression coefficients with p values.

17. Review Practice Problem 7; then carry the analysis further by

a. establishing a 95 percent confidence interval for $\mu_{Y \cdot 12}$, given $X_1 = 5$ and $X_2 = 2$.

b. establishing a 95 percent prediction interval for $I_{Y \cdot 12}$, given $X_1 = 5$ and $X_2 = 2$.

c. establishing 95 percent confidence intervals for β_1 and β_2.

d. testing the significance of the regression coefficients with t values.

e. testing the significance of the regression coefficients with p values.

18. Review Practice Problem 8; then carry the analysis further by

a. establishing a 95 percent confidence interval for $\mu_{Y\cdot12}$, given $X_1 = 80$ and $X_2 = 100$.

b. establishing a 95 percent prediction interval for $I_{Y\cdot12}$, given $X_1 = 80$ and $X_2 = 100$.

c. establishing 95 percent confidence intervals for β_1 and β_2.

d. testing the significance of the regression coefficients with t values.

e. testing the significance of the regression coefficients with p values.

19. Review Practice Problem 9; then carry the analysis further by

a. establishing a 95 percent confidence interval for $\mu_{Y\cdot12}$, given $X_1 = 75$ and $X_2 = 7$.

b. establishing a 95 percent prediction interval for $I_{Y\cdot12}$, given $X_1 = 75$ and $X_2 = 7$.

c. establishing 95 percent confidence intervals for β_1 and β_2.

d. testing the significance of the regression coefficients with t values.

e. testing the significance of the regression coefficients with p values.

20. Review Practice Problem 10; then carry the analysis further by

a. establishing a 95 percent confidence interval for $\mu_{Y\cdot12}$, given $X_1 = 30$ and $X_2 = 25$.

b. establishing a 95 percent prediction interval for $I_{Y\cdot12}$, given $X_1 = 30$ and $X_2 = 25$.

c. establishing 95 percent confidence intervals for β_1 and β_2.

d. testing the significance of the regression coefficients with t values.

e. testing the significance of the regression coefficients with p values.

Section 17.5 ANOVA Revisited: Testing the Overall Significance of a Regression

Section 17.6 Multiple Correlation Analysis

21. Review Practice Problem 1; then carry the analysis further by

a. conducting an ANOVA test of the overall significance of the regression.

b. computing the sample coefficient of multiple determination, R^2.

c. computing and interpreting the adjusted sample coefficient of multiple determination, R^2(adj.).

22. Review Practice Problem 2; then carry the analysis further by

a. conducting an ANOVA test of the overall significance of the regression.

b. computing the sample coefficient of multiple determination, R^2.

c. computing and interpreting the adjusted sample coefficient of multiple determination, R^2(adj.).

23. Review Practice Problem 3; then carry the analysis further by

a. conducting an ANOVA test of the overall significance of the regression.

b. computing the sample coefficient of multiple determination, R^2.

c. computing and interpreting the adjusted sample coefficient of multiple determination, R^2(adj.).

24. Review Practice Problem 4; then carry the analysis further by

a. conducting an ANOVA test of the overall significance of the regression.

b. computing the sample coefficient of multiple determination, R^2.

c. computing and interpreting the adjusted sample coefficient of multiple determination, R^2(adj.).

25. Review Practice Problem 5; then carry the analysis further by

a. conducting an ANOVA test of the overall significance of the regression.

b. computing the sample coefficient of multiple determination, R^2.

c. computing and interpreting the adjusted sample coefficient of multiple determination, R^2(adj.).

26. Review Practice Problem 6; then carry the analysis further by

a. conducting an ANOVA test of the overall significance of the regression.

b. computing the sample coefficient of multiple determination, R^2.

c. computing and interpreting the adjusted sample coefficient of multiple determination, R^2(adj.).

27. Review Practice Problem 7; then carry the analysis further by

a. conducting an ANOVA test of the overall significance of the regression.

b. computing the sample coefficient of multiple determination, R^2.

c. computing and interpreting the adjusted sample coefficient of multiple determination, R^2(adj.).

28. Review Practice Problem 8; then carry the analysis further by

a. conducting an ANOVA test of the overall significance of the regression.

b. computing the sample coefficient of multiple determination, R^2.

c. computing and interpreting the adjusted sample coefficient of multiple determination, R^2(adj.).

29. Review Practice Problem 9; then carry the analysis further by

a. conducting an ANOVA test of the overall significance of the regression.

b. computing the sample coefficient of multiple determination, R^2.

c. computing and interpreting the adjusted sample coefficient of multiple determination, R^2(adj.).

30. Review Practice Problem 10; then carry the analysis further by

a. conducting an ANOVA test of the overall significance of the regression.

b. computing the sample coefficient of multiple determination, R^2.

c. computing and interpreting the adjusted sample coefficient of multiple determination, R^2(adj.).

Section 17.7 Linear Multiple Regression with Three or More Explanatory Variables

31. A textbook publisher wants to assess the relationship between the number of book copies sold, Y, and a number of possible determinants, including the number of pages in the book, X_1, the age of the author, X_2, the advertising expenditure made, X_3, and the number of similar books on the market, X_4. Given the data of Table 17.6, compute and interpret

a. a multiple regression equation, including t values.

b. the values of R^2 and R^2(adj.).

TABLE 17.6

Copies Sold (thousands), Y	Pages (number), X_1	Author's Age (years), X_2	Ad Expenses ($ thousands), X_3	Competing Books (number), X_4
5	352	22	5	7
13	490	29	9	3
23	250	38	5	20
36	670	67	7	39
57	805	70	8	61
72	390	52	6	10
98	510	50	12	7
102	711	31	22	2
122	905	29	39	5
190	472	75	30	0

32. Review Practice Problem 31; then carry the analysis further by

a. conducting an ANOVA test of the overall significance of the regression.

b. making a point estimate of sales for an 800-page book with a 60-year-old author, $30,000 in advertising expenses, and 8 competitive books on the market.

c. creating a 95 percent prediction interval for the next occasion on which the circumstances described in (b) occur (MINITAB users only).

33. A textbook publisher wants to assess the relationship between the number of book copies sold, Y, and certain book characteristics, including the number of pages in the book, X_1, the number of Applications, X_2, the number of Practice Problems, X_3, and the ratio of favorable to unfavorable reviews, X_4. Given the data of Table 17.7, compute and interpret

a. a multiple regression equation, including t values.

b. the values of R^2 and R^2(adj.).

TABLE 17.7

Copies Sold (thousands), Y	Pages (number), X_1	Applications (number), X_2	Practice Problems (number), X_3	Review Ratio (fav./unfav.), X_4
7	390	0	0	5.1
11	472	0	0	4.6
14	512	0	0	6.0
17	408	15	100	2.0
29	610	15	100	3.1
39	830	30	900	.2
52	310	15	500	.1
6	910	92	900	10.3
3	211	0	10	5.0
2	172	0	0	12.0

34. Review Practice Problem 33; then carry the analysis further by

a. conducting an ANOVA test of the overall significance of the regression.

b. making a point estimate of sales for an 800-page book with 60 Applications, 300 Practice Problems, and a review ratio of 10.

c. creating a 95 percent prediction interval for the next occasion on which the circumstances described in (b) occur (MINITAB users only).

35. A marketing manager wants to assess the relationship between average monthly purchases with a company's credit card, Y, and a number of possible determinants, including cardholder family income, X_1, cardholder family size, X_2, and the interest rate charged, X_3. Given the data of Table 17.8 on the next page, compute and interpret

a. a multiple regression equation, including t values.

b. the values of R^2 and R^2(adj.).

36. Review Practice Problem 35; then carry the analysis further by

a. conducting an ANOVA test of the overall significance of the regression.

b. making a point estimate of purchases for a $5,000 income, a family size of 2, and an interest rate of 12 percent.

c. creating a 95 percent prediction interval for the next occasion on which the circumstances described in (b) occur (MINITAB users only).

TABLE 17.8

Average Purchases ($/month), Y	Family Income (thousands of $/month), X_1	Family Size (number of persons), X_2	Interest Rate (percent/year), X_3
22.50	1.1	1	15.0
33.77	1.4	1	15.0
52.41	2.3	2	18.9
156.77	1.3	3	22.0
233.56	2.7	2	12.9
457.34	4.0	1	3.9
600.56	3.4	2	2.9
750.33	2.9	3	15.0
899.32	3.6	1	15.0
1,122.56	5.8	4	18.9
1,500.77	3.9	2	10.0
1,600.39	6.1	1	9.0
1,677.99	4.8	2	5.9
1,899.44	8.9	3	6.9
2,344.79	6.9	3	17.0

37. An executive of a shoe manufacturing company wants to assess the relationship between average daily sales at the firm's factory outlet stores, Y, and a number of possible determinants, including the number of competitors within a 3-mile radius, X_1, per capita annual income in the county, X_2, and the average price per pair of shoes, X_3. Given the data of Table 17.9, compute and interpret

a. a multiple regression equation, including t values.

b. the values of R^2 and R^2(adj.).

38. Review Practice Problem 37; then carry the analysis further by

a. conducting an ANOVA test of the overall significance of the regression.

b. making a point estimate of sales with 5 competitors, a per capita income of $10,000 and a price of $50.

c. creating a 95 percent prediction interval for the next occasion on which the circumstances described in (b) occur (MINITAB users only).

39. A quality inspector wants to assess the relationship between the tensile strength of plastic sheets, Y, and a number of possible determinants, including the quantity of ingredient #1, X_1, the quantity of ingredient #2, X_2, and the production temperature, X_3. Given the data of Table 17.10, compute and interpret

a. a multiple regression equation, including t values.

b. the values of R^2 and R^2(adj.).

40. Review Practice Problem 39; then carry the analysis further by

a. conducting an ANOVA test of the overall significance of the regression.

b. making a point estimate of tensile strength with 15 units of #1, 100 units of #2, and 200 degrees.

c. creating a 95 percent prediction interval for the next occasion on which the circumstances described in (b) occur (MINITAB users only).

TABLE 17.9

Average Daily Sales ($1,000s), Y	Competitors within 3 Miles (number), X_1	Per Capita Income in County ($1,000/year), X_2	Average Price of Shoes ($/pair), X_3
2.8	0	3.1	28
3.1	0	4.0	31
.6	4	2.9	67
1.9	1	5.9	44
1.9	1	6.9	47
1.4	1	4.9	43
.6	6	2.7	78
2.5	3	4.7	34
1.7	1	4.2	23
2.9	2	6.0	33
4.8	2	7.3	55
3.9	3	7.2	66
5.1	0	8.0	43
8.6	0	14.7	83

TABLE 17.10

Tensile Strength (psi), Y	Quantity of Ingredient #1 (units), X_1	Quantity of Ingredient #2 (units), X_2	Production Temperature (degrees F), X_3
31.7	12	66	170
52.0	13	99	200
45.6	14	89	170
29.1	15	60	170
49.3	16	99	170
37.0	17	77	170
48.0	18	99	170
88.9	19	157	250
66.3	20	123	200
12.9	21	20	134

SECTION 17.8 DISCOVERING POSSIBLE VIOLATIONS OF ASSUMPTIONS

41. Review Practice Problem 1; then carry the analysis further by

a. plotting residuals against fitted values to test the normality and homoscedasticity assumptions.

b. conducting a Durbin-Watson test to validate the statistical independence assumption.

c. checking on the multicollinearity problem by setting up a correlation matrix and computing VIF values.

42. Review Practice Problem 3; then carry the analysis further by

a. plotting residuals against fitted values to test the normality and homoscedasticity assumptions.

b. conducting a Durbin-Watson test to validate the statistical independence assumption.

c. checking on the multicollinearity problem by setting up a correlation matrix and computing VIF values.

43. Review Practice Problem 5; then carry the analysis further by

a. plotting residuals against fitted values to test the normality and homoscedasticity assumptions.

b. conducting a Durbin-Watson test to validate the statistical independence assumption.

c. checking on the multicollinearity problem by setting up a correlation matrix and computing VIF values.

44. Review Practice Problem 7; then carry the analysis further by

a. plotting residuals against fitted values to test the normality and homoscedasticity assumptions.

b. conducting a Durbin-Watson test to validate the statistical independence assumption.

c. checking on the multicollinearity problem by setting up a correlation matrix and computing VIF values.

45. Review Practice Problem 9; then carry the analysis further by

a. plotting residuals against fitted values to test the normality and homoscedasticity assumptions.

b. conducting a Durbin-Watson test to validate the statistical independence assumption.

c. checking on the multicollinearity problem by setting up a correlation matrix and computing VIF values.

46. Review Practice Problem 31; then carry the analysis further by

a. plotting residuals against fitted values to test the normality and homoscedasticity assumptions.

b. conducting a Durbin-Watson test to validate the statistical independence assumption.

c. checking on the multicollinearity problem by setting up a correlation matrix and computing VIF values.

47. Review Practice Problem 33; then carry the analysis further by

a. plotting residuals against fitted values to test the normality and homoscedasticity assumptions.

b. conducting a Durbin-Watson test to validate the statistical independence assumption.

c. checking on the multicollinearity problem by setting up a correlation matrix and computing VIF values.

48. Review Practice Problem 35; then carry the analysis further by

a. plotting residuals against fitted values to test the normality and homoscedasticity assumptions.

b. conducting a Durbin-Watson test to validate the statistical independence assumption.

c. checking on the multicollinearity problem by setting up a correlation matrix and computing VIF values.

49. Review Practice Problem 37; then carry the analysis further by

a. plotting residuals against fitted values to test the normality and homoscedasticity assumptions.

b. conducting a Durbin-Watson test to validate the statistical independence assumption.

c. checking on the multicollinearity problem by setting up a correlation matrix and computing VIF values.

50. Review Practice Problem 39; then carry the analysis further by

a. plotting residuals against fitted values to test the normality and homoscedasticity assumptions.

b. conducting a Durbin-Watson test to validate the statistical independence assumption.

c. checking on the multicollinearity problem by setting up a correlation matrix and computing VIF values.

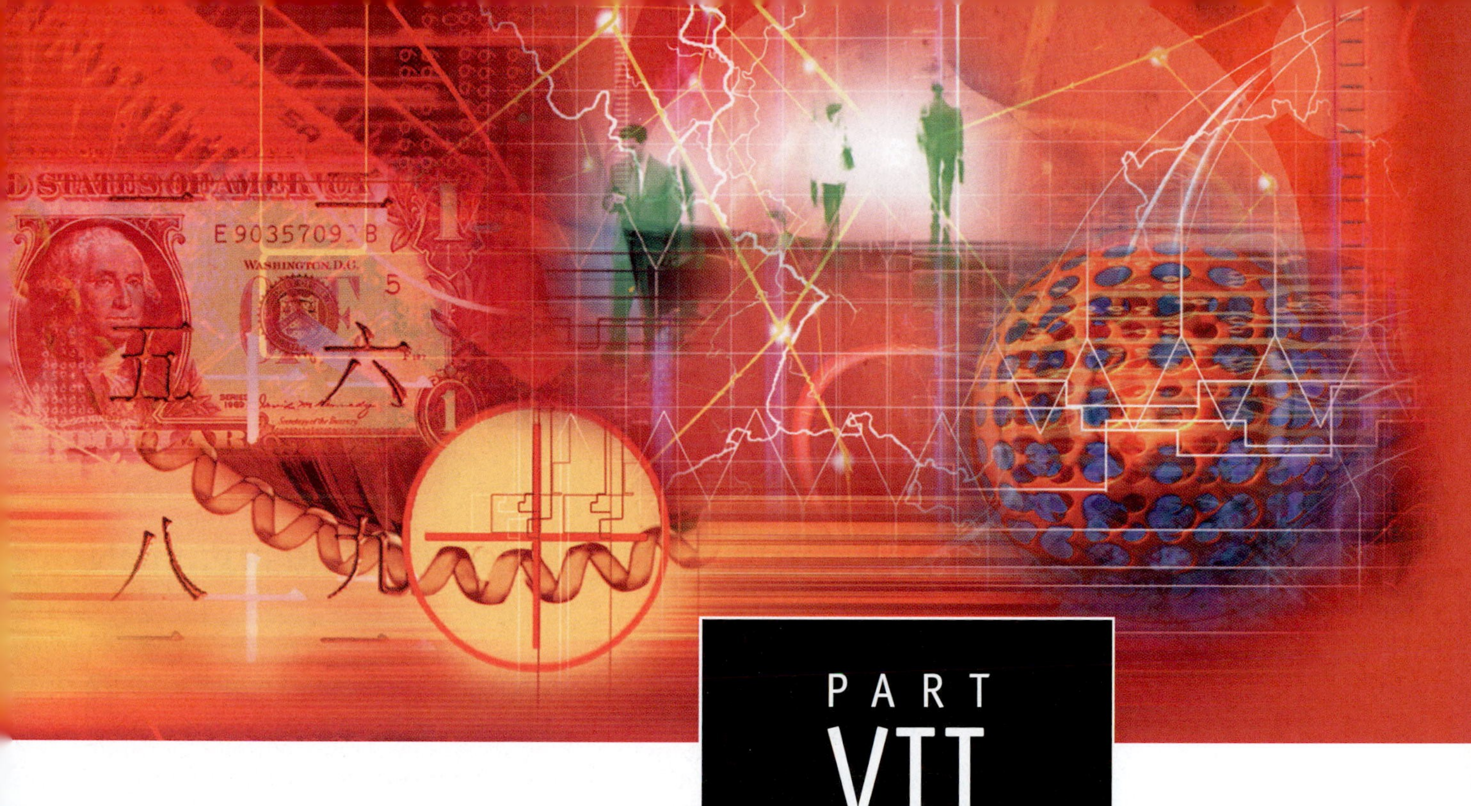

PART VII

SUPPLEMENTARY TOPICS FOR ECONOMICS

Chapter 18

MODEL BUILDING WITH MULTIPLE REGRESSION

LOOKING AHEAD

After reading this chapter, you will be able to employ multiple regression techniques in a variety of sophisticated ways. Among other things, you will learn to:

1. explain the behavior of a dependent variable not only via quantitative independent variables, but also by introducing *qualitative* independent variables, known as *dummy variables,*
2. use *forward-selection, backward-elimination,* and *best subset* techniques to select the best set of independent variables from among numerous candidates,
3. build *simultaneous equations models* containing *n* unknowns and *n* independent equations rather than a single equation,
4. recognize *simultaneous equations bias* in such multiple-equations models,
5. deal with the bias problem by applying the *indirect least-squares (ILS) method,*
6. recognize the *identification problem* that often plagues ILS procedures, and
7. overcome that problem, in turn, with the help of *instrumental variable (IV) methods,* such as the *two-stage least-squares technique.*

AND HERE IS A TYPICAL PROBLEM YOU WILL BE ABLE TO SOLVE:

Consider the following demand and supply model:

$$Q_D = \alpha_0 + \beta_1 P + \beta_2 DI + \varepsilon_0$$
$$Q_S = \alpha_1 + \beta_3 P + \beta_4 D + \varepsilon_1$$
$$Q_D = Q_S$$

Among the right-hand side explanatory variables, the good's price, *P,* is endogenous. The disposable income of consumers, *DI,* and a dummy variable, *D,* denoting the existence or absence of import restrictions, are predetermined. Can each equation be identified? Can unique estimators be computed for the model's structural parameters? If the answers are *yes,* do so now.

PREVIEW

During the last two decades of the 20th century, various court decisions and administrative rulings by the Federal Trade Commission (FTC) put an end to an old practice. Professional societies and legal statutes had long insisted that *advertising* by dentists, lawyers, physicians, and other professionals was "unethical." Allegedly, such ads would not only besmirch the dignity of the professions, but would also lead to higher prices as unscrupulous advertisers achieved market positions of "near monopoly." It was also argued that the winners of all this undignified competition would be swamped with clients, become less careful in their work, and pull down service quality. In contrast, economists had long argued that advertising might be a weapon by which newcomers could challenge established providers and that the newcomers' market entry would lower prices without affecting quality.

A number of studies have now confirmed the economists' hunch. One study compared package prices of eye exams plus eyeglasses in states such as North Carolina, where government or professional societies forbade advertising, with package prices in other states such as Texas, where there had been a long tradition of open advertising. In the 1960s, the price in the restricted states was $50.73; in the unrestricted states, it was $29.97. Other studies noted how the prices of legal services, such as divorces, title searches, and wills, plummeted whenever lawyers began to advertise. More recently, an economist examined the contact lens industry.

Getting contact lenses involves three steps: a refractive eye exam that leads to a lens prescription, a keratometric or fitting exam that measures the curvature of the cornea, and the purchase of the lens itself. When the study was initiated, some states, such as Missouri, New Jersey, New Mexico, and Vermont, forbade opticians to perform fitting exams and required consumers to get such exams from ophthalmologists or optometrists. Other states restricted advertising by mere opticians. Still others restricted the number of optician offices or their locations. The question of interest to the economist was: How has the presence or absence of such restrictions affected the prices of contact lenses and the quality of eye health care?

A proper answer to the question, the economist argued, required more sophisticated procedures than those introduced in the two preceding chapters of this text. First, she noted that many relevant explanatory variables are not *quantitative* but *qualitative* in nature. Therefore, instead of relying entirely on quantitative variables that are naturally measured numerically, she also made use of qualitative variables that are normally expressed in words. (When coded as nominal data and entered into a regression analysis, the latter are referred to as "dummy" variables.) Second, the economist decided not to be tied to a single-equation model but to specify *two* regression equations. One of these related product price to an index of service quality (measured by the frequency of various pathological conditions associated with poorly fitted contact lenses) and to dummy variables indicating restrictions on who was allowed to fit lenses, to advertise, and so on. Another equation related service quality to product price, the characteristics of lens wearers (such as age, sex, and hours of wearing), the characteristics of lenses (such as type, cleanliness, and warpage), and more.

Such a sophisticated form of multiple-equations modeling, however, is tricky business. Whenever the *dependent* variable of one equation, such as price in the first equation at the beginning of this chapter or quality in the second, also appears as an *independent* variable in another equation, a problem arises. The equations cannot be estimated reliably by the "ordinary least-squares" (OLS) techniques introduced in earlier chapters of this text. In an interdependent system of equations, these techniques yield parameter estimates that are seriously biased and inconsistent. Therefore, as the current chapter will explain, researchers must estimate these equations differently.

One of these alternative approaches is called *two-stage least squares;* it is the approach taken by the author of the contact lens study. The result: Rules as to who may fit lenses, who may advertise, and other restrictive governmental practices all increased prices. The abolition of these restrictions lowered prices, while leaving the quality of service unaffected.[1]

[1] For the contact lens study, see Deborah Haas-Wilson, "Tying Requirements in Markets with Many Sellers: The Contact Lens Industry," *The Review of Economics and Statistics,* February 1987, pp. 170–175. Some of the other studies are described in Lee Benham, "The Effect of Advertising on the Price of Eyeglasses," *The Journal of Law and Economics,* October 1972, pp. 337–352; John E. Kwoka, Jr., "Advertising and the Price and Quality of Optometric Services," *The American Economic Review,* March 1984, pp. 211–216; and Warren Weaver, Jr., "Court Rules Lawyer May Advertise Fee for Routine Service," *The New York Times,* June 28, 1977, pp. A1 and 14.

18.1 Economic Theory and Econometrics

Business executives and economists are always eager to understand and predict people's economic behavior. Yet the determinants of any individual's behavior are numerous and complex. Equally numerous and complex are the factors that account for the behavior of groups of people, such as all the buyers of apples, all the producers of steel, or all the suppliers of labor. As a result, it is impossible to explain such microeconomic variables as the price of apples and the quantity of steel produced, or such macroeconomic aggregates as the general price level and the total of consumer expenditures, by noting *all* the relevant influences in detail. If we tried, we would have to recognize that any given variable, Y, depends on dozens, hundreds, even millions of variables, X. Any truly detailed description of all that is going on in a given market or given economy would lead to confusion rather than enlightenment. Contrary to the often-heard cliché, facts, even volumes of them, do *not* speak for themselves. In a complex world, paradoxically, understanding comes with a deliberate *loss* of detail, which is the very purpose of economic theorizing.

DEFINITION 18.1 An **economic theory** is a deliberately simplified and, thus, inevitably unrealistic representation or *model* of economic reality. Such a model can be extremely useful for those seeking to understand economic relationships and predict economic events—precisely because it ignores detail and focuses on essentials.

Good economic theory is often likened to a good geographic map, which is so very useful despite its inherent lack of realism. Geographers never provide us with a truly detailed picture of the physical world. Like economic theorists, they focus on the most essential features. Nowadays, their maps are drawn from satellite pictures that bring the broad outlines of reality into sharp focus. Before we know it, all of North America is shown on a piece of paper 6 inches square! Could anything be more unrealistic? Entire cities are missing, as are many mountains, rivers, highways, houses, and certainly millions of trees. Yet, precisely because such detail is omitted, geographers can create a useful image of the reality in which we live. Building regression models, as we did in the previous two chapters of this text, involves an analogous activity. It involves drawing maps of the economic world by endowing rather vague economic theory (about, say, a suspected relationship between Y and X) with empirical content (the precise regression equation). Indeed, regression analysis takes us into the world of *econometrics,* which literally means *economic measurement.*

DEFINITION 18.2 The study of **econometrics** involves the application of statistical methods to economic data so as to endow economic theories with empirical content. (While economic theory might merely suggest that aggregate consumption expenditures, *C,* rise with aggregate disposable income, *DI,* econometrics might tell us that in the United States of 2001, all else being equal and measured in billions of dollars of 1992 purchasing power, $C = 500 + .71\ DI$.)

This chapter carries our foray into econometrics considerably further than the previous two chapters did. Chapter 16 introduced simple regression analysis, a method that models real-world phenomena by mathematically relating the value of a dependent variable, *Y,* to that of a *single* independent variable, *X*. Chapter 17 turned to multiple regression analysis and showed how a dependent variable, *Y,* might relate to *several* independent variables, X_1, X_2, X_3, and so forth. Yet despite this difference, these chapters were quite similar. In both chapters, the independent variables were *quantitative* variables that are naturally measured numerically. In both chapters, the relationships being modeled were expressed by *single* equations. In the current chapter, we learn to build more sophisticated models.

First, we find out how *qualitative* variables, which are ordinarily expressed in words, can enter regressions after being coded as nominal data. (For a quick review of different data types, see Section 1.7 on page 18.)

Second, we become familiar with a variety of techniques that help us decide which among numerous *X* variables should be included in any given regression model and which should be discarded.

Third, we turn to building *multiple-equation* models of complex, interdependent relationships that cannot be captured by the overly simple representation of reality that a single regression equation provides. In the process, we learn why our single-equation *ordinary least-squares* regression techniques, generally known as **OLS techniques,** cannot be used to estimate *reliable* coefficients for the explanatory variables found in a *whole series* of interdependent equations. The solution to that problem will concern us as well.

18.2 Dummy Variables

The type of regression analysis we have conducted so far requires that all variables be quantitative. But sometimes we may have reason to believe that the dependent variable under study is influenced in some important way by one or more independent variables that are *qualitative* in nature. Such variables cannot be measured numerically (as so many thousands of dollars of income or so many years of education) but can only be described categorically (as male/female; black/white; homeowner/renter; urban/rural; wartime/peacetime; recession/prosperity; Catholic/Protestant/Jewish). Under such circumstances, all is not lost; we can incorporate any qualitative variable into regression analysis by creating one or more **dummy variables.** These are also known as **binary variables, categorical variables,** or **indicator variables.** These variables take on only two values, namely 0 or 1, and those values are used to indicate the absence or presence of a particular qualitative characteristic. If the qualitative variable of interest has two categories only (is binomial), a single dummy variable will do; we might code "male" as 0 and "female" as 1, for instance. Or if the qualitative variable of interest has more than two categories, we represent it by several dummy variables, as will be shown below.

A QUALITATIVE VARIABLE WITH TWO CATEGORIES

Consider the sample data contained in columns 1–4 of Table 18.1 on the next page. If we believe that income is influenced not only by education, but also by sex, we do not have to

TABLE 18.1 | Sample Data on Income, Using Education and Sex as Independent Variables

Individual (1)	Income, Y (thousands of dollars/year) (2)	Education, X_1 (years) (3)	Sex (4)	Sex Dummy, D_1 (male = 0, female = 1) (5)
A	5.012	2	male	0
B	9.680	4	female	1
C	28.432	8	male	0
D	8.774	8	female	1
E	21.008	8	male	0
F	26.565	10	male	0
G	25.428	12	male	0
H	23.113	12	male	0
I	22.500	12	male	0
J	19.456	12	female	1
K	21.690	12	female	1
L	24.750	13	male	0
M	30.100	14	male	0
N	24.798	14	female	1
O	28.532	15	male	0
P	26.000	15	female	1
Q	38.908	16	male	0
R	22.050	16	female	1
S	33.060	17	male	0
T	48.276	21	male	0

abandon the sex issue just because the column 4 data are qualitative. We can create the column 5 *nominal* data and develop a multiple regression equation of the form

$$\hat{Y} = a + b_1X_1 + b_2D_1$$

where D_1 represents the dummy variable. This multiple regression equation predicts the income of any male as $\hat{Y}_M = a + b_1X_1$ (because D_1 then equals 0) and that of any female as $\hat{Y}_F = a + b_1X_1 + b_2 = (a + b_2) + b_1X_1$ (because D_1 then equals 1). Using relevant data from Table 18.1, the computer estimates the multiple regression equation as

$$\begin{aligned}\hat{Y} = \underset{(1.89)}{5.393} + \underset{(8.39)}{1.785X_1} - \underset{(-3.66)}{7.125D_1}\end{aligned}$$

The t values are given in parentheses. Our newly found information is graphed in Figure 18.1.

We can view our dummy variable as a switch. It is "on" when we are estimating the income of women; the lower broken regression line then applies. It is "off" when we are estimating the income of men; the upper solid regression line applies. Note also that the accuracy of the

FIGURE 18.1 | Scatter Diagram and Multiple Regression with Dummy Variable

The scatter of points in this graph depicts the data of columns (2)–(4) of Table 18.1. The income and education data are precisely the same as in Figure 16.5 (on p. 714), but those pertaining to women have been highlighted by the red crosses. This time, furthermore, a multiple regression equation has been estimated, including sex as a dummy variable, D_1. Income estimates for males can be made by the upper line ($D_1 = 0$); incomes for females can be estimated by the lower line ($D_1 = 1$). Thus, a woman's income is estimated at \$7,125 less than that of a comparably educated man.

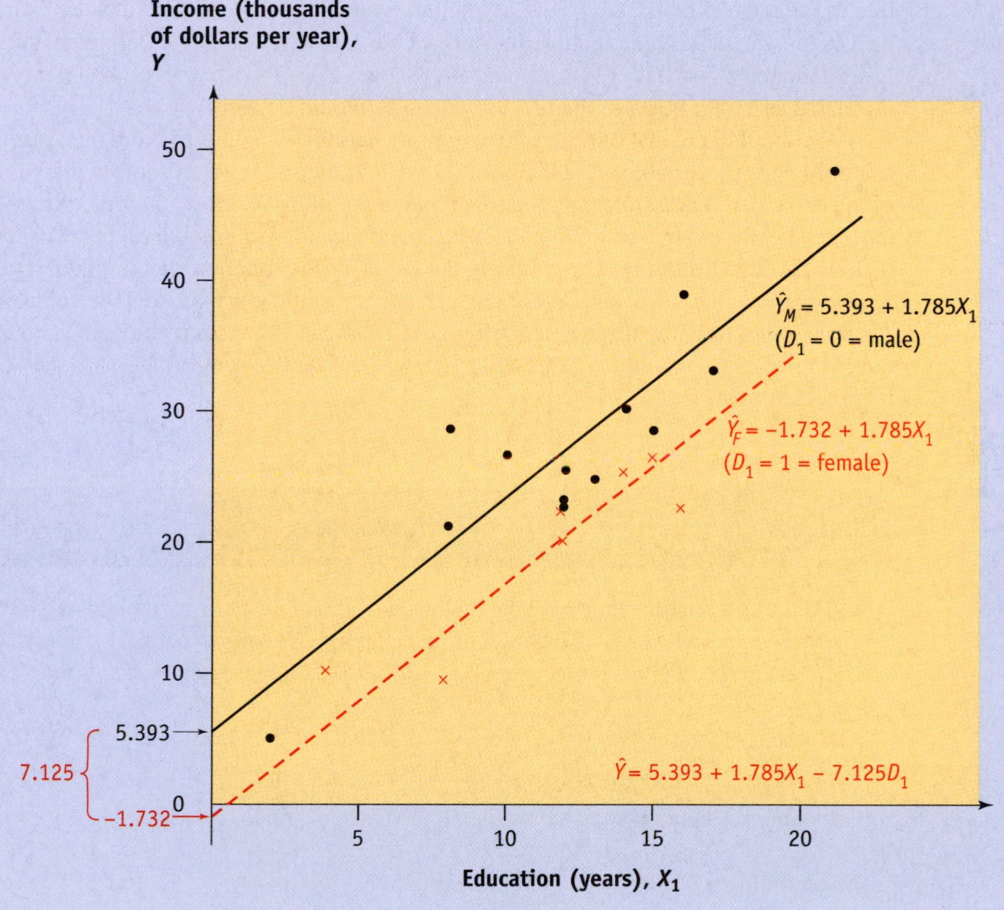

estimates improves considerably when sex is added to education as a second explanatory variable: The standard error of the estimate of Y falls from $s_{Y \cdot X_1} = \$5,377$ to $s_{Y \cdot X_1 D_1} = \$4,137$. The coefficient of determination rises from $r^2(\text{adj.}) = .698$ to $R^2(\text{adj.}) = .821$.

Note: These results merely tell us that adding sex to education improves our ability to estimate income. We should *not* jump to the conclusion that our data prove discrimination against women in the job market. Our sample data are quite consistent with the absence of discrimination. For all we know, all the women in our sample are young, while all the men are older, and our results merely show that experienced employees of either sex tend to be paid more. Or the women in our sample may be in lower-paying occupations than the sampled men, although men and women are paid the same in any given line of work.

A QUALITATIVE VARIABLE WITH MORE THAN TWO CATEGORIES

We can incorporate even qualitative variables with multiple categories (such as first/second/third/fourth quarter of the year, Catholic/Protestant/Jewish, or extremely interested/somewhat interested/not interested) into a multiple regression equation using the dummy-variables technique. In that case, given k categories, we must use $k - 1$ dummy variables.

Suppose, for example, that we wanted to investigate someone's claim that income, Y, can be explained solely by religion. If there were $k = 3$ religions (say, Catholicism, Protestantism, and Judaism), we could create $k - 1 = 2$ dummy variables and specify a multiple regression equation of the form $\hat{Y} = a + b_1D_1 + b_2D_2$. In this equation, both of the independent variables would be dummy variables, such that, perhaps, $D_1 = 1$ if Catholic and $D_1 = 0$ if not Catholic; $D_2 = 1$ if Protestant and $D_2 = 0$ if not Protestant. If someone were Jewish, that person's income would be estimated as $\hat{Y} = a$ because then D_1 as well as D_2 would be zero.

You should note that our use of two dummy variables appeals to more than just convenience. If a third dummy variable were included ($D_3 = 1$ if Jewish, $D_3 = 0$ if not Jewish), the parameters of the expanded regression equation (then including "$+ b_3D_3$" as well) could not be uniquely determined because our assumption about independence (Assumption 5 on page 797) would be violated. The third dummy, D_3, would be an exact linear function of the other two, D_1 and D_2. Knowing the values of D_1 and D_2 for any person, we would always know the value for D_3 as well. Assuming that only the three noted religious affiliations exist, someone who is not-Catholic and not-Protestant, for example, necessarily is Jewish. When Assumption 5 is violated, proper estimation is impossible.

TECHNICAL DETAIL

A dummy variable can even take the place of the *dependent* variable! Consider the hypothesis that poverty is a function of race and sex. We might collect sample data on the subject and code the results using *three* dummy variables such that

- $D_1 = 1$ means "poverty," while $D_1 = 0$ means "the absence of poverty"
- $D_2 = 1$ means "black," while $D_2 = 0$ means "white"
- $D_3 = 1$ means "female," while $D_3 = 0$ means "male"

The multiple regression equation might read

$$\hat{D}_1 = .06 + .25D_2 + .50D_3$$

or

$$\text{Poverty} = .06 + .25 \text{ Race} + .50 \text{ Sex}$$

This equation would give us the *probability* of being poor—equal to .06 for a white male and .06 + .25 + .50 = .81 for a black female, for example. However, extreme caution is advised. Such *linear probability models* violate some of the assumptions of linear regression analysis (for example, the assumption concerning homoscedasticity), and there is no guarantee that the estimated probability number lies between 0 and 1. One can deal with these problems, but we must leave that resolution to more advanced texts.

Application 18.1 *Whom Do Regulators Serve? The Case of the Education Industry*
http://www.harcourtcollege.com/business_stats/kohler/siteresources.html

Do Consumer Products Safety Regulators Reduce Injuries and Deaths?

Every year, some 30,000 Americans are killed while using consumer products at home. Have government regulators of health and safety managed to make a significant difference? The question was investigated with respect to the Consumer Product Safety Commission (CPSC), created in the 1970s.

Case 1. One multiple regression equation using 1949–1981 data related the year *t* home accident rate, HAR_t, to a number of independent variables, including (among others):

- the lagged value of that rate, HAR_{t-1} (that is, the rate in the preceding year)
- real per capita consumption, *RPCC*
- a dummy variable, *CPSC,* denoting the existence (1973–1981 = 1) or absence (1949–1972 = 0) of the Commission
- the percentage of children under 5, *%UNDER5*

HAR_{t-1} was included because any one year's accident rate is affected not only by newly purchased products, but also by the continued use of a large stock of preexisting products that produced last year's accident rate. *RPCC* was included because rising consumer affluence can give rise to a greater demand for safety, which will reduce the accident rate. Finally, *%UNDER5* was included because this demographic group is particularly vulnerable to death by fire, ingestion, poisoning, and so forth.

The equation (with *t* values in parentheses) was

$$HAR_t = \underset{(1.79)}{17.79} + \underset{(3.15)}{.548}HAR_{t-1} - \underset{(-2.00)}{.002}RPCC$$

$$- \underset{(-.90)}{.333}CPSC - \underset{(-1.28)}{53.80}\%UNDER5 \text{ . . . and so on}$$

$$R^2 = .97$$

The effects of HAR_{t-1} and *RPCC* on the current home accident rate were positive and negative, respectively (as expected), and were significant (given the *t* values). The effect of the *CPSC* was negative (as one would hope), but not much and it was not statistically significant. Taken at face value, the coefficient of −.333 suggested that—all else being equal—the *CPSC* reduced the 1981 home accident rate, for example, from 9.5 deaths to 9.2 deaths per 100,000.

Case 2. The study also related PDR_t (the year *t* aspirin poisoning death rate of children under 5) to these variables:

- the same variable's lagged value, PDR_{t-1}
- real per capita consumption, *RPCC*
- *SAFETYCAPS* (the fraction of aspirin sold with safety caps)
- *PROD* (the per capita production of aspirin tablets, which had shown a declining trend as a result of the use of substitutes, such as Tylenol)

The equation (with *t* values in parentheses) was

$$PDR_t = \underset{(2.17)}{9.500} + \underset{(2.15)}{.483}PDR_{t-1} - \underset{(-2.00)}{.002}RPCC$$

$$+ \underset{(.10)}{.100}SAFETYCAPS - \underset{(-.31)}{.032}PROD$$

$$R^2 = .95$$

The *SAFETYCAPS* coefficient was not statistically significant. The poison rate showed no downward shift attributable to safety caps! According to the author of the study, this can be explained in large part by a wholly unjustified lulling effect on consumers who thought all was well with the advent of the caps. In fact, an ever-increasing percentage of poisonings has come from safety cap bottles; fully half of all poisonings came from bottles with the cap left off, because consumers were tired of grappling with the troublesome caps. (A similar effect has been noted with respect to auto fatality rates and seat belts. Drivers with seat belts have exercised less care in driving, thus offsetting the seat-belt safety effect.)

SOURCE: Adapted from W. Kip Viscusi, "Consumer Behavior and the Safety Effects of Product Safety Regulation," *Journal of Law and Economics,* October 1985, pp. 527–553.

APPLICATION 18.3

Does Photocopying Harm Authors and Publishers?

Creators and owners of intellectual properties have become increasingly alarmed by technologies, such as copy machines or scanners, that make it easy to copy texts, graphics, musical scores, and the like. Yet some economists have argued that unauthorized copying of intellectual properties need not be harmful, and may actually be beneficial, because authors and publishers can *indirectly* appropriate revenues from users who are not original purchasers.

The issue was addressed by one economist who argued that academic journals, for example, are most heavily photocopied in libraries and that publishers were getting revenue for this service by *price discrimination*. (Publishers routinely charge libraries considerably more than they charge individuals.) One economist gathered data on institutional and individual subscription prices for 80 economics journals in 1959 and 1982. A multiple regression equation was estimated relating P_{LIB}/P_{IND} (the ratio of library price to individual price) to the following:

- *CIT* (the number of citations per page received by each journal in 1981 to articles written between 1975 and 1979—a proxy for popularity and, hence, photocopying activity)
- D_{PUB} (a dummy variable = 1, if the publisher was a commercial firm presumably interested in profit maximization)
- D_{AGE} (a dummy variable = 1, if the journal was in existence prior to 1959, the year the Xerox machine came into use)

The result (with *t* values in parentheses) was

$$P_{LIB}/P_{IND} = \underset{}{1.38} + \underset{(2.14)}{.0071CIT} + \underset{(3.36)}{.578D_{PUB}} - \underset{(-1.01)}{.160D_{AGE}}$$

$$R^2(\text{adj.}) = .17$$

The coefficient of *CIT* is of greatest interest. It has the expected positive sign (more photocopying leads to a higher ratio of library-to-individual price), and it is statistically significant ($t = 2.14$). In addition, the coefficient and *t* value of D_{PUB} shows that pricing by commercial publishers is significantly more discriminatory than that of noncommercial publishers.

Indirect evidence is interesting as well: In 1959, only 3 of 38 economics journals then in existence price-discriminated between institutions and individuals. In 1983, 59 out of 80 journals did. On the other hand, the ratio of expenditures on periodicals to expenditures on books for American academic libraries was .41 in 1959; it was .88 in 1981.

SOURCE: Adapted from S. J. Liebowitz, "Copying and Indirect Appropriability: Photo-Copying of Journals," *Journal of Political Economy,* October 1985, pp. 945–957.

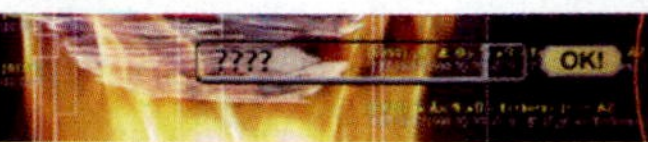

APPLICATION 18.4

Determinants of Air Fares

When passing the 1978 Airline Deregulation Act, Congress decided that operational decisions about flying, such as where planes can fly and what fares they can charge, are best left to airlines, not government regulators. Since that time, air fares have plummeted and air traffic has boomed. One study investigated direct flights to Cleveland in order to explore factors that determine ticket prices. Table 18.A on pages 850–851 summarizes the results of this multiple regression analysis. In all cases, the *dependent variable, Y,* was the one-way fare to Cleveland; 323 different places of origin were examined.

(continued on pages 850–851)

APPLICATION 18.5

WOMEN'S WAGES AND THE CROWDING HYPOTHESIS

In the recent past, women's wages in the United States have risen substantially relative to men's wages. Still, even in the 1990s, the median earnings of full-time female workers only came to 70 percent of those received by full-time male workers. One possible explanation is the *crowding hypothesis:* Employers exclude women from some occupations considered "men's work." These women crowd into other occupations considered "women's work." As the supply in the former fields falls and the supply in the latter fields rises, a wage differential develops. Compared to what would otherwise occur, wages rise for all those doing "men's work," while wages fall for those doing "women's work."

Researchers tested the hypothesis with data provided by the 1983 Current Population Survey (CPS), which sampled 9,158 men and 8,027 women, as well as by the 1984 Panel Study of Income Dynamics (PSID), which sampled 2,619 men and 2,411 women. A multiple regression analysis defined the natural log of hourly earnings as the independent variable, *Y.* It also defined a large number of independent variables that might explain hourly earnings. These *X* variables included:

- the proportion of women in an occupation
- a number of job attributes (including general education requirements, specific vocational preparation requirements, strength requirements, possible undesirable environmental conditions associated with jobs)
- human capital variables (including years of schooling completed, B.A. degree, advanced degree, work experience)
- other worker attributes (including marital status, children, union status, race/ethnicity)
- 42 industry *dummy variables* that might take account of different economic circumstances associated with different industries

Multiple regression equations were estimated from each data source, separately for male and female workers. These equations took the form

$$\hat{Y} = a + b_1X_1 + b_2X_2 + b_3X_3 + \ldots$$

where Y = hourly earnings; X_1 = the proportion of women in the occupation; and X_2, X_3, and so forth were the other explanatory variables.

The crucial coefficient b_1, attached to the crowding hypothesis, is given in Table 18.B, along with associated t values.

TABLE 18.B | Regression Results on Labor Market Crowding

	Value of b_1	
	CPS	**PSID**
Women	−.150	−.227
	(−5.75)	(−6.97)
Men	−.246	−.237
	(−8.53)	(−5.98)

PARTIAL INTERPRETATION. The negative signs indicate that both women's and men's wages in an occupation *decline* as the proportion of female workers in it rises. Depending on the data source, the percentage of the female/male earnings gap explained by occupational segregation of the sexes ranged from 15 to 23 percent for women doing "women's work" and equaled about 24 percent for men doing "women's work." The same study attributed between 12 and 17 percent of the gap to industrial differences and between 25 and 37 percent to other differences, and it could not explain between 22 and 43 percent of the gap.

SOURCE: Adapted from Elaine Sorensen, "The Crowding Hypothesis and Comparable Worth," *The Journal of Human Resources,* Winter 1990, pp. 55–89.

Application 18.4 (continued from page 848)

TABLE 18.A | Regression Results on the Determinants of Air Fares

	First Class (R^2 = .863)		Coach (R^2 = .871)		Discount (R^2 = .799)	
Independent Variable	**Coefficient**	***t* Value**	**Coefficient**	***t* Value**	**Coefficient**	***t* Value**
CONSTANT	212.00	5.21	126.00	5.75	113.00	12.40
CARRIERS (number of carriers)	−19.50	−.878	−23.00	−1.99	−17.50	−3.67
CARRIERS^2 (squared number of carriers)	2.79	.632	4.00	1.83	2.19	2.42
PASS (number of passengers flown on route by all carriers)	−.818E−3	−.771	−.275E−3	−.527	.853	3.93
MILES (mileage from origin city to Cleveland)	.233	5.13	.277	12.00	.791E−1	8.24
MILES^2 (squared mileage)	−.974E−5	−.495	−.520E−4	−4.98	−.140E−4	−3.23
POP (population of origin city)	−.598E−2	−1.67	−.114E−2	−.570	−.868E−3	−1.05
INC (per capita income in origin city)	−.195E−2	−.686	−.178E−2	−1.06	−.411E−2	−6.05
CORP (proxy for potential business traffic from origin city)	3.62	3.45	1.22	2.51	−1.06	−5.22
SLOT (dummy variable, = 1, if origin city had FAA slot-restricted airport; = 0 otherwise)	12.50	.299	−.746	−.667E−1	17.70	3.82
STOP (number of on-flight stops)	7.13	1.36	7.64	2.13	−3.85	−2.60

(continued)

Application 18.4 (continued)

TABLE 18.A (*continued*)

	First Class (R^2 = .863)		Coach (R^2 = .871)		Discount (R^2 = .799)	
Independent Variable	**Coefficient**	***t* Value**	**Coefficient**	***t* Value**	**Coefficient**	***t* Value**
MEAL (dummy variable, = 1, if meal was served; = 0 otherwise)	11.20	1.07	.945	.177	1.80	.813
HUB (dummy variable, = 1, if origin city had hub airline, = 0 otherwise)	11.30	.900	4.18	.810	−3.50	−1.62
EA (dummy variable, = 1, if carrier was Eastern Airlines, = 0 otherwise)	−18.30	−1.60	5.80	.775	−10.60	−3.49
CA (dummy variable, = 1, if carrier was Continental Airlines, = 0 otherwise)	−66.40	−5.72	−56.50	−7.61	−4.17	−1.35

Note: A number such as −.818E-3 is shorthand for −.000818. Thus, E-3 calls for moving the decimal point three positions to the left.

Partial Interpretation. The basic fare, the first row tells us, was $212 for first class, $126 for coach, and $113 for discount passengers. The three associated *t* values confirm the statistical significance of these constants. According to the remaining rows of our table, the basic fare was raised or lowered by 14 other factors. Considering only the number of carriers on a given route, for example, the monopoly price for a coach passenger would be $126 − 23(1) + 4(1^2) = $107. The appearance of a second carrier on the same route—all else being ignored—would change the price to $126 − 23(2) + 4(2^2) = $96. The appearance of a third carrier, still ignoring all other factors, would change the price to $126 − 23(3) + 4(3^2) = $93. Each additional carrier lowers fares less than the one before. By the time three to four carriers operate on a route, fares are no longer affected by additional competitors. However, other factors do play a role.

Notice how longer distances, shown by the positive MILES coefficients, raise all types of fares. So do FAA-imposed airport capacity constraints (SLOT), at least for first class and discount travelers. So do on-flight stops (except for discount passengers) and the serving of meals (for all). But note that not all coefficients are significant at the 95 percent level of confidence, as *t* values below absolute 2 indicate.

SOURCE: Paul W. Bauer and Thomas J. Zlatoper, "The Determinants of Direct Air Fares to Cleveland: How Competitive?" Federal Reserve Bank of Cleveland, *Economic Review,* 1, 1989, pp. 2–9.

18.3 Selecting an Ideal Set of Predictor Variables

Modern computers enable us to perform easily a complicated procedure that, in the view of some statisticians, should not be performed at all. This controversial procedure is **stepwise multiple regression,** and, as the name implies, it develops a multiple regression equation in carefully delineated steps. The following discussion will explain why some statisticians disapprove of the procedure. We have a look at it, nevertheless, because it is, in fact, widely used. (In the view of this author, a textbook should make students *aware* of controversies rather than keep students ignorant of them.) Two versions of stepwise multiple regression exist, the *forward-selection method* and the *backward-elimination method.*

THE FORWARD-SELECTION METHOD

The **step-up method** or **forward-selection method** starts with *no* independent X variables in a model designed to explain the behavior of the dependent variable, Y, and then adds one X variable at a time. Given a possibly long list of potential explanatory variables, one such variable is selected for inclusion in the analysis in each successive step—namely, the one that provides the greatest decrease in the hitherto unexplained variation in Y. The newly added variable, thus, has the highest coefficient of partial determination and promises to make the greatest marginal contribution to explaining the variation found in Y.

At the first stage, the computer performs simple regressions separately for each potential independent variable, identifies the most promising of these (the one that produces the highest regression sum of squares and, therefore, the lowest error sum of squares), and prints these results only. At the second stage, the computer performs multiple regressions separately for each combination of the previously selected independent variable and one of the remaining independent-variable candidates. Once again, the combination that reduces the unexplained variation of Y the most is chosen. This process continues until all potential independent variables appear in the equation or until further reductions in the unexplained variation of Y prove impossible. In this way, statisticians can determine which among all the potential independent variables provide the best explanation of the behavior of the dependent variable.

CAUTION

The list of potential independent variables to be included in a regression analysis must not be drawn up indiscriminately. It is important to have good *a priori* reasons (that is, meaningful common sense explanations) for potentially including each of the independent variables in the analysis. After all, given the ease with which modern computer technology allows us to perform stepwise multiple regression analysis, we could possibly search for an ever better-fitting regression equation until we found some set of independent variables that explained almost all of the variation in the dependent variable *even if these independent variables had no causal connection whatsoever to the dependent variable.* Some variables are highly correlated with others by pure chance; recall Application 16.5, *Snowfall and Unemployment,* on page 758. In addition, two variables can both be influenced by some third factor without being causally related to each other. The number of ministers and the volume of whiskey consumption, for example, may be higher in one state than in another simply because that state has a larger population and *not* because ministers do most of the drinking! When such is the case, the selection of a coincidentally correlated variable (snowfall or number of ministers) as the independent variable may well "explain" perfectly the dependent variable (unemployment or whiskey consumption), yet the relationship is nonsensical because no logical connection between the variables exists. Nevertheless, if we use the computer to hunt long enough, we are likely to find such a nonsensical, yet well-fitting regression equation. Only a good dose of plain common sense can ultimately prevent such foolishness.

This explains why some statisticians would rather not employ this procedure at all. They argue that we should

(continued)

Caution (continued)

specify on theoretical grounds, and *in advance of data selection and computer analysis,* which independent variables are logically capable of explaining the behavior of the dependent variable. *Following* such a one-time specification of the model, we should select and analyze data, accept or reject the model, and that should be the end of it! Statisticians who hold this view reject the forward-selection method and the backward-elimination method, to be discussed below, as unscientific "data mining," "fishing expeditions," and "cooking the data."

The following computer application illustrates the forward-selection method, using the data of Table 18.2.

EXCEL Example 18.1

Arguing on *a priori* grounds that it is reasonable to assume that income might be explained by education, job experience, age, and sex, apply the *forward-selection method* to the data of Table 18.2.

TABLE 18.2 | Sample Data on Income, Using Education, Job Experience, Age, and Sex as Potential Independent Variables

Individual (1)	Income (thousands of $/year) (2)	Education (years) (3)	Job Experience (years) (4)	Age (years) (5)	Sex Dummy (male = 0, female = 1) (6)
A	5.012	2	9	29	0
B	9.680	4	18	50	1
C	28.432	8	21	41	0
D	8.774	8	12	55	1
E	21.008	8	14	34	0
F	26.565	10	16	36	0
G	25.428	12	16	61	0
H	23.113	12	9	29	0
I	22.500	12	18	64	0
J	19.456	12	5	30	1
K	21.690	12	7	28	1
L	24.750	13	9	29	0
M	30.100	14	12	35	0
N	24.798	14	17	59	1
O	28.532	15	19	65	0
P	26.000	15	6	30	1
Q	38.908	16	17	40	0
R	22.050	16	1	23	1
S	33.060	17	10	58	0
T	48.276	21	17	44	0

SOLUTION: EXCEL is not equipped to perform automatically the *forward-selection method* described above. However, consider how we can use EXCEL to perform a similar procedure:

1. Enter the Table 18.2 income, education, job experience, age, and sex data, inclusive of column headings, into columns A–E, respectively, of a new worksheet. (You can also copy and paste the data from columns U–Y of the file HKMISC.)
2. Enter the first four column heads of Table 18.3 in the range G1–J1; then enter the remainder of that table's first two columns in G2–H6.

Step 0

3. Select cell I2, click the **Function Wizard (*fx*)** > **Statistical** > **STDEV** > **OK**.
4. In the dialog box, under *Number 1,* enter **A2:A21** and click **OK** to get the standard error of the estimate of *Y* in the absence of any regression. Enter a dash into J2.

Step 1

5. Click **Tools** > **Data Analysis** > **Regression** > **OK** to open the *Regression* dialog box.
6. Under *Input Y Range,* enter **A2:A21**
7. Under *Input X Range,* enter **B2:B21**
8. Check *New Worksheet Ply,* and click **OK**.
9. Copy the standard error from the income-versus-education output and paste it into cell I3. Copy the R-square value and paste it into J3.

Step 2

10. Click **Tools** > **Data Analysis** > **Regression** > **OK** to open the *Regression* dialog box.
11. Under *Input Y Range,* enter **A2:A21**
12. Under *Input X Range,* enter **B2:C21**
13. Check *New Worksheet Ply,* and click **OK**.
14. Copy the standard error from the income-versus-education-and job-experience output and paste it into cell I4. Copy the R-square value and paste it into J4.

TABLE 18.3 | The Influence of Successively Higher-Dimensional Regressions on the Proportion of Explained Variation in *Y*

Step	Independent *X* Variables Added	Standard Error of the Estimate of *Y*	Proportion of Variation in *Y* Explained by Regression	Proportional Reduction in Previously Unexplained Variation in *Y* Resulting from Additional *X*
0	none	$s_Y = 9{,}789$	0	–
1	education, X_1	$s_{Y\cdot 1} = 5{,}377$	$r^2_{Y\cdot 1} = .7141$	$r^2_{Y\cdot 1} = .7141$
2	job exp., X_2	$s_{Y\cdot 12} = 4{,}076$	$R^2_{Y\cdot 12} = .8448$	$r^2_{Y2\cdot 1} = .4572$
3	age, X_3	$s_{Y\cdot 123} = 2{,}507$	$R^2_{Y\cdot 123} = .9448$	$r^2_{Y3\cdot 12} = .6443$
4	sex, X_4	$s_{Y\cdot 1234} = 2{,}146$	$R^2_{Y\cdot 1234} = .9621$	$r^2_{Y4\cdot 123} = .3134$

Step 3

15. Click **Tools > Data Analysis > Regression > OK** to open the *Regression* dialog box.

16. Under *Input Y Range,* enter **A2:A21**

17. Under *Input X Range,* enter **B2:D21**

18. Check *New Worksheet Ply,* and click **OK**.

19. Copy the standard error from the income versus education, job experience, and age output and paste it into cell I5. Copy the R-square value and paste it into J5.

Step 4

20. Click **Tools > Data Analysis > Regression > OK** to open the *Regression* dialog box.

21. Under *Input Y Range,* enter **A2:A21**

22. Under *Input X Range,* enter **B2:E21**

23. Check *New Worksheet Ply,* and click **OK**.

24. Copy the standard error from the income versus education, job experience, age, and sex output and paste it into cell I6. Copy the R-square value and paste it into J6.

The result confirms Table 18.3:

G	H	I	J
Step	X Variable Added	Standard Error of the Estimate of Y	R-squ.
0	none	9789.286	—
1	education	5377.376	0.7141
2	job experience	4076.462	0.8448
3	age	2507.239	0.9448
4	sex	2145.681	0.9621

THE BACKWARD-ELIMINATION METHOD

As noted in the Caution box on pages 852–853, the alternative stepwise approach discussed in this section is equally disdained by many statisticians. But it is employed just as often, so we explain it. The **step-down method** or **backward-elimination method** starts by including *all* potential independent *X* variables in a regression model and then eliminates one *X* at a time. In step 1, the computer estimates a multiple regression equation containing all independent variables under consideration. In step 2, the computer identifies all explanatory variables with insignificant *t* values, removes the variable with a *t* value closest to zero from this group, and estimates another regression equation with the remaining independent variables. (The coefficient of the removed variable, thus, has the largest *p* value among all those in excess of some designated level of significance.) In successive steps, this process continues until all the independent variables remaining in the analysis have coefficients that are significantly different from zero.

EXCEL Example 18.2

Arguing on *a priori* grounds that it is reasonable to assume that income might be explained by education, job experience, age, and sex, apply the *backward-elimination method* to the data of Table 18.2 on page 853.

SOLUTION: EXCEL is not equipped to perform automatically the *backward-elimination method* described above. However, consider how we can use EXCEL to perform such a procedure, nevertheless:

1. Enter the Table 18.2 income, education, job experience, age, and sex data, inclusive of column headings, into columns A–E, respectively, of a new worksheet. (You can also copy and paste the data from columns U–Y of the file HKMISC.)
2. To estimate a regression including *all* potential independent variables, click **Tools** > **Data Analysis** > **Regression** > **OK** to open the *Regression* dialog box.
3. Under *Input Y Range,* enter **A1:A21**
4. Under *Input X Range,* enter **B1:E21**
5. Check *Labels* and *New Worksheet Ply,* and click **OK**.

Among other things, the output includes the following:

	Coefficients	*Standard Error*	*t Stat*
Intercept	−290.3209	2270.77116	−0.12785
Education	2035.1142	116.2376736	17.50822
Job Experience	1008.17	145.6488744	6.921921
Age	−273.78388	51.424977	−5.32395
Sex	−3087.5226	1179.986377	−2.61657

Because none of the relevant t values is insignificant, we do not proceed to Step 2.

Note: The result is the same as in EXCEL Example 18.1. However, the step-up and step-down methods cannot be relied upon to produce the same end result. It is possible that the regression model ultimately chosen contains a different subset of the original list of Xs in one case than in the other.

THE BEST SUBSETS APPROACH

The **best subsets approach** generates regression models using the maximum R^2 criterion. Suppose you specify m predictors. Typically, the computer first creates all possible one-predictor regression models and then selects the two models with the largest R^2. Subsequently, the computer finds the two-predictor model with the largest R^2, and prints information on it and the next best. The process continues until all m predictors are used.

EXCEL Example 18.3

Arguing on *a priori* grounds that it is reasonable to assume that income might be explained by education, job experience, age, and sex, apply the *best subsets approach* to the data of Table 18.2.

SOLUTION: EXCEL is not equipped to perform automatically the *best-subsets approach* described above. However, consider how we can use EXCEL to perform such a procedure, nevertheless:

1. Enter the Table 18.2 income, education, job experience, age, and sex data, inclusive of column headings, into columns A–E, respectively, of a new worksheet. (You can also copy and paste the data from columns U–Y of the file HKMISC.)
2. In cell G1, enter the label *Regression of Income versus*, followed in G2-G5 by labels for individual *X* variables *education, job experience, age*, and *sex,* respectively.
3. In cells G6-G11, enter labels for all six possible combinations of two *X* variables.
4. In cells G12-G15, enter labels for all four possible combinations of three *X* variables.
5. In cell G16, enter the label for the only possible combination of four *X* variables.
6. In cells H1 and I1, respectively, enter *R-squared* and *Standard Error*.

Section I: Performing regressions with one *X* variable

1. Click **Tools** > **Data Analysis** > **Regression** > **OK** to open the *Regression* dialog box.
2. Under *Input Y Range*, enter **A1:A21**.
3. Under *Input X Range*, enter **B1:B21** (for education).
4. Check *Labels* and *New Worksheet Ply*, and click **OK**.
5. Copy and paste the values of R^2 and the standard error into cells H2 and I2, respectively.
6. Repeat Steps 1–5 of Section I, except for using the *X* range C1:C21 (for job experience) and pasting the results into cells H3 and I3, respectively.
7. Repeat Steps 1–5 of Section I, except for using the *X* range D1:D21 (for age) and pasting the results into cells H4 and I4, respectively.
8. Repeat Steps 1–5 of Section I, except for using the *X* range E1:E21 (for sex) and pasting the results into cells H5 and I5, respectively.

Section II: Performing regressions with two *X* variables

1. Repeat Steps 1–5 of Section I, except for using the *X* range B1:C21 (for education and job experience) and pasting the results into cells H6 and I6, respectively.
2. Move the job-experience column from C to F and the age column to C. Repeat Steps 1–5 of Section I, except for using the *X* range B1:C21 (for education and age) and pasting the results into cells H7 and I7, respectively.
3. Clear the duplicate column C age data; then copy and paste the sex column from E to C. Repeat Steps 1–5 of Section I, except for using the *X* range B1:C21 (for education and sex) and pasting the results into cells H8 and I8, respectively.
4. Clear the duplicate column E sex data; then copy and paste the job experience column from F to E. Repeat Steps 1–5 of Section I, except for using the *X* range D1:E21 (for job experience and age) and pasting the results into cells H9 and I9, respectively.

5. Clear the duplicate column F job experience data; then copy and paste the sex column from C to F. Repeat Steps 1–5 of Section I, except for using the *X* range E1:F21 (for job experience and sex) and pasting the results into cells H10 and I10, respectively.
6. Repeat Steps 1–5 of Section I, except for using the *X* range C1:D21 (for age and sex) and pasting the results into cells H11 and I11, respectively.

Section III: Performing regressions with three *X* variables

1. Clear the duplicate column C sex data; then copy and paste the job experience column from E to C. Repeat Steps 1–5 of Section I, except for using the *X* range B1:D21 (for education, job experience, and age) and pasting the results into cells H12 and I12, respectively.
2. Clear the duplicate column E job experience data; then copy and paste the age column from D to E. Clear the duplicate column D age data; then copy and paste the sex column from F to D. Repeat Steps 1–5 of Section I, except for using the *X* range B1:D21 (for education, job experience, and sex) and pasting the results into cells H13 and I13, respectively.
3. Clear the duplicate column F sex data; then copy and paste the job experience column from C to F. Clear the duplicate column C job experience data; then copy and paste the age column from E to C. Repeat Steps 1–5 of Section I, except for using the *X* range B1:D21 (for education, job experience, and sex) and pasting the results into cells H14 and I14, respectively.
4. Repeat Steps 1–5 of Section I, except for using the *X* range D1:F21 (for job experience, age, and sex) and pasting the results into cells H15 and I15, respectively.

Section IV: Performing the regression with all four *X* variables

1. Clear the duplicate column C age data; then copy and paste the job experience column from F to C. Repeat Steps 1–5 of Section I, except for using the *X* range B1:E21 (for education, job experience, age, and sex) and pasting the results into cells H16 and I16, respectively.

End result

G Regression of Income versus	H R-squared	I Standard Error
Education	0.7141	5377.38
Job Experience	0.0724	9686.39
Age	0.0112	10001.13
Sex	0.178	9118.73
Education and Job Experience	0.8448	4076.46
Education and Age	0.7147	5528.21
Education and Sex	0.8402	4137.35
Job Experience and Age	0.0831	9909.88
Job Experience and Sex	0.1863	9335.42
Age and Sex	0.1799	9371.97
Education, Job Experience, and Age	0.9448	2507.24
Education, Job Experience, and Sex	0.8904	3531.6
Education, Age, and Sex	0.8409	4254.76
Job Experience, Age, and Sex	0.187	9618.8
Education, Job Experience, Age, and Sex	0.9621	2145.68

The best *one-variable, two-variable, three-variable,* and *four variable* regressions (as judged by highest R-squared and lowest standard error within each group) are highlighted in red. Overall, clearly, the last of these regressions is best.

18.4 Multiple-Equations Models

The single-equation econometric models discussed so far are simple in the sense that they clearly distinguish between the explained variable and explanatory variables. All of these models contain a single unknown—the dependent, explained, or predicted variable, Y. All of them contain at least one known—the independent, explanatory, or predictor variable, X. And X *explains* Y. (In addition, model builders often suspect a cause-and-effect relationship such that X *causes* Y, but strictly speaking, such can only be established by the types of controlled experiments discussed in Chapter 5.)

Multi-equation econometric models are more complex. First, they contain more than one unknown. Second, any given unknown is likely to appear in more than one equation. Third, any given unknown may be the variable to be explained in one equation, while playing the role of explanatory variable in another equation. The distinction between dependent and independent variables then becomes fuzzy.

The three points just noted are reflected in the following definition:

DEFINITION 18.3 A **simultaneous equations model** is an econometric model containing n unknowns and n independent equations, which must be used jointly to find the values of the unknowns.

Note how the values of the unknowns must be determined jointly, by simultaneously solving all the equations. This feat can usually be accomplished, provided the number of unknowns precisely matches the number of independent equations contained in the model.

THE GENERAL MODEL OF DEMAND AND SUPPLY

Consider the well-known model of demand and supply, designed to explain a good's price and quantity traded.

DEMAND Someone trying to model the demand side of the apple market, for example, might postulate that the quantity of apples demanded, Q_{Da}, varies with the price of apples, P_a, such that higher price discourages and lower price encourages purchases. In addition, however, the quantity demanded might vary with consumer disposable income, DI, in such a way that higher income encourages and lower income discourages desired purchases (which, as economists put it, make apples a "normal" good). Yet, other factors could be at work as well. Consider the price of some substitute, P_s, such as peaches, that consumers might choose *instead of* apples. We could easily imagine that a higher price of peaches would discourage the quantity of peaches demanded and, for that very reason, increase the quantity of apples demanded. By analogy, a lower price of peaches might lower the quantity of apples demanded.

Or consider the price of a complement, P_c, such as piecrust, that might be purchased *together with* apples. We can easily see that a higher price of piecrust might discourage the baking of apple pies and, thus, the desired purchases of apples. By analogy, a lower price of piecrust would probably increase the quantity of piecrust *as well as* that of apples demanded.

Consider, finally, that hard-to-measure factor known as consumer tastes, T. A news story about apples curing cancer might bring about a stronger inclination to buy apples. ("An apple a day keeps the doctor away.") A government announcement about apples *causing* cancer would, presumably, have just the opposite effect and would drastically reduce the demand for apples.

Proceeding along this path, a theorist could easily come up with a lengthy list of possible factors that might influence the annual quantity of apples demanded. Indeed, even the price of gasoline might play a role—if higher gas prices left commuters with fewer funds to buy fruit!

A formal representation of our demand theory might be equation (1):

$$Q_{Da} = f(P_a, DI, P_s, P_c, T, \ldots) \tag{1}$$

The quantity of apples demanded in a given year, this equation says, varies with or "is a function of" the price of apples, consumers' disposable income, the price of a substitute, the price of a complement, consumer taste, and possibly much more. Yet an economic model builder would not care to fill in the dots in equation (1). Like a mapmaker, such a theorist would want to eliminate detail and focus only on the most essential features, which might turn equation (1) into equation (2):

$$Q_{Da} = f(P_a, DI) \tag{2}$$

SUPPLY And the theorist might make a similarly compact statement about the supply side of the apple market:

$$Q_{Sa} = f(P_a, R) \tag{3}$$

The annual quantity of apples supplied, Q_{Sa}, says equation (3), is a function of the price of apples, P_a, and of the amount of rainfall, R. Other influences, such as the prices of fertilizer, labor, and land or the technical know-how of apple growers, undoubtedly play a role as well, but this theorist has singled out P_a and R as the most important factors at work. This approach corresponds precisely to the mapmaker's choice to indicate only Boston and Springfield on a Massachusetts map.

EQUILIBRIUM Finally, our economic theorist might add information on how crucial variables are likely to interact. In our case, this would involve the well-known equilibrium condition that quantity demanded and quantity supplied will change until they are equal to one another. In equilibrium:

$$Q_{Da} = Q_{Sa} \tag{4}$$

The final touches will also involve the specification of partial derivatives, which indicate how the theorist expects any given variable to change with the change in another variable, given unchanged values of all remaining variables. In our case, as already noted, the quantity of apples demanded would be expected to go down with a rise in the apple price (or go up with a fall in that price). This is expressed formally as

$$\frac{\partial Q_{Da}}{\partial P_a} < 0$$

where ∂Q_{Da} represents a small change in the apple quantity demanded and ∂P_a an associated change in the apple price—given no change in all other factors. Similarly, the theorist might specify

$$\frac{\partial Q_{Da}}{\partial DI} > 0 \quad \text{and} \quad \frac{\partial Q_{Sa}}{\partial P_a} > 0 \quad \text{and} \quad \frac{\partial Q_{Sa}}{\partial R} > 0$$

These notations express the belief that the apple quantity demanded will vary directly with disposable income (rise with higher income and fall with lower income), while the apple quantity supplied will vary directly with the apple price and also with the amount of rain.

AN ECONOMETRIC MODEL OF DEMAND AND SUPPLY

Equations 2 to 4 above neatly summarize the economic theory of demand and supply, but they are fairly vague. They tell us that the price of apples and consumer income *somehow* determine the quantity of apples demanded, but if we knew that the price equals $5/bushel and annual income equals $4,500 billion, could we predict the annual quantity of apples demanded? The answer is *no*. Could we predict the annual quantity of apples supplied from a knowledge of a $5/bushel apple price and an annual rainfall amount of 47 inches? Again, the answer is *no*. Even the partial derivatives are of no help. If $\partial Q_{Da} / \partial P_a$ is less than zero, we know that a fall in the apple price will raise the quantity demanded, but we cannot predict how many extra bushels will be demanded when the price drops from $5 to $4.33 per bushel.

In order to give specific answers to the kinds of questions just posed, we need an **econometric model,** a set of equations that precisely quantify the basic relationships suggested by a general economic model. Our demand and supply model of equations (2) to (4), for example, might be expressed by the following set of econometric equations:

$$Q_D = \alpha_0 + \beta_1 P + \beta_2 DI + \varepsilon_0 \qquad (5)$$

$$Q_S = \alpha_1 + \beta_3 P + \beta_4 R + \varepsilon_1 \qquad (6)$$

$$Q_D = Q_S \qquad (7)$$

where $\beta_1 < 0$, $\beta_2 > 0$, $\beta_3 > 0$, and $\beta_4 > 0$, while Q refers to quantities of apples demanded or supplied, P is the apple price, DI is disposable income, and R is rainfall.

Econometric equations such as equations 5 to 7 are called **structural equations** because they reveal the structure or essential nature of an economic model. Structural equations can be categorized in various ways. Our equations 5 and 6 are *behavioral equations* because they describe the behavior of economic decision makers, in this case of people who demand and supply apples. Other structural equations include *equilibrium conditions,* such as equation 7, *definitional identities* (not shown here, such as the macroeconomic $S \equiv I$, where the terms refer to realized rather than intended saving and investment), and *technical equations,* which specify the outputs producible from alternative input combinations.

The coefficients found in structural equations, such as the α's and β's here, are called **structural parameters.** They express the direct effect of any change in an explanatory variable (such as the apple price, P) on the variable to be explained (such as the apple quantity demanded, Q_D), all else being equal. Thus, if $\beta_1 = -25$ and P changes by $+10$ units—all else being equal—equation 5 predicts a change in quantity demanded of -250 units.

Notice that many structural equations contain a **random error term** or a **random disturbance term,** here designated by the Greek letter epsilon, ε. This is a catchall for the effects of all other variables ignored by the model builder and for the effects of unforeseen events. Thus, the term accounts for every error, avoidable or not, that is inherent in the use of the equation. The ε term reminds us that the equation is not deterministic: The value of the dependent variable, such as Q_D in equation (5), is not uniquely determined from specified values of the explanatory variables, such as P and DI. Instead, such an equation is *stochastic:* Many possible values of the dependent variable can be associated with any given set of values of the explanatory variables—depending entirely on the value of ε.

ENDOGENOUS VARIABLES AND PREDETERMINED VARIABLES

We traditionally classify the variables that appear in a simultaneous equations model, such as our equations (5) to (7), into two groups. How we make this classification depends entirely on the economic theory underlying the econometric model. The unknowns that are jointly determined by the equations of the model are called *endogenous variables.* In the model just cited, Q_D, Q_S, and P are usually so categorized. Variables with known values, on the other hand, are called *predetermined variables.* These variables help determine the endogenous variables, but are independent of them. Predetermined variables are either past values of endogenous variables (which are, therefore, known in the period under study), or they are values determined by forces entirely alien to the model. In the latter case, the variables are said to be "determined outside the model," which makes them *exogenous variables.* In our demand and supply model, *DI* and *R* might be so categorized. The following definition summarizes our discussion:

DEFINITION 18.4 In a simultaneous equations model, the n unknowns that are jointly determined by the system of n independent equations are **endogenous variables.** The variables with known values, on the other hand, are **predetermined variables.** The latter are either past values of endogenous variables or they are **exogenous variables,** determined by forces not considered by the model builder and in that sense "outside the model."

EXAMPLE PROBLEM 18.1

Consider the following macroeconomic model:

$$C_t = \alpha_0 + \beta_1 Y_t + \beta_2 C_{t-1} + \varepsilon_0 \quad (8)$$

$$I_t = \alpha_1 + \beta_3 r_t + \beta_4 I_{t-1} + \varepsilon_1 \quad (9)$$

$$r_t = \alpha_2 + \beta_5 Y_t + \beta_6 MS_t + \varepsilon_2 \quad (10)$$

$$Y_t \equiv C_t + I_t + G_t + NX_t \quad (11)$$

where

- *C* is consumption expenditures
- *I* is investment expenditures
- *G* is government expenditures
- *NX* is net exports
- *Y* is the national income
- *r* is the interest rate
- *MS* is the money supply

The subscript t refers to the current time period, $t - 1$ refers to the prior time period. From your knowledge of macroeconomic theory, identify

a. the likely endogenous variables.

b. the likely predetermined variables.

c. the meaning of β_1 and its likely value.

SOLUTION:

a. The endogenous variables are probably C_t, I_t, r_t, and Y_t, which makes for 4 unknowns and 4 independent equations.

b. The predetermined variables are past endogenous variables, C_{t-1} and I_{t-1}, plus exogenous variables MS_t, G_t, and NX_t.

c. β_1 is the marginal propensity to consume (the change in consumption expenditures divided by the associated change in national income); typically, its value is expected to exceed 0 but to fall short of 1.

Note: The model of equations (8)–(11) is an adaptation of the basic Keynesian model that relates consumption expenditures to the national income, investment expenditures to the interest rate, and the interest rate to the demand for money (itself a function of the national income) and the supply of money.

18.5 Simultaneous Equations Bias

Once an econometric model has been specified in a fashion similar to our micro-model (equations 5 to 7) or macro-model (equations 8 to 11), we may be tempted simply to collect relevant data and separately estimate the parameters of each equation via the simple or multiple regression technique introduced in the preceding chapters. But with simultaneous equations models, such an ordinary least-squares (OLS) procedure is not legitimate because regression coefficients so estimated would be biased and inconsistent. (For a review of these concepts, see pages 484–489.)

For example, if we applied the multiple regression technique to sample data on Q, P, and DI to estimate demand equation (5) as $\hat{Q} = a_0 + b_1P + b_2DI$, we could *not* be sure that ever-larger samples would produce ever-new estimated coefficients (a_0, b_1, b_2) that would get ever-closer to their true population values (α_0, β_1, β_2). Why would such inconsistency occur? It would occur because, in the context of a simultaneous equations model, explanatory variables are frequently correlated with error terms found in equations. Such a correlation violates a crucial assumption to the contrary that underlies regression analysis. In this case, the values of explanatory variables are *not* known without error. (See Assumption 3 on page 797.)

CORRELATION BETWEEN EXPLANATORY VARIABLE AND ERROR TERM

Reconsider our demand and supply model:

$$Q_D = \alpha_0 + \beta_1 P + \beta_2 DI + \varepsilon_0 \quad \textbf{(5)}$$

$$Q_S = \alpha_1 + \beta_3 P + \beta_4 R + \varepsilon_1 \quad \textbf{(6)}$$

$$Q_D = Q_S \quad \textbf{(7)}$$

CASE 1: EXPLANATORY VARIABLE CORRELATES POSITIVELY WITH ε_0 Let there be a decrease in the price of a complement, an increase in the price of a substitute, or a strengthening of consumer taste. All else being equal, any one of these events might raise the quantity of apples demanded, Q_D. This can be shown mathematically in equation (5): An increase in ε_0, due to any one of the "disturbances" just noted, raises Q_D, given P and DI.

We can also show this graphically, as in panel (a) of Figure 18.2: An increase in ε_0 shifts demand line D to D^*. But this is not the end of the story. Mathematically, according to equation (7), higher Q_D requires higher Q_S but that, according to equation (6), requires higher P, given R and ε_1. Thus, an increase in ε_0 causes an increase in P. Panel (a) of Figure 18.2 on the next page shows the same thing: An increase in ε_0 that shifts D to D^* also raises price from P_e to P_e^*. Conclusion: Explanatory variable P is (positively) correlated with ε_0.

CASE 2: EXPLANATORY VARIABLE CORRELATES NEGATIVELY WITH ε_0 Let there be a strike, a rise in input prices, or a restriction of foreign imports. All else being equal, any one of

FIGURE 18.2 | The Model of Demand and Supply

These graphs illustrate how a good's quantity demanded and quantity supplied might be explained by the good's price, all else being equal. In equilibrium, according to intersection e in each panel, price will settle at P_e and quantity at Q_e. Other explanatory factors are not explicitly shown, but changes in their values can be incorporated in the graph. Panel (a) shows the effects of events (such as a rise in the price of a substitute) that raise the quantity demanded at any given price. Equilibrium price and quantity both rise. Panel (b) shows the effects of events (such as a rise in input prices) that lower the quantity supplied at any given price. Equilibrium quantity falls, but price rises.

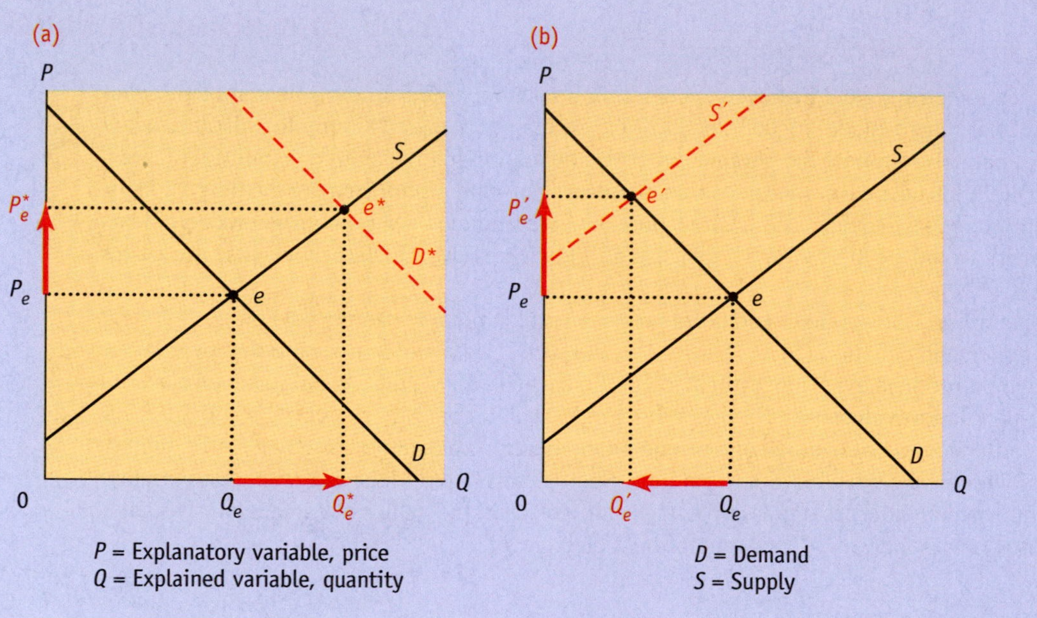

these events might lower the good's quantity supplied, Q_S. This can be shown mathematically in equation (6): A decrease in ε_1 (that reflects any one of the "disturbances" just noted) lowers Q_S, given P and R.

This can also be shown graphically, as in panel (b) of Figure 18.2: A decrease in ε_1 shifts supply line S to S'. But, again, this is not the end of the story. Mathematically, according to equation (7), lower Q_S requires lower Q_D, but that, according to equation (5), requires higher P, given DI and ε_0. Thus, a decrease in ε_1 causes a rise in P. (Remember that β_1, the slope of the demand line, is expected to be negative). Panel (b) of Figure 18.2 shows the same thing: A decrease in ε_1 that shifts S to S' also raises price from P_e to P'_e. Conclusion: Explanatory variable P is (negatively) correlated with ε_1.

The correlation between explanatory variables and error terms found in a system of simultaneous equations is common, but not a logical necessity. Figure 18.3 illustrates two exceptions in which such correlation does not arise.

In panel (a), the supply line is horizontal: Firms are willing to sell, at a fixed price, whatever quantity is demanded. A disturbance that raises ε_0 changes D to D^* and moves equilibrium e to e^*. While Q_D rises, price is unaffected.

In panel (b), the demand line is horizontal: Consumers are willing to buy, at a fixed price, whatever quantity is supplied. A disturbance that lowers ε_1 changes S to S' and moves equilibrium e to e'. While Q_S falls, price is unaffected.

(continued)

Caution (continued)

FIGURE 18.3 | Cases of No Correlation between Explanatory Variable *P* and Error Terms

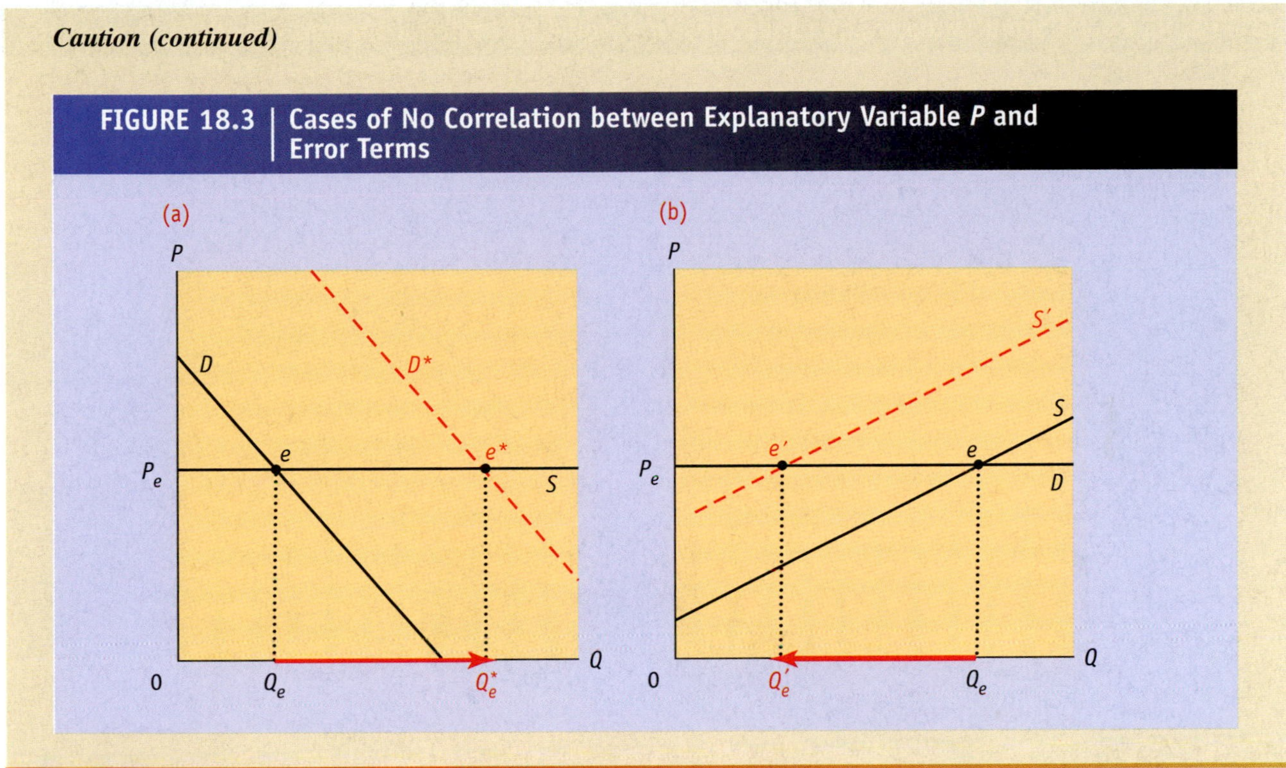

Whenever explanatory variables *are* correlated with error terms, a serious problem arises. The following definition explains:

DEFINITION 18.5 When the ordinary least-squares (OLS) regression technique is used to estimate the parameter contained in a simultaneous equations model, **simultaneous equations bias** occurs if error terms in equations are correlated with explanatory variables. In that case, estimated regression coefficients are biased and inconsistent; they are higher or lower than the true coefficients, and even ever-larger sample sizes will not make the estimated coefficients converge to the values of the true coefficients.

A GRAPHICAL ILLUSTRATION OF SIMULTANEOUS EQUATIONS BIAS

Figure 18.4 on the next page provides a graphical illustration of simultaneous equations bias. It features a simplified macroeconomic model that includes only a consumption function and the national income identity. Consumption expenditures, *C*, and national income, *Y*, are endogenous and investment expenditures are exogenous:

$$C = \alpha_0 + \beta_1 Y + \varepsilon_0 \quad \textbf{(12)}$$

$$Y \equiv C + I \quad \textbf{(13)}$$

Assume that an economist wants to estimate the consumption function of equation (12) and collects sample data of *C* and *Y* for a number of past years. Given the above simultaneous equations model, all of these data must satisfy both equations.

FIGURE 18.4 | Simultaneous Equations Bias in a Model of National Income Determination

When error terms are correlated with explanatory variables in a simultaneous equations model, the ordinary least-squares (OLS) regression technique produces estimated regression coefficients, such as a and b here, that are biased and inconsistent and, thus, diverge from true coefficients, such as α_0 and β_1. Even larger sample sizes cannot correct the problem.

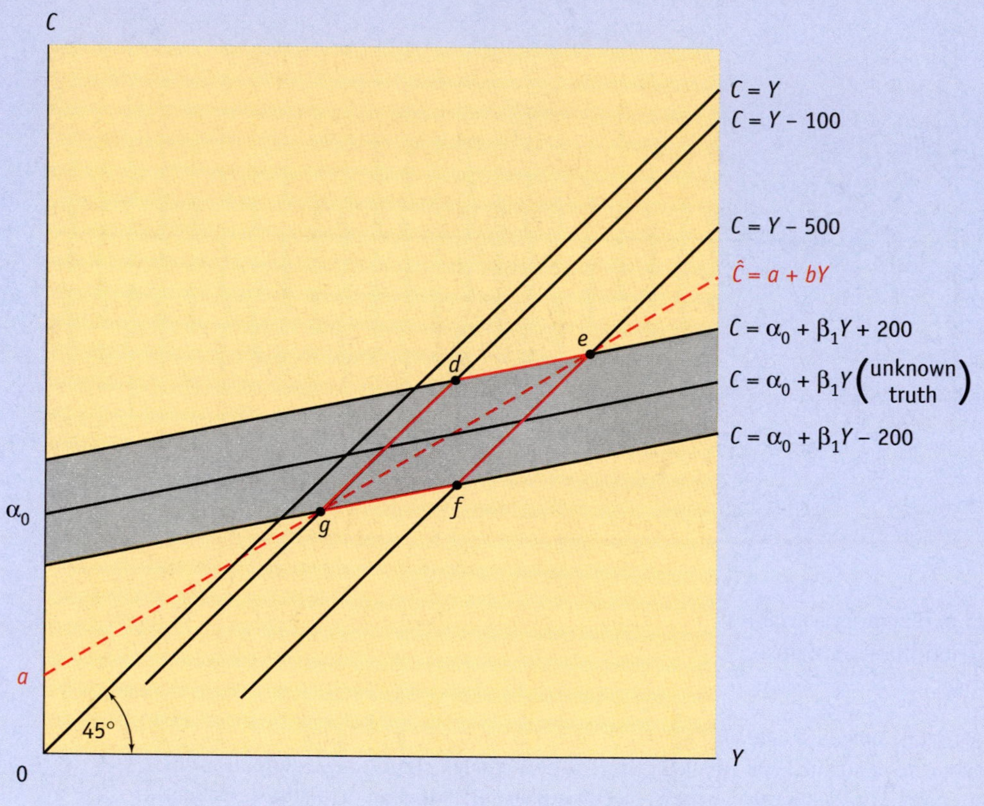

Now let the true but unknown relationship between consumption and income be represented by the line $C = \alpha_0 + \beta_1 Y$. If $\varepsilon_0 = 0$, the economist's plot of any given year's C versus Y combination will be found precisely on this true consumption function. If $\varepsilon_0 = +200$, the plot will appear on the line $C = \alpha_0 + \beta_1 Y + 200$. If $\varepsilon_0 = -200$, the plot will appear on the line $C = \alpha_0 + \beta_1 Y - 200$. If, as we shall henceforth assume, ε_0 is equally likely to take on any value between +200 and −200, all dots in the economist's C versus Y scatter diagram will appear somewhere in the shaded area of the graph.

But remember: In a simultaneous equations model, we cannot focus on one equation alone. We must also take account of the information provided by all the other equations. In this case, every C versus Y combination must satisfy not only equation (12) but also the national income identity of equation (13). If $I = 0$, then $C = Y$ and the C versus Y plot will appear on the 45° line so labeled. If $I = 100$, the plot must lie on the line $C = Y - 100$. If $I = 500$, the plot must lie on the line $C = Y - 500$. And if, as we shall henceforth assume, I is equally likely to equal any value between 100 and 500, all the C versus Y combinations will lie between the $C = Y - 100$ and $C = Y - 500$ lines.

Because our macro-model requires simultaneous fulfillment of *both* equations, our assumptions will produce this effect: All the sample plots will be *uniformly* distributed in the area of the parallelogram *defg* in Figure 18.4. Anyone estimating the consumption function via the OLS technique will, therefore, produce the dashed red regression line $\hat{C} = a + bY$. That line, clearly, is a bad estimate of the truth. Its intercept a underestimates the true intercept α_0. Its slope b overestimates the true slope β_1 (which is the marginal propensity to consume—a crucial concept in any macroeconomic analysis). The downward bias of the intercept and the upward bias of the slope remain intact even if we increase sample size indefinitely—because the error term ε_0 is correlated with the explanatory income variable Y.

18.6 Indirect Least Squares—An Introduction

Given the simultaneous equations bias associated with the OLS technique, statisticians have developed a variety of alternative procedures that allow them to make at least *consistent* estimates of parameters contained in simultaneous equations models. (They remain biased.) One of these alternatives is the **indirect least-squares (ILS) method.**

THE RATIONALE FOR ILS

Simultaneous equations bias arises whenever the explanatory variables of an econometric model include not only predetermined variables, but also endogenous variables. In that case, a structural equation may well explain the value of any one endogenous variable by that of another endogenous variable, at least in part, and if the value of the latter correlates with the equation's error term, simultaneous equations bias results. Consider how, in equation (5), endogenous variable Q_D is explained by a combination of endogenous variable P, predetermined variable DI, and the error term. We can avert the problem by rewriting each of the structural equations in such a way that (1) endogenous variables disappear from among the explanatory variables and (2) each endogenous variable is represented only as function of predetermined variables and error terms. This procedure turns the structural equations into *reduced-form equations* and turns structural parameters into *reduced-form parameters.*

DEFINITION 18.6 Equations of an econometric model that represent each endogenous variable as a function of predetermined variables and error terms only (and never as a function of other endogenous variables) are **reduced-form equations.** The coefficients attached to the (predetermined) explanatory variables in these equations are **reduced-form parameters.**

Once we have specified an econometric model by reduced-form equations, its explanatory variables (all of them predetermined) cease to correlate with the equations' error terms, and we can apply the OLS technique to compute *consistent* estimators of reduced-form parameters. Subsequently, we can sometimes work backward from the reduced-form equations to the structural equations and find consistent estimators of the structural parameters with the help of the estimated reduced-form parameters.

CAUTION

The indirect least-squares procedure, as the word "sometimes" in the previous sentence implies, does not always work. A crucial requirement for success is that the structural equations can be properly identified. If an estimated equation relates quantity to price, for example, how do we know that it is a demand function? Might it not be a supply function instead? We take up his so-called *identification problem* below.

FINDING REDUCED-FORM EQUATIONS

Reconsider our demand and supply model:

$$Q_D = \alpha_0 + \beta_1 P + \beta_2 DI + \varepsilon_0 \qquad \textbf{(5)}$$

$$Q_S = \alpha_1 + \beta_3 P + \beta_4 R + \varepsilon_1 \qquad \textbf{(6)}$$

$$Q_D = Q_S \qquad \textbf{(7)}$$

Both of the behavioral equations explain an endogenous variable on the left-hand side by a combination, on the right-hand side, of one explanatory variable that is endogenous (P) and another that is predetermined (DI or R). In order to remove the endogenous P variable from among the explanatory variables, we can create reduced-form equations for the equilibrium values of the endogenous P and Q variables. The accompanying Technical Detail box explains.

TECHNICAL DETAIL

First, because $Q_D = Q_S$ in equilibrium, we can equate equations (5) and (6) and solve for P:

$$\alpha_0 + \beta_1 P + \beta_2 DI + \varepsilon_0 = \alpha_1 + \beta_3 P + \beta_4 R + \varepsilon_1$$

$$\beta_1 P - \beta_3 P = \alpha_1 - \alpha_0 - \beta_2 DI + \beta_4 R + \varepsilon_1 - \varepsilon_0$$

$$(\beta_1 - \beta_3) P = \alpha_1 - \alpha_0 - \beta_2 DI + \beta_4 R + \varepsilon_1 - \varepsilon_0$$

$$P = \left(\frac{\alpha_1 - \alpha_0}{\beta_1 - \beta_3}\right) + \left(\frac{-\beta_2}{\beta_1 - \beta_3}\right)DI + \left(\frac{\beta_4}{\beta_1 - \beta_3}\right)R + \varepsilon_2 \qquad \textbf{(14)}$$

where $\varepsilon_2 = \dfrac{\varepsilon_1 - \varepsilon_0}{\beta_1 - \beta_3}$.

Second, we can substitute the newly found value of P into equation (6), which yields:

$$Q = \alpha_1 + \beta_3\left(\frac{\alpha_1 - \alpha_0}{\beta_1 - \beta_3}\right) + \beta_3\left(\frac{-\beta_2}{\beta_1 - \beta_3}\right)DI + \beta_3\left(\frac{\beta_4}{\beta_1 - \beta_3}\right)R + \beta_3\varepsilon_2 + \beta_4 R + \varepsilon_1$$

$$Q = \left[\frac{\alpha_1(\beta_1 - \beta_3) + \beta_3(\alpha_1 - \alpha_0)}{\beta_1 - \beta_3}\right] + \left(\frac{-\beta_2\beta_3}{\beta_1 - \beta_3}\right)DI + \left[\frac{\beta_3\beta_4 + \beta_4(\beta_1 - \beta_3)}{\beta_1 - \beta_3}\right]R + \beta_3\varepsilon_2 + \varepsilon_1$$

$$Q = \left(\frac{\alpha_1\beta_1 - \alpha_0\beta_3}{\beta_1 - \beta_3}\right) + \left(\frac{-\beta_2\beta_3}{\beta_1 - \beta_3}\right)DI + \left(\frac{\beta_1\beta_4}{\beta_1 - \beta_3}\right)R + \varepsilon_3 \qquad \textbf{(15)}$$

where $\varepsilon_3 = \beta_3\varepsilon_2 + \varepsilon_1$.

(continued)

Technical Details (continued)

These reduced-form equations are traditionally written in the form

$$P = \Pi_1 + \Pi_2 DI + \Pi_3 R + \varepsilon_2 \quad (16)$$

$$Q = \Pi_4 + \Pi_5 DI + \Pi_6 R + \varepsilon_3 \quad (17)$$

where the Π's are the reduced-form parameters, such that (in this case)

$$\Pi_1 = \frac{\alpha_1 - \alpha_0}{\beta_1 - \beta_3} \qquad \Pi_2 = \frac{-\beta_2}{\beta_1 - \beta_3} \qquad \Pi_3 = \frac{\beta_4}{\beta_1 - \beta_3}$$

$$\Pi_4 = \frac{\alpha_1\beta_1 - \alpha_0\beta_3}{\beta_1 - \beta_3} \qquad \Pi_5 = \frac{-\beta_2\beta_3}{\beta_1 - \beta_3} \qquad \Pi_6 = \frac{\beta_1\beta_4}{\beta_1 - \beta_3}$$

The OLS technique will then produce consistent estimators of the Π's because the reduced-form equations (16) and (17) explain each endogenous variable solely by a combination of error terms and predetermined variables. The latter, by definition, are uncorrelated with the error terms. Under certain conditions, the Π's can then be used to estimate the structural parameters in which we are really interested. The conditions for success in this endeavor will be spelled out presently.

18.7 The Identification Problem

The problem of working backward from consistent estimators that reduced-form parameters provide to consistent estimators of structural parameters and of, thus, correctly identifying the structural equations of a simultaneous equations model is known as the **identification problem.** The nature of this problem can be conveyed best by example.

1. Suppose the demand and supply functions contained in an econometric model of the apple market are represented by the following structural equations:

$$Q_D = 200 - 4P + 2DI \quad (18)$$

$$Q_S = -40 + 2P \quad (19)$$

The corresponding reduced-form equations give us the (demand and supply equating) equilibrium values of the two endogenous variables:

$$P = 40 + .33DI \quad (20)$$

$$Q = 40 + .67DI \quad (21)$$

2. Let the structural equations instead be these:

$$Q_D = 80 - P + DI \quad (22)$$

$$Q_S = -40 + 2P \quad (23)$$

The corresponding reduced-form equations are precisely the same as equations (20) and (21).

3. Finally, consider structural equations such as these:

$$Q_D = 320 - 7P + 3DI \tag{24}$$

$$Q_S = -40 + 2P \tag{25}$$

Once again, the reduced-form equations are the same as before, equations (20) and (21).

CONCLUSION *An infinite number of different structures could have the same reduced form.* This presents a problem. If we manage to find consistent estimators of the reduced-form parameters, how can we deduce from these estimators consistent estimators of the underlying structural equations? In the example just cited, the reduced-form equations (20) and (21) might be associated with structural equations (18) and (19) *or* with structural equations (22) and (23) *or* with structural equations (24) and (25) *or* with all kinds of others not even shown!

THE COUNTING RULE

Although we must leave its proof to more advanced econometrics texts, the so-called **counting rule** or **order condition,** explained in Formula 18.A, can help us deal with the problem noted in the preceding paragraph.

FORMULA 18.A | The Counting Rule

A necessary condition for being able to identify a structural equation with the help of reduced-form equations is this:

$$k \geq g - 1$$

where k is the number of predetermined variables in an econometric model that are *excluded* from the structural equation in question, while g is the number of endogenous variables *included* in that equation.

Notes:

1. If $k = g - 1$, the structural equation can be *exactly identified* (a unique consistent estimator for each structural parameter can be found).
2. If $k > g - 1$, the structural equation is *overidentified* (multiple consistent estimators for each structural parameter can be found).
3. If $k < g - 1$, the structural equation is *underidentified* (it is impossible to find consistent estimators for the structural parameters).

CAUTION

As noted in Formula 18.A, the counting rule states a *necessary* condition for identification. As more advanced texts show, additional considerations come into play as well. For example, a so-called **rank condition,** not discussed here, is based on the structure of missing variables in the other equations of the simultaneous equations model and provides a necessary and sufficient condition for the identification of a structural equation.

EXAMPLE PROBLEM 18.2

Consider structural equations (18) and (19). In each case, can the equation be identified?

SOLUTION: *Equation (18):* The model contains only one predetermined variable (*DI*), which is *not* excluded from equation (18); hence, $k = 0$. The equation contains two endogenous variables (Q_D and P); hence, $g = 2$. Thus, $k < g - 1$ and the demand equation *cannot* be identified.

Equation (19): The model's only predetermined variable (*DI*) is excluded from the equation; hence, $k = 1$. The equation contains two endogenous variables (Q_S and P); hence, $g = 2$. Because $k = g - 1$, the supply equation can be precisely identified.

A GRAPHICAL ILLUSTRATION OF THE IDENTIFICATION PROBLEM

The conclusions reached in Example Problem 18.2—that our supply line can be identified, while our demand line cannot—are illustrated graphically in Figure 18.5. The supply function of equation (19) is drawn as the upward-sloping line *S* in our *P* versus *Q* system of coordinates. Alternative demand functions can be drawn—a different one for each level of disposable income, *DI*.

FIGURE 18.5 | The Identification Problem

This graph pictures the econometric model of equations (18) and (19). While the supply function is uniquely identified by points such as a, b, and c, the precise position of the demand function remains uncertain—no matter what the income level—because only one point on each line (a, b, or c, respectively) is known. If D_2, for instance, took on the shape of either one of the dashed lines, equilibrium b would remain intact.

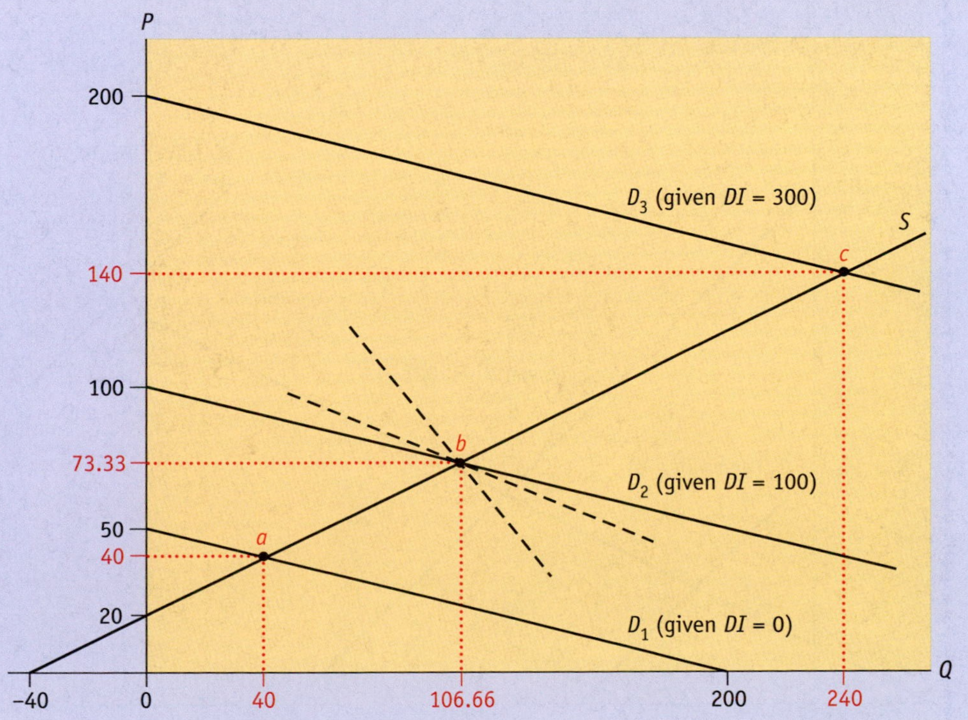

If $DI = 0$, demand line D_1 prevails. Equilibrium is established at *a,* and the associated values of $P = 40$ and $Q = 40$ are confirmed by reduced-form equations (20) and (21), given $DI = 0$. If $DI = 100$, demand line D_2 prevails. Equilibrium is established at *b,* and the associated values of $P = 73.33$ and $Q = 106.66$ again follow from the reduced-form equations, given $DI = 100$.

Finally, if $DI = 300$, demand line D_3 prevails. Equilibrium is established at *c,* and the associated values of $P = 140$ and $Q = 240$ once again satisfy our reduced-form equations, given $DI = 300$.

Now note that we could draw an infinite number of alternative demand lines—one for each conceivable level of disposable income—and every time we would find a different point on the supply line, such as *a, b,* or *c.* These equilibrium points would trace out and, thus, *identify* the precise position of the *supply line.* On the other hand, no matter how many equilibrium points we found with our reduced-form equations, we would never have more than a single point on a given *demand line.* This would be insufficient to identify its precise position. Demand line D_1, for example, as long as it passed through point *a,* could easily have a completely different slope. The same could be true of line D_2 with respect to point *b* and of line D_3 with respect to point *c.* Such alternative demand lines that nevertheless trace out the identical supply line are implied by structural equation sets (22)–(23) and again by (24)–(25).

Figure 18.6 provides a graphical illustration that should be compared with Figure 18.5 on the previous page.

FIGURE 18.6 | The Identification Problem Revisited

This graph pictures the econometric model of equations (22) and (23), which has the same reduced form as that pictured in Figure 18.5. Again, the supply function is identified by equilibrium points such as a, b, and c, but the precise shape of demand at any given income level is uncertain. Given reduced-form equations (20) and (21) and, thus, identical points a, b, and c, will the demand function be represented by lines D_3, D_4, and D_5 here or by lines D_1, D_2, and D_3 in Figure 18.5? Or will, perhaps, a still different set of demand lines apply, such as the set (not shown) that is implied by equations (24) and (25)?

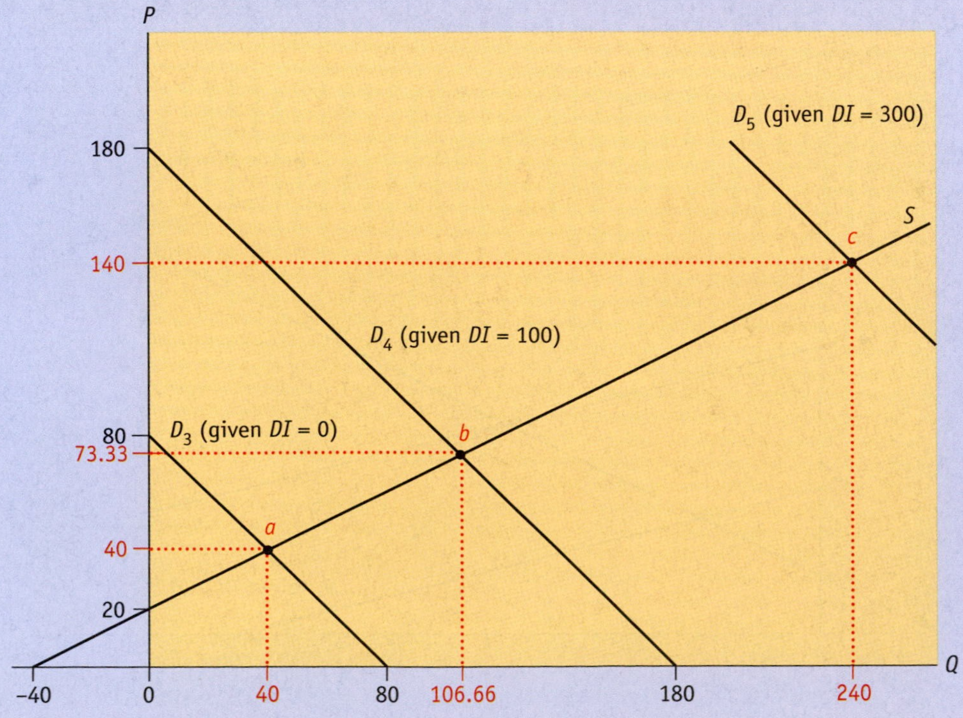

Note how the different demand lines in Figure 18.6, D_3 through D_5, nevertheless, produce identical equilibrium points, *a* through *c*, and, thus, trace out an identical supply line, *S*.

18.8 Indirect Least Squares—An Extended Example

Having become aware of the identification problem, we can pursue our earlier discussion of the ILS technique, focusing again on our original demand and supply model:

$$Q_D = \alpha_0 + \beta_1 P + \beta_2 DI + \varepsilon_0 \quad (5)$$

$$Q_S = \alpha_1 + \beta_3 P + \beta_4 R + \varepsilon_1 \quad (6)$$

$$Q_D = Q_S \quad (7)$$

We begin by quickly solving a problem.

EXAMPLE PROBLEM 18.3

Consider equations (5)–(7). Are the model's two behavioral equations identifiable?

SOLUTION: The answer can be found by applying the Formula 18.A counting rule. Equation (5) *excludes* one of the model's predetermined variables (R); hence, $k = 1$. The equation *includes* two endogenous variables (Q_D and P); hence, $g = 2$. Thus, $k = g - 1$; the equation is exactly identified.

Equation 6 excludes one of the model's predetermined variables as well (DI); again, $k = 1$. This equation, too, includes two endogenous variables (Q_S and P); hence, $g = 2$. Again, $k = g - 1$; the equation is exactly identified.

TECHNICAL DETAIL

The answer to Example Problem 18.3 implies that unique estimators can be computed for our model's structural parameters. Assume we have applied the OLS technique to reduced-form equations (16) and (17) and have derived estimates, $\hat{\Pi}$, for all the Π's noted on page 869. Then we can find similar estimates of the structural parameters ($\hat{\alpha}_0$, $\hat{\beta}_1$, etc.) as follows:

$$\hat{\beta}_1 = \frac{\hat{\Pi}_6}{\hat{\Pi}_3} \quad \text{because} \quad \frac{\Pi_6}{\Pi_3} = \frac{\dfrac{\beta_1\beta_4}{\beta_1 - \beta_3}}{\dfrac{\beta_4}{\beta_1 - \beta_3}} = \frac{\beta_1\beta_4}{\beta_1 - \beta_3} \cdot \frac{\beta_1 - \beta_3}{\beta_4} = \beta_1$$

$$\hat{\beta}_3 = \frac{\hat{\Pi}_5}{\hat{\Pi}_2} \quad \text{because} \quad \frac{\Pi_5}{\Pi_2} = \frac{\dfrac{-\beta_2\beta_3}{\beta_1 - \beta_3}}{\dfrac{-\beta_2}{\beta_1 - \beta_3}} = \frac{-\beta_2\beta_3}{\beta_1 - \beta_3} \cdot \frac{\beta_1 - \beta_3}{-\beta_2} = \beta_3$$

(continued)

Technical Detail (continued)

$$\hat{\beta}_2 = -\hat{\Pi}_2(\hat{\beta}_1 - \hat{\beta}_3) \quad \text{because} \quad -\Pi_2(\beta_1 - \beta_3) = \frac{\beta_2}{\beta_1 - \beta_3} \cdot (\beta_1 - \beta_3) = \beta_2$$

$$\hat{\beta}_4 = \hat{\Pi}_3(\hat{\beta}_1 - \hat{\beta}_3) \quad \text{because} \quad \Pi_3(\beta_1 - \beta_3) = \frac{\beta_4}{\beta_1 - \beta_3} \cdot (\beta_1 - \beta_3) = \beta_4$$

$$\hat{\alpha}_0 = \hat{\Pi}_4 - \hat{\beta}_1\hat{\Pi}_1 \quad \text{because}$$

$$\Pi_4 - \beta_1\Pi_1 = \frac{\alpha_1\beta_1 - \alpha_0\beta_3}{\beta_1 - \beta_3} - \beta_1\frac{\alpha_1 - \alpha_0}{\beta_1 - \beta_3} = \frac{\alpha_1\beta_1 - \alpha_0\beta_3 - \beta_1\alpha_1 + \beta_1\alpha_0}{\beta_1 - \beta_3}$$
$$= \frac{-\alpha_0\beta_3 + \beta_1\alpha_0}{\beta_1 - \beta_3} = \frac{\alpha_0(\beta_1 - \beta_3)}{\beta_1 - \beta_3} = \alpha_0$$

$$\hat{\alpha}_1 = \hat{\Pi}_4 - \hat{\beta}_3\hat{\Pi}_1 \quad \text{because}$$

$$\Pi_4 - \beta_3\Pi_1 = \frac{\alpha_1\beta_1 - \alpha_0\beta_3}{\beta_1 - \beta_3} - \beta_3\frac{\alpha_1 - \alpha_0}{\beta_1 - \beta_3} = \frac{\alpha_1\beta_1 - \alpha_0\beta_3 - \beta_3\alpha_1 + \beta_3\alpha_0}{\beta_1 - \beta_3}$$
$$= \frac{\alpha_1\beta_1 - \beta_3\alpha_1}{\beta_1 - \beta_3} = \frac{\alpha_1(\beta_1 - \beta_3)}{\beta_1 - \beta_3} = \alpha_1$$

These estimates of the structural parameters are consistent estimators of those parameters, which concludes the ILS procedure.

Note: As more advanced texts show, the estimators of structural parameters derived by the ILS procedure are consistent but still biased. See, for instance, Ralph E. Beals, *Statistics for Economists* (Chicago: Rand McNally and Co., 1972), p. 377.

EXAMPLE PROBLEM 18.4

Given the sample data provided in Table 18.4, use the ILS procedure to estimate the parameters of equations (5) and (6).

SOLUTION:

1. An OLS computer calculation applied to reduced-form equations (16) and (17) provides the following equations, with t values in parentheses:

$$\hat{P} = \underset{(4.87)}{5.557} + \underset{(2.62)}{.8241}DI - \underset{(-7.61)}{.09761}R \qquad \textbf{(26)}$$

$$R^2(\text{adj.}) = .809$$

$$\hat{Q} = \underset{(6.52)}{67.03} + \underset{(3.68)}{10.417}DI + \underset{(8.82)}{1.0183}R \qquad \textbf{(27)}$$

$$R^2(\text{adj.}) = .874$$

2. The estimated reduced-form parameters of equations (26) and (27) can then be used to estimate the structural parameters:

TABLE 18.4 | Sample Data for the Apple Market

Year	Quantity Traded (millions of bushels)	Price (dollars per bushel)	Disposable Income (trillions of dollars)	Rainfall (inches per year)
1	110.2	7.00	2.50	12.1
2	127.5	3.17	2.60	37.9
3	117.9	6.55	2.73	16.2
4	121.5	5.44	2.81	29.7
5	144.3	2.41	2.92	45.6
6	149.4	3.12	3.03	55.6
7	170.4	2.04	3.19	65.0
8	125.6	5.10	3.39	27.3
9	138.1	6.01	3.91	28.8
10	140.5	5.53	3.80	32.6
11	163.2	4.88	3.71	47.2
12	146.6	3.26	3.96	47.0
13	171.5	4.73	4.02	52.1
14	133.0	5.44	4.20	29.3
15	134.8	7.44	4.35	20.2

$$\hat{\beta}_1 = \frac{\hat{\Pi}_6}{\hat{\Pi}_3} = \frac{1.0183}{-.09761} = -10.43$$

$$\hat{\beta}_3 = \frac{\hat{\Pi}_5}{\hat{\Pi}_2} = \frac{10.417}{.8241} = 12.64$$

$$\hat{\beta}_2 = -\hat{\Pi}_2(\hat{\beta}_1 - \hat{\beta}_3) = -.8241(-10.42 - 12.64) = 19.00$$

$$\hat{\beta}_4 = \hat{\Pi}_3(\hat{\beta}_1 - \hat{\beta}_3) = -.09761(-10.42 - 12.64) = 2.25$$

$$\hat{\alpha}_0 = \hat{\Pi}_4 - \hat{\beta}_1\hat{\Pi}_1 = 67.03 - (-10.43)5.557 = 124.99$$

$$\hat{\alpha}_1 = \hat{\Pi}_4 - \hat{\beta}_3\hat{\Pi}_1 = 67.03 - 12.64(5.557) = -3.21$$

3. Inserting the estimated structural parameters into equations (5) and (6) yields the result we seek:

$$\hat{Q}_D = 124.99 - 10.43P + 19.00DI \quad \textbf{(28)}$$

$$\hat{Q}_S = -3.21 + 12.64P + 2.25R \quad \textbf{(29)}$$

Notice that the signs of the coefficients make sense: In equation (28), we would expect a positive quantity to be demanded at zero price and zero income. We would also expect Q_D to fall with higher price and to rise with higher income. In equation (29), it seems reasonable that a higher price coaxes out higher Q_S and that more rainfall, by increasing the crop perhaps, raises supply as well. However, we must leave the computation of the coefficients' standard errors and, thus, their *t* values to more advanced texts.

4. It is interesting to compare the estimated demand and supply functions of equations (28) and (29) with the results reached when the *inappropriate* OLS technique is applied to our Table 18.4 data and the structural equations are estimated directly. Once again, t values appear in parentheses:

$$\hat{Q}_D = \underset{(6.26)}{116.97} - \underset{(-3.85)}{7.584P} + \underset{(3.28)}{17.348DI} \tag{30}$$

$$R^2(\text{adj.}) = .577$$

$$\hat{Q}_S = \underset{(2.05)}{30.67} + \underset{(4.86)}{8.53P} + \underset{(9.72)}{1.8647R} \tag{31}$$

$$R^2(\text{adj.}) = .910$$

Application 18.6
An Econometric Model of the U.S. Economy
http://www.harcourtcollege.com/business_stats/kohler/siteresources.html

The coefficients of these equations have the same reasonable signs as those in equations (28) and (29), but do not be fooled by the high t values. These coefficients are biased and inconsistent.

18.9 Two-Stage Least Squares

As the preceding sections have shown, the ILS technique allows us to estimate a unique set of consistent structural parameters, provided the equations in question are exactly identified. When some or all equations are overidentified, however, the technique fails and we must employ a different remedy, as we shall see presently.

OVERIDENTIFICATION

Recall from Formula 18.A that overidentification refers to a situation in which $k > g - 1$, where k is the number of predetermined variables in a model that are *excluded* from the structural equation in question, while g is the number of endogenous variables *included* in that equation.

Consider the following econometric model of the apple market:

$$Q_{Da} = \alpha_0 + \beta_1 P_a + \beta_2 DI + \beta_3 P_s + \varepsilon_0 \tag{32}$$

$$Q_{Sa} = \alpha_1 + \beta_4 P_a + \beta_5 R + \varepsilon_1 \tag{33}$$

$$Q_{Da} = Q_{Sa} \tag{34}$$

The model corresponds to our earlier equations (5) to (7), except that we now treat demand as dependent on an additional (predetermined) variable: the price of a substitute, P_s. Thus, we have three endogenous variables (Q_{Da}, Q_{Sa}, P_a) as well as three predetermined variables (DI, P_s, R). With the help of Formula 18.A, we can assess the identification issue.

EXAMPLE PROBLEM 18.5

Consider the structural equations (32) and (33). In each case, can the equation be identified?

SOLUTION: *Equation 32:* Only one of the model's predetermined variables (R) is excluded from the equation; hence, $k = 1$. The equation contains two endogenous variables (Q_{Da} and P_a); hence, $g = 2$. Thus, $k = g - 1$ and the demand equation is exactly identified.

Equation 33: Two of the model's predetermined variables (DI and P_s) are excluded from the equation; hence, $k = 2$. The equation contains two endogenous variables (Q_{Sa} and P_a); hence, $g = 2$. Accordingly, $k > g - 1$ and the equation is overidentified.

TECHNICAL DETAIL

The overidentification problem can be made visible in another way. Consider the reduced-form equations implied by our model:

$$P_a = \Pi_1 + \Pi_2 DI + \Pi_3 P_s + \Pi_4 R + \varepsilon_2 \quad \textbf{(35)}$$

$$Q_a = \Pi_5 + \Pi_6 DI + \Pi_7 P_s + \Pi_8 R + \varepsilon_3 \quad \textbf{(36)}$$

where

$$\Pi_1 = \frac{\alpha_1 - \alpha_0}{\beta_1 - \beta_4} \qquad \Pi_2 = \frac{-\beta_2}{\beta_1 - \beta_4} \qquad \Pi_3 = \frac{-\beta_3}{\beta_1 - \beta_4} \qquad \Pi_4 = \frac{\beta_5}{\beta_1 - \beta_4}$$

$$\Pi_5 = \frac{\alpha_1\beta_1 - \alpha_0\beta_4}{\beta_1 - \beta_4} \qquad \Pi_6 = \frac{-\beta_2\beta_4}{\beta_1 - \beta_4} \qquad \Pi_7 = \frac{-\beta_3\beta_4}{\beta_1 - \beta_4} \qquad \Pi_8 = \frac{\beta_1\beta_5}{\beta_1 - \beta_4}$$

From these equations, we obtain

$$\beta_4 = \frac{\Pi_6}{\Pi_2} \quad \text{or} \quad \beta_4 = \frac{\Pi_7}{\Pi_3}$$

which means there are two (consistent) estimates of the price coefficient in the supply function. There is, however, no reason to believe that the two estimates will be identical. Moreover, because β_4 appears in the denominators of all the reduced-form coefficients, the ambiguity as to β_4 will be transmitted to all the Π's. Thus, use of the ILS technique is not recommended here.

INSTRUMENTAL VARIABLE TECHNIQUES

Statisticians have developed alternative estimation techniques in order to escape the ILS ambiguities associated with overidentification. One general approach removes, from the structural equations of the model, all those annoying endogenous explanatory variables that correlated with error terms and, therefore, cause simultaneous equations bias. It then replaces each of these variables with a proxy or **instrumental variable** that (1) is uncorrelated with the equation's error term, but (2) is highly correlated with the right-hand side endogenous variable just removed. Not surprisingly, the technique is called the **instrumental variable (IV) method,** and it comes in various forms. We focus on a variant known as *two-stage least squares:*

DEFINITION 18.7 The **two-stage least-squares (2SLS) method** is a technique for estimating a unique set of consistent structural parameters for overidentified or exactly identified equations of a simultaneous equations system. (For exactly identified equations, the 2SLS method gives the same result as the ILS technique.)

The basic idea of the 2SLS method is this: Any stochastic endogenous explanatory variable found in an equation of a multiple-equations model is replaced not by a single proxy variable, but by a linear combination of several variables—namely, *all* of the model's nonstochastic predetermined variables. This combination is then used as a proxy for the deleted explanatory variable, which explains why 2SLS is frequently called a "weighted IV method." Because predetermined variables are known with certainty and are thus uncorrelated with the equations' error terms, the cause of simultaneous equations bias is purged from the model. Just as ILS applied to exactly identified equations, 2SLS produces unique consistent estimators of the parameters: As sample size increases indefinitely, the estimated regression coefficients tend toward the true population values.

AN EXTENDED EXAMPLE OF 2SLS

The 2SLS technique, unlike ILS, provides us not with multiple estimates of parameters in overidentified equations but with one estimate per parameter. The method is best introduced with the help of an extended example.

EXAMPLE PROBLEM 18.6

Estimate the coefficients of supply equation (33) with the data of Table 18.4 on page 875, supplemented with the following year 1–15 data on the dollar-per-bushel price of peaches, an apple substitute: 10.00, 8.50, 9.71, 9.28, 8.50, 10.00, 13.10, 9.80, 9.75, 9.72, 12.87, 9.98, 13.72, 10.20, 10.00.

SOLUTION: As the name suggests, the two-stage least-squares technique proceeds in two steps:

Stage 1: To get rid of the likely correlation between endogenous explanatory variable P_a and ε_1, we must generate a new explanatory variable. Accordingly, we replace variable P_a with a combination of *all* the predetermined variables in the entire system of equations, here DI, P_s, and R. Regressing P_a on DI, P_s, and R, a computer produces this equation, with t values in parentheses:

$$\hat{P}_a = \underset{(3.26)}{3.2074} + \underset{(2.20)}{.5038DI} + \underset{(3.88)}{.4050P_s} - \underset{(-11.61)}{.11812R} \qquad (37)$$

$$R^2(\text{adj.}) = .912$$

Note that equation (37) is a reduced-form equation. It shows the dependent variable, P_a, solely as a function of predetermined variables, which allows us to estimate the value of $\hat{P}_a$, the mean value of P_a for each year's set of DI, P_s, and R. Based on relevant data from Table 18.4, these $\hat{P}_a$ estimates appear in Table 18.5, along with the actual Table 18.4 values of P_a.

It is crucial that the value of R^2 (adj.) computed in the first stage of the 2SLS procedure not be unreasonably low. Our R^2(adj.) = .912 seems "high enough," and we proceed to Stage 2. In general, however, a low R^2(adj.) in the first-stage regression would make the second stage rather meaningless. Such a low R^2(adj.) would indicate that the proxy being introduced (such as the proxy of linear combination DI, P_s, and R in place of P_a) was a poor choice. If much of the variation in P_a were *not* explained by the variation in DI, P_s, and R [which is what a low R^2(adj.) would indicate], we would be replacing the original values of P_a (the correlation of which with the error term bothers us so much) by values of $\hat{P}_a$ that would mostly represent the effects of the very disturbances we want to escape. In our present example, 91.2 percent of the variation in P_a is explained by the variation in DI, P_s, and R; 7 percent is not so explained and is attributable to factors other than our chosen proxy variables.

TABLE 18.5 | Actual Values of Endogenous Explanatory Variable P_a and Estimated Values Based on Equation (37)

Year	P_a	$\hat{P}_a$
1	7.00	7.087
2	3.17	3.483
3	6.55	6.601
4	5.44	4.873
5	2.41	2.734
6	3.12	2.216
7	2.04	2.441
8	5.10	5.659
9	6.01	5.724
10	5.53	5.207
11	4.88	4.713
12	3.26	3.692
13	4.73	4.634
14	5.44	5.993
15	7.44	7.062

Stage 2: We now use the OLS technique to estimate supply equation (33) directly, regressing Q against the values of $\hat{P}_a$ derived in Stage 1 and the remaining predetermined variable R. A computer produces the following equation, with t values in parentheses:

$$\hat{Q}_{S_a} = \underset{(.82)}{11.24} + \underset{(6.73)}{10.887}\hat{P}_a + \underset{(12.22)}{2.0869}R \qquad \textbf{(38)}$$

$$R^2(\text{adj.}) = .944$$

The estimated parameters of this structural equation are *consistent* estimates, but note the Caution box about the t values:

The OLS procedure used in Stage 2 does provide standard errors for the estimated coefficients and, thus, t values as shown. However, these values should be modified somewhat by a procedure that goes beyond the intended scope of this text. The required modification has to do with the fact that the error terms of reduced-form equations are different from those of the structural equations, just as in our earlier examples ε_2 and ε_3 differed from ε_0 and ε_1. For further detail, consult, for instance, Damodar Gujarati, *Basic Econometrics* (New York: McGraw-Hill, 1978), Appendix 18A.2, pp. 386–387.

EXAMPLE PROBLEM 18.7

Using the 2SLS technique, estimate the coefficients of demand equation (32) with the data used in Example Problem 18.6.

SOLUTION:

Stage 1: To eliminate P_a, we must regress P_a on DI, P_s, and R. That work has already been done; see equation (37).

Stage 2: We regress Q on $\hat{P}_a$, DI, and P_s. The result is as follows (with unadjusted t values in parentheses):

$$\begin{array}{l} \hat{Q}_{D_a} = 68.095 - 7.032\,\hat{P}_a + 11.03DI + 6.5519P_s \\ \qquad\quad (7.38) \qquad (-9.28) \qquad (5.28) \qquad (8.17) \\ \qquad\qquad R^2(\text{adj.}) = .945 \end{array} \tag{39}$$

As was noted earlier, the 2SLS technique produces the same result as the ILS technique does in the case of exactly identified equations. This, too, can most easily be seen by example.

EXAMPLE PROBLEM 18.8

Reconsider Example Problem 18.4, which estimated (exactly identified) structural equations (5) and (6) via the ILS technique. Confirm the result obtained in equations (28) and (29) via the 2SLS technique.

SOLUTION:

Stage 1: We must express the explanatory variable P as a function of the model's two predetermined variables, DI and R. The result was found earlier as equation (26). From that equation, we can find estimated values of P for each of the 15 combinations of DI and R in our sample, as in Table 18.6.

Stage 2: We estimate equations (5) and (6) directly, with the Table 18.4 data, but replacing P by $\hat{P}$ found in Stage 1. The result, with (unadjusted) t values in parentheses:

$$\begin{array}{l} \hat{Q}_D = 125.00 - 10.432\,\hat{P} + 19.012DI \\ \qquad (12.13) \qquad (-8.82) \qquad (6.55) \\ \qquad R^2(\text{adj.}) = .874 \end{array} \tag{40}$$

$$\begin{array}{l} \hat{Q}_S = -3.26 + 12.646\,\hat{P} + 2.2526R \\ \qquad (-.11) \qquad (3.68) \qquad (6.56) \\ \qquad R^2(\text{adj.}) = .874 \end{array} \tag{41}$$

Except for rounding errors, equations (40) and (41) equal equations (28) and (29), as expected.

TABLE 18.6 | Actual Values of Endogenous Explanatory Variable P_a and Estimated Values Based on Equation (26)

Year	P	$\hat{P}$
1	7.00	6.436
2	3.17	4.000
3	6.55	6.225
4	5.44	4.973
5	2.41	3.512
6	3.12	2.626
7	2.04	1.841
8	5.10	5.685
9	6.01	5.967
10	5.53	5.506
11	4.88	4.007
12	3.26	4.232
13	4.73	3.784
14	5.44	6.158
15	7.44	7.169

APPLICATION 18.7

CEO Incentive Contracts and Corporate Performance

During the last two decades of the 20th century, the after-tax real wage of the average U.S. worker fell 13 percent, while the average chief executive officer received a pay raise of over 300 percent. This glaring contrast sparked a flood of papers about one of the main justifications for the extraordinary pay of top CEOs—namely, that their pay must be linked to the performance of their firms. One recent study, using the *instrumental variable method,* examined the response of CEO pay to firm performance.

One two-stage least-squares estimation used 228 observations and regressed CEO salary and bonus against two performance measures of the firm: sales and stock price. With t values in parentheses, the equation was

$$\Delta \log(\text{Salary and Bonus}) = \underset{(2.05)}{2.52}\,\Delta \log(\text{Sales}) + \underset{(.36)}{.42}\,\Delta \log(\text{Stock Price})$$

According to this regression, holding the stock price constant, a 10 percent increase in sales yields a 25.2 percent increase in CEO compensation, while a 10 percent increase in the stock price, holding sales constant, raises CEO compensation by 4.2 percent. According to the t statistic, the latter coefficient, however, is not statistically significant.

Concludes the author, "performance of the firm has a very large effect on CEO compensation. By rewarding CEOs for increased performance, shareholders align the interests of the CEO with their own and ensure that the CEO is choosing actions that optimize performance for both."

SOURCE: Adapted from Stacey Tevlin, "CEO Incentive Contracts, Monitoring Costs, and Corporate Performance," Federal Reserve Bank of Boston, *New England Economic Review,* January/February 1996, pp. 39–50.

18.10 Second Thoughts on Ordinary Least Squares

As our discussion of the ILS and 2SLS techniques has shown, any straightforward application of OLS when estimating simultaneous equations models is fraught with danger. At the very least, parameter estimates so derived will be biased and inconsistent. Yet, our discussion has also shown something else. On occasion, even the inappropriate application of the OLS technique will produce estimates of structural parameters that differ very little from those yielded by more sophisticated, and theoretically purer, techniques.

SIMILAR RESULTS FROM OLS

Recall Example Problem 18.4 and its correct answer given by equations (28) and (29). Then compare the roughly similar answer found in equations (30) and (31). Or consider the application of OLS in Example Problem 18.8 to estimate the supply and demand functions already computed in Example Problems 18.6 and 18.7. Example Problem 18.9 provides another case in point.

EXAMPLE PROBLEM 18.9

Although the procedure is inappropriate, estimate the supply function of equation (33) and the demand function of equation (32) directly via OLS. Then compare your answers to the correct estimation noted in equations (38) and (39).

SOLUTION: Regressing Q against P_a and R with the help of Table 18.4 data, yields

$$\begin{aligned}\hat{Q}_S = {} & \underset{(2.05)}{30.67} + \underset{(4.86)}{8.530P_a} + \underset{(9.72)}{1.8647R} \\ & R^2(\text{adj.}) = .910\end{aligned} \tag{42}$$

Regressing Q against P_a, DI, and P_s with the help of the above data, yields

$$\begin{aligned}\hat{Q}_D = {} & \underset{(5.09)}{65.03} - \underset{(-6.25)}{6.342P_a} + \underset{(3.62)}{10.485DI} + \underset{(6.01)}{6.707P_s} \\ & R^2(\text{adj.}) = .892\end{aligned} \tag{43}$$

Although the results differ (the estimated coefficients here are biased and inconsistent), they do not differ drastically.

Note: Such similarities are not guaranteed in every application.

The foregoing examples go a long way toward explaining why we can still encounter instances of OLS use when ILS or 2SLS (or any one of many other techniques not discussed here) would be more appropriate. Using OLS is so simple; the use of alternative procedures often is not.

ILS DRAWBACKS ILS calculations turn very cumbersome, for example, when the number of simultaneous equations is extremely large. Just recall the awkward calculation, even in our simple examples, of structural parameter estimates ($\hat{\alpha}_0$, $\hat{\beta}_1$, etc.) from reduced-form parameter estimates ($\hat{\Pi}_1$, $\hat{\Pi}_2$, etc.). When all this gets too time-consuming and costly, econometricians turn to OLS instead.

Usually, when the R^2(adj.) value in reduced-form equations is very high, the result of the inappropriate OLS procedure is very similar to that achieved by the appropriate ILS method. This is not surprising. When the values of an endogenous variable that are being estimated by the predetermined variables are very close to the actual values, the endogenous variable is less likely to be correlated with stochastic disturbances. Hence, simultaneous equations bias is less of a problem, and OLS gives roughly correct results.

2SLS DRAWBACKS The 2SLS procedure has its drawbacks as well. One of them, not noted so far, is the fact that parameter estimates for an overidentified structural equation differ depending on *how* the equations are "normalized." Typically, a structural equation is written in such a way that one endogenous variable appears on the left-hand side with a (usually invisible) coefficient of 1. Then the equation is said to be normalized with respect to that variable. The demand function of equation (5), for example, was normalized with respect to quantity:

$$Q_D = \alpha_0 + \beta_1 P + \beta_2 DI + \varepsilon_0 \qquad (5)$$

The function could have been normalized with respect to price. Rewriting equation (5),

$$-\beta_1 P = \alpha_0 - 1Q_D + \beta_2 DI + \varepsilon_0 \qquad (44)$$

$$1P = \frac{\alpha_0}{-\beta_1} + \frac{1}{\beta_1} Q_D + \frac{\beta_2}{-\beta_1} DI + \frac{\varepsilon_0}{-\beta_1} \qquad (45)$$

$$P = \alpha_1 + \beta_3 Q_D + \beta_4 DI + \varepsilon_1 \qquad (46)$$

Now consider this: If a 2SLS procedure begins with equation (5), P is the variable eliminated in Stage 1; if it begins with equation (46), Q_D is so eliminated, which leads, ultimately, to different results. Again, this leads some statisticians to prefer the OLS method—imperfect as it is. Application 18.8, *A Macroeconomic Model of the Chinese Economy* on the next page, provides a case in point.

RECURSIVE MODELS

On some occasions, the direct application of OLS to each equation of a multiple-equations model is perfectly legitimate. Such is the case with a *recursive* or *causal model.*

DEFINITION 18.8 A **recursive model** or **causal model** is a multiple-equations system that is free of simultaneous equations bias because there is no interdependence among the endogenous variables. There is only a one-directional causal dependence: Y_0 influences Y_1, Y_1 influences Y_2, and so on, but not the reverse. The OLS method can be applied *sequentially* to each equation of such a model, and it will yield consistent parameter estimates.

Consider the following model with three endogenous variables (Y_0, Y_1, and Y_2) and one predetermined variable (X_0):

$$Y_0 = \alpha_0 + \beta_1 X_0 + \varepsilon_0 \qquad (47)$$

$$Y_1 = \alpha_1 + \beta_2 Y_0 + \beta_3 X_0 + \varepsilon_1 \qquad (48)$$

$$Y_2 = \alpha_2 + \beta_4 Y_1 + \beta_5 X_0 + \varepsilon_2 \qquad (49)$$

In this model, Y_1 is a function of Y_0, but Y_0 is not a function of Y_1. Similarly, although Y_2 is a function of Y_1, Y_1 is not a function of Y_2. The line of causation runs clearly in one direction only, from Y_0 to Y_1 to Y_2; it does not run in both directions.

In equation (47), the predetermined X_0 is uncorrelated with the error term ε_0; hence, OLS gives consistent estimates for parameters α_0 and β_1, allowing us to estimate Y_0 for every conceivable value of X_0. Note that Y_0 will be correlated with ε_0, but, like X_0, it will be uncorrelated with ε_1. Hence, Y_0 can be used, together with X_0, to make consistent OLS estimates for parameters α_1, β_2, and β_3 in equation (48). Once again, because Y_1 is correlated with ε_1, but, like X_0, is not correlated with ε_2, Y_1 from equation (48) can be used, together with X_0, to make consistent OLS estimates for parameters α_2, β_4, and β_5 in equation (49). Thus, the equations of a recursive model can be estimated by the *sequential* application of OLS.

APPLICATION 18.8

A Macroeconomic Model of the Chinese Economy

One economist, Gregory C. Chow, estimated a macroeconomic model of the Chinese economy, using data for 1953–1981. The model explained seven endogenous variables: national income, consumption, enterprise investment, taxes, interest rate, price level, and government bonds issued. It included two exogenous variables: government investment and money supply.

A consumption function, with *t* values in parentheses, was estimated as

$$C_t = -.7323 + .2294Y_t + .7261C_{t-1}$$
$$(-.2541) \quad (3.1685) \quad (5.9565)$$

$$R^2 = .99$$

where C_t is consumption in year *t*, Y_t is the national income in year *t*, and C_{t-1} is lagged consumption.

An investment function took the form

$$I_t = 2.1744 + .7549(Y_t - Y_{t-1}) + .8496I_{t-1}$$
$$(1.0419) \quad (8.9337) \qquad\qquad (22.5957)$$

$$R^2 = .97$$

where I_t is investment in year *t* and I_{t-1} is lagged investment.

A number of other equations (not shown here) explained the other endogenous variables noted, including the national income, *Y*, that appears as an explanatory variable in both the consumption equation and investment equation. But note that despite this fact, the equations of the model were not estimated by ILS or 2SLS or any of the other sophisticated methods that should be used to deal with simultaneous equations bias. Each equation was estimated by the ordinary least-squares technique (OLS) introduced in the previous chapter.

Said the author: "In the econometric literature other methods than least squares have been suggested when a right-hand side variable (national income in our case) is endogenous, but we cannot deal with this technical problem here." Given the low quality of Chinese data, this choice was certainly reasonable.

SOURCE: Adapted from Gregory C. Chow, *The Chinese Economy* (New York: Harper & Row, 1985), Chapter 6. The author is professor of economics and director of the econometric research program at Princeton University. Equations reprinted by permission from Gregory C. Chow.

Summary

1. The worlds of business and economics are filled with complex, interdependent relationships. This complex reality is modeled by *economic theories.* The application of statistical methods to economic data for the purpose of endowing economic theories with empirical content is called *econometrics.*
2. Single-equation regression models that relate some dependent variable, *Y,* to some *quantitative* independent variable, *X,* or to several such *X* variables, provide examples of econometrics at work, but are often inadequate for capturing complex reality. More often than not, such reality is modeled better by incorporating *qualitative* independent variables in regression analysis. These are *dummy variables* that can take on only two values (0 or 1).

3. In order to identify the best set of independent variables from among numerous candidates, one can employ a procedure known as *stepwise multiple regression*. Here one develops a multiple regression equation in carefully delineated steps, by means of the *forward-selection method,* the *backward-elimination method,* or the *best subsets approach.*
4. A still better approach to modeling a complex reality involves the creation of *simultaneous equations models* containing *n* unknowns and *n* independent equations that must be used jointly to find the values of the unknowns. The variables appearing in a simultaneous equations model are traditionally classified into two groups: *endogenous and predetermined.* The values of endogenous variables are jointly determined by the equations of the model; those of predetermined variables are already known. Either type of variable can play the role of explanatory variable.
5. Once an econometric model has been specified by a set of *structural equations,* it is tempting simply to collect relevant data and separately estimate the parameters of each equation via the *ordinary least-squares (OLS) regression technique.* Such procedure, however, is illegitimate if error terms in equations are correlated with explanatory variables, which is often true when these variables are endogenous. In that case, use of the OLS technique produces *simultaneous equations bias:* Estimated regression coefficients are biased and inconsistent.
6. Statisticians have developed a variety of alternative procedures that allow them to make *consistent* estimates of parameters contained in simultaneous equations models. One of these is the *indirect least-squares (ILS) method.* It replaces structural equations by *reduced-form equations* that define each endogenous variable only as a function of predetermined variables and error terms. The OLS technique is then applied to these reduced-form equations, and their consistently estimated parameters are used to find consistent estimates of the model's *structural parameters.*
7. It is not always possible to work backward from consistent estimators of *reduced-form parameters* to consistent estimators of structural parameters, which is due to the *identification problem.* The ILS method requires that structural equations be exactly identified rather than overidentified or underidentified.
8. When a simultaneous equations model contains overidentified equations, consistent structural parameters can still be estimated by an *instrumental variable (IV) technique,* such as *the two-stage least-squares (2SLS) method.* It modifies the structural equations (Stage 1) by replacing any endogenous explanatory variable by a proxy variable that is uncorrelated with the equation's error term—to wit, by a linear combination of all the predetermined variables in the model. The OLS technique is then applied (Stage 2) to the modified structural equation.
9. There are occasions when the OLS technique provides results that differ little from those yielded by ILS or 2SLS; such similarities are not guaranteed. The OLS method can, however, be trusted to provide consistent parameter estimates for any *recursive model.*

Key Terms

backward-elimination method
best subsets approach
binary variables
categorical variables
causal model
counting rule
dummy variables
econometric model
econometrics
economic theory
endogenous variables
exogenous variables
forward-selection method
identification problem
indicator variables
indirect least-squares (ILS) method
instrumental variable
instrumental variable (IV) method
OLS techniques
order condition
predetermined variables
random disturbance term
random error term
rank condition
recursive model
reduced-form equations
reduced-form parameters
simultaneous equations bias
simultaneous equations model
step-down method
step-up method
stepwise multiple regression
structural equations
structural parameters
two-stage least-squares (2SLS) method

Practice Problems

NOTE

Some problems require the use of a statistical program, EXCEL or MINITAB. The program's major features are explained in text Chapter 2; plenty of additional advice is available via the program's built-in Help feature.

SECTION 18.2 DUMMY VARIABLES

1. A realty executive has collected the data of Table 18.7.

a. Create a multiple regression equation that relates weeks-to-sale to asking price and realtor's sex, while showing t values and R^2(adj.).

b. Interpret the estimated regression coefficient of the dummy variable.

c. Conduct an ANOVA test about the overall significance of the regression, using a critical value of $F_{.05}$.

TABLE 18.7 | Sample Data on Recent Home Sales

Weeks to Sale, Y	Asking Price ($1,000s), X_1	Realtor's Sex (= 0 if male; = 1 if female), D_1
6.5	20	1
6.8	80	1
7.0	100	1
8.6	99	1
12.1	125	0
9.0	140	1
9.5	110	1
8.6	99	1
10.6	99	0
15.0	125	0
15.0	130	0
19.0	180	0
12.5	120	0
27.0	200	0

2. A railroad executive has collected the data of Table 18.8.

a. Create a multiple regression equation that relates fuel costs to cars on train and terrain, while showing t values and R^2(adj.).

b. Interpret the estimated regression coefficient of the dummy variable.

c. Conduct an ANOVA test about the overall significance of the regression, using a critical value of $F_{.05}$.

3. A wholesale executive has collected the data of Table 18.9.

a. Create a multiple regression equation that relates year-2 sales to year-1 sales and sales territory, while showing t values and R^2(adj.).

b. Interpret the estimated regression coefficient of the dummy variable.

c. Conduct an ANOVA test about the overall significance of the regression, using a critical value of $F_{.05}$.

TABLE 18.8 | Sample Data on Railroad Fuel Costs

Fuel Costs (cents/ton-mile), Y	Cars on Train (number), X_1	Terrain (= 0 if flat; = 1 if mountainous), D_1
16.3	20	1
15.0	30	1
14.3	36	1
13.0	40	1
15.1	49	1
12.0	51	0
12.0	60	0
12.1	63	0
14.7	70	1
15.2	70	1
12.1	81	0
11.0	97	0
9.2	100	0
10.1	120	0
6.2	152	0
4.8	156	0

TABLE 18.9 | Sample Data on Sales

Year 2 Sales, Y	Year 1 Sales, X_1	Sales Territory (= 0 if North; = 1 if South), D_1
69	170	0
75	133	0
86	86	0
111	161	0
129	112	1
133	133	0
134	136	0
136	82	1
140	60	1
152	152	0
161	83	1
170	97	1

TABLE 18.10 | Sample Data on Grievances Filed

Grievances Filed (number/week), Y	Humidity Index (weekly average), X_1	Type of Plant (= 0 if new; = 1 if old), D_1
11	0.7	0
9	1.4	0
11	2.1	0
13	2.7	0
22	3.7	0
18	4.2	0
22	5.0	0
41	5.6	0
62	6.9	0
50	7.3	0
88	7.7	1
68	7.8	1
109	8.1	1
125	8.4	1
142	8.5	1
96	8.6	1
112	8.8	1
132	9.0	1

4. A personnel manager has collected the data of Table 18.10.

a. Create a multiple regression equation that relates grievances filed to humidity index and type of plant, while showing t values and R^2(adj.).

b. Interpret the estimated regression coefficient of the dummy variable.

c. Conduct an ANOVA test about the overall significance of the regression, using a critical value of $F_{.05}$.

5. An auto industry executive has collected the data of Table 18.11.

a. Create a multiple regression equation that relates new car sales to the old car stock and import quotas, while showing t values and R^2(adj.).

b. Interpret the estimated regression coefficient of the dummy variable.

c. Conduct an ANOVA test about the overall significance of the regression, using a critical value of $F_{.05}$.

6. An insurance company executive has collected the data of Table 18.12.

a. Create a multiple regression equation that relates fire damage to fire station distance and property type, while showing t values and R^2(adj.).

b. Interpret the estimated regression coefficient of the dummy variable.

c. Conduct an ANOVA test about the overall significance of the regression, using a critical value of $F_{.05}$.

TABLE 18.11 | Sample Data on Car Sales

New Car Sales (millions/year), Y	Old Car Stock (millions at mid-year), X_1	Import Quota (= 0 if not in effect; = 1 if in effect), D_1
9.3	68.9	0
8.4	80.4	0
8.6	95.2	0
10.7	104.7	1
9.0	104.6	1
8.5	105.8	1
8.0	106.9	1
11.9	100.5	0
15.6	98.1	0

TABLE 18.12 | Sample Data on Fire Damage

Fire Damage ($1,000s), Y	Distance to Fire Station (miles), X_1	Property Type (= 0 if commercial; = 1 if residential), D_1
12.6	1.1	1
18.9	0.9	1
33.0	2.0	0
4.1	0.7	1
150.0	1.2	0
77.0	0.8	0
6.1	3.1	1
9.2	3.2	1
10.2	7.0	1
300.0	1.3	0
78.9	12.3	1

7. A small-aircraft manufacturing company executive has collected the data of Table 18.13 on page 890.

a. Create a multiple regression equation that relates airplanes sold to price and aircraft type, while showing t values and R^2(adj.).

b. Interpret the estimated regression coefficient of the dummy variable.

c. Conduct an ANOVA test about the overall significance of the regression, using a critical value of $F_{.05}$.

TABLE 18.13 | Sample Data on Aircraft Sales

Aircraft Sold (number/year), Y	Price ($1,000/plane), X_1	Aircraft Type (= 0 if single-engine; = 1 if multi-engine), D_1
451	49	0
437	63	0
411	89	0
389	111	0
359	141	1
350	150	1
345	155	1
331	169	1
267	233	1
207	293	1
87	413	1
98	415	1

8. The manager of an art gallery has collected the data of Table 18.14.

a. Create a multiple regression equation that relates the auction price of paintings to the number of bidders and the type of painting, while showing t values and R^2(adj.).

b. Interpret the estimated regression coefficient of the dummy variable.

c. Conduct an ANOVA test about the overall significance of the regression, using a critical value of $F_{.05}$.

TABLE 18.14 | Sample Data on Auctioned Paintings

Auction Price ($1,000s), Y	Bidders (number), X_1	Painting Type (= 0 if modern art; = 1 if Old Masters), D_1
150	12	0
147	7	0
299	8	1
500	3	0
840	7	1
77	12	0
22	9	1
179	15	1
200	33	0
20	3	0

9. A textbook publisher has collected the data of Table 18.15.

a. Create a multiple regression equation that relates copies sold to the review ratio and Web site availability, while showing *t* values and R^2(adj.).

b. Interpret the estimated regression coefficient of the dummy variable.

c. Conduct an ANOVA test about the overall significance of the regression, using a critical value of $F_{.05}$.

TABLE 18.15 | Sample Data on Textbook Sales

Copies Sold (1,000s/year), Y	Favorable-to-Unfavorable Review Ratio, X_1	Web Site (= 0 if unavailable; = 1 if available), D_1
7	5.1	0
11	4.6	0
14	6.0	0
17	2.0	0
29	3.1	1
39	0.2	1
52	0.1	1
6	10.3	0
3	5.0	0
2	12.0	0

10. A local tax assessor wants to develop a regression model that can explain the value of houses (Y) measured in thousands of dollars, by the age of houses (X_1), by their square footage (X_2), by the number of bathrooms (X_3), by the absence (0) or presence (1) of an attached garage (D_1), and by the absence (0) or presence (1) of a view (D_2). A random sample of 15 houses is used to gather observations, with these results (*standard errors* in parentheses):

$$\hat{Y} = \underset{(40.54)}{64.42} - \underset{(.5060)}{.5415X_1} + \underset{(.02166)}{.00845X_2} + \underset{(12.01)}{.76X_3} - \underset{(18.77)}{5.22D_1} + \underset{(18.15)}{12.16D_2}$$

The error sum of squares is 8,337; the total sum of squares is 9,773.

a. Comment on the significance of the regression coefficients.

b. Comment on the overall significance of this regression.

11. Text Section 18.2 contains the following multiple regression equation (with t values in parentheses) relating income (Y) to education (X_1) and sex (D_1):

$$\hat{Y} = \underset{(1.89)}{5.393} + \underset{(8.39)}{1.785X_1} - \underset{(-3.66)}{7.125D_1}$$

With the help of the Table 18.1 data on page 844,

a. determine the standard error of the estimate of Y.

b. make a point estimate of the annual income of a woman with 10 years' education.

c. find a 99 percent confidence interval for the annual income of the average woman in the sampled population who has 10 years' education.

d. find such a prediction interval for the next woman sampled who has 10 years' education.

e. find 98 percent confidence intervals for β_1 (the population coefficient of X_1) and β_2 (the population coefficient of D_1). What is the meaning of the β_2 interval?

f. set up an ANOVA table and comment on the overall significance of the regression.

g. use the ANOVA table to determine $R^2_{Y \cdot X_1 D_1}$.

12. Reconsider Application 18.2, *Do Consumer Product Safety Regulators Reduce Injuries and Deaths?* Let the poisoning death rate of children under age 5 equal 5 per 100,000 when 10 percent of aspirin tablets are sold in bottles with safety caps. According to the equation as it stands (and ignoring the issue of significance of its coefficients), what would happen to PDR_t if the percentage of safety cap bottles changed from 10 to 80?

13. Reconsider Application 18.3, *Does Photocopying Harm Authors and Publishers?* Let the ratio of library price to individual price be 10/1 when the citations per page equal .5. What would happen to P_{LIB}/P_{IND} if the journal's popularity rose such that .5 became 1.0?

14. Have another look at Table 18.A on pages 850–851, which is part of Application 18.4, *Determinants of Air Fares.* Do you see any problem with the study?

SECTION 18.3 SELECTING AN IDEAL SET OF PREDICTOR VARIABLES

15. Start EXCEL or MINITAB and activate the file HK99F500, which contains 1998 data about all *Fortune 500* companies. Then investigate someone's claim that the 500 firms' market values are directly related to and easily predictable from their revenue, profit, assets, and equity. Use the *forward-selection method* to look for a useful multiple regression equation.

16. Start EXCEL or MINITAB and activate the file HK99F500, which contains 1998 data about all *Fortune 500* companies. Then investigate someone's claim that the 500 firms' market values are directly related to and easily predictable from their revenue, profit, assets, and equity. Use the *backward-elimination method* to look for a useful multiple regression equation.

17. Start EXCEL or MINITAB and activate the file HK99F500, which contains 1998 data about all *Fortune 500* companies. Then investigate someone's claim that the 500 firms' market values are directly related to and easily predictable from their revenue, profit, assets, and equity. Use the *best subsets approach* to look for a useful multiple regression equation.

18. Review Table 17.7 on page 835. Could copies sold be explained by one or more of the X variables listed? Use the *best subsets approach* to look for a useful multiple regression equation.

19. Review Table 17.8 on page 836. Could credit card purchases be explained by one or more of the X variables listed? Use the *best subsets approach* to look for a useful multiple regression equation.

20. Review Table 17.9 on page 837. Could sales be explained by one or more of the X variables listed? Use the *best subsets approach* to look for a useful multiple regression equation.

21. Review Table 17.10 on page 837. Could tensile strength be explained by one or more of the X variables listed? Use the *best subsets approach* to look for a useful multiple regression equation.

SECTION 18.5 SIMULTANEOUS EQUATIONS BIAS

22. Reconsider the macro-model of equations (12) and (13). The text alleges that the error term, ε_0, is correlated with the explanatory variable, *Y*. Prove it.

23. Text Section 18.5 discusses simultaneous equations bias arising from a correlation between explanatory variable and error term. Case 1, graphed in panel (a) of Figure 18.2, illustrates the problem in the demand and supply model when demand rises. Explain the problem with the help of a similar graph in which demand *falls*.

24. Text Section 18.5 discusses simultaneous equations bias arising from a correlation between explanatory variable and error term. Case 2, graphed in panel (b) of Figure 18.2, illustrates the problem in the demand and supply model when supply falls. Explain the problem with the help of a similar graph in which supply *rises*.

25. The Caution box in Section 18.5 shows that an endogenous explanatory variable need not always be correlated with the equation's error term. Panel (a) of Figure 18.3 illustrates that point with a horizontal supply line in the demand and supply model. Can the point also be made with a *vertical* supply line? Graph your answer, then explain it.

26. The Caution box in Section 18.5 shows that an endogenous explanatory variable need not always be correlated with the equation's error term. Panel (b) of Figure 18.3 illustrates that point with a horizontal demand line in the demand and supply model. Can the point also be made with a *vertical* demand line? Graph your answer, then explain it.

SECTION 18.6 INDIRECT LEAST SQUARES—AN INTRODUCTION

27. Study the coefficients of equation (14) in conjunction with the econometric model of equations (5) to (7). Do the *signs* of the coefficients make sense? Explain.

28. Study the coefficients of equation (15) in conjunction with the econometric model of equations (5) to (7). Do the *signs* of the coefficients make sense? Explain.

29. According to the text, structural equations (22) and (23) imply reduced-form equations (20) and (21). Prove it.

30. According to the text, structural equations (18) and (19) imply reduced-form equations (20) and (21). Prove it.

31. According to the text, structural equations (24) and (25) imply reduced-form equations (20) and (21). Prove it.

32. Reduced-form equations (35) and (36) were derived from structural equations (32) to (34). Prove that they are correct.

SECTION 18.7 THE IDENTIFICATION PROBLEM

33. Draw a graph that illustrates the econometric model of equations (24) and (25) for disposable income levels of 0, 100, and 300. Explain the identification problem.

34. Consider the following demand and supply model:

$$Q_D = \alpha_0 + \beta_1 P + \beta_2 DI + \varepsilon_0$$
$$Q_S = \alpha_1 + \beta_3 P + \beta_4 D + \varepsilon_1$$
$$Q_D = Q_S$$

Among the right-hand side explanatory variables, the good's price, *P*, is endogenous; the disposable income of consumers, *DI*, and a dummy variable, *D*, denoting the existence or absence of import restrictions, are predetermined.

a. Can each equation be identified?

b. Can unique estimators be computed for the model's structural parameters?

35. Consider the following demand and supply model:

$$Q_D = \alpha_0 + \beta_1 P + \beta_2 DI + \beta_3 P_c + \varepsilon_0$$
$$Q_S = \alpha_1 + \beta_4 P + \beta_5 D + \varepsilon_1$$
$$Q_D = Q_S$$

Among the right-hand side explanatory variables, the good's price, *P*, is endogenous; the disposable income of consumers, *DI*, the price of a complement, P_c, and a dummy variable, *D*, denoting the existence or absence of import restrictions, are predetermined. Can each equation be identified?

SECTION 18.8 INDIRECT LEAST SQUARES—AN EXTENDED EXAMPLE

36. Use equations (28) and (29) and the Table 18.4 data on page 875 to predict, respectively, quantity demanded and quantity supplied for years 1, 6, and 13. In any given year, do the results computed by the two equations differ? Why or why not?

37. Use equations (30) and (31) to check the results reached in Practice Problem 36. If these answers differ, explain.

38. Consider the exactly identified econometric model of the apple market given by equations (5) to (7). With the help of relevant data from Table 18.16, estimate the reduced-form equations.

TABLE 18.16 | Sample Data for the Apple Market

Year	Quantity Traded (millions of bushels)	Price (dollars per bushel)	Disposable Income (trillions of dollars)	Rainfall (inches per year)	Wealth (trillions of dollars)
1	87.1	5.56	2.500	12.1	21.8
2	120.9	4.92	2.603	37.9	22.2
3	93.2	5.81	2.733	16.2	22.7
4	130.6	5.52	2.813	29.7	23.1
5	124.3	5.47	2.922	45.6	23.6
6	136.4	5.82	3.025	55.6	24.1
7	161.0	5.18	3.192	65.0	24.6
8	111.7	6.39	3.390	27.3	25.0
9	115.5	6.22	3.905	28.8	25.5
10	148.3	6.48	3.802	32.6	26.1
11	144.4	5.99	3.706	47.2	26.6
12	137.8	6.49	3.960	47.0	27.1
13	142.9	6.51	4.022	52.1	27.6
14	121.2	4.82	4.199	29.3	28.2
15	141.7	7.00	4.350	47.0	28.8
16	152.3	6.83	4.400	57.1	29.3
17	141.9	6.90	4.502	60.3	29.9
18	119.0	5.89	4.301	20.2	30.5
19	117.6	7.29	4.517	22.3	31.1
20	118.9	7.38	4.698	31.9	31.8

39. Given your answer to Practice Problem 38, estimate the structural parameters of equations (5) and (6).

40. Using data from Table 18.16, estimate structural equations (5) and (6) directly by the OLS technique and compare the result with that yielded by ILS in Practice Problem 39. Comment on the difference.

41. Consider the exactly identified econometric model of the apple market given by equations (5) to (7). With the help of relevant data from Table 18.17, estimate the reduced-form equations.

42. Given your answer to Practice Problem 41, estimate the structural parameters of equations (5) and (6).

43. Consider the following demand and supply model:

$$Q_D = \alpha_0 + \beta_1 P + \beta_2 DI + \varepsilon_0$$
$$Q_S = \alpha_1 + \beta_3 P + \beta_4 D + \varepsilon_1$$
$$Q_D = Q_S$$

Estimate the parameters of these equations via the ILS procedure, using the data of Table 18.18.

TABLE 18.17 | Sample Data for the Apple Market

Year	Quantity Traded (millions of bushels)	Price (dollars per bushel)	Disposable Income (trillions of dollars)	Rainfall (inches per year)	Wealth (trillions of dollars)
1	37.1	6.29	2.500	12.1	21.8
2	64.0	3.89	2.603	37.9	22.2
3	43.2	6.08	2.733	16.2	22.7
4	87.1	4.83	2.813	29.7	23.1
5	75.8	3.54	2.922	45.6	23.6
6	85.9	2.45	3.025	55.6	24.1
7	97.3	2.01	3.192	65.0	24.6
8	61.7	5.66	3.390	27.3	25.0
9	68.6	6.03	3.905	28.8	25.5
10	91.4	5.54	3.802	32.6	26.1
11	84.2	3.99	3.706	47.2	26.6
12	87.5	4.86	3.960	47.0	27.1
13	92.6	3.81	4.022	52.1	27.6
14	71.3	6.26	4.199	29.3	28.2
15	90.5	4.62	4.350	47.0	28.8
16	101.4	3.69	4.400	57.1	29.3
17	105.7	3.97	4.502	60.3	29.9
18	68.0	7.28	4.301	20.2	30.5
19	67.8	7.27	4.517	22.3	31.1
20	79.9	6.51	4.698	31.9	31.8

TABLE 18.18 | Sample Data for the Tomato Market

Year	Quantity Traded (million units)	Price (dollars per unit)	Disposable Income (trillions of dollars)	Dummy Variable (= 0 if no import quota; = 1 if quota)
1	27	106	5.6	0
2	27	107	5.9	0
3	29	110	6.2	0
4	23	145	7.5	1
5	22	139	7.5	1
6	20	139	6.9	1
7	20	133	5.1	1
8	21	127	6.0	1
9	29	122	7.5	0
10	31	119	8.0	0

Section 18.9 Two-Stage Least Squares

44. Consider the overidentified econometric model of the apple market given by equations (32) to (34), but replace P_s by consumer wealth, W. Then use the Table 18.16 data on page 894 to make a 2SLS estimate of the model.

45. Consider the overidentified econometric model of the apple market given by equations (32) to (34), but replace P_s by consumer wealth, W. Then use the Table 18.17 data on page 895 to make a 2SLS estimate of the model.

46. Review Practice Problem 35. Using two-stage least squares, estimate the coefficients of the overidentified supply equation. Employ the data of Table 18.18 on page 895 and these additional data on the price of a complementary good: 30, 28, 25, 31, 33, 35, 34, 33, 23, 21.

47. Using 2SLS and the same data as in the previous problem, estimate the Practice Problem 35 demand equation.

Section 18.10 Second Thoughts on Ordinary Least Squares

48. Review the estimated demand and supply functions derived in Practice Problem 43. Then estimate them by applying the inappropriate OLS procedure to the Table 18.18 data on page 895. Comment on the result.

49. Consider the econometric model of equations (47) to (49). Given the sample data of Table 18.19, use any appropriate technique to

a. make consistent estimates of the model's parameters.

b. assess the significance of each of the estimated regression coefficients.

c. assess the overall significance of each of the three regressions.

TABLE 18.19 | Sample Data

Year	Y_0	Y_1	Y_2	X_0
1	50	60	14	97
2	55	62	22	22
3	69	65	79	33
4	72	79	99	72
5	78	76	36	78
6	70	71	18	66
7	62	62	47	62
8	85	73	56	85
9	89	85	36	41
10	92	89	22	53

50. Assess the value of the model estimated in Practice Problem 49.

Chapter 19

TIME SERIES AND FORECASTING

LOOKING AHEAD

After reading this chapter, you will understand the connection between time-series analysis and a variety of popular business and economic forecasting techniques. Among other things, you will learn to:

1. recognize the major components of time series: trend, cyclical, seasonal, and irregular,
2. construct *moving-averages series* and develop forecasts on that basis,
3. subject time series to *exponential smoothing* and develop forecasts on that basis,
4. employ the *least-squares regression technique* for forecasting purposes,
5. compute *seasonal indexes* and use them to make forecasts, and
6. appreciate the usefulness of *barometric indicators* in forecasting.

AND HERE IS A TYPICAL PROBLEM YOU WILL BE ABLE TO SOLVE:

Many economic time series behave in a predictable fashion near the turning points of the business cycle, which makes them extremely useful for forecasting purposes. Originally, such series were collected and studied systematically at the National Bureau of Economic Research. The Bureau's detailed examination of the behavior of time series, many of which were 100 years long or even longer, led to an important discovery. Some economic time series, now called *leading economic indicators,* anticipate business-cycle turns. They turn down just before the GDP reaches its cyclical peak and turn up just before the cycle reaches its trough.

a. Identify the most recent behavior of the leading economic indicators, now published by the Conference Board.

b. Explain how the *diffusion index* helps us deal with situations in which some leading indicators point to a change, while others do not.

PREVIEW

Open almost any magazine or newspaper on almost any day, and you are likely to run into a story that projects some past series of data into the future. U.S. trade deficits, some writer might note, were nonexistent a decade ago, then rose to $1 billion a year later, to $2 billion the next year, to $4 billion after that, and so on, year after year. Given present trends, the writer then concludes, the deficit will reach $64 billion by the year 2005 and $2,048 billion a decade after that. Similar stories abound: Because the Japanese market share has been rising, their complete takeover of the world's aerospace industry is inevitable. Before too long, health care will swallow up the entire national income. Our grandchildren will be buried by an exponentially growing volume of junk mail or bankrupted by the mere interest on the national debt. Before long, writers warn, the ever-growing list of endangered species will include every living thing on Earth, the federal prison population will include the entire population of the country, and *everyone* will have AIDS.

The prognosticators are equally apt to embrace downward trends. Labor productivity will continue to fall, reach zero, and turn negative. The average cost per million computations, having halved decade after decade, will be zero by the year 2010. The reserves of natural resources, once so abundant, will be gone by the middle of the 21st century. Indeed, in 1980, Paul H. Ehrlich, a Stanford University ecologist, and Julian L. Simon, a University of Maryland economist, made a bet about the latter type of forecast. Ehrlich, author of *The Population Bomb,* had argued that the world was moving toward disaster. He saw population growth outstripping the food supply, topsoil eroding, pesticides poisoning the groundwater, farmland being paved over, fisheries dying, and minerals becoming exhausted. Accordingly, he predicted ever-rising prices of resources about to disappear. Simon, author of *The Ultimate Resource,* had painted a different scenario: silos brimming with record harvests, people living longer, technical progress finding substitutes for scarcer resources, and economic incentives stimulating new discoveries of seemingly vanishing resources. If anything, argued Simon, Ehrlich's vanishing resources, such as copper, chrome, nickel, tin, and tungsten, would become more abundant *and cheaper* over time instead of ever-scarcer and more expensive. Thus, the two made a bet: Using dollars of constant purchasing power, they defined a market basket of the five noted metals, containing 196.56 pounds of copper, 51.28 pounds of chrome, and so on. Its value in 1980 was $1,000. If the value was higher in 1990, Simon would pay Ehrlich the difference; if it was lower, Ehrlich would have to pay Simon. In 1990, the basket's value was $618. Ehrlich paid up, but he likened Simon to a man falling off the top of a skyscraper and, while passing the tenth floor, shouting *"so far, so good."*

If there is one lesson to be learned from the above, it is this: Whenever someone says "given present trends . . . variable X will do this or that," you better watch out. Predictions about the future have a nasty habit of turning out wrong. Yet, sometimes such predictions have to be made. The producers of electric power, for instance, have to forecast future demand, because production facilities must be built decades in advance. Under such circumstances, some method must be devised to make reasonable projections of time-series into the future. This chapter considers some of the possibilities, but success is never guaranteed.[1]

---

[1]Adapted from "America Extrapolated: Tomorrow Will Be Different," *The Economist,* December 21, 1991–January 3, 1992, pp. 25–27; and John Tierney, "Betting the Planet," *The New York Times Magazine,* December 2, 1990, pp. 52–81.

19.1 Basic Concepts

Every organization must plan for the future. Businesses and governments are no exception. Implicitly or explicitly, all such planning involves making predictions, and such predictions are inevitably linked to experiences gained in the past. An electric power producer, for example, may study how demand has grown in the past decades, project this growth into the future, and on that basis plan the construction of new generating capacity. A clothing manufacturer, likewise, may use past sales data as a guide to what it can expect and place new orders for raw materials and equipment accordingly. A government agency may study the past behavior of national income to estimate its future course and, thus, the tax revenues likely to be available.

The business and economic data about the past that are available to decision makers usually fall into one of two categories. Most of them are either *cross-section* or *time-series* data.

DEFINITION 19.1 **Cross-section data** are numerical values pertaining to units of *different* populations that have been observed simultaneously at the same point in time (in the case of a *stock variable*) or during the same period of time (in the case of a *flow variable*).

DEFINITION 19.2 **Time-series data,** also called **longitudinal data,** are chronological sequences of numerical values that pertain to units of a *given* population, which has been observed repeatedly at different points in time or during different periods of time.

The June 29, 2001, individual closing prices of all the securities traded at the New York Stock Exchange are cross-section data. They are also data about a stock variable, not because they happen to convey information about corporate stocks, but because they refer to a particular *point* in time. The year 2001 individual profits earned by all U.S.-based multinationals are cross-section data as well. These data, in contrast, describe a flow variable, because they refer to a *period* of time. Cross-section data, however, will *not* concern us in this chapter.

This chapter deals with data pertaining to a *given* population that has been observed repeatedly at different points in time (in the case of a stock variable) or during different periods of time (in the case of a flow variable). Consider a listing of the closing prices of a single security, such as IBM stock, at the end of each of 30 successive business days or a listing of the profits of a given multinational company, such as General Motors, for each of the last 50 years. It is precisely the latter type of chronological sequence of numerical data that becomes the raw material for our analysis here.

DEFINITION 19.3 **Time-series analysis** is a statistical procedure that employs time-series data, usually for the purpose of explaining past events or forecasting future events.

19.2 The Composition of a Time Series

Several models seek to describe the typical time series. Most popular, no doubt, is the **classical time-series model.** It attempts to explain the pattern observed in an actual time series by the presence of four components: trend, cyclical, seasonal, and irregular. As we show below, all four components are likely to appear in data that pertain to periods shorter than a year, such as weekly, monthly, or quarterly data. When data pertaining to periods of a year or longer are being used, however, the seasonal component disappears from the model.

DEFINITION 19.4 The classical time-series model recognizes four time-series components:

1. The **trend component** is a relatively smooth, progressively upward or downward movement of a variable over an extended period of many years.
2. The **cyclical component** consists of wide up-and-down swings of a variable around the trend, lasting from one to several years each and typically differing in length and amplitude from one occurrence to the next.
3. The **seasonal component** is defined by narrow up-and-down swings of a variable around the trend/cyclical components, with the swings predictably repeating each other within periods of one year or less.
4. The **irregular component** is made up of random movements of a variable around all the other trend/cyclical/seasonal components.

Note: In time-series graphs, it is customary to measure the variable of interest on the vertical axis and time on the horizontal axis.

THE TREND

The *trend component* of a time series, denoted by *T*, is a relatively smooth, progressively upward or downward movement of a variable, *Y*, over an extended period of time. The trend is viewed as the consequence of long-range gradual changes in such factors as population size or composition, technology, or consumer preferences. It is typically computed from data that cover a minimum of 20 years. If the observed data grow larger as time passes, the trend is said to be positive. If the data drift downward over time, the trend is negative.

As a result of this trend factor, a firm's sales of avionics equipment, say, may be rising steadily at a rate of 50 units per year. *(Avionics equipment* is electronic instruments used by aircraft, such as communication and navigation units, distance-measuring units, radar transponders, and more.) Figure 19.1 illustrates this trend component in a firm's sales (with trend sales, *T*, measured vertically and time, *t*, measured horizontally).

Note how anyone with a knowledge of initial sales of 100 units during the winter of 1995 (point *a*) would, on the basis of this trend line, have predicted quarterly sales of 300 units four years hence—that is, in the winter of 1999 (point *b*). Yet this may not be what actually happened. We also have to take into account the cyclical component in the firm's sales.

CYCLICAL FLUCTUATIONS

The *cyclical component* of a time series, denoted by *C*, appears as up-and-down swings of a variable around the trend. Typically, the swings last from one to several years each and differ in length and amplitude from one cycle to the next. Such irregular (but recurring) swings reflect the endless ebb and flow of economic activity in general, the eternal *business cycle* of boom and bust, that is bound to affect any particular variable in the economy.

Consider the influence of the business cycle on avionics sales. If such cyclical swings occurred, avionics sales might lie above the trend in "good" years (that is, years of economic expansion) and below it in "bad" years (that is, years of economic contraction), as depicted in panel (a) of Figure 19.2 on page 902.

The cyclical component is measured as a proportion of the trend, which is now depicted as the horizontal line. Thus, "booms" raise avionics sales to 1.3 times the expected level in the winter of 1995 (point *a*), and again to well above the trend in late 1997 (point *c*) and in the winter of 2002 (point *f*). Yet, by the same token, economic "busts" lower sales below their trend, to 82 and 61 percent of the trend, respectively, in mid-1996 and mid-1999 (points *b* and *e*).

FIGURE 19.1 | Trend Component in Avionics Sales

The line in this graph illustrates the trend component in a firm's sales that has been determined, we assume, on the basis of data pertaining to at least 20 years, but only some of which are shown here. Taking into account the trend only, sales of 100 units in the winter of 1995 (point a) rise by 50 units per year—for example, to 450 units in the winter of 2002 (point c). (W, S, S, and F refer to the winter, spring, summer, and fall quarters of the various years.)

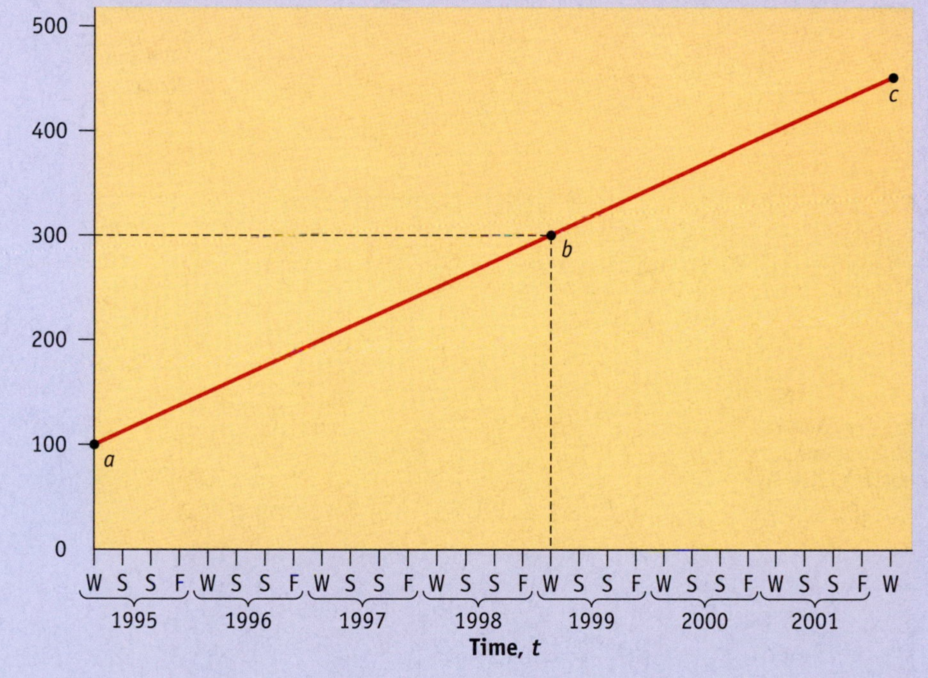

By combining the information in panel (a) with that given in Figure 19.1, we can produce the trend/cyclical time series of sales given in panel (b). Note how the trend sales for the winter of 1999 (300 units according to point *b* of either Figure 19.1 or Figure 19.2) do not materialize. Panel (a) of Figure 19.2 shows how the (assumed) business cycle trough at that time depresses sales to 64 percent of their trend level (point *d*). Thus, trend and cycle together produce sales of $300(.64) = 192$ units only, as represented by point *c* in panel (b) of Figure 19.2. The combined trend/cyclical component of our time series can always be found by multiplying T_t (expressed in physical units sold) by C_t (expressed as a proportion of T_t). Trend and cycle do not tell the whole story yet. Seasonal fluctuations play a role as well.

SEASONAL FLUCTUATIONS

The *seasonal component* of a time series, denoted by *S*, is evidenced by narrow up-and-down swings of a variable around the trend/cyclical components, with the swings predictably

FIGURE 19.2 | Recognizing a Cyclical Component in Avionics Sales

The influence of the business cycle on a particular time series, shown in panel (a), will make the movement of the series over time diverge from the trend. Compare the red line in panel (b) with the black line representing the trend.

(a) The Cyclical Component in Sales

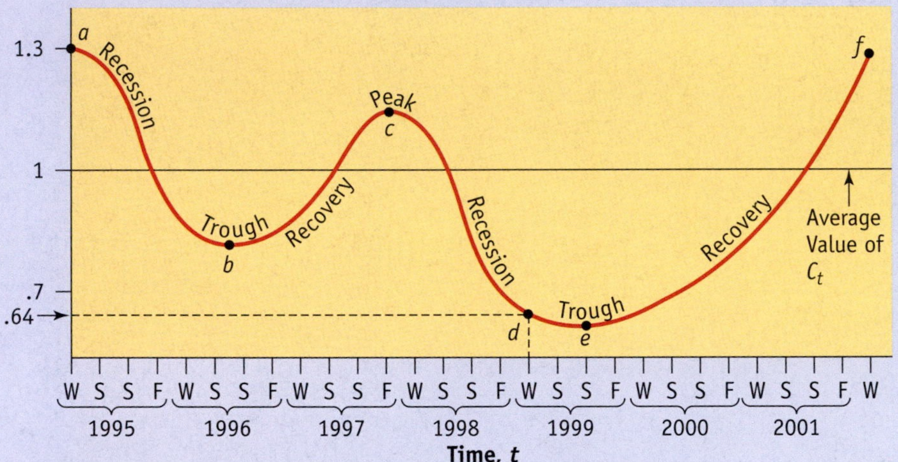

(b) The Trend/Cyclical Component in Sales

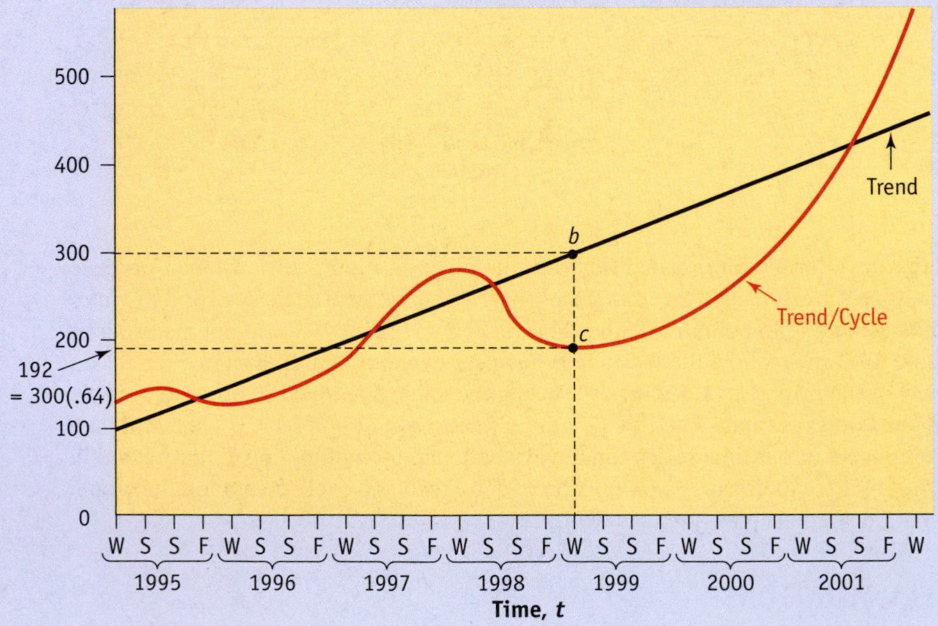

repeating within periods of one year or less. Such regularly recurring intrayear variations often reflect the influence of the weather or the calendar on economic activity. Consider how the sales of coal, gas, and oil (or heavy clothing and snow-removal equipment) rise predictably each winter but decline during other seasons. Consider how the sales of air conditioners, gardening supplies, and swimming pools rise during the spring and summer and stagnate in the fall and winter. Consider the booming activity of tax-preparation firms just before April 15, of resorts after schools let out, of caterers of June weddings, or of sellers of Christmas tree ornaments before December 25.

Once again we can depict the story graphically, as in Figure 19.3 on the next page. Panel (a) shows (assumed) seasonal fluctuations in avionics sales, this time around the longer-term trend/cyclical component of the time series. Note how winter sales always are 80 percent of average quarterly sales, while spring and summer sales rise to 100 and 120 percent, respectively, with fall sales returning to the average.

The red line in panel (b) shows the actual time series, taking into account trend, cycle, and seasonal factors. The trend-only sales and the trend/cycle components are shown in black for comparison. Note how neither the 300-unit trend sales for the winter of 1999 (point *b*) nor the 192-unit trend/cycle sales (point *c*) materialize. The assumed seasonal low at that time, represented by point *a* in panel (a) of Figure 19.3, depresses sales to 80 percent of their trend/cyclical level. Thus, trend, cycle, and season together produce sales of $300(.64)(.8) = 154$ units (rounded), which is represented by point *d* in panel (b) of Figure 19.3. The combined trend/cycle/seasonal component of our time series can always be found by multiplying T_t (expressed in physical units sold) by C_t (expressed as a proportion of T_t) and by S_t (expressed as a proportion of $T_t \cdot C_t$). Still, there is more to the story than trends, cycles, and seasons can tell, as we will see presently.

IRREGULAR VARIATIONS

The *irregular component* of a time series, denoted by *I*, is evidenced by random movements of a variable around the trend/cyclical/seasonal components. Such movements are viewed as arising from completely unpredictable and probably nonrecurring chance events, such as fads in fashion, strikes, natural disasters, or wars.

The effects of such unsystematic influences on our avionics sales might be summarized by panel (a) of Figure 19.4 on page 905. We assume that these factors average to zero in the long run.

Note how the winter 1999 sales are only 95 percent of what we would expect as a result of trend, cyclical, and seasonal factors, perhaps because of a strike in the industry (point *a*). The red line in panel (b) shows the actual time series, taking into account all the components considered in the classical model. This line differs from the red line in panel (b) of Figure 19.3 by the inclusion of the irregular factors.

Thus, in the winter of 1999, neither the 300-unit trend sales materialize (point *b*), nor the 192-unit trend/cycle sales (point *c*), nor even the 154-unit trend/cycle/seasonal sales (point *d*). Actual sales are 146 units (point *e*). The winter of 1999 is a bad time for avionics sales, indeed: The recession depresses sales to 64 percent below the trend (from *b* to *c*), the winter season, as usual, depresses sales to 80 percent of that (from *c* to *d*), and the strike reduces them further to 95 percent of that (from *d* to *e*). Thus, the classical time-series model asserts, the actual value, Y_t, of a time series at time *t* can always be found by multiplying its trend value, T_t (expressed in physical units), by C_t (expressed as a proportion of T_t), by S_t (expressed as a proportion of $T_t \cdot C_t$), and by I_t (expressed as a proportion of $T_t \cdot C_t \cdot S_t$). Indeed, for this reason, the classical time-series model discussed here is called a **multiplicative time-series model.**

Formula 19.A on page 906 summarizes our discussion, but the subsequent Caution box reminds us that other types of time-series models can be created as well.

FIGURE 19.3 | Recognizing a Seasonal Component in Avionics Sales

The influence of seasonal factors on a particular time series, shown in panel (a), will make the movement of the series over time diverge from the path that trend alone or trend plus cyclical factors alone would suggest. Compare the red line in panel (b) with the solid and dashed black lines that represent, respectively, trend sales alone or trend/cyclical sales alone.

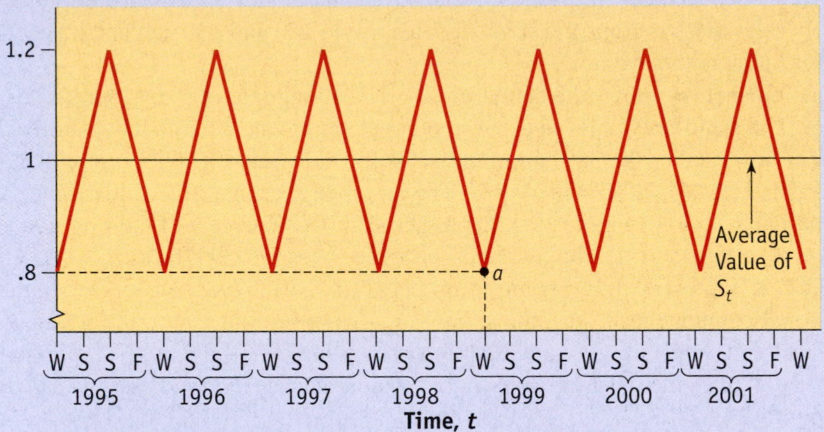

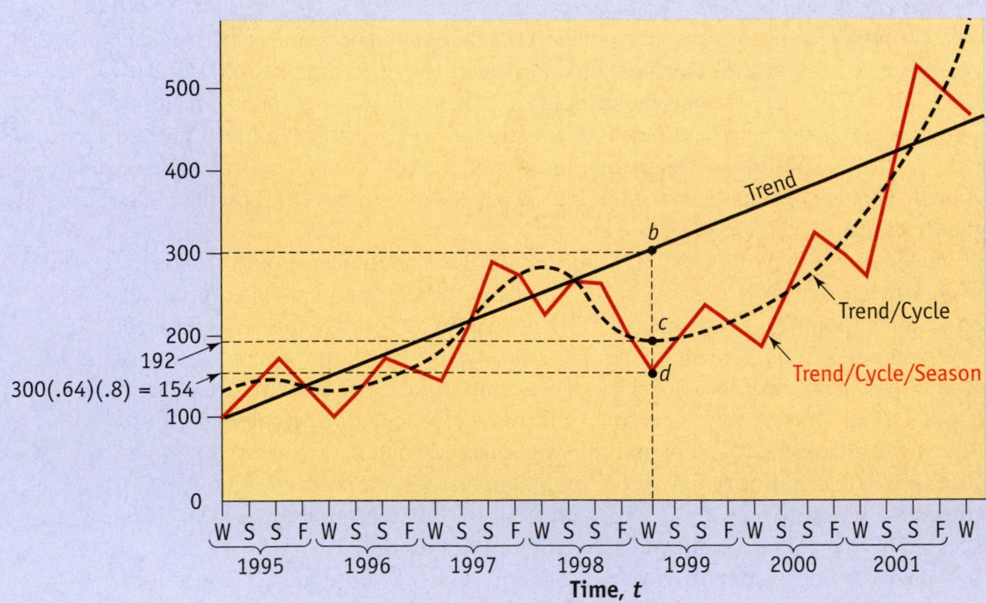

FIGURE 19.4 | Recognizing an Irregular Component in Avionics Sales

The influence of irregular factors, such as strikes, on a particular time series will make the movement of the series over time diverge from the path that trend, cyclical, and seasonal factors alone would suggest [and that is depicted by the red line in panel (b) of Figure 19.3]. Note in panel (a) how a strike depresses winter 1999 sales to 95 percent of otherwise expected sales. The red line in panel (b) shows the actual avionics sales that a company statistician would record. In the winter of 1999, they equal 146 units (point e). Trend sales, b, have been reduced by a recession to c, by seasonal factors to d, and by a strike to e.

(a) The Irregular Component of Sales

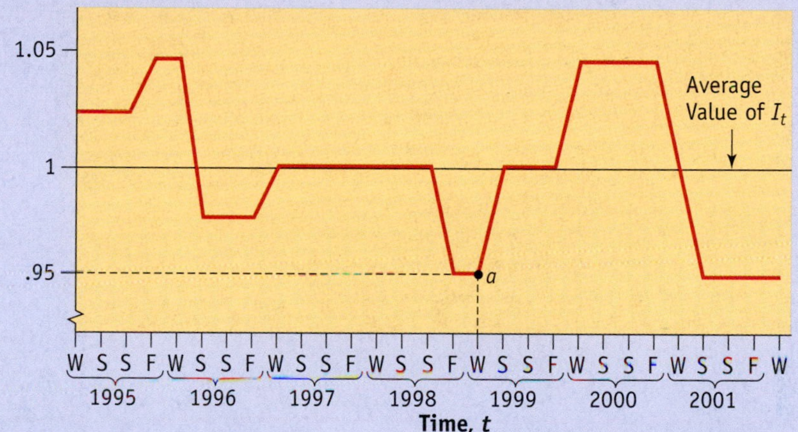

(b) The Actual Value of the Time Series of Sales

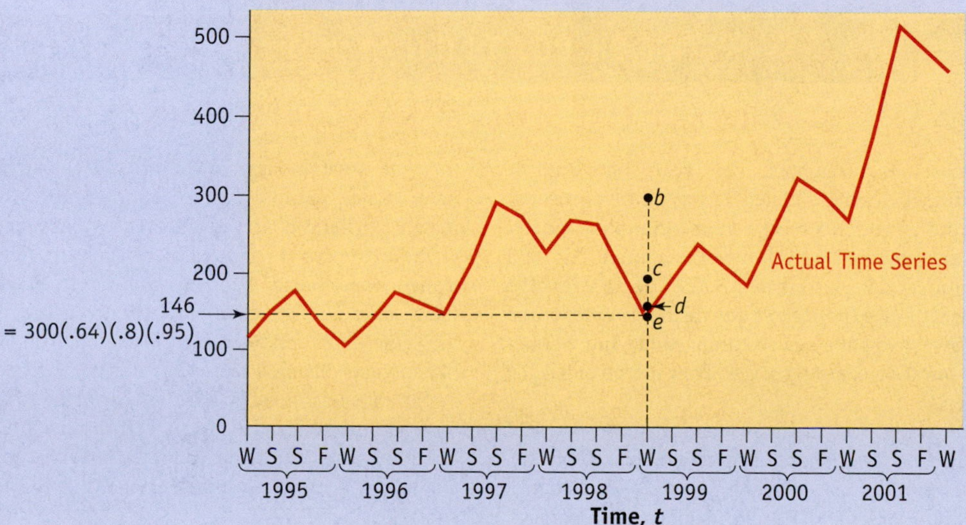

FORMULA 19.A | The Classical Multiplicative Time-Series Model

$$Y_t = T_t \cdot C_t \cdot S_t \cdot I_t$$

where Y_t is the actual value of the time series, while T_t is its trend component (expressed in physical units), C_t is its cyclical component (expressed as a proportion of T_t), S_t is its seasonal component (expressed as a proportion of $T_t \cdot C_t$), and I_t is its irregular component (expressed as a proportion of $T_t \cdot C_t \cdot S_t$), all with respect to time t.

The multiplicative time-series model is well suited for a great variety of business and economic data and, therefore, has been widely accepted as the standard for analyzing time series. Yet, on occasion, time series are better represented by alternative models that allow for the possibility of components interacting in additive fashion or in a mixture of additive and multiplicative ways. In the **additive time-series model,**

$$Y_t = T_t + C_t + S_t + I_t$$

and all the components are expressed in the same physical units.

Examples of **mixed time-series models** are

$$Y_t = T_t \cdot C_t + S_t \cdot I_t$$

and

$$Y_t = T_t \cdot C_t \cdot S_t + I_t$$

Application 19.1, *The Role of Time Series in Social Experiments,* provides an example of the usefulness of time-series analysis; Application 19.2, *The Importance of Proper Timing,* illustrates vividly why time-series analysis must be practiced with great caution.

APPLICATION 19.1

The Role of Time Series in Social Experiments

On many occasions throughout every year, some kind of social experiment is being initiated. It may involve a tax cut designed to put an end to a recession or a cut in the money supply to stop inflation. It may involve a price cut or a change in product design to increase sales. It may involve the assignment of more police to a city district to deter crime or to the freeways to put an end to drunken driving. Sooner or later, one question naturally arises: How effective has the program been?

Unfortunately, we can rarely conduct these types of social experiments like laboratory experiments. Typically, we cannot assign human subjects randomly to a control group or to an experimental group, supply a "treatment" (tax cut, tight money, lower price, new product design, more police patrols) to the latter group only, and ultimately attribute observed differences between the groups to the treatment. In the realm of social policy, such controlled experiments happen only rarely, if at all. More likely than not, for example, all citizens get a tax cut at the same time, and later on it is difficult to know whether the subjects changed their behavior because of the tax cut or for all kinds of other reasons. Nevertheless, a comparison of time-series data from before and after the introduction of a new social policy is usually employed to evaluate the effectiveness of that policy. Clearly, this is tricky business.

(continued)

Application 19.1 (continued)

Consider the case of Connecticut's crackdown on speeding that began on December 23, 1955. Traffic deaths in 1955 had been 324; in 1956, they dropped to 284, as shown in panel (a) of Figure 19.A.

The governor attributed the saving of 40 lives to the crackdown. But he implicitly assumed that there would have been no change in traffic deaths in the absence of his program, and he was surely wrong on that, as panel (b) indicates. Throughout the 1950s, Connecticut traffic deaths had been zigzagging up and down. The 1955 figure had been an all-time high. Thus, chances were high that the number would drop in the next year even without any crackdown (once again, the regression effect!).

Thus, any evaluation of social quasi experiments by means of time-series analysis must carefully consider the observed effect—panel (a) of Figure 19.A—*in the context of the general trend*—panel (b) of Figure 19.A. Any single rise or fall in a variable that is part of a zigzagging time series can hardly be attributed to a policy in place when that rise or fall happens to occur. The same is true for any rise embedded in a generally upward trend or any decline that is part of a generally downward trend. A rise, at the time of a policy change, in a long-standing downward trend is quite another matter. So is a decline at such a time in a long-term upward trend. Thus, time-series analysis is far from useless when it comes to evaluating social experiments, but it must be applied with caution.

SOURCE: Adapted from Donald T. Campbell, "Measuring the Effects of Social Innovations by Means of Time Series," in Judith A. Tanur et al., eds., *Statistics: A Guide to the Unknown* (San Francisco: Holden-Day, 1972), pp. 120–129. Figure 19.A copyright © 1972 by Holden-Day, Inc. Reprinted by permission of Holden-Day, Inc.

FIGURE 19.A

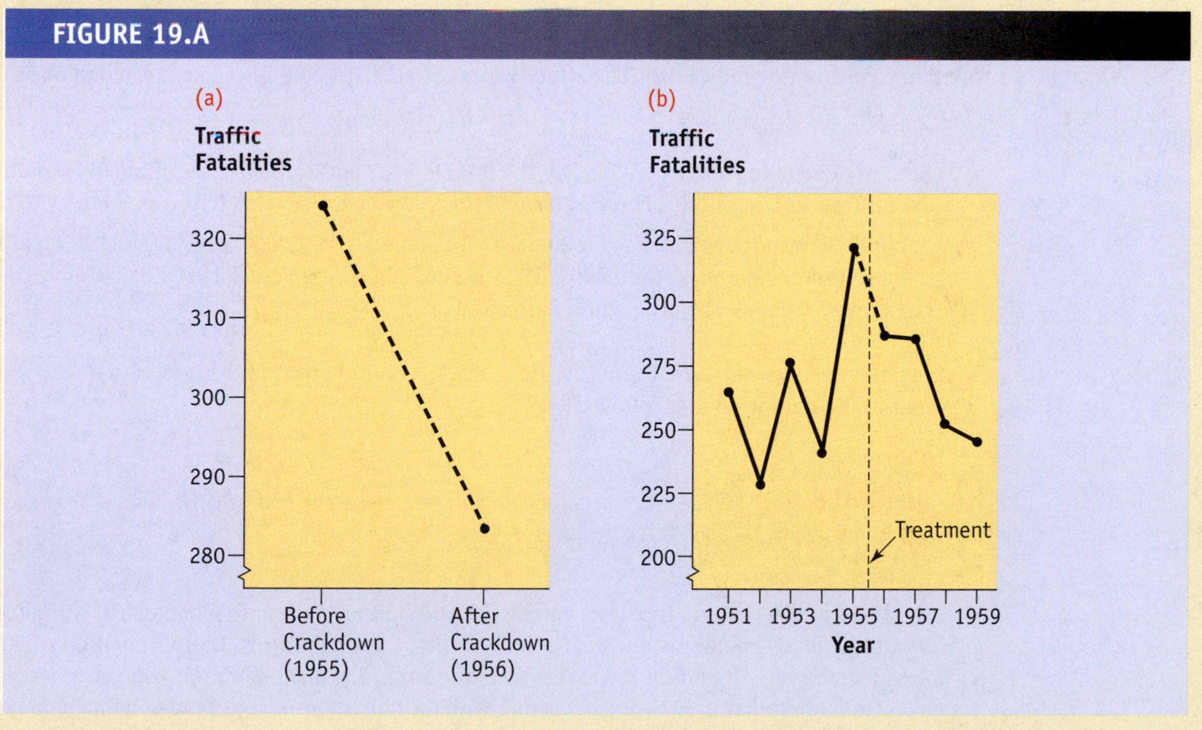

APPLICATION 19.2

THE IMPORTANCE OF PROPER TIMING

The importance of meticulously associating time-series values with the proper moment or period of time, lest false conclusions be drawn, is illustrated nicely by a story about an agricultural census in Bulgaria. On January 1, 1910, that census counted 527,311 pigs (note the precision!). Ten years later, on January 1, 1920, the count was 1,089,699 pigs. It was concluded that pig raising had expanded mightily in the intervening decade.

Yet during World War I, Bulgaria's government had abandoned the "old" Julian for the "new" Gregorian calendar, while the church continued to celebrate religious holidays on the old dates, which were then 13 days later. As a result, January 1, 1910, came after Christmas, a time at which half of Bulgaria's pigs were traditionally slaughtered, while January 1, 1920, came before Christmas, when the about-to-be-slaughtered pigs were still alive and present to be counted. Bulgarians had enjoyed no pig-raising boom after all.

SOURCE: Adapted from Oskar Morgenstern, *On the Accuracy of Economic Observations* (Princeton, N.J.: Princeton University Press, 1963), pp. 46–47.

19.3 Forecasting and Moving Averages

Business managers and economists are always interested in developing procedures that help them make accurate predictions. The effectiveness of such procedures can be tested in one of two ways:

- First, we can take known data for, say, the last 20 years and somehow use them to predict events 5 years from now. Then we can wait for 5 years and see what happens.
- Second, we can focus entirely on the past. We can take data, say, for 1960 to 1989 and use them to predict events in the 1990s. Then we can check the actual 1990s data to discover right away whether the procedure seems to work.

Making forecasts about *past* events is, thus, not a contradiction and gives rise to the careful wording in the definition that follows.

DEFINITION 19.5 Making statements about unknown, uncertain, and usually (but not necessarily) future events is called **forecasting.**

Business and economic forecasts can be derived in many ways. In Chapter 18, we noted the use of simultaneous equations models for forecasting. (Application 18.6, *An Econometric Model of the U.S. Economy*, found on the text's Web site provides an illustration.) In this chapter, we focus on other approaches, such as forecasting with the help of time-series data. In that context, the trend component of a time series is often considered the most valuable forecasting tool, especially for long-term projections. If we have a trend line available that summarizes the historical movement of a time series over an extended period of time, it is tempting to predict the future by simple **extrapolation.** Such a procedure estimates values outside a known range by assuming that unknown values outside the range behave just like the known values within that range. Given a trend line, this involves nothing more complicated than extending the slope of that line beyond the range of past and current data. Initially, however, such a trend line is rarely available. Usually, the forecaster begins the analysis with raw data.

THE RAW DATA

Every forecaster begins work with an actual time series, such as, perhaps the quarterly data embodied in the red line of Figure 19.4, panel (b). Unfortunately, quarterly data reflect a mixture of trend, cyclical, seasonal, and irregular influences. To the extent that we wish to make forecasts by means of a *trend line,* therefore, we should seek annual data. They have the advantage of automatically excluding all the seasonal fluctuations that, by definition, arise *within* years only, and they exclude many short-term irregular fluctuations as well. The first two columns of Table 19.1 on the next page might represent such an annual time series available to a would-be forecaster. (In order to simplify calculations, the example is restricted to 20 years; in real-life cases, trend calculations are preferably performed with much longer time series.)

COMPUTING MOVING AVERAGES

One way to portray a trend is to construct a series of *moving averages.* The averages are "moving" because we successively compute an ever-new average by adding a more recent time-series value to a group of such values and dropping the oldest value in the group.

DEFINITION 19.6 Forecasting can be facilitated by constructing a **moving-averages series,** which is a series of numbers obtained by successively averaging overlapping groups of two or more consecutive values in a time series and replacing the central value in each group by the group's average.

EXAMPLE PROBLEM 19.1

Construct a 3-year moving averages series for the data given in columns 1 and 2 of Table 19.1.

SOLUTION: See column 3 of Table 19.1. The first three column 2 numbers (330, 241, and 200) are averaged first, and their average (257) replaces the central value of the group (241). This explains the first numerical entry in column 3. Then a new average is calculated, this time after adding to the group of three the 1987 time series value (499), while dropping the 1984 value (330). The (rounded) average of the new group (241, 200, and 499) equals 313, and it replaces the central value of the new group (200), which accounts for the second numerical entry in column 3. And so it goes.

Let us visualize what Example Problem 19.1 has accomplished. We graph the original time series, along with the moving-averages series, in Figure 19.5 on page 911. The moving-averages line displays considerably fewer fluctuations, which explains why any statistical procedure that dampens (or averages out) fluctuations in a time series is referred to as a **smoothing technique.** Having used the technique, we are free to imagine that the line of moving averages, such as the red line in Figure 19.5, reflects the trend of the underlying series. And we are free to forecast values lying in the (shaded) realm of the future by projecting that red line to points such as *a* or *b.*

TABLE 19.1 | Avionics Sales of Butler Aviation and the Moving-Averages Method

Year, t (1)	Units Sold, Y_t (2)	3-Year Moving Averages (3)	8-Year Moving Averages	
			Unadjusted (4)	Adjusted (5)
1984	330	—		—
			—	
1985	241	257		—
			—	
1986	200	313		—
			—	
1987	499	340		—
			387	
1988	322	440		392
			396	
1989	500	474		437
			478	
1990	601	501		503
			528	
1991	401	468		546
			564	
1992	401	567		586
			607	
1993	899	633		611
			615	
1994	598	761		613
			610	
1995	787	684		643
			675	
1996	666	674		709
			743	
1997	569	599		736
			729	
1998	561	682		762
			794	
1999	915	808		844
			894	
2000	947	884		—
			—	
2001	791	951		—
			—	
2002	1,114	1,165		—
			—	
2003	1,591	—		—

FIGURE 19.5 | A 20-Year Time Series of Avionics Sales and 3-Year Moving Averages

The original 20-year time series of avionics sales—given in columns 1 and 2 of Table 19.1 and plotted here as the black line—shows considerably more fluctuations than the red 3-year moving-averages series constructed with its help. For this reason, the construction of a moving-averages series is referred to as a ***smoothing technique.*** *The red line may be interpreted as a trend. With the help of such trends, we might forecast values of future years (shaded). (Note the projection of the red line by the forecaster to some point such as a or b.)*

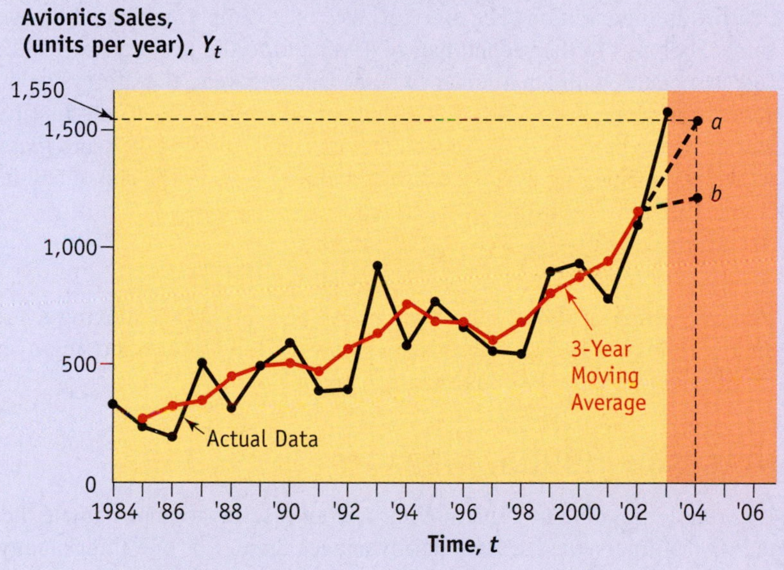

CAUTION

Our original series of annual data (column 2 of Table 19.1), by definition, is free of seasonal fluctuations because such fluctuations are intrayear changes. Our series, perhaps, is free of most irregular fluctuations as well because such fluctuations are often short-lived. Given these facts, if our annual data series contained a *regular* 3-year cycle, averaging these recurring cycles out by constructing a 3-year moving-averages series would make sense. Yet cycles are not that regular. Their periodicity could vary from 3 years in the 1960s and 1970s to 8 years in the 1980s and 1990s, and in that case we could not conclude that the Figure 19.5 red line has accurately captured the underlying trend. Nor would the result be any more certain if we constructed an 8-year moving-averages series instead, but when we do, we learn two additional lessons:

First, as we construct moving averages for even-numbered sets of time-series data, rather than odd-numbered sets, the procedure gets more complicated, because it becomes unclear to which time period we should assign the average. (It makes sense to assign the average value of periods 1, 2, and 3 to period 2, but how do we assign the average value of periods 1, 2, 3, and 4, the center of which is nonexisting period 2.5?)

Second, as we construct moving averages for larger sets of data, the resulting series becomes even smoother.

Example Problem 19.2 and Figure 19.6 on the following pages illustrate these points.

EXAMPLE PROBLEM 19.2

Construct an 8-year moving averages series for the data given in columns 1 and 2 of Table 19.1.

SOLUTION: See columns 4 and 5 of Table 19.1. As we average the first group of 8 data—the 1984–1991 values of column 2—we derive an average of 387, but placing it in the center of the set of 1984–1991 values puts it right in the middle between 1987 and 1988. To which of these two years does the average belong? As Application 19.2 shows, the assignment of time-series values to proper times is crucial. In our present case, the calculated average really belongs to a year that includes the second half of 1987 and the first half of 1988; therefore, the entry of 387 in column 4 is printed *between* the other rows of our table. The same is true of all the other, similarly derived entries in that column. The entry of 396, for example, which is the average of the 1985–1992 values, belongs to the second half of 1988 and to the first half of 1989. To find the moving average associated with a particular (whole) calendar year, therefore, one must average adjacent averages! Thus, the averaging of 387 (half of which belongs to the first half of 1988) and of 396 (half of which belongs to the second half of 1988) gives us 392, and *that* number can be regarded as the 8-year-moving average properly belonging to 1988. The remaining entries in column 5 of Table 19.1 have been similarly derived.

Figure 19.6 is a graph of the original time series and the 8-year moving-averages series. When compared with Figure 19.5, it clearly shows how the longer-term moving-averages series produces an even smoother picture of long-term change.

DISADVANTAGES OF MOVING AVERAGES

Although it is certainly possible to use a moving-averages series to approximate the underlying trend component of a time series, several disadvantages arise. For one thing, many a moving-averages series still is quite irregular in appearance; the 3-year series of Figure 19.5 exemplifies this fact. Worse yet, it is possible for a moving-averages series to exhibit strong cyclical fluctuations even though there are no fluctuations whatsoever in the original time-series data. Application 19.3 on the next page describes this so-called **Slutsky-Yule effect.** Indeed, a moving-averages series can produce all kinds of false impressions about the underlying data. Consider these points:

- A moving-averages series can lie consistently above or below the original data—namely, when they are growing or declining exponentially.
- Such a series will anticipate or prolong changes in the original data and, thus, show a different timing of turning points.
- Such a series will be extremely sensitive to unusually large or small values in the time series, as any average is bound to be.

Worst of all, the very procedure of calculating moving averages makes it impossible to construct this "trend line" for the earliest and latest years of a time series, because the average centered on any one year must be calculated with the help of a number of preceding and following values. Note how Table 19.1 contains no entry in the first and last rows of column 3, nor in the first and last four rows of column 5. Accordingly, the moving-averages lines in Figures 19.5 and 19.6 are considerably shorter than the 20-year period for which the original time-series data are available. This fact leads directly to the most serious disadvantage of all: There exists no reliable method for making *reproducible* forecasts with a moving-averages series, which is a point taken up in the next section.

FIGURE 19.6 | A 20-Year Time Series of Avionics Sales and 8-Year Moving Averages

The original 20-year time series of avionics sales—given in Table 19.1 and plotted here as the black line—shows considerably more fluctuations than the red 8-year moving-averages series constructed with its help. Note that the 8-year series, in turn, is even smoother than the 3-year series depicted in Figure 19.5. Unfortunately, it is also shorter. As a result, it is all the more risky to "cast forward," by means of the dashed lines, the past movement of the red "trend" into the (shaded) future.

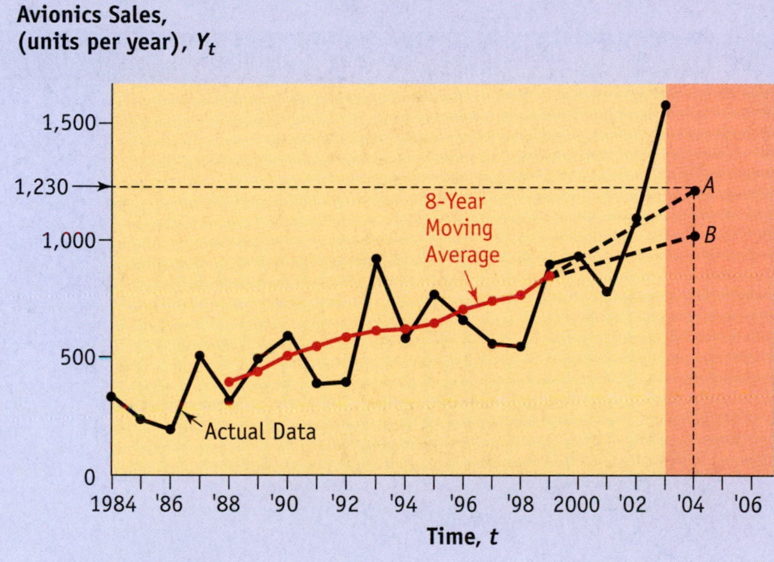

APPLICATION 19.3

THE SLUTSKY-YULE EFFECT

The moving-averages method produces a fairly reliable estimate of a time-series value at any particular time. But it also produces a misleading *pattern* of points over an extended period of time. It *creates* periodicities where the original data show no repetitive fluctuations at all. This *Slutsky-Yule effect* can be illustrated most effectively by noting how a time series that consists of nothing but random numbers (and, therefore, contains no oscillations) can give birth to an oscillatory moving-averages series that shows clearly visible, yet artificially created and therefore misleading, waves.

Consider the hypothetical time series plotted in panel (a) of Figure 19.B. It is nothing but a plot of the 50 digits found in row 1 of Appendix Table A, *Random Numbers,* or, what time-series analysts refer to as patternless "white noise."

Now imagine taking 10-period moving averages of this series and plotting these, as in panel (b). The oscillations are obvious, yet it would be wrong to look for any causal link here, such as the influence of strikes or holidays on our time series.

In fact, the reason for the waves is fairly simple. Because the original numbers vary randomly, the sum of

(continued)

Application 19.3 (continued)

any 10 of these (and the average of that group) is bound to fluctuate. When that sum is unusually high, there are lots of large numbers in the group; chances are lower that a larger number will be added next than that a smaller number will be added next. But a large number will be dropped, so the sum (and average) probably decline after a peak. The reverse is true when we start with an unusually small sum (and average); thus, the two probably rise after a trough. If all this reminds you of the *regression effect,* discussed on page 709, it should.

SOURCE: Adapted from Eugen E. Slutsky, "The Summation of Random Causes as the Source of Cyclic Processes," *Econometrica,* 5 (1937), pp.105–146; G. Udny Yule, "On a Method of Investigating Periodicities in Disturbed Series, with Special Reference to Wolfer's Sunspot Numbers," Royal Society of London, *Philosophical Transactions* (1927), pp. 267–298.

FIGURE 19.B

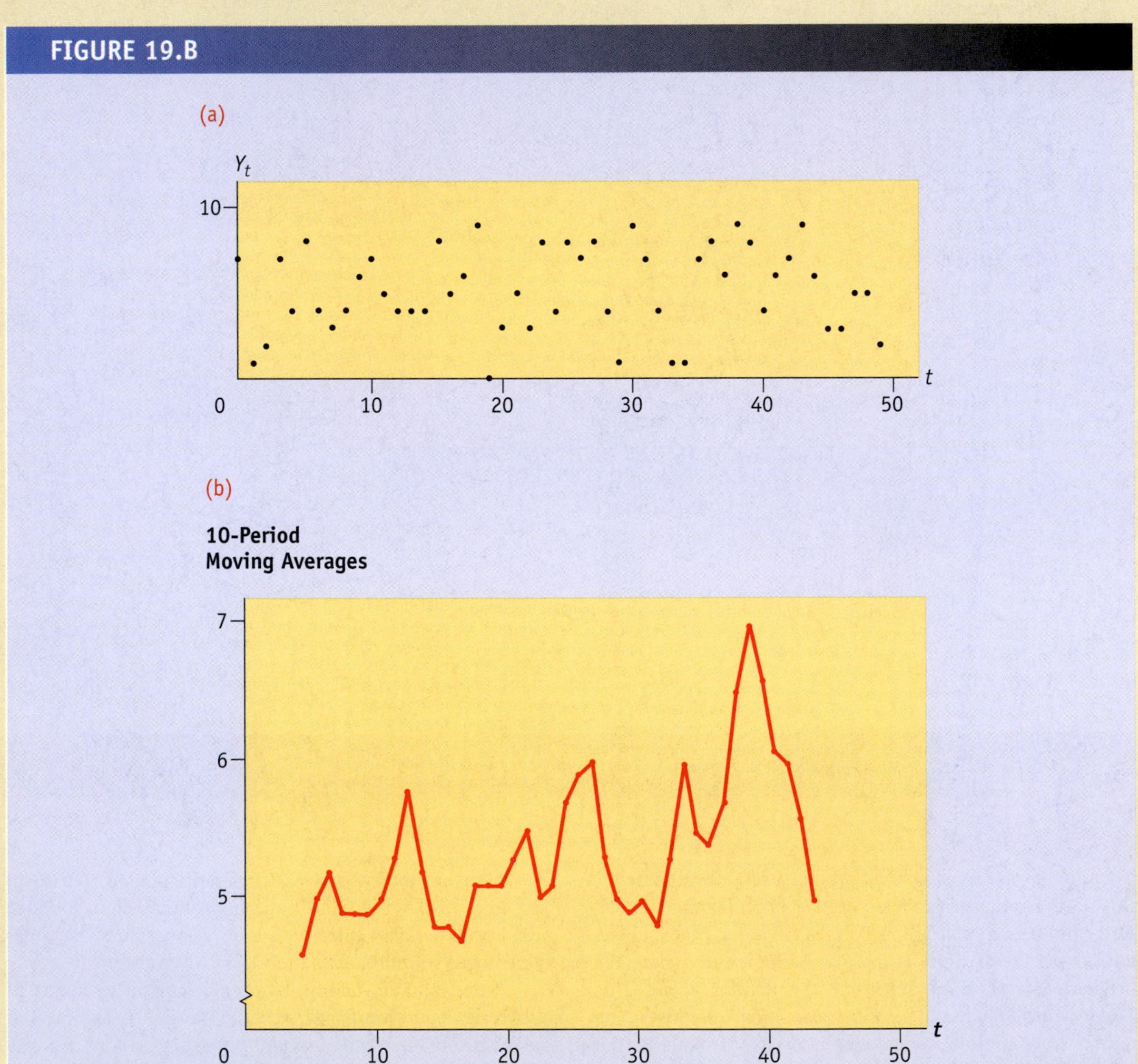

FORECASTING WITH MOVING AVERAGES

Suppose we wanted to forecast, in 2003, avionics sales for 2004 or later years. How would we do so with the help of our 3-year moving-averages series (that ends in 2002) or with the help of our 8-year moving-averages series (that ends in 1999)? Would we dare project our red "trend line" straight into the (shaded) future region depicted in our graphs? Note how such a projection of the 3-year moving-averages series brings us to point *a* in Figure 19.5, leading us to forecast 2004 trend sales of 1,550 units, if we project the last segment of the red line by means of the upper dashed arrow. (This procedure is nothing more complicated than extending the last segment of the red line, while leaving its slope unchanged.) Yet we could just as well project sales to point *b,* if we took into account the generally lower slope of the entire red line.

On the other hand, a projection of the last segment of the 8-year moving-averages series brings us to point *A* in Figure 19.6, leading us to forecast 2004 trend sales of 1,230 units, while a projection of the general slope of *that* line leads us perhaps, to point *B*. Even assuming we had good reason to choose one of these "trend lines" over the other, how reliable would such a forecast be? It would be excellent if we could assume that the behavior of the "trend" observed in the past will not change in the near future, but such is never true with certainty. Application 19.4, *The Dangers of Extrapolation,* issues an important warning on the subject.

APPLICATION 19.4

THE DANGERS OF EXTRAPOLATION

Even when the past data of a time series exhibit a clearly visible trend, forecasting the future on that basis (or, for that matter, making inferences about a more distant and unknown past) is dangerous business. Thus, President Lincoln, upon observing the 1790–1860 trend in U.S. population, predicted a U.S. population of 252 million by 1930. In fact, the actual 1930 population was 123 million. On the other hand, a 1938 presidential commission doubted that the U.S. population would ever reach 140 million, yet that figure was reached and surpassed by 1945.

No one, perhaps, has ever put the matter more clearly than Mark Twain when he wrote these lines in 1874 in *Life on the Mississippi:*

> In the space of one hundred and seventy-six years the Lower Mississippi has shortened itself two hundred and forty-two miles. That is an average of a trifle over one mile and a third per year. Therefore, any calm person, who is not blind or idiotic, can see that in the Old Oölitic Silurian Period, just a million years ago next November, the Lower Mississippi River was upward of one million three hundred thousand miles long, and stuck out over the Gulf of Mexico like a fishing-rod. And by the same token any person can see that seven hundred and forty-two years from now the Lower Mississippi will be only a mile and three-quarters long, and Cairo [Illinois] and New Orleans will have joined their streets together, and be plodding comfortably along under a single mayor and a mutual board of aldermen. There is something fascinating about science. One gets such wholesale returns of conjecture out of such a trifling investment of fact.

SOURCE: Adapted from Darrell Huff, *How to Lie with Statistics* (New York: Norton, 1954), p. 142.

EXCEL Example 19.1

Using the data of Table 19.1, column 2, on page 910, let a computer

a. create a 3-year moving averages series and make a 1-period forecast on that basis.

b. create an 8-year moving averages series and make a 1-period forecast on that basis.

SOLUTION:

Part (a)

1. Enter the Table 19.1, column 2, data into column A of a new EXCEL worksheet and name it *Sales*. (You can also copy and paste column A of the file HK19MISC.)
2. Enter labels *Moving Average* and *Forecast* into cells B1 and C1, respectively.
3. Click **Tools** > **Data Analysis** > **Moving Average** > **OK** to activate the *Moving Average* dialog box.
4. Under *Input Range*, enter **A1:A21** and check *Labels in First Row*.
5. Under *Interval*, enter **3**.
6. Under *Output Range*, enter **B2**.
7. Choose *Chart Output* and click **OK**.
8. One common practice (which is not the only possibility) makes each period's forecast equal to the latest moving average available for a prior period. To create such forecasts, enter = **B4** into C5, select C5, and drag to C22. The result:

Sales	Moving Average	Forecast
330	#N/A	
241	#N/A	
200	257	
499	313.3333	257
322	340.3333	313.3333
500	440.3333	340.3333
601	474.3333	440.3333
401	500.6667	474.3333
401	467.6667	500.6667
899	567	467.6667
598	632.6667	567
787	761.3333	632.6667
666	683.6667	761.3333
569	674	683.6667
561	598.6667	674
915	681.6667	598.6667
947	807.6667	681.6667
791	884.3333	807.6667
1114	950.6667	884.3333
1591	1165.333	950.6667
		1165.333

Note: EXCEL associates the moving average with the *last* of the original values that are being averaged rather than with the *central* value, as in columns 3 of Table 19.1. (We could, however, manipulate the display to achieve a different result. Select, for example, B2, click **Edit > Delete**, choose *Shift cells up*, and click **OK**.)

Compare Figure 19.5 on page 911 with EXCEL'S 3-Year Moving Averages chart on the next page (which has been edited for aesthetic reasons):

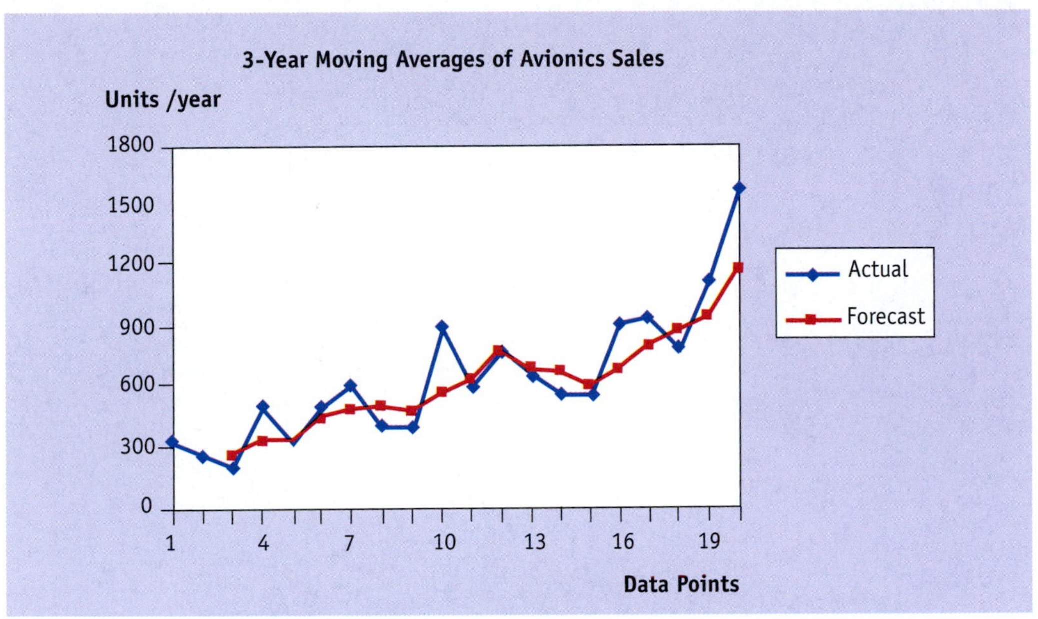

Part (b)

1. Repeat Steps 1-7 of Part (a), but enter **8** in Step 5.
2. To create forecasts, enter =**B9** into C10, select C10, and drag to C22. The result:

Sales	Moving Average	Forecast
330	#N/A	
241	#N/A	
200	#N/A	
499	#N/A	
322	#N/A	
500	#N/A	
601	#N/A	
401	386.75	
401	395.625	386.75
899	477.875	395.625
598	527.625	477.875
787	563.625	527.625
666	606.625	563.625
569	615.25	606.625
561	610.25	615.25
915	674.5	610.25
947	742.75	674.5
791	729.25	742.75
1114	793.75	729.25
1591	894.25	793.75
		894.25

Note: EXCEL again associates the moving average with the *last* of the original values that are being averaged rather than with the *central* value (as in column 5 of Table 19.1.) Compare Figure 19.6 on page 913 with EXCEL'S 8-Year Moving Averages chart on the next page (which has been edited for aesthetic reasons):

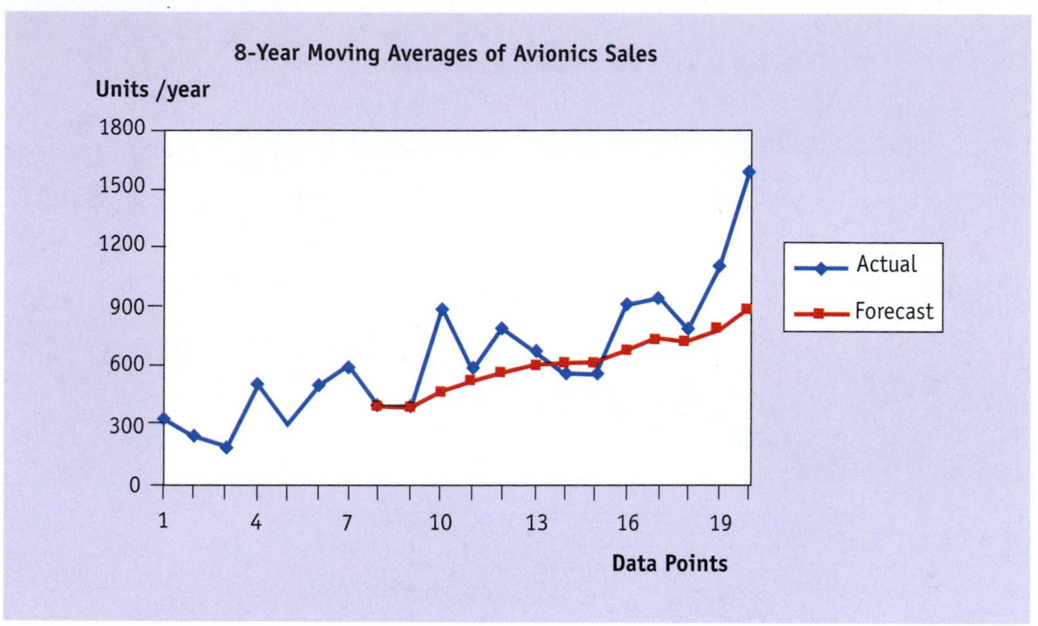

19.4 Forecasting and Exponential Smoothing

We can eliminate much of the uncertainty that is connected with the moving-averages method by employing another forecasting procedure, called **exponential smoothing.** It operates like a thermostat and produces self-correcting forecasts by means of a built-in adjustment mechanism that corrects for earlier forecasting errors. We consider two versions of this procedure: *single-parameter exponential smoothing* and *two-parameter exponential smoothing.*

SINGLE-PARAMETER EXPONENTIAL SMOOTHING

The simplest approach to exponential smoothing produces the next period's forecast value, F_{t+1}, directly from the current actual value of the time series, Y_t, and the current forecast value, F_t, by using a **smoothing constant,** α, as shown in Formula 19.B. As long as only one such parameter is being employed, the procedure is called **single-parameter exponential smoothing.**

FORMULA 19.B | Single-Parameter Exponential Smoothing

$$F_{t+1} = \alpha Y_t + (1 - \alpha)F_t$$

where F_{t+1} is next period's forecast value, Y_t is the current actual value of the time series, F_t is the current forecast value, and α is a smoothing constant.

The parameter, α, is a value between 0 and 1 that forecasters choose to indicate the weight they want to attach to the most recent value of the time series. By implication, it also indicates the weight, $1 - \alpha$, they want to attach to the current forecast value.

Look at Formula 19.B. If α were 0, the expression αY_t would equal zero, which would indicate the forecaster's desire to attach no weight whatsoever to the current actual value of the time series when making next period's forecast. (By implication, next period's forecast would equal this period's forecast.) At the other extreme, if α were 1, the expression $(1 - \alpha)F_t$ would equal zero, which would indicate the forecaster's desire to attach no weight whatsoever to the current forecast value of the time series and to use only the current actual value when making next period's forecast. Clearly, all kinds of possibilities exist in between. A value of $\alpha = .5$, for example, would create next period's forecast by summing *half* the current actual value of the time series and *half* the current forecast value.

At least one exception to the preceding discussion exists. Unlike EXCEL, the MINITAB computer program gives users the choice not to provide an α value and to let the computer find an *optimal* smoothing constant that minimizes forecast errors. The computer then experiments with numerous α values until the exponentially smoothed series matches the actual data series as closely as possible. On occasion, this procedure picks an α value outside the range from 0 to 1.

EXAMPLE PROBLEM 19.3

Review Table 19.1, then picture yourself in 1984 ($t = 1$) knowing only that current sales equal $Y_t = 330$ units, that current sales had been forecast as $F_t = 320$ units, and that 1984 sales, thus, exceed the forecast by 10 units, as in row 1 of Table 19.2 on the next page. If you choose $\alpha = .20$ as your smoothing constant, you can use the Formula 19.B equation to forecast 1985 sales as

$$F_2 = \alpha Y_1 + (1 - \alpha)F_1 = .20(330) + (1 - .20)320 = 322$$

This value is the second entry in column 3. Note that the previous error of +10 has raised the subsequent forecast by α times the error, or by +2. Thus, the next forecast is being adjusted by a fraction of and in the direction of the previous forecast error. Given actual sales data of column 2, make similar forecasts through 2004 by

a. using $\alpha = .20$.

b. using $\alpha = .50$.

SOLUTION:

a. See Table 19.2.You find actual 1985 ($t = 2$) sales of 241. Accordingly, you record an error of −81 and make a new forecast for 1986 of

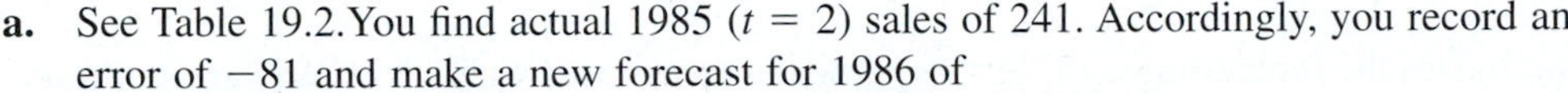

$$F_3 = \alpha Y_2 + (1 - \alpha)F_2 = .20(241) + (1 - .20)322 = 305.8$$

Once again, you have adjusted the previous forecast (of 322) by α times the previous error (of −81), or by −16.2 in this case. The remainder of columns 3 and 4 have been filled out in similar fashion; all entries have been rounded.

Note: If no forecast had existed for 1984, the actual 1984 value of 330 would have been used as the 1985 forecast, and the equation would have been employed thereafter.

b. See Table 19.2. As an inspection of column 4 indicates, many forecasts made in (a) were fairly wide off the mark; that is, they differed significantly from actual sales. Whenever this happens, forecasters adjust the value of α, increasing it when they want to give more weight to current experience and less to the past, or decreasing it when they want to do the opposite. By trial and error, they can in this way select a smoothing constant that

TABLE 19.2 | Forecasting Avionics Sales by Single-Parameter Exponential Smoothing

		α = .20		α = .50	
Year, t (1)	Actual Sales, Y_t (2)	Forecast Sales, F_t (3)	Forecasting Error, $Y_t - F_t$ (4) = (2) − (3)	Forecast Sales, F_t (5)	Forecasting Error, $Y_t - F_t$ (6) = (2) − (5)
1984	330	320	10	320	10
1985	241	322	−81	325	−84
1986	200	306	−106	283	−83
1987	499	285	214	242	257
1988	322	328	−6	371	−49
1989	500	327	173	347	153
1990	601	362	239	424	177
1991	401	410	−9	513	−112
1992	401	408	−7	457	−56
1993	899	407	492	429	470
1994	598	505	93	664	−66
1995	787	524	263	631	156
1996	666	577	89	709	−43
1997	569	595	−26	688	−119
1998	561	590	−29	629	−68
1999	915	584	331	595	320
2000	947	650	297	755	192
2001	791	709	82	851	−60
2002	1,114	725	389	821	293
2003	1,591	803	788	968	623
2004	—	961	—	1,280	—

minimizes the forecasting error for the particular time series with which they are working. Typically, a very stable time series calls for the use of a large α; an extremely volatile series calls for a smaller α. It is easy to see why: In a stable series, we want to give a large weight to the current actual value (because actual values are changing little over time). In a volatile series, we want to attach little weight to the current actual value (because actual values are changing frequently over time). Columns 5 and 6 of Table 19.2 indicate the forecasting record that can be achieved with $\alpha = .5$.

A GRAPHICAL EXPOSITION OF SINGLE-PARAMETER EXPONENTIAL SMOOTHING

Figure 19.7 shows graphically how actual and forecast values behave when using the alternative smoothing constants of Example Problem 19.3.

FIGURE 19.7 | Avionics Sales: Actual and Single-Parameter Exponentially Smoothed

This graph indicates how a time series might be smoothed exponentially—in this case, by employing a smoothing constant of α = .2 or α = .5, respectively. The method can also be employed to make forecasts—for example, of A or B in 2004.

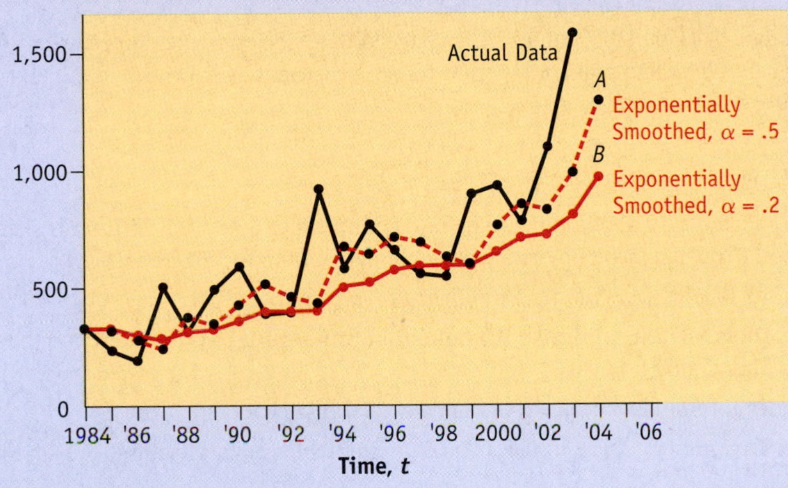

ADVANTAGES OF EXPONENTIAL SMOOTHING

Forecasting with the help of exponentially smoothed times series is popular. This popularity arises from two facts: (1) the calculations are simple, and (2) next to no data storage is required. To appreciate the latter, consider that only one number, namely, F_{t+1}, the most recent forecast made, has to be remembered, because any given forecast embodies the entire time series in it. As we have noted,

$$F_{t+1} = \alpha Y_t + (1 - \alpha)F_t$$

but, in turn,

$$F_t = \alpha Y_{t-1} + (1 - \alpha)F_{t-1}$$

Thus,

$$\begin{aligned} F_{t+1} &= \alpha Y_t + (1 - \alpha)[\alpha Y_{t-1} + (1 - \alpha)F_{t-1}] \\ &= \alpha Y_t + \alpha(1 - \alpha)Y_{t-1} + (1 - \alpha)^2 F_{t-1} \end{aligned}$$

If we continued this breakdown for ever-earlier periods, we would discover all the preceding Y values (Y_t, Y_{t-1}, Y_{t-2}, Y_{t-3}, and so on) hidden in the most recent forecast, and they would appear with successive weights of α, $\alpha(1 - \alpha)$, $\alpha(1 - \alpha)^2$, $\alpha(1 - \alpha)^3$, and so on. These weights decrease *exponentially* (the more distant the value of the time series, the less its forecasting weight), which explains the name of this technique.

To sum up, the exponential-smoothing technique produces a weighted average of all past time-series values with weights decreasing exponentially as one goes back in time, and the average so constructed serves as a forecast for the next period. The method is cheap and fast and is often employed when multiple forecasts for a large set of items are required—as, perhaps, in a firm's inventory-control system, which might require demand forecasts for tens of thousands of items.

EXCEL Example 19.2

Using the data of Table 19.2, column 2, on page 920, let the computer apply *single-parameter exponential smoothing* and make a 1-period forecast on that basis. Unlike in the text earlier, apply a smoothing constant of $\alpha = .6$.

SOLUTION:

1. Enter the Table 19.2, column 2, data into column A of a new EXCEL worksheet and name it *Sales*. (You can also copy and paste column A of the file HK19MISC.)
2. Enter the label *Exponentially Smoothed Forecast* into cell B1.
3. Click **Tools** > **Data Analysis** > **Exponential Smoothing** > **OK** to activate the *Exponential Smoothing* dialog box.
4. Under *Input Range*, enter **A1:A21** and check the *Labels* box.
5. Under *Damping factor*, enter **.4**. (The damping factor equals 1 minus the smoothing constant.)
6. Under *Output Range*, enter **B2**.
7. Choose *Chart Output* and click **OK**.
8. To make the forecast, select B21 and drag to B22. The result:

Sales	Exp. Smoothed Forecast
330	#N/A
241	330
200	276.6
499	230.64
322	391.656
500	349.8624
601	439.94496
401	536.577984
401	455.2311936
899	422.6924774
598	708.476991
787	642.1907964
666	729.0763186
569	691.2305274
561	617.892211
915	583.7568844
947	782.5027538
791	881.2011015
1114	827.0804406

1591	999.2321762
	1354.29287

Compare Figure 19.7 on page 921 with EXCEL'S chart here (which has been edited for aesthetic reasons):

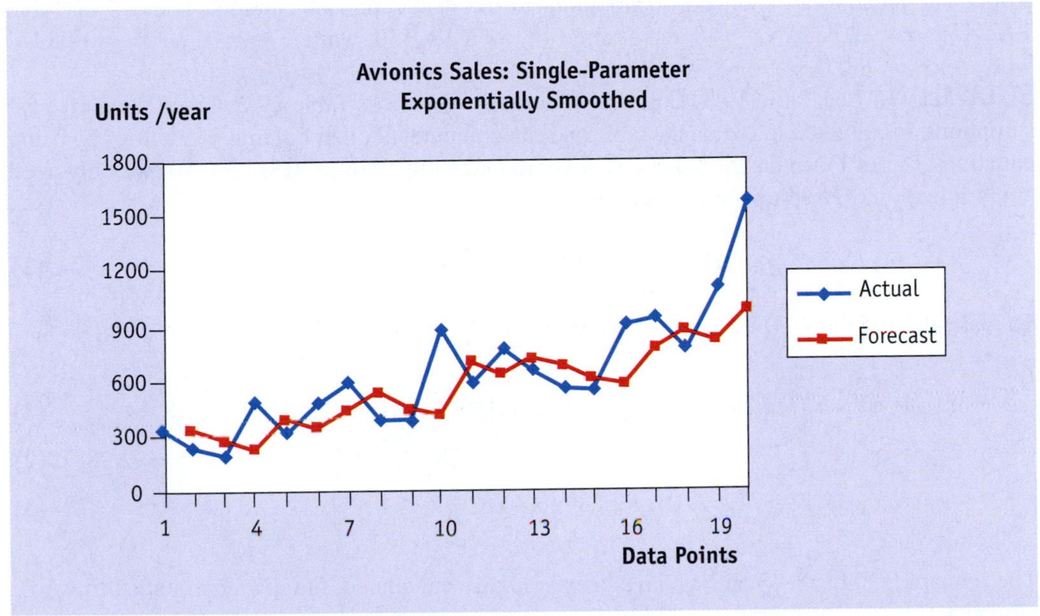

TWO-PARAMETER EXPONENTIAL SMOOTHING

Whenever a time series exhibits a strong upward trend, single-parameter exponential smoothing will produce generally-too-low forecasts, as is evident from an inspection of Figure 19.7. An alternative, **two-parameter exponential smoothing,** might eliminate this problem by explicitly taking into account the influence of the trend. The technique employs three equations: (1) to produce a smoothed time-series value, Y_t^*, for the current time period, (2) to produce a smoothed trend-component value, T_t^*, for the current time period, and (3) to produce a forecast, F_{t+1}, for the next time period. These equations appear in Formula 19.C.

FORMULA 19.C | Two-Parameter Exponential Smoothing

$$Y_t^* = \alpha Y_t + (1 - \alpha)(Y^*_{t-1} + T^*_{t-1}) \quad (1)$$

$$T^*_t = \gamma(Y^*_t - Y^*_{t-1}) + (1 - \gamma)T^*_{t-1} \quad (2)$$

$$F_{t+1} = Y^*_t + T^*_t \quad (3)$$

where Y^* is a smoothed time series value, while Y is the actual value, T^* is the smoothed trend component, α and γ are smoothing constants, and the subscripts t define the time periods.

Note: To start the computations, we typically assume that $Y^*_2 = Y_1$, while $T^*_2 = Y_2 - Y_1$.

In Formula 19.C, the parameter γ (the lowercase Greek gamma) is the trend smoothing constant, also chosen to lie between 0 and 1, while the current trend is defined as the difference between the current and preceding smoothed value of the series, $Y^*_t - Y^*_{t-1}$.

EXAMPLE PROBLEM 19.4

Apply two-parameter exponential smoothing to the data found in columns 1 and 2 of Table 19.2. Use $\alpha = .20$ and $\gamma = .40$ and assume $Y^*_2 = Y_1 = 330$, while $T^*_2 = Y_2 - Y_1 = -89$.

SOLUTION: See Table 19.3. Columns 1 and 2 are copies of Table 19.2. Given the above assumptions, highlighted in red on the table, we can compute all other column 3–5 entries by using equations 1–3 of Formula 19.C. For example, to make the 1986 ($t = 3$) forecast, we only need apply Equation (3) to the values in red to find

$$F_3 = Y^*_2 + T^*_2 = 330 - 89 = 241 \quad \textbf{(3)}$$

To make the 1987 ($t = 4$) forecast, we figure $F_4 = Y^*_3 + T^*_3$ and

$$Y^*_3 = \alpha Y_3 + (1 - \alpha)(Y^*_2 + T^*_2) = .20(200) + .80(330 - 89) = 232.8 \quad \textbf{(1)}$$

$$T^*_3 = \gamma(Y^*_3 - Y^*_2) + (1 - \gamma)T^*_2 = .40(232.8 - 330) + .60(-89) = -92.28 \quad \textbf{(2)}$$

$$F_4 = Y^*_3 + T^*_3 = 232.8 - 92.28 = 140.52 \quad \textbf{(3)}$$

The remaining Table 19.3 entries have been similarly calculated, but always rounded to whole numbers.

A GRAPHICAL EXPOSITION OF TWO-PARAMETER EXPONENTIAL SMOOTHING

We can also draw a picture of our forecasting record, as in Figure 19.8 on page 926. The graph vividly shows what column (6) of Table 19.3 indicates: The forecasting record is not too good and certainly makes us wonder whether we should trust the 2004 forecast of 1,249 units (point *A* in the graph).

The use of different smoothing constants might improve the Figure 19.8 forecasting record, however, and this outcome could be determined by trial and error. In addition, a great variety of other exponential-smoothing procedures exist. These include **three-parameter exponential smoothing** (a method that adds seasonal smoothing to trend smoothing), adjusting the smoothing constant, α, from one period to the next, and even considering nonlinear relationships between values.

EXCEL Example 19.3

Using the data of column 2 of Table 19.3, along with smoothing constants of $\alpha = .425$ and $\gamma = .158$, apply two-parameter exponential smoothing and

a. make a 1-period forecast on that basis.

b. contrast the actual and smoothed data series in a graph.

TABLE 19.3 | Forecasting Avionics Sales by Two-Parameter Exponential Smoothing ($\alpha = .20$ and $\gamma = .40$)

Year, t (1)	Actual Sales, Y_t (2)	Equation (1): Smoothed Sales, Y^*_t (3)	Equation (2): Smoothed Trend, T^*_t (4)	Equation (3): Forecast Sales, F_t (5)	Forecasting Error, $Y_t - F_t$ (6) = (2) − (5)
1984	330	—	—	—	—
1985	241	330	−89	—	—
1986	200	233	−92	241	−41
1987	499	213	−63	141	358
1988	322	184	−49	150	172
1989	500	208	−20	135	365
1990	601	271	13	188	413
1991	401	307	22	284	117
1992	401	343	28	329	72
1993	899	477	70	371	528
1994	598	557	74	547	51
1995	787	662	86	631	156
1996	666	732	80	748	−82
1997	569	763	60	812	−243
1998	561	771	39	823	−262
1999	915	831	47	810	105
2000	947	892	53	878	69
2001	791	914	41	945	−154
2002	1,114	987	54	955	159
2003	1,591	1,151	98	1,041	550
2004	—	—	—	1,249	—

SOLUTION:

Part (a)

EXCEL is not equipped to make the computations automatically, but you can proceed as follows:

1. Enter the label *Sales* into A1 of a new EXCEL worksheet, followed by numerical data in A2 and below. (You can also copy and paste the data from column A of the file HK19MISC.)
2. Enter the alpha and gamma smoothing constants into C3 and C4.
3. Enter labels *Equation 1: Smoothed Y**, *Equation 2: Smoothed T**, and *Equation 3: Forecast F*, respectively, into D2:F2.
4. Into D3, enter the formula = **A2**
5. Into E3, enter the formula = **A3−A2**
6. Into D4, enter the equation 1 formula = **$C$3*A4+(1−$C$3)*(D3+E3)**

FIGURE 19.8 | Avionics Sales: Actual and Two-Parameter Exponentially Smoothed

This graph indicates how a time series might be smoothed exponentially by employing two parameters (here $\alpha = .2$, $\gamma = .4$). The method can also be employed to make forecasts—as of 1,249 units (point A) in 2004.

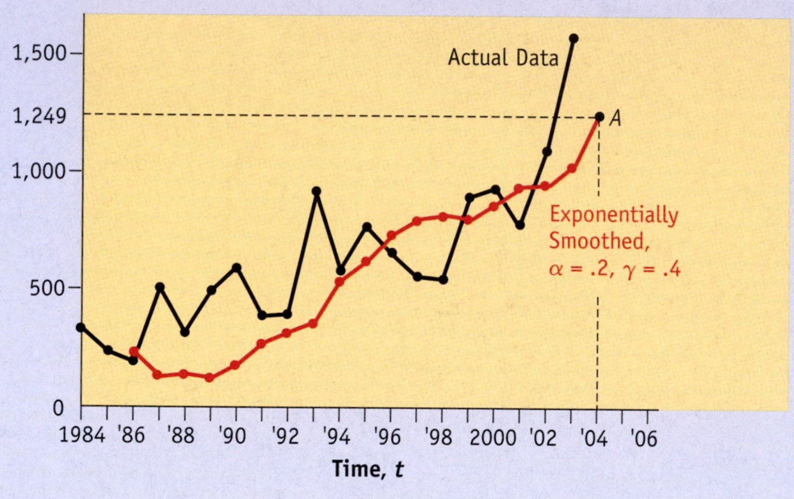

7. Into E4, enter the equation 2 formula = **\$C\$4*(D4−D3)+(1−\$C\$4)*E3**
8. Into F4, enter the equation 3 formula = **D3+E3**
9. Select D4:F4 and drag downwards to your last data row.
10. To find one additional forecast, select cell F in your last data row and drag down one row.

The first three and last three rows of output are reproduced here; the 1-period forecast beyond the known data range is highlighted in red:

Equation 1: Smoothed Y^*	Equation 2: Smoothed T^*	Equation 3: Forecast F
330	−89	
223.575	−91.75315	241
287.8725638	−67.0971372	131.82185
263.7958703	−60.2999071	220.7754265
329.5101788	−40.389661	203.4959631
848.7145985	36.74235569	776.068867
845.3127487	30.39957122	885.4569542
976.9845839	46.40058894	875.7123199
1264.621474	84.51592458	1023.385173
		1349.137399

Note: For quicker results, you can use HKStat, Sheet 45.

Part (b)

To plot the actual Y data versus the forecast F values, click the **Chart Wizard > Standard Types > Chart type: Line. . .** , follow the prompts, and edit the result:

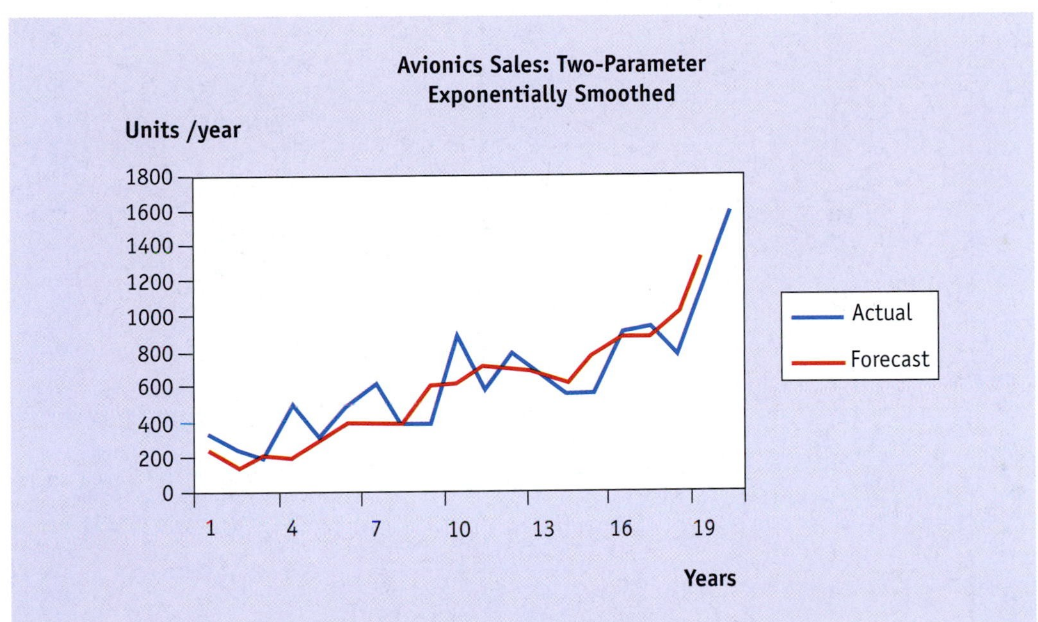

19.5 Forecasting and Least-Squares Regression

We can also estimate a trend, and then make forecasts with its help, by fitting a least-squares regression line to the available time-series data. This approach is dangerous business, however, because the crucial assumptions underlying that procedure (and noted in Chapters 16 and 17) may not be met. In that case, we may still be able to estimate unbiased regression coefficients, but all kinds of inferences are no longer appropriate. Yet such inferences would be particularly useful in a forecasting situation. Precarious as it is, the projection of the dependent variable (for example, of avionics sales) by means of a regression line to time periods beyond the range of data from which that line was calculated is, in this case, the whole point of estimating the regression line in the first place. Thus, we would like to have reliable confidence intervals for any estimated future values precisely when such intervals are unlikely to be available. Nevertheless, because the procedure is frequently employed, let us consider how we might use regression analysis to forecast future Y values.

CONSULTING A SCATTER DIAGRAM

In all cases, good judgment suggests first drawing a scatter diagram of the variable of interest against time. Such a diagram will suggest a basic type of trend line that is likely to fit the data best; Figure 19.9 shows several possibilities.

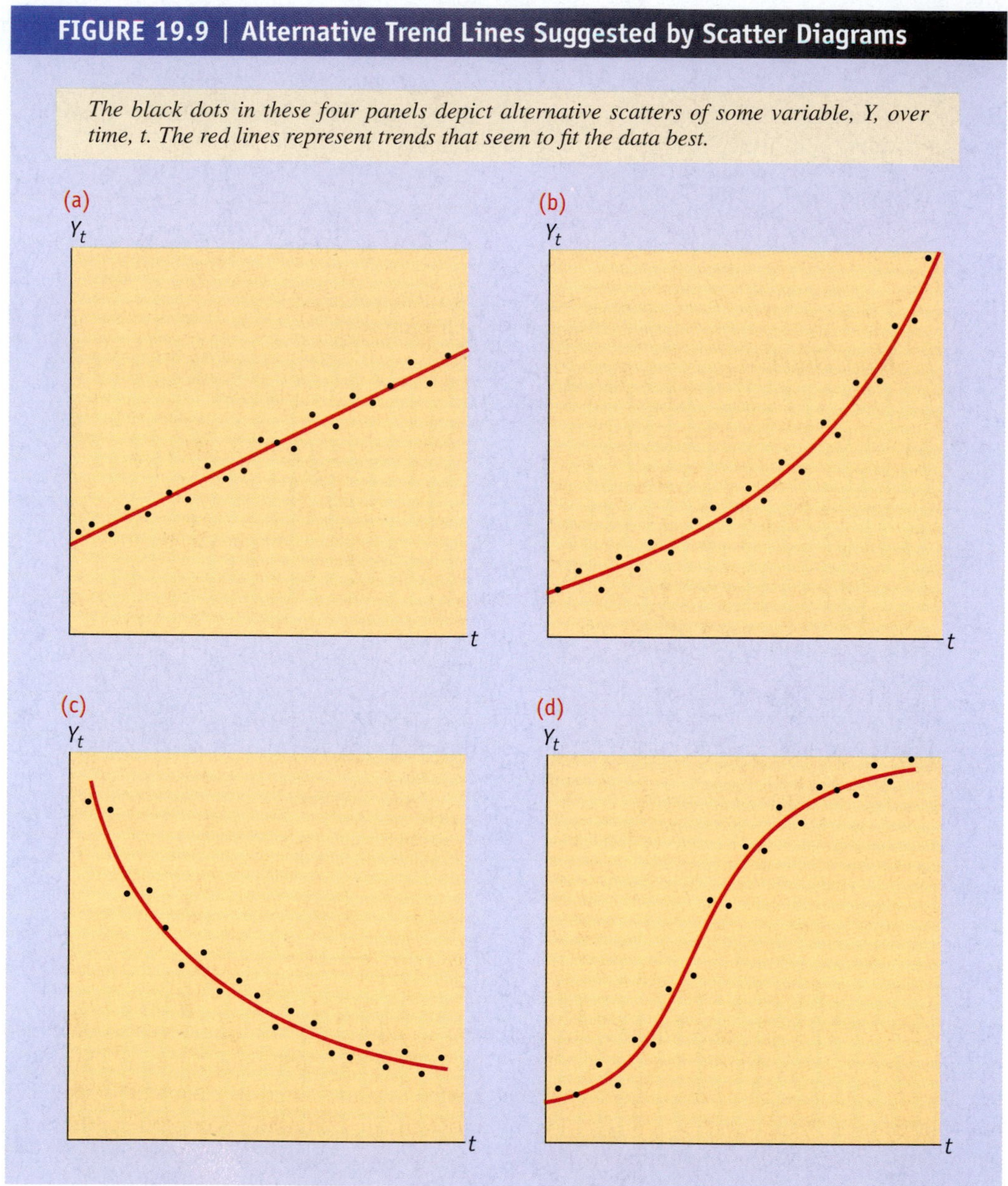

Panel (a) might represent the steady *absolute* growth in a firm's sales (at a rate of 50 units per year). Panel (b) might depict a steady *percentage* growth of sales (at a rate of 2 percent per year), and panel (c) might show a steady percentage decline in sales (at a rate of 3 percent a year). Panel (d) shows a mixture, with growth at an increasing rate followed by growth at a decreasing rate.

Panel (b) depicts well the trend in such time series as the U.S. population, the U.S. GDP, the number of passengers carried by U.S. airlines, or the U.S. per capita consumption of synthetic fibers or that of frozen vegetables. Panel (c) depicts well the trend in such time series as the number of passengers carried by U.S. railroads or the U.S. per capita consumption of cotton or that of fresh vegetables. Panel (d) might be a so-called Gompertz or logistic (Pearl-Reed) growth curve; it depicts the production and sales behavior of many a new product that experiences spectacular growth, followed by market saturation.

FORECASTING WITH A LINEAR REGRESSION LINE

A scatter diagram of our avionics sales data against time indicates that a *linear* representation of this relationship is not unreasonable. Accordingly, we may be tempted to use a linear regression line to make forecasts of future sales. Example Problem 19.5 explains. (For the time being, we are ignoring possible violations of crucial assumptions here, but we will return to that subject in a later section.)

EXAMPLE PROBLEM 19.5

Review the avionics sales data from column 2 of Table 19.1 on page 910. If you let $X = 0$ stand for mid-1984, $X = 1$ for mid-1985, and so on, until $X = 19$ stands for mid-2003, you can derive the following linear regression equation (with t values in parentheses):

$$\text{Sales} = \underset{(2.43)}{200.09} + \underset{(6.33)}{47.007X}$$

$$R^2(\text{adj.}) = .673$$

a. Plot the data and the equation in a scatter diagram.

b. Make a forecast of trend sales in 2006.

SOLUTION:

a. Figure 19.10 is the diagram.

FIGURE 19.10 | Scatter Diagram of Avionics Sales and Fitted Regression Line

This scatter diagram is based on the data in columns 1 and 2 of Tables 19.1–19.3. Using the solid red line, fitted by the method of least squares, we forecast 2006 trend sales of 1,234 units (point a).

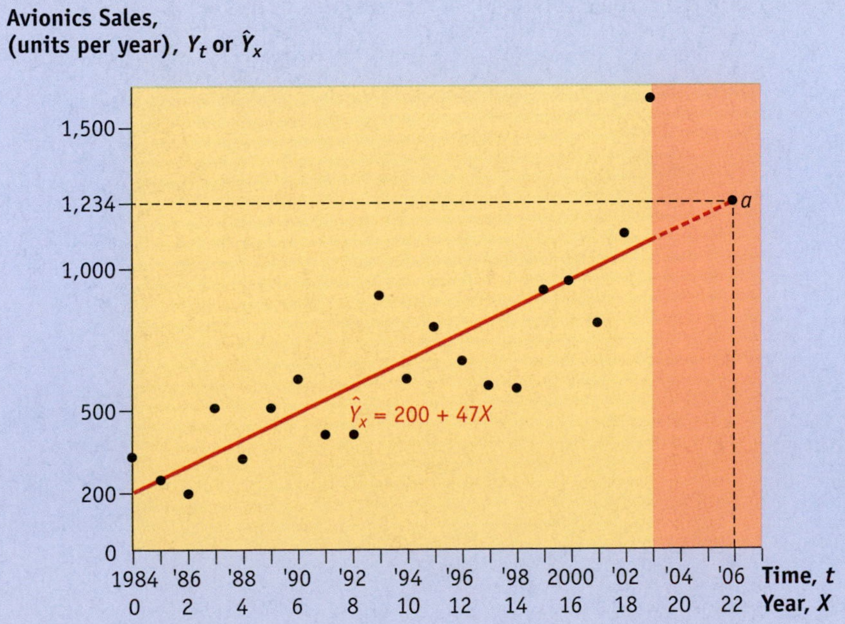

b. The 2006 forecast is

$$\text{Sales}_{2006} = 200.09 + 47.007(22) = 1{,}234 \text{ (rounded)}$$

EXCEL Example 19.4

Retrieve the avionics sales data of columns 1 and 2, Table 19.1 on page 910. Let $X = 0$ stand for mid-1984, $X = 1$ for mid-1985, and so on, until $X = 19$ stands for mid-2003. Then use your computer to

a. confirm the regression of Y = sales against X = years in Example Problem 19.5.

b. create a graph similar to Figure 19.10.

SOLUTION:

1. Enter the label *Years* into cell A1 of a new EXCEL worksheet and the numbers 0-19 below it.
2. Enter the label *Sales* into cell B1 and the Table 19.1, column 2, data below it. (You can also copy and paste column A of the file HK19MISC.)
3. Select A1:B21; then click the **Chart Wizard** > **XY(Scatter)** > **Next** > **Next**.
4. Click the *Titles* tab in the *Chart Options* dialog box.
5. Under *Chart title*, enter **Avionics Sales Regression** and press TAB.
6. Under *Value (X) axis*, enter **Years** and press TAB.
7. Under *Value (Y)* axis, enter **Units/year**.
8. Click the *Gridlines* and *Legend* tabs and remove all check marks.
9. Click **Next** > **Finish**; then enlarge and edit the graph as desired.
10. Click on the chart. On the menu bar, click **Chart** > **Add Trendline** > **Type** > **Linear**.
11. Click the *Options tab*, choose *Automatic, Forward* **3**, *Display equation on chart*, and click **OK**.
12. Once again, edit the graph as you like for a result such as this:

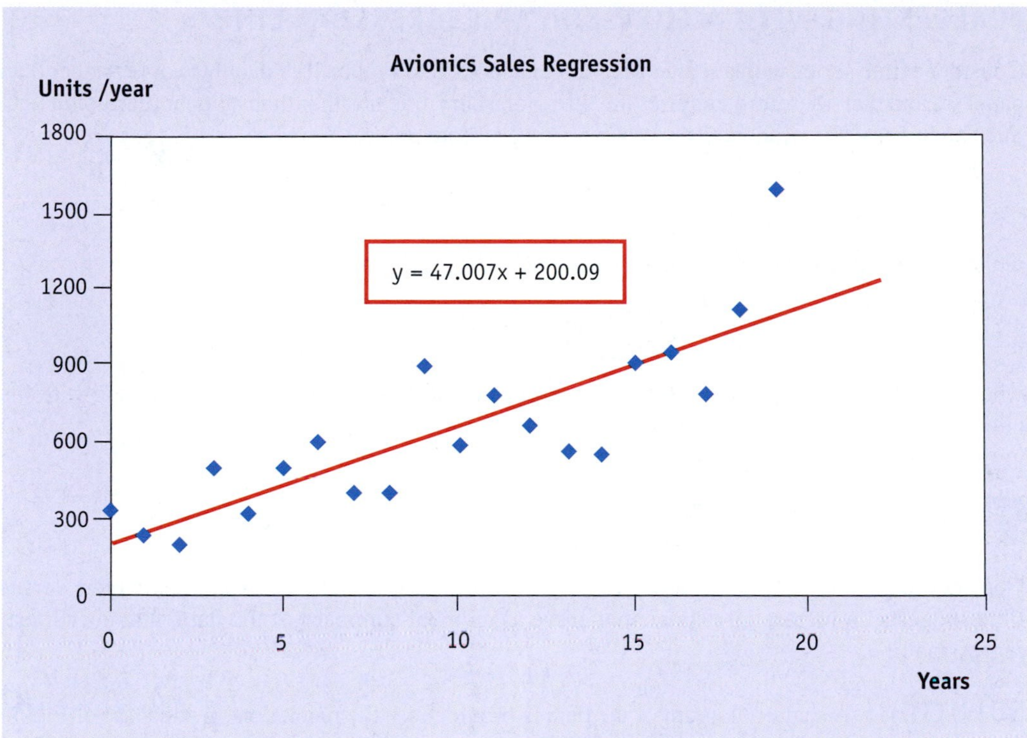

Note that the year 2006 corresponds to $X = 22$, from which a forecast of $47.007(22) + 200.09 =$ 1,234 units can be derived.

FROM ANNUAL TO QUARTERLY DATA

Most trend lines are fitted to annual data, but we may also wish to examine quarterly or even monthly trend values. These can be determined by modifying our above regression equation. Suppose our manager required quarterly information on sales (at annual rates). In that case, we would need X values measured in quarters from a zero base, each of them centered in the middle of a quarter. If $X = 0$ were placed in the middle of the first or winter quarter of 1984 (that is, at mid-February 1984), the base would shift backward in time by 1.5 quarters (the original base was mid-1984, at the end of the second or spring quarter). Our earlier calculation showed sales rising annually by $b = 47$ units; hence, they are rising by $b/4$ or 11.75 units per quarter, which would be the slope of our new regression line for quarterly data. Hence, the new line's intercept would have to equal 200 (or mid-1984 trend sales) minus 1.5(11.75), or 182.375. Thus, the transformed regression line, measuring *quarterly* sales at annual rates, is

$$\text{Sales} = 182.375 + 11.75X$$

where X is measured in quarters and $X = 0$ is located at the middle of the first or winter quarter of 1984. Note how this equation accurately predicts the 200-unit annual trend sales of 1984 that constitutes the intercept of the annual-data regression line in Figure 19.10:

$$\text{Sales} = 182.375 + 11.75(1.5) = 200$$

FORECASTING WITH A CURVILINEAR REGRESSION LINE

Consider a time series with a scatter diagram that looks like Figure 19.9 panel (b) or (c) rather than panel (a) and that, therefore, requires the fitting of a curvilinear rather than a linear regression line. Such an increasing exponential curve would have an equation of

$$\hat{Y}_X = a \cdot b^X$$

while a decreasing exponential curve would be described by

$$\hat{Y}_X = a \cdot b^{-X}$$

where a and b are positive constants. We can develop such a curvilinear regression line with the help of an appropriate data transformation.

EXAMPLE PROBLEM 19.6

Consider the actual historical data of Table 19.4. Because a scatter diagram of passengers versus time suggests an increasing exponential curve as an ideal summary of the data, fit a curvilinear regression line.

SOLUTION: A scatter diagram of the data is provided by the black dots in panel (a) of Figure 19.11 on page 934. It suggests that the equation $\hat{Y}_X = a \cdot b^X$ might best summarize the data. If we take the logarithms of both sides, the equation becomes

$$\log \hat{Y}_X = \log a + X \log b$$

which is the equation of a straight regression line with $\log \hat{Y}_X$ on the vertical axis, $\log a$ as the intercept, and $\log b$ as the slope. If we fit the Table 19.4 data accordingly (by regressing $\log Y_t$ against X), we find this result (with t values in parentheses):

$$\log \hat{Y}_X = \underset{(77.93)}{1.5194} + \underset{(26.28)}{.0338X} \quad \textbf{(1)}$$

$$R^2(\text{adj.}) = .964$$

TABLE 19.4 | Millions of Domestic Revenue Passengers Carried by Major U.S. Airlines

Year, t	X	Passengers, Y_t
1955	0	34
1956	1	38
1957	2	40
1958	3	40
1959	4	44

(continued)

TABLE 19.4 (continued)

Year, t	X	Passengers, Y_t
1960	5	45
1961	6	45
1962	7	47
1963	8	53
1964	9	61
1965	10	70
1966	11	79
1967	12	97
1968	13	119
1969	14	126
1970	15	123
1971	16	124
1972	17	137
1973	18	145
1974	19	148
1975	20	147
1976	21	160
1977	22	172
1978	23	196
1979	24	212
1980	25	222
1981	26	205

SOURCE: *Moody's Transportation Manual* (New York: Investor's Service, 1982), p. a.39. Reprinted by permission.

Given that antilog 1.5194 = 33.0674 and antilog .0338 = 1.08094, we can rewrite equation (1) as

$$\log \hat{Y}_X = \log 33.07 + X \log 1.081 \quad \textbf{(2)}$$

which implies

$$\hat{Y}_X = 33.07\,(1.081)^X \quad \textbf{(3)}$$

Panel (a). Equation (3) has been graphed as the red line in panel (a) of Figure 19.11. Note how it estimates 1970 passengers (the *actual* number was 123 million) as

$$\hat{Y}_{15} = 33.07\,(1.081)^{15} = 106.37 \text{ million (point } A\text{)}$$

Notice also that the value of b indicates an annual passenger-growth rate of 8.1 percent.

FIGURE 19.11 | Exponential Trend Line and Its Logarithmic Transformation

A scatter diagram of the Table 19.4 data, shown in panel (a), suggests an exponential trend line as the best fit, and such a line is shown there. The same information, however, is embodied in panel (b), which contains a scatter diagram of the dependent variable, logarithmically transformed, against time, along with a straight-line logarithmic trend. Note how estimating, say, year 15 trend passengers yields the same result (point A or B), regardless of which of the two trend equations is used. (Except for rounding error, log 106.37 = 2.0264.)

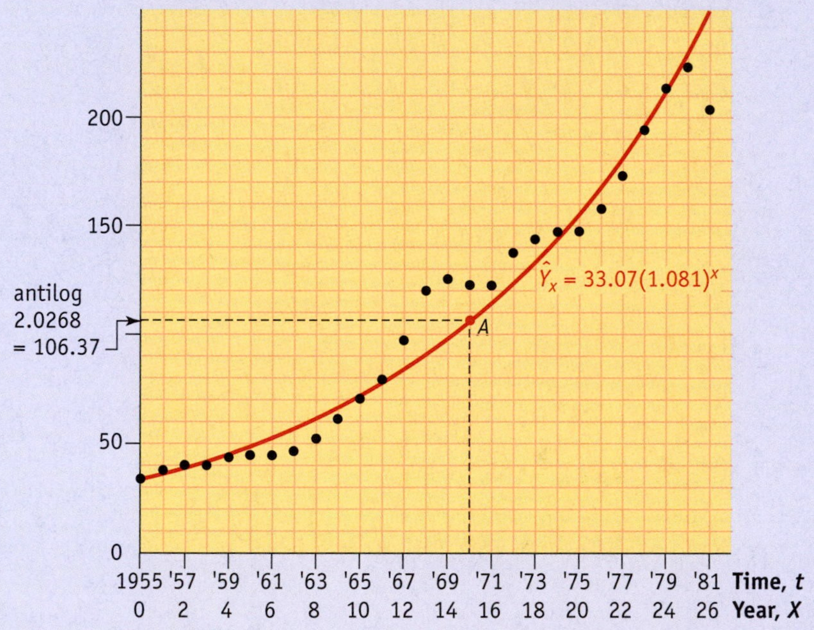

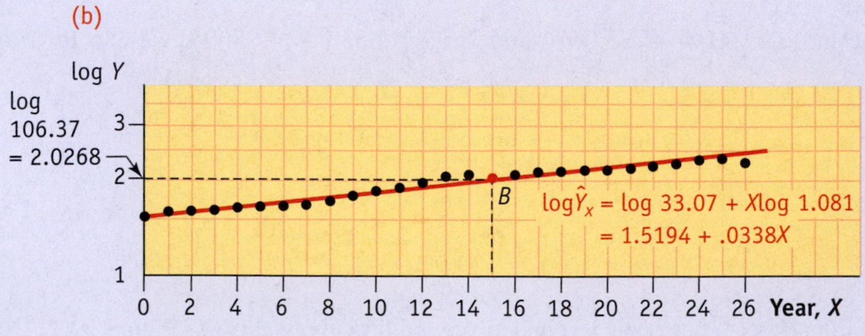

Panel (b). Equation (1) has been graphed as the red line in panel (b) of Figure 19.11, which also contains a scatter diagram of log Y values against X. This equation estimates the logarithm of 1970 passengers as

$$\log \hat{Y}_{15} = 1.5194 + .0338\,(15) = 2.0264 \text{ (point } B\text{)}$$

which makes for a passenger number of 106.27 million (because log 106.27 = 2.0264). Except for rounding error, the result corresponds to that found in panel (a).

EXAMPLE PROBLEM 19.7

Review the forecasting model derived and tested in Example Problem 19.6. Then forecast 1988 passenger levels, using

a. equation (3).

b. equation (1).

SOLUTION: The year 1988 corresponds to $t = 33$.

a. According to equation (3),

$$\hat{Y}_{33} = 33.07\,(1.081)^{33} = 432.2 \text{ (million passengers)}$$

b. According to equation (1),

$$\log \hat{Y}_{33} = 1.5194 + .0338(33) = 2.6348$$

and

$$\text{antilog } 2.6348 = 431.3 \text{ (million passengers)}$$

The answers differ slightly because of rounding.

Note: According to the U.S. Department of Transportation, the actual 1988 passenger level was 454.6 million, slightly more than here estimated. By 1999, however, there were 635.4 million actual passengers, but this model predicts 1,018 million.

EXCEL Example 19.5

Review the airline-passengers data of Table 19.4 on pages 932–933. Make a forecast for 1988 (or $X = 33$) with the help of

a. an exponential trend line.

b. logarithmically transformed passenger data.

SOLUTION:

Part (a)

1. Enter the label *X* into cell A1 of a new EXCEL worksheet and the numbers 0-26 below it.
2. Enter the label *Passengers* into cell B1 and the corresponding Table 19.4 data below it. (You can also copy and paste column AA of the file HKMISC.)

3. Select A1:B28; then click the **Chart Wizard** > **XY(Scatter)** > **Next** > **Next**.
4. Click the *Titles* tab in the *Chart Options* dialog box.
5. Under *Chart title*, enter **Exponential Trend Line** and press TAB.
6. Under *Value (X) axis*, enter **Years** and press TAB.
7. Under *Value (Y)* axis, enter **Airline Passengers (millions)**.
8. Click the *Gridlines* and *Legend* tabs and remove all check marks.
9. Click **Next** > **Finish**; then enlarge and edit the graph as desired.
10. Click on the chart. On the menu bar, click **Chart** > **Add Trendline** > **Type** > **Exponential**.
11. Click the *Options tab*, choose *Automatic, Forward 7, Display equation on chart*, and click **OK**.
12. Once again, edit the graph as you like for a result such as this:

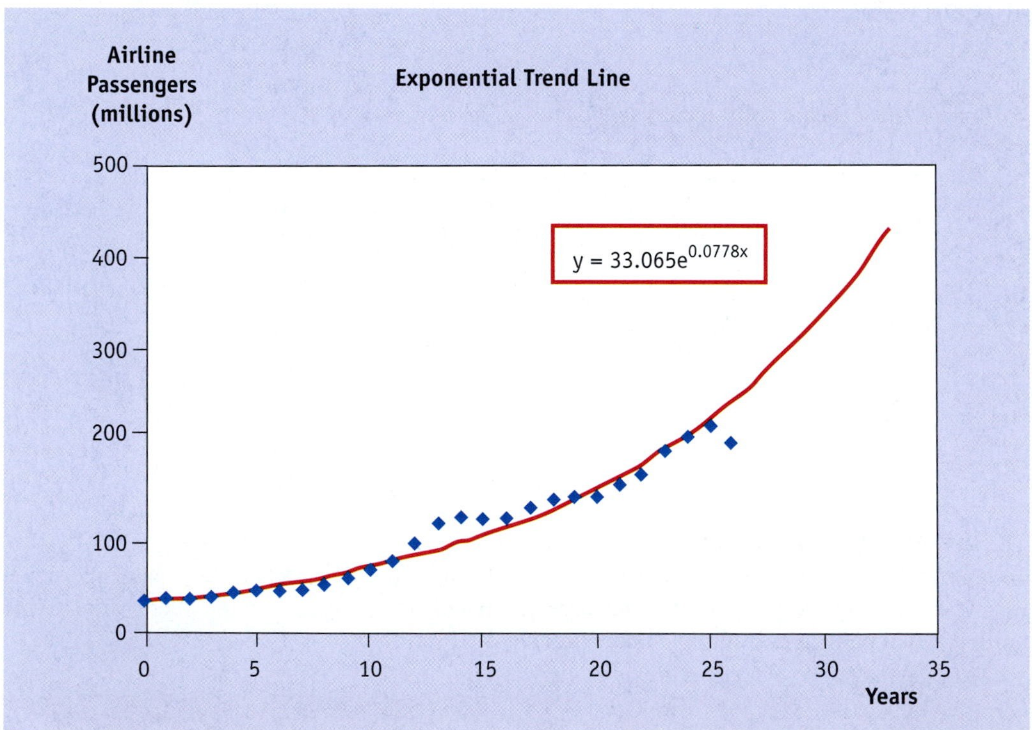

Note: Given that e = 2.7183, the value of $e^{.0778}$ = 1.0809, which makes the equation shown here identical to that given in part (a) of Figure 19.11. Accordingly, the forecast for $X = 33$ can be found by entering **= 33.065*1.0809^33** into any empty cell. The result: **430.815** (million passengers), which is depicted by a point at the upper right end of the red line in our graph.

Part (b)

1. Repeat Steps 1 and 2 of Part (a); then copy column A to column C.
2. Enter the label **log Y** into D1, enter **=LOG10(B2)** into D2, select D2, and drag to D28.
3. Select C1:D28; then click the **Chart Wizard** > **XY(Scatter)** > **Next** > **Next**.
4. Click the *Titles* tab in the *Chart Options* dialog box.
5. Under *Chart title*, enter **Logarithmic Transformation of Y** and press TAB.

6. Under *Value (X) axis*, enter **Years** and press TAB.
7. Under *Value (Y)* axis, enter **log Y**.
8. Click the *Gridlines* and *Legend* tabs and remove all check marks.
9. Click **Next** > **Finish**; then enlarge and edit the graph as desired.
10. Click on the chart. On the menu bar, click **Chart** > **Add Trendline** > **Type** > **Linear**.
11. Click the *Options tab*, choose *Automatic, Forward* 7, *Display equation on chart*, and click **OK**.
12. Once again, edit the graph as you like for a result such as this:

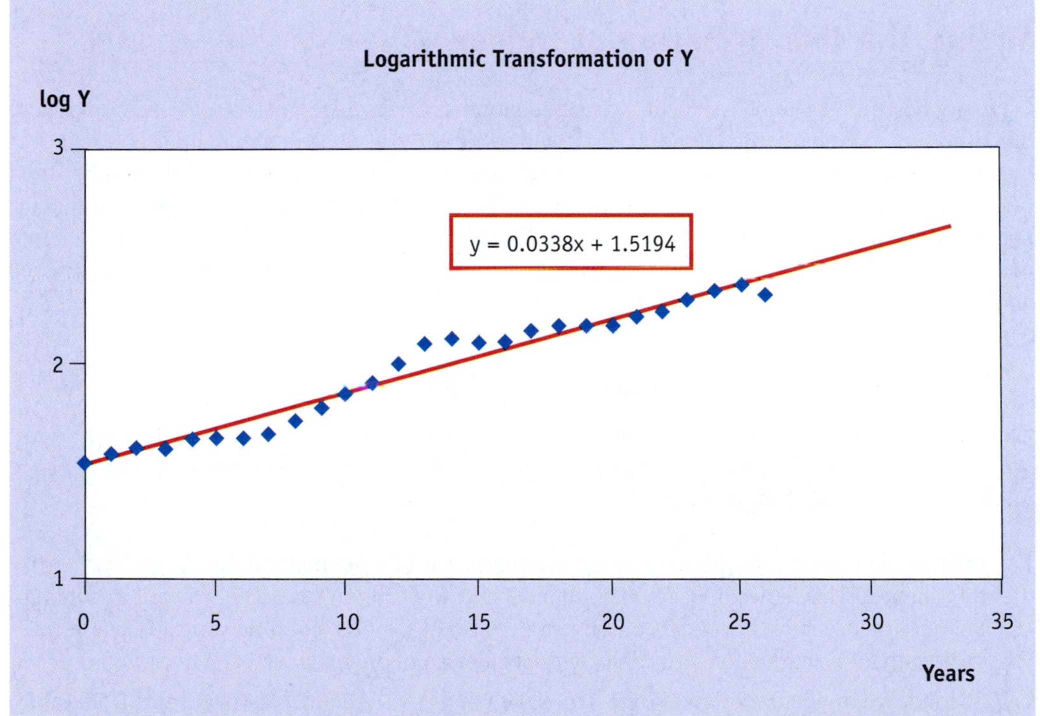

Note: The equation shown here identical to that given in part (b) of Figure 19.11. Accordingly, the forecast for $X = 33$ can be found by entering **=.0338*33+1.5194** into any empty cell, which provides the forecast log Y **=2.6348**. The antilog of that number comes to 431.3 (million passengers), which equals the Part (a) result, except for rounding. The log Y forecast is depicted by a point at the upper right end of the red line in our graph

Application 19.5
Fitting Trends with Logarithms
http://www.harcourtcollege.com/business_stats/kohler/siteresources.html

DEALING WITH SERIAL CORRELATION

We have already noted that time-series data are *unlikely* to be a string of random numbers, each independent of the others. More likely than not, they are serially correlated. In fact, an inspection of (either panel of) Figure 19.11 should make us suspicious. Note how the first three data points lie above their regression line estimates; thus, we have three positive errors (of $Y_X - \hat{Y}_X$) in a row. This string is followed by strings of eight negative errors, nine positive errors, and seven negative errors, which certainly suggests the presence of *positive* serial correlation. Indeed, we can apply what we learned in Chapter 17 and perform the Durbin-Watson test with respect to the data in Table 19.4. If we test the hypothesis H_0: "No serial correlation exists" against the alternative

H_A: "Positive serial correlation exists," we find $d = .44$. If we then consult Appendix Table P for $\alpha = .05$, we find that H_0 should be resoundingly *rejected.*

One common approach to dealing with serial correlation is to compute regressions for time series not with the help of the original data, but on the basis of their *first differences.* In this case, a regression would be derived not on the basis of annual passenger numbers, but of year-to-year changes in these numbers. (Can you see, in Table 19.4 on pages 932–933, how the last column of numbers, now beginning in 1956, would be transformed into the series +4, +2, 0, +4, +1, and so on?) If such first differences are used, first-order serial correlation often disappears, and better forecasts result. (Some analysts even use *second differences* to escape the problem, recording year-to-year changes in the changes!)

19.6 Forecasting and the Use of Seasonal Indexes

On many occasions, business executives and economists want to isolate the seasonal component of a time series rather than its trend. If first-quarter (or winter) sales are typically low, a manager who is aware of this fact will not worry when January sales figures start to slip. If December food prices are typically high, an economist who is aware of this fact will not falsely conclude that inflation is accelerating when the month's price index begins to climb. We will consider two methods of isolating the seasonal component in a time series, the *ratio-to-moving-average method* and the *dummy-variable method.*

THE RATIO-TO-MOVING-AVERAGE METHOD

Consider the quarterly time series given in columns 1 and 2 of Table 19.5 on the following pages. We will show how its seasonal component can be isolated by the **ratio-to-moving-average method,** which involves four steps:

1. First, we construct a 4-quarter moving-averages series by the method introduced earlier in this chapter. This series appears in columns 3 and 4 of Table 19.5 and is viewed as containing only the trend and cyclical component ($T_t \cdot C_t$) of the original time series (because the shorter-than-4-quarter-long seasonal and irregular components have been averaged out).
2. Second, we divide the original time-series data of $Y_t = T_t \cdot C_t \cdot S_t \cdot I_t$ (in column 2 of Table 19.5) by the associated 4-quarter moving averages of $T_t \cdot C_t$ (in column 4), which isolates $S_t \cdot I_t$ (in column 5). Note how, in the summer of 1997, actual sales were $Y_t = 177$, but the average quarterly sales for the 4 quarters centered in midsummer 1997 (and presumably reflecting trend and cyclical factors only) were $T_t \cdot C_t = 143$. At this point, the *ratio* of actual sales *to* the associated *moving-average* sales was 1.24, which accounts for the strange name of this procedure. Thus, actual summer 1997 sales were 1.24 times, or 124 percent of, the level we would expect from trend and cyclical factors alone. The divergence must be attributed to seasonal and irregular factors.
3. Third, we remove the irregular component by grouping, as in Table 19.6 on page 930, all the available actual-to-moving-average sales ratios (from column 5 of Table 19.5) by season and finding an average ratio for each season. That average, which might be the arithmetic mean or the median of the entries found in any given column, is believed to show the "typical" seasonal influence only, free of the irregular component.
4. Fourth, we expect that the quarterly seasonal time-series components, S_t (which we calculated in step 3 and which appear in row A of Table 19.6), will average to 1 over the course of a year; thus, their sum must equal 4. If it does not, we make an appropriate adjustment. In our case, the sum of the row A entries equals 3.925; hence, we multiply each S_t by

TABLE 19.5 | **Avionics Sales of Butler Aviation and the Construction of Seasonal Indexes by the Ratio-to-Moving-Average Method**

Time, t (1)	Actual Units Sold, $Y_t = T_t \cdot C_t \cdot S_t \cdot I_t$ (2)	4-Quarter Moving Average, $T_t \cdot C_t$		Ratio of Actual to Moving-Average Sales, $S_t \cdot I_t$ (5) = (2)/(4)	Seasonal Index, S_t (6)	Deseasonalized Units Sold, $T_t \cdot C_t \cdot I_t$ (7) = (2)/(6)
		Not Adjusted (3)	Adjusted (4)			
1997 Winter	107		—	—	.80	133.75
		—				
Spring	146		—	—	1.00	146
		142				
Summer	177		143	1.24	1.20	147.5
		143				
Fall	139		141	.99	1.00	139
		139				
1998 Winter	108		138	.78	.80	135
		137				
Spring	130		139	.94	1.00	130
		140				
Summer	169		145	1.17	1.20	140.8
		149				
Fall	154		159	.97	1.00	154
		169				
1999 Winter	144		185	.78	.80	180
		200				
Spring	208		215	.97	1.00	208
		229				
Summer	292		239	1.22	1.20	243.3
		249				
Fall	271		257	1.05	1.00	271
		264				
2000 Winter	224		261	.86	.80	280
		257				
Spring	268		247	1.09	1.00	268
		237				
Summer	264		227	1.16	1.20	220
		217				
Fall	191		208	.92	1.00	191
		199				
2001 Winter	146		196	.74	.80	182.5
		192				
Spring	194		195	.99	1.00	194
		198				
Summer	238		204	1.17	1.20	198.3
		210				
Fall	213		219	.97	1.00	213
		227				

(continued)

TABLE 19.5 *(continued)*

Time, t (1)		Actual Units Sold, $Y_t = T_t \cdot C_t \cdot S_t \cdot I_t$ (2)	4-Quarter Moving Average, $T_t \cdot C_t$: Not Adjusted (3)	4-Quarter Moving Average, $T_t \cdot C_t$: Adjusted (4)	Ratio of Actual to Moving-Average Sales, $S_t \cdot I_t$ (5) = (2)/(4)	Seasonal Index, S_t (6)	Deseasonalized Units Sold, $T_t \cdot C_t \cdot I_t$ (7) = (2)/(6)
2002	Winter	194		240	.81	.80	242.5
			253				
	Spring	263		266	.99	1.00	263
			279				
	Summer	340		288	1.18	1.20	283.3
			297				
	Fall	317		310	1.02	1.00	317
			322				
2003	Winter	269		342	.79	.80	336.25
			361				
	Spring	361		380	.95	1.00	361
			398				
	Summer	495		419	1.18	1.20	412.5
			440				
	Fall	466		—	—	1.00	466
			—				
2004	Winter	438		—	—	.80	547.5

TABLE 19.6 | **Calculating Seasonal Indexes from Groupings of Actual-to-Moving-Average Ratios ($S_t \cdot I_t$ data)**

Year	Quarter: Winter	Spring	Summer	Fall
1997	—	—	1.24	.99
1998	.78	.94	1.17	.97
1999	.78	.97	1.22	1.05
2000	.86	1.09	1.16	.92
2001	.74	.99	1.17	.97
2002	.81	.99	1.18	1.02
2003	.79	.95	1.18	—
A. Median Ratio = Unadjusted S_t	.785	.98	1.18	.98
B. Seasonal Index = Adjusted S_t	.80	1.00	1.20	1.00

4/3.925. The result is given in row B. In our example, these **seasonal indexes** indicate that seasonal factors alone typically depress winter sales to 80 percent, but raise summer sales to 120 percent, of the level that could be accounted for by trend, cycle, and irregular factors. Spring and fall sales, on the other hand, are fully explained by those factors and, thus, equal the quarterly average.

DESEASONALIZING DATA

We can divide any original time series by the kind of seasonal indexes found in row B of Table 19.6 to produce a **deseasonalized time series,** also known as a **seasonally adjusted time series.** The seasonal adjustment of the data on avionics sales appears in columns 6 and 7 of Table 19.5. Because the division of $Y_t = T_t \cdot C_t \cdot S_t \cdot I_t$ by S_t produces $T_t \cdot C_t \cdot I_t$, a seasonally adjusted time series is one that contains all influences except the seasonal factor. Thus, the manager of Butler Aviation who sadly contemplates low winter 1997 avionics sales of 107 units (column 1 of Table 19.5) can take comfort in the fact that underlying nonseasonal factors are producing sales of 133.75 units per quarter (column 7 of Table 19.5) and that usual seasonal factors are depressing this number. By the same token, that manager should not be overly elated by the brisk summer 1997 sales of 177 units; the seasonal factor explains almost 17 percent of this, and the underlying nonseasonal factors are producing sales of only 147.5 units per quarter. Figure 19.12 on the next page indicates visually what a different picture a decision maker can get from seasonally adjusted as opposed to original, unadjusted data.

MAKING FORECASTS

Seasonal indexes are ideally suited for making short-term forecasts—for example, of quarterly sales at annual rates.

EXAMPLE PROBLEM 19.8

Consider the quarterly trend equation derived earlier on page 931:

$$\text{Sales} = 182.375 + 11.75X$$

where X is measured in quarters and $X = 0$ is located in the middle of the 1984 winter quarter.

a. On the basis of this equation alone (and rounding to whole numbers), forecast 2006 and 2007 quarterly trend sales (at annual rates).

b. Then make a quarterly forecast that takes seasonality into account by applying the seasonal indexes of Table 19.6.

SOLUTION:

a. See column 4 of Table 19.7 on the next page.

b. See column 5 of Table 19.7 on the next page.

FIGURE 19.12 | Avionics Sales: Unadjusted versus Deseasonalized Data

This graph is based on columns 1, 2, and 7 of Table 19.5 and vividly shows the difference between time series that do and do not contain a seasonal component. The fluctuations of the black line (that represents $Y_t = T_t \cdot C_t \cdot S_t \cdot I_t$) about the red line (that represents Y_t/S_t or $T_t \cdot C_t \cdot I_t$) are accounted for by seasonal factors alone (S_t).

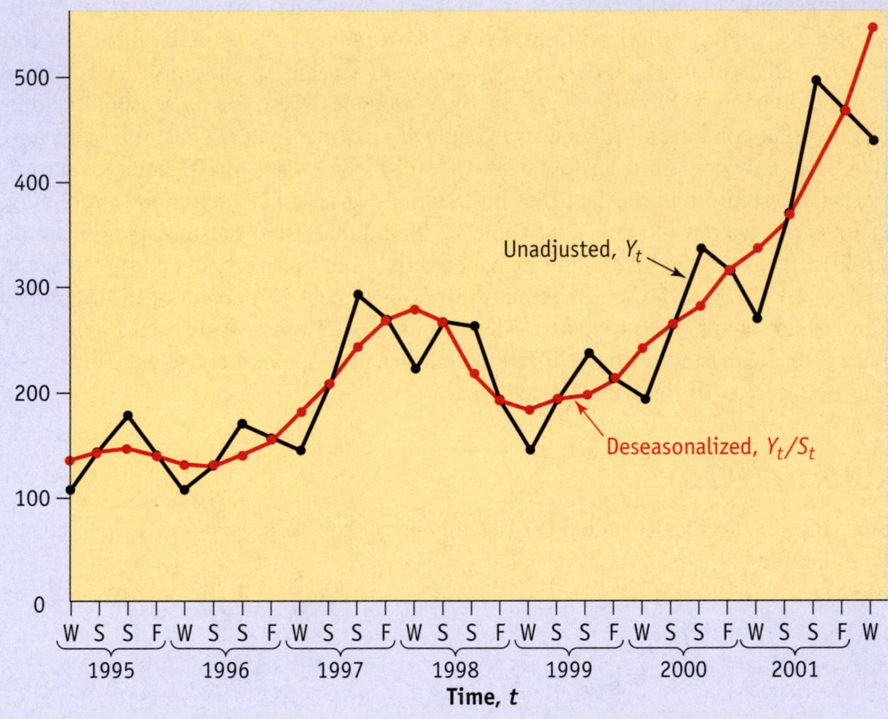

TABLE 19.7 | Making Quarterly Forecasts of Butler Avionics Sales ($X = 0$ at mid-winter 1984)

Time t (1)		X (2)	Seasonal Index (3)	Quarterly Sales Forecast: Trend Only (4)	Quarterly Sales Forecast: Trend/Season (5) = (3) · (4)
2006	Winter	88	.80	1,216	973
	Spring	89	1.00	1,228	1,228
	Summer	90	1.20	1,240	1,488
	Fall	91	1.00	1,252	1,252
2007	Winter	92	.80	1,263	1,010
	Spring	93	1.00	1,275	1,275
	Summer	94	1.20	1,287	1,544
	Fall	95	1.00	1,299	1,299

COMPUTER APPLICATIONS

The ratio-to-moving-average method was introduced in 1922 by Frederick R. Macaulay at the National Bureau of Economic Research. It was then adopted by the U.S. Bureau of the Census in 1954 under the leadership of Julius Shiskin (1912–1978), and is now commonly used worldwide. As a result, the method has found its way into many computer programs. Although the above example has focused on quarterly data, many business and economic applications require monthly data, and computers are often programmed to deseasonalize monthly data in an analogous fashion.

EXCEL Example 19.6

EXCEL is not equipped to deseasonalize data series automatically. Nevertheless, you can use it to do such work, albeit somewhat awkwardly. Enter the column 2, Table 19.5 units-sold data (found on pages 939–940) into a new EXCEL worksheet. Then use EXCEL to derive the column 7 series of deseasonalized units sold.

SOLUTION:

1. Enter the label *Sales* into A1. Then enter the actual sales data into A2 and below. (You can also copy and paste column B of the file HK19MISC.)
   To produce the Table 19.5, column 3 (unadjusted 4-quarter moving-average) data
2. Click **Tools** > **Data Analysis** > **Moving Average** > **OK**
3. In *Input Range*, enter **A2:A30** and clear *Labels in First Row*
4. In *Interval*, enter **4**
5. In *Output Range*, enter **B2:B30**
6. Click **OK**
   To produce the Table 19.5, column 4 (adjusted 4-quarter moving-average) data
7. Enter the label *4-Quarter Moving Average (adj.)* into C1.
8. Select C4 and enter the formula **=AVERAGE(B5:B6)**
9. Select C4 and drag the result to C29
   To produce the Table 19.5, column 5 (ratio of actual to moving-average sales) data
10. Enter the label *Ratio of Actual to Moving-Average Sales* into D1.
11. Select D4 and enter the formula = **A4/C4**
12. Select D4 and drag the result to D29
    To find the Table 19.6 seasonal indexes and produce the Table 19.5, column 6 data
13. Enter the labels *Summer, Fall, Winter, Spring, Sum* into I2:I6
14. Select J2 and enter the formula **=AVERAGE(D4,D8,D12,D16,D20,D24,D28)**
15. Select J2 and drag the result to J5
16. Select J6 and enter the formula **=SUM(J2:J5)**
17. Select K2 and enter the formula **=J2*4/$J$6**
18. Select K2 and drag the result to K6.

Column K now contains the adjusted seasonal indexes:

I	J	K
Summer	1.189666	1.197704
Fall	0.998917	1.005666
Winter	0.795465	0.80084
Spring	0.989106	0.99579
Sum	**3.973154**	**4**

19. Enter the label *Seasonal Index* into E1.

20. Starting with E2, enter successive groups of indexes (.8, 1, 1.2, 1) into the remainder of the column until you reach E30.
To produce the Table 19.5, column 6 (deseasonalized sales) data

21. Enter the label *Deseasonalized Sales* into F1.

22. Select F2 and enter the formula **=A2/E2**

23. Select F2 and drag the result to F30, which provides us with the data sought.

A	B	C	D	E	F
Sales	4-Quarter Moving Average (unadj.)	4-Quarter Moving Average (adj.)	Ratio of Actual to Moving Average Sales	Seasonal Index	Deseasonalized Sales
107	#N/A			0.8	133.75
146	#N/A			1	146
177	#N/A	142.375	1.243196	1.2	147.5
139	142.25	140.5	0.989324	1	139
108	142.5	137.5	0.785455	0.8	135
130	138.5	138.375	0.939476	1	130
169	136.5	144.75	1.16753	1.2	140.8333333
154	140.25	159	0.968553	1	154
144	149.25	184.125	0.782077	0.8	180
208	168.75	214.125	0.971395	1	208
292	199.5	238.75	1.223037	1.2	243.3333333
271	228.75	256.25	1.057561	1	271
224	248.75	260.25	0.860711	0.8	280
268	263.75	246.75	1.08612	1	268
264	256.75	227	1.162996	1.2	220
191	236.75	208	0.918269	1	191
146	217.25	195.5	0.746803	0.8	182.5
194	198.75	195	0.994872	1	194
238	192.25	203.75	1.168098	1.2	198.3333333
213	197.75	218.375	0.975386	1	213
194	209.75	239.75	0.809176	0.8	242.5
263	227	265.5	0.990584	1	263

340	252.5	287.875	1.181068	1.2	283.3333333
317	278.5	309.5	1.024233	1	317
269	297.25	341.125	0.788567	0.8	336.25
361	321.75	379.125	0.952193	1	361
495	360.5	418.875	1.181737	1.2	412.5
466	397.75	440	1.059091	1	466
438	440			0.8	547.5

THE DUMMY-VARIABLE METHOD

On occasion, we may wish to estimate a multiple regression equation that takes the seasonal factor into account. For a quarterly time series such as the one in Table 19.5, the equation might take the form

$$\hat{Y}_t = a + b_1 t + c_1 Q_1 + c_2 Q_2 + c_3 Q_3$$

where Q_1, Q_2, and Q_3 are dummies equal to 1 if t is the first, second, or third quarter, respectively; they are equal to 0 otherwise. Note that for a fourth-quarter observation, $\hat{Y}_t = a + b_1 t$, while for a first (or second or third) quarter observation it equals $\hat{Y}_t = a + b_1 t + c_1$ (or c_2 or c_3). Thus, c_1, c_2, or c_3, respectively, gives the difference in the expected value of the time series between the fourth quarter on the one hand and the first, second, or third quarter on the other, and these coefficients can be used to represent the seasonal variation.

CAUTION

In this model, the seasonal effects are *added* to the linear trend of $a + b_1 t$; thus, the model differs from the classical multiplicative model. In addition, any performance of such a multiple regression in the presence of a likely violation of crucial assumptions can lead to absurd results.

19.7 Forecasting and Barometric Indicators

Many forecasters make use of qualitative indicators of business and economic conditions, known as **barometric indicators.** These include (1) the results of anticipatory surveys and (2) leading economic indicators.

ANTICIPATORY SURVEYS

A number of agencies make forecasts by the eminently sensible method of *asking* the economic actors involved about their intentions. Several anticipatory surveys of households, businesses, or governments are conducted on a regular basis to determine economic intentions. The Survey Research Center of the University of Michigan, for instance, develops quarterly data on consumer spending plans. The U.S. Department of Commerce, together with the Securities and Exchange Commission, produces surveys on business investment plans; so do the McGraw-Hill Publishing Company, *Fortune* magazine, and others. The oldest of these surveys, the Railroad Shippers' Forecast, has provided data on quarterly anticipated carloadings, differentiated by commodities, ever since 1927.

BUSINESS-CYCLE INDICATORS

Many economic time series behave in a predictable fashion near the turning points of the business cycle, which makes them extremely useful for forecasting purposes. Originally, such series were collected and studied systematically at the National Bureau of Economic Research (by such researchers as Wesley C. Mitchell, Arthur F. Burns, Geoffrey H. Moore, and Julius Shiskin), and the bureau still follows the behavior of many hundreds of monthly and quarterly series. The National Bureau's detailed examination of the behavior of time series (many of which were 100 years long or even longer) led to an important discovery. Some economic time series, which are now called **leading economic indicators,** anticipate business-cycle turns. They turn down just before the GDP reaches its cyclical peak and turn up just before it reaches its trough. Other series, known as **coincident economic indicators,** precisely coincide with the business cycle. They turn down at the GDP peak and up at its trough. Still other series, called **lagging economic indicators,** lag behind the cyclical turns. They turn down only after the GDP has begun its cyclical decline, while turning up only after the GDP has begun to rise.

For decades, the Bureau of Economic Analysis of the U.S. Department of Commerce published these indicators monthly, along with several hundred time series of interest to economic analysts and forecasters. In 1995, however, in a cost-saving move hailed as the first privatization of a government statistical series, the Commerce Department bid farewell to the economic forecasting business. It picked the Conference Board, a leading business-research organization, to disseminate its business-cycle indicators. You can find them at its Web site, http://www.conference-board.org, from which the Table 19.8 list of currently used indicators has been derived.

Table 19.8 contains the so-called short list of business-cycle indicators. However, despite many historical successes, that list is not totally reliable and, therefore, subject to revision. For example, in 1952 and again in 1962 and 1995, the leading indicators turned down, but the economy did not follow. Nor did they predict the recession of the early 1990s. In addition, there are times when some leading indicators point to a change, while others do not. To deal with that situation, a **diffusion index** is published for each category of indicators in Table 19.8. The diffusion index for the 10 leading indicators, for example, equals the percentage of these indicators that have increased in a given month. Thus, the index lies between 0 and 100. If 8 of these indicators are higher this month than last month, the diffusion index is (8/10)100, or 80 (percent). Other such indexes, covering the previous six months, are published as well.

TABLE 19.8 | The Year 2000 Short List of Business-Cycle Indicators

Leading Indicators
Average weekly hours, production workers, manufacturing
Average weekly initial claims for unemployment insurance
Manufacturers' new orders for consumer goods and materials, 1996 dollars
Vendor performance, percentage of companies receiving slower deliveries
Manufacturers' new orders, nondefense capital goods, 1996 dollars
Building permits, new private housing units, index: 1967 = 100
Stock prices, 500 common stocks, index: 1941–1943 = 10
Money supply (M2), 1996 dollars
Interest rate spread, 10-year Treasury bonds less federal funds rate
Index of consumer expectations, University of Michigan, 1966: I = 100
Coincident Indicators
Employees on nonagricultural payrolls
Personal income less transfer payments, 1996 dollars
Industrial production, total, index: 1987 = 100
Manufacturing and trade sales, 1996 dollars
Lagging Indicators
Average duration of unemployment, weeks
Inventories-to-sales ratio, manufacturing and trade
Labor cost per unit of output, manufacturing, percentage change
Average prime rate charged by banks
Commercial and industrial loans outstanding, 1996 dollars
Consumer installment credit to personal income ratio
Consumer price index for services, percentage change

SOURCE: http://www.tcb-indicators.org/lei/component_description.htm

Summary

1. All economic organizations must plan for the future. Inevitably, this planning requires the making of predictions that, in turn, are linked to experiences gained and data gathered in the past. Most business and economic data are either *cross-section data,* which come from different populations observed at the same time, or *time-series data,* which come from the same population observed at different times. This chapter's *time-series analysis* employs time-series data for the purpose of explaining past or forecasting future events.
2. The *classical time-series model* attempts to explain the pattern observed in an actual time series by the presence of four components: trend, cyclical, seasonal, and irregular. The *trend component, T,* is a relatively smooth, progressively upward or downward movement of a variable over an extended period of time. The *cyclical component, C,* is evidenced by up-and-down swings of a variable around its trend, with the swings typically lasting from one to several years each and differing in length and amplitude from one cycle to the next. The *seasonal component, S,* is evidenced by narrow up-and-down swings of a variable around its trend/cyclical components, with the swings predictably repeating each other within periods of one year or less. The *irregular component, I,* finally, adds random movements to all of the above. Because the classical model expresses the actual time-series value, *Y,* as the product of the four components just noted (making $Y = T \cdot C \cdot S \cdot I$), this model is a *multiplicative* time-series model.
3. Business and economic forecasting is making statements about unknown, uncertain, and, typically, future events. Many such statements are derived with the help of time-series data. The trend component is often considered the most valuable forecasting tool, especially for long-term projections. The trend can be estimated in a variety of ways, one favorite being the construction of a *moving-averages series* by successively averaging overlapping groups of two or more consecutive values in a time series and replacing the central value in each group by the group's average.
4. A second method of trend construction involves the employment of single or multiple-parameter *exponential-smoothing techniques.* They produce self-correcting forecasts in the form of weighted averages of all past time-series values, with weights decreasing exponentially as one goes back in time.
5. A third method of trend construction involves the fitting of least-squares linear or curvilinear regression lines, which can be problematic because of serial correlation.
6. On many occasions, especially when short-term forecasts are desired, business executives and economists are interested in isolating not the trend, but the seasonal component of a time series. Two favorite approaches are (1) the *ratio-to-moving-average method* that leads to the computation of seasonal indexes and (2) the computation of a multiple regression equation in which dummy variables represent the seasonal factor.
7. Many forecasters make use of qualitative *barometric indicators;* these include the results of *anticipatory surveys* (for example, of consumer spending plans) and a variety of *leading economic indicators* (time series that have been found to anticipate business-cycle turning points).

Key Terms

additive time-series model
barometric indicators
classical time-series model
coincident economic indicators
cross-section data
cyclical component
deseasonalized time series
diffusion index
exponential smoothing
extrapolation
forecasting
irregular component
lagging economic indicators
leading economic indicators
longitudinal data
mixed time-series model
moving-averages series
multiplicative time-series model
ratio-to-moving-average method
seasonal component
seasonal indexes
seasonally adjusted time series
single-parameter exponential smoothing
Slutsky-Yule effect
smoothing constant
smoothing technique
three-parameter exponential smoothing
time-series analysis
time-series data
trend component
two-parameter exponential smoothing

Practice Problems

NOTE

Some problems require the use of a statistical program, EXCEL or MINITAB. The program's major features are explained in text Chapter 2; plenty of additional advice is available via the program's built-in Help feature.

SECTION 19.2 THE COMPOSITION OF A TIME SERIES

1. An analyst has put together the data given in Table 19.9. Assuming the classical multiplicative time-series model applies,

a. find the missing values.

b. explain how you found them.

TABLE 19.9 | Analysis of Recent Avionics Sales, Butler Aviation

Quarter, t	Actual Sales, Y_t	Trend Component, T_t	Cyclical Component, C_t	Seasonal Component, S_t	Irregular Component, I_t
Winter	$93,060	$50,000	.99	2.00	
Spring		55,000	.95	.50	1.02
Summer	22,344	60,000	.95		.98
Fall	69,998.5	65,000		1.10	1.10

2. An analyst has put together the data given in Table 19.10. Assuming the classical multiplicative time-series model applies,

a. find the missing values.

b. explain how you found them.

TABLE 19.10 | Analysis of Recent Tax Receipts, U.S. Government

Quarter, t	Tax Receipts (billions), Y_t	Trend Component (billions), T_t	Cyclical Component, C_t	Seasonal Component, S_t	Irregular Component, I_t
Winter	$75	$80		.8	1.1
Spring	82	85		1.1	.9
Summer	110			.9	1.0
Fall		95	1.1		.8

3. An analyst has put together the data given in Table 19.11. Assuming the classical multiplicative time-series model applies,

   a. find the missing values.

   b. explain how you found them.

TABLE 19.11 | Analysis of Current Liabilities, Butler Aviation

Quarter, t	Average Daily Debt, Y_t	Trend Component, T_t	Cyclical Component, C_t	Seasonal Component, S_t	Irregular Component, I_t
Winter	$193,000	$190,000	1.00	.9	
Spring	256,000	240,000	.95	1.0	
Summer	312,000	290,000	.90		
Fall			.85	1.0	1.700

4. An analyst has put together the data given in Table 19.12. Assuming the classical multiplicative time-series model applies,

   a. find the missing values.

   b. explain how you found them.

TABLE 19.12 | Analysis of Recent Net Profits, Butler Aviation

Quarter, t	Net Profits, Y_t	Trend Component, T_t	Cyclical Component, C_t	Seasonal Component, S_t	Irregular Component, I_t
Winter	$233,987	$200,000	.99	2.00	
Spring		250,000	.95	.50	1.02
Summer	257,123				.98
Fall	299,387	350,000		1.10	1.10

5. An analyst has put together the data given in Table 19.13. Assuming the classical multiplicative time-series model applies,

   a. find the missing values.

   b. explain how you found them.

6. An analyst has put together the data given in Table 19.14. Assuming the classical multiplicative time-series model applies,

   a. find the missing values.

   b. explain how you found them.

7. An analyst has put together the data given in Table 19.15. Assuming the classical multiplicative time-series model applies,

   a. find the missing values.

   b. explain how you found them.

TABLE 19.13 | Analysis of Recent Food Stamp Expenditures, U.S. Government

Quarter, t	Expenditures (billions), Y_t	Trend Component (billions), T_t	Cyclical Component, C_t	Seasonal Component, S_t	Irregular Component, I_t
Winter	$75	$80		1.3	1.1
Spring	82			1.1	.9
Summer	110	90		.9	1.0
Fall		95	1.1		.8

TABLE 19.14 | Analysis of Accounts Receivable, Butler Aviation

Quarter, t	Average Daily Accounts Receivable, Y_t	Trend Component, T_t	Cyclical Component, C_t	Seasonal Component, S_t	Irregular Component, I_t
Winter		$290,000	1.00	.9	3.477
Spring		280,000	.95	1.5	2.900
Summer		270,000	.90		1.999
Fall			.85	.6	1.700

TABLE 19.15 | Analysis of Accounts Payable, Butler Aviation

Quarter, t	Average Daily Accounts Payable, Y_t	Trend Component, T_t	Cyclical Component, C_t	Seasonal Component, S_t	Irregular Component, I_t
Winter	$34,789		1.00	.9	.477
Spring	56,980		.95	1.5	.900
Summer	33,237		.90		.999
Fall	76,895		.85	.6	.700

8. An analyst has put together the data given in Table 19.16 on the next page. Assuming the classical multiplicative time-series model applies,

a. find the missing values.

b. explain how you found them.

TABLE 19.16 | Analysis of Wage Bill, Butler Aviation

Quarter, t	Average Daily Wage Bill, Y_t	Trend Component, T_t	Cyclical Component, C_t	Seasonal Component, S_t	Irregular Component, I_t
Winter	$55,789	$50,000	1.00	1.00	
Spring	45,678	60,000	.95	.75	
Summer	34,890	70,000	.70	.75	
Fall	89,677	80,000	.55	1.50	

9. An analyst has put together the data given in Table 19.17. Assuming the classical multiplicative time-series model applies,

a. find the missing values.

b. explain how you found them.

TABLE 19.17 | Analysis of Exports, Butler Aviation

Quarter, t	Exports (millions), Y_t	Trend Component (millions), T_t	Cyclical Component, C_t	Seasonal Component, S_t	Irregular Component, I_t
Winter	$55.7	$50		1.00	1.2
Spring	45.7	60		.25	1.0
Summer	34.9	70		.75	.7
Fall	89.9	80		2.00	1.9

10. An analyst has put together the data given in Table 19.18. Assuming the classical multiplicative time-series model applies,

a. find the missing values.

b. explain how you found them.

TABLE 19.18 | Analysis of Internet Sales, Butler Aviation

Quarter, t	Internet Sales (millions), Y_t	Trend Component (millions), T_t	Cyclical Component, C_t	Seasonal Component, S_t	Irregular Component, I_t
Winter	$55.7	$50	1.0	1.00	
Spring	75.7	60	1.2	.25	
Summer	84.9	70	1.4	.75	
Fall	99.9	80	1.6	2.00	

SECTION 19.3 FORECASTING AND MOVING AVERAGES

11. The following time series represents the U.S. gross federal debt at the end of fiscal years 1939–2000 (in billions of dollars):

48.2–50.7–57.5–79.2–142.6–204.1–260.1–271.0–257.1–252.0–252.6–256.9–255.3–259.1–266.0–270.8–274.4–272.7–272.3–279.7–287.5–290.5–292.6–302.9–310.3–316.1–322.3–328.5–340.4–368.7–365.8–380.9–408.2–435.9–466.3–483.9–541.9–629.0–706.4–776.6–829.5–909.1–994.8–1,137.3–1,371.7–1,564.7–1,817.5–2,120.6–2,346.1–2,601.3–2,868.0–3,206.6–3,598.5–4,002.1–4,351.4–4,643.7–4,921.0–5,181.9–5,369.7–5,478.7–5,614.9–5,711.4

a. Estimate the trend in the form of a 5-year moving-averages series.

b. On the basis of the slope of the trend line between the last two numbers estimated in (a), forecast the U.S. gross federal debt at the end of fiscal 2001.

12. Using the data of Practice Problem 11, let a computer

a. make a forecast for 2001 based on 5-year moving averages.

b. create a plot of the original data and the 5-year moving averages.

13. Using the data of Practice Problem 11,

a. estimate the trend in the form of a 10-year moving-averages series.

b. on the basis of the slope of the trend line between the last two numbers estimated in (a), forecast the U.S. gross federal debt at the end of fiscal 2001.

14. Using the data of Practice Problem 11, let a computer

a. make a forecast for 2001 based on 10-year moving averages.

b. create a plot of the original data and the 10-year moving averages.

15. The following time series represents new U.S. (farm and nonfarm) housing units started in 1959–1998 (in thousands):

1,517.0–1,252.2–1,313.0–1,462.9–1,603.2–1,528.8–1,472.8–1,164.9–1,291.6–1,507.6–1,466.8–1,433.6–2,052.2–2,356.6–2,045.3–1,337.7–1,160.4–1,537.5–1,987.1–2,020.3–1,745.1–1,292.2–1,084.2–1,062.2–1,703.0–1,741.8–1,805.4–1,620.5–1,488.1–1,376.1–1,192.7–1,013.9–1,199.7–1,287.6–1,457.0–1,354.1–1,476.8–1,474.0–1,615.6

a. Estimate the trend in the form of a 3-year moving-averages series.

b. On the basis of the slope of the trend line between the last two numbers estimated in (a), forecast the U.S. housing starts in 2004.

16. Using the data of Practice Problem 15, let a computer

a. make a forecast for 2004 based on 3-year moving averages.

b. create a plot of the original data and the 3-year moving averages.

17. Using the data of Practice Problem 15,

a. estimate the trend in the form of a 6-year moving-averages series.

b. on the basis of the slope of the trend line between the last two numbers estimated in (a), forecast the U.S. housing starts in 2004.

18. Using the data of Practice Problem 15, let a computer

a. make a forecast for 2004 based on 6-year moving averages.

b. create a plot of the original data and the 6-year moving averages.

19. The following time series represents U.S. corporate tax liabilities from 1959 to 1997 (in billions of dollars):

23.6–22.7–22.8–24.0–26.2–28.0–30.9–33.7–32.7–39.4–39.7–34.4–37.7–41.9–49.3–51.8–50.9–64.2–73.0–83.5–88.0–84.8–81.1–63.1–77.2–94.0–96.5–106.5–127.1–137.0–141.3–140.5–133.4–143.0–165.2–186.6–211.0–226.1–246.1

a. Estimate the trend in the form of a 7-year moving-averages series.

b. On the basis of the slope of the trend line between the last two numbers estimated in (a), forecast corporate taxes in 2004.

c. Let the computer create an automatic plot of the original data and 7-year moving averages.

20. The following time series represents the net-profit-to-equity ratio for all U.S. manufacturing corporations from 1947-1997 (in percent):

15.6–16.0–11.6–15.4–12.1–10.3–10.5–9.9–12.6–12.3–10.9–8.6–10.4–9.2–8.9–9.8–10.3–11.6–13.0–13.4–11.7–12.1–11.5–9.3–9.7–10.6–12.8–14.9–11.6–13.9–14.2–15.0–16.4–13.9–13.6–9.2–10.6–12.5–10.1–9.5–12.8–16.1–13.5–10.6–6.2–2.1–8.0–15.8–16.0–16.7–16.7

a. Estimate the trend in the form of a 7-year moving-averages series.

b. On the basis of the slope of the trend line between the last two numbers estimated in (a), forecast the ratio in 2004.

c. Let the computer create an automatic plot of the original data and 7-year moving averages.

Section 19.4 Forecasting and Exponential Smoothing

21. Review the corporate tax liability data of Practice Problem 19. Let a computer apply single-parameter exponential smoothing and make a forecast for 2004, given $\alpha = .5$.

22. Review the corporate tax liability data of Practice Problem 19. Let a computer apply single-parameter exponential smoothing and make a forecast for 2004 with an optimal α that minimizes forecasting errors. (According to MINITAB, forecast errors in this example are minimized by using an α value of 1.71423. In EXCEL, which does not allow α values of 1 or above, and hence does not allow damping factors of 0 or below, use $\alpha = .99$.)

23. Review the net-profit-to-equity data of Practice Problem 20. Let a computer apply single-parameter exponential smoothing and make a forecast for 2004, given $\alpha = .5$.

24. Review the net-profit-to-equity data of Practice Problem 20. Let a computer apply single-parameter exponential smoothing and make a forecast for 2004 with an optimal α that minimizes forecasting errors. (According to MINITAB, forecast errors in this example are minimized by using an α value of 1.09396. In EXCEL, which does not allow α values of 1 or above, and hence does not allow damping factors of 0 or below, use $\alpha = .99$.)

25. The following time series represents the New York Stock Exchange Composite Index for 1956–1998 (December 31, 1965 = 50):

24.40–23.67–24.56–30.73–30.01–35.37–33.49–37.51–43.76–47.39–46.15–50.77–55.37–54.67–45.72–54.22–60.29–57.42–43.84–45.73–54.46–53.69–53.70–58.32–68.10–74.02–68.93–92.63–92.46–108.09–136.00–161.70–149.91–180.02–183.46–206.33–229.01–249.58–254.12–291.15–358.17–456.54–550.26

Let a computer apply single-parameter exponential smoothing and make a forecast for 2004,

a. given $\alpha = .5$.

b. given an optimal α that minimizes forecasting errors. (According to MINITAB, forecast errors in this example are minimized by using an α value of 1.54138. In EXCEL, which does not allow α values of 1 or above, and hence does not allow damping factors of 0 or below, use $\alpha = .99$.)

26. Review the corporate tax liability data of Practice Problem 19. Let a computer apply two-parameter exponential smoothing and make a forecast for 2004, given $\alpha = .5$ and $\gamma = .3$.

27. Review the corporate tax liability data of Practice Problem 19. Let a computer apply two-parameter exponential smoothing and make a forecast for 2004 with an optimal set of α and γ that minimizes forecasting errors. (According to MINITAB, forecast errors in this example are minimized by using $\alpha = 1.47898$ and $\gamma = .12446$. You can use the same values in EXCEL, HKStat, Sheet 45.)

28. Review the net-profit-to-equity data of Practice Problem 20. Let a computer apply two-parameter exponential smoothing and make a forecast for 2004, given $\alpha = .5$ and $\gamma = .3$.

29. Review the net-profit-to-equity data of Practice Problem 20. Let a computer apply two-parameter exponential smoothing and make a forecast for 2004 with an optimal set of α and γ that minimizes forecasting errors. (According to MINITAB, forecast errors in this example are minimized by using $\alpha = 1.08549$ and $\gamma = .01$. You can use the same values in EXCEL, HKStat, Sheet 45.)

30. Review the stock index data of Practice Problem 25. Let a computer apply two-parameter exponential smoothing and make a forecast for 2004,

a. given $\alpha = .5$ and $\gamma = .3$.

b. with an optimal set of α and γ that minimizes forecasting errors. (According to MINITAB, forecast errors in this example are minimized by using $\alpha = .925996$ and $\gamma = .825073$. You can use the same values in EXCEL, HKStat, Sheet 45.)

Section 19.5 Forecasting and Least-Squares Regression

31. The following time series represents the U.S. index of net business formation during 1955–1994 (1967 = 100):

96.6–94.6–90.3–90.2–97.9–94.5–90.8–92.6–94.4–98.2–99.8–99.3–100–108.3–115.8–108.8–111.1–119.3–119.1–113.2–109.9–120.4–130.8–138.1–138.3–129.9–124.8–116.4–117.5–121.3–120.9–120.4–121.2–124.1–124.8–120.7–115.2–116.3–121.1–125.5

Using your computer as necessary,

a. develop a linear regression equation of net business formation versus time, X, letting $X = 0$ stand for mid-1955.

b. depict the regression equation for the two variables in a scatter diagram.

c. make forecasts of net business formation for the years 1995–2000 (because the series was discontinued in 1995).

32. The following time series represents the Dow Jones industrial average of common stock prices for 1956–1998:

493.01–475.71–491.66–632.12–618.04–691.55–639.76–714.81–834.05–910.88–873.60–879.12–906.00–876.72–753.19–884.76–950.71–923.88–759.37–802.49–974.92–894.63–820.23–844.40–891.41–932.92–884.36–1,190.34–1,178.48–1,328.23–1,792.76–2,275.99–2,060.82–2,508.91–2,678.94–2,929.33–3,284.29–3,522.06–3,793.77–4,493.76–5,742.89–7,441.15–8,625.52

Using your computer as necessary,

a. develop a linear regression equation of the Dow versus time, X, letting $X = 0$ stand for mid-1956.

b. depict the regression equation for the two variables in a scatter diagram.

c. make forecasts of the Dow for 1999–2004.

33. The scatter diagram developed in Practice Problem 32 certainly does not suggest a linear relationship between the Dow and time. Accordingly, the linear regression line indicates a bad fit. In an effort to do better, repeat the exercise and

a. develop a linear regression equation of the *logarithm* of the Dow versus time, X, letting $X = 0$ stand for mid-1956.

b. depict the regression equation for the two variables in a scatter diagram.

c. make forecasts of the Dow for 1999–2004.

34. The following time series represents the U.S. real gross private domestic investment for 1959-1998 (in billions of 1992 dollars):

271.7–270.5–267.6–302.1–321.6–348.3–397.2–430.6–411.8–433.3–458.3–426.1–474.9–531.8–595.5–546.5–446.6–537.4–622.1–693.4–709.7–628.3–686.0–587.2–642.1–833.4–823.8–811.8–821.5–828.2–863.5–815.0–738.1–790.4–863.6–975.7–996.1–1,084.1–1,206.4–1,329.4

Using your computer as necessary,

a. develop a linear regression equation of real gross private domestic investment versus time, X, letting $X = 0$ stand for mid-1959.

b. depict the regression equation for the two variables in a scatter diagram.

c. make forecasts of the variable for 1999–2004.

35. The following time series represents the U.S. real exports of goods and services for 1959–1998 (in billions of 1992 dollars):

71.9–86.8–88.3–93.0–100.0–113.3–115.6–123.4–126.1–135.3–142.7–158.1–159.2–172.0–209.6–229.8–228.2–241.6–247.4–273.1–299.0–331.4–335.3–311.4–303.3–328.4–337.3–362.2–402.0–465.8–520.2–564.4–599.9–639.4–658.2–712.4–792.6–860.0–970.0–976.2

Using your computer as necessary,

a. develop a linear regression equation of real exports versus time, X, letting $X = 0$ stand for mid-1959.

b. depict the regression equation for the two variables in a scatter diagram.

c. make forecasts of the variable for 1999–2004.

36. Review Practice Problem 11. Using the data about the U.S. gross federal debt at the end of fiscal years 1939–2000,

a. develop a linear regression equation of debt versus time, X, letting $X = 0$ stand for mid-1939.

b. depict the regression equation for the two variables in a scatter diagram.

c. make a forecast of the variable for the end of fiscal year 2001.

37. Review Practice Problem 15. Using the data about U.S. (farm and nonfarm) housing starts in 1959–1998,

a. develop a linear regression equation of housing starts versus time, X, letting $X = 0$ stand for mid-1959.

b. depict the regression equation for the two variables in a scatter diagram.

c. make a forecast of the variable for 2004.

38. Review Practice Problem 19. Using the data about U.S. corporate tax liabilities from 1959–1997,

a. develop a linear regression equation of corporate taxes versus time, X, letting $X = 0$ stand for mid-1959.

b. depict the regression equation for the two variables in a scatter diagram.

c. make a forecast of the variable for 2004.

39. Review Practice Problem 20. Using the data about the net-profit-to-equity ratio for all U.S. manufacturing corporations from 1947–1997,

a. develop a linear regression equation of the ratio versus time, X, letting $X = 0$ stand for mid-1947.

b. depict the regression equation for the two variables in a scatter diagram.

c. make a forecast of the variable for 2004.

40. Review Practice Problem 25. Using the data about the New York Stock Exchange Composite Index for 1956–1998,

a. develop a linear regression equation of the stock price index versus time, X, letting $X = 0$ stand for mid-1956.

b. depict the regression equation for the two variables in a scatter diagram.

c. make a forecast of the variable for 2004.

41. Figure 19.10 on page 929 gives an annual trend equation. Convert it to a monthly equation (that gives month-to-month trend sales at annual rates).

42. The answer to Practice Problem 31 contains the following annual trend equation:

$$\text{Net Business Formation Index} = 94.085 + .9346X \quad (\text{with } X = 0 \text{ at mid-1955})$$

Convert it to a monthly equation (that gives month-to-month trend business formations at annual rates).

43. The answer to Practice Problem 34 contains the following annual trend equation:

$$\text{GPDI} = 230.24 + 21.297X \quad (\text{with } X = 0 \text{ at mid-1959})$$

Convert it to a quarterly equation (that gives quarter-to-quarter trend investment at annual rates).

44. The answer to Practice Problem 35 contains the following annual trend equation:

$$\text{Exports} = -47.68 + 20.246X \quad (\text{with } X = 0 \text{ at mid-1959})$$

Convert it to a quarterly equation (that gives quarter-to-quarter trend exports at annual rates).

45. A look at the scatter diagrams produced in many of the preceding practice problems suggests that linear regression analysis (and subsequent forecasts based thereon) may well have been inappropriate due to the likely presence of *serial correlation.* Conduct an appropriate test with respect to

a. the net business formation data of Practice Problem 31.

b. the Dow Jones stock index data of Practice Problem 32.

46. A look at the scatter diagrams produced in many of the preceding practice problems suggests that linear regression analysis (and subsequent forecasts based thereon) may well have been inappropriate due to the likely presence of *serial correlation.* Conduct an appropriate test with respect to

a. the gross private domestic investment data of Practice Problem 34.

b. the export data of Practice Problem 35.

47. A look at the scatter diagrams produced in many of the preceding practice problems suggests that linear regression analysis (and subsequent forecasts based thereon) may well have been inappropriate due to the likely presence of *serial correlation.* Conduct an appropriate test with respect to

a. the federal debt data of Practice Problem 36.

b. the corporate tax data of Practice Problem 38.

48. A look at the scatter diagrams produced in many of the preceding practice problems suggests that linear regression analysis (and subsequent forecasts based thereon) may well have been inappropriate due to the likely presence of *serial correlation.* Conduct an appropriate test with respect to the New York Stock Exchange data of Practice Problem 40.

Section 19.6 Forecasting and the Use of Seasonal Indexes

49. Table 19.19 gives average weekly carloadings of all commodities carried by major U.S. railroads. Determine a set of monthly seasonal indexes. (Normally, these would be determined from a considerably larger set of data, but this is only an exercise.)

50. Table 19.20 shows the monthly demand for electricity at a power station. Determine a set of monthly seasonal indexes. (Normally, these would be determined from a considerably larger set of data, but this is only an exercise.)

TABLE 19.19 | Average Weekly Carloadings (thousands)

Month	Year 1999	2000	2001
January	392	426	410
February	407	439	437
March	584	457	456
April	478	442	382
May	494	435	385
June	611	450	424
July	446	387	411
August	476	434	439
September	476	436	435
October	488	454	441
November	459	439	403
December	399	410	360

TABLE 19.20 | Monthly Electricity Demand (megawatts)

Month	Year 1999	2000	2001
January	65	73	83
February	66	74	83
March	66	75	85
April	65	72	81
May	63	70	78
June	60	69	75
July	69	77	88
August	70	79	88
September	70	80	93
October	65	78	90
November	66	76	87
December	73	81	85

Chapter 20

INDEX NUMBERS

LOOKING AHEAD

After reading this chapter, you will know a great deal about price indexes and quantity indexes, both of which are commonly used in business and economics. Among other things, you will learn to:

1. construct *simple price indexes* that compare the price of a single item at one time or place with the price of the same item at another time or place,
2. construct *composite price indexes* that compare entire sets of prices for a variety of items at one time or place with sets for the same items at another time or place,
3. distinguish between unweighted and weighted composite price indexes and construct unweighted averages of simple price indexes, unweighted aggregative price indexes, and weighted aggregative price indexes developed by Laspeyres, Paasche, and others,
4. appreciate the *index-number problem,* which is the most serious flaw of most index numbers,
5. administer Fisher's price index quality tests and construct Fisher's own *ideal price index,*
6. manipulate series of price index numbers by shifting their base, splicing, combining, and chaining them,
7. use major U.S. price index series—including the Consumer Price Index, the Producer Price Index, various stock price indexes, and the implicit GDP deflator—for such purposes as evaluating economic policy, deflating current-dollar series into constant-dollar series, and more,
8. understand the nature and construction of *quantity* indexes, such as the Federal Reserve index of industrial production, and
9. refrain from index-number construction when the task cannot possibly succeed—a lesson exemplified by a case study of the United Nations *human development index.*

AND HERE IS A TYPICAL PROBLEM YOU WILL BE ABLE TO SOLVE:

Seen in a 1998 newspaper:

a. "For Sale 1960 Cadillac. $100 (1960 dollars)." What was the car's current-dollar price?

b. "For Sale 1970 Piper Cherokee. $12,000 (1970 dollars)." What was the plane's current-dollar price?

PREVIEW

We can highlight the subject matter of this chapter neatly with the help of two historical examples. The first of these features the use of price indexes; the second illustrates the role of quantity indexes.

Case 1: In the autumn of 1992, during the waning weeks of the U.S. presidential election campaign, the Republicans asked voters to give them "four more years." They pointed with pride to the Reagan–Bush years, during which average weekly earnings of workers in private nonagricultural industries had risen from $235.10 in 1980 to $354.66 in 1991. Before long, however, supporters of Democratic challenger Bill Clinton trailed incumbent President Bush with signs reading "four more months." As they saw it, the 50 percent rise in nominal wages during the Reagan–Bush years had been more than negated by higher prices that workers had to pay for the goods they bought; therefore, it was time for a change.

Looking back in 1992, anyone who surveyed the prices of consumer goods during the 1980s could easily point out many examples of rising prices. Such a person, however, encountered just as many individual prices that had stayed the same or even fallen. Finding a trustworthy answer to the question of whether Americans had become better or worse off during the Reagan–Bush years, therefore, involved the difficult task of creating a meaningful indicator or *index* of what *average* prices had done. This chapter introduces methods to accomplish this type of goal.

Indeed, if we create a consumer price index for urban wage and clerical workers and then apply it to the dollar figures noted above, the Democrats are vindicated. Measured in dollars of 1982 purchasing power, the average weekly earnings of U.S. workers in private nonagricultural industries *fell* from $274.65 in 1980 to $255.89 in 1991.

Case 2: Now envision the presidential campaign of 1960 when the Cold War was in full swing. The Soviets, under Nikita Khrushchev, had recently launched *Sputnik,* the first artificial earth satellite. Similar U.S. attempts had failed. The Soviet economy, measured by the aggregate of commodities and services produced each year, seemed to grow by leaps and bounds. The U.S. economy was mired in a recession. Khrushchev promised "to bury the United States," not in a hail of nuclear bombs, but by outproducing her in everything and making the Soviet Union a magnet to which people from all over the world would flock. Economists asked: How large was the Soviet national output compared to that of the United States? Was it 33 percent and growing at 7 percent per year? Was it 62 percent and growing even faster? Once again, the problem was this: How can we meaningfully add together a vast array of disparate things, now ranging from bread, meat, and television sets to highway bridges, education, and medical care? The construction of *quantity* indexes deals with questions like these.

20.1 The Nature of Index Numbers

On one occasion or another, almost everyone is interested in comparing economic conditions over time or space.

- Consider the consumer who wants to know whether and to what extent the cost of living now is higher or lower than in the past, or how it differs now between Boston and Detroit.
- Consider the worker who wants to contrast current wages with wages 10 years ago, or wages now and here with wages now and elsewhere.

- Consider the business executive who looks at the prices currently paid or received versus those paid or received in the past, or who wishes to compare the firm's vast inventory of items in the U.S. with a similar inventory abroad.
- Consider, finally, the government official running for reelection, who ponders differences between the general price level now and four years ago, between the physical volume of national output now and then, or even between the levels of national output here and abroad.

In all these cases and a million more, a certain kind of yardstick can greatly facilitate the desired comparison. Such a yardstick is provided by *index numbers.*

DEFINITION 20.1 Numbers that measure a variable's magnitude at one time or place relative to the same variable's magnitude at another time or place are called **index numbers.** Comparisons between one time and another produce **intertemporal index numbers.** In contrast, comparisons between one geographic location and another yield **interspatial index numbers.**

The variable in question can be an individual price, quantity, or value figure. More often, however, entire sets of these prices, quantities, or values are being compared. When we compare single items rather than sets of them, index construction is simple. When we attempt to compare the prices or quantities of hundreds or even thousands of items, things quickly become more complicated. This chapter discusses the construction of index numbers and also introduces the major types of business and economic index numbers that are regularly published and used in the United States.

We begin our discussion by considering a variety of methods that are commonly used to construct **price indexes,** which are numbers that measure the level of either a single price or of a set of prices at one time or place relative to another time or place. Later in the chapter, we turn to **quantity indexes,** which are analogously defined as numbers that measure the magnitude of a single quantity or of a set of quantities at one time or place relative to another time or place.

20.2 Simple Price Indexes

A **simple price index** or **price-relative index** is a number that compares the price of a single item at one time or place with the price of the same item at another time or place. We consider the intertemporal as well as the interspatial version of this index.

AN INTERTEMPORAL INDEX

Table 20.1 illustrates the computation of a simple intertemporal price index series.

Columns 1 and 2 contain data about the average price of grade-A eggs in Boston, Massachusetts, during a number of recent years. We might view each column 2 entry as an average of daily egg prices observed in a sample of Boston stores during the year. Accordingly, we can calculate a simple (intertemporal) price index series in two steps, as noted in columns 3 and 4.

First, we relate the price of each period, P_t, to the price, P_0, of an *arbitrarily chosen* **base period** or **reference period,** which is 1995 in this example. For 1996, for instance, this ratio or **price relative** equals \$.88/\$.80 or 1.10, as column 3 indicates. We can find all other entries in column 3 in the same manner, always by dividing the given year's price by the base-year price. Naturally, this procedure makes the price relative for the base period itself equal to 1.00 (in our case, as a result of dividing \$.80 by \$.80).

TABLE 20.1 | Constructing Simple Intertemporal Price Indexes

Year (1)	Average Price of Grade-A Eggs in Boston (dollars/dozen) (2)	Current Price, P_t, Relative to 1995 Base Period Price, P_0 (3)	Simple Price Index (1995 = 100) (4) = (3) · 100
1995	.80	(.80/.80) = 1.00	100
1996	.88	(.88/.80) = 1.10	110
1997	.96	(.96/.80) = 1.20	120
1998	1.08	(1.08/.80) = 1.35	135
1999	1.12	(1.12/.80) = 1.40	140
2000	1.20	(1.20/.80) = 1.50	150

Second, we quickly convert all the column 3 price relatives into the simple price indexes of column 4. In doing so, we follow tradition and express the base-year index as 100, which can be thought of as a pure number or as 100 percent.

Formula 20.A summarizes the procedure.

FORMULA 20.A | The Simple (Intertemporal) Price Index

$$PI_{t,0} = \frac{P_t}{P_0} \cdot 100$$

where P_t is the price in period t and P_0 is the price in (arbitrarily chosen) base period 0.

EXAMPLE PROBLEM 20.1

Using Formula 20.A, confirm the 1999 price index found in Table 20.1; then interpret it.

SOLUTION: Using calendar-year subscripts, the formula gives us the 1999 price index, with 1995 base, as

$$PI_{99,\,95} = \frac{P_{99}}{P_{95}} \cdot 100 = \frac{\$1.12}{\$.80} \cdot 100 = 140$$

The result means that the 1999 Boston average price of grade-A eggs equaled 140 percent of (or was 40 percent higher than) the corresponding 1995 price.

AN INTERSPATIAL INDEX

We can derive a simple interspatial price index in an analogous manner. Imagine that column 1 of Table 20.1, instead of listing various years, contained the names of various cities, such as Boston, Detroit, New York, and so on, while column 2 listed the average egg prices in these cities for a *given* year, such as 2001. In that case, we might choose a base *location* (such as Boston) and then relate the price in each city, P_x, to that of the base city (P_b). For the Detroit-to-Boston comparison, the price relative might equal (P_x/P_b) = (\$.88/\$.80) = 1.10, and the corresponding simple (interspatial) price index would equal 110. This index number would indicate that the 2001 Detroit price of eggs was, on the average, 10 percent above the 2001 Boston price.

Because this kind of analogy works for all other price indexes as well, we will henceforth focus our attention on intertemporal indexes entirely, but keep in mind that you can construct interspatial price indexes using the same procedures.

20.3 Unweighted Composite Price Indexes

Typically, economic decision makers are concerned with comparisons that are considerably more complex than those discussed so far. Consider their need to compare an *entire set* of prices prevailing at a given place at one time with a corresponding set of prices prevailing at the same place at a different time. Table 20.2 helps us visualize the problem.

Given the indicated price quotations, we can easily calculate a simple price index separately for each row of the table and note the degree to which the price of any one food item has risen, remained unchanged, or fallen. But what has happened over time to the Boston price of breakfast food *in general?* Or how do such Boston prices in general compare to those in Detroit? Answers to these questions can be found by calculating a **composite price index,** a number that compares a set of prices for a variety of items at one time or place with such a set for the same items at another time or place. Several possible approaches to such a calculation exist. In this section, we consider the construction of *unweighted* composite price indexes, along with the flaws associated with each construction.

AN UNWEIGHTED AVERAGE OF SIMPLE PRICE INDEXES

One way to construct a composite price index that combines the possibly divergent price movements of different items in a single number is to compute an *unweighted average* of the separate simple price indexes for all the items in question. Such an average is constructed on the

TABLE 20.2 | Constructing a Composite Price Index by Averaging Simple Price Indexes

	Price in Boston (dollars per unit)		
Market Basket Components (1)	in 2000, P_{00} (2)	in 2001, P_{01} (3)	Simple Price Index, $\frac{P_{01}}{P_{00}} \cdot 100$ (4) = [(3)/(2)] · 100
Small eggs (dozen)	1.00	1.21	121
Whole milk (gallon)	1.40	1.54	110
Wheat bread (loaf)	.88	.88	100
Margarine (pound)	1.80	1.71	95
Grape jelly (18 oz.)	1.50	2.01	134
Corn flakes (12 oz.)	.93	.93	100
			Sum: 660

(often questionable) assumption that all items are equally important. Formula 20.B summarizes the procedure.

FORMULA 20.B | The Composite (Intertemporal) Price Index as an Unweighted Average of Simple Price Indexes

$$PI_{t,0} = \frac{\Sigma\left(\frac{P_t}{P_0} \cdot 100\right)}{n}$$

where P_t is the price in period t, P_0 is the price in an (arbitrarily chosen) base period 0, n is the number of simple price indexes being averaged, and Σ is the summation sign.

EXAMPLE PROBLEM 20.2

Using Formula 20.B, compute a composite price index for 2001 from the data of columns 2 and 3 of Table 20.2.

SOLUTION: After computing the price-relative indexes of column 4, we can derive the composite index as

$$PI_{01,00} = \frac{\Sigma\left(\frac{P_{01}}{P_{00}} \cdot 100\right)}{n} = \frac{660}{6} = 110$$

This result indicates that Boston breakfast-food items in 2001 were, in general, 10 percent more expensive than in 2000.

Indeed, this method of price indexation was the first one employed historically: In 1764, Giovanni R. Carli, an Italian nobleman, set out to measure the effect on European prices of the influx of precious metals following the discovery of the New World. He applied Formula 20.B to the prices of grain, oil, and wine in 1500 and 1750.

The construction of a composite price index with the help of Formula 20.B embodies one major flaw: Implicitly, every item is treated as if it had the same importance as every other item. This may, in fact, not be the case. Eggs and milk, for example, may be less important in people's diets than bread, jelly, and margarine.

Therefore, as we will show in Section 20.4, statisticians attempt to account for the possibly different importance of the various items entering an index by *weighting* each item by some appropriate measure of "importance." In the case of price indexes, the typical measure used is the set of quantities (Q) or values ($P \cdot Q = V$) associated with the set of prices for which the index is being constructed.

AN UNWEIGHTED AGGREGATIVE PRICE INDEX

An altogether different approach to constructing a composite price index does not require the prior computation of individual price relatives at all. In its simplest form, this method constructs an unweighted aggregative price index by simply summing the prices of all relevant products in the year for which the index is desired and relating that sum to a similar sum of all the base-year prices. Formula 20.C explains.

FORMULA 20.C | The Composite (Intertemporal) Price Index as an Unweighted Aggregative Index

$$PI_{t,0} = \frac{\Sigma P_t}{\Sigma P_0} \cdot 100$$

where ΣP_t is the sum of all prices in period t and ΣP_0 is the sum of all prices in an (arbitrarily chosen) base period 0.

EXAMPLE PROBLEM 20.3

Consider Part A of Table 20.3. Use it to calculate a composite price index in the form of an unweighted aggregative index for 2001 with a year 2000 base.

TABLE 20.3 | Constructing a Composite Price Index as an Unweighted Aggregative Index

Market Basket Components	Price in Boston (dollars per unit)					
	Part A			Part B		
	Unit	P_{00}	P_{01}	Unit	P_{00}	P_{01}
Small eggs	dozen	1.00	1.21	1,000	83.33	100.83
Whole milk	gallon	1.40	1.54	10 gallons	14.00	15.40
Wheat bread	loaf	.88	.88	loaf	.88	.88
Margarine	pound	1.80	1.71	pound	1.80	1.71
Grape jelly	18 oz.	1.50	2.01	pound	1.33	1.79
Corn flakes	12 oz.	.93	.93	pound	1.24	1.24
		7.51	**8.28**		**102.58**	**121.85**

SOLUTION: Using Formula 20.C, we derive

$$PI_{01,00} = \frac{\Sigma P_{01}}{\Sigma P_{00}} \cdot 100 = \frac{8.28}{7.51} \cdot 100 = 110.25$$

This result indicates that Boston breakfast-food items in 2001 were, in general, 10.25 percent more expensive than in 2000.

The construction of a composite price index with the help of Formula 20.C is flawed as well. Just consider what happens if we consider the price data of Table 20.3, Part A, but express the *identical* prices with respect to different quantity units, as in Part B. Note, for example, that a price of $1 per dozen eggs is the same thing as a price of $83.33 per 1,000 eggs. If we apply Formula 20.C in Part B, we can compute an entirely different index:

$$PI_{01,00} = \frac{\Sigma P_{01}}{\Sigma P_{00}} \cdot 100 = \frac{121.85}{102.58} \cdot 100 = 118.47$$

This result suggests that breakfast-food prices have risen not by 10.25, but by 18.47 percent!

Thus, an unweighted aggregative price index is a poor index because the physical units in which goods happen to be priced affect its magnitude. In addition, like the Formula 20.B unweighted average of simple price indexes, this index, too, treats all goods as equally important, which is unlikely to be true. Both problems are avoided by introducing *quantity* weights into Formula 20.C, as we will see presently.

20.4 Weighted Aggregative Price Indexes

Numerous weighted aggregative price indexes exist; some are more popular than others. Each of them computes a sum of quantity-weighted prices for the current year and then relates that sum to a similar sum for the base year. The indexes differ from one another with respect to the way in which the quantity weights are chosen.

THE LASPEYRES PRICE INDEX

The most commonly used price index nowadays is probably the weighted aggregative index introduced in 1864 by Étienne Laspeyres.

DEFINITION 20.2 The **Laspeyres price index** is a weighted aggregative price index that uses base-year quantity weights, Q_0, in both the numerator and denominator of the price index formula.

FORMULA 20.D | The Composite (Intertemporal) Price Index as the Weighted Aggregative Index of Laspeyres

$$PI^{Laspeyres}_{t,0} = \frac{\Sigma P_t \cdot Q_0}{\Sigma P_0 \cdot Q_0} \cdot 100$$

where $\Sigma P_t \cdot Q_0$ is the sum of all prices in period t multiplied by the corresponding quantities of an (arbitrarily chosen) base period 0, while $\Sigma P_0 \cdot Q_0$ is the sum of all prices in base period 0 multiplied by the corresponding quantities in base period 0.

It is easy to see how this simple weighting device instantly eliminates both objections to the unweighted aggregative index that we noted earlier.

First, the fact that each price is multiplied by quantity makes the choice of quantity units unproblematic because the quantity units cancel. Thus, a price of \$1 *per dozen* eggs, when multiplied by a quantity of, say, 100 *dozens,* simply yields \$100 (the "dozens" have disappeared). An equivalent price of \$83.33 *per thousand* eggs, when multiplied by the equivalent quantity of 1.2 *thousand* eggs, also yields \$100 (the "thousands" have disappeared).

Second, the use of differentiated quantity weights eliminates the equal treatment of all goods. It allows us to take account of the importance of each product relative to the entire set of products.

EXAMPLE PROBLEM 20.4

Consider the data of columns 1–4 of Table 20.4. Compute a Laspeyres price index for 2001, based on 2000.

TABLE 20.4 | Constructing a Composite Price Index: The Weighted Aggregative Index of Laspeyres

Market Basket Components	Price in Boston (dollars per unit)		Quantity (number of units bought by average family in base year)	Prices Weighted by Base-Year Quantities (dollars)	
(1)	P_{00} (2)	P_{01} (3)	Q_{00} (4)	$P_{00} \cdot Q_{00}$ (5) = (2) · (4)	$P_{01} \cdot Q_{00}$ (6) = (3) · (4)
Small eggs (dozen)	1.00	1.21	50	50	60.5
Whole milk (gallon)	1.40	1.54	100	140	154.0
Wheat bread (loaf)	.88	.88	400	352	352.0
Margarine (pound)	1.80	1.71	50	90	85.5
Grape jelly (18 oz.)	1.50	2.01	100	150	201.0
Corn flakes (12 oz.)	.93	.93	300	279	279.0
				1,061	**1,132.0**

SOLUTION: Applying Formula 20.D, we derive columns 5 and 6. Thus,

$$PI_{01,00}^{Laspeyres} = \frac{\Sigma P_{01} \cdot Q_{00}}{\Sigma P_{00} \cdot Q_{00}} \cdot 100 = \frac{\$1{,}132}{\$1{,}061} \cdot 100 = 106.7$$

According to the Laspeyres formula, Boston breakfast-food items in 2001 were, in general, 6.7 percent more expensive than in 2000.

THE PAASCHE PRICE INDEX

An alternative type of weighted aggregative index was introduced in 1874 by Hermann Paasche.

DEFINITION 20.3 The **Paasche price index** is a weighted aggregative price index that uses current-year quantity weights, Q_t, in both the numerator and denominator of the price index formula.

FORMULA 20.E | The Composite (Intertemporal) Price Index as the Weighted Aggregative Index of Paasche

$$PI_{t,0}^{Paasche} = \frac{\Sigma P_t \cdot Q_t}{\Sigma P_0 \cdot Q_t} \cdot 100$$

where $\Sigma P_t \cdot Q_t$ is the sum of all prices in period t multiplied by the corresponding quantities of period t, while $\Sigma P_0 \cdot Q_t$ is the sum of all prices in an (arbitrarily chosen) base period 0 multiplied by the corresponding quantities in period t.

EXAMPLE PROBLEM 20.5

Consider the data of columns 1–4 of Table 20.5. Compute a Paasche price index for 2001, based on 2000.

TABLE 20.5 | Constructing a Composite Price Index: The Weighted Aggregative Index of Paasche

Market Basket Components	Price in Boston (dollars per unit)		Quantity (number of units bought by average family in current year),	Prices Weighted by Current-Year Quantities (dollars)	
	P_{00}	P_{01}	Q_{01}	$P_{00} \cdot Q_{01}$	$P_{01} \cdot Q_{01}$
(1)	(2)	(3)	(4)	(5) = (2) · (4)	(6) = (3) · (4)
Small eggs (dozen)	1.00	1.21	40	40	48.4
Whole milk (gallon)	1.40	1.54	90	126	138.6
Wheat bread (loaf)	.88	.88	450	396	396.0
Margarine (pound)	1.80	1.71	60	108	102.6
Grape jelly (18 oz.)	1.50	2.01	90	135	180.9
Corn flakes (12 oz.)	.93	.93	600	558	558.0
				1,363	**1,424.5**

SOLUTION: Applying Formula 20.E, we derive columns 5 and 6. Thus,

$$PI_{01,00}^{Paasche} = \frac{\Sigma P_{01} \cdot Q_{01}}{\Sigma P_{00} \cdot Q_{01}} \cdot 100 = \frac{\$1{,}424.5}{\$1{,}363} \cdot 100 = 104.5$$

According to the Paasche formula, Boston breakfast-food items in 2001 were, in general, 4.5 percent more expensive than in 2000.

EXCEL Example 20.1

Use the computer to check

a. the value of the Laspeyres index found in Example Problem 20.4.

b. the value of the Paasche index found in Example Problem 20.5.

SOLUTION:

1. Enter labels *P0*, *P1*, *Q0*, and *Q1* into cells A1–D1 of a new worksheet.
2. Enter relevant data from columns 2-4 of Table 20.4 and column 4 of Table 20.5 just below the labels.
3. Enter the labels *Laspeyres Price Index (1,0)* and *Paasche Price Index (1,0)* into cells E1 and E2, respectively.
4. Enter the Laspeyres formula into cell F1 as **=(SUMPRODUCT(B2:B7*C2:C7)/SUMPRODUCT(A2:A7*C2:C7))*100**
5. Enter the Paasche formula into cell F2 as **=(SUMPRODUCT(B2:B7*D2:D7)/SUMPRODUCT(A2:A7*D2:D7))*100**

The result:

A	B	C	D	E	F
P0	P1	Q0	Q1	Laspeyres Price Index (1,0)	106.6918
1	1.21	50	40	Paasche Price Index (1,0)	104.5121
1.4	1.54	100	90		
0.88	0.88	400	450		
1.8	1.71	50	60		
1.5	2.01	100	90		
0.93	0.93	300	600		

For even quicker results, use HKStat, Sheet 46.

THE INDEX-NUMBER PROBLEM

Note how the outcome of Example Problem 20.4, based on the Laspeyres formula, differs from that of Example Problem 20.5, based on the Paasche formula. Neither result is more correct or faulty than the other. Despite the fact that the two indexes attempt to measure the same thing—namely, price level changes between 2000 and 2001—they actually measure two different things.

Laspeyres tells us how much more or less money people would have had to spend in 2001, compared to 2000, if they had tried to buy in both years the physical quantities that they in fact bought in 2000. (The answer is "6.7 percent more"; thus, we conclude that prices on the average rose by 6.7 percent.)

Paasche tells us how much more or less money people would have had to spend in 2001, compared to 2000, if they had tried to buy in both years the physical quantities that they in fact bought in 2001. (The answer is "4.5 percent more"; thus, we conclude that prices, on the average, rose by 4.5 percent.)

The truth is that both of these stories are *pure fiction.* Each serves the sole purpose of constructing two value figures (found in the numerator and denominator of the respective formulas) that (1) conveniently contain the same quantity component, (2) can, therefore, differ from one another only as a result of intertemporal differences in prices, and (3) can, thus, be used to estimate price change.

Yet, in truth, people bought year 2000 quantities in 2000 and different year 2001 quantities in 2001! What then is the *true* price level change between our two years? Sadly, we cannot answer that question because, when comparing a 2001 price set with a 2000 price set, it is equally logical to follow the Laspeyres procedure of using year 2000 quantity weights as to follow the Paasche procedure of using year 2001 quantity weights. Indeed, good reasons may even exist for using 1980 quantity weights if, say, consumer spending patterns near the turn of the century were in some way abnormal and distorted as a result, perhaps, of such unusual conditions as a war, a depression, a hyperinflation, or bizarre Y2K expectations.

The problem of being able to construct different indexes for a given phenomenon (such as price changes in Boston between 2000 and 2001), depending on which of several *equally logical* sets of weights is being employed, has a special name. Definition 20.4 explains.

DEFINITION 20.4 The **index-number problem** is an insoluble problem, which refers to the fact that it is often possible to construct different indexes for a given phenomenon, depending on which one of several equally logical sets of weights is applied to individual index components.

Indeed, the discrepancy between the Laspeyres and Paasche indexes will likely widen as the distance between the base period and the current period increases. Suppose we tried to measure price changes between 1900 and 2000. First, people's tastes often change drastically over such long periods; the discovery of cholesterol in eggs and whole milk, for example, might make modern health-conscious consumers buy relatively lower quantities than their ancestors did a century earlier. Second, the discrepancy would be large because consumers change their buying patterns in response to changes in relative prices. A century of improvements in agricultural productivity, for example, might drastically reduce the relative prices of wheat and corn products and make consumers buy relatively larger quantities of these even if their tastes did not change. As a result of these and other factors, a year 1900 quantity set (which Laspeyres would use) would hardly resemble the year 2000 quantity set (which Paasche would use), and the indexes would differ from one another accordingly.

CAUTION

The index-number problem, although common, is not inevitable. It arises whenever the relative magnitudes of the weights contained in one set of weights, such as our year 2000 quantities, differ from the relative magnitudes of the weights contained in another set, such as our year 2001 quantities. Unfortunately, this difference is usually present. We can show, however, that the index-number problem disappears when the relative magnitudes of weights contained in alternative sets of weights are the same. Thus, the same composite price index would have been computed in Example Problems 20.4 and 20.5 if, compared to the year 2000 quantity weights, all year 2001 quantity weights had been, say, precisely 10 percent higher or precisely 40 percent lower.

OTHER WEIGHTED AGGREGATIVE PRICE INDEXES

The Laspeyres and Paasche indexes are by no means the only types of weighted aggregative price indexes. There is literally no end to the possibilities of constructing such indexes once we realize that all kinds of other weighting schemes can be used as well. Two common alternatives are introduced here:

1. A **typical-year aggregative price index** is constructed in the manner of the Laspeyres and Paasche indexes, except that neither a base-year nor a current-year quantity set is employed. Instead, quantity weights (Q_a) of another arbitrarily selected but "typical" year are substituted. Sometimes this index is also referred to as the "fixed-weight" aggregative index, but that name is a most unfortunate one. The other weighted indexes discussed here have fixed weights, too; they just refer to a different kind of year.
2. Another version of a weighted aggregative price index was suggested by Alfred Marshall (1842–1924) and popularized by Francis Y. Edgeworth (1845–1926), both renowned British economists. The **Edgeworth price index,** as it is now called, combines features of the Laspeyres and Paasche indexes by using the sum of base-year and current-year quantities ($Q_0 + Q_t$) as weights.

20.5 Fisher's Quality Tests and His Ideal Index

With so many indexes from which to choose, the index maker naturally looks for guidance to facilitate the inevitable choice. We may well ask: What would make one index number better than another? Or is it simply impossible to rank different types of index numbers on a quality scale?

In a now classic work, *The Making of Index Numbers,* first published in 1922, the American economist Irving Fisher (1867–1947) set out to provide general principles according to which superior index numbers could be distinguished from inferior ones. Although he did not consider them equally important, we shall consider three of his index-number quality tests: the time-reversal test, the factor-reversal test, and the circularity test. We shall also consider the ideal index-number formula suggested by Fisher himself.

THE TIME-REVERSAL TEST

Consider the price of a single item, such as a loaf of bread. If the loaf costs \$1 in year 0 and \$2 in year 1, we can describe the matter in one of two ways:

- We can say that the year 1 price is *double* the year 0 price.
- We can say that the year 0 price is *half* the year 1 price.

Either way, we are telling the same story. Fisher argued that price index numbers, which combine the prices of many items, should be able to tell an equally consistent story, regardless of whether we use year 0 or year 1 as the basis of comparison. Accordingly, a price index formula passes Fisher's **time-reversal test** if, in a comparison of prices at two dates, we get consistent (reciprocal) results regardless of which date we choose as the base. For example, if the formula indicates that year 2000 prices are twice as high as 1990 prices when 1990 is used as a base, then it should also indicate that 1990 prices are half as high as 2000 prices when 2000 is used as a base. Denoting the price index by *PI* and the two dates by 0 and 1, passing the test requires that

$$\frac{PI_{1,0}}{100} = \frac{100}{PI_{0,1}}$$

or that

$$\frac{PI_{1,0}}{100} \cdot \frac{PI_{0,1}}{100} = 1$$

THE FACTOR-REVERSAL TEST

Now consider the price *and* quantity of a single item, such as bread. If a loaf costs \$1 and you buy 4 loaves, we can figure the value of your purchase as \$1 × 4 = \$4. For individual items, we take it for granted that

$$\text{Price} \times \text{Quantity} = \text{Value}$$

Fisher argued that index numbers that combine the prices *or* the quantities *or* the values of many items (whichever the case may be) should indicate the same logical relationship. An index of prices, multiplied by an index of quantities, should equal an index of values.

Fisher's **factor-reversal test** presupposes that the weights used in a price index formula are quantity weights and that a corresponding quantity index is derived by interchanging the *P*'s and *Q*'s in the formula. This being so, a price index formula passes the test if division of the price index by 100, and subsequent multiplication by a corresponding quantity index, produces a number that equals an independently derived value index. Denoting the price index by *PI* and the quantity index by *QI*, passing the test requires that

$$\frac{PI_{1,0}}{100} \cdot QI_{1,0} = \frac{\Sigma P_1 Q_1}{\Sigma P_0 Q_0} \cdot 100$$

THE CIRCULARITY TEST

Consider once again the price of a single item, such as a loaf of bread. If the loaf costs \$1 in year 0, \$2 in year 1, and \$4 in year 2, we can describe the matter as follows:

- We can say that the year 1 price is *double* the year 0 price.
- We can say that the year 2 price is *double* the year 1 price.
- We can say that the year 2 price is *quadruple* the year 0 price.

Note that we could have derived the last statement without looking at the original year 0 and year 2 prices and by simply multiplying the key numbers found in the first two comparisons:

$2 \times 2 = 4$. Fisher argued that index numbers that combine the prices of many items should indicate the same logical relationship.

Accordingly, a price index formula passes Fisher's **circularity test** if the price index of year 1 with year 0 base, when multiplied by the price index of year 2 with year 1 base (and divided by 100), equals the independently calculated price index of year 2 with year 0 base. For example, if the formula indicates that prices have doubled between 1990 and 1995 and then have doubled again between 1995 and 2000, it should also indicate that prices have quadrupled between 1990 and 2000 when the prices of the latter two years are compared directly. Thus, passing the test requires that

$$\frac{PI_{1,0} \cdot PI_{2,1}}{100} = PI_{2,0}$$

TESTING THE LASPEYRES INDEX

All of Fisher's quality tests make eminent sense. Surely, if A is twice as big as B, an examination of B should reveal it as being half as big as A (the time-reversal test). Surely, if A times B equals C, the aggregation of lots of A's times the aggregation of lots of B's should equal the aggregation of lots of C's (the factor-reversal test). Surely, if B is twice A and C is twice B, C should be found to equal four times A (the circularity test). Yet, surprisingly, many index numbers in common use—including the Laspeyres and Paasche indexes—fail to meet these tests! The following calculations illustrate this sad truth with respect to the first of these.

EXAMPLE PROBLEM 20.6

Review the price and quantity data for the years 2000 and 2001 that are found in Example Problems 20.4 and 20.5. Assume the following additional data for the year 2002:

P_{02}:	2.00	1.75	1.00	2.00	2.50	1.00
Q_{02}:	45	100	400	80	120	500

Then subject the Laspeyres price index to Fisher's three quality tests.

SOLUTION:

The time-reversal test: Laspeyres. We already found in Example Problem 20.4 that

$$PI^{Laspeyres}_{01,\,00} = \frac{\Sigma P_{01} \cdot Q_{00}}{\Sigma P_{00} \cdot Q_{00}} \cdot 100 = \frac{\$1{,}132}{\$1{,}061} \cdot 100 = 106.7$$

By using calculations already made in Table 20.5, we can compute a corresponding Laspeyres price index for 2000 with 2001 base as

$$PI^{Laspeyres}_{00,\,01} = \frac{\Sigma P_{00} \cdot Q_{01}}{\Sigma P_{01} \cdot Q_{01}} \cdot 100 = \frac{\$1{,}363}{\$1{,}424.5} \cdot 100 = 95.7$$

The Laspeyres price index does *not* pass the time-reversal test because

$$\frac{PI_{1,0}}{100} \cdot \frac{PI_{0,1}}{100} = \frac{106.7}{100} \cdot \frac{95.7}{100} = 1.021 \neq 1$$

The factor-reversal test: Laspeyres. We already found in Example Problem 20.4 that

$$PI^{Laspeyres}_{01,00} = \frac{\Sigma P_{01} \cdot Q_{00}}{\Sigma P_{00} \cdot Q_{00}} \cdot 100 = \frac{\$1{,}132}{\$1{,}061} \cdot 100 = 106.7$$

We find the corresponding Laspeyres *quantity* index by interchanging the price and quantity entries in the formula and using the calculations already available in Tables 20.4 and 20.5:

$$QI^{Laspeyres}_{01,00} = \frac{\Sigma Q_{01} \cdot P_{00}}{\Sigma Q_{00} \cdot P_{00}} \cdot 100 = \frac{\$1{,}363}{\$1{,}061} \cdot 100 = 128.5$$

This result indicates that year 2001 quantities were, on average, 28.5 percent above year 2000 quantities, provided that we aggregate both sets with the help of year 2000 prices. Using Table 20.4 and 20.5 calculations, the corresponding *value index, VI,* is found to equal

$$VI_{01,00} = \frac{\Sigma P_{01} \cdot Q_{01}}{\Sigma P_{00} \cdot Q_{00}} \cdot 100 = \frac{\$1{,}424.5}{\$1{,}061} \cdot 100 = 134.3$$

This result indicates that 2001 actual-dollar expenditures exceeded 2000 expenditures by 34.3 percent. The Laspeyres price index does *not* pass the factor-reversal test because

$$\frac{PI_{1,0}}{100} \cdot QI_{1,0} = \frac{106.7}{100} \cdot 128.5 = 137.1 \neq \frac{\Sigma P_1 Q_1}{\Sigma P_0 Q_0} \cdot 100 = 134.3$$

The circularity test: Laspeyres. We already found in Example Problem 20.4 that

$$PI^{Laspeyres}_{01,00} = \frac{\Sigma P_{01} \cdot Q_{00}}{\Sigma P_{00} \cdot Q_{00}} \cdot 100 = \frac{\$1{,}132}{\$1{,}061} \cdot 100 = 106.7$$

Using the new data and those in Tables 20.4 and 20.5, we can compute corresponding Laspeyres price indexes of

$$PI^{Laspeyres}_{02,01} = \frac{\Sigma P_{02} \cdot Q_{01}}{\Sigma P_{01} \cdot Q_{01}} \cdot 100 = \frac{\$1{,}632.5}{\$1{,}424.5} \cdot 100 = 114.6$$

and

$$PI^{Laspeyres}_{02,00} = \frac{\Sigma P_{02} \cdot Q_{00}}{\Sigma P_{00} \cdot Q_{00}} \cdot 100 = \frac{\$1{,}325}{\$1{,}061} \cdot 100 = 124.9$$

The Laspeyres price index does *not* pass the circularity test because

$$\frac{PI_{1,0} \cdot PI_{2,1}}{100} = \frac{106.7(114.6)}{100} = 122.3 \neq PI_{2,0} = 124.9$$

FISHER'S IDEAL INDEX

The logic of Fisher's three tests is so compelling, yet it seems impossible to devise an index that passes all of the tests. Fisher himself suggested as ideal an index of his own that passes only the time-reversal and factor-reversal tests. **Fisher's ideal index** can be calculated for prices or quantities and equals the geometric mean of the Laspeyres and Paasche indexes. (The *geometric mean* of two positive values, a and b, equals the square root of their product, $\sqrt{a \cdot b}$.)

FORMULA 20.F | Fisher's Ideal Index

$$I_{t,0}^{Fisher} = \sqrt{I_{t,0}^{Laspeyres} \cdot I_{t,0}^{Paasche}}$$

where $I_{t,0}$ is a price or quantity index for time period t, with base period 0.

EXAMPLE PROBLEM 20.7

Reconsider Example Problems 20.4 and 20.5. Compute Fisher's ideal price index for 2001, based on 2000.

SOLUTION:

Given a Laspeyres price index of 106.7 and a Paasche price index of 104.5, Fisher's price index equals

$$PI_{01,00}^{Fisher} = \sqrt{PI_{01,00}^{Laspeyres} \cdot PI_{01,00}^{Paasche}} = \sqrt{106.7(104.5)} = 105.6$$

EXAMPLE PROBLEM 20.8

Reconsider Example Problem 20.7 and the Fisher price index calculated there. Subject the index to Fisher's three quality tests.

SOLUTION:

The time-reversal test: Fisher. According to Example Problem 20.6, the Laspeyres price index for 2000 with a 2001 base equals 95.7. A corresponding Paasche index equals 93.7. Hence, the Fisher price index for 2000 with a 2001 base is

$$PI_{00,01}^{Fisher} = \sqrt{PI_{00,01}^{Laspeyres} \cdot PI_{00,01}^{Paasche}} = \sqrt{95.7(93.7)} = 94.7$$

Fisher's ideal price index *passes* the time-reversal test because

$$\frac{PI_{1,0}}{100} \cdot \frac{PI_{0,1}}{100} = \frac{105.6}{100} \cdot \frac{94.7}{100} = 1$$

The factor-reversal test: Fisher. According to Example Problem 20.7, Fisher's ideal price index for 2001 with a 2000 base is 105.6. The corresponding Fisher *quantity* index makes use of the corresponding Laspeyres quantity index of 128.5 (found in Example Problem 20.6) and the corresponding Paasche quantity index of 125.8 (analogously calculated). It equals

$$QI_{01,00}^{Fisher} = \sqrt{QI_{01,00}^{Laspeyres} \cdot QI_{01,00}^{Paasche}} = \sqrt{128.5(125.8)} = 127.1$$

Fisher's price index *passes* the factor-reversal test because

$$\frac{PI_{1,0}}{100} \cdot QI_{1,0} = \frac{105.6}{100} \cdot 127.1 = 134.3 = \frac{\Sigma P_1 Q_1}{\Sigma P_0 Q_0} \cdot 100 = 134.3$$

(slight differences, not shown here, being due to rounding error).

The circularity test: Fisher. According to Example Problem 20.7, Fisher's ideal price index for 2001 with a 2000 base is 105.6. Given the above data, we can also compute

$$PI^{Fisher}_{02,\,01} = \sqrt{PI^{Laspeyres}_{02,\,01} \cdot PI^{Paasche}_{02,\,01}} = \sqrt{114.6(115.8)} = 115.2$$

and

$$PI^{Fisher}_{02,\,00} = \sqrt{PI^{Laspeyres}_{02,\,00} \cdot PI^{Paasche}_{02,\,00}} = \sqrt{124.9(122.5)} = 123.7$$

Fisher's price index does *not* pass the circularity test because

$$\frac{PI_{1,0} \cdot PI_{2,1}}{100} = \frac{105.6(115.2)}{100} = 121.7 \neq PI_{2,0} = 123.7$$

20.6 Manipulating Index-Number Time Series

On occasion, it is desirable to manipulate index-number times series in various ways. Four of the most common procedures are *shifting, splicing, combining,* and *chaining.*

SHIFTING THE BASE

Imagine the availability of an index-number time series with a common base, such as the one given in column 2 of Table 20.6 on the next page. This series is in fact the official *U.S. Consumer Price Index* that we discuss below. Over time, users of such an index may be less and less able to relate to the base period because it moves further and further away from the realm of their personal experience. For example, the fact that 1999 prices were about five times as high as 1967 prices may not mean very much to someone who was not an adult in 1967 and who has no concept of the meaning of "1967 purchasing power." Under such circumstances, we may wish to shift the base of the index series to a more recent date, such as 1985.

Another reason for wanting to shift the base is that we may want to compare one index-number series, such as a series of U.S. price indexes based on 1967, with another series that has a different base, such as a series of U.S. *quantity* indexes or *French* price indexes based on 1985. Such side-by-side comparisons are eased considerably by having identical base periods.

We can convert one index-number series into another one with a new base by a process called **base shifting.** We successively divide each value of the original series by the original index number (such as the red 322.2 in Table 20.6) for the year that is to become the new base (here 1985) and multiply each result by 100. The results are shown in column 3 of Table 20.6. Note how the 1960 value of 88.7, when divided by the red 1985 value of 322.2 and multiplied by 100, yields the first entry of 27.5 in column 3. Changing the 88.7 figure to 27.5 means that 1960 prices, which had been listed as 88.7 percent of 1967 prices (then equal to 100) are now expressed as 27.5 percent of 1985 prices. All other column 3 entries are similarly calculated, and the 1985 value turns into the new (red) base value of 100.

TABLE 20.6 | Shifting the Base of an Index-Number Time Series

Year (1)	Original Price Index (1967 = 100) (2)	Price Index with Shifted Base (1985 = 100) (3)
1960	88.7	27.5
1961	89.6	27.8
1962	90.6	28.1
1963	91.7	28.5
1964	92.9	28.8
1965	94.5	29.3
1966	97.2	30.2
1967	100.0	31.0
1968	104.2	32.3
1969	109.8	34.1
1970	116.3	36.1
1971	121.3	37.6
1972	125.3	38.9
1973	133.1	41.3
1974	147.7	45.8
1975	161.2	50.0
1976	170.5	52.9
1977	181.5	56.3
1978	195.4	60.6
1979	217.4	67.5
1980	246.8	76.6
1981	272.4	84.5
1982	289.1	89.7
1983	298.4	92.6
1984	311.1	96.6
1985	**322.2**	**100.0**
1986	328.4	101.9
1987	340.1	105.6
1988	354.2	109.9
1989	371.3	115.2
1990	391.3	121.4
1991	407.8	126.6
1992	419.7	130.3
1993	432.3	134.2
1994	443.3	137.6
1995	455.9	141.5
1996	469.4	145.7
1997	480.1	149.0
1998	487.6	151.3
1999	499.6	155.1

Note how much easier it might be for a younger person to relate to the new base. The fact that 1999 prices were 155 percent of 1985 prices may well conjure up a more concrete image than the equivalent statement that 1999 prices were 500 percent of 1967 prices. Note also that the two index-number series provide the same year-to-year percentage changes. Column 2 tells us, for example, that prices between 1985 and 1999 rose by [(499.6/322.2)100] − 100 = 55.1 percent; column 3 tells us the same.

SPLICING TWO SHORT SERIES INTO A LONGER SERIES

Sometimes two or more index-number time series are available that cover different ranges of time. Columns 1–3 of Table 20.7 provide a hypothetical example that represents a fairly common experience.

The publication of one index-number series may be abandoned because a new formula is being applied, because a major change in weights has been made, or because new goods are being included. A new, revised series may be published instead. A user of the index in question may, however, require a series that covers a range of time that includes years covered by both series. In the absence of any better alternative, the user may have to resort to the process of **splicing index-number series,** which involves uniting two index-number time series that cover different ranges of time into a single and longer series. Such splicing is not very satisfactory

TABLE 20.7 | Splicing Two Short Index-Number Series into a Longer Series

Year (1)	Old Price Index (1985 = 100) (2)	Revised Price Index (1995 = 100) (3)	Spliced Price Index (1995 = 100) (4)
1985	100.0	—	61.3
1986	105.2	—	64.5
1987	111.3	—	68.2
1988	117.9	—	72.3
1989	129.1	—	79.2
1990	136.8	—	83.9
1991	142.4	—	87.3
1992	146.5	—	89.8
1993	150.6	—	92.3
1994	155.9	—	95.6
1995	**163.1**	**100.0**	100.0
1996	—	102.3	102.3
1997	—	104.7	104.7
1998	—	106.4	106.4
1999	—	112.6	112.6
2000	—	122.5	122.5
2001	—	131.9	131.9
2002	—	137.3	137.3
2003	—	142.9	142.9

because the two series clearly measure different things, but it can be done as long as the two series contain at least one overlapping period. Our example shows how we might retain the values of the new series (the column 4 entries below the red horizontal line), while making the old series conform to the new one by shifting its base to the base of the new series. This base shifting requires, in our case, the division of each old-series index-number by 163.1 (in red on the table) and multiplication of the result by 100.

COMBINING TWO SPECIALIZED SERIES INTO A MORE COMPREHENSIVE SERIES

Sometimes two (or more) index-number time series are available that cover different items rather than different ranges of time. Columns 1–3 of Table 20.8 provide an example. The user of such indexes (a car dealer, perhaps) may wish to combine them into a more comprehensive measure (for new *and* used cars, for example). The process of **combining index-number series** involves uniting two specialized index-number series into a single, more comprehensive series by computing a weighted average of the separate indexes for each year. If our car dealer's sales included 70 percent new cars and 30 percent used cars, the published national indexes of any one year might be combined accordingly, as is shown in column 4. Each entry in column 4 equals .7 times the column 2 index plus .3 times the column 3 index. The dealer can now compare personal experience with the national experience given in column 4.

TABLE 20.8 | Combining Two Specialized Index-Number Series into a More Comprehensive Series

Year (1)	Price Index for New Cars (1992 = 100) (2)	Price Index for Used Cars (1992 = 100) (3)	Price Index for New and Used Cars (1992 = 100) (4) = [.7 × (2)] + [.3 × (3)]
1992	100.0	100.0	100.0
1993	107.9	107.8	107.9
1994	116.6	111.6	115.1
1995	123.7	137.7	127.9
1996	128.5	158.9	137.6
1997	133.4	183.3	148.4
1998	140.1	210.8	161.3
1999	147.1	242.4	175.7
2000	154.4	278.8	191.7
2001	159.0	300.8	201.5
2002	161.6	318.9	208.8

CREATING CHAIN INDEXES

All the price-index formulas discussed so far have involved comparisons between two dates only, a current period and a base period. In many cases, when price indexes are constructed repeatedly (month after month, quarter after quarter, or year after year), the base is not just shifted occasionally but is *continually* moved forward. When this procedure is used, the prices of each period always relate to those of the immediately preceding period. Thus, we might create (as we did above) a Laspeyres price index for 2001, *with 2000 base,* of 106.7, followed a year hence by an index for 2002, *with 2001 base,* of 114.6, and so on indefinitely. Such index numbers, each of which uses the immediately preceding period as a base, rather than a common base, are called **chain indexes.**

On occasion, in order to facilitate longer-term comparisons, we may wish to convert chain indexes to a common base, yet caution is advised. If the index-number formula in question does not meet the circularity test, we cannot multiply, say, $PI_{01,00} = 106.7$ by $PI_{02,01} = 114.6$, divide by 100, and expect to find $PI_{02,00} = 124.9$. (Recall the above section *The circularity test: Laspeyres* on page 973.) Still, chain indexes *can* be converted into a series with a common base. The usual procedure employs Formula 20.G, wherein Q_a is an arbitrary set of quantity weights that must be applied to all indexes alike.

FORMULA 20.G | Converting Chain Price Indexes to a Common Base

$$PI_{t,0} = PI_{t-1,0}\left(\frac{\Sigma P_t \cdot Q_a}{\Sigma P_{t-1} \cdot Q_a}\right)$$

where $PI_{t,0}$ is the price index of period t with respect to base period 0 and $PI_{t-1,0}$ is the price index of preceding period $t - 1$ with respect to base period 0, while P_t is the price in period t, P_{t-1} is the price in period $t - 1$, and Q_a is the quantity in arbitrary period a.

EXAMPLE PROBLEM 20.9

Review the price and quantity data found in Table 20.4 on page 966 and assume the following additional price data for the year 2002:

P_{02}: 2.00 1.75 1.00 2.00 2.50 1.00

Given the implied Laspeyres price index of 2001 with 2000 base of 106.7 and the quantity set of Table 20.4, use Formula 20.G to compute a Laspeyres price index of 2002 with 2000 base.

SOLUTION:

$$PI_{02,00} = PI_{01,00}\left(\frac{\Sigma P_{02} \cdot Q_{00}}{\Sigma P_{01} \cdot Q_{00}}\right) = 106.7\left(\frac{1{,}325}{1{,}132}\right) = 124.9$$

which is the number calculated independently in Example Problem 20.6. Thus, our short series of 2000, 2001, and 2002 price indexes *with a common 2000 base* is 100, 106.7, and 124.9.

20.7 Major U.S. Price Indexes

Having discussed the procedures that might be employed in index-number construction, it is time to consider some of the actual price indexes regularly published in the United States. These include the Consumer Price Index, the Producer Price Index, various stock price indexes, and a variety of other price indexes, such as implicit price deflators.

THE CONSUMER PRICE INDEX

The **Consumer Price Index,** usually referred to as the **CPI,** is published monthly by the Bureau of Labor Statistics of the U.S. Department of Labor and is readily available in such government publications as the *Monthly Labor Review,* the *Survey of Current Business,* the *Economic Report of the President,* and on the Internet. The index measures the average change in U.S. consumer prices over time. It is an aggregative chain index that is converted to a common base. Column 2 of Table 20.6 contains data for the last four decades of the 20th century; they also appear as panel (a) of Figure 20.1. Note that this particular rendition of the index is based on 1967 = 100, but the base year is changed about once per decade. (Base periods employed in recent times have included 1947–1949, 1957–1959, and 1982–1984.)

FIGURE 20.1 | The Recent Behavior of Selected U.S. Prices

These four panels picture the movements of four major price-index time series that are regularly published in the United States.

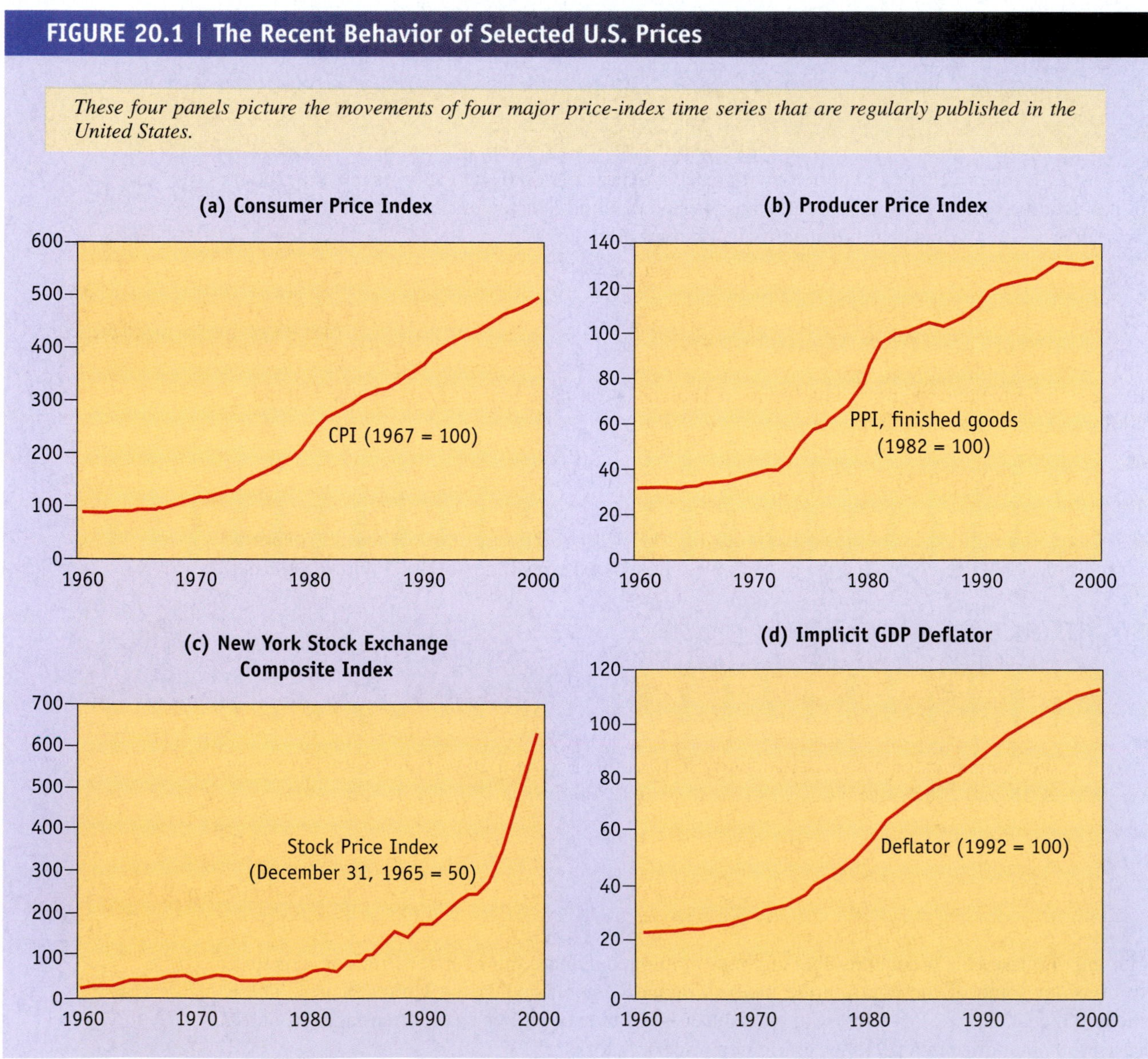

TABLE 20.9 | The 1990 Relative Importance of Various Groups of Commodities and Services Priced for the CPI (all urban consumers)

Major Group	Relative Importance	Major Group	Relative Importance
All items	100.000	Apparel and upkeep	6.073
Food and beverages	17.706	Apparel commodities	5.512
Food	16.188	Mens' and boys'	1.451
Food at home	10.094	Womens' and girls'	2.495
Cereals and bakery products	1.420	Infants' and toddlers'	.219
Meats, poultry, fish, and eggs	3.169	Footwear	.801
Dairy products	1.258	Other apparel commodities	.547
Fruits and vegetables	1.830	Apparel services	.561
Sugar and sweets	.343	Transportation	17.796
Fats and oils	.271	Private transportation	16.214
Nonalcoholic beverages	.765	New cars	4.043
Other prepared food	1.039	Used cars	1.139
Food away from home	6.094	Gasoline	4.051
Alcoholic beverages	1.518	Maintenance and repair	1.498
Housing	41.356	Other private transport	4.507
Shelter	27.657	Commodities	.688
Rent, residential	5.840	Services	3.819
Other rental costs	2.065	Public transportation	1.582
Homeownership	19.544	Medical care	6.387
Owners' equivalent rent	19.163	Medical-care commodities	1.203
Household insurance	.382	Medical-care services	5.184
Maintenance, repairs	.207	Professional services	3.119
Services	.127	Other medical-care services	.166
Commodities	.080	Entertainment	4.316
Fuel and other utilities	7.327	Entertainment commodities	2.016
Fuels	4.140	Entertainment services	2.300
Fuel oil, coal, and bottled gas	.520	Other goods and services	6.367
Piped gas, electricity	3.619	Tobacco products	1.542
Other utilities	3.188	Personal care	1.194
Household furnishings and operation	6.371	Toilet goods, personal care goods	.634
House furnishings	3.773	Personal-care services	.559
Housekeeping supplies	1.168	Personal and educational expenses	3.631
Housekeeping services	1.431	School books and supplies	.237
Appliances, electronics	1.015	Personal and educational services	3.395

SOURCE: Bureau of Labor Statistics, U.S. Department of Labor, *Relative Importance of Components in the Consumer Price Indexes 1990* (Washington, D.C.: U.S. Government Printing Office, 1991), pp. 2–7.

PRODUCING THE CPI How is the CPI produced? It is clearly impossible to monitor *all* the transactions U.S. consumers make. Therefore, the index uses data derived from a complex series of samples. In the 1990s, price data were collected in 85 urban areas across the country, ranging from New York City (the prices of which were given a weight of 9.585 out of 100) to Anchorage, Alaska (the prices of which were given a weight of only .102 because fewer people paid them). In addition, price data were collected only for a fixed *market basket* of about 400 commodities and services. The content of this basket was established by a 1982–1984 Consumer Expenditure Survey during which some 20,000 randomly selected families kept two-week diaries of everything they bought. As we might expect, the basket does not contain van Gogh paintings, but it does include major items of food, clothing, shelter, fuel, medical care, and more. Table 20.9 on the preceding page shows the relative importance of the major groups of commodities and services that were recently being priced for the CPI.

The prices of 400 specific items included in the fixed market basket are being gathered in a variety of ways. Mail questionnaires establish a few prices, such as transportation costs, public-utility rates, and newspaper prices. Most prices, however, are found by bureau representatives who regularly visit 24,000 retail stores and service establishments, 18,000 tenants (for rent), and another 18,000 housing units (for property taxes). The list of those to be visited was also established by sampling, based on such frames as the Census of Retail Trade. Bureau representatives attempt to price identical quantities of identical items at each visit, and, for that purpose, they follow detailed instructions. A dress may be described not only by size, but also by width in hem and seams, seams pressed open, taping on inside of hem, type of stitching, number of loose threads, and the presence of thread belt loops! When all is said and done, price data for any given location are combined into a weighted average (a popular store's price counting more than one from a store with few customers) and then into a weighted average of all sampled locations and, ultimately, all sampled goods.

In the process, a variety of consumer price indexes emerge. There are two overall indexes, one for urban wage and clerical workers only (the CPI-W), another for all urban consumers (the CPI-U). The CPI-W excludes not only the prices paid by rural Americans, but also those paid by some urban Americans, such as professional, managerial, and technical workers, the self-employed, short-term workers, the retired, and the (voluntarily or involuntarily) unemployed. Thus, it applies to only about 32 percent of the U.S. population. The CPI-U, in contrast, covers 80 percent of the population; it is the most commonly cited index. In addition to the two overall indexes, separate indexes are published for many categories of goods and localities, and there are also seasonally adjusted CPI series.

CRITICISMS Criticizing the CPI is child's play, but there is no better index of the prices U.S. consumers pay. Among the criticisms are these:

1. The fixed market basket of 400 goods is always out of date. People in the 1990s were in fact already buying different quantities and qualities of goods than the 1982–1984 survey found. Indeed, they were buying all kinds of goods that didn't even exist at the earlier time.
2. Bureau agents may not find the prices people actually pay. The agents may "shop" on Tuesdays, while most people buy goods on Saturdays, taking advantage of cheaper weekend specials. The agents may miss the presence of secret kickbacks, side payments, and quantity discounts. The agents will persist in pricing at a fixed sample of stores, while real shoppers are abandoning these for other, cheaper, or newer stores that may not be in the sample at all.
3. Bureau agents may miss quality changes. The nickel candy bar that shrinks in size has surely risen in price (more cents per gram), while the $50 tire that gives more mileage has

surely fallen in price (fewer cents per mile). Similarly, equal-priced medical care that can cure formerly incurable diseases is really cheaper, while equal-priced city bus rides that are dirtier, slower, and more crowded are surely more expensive.

4. The CPI is still irrelevant for the 20 percent of rural Americans whose goods are not being priced at all.

This list is by no means an exhaustive one.

THE PRODUCER PRICE INDEX

Like the CPI, the **Producer Price Index,** formerly called the *Wholesale Price Index,* is also a monthly product of the Bureau of Labor Statistics. It can be found in the same publications as the CPI. The index measures average price changes over time in U.S. primary (nonretail) markets. It is a value-weighted average of simple price indexes; the weights are 1982 shipments. Each month, bureau agents price more than 3,000 domestically produced and imported products in U.S. nonretail markets. Ultimately, a number of indexes emerge: by stage of processing (for finished goods, intermediate materials, and crude materials) and by major commodity groups (for farm products, chemicals, fuels, machinery, and many more). Panel (b) of Figure 20.1 on page 980 shows the recent behavior of the Producer Price Index for finished goods, which is regarded as a leading indicator of the future behavior of consumer prices.

STOCK PRICE INDEXES

A variety of common-stock indexes are published regularly by the New York Stock Exchange (NYSE), by Dow Jones and Co., and by Standard & Poor's Corporation. All of them are computed from average daily closing prices, but coverages and base periods vary. The NYSE composite index—the behavior of which is shown in panel (c) of Figure 20.1 on page 980—is based on December 31, 1965 = 50 and covers all of the more than 3,500 issues listed on the New York Stock Exchange; other NYSE indexes cover industrial, transportation, utilities, or finance stocks only. Standard & Poor's composite or "500 index" is based on 1941–1943 = 10 and, as the name suggests, covers 500 stocks. The famous Dow Jones Industrial Average, finally, is simply a weighted average of 30 stock prices; it is not even expressed as a percentage of any base-period average.

IMPLICIT PRICE DEFLATORS

The U.S. government publishes a multitude of economic time series (for example, in the annual *Economic Report of the President* or the Commerce Department's *Survey of Current Business*) that are expressed both in current dollars and constant (recently 1992) dollars. Such series include the Gross Domestic Product, shown in Table 20.10 on the next page.

Similar series include many of the GDP's expenditure subdivisions (consumption, investment, government, net exports), its industry subdivisions (such as agriculture, mining, manufacturing, services), and its product subdivisions (such as commodities, structures, and even autos). Given any current-dollar figure and a corresponding constant-dollar figure, we can divide the former by the latter, multiply by 100, and, thus, produce an **implicit price deflator.** The deflator is a price index for the item and period in question relative to the base period of the constant-dollar series.

Consider columns 1–3 of Table 20.10. They give data for the U.S. GDP at current and 1992 prices for the period from 1985 to 1999. Successively dividing each column 1 figure by the associated column 2 figure, and multiplying by 100, yields the price-index series of column 4. This implicit GDP deflator series measures the change, relative to 1992, in the general price level of

TABLE 20.10 | Finding the Implicit GDP Deflator

Year (1)	GDP at Current Prices (billions of dollars) (2)	GDP at Constant Prices (billions of 1992 dollars) (3)	Implicit GDP Deflator (4) = [(2)/(3)] · 100
1985	4,180.7	5,323.5	78.53
1986	4,422.2	5,487.7	80.58
1987	4,692.3	5,649.5	83.06
1988	5,049.6	5,865.2	86.09
1989	5,438.7	6,062.0	89.72
1990	5,743.8	6,136.3	93.60
1991	5,916.7	6,079.4	97.32
1992	6,244.4	6,244.4	100.00
1993	6,558.1	6,389.6	102.64
1994	6,947.0	6,610.7	105.09
1995	7,269.6	6,761.7	107.51
1996	7,661.6	6,994.8	109.53
1997	8,110.9	7,269.8	111.57
1998	8,511.0	7,551.9	112.70
1999	8,905.8	7,806.1	114.09

all the commodities and services entering the GDP. Thus, if we call the general U.S. price level 100 in 1992, column 4 tells us, the price level was 78.53 in 1985 (roughly 21 percent lower) and it was 114.09 in 1999 (roughly 14 percent higher). Panel (d) of Figure 20.1 on page 980 shows these and earlier data graphically.

Note that we can use the column 4 data to calculate the rate of inflation from any one year to the next. Between 1996 and 1997, for example, the general price level rose from 109.53 to 111.57, which suggests an annual inflation rate of 1.86 percent, because 111.57 is that much larger than 109.53.

20.8 Major Uses of Price Indexes

Price indexes are regularly put to use by all kinds of people. This section describes some of these possible uses.

EVALUATING ECONOMIC POLICY

The most obvious use for price indexes is to help evaluate the success or failure of economic policy. If a chairman of the Federal Reserve Board or a president of the United States proclaims in 1970 that "inflation can and must be stopped during this decade," we can wait 10 years, look at price-index series such as those pictured in Figure 20.1, and pronounce the policy a failure. Given the fact that any price index can never be more than a rough estimate of the underlying phenomenon, we should be less hasty, however, about drawing conclusions from minute changes of an index from one month to the next. Nevertheless, newspapers never fail to make headlines when the CPI or a similar price index quivers by a decimal point.

DEFLATING CURRENT-DOLLAR TIME SERIES

A less obvious but important use of price indexes is their role as deflators of economic time series that are expressed in current dollars. Such **deflation** is a process that removes the effect of price level changes from a current-dollar time series and, thus, restates the series in dollars of constant purchasing power, known as *constant dollars.* In 2000, the members of a labor union, for example, might be pondering the column 2 data of Table 20.11 just published by the U.S. government. Yet they might fail to be impressed by the 2.9-fold increase in their hourly earnings since 1975. They might divide each entry in that column by the column 3 Consumer Price Index, multiply by 100 and, thus, compute the column 4 time series of their *real* hourly earnings, which *declined* by 7 percent.

In the same way, a business executive might deflate current-dollar time series of company sales, production, inventory, or profit by some appropriate price index (a producer price index,

TABLE 20.11 | Deflating a Time Series with the Help of Index Numbers

Year (1)	Average Hourly Earnings in Manufacturing (current dollars) (2)	Consumer Price Index (1982–1984 = 100) (3)	Average Hourly Earnings in Manufacturing (1982–1984 dollars) (4)
1975	4.83	53.8	8.98
1976	5.22	56.9	9.17
1977	5.68	60.6	9.37
1978	6.17	65.2	9.46
1979	6.70	72.6	9.23
1980	7.27	82.4	8.82
1981	7.99	90.9	8.79
1982	8.49	96.5	8.80
1983	8.83	99.6	8.87
1984	9.19	103.9	8.85
1985	9.54	107.6	8.87
1986	9.73	109.6	8.88
1987	9.91	113.6	8.72
1988	10.19	118.3	8.61
1989	10.48	124.0	8.45
1990	10.83	130.7	8.27
1991	11.18	136.2	8.21
1992	11.46	140.3	8.17
1993	11.74	144.5	8.12
1994	12.07	148.2	8.14
1995	12.37	152.4	8.12
1996	12.77	156.9	8.14
1997	13.17	160.5	8.21
1998	13.49	163.0	8.28
1999	13.91	166.6	8.35

perhaps) to discover the underlying change in physical volume or real purchasing power. Similarly, economists invariably deflate current-dollar series of national output, consumption, money supply, and a host of other variables because a knowledge of *real* change (undistorted by price level movements) is more important to them.

ESCALATORS

In recent years, ever more legal contracts have come to contain **escalator clauses.** Such provisions specify that nominal monetary payments must be raised periodically in accordance with increases in the Consumer Price Index so as to preserve the real purchasing power of these payments. Escalator clauses are part of the labor contracts of millions of union members who seek to get nominal pay raises of, say, 6.9 percent when the CPI rises by 6.9 percent so that the purchasing power of their pay remains unchanged. Similar clauses can be found in divorce settlements (with respect to alimony payments), in insurance contracts (with respect to premiums and benefits), and in long-term leases on commercial land and buildings (with respect to rents). Even the rents of some Chicago penthouse apartments have recently been tied to the index, as have been pensions, Social Security benefits, and certain welfare payments and taxes.

CAUTION

Pay increases in strict accordance with the CPI are not necessarily required to protect an income recipient's current welfare from inflation. For one thing, people do not consume all of their income; some of it is taxed away or saved. Thus, a 6.9 percent increase in the CPI, together with a much smaller (escalator-induced) increase in money income, could easily be sufficient to raise the amount of money available for consumption by 6.9 percent.

More important, inflation is never uniform, with all prices moving in the same direction and by the same percentage. While the CPI rises by 6.9 percent, some individual prices fall, others stay unchanged, and yet others rise. Consumers can and do adjust their purchases to these changes in *relative* prices: They buy more of relatively cheaper goods and less of relatively more expensive goods. They certainly do not continue to buy a fixed basket of goods forever, which is what the advocates of escalator clauses often assume. These facts have an interesting implication.

Consider consumers who, following a rise in the CPI, are given enough extra dollars to be able to buy the very set of goods that they bought at the relative prices prevailing in the past. Then picture them in fact substituting a different set of goods because of the changed relative prices prevailing in the present. Can you see that these consumers will actually be better off, not equally well off? Thus, it is possible for consumers to keep a *constant* level of welfare (or utility), while spending *even on consumption goods* an added percentage that falls short of the rise in the CPI.

Economists (in contrast to statisticians), therefore, have long been interested in establishing a *constant-utility index.* In the face of a given increase (of, say, 6.9 percent) in the Consumer Price Index, such a measure would indicate the extra amount of money people would require (say, only 3.1 percent) to keep their *utility* constant (as opposed to their ability to buy an unchanged set of goods).

Note: For a brief discussion of the economic theory involved, see Heinz Kohler, *Intermediate Microeconomics: Theory and Applications,* 1st ed. (Glenview, Ill.: Scott, Foresman and Company, 1982), pp. 68–72. For further readings see Melville J. Ulmer, *The Economic Theory of Cost of Living Index Numbers* (New York: Columbia University Press, 1950).

20.9 Quantity Indexes

While the major part of this chapter has been concerned with price indexes, quantity indexes are no less important. However, we need not discuss the theory of constructing them because all the above formulas apply fully if we simply switch the roles of P and Q. For example, a Laspeyres (intertemporal) *quantity* index equals

$$QI_{t,0}^{Laspeyres} = \frac{\Sigma Q_t \cdot P_0}{\Sigma Q_0 \cdot P_0} \cdot 100$$

which is nothing else but a transformation of Formula 20.D. The index is constructed by aggregating time t and time 0 quantity sets, using time 0 (or base-year) price weights. All other index formulas can be similarly transformed. A Paasche quantity index, for instance, would use time t (or current-year) price weights.

THE INDEX OF INDUSTRIAL PRODUCTION

The most important quantity index used in the United States, perhaps, is the monthly (Federal Reserve) **index of industrial production,** published in the *Federal Reserve Bulletin* and on the Internet. It seeks to measure changes over time in the physical volume of industrial goods produced in the United States. The index uses *value added per unit of output* as weights. In addition to the overall index, separate indexes are computed for major industry divisions (such as manufacturing, mining, and utilities) and also for major market groupings (such as final products, intermediate products, and materials). Further subdivisions are available; final products, for example, are divided into automotive products, other durable consumer goods, nondurable consumer goods, business equipment, and more. Figure 20.2 shows the movement of the overall index since 1948. Note the clear impact of the seven post–World War II recessions.

THE INDEX-NUMBER PROBLEM REVISITED

Just like price indexes, quantity indexes can be plagued by the index-number problem. Suppose we wanted to compare a year 2000 set of physical output quantities with a similar set of goods

FIGURE 20.2 | The Federal Reserve Index of Industrial Production

The physical volume of U.S. industrial production has grown significantly since World War II but not without the interruption of seven major recessions (arrows).

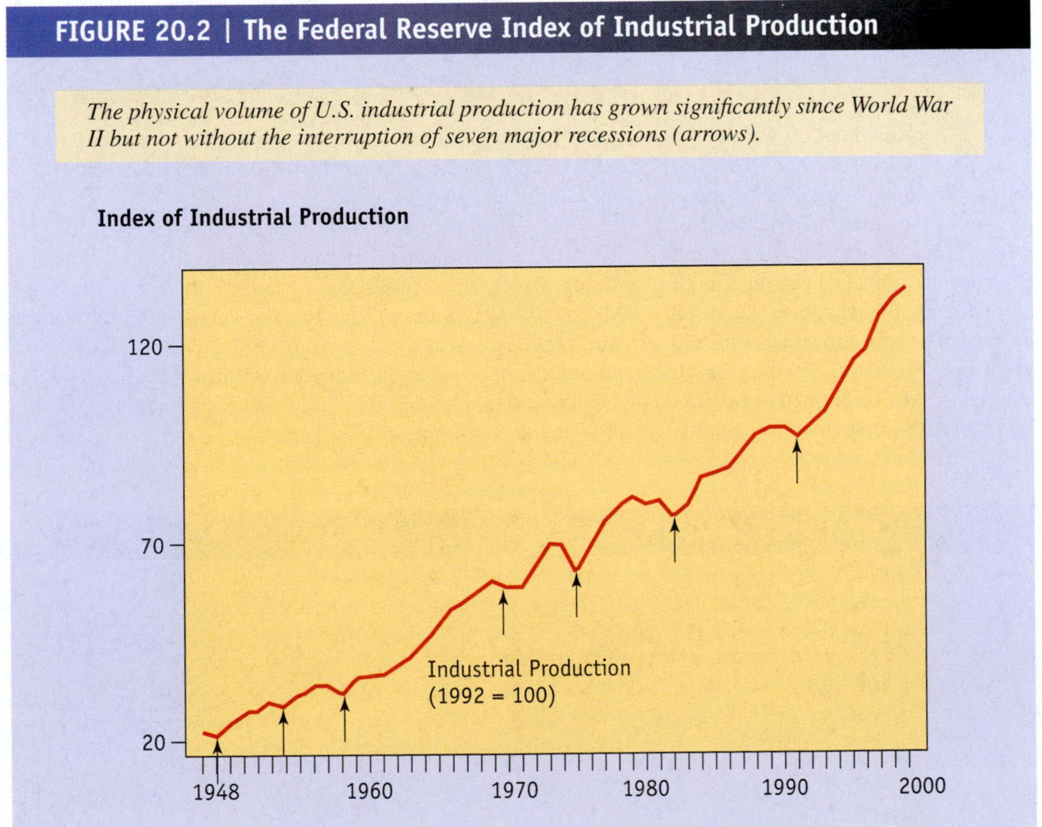

produced in 1990. We might add together each year's set of apples, oranges, and all the rest by using 1990 prices, compare the two constant-dollar aggregates, and compute a real-output growth rate of 3.6 percent. Yet, if we repeated the exercise with year 2000 prices, which would be just as logical, we might derive a growth rate of 2.9 or even 4.1 percent. Which computation would be correct? Once again, no answer exists. But all sorts of people make quantity comparisons such as these every day! Typically, they are quite unaware of the index-number problem.

Applications 20.1, *Measuring Soviet Economic Growth,* and 20.2, *Comparing U.S. with Soviet Real GNP,* provide two historical examples. Both of them take us back to the days of the Cold War when the United States and the Soviet Union were competing for world supremacy. But do not be misled by the historical nature of these examples. The index-number problem that they identify is just as relevant to modern-day comparisons of economic growth—whether you find them in the World Bank's latest *World Development Report,* the United Nations' latest *Human Development Report,* or even the latest *Economic Report of the President*. All these publications and many more continually contrast *real* GDP growth rates:

- between the United States now and the United States during various past periods of time
- between the United States and all sorts of other countries: the developed market economies of Canada, Western Europe, and Japan; the transition economies of post-Soviet Russia and Eastern Europe; the Islamic countries; sub-Saharan Africa, India, China, and Latin America . . . the list goes on

Yet every one of these comparisons may well be seriously flawed by the problem about to be reviewed!

Measuring Soviet Economic Growth

The index-number problem emerges whenever we attempt to compare, over time or space, heterogeneous aggregates of prices or output. Various sections of this chapter noted the difficulties associated with comparing price levels over time; consider the similar difficulty of comparing output levels over time. Heterogeneous outputs of apples, blast furnaces, medical care, and steel, for example, cannot be compared directly; they have to be added together using the common denominator of money. To yield meaningful results, the same price weights must be applied to the lists of quantities produced in two different periods, but the prices of one year work just as easily as those of another. If (as is likely) relative prices come to differ over time, different results can emerge.

Thus, Raymond P. Powell once attempted to measure the growth of Soviet GNP from 1928 to 1937, a time during which the Soviets industrialized their economy. Measured in 1928 prices, the average annual growth rate was 11.9 percent, but measured in 1937 prices, it was 6.2 percent. Neither answer is more correct than the other. The hypothetical example in Table 20.A highlights the problem.

TABLE 20.A

Type of Output	1928		1937	
	Quantity	Price	Quantity	Price
Food	100	1	90	2.0
Machinery	50	1	300	0.5

(continued)

Application 20.1 (continued)

Evaluate each year's physical output at earlier 1928 prices (as a Laspeyres *quantity* index would), and aggregate output is seen to have risen from (100 × 1) + (50 × 1) = 150 rubles to (90 × 1) + (300 × 1) = 390 rubles—at an average rate of more than 11 percent per year. Now evaluate each year's physical output at later 1937 prices (as a Paasche quantity index would), and aggregate output can be seen to have risen from (100 × 2) + (50 × 0.5) = 225 rubles to (90 × 2) + (300 × 0.5) = 330 rubles—at an average rate of less than 5 percent per year. There is no logical way to escape the problem.

SOURCES: Adapted from Heinz Kohler, *Intermediate Microeconomics: Theory and Applications,* lst ed. (Glenview, Ill.: Scott, Foresman and Company, 1982), p. 71; Raymond P. Powell, "Economic Growth in the U.S.S.R.," *Scientific American,* December 1968, pp. 17–23.

APPLICATION 20.2

Comparing U.S. with Soviet Real GNP

The index-number problem is just as serious with respect to interspatial comparisons as it is with respect to intertemporal comparisons. One favorite type of interspatial comparison, which is continually being made by economists and politicians all over the world, involves the real GNPs of different countries. Thus, the author of this book once noted, *measured in U.S. prices,* the Soviet real GNP grew tenfold between 1928 and 1975, while its U.S. counterpart grew only fourfold. As a result, the Soviet real GNP (which had equaled 25 percent of U.S. real GNP in 1928) rose to 40 percent of U.S. real GNP by 1955 and to 61 percent by 1975, making the Soviet Union the world's second largest economic power at that time. The hypothetical example in Table 20.B once again highlights the (unavoidable) problem with this kind of statement.

TABLE 20.B

Type of Output Price	1975 United States		1975 Soviet Union	
	Quantity	Dollar Price	Quantity	Ruble
Food	200	1	44	1

Evaluate each country's physical output at U.S. prices, and Soviet output is seen to equal (44 × 1) + (200 × 1) = 244 dollars as opposed to U.S. output of (200 × 1) + (200 × 1) = 400 dollars. Hence, Soviet output equals 61 percent of U.S. output. Now evaluate each country's physical output at Soviet prices (which is just as logical) and Soviet output is seen to equal (44 × 1) + (200 × 100) = 20,044 rubles as opposed to a U.S. output of (200 × 1) + (200 × 100) = 20,200 rubles. Therefore, the Soviet output equals 99 percent of U.S. output. Both statements cannot be true at the same time.

It is interesting to note that the Central Intelligence Agency has recently been blamed for not correctly predicting the economic collapse and political disintegration of the Soviet Union—precisely because it did not pay attention to the index-number problem and vastly overestimated Soviet economic strength.

SOURCE: Adapted from Heinz Kohler, *Scarcity and Freedom: An Introduction to Economics* (Lexington, Mass.: D. C. Heath, 1977), p. 449.

20.10 The Vain Pursuit of the Unquantifiable

On all too many occasions, those who construct index numbers are driven by an urgent desire to quantify what cannot possibly be quantified in a meaningful way. This section provides a vivid example of how indexes should *not* be constructed.

THE UNITED NATIONS HUMAN DEVELOPMENT INDEX

Economists are fond of comparing human welfare over time and space with the help of data on the per capita real GDP. United Nations analysts have been unhappy with this approach, arguing that there is so much more to life than the availability of mere commodities and services to people. Accordingly, they have developed a more comprehensive **human development index (HDI).** It is designed to be a composite measure of human welfare containing indicators of three equally weighted dimensions of human development: longevity, knowledge, and standard of living. Let us consider each of these components in turn.

LONGEVITY People's longevity is measured by their life expectancy at birth, which is the number of years a newborn would live if prevailing patterns of mortality at the time of its birth were to stay the same throughout its life. For the United States in 1995, for instance, the figure was 76.4 years.

KNOWLEDGE People's knowledge is measured by the adult literacy rate (given a weight of 2/3) and the combined school enrollment ratio (with a weight of 1/3). The adult literacy rate is defined as the percentage of persons age 15 and over who can, with understanding, both read and write a short, simple statement on their everyday life. The combined school enrollment ratio, in turn, is defined as the number of students enrolled in primary, secondary, and tertiary (college) education as a percentage of the population under age 24 in relevant age groups. For the United States in 1995, the adult literacy rate was 99 percent, and the combined school enrollment ratio was 96 percent.

STANDARD OF LIVING People's standard of living is measured by per capita real GDP data that are (1) expressed in purchasing power parity dollars (PPP$) and (2) adjusted for the declining marginal utility of higher income. The purchasing power parity adjustment changes per capita real GDP figures that are based on current market exchange rates in such a way that the adjusted figures reflect identical purchasing power around the world. Consider a market basket of commodities and services costing $800 in the United States. If an identical basket in Angola can be bought in local markets with the country's per capita GDP of 20,000 kwanzas, then the Angolan per capita GDP in purchasing power parity dollars is recorded as $800. This would happen even if the official exchange rate were, say 60 kwanzas/$1 and an Angolan who wanted to get *U.S. dollars* (rather than goods in Angolan markets) would get only $333.33 for 20,000 kwanzas spent at the bank.

The marginal utility adjustment, in turn, heavily discounts PPP$-denominated per capita real GDP figures in excess of PPP$5,990, which are deemed to provide a "decent standard of living." Dollar figures up to $5,990 are accepted at face value, but higher ones are discounted on the grounds that the marginal utility of income then rapidly declines and a person with, say, an $11,980 income will enjoy a total utility far less than twice that associated with a $5,990 income.

For the United States in 1995, the unadjusted purchasing power parity estimate of per capita GDP, with which the local purchasing power of the per capita GDPs of all other countries were compared, was recorded as PPP$26,977, but that figure was adjusted to PPP$6,259. (In that year the adjusted per capita GDPs of the world's nations ranged from a low of $355 in the Democratic Republic of the Congo to a high of $6,287 in Luxembourg.)

CONSTRUCTING THE INDEX

How does the United Nations combine disparate figures about life expectancy, knowledge, and standard of living into a *single* number? Consider its 1998 computation of 1995 HDIs:

- First, the U.N. statisticians determined a minimum and maximum for each of the components and then set the minimum equal to 0, the maximum equal to 1, and the actual figure proportionately in between.
- Second, they combined the three components by weighting them equally, which yielded an HDI index number lying between 0 and 1.
- Third, they ranked all the world's countries for which complete data were available in accordance with the HDI index. The country with the highest HDI index received a ranking of 1. In 1995, the country with the lowest index received a ranking of 174 (because that was the number of countries with relevant data in that year).

Table 20.12 provides an illustration of the minima and maxima involved, along with the 1995 index construction for the United States.

TABLE 20.12 | Constructing the 1995 Human Development Index

The first three index components are calculated with the help of simple proportions; the computation of the last component is slightly more complicated. In the life expectancy case, the index rises by 1 (above 0) when life expectancy rises by 60 years (above the 25-year minimum). Hence the index for the United States rises by x above zero when U.S. life expectancy rises by 51.4 years above the 25-year minimum. Thus 1:60 = x:51.4, and x = .857, as shown. Subsequent to calculating all components of the index, they are combined into the HDI with the help of the weights shown. For the United States in 1995,

$$HDI = \frac{.857(1) + .990(2/3) + .960(1/3) + .992(1)}{3} = .943$$

which ranked fourth among the 174 nations of the world so analyzed.

Category	Weight	Minimum (set equal to 0)	Maximum (set equal to 1)	U.S. Example: Actual Figure	U.S. Example: Index Component
Life Expectancy at Birth	1	25 years	85 years	76.4	.857
Knowledge					
Adult Literacy Rate	2/3	0%	100%	99%	.990
Combined School Enrollment Ratio	1/3	0%	100%	96%	.960
Standard of Living	1	adjusted PPP$100	adjusted PPP$6,311	adjusted PPP$6,259	.992

SOURCE: United Nations, *Human Development Report 1998* (New York: Oxford University Press, 1998), pp. 107 and 128.

HDI DATA FROM AROUND THE WORLD

In its human development index, the United Nations believes to have found a viable alternative way of comparing human welfare across the globe. Table 20.13 lists the ten worst and best countries in which to live, according to the HDI criterion.

A WORD OF CAUTION

It is important to understand that the United Nations' attempt to find a more comprehensive substitute for traditional measures of per capita GDP is subject to plenty of criticisms.

To begin with, life expectancy is closely related to per capita GDP; surely the same is true of adult literacy and the combined school enrollment ratio. This is so because people who have high incomes are more likely to buy larger quantities of normal goods than low-income people do. Such normal goods include health care and education—the purchase of which affects life expectancy, literacy rates, and school enrollment. As a result, an index that puts together life expectancy *and* literacy rates *and* school enrollment ratios *and* per capita income is apt to do nothing more than measure the same thing over and over again! (Indeed, if we take the United Nations' detailed 174-country data and subject them to a simple statistical test, we find correlation coefficients of .833, .657, and .746, respectively, between adjusted per capita real GDP on the one hand and life expectancy at birth, adult literacy, and the combined school enrollment ratio on the other hand. Not surprisingly, the remaining correlations are just as high: .837 and .844 between school enrollment on the one hand and life expectancy and literacy on the other, and .810 between literacy and life expectancy.) This is why the HDI data in Table 20.13 contain no surprises; we could have guessed as much from merely studying the per capita GDPs of the countries involved.

In addition, the list of particular index components used and the weighting scheme attached to them in the HDI construction are necessarily arbitrary. By adding other components of human welfare, such as rates of homicide, female labor force participation, and pollution, or by changing the weights noted in Table 20.12, totally different index values could be derived. They might turn even Sierra Leone into the best place on earth and Canada into a country everyone should

TABLE 20.13 | HDI Rankings of Nations: The Best and the Worst in 1995

The Top Ten	The Bottom Ten
1. Canada	165. Gambia
2. France	166. Mozambique
3. Norway	167. Guinea
4. United States	168. Eritrea
5. Iceland	169. Ethiopia
6. Finland	170. Burundi
7. Netherlands	171. Mali
8. Japan	172. Burkina Faso
9. New Zealand	173. Niger
10. Sweden	174. Sierra Leone

SOURCE: United Nations, *Human Development Report 1998* (New York: Oxford University Press, 1998), pp. 128 and 130.

avoid. (Indeed, over the years, the United Nations has published a series of indexes coming to vastly different conclusions for exactly this reason.)

In the end, we have to recognize that the ability to quantify the unquantifiable will forever elude us. The message contained in data on per capita GDP is likely to be the best we are going to get. No fancy human welfare index is likely to improve matters.

Summary

1. *Index numbers* measure the magnitude of a variable at one time or place relative to the magnitude of the same variable at another time or place. The variable in question can be an individual price, quantity, or value figure; more often, entire sets of these prices, quantities, or values are being compared. Thus, *price indexes* measure the level of either a single price or of a set of prices at one time or place relative to another time or place, while *quantity indexes* measure the magnitude of either a single quantity or of a set of quantities at one time or place relative to another time or place.

2. A *simple price index* compares the price of a single item at one time or place with the price of the same item at another time or place. The period to which a given price is related is the *base period;* its index is expressed as 100.

3. *A composite price index* compares a set of prices for a variety of items at one time or place with such a set for the same items at another time or place. Such an index can be constructed in many ways—for example, as an *unweighted average of simple price indexes,* as an *unweighted aggregative price index,* or as a *weighted aggregative price index.*

4. Versions of the weighted aggregative price index, such as the *Laspeyres price index,* the *Paasche price index*, the *typical-year aggregative price index,* or the *Edgeworth price index,* are distinguished by the way in which the weights are chosen. Weighted indexes are usually considered superior to unweighted indexes because the latter treat all prices (or quantities) as equally important, which is rarely correct. However, weighting gives rise to the *index-number problem,* which occurs when one is able to construct different indexes for a given phenomenon depending on which of several, equally logical sets of weights is being employed.

5. Irving Fisher suggested a number of quality tests designed to distinguish superior from inferior index numbers, including the time-reversal test, the factor-reversal test, and the circularity test. A price index formula, for instance, passes the *time-reversal test* if, in a comparison of prices at two dates, the same result is obtained regardless of which of the two dates is chosen as a base. Similarly, a (quantity-weighted) price index formula passes the *factor-reversal test* if division of the price index by 100, and subsequent multiplication by a corresponding quantity index, produces a value equal to an independently derived value index. A price index formula passes the *circularity test* if the price index of year 1 with year 0 base, when multiplied by the price index of year 2 with year 1 base and divided by 100, equals the independently calculated price index of year 2 with year 0 base. The Laspeyres and Paasche indexes, although commonly used, fail all of these tests. *Fisher's ideal index,* which equals the geometric mean of the Laspeyres and Paasche indexes, passes the time-reversal test and the factor-reversal test.

6. Index-number time series can be manipulated in a variety of ways—for example, by shifting the base, by splicing two short series into a longer series, by combining two specialized series into a more comprehensive series, and by chaining index numbers together. (Series of index numbers each of which uses the immediately preceding period as a base, rather than a common base, are called *chain indexes.* They can be converted into a single series with a common base to facilitate longer-term comparisons. Such conversion must, however, proceed with caution when the index-number formula in question fails to pass the circularity test.)

7. Major price indexes that are regularly published and used in the United States include the *Consumer Price Index,* the *Producer Price Index,* various stock price indexes, and *implicit price deflators.*

8. Price indexes serve a number of purposes. They are used to evaluate economic policy, to deflate current-dollar time series, and to facilitate computations required by *escalator clauses* of legal contracts. Escalator clauses that raise nominal income payments in strict accordance with increases in the Consumer Price Index (ostensibly to keep real income unchanged) probably *raise* the recipient's welfare.

9. Quantity indexes are no less important than price indexes. They can easily be constructed by reversing the roles of P and Q in price index formulas. The Federal Reserve index of industrial production is one of the more important quantity indexes used in the United States. Just like price indexes, quantity indexes suffer from the index-number problem.

10. It is important to recognize instances in which those who construct index numbers get carried away by their desire to quantify the unquantifiable. More likely than not, the resultant indexes make no sense at all. The United Nations *human development index* is a case in point.

Key Terms

base period
base shifting
chain indexes
circularity test
combining index-number series
composite price index
Consumer Price Index (CPI)
deflation
Edgeworth price index
escalator clauses
factor-reversal test
Fisher's ideal index
human development index (HDI)
implicit price deflator
index-number problem
index numbers
index of industrial production
interspatial index numbers
intertemporal index numbers
Laspeyres price index
Paasche price index
price indexes
price relative
price-relative index
Producer Price Index
quantity indexes
reference period
simple price index
splicing index-number series
time-reversal test
typical-year aggregative price index

Practice Problems

NOTE

Some problems require the use of a statistical program, EXCEL or MINITAB. The program's major features are explained in text Chapter 2; plenty of additional advice is available via the program's built-in Help feature.

Section 20.2 Simple Price Indexes

1. Using the data of Table 20.14,
   a. create a series of intertemporal simple price indexes based on 1990.
   b. interpret the 1995 index.

TABLE 20.14 | Wholesale Coffee Prices, Premium-Grade Beans

Year	Price (dollars/pound)
1990	.91
1991	.80
1992	.55
1993	.75
1994	1.60
1995	1.50
1996	1.25
1997	2.60
1998	1.20
1999	1.06

2. Using the Oracle data of Table 20.15,
   a. create a series of intertemporal simple price indexes based on January 1999.
   b. interpret the November index.
3. Using the Sony data of Table 20.15,
   a. create a series of intertemporal simple price indexes based on January 1999.
   b. interpret the November index.

TABLE 20.15 | 1999 Stock Prices

Month	Price (dollars/share)	
	Oracle	Sony
January	31	70
February	38	74
March	28	90
April	25	105
May	24	94
June	25	91
July	40	117
August	38	122
September	46	133
October	45	156
November	76	177

4. Using the data of Table 20.16,

a. create a series of simple quantity indexes based on Amazon.

b. interpret the AOL index.

TABLE 20.16 | October 1999 Web Site Visitors

Web Site	Visitors (millions)
AOL	42.1
Yahoo	40.1
Microsoft	37.7
Lycos	29.2
Go Network	21.7
Excite	15.0
Amazon	12.9
Time Warner Online	12.5
Go2Net Network	11.3
BlueMountainArt.com	11.0
AltaVista	10.3
eBay	9.7
CNET	9.6
RealSite Portfolio	9.6
LookSmart	9.3
Snap	9.0
About.com	8.8
Xoom.com	8.4
ZDNet	8.3
GoTo.com	7.2

5. Using the data of Table 20.17,

a. create a series of simple quantity indexes based on Toyota.

b. interpret the Ford index.

TABLE 20.17 | July 1999 U.S. Light-Truck Sales

Company	Number (thousands)
G.M.	202.1
Ford	197.9
Daimler-Chrysler	176.0
Toyota	56.1
Nissan	30.5
Honda	18.4

6. Using the data of Table 20.18,

a. create a series of interspatial simple quantity indexes based on Brazil.

b. interpret the Guatemalan index.

TABLE 20.18 | World Coffee Production, 1999–2000 Season

Grower	Quantity (million bags of 132 lb.)
Brazil	26.5
Colombia	12.7
Indonesia	7.2
Vietnam	7.0
Mexico	5.2
Côte d'Ivoire	5.0
India	4.5
Guatemala	3.3
Honduras	2.9
Costa Rica	2.6

7. Using the data of Table 20.19,

a. create a series of simple quantity indexes based on the Ford Taurus.

b. interpret the Toyota Camry and Dodge Caravan indexes.

8. Using the data of Table 20.20,

a. create a series of simple value indexes based on Wal-Mart.

b. interpret the Ames index.

9. Using the data of Table 20.21,

a. create a series of simple value indexes based on J. C. Penney.

b. interpret the Sears and Saks indexes.

TABLE 20.19 | July 1999 Top-Selling Vehicles in the U.S.

Vehicle	Number (thousands)
Ford F-Series pickup	64.3
Chevrolet Silverado	45.7
Dodge Ram pickup	44.6
Toyota Camry	44.5
Honda Accord	38.4
Ford Explorer	35.8
Ford Taurus	32.0
Honda Civic	31.5
Jeep Grand Cherokee	29.2
Ford Escort	28.6
Ford Ranger	28.5
Dodge Caravan	27.3

TABLE 20.20 | November 1999 Retail Sales

Company	Sales (million dollars)
Wal-Mart	15,023
Kmart	2,961
Dayton Hudson	2,908
Costco	2,460
Ames	429
Dollar General	342

TABLE 20.21 | November 1999 Retail Sales

Company	Sales (million dollars)
Sears	2,748
Federated	1,536
J. C. Penney	1,459
May	1,269
Saks	650
Dillard's	650
Neiman Marcus	256

10. Using the data of Table 20.22 on the next page,

a. create a series of simple value indexes based on Lake Tahoe, California.

b. interpret the Southampton, N.Y., and Naples, Fla., indexes.

TABLE 20.22 | Average Vacation Home Prices in 1999

Area	Price (thousands of dollars)
Southampton, N.Y.	1,400
Litchfield County, Conn.	857
Key West, Fla.	826
Vail, Colo.	740
Kennebunkport, Maine	706
Park City, Utah	580
Santa Barbara, Calif.	475
Hilton Head, S.C.	460
Lake Tahoe, Calif.	417
Stone Harbor, N.J.	408
Sedona, Ariz.	350
Maui, Hawaii	345
Rehoboth Beach, Del.	343
Big Sky, Mont.	324
Naples, Fla.	311

SECTION 20.3 UNWEIGHTED COMPOSITE PRICE INDEXES

11. Using the data of Table 20.23, calculate

a. separate 1999 simple price indexes for the 30 teams, using 1998 as a base.

b. the unweighted average of the simple price indexes computed in (a) and interpret it.

12. Using the data of Table 20.23, calculate

a. separate 1998 simple price indexes for the 30 teams, using 1999 as a base.

b. the unweighted average of the simple price indexes computed in (a) and interpret it.

13. Using the data of Table 20.24 on page 1000, calculate

a. separate 1999 simple price indexes for the stocks of the 4 companies, using 1998 as a base.

b. the unweighted average of the simple price indexes computed in (a) and interpret it.

14. Using the data of Table 20.24 on page 1000, calculate

a. separate 1998 simple price indexes for the stocks of the 4 companies, using 1999 as a base.

b. the unweighted average of the simple price indexes computed in (a) and interpret it.

15. Using the data of Table 20.25 on page 1000, calculate

a. separate 1999 simple price indexes for the 30 teams, using 1998 as a base.

b. the unweighted average of the simple price indexes computed in (a) and interpret it.

16. Using the data of Table 20.25 on page 1000, calculate

a. separate 1998 simple price indexes for the 30 teams, using 1999 as a base.

b. the unweighted average of the simple price indexes computed in (a) and interpret it.

17. Review Practice Problem 11; then calculate an unweighted aggregative price index for 1999 based on 1998 and interpret it.

18. Review Practice Problem 12; then calculate an unweighted aggregative price index for 1998 based on 1999 and interpret it.

TABLE 20.23 | The Prices of Major League Baseball Teams

Team	1998 Price (million dollars)	1999 Price (million dollars)
New York Yankees	361	491
Cleveland Indians	321	359
Atlanta Braves	300	357
Baltimore Orioles	322	351
Colorado Rockies	302	311
Arizona Diamondbacks	291	291
Texas Rangers	253	281
Los Angeles Dodgers	237	270
Boston Red Sox	229	256
New York Mets	193	249
Houston Astros	190	239
Seattle Mariners	251	236
Tampa Bay Devil Rays	225	225
Chicago Cubs	204	224
San Francisco Giants	188	213
St. Louis Cardinals	174	205
San Diego Padres	161	205
Anaheim Angels	157	195
Chicago White Sox	214	178
Cincinnati Reds	136	163
Toronto Blue Jays	141	162
Milwaukee Brewers	127	155
Florida Marlins	159	153
Detroit Tigers	137	152
Philadelphia Phillies	131	145
Pittsburgh Pirates	133	145
Oakland Athletics	118	125
Kansas City Royals	108	96
Minnesota Twins	94	89
Montreal Expos	88	84

SOURCE: Adapted from *Forbes,* May 31, 1999, p. 114.

19. Review Practice Problem 13; then calculate an unweighted aggregative price index for 1999 based on 1998 and interpret it.

20. Review Practice Problem 14; then calculate an unweighted aggregative price index for 1998 based on 1999 and interpret it.

21. Review Practice Problem 15; then calculate an unweighted aggregative price index for 1999 based on 1998 and interpret it.

22. Review Practice Problem 16; then calculate an unweighted aggregative price index for 1998 based on 1999 and interpret it.

TABLE 20.24 | The Stock Prices of Major Racing Companies

Company	1998 Stock Price (dollars per share)	1999 Stock Price (dollars per share)
International Speedway	30.37	48.50
Speedway Motorsports	26.26	34.50
Penske Motorsports	32.27	34.88
Action Performance	35.27	32.28

SOURCE: Adapted from *Fortune,* April 12, 1999, p. 68.

TABLE 20.25 | The Prices of National Football League Teams

Team	1998 Price (million dollars)	1999 Price (million dollars)
Dallas Cowboys	412	663
Washington Redskins	402	607
Tampa Bay Buccaneers	346	502
Carolina Panthers	364	488
New England Patriots	251	460
Miami Dolphins	340	446
Denver Broncos	321	427
Jacksonville Jaguars	293	419
Baltimore Ravens	329	408
Seattle Seahawks	324	399
Pittsburgh Steelers	301	397
Cincinnati Bengals	310	394
St. Louis Rams	322	390
New York Giants	287	376
San Francisco 49ers	254	371
Tennessee Titans	321	369
New York Jets	259	363
Kansas City Chiefs	256	353
Buffalo Bills	251	326
San Diego Chargers	247	323
Green Bay Packers	244	320
Philadelphia Eagles	248	318
New Orleans Saints	242	315
Chicago Bears	237	313
Minnesota Vikings	232	309
Atlanta Falcons	234	306
Indianapolis Colts	228	305
Arizona Cardinals	230	301
Oakland Raiders	235	299
Detroit Lions	312	293

SOURCE: Adapted from *Forbes,* September 20, 1999, p. 177.

SECTION 20.4 WEIGHTED AGGREGATIVE PRICE INDEXES

23. Using the data of Table 20.26, compute a Laspeyres price index of automobile operating costs for 2000, based on 1990.

24. Using the data of Table 20.26, compute a Paasche price index of automobile operating costs for 2000, based on 1990.

25. Review the answers to Practice Problems 23 and 24 and identify the index-number problem. Then

a. propose changes to the year 2000 quantity data that would eliminate the problem.

b. recalculate the Paasche price index with your new quantity set to prove that the problem has disappeared.

26. Using the data of Table 20.26, compute an Edgeworth price index of automobile operating costs for 2000, based on 1990.

TABLE 20.26 | Automobile Operating Costs in Boston

Market Basket Components	Price (dollars per unit)		Quantity (number of units bought by average car owner)	
	1990	2000	1990	2000
Gasoline (gallons)	1.09	1.34	500.0	700
Oil (quarts)	1.00	1.25	12	20
Insurance (annual)	950.00	800.00	1.3	2
Repairs (hours)	32.00	52.00	12	23
Tires (number)	55.00	55.00	5	3
Taxes (annual)	155.00	140.00	1.3	2

27. Using the data of Table 20.27, compute a Laspeyres price index of aircraft accessories for 2000, based on 1990.

TABLE 20.27 | Aircraft Accessory Data

Market Basket Components	Price (dollars per unit)		Quantity (number of units sold by Sporty's Pilot Shop)	
	1990	2000	1990	2000
Altimeter	533	197	173	158
Battery charger	35	36	39	60
Flight case	125	152	20	23
Flight-plan computer	695	258	15	233
Life raft	999	629	1	5
Oxygen system	521	460	10	12
Tire (nose wheel)	182	170	622	499
Transceiver	999	495	5	49
Transponder	980	621	120	378
Xenon strobe	120	65	7	77

28. Using the data of Table 20.27 on the preceding page, compute a Paasche price index of aircraft accessories for 2000, based on 1990.

29. Review the answers to Practice Problems 27 and 28 and identify the index-number problem. Then
    a. propose changes to the year 2000 quantity data that would eliminate the problem.
    b. recalculate the Paasche price index with your new quantity set to prove that the problem has disappeared.

30. Using the data of Table 20.27 on the preceding page, compute an Edgeworth price index of aircraft accessories for 2000, based on 1990.

31. Show your understanding of the *index-number problem* by indicating what change in Soviet 1928 prices, in Application 20.1 on page 988, would eliminate the index-number problem encountered there.

32. Show your understanding of the *index-number problem* by indicating what change in Application 20.2 on page 989 would eliminate the index-number problem encountered there.

33. Review Example Problems 20.4 and 20.5 on pages 966 and 967. Using the same data, compute an Edgeworth price index for 2001 based on 2000.

SECTION 20.5 FISHER'S QUALITY TESTS AND HIS IDEAL INDEX

34. Example Problem 20.4 computed a Laspeyres price index; in Example Problem 20.6, it was subjected to Fisher's *time-reversal test*. Using the same data, make the same test for the Paasche price index computed in Example Problem 20.5.

35. Example Problem 20.4 computed a Laspeyres price index; in Example Problem 20.6, it was subjected to Fisher's *factor-reversal test*. Using the same data, make the same test for the Paasche price index computed in Example Problem 20.5.

36. Example Problem 20.4 computed a Laspeyres price index; in Example Problem 20.6, it was subjected to Fisher's *circularity test*. Using the same data, make the same test for the Paasche price index computed in Example Problem 20.5.

37. Using the automobile-operating data of Table 20.26 on the preceding page, compute Fisher's ideal price index for 2000 based on 1990.

TABLE 20.28 | Historical Index Series

Part A			Part B	
Year	Old Index (1955 = 100)	Revised Index (1979 = 100)	Place	U.S. State Department 1985 Cost-of-Living Index
1976	293	—	Washington, D.C.	100
1977	301	—	London	110
1978	311	—	Paris	139
1979	317	100	Bonn	120
1980	—	105	Moscow	80
1981	—	111	Nairobi	60
1982	—	97		
1983	—	95		
1984	—	103		
1985	—	115		

38. Using the aircraft-accessory data of Table 20.27 on page 1001, compute Fisher's ideal price index for 2000 based on 1990.

SECTION 20.6 MANIPULATING INDEX-NUMBER TIME SERIES

39. Review Table 20.1 on page 961. Rearrange the column 4 price index series by shifting the base to 1998. Round your answers to whole numbers.

40. Review Table 20.8 on page 978. Rearrange the column 4 price index series by shifting the base to 2000. Round your answers to whole numbers.

41. Consider the index-number series in Table 20.28 to solve the following problems (in all cases, round to whole numbers):

a. Splice the two series in Part A together into a combined series with 1979 = 100 as a base.

b. Shift the base of your spliced series to 1985 = 100.

c. Shift the base of the Part B series from Washington, D.C. = 100 to Moscow = 100.

SECTION 20.7 MAJOR U.S. PRICE INDEXES

SECTION 20.8 MAJOR USES OF PRICE INDEXES

42. Consider the data of Table 20.29. Use them to create a price index series for mining products based on 1992 = 100.

TABLE 20.29 | The Mining Industry Component of U.S. GDP

Year	Billions of Current Dollars	Billions of 1992 Dollars
1980	112.7	82.0
1981	151.7	81.4
1982	149.5	78.8
1983	127.5	73.7
1984	134.2	82.0
1985	132.8	87.1
1986	86.3	83.6
1987	88.3	86.4
1988	99.9	104.4
1989	96.3	92.8
1990	112.3	96.9
1991	101.1	97.5
1992	92.2	92.2
1993	94.6	96.4
1994	94.9	102.5
1995	98.7	107.4
1996	113.8	103.0
1997	120.5	109.9

43. Consider the data of Table 20.30 on the next page. Use them to create a price index series for the medical-care component of personal consumption expenditures based on 1992 = 100.

TABLE 20.30 | The Medical-Care Component of U.S. Consumption

Year	Billions of Current Dollars	Billions of 1992 Dollars
1982	239.4	442.2
1983	267.8	459.7
1984	294.1	472.4
1985	321.8	490.7
1986	346.1	510.3
1987	381.1	537.3
1988	428.7	561.3
1989	477.1	575.8
1990	537.7	602.8
1991	586.5	621.6
1992	646.6	646.6
1993	695.6	655.3
1994	731.6	662.1
1995	776.2	675.0
1996	806.8	686.6
1997	843.4	701.7
1998	893.0	725.3

TABLE 20.31 | The Residential Construction Component of U.S. Investment

Year	Billions of Current Dollars	Billions of 1992 Dollars
1982	105.7	140.1
1983	152.5	197.6
1984	179.8	226.4
1985	186.9	229.5
1986	218.1	257.0
1987	277.6	257.6
1988	232.5	252.5
1989	231.3	243.2
1990	215.7	220.6
1991	191.2	193.4
1992	225.6	225.6
1993	251.6	242.6
1994	286.0	267.0
1995	284.8	256.8
1996	311.8	275.9
1997	327.9	282.8
1998	375.8	316.5

44. Consider the data of Table 20.31. Use them to create a price index series for the residential construction component of investment expenditures based on 1992 = 100.

45. Consider the data of Table 20.32. Use the implicit GDP deflators found in Table 20.10 on page 984 to compute the *real* money stock, reflecting 1992 purchasing power.

TABLE 20.32 | The U.S. M1 Money Stock (average of daily figures)

Year	Billions of Current Dollars
1990	825.8
1991	897.3
1992	1,025.0
1993	1,129.9
1994	1,150.7
1995	1,128.7
1996	1,082.8
1997	1,076.0
1998	1,092.3

46. Consider the data of Table 20.33. In real terms, which was the best offer? Which the worst?

TABLE 20.33 | Average Salary Offers Received by Graduating Students

Year	Dollars per Year	CPI (1982–1984 = 100)
1960	7,000	29.6
1970	11,000	38.8
1980	19,000	82.4
1990	28,000	130.7
1998	35,000	163.0

47. Seen in a 1998 newspaper:

a. "For Sale 1960 Cadillac. $100 (1960 dollars)." What was the car's current-dollar price?

b. "For Sale 1970 Piper Cherokee. $12,000 (1970 dollars)." What was the plane's current-dollar price?

SECTION 20.9 QUANTITY INDEXES

48. The manager of an orchard has collected the data of Table 20.34. Compute a 1995 *Laspeyres quantity index* for the orchard's output, based on 1985.

49. The manager of an orchard has collected the data of Table 20.34. Compute a 1995 *Paasche quantity index* for the orchard's output, based on 1985.

50. The manager of an orchard has collected the data of Table 20.34. Compute a 1995 *Fisher ideal quantity index* for the orchard's output, based on 1985.

TABLE 20.34 | Orchard Data

	Output (thousands of bushels)				Price (dollars per bushel)			
Item	**1985**	**1990**	**1995**	**2000**	**1985**	**1990**	**1995**	**2000**
Almonds	12	13	15	9	20	19	15	26
Apricots	4	5	8	6	10	10	9	12
Cherries	20	15	16	25	25	28	30	15
Peaches	6	6	6	7	15	12	12	12

PART VIII

SUPPLEMENTARY TOPICS FOR BUSINESS

HYPOTHESIS TESTING: NONPARAMETRIC TECHNIQUES

LOOKING AHEAD

After reading this chapter, you will know a great deal about nonparametric tests that make no assumptions about the probability distributions of population values or about the sizes of population parameters. Among other things, you will learn to apply:

1. the *Wilcoxon rank-sum test,* which seeks to determine whether the relative frequency distributions of two statistical populations are identical,
2. the *Mann-Whitney test,* an alternative to the rank-sum test that pursues the same goal and is often favored in business and economics applications,
3. the *sign test,* which examines matched-pair samples to determine whether the relative frequency distributions of two statistical populations are identical (and which can also be used to determine whether a sample comes from a population with a specified median),
4. the *Wilcoxon signed-rank test,* which, like the sign test, uses matched-pair samples to determine whether the relative frequency distributions of two statistical populations are identical, but uses more of the available sample information than the sign test,
5. the *number-of-runs test,* which determines whether the elements of a sequence appear in random order,
6. the *Kruskal-Wallis test,* which extends the Wilcoxon rank-sum test from two to more than two populations,
7. the *Kolmogorov-Smirnov test,* an alternative to the χ^2 test for goodness of fit, which allows us to ascertain the nature of a population's probability distribution and can serve as a screening device for parametric tests that require a particular population distribution (often the normal distribution) in order to lead to valid results, and
8. the *Spearman rank-correlation test,* which measures the degree of association between two variables for which only rank-order data are available.

AND HERE IS A TYPICAL PROBLEM YOU WILL BE ABLE TO SOLVE:

A manufacturer advertised the median life of an aircraft spark plug as 800 service hours. The FAA doubted the claim and checked a random sample of logbooks on 50 types of planes using this type of plug. In 12 types of airplanes, the spark plugs lasted more than 800 hours (+), but they lasted fewer hours (−) in the remaining 38 airplane types. Was the advertising claim correct? Conduct an appropriate hypothesis test at the 5 percent level of significance.

PREVIEW

In 1999, a government economist wanted to compare average monthly salaries received by workers in two industries. Relevant data from two small random samples, taken independently, were available. Yet, the economist hesitated to employ the kind of hypothesis test about the difference of two means that was introduced in Chapter 13. The hesitation was well advised, because any hypothesis test based on the t statistic is only valid if certain conditions hold: In a two-sample test, the sampled populations *must* be normally distributed and *must* have equal variances. Salary populations, however, are almost certainly skewed to the right and not normally distributed.

At about the same time, a management-consulting firm hired by the FAA set out to determine whether the training given to future air traffic controllers was equally effective at four locations. The same test had been administered everywhere to the most recent air traffic controller class. Seven test scores were available for regions A, C, and D and six scores from region B. Yet, this analyst, too, was reluctant to employ what *seemed* to be the best test for the data involved: the one-way ANOVA procedure. True enough, the ANOVA F test helps us compare numerous means, but it also requires sampled populations to be normally distributed and to have equal variances. It was unclear whether such stringent assumptions could be made about the test score populations involved.

Meanwhile, a business executive had encountered a problem of her own. The firm's quality inspector had been recording the sequence of satisfactory (S) and defective (D) items coming off the assembly line, collecting data such as S, S, S, D, S, S, D, S, S. . . . Perusing these nominal data, the executive wondered whether the appearance of defective items in the continuous production process was entirely random or whether it exhibited some kind of pattern traceable to a particular worker or machine. Yet the executive was stumped. What kind of statistical test of such an S and D sequence could possibly answer the question raised?

The current chapter deals precisely with situations such as these. Unlike the classical hypothesis tests introduced in earlier chapters, none of this chapter's tests requires particular assumptions about the sampled populations or their parameters. Nor do these tests necessarily require the use of interval or ratio data. Indeed, in these *nonparametric tests,* the probability distributions and parameters of the sampled populations can be unknown. In addition, many of these tests can be undertaken with *ordinal* data or even with more primitive *nominal* data.

21.1 Parametric versus Nonparametric Tests

Many traditional hypothesis tests rely on strict assumptions concerning the underlying populations that we sample. Our view of the sampling distributions of the test statistics that we employ is only accurate if these assumptions are fulfilled. Consider our use of Student's t statistic in an independent-sample test of the difference between two population means. The validity of the entire test rests on an assumption about the shape of the population distributions (namely, that they are normal) and on a further assumption about the values of certain population parameters (namely, that the two population variances are equal). Whenever a hypothesis test depends in this way on certain specific assumptions about the probability distribution of population values or the sizes of population parameters, we refer to it as a **parametric test** and call the test statistic a **parametric statistic.** All too often, however, we cannot fulfill such assumptions, especially if they are demanding and narrow. Not surprisingly, therefore, statisticians are keenly interested in how sensitive their tests are to deviations from basic assumptions. Some tests show a great deal of **robustness;** their degree of sensitivity to errors in assumptions is low. Other tests are not so robust; any violation of assumptions in such situations causes the tests to grind out nonsense. In such cases, we want to find inferential procedures that are free from restrictive assumptions about the sampled populations. Such methods of inference are the focus of this chapter.

DEFINITION 21.1 Methods of inference that make no assumptions whatsoever about the nature of underlying population distributions or their parameters are **nonparametric tests.** Their test statistics are **nonparametric statistics.**

Nonparametric tests are also referred to as **distribution-free tests,** because no assumption about the nature of the *population* distribution is being made. But this term can easily lead to confusion, because these tests make very definite assumptions about the *sampling* distributions of their test statistics.

ADVANTAGES OF NONPARAMETRIC TESTS

The most important advantage of any nonparametric test is that we can safely employ it even when we know nothing at all about the population from which sample data are being drawn. The use of a parametric test in such circumstances would carry with it the risk of possibly violating crucial assumptions and generating erroneous or misleading results.

Another advantage is the fact that we can conduct nonparametric tests with nominal and ordinal data, while parametric tests require data of a higher order. (For a review of these data concepts, see pages 18-23 in Chapter 1.)

DISADVANTAGES OF NONPARAMETRIC TESTS

Nonparametric tests have disadvantages, too. For example, when parametric assumptions are valid and, therefore, either type of test could be used, nonparametric tests are less powerful than parametric tests. Given sample size and a specified significance level (that is, a specified type I error probability of erroneously rejecting a null hypothesis that is in fact true), the probability of a type II error (of erroneously accepting a null hypothesis that is in fact false) is larger for a nonparametric test.

In addition, using a nonparametric test when we could employ a parametric test can be less efficient: A nonparametric test often tends to ignore available sample information—for example, by focusing only on the directions rather than the sizes of observed differences.

This list of shortcomings provides sufficient reason to use parametric tests whenever conditions warrant. However, we should use nonparametric tests whenever our data are merely nominal or ordinal or, if interval or ratio data are available, whenever we know that crucial parametric test assumptions cannot be upheld.

TYPES OF NONPARAMETRIC TESTS

Innumerable nonparametric tests exist; an entire book could easily be devoted to them. In the following sections, we meet eight of the more popular tests. Table 21.1 tells us about them.

TABLE 21.1 | Selected Nonparametric Tests

Test	General Nature	Example
Wilcoxon rank-sum test	Uses two independent simple random samples to determine whether the relative frequency distributions of two statistical populations of continuous values are identical to or different from one another	Comparing the output of strawberries grown on plots using fertilizer A with that grown on otherwise identical plots using fertilizer B in order to make a general assessment of relative fertilizer effectiveness
Mann-Whitney test	Same as Wilcoxon rank-sum test	Comparing the hours of relief experienced by a sample of patients using drug A with hours of relief experienced by a sample of otherwise identical patients using drug B in order to make a general assessment of relative drug effectiveness
Sign test	(1) Uses the directions of differences observed in a matched-pairs sample to determine whether the relative frequency distributions of two statistical populations are identical to or different from one another, and (2) determines whether a sample comes from a population with a specified median	(1) Using a 100-day string of pluses (+) and minuses (−) to determine whether work accidents are generally more or less numerous during the night shift than the day shift; (2) using a 100-city string of pluses (+) and minuses (−) to determine whether the national median house price equals $160,000
Wilcoxon signed-rank test	Uses the directions *and* magnitudes of differences observed in a matched-pairs sample to determine whether the relative frequency distributions of two statistical populations are identical to or different from one another	Comparing dollar sales at identical stores during weeks when a product was displayed at eye level and weeks when it was displayed above/below eye level in order to make a general assessment of relative display effectiveness
Number-of-runs test	Determines whether the elements of a sequence appear in random order	Deciding whether a 60-day sequence of A's and B's is random or attributable to the actions of a suspected polluter, where A measures a lake's above-average acidity and B measures the lake's below-average acidity
Kruskal-Wallis test	An extension of the Wilcoxon rank-sum test from two to more than two statistical populations	Comparing the times-to-failure of radar transponders made by firms A, B, and C, based on an airline's sample experience with the three types of instruments
Kolmogorov-Smirnov one-sample test	Checks the nature of a statistical population's relative frequency distribution	Using an oil company's past experience to determine whether the number of promising oil wells, x, out of $n = 3$ drillings per site is generally well described as a binomially distributed random variable with $\pi = .2$
Spearman rank-correlation test	Measures the degree of association between two variables for which only rank-order data are available	Measuring the association between TV preference scores of men and women in general, given these sample rankings by 20 persons: TV show: A B C D E F G H I J Men: 1 2 3 4 5 6 7 8 9 10 Women: 10 1 9 2 8 3 7 4 6 5

21.2 The Wilcoxon Rank-Sum Test

The **Wilcoxon rank-sum test** is a nonparametric test based on two independent simple random samples. It is designed to determine whether the relative frequency distributions of two statistical populations of continuous values are identical to or different from one another. If the answer is *yes,* we would conclude that the two means are equal as well, and in this sense the Wilcoxon rank-sum test is the equivalent to a parametric t test of the difference between two means. If the answer is *no,* however, this test does not tell us how the two populations differ. The test is named after Frank Wilcoxon (1882–1965) and is also called the ***W* test.**

THE TEST STATISTIC

The Wilcoxon rank-sum test uses a test statistic, symbolized by W, that is derived in a series of steps:

1. pooling the data contained in two independent samples, the sizes of which can be called n_A and n_B;
2. ranking the combined data from the smallest value, to be called 1, to the largest value, equal to $n_A + n_B$;
3. recreating the original two samples with the rank data;
4. summing the ranks in each sample; and, finally,
5. designating *either one* of these rank sums, typically that of sample A, as the test statistic.

FORMULA 21.A | The Wilcoxon Rank-Sum Test Statistic

$$W = \text{rank sum of sample A}$$

Note: In this text, W is defined as the rank sum of sample A, but, in principle, it could also be the rank sum of sample B.

AN ILLUSTRATION

We can most easily illustrate the derivation of W by considering the results of two samples, given in Table 21.2. The two samples show randomly selected average monthly checking-account balances in two hypothetical banks, A and B.

Step 1: The Table 21.2 sample data have been pooled, in order of their magnitude, in column 1 of Table 21.3 on page 1014; for each value, the sample of origin has been noted in column 2.

Step 2: In column 3 of Table 21.3, the pooled data have been ranked by assigning a value of 1 to the lowest number, a value of 2 to the next one, and so on, until the highest number contained in the sample receives a rank of $n_A + n_B$, equal to $10 + 12 = 22$ in this case. (Tied values in column 1, such as the two \$201 values and again the two \$950 values in this example, were given the mean of the next ranks about to be assigned in column 3.)

Steps 3–4: As Table 21.3 shows, by using the column 2 information about the origin of any column 1 value, the column 3 pooled rank data can easily be separated, as in columns 4 and 5,

TABLE 21.2 | Average Monthly Checking-Account Balances in Two Banks

The average monthly checking-account balances found in two independent samples might equal the values shown here. As this example indicates, the two samples need not be of equal size (here $n_A = 10$, but $n_B = 12$).

Bank A		Bank B	
Sampled Account Number	Average Balance Last Month (dollars)	Sampled Account Number	Average Balance Last Month (dollars)
33552	201	15432	3,362
38174	950	12987	129
24677	1,209	97433	201
30876	367	64739	1,579
22654	792	08765	485
34897	804	81486	2,639
30674	42	98564	79
88455	950	44298	92
12598	505	23098	3,010
29600	4,099	92653	3,159
		89655	3,412
		52119	2,910

into sample A ranks and sample B ranks, and a sum of ranks can then be calculated for each sample.

Step 5: As Formula 21.A indicates, in principle, either one of these rank sums can be used as the test statistic; the sample A rank sum, highlighted in red, will be used here.

CAUTION

Because this type of test deals with continuous data, values of equal size in the original sample data—column 1—are highly unlikely in theory, but in practice such ties do occur, mainly as a result of rounding. In our example (Table 21.3 on the next page), average balances of $201 and $950 each occur twice; in the absence of rounding to whole dollars, this duplication probably would not have occurred.

When assigning ranks—column 3—tied values are each given the mean of the next ranks to be assigned. Note how the two values of $201 are made to share ranks 5 and 6 and are both ranked as 5.5. Similarly, the two values of $950 are made to share ranks 12 and 13 and are both ranked as 12.5. This procedure is crucial when the tied values belong to different samples, as is the case here for the two balances of $201. In the absence of this procedure, depending on whether one rank (say, 5) was assigned to the sample A figure and the next rank (say, 6) to the sample B figure or whether rank 6 went to the A figure and 5 to the B figure, we would produce a different sum of ranks for the two samples. The averaging procedure avoids such arbitrariness. For the same reason, the procedure, although employed here, is not crucial (and an arbitrary assignment of ranks to tied values would be acceptable) when the tied values belong to the same sample, as is true for the two balances of $950. Note how the two rank sums remain the same whether the two $950 values are each ranked 12.5 or whether they are ranked 12 and 13.

TABLE 21.3 | Finding the Wilcoxon Rank Sums

After pooling the original sample data in column 1 and ranking them in column 3, the rank data can again be separated by noting, in column 2, the sample that contained the original data. The separation of rank data, in columns 4 and 5, in turn, allows us to calculate a sum of ranks for each sample. One of these Wilcoxon rank sums, typically that of sample A, is used as the test statistic. In this case, the computed value of the rank sum of sample A is W = 104.5.

Average Balance Last Month (dollars) (1)	Sample of Origin (2)	Rank (3)	Sample A Ranks (4)	Sample (B) Ranks (5)
42	A	1	1	
79	B	2		2
92	B	3		3
129	B	4		4
201	A	5.5	5.5	
201	B	5.5		5.5
367	A	7	7	
485	B	8		8
505	A	9	9	
792	A	10	10	
804	A	11	11	
950	A	12.5	12.5	
950	A	12.5	12.5	
1,209	A	14	14	
1,579	B	15		15
2,639	B	16		16
2,910	B	17		17
3,010	B	18		18
3,159	B	19		19
3,362	B	20		20
3,412	B	21		21
4,099	A	22	22	
		Rank sums:	**W = 104.5**	**148.5**

THE SAMPLING DISTRIBUTION OF *W*

Knowing how to calculate the observed value of our rank-sum test statistic is one thing; knowing how to interpret it is another. Consider the following set of hypotheses:

H_0: The relative frequency distributions of the two sampled populations are identical.

H_A: The relative frequency distributions of the two sampled populations differ.

Wilcoxon argued thusly:

1. If the null hypothesis were *not true,* the value of W (the rank sum of sample A) would either be very small or very large. The precise outcome would depend on whether the pop-

ulation A data (and thus the original *sample* A data) were generally smaller or larger than the population B data (and thus the original *sample* B data). In our example, the smallest possible value of W equals $1 + 2 + 3 + \ldots + 10 = 55$ (and that value would occur if every single dollar balance in sample A were smaller than every single balance in sample B). The largest possible value of W, on the other hand, equals $13 + 14 + 15 + \ldots + 22 = 175$ (and that value would occur if every single dollar balance in sample A were larger than every single balance in sample B).

2. If, in contrast, the null hypothesis of identical populations were *true,* we would expect sample A to produce about as many low ranks as high ranks, making the expected value of W the mean of the minimum and maximum values just noted, or $[(55 + 175)/2] = 115$. Indeed, argued Wilcoxon, if the sample sizes were at least equal to 10 each and if the identical-population hypothesis were true, the entire sampling distribution of W could be approximated by the normal curve and would have the mean and standard deviation given in Formula 21.B.

FORMULA 21.B | Mean and Standard Deviation of the Sampling Distribution of W (Given H_0: The Sampled Populations Are Identical)

$$\mu_W = \frac{n_A(n_A + n_B + 1)}{2}$$

$$\sigma_W = \sqrt{\frac{n_A \cdot n_B(n_A + n_B + 1)}{12}}$$

where n_A is the size of sample A and n_B is the size of sample B, and it is assumed that $n_A \geq 10$ and $n_B \geq 10$.

Note: If W were defined as the rank sum of sample B, one would have to interchange subscripts A and B in the μ_W formula.

Formula 21.B produces an expected value of $W = 115$, which is the value calculated above by averaging the smallest possible value of $W = 55$ and the largest possible value of $W = 175$:

$$\mu_W = \frac{n_A(n_A + n_B + 1)}{2} = \frac{10(10 + 12 + 1)}{2} = 115$$

Formula 21.C gives the formula for calculating the normal deviate (or z-score) of W, which can also be used as a test statistic instead of W itself.

FORMULA 21.C | Normal Deviate for the Wilcoxon Rank-Sum Test

$$z = \frac{W - \mu_W}{\sigma_W}$$

Assumption: $n_A \geq 10$ and $n_B \geq 10$

EXAMPLE PROBLEM 21.1

The manager of a bank holding company wants to know quickly whether the average monthly balance in customers' checking accounts is the same in two banks, A and B. Two small simple random samples are to be taken: one from the accounts in bank A and another from those in bank B. A test at the 5 percent significance level is to be conducted. A statistician eventually collects the data already noted in Table 21.2 on page 1013.

SOLUTION: As we did in Chapters 13 and 14, we can proceed in four steps:

Step 1: *Formulating two opposing hypotheses.*

H_0: The average balance is identical in the two banks.

H_A: The average balance differs in the two banks.

Step 2: *Selecting a test statistic.*

Conceivably, the statistician could conduct a parametric test, using the t statistic as in the Chapter 13 section that introduced small-sample hypothesis tests of the difference between two population means (pages 578–583). But suppose our statistician was far from certain that the requirements for such a test were met—namely, that the two populations of average monthly bank balances were normally distributed and also had identical variances. In that case, the statistician could turn to the Wilcoxon rank-sum test and choose the test statistic from Formula 21.A or 21.C:

$$W = \text{rank sum of sample A}$$

or

$$z = \frac{W - \mu_W}{\sigma_W}$$

For illustrative purposes, we shall employ both W and z in this solution.

Step 3: *Deriving a decision rule.*

Given a desired significance level of $\alpha = .05$, and this being a two-tailed test because we are interested in possible differences in both directions, we find in Appendix Table J critical normal deviate values of $\pm z_{\alpha/2} = \pm 1.96$. Thus, the decision rule must be

a. Accept H_0 if $[\mu_W - 1.96\,\sigma_W] \leq W \leq [\mu_W + 1.96\sigma_W]$

or

b. Accept H_0 if $-1.96 \leq z \leq +1.96$

With the help of Formula 21.B, we can compute $\mu_W = 115$ and $\sigma_W = 15.16575$. Therefore, we can calculate the critical rank sums given in decision rule (a) as 85.28 and 144.72. The critical values are encircled in Figure 21.1.

FIGURE 21.1 | Wilcoxon Rank-Sum Test of Account Balances

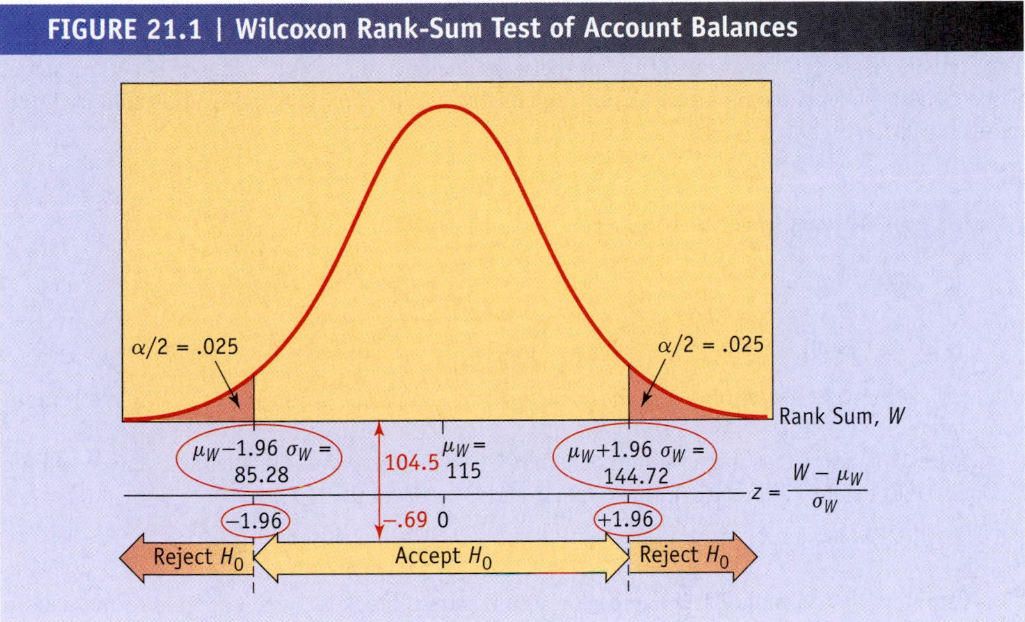

Step 4: *Using sample data to compute the test statistic and confronting it with the decision rule.*

At this point, the statistician would select the data we have already met in Table 21.2 and would calculate, as in Table 21.3, the observed value of W as

$$W = 104.5$$

or would employ Formula 21.C to compute the normal deviate of

$$z = \frac{W - \mu_W}{\sigma_W} = \frac{104.5 - 115}{15.16575} = -.69$$

These values correspond to those marked by the red arrow in Figure 21.1. They suggest that the null hypothesis should be *accepted.* Although the sample A rank sum is smaller than the value to be expected if H_0 is true, the sample result is not statistically significant. At the 5 percent significance level, it is quite likely that the populations of average monthly balances in the two banks are identical and that sampling error alone accounts for the deviation of W from its expected value.

21.3 The Mann-Whitney Test

The **Mann-Whitney test** is a nonparametric test that is equivalent to the Wilcoxon rank-sum test that uses two independent simple random samples to determine whether the relative frequency distributions of two statistical populations of continuous values are identical to or different from one another. The test discussed in this section is named after Henry B. Mann and D. R. Whitney; it is often referred to as the ***U* test** because U is the symbol employed for its test statistic.

THE TEST STATISTIC

The statistic, U, is defined as the difference between the largest possible value of W and its actual value (where W, as in the previous section, equals the sum of sample A ranks). Formula 21.D explains.

FORMULA 21.D | The Mann-Whitney Test Statistic

$$U = \left[(n_A \cdot n_B) + \frac{n_A(n_A + 1)}{2}\right] - W$$

where n_A is the size of sample A and n_B is the size of sample B, while W is the Wilcoxon rank-sum statistic.

Note: W is defined as the rank sum of sample A. If it were defined as the rank sum of sample B, one would have to interchange subscripts A and B in Formula 21.D.

Note how the Formula 21.D expression in the square brackets, when applied to the data in Table 21.3, does indeed produce the largest possible value of W calculated earlier:

$$\left[(n_A \cdot n_B) + \frac{n_A(n_A + 1)}{2}\right] = (10 \cdot 12) + \frac{10(10 + 1)}{2} = 175$$

THE SAMPLING DISTRIBUTION OF *U*

When the sizes of the two independent samples are equal to at least 10 each and the identical-population hypothesis is true, the sampling distribution of U can also be approximated by the normal curve (as is true for W). The mean and standard deviation of the sampling distribution of U appear in Formula 21.E. Accordingly, the normal deviate (or z-score) of U can be calculated as in Formula 21.F.

FORMULA 21.E | Mean and Standard Deviation of the Sampling Distribution of *U* (Given H_0: The Sampled Populations Are Identical)

$$\mu_U = \frac{n_A \cdot n_B}{2}$$

$$\sigma_U = \sqrt{\frac{n_A \cdot n_B(n_A + n_B + 1)}{12}} = \sigma_W$$

where n_A is the size of sample A and n_B is the size of sample B, and $n_A \geq 10$ and $n_B \geq 10$.

FORMULA 21.F | Normal Deviate for the Mann-Whitney Test

$$z = \frac{U - \mu_U}{\sigma_U}$$

Assumption: $n_A \geq 10$ and $n_B \geq 10$

EXAMPLE PROBLEM 21.2

Rework Example Problem 21.1; this time, however, apply the U test.

SOLUTION:

Step 1: *Formulating two opposing hypotheses.*

H_0: The average balance is identical in the two banks.
H_A: The average balance differs in the two banks.

Step 2: *Selecting a test statistic.*

$$U = \left[(n_A \cdot n_B) + \frac{n_A(n_A + 1)}{2} \right] - W$$

or

$$z = \frac{U - \mu_U}{\sigma_U}$$

Step 3: *Deriving a decision rule.*

Given a desired significance level of $\alpha = .05$, and this being a two-tailed test, we find in Appendix Table J critical normal deviate values of $\pm z_{\alpha/2} = \pm 1.96$. Thus, the decision rule must be

a. Accept H_0 if $[\mu_U - 1.96\sigma_U] \leq U \leq [\mu_U + 1.96\,\sigma_U]$

or

b. Accept H_0 if $-1.96 \leq z \leq +1.96$

With the help of Formula 21.E, we can compute $\mu_U = 60$ and $\sigma_U = 15.16575$. Therefore, we can calculate the critical values given in decision rule (a) as 30.28 and 89.72.

Step 4: *Using sample data to compute the test statistic and confronting it with the decision rule.*

Given $W = 104.5$ (from Table 21.3) we find

$$U = 175 - 104.5 = 70.5$$

or its normal deviate of

$$z = \frac{U - \mu_U}{\sigma_U} = \frac{70.5 - 60}{15.16575} = .69$$

Given the decision rule, either number indicates that H_0 should be *accepted,* just as the W test did.

The earlier W test (Example Problem 21.1) produced a z value of $-.69$ when W was defined as the sum of sample A ranks. Yet the U test here, which *utilizes*, in Formula 21.D, a value of W defined as the sum of sample A ranks, produces a z value of $+.69$, just as a W test would if W were the sum of sample B ranks. In a two-tailed test, the sign of the test statistic makes little difference. If H_0 is accepted for $z = -.69$ (as in our W test), it is equally accepted for $z = +.69$ (as in our U test).

In a one-tailed test, on the other hand, watch out. A test statistic of -2.14 might spell acceptance of H_0, while a test statistic of $+2.14$ might indicate rejection. In *one-tailed U* tests, therefore, correct test results are found only if the decision rule is confronted with the *negative* of whatever z value emerges from Formula 21.F.

EXCEL Example 21.1

Check the result of Example Problems 21.1 and 21.2 with the help of a computer application of the *Wilcoxon's rank sum test.*

SOLUTION: EXCEL is not programmed to conduct such a test automatically, but we can use it to make the test, nevertheless. The following commands produce a *two-tailed W test:*

1. Enter labels *Bank A Sample* and *Bank B Sample* into cells A1 and B1, respectively, of a new worksheet.
2. Enter average-balance data from Table 21.2 below the labels. (If you prefer, you can copy and paste columns AB and AC from the file HKMISC.)
3. Enter the labels *Combined, Population,* and *Rank* into cells C1–E1, respectively.
4. Copy the Bank A Sample data from A2:A11 and paste them into C2:C11.
5. Copy the Bank B Sample data from B2:B13 and paste them into C12:C23.
6. Enter population indicator **A** into D2:D11 and **B** into D12:D23.
7. Enter the values **1–22** into E2:E23.
8. Select C2:D23 and click **Data** > **Sort**.
9. In the dialog box, choose *Sort by Column C Ascending* and *No header row* and click **OK**. (Columns C-E now look like columns 1–3 of Table 21.2.)
10. Enter labels *alpha, n1, n2, W, mu, sigma, computed z, critical z, decision,* and *p-value*, respectively, into cells F2:F11.
11. Enter formulas or known values into adjacent column G cells as follows:

    .05 into G2

    10 into G3

    12 into G4

    =SUMIF(D2:D23, "=A", E2:E23) into G5

    =G3*(G3+G4+1)/2 into G6

    =SQRT(G3*G4*(G3+G4+1)/12) into G7

    =(G5−G6)/G7 into G8

    =ABS(NORMSINV(G2/2)) into G9

    =IF(ABS(G8)>G9, "Reject Ho", "Accept Ho") into G10

    =2*(1−NORMSDIST(ABS(G8))) into G11

The result confirms the Figure 21.1 computations; slight differences are due to rounding.

F	G
alpha	0.05
n1	10
n2	12
W	104
mu	115
sigma	15.16575
computed z	−0.725319
critical z	1.959961
decision	Accept Ho
p-value	0.468256

Note: For a quicker result, use HKStat, Sheet 47 for the W test or Sheet 48 for the U test. For lower and upper-tailed tests, see Sheets 49–52.

21.4 The Sign Test

The history of nonparametric statistics dates back to the invention, by J. Arbuthnott in 1710, of the **sign test.** This nonparametric test has two major applications:

1. It uses the directions of differences observed in a matched-pairs sample to determine whether the relative frequency distributions of two statistical populations are identical to or different from one another.
2. It determines whether a sample comes from a population with a specified median.

We begin by looking at the first of these applications.

THE TEST STATISTIC

Unlike the W test and the U test, this version of the sign test is not based on two independent samples, but on a matched-pairs sample. In addition, and unlike the matched-pairs tests discussed in Chapter 13, the sign test does not consider the absolute sizes of differences between the sample pairs but notes only the direction of these differences, initially expressed by a zero (0), a plus sign (+), or a minus sign (−). Subsequently, matched pairs with a zero difference are omitted from the analysis, while the number of plus signs (+) among the remaining n matched pairs is used as the test statistic, S.

FORMULA 21.G | The Sign Test Statistic

S = number of plus signs (+) among the n matched pairs with nonzero differences

The sign test is the simplest of all the nonparametric tests, but is also considerably less discriminating than a t test. It is less certain to tell us correctly whether the relative frequency distributions of two statistical populations, and therefore their means, are identical to or different from one another. This happens precisely because the sign test, as its name suggests, focuses on signs. It often discards available sample information, while the t test uses it. (In a sign test, for example, differences of $+2.3$ and $+230$ are treated alike, as simply $+$ and $+$. Likewise, values of $-.3$ and $-3{,}000$ enter the test as merely $-$ and $-$.) Therefore, whenever *quantitative* measures of matched-pair differences are available and whenever we can assume that the population of all such potential differences is normally distributed, we should employ the more powerful t test. The sign test then is a definite second choice. However, when quantitative measures cannot be acquired or when the above assumption of normality cannot be made, the t test cannot be employed, and the sign test is most useful.

THE SAMPLING DISTRIBUTION OF *S*

If the null hypothesis of no differences is true, the sampling distribution of S is binomial and the probability of "success" (finding a plus sign) equals $\pi = .5$ in any one of the n trials. Accordingly, the mean and standard deviation of the sampling distribution of S can be derived from Chapter 9 as now shown in Formula 21.H.

FORMULA 21.H | Mean and Standard Deviation of the Sampling Distribution of S (Given H_0: There Are No Population Differences)

$$\mu_S = n(.5)$$

$$\sigma_S = \sqrt{n(.5)(.5)}$$

where n is the number of matched pairs in the sample with nonzero differences and $n \geq 10$.

Yet, as we noted in Chapter 9, when both $n\,\pi$ and $n(1 - \pi) \geq 5$, the normal distribution becomes a good approximation of the binomial distribution. Given $\pi = 1 - \pi = .5$, this condition is fulfilled whenever $n \geq 10$. Accordingly, the normal deviate (or z-score) of S, given in Formula 21.I, can replace S as the test statistic when $n \geq 10$.

FORMULA 21.I | Normal Deviate for the Sign Test

$$z = \frac{S - \mu_S}{\sigma_S}$$

Assumption: $n \geq 10$

EXAMPLE PROBLEM 21.3

A manufacturer of house paint wants to determine whether the company's paint (A) is of the same quality as that of a competitor (B). Each of 100 wooden planks is painted half with A and half with B. Accordingly, the two halves of each individual plank constitute a matched pair. The planks are then placed outdoors. Eventually, a plus, minus, or zero is recorded for each plank depending on whether the portion painted with A, compared to that painted with B, lasts a longer time (+), a shorter time (−), or the same time (0) before the first signs of cracking or peeling appear. A test at the 5 percent level of significance is desired. A company statistician eventually records 60 pluses and 34 minuses.

SOLUTION:

Step 1: *Formulating two opposing hypotheses.*

H_0: There are no differences in quality.

H_A: There are differences in quality.

Step 2: *Selecting a test statistic.*

Because the test procedure does not call for any recording of actual time differences (such as the A portion of a plank lasting 9 months longer than, 3 months less than, or the same time as the B portion) and also because there is no information about the probability distribution of all such potential time differences, the statistician employs the sign test. Accordingly, the test statistic can be:

S = the number of plus signs (+) among the n matched pairs remaining after pairs with a zero difference are omitted from the analysis

or

the normal deviate of S: $$z = \frac{S - \mu_S}{\sigma_S}$$

For illustrative purposes, we shall employ both S and z.

Step 3: *Deriving a decision rule.*

Given a desired significance level of $\alpha = .05$, and this being a two-tailed test, we find in Appendix Table J critical normal deviate values of $\pm z_{\alpha/2} = \pm 1.96$. Thus, the decision rule must be

a. Accept H_0 if $[\mu_S - 1.96\sigma_S] \leq S \leq [\mu_S + 1.96\sigma_S]$

or

b. Accept H_0 if $-1.96 \leq z \leq +1.96$

The critical values are encircled in Figure 21.2 on the next page.

Step 4: *Using sample data to compute the test statistic and confronting it with the decision rule.*

At this point, the statistician would consider the data provided by the experiment: a plus (+) 60 times, a minus (−) 34 times, and a zero (0) 6 times, making $n = 60 + 34 = 94$. This information allows the calculation, with Formula 21.H, of the encircled critical values of S, as shown in Figure 21.2. Because $\mu_S = 47$ and $\sigma_S = 4.8477$, we find

$$[\mu_S - 1.96\sigma_S] = 37.50 \quad \text{and} \quad [\mu_S + 1.96\sigma_S] = 56.50$$

On the other hand, given the actual value of $S = 60$, the above summary measures imply a normal deviate of

$$z = \frac{S - \mu_S}{\sigma_S} = \frac{60 - 47}{4.8477} = 2.68$$

FIGURE 21.2 | Sign Test Of Paint Quality

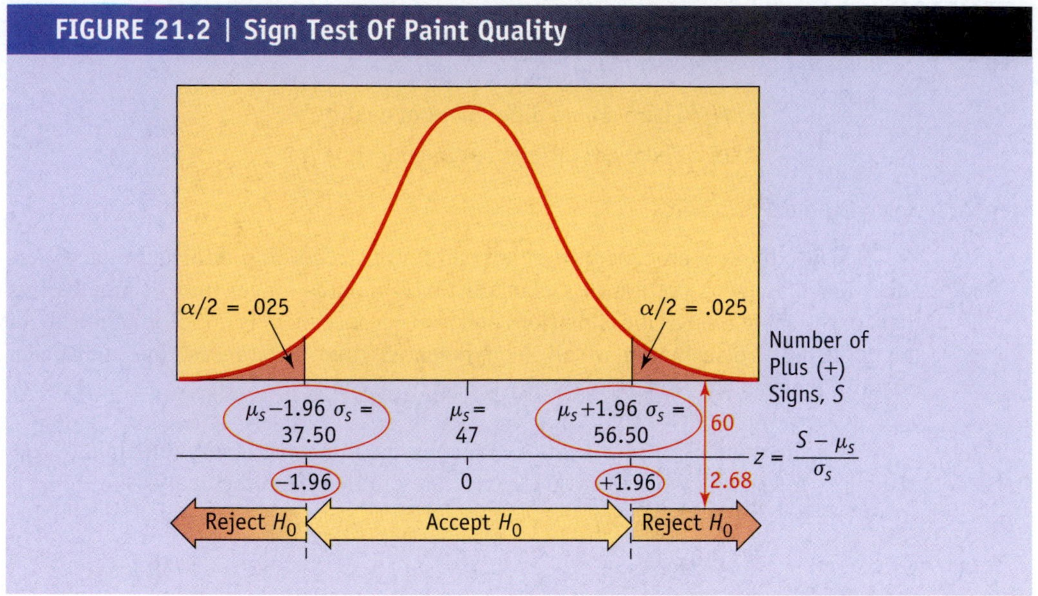

These actual values are marked by the red arrow in Figure 21.2. They suggest that the null hypothesis should be *rejected.* At the 5 percent level, the sample result is statistically significant. It is unlikely that the observed better performance of paint A is a result of sampling error. Paint A is of better quality.

AN IMPORTANT VARIATION: A SIGN TEST CONCERNING THE POPULATION MEDIAN

The sign test lends itself admirably to answering another kind of question—namely, whether a sample comes from a population with a specified median. In this case, the null hypothesis asserts "H_0: The sample comes from a population with a median of x."

EXAMPLE PROBLEM 21.4

A tire manufacturer asserts that the firm's tires have a median life of 25,000 miles. If the claim is true, we would expect that half of a random sample of the firm's tires last a longer time (+), while half last a shorter time (−). What if 100 tires are tested and 40 are found to last a longer time ($S = 40$), while 60 are found to last a shorter time? Can this result be attributed to sampling error or does it suggest that the tires do *not* come from a population with a median life of 25,000 miles (but come from a population with a lower median)? A two-tailed test at the 5 percent level of significance is desired.

SOLUTION: We can adopt this decision rule: "Accept H_0 (The sample comes from a population with a median of 25,000 miles) if $-1.96 \leq z \leq +1.96$."

The value of the test statistic can, in turn, be calculated as follows: Given $n = 100$ and $S = 40$, we find $\mu_S = 50$ and $\sigma_S = 5$ and

$$z = \frac{S - \mu_S}{\sigma_S} = \frac{40 - 50}{5} = -2.00$$

Accordingly, the null hypothesis should be *rejected.* The median life of this type of tire is less than 25,000 miles.

EXCEL Example 21.2

Rework the Example Problem 21.4 *sign test* with the help of a computer. Assume that 40 of the sampled tires lasted 26,000 miles, while 60 of them lasted 24,000 miles.

SOLUTION: EXCEL is not programmed to conduct such a test automatically, but we can use it to make the test, nevertheless:

1. In cells A1:A8 of a new worksheet, enter the labels *alpha, n, S, mu, sigma, computed z, critical z,* and *decision,* respectively.
2. Enter formulas or known values into adjacent column B cells as follows:

   .05 into B1

   100 into B2

   40 into B3

   =B2*.5 into B4

   =SQRT(B2*.5*.5) into B5

   =(B3−B4)/B5 into B6

   =ABS(NORMSINV(B1/2)) into B7

   =IF(ABS(B6)>B7, "Reject Ho", "Accept Ho") into B8

   The result confirms the Example Problem 21.4 computations:

A	B
alpha	0.05
n	100
S	40
mu	50
sigma	5
computed z	−2
critical z	1.959961
decision	Reject Ho

Note: For a quicker result, use HKStat, Sheet 53.

21.5 The Wilcoxon Signed-Rank Test

The **Wilcoxon signed-rank test** is a more powerful alternative to the sign test. It uses the directions *and* magnitudes of differences observed in a matched-pairs sample to determine whether the relative frequency distributions of two statistical populations are identical to or different from one another. Because the test considers not only the direction, but also the magnitude of differences between the matched sample pairs, it uses more of the information contained in sample data and is more efficient for a given sample size. Thus, if the magnitude of differences is known, it pays to use this more discriminating test.

THE TEST STATISTIC

After collecting data for each sample pair, the procedure involves these steps:

1. Calculating the difference between the sample data for each matched pair. (Pairs with zero differences are eliminated from the test at this stage, and sample size, n, is reduced to the remaining number of pairs with nonzero differences.)
2. Ranking the absolute values of the (nonzero) differences from the smallest (rank $= 1$) to the largest (rank $= n$).
3. Attaching to each rank the sign of the original difference corresponding to it.
4. Calculating the sum of these signed ranks and designating it as the test statistic, T.

FORMULA 21.J | The Wilcoxon Signed-Rank Test Statistic

$T =$ sum of signed ranks among the n matched pairs with nonzero differences

THE SAMPLING DISTRIBUTION OF *T*

If the null hypothesis—stating that the two populations are identical—is true, half of the matched-pair differences will be positive and half will be negative. In addition, positive or negative differences of a given magnitude will be equally likely. (A value of -3, for example, will then have an equal probability as a $+3$.) As a result, the sum of signed ranks, T, has an expected value of zero. Given sufficient sample size ($n \geq 10$), the entire sampling distribution of T can again be approximated by the normal curve; the mean and standard deviation are given in Formula 21.K, and the normal deviate (or z-score) of T appears in Formula 21.L.

FORMULA 21.K | Mean and Standard Deviation of the Sampling Distribution of T (Given H_0: There Are No Population Differences)

$$\mu_T = 0$$

$$\sigma_T = \sqrt{\frac{n(n+1)(2n+1)}{6}}$$

where n is the number of matched pairs in the sample with nonzero differences and $n \geq 10$.

FORMULA 21.L | Normal Deviate for the Wilcoxon Signed-Rank Test

$$z = \frac{T - \mu_T}{\sigma_T} = \frac{T}{\sigma_T}$$

Assumption: $n \geq 10$

EXAMPLE PROBLEM 21.5

A government agency wants to test a refining company's claim that the mileage achieved with its unleaded gasoline (A) is at most equal to (and probably less than) that achieved with its leaded gasoline (B). The agency chooses 15 car models; a given driver drives each model twice over the identical route. At random, each driver is given brand A or brand B first, then drives with the other brand during the second trip. This procedure is designed to assure that neither brand of gasoline is favored or handicapped by all drivers being fresh or tired, respectively. A Wilcoxon signed-rank test at the 2.5 percent level of significance is to be conducted on the basis of the observed differences in miles per gallon. Eventually, the data given in columns 1–3 of Table 21.4 become available.

SOLUTION:

Step 1: *Formulating two opposing hypotheses.*

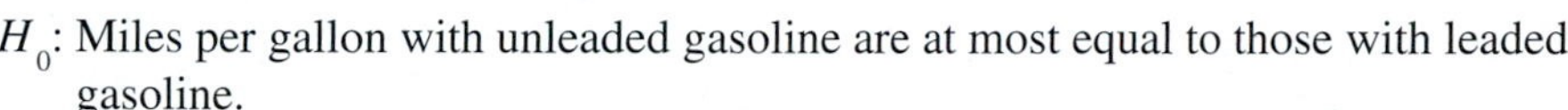

H_0: Miles per gallon with unleaded gasoline are at most equal to those with leaded gasoline.

H_A: Miles per gallon with unleaded gasoline exceed those with leaded gasoline.

Step 2: *Selecting a test statistic.*

$$z = \frac{T - \mu_T}{\sigma_T} = \frac{T}{\sigma_T}$$

Step 3: *Deriving a decision rule.*

Given a desired significance level of $\alpha = .025$, and this being a one-tailed test, we find in Appendix Table J a critical normal deviate value of $z_\alpha = 1.96$. Thus, the

TABLE 21.4 | Gasoline Experiment

Car Model	Miles per Gallon: Unleaded Gas (A)	Miles per Gallon: Leaded Gas (B)
1	22.1	23.7
2	15.7	16.1
3	18.2	19.0
4	19.0	19.0
5	25.7	24.2
6	19.2	22.0
7	11.9	12.1
8	28.0	30.2
9	35.0	37.8
10	27.0	30.0
11	19.7	19.0
12	16.3	15.1
13	21.2	23.4
14	22.2	20.7
15	27.8	28.1

FIGURE 21.3 | Wilcoxon Signed-Rank Test of Gas Mileage

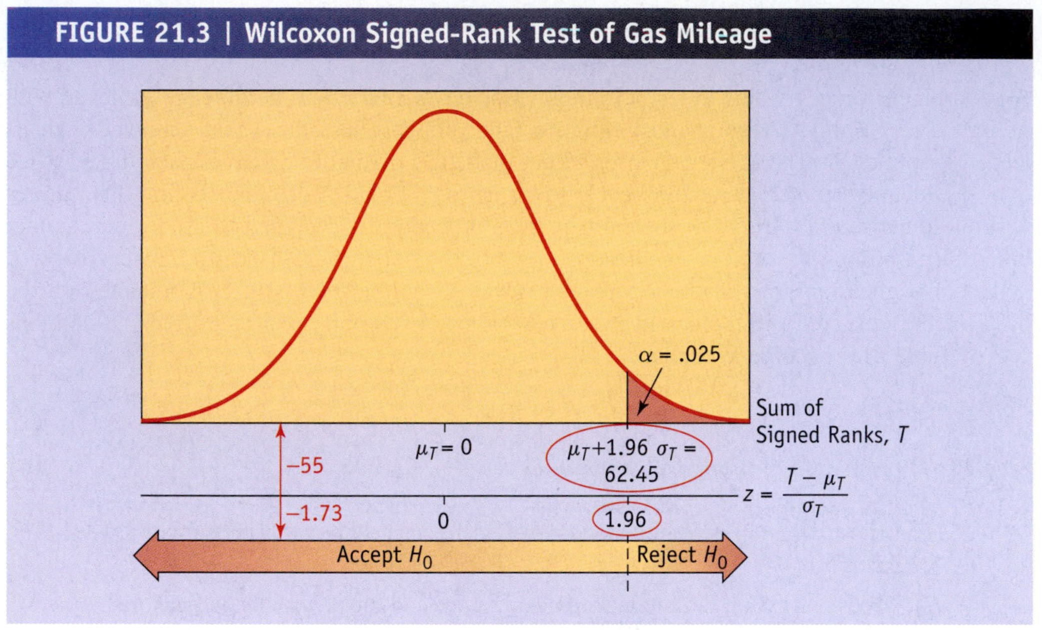

TABLE 21.5 | Finding the Wilcoxon Signed-Rank Statistic

Car Model	Miles per Gallon: Unleaded Gas (A)	Miles per Gallon: Leaded Gas (B)	Difference (A − B)	Absolute Value of Nonzero Difference	Rank of Absolute Nonzero Difference	Signed Rank
1	22.1	23.7	−1.6	1.6	9	−9
2	15.7	16.1	−.4	.4	3	−3
3	18.2	19.0	−.8	.8	5	−5
4	19.0	19.0	0	—	—	—
5	25.7	24.2	+1.5	1.5	7.5	+7.5
6	19.2	22.0	−2.8	2.8	12.5	−12.5
7	11.9	12.1	−.2	.2	1	−1
8	28.0	30.2	−2.2	2.2	10.5	−10.5
9	35.0	37.8	−2.8	2.8	12.5	−12.5
10	27.0	30.0	−3.0	3.0	14	−14
11	19.7	19.0	+.7	.7	4	+4
12	16.3	15.1	+1.2	1.2	6	+6
13	21.2	23.4	−2.2	2.2	10.5	−10.5
14	22.2	20.7	+1.5	1.5	7.5	+7.5
15	27.8	28.1	−.3	.3	2	−2

Sum of Signed Ranks: T = −55

decision rule must be "Accept H_0 if $z \leq +1.96$." The critical value is encircled in Figure 21.3.

Step 4: *Using sample data to compute the test statistic and confronting it with the decision rule.*

The necessary calculations, based on the sample data, are given in Table 21.5, which reveals the value of $T = -55$.

Because one pair (with zero difference) is eliminated, $n = 14$ and (according to Formula 21.K) $\sigma_T = 31.86$. Hence, we can find the critical value of T in Figure 21.3 as 62.45 and compute the normal deviate of the observed T value as $z = -1.73$ (using Formula 21.L). As the position of the red arrow in Figure 21.3 indicates, H_0 should be *accepted.*

Note: Had we employed the simpler sign test in this particular example, we would have reached the same conclusion, but it can easily happen that the more discriminating signed-rank test, because it uses more information, reverses the judgment of the sign test, which may well discard available information. Whenever either test could be used, the signed-rank test, therefore, is the one to apply.

APPLICATION 21.1

The Gains from Takeover Deregulation

Imagine an economy in which strict government regulation prohibits all corporate takeover activity. Firms seeking to gain profit from economies of scale and scope would be forbidden to acquire other firms or to merge with them. Poor managers would not have to worry about losing their jobs as a result of hostile takeovers designed to eliminate internal inefficiencies. And then, suddenly, the government announces its intention to eliminate all these restrictions within a year. The story is not a fairy tale, but describes the U.S. banking industry that was so regulated by the McFadden Act of 1927 (and subsequent amendments) and that was suddenly freed by the Interstate Banking and Branching Efficiency Act of 1994.

Three economists set out to investigate the likely capital market response. They imagined that the threat of takeovers would quickly motivate managers to run their banks more efficiently and to use the potential of economies of scale and scope by merging with other firms. As a result, revenues would rise, costs would fall, and the resulting increased profitability would raise the affected firms' stock prices and market values. Accordingly, they sampled 290 publicly traded banks jointly holding 68 percent of U.S. banking assets. They recorded the banks' stock prices during the 107-day period (from February 23 to July 26, 1994) during which the new law made its way though Congress. And they regressed daily changes in stock prices on a number of variables, including market conditions, interest rate trends, and the enactment of the new law. The result: During the period in question, an average daily "abnormal" return of 0.18 percent appeared, not explainable by other factors, accumulating to 21.1 percent eventually. This increased the equity values of the sampled banks by $59 billion and those of the banking industry as a whole by $85 billion.

A *signed-rank test* was conducted to test the null hypothesis that the median regression coefficient associated with the abnormal return variable was in fact zero. The hypothesis was *rejected* at the $\alpha = .01$ level. The abnormal return coefficient significantly exceeded zero—not only for the legislative passage period as a whole, but also for every 2-day stretch within that period as the capital market gradually absorbed the legislative news and its implications for the banking industry.

SOURCE: Adapted from Yaron Brook, Robert Hendershott, and Darrell Lee, "The Gains from Takeover Deregulation: Evidence from the End of Interstate Banking Restrictions," *The Journal of Finance*, December 1998, pp. 2185–2204.

21.6 The Number-of-Runs Test

An unbroken succession of like observations in a sequence containing potentially different types of observations is referred to as a **run.** Consider tossing a coin 10 times and recording the appearance of heads (H) or tails (T). The result may be sequence 1:

Sequence 1: $\underline{H\,H}\,\overline{T\,T\,T}\,\underline{H\,H}\,\overline{T}\,\underline{H\,H}$

As the horizontal lines below or above the letters indicate, this sequence contains 3 runs of heads and 2 runs of tails. As the example also indicates, a run may be as short as a single observation that is preceded or followed by a different type of observation. If the observations are generated by a random process, some sequences, such as sequence 1, will instantly appear more probable than others, such as sequence 2 or 3 below:

Sequence 2: $\overline{T\,T\,T\,T\,T}\,\underline{H\,H\,H\,H\,H}$

Sequence 3: $\underline{H}\,\overline{T}\,\underline{H}\,\overline{T}\,\underline{H}\,\overline{T}\,\underline{H}\,\overline{T}\,\underline{H}\,\overline{T}$

The **number-of-runs test** is a procedure designed to discover whether the elements of a sequence appear in random order. Whenever sample data can be separated into two categories, such as heads or tails (including such symbolic "heads" or "tails" as fatal versus nonfatal accidents, income below $3,000 versus income of $3,000 and above, defective versus nondefective parts, and so on), they can be represented by a string of letters (H and T) appearing in the chronological order in which the data were collected or in the order in which the events that they represent occurred. The test to be discussed in this section is designed to determine whether occurrences describe a random pattern or whether instead some form of nonrandomness exists. An example of the latter is **serial dependency,** a series of different types of events such that the order of occurrences is affected by previous events. Note how, in sequence 3, each T is preceded by an H—which suggests something other than randomness. Sequence 2, similarly, does not exactly conjure up the image of a random process at work.

THE TEST STATISTIC

The runs test begins with the null hypothesis that the elements of the sequence appear randomly. The test is two-sided: If the null hypothesis is true, too few runs, as in sequence 2, are considered just as unlikely as too many, as in sequence 3. The number of runs of a given category (such as "heads") is typically used as the test statistic and is denoted by R_H. For the three above sequences, R_H equals 3, 1, and 5, respectively. It would also be possible to define the test statistic as R_T, the number of runs of some other category, such as "tails," or simply as R, the total number of all types of runs.

FORMULA 21.M | The Number-of-Runs Test Statistic

$$R_H = \text{number of runs in category } H$$

or

$$R_T = \text{number of runs in category } T$$

or

$$R = \text{total number of runs in all types of categories}$$

THE SAMPLING DISTRIBUTION OF R_H

The sampling distribution of R_H can be approximated by the normal distribution under certain conditions. If n_H and n_T are defined, respectively, as the number of "heads" and "tails" in the sample (not to be confused with the number of runs), the summary measures of the sampling distribution of R_H are those found in Formula 21.N. Accordingly, the normal deviate (or z-score) of R_H can be calculated as in Formula 21.O.

FORMULA 21.N | Mean and Standard Deviation of the Sampling Distribution of R_H (Given H_0: Sampling Is Random)

$$\mu_{R_H} = \frac{n_H(n_T + 1)}{n_H + n_T}$$

$$\sigma_{R_H} = \sqrt{\frac{n_H(n_T + 1)(n_H - 1)}{(n_H + n_T)^2}\left(\frac{n_T}{n_H + n_T - 1}\right)}$$

where n_H and n_T are defined, respectively, as the number of "heads" and "tails" in the sample.

FORMULA 21.O | Normal Deviate for the Number-of-Runs Test

$$z = \frac{R_H - \mu_{R_H}}{\sigma_{R_H}}$$

EXAMPLE PROBLEM 21.6

Apply the number-of-runs test to each of the three sequences given on page 1030, using a significance level of $\alpha = .05$. (When performing the test, remember that *heads* and *tails* can symbolize all kinds of things besides the actual sides of coins observed in a coin-tossing experiment.)

SOLUTION: In each of these cases, the first three steps of the hypothesis test are the same.

Step 1: *Formulating two opposing hypotheses.*

H_0: The different types of sample elements in the sequence are distributed randomly.

H_A: The different types of sample elements in the sequence are not distributed randomly.

Step 2: *Selecting a test statistic.*

We select the normal deviate for the number-of-runs test from Formula 21.O.

Step 3: *Deriving a decision rule.*

Given a significance level of $\alpha = .05$, and this being a two-tailed test, we find in Appendix Table J critical normal deviate values of $\pm z_{\alpha/2} = \pm 1.96$. Thus, the decision rule is: "Accept H_0 if $-1.96 \le z \le +1.96$." The critical values are encircled in Figure 21.4 on the next page.

FIGURE 21.4 | Runs Test of Coin Tosses

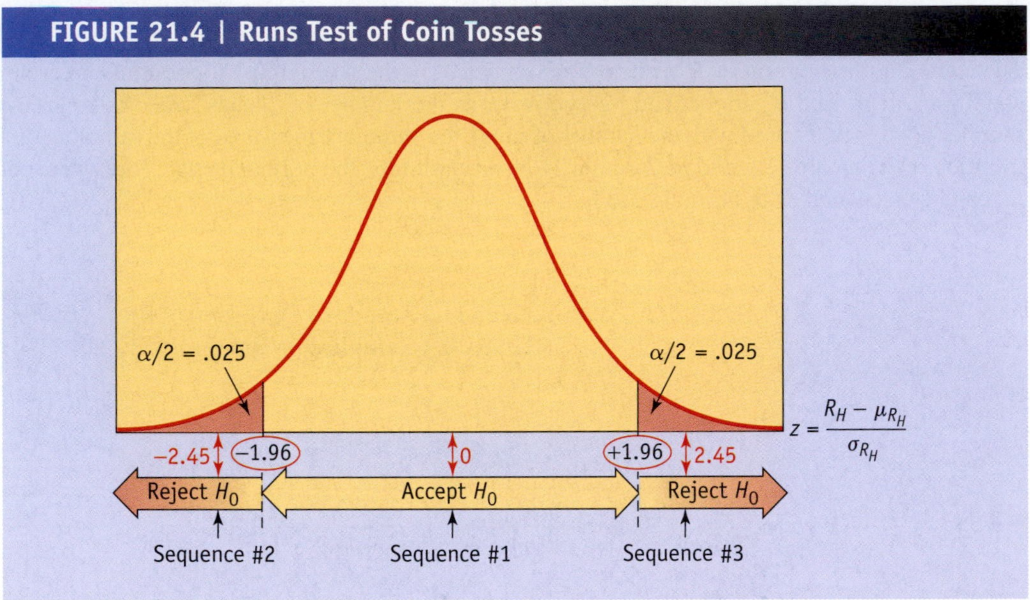

Step 4: *Using sample data to compute the test statistic and confronting it with the decision rule.*

This final step in our procedure differs depending on which of the three sequences is being tested for randomness. The observed normal deviates calculated below for sequences 1–3 are marked by the three red arrows in Figure 21.4.

Sequence 1: $n_H = 6, n_T = 4, R_H = 3$

$$\mu_{R_H} = \frac{6(4+1)}{6+4} = 3$$

$$\sigma_{R_H} = \sqrt{\frac{6(4+1)(6-1)}{(6+4)^2}\left(\frac{4}{6+4-1}\right)} = .8165$$

$$z = \frac{3-3}{.8165} = 0$$

Accordingly, H_0 should be *accepted* in the case of sequence 1.

Sequence 2: $n_H = 5, n_T = 5, R_H = 1$

$$\mu_{R_H} = \frac{5(5+1)}{5+5} = 3$$

$$\sigma_{R_H} = \sqrt{\frac{5(5+1)(5-1)}{(5+5)^2}\left(\frac{5}{5+5-1}\right)} = .8165$$

$$z = \frac{1-3}{.8165} = -2.45$$

Accordingly, H_0 should be *rejected* in the case of sequence 2. There are too few runs to make randomness believable.

Sequence 3: $n_H = 5, n_T = 5, R_H = 5$

$$\mu_{R_H} = \frac{5(5+1)}{5+5} = 3$$

$$\sigma_{R_H} = \sqrt{\frac{5(5+1)(5-1)}{(5+5)^2}\left(\frac{5}{5+5-1}\right)} = .8165$$

$$z = \frac{5-3}{.8165} = 2.45$$

Accordingly, H_0 should be *rejected* in the case of sequence 3. There are too many runs to make randomness believable.

EXCEL Example 21.3

Review Example Problem 21.6; then check the Sequence 1 *number-of-runs test* by computer.

SOLUTION: EXCEL is not programmed to conduct such a test automatically, but we can use it to make the test, nevertheless:

1. In cells A1:A9 of a new worksheet, enter the labels *alpha, nH, nT, RH, mu, sigma, computed z, critical z,* and *decision,* respectively.
2. Enter formulas or known values into adjacent column B cells as follows:

   .05 into B1

   6 into B2

   4 into B3

   3 into B4

   =(B2*(B3+1))/(B2+B3) into B5

   =SQRT(((B2*(B3+1)*(B2−1))/(B2+B3)^2)*(B3/(B2+B3−1))) into B6

   =(B4−B5)/B6 into B7

   =ABS(NORMSINV(B1/2)) into B8

   =IF(ABS(B7)>B8, "Reject Ho", "Accept Ho") into B9

   The result confirms the Example Problem 21.6 computations for Sequence 1:

A	B
alpha	0.05
nH	6
nT	4
RH	3
mu	3
sigma	0.816497
computed z	0
critical z	1.959961
decision	Accept Ho

Note: For a quicker result, use HKStat, Sheet 55.

21.7 The Kruskal-Wallis Test

The **Kruskal-Wallis test** extends the Wilcoxon rank-sum test from two to more than two statistical populations. The purpose of the test, named after W. H. Kruskal and W. A. Wallis, remains the same: to determine whether the relative frequency distributions of populations of interest are identical to or different from one another. The Kruskal-Wallis test accomplishes this goal by drawing independent simple random samples from more than two populations and analyzing these samples or by analyzing appropriate experimental data. The test is usually employed in place of the one-way ANOVA test when the crucial assumptions of the *F* test cannot be validated. As in the *W* test, the observations contained in the various samples are pooled and ranked, and a rank sum is computed for each original sample. A test statistic, *K*, is computed on that basis, as given in Formula 21.P on page 1036.

APPLICATION 21.2

EXAMINING THE 1971 DRAFT LOTTERY

This application returns us to a time long ago when young men were routinely drafted into the military. Application 4.3, *The 1970 Draft Lottery Fiasco* on page 117 described how that year's determination of draft priority birthdates was anything but random. Was the 1971 lottery any better? We can apply the *number-of-runs test* to the lottery results to see for ourselves. The result of the 1971 lottery is given in Table 21.A on the next page.

If the lottery had been truly random, we would expect each month to contain an equal number of draft priority numbers that are "dangerously low" and "safely high." Because half the number of days in 1971 is 182.5, we might classify numbers between 1 and 182 as "dangerous" (more likely to lead to the draft) and those between 183 and 365 as "safe" (less likely to lead to the draft). The "dangerous" numbers have been printed in the table in red. Let us apply the number-of-runs test to answer the question posed in the previous paragraph.

Step 1:

H_0: "Dangerous" and "safe" numbers are randomly distributed over the dates of the year.

H_A: The randomness asserted in H_0 does not exist.

Step 2:

We select the normal deviate for the number-of-runs test (Formula 21.O).

Step 3:

We select a significance level of $\alpha = .05$; hence, the decision rule is:

"Accept H_0 if $-1.96 \le z \le +1.96$."

Step 4:

We inspect our data, and calling "dangerous" numbers "heads" and "safe" numbers "tails," we find $n_H = 182$, $n_T = 183$, $R_H = 95$. (We find the latter number by counting the runs of red numbers, going down successive columns of the table.) Thus, according to Formulas 21.N and 21.O,

$$\mu_{R_H} = \frac{182(183 + 1)}{365} = 91.75$$

$$\sigma_{R_H} = \sqrt{\frac{182(183 + 1)(182 - 1)}{(182 + 183)^2}\left(\frac{183}{182 + 183 - 1}\right)}$$

$$= 4.7826$$

$$z = \frac{95 - 91.75}{4.7826} = .68$$

We should *accept* H_0. The 1971 draft lottery results *were* random.

(continued)

Application 21.2 (continued)

TABLE 21.A | 1971 Draft Priority Numbers

Birth-day	Jan.	Feb.	Mar.	Apr.	May	Jun.	Jul.	Aug.	Sep.	Oct.	Nov.	Dec.
1	133	335	14	224	179	65	104	326	283	306	243	347
2	195	354	77	216	96	304	322	102	161	191	205	321
3	336	186	207	297	171	135	30	279	183	134	294	110
4	99	94	117	37	240	42	59	300	231	266	39	305
5	33	97	299	124	301	233	287	64	295	166	286	27
6	285	16	296	312	268	153	164	251	21	78	245	198
7	159	25	141	142	29	169	365	263	265	131	72	162
8	116	127	79	267	105	7	106	49	108	45	119	323
9	53	187	278	223	357	352	1	125	313	302	176	114
10	101	46	150	165	146	76	158	359	130	160	63	204
11	144	227	317	178	293	355	174	230	288	84	123	73
12	152	262	24	89	210	51	257	320	314	70	255	19
13	330	13	241	143	353	342	349	58	238	92	272	151
14	71	260	12	202	40	363	156	103	247	115	11	348
15	75	201	157	182	344	276	273	270	291	310	362	87
16	136	334	258	31	175	229	284	329	139	34	197	41
17	54	345	220	264	212	289	341	343	200	290	6	315
18	185	337	319	138	180	214	90	109	333	340	280	208
19	188	331	189	62	155	163	316	83	228	74	252	249
20	211	20	170	118	242	43	120	69	261	196	98	218
21	129	213	246	8	225	113	356	50	68	5	35	181
22	132	271	269	256	199	307	282	250	88	36	253	194
23	48	351	281	292	222	44	172	10	206	339	193	219
24	177	226	203	244	22	236	360	274	237	149	81	2
25	57	325	298	328	26	327	3	364	107	17	23	361
26	140	86	121	137	148	308	47	91	93	184	52	80
27	173	66	254	235	122	55	85	232	338	318	168	239
28	346	234	95	82	9	215	190	248	309	28	324	128
29	277		147	111	61	154	4	32	303	259	100	145
30	112		56	358	209	217	15	167	18	332	67	192
31	60		38		350		221	275		311		126

SOURCE: U.S. Department of Defense

FORMULA 21.P | The Kruskal-Wallis Test Statistic

$$K = \left[\frac{12}{n(n+1)}\left(\sum \frac{W_i^2}{n_i}\right)\right] - [3(n+1)]$$

where n is the number of observations in all samples, W_i is the rank sum of an individual sample, and n_i is the number of observations in that sample.

We can determine a precise sampling distribution of K from the knowledge that the rank assigned to any particular observation has an equal chance of being any number between 1 and n, regardless of the sample to which the observation belongs, provided the null hypothesis of identical populations is true. Furthermore, if each of these x samples contains more than 5 observations, the sampling distribution of K can be approximated by a χ^2 distribution with $x - 1$ degrees of freedom. Example Problem 21.7 illustrates how the Kruskal-Wallis test is conducted.

EXAMPLE PROBLEM 21.7

An advertising agency has been running one of four distinctly different advertisements, A–D, in four different cities. It wishes to test, at the 5 percent level of significance, whether these ads are equally effective in stimulating sales. For this purpose, monthly extra sales figures (compared to a year ago) are collected for half a year, as shown in the "Extra Units Sold" columns of Table 21.6. Conduct a K test; then comment on the general validity of the results.

SOLUTION:

Step 1: *Formulating two opposing hypotheses.*

H_0: There are no differences in the effectiveness of the ads. (The four populations of extra units sold are identical.)

H_A: There are differences in the effectiveness of the ads.

TABLE 21.6 | The Effectiveness of Four Advertisements

Month	Ad #A		Ad #B		Ad #C		Ad #D	
	Extra Units Sold	Rank of Sales	Extra Units Sold	Rank of Sales	Extra Units Sold	Rank of Sales	Extra Units Sold	Rank of Sales
May	80	18.5	25	4	97	24	78	16
June	66	13	62	10	15	2	75	15
July	66	13	22	3	43	7	85	20
August	80	18.5	87	21	27	5	94	23
September	50	8	63	11	42	6	52	9
October	79	17	66	13	12	1	93	22
	$W_A = 88$		$W_B = 62$		$W_C = 45$		$W_D = 105$	
	$\frac{W_A^2}{n_A} = 1{,}290.67$		$\frac{W_B^2}{n_B} = 640.67$		$\frac{W_C^2}{n_C} = 337.5$		$\frac{W_D^2}{n_D} = 1{,}837.5$	

FIGURE 21.5 | Kruskal-Wallis Test on Advertising

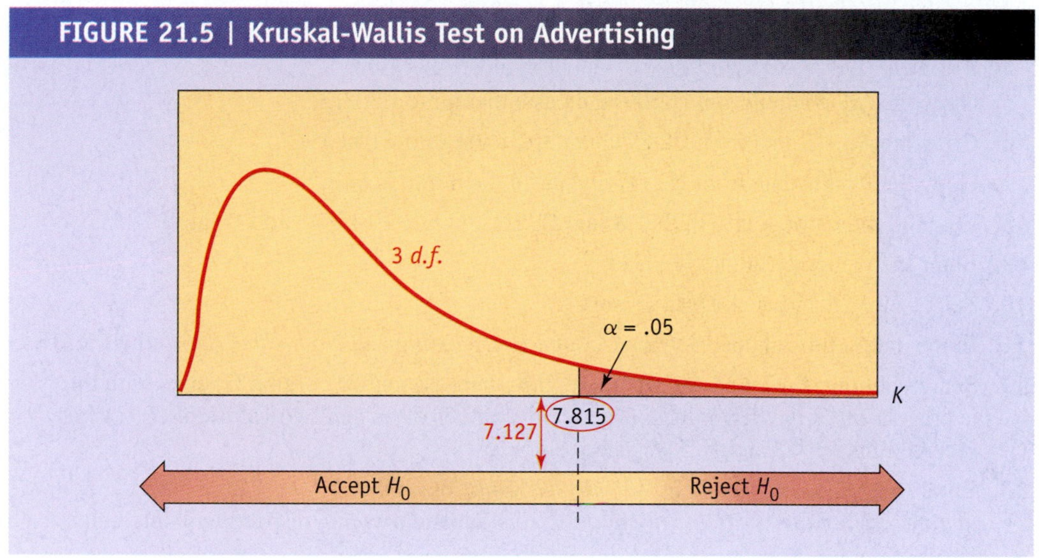

Step 2: *Selecting a test statistic.*

The agency selects the K statistic (Formula 21.P).

Step 3: *Deriving a decision rule.*

Because there are $x = 4$ samples, we have $x - 1 = 3$ degrees of freedom. According to Appendix Table M, the critical value of $\chi^2_{.05,3} = 7.815$. Thus, the decision rule is: "Accept H_0 if $K \leq 7.815$." The critical value is encircled in Figure 21.5.

Step 4: *Using sample data to compute the test statistic and confronting it with the decision rule.*

In the "Rank of Sales" columns of Table 21.6, ranks for the pooled sample data have been inserted, and the separate sample rank sums, W_A to W_D, have been calculated. Each of these values has, in turn, been squared and divided by the corresponding sample size, n_A to n_D, as noted in the last row of the table. Thus, the observed value of the test statistic (which makes use of the *sum* of these values) is

$$K = \left[\frac{12}{24(24 + 1)}(4{,}106.34)\right] - [3(24 + 1)] = 7.1268$$

Accordingly, H_0 should be *accepted*. There are no differences in the effectiveness of the ads.

EXCEL Example 21.4

Check the result of Example Problem 21.7 with the help of the computer.

SOLUTION: EXCEL is not programmed to conduct such a test automatically, but we can use it to make the test, nevertheless:

1. Enter labels *Ad #A, Ad #B, Ad #C*, and *Ad #D* into cells A1:D1 of a new worksheet.
2. Enter the associated *Extra Units Sold* data from Table 21.6 underneath each label. (You can also copy and paste columns AD–AG from the file HKMISC.)

3. Enter the labels *Combined, Population,* and *Rank* into cells E1:G1, respectively.
4. Copy the Ad #A data from A2:A7 and paste them into E2:E7.
5. Copy the Ad #B data from B2:B7 and paste them into E8:E13.
6. Copy the Ad #C data from C2:C7 and paste them into E14:E19.
7. Copy the Ad #D data from D2:D7 and paste them into E20:E25.
8. Enter ad indicator **A** into F2:F7, **B** into F8:F13, **C** into F14:F19, and **D** into F20:F25.
9. Enter the values **1–24** into G2:G25.
10. Select E2:F25 and click **Data** > **Sort**.
11. In the dialog box, choose *Sort by Column E Ascending* and *No header row* and click **OK**.
12. Search column E for tied values and replace their associated column G ranks with the average rank of the tied values. (There are 3 values of 66 and two values of 80. They receive ranks of 13 and 18.5, respectively.)
13. Enter labels *Wa, na, Wa^2/na, Wb, nb, Wb^2/nb, Wc, nc, Wc^2/nc, Wd, nd, Wd^2/nd, n, K, degrees of freedom, critical chi-square, decision*, and *p-value*, respectively, into cells H1:H18.
14. Enter formulas or known values into adjacent column I cells as follows:

    =SUMIF(F2:F25,"=A", G2:G25) into I1

    6 into I2

    =I1^2/I2 into I3

    =SUMIF(F2:F25,"=B", G2:G25) into I4

    6 into I5

    =I4^2/I5 into I6

    =SUMIF(F2:F25,"=C", G2:G25) into I7

    6 into I8

    =I7^2/I8 into I9

    =SUMIF(F2:F25,"=D", G2:G25) into I10

    6 into I11

    =I10^2/I11 into I12

    =I2+I5+I8+I11 into I13

    =(12/(I13*(I13+1))*(I3+I6+I9+I12))−(3*(I13+1)) into I14

    3 into I15

    =CHIINV(.05,I15) into I16

    =IF(ABS(I14)>I16, "Reject Ho", "Accept Ho") into I17

    =CHIDIST(I14,I15) into I18

The result confirms the Example Problem 21.7 computations:

H	I
Wa	88
na	6
Wa^2/na	1290.6667
Wb	62

nb	6
Wb^2/nb	640.66667
Wc	45
nc	6
Wc^2/nc	337.5
Wd	105
nd	6
Wd^2/nd	1837.5
n	24
K	7.1266667
degrees of freedom	3
critical chi-square	7.8147247
decision	Accept Ho
p-value	0.0679682

The null hypothesis (there are no differences in the effectiveness of the ads) is *accepted* for α levels below the p-value of 0.068.

Note: For a quicker result, use HKStat, Sheet 56.

21.8 The Kolmogorov-Smirnov One-Sample Test

The **Kolmogorov-Smirnov one-sample test** is an alternative to the chi-square test for goodness of fit. It enables us to check the nature of a statistical population's relative frequency distribution. Thus, the test can serve as a screening device for the possible use of parametric procedures that require, say, a normally distributed population in order to lead to valid results. The test is named after A. N. Kolmogorov, who proposed it in 1933, and N. V. Smirnov, who later tabulated critical values and also extended the test to the two-sample case. As was shown in Chapter 14, the χ^2 test requires that each expected frequency equal at least 5. This condition can often be achieved only by taking large samples, which is costly, or by combining classes with low frequencies, which results in a loss of valuable information. The Kolmogorov-Smirnov test does not impose lower limits on class frequencies and, thus, avoids this difficulty.

The test compares a *cumulative* relative frequency distribution derived from sample data with a corresponding theoretical distribution that pertains to a specified type of population from which, the null hypothesis claims, the sample was drawn. The test statistic, D, is the absolute value of the maximum deviation between the observed cumulative relative frequency distribution (F_o) and the expected cumulative relative frequency distribution (F_e), as noted in Formula 21.Q. Depending on the probability that such a deviation would occur if the sample data really came from the specified type of population, the null hypothesis is accepted or rejected.

FORMULA 21.Q | The Kolmogorov-Smirnov One-Sample Test Statistic

$$D = \max |F_o - F_e|$$

where D is the absolute value of the maximum difference between an observed cumulative relative frequency distribution, F_o, and an expected cumulative relative frequency distribution, F_e, which is derived on the assumption that the null hypothesis (concerning the type of population from which sample data were drawn) is true.

GOODNESS OF FIT TO THE BINOMIAL DISTRIBUTION

EXAMPLE PROBLEM 21.8

Conduct a Kolmogorov-Smirnov test (rather than a χ^2 test) on Example Problem 14.9 (page 622) concerning housing code violations in order to determine whether the data fit a binomial distribution.

SOLUTION:

Step 1: *Formulating two opposing hypotheses.*

H_0: The number of violations per apartment in the population of all city apartments is binomially distributed with a probability of success in any one trial of $\pi = .3$.

H_A: The number of violations per apartment in the population of all city apartments is not correctly described by H_0.

Step 2: *Selecting a test statistic.*

We select the Kolmogorov-Smirnov test statistic, D.

Step 3: *Deriving a decision rule.*

Given a desired significance level of $\alpha = .05$ (as in the Chapter 14 computation) and a sample size of $n = 200$ observations (from Table 14.10), we establish a critical value of D_α by consulting Appendix Table Q. It suggests that $D_{.05}$ be calculated as $1.36/\sqrt{n}$; thus, it equals $1.36/\sqrt{200}$, or .09617. Therefore, when H_0 is true, the probability is .05 that an observed value of D equals or exceeds .09617. Accordingly, the decision rule must be: "Accept H_0 if $D \leq .09617$."

Step 4: *Using sample data to compute the test statistic and confronting it with the decision rule.*

Table 21.7 on the next page helps us see how the value of D is computed. The entries in columns 1, 2, and 5 have been taken from Table 14.10; note how the current test does not require that data be combined in expected-frequency column 5. The entries in the remaining columns are computed from the original data in a fashion indicated by the column headings: Absolute values in columns 2 and 5 are converted into relative values in columns 3 and 6 by means of division by sample size ($n = 200$), and these relative values are then cumulated in columns 4 and 7. After compiling the absolute deviations between the cumulative values, the maximum deviation—and, thus, the size of the test statistic—immediately emerges as $D = .0374$. Accordingly, H_0 should be *accepted* (exactly as in Chapter 14's χ^2 test).

The Kolmogorov-Smirnov test has one major disadvantage. It does not allow us to estimate population parameters from sample data; these must be specified in advance of testing. In the above null hypothesis, $\pi = .3$ must be based on information other than that contained in the sample, such as previous experience. In contrast, a χ^2 test allows such estimation from a sample, provided the degrees of freedom are appropriately reduced.

TABLE 21.7 | Goodness of Fit to the Binomial Distribution

	Observed Frequencies			Expected Frequencies (if H_0 is true)			
Number of Possible Violations per Apartment (1)	Absolute Values f_o (2)	Relative Values $f_o/200$ (3)	Cumulative Relative Values F_o (4)	Absolute Values f_e (5)	Relative Values $f_e/200$ (6)	Cumulative Relative Values F_e (7)	Absolute Deviations $\|F_o - F_e\|$ (8)
0	31	.155	.155	23.52	.1176	.1176	.0374 = D
1	51	.255	.410	60.50	.3025	.4201	.0101
2	70	.350	.760	64.82	.3241	.7442	.0158
3	32	.160	.920	37.04	.1852	.9294	.0094
4	9	.045	.965	11.90	.0595	.9889	.0239
5	5	.025	.990	2.04	.0102	.9991	.0091
6	2	.010	1.000	.14	.0007	1.0000	0
Total	**200**	**1.000**		**200**	**1.0000**		

Note: Detail may not always add to totals due to rounding.

GOODNESS OF FIT TO THE POISSON DISTRIBUTION

EXAMPLE PROBLEM 21.9

Conduct a Kolmogorov-Smirnov test on Example Problem 14.10 (page 625) concerning outpatient arrivals in order to test whether the data fit a Poisson distribution.

SOLUTION: Step 1 can take the same form as in the earlier χ^2 test; Step 2 now selects the D statistic.

In Step 3, we establish a critical value of $D = .21068$ with the help of Appendix Table Q, using $\alpha = .01$ (as before) and noting that $n = 50$ (from Table 14.11). Hence, the decision rule is: "Accept H_0 if $D \leq .21068$."

In Step 4, we compute the value of D with the help of Table 21.8 on the next page. The entries in columns 1, 2, and 5 come from Table 14.11; the remaining entries are computed on that basis. Given $D = .1935$, H_0 should be *accepted* (as in Chapter 14's χ^2 test).

GOODNESS OF FIT TO THE NORMAL DISTRIBUTION

EXAMPLE PROBLEM 21.10

Conduct a Kolmogorov-Smirnov test on Example Problem 14.11 (page 627) about trading in the futures market in order to test whether the data fit a normal distribution. The original data from Table 14.12 reappear as columns 1 and 2 of Table 21.9 on the next page.

TABLE 21.8 | Goodness of Fit to the Poisson Distribution

	Observed Frequencies			Expected Frequencies (if H_0 is true)			
Number of Possible Outpatient Arrivals per Hour (1)	Absolute Values f_o (2)	Relative Values $f_o/50$ (3)	Cumulative Relative Values F_o (4)	Absolute Values f_e (5)	Relative Values $f_e/50$ (6)	Cumulative Relative Values F_e (7)	Absolute Deviations $\|F_o - F_e\|$ (8)
0	0	0	0	1.12	.0224	.0224	.0224
1	1	.02	.02	4.25	.0850	.1074	.0874
2	5	.10	.12	8.075	.1615	.2689	.1489
3	8	.16	.28	10.23	.2046	.4735	.1935 = D
4	15	.30	.58	9.72	.1944	.6679	.0879
5	9	.18	.76	7.385	.1477	.8156	.0556
6	7	.14	.90	4.68	.0936	.9092	.0092
7	3	.06	.96	2.54	.0508	.9600	0
8 and more	2	.04	1.00	2.00	.0400	1.0000	0
	50	**1.00**		**50**	**1.0000**		

TABLE 21.9 | Goodness of Fit to the Normal Distribution

	Observed Frequencies			Expected Frequencies (if H_0 is true)			
Millions of Futures Contracts Traded per Day (1)	Absolute Values f_o (2)	Relative Values $f_o/90$ (3)	Cumulative Relative Values F_o (4)	Absolute Values f_e (5)	Relative Values $f_e/90$ (6)	Cumulative Relative Values F_e (7)	Absolute Deviations $\|F_o - F_e\|$ (8)
under 10	5	.0556	.0556	0	0	0	.0556
10 to under 20	9	.1000	.1556	.126	.0014	.0014	.1542
20 to under 30	15	.1667	.3223	1.926	.0214	.0228	.2995
30 to under 40	23	.2556	.5779	12.231	.1359	.1587	.4192 = D
40 to under 50	20	.2222	.8001	30.717	.3413	.5000	.3001
50 to under 60	8	.0889	.8890	30.717	.3413	.8413	.0477
60 to under 70	6	.0667	.9557	12.231	.1359	.9772	.0215
70 to under 80	3	.0333	.9890	1.926	.0214	.9986	.0096
80 and above	1	.0111	1.0000	.126	.0014	1.0000	0
	90	**1.0000**		**90**	**1.0000**		

SOLUTION: Step 1 remains unchanged; Step 2 selects the D statistic. In Step 3, we establish a critical value of $D = .14117$ with the help of Appendix Table Q, using $\alpha = .025$ (the closest available value to the earlier .02) and noting that $n = 90$ (from Table 14.12). Hence, the decision rule is: "Accept H_0 if $D \leq .14117$."

In Step 4, we compute the value of D with the help of Table 21.9. The entries in columns 1, 2, and 5 come from Tables 14.12; and 14.13, respectively; the remaining entries are computed on that basis. Given $D = .4192$, H_0 should be *rejected* (as in Chapter 14's χ^2 test).

FIGURE 21.6 | The Kolmogorov-Smirnov Maximum Deviation Test for Goodness of Fit

This graph is based on columns 4 and 7 of Table 21.9, with smooth curves approximating what would, strictly speaking, be a step function. The graph, thus, provides a visual picture of what the Kolmogorov-Smirnov test accomplishes. In Example Problem 21.10, it determines that the maximum deviation, D, between the observed and expected distributions is too large to be attributed to sampling error alone. Thus, the null hypothesis, stating that the sample has come from a population with the expected distribution shown here, should be rejected.

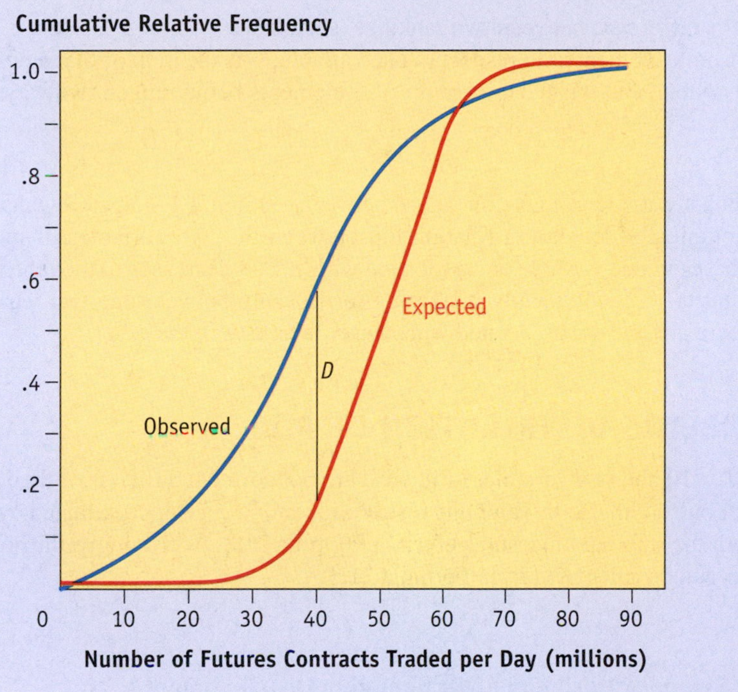

Note the bad fit of the observed distribution to the expected distribution in Table 21.9 by comparing the F_o values in column 4 with the F_e values in column 7 or by inspecting the absolute differences in column 8. All this is made visually obvious in Figure 21.6, which also shows the value of the test statistic graphically.

21.9 Spearman's Rank-Correlation Test

The **Spearman rank-correlation test** is a popular nonparametric test introduced by C. E. Spearman (1863–1945). It measures the degree of association between two variables for which only rank-order data are available. (Chapters 16 and 17 introduced other correlation measures that focus on the association between two variables for which quantitative data are available.)

THE TEST STATISTIC

The test statistic produced by this test is the **Spearman rank-correlation coefficient,** symbolized by ρ (the lowercase Greek rho). Spearman's measure is defined in Formula 21.R.

FORMULA 21.R | Spearman's Rank-Correlation Coefficient

$$\rho = 1 - \frac{6\Sigma d_i^2}{n(n^2 - 1)}$$

where d_i is the difference between two rankings (such that $d_i = x_i - y_i$), while x_i is the rank of an individual sample element with respect to one variable, y_i is the rank of that element with respect to another variable, and n is the total number of elements being ranked two ways.

Spearman's statistic can take on values between -1 and $+1$. Negative values near -1 indicate a monotonically decreasing relationship between the two variables of interest, such that steady decreases in one variable are associated with steady decreases in the other. Positive values near $+1$ point to a monotonically increasing relationship between the two variables, such that steady increases in one are associated with steady increases in the other.

THE SAMPLING DISTRIBUTION OF RHO

Whenever $n \geq 10$ and two variables of interest are not correlated (that is, if their rankings are independent of one another), the sampling distribution of ρ can be approximated by the normal distribution with the summary measures given in Formula 21.S. Accordingly, the normal deviate (or z-score) of ρ can be calculated as in Formula 21.T.

FORMULA 21.S | Mean and Standard Deviation of the Sampling Distribution of ρ (Given H_0: There Exists No Rank Correlation)

$$\mu_\rho = 0$$

$$\sigma_\rho = \sqrt{\frac{1}{n - 1}}$$

where n is the total number of elements being ranked in two ways and $n \geq 10$.

FORMULA 21.T | Normal Deviate for Spearman's Rank-Correlation Test

$$z = \frac{\rho - \mu_\rho}{\sigma_\rho} = \frac{\rho}{\sigma_\rho}$$

Assumption: $n \geq 10$

EXAMPLE PROBLEM 21.11

Consider the data of columns 1–3 of Table 21.10. Determine, at the 5 percent level of significance, whether a significant rank correlation exists between the speed and price of airplanes.

SOLUTION:

Step 1: *Formulating two opposing hypotheses.*

H_0: The speed and price rankings are not correlated.
H_A: The speed and price rankings are correlated.

Step 2: *Selecting a test statistic.*

We select the normal deviate for Spearman's rank-correlation coefficient, using Formula 21.T.

Step 3: *Deriving a decision rule.*

Given a significance level of $\alpha = .05$ and this being a two-tailed test (either a negative or a positive correlation might exist), we find in Appendix Table J critical normal deviate values of $\pm za_{\alpha/2} = \pm 1.96$. Thus, the decision rule is "Accept H_0 if $-1.96 \leq z \leq +1.96$." The critical values are encircled in Figure 21.7 on the next page.

TABLE 21.10 | Speed versus Price of Airplanes

Airplane Model (1)	Rank According to Speed, x_i (2)	Rank According to Price, y_i (3)	Rank Difference $d_i = x_i - y_i$ (4)	d_i^2 (5)
A	1	2	−1	1
B	2	1	+1	1
C	3	5	−2	4
D	4	4	0	0
E	5	3	+2	4
F	6	9	−3	9
G	7	7	0	0
H	8	8	0	0
I	9	6	+3	9
J	10	10	0	0
			Sum:	28

FIGURE 21.7 | Rank-Correlation Test on Airplanes

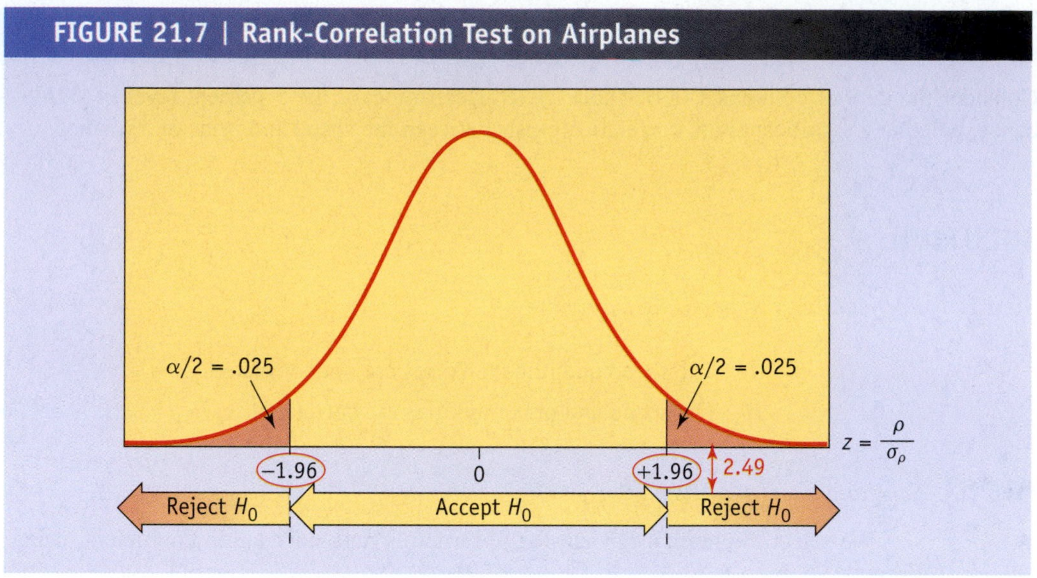

Step 4: *Using sample data to compute the test statistic and confronting it with the decision rule.*

We proceed on the assumption that a sample of $n = 10$ airplane types reveals the rank data given in columns 1–3 of Table 21.10. Thus,

$$\rho = 1 - \frac{6\Sigma d_i^2}{n(n^2 - 1)} = 1 - \frac{6(28)}{10(100 - 1)} = 1 - .1697 = +.8303$$

Furthermore,

$$\sigma_\rho = \sqrt{\frac{1}{n - 1}} = \sqrt{\frac{1}{10 - 1}} = .3333$$

Accordingly,

$$z = \frac{\rho}{\sigma_\rho} = \frac{.8303}{.3333} = 2.49$$

as indicated by the red arrow in Figure 21.7. Thus, H_0 should be *rejected.* A significant degree of (positive) rank correlation between speed and price exists.

EXCEL Example 21.5

Review Example Problem 21.11; check the correlation coefficient by computer.

SOLUTION:

1. Enter the Table 21.10, column 2 and 3 rank data, exclusive of column heads, into columns A and B of a new EXCEL worksheet. Place the cursor into any empty cell.
2. Click the **Function Wizard** > **Statistical** > **CORREL** > **OK** to activate the *Correlation* dialog box.

3. Under *Array 1,* enter **A1:A10** and press TAB.
4. Under *Array 2,* enter **B1:B10** and click **OK**.

The correlation coefficient of **.8303** appears in the selected cell.

SEARCHING FOR LEVIATHAN

Two economists, Geoffrey Brennan and James Buchanan, once put forth a striking and controversial view of the economy's public sector. As they saw it, just as monopoly in the private sector tends to harm people by decreasing output and raising prices (compared to competitive conditions), so a monolithic government (Leviathan) tends to harm its citizenry by maximizing the tax revenues that it extracts from the economy. (In the Bible and other writings, Leviathan appears as an unusually large and monstrous sea creature.) Yet Leviathan can be constrained! The authors predicted that "total government intrusion into the economy should be smaller, *ceteris paribus,* the greater the extent to which taxes and expenditures are decentralized."

Another economist, Wallace E. Oates, decided to test the Leviathan thesis, one implication of which is that the size of the economy's public sector should vary inversely with the extent of fiscal decentralization: If making more fiscal decisions locally limits the capacity of government to tax and spend, less tax revenue and less government spending should go hand in hand with more decentralization. However, in order not to prejudge the issue of whether decentralization constrains or expands the public sector, a two-tailed test was designed. Its null hypothesis was

> H_0: The size of the public sector and the extent of government decentralization are not correlated.

Three sets of data were explored, a U.S. sample and two international samples.

THE U.S. SAMPLE. Data were assembled for the 48 contiguous states: The size of each state's state-local public sector, *G,* was measured by state-local tax receipts as a fraction of state personal income. The degree of government decentralization within each state was then measured in three alternative ways: (1) as *R,* the state government's share in state-local government revenue; (2) as *E,* the state government's share in state-local government expenditures; and (3) as *L,* the absolute number of local government units in the state. If the Leviathan thesis were true, we would expect a positive correlation between *G* and *R* and between *G* and *E,* but a negative correlation between *G* and *L.* We would expect H_0 to be rejected in all three cases. However, as the Table 21.B test results show, at a significance level of α = .05, H_0 was *accepted.* The size of the public sector and the extent of government decentralization were *not* correlated.

TABLE 21.B | Sample of 48 U.S. States

Variable	Spearman's Rank-Correlation Coefficient, ρ	*z* Value
G versus *R*	−.22	−1.50
G versus *E*	−.25	−1.73
G versus *L*	−.06	−.41

SAMPLE OF 18 INDUSTRIALIZED COUNTRIES. Data were available for 18 industrialized countries. The size of each county's public sector, *G,* was now measured by total government tax receipts as a fraction of gross domestic product. The degree of government decentralization within each country was measured (1) as *R,* the central government's share of all government revenues; and (2) as *E,* the central government's share of all government expenditures. Once, again, if the Leviathan thesis were true, we would

(continued)

Application 21.3 (continued)

TABLE 21.C | Sample of 18 Industrialized Countries

Variable	Spearman's Rank-Correlation Coefficient, ρ	z Value
G versus R	−.02	−.08
G versus E	−.15	−.61

TABLE 21.D | Sample of 25 Developing Countries

Variable	Spearman's Rank-Correlation Coefficient, ρ	z Value
G versus R	.20	.98
G versus E	.12	.58

expect a positive correlation between G and R and also between G and E and a rejection of H_0. As Table 21.C shows, however, H_0 was *accepted.*

SAMPLE OF 25 DEVELOPING COUNTRIES. Data were also available for 25 developing countries. Using the same variables as for the industrialized countries, the test results are given in Table 21.D; once again, H_0 was *accepted.*

CONCLUSION. Because Spearman's rank-correlation test is a crude test that fails to hold constant the possible influence of other variables on the size of the public sector, further tests were performed. The conclusion, however, remained the same: "Perhaps, after all, Leviathan is a mythical beast."

SOURCES: Adapted from Geoffrey Brennan and James Buchanan, *The Power to Tax: Analytical Foundations of a Fiscal Constitution* (Cambridge: Cambridge University Press, 1980), p. 185; Wallace E. Oates, "Searching for Leviathan: An Empirical Study," *The American Economic Review,* September 1985, pp. 748–757. For a fascinating set of follow-up studies, see Jeffrey S. Zax, "Is There a Leviathan in Your Neighborhood?" *The American Economic Review,* June 1989, pp. 560–567; Kevin F. Forbes and Ernest M. Zampelli, "Is Leviathan a Mythical Beast?" *ibid.,* pp. 568–577; and Wallace E. Oates, "Searching for Leviathan: A Reply and Some Further Reflections," *ibid.,* pp. 578–583.

Summary

1. Whenever a hypothesis test is based on specific assumptions about the probability distribution of population values or about the sizes of population parameters, it is a *parametric test.* In contrast, any test that makes no such assumptions is a *nonparametric test.* When nothing is known about the statistical populations from which samples are being drawn, nonparametric tests alone can be employed. In addition, such tests are often capable of analyzing primitive data, such as nominal and ordinal data, while parametric tests usually require interval or ratio data.

2. Innumerable nonparametric tests exist; this chapter focuses on eight of the more popular tests:

a. The *Wilcoxon rank-sum test* (or *W test*) uses two independent simple random samples to determine whether the relative frequency distributions of two statistical populations of continuous values are identical to or different from one another.

b. The *Mann-Whitney test* (or *U test*) is equivalent to the Wilcoxon rank-sum test and serves the same goal.

c. The *sign test* uses the directions of differences observed in a matched-pairs sample to determine whether the relative frequency distributions of two statistical populations are identical to or different from one another. It can also be employed to test whether a sample comes from a population with a specified median.

d. The *Wilcoxon signed-rank test* uses the directions and magnitudes of differences observed in a matched-pairs sample to determine whether the relative frequency distributions of two statistical populations are identical to or different from one another. Thus, it uses more of the available sample information than the sign test.

e. The *number-of-runs test* determines whether the elements of a sequence appear in random order.

f. The *Kruskal-Wallis test* extends the W test from two to more than two statistical populations.

g. The *Kolmogorov-Smirnov one-sample test* is an alternative to the χ^2 test for goodness of fit. It checks the nature of a statistical population's relative frequency distribution.

h. The *Spearman's rank-correlation test* measures the degree of association between two variables for which only rank-order data are available.

Key Terms

distribution-free tests
Kolmogorov-Smirnov one-sample test
Kruskal-Wallis test
Mann-Whitney test
nonparametric statistics
nonparametric tests
number-of-runs test
parametric statistic
parametric test
robustness
run
serial dependency
sign test
Spearman rank-correlation coefficient
Spearman rank-correlation test
U test
W test
Wilcoxon rank-sum test
Wilcoxon signed-rank test

Practice Problems

NOTE

Some problems require the use of a statistical program, EXCEL or MINITAB. The program's major features are explained in text Chapter 2; plenty of additional advice is available via the program's built-in Help feature.

SECTION 21.2 THE WILCOXON RANK-SUM TEST

1. Review Example Problem 21.1 on page 1016. Then solve it by defining *W* as the rank sum not of sample A, but of sample B.
2. A farm manager wants to test a manufacturer's claim that cheaper fertilizer A is at least as effective as more expensive fertilizer B. Twenty identical plots of strawberries are randomly selected. Half are fertilized with A and half with B. The yields are to be recorded and a statistical test at the 5 percent significance level is to be made. The eventual results of the experiment appear in Table 21.11.

TABLE 21.11 | Fertilizer Experiment

Fertilizer A		Fertilizer B	
Plot Number	Strawberry Output (quarts)	Plot Number	Strawberry Output (quarts)
3	91	1	79
4	97	2	90
7	85	5	80
9	88	6	95
11	86	8	83
12	93	10	93
13	80	14	85
15	81	16	80
18	81	17	82
20	90	19	84

3. The information in Table 21.12 was gathered in two random samples of recent engineering graduates. Test at the 10 percent significance level whether starting salaries are the same for graduates of the two institutions.

TABLE 21.12 | Starting Salaries of Engineers

University A		University B	
Student	**Dollars/Week**	**Student**	**Dollars/Week**
Abrams	1,200	Adler	1,390
Bak	1,500	Bacon	1,750
Cotter	2,000	Conrad	1,250
Derin	1,850	Heber	2,350
Ford	1,900	Kott	2,100
McRae	2,200	Noke	2,050
Topa	2,300	Ryan	1,710
Torok	1,450	Trane	1,490
Upton	1,600	Vogel	1,410
Weber	1,800	Weise	2,200

4. Given the sample information in Table 21.13, a pharmaceutical company researcher wants to test the claim that drug A really provides at least as much relief as drug B. Make the test at the 5 percent significance level.

TABLE 21.13 | Hours of Relief Experienced by 25 Patients

Drug A	Drug B
3.0	3.8
5.9	8.3
4.7	7.9
3.3	6.5
3.8	4.5
4.2	6.1
4.5	5.9
6.1	7.6
8.0	4.2
7.1	3.3
	8.1
	8.2
	7.0
	5.0
	6.9

5. A personnel manager wants to test the claim, at the 1 percent significance level, that output per worker under an hourly pay plan (A) is less than or at most equal to that under a piecework plan (B). A four-week experiment provides the information shown in Table 21.14. Make the test.

TABLE 21.14 | Output per Worker (units per day)

Under Plan A (hourly pay)	Under Plan B (piecework pay)
552	751
274	252
241	917
547	981
651	492
492	517
631	707
602	908
510	937
278	199

6. A government agency wants to test an oil company's advertising claim according to which cars will run at least as many miles on a tankful of its regular gas as on a tankful of a competitor's (more expensive and allegedly superior) gasohol. Twenty identical cars are randomly selected. Half are filled with gasoline and half with gasohol. The resulting mileages appear in Table 21.15. Make a *W* test at the 5 percent level of significance.

TABLE 21.15 | Miles Driven before Fuel Exhaustion

On Gasoline (A)	On Gasohol (B)
350	352
372	375
348	351
371	375
381	391
392	390
353	360
388	393
388	394
373	379

SECTION 21.3 THE MANN-WHITNEY TEST

7. You are given the sample information of Table 21.16. Make a *U* test at the 10 percent level of significance on whether now-bankrupt firms were in business about equally long in the two industries. Do not use a computer, and show your calculations.

TABLE 21.16 | Lifetimes of Now-Bankrupt Firms (years)

Industry A	Industry B
2.3	30.6
3.7	25.5
10.6	3.3
8.9	7.0
27.0	6.7
16.5	5.8
9.2	.6
.6	.2
.9	.3
1.3	8.9
2.5	
3.1	
1.0	

8. Review Practice Problem 7. Check its result by computer.
9. You are given the sample information in Table 21.17. Make a *U* test at the 5 percent level of significance on whether your company's job application test scores are at least as high for high school dropouts as for high school graduates. Do not use a computer, and show your calculations.

TABLE 21.17 | Job Application Test Scores

High School Dropouts (A)	High School Graduates (B)
66	88
82	83
93	84
50	85
50	86
72	89
73	91
77	62
69	69
85	75
91	69
	71
	75
	75

10. Review Practice Problem 9 on the preceding page. Check its result by computer.

11. You are given the sample information in Table 21.18. Make a U test at the 2.5 percent level of significance on whether the daily memory sales at computer store A are at most equal to those at store B. Do not use a computer, and show your calculations.

TABLE 21.18 | RAM Sales (megabytes)

Store A	Store B
64	128
192	256
384	192
576	0
896	64
704	320
192	640
0	896
384	1,088
128	0

12. Review Practice Problem 11. Check its result by computer.

Section 21.4 The Sign Test

13. A government agency wants to test a refining company's claim that the mileage achieved with its unleaded gasoline (A) is at most equal to and probably less than that achieved with its leaded gasoline (B). Fifteen car models are chosen; a given driver drives each model twice over the identical route. At random, each driver is given brand A or brand B first, then drives with the other brand during the second trip. This procedure is designed to assure that neither brand of gasoline is favored or handicapped by all drivers being fresh or tired, respectively. Because the agency statistician knows nothing about the probability distribution of the population of miles-per-gallon differences, a sign test at the 2.5 percent level of significance is chosen. Make the test, using the government's Table 21.19 data.

14. The Federal Aviation Administration creates 30 pairs of similar individuals who are about to take its air traffic controller course. One member of each pair is subjected to a new curriculum (A), the other member to an old one (B). Then both take the same test, and the difference in scores is recorded. It is hypothesized that the new curriculum will produce equal or better scores. In fact, there are 20 better scores (+) and no ties. Make an appropriate hypothesis test at the 5 percent level of significance.

15. A plant manager believes that in general fewer accidents occur during the day shift than during the night shift. The difference in the number of accidents is recorded for 100 days; more accidents during the day than night are recorded as (+), fewer during the day are recorded as (−). There are 8 ties and 50 pluses. Make an appropriate hypothesis test at the 5 percent level of significance.

16. A department store executive wants to assess the company's in-store sales campaign. Are sales of children's clothing promoted more effectively by periodic loudspeaker announcements or visual displays? A simple random sample of 12 stores is selected. In each, sales are recorded during one week of loudspeaker announcements (A), then during a second week of visual displays (B). In the end, sales were the same in one store, higher (+) in 7 stores under A, lower (−) in 4 stores under A. Make an appropriate hypothesis test at the 2.5 percent level of significance.

TABLE 21.19 | Gasoline Experiment

	Miles per Gallon		
Car Model	Unleaded Gas (A)	Leaded Gas (B)	Signs of Difference (A − B)
1	22.1	23.7	−
2	15.7	16.1	−
3	18.2	19.0	−
4	19.0	19.0	0
5	25.7	24.2	+
6	19.2	22.0	−
7	11.9	12.1	−
8	28.0	30.2	−
9	35.0	37.8	−
10	27.0	30.0	−
11	19.7	19.0	+
12	16.3	15.1	+
13	21.2	23.4	−
14	22.2	20.7	+
15	27.8	28.1	−

17. At a time when the median price of a single-family home was alleged to be $153,000 nationally, a large real estate firm investigated the median prices in the 100 largest cities. Of these, 30 exceeded the above figure (+) and 70 were below it (−). Did the 100 largest cities belong to a population with a $153,000 median price? Make an appropriate hypothesis test at the 5 percent level of significance.

18. A manufacturer advertised the median life of an aircraft spark plug as 800 service hours. The FAA doubted the claim and checked a random sample of logbooks on 50 types of planes using this type of plug. In 12 types of airplanes, the spark plugs lasted more than 800 hours (+), but they lasted fewer hours (−) in the remaining 38 airplane types. Was the advertising claim correct? Make an appropriate hypothesis test at the 5 percent level of significance.

SECTION 21.5 THE WILCOXON SIGNED-RANK TEST

19. An advertising agency wonders whether a national ad campaign has been successful in boosting sales. A simple random sample of 10 urban areas reveals the data in Table 21.20 on the next page. Assuming that observed differences are attributable solely to the campaign, make an appropriate hypothesis test at the 1 percent level of significance.

20. The Food and Drug Administration wants to test a meat packer's claim that luncheon meats have a shorter shelf life with a traditional preservative than with a newly developed one. A random sample of meats from 12 suppliers reveals the information in Table 21.21 on the next page. Make an appropriate hypothesis test at the 1 percent level of significance.

TABLE 21.20 | Advertising and Sales

City	Sales (millions of dollars)	
	Before Campaign	After Campaign
Atlanta	100	110
Boston	120	130
Cincinnati	27	25
Detroit	35	30
Houston	51	70
Los Angeles	75	82
Sacramento	12	19
Seattle	80	75
Toledo	60	58
Washington	34	64

TABLE 21.21 | The Shelf Life of Meat

Supplier	Shelf Life (days)	
	With Old Preservatives	With New Preservatives
A	4.2	4.8
B	6.1	6.3
C	5.3	5.0
D	3.9	4.5
E	4.5	4.2
F	6.0	5.5
G	5.8	5.9
H	4.9	4.9
I	5.3	5.0
J	5.5	5.5
K	5.2	5.5
L	4.8	4.0

21. A marketing manager wants to test whether a particular product's sales differ depending on whether it is displayed at eye level or above/below eye level on supermarket shelves. A random sample of 20 stores is taken. They are grouped in pairs according to similarity of weekly sales in the past, and the data of Table 21.22 are collected. Make an appropriate hypothesis test at the 5 percent level of significance.

22. The personnel manager of a multinational company wonders whether the salaries of economists in a foreign country differ between academic and nonacademic employment. Two random samples of 15 economists are taken—one sample in each field of employment—and the 30 individuals are grouped into 15 pairs in accordance with years of experience. Based on the data in Table 21.23, make an appropriate hypothesis test at the 2.5 percent level of significance.

TABLE 21.22 | Display Position and Sales

	Weekly Sales (dollars)	
Store Pair	**Product at Eye Level**	**Product above or below Eye Level**
A	52	17
B	79	29
C	26	28
D	197	120
E	220	190
F	92	120
G	105	85
H	69	70
I	97	70
J	53	23

TABLE 21.23 | The Pay of Economists Abroad

	Annual Salary (thousands of dollars)	
Economist Pair	**Academic Employment**	**Nonacademic Employment**
A	52.7	81.3
B	33.8	75.0
C	21.5	32.9
D	25.7	38.6
E	32.1	42.6
F	40.0	41.2
G	45.0	38.6
H	35.4	38.9
I	42.6	52.1
J	31.9	42.7
K	50.0	48.0
L	56.0	62.7
M	52.0	66.6
N	39.0	75.0
O	27.8	42.0

23. A corporate lawyer wonders whether the vigor of antitrust enforcement differed in the 1990s compared to the 1980s. A sample of 10 firms is selected from the *Fortune 500* list, and the data of Table 21.24 are collected. Make an appropriate hypothesis test at the 5 percent level of significance.

TABLE 21.24 | The Vigor of Antitrust Enforcement

Firm	Number of Indictments	
	1980s	1990s
A	5	7
B	6	8
C	2	3
D	7	9
E	10	9
F	15	20
G	9	18
H	12	7
I	8	12
J	3	7

24. A hospital administrator, who is your boss, wants you to check the result of a signed-rank test that someone else has performed. As was done before, you are to use a 1 percent level of significance and the sample data of Table 21.25. Do you agree with the previous statistician's claim that penicillin is basically inferior to the sulfa drug because it takes longer, or at best the same time, to effect a cure?

TABLE 21.25 | Penicillin versus Sulfa Drug

Matched-Patient Pair	Days to Effect Cure	
	Penicillin	Sulfa Drug
A	4.2	4.0
B	6.1	6.0
C	5.3	5.1
D	3.9	3.7
E	4.5	4.4
F	6.0	5.9
G	5.8	5.6
H	5.5	5.8
I	4.8	4.5
J	4.8	4.4

Section 21.6 The Number-of-Runs Test

25. The Environmental Protection Agency suspects a firm of polluting a lake. It needs to test, therefore, whether the lake's acidity level varies randomly over time. The acidity is measured on 60 days, its average level is computed, and each day's measurement is then designated to be above average (A) or below average (B). The results appear in Table 21.26. Make an appropriate hypothesis test at the 5 percent significance level.

TABLE 21.26 | The Acidity Level of a Lake

Day	Acidity	Day	Acidity	Day	Acidity	Day	Acidity
1	B	16	B	31	B	46	A
2	B	17	B	32	B	47	A
3	B	18	B	33	B	48	A
4	A	19	B	34	B	49	A
5	A	20	B	35	B	50	A
6	A	21	B	36	B	51	B
7	A	22	A	37	B	52	B
8	A	23	A	38	B	53	A
9	A	24	A	39	B	54	A
10	A	25	A	40	A	55	A
11	A	26	A	41	A	56	B
12	A	27	A	42	A	57	B
13	B	28	A	43	A	58	A
14	B	29	A	44	A	59	A
15	B	30	A	45	A	60	A

26. A stock-market analyst wants to test the *random-walk hypothesis,* according to which stock prices move randomly over time with no discernible pattern whatsoever. A test at the 1 percent significance level is to be conducted, based on the information about a given stock in Table 21.27. [*Hint:* First, calculate the average closing price and classify each day according to whether its price was above (A) or below (B) that average. Then make an appropriate hypothesis test.]

TABLE 21.27 | The Closing Prices of a Stock

Day	Dollars per Share	Day	Dollars per Share	Day	Dollars per Share
1	41	9	23	17	23
2	43	10	39	18	42
3	37	11	61	19	57
4	51	12	48	20	51
5	63	13	48	21	47
6	39	14	60	22	41
7	43	15	33	23	39
8	58	16	39	24	50

27. A business-school admissions board stands accused of manipulating admissions on a daily basis according to a secret quota system based on sex. The board denies the charge and claims that sex is determined randomly for each succeeding admission, because sex is never even considered during the admission process. Investigators acquire the Table 21.28 information on 60 successive admissions. (M = male, F = female, and data are to be read in successive rows.)

a. Make an appropriate hypothesis test at the 2.5 percent level of significance.

b. Ask yourself this: Would your answer be different if a 5 percent significance level had been specified?

TABLE 21.28 | Business School Admissions

Order of Admission	Sex of Admission
1–10	M M M M M F F M M M
11–20	M M F F F M M M M M
21–30	F F M F M M M M M F
31–40	F F M M M M M M M F
41–50	F F M F M M M M M M
51–60	M M F F M M F F M M

28. A quality inspector wonders whether the appearance of defective items in a continuous production process is random. Make an appropriate test, at the 5 percent significance level, using the inspector's Table 21.29 data. (S = satisfactory, D = defective, and data are to be read in successive rows.)

TABLE 21.29 | Satisfactory and Defective Items in a Production Process

S S S S S S D S S S D S S S S S S D S S
S D S S S S S S D S S S D S S S S S S D
S S S D S S S S S S D S S S D S S S S S

29. Review Example Problem 21.6 on page 1031. Then check the sequence 2 *number-of-runs test* by computer. (Sequence 2: $\overline{T\,T\,T\,T\,T}\,\underline{H\,H\,H\,H\,H}$)

30. Review Example Problem 21.6 on page 1031. Then check the sequence 3 *number-of-runs test* by computer. (Sequence 3: $\underline{H}\,\overline{T}\,\underline{H}\,\overline{T}\,\underline{H}\,\overline{T}\,\underline{H}\,\overline{T}\,\underline{H}\,\overline{T}$)

SECTION 21.7 THE KRUSKAL-WALLIS TEST

31. An airline executive wants to test, at the 1 percent level of significance, whether there is any difference in the times to failure of three types of radar transponders. Random samples of new units installed in the airline's fleet yield the months-of-service data in Table 21.30. Make the test without using a computer.

TABLE 21.30 | Transponder Times to Failure

Type A	Type B	Type C
48.1	40.3	13.8
26.5	43.7	20.4
41.8	50.1	19.1
38.1	40.4	21.8
36.3	36.0	24.7
40.7	28.8	26.8
26.6		19.8
28.8		

32. An auto executive wants to determine, at the 5 percent level of significance, whether the training given to newly hired workers is equally effective at four locations. The same test is administered everywhere to the most recent class; the scores are given in Table 21.31. Make the test without using a computer.

TABLE 21.31 | Test Scores at Four Locations

A	B	C	D
96	65	60	95
82	74	73	93
88	72	85	90
70	66	61	88
90	79	79	91
91	82	85	87
87		88	90

33. A corporate executive wants to test, at the 2 percent level of significance, whether the percentage of overdue customer accounts differs from one region of the country to another. Random samples of sales outlets in regions A–D reveal the information given in Table 21.32. Make the test without using a computer.

TABLE 21.32 | Percentage of Overdue Accounts in Four Regions

A	B	C	D
10.1	7.2	20.7	4.1
7.2	8.5	19.0	3.0
8.5	9.1	18.0	2.7
9.0	6.3	13.7	8.3
7.0	5.9	21.2	7.1
5.2	7.3		1.0
			1.5

34. Check the result of Practice Problem 31 with the help of the computer.

35. Check the result of Practice Problem 32 with the help of the computer.

36. Check the result of Practice Problem 33 with the help of the computer.

SECTION 21.8 THE KOLMOGOROV-SMIRNOV ONE-SAMPLE TEST

37. An oil company has been drilling 3 wells each at 500 sites around the world. The number of promising wells per site was 0 in 250 tries, 1 in 198 tries, 2 in 47 tries, and 3 in 5 tries. The company wants to test the hypothesis that the number of promising wells (out of 3 drillings per site) is a binomially distributed random variable with a probability of success in any one trial of $\pi = .2$, which is what past experience suggests. Make the test at the 1 percent significance level.

38. Apply the *Kolmogorov-Smirnov one-sample test* to Chapter 14, Practice Problem 42, on page 644, but use $\alpha = .025$.

39. An insurance company executive believes that a Poisson distribution nicely describes the population of yearly auto accidents per driver. To test this proposition at the 10 percent significance level, apply the *Kolmogorov-Smirnov one-sample test* to the data of Table 21.33.

TABLE 21.33 | Auto Accidents per Driver

Yearly Accidents per Driver	Observed Frequency
0	103,628
1	7,389
2	1,910
3	29
Total	**112,956**

TABLE 21.34 | Pilot Errors

Errors per Hour	Observed Frequency
0	3
1	8
2	5
3	7
4	2
5	1
6	2
7	1
8	0
9	0
10	1
Total	**30**

40. An airline flight instructor wonders whether a Poisson distribution can describe the hourly number of errors made by pilots operating a flight simulator. To test this proposition at the 1 percent significance level, apply the *Kolmogorov-Smirnov one-sample test* to the data of Table 21.34.

41. An executive of a multinational corporation wants to test the allegation that a normal curve with a mean of $45,000 and a standard deviation of $10,000 nicely describes the annual incomes of lawyers in a foreign country. A simple random sample of 100 lawyers yields Table 21.35. Apply the *Kolmogorov-Smirnov one-sample test* to the data, using a significance level of 5 percent.

TABLE 21.35 | The Income of Foreign Lawyers

Annual Income (thousands of dollars)	Observed Frequency
under 20	2
20 to under 30	5
30 to under 40	10
40 to under 50	60
50 to under 60	10
60 to under 70	5
70 to under 80	3
80 to under 90	0
90 and above	5
Total	**100**

42. An advertising agency asks a random sample of 500 people to taste 5 brands of coffee and records the brand most preferred. Given the data of Table 21.36, and using a significance level of 10 percent, make a *Kolmogorov-Smirnov one-sample test* of the agency's claim that the preferences of coffee drinkers in general are uniformly distributed among the sampled brands.

TABLE 21.36 | Consumer Coffee Survey

Most Preferred Brand	Observed Frequency
A	91
B	109
C	85
D	100
E	115
Total	**500**

Section 21.9 Spearman's Rank-Correlation Test

43. In each of the following cases, determine whether a significant degree of *rank correlation* exists, using $\alpha = .10$ as the desired significance level.

a. These are the ranks of exam scores received by 10 students:

Student:	A	B	C	D	E	F	G	H	I	J
Midterm:	1	2	3	4	5	6	7	8	9	10
Final:	10	9	8	7	6	5	4	3	2	1

b. These are the ranks of evaluation scores given to 10 salespeople:

Salesperson:	A	B	C	D	E	F	G	H	I	J
When hired:	1	2	3	4	5	6	7	8	9	10
After 2 years:	1	2	3	4	5	6	7	8	9	10

44. These are the ranks of preference scores given to 10 TV shows:

TV show:	A	B	C	D	E	F	G	H	I	J
Men:	1	2	3	4	5	6	7	8	9	10
Women:	10	1	9	2	8	3	7	4	6	5

Determine whether a significant degree of *rank correlation* exists, using $\alpha = .10$ as the desired significance level.

45. These are the ranks of 10 firms by two criteria:

Firm:	A	B	C	D	E	F	G	H	I	J
Advertising expenditure:	1	2	3	4	5	6	7	8	9	10
Sales:	3	7	5	9	1	6	10	8	2	4

Determine whether a significant degree of *rank correlation* exists, using $\alpha = .10$ as the desired significance level.

46. These are the evaluation scores given by two critics to 10 paintings at an exhibition:

Painting:	A	B	C	D	E	F	G	H	I	J
Critic A:	1	2	3	4	5	6	7	8	9	10
Critic B:	3	7	1	5	8	2	6	10	4	9

Determine whether a significant degree of *rank correlation* exists, using $\alpha = .05$ as the desired significance level.

47. The average monthly draft priority numbers picked during the 1970 draft lottery (discussed in Application 4.3 on page 117) are given in Table 21.37. Determine whether a significant degree of *rank correlation* exists, using $\alpha = .10$ as the desired significance level.

TABLE 21.37 | 1970 Draft Lottery

Month	Average Number Picked	Month	Average Number Picked
January	201.2	July	181.5
February	203.0	August	173.5
March	225.8	September	157.3
April	203.7	October	182.5
May	208.0	November	148.7
June	195.7	December	121.5

48. Table 21.38 shows the world's 10 richest countries according to the World Bank's 1997 ranking by per capita GNP. It also shows the same countries' rankings by the United Nations' human development index. Determine whether a significant degree of *rank correlation* exists, using $\alpha = .05$ as the desired significance level.

TABLE 21.38 | 1997 Country Rankings

Country	Per Capita GNP Rank	HDI Rank
Switzerland	1	7
Japan	2	3
Norway	3	1
Singapore	4	10
Denmark	5	8
United States	6	2
Germany	7	9
Austria	8	6
Belgium	9	5
Sweden	10	4

Entire Chapter

49. For each of the following sampling situations, specify an appropriate nonparametric hypothesis test.

a. After running its vehicles with ordinary gasoline for half a year and then with gasohol, United Parcel Service wants to determine the relative performance of the two types of fuel.

b. An advertising agency asks a group of men to shave with one shaver for a while and then to shave with another (although the order is varied from man to man). It wants to determine which shaver is perceived to give a closer shave.

c. An economist wants to determine whether the past movements of silver futures prices have been random over time.

d. An economist wants to determine whether the median house price in an area equals an alleged number.

e. A researcher wants to determine which of two drugs cures a disease faster.

f. An executive wants to compare the delivery times of steel coming from two mills; relevant times are available for the last 50 shipments received.

g. An executive wants to know whether output is higher without or with piped-in music at the workplace; data are available for the performance of 15 employees.

50. For each of the following sampling situations, specify an appropriate nonparametric hypothesis test.

a. A union official wants to determine the preferences of union members between two proposed labor contracts.

b. After running 25 military vehicles with regular gasoline for half a year, then with unleaded gasoline, then with gasohol, and then with a new top-secret type of fuel, the Pentagon wants to determine the relative performance of the four types of fuel.

c. An executive wants to know whether brand preference and price are related.

d. A quality inspector wants to determine whether the appearance of defective items in a continuous production process is random.

e. An economist wants to know whether riskiness and salaries of different jobs are related.

f. An executive wants to compare the delivery times of steel coming from seven mills; times are available for the last 50 shipments received.

g. An executive wants to study the relationship between newspaper advertising and sales results; data are available for the last 17 weeks.

Chapter 22

QUALITY CONTROL

LOOKING AHEAD

After reading this chapter, you will know a great deal about quality control. Among other things, you will learn to:

1. recognize the many places in a production process—ranging from product design to manufacturing and even customer billing—at which quality control measures can be implemented,
2. execute *acceptance sampling* to ensure the quality of materials used and end products created,
3. utilize *control charts* to monitor the behavior of crucial data series reflecting different aspects of the production process, and
4. appreciate the nature of the *total quality movement* that seeks to achieve near perfection via the Six Sigma approach.

AND HERE IS A TYPICAL PROBLEM YOU WILL BE ABLE TO SOLVE:

A properly working production process fills bottles with an average 16.5 ounces of liquid detergent. The population of filling weights is normally distributed with a standard deviation of 0.8 oz. Inspectors take periodic samples of 35 bottles. One sample yields a mean filling weight of 16.2 oz., the next two samples yield 15.8 oz. and 17.3 oz. Is the production process out of control?

PREVIEW

In the late 1980s, the following true story made the rounds in American management circles. A Canadian subsidiary of IBM had ordered 1,000 parts from a Japanese supplier. IBM's purchasing order made it clear that the parts had to be 95 percent defect-free and that no more than 5 percent defective parts would be deemed acceptable. Before long, the shipment arrived. It contained 950 parts in one package and 50 parts in another. There was also a note, stating "enclosed are the 950 perfect parts, as requested; although we don't know why you would want them, we have packed the 50 defective parts separately for your convenience." The story tells a lot about American and Japanese attitudes concerning quality. While American managers have long been striving for products that are *good enough,* their Japanese counterparts have been insisting on *perfection.*

Keep in mind that Japan's productive capacity was almost nonexistent at the end of World War II. Yet a mere four decades later, Japan had become a dominant manufacturing power, and its high-quality products inspired admiration around the world. Interestingly, this amazing development can be traced to an American professor and management consultant, William Edwards Deming (1900–1993), who worked with the Supreme Command of the Allied Powers in Japan in the 1950s. During his stay in Japan, Deming imparted his philosophy of management, which had been treated with disdain in the United States, to top Japanese executives, who received it with enthusiasm.

Deming's ideas are often summarized in a number of rather folksy rules; their style is reminiscent of the once-famous exhortations of China's Chairman Mao that were enshrined in his equally famous *Little Red Book.* Here are *some* of Deming's 14 rules, along with brief interpretations:

1. *Create constancy of purpose toward improvement of product and service, with the aim of becoming competitive, staying in business, and providing jobs.* Continuous quality improvement must be a firm's overriding goal; day in and day out, all employees must make this their first priority.
2. *Adopt the new philosophy.* Reject the old approach that relies on detecting quality problems at the end of the production process or through customer complaints and then reacts by making appropriate adjustments. Instead, implement a preventative management style that is obsessed with never-ending quality improvement.
3. *Cease dependence on mass inspection of finished products.* Such inspection is not needed if quality is designed into products, good materials are used, and the production process itself is continually monitored with a view to achieving high quality.
4. *End the practice of awarding business to lowest-bid vendors.* Low price tag often means low quality. Establish long-term relations with a single supplier based on loyalty and trust.
5. *Improve constantly and forever the system of production and service, to improve quality and productivity and, thus, constantly decrease cost.* Higher quality decreases costs as fewer items need reworking; it raises labor productivity as there are fewer delays. Ultimately, it helps a firm lower prices and gain market share.
6. *Institute a vigorous program of worker education and training.* Workers must be properly trained, by knowledgeable persons, to do their job right. They must be provided with ever-new skills as the need arises, including the ability to understand and use statistical methods of quality control.
7. *Institute high-quality leadership.* Supervisors should help workers do a better job, not order them around or punish them.
8. *Drive out fear.* Workers should not be passive and afraid to ask questions. They should feel secure in reporting out-of-control processes to management.
9. *Break down barriers among departments.* Everyone in the firm should work as a team for the same goal, not compete against one another.
10. *Remove barriers that rob employees of their pride of workmanship.* Treat workers with respect, improve working conditions, and provide employees with good materials and tools to enable them to produce what makes them proud.

Although these and other rules point to issues that go far beyond the discipline of statistics, this chapter introduces quality control, with special emphasis on the statistical methods involved.[1]

[1]Various listings of the Deming rules can be found in the literature cited on the text's Web site. The story introducing this Preview was first reported by Patrick Lush in the June 15, 1988, issue of *The Globe and Mail* of Toronto.

22.1 Introduction

In the 1990s, many markets for inputs and outputs turned international in scope. At some time during the 21st century, many markets may well encompass the entire earth. Already nations are dismantling all kinds of artificial restrictions to the international mobility of labor and capital resources and to the free trade of commodities and services that these inputs help produce. Consider the easing of emigration and immigration laws, the enactment of laws promoting international investment flows, and the continuing efforts worldwide to remove tariffs and quotas that restrict trade. Consider the 1992 elimination of the last remaining economic boundaries among the members of the European Community. Consider the eagerness of new nations—remnants of the former Soviet empire—to join that community. Consider the creation of the North American Free Trade Area, combining the already giant economies of Canada, the United States, and Mexico. And think of the recent spectacular economic growth of Japan and other countries of the Pacific rim. Their growth has been export-driven, fueled by products *outcompeting* those of European and American firms in markets throughout the world. Interestingly, as newspaper headlines never fail to remind us, persistent U.S. trade deficits with Japan and ever-growing Japanese investments in the United States, financed with the surplus dollars so earned, can be linked to a fierce Japanese commitment to supply consumers with products of consistently *high quality*. U.S. consumers' response is evidenced by facts such as these: In 1989, for the first time ever, the top-selling car in the U.S. market was foreign made (Japan's Honda Accord)—a feat that has been repeated in later years—and by now virtually all television sets and VCRs come from Japan as well. No wonder American firms are becoming increasingly concerned with meeting the quality challenge, which accounts for the subject matter of this chapter.

Producers who want to meet the challenge of the global marketplace must institute **quality control,** a series of production-process investigations and analyses that (1) determine whether emerging products meet the quality standards demanded by consumers and (2) trigger remedial actions, when necessary, to achieve and maintain that desired quality level.

22.2 The Production Process

In order to understand the actions that firms might take to enhance product quality and the role that statisticians can play in this quest, we must look at various stages that are typically associated with the production of a product. Consider the production of aircraft emergency locator transmitters (ELTs). According to government regulations, an ELT must be attached to every aircraft and must be capable of transmitting an automatically activated, continuous signal that can help search parties locate crashed aircraft. Yet such a product would be of low quality if it did not have all of the characteristics that users consider crucial: low weight, small size, indestructibility, visual attractiveness, and the power to emit clear signals (say, within a 100-mile radius) continuously for seven days. Figure 22.1 can guide our thinking about the creation of such a product.

At Stage 1, possibly far removed from the actual product manufacture, consumer research identifies the preferences of potential customers. Regardless of whether firms establish focus groups or send questionnaires in the mail, statisticians inevitably are involved in the design and execution of random samples and the subsequent analysis of the results. Initially, they use sampling techniques described in Chapter 4; later, they subject their results to methods such as those encountered in Chapters 11–13.

At Stage 2, design engineers translate the information gained in consumer research into precise product specifications. They might design an ELT in the form of a box, weighing 10 ounces ± 5 percent and sized 1 inch by 2 inches by 6 inches plus a 2-foot antenna. The box might be capable of withstanding 6.7 Gs (impact forces of 6.7 times the force of gravity), while being impervious to fire and submersion in water. Engineering specs may call for a smooth,

FIGURE 22.1 | Typical Stages of Production

We can break down the process of producing most products, such as aircraft emergency locator transmitters (ELTs) considered here, into a number of distinct stages. Firms can address quality at any one of the stages shown; each time, statisticians are likely to be involved.

1. Consumer Research → Customer preferences are identified. Statisticians design and conduct random samples, then analyze the results.

2. Product Design → Engineers translate Stage 1 results into precise product specifications. Statisticians help identify **design quality.**

3. Materials Purchase → Based on Stage 2 requirements, material inputs are acquired from outside suppliers. Statisticians perform **acceptance sampling.**

4. Manufacture → The materials purchased at Stage 3 are combined with labor and machinery to create the product designed at Stage 2. Statisticians monitor the process by repetitive sampling, with results highlighted in **control charts.**

5. Warehousing → Finished products are shipped to the warehouse. Statisticians perform **acceptance sampling.**

6. Marketing → The product is advertised and sold, post-sale service is provided. Statisticians employ random sampling to monitor sales and customer satisfaction.

painted surface, free of visible blemishes. And the ELT's transmission quality may be designed to equal that of the best aircraft radios typically used for voice communications. Even here, statisticians can play a role. They can subject the prototype transmitter to all kinds of experiments and hypothesis tests, perhaps like those noted in Chapters 13–15, and thus establish the product's **design quality,** the level of quality that the product would have if engineering specifications were precisely met. The mean time between failures (MTBF) of the fire and waterproof battery pack, for example, might be established at 1.9 years. All kinds of probabilities might be computed for possible failure at earlier or later times. Application 22.1, *Striving for Reliability—The Case of the Apollo Mission,* at the end of this section, provides a famous example of an attempt to create high quality *by design.*

At Stage 3, company buyers acquire material inputs, such as raw materials and parts, from outside suppliers. The buyers are guided by engineering specs established at Stage 2. Statisticians test samples of incoming shipments for stated quality, as, for example, the thickness of aluminum sheets, the lifespan of batteries, the durability of paint. This type of *acceptance sampling* is discussed (and defined) in Section 22.3.

At Stage 4, labor and machinery are applied to the purchased materials to create the product designed at Stage 2. The **manufactured quality,** which is the level of quality that the product in fact exhibits, might vary from the design quality for innumerable reasons, including the nature of materials, manpower, and machines. Materials may fail to meet the specs, workers may be badly motivated or fatigued, and machines may be wearing out. Statisticians frequently monitor various aspects of manufactured quality by repetitive sampling during the production process. Their favorite method involves *control charts,* already encountered in Application 7.2 on page 255, and discussed (and defined) in detail in Section 22.4.

At Stage 5, finished products emerge from the manufacturing stage and are shipped to the warehouse. Once again, statisticians perform *acceptance sampling,* discussed in Section 22.3, to assure that the ultimate manufactured quality comes close to the consumer preferences that were specified in product design.

At Stage 6, the finished product is advertised and sold. In addition, post-sale support is provided. In the case of our ELTs, for example, this may involve customer 800-number hotlines and the establishment, at all major airports, of repair centers with 1-hour turnaround. Statisticians monitor all of these processes and, thus, measure customer satisfaction levels.

CAUTION

The preceding discussion of Figure 22.1 must not be misunderstood. It does not imply that *professional* statisticians must carry out the statistical work noted and that professional statisticians alone are responsible for the achievement of quality goals. Rather, the sketch merely illustrates the kinds of quality issues that must be addressed. It would be quite feasible to train workers and supervisors at all stages of the production process to carry out this type of statistical work and to make them responsible for quality.

Likewise, Figure 22.1 does not imply that each department should do its work in isolation from all other company employees. On the contrary, those engaged in product design would surely be consulting and cooperating with many others throughout the firm: with employees engaged in consumer research; with materials buyers who know what kinds of materials are available from suppliers; with manufacturing workers who have all kinds of experiences to share about how materials, people, and machines interact at the assembly line; and, last but not least, with marketing and sales people who, better than all others, come to know the level of customer satisfaction and complaints.

In short, Figure 22.1 indicates the kinds of tasks that have to be performed; it does not suggest that everyone can work in isolation or everyone can ignore quality as long as professional statisticians have been put to work on that front. In fact, Deming's points, noted in the Preview, suggest that *all* employees be involved with assessing quality.

APPLICATION 22.1

STRIVING FOR RELIABILITY—THE CASE OF THE APOLLO MISSION

As is so often the case, we can learn much from history. Consider the Apollo mission, which was to land Americans on the moon. It required the cooperation of a large number of private firms and government agencies toward a single goal: the creation of a complex artificial world to sustain three astronauts in a hostile environment for two weeks. Because the failure of any one component of the Apollo system could ruin the entire mission, the reliability problem was the greatest challenge facing the program. Because *reliability* of components is closely linked with the *probability* of their success or failure, the entire issue had to be dealt with by probability theory.

First, the mission planners developed a mathematical model of the Apollo system showing the location in various subsystems of 2 *million* functional parts, miles of wiring, and thousands of joints. Such a simplified model is given in panel (a) of Figure 22.A; an even more simplified model appears in panel (b).

Second, mission planners estimated the reliability of each subsystem from experimental data and then used the laws of probability to predict the reliability of the Apollo system as a whole.

PROBABILITIES AND A SERIES SYSTEM. Figure 22.A is a typical example of a *series system:* If any component fails, the entire system fails (just as, in the case of old-fashioned strings of Christmas tree lights, the entire tree was darkened whenever a single bulb failed). Assuming that the components operate independently and that the individual probability-of-success values are $p(A)$, $p(B)$, $p(C)$, $p(D)$, and $p(E)$, respectively, the reliability of the entire system, $p(S)$, can be calculated by the *special* multiplication law for independent events (see page 319) as $p(S) = p(A) \cdot p(B) \cdot p(C) \cdot p(D) \cdot p(E)$. Thus, if each component has a reliability of .95, the probability of success for the entire system shown in Figure 22.A is given by $p(S) = (.95)^5 = .774$, which is not too encouraging. If the performance of each subsystem is not independent of that of the others (and, say, the successful performance of A portends the successful performance of E or if the failure of B puts a high load on other subsystems and causes the failure of D), the *general* multiplication law must be used to calculate $p(S)$.

PROBABILITIES AND PARALLEL CONFIGURATIONS. The Apollo planners were also aware, however, of the implications of *parallel configurations*—of replacing, say, the large main engine A by two smaller engines, A_1 and A_2. If, then, failure occurs only if *both* A_1 and A_2 fail (or only if an intersection of two events occurs), reliability might be increased. Such a possible new engine configuration is shown in panel (a) of Figure 22.B.

FIGURE 22.A | Series Systems

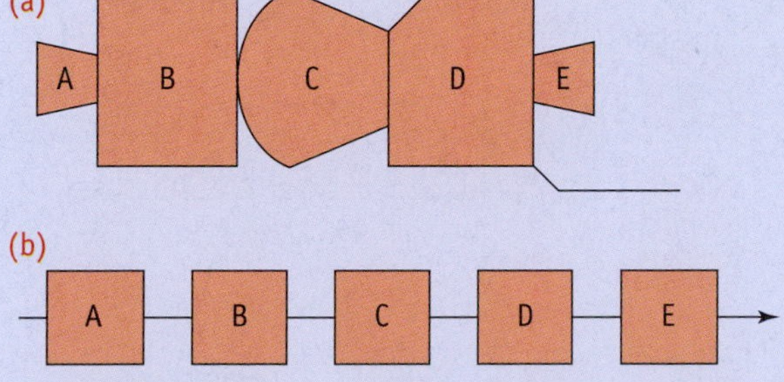

(continued)

Application 22.1 (continued)

Under this scheme, the probability of success for the engine function now equals the probability of success for engine A_1 *or* A_2; that is,

$$p(A) = p(A_1 \text{ or } A_2)$$

According to the general addition law, this equation can also be written as

$$p(A) = p(A_1) + p(A_2) - p(A_1 \text{ and } A_2)$$

Assuming again independence of engines A_1 and A_2, the latter term can be replaced by $p(A_1) \cdot p(A_2)$ in accordance with the special multiplication law, yielding

$$p(A) = p(A_1) + p(A_2) - [p(A_1) \cdot p(A_2)]$$

Assuming the same probability of success for the smaller engine as for the larger one—that is, $p(A_1) = .95$ and $p(A_2) = .95$—the success probability for the engine function becomes

$$p(A) = .95 + .95 - (.95)^2 = 1.9 - .9025 = .9975$$

which is a great improvement over the original .95. Together with the other components, this engine setup raises the probability of success for the entire mission from .774 to

$$p(S) = .9975\,(.95)^4 = .8125$$

Indeed, one can do better than that! Consider parallel configurations for all of the subsystems, as shown in panel (b) of Figure 22.B. Assuming probabilities of success of .95 for all the components, and applying the same reasoning, one can raise the probabilities of success for all the other subsystems to .9975 as well.

Thus, the probability of success for the entire system to sustain the three astronauts, shown in panel (b) of Figure 22.B, becomes

$$p(S) = (.9975)^5 = .9876$$

which is a dramatic improvement over the original .774. Further improvements of the same type can also be made as well—for example, by the substitution of two engines for A_1 and of two more engines for A_2. Nor is this idle speculation: During the *Apollo 13* launch, the center engine of the second stage of the Saturn rocket failed, yet a satisfactory earth orbit was achieved with the remaining *four* rocket motors.

OTHER APPLICATIONS. The same principle of reliability control or of assuring quality *by design* applies in the case

FIGURE 22.B | Parallel Configurations

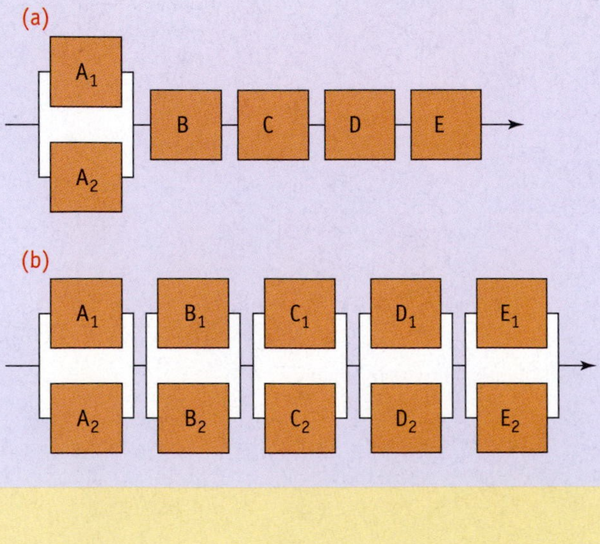

(continued)

Application 22.1 (continued)

of other and possibly less complex systems, be they automobiles, household appliances, power supplies, or telephones. Indeed, auto manufacturers introduced the five-year unconditional guarantee after examining the reliability of the affected components and determining the overall reliability of their cars in the fashion indicated here.

SOURCE: Adapted from Gerald J. Lieberman, "Striving for Reliability," in Judith M. Tanur et al., eds., *Statistics: A Guide to the Unknown* (San Francisco: Holden-Day, 1972), pp. 400–406. Figures 22.A and 22.B copyright © 1972 by Holden-Day, Inc. Reprinted by permission of Holden-Day, Inc.

22.3 Acceptance Sampling

As Figure 22.1 indicates, statisticians are likely to perform acceptance sampling at two points in the production process: when materials purchased from other firms are being received (Stage 3), and again when the finished product emerges from the manufacturing division and is about to be sold to intermediate users, such as other firms, or to final users, such as households or governments (Stage 5). At each of these two points, the assurance of an acceptable quality level is crucial for the firm's ultimate survival. The foregoing explains the commonly employed definition given here:

DEFINITION 22.1 **Acceptance sampling** is a form of statistical quality control that involves taking one or more samples from a group of incoming or outgoing items, called a *lot,* and deciding, on the basis of the observed sample quality, to accept or reject the entire lot.

TYPES OF SAMPLING PLANS

Those who are about to engage in acceptance sampling must have some kind of prearranged plan or rule to determine whether a given lot is to be accepted or rejected. Typically, the rule comes in four parts, specifying

1. the number of samples to be taken from a given lot,
2. the size of each sample,
3. a decision variable, and
4. an acceptance criterion.

The rule just discussed has a special name:

DEFINITION 22.2 A **sampling plan** is a detailed rule to determine whether a given lot encountered in acceptance sampling is to be accepted or rejected. Typically, this rule specifies the number of samples to be taken from a given lot, the size of each sample, a decision variable, and an acceptance criterion.

THE NUMBER OF SAMPLES Numerous possibilities exist with respect to the number of samples in a sampling plan. The simplest case involves only one sample. Whenever a single sample is taken from a given lot, we talk of a **single-stage sampling plan.** Its general nature is illustrated in Figure 22.2.

FIGURE 22.2 | A Single-Stage Sampling Plan

This sketch illustrates the general nature of a ***single-stage sampling plan*** *that might be applied at Stage 3 or Stage 5 of the production process noted in Figure 22.1.*

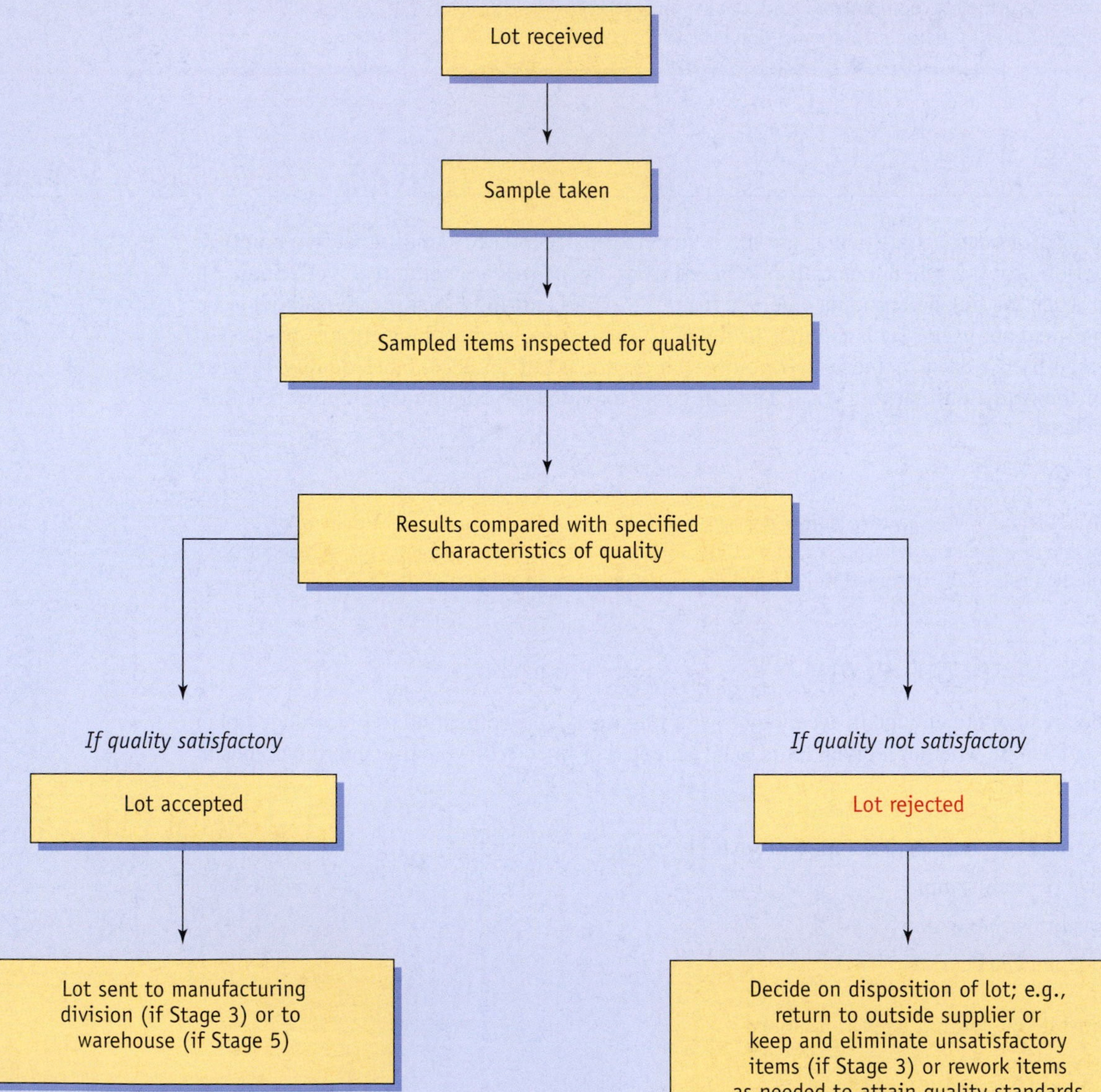

An alternative is provided by the **two-stage sampling plan,** in which a first sample is expected to lead to one of *three* decisions: acceptance, rejection, or uncertainty. The last alternative then leads to the taking of a second sample. The results of the second sample, however, are acceptance or rejection of the lot, as illustrated in Figure 22.2 for the single-stage sampling case.

Another possibility is the **multiple-sampling plan,** a form of acceptance sampling that specifies a preselected number of samples greater than two. In this case, a given lot might get five chances. For example, if acceptance, rejection, and uncertainty are possible outcomes in the first four samples taken, the fifth round leads to a clear accept-or-reject decision.

Finally, we can even follow a **sequential-sampling plan,** in which no maximum number of samples is specified and each sample always allows for three possible outcomes, with uncertainty leading to yet another sample.

THE SIZE OF THE SAMPLE Every sampling plan must specify the size of the sample to be taken. This size is designated by n. In two-stage, multiple, and sequential-sampling plans, the sizes of successive samples (n_1, n_2, n_3, and so on) need not be equal.

THE DECISION VARIABLE When the decision to accept or reject is based on observing a qualitative variable, such as counting defective and satisfactory items, the procedure is called an **attribute-sampling plan.** When the decision depends on some kind of quantitative measurement, it is a **variables-sampling plan.**

THE ACCEPTANCE CRITERION Finally, a complete sampling plan specifies a specific criterion (typically designated by c) that leads to acceptance of the lot. In the case of an attribute-sampling plan, c might, for example, specify the maximum number of defective items that may be found in a sample without causing the lot to be rejected.

PRODUCER'S RISK AND CONSUMER'S RISK

When statisticians engage in acceptance sampling, they are conducting this hypothesis test:

H_0: The sampled lot is of good quality.
H_A: The sampled lot is of poor quality.

Yet, as we learned in Chapter 13, any hypothesis testing procedure carries with it the possibility of error. After the sampling plan has been carried out, the decision made can be correct (a good-quality lot is accepted, a poor-quality lot is rejected), but it can also be erroneous (as when a good-quality lot is rejected and a poor-quality lot is accepted). These possibilities are summarized in Table 22.1.

Producers are particularly annoyed by the type I error: They have produced a good-quality lot, yet it is rejected. This type of error, therefore, is called the *producer's risk.* The probability of its occurrence is designated by α. Thus, if $\alpha = .05$, a particular acceptance sampling plan carries with it a 5 percent chance of rejecting a perfectly good lot.

Consumers are similarly annoyed by the type II error: They have received a poor-quality lot, yet it is accepted. This type of error is called the *consumer's risk.* The probability of its occurrence is designated by β. Thus, if $\beta = .07$, a particular sampling plan carries with it a 7 percent chance of accepting a poor-quality lot.

DEFINITION 22.3 In acceptance sampling, **producer's risk** is the risk of erroneously rejecting a good-quality lot; the probability of this event is α. In contrast, **consumer's risk** is the risk of erroneously accepting a poor-quality lot; the probability of this event is β.

TABLE 22.1 | Possible Outcomes of Acceptance Sampling

The acceptance sampling procedure inevitably leads to one of four possible results: The decision, respectively, to accept or reject a given lot is correct when the lot is in fact of good quality (a) or of poor quality (d). The decision is mistaken when a good-quality lot is erroneously rejected (b) or a poor-quality lot is erroneously accepted (c).

True State of the World	Decision Reached: Accept Lot	Decision Reached: Reject Lot
H_0 is true (The lot is of good quality)	**(a)** Correct	**(b)** Type I error (producer's risk = α risk)
H_0 is false (The lot is of poor quality)	**(c)** Type II error (consumer's risk = β risk)	**(d)** Correct

MANAGING RISK LEVELS

Those who engage in acceptance sampling naturally want to keep the associated risks at reasonable levels. Therefore, they must assess the α and β risks inherent in any given sampling plan. Let us reflect on how this might be done.

Consider the case of a single-stage attribute-sampling plan that is to be applied to large incoming lots. The plan, let us assume, calls for sampling $n = 20$ items per lot. It defines the acceptance criterion as the *maximum* number of defectives that can be found in a sample without triggering rejection of the lot and designates $c = 0$.

Given any actual percentage of defectives, π, contained in a lot, we can compute the probability of finding $X = 0$ defectives in a sample of $n = 20$ with the help of binomial Formula 9.D (on page 346) or we can look up the probability number directly in Appendix Table C. (Strictly speaking, as a review of Chapter 9 can show, the more complex hypergeometric formula should be applied, but the binomial formula provides a close approximation when n/N is small.) Thus, for a lot that in fact contains 5 percent defectives, we can figure the likelihood of finding zero defectives with our sampling plan (and, thus, the likelihood of *accepting* the lot) as

$$p(X = 0 \mid n = 20, \pi = .05) = \frac{20!}{0!\,20!}(.05)^0(.95)^{20} = .3585$$

Our plan implies a probability of .3585 of accepting a lot containing 5 percent defectives and a probability of 1 – .3585 = .6415 of rejecting such a lot. We can find similar numbers for other potential values of π, as noted in Table 22.2 on the next page.

We can, in turn, graph the information of Table 22.2, as in Figure 22.3 on page 1078. This graph has a special name:

DEFINITION 22.4 In acceptance sampling, an **operating-characteristic *(OC)* curve** indicates, for all possible proportions, π, of defectives in a lot, the probability of accepting the lot if a given sampling plan is implemented. Reading the curve allows the user quickly to assess the levels of producer's risk and consumer's risk associated with any given value of π.

We can use a graph, such as Figure 22.3, to determine whether a particular acceptance sampling plan sufficiently controls risk for both the producer and the consumer of the sampled lot.

TABLE 22.2 | Implications of Acceptance Sampling Plan $n = 20, c = 0$

This table provides probabilities of lot acceptance for alternative lot qualities, provided random samples of $n = 20$ items are taken per lot and the maximum number of defectives that can be found in a sample without triggering rejection of the lot is $c = 0$.

Actual Proportion of Defectives in Lot, π	Probability of Accepting Lot, p_a
.01	.8179
.02	.6676
.03	.5438
.04	.4420
.05	.3585
.06	.2901
.07	.2342
.08	.1887
.09	.1516
.10	.1216
.15	.0388
.20	.0115
.25	.0032
.30	.0008
.35	.0002

THE PRODUCER'S RISK Suppose, for example, that a producer is willing to accept a lot that contains a maximum proportion of defectives equal to $\pi = .05$. This limiting value is often called the **acceptable quality level *(AQL)*.** Given the acceptance sampling plan summarized by Figure 22.3, the probability that quality inspectors accept a lot with precisely 5 percent defectives is $p_a = .3585$ (note point B). Accordingly, the probability of *rejecting* such a good-quality lot (and committing a type I error) is $1 - p_a = .6415$ (distance AB, which is the producer's risk for $AQL = .05$). A producer may not be happy with a sampling plan that implies a producer's risk that may be as large as this. If management desires a maximum producer's risk of, say, .10, this particular acceptance sampling plan won't do.

THE CONSUMER'S RISK Now suppose that consumers are determined to reject all lots with proportions of defectives equal to $\pi = .10$ or higher. This limiting value is often called the **rejectable quality level *(RQL)*.** Given the acceptance sampling plan summarized by Figure 22.3, the probability that quality inspectors nevertheless accept a lot with precisely 10 percent defectives (and, thus, commit a type II error) is $p_a = .1216$ (note point C). A consumer may not be happy with a sampling plan that implies such a large consumer's risk. If the desired maximum consumer's risk equals, say, .05, this particular acceptance sampling plan will not be usable.

ALTERNATIVE SAMPLING PLANS There is a way out of this dilemma, however. We can change the sampling plan. Table 22.3 on page 1079 provides a number of alternatives, which are then graphed in Figure 22.4 on page 1080.

The red lines in the graph show *OC* curves for samples of $n = 20$, but differ because the acceptance criterion, c, changes from 0 to 1 and then to 2. The dashed black lines show *OC* curves

FIGURE 22.3 | The Operating-Characteristic *(OC)* Curve for Acceptance Sampling Plan $n = 20$, $c = 0$

The implications of an acceptance sampling plan that samples 20 items per lot and only accepts the lot if 0 defectives are found can be summarized by an operating-characteristic curve, such as the red line shown here. That line, in turn, can be used to assess the producer's risk and the consumer's risk associated with any given quality level. The graph here is based on the data of Table 22.2.

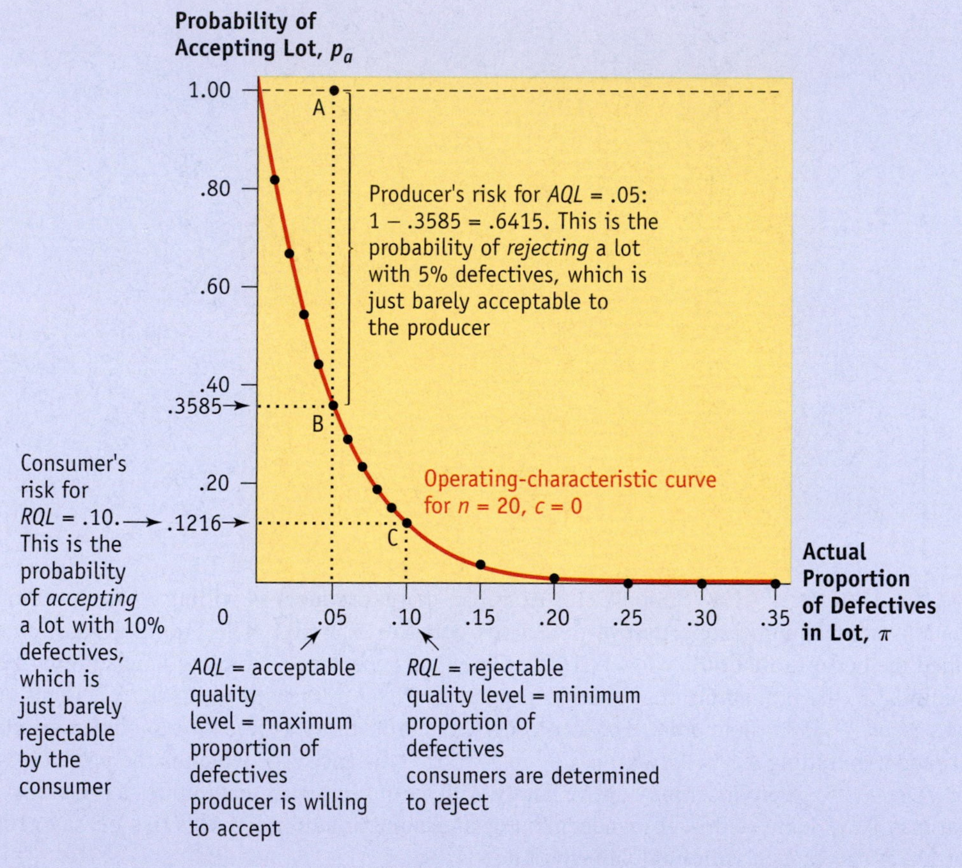

for samples of $n = 15$, given $c = 0$ or $c = 1$. Finally, the solid black line shows one of many possible *OC* curves for $n = 10$, here given $c = 0$.

You can easily see how the producer's risk at any given level of π (and measured by distance AB in Figure 22.3) will vary, depending on the sampling plan selected. In our example, at $\pi = .05$, *all* of the plans that are alternatives to $n = 20$, $c = 0$, imply a lower producer's risk. The consumer's risk, at any given level of π (measured by point C in Figure 22.3) varies as well. In our case, at $\pi = .10$, all the alternative plans presented here imply a larger consumer's risk. To reduce producer's risk as well as consumer's risk, a larger value of n may be necessary.

Innumerable alternative acceptance sampling plans can be devised, however, and one of them may well accommodate both producer and consumer. Yet, making the types of calculations shown in Tables 22.2 and 22.3 in order to find the ideal sampling plan is extremely awkward. Graphs

TABLE 22.3 | Implications of Alternative Acceptance Sampling Plans

This table provides probabilities of lot acceptance for alternative lot qualities, provided random samples of size n are taken and the number of defectives that can be found in a sample without triggering rejection of the lot is c or less.

Actual Proportion of Defectives in Lot, π	Probability of Accepting Lot, p_a for Specified Sampling Plan				
	$n = 20$ $c = 1$	$n = 20$ $c = 2$	$n = 15$ $c = 0$	$n = 15$ $c = 1$	$n = 10$ $c = 0$
.01	.9831	.9990	.8601	.9904	.9044
.02	.9401	.9929	.7386	.9647	.8171
.03	.8802	.9790	.6333	.9271	.7374
.04	.8103	.9561	.5421	.8809	.6648
.05	.7358	.9245	.4633	.8290	.5987
.06	.6604	.8850	.3953	.7738	.5386
.07	.5868	.8390	.3367	.7168	.4840
.08	.5169	.7880	.2863	.6597	.4344
.09	.4516	.7334	.2430	.6035	.3894
.10	.3917	.6769	.2059	.5490	.3487
.15	.1756	.4049	.0874	.3186	.1969
.20	.0692	.2061	.0352	.1671	.1074
.25	.0243	.0913	.0134	.0802	.0563
.30	.0076	.0355	.0047	.0353	.0282
.35	.0022	.0121	.0016	.0142	.0135

even more elaborate than Figure 22.4 are often hard to read. Statisticians, therefore, have developed handbooks of tables that help quality controllers quickly find values for n and c that assure desired maximum levels of both producer's risk and consumer's risk. A much-used table for attribute sampling, noted in this chapter's Recommended Readings on the text's Web site, was developed by the military and is called MIL-STD-105D. Civilian counterparts include ANSI Z 1.4 (issued by the American National Standards Institute) and the international standard ISO 2859.

22.4 Statistical Process Control

As Figure 22.1 indicates, firms also monitor the *manufacturing* process (Stage 4) by repetitive sampling. Their goal is to determine whether the ongoing process should be continued or adjusted in order to achieve a desired quality level. In this connection, statisticians use control charts, which we have already encountered in Application 7.2 on page 255.

DEFINITION 22.5 **Control charts** are graphical displays that highlight the average performance of a data series and the dispersion around this average so that average and dispersion of the past, if deemed acceptable, become standards for controlling performance in the present.

FIGURE 22.4 | Operating-Characteristic *(OC)* Curves for Alternative Acceptance Sampling Plans

Alternative acceptance sampling plans can be defined by sample size n and acceptance criterion c, here denoting the ***maximum*** *number of defectives that can be encountered in a sample without triggering rejection of the sampled lot. Each plan implies a different operating-characteristic curve and, thus, different levels of producer's risk and consumer's risk for any given value of π.*

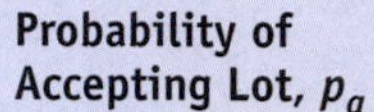

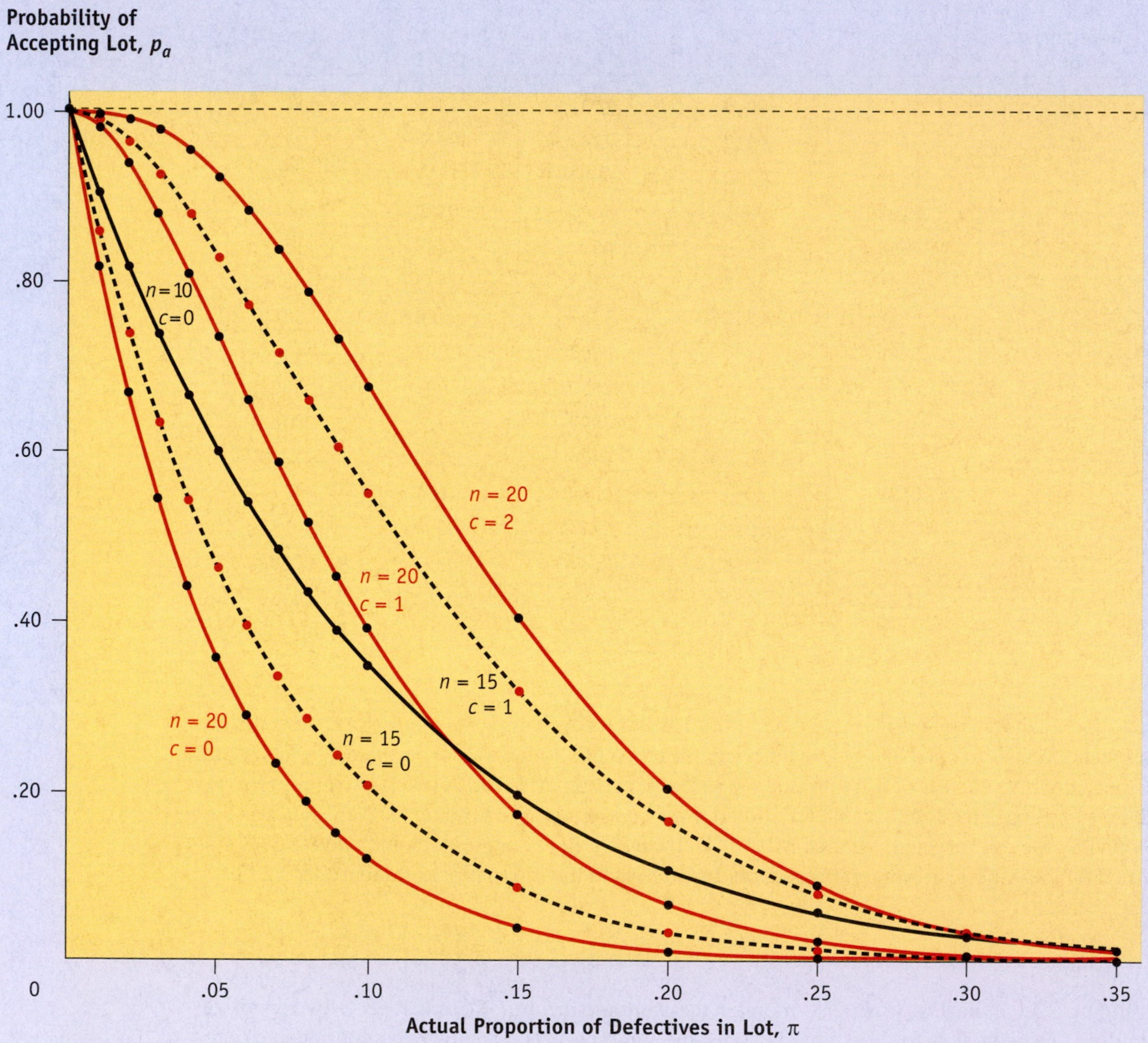

THE INEVITABILITY OF VARIATION

In any manufacturing process, variation in output quality is an inescapable fact of life. As strange as it may seem, no two items are ever *precisely* alike. Two major types of reasons can be given: common causes and assignable causes.

COMMON CAUSES Some product variations are inherent to a given process and, therefore, unavoidable and not correctable. Their causes are known as **common causes** of variation. The weather is a good example. It brings ever-changing levels of humidity and temperature, which, in turn, produce variations in product quality. Unless we substitute completely different manufacturing processes, such as producing everything in humidity- and temperature-controlled buildings or even in outer space, we cannot eliminate such common causes.

ASSIGNABLE CAUSES So-called **assignable causes,** also known as **special causes,** of product variation can be traced to materials, manpower, machines, and methods of production (often called the four M's). All of these are, in principle, correctable.

Materials used, for example, are likely to vary in quality from one supplier to the next. Even for a given supplier, they vary from one shipment to the next. As a result, as the nature of materials varies—possibly from hour to hour—so does the nature of the product being produced.

The people engaged in the production process are just as varied as the materials they use. Worker A differs from worker B in general education, specific job training, work experience, and motivation. Even if all these factors are the same (a highly unlikely case), worker A may be particularly upset or fatigued on a particular day and on that account is surely more likely to make mistakes than is worker B. In any case, all workers are more likely to make mistakes toward the end of a long workday than at the beginning, when they are more alert.

Variation in quality can also be traced to machines. Like people, machines wear out. Saw blades become dull. Oil has to be replaced. Vibrations shift machine settings, however imperceptibly, and unless adjustments are made quickly, product quality plummets. One well-known example occurred in 1986 when slightly faulty O-rings caused the *Challenger* space shuttle disaster. Similarly, in 1990, a spacing error of a mere 1.3 millimeters caused the $1.5 billion Hubble space telescope to send back blurry images instead of the expected clear pictures.

HYPOTHESIS TESTING FOR QUALITY

Quality inspectors who monitor production processes by repeated random sampling of output seek to determine whether quality variations are due to common causes or assignable causes. In the first case, the production process is said to be "in (statistical) control," and no remedial action is required. In the latter case, when quality variations can be traced to assignable causes, the production process is said to be "out of control," and adjustments are initiated. Over time, as quality inspectors repeatedly make this determination, they are, in effect, performing a series of hypothesis tests. Each test can be stated as follows:

H_0: The production process is in control.

H_A: The production process is out of control.

Once again, there are four possible outcomes of each hypothesis test, as Table 22.4 indicates.

Naturally, quality inspectors want to avoid costly type I and type II errors. Halting a production process and making adjustments that need not be made is an expensive proposition. It raises costs unnecessarily and thus lowers profits. The likelihood of its occurrence is called the α risk. On the other hand, continuing a production process that is out of control is just as undesirable.

TABLE 22.4 | Possible Outcomes of Process Control Sampling

Statistical process control inevitably leads to one of four possible results: The decision, respectively, to continue the production process or to halt it and make adjustments is correct when the process is in control (a) or out of control (d). The decision is mistaken when an in-control process is erroneously halted and adjusted (b) or an out-of-control process is erroneously allowed to continue (c).

	Decision Reached	
True State of the World	**Continue Process**	**Halt Process, Make Adjustments**
H_0 is true (Process in control)	**(a)** Correct	**(b)** Type I error (α risk)
H_0 is false (Process out of control)	**(c)** Type II error (β risk)	**(d)** Correct

Low-quality output then continues to be produced and alienates customers. Eventually, revenues and profits plummet. The likelihood of this occurring is called the β risk. Control charts, as we will see presently, help firms manage these risks.

Throughout our discussion, the term *quality inspector* refers to a person performing a particular function of monitoring quality. It does not necessarily refer to a person who does nothing else. Quite possibly, as Deming might suggest, quality inspection may be carried out, part-time, by the same workers who produce the product that is being inspected or who run the process that is being monitored.

ALTERNATIVE TYPES OF CONTROL CHARTS

Our discussion of control charts so far has been rather general. Definition 22.5, for example, tells us nothing about the kinds of data that quality inspectors might use to measure performance. The reason for this lack of verbal precision is not difficult to see: *Quality* encompasses many aspects and what constitutes acceptable performance varies from one production process to the next. If a firm is engaged in filling cans of green peas and the labels claim that each can contains 8 ounces, a production process that manages to put 8 ounces into the *average* can may be considered to be "in control." Inspectors, therefore, may wish to focus on the mean weight of peas found in sampled cans and make their decision to continue or to interrupt the production on the basis of the sample mean, $\overline{X}$. Accordingly, control charts used when inspectors assess production processes with the help of sample means are called **$\overline{X}$ charts.**

On the other hand, if a firm is engaged in producing computer chips, their average weight is probably of little interest. Managers and consumers alike are much more interested in, say, the *proportion* of defective chips in a lot. Inspectors, therefore, focus their attention on the proportion of defectives found in their samples. Accordingly, control charts used when inspectors assess production processes with the help of sample proportions are called ***P* charts.**

Other types of control charts include:

- ***nP* charts,** which focus on *absolute numbers* (rather than proportions) of defectives found in samples
- ***R* charts,** which monitor *ranges* of measurements found in samples
- ***s* charts,** which monitor sample *standard deviations*
- ***c* charts,** which monitor *counts of defects per sampled item,* such as the number of blemishes found on each sampled piece of furniture

All of these control charts, and others still, have this in common:

1. They plot the variable of interest, such as $\overline{X}$, P, and so forth, measured vertically, against time, measured horizontally. Thus, the variation of the quality variable can be watched as time passes and more and more samples are taken.
2. They compare each data plot with the variable's expected value—that is, the average value of the variable when the production process is in control. An excessive deviation above or below the expected process average then indicates a process out of control.

The following sections explain.

$\overline{X}$ CHARTS: PARAMETERS KNOWN

Consider a production process that is designed to fill 8-ounce cans of peas. Let us assume that we happen to *know* the crucial parameters associated with the filling process when it is in control:

FIGURE 22.5 | A Population of Filling Weights

This normal curve illustrates the population of filling weights of 8-ounce cans of peas that is associated with an ongoing production process that is in control.

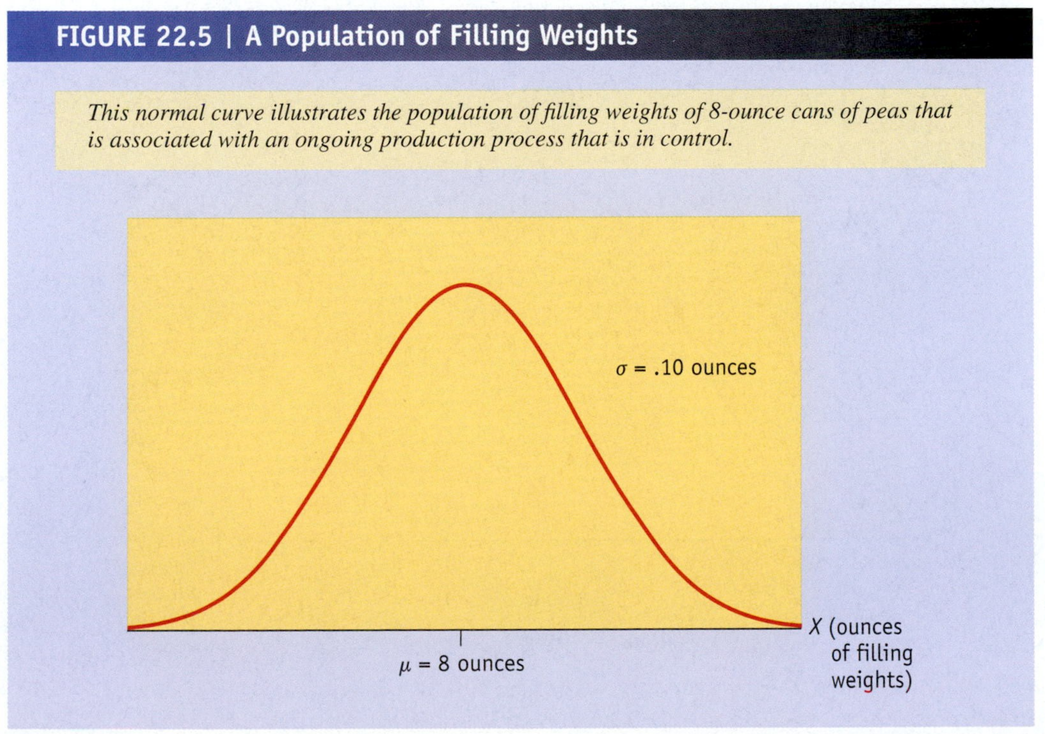

When the process is in control, the population of filling weights is normally distributed, with a mean of $\mu = 8$ oz. and a standard deviation of $\sigma = .10$ oz., which is illustrated in Figure 22.5.

Under the circumstances (for reasons noted in Chapter 11) the sampling distribution of filling weights is normally distributed as well, with a mean of $\mu_{\overline{X}} = \mu = 8$ oz. and a standard deviation of $\sigma_{\overline{X}} = \sigma/\sqrt{n}$, as illustrated in Figure 22.6.

We can use Figure 22.6 to determine which $\overline{X}$ values that quality inspectors might encounter in sampling can reasonably be taken as evidence that the production process is in control. The answer is arbitrary, but most quality controllers use this rule of thumb:

1. Any $\overline{X}$ value that lies within 3 standard deviations of the sampling distribution's mean is considered sufficiently reasonable to uphold the null hypothesis of a production process in control. (As a quick review of the normal curve can show, 99.7 percent of all $\overline{X}$ values that could occur when the production process is in control will be found within 3 standard deviations of the mean. See Application 7.1, *Standard Scores,* on page 254 or consult Appendix Table H for a z value of 3.0.)
2. Any $\overline{X}$ value that lies outside the limits of $\mu_{\overline{X}} \pm 3\sigma_{\overline{X}}$ is considered strong evidence that the production process is out of control and should be adjusted. Accordingly, a typical $\overline{X}$ chart is constructed as shown in Figure 22.7 on the next page.

FIGURE 22.6 | A Sampling Distribution of Filling Weights

Given an in-control production process that generates the normally distributed population of filling weights illustrated in Figure 22.5, the sampling distribution of filling weights is also normally distributed, as shown here. Indeed, the sampling distribution would be normal, even if the underlying population distribution were not, as long as sampling procedures assured the conditions validating the central limit theorem.

Note: *The horizontal scale of this graph differs from that in Figure 22.5, because $\sigma_{\overline{X}}$ is smaller than σ.*

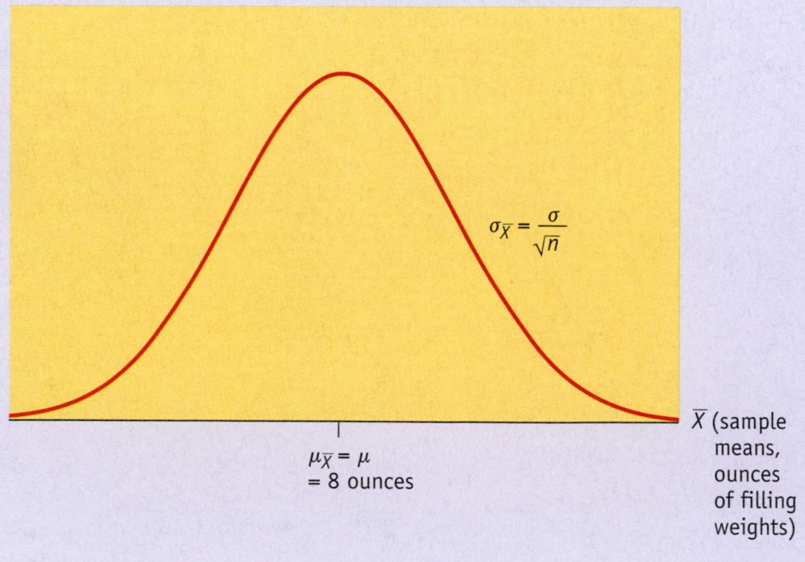

FIGURE 22.7 | A Typical $\overline{X}$ Chart

A typical $\overline{X}$ chart shows the mean value, μ, of some quality variable when the production process is proceeding normally. It defines upper and lower control limits (UCL and LCL) between which sample values are likely to appear as long as the process remains in control. Quality inspectors plot $\overline{X}$ values found in various samples taken at different times during the production process. As long as these sample means (represented by the red dots) lie within the upper and lower control limits, the null hypothesis of "H_0: The production process is in control" is accepted. When a sample mean falls outside the UCL or LCL (as for samples 4 and 10 here), H_0 is rejected and the production process is considered out of control.

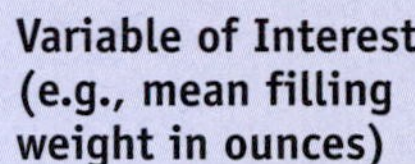

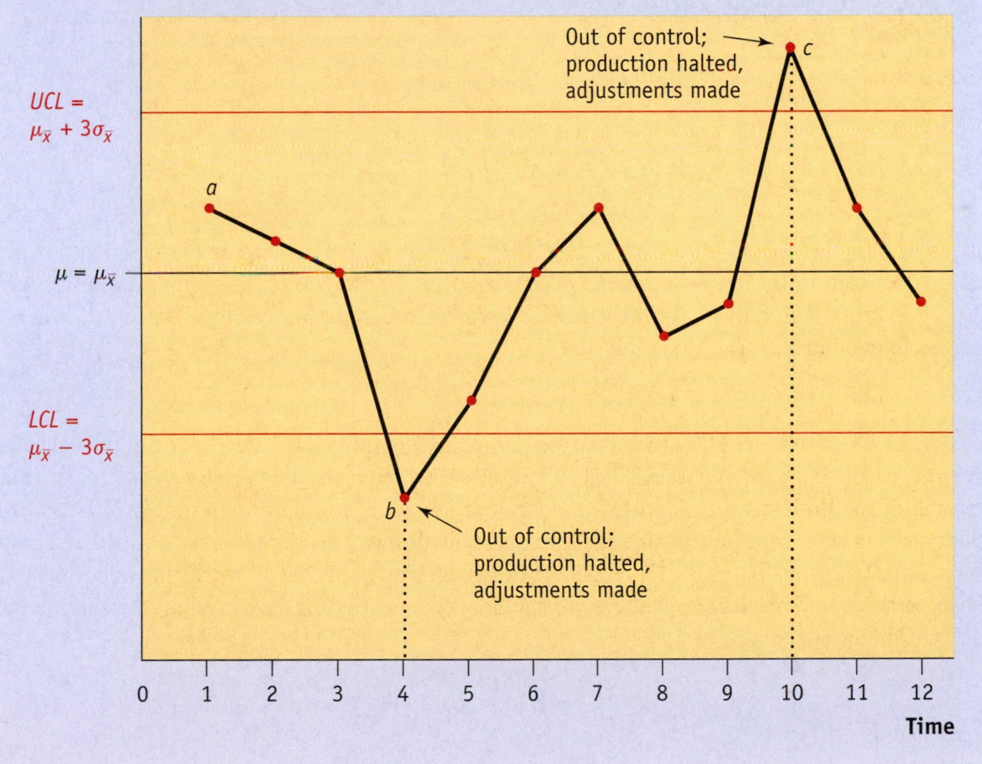

THREE HORIZONTAL LINES Like every control chart, Figure 22.7 contains three crucial horizontal lines. We discuss each of them in turn.

1. The horizontal **centerline** shows a series of hypothetical sample values equal to the process mean when the production process is in control and no adjustments are needed. In the case of an $\overline{X}$ chart, the height of the line equals $\mu = \mu_{\overline{X}}$.
2. The upper red line represents the **upper control limit *(UCL)*,** a series of hypothetical sample values lying 3 standard deviations above the mean. Inspectors are extremely un-

likely to encounter actual sample values above this limit when the production process is in control. Hence they interpret the appearance of such above-limit values as strong evidence of a process out of control. In the case of an $\overline{X}$ chart, this upper control limit equals $\mu_{\overline{X}} + 3\sigma_{\overline{X}}$. (As Appendix Table H can show, when the production process is in control, the probability of nevertheless encountering a sample mean above the *UCL* equals a mere 1 − .4986 = .0014.)

3. The lower red line represents the **lower control limit *(LCL),*** a series of hypothetical sample values lying 3 standard deviations below the mean. Inspectors are extremely unlikely to encounter actual sample values below this limit when the production process is in control. Hence they interpret the appearance of such below-limit values as strong evidence of a process out of control. In the case of an $\overline{X}$ chart, this lower control limit equals $\mu_{\overline{X}} - 3\sigma_{\overline{X}}$. (Again, the probability of encountering such a low $\overline{X}$ when the process *is* in control is a mere .0014.)

FORMULA 22.A | $\overline{X}$ Chart Control Limits (μ and σ known)

$$UCL = \mu_{\overline{X}} + 3\sigma_{\overline{X}} = \mu + 3\frac{\sigma}{\sqrt{n}}$$

$$LCL = \mu_{\overline{X}} - 3\sigma_{\overline{X}} = \mu - 3\frac{\sigma}{\sqrt{n}}$$

where *UCL* is the upper control limit, *LCL* is the lower control limit, μ is the mean and σ is the standard deviation of quality variable X when the production process is functioning properly, $\mu_{\overline{X}} = \mu$ is the mean and $\sigma_{\overline{X}}$ is the standard error of the sampling distribution of $\overline{X}$ when the process is in control, and n is sample size.

A SERIES OF HYPOTHESIS TESTS As the Figure 22.7 caption indicates, each additional sample gives occasion to a new hypothesis test. As long as the result, shown here by a red dot, such as *a*, lies within the limits of *UCL* and *LCL*, H_0 is accepted and production continues. Whenever the result, as at point *b* or *c*, lies outside the limits, production is considered out of control and adjustments must be made. In this example, underfilling occurred in period 4, overfilling in period 10. As subsequent sample results show, the adjustments were successful; they brought the sample mean back within the acceptable range.

EXAMPLE PROBLEM 22.1

A properly functioning production process fills bottles with an average 64 ounces of ketchup. The population of filling weights is normally distributed and has a standard deviation of 1 oz. Inspectors take periodic samples of 36 bottles. One sample yields a mean filling weight of 63.0 oz., the next two yield 64.9 and 64.1 oz. Is the production process in control?

SOLUTION:

$$\text{Given } \mu = 64, \mu_{\overline{X}} = 64$$

$$\text{Given } \sigma = 1 \text{ and } n = 36, \sigma_{\overline{X}} = \frac{\sigma}{\sqrt{n}} = \frac{1}{\sqrt{36}} = .1667$$

Therefore,

$$UCL = \mu_{\bar{X}} + 3\sigma_{\bar{X}} = 64 + 3(.1667) = 64.50$$

$$LCL = \mu_{\bar{X}} - 3\sigma_{\bar{X}} = 64 - 3(.1667) = 63.50$$

Implications: $\bar{X} = 63.0$ indicates out-of-control underfilling

$\bar{X} = 64.9$ indicates out-of-control overfilling

$\bar{X} = 64.1$ indicates process in control

$\bar{X}$ CHARTS: PARAMETERS UNKNOWN

The preceding examples assumed that we knew the crucial parameters, μ and σ, of some production process when it was in control. In reality, this is often not the case and we must *estimate* these values. Several approaches are widely used; let us illustrate the most popular one.

A quality inspector, we assume, has been assigned to monitor the filling of mustard jars, labeled to contain 8 oz. each. At a time when the process is believed to be in control, the inspector takes 10 samples of 5 jars each and weighs the contents. The results appear in the first six columns of Table 22.5.

TABLE 22.5 | A Quality Inspector's Sample Data

When the key parameters, μ and σ, of an in-control production process are unknown, we can estimate them by taking a series of samples at a time when the process is believed to be in control. In this example, $k = 10$ samples of size $n = 5$ are taken. The average of the sample means, here $\bar{\bar{X}} = 8.033$, serves as an estimate of μ. The average of the sample ranges, here $\bar{R} = .323$, is one of two factors that help us estimate σ.

Sample Number	Sample Observations (ounces of mustard per jar)					Sample Mean, $\bar{X}$	Sample Range, R
1	8.234	7.890	8.002	7.990	8.009	8.025	.344
2	8.137	7.999	7.904	7.926	8.099	8.013	.233
3	8.178	7.980	7.804	7.888	8.087	7.987	.374
4	8.008	7.899	7.999	7.899	8.044	7.970	.145
5	8.256	8.245	8.003	7.934	7.700	8.028	.556
6	7.906	8.003	8.099	7.956	8.356	8.064	.450
7	8.178	8.123	8.089	7.988	8.099	8.095	.190
8	7.899	8.111	8.255	7.980	8.179	8.085	.356
9	8.000	8.234	8.233	7.867	8.055	8.078	.367
10	8.036	7.889	8.099	8.009	7.894	7.985	.210
						$\bar{\bar{X}} = 8.033$	$\bar{R} = .323$

ESTIMATING μ Because the mean content weight, μ, of the in-control filling process is unknown, the inspector:

- computes the 10 sample means, $\overline{X}$
- finds the mean of these sample means, $\overline{\overline{X}} = 8.033$
- and henceforth uses this $\overline{\overline{X}}$ value as the estimate of the unknown μ (and, thus, as the control-chart centerline)

ESTIMATING σ Because the standard deviation of the content weight, σ, of the in-control filling process is also unknown, the inspector might similarly compute the 10 sample standard deviations and average them. Following a more popular (and computationally easier) approach, the inspector:

- computes the 10 sample ranges, R (each being the difference between the largest and smallest sample observations)
- finds the mean of these sample ranges, $\overline{R} = .323$
- and estimates σ as $\overline{R}/d_2$, where d_2 is a factor that varies with sample size, n, and facilitates the best possible estimate of σ

The American Society for Testing and Materials has prepared values of d_2 for numerous sample sizes; some of these values appear in Appendix Table R. For a sample of size $n = 5$, the value of d_2 equals 2.326. Thus, the best estimate of filling weight variability in our example comes to

$$\sigma \cong \frac{\overline{R}}{d_2} = \frac{.323}{2.326} = .139$$

FINDING THE CONTROL LIMITS Having estimated the values of μ and σ, our inspector can quickly determine the upper and lower control limits of the production process. Formula 22.B summarizes the procedure.

FORMULA 22.B | $\overline{X}$ Chart Control Limits (μ and σ unknown)

$$UCL \cong \overline{\overline{X}} + 3\frac{\overline{R}/d_2}{\sqrt{n}} = \overline{\overline{X}} + \frac{3}{d_2\sqrt{n}}\overline{R} = \overline{\overline{X}} + A_2\overline{R}$$

$$LCL \cong \overline{\overline{X}} - 3\frac{\overline{R}/d_2}{\sqrt{n}} = \overline{\overline{X}} - \frac{3}{d_2\sqrt{n}}\overline{R} = \overline{\overline{X}} - A_2\overline{R}$$

where UCL is the upper control limit, LCL is the lower control limit, μ is the mean and σ is the standard deviation of quality variable X when the production process is functioning properly, $\overline{\overline{X}}$ is the mean of all sample means and serves as the estimator of μ, $\overline{R}$ is the mean of all sample ranges, d_2 is a factor dependent on sample size (found in Appendix Table R), $\overline{R}/d_2$ is the estimator of σ, and n is sample size.

Note: The expression $\dfrac{3}{d_2\sqrt{n}}$ is often denoted by A_2 and found in tables, such as Appendix Table R.

In our example, $\overline{\overline{X}} = 8.033$, $d_2 = 2.326$, $n = 5$, and $\overline{R} = .323$. Thus, the expression $\dfrac{3}{d_2\sqrt{n}} = .577$, which is also the value of A_2 found in the $n = 5$ row of Appendix Table R. Accordingly,

$$UCL \cong \overline{\overline{X}} + \frac{3}{d_2\sqrt{n}}\overline{R} = 8.033 + .577\,(.323) = 8.219$$

$$LCL \cong \overline{\overline{X}} - \frac{3}{d_2\sqrt{n}}\overline{R} = 8.033 - .577\,(.323) = 7.847$$

EXCEL Example 22.1

Review the sample data in Table 22.5. Let a computer create an $\overline{X}$ chart.

SOLUTION:

1. Enter the labels *Sample Means, Grand Mean, UCL,* and *LCL* into cells A1:D1 of a new worksheet.
2. Enter the 10 sample means into A2:A11. (You can also copy and paste data from column B of the file HK22MISC.)
3. In B2, enter the formula **=AVERAGE($A$2:$A$11)** and drag the result to B11.
4. In C2, enter the formula **=B2+(.577*.323)** and drag the result to C11.
5. In D2, enter the formula **=B2−(.577*.323)** and drag the result to D11.
6. Click the **Chart Wizard** > **Standard Types** > **Line**; then click the first choice in **Chart sub-type** and **Next**.
7. In *Data range,* enter **A2:D11**, choose *Series in Columns,* click **Next**.
8. In the third dialog box, click **Titles**. Enter *X-bar Chart for Mustard, Sample Number,* and *Sample Means,* respectively, in the first three boxes.
9. Remove all check marks under the *Gridlines* and *Legend* tabs and click **Next** > **Finish**.
10. Finally, enlarge and edit the graph with a result such as that found on the next page.

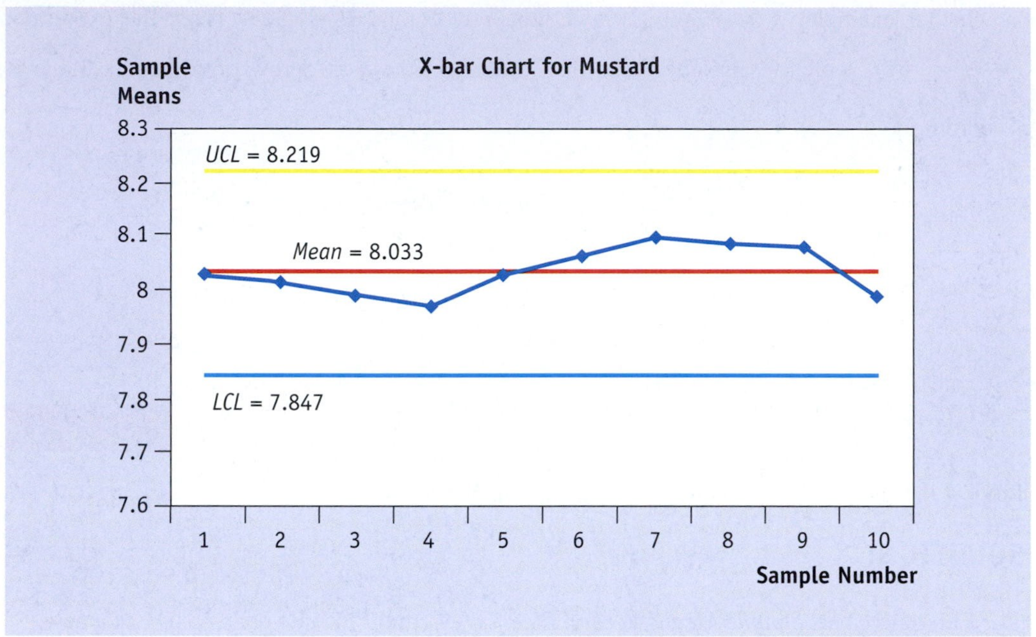

The graph shows no $\overline{X}$ values outside the 3 sigma limits, which indicates a process in control.

P CHARTS

Control charts in use when the production process is being assessed by sample proportions are called *P charts.* Consider a process that produces computer chips. We assume numerous samples have been taken when the process was judged to be in control. Even at its best, the process seems to yield a certain small percentage of defectives in the long run; this population proportion of defectives is π. Let us assume that sufficiently large samples are taken so that $n\pi \geq 5$ and also $n(1 - \pi) \geq 5$. Under these conditions, the sampling distribution of the sample proportion P approaches a normal distribution, with $\mu_P = \pi$ and $\sigma_P = \sqrt{\frac{\pi(1 - \pi)}{n}}$. Such a sampling distribution would look just like Figure 22.6.

Formula 22.C defines the control limits for the *P* chart. A corresponding control chart, analogous to Figure 22.7, is illustrated by Figure 22.8 on the next page.

FORMULA 22.C | *P* Chart Control Limits [$n\pi \geq 5$ and also $n(1 - \pi) \geq 5$]

$$UCL = \mu_P + 3\sigma_P = \pi + 3\sqrt{\frac{\pi(1 - \pi)}{n}}$$

$$LCL = \mu_P - 3\sigma_P = \pi - 3\sqrt{\frac{\pi(1 - \pi)}{n}} \text{ if } >0, \text{ otherwise } 0$$

where *UCL* is the upper control limit, *LCL* is the lower control limit, π is the population proportion of the quality variable when the production process is functioning properly, $\mu_P = \pi$ is the mean and σ_P is the standard error of the sampling distribution of P when the process is in control, and n is sample size.

Note: The value of π is often estimated as the average sample proportion, $\overline{P}$, found in numerous samples taken at times when the production process was believed to be in control.

FIGURE 22.8 | A Typical *P* Chart

A typical P chart has a centerline that shows the proportion of defectives, π, when the production process is proceeding normally. It also has upper and lower control limits (UCL and LCL), defined as $\mu_P \pm 3\sigma_P$, in analogy to the procedure used in the $\overline{X}$ chart. Quality inspectors plot P values found in various samples taken at different times during the production process. As long as these sample proportions (represented by the red dots) lie within the upper and lower control limits, the null hypothesis of "H_0: The production process is in control" is accepted. When a proportion falls outside the UCL or LCL (as for sample 2 here), H_0 is rejected and the production process is considered out of control.

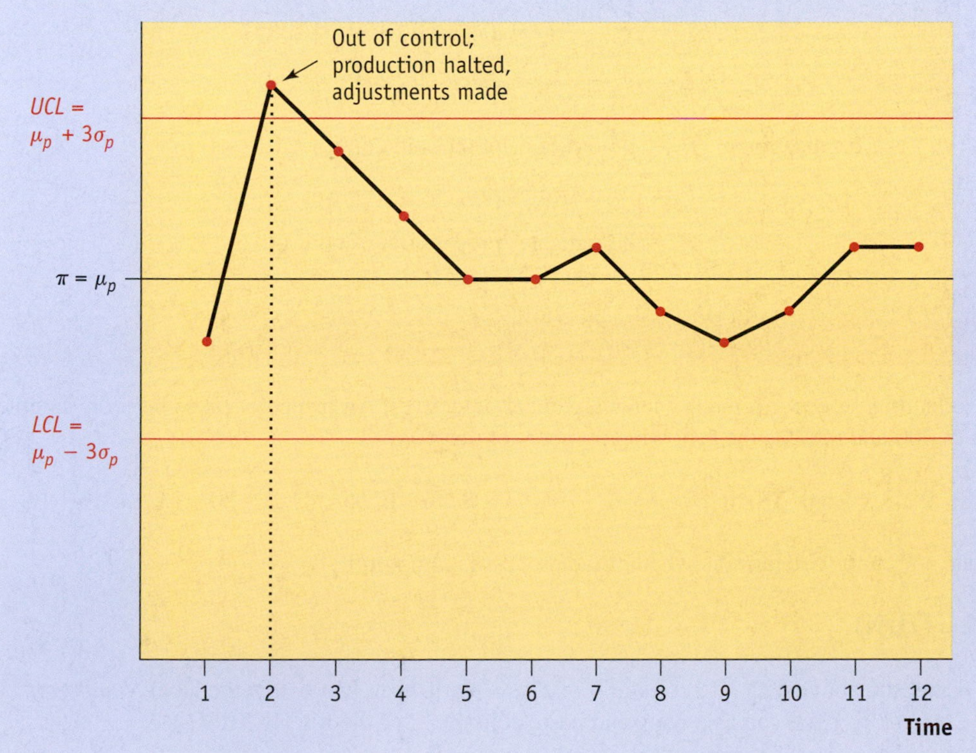

In actual applications, the lower control limit in the P chart is never set below zero, although the value of $\mu_P - 3\sigma_P$ might conceivably be negative.

When the LCL is positive, a proportion of defectives lower than LCL might be found in a sample, which would make the proportion "excessively low." Yet such designation seems strange. Why would anyone complain about too few defectives or, put differently, about excessively high quality? Too high a quality can be a problem because the product's consumers may not require that level of quality, yet it is costly to achieve.

EXAMPLE PROBLEM 22.2

A production process normally yields 4 percent defectives. Inspectors take periodic samples of $n = 200$. One sample yields a proportion of defectives of $P = .06$, the next two yield $P = .01$ and $P = .83$. Is the production process in control?

SOLUTION:

Given $\pi = .04$, $\mu_P = .04$

Given $n = 200$, $n\pi \geq 5$ and $n(1 - \pi) \geq 5$ and $\sigma_P = \sqrt{\dfrac{\pi(1-\pi)}{n}} = \sqrt{\dfrac{.04\,(.96)}{200}} = .0139$

Therefore,

$$UCL = \mu_P + 3\sigma_P = .04 + 3(.0139) = .0817$$
$$LCL = \mu_P - 3\sigma_P = .04 - 3(.0139) = -.0017. \text{ Use } 0.$$

Implications: $P = .06$ indicates process in control.

$P = .01$ indicates process in control.

$P = .83$ indicates process out of control.

EXCEL Example 22.2

A production process normally yields 2 percent defectives. An inspector takes periodic samples of $n = 300$ and records the following numbers of defectives:

6 8 9 3 1 0 5 6 7 8 9 10 11 8 6 6 5 4 3 20 23 4 6 18 9

Create a P chart to determine whether the process is in control.

SOLUTION:

1. Enter the above data into column A of a new worksheet, just below the label *Number of Defectives.* (You can also copy and paste column AI of the file HKMISC.)
2. Enter the label *Proportion of Defectives* into cell B1.

3. Enter the formula **=A2/300** into B2, select the result, and drag to B26.
4. Enter labels *Average proportion, Standard deviation of proportion, Upper control limit,* and *Lower control limit,* respectively, into cells F2:F5.
5. In adjacent column G cells, enter known values or appropriate formulas:

   .02 into G2

   =SQRT((G2*(1−G2))/300) into G3

   =G2+3*G3 into G4

   =IF(G2−3*G3<0,0,G2−3*G3) into G5
   (which creates a lower control limit that cannot be negative)

   The result:

F	G
Average proportion	0.02
Standard deviation of proportion	0.00808
Upper control limit	0.04425
Lower control limit	0

6. Enter labels *Upper control limit, Centerline,* and *Lower control limit,* respectively, into cells C1:E1.
7. Enter the *Upper control limit* value into C2, the *Average proportion* value into D2, and the *Lower control limit* value into E2. Select C2:E2 and drag to row 26. In columns B–E, you now have the data needed to create the control chart.
8. Click the **Chart Wizard** > **Standard Types** > **Line**; then click the first choice in **Chart sub-type** and **Next**.
9. In *Data range,* enter **B2:E26**, choose *Series in Columns,* click **Next**.
10. In the third dialog box, click **Titles**. Enter *P Chart, Sample Number,* and *Sample Proportion,* respectively, in the first three boxes.
11. Remove all check marks under the *Gridlines* and *Legend* tabs and click **Next** > **Finish**.
12. Finally, enlarge and edit the graph with a result such as that found on the next page.

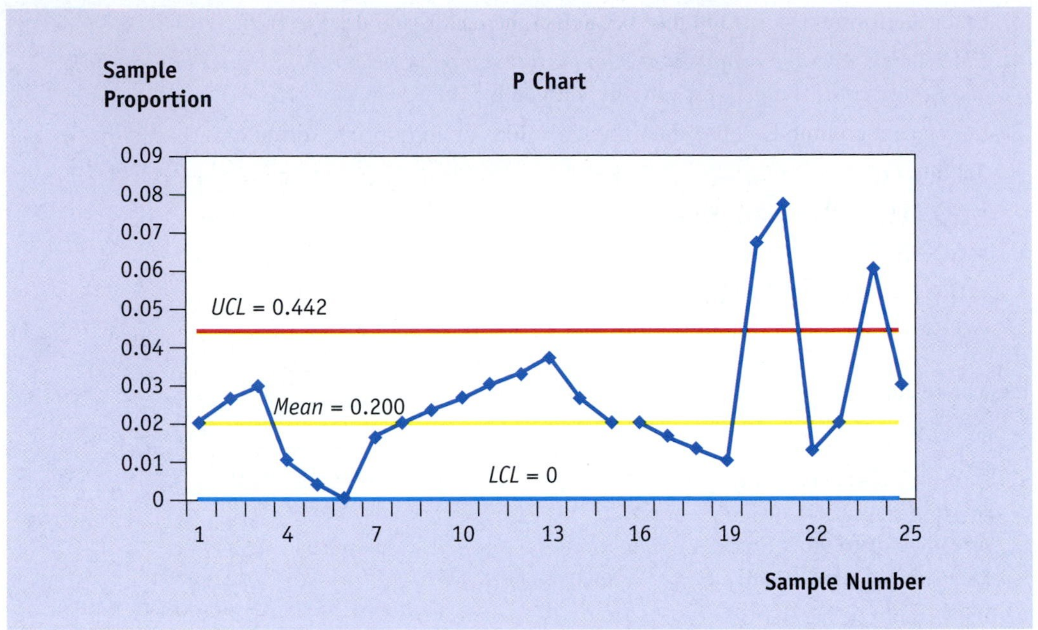

INTERPRETATION Samples 20, 21, and 24 show P values more than 3 sigmas above the historical P centerline and, thus, indicate a process out of control.

nP CHARTS, *R* CHARTS, AND *c* CHARTS

Quality inspectors construct other types of control charts in a manner that is similar to the procedures just discussed. Each time, large enough samples are taken to validate the central limit theorem and to assure that the quality variable's sampling distribution is normal. Formulas 22.D–22.F summarize the most popular procedures.

FORMULAS 22.D–22.F | Selected Control Chart Limits

22.D ***nP* Chart**

$$UCL = n\pi + 3\sqrt{n\pi(1-\pi)}$$

$$LCL = n\pi - 3\sqrt{n\pi(1-\pi)} \text{ if } >0\text{, otherwise } 0$$

22.E ***R* Chart**

$$UCL = \overline{R} + 3\frac{d_3}{d_2}\overline{R} = D_4\overline{R}$$

$$LCL = \overline{R} - 3\frac{d_3}{d_2}\overline{R} = D_3\overline{R}$$

22.F ***c* Chart**

$$UCL = \overline{c} + 3\sqrt{\overline{c}}$$

$$LCL = \overline{c} - 3\sqrt{\overline{c}} \text{ if } > 0\text{, otherwise } 0$$

where UCL is the upper control limit, LCL is the lower control limit, n is sample size, P is the sample proportion, π is the population proportion, R is the range of sample data (maximum minus minimum observation), $\bar{R}$ is the mean of all sample ranges, c is the count of defects in a single sampled item, and $\bar{c}$ is the mean of such counts.

Symbols d_2 and d_3 are factors dependent on sample size (found in Appendix Table R). The expressions D_3 and D_4, as Appendix Table R notes, are derived from these terms such that

$$D_3 = 1 - 3\frac{d_3}{d_2} \text{ (but never} < 0) \quad \text{and} \quad D_4 = 1 + 3\frac{d_3}{d_2}$$

Notes:

1. The value of π is often estimated as the average sample proportion, $\bar{P}$, found in numerous samples taken at times when the production process was believed to be in control.
2. As more advanced texts show, Formula 22.D is based on summary measures of the binomial probability distribution (Formulas 9.E–9.G on page 348), which deals with probabilities of finding x among n. Formula 22.F is based on summary measures of the Poisson probability distribution (Formulas 9.I–9.K on page 367), which finds probabilities for rare events. Review Section 10.6 on page 418 on how the normal probability distribution can be used to approximate such discrete probability distributions.

EXCEL Example 22.3

Review EXCEL Example 22.2. Using the same data, examine the production process with the help of an *nP chart* that plots the plots absolute numbers (rather than proportions) of defectives found in samples.

SOLUTION:

1. Enter the data into column A of a new worksheet, just below the label *Number of Defectives.* (You can also copy and paste column AI of the file HKMISC.)
2. Enter labels *Sample size, pi, Mean, Standard deviation, Upper control limit,* and *Lower control limit,* respectively, into cells F2:F7.
3. In adjacent column G cells, enter appropriate known values or formulas:

   300 into G2

   .02 into G3

   =G2*G3 into G4

   =SQRT(G2*G3*(1−G3)) into G5

   =G4+3*G5 into G6

   =IF(G4−3*G5<0,0,G4−3*G5) into G7
   (which creates a lower control limit that cannot be negative)

The result:

Sample size	300
pi	0.02
Mean	6
Standard deviation	2.4249
Upper control limit	13.275
Lower control limit	0

4. Enter labels *Upper control limit, Centerline,* and *Lower control limit,* respectively, into cells B1:D1.
5. Enter the *Upper control limit* value into B2, the *Mean* value into C2, and the *Lower control limit* value into D2. Select B2:D2 and drag to row 26. In columns A–D, you now have the data needed to create the control chart.
6. Click the **Chart Wizard** > **Standard Types** > **Line**; then click the first choice in **Chart sub-type** and **Next**.
7. In *Data range,* enter **A2:D26**, choose *Series in Columns,* click **Next**.
8. In the third dialog box, click **Titles**. Enter *C Chart, Sample Number,* and *Number of Defectives,* respectively, in the first three boxes.
9. Remove all check marks under the *Gridlines* and *Legend* tabs and click **Next** > **Finish**.
10. Finally, enlarge and edit the graph with a result such as this:

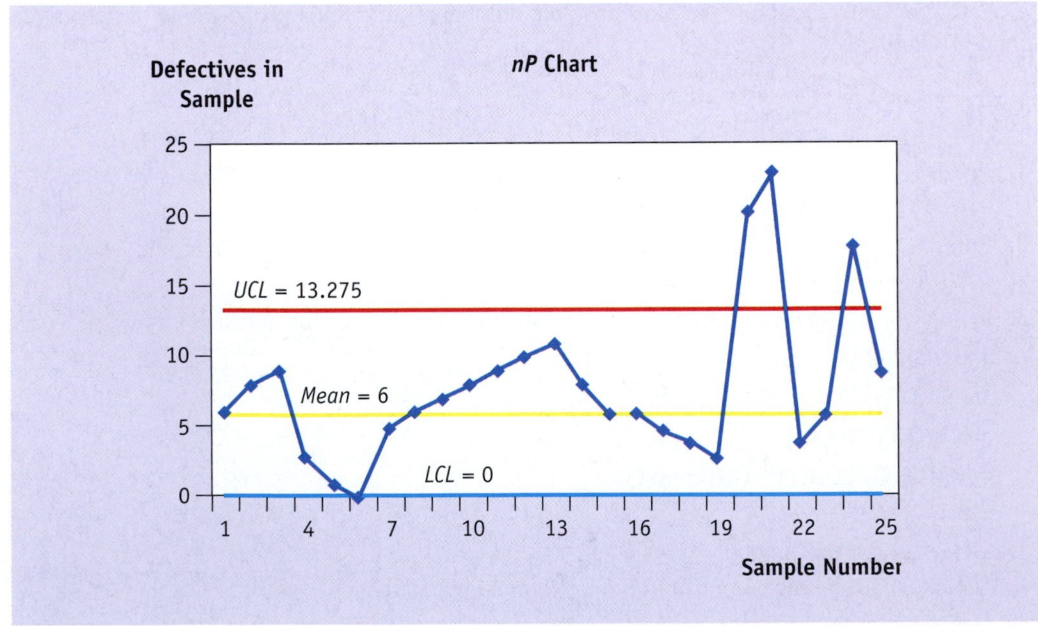

INTERPRETATION Samples 20, 21, and 24 show *nP* values more than 3 sigmas above the historical centerline and, thus, indicate a process out of control.

Note: It is no accident that the three labels within the graph equal $n = 300$ times the corresponding values in EXCEL Example 22.2.

EXCEL Example 22.4

Review the sample data in Table 22.5 on page 1087. Let a computer create an *R* chart.

SOLUTION:

1. Enter the labels *Ranges, Range Mean, UCL,* and *LCL* into cells A1:D1 of a new worksheet.
2. Enter the 10 sample ranges into A2:A11. (You can also copy and paste data from column E of the file HK22MISC.)
3. In B2, enter the formula **=AVERAGE($A$2:$A$11)** and drag the result to B11.
4. In C2, enter the formula **=2.114*B2** and drag the result to C11.
5. In D2, enter the formula **=0*B2** and drag the result to D11.
6. Click the **Chart Wizard** > **Standard Types** > **Line**; then click the first choice in **Chart sub-type** and **Next**.
7. In *Data range,* enter **A2:D11**, choose *Series in Columns,* click **Next**.
8. In the third dialog box, click **Titles**. Enter *R Chart for Mustard, Sample Number,* and *Sample Ranges,* respectively, in the first three boxes.
9. Remove all check marks under the *Gridlines* and *Legend* tabs and click **Next** > **Finish**.
10. Finally, enlarge and edit the graph with a result such as this:

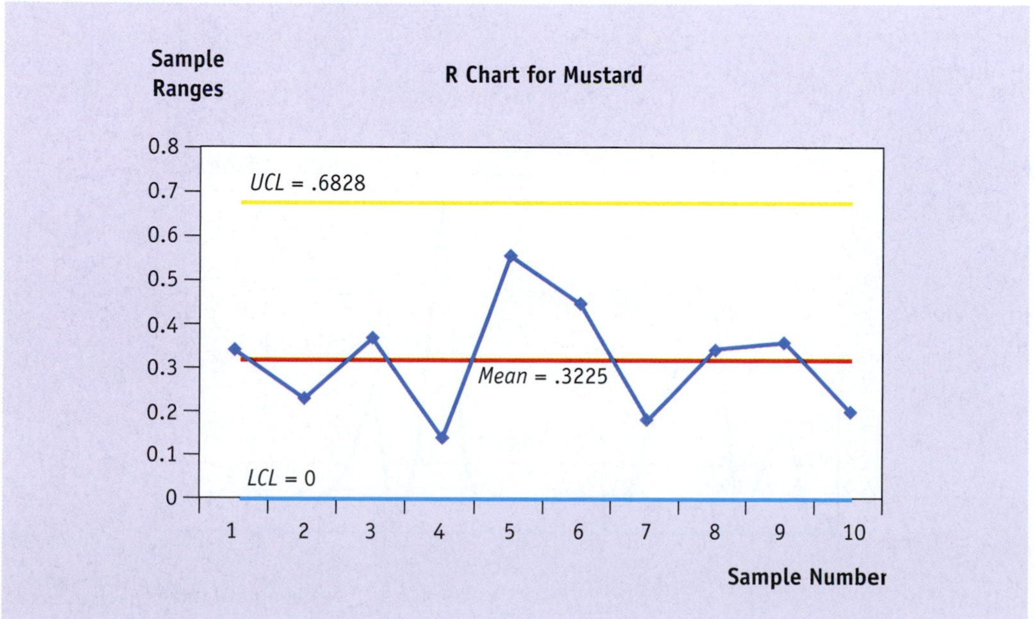

INTERPRETATION The graph shows no range values outside the 3 sigma limits, which indicates a process in control.

EXCEL Example 22.5

A quality inspector at a furniture company sets aside every 25th piece of furniture produced and checks it for blemishes. The count of blemishes on the last 30 pieces was as follows:

0–0–3–2–0–6–7–4–3–1–1–1–1–0–0–0–2–9–2–0–4–2–1–1–0–0–0–1–1–4.

Let a computer create a *c* chart.

SOLUTION:

1. Enter the labels *Counts, Count Mean, UCL,* and *LCL* into cells A1:D1 of a new worksheet.
2. Enter the 30 counts into A2:A31. (You can also copy and paste data from column F of the file HK22MISC.)
3. In B2, enter the formula **=AVERAGE($A$2:$A$31)** and drag the result to B31.
4. In C2, enter the formula **=B2+3*SQRT(B2)** and drag the result to C31.
5. In D2, enter the formula **=IF(B2−3*SQRT(B2)<0,0,B2−3*SQRT(B2))** and drag the result to D31.
6. Click the **Chart Wizard** > **Standard Types** > **Line**; then click the first choice in **Chart sub-type** and **Next**.
7. In *Data range,* enter **A2:D31**, choose *Series in Columns,* click **Next**.
8. In the third dialog box, click **Titles**. Enter *c Chart for Blemishes, Sample Number,* and *Count per Item,* respectively, in the first three boxes.
9. Remove all check marks under the *Gridlines* and *Legend* tabs and click **Next** > **Finish**.
10. Finally, enlarge and edit the graph with a result such as this:

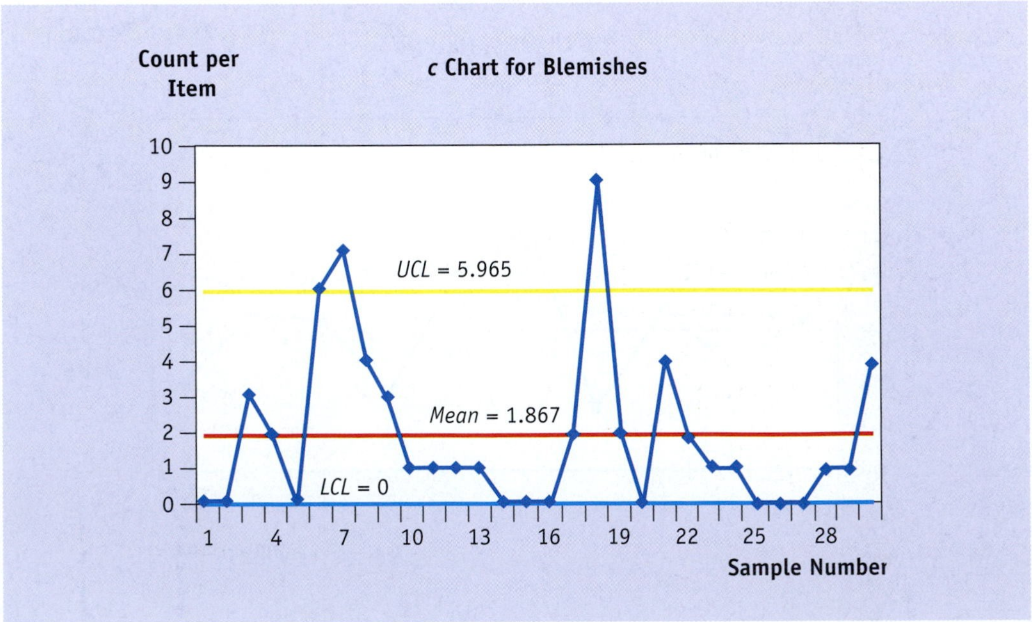

INTERPRETATION At samples 6, 7, and 18, the process is out of control.

INTERPRETING CONTROL CHARTS

Our discussion of Figures 22.7 and 22.8 has already indicated one way in which firms use control charts. Whenever the production process is out of control, as evidenced by crucial sample results failing outside the control limits, production can be halted and appropriate adjustments can be made.

However, there are other uses as well, as Figure 22.9 illustrates.

Even if all sample results lie within the two control limits, quality inspectors are well advised to study the *pattern* of points. Panel (a) shows many more sample results above than below the centerline. This may point to some kind of problem about to occur, such as the imminent failure of equipment that is wearing out. Panel (b) shows a clear trend toward one of the control limits, which, again, may herald a serious problem in the near future, such as the

FIGURE 22.9 | Reading Control Charts

*Even when all sample results fall **within** the bounds of a control chart's upper and lower control limits, the **pattern** of results may point to hidden factors that good managers may wish to explore.*

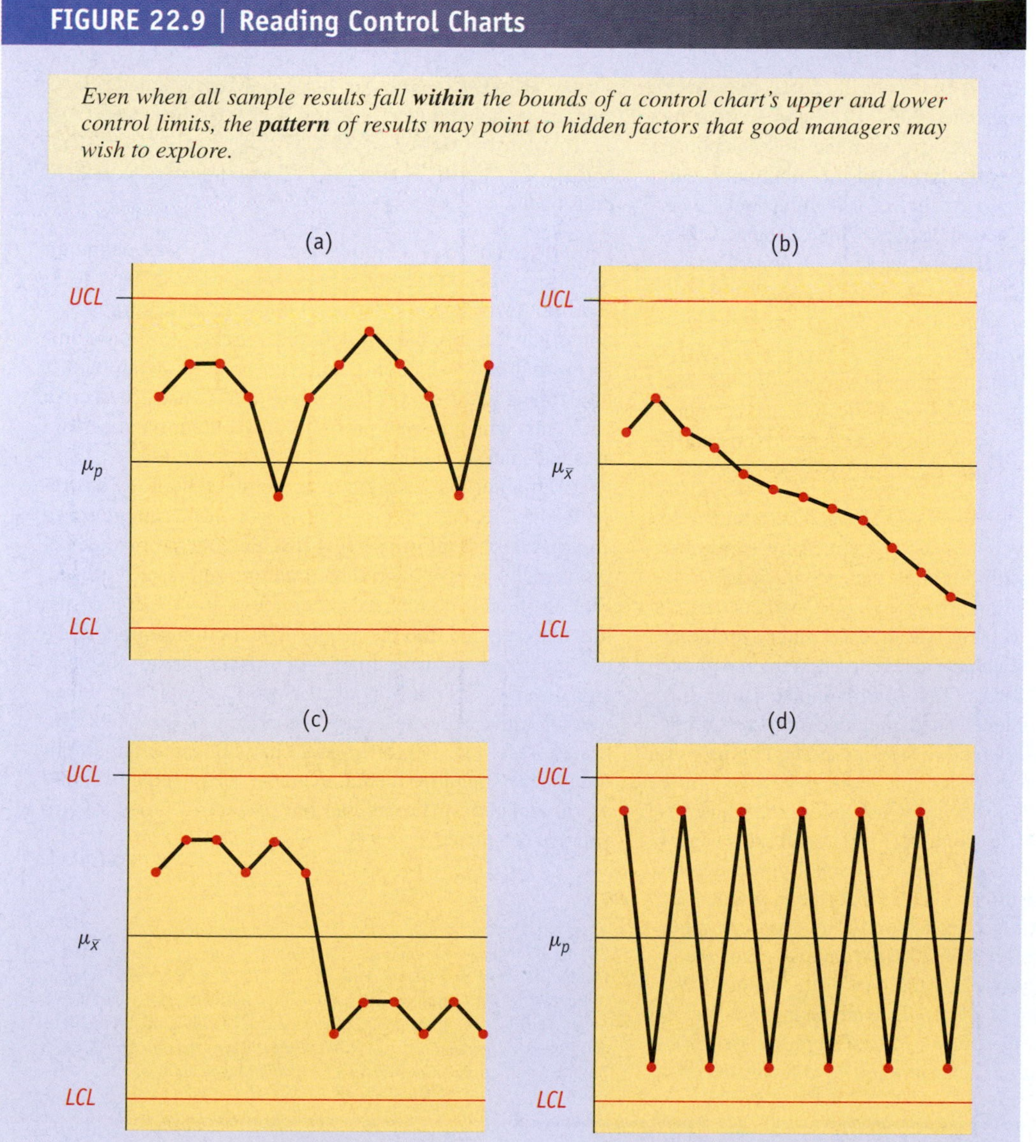

breakdown of a machine hampered by the buildup of dirt or even the imminent collapse of the human operator who is slowly being poisoned by fumes. Panel (c) shows a sudden shift in the general level of sample measurements, which may well be worth investigating. The shift may be traceable to the hiring of a new worker, the use of a different raw materials supplier, or even the installation of an allegedly superior machine. Finally, panel (d) shows a strange cyclical pattern that a good manager may wish to understand. The pattern may reflect the different work of two workers between whom the quality inspector just happens to alternate when collecting samples. Or it may be caused by a factor nobody has ever thought of before.

APPLICATION 22.2

CONTROL CHARTS—A BRIEF HISTORICAL TOUR

Quality control, with the help of control charts, goes back to a now-famous memo dated May 1924 and written by Walter A. Shewhart, then a researcher at the Bell Telephone Laboratories. His work greatly helped the monopoly telephone system improve the quality of its output, but it was ignored by firms in other industries. This changed somewhat during World War II when the U.S. Defense Department insisted that its suppliers become familiar with and employ procedures of statistical quality control, such as those introduced in this text.

Yet, U.S. manufacturing firms in general did not take a keen interest in the subject until the late 1970s when confronted with Japan's competitive challenge. Apparently, they still have much to learn. Consider two cases in point.

AUTOMOBILES. In the 1990s, Japanese cars continued to dominate the list of vehicles recommended by *Consumer Reports.* The quality differential that so intrigues consumers was neatly summarized by auto makers' *recall rates,* the number of vehicles recalled for safety problems as a percentage of total vehicle sales. In 1991, the recall rate was 60 for General Motors, 77 for Ford, and an astounding 89 for Chrysler. Problems cited included malfunctioning brakes and seat belts, defective steering bolts, engine fires caused by leaking power-steering fluid, defective cruise controls, and cars rolling away when automatic transmissions were set to *Park.* In contrast, 1991 recall rates were 4 for Honda, 5 for Toyota, and 35 for Nissan. Typical defects in Japanese cars were minor, such as incorrectly worded tire inflation stickers. Altogether 6.2 million American-made cars were recalled; fewer than 300,000 Japanese cars were.

Had matters improved by the turn of the century? Not really. Despite years of effort, Detroit hadn't shaken its poor-quality image. *Consumer Reports* grades for 2000-model vehicles pretty much summed up the results of a survey of 41,000 new-car buyers. Models rated *above* average included 5 of 6 Nissans, 8 of 9 Hondas, and 10 of 11 Toyotas, but only 7 of 35 GM cars, 3 of 22 Chryslers, and 10 of 20 Fords. The Firestone/Ford tire debacle in 2000 didn't help.

CLOTHING. The U.S. clothing industry has been declining for a long time; imports of foreign-made clothing have been soaring. According to the U.S. Defense Logistics Agency, a unit of the Defense Department that purchases military uniforms and other apparel, quality differences are to blame. U.S. manufacturing processes yield too many defective garments, which lowers profit because output must be sold at a discount, discarded, or reworked.

But note: The Georgia Institute of Technology has recently developed a device that is akin to a *computerized control chart.* It allows sewing machine operators to detect problems in needles and thread before defects are caused. First, a thread motion sensor monitors the motion of the thread as it is fed into the needle. The motion is plotted in a computerized control chart. A broken thread instantly signals a process out of control. Second, a vibration sensor measures the acoustic energy generated as the needle vibrates. This, too, is plotted in a chart. Because the amplitude of the sound frequency increases as a needle becomes worn, chipped, or broken, an out-of-control process is instantly recognized.

SOURCES: Adapted from Frederik Eliason, "Keeping Clothes Defect-Free," *The New York Times,* February 16, 1992, p. F7; Neal Templin, "Despite Big 3's Claims of Higher Quality, Japanese Still Boast Fewer Safety Recalls," *The Wall Street Journal,* March 24, 1992, pp. B1 and B10; and Robert L. Simison and Joseph B. White, "Reputation for Poor Quality Still Plagues Detroit," *The Wall Street Journal,* May 4, 2000, pp. B1 and B4.

22.5 Other Methods of Quality Control

Have another look at Figure 22.1 and notice that measures to improve quality might be taken at many points in the production process; they need not be confined to acceptance sampling and the use of control charts. In this section, we consider some of the broader alternatives.

QUALITY CIRCLES AND TEAM WORK

Under the influence of William E. Deming, Japanese and Swedish firms have paid particular attention to factors that *motivate* workers to achieve and maintain high quality. The Japanese have instituted **quality circles,** voluntary groups of 5 to 10 workers from a common work area who meet regularly with a trained leader to identify problems and suggest solutions with respect to product quality. Firms then guarantee subsequent management action in response to such suggestions. In addition, firms recognize involved workers by internal company publicity, certificates, trophies, and possibly, promotion, but never by cash payments. The goal is to engender pride and greater job satisfaction and to raise morale so as to foster an ideal work climate in which quality can flourish. Application 22.3, *Team Work in Sweden,* found on the Web site, has more to say on the subject.

Application 22.3
Team Work in Sweden
http://www.harcourtcollege.com/business_stats/kohler/siteresources.html

GUARANTEED EMPLOYMENT

In most firms around the world, workers are treated like raw materials or machines in the sense that management shows no hesitation in disposing of them once market conditions change and their continued employment becomes unprofitable. Under the circumstances, critics say, one cannot expect workers to be fiercely loyal to their firm and to give their all, minute by minute, in order to produce products of the highest possible quality. Such devotion, however, could be generated, it is said, if each worker developed a lifelong attachment to a firm. Therefore, high-quality output requires, ultimately, a complete change in labor relations so that workers' jobs are *guaranteed.* Application 22.4, *Guaranteed Employment in Japan,* found on the Web site, elaborates.

Application 22.4
Guaranteed Employment in Japan
http://www.harcourtcollege.com/business_stats/kohler/siteresources.html

THE TOTAL-QUALITY MOVEMENT

In recent years, traditional methods of statistical process control discussed in Section 22.4 have been challenged. Genichi Taguchi, a Japanese engineer, disdains the setting of upper and lower control limits and preaches an alternative gospel of *perfection.* As he puts it, "Good enough [achieving quality within stated tolerance limits] is *not* good enough." According to Taguchi, the only acceptable outcome is one that achieves excellence and tolerates no variation from the ideal depicted by the control chart's centerline. Thus, *continuous* improvement is in order, not merely occasional action when the production process is out of control in the sense depicted in Figure 22.7. Similar ideas have been voiced by Robert Galvin, chairman of Motorola, a firm that won the U.S. Commerce Department's 1988 Malcolm Baldrige Award for Quality. Galvin measures product quality on a *sigma scale,* from 0 to about 6. Each sigma level is defined on the basis of defects per million opportunities for error. Quality level 3, for example, describes a production process typical of U.S. manufacturing in the early 1990s, which generated 66,810 defects per million opportunities. Quality level 6 is the ideal and generates a mere 3.4 errors per million. Figure 22.10 gives recent estimates of the quality of some U.S. production processes. Galvin,

FIGURE 22.10 | Estimated Quality of Selected U.S. Production Processes, 1990

The new philosophy of flawlessness urges organizations to seek Six Sigma, a state of affairs in which no more than 3.4 defects per million opportunities occur. Put differently, in such a state of affairs, all processes and products are 99.99966 percent defect-free.

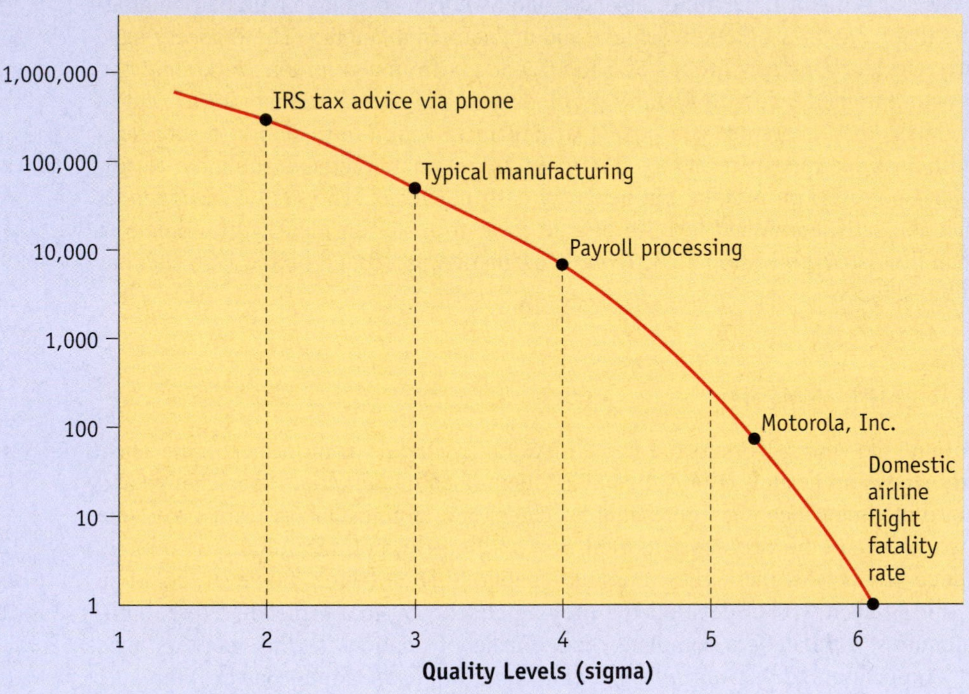

like Taguchi, urges firms to make a *continuous* effort to eliminate all variation from the ideal and achieve Six Sigma.

Application 22.5, *U.S. Quality Programs Show Mixed Results,* indicates that U.S. firms have a long way to go on the quality improvement path. Nevertheless, many U.S. managers are clearly questioning old-style, hierarchical management practices that put top managers in charge of everything and require production workers merely to obey orders. That traditional approach employs full-time quality inspectors and statisticians to detect defects and then find a way of correcting them. In contrast, new-style business managers focus on preventing the production of inferior-quality products in the first place. This approach rejects the notions that one only need correct defects caught by quality inspectors and that one can be proud of a "low" 5 percent defect rate. This new approach pursues *zero* defects by involving employees throughout the process and continually setting new targets. Once defects have been reduced to 3 percent, a new target of 1 percent is set. Even a production process that is 99.9 percent defect-free is not good enough. Indeed, think of this: Such a seemingly strict standard would still tolerate two unsafe landings *per day* at New York's Kennedy Airport. It would permit the loss of 650,000 pieces of mail *per day* by the U.S. Postal Service. And it would allow 528,000 checks to be deducted from the wrong account *per day* in the U.S. banking system.

APPLICATION 22.5

U.S. Quality Programs Show Mixed Results

In recent years, the "total-quality movement" has become the biggest fad in U.S. corporate management. Well-known companies like AT&T, Ford, and Xerox claim to have adopted Taguchi methods, while Boeing, Caterpillar, Corning, Digital, General Electric, IBM, Northern Telecom, Raytheon, and others have initiated company-wide Six Sigma programs.

Under the chairmanship of John W. Welch, General Electric, for example, converted all of its divisions to the Six Sigma faith. A typical success story involved the company's Medical Systems Division, which recreated its $1.25 million diagnostic CT scanner on the basis of the new principle. The superfast scanner, known as the Lightspeed, was subjected to 250 separate quality analyses, ultimately leading to changes such as these:

1. In the old device, lead-based paint inside a chamber contaminated oil, causing all kinds of problems. A new type of paint solved them.
2. In the old device, a crucial vacuum was compromised as air leaked in. The problem was traced to a metal pin that tarnished over time. The problem was solved by roughening the metal before assembly to create a better seal.
3. In the old device, excessive heat caused printed circuit boards to overload. The problem was solved by perforating a metal box, allowing heat to dissipate.

Ultimately, significant increases in profits were traced to changes inspired by Six Sigma efforts.

While examples such as these can be multiplied manifold, not everything that glitters is gold. According to a comprehensive study undertaken by Ernst & Young and the American Quality Foundation, many U.S. quality management programs are stumbling.

The researchers surveyed 584 companies in the United States, Canada, Germany, and Japan. The firms ranged widely across industries, from automakers and banks to computer makers and hospitals. A total of 945 quality management approaches were identified; everyone, apparently, used a different pet strategy.

Among the findings:

1. U.S. firms rarely involved workers in idea-suggestion programs. In such programs, workers are urged to contact management with ideas for quality improvements. The degree of involvement was highest among U.S. automakers, which involved 28 percent of their employees in quality programs; in Japan, the carmakers' percentage was 78.
2. Only 26 percent of U.S. firms considered customer complaints an important source of ideas to improve quality; in Germany, the percentage was 60; in Japan, it was 73. Fewer than 20 percent of U.S. firms tied executive pay to the firm's output quality as measured by defect rates or customer satisfaction indexes. Many more foreign firms did.

SOURCES: Adapted from John Holusha, "Improving Quality, the Japanese Way," *The New York Times*, July 20, 1988, p. D7; Glenn Rifkin, "Pursuing Zero Defects under the Six Sygma Banner," *The New York Times*, January 13, 1991, p. F9; Gilbert Fuchsberg, "Quality Programs Show Shoddy Results," *The Wall Street Journal*, May 14, 1992, pp. B1 and 7; Claudia H. Deutsch, "Six Sigma Enlightenment," *The New York Times*, December 7, 1998, pp. C1 and 7.

Summary

1. *Quality control* is a series of production-process investigations and analyses that (1) determine whether emerging products meet the quality standards demanded by consumers and (2) trigger remedial actions, when necessary, to achieve and maintain that desired quality level.
2. The production process can be divided into a number of stages, leading from research regarding customer preferences to the marketing and servicing of a final product. Measures to assure quality can be taken at each of these stages.
3. A common form of statistical quality control involves taking one or more samples from a group of incoming or outgoing items, called a *lot,* and deciding, on the basis of the observed sample quality, to accept or reject the entire lot. Such *acceptance sampling* proceeds according to a sampling plan that specifies the number of samples to be taken from a given lot, the size of each sample, a decision variable, and an acceptance criterion.
4. Acceptance sampling is akin to performing a hypothesis test about the quality of the sampled lot. Accordingly, it is possible to make a type I error and reject a good-quality lot. It is also possible to make a type II error and accept a poor-quality lot. Different sampling plans imply different degrees of *producer's risk* (type I error) and *consumer's risk* (type II error).
5. The implications of a particular sampling plan can be summarized by an *operating-characteristic* (*OC*) *curve.* It indicates, for all possible proportions, π, of defectives in a lot, the probability of accepting the lot if the particular sampling plan is implemented. It also allows a quick assessment of producer's risk and consumer's risk at any given value of π. If the risk levels are unacceptable, a different sampling plan, with a different *OC* curve, can be selected.
6. Statisticians also monitor the manufacturing process by repetitive sampling, thereby performing hypothesis tests on whether the production process is "in control" or "out of control." For this purpose, they use *control charts,* graphical displays that highlight the average performance of a data series and the dispersion around this average so that average and dispersion of the past, if deemed acceptable, become standards for controlling performance in the present.
7. Many types of control charts exist, including $\overline{X}$ *charts, P charts, nP charts, R charts, c charts,* and more. This variety reflects the fact that the concept of quality has many dimensions. Accordingly, it may be measured by sample means, sample proportions, sample ranges, and more.
8. Patterns of sample results found in control charts can be useful predictors of trouble to come even if all results fall within the bounds of the chart's *upper* and *lower control limits.*
9. Quality control can clearly go beyond acceptance sampling and control charts. Recent proposals associated with the *total-quality movement* seek to *motivate* workers better—for example, by involving them in *quality circles,* substituting team work for the assembly line, providing guaranteed employment, and involving them in company-wide Six Sigma campaigns.

Key Terms

acceptable quality level *(AQL)*
acceptance sampling
assignable causes
attribute-sampling plan
c charts
centerline
common causes
consumer's risk
control charts
design quality
lower control limit *(LCL)*
manufactured quality
multiple-sampling plan
nP charts
operating-characteristic *(OC)* curve
P charts
producer's risk
quality circles
quality control
R charts
rejectable quality level *(RQL)*
sampling plan
s charts
sequential-sampling plan
single-stage sampling plan
special causes
two-stage sampling plan
upper control limit *(UCL)*
variables-sampling plan
$\overline{X}$ charts

Practice Problems

NOTE

Some problems require the use of a statistical program, EXCEL or MINITAB. The program's major features are explained in text Chapter 2; plenty of additional advice is available via the program's built-in Help feature.

Section 22.3 Acceptance Sampling

1. Table 22.2 shows a probability of acceptance of .2901, given $\pi = .06$.

a. Show how this value is derived.

b. Determine the associated producer's risk.

2. Table 22.2 shows a probability of acceptance of .6676, given $\pi = .02$.

a. Show how this value is derived.

b. Determine the associated producer's risk.

3. Consider Table 22.2. Find the producer's risk for AQL = .02, .09, and .30.

4. Table 22.3 shows the value of p_a for various sampling plans. Prove the correctness of the entries in the $\pi = .09$ row, using the formula noted in the text.

5. Table 22.3 shows the value of p_a for various sampling plans. Prove the correctness of the entries in the $\pi = .01$ row, using the computer.

6. Table 22.3 shows the value of p_a for various sampling plans. Prove the correctness of the entries in the $\pi = .05$ row, using the computer.

7. Table 22.3 shows the value of p_a for various sampling plans. Create a new row for $\pi = .005$, using the computer.

8. Table 22.3 shows the value of p_a for various sampling plans. Create a new row for $\pi = .025$, using the computer.

9. A production process has an actual proportion of defectives of $\pi = .03$. Using the computer, find out what happens to the producer's risk in alternative acceptance sampling plans defined by $n = 50$ and $c = 0$, 1, and 2, respectively.

10. A production process has an actual proportion of defectives of $\pi = .015$. Using the computer, find out what happens to the producer's risk in alternative acceptance sampling plans defined by $n = 40$ and $c = 0$, 1, 2, and 3, respectively.

11. Consider Table 22.3 and sampling plan $n = 15$, $c = 0$. A manager seeks a maximum producer's risk of .08 at $AQL = .05$ and also a maximum consumer's risk of .10 at $RQL = .15$. Is this possible?

12. A manager considers alternative sampling plans with n = 10, 20, or 50. Use Appendix Table D to find a plan that provides (a) a producer's risk of .03, given AQL = .05, and also (b) a consumer's risk of .12, given RQL = .30.

13. A manager considers alternative sampling plans with n = 15, 20, 50, or 100. Use Appendix Table D to find a plan that provides (a) a producer's risk of .13, given $AQL = .05$, and also (b) a consumer's risk of .21, given $RQL = .10$.

14. A domestic manufacturer of aircraft navigation equipment buys parts from a German firm. These come in lots of 5,000. The manufacturer plans on sampling $n = 50$ items per lot. Construct a table similar to Table 22.3 for values of $c = 0$, 2, and 5 and values of $\pi = .01, .02 \ldots$ and .10.

15. For each of the three sampling plans developed in Practice Problem 14,

a. determine the producer's risk and the consumer's risk at $\pi = .02$, .08, and .09.

b. let a computer draw relevant OC curves similar to Figure 22.4.

16. A domestic manufacturer of microwave ovens buys parts from a Japanese firm. These come in lots of 5,000. The manufacturer plans on sampling $n = 100$ items per lot. Construct a table similar to Table 22.3 for values of $c = 0$, 3, and 5 and values of $\pi = .01, .02 \ldots$ and .12.

17. For each of the three sampling plans developed in Practice Problem 16,

a. determine the producer's risk and the consumer's risk at $\pi = .03$, .07, and .12.

b. let a computer draw relevant OC curves similar to Figure 22.4.

Section 22.4 Statistical Process Control

18. A production process is designed to fill bottles with an average 64.1 ounces of fruit juice. The population of filling weights is normally distributed with a standard deviation of 1.3 oz. Inspectors take periodic samples of 20 bottles. One sample yields a mean filling weight of 62 oz., the next two samples yield 64.9 oz. and 60.5 oz. Is the production process in control?

19. Illustrate Practice Problem 18 with an appropriate $\overline{X}$ chart. If the next sample yields 62.7 oz., is the production process in control?

20. A production process is designed to fill bottles with an average 16.5 ounces of liquid detergent. The population of filling weights is normally distributed with a standard deviation of 0.8 oz. Inspectors take periodic samples of 35 bottles. One sample yields a mean filling weight of 16.2 oz., the next two samples yield 15.8 oz. and 17.3 oz. Is the production process out of control?

21. Illustrate Practice Problem 20 with an appropriate $\overline{X}$ chart. If the next sample yields 15.9 oz., is the production process in control?

22. A quality inspector takes 8 samples of $n = 10$ boxes of wild rice at a time when the production process is believed to be in control. Measured in ounces, the filling weights appear in Table 22.6.

a. Use a computer to construct an $\overline{X}$ control chart.

b. If another sample of $n = 10$ yields a mean of 84.96, is the process in control?

TABLE 22.6 | Wild Rice Samples

#1	#2	#3	#4	#5	#6	#7	#8
80.07	85.16	85.17	84.23	81.55	81.98	80.00	78.59
77.00	77.01	78.45	79.56	80.34	79.99	80.03	83.45
80.02	80.09	80.97	80.77	84.33	82.22	81.45	83.30
80.00	80.02	80.45	80.34	80.56	80.77	80.89	80.99
81.34	81.34	83.33	82.33	82.99	83.99	82.89	80.00
78.99	78.56	78.56	78.33	78.99	79.03	79.04	79.95
82.33	82.46	82.44	82.99	82.10	82.77	83.22	84.00
76.00	79.00	79.86	79.56	79.56	78.84	78.66	78.99
80.00	80.00	80.00	80.99	80.99	80.99	80.56	82.99
77.99	78.99	78.66	81.00	81.22	82.99	82.84	82.73

23. A quality inspector takes 11 samples of $n = 10$ locking bolts at a time when the production process is believed to be in control. The raw measurement data appear in Table 22.7.

a. Use a computer to construct an $\overline{X}$ control chart.

b. If another sample of $n = 10$ yields a mean of 3.34, is the process in control?

TABLE 22.7 | Locking Bolt Samples

Sample Number	Inches									
1	2.30	2.33	2.34	2.35	2.36	2.33	2.21	2.38	2.89	3.01
2	2.29	2.56	2.57	2.38	2.45	2.56	2.67	2.33	2.45	2.90
3	2.11	2.23	2.40	2.34	2.45	3.90	2.56	2.24	2.35	2.56
4	2.11	2.33	2.34	3.00	2.11	2.22	2.33	2.45	2.53	2.19
5	2.34	2.45	2.43	2.33	2.37	2.39	2.45	2.67	2.99	3.06
6	2.33	2.45	2.78	3.02	3.99	2.33	2.33	2.35	2.49	1.98
7	2.34	2.56	2.78	2.90	2.11	2.13	2.11	2.11	2.18	1.79
8	3.00	3.03	3.05	3.08	3.09	2.45	2.55	2.66	2.88	3.06
9	3.09	3.99	2.33	2.44	2.33	2.11	2.34	2.38	2.45	2.77
10	2.30	2.32	2.39	2.38	2.37	2.40	2.45	2.78	2.56	2.33
11	2.33	2.56	2.33	2.35	3.09	2.98	2.87	3.19	3.99	2.38

24. A machine fastens screw-on caps to bottles of mouthwash. If it applies too much torque, the cap breaks. Historically, the proper mean was 8 psi, with a standard deviation of .3 psi. During the production process, a quality inspector is to take a sample of 10 capping operations every half hour.

a. Compute relevant values for an appropriate control chart.

b. Assess the next sample mean of 9.2 psi.

25. The controls of an air conditioner are supposed to turn on at 75 degrees Fahrenheit, with a standard deviation of .5 degree. During the production process, a quality inspector is to take a sample of 10 air conditioners every half hour and test the turn-on temperature setting.

a. Compute relevant values for an appropriate control chart.

b. Assess the next sample mean of 78.1 degrees.

26. An executive of a hotel chain has specified a maximum waiting time for telephone reservations of 1 minute, with a standard deviation of .5 minute. A quality inspector is to take random samples of the reservation process 10 times per day and record the times involved.

a. Compute relevant values for an appropriate control chart.

b. Assess the next sample mean of 8.8 minutes.

27. A tire manufacturer has specified that a certain tread wear test should, on average, take off no more than 25 hundredths of an inch, with a standard deviation of 5 hundredths. A quality inspector is to take random samples of 10 new tires per day and test them.

a. Compute relevant values for an appropriate control chart.

b. Assess the next sample mean of 26 hundredths of an inch.

28. Review the data of Table 6.10 on page 215 and assume that each of the first 9 columns represents a separate sample of $n = 8$ cans of peas.

a. Create an $\overline{X}$ chart on the assumption that the population of filling weights is normally distributed, with a mean of 16 ounces and a standard deviation of .3 ounce.

b. Assess a next sample of 8 cans with an average weight of 14.4 ounce.

29. A production process normally yields 2 percent defectives. Inspectors take periodic samples of $n = 250$. One sample yields a proportion of defectives of $P = .030$; the next two yield $P = .018$ and $P = .027$. Is the production process in control?

30. A production process normally yields 5 percent defectives. Inspectors take periodic samples of $n = 120$. One sample yields a proportion of defectives of $P = .043$; the next two yield $P = .056$ and $P = .071$. Is the production process in control?

31. Illustrate Practice Problem 29 with an appropriate P chart. If the next sample yields $P = .025$, is the production process in control?

32. Illustrate Practice Problem 30 with an appropriate P chart. If the next sample yields $P = .059$, is the production process in control?

33. A quality inspector takes 30 samples of $n = 50$ each at a time when the production process is believed to be in control. A total of 165 defectives is found.

a. Estimate the value of π when the process is in control.

b. Figure the limits of an appropriate P chart.

c. If a new sample of $n = 50$ yields 7 defectives, is the process in control?

34. A manufacturing process seals aircraft fuel tanks, then paints them. One control chart measures the proportion of fuel tanks with faulty rivets as equal to .01 when the process is in control. Another control chart measures the proportion of tanks with blemishes on the paint job as equal to .02 when the process is in control. Samples of $n = 500$ tanks are taken during the day shift and during the night shift. The results are summarized in Table 22.8 on the next page. Are the two processes in control?

TABLE 22.8 | Fuel Tank Study

Number of Tanks With	Day Shift	Night Shift
Faulty Rivets	7	9
Blemishes	9	13

35. Historically, a sawmill's output has contained 10 percent defectives. A concerned quality inspector takes daily samples of $n = 100$ pieces of lumber. The last 30 samples contain the following numbers of defective planks:

14 15 3 21 26 14 17 6 9 10 10 11 16 22 17
12 15 27 19 9 7 9 9 12 13 17 20 11 1 8

Create a *P* chart that indicates whether the production process in control.

36. Rework Practice Problem 35, but this time create an *nP* chart.

37. Historically, an airline has lost 2 percent of its passengers' baggage. A concerned executive takes daily samples of $n = 100$ passengers. The last 30 samples contain the following numbers of lost baggage claims:

0 0 0 4 0 3 1 0 0 6 1 1 1 3 9
0 1 3 2 2 2 2 2 3 6 1 1 0 0 0

a. Create a *P* chart that indicates whether the production process in control.

b. Create an *nP* chart that indicates whether the production process in control.

38. Historically, an overnight delivery service has failed to deliver 1 percent of its parcels by the next day noon deadline. A concerned executive takes daily samples of $n = 100$ parcels. The last 30 samples contain the following numbers of late deliveries:

0 0 0 4 0 3 1 0 0 6 1 1 1 3 9
0 1 3 2 2 2 2 2 3 6 1 1 0 0 0

Create a *P* chart that indicates whether the production process in control.

39. Review Practice Problem 38. Using the same data, create an *nP* chart that indicates whether the production process in control.

40. Review the Table 22.6 wild rice samples on page 1106. Produce an *R* chart for the sample ranges.

41. Review the Table 22.7 locking bolt samples on page 1106. Produce an *R* chart for the sample ranges.

42. Review the data of Table 6.10 on page 215 and assume that each of the first 9 columns represents a separate sample of $n = 8$ cans of peas. Produce an *R* chart for the sample ranges.

43. A quality inspector at a carpet factory inspects every 25th carpet for flaws. The count of flaws on the last 40 inspected carpets was as follows:

1 4 3 5 6 3 2 8 5 3 5 4 2 5 8 9 3 5 7 3 9
12 13 2 3 6 7 9 10 3 4 5 7 2 3 5 6 6 8 9

Let a computer create a *c* chart.

44. A quality inspector at a glass factory inspects every 25th sheet of Plexiglas for flaws. The count of flaws on the last 42 inspected sheets was as follows:

0 0 0 3 4 5 6 0 0 3 5 1 2 1 2 0 0 2 3 4 1
1 1 0 0 0 0 1 2 0 3 8 9 2 1 0 0 0 0 0 0 1

Let a computer create a *c* chart.

45. Even though a process may be in control, as was illustrated in text Figure 22.9, it is often of great interest to quality inspectors to detect patterns in data that suggest nonrandom behavior. A *run chart* serves precisely this purpose and can easily be created by MINITAB. Do so for the filling weight data of Practice Problem 28, which involved nine samples of $n = 8$ cans of peas.

46. Practice Problem 28 investigated 9 samples of $n = 8$ cans of peas with the help of an $\overline{X}$ chart. However, in MINITAB it is also easy to investigate the behavior of the 72 observations directly, as if they came from a single sample, with the help of an *individuals chart.* Do so now, once again assuming historical values of mean = 16 oz. and standard deviation = .3 oz.

SECTION 22.5 OTHER METHODS OF QUALITY CONTROL

47. Workers cooperating in teams often have trouble deciding which of numerous alternative projects to tackle first. Those seeking to make quality improvements are no exception. In such a situation, a *Pareto chart* can be of help because it identifies which problem is most significant and, thus, guides workers to focus their efforts on an area in which the largest gains can be made. Such a *Pareto chart* is a bar chart in which the horizontal axis represents (noncontiguous) categories of interest, such as types of defects about which consumers of the firm's products have complained. The chart orders these categories from largest to smallest, which makes it easy to distinguish the vital few concerns from the trivial many. The chart also contains a line that shows the cumulative importance of categories.

Use a computer to illustrate the following data with a *Pareto chart:* During the last year, pilots using a new radar altimeter made a total of 985 complaints to the manufacturer via the FAA: In 123 cases, the readout was illegible in bright sunlight; in 534 cases, the instrument failed in severe turbulence; in 71 cases, the readout flickered annoyingly at night; in 23 cases, the instrument failed in icing conditions; in 234 cases, the instrument failed in high temperatures.

48. Review Practice Problem 47 as needed to learn about the *Pareto chart.* Then use a computer to illustrate the following data with a *Pareto chart:* During the last year, patients using a new drug made a total of 1,113 complaints about side effects to the manufacturer via the FDA: In 288 cases, there was nausea; in 629 cases, dizziness; in 125 cases, fainting; in 71 cases, arrhythmia.

49. Visit http://www.minitab.com, the home page of the MINITAB statistical software company.

a. Click **Resources** > **Customer Success Stories** and read about major companies using MINITAB for quality control.

b. Click **Search**, enter *Quality,* and pursue some of the leads.

50. Visit http://www.sixsigmaqualtec.com, the home page of Six Sigma Qualtec, a premier provider of training and implementation services that help companies develop Six Sigma programs. The firm's clients, such as General Electric, BMW, Navistar, GenCorp, and Thermo King, have added billions to their bottom lines through Six Sigma performance improvement methodologies. Learn all you can about the firm.

Chapter 23

DECISION THEORY

LOOKING AHEAD

After reading this chapter, you will know a great deal about decision making under uncertainty. Among other things, you will learn to:

1. make decisions even when nothing is known about the likelihood of alternative future events that are certain to affect the eventual outcome of a present decision, employing decision criteria with fancy names such as *maximin, minimax, maximax, minimin,* and even *minimax regret,*
2. engage in *prior analysis,* a form of decision making that employs whatever probabilities are available prior to gathering new experimental or sample evidence and that uses such alternative decision criteria as *maximum likelihood, expected monetary value, expected opportunity loss,* and *expected utility,*
3. carry out *posterior analysis,* a form of decision making that starts out with prior probabilities, proceeds to gather additional evidence about the probabilities of future events, and then uses this new evidence (by means of Bayes' theorem) to transform prior probabilities into a revised set of posterior probabilities with the help of which a final decision is reached,
4. figure the maximum amount of money a decision maker can be expected to pay for obtaining perfect (and even imperfect) information about future events, and
5. engage in *preposterior analysis,* a form of decision making that decides the worth of obtaining additional information before proceeding to prior or posterior analysis, and thus combines the two—more often than not, in an easy-to-read *decision tree.*

AND HERE IS A TYPICAL PROBLEM YOU WILL BE ABLE TO SOLVE:

A firm has just produced 10 million copies of a new game for the Christmas market. It can sell the entire batch to a distributor for a net return of $20 million in 6 months. It can instead market the games on its own to individual buyers with a 40 percent chance of encountering weak demand (and getting a net return of $2 million in 6 months) and a 60 percent chance of encountering strong demand (and getting a net return of $40 million in 6 months). For a $2 million fee, a consulting firm is offering advice on the likely demand situation. The consulting firm's track record is mixed: In similar situations in the past, when demand turned out to be weak, the firm had made a correct prediction 70 percent of the time (but had falsely predicted strong demand in the other 30 percent of cases). When demand turned out to be strong, the firm had made a correct prediction 80 percent of the time (but had made a wrong prediction in the remaining 20 percent of cases). Use a decision tree to determine the optimal strategy that maximizes your *expected monetary value.*

PREVIEW

In 1999, as hurricane Floyd moved toward the southeastern seaboard of the United States with some of the deadliest winds in recent years, homeowners were not the only ones holding their breath. So were insurance company executives and multitudes of bondholders throughout the world. The connection is not too difficult to see.

It all started in 1992, when the United States experienced its costliest natural disaster in history. When hurricane Andrew blasted its way through southern Florida and Louisiana, it killed a relatively small number of people, but it caused over $27 billion in property damage and, ultimately, some $17 billion in insurance company losses. No wonder the industry looked for ways to insure itself against a repeat performance. Thus, amidst much fanfare, "catastrophe bonds" or "act-of-God securities" were born. Rated at junk-bond levels, these new securities promised annual yields close to 10 percent, and almost $2 billion dollars' worth were sold during the late 1990s. The drawback: If a new hurricane should cause damage above a predefined level, investors could lose not only promised interest payments but also their original capital. Thus, as Floyd approached, Moody's Investors Service placed the new types of bonds on watch for a possible downgrade. Instantly, markets for high-grade corporate and government bonds reacted as well: As they pictured insurance companies dumping securities to pay claims, other investors quickly tried to reduce their holdings, and bond prices tumbled even before the hurricane's landfall.

This story leads us directly to the main issue of this chapter: *How can businesses or governments make wise decisions in the face of uncertainty?* To appreciate, for example, the kinds of decisions that hurricanes require, it is important to recognize a trend that began a century ago. Probably as a result of better weather forecasts (which allow timely evacuations), the human death toll from hurricanes in the United States has been declining steadily, from over 8,000 during 1901–1910 to fewer than 200 during the 1990s. On the other hand, as a result of increasing economic development in the southeastern United States—which has turned swamplands into beachfront malls, luxury hotels, and sprawling suburban subdivisions—property damage has been steadily climbing. Measured in 1990 dollars, it amounted to less than $1 billion during the 20th century's first decade, then climbed to almost $50 billion in the 1990s. Are humans helpless in the face of such fury? Not entirely.

Recall Application 10.3, which used the normal curve to analyze the decision to *tame* hurricanes by seeding them with silver iodide. This chapter explains how crucial decisions like this can be made systematically rather than haphazardly, despite the uncertainty that inevitably surrounds them. When a new hurricane is discovered, government decision makers have a choice: to seed or not to seed. The question is, which is the least costly path to pursue? If they take no action, the newly born hurricane can act in any one of many different ways. The hurricane may suddenly fizzle out or turn away from vulnerable population centers. The hurricane may increase in strength, roaring toward the coast at 111 to 130 miles per hour, as Gabrielle did in 1989, Gustav in 1990, or Bob in 1991. The hurricane may even reach a more dangerous force, carrying winds anywhere from 131 to 155 mph, as Helene and Joan did in 1988, followed by Claudette in 1991, and by Andrew in 1992. Indeed, a maximal hurricane with winds in excess of 155 mph is even in the cards; Gilbert in 1988 and Hugo in 1989 are examples. Each of these possibilities carries with it not only a different probability of occurring, but also the likelihood of different levels of death and destruction. On the other hand, if decision makers do commit resources to seed a hurricane, they can pursue that option to varying degrees, and each of these decisions will, in turn, slow down the storm and reduce the damage to different extents. How to choose among numerous options such as these is what this chapter is all about, because complicated decisions of this type are common not only in circumstances that government officials must deal with but also in situations that business executives and economists face every day.[1]

[1]Adapted from Peter Applebome, "Storm Cycles and Coastal Growth Could Make Disaster a Way of Life," *The New York Times,* August 30, 1992, pp. E1 and 3; Gregory Zuckerman, "Hurricane Poses Risks for Bonds: Catastrophe Securities Get First Major Test," *The Wall Street Journal,* September 15, 1999, pp. C1 and 21.

23.1 Introduction

In countless situations, business and economic decision makers face a serious problem: They are called upon to choose among alternative courses of action at a time when they cannot foresee the consequences of those actions with certainty. More often than not, these consequences depend on future events over which the decision makers have no control. Under such circumstances, it is difficult to make a rational decision. Consider:

- the farmer who must choose now among plantings of alternative crops but knows that some of these crops will flourish if the season turns out to be cool and dry, while others will do so only if it is hot and wet
- the manufacturer who must decide now whether to introduce a new production process or to continue using the old one, but who also knows that the profit consequences of this decision will differ greatly, depending on whether future oil prices (or future wages) are low or high
- the marketing manager who must give advice now about introducing a new product, or modifying the style, packaging, or labeling of an old product, but who knows the consequences of any of these actions depend on as-yet-unknown levels of future demand

Think of the real estate developer who must make a commitment now to a small, medium-sized, or large-scale project; the consulting firm that must decide now whether to install a small or a large computer; the oil company that must drill now or sell its rights; the record producer who must initiate a major sales campaign now or abort the production of a record altogether; the independent TV producer who can submit the pilot of a new program to a network now or sell the rights to someone else; the job applicant who must decide now whether to work for a fixed salary or on a commission basis. Examples such as these can be multiplied without end because the ultimate outcome of any *choice* is likely to be affected by *chance.*

Thus, the wisdom or foolishness of any present decision will be determined by (uncontrollable) future events: by whether the demand for housing (or consulting services) turns out to be high or low, by whether oil is found at the drilling site or the test hole is dry, by whether the new record (or TV show) becomes a hit or fails, by whether the new employee is successful at making sales or not. The following definition summarizes the subject matter of this chapter:

DEFINITION 23.1 Certain decision-making problems arise because uncertainty exists about future events over which the decision maker has no control, but which are bound to influence the ultimate outcome of a decision. Various methods that can be employed in the systematic analysis and solution of such problems are collectively known as **decision theory.**

Some writers, such as the economist Frank Knight (1885–1972), have introduced a fine distinction between decision making under *uncertainty* and decision making under *risk*. In either case, the ultimate outcome of a present decision is affected by future random events. In the case of decision making under uncertainty, the probabilities associated with all of these events, or even the nature of the events themselves, are unknown at the time of decision making. In the case of decision making under risk, both the nature and the probabilities of these events are known in advance. Like most writers, we make no such distinction here and refer to all situations in which the ultimate outcome of a decision maker's choice depends on chance as **decision making under uncertainty.**

23.2 Basic Concepts

Whenever we make decisions in the context of uncertainty, certain identical elements are present. It helps to focus on these elements systematically when searching for a solution to a decision-making problem.

ACTIONS, EVENTS, PAYOFFS

First, each decision maker has specific decision alternatives available. In the language of decision theory, the decision maker must choose among various mutually exclusive *actions,* a complete list of which is symbolized by $A_1, A_2, \ldots A_n$. A business executive, for example, might be called upon to manufacture and market a new product by taking one of two actions: A_1 = constructing a small plant; A_2 = constructing a large plant.

DEFINITION 23.2 Mutually exclusive decision alternatives open to a decision maker are called **actions;** they are symbolized by $A_1, A_2, \ldots A_n$.

Second, future occurrences not under the control of the decision maker will affect the outcome of any present action taken by the decision maker. These occurrences are commonly referred to as *events* or *states of nature.* A collectively exhaustive list of mutually exclusive events is symbolized by $E_1, E_2, \ldots E_n$. The production and marketing of a new product, for example, might be linked with one of two events: E_1 = an environment of weak demand; E_2 = an environment of strong demand. As we shall see, decision makers may or may not employ probability values attached to such events at the time when a choice among actions is taken.

DEFINITION 23.3 Mutually exclusive future occurrences that will affect the outcome of any present action taken, but that are not under the control of the decision maker, are called **events** or **states of nature.** They are symbolized by $E_1, E_2, \ldots E_n$.

Third, positive or negative net benefits are associated with each possible action/event combination. These net benefits have a special name as well:

DEFINITION 23.4 The positive or negative net benefits that are associated with each possible action/event combination, which are thus the joint outcome of choice and chance, are called **payoffs.**

Payoffs can be measured in any kind of unit appropriate to the problem at hand: in units of money, time, or even utility. The payoffs from constructing a *small* plant, for example, might be annual profits of $8 million if demand is weak or $5 million if demand is strong. The smaller payoff associated with strong demand might result from the need to run the small plant above its designed capacity, which leads to higher unit costs of production. The corresponding payoffs from a *large* plant might be −$2 million or +$12 million instead. This time, the smaller payoff might occur because running a large plant *below* its capacity also involves unusually high unit costs.

THE PAYOFF TABLE

We can summarize a decision-making situation in the context of uncertainty in a variety of ways. One popular summary is the **payoff table,** a tabular listing of the payoffs associated with all possible combinations of actions and events. Table 23.1 is such a tabular summary for our example. Each row corresponds to one of the two possible actions. Each column corresponds to one of the two possible events.

TABLE 23.1 | A Payoff Table

This table shows the annual profits (in millions of dollars) associated with four possible action/event combinations.

	Events	
Actions	E_1 = weak demand for new product	E_2 = strong demand for new product
A_1 = constructing a small plant	8	5
A_2 = constructing a large plant	−2	12

In this payoff table, neither action is unambiguously superior to the other in the sense that it produces payoffs that are as good as or better than those of the alternative action, no matter which event occurs. If such an unambiguously superior action existed, it would be a **dominant action.** The existence of a dominant action turns the alternative into an **inadmissible action** that need not be considered further because of its obvious inferiority. In our example, A_1 would be dominant if, all else being equal, the A_1/E_2 cell contained an entry of 12 instead of 5. If A_1 were so dominant, A_2 would be inadmissible. Under those circumstances, the decision maker could choose A_1 without hesitation and would reap a profit of $8 million if E_1 occurred or of $12 million if E_2 occurred. The choice of A_2 would lead to worse or at best equally good results, as the A_2 row shows.

THE DECISION TREE

Another popular summary of a decision-making situation is similar to the tree diagram encountered in Chapter 8. As Figure 23.1 shows, it has a similar name as well.

DEFINITION 23.5 A **decision tree** is a graphical device that summarizes a decision-making problem under uncertainty by listing in chronological order, from left to right, every potential action, event, and payoff. A decision-tree diagram is particularly useful when a decision problem involves a sequence of many decisions that extend over a long stretch of time.

FIGURE 23.1 | A Decision Tree

The possible payoffs associated with a decision made under uncertainty result from a mixture of choice (square symbol) and chance (circular symbols). Note that the information contained in this diagram is precisely the same as that found in the payoff table (Table 23.1).

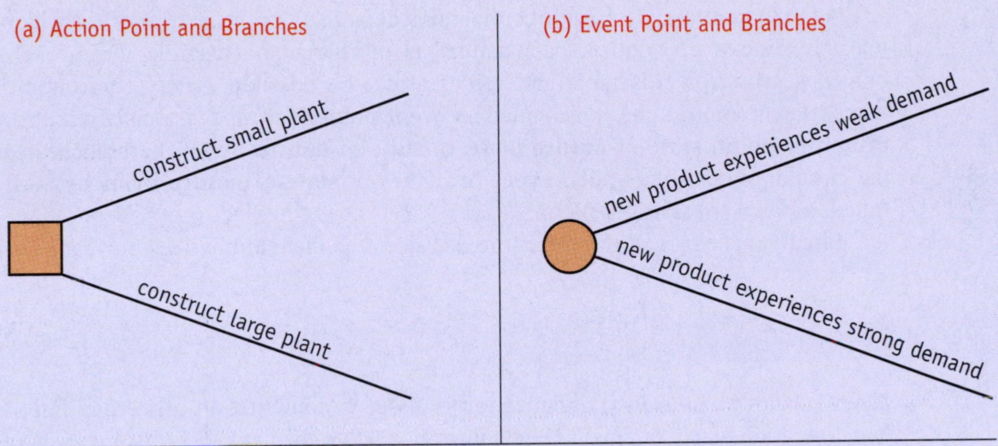

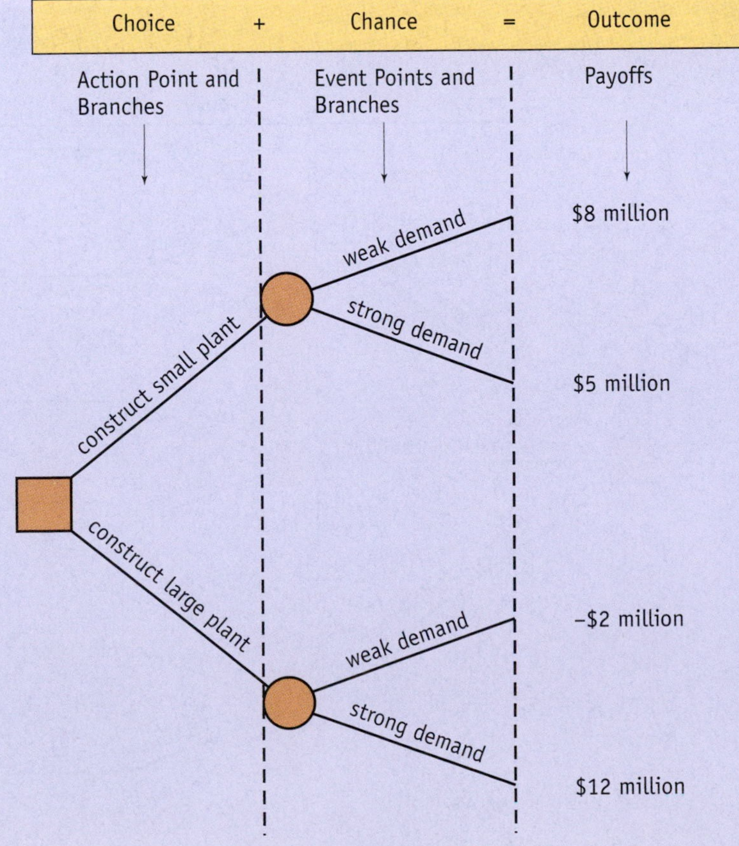

SQUARES Customarily, decision-tree diagrams denote any point of *choice* (at which the decision maker is in control) by a square symbol. From each square, branches representing the possible actions of the decision maker grow toward the right. Each point of choice is called an **action point.** It is also variously referred to as a **decision point, decision node,** or even **decision fork.** The branches sprouting from the square symbol are called **action branches** or **decision branches.** All this is illustrated in panel (a) of Figure 23.1.

CIRCLES In contrast, decision-tree diagrams depict any point of *chance* (at which the decision maker exercises no control, but "nature" is in charge) by a circle. From each circle, other branches grow towards the right, representing the possible *events* confronting the decision maker. Each point of chance is called an **event point.** It is also variously referred to as a **state-of-nature point, state-of-nature node,** or **state-of-nature fork.** The branches sprouting from the circular symbol are called **event branches** or **state-of-nature branches.** All this is illustrated in panel (b) of Figure 23.1.

Finally, panel (c) shows the entire decision tree that summarizes our Table 23.1 example.

EXAMPLE PROBLEM 23.1

A new health maintenance organization is about to construct an office building, which can be large, medium-sized, or small. Depending on whether the next 10 years are years of recession or inflation, profits are expected to be $10 million or $20 million with the large building. They are

FIGURE 23.2 | The HMO Dilemma

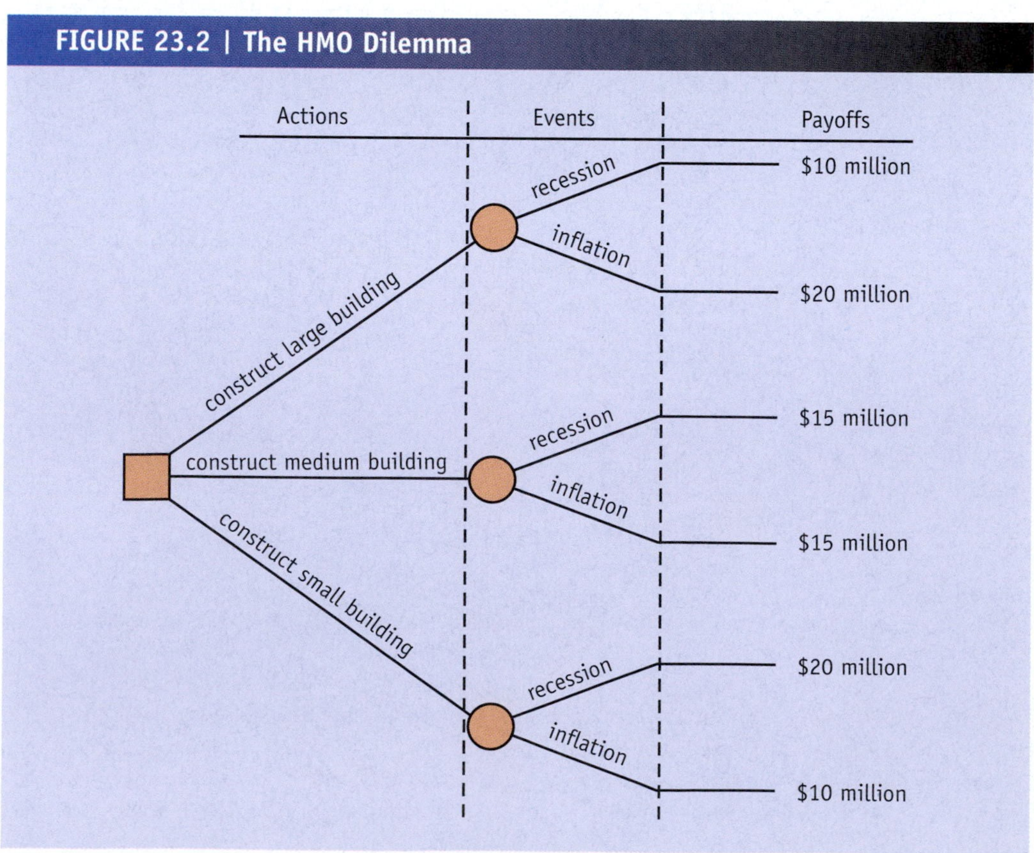

likely to be $15 million with the medium-sized building regardless of the economy. They are likely to be $20 million or $10 million with a small building.

a. Summarize the decision-making problem with a *decision tree.*

b. If maximum profit is desired, is the solution obvious?

SOLUTION:

a. See Figure 23.2.

b. No, it is far from obvious. Summarizing a decision problem, either with the help of a payoff table or a decision tree, is helpful, but it represents only the first step toward a solution. A best plan of action still remains to be chosen (and the following sections consider some of the criteria that might be employed to find it).

23.3 Decision Making without Probabilities

Consider a situation such as that summarized by Table 23.1 or Figure 23.1, in which a decision must be made but nothing is known about the likelihood of occurrence of those alternative future events that are certain to affect the eventual outcome of the present decision. Imagine that the decision maker does not even care to guess what the event probabilities might be. In such a case, it is common practice to employ one of three nonprobabilistic decision criteria: *maximin* (or *minimax*), *maximax* (or *minimin*), or *minimax regret.*

MAXIMIN OR MINIMAX

The first of the nonprobabilistic criteria embodies a decidedly conservative approach to decision making. It guarantees that the decision maker does no worse than achieve the best among the poorest possible outcomes. This criterion takes one of two forms, depending on whether the decision maker aims to maximize benefit or minimize cost.

MAXIMIN If maximization of benefit is the objective, the criterion is called **maximin.** In this case, the decision maker identifies the lowest possible (or minimum) benefit associated with each possible action, finds the highest (or maximum) benefit among these minima, and then chooses the action associated with this maximum of minima, which explains the name given to this criterion.

EXAMPLE PROBLEM 23.2

Consider the decision-making problem summarized by Table 23.1. Solve it by applying the *maximin* criterion.

SOLUTION: See Table 23.2 on the next page.

MINIMAX If minimization of cost is the objective, as when a firm must choose between alternative antipollution devices, the analogous criterion is often referred to as **minimax.** In this case, the decision maker identifies the highest possible (or maximum) cost associated with each possible action, finds the lowest (or minimum) cost among these maxima, and then chooses the action associated with this minimum of maxima, which explains the name given to the criterion in this instance.

TABLE 23.2 | Maximizing Benefit: The Maximin Criterion

This table shows the annual profits (in millions of dollars) associated with four possible action/event combinations. The lowest of the possible profits associated with each action is shown in the last column. The maximin criterion suggests taking the best of these (highlighted in red), or action A_1. Under the circumstances, the firm can do no worse than earn a profit of \$5 million. It might even earn \$8 million, if E_1 rather than E_2 occurs.

Actions	Events		Row Minimum
	E_1 = weak demand for new product	E_2 = strong demand for new product	
A_1 = constructing a small plant	8	5	**5 Maximin**
A_2 = constructing a large plant	−2	12	−2

EXAMPLE PROBLEM 23.3

A firm must install one of two antipollution systems, small or large. If the level of demand and production is low, the former imposes annual costs of \$5 million; the latter, \$10 million. If the level of demand and production is high, the corresponding cost figures are \$8 million and \$4 million. Use the *minimax* criterion to make the decision.

SOLUTION: See Table 23.3.

TABLE 23.3 | Minimizing Cost: The Minimax Criterion

This table shows the annual costs (in millions of dollars) associated with four possible action/event combinations. The highest of the possible costs associated with each action is shown in the last column. The minimax criterion suggests taking the best of these (highlighted in red), or action A_1. Under the circumstances, the firm can do no worse than incur a cost of \$8 million. It might even pay as little as \$5 million, if E_1 rather than E_2 occurs.

Actions	Events		Row Maximum
	E_1 = low level of demand and production	E_2 = high level of demand and production	
A_1 = install small antipollution system	5	8	**8 Minimax**
A_2 = install large antipollution system	10	4	10

CONCLUSION The maximin (or minimax) criterion is ideally suited to the born pessimist. If you always expect the worst, if you always suspect that "nature" or chance will work against you, then you cannot do better than employ this criterion. It will give you the best among all the worst things that can happen: the highest of the lowest possible profits that are listed in the last column of Table 23.2 and the lowest of the highest possible costs that are listed in the last column of Table 23.3. These best outcomes among the worst possible outcomes are highlighted in red.

MAXIMAX OR MINIMIN

The second among the nonprobabilistic criteria goes to the other extreme and seeks to achieve the best of the best possible outcomes. This criterion, too, comes in two forms.

MAXIMAX If maximization of benefit is the objective, the criterion is called **maximax.** In this case, the decision maker identifies the highest possible (or maximum) benefit associated with each possible action, finds the highest (or maximum) benefit among these maxima, and then chooses the action associated with this maximum of maxima, as the name suggests.

EXAMPLE PROBLEM 23.4

Once again, consider the decision-making problem summarized by Table 23.1. Solve it now by applying the *maximax* criterion.

SOLUTION: See Table 23.4.

TABLE 23.4 | Maximizing Benefit: The Maximax Criterion

This table shows the annual profits (in millions of dollars) associated with four possible action/event combinations. The highest of the possible profits associated with each action is shown in the last column. The maximax criterion suggests taking the best of these (highlighted in red), or action A_2. Under the circumstances, the firm might earn a profit of \$12 million, but it might also have a loss of \$2 million, if E_1 rather than E_2 occurs.

Actions	Events: E_1 = weak demand for new product	Events: E_2 = strong demand for new product	Row Maximum
A_1 = constructing a small plant	8	5	8
A_2 = constructing a large plant	−2	12	**12 Maximax**

MINIMIN If minimization of cost is the objective, the analogous criterion is often referred to as **minimin.** In this case, the decision maker identifies the lowest possible (or minimum) cost associated with each possible action, finds the lowest (or minimum) cost among these minima, and then chooses the action associated with this minimum of minima, as the name suggests.

EXAMPLE PROBLEM 23.5

Rework Example Problem 23.3, using the *minimin* criterion.

SOLUTION: See Table 23.5.

TABLE 23.5 | Minimizing Cost: The Minimin Criterion

This table shows the annual costs (in millions of dollars) associated with four possible action/event combinations. The lowest of the possible costs associated with each action is shown in the last column. The minimin criterion suggests taking the best of these (highlighted in red), or action A_2. Under the circumstances, the firm might incur costs as low as \$4 million, but it might also have costs of \$10 million, if E_1 rather than E_2 occurs.

	Events		
Actions	E_1 = low level of demand and production	E_2 = high level of demand and production	Row Minimum
A_1 = install small antipollution system	5	8	5
A_2 = install large antipollution system	10	4	**4 Minimin**

CONCLUSION The maximax (or minimin) criterion is ideally suited to the born optimist. If you always expect the best, if you are always convinced that "nature" or chance will be on your side, then you might go after the best of the best in the fashion just shown: the highest of the highest possible profits in Table 23.4 and the lowest of the lowest possible costs in Table 23.5.

MINIMAX REGRET

The third one among the nonprobabilistic criteria is just a bit more complicated. To understand it, we must first define the concept of **opportunity loss *(OL)*** or **regret.** It differs slightly depending on whether we seek to maximize some benefit or minimize some cost.

MAXIMIZING BENEFIT When the decision maker aims to maximize benefit, the opportunity loss equals the difference between (1) the optimal payoff for a given event (the highest benefit in a given event column of our tables) and (2) the actual payoff achieved as a result of taking a specified action and the subsequent occurrence of that event. Consider, for example, the E_1 column of Table 23.4 on the preceding page. If E_1 occurs, the optimal payoff is \$8 million.

- If the decision maker has previously chosen A_1, the actual payoff will equal \$8 million as well. Hence, the opportunity loss will equal \$8 million − \$8 million = 0. The decision maker has no reason to regret anything. Given the occurrence of E_1, the best possible action had, in fact, been taken.

- On the other hand, if the decision maker has previously chosen A_2, the actual payoff will equal −\$2 million. Hence, the opportunity loss will equal \$8 million − (−\$2 million) = \$10 million. The decision maker has plenty of reason for regret. Given the occurrence of E_1, if only A_1 had been chosen instead of A_2! The decision maker would be better off by \$10 million, having a gain of \$8 million instead of a loss of \$2 million.

Similar opportunity-loss values can be calculated for the E_2 column, as is shown in Table 23.6, which is also referred to as a **regret table.**

TABLE 23.6 | Maximizing Benefit: The Minimax-Regret Criterion

This table, based on Table 23.4, shows the opportunity loss or regret values (in millions of dollars) associated with four possible action/event combinations. The highest of the possible regret values associated with each action is shown in the last column. The minimax-regret criterion suggests taking the least painful of these (highlighted in red), or action A_1. Under the circumstances, the decision maker might come to regret the lost opportunity of earning \$7 million in extra profit, but the regret might also be zero (if E_1 rather than E_2 occurs), and it could not be worse than \$7 million (as it would be if A_2 were chosen and E_1 were to occur).

Actions	Events: E_1 = weak demand for new product	Events: E_2 = strong demand for new product	Row Maximum
A_1 = constructing a small plant	8 − 8 = 0	12 − 5 = 7	**7 Minimax regret**
A_2 = constructing a large plant	8 − (−2) = 10	12 − 12 = 0	10

The application of the criterion of **minimax regret** is also illustrated in that table. According to this criterion, the decision maker identifies the highest possible (or maximum) regret value associated with each possible action, finds the lowest (or minimum) value among these maxima, and then chooses the action associated with this minimum of maximum regret values. (Note the highlighted figure in Table 23.6.)

MINIMIZING COST The minimax-regret criterion is applied similarly to cost-minimization problems, but the regret table itself is computed in a slightly different way. When the decision maker aims to minimize cost, the opportunity loss equals the difference between (1) the actual cost incurred as a result of taking a specified action and the subsequent occurrence of an event and (2) the minimum cost achievable for that event (the lowest cost in a given event column of our tables).

EXAMPLE PROBLEM 23.6

Rework Example Problem 23.3, using the criterion of *minimax regret.*

SOLUTION: See Table 23.7 on the next page.

TABLE 23.7 | Minimizing Cost: The Minimax-Regret Criterion

This table, based on Table 23.3, shows the opportunity loss or regret values (in millions of dollars) associated with four possible action/event combinations. The highest of the possible regret values associated with each action is shown in the last column. The minimax-regret criterion suggests taking the least painful of these (highlighted in red), or action A_1. Under the circumstances, the decision maker might come to regret the lost opportunity of reducing costs by \$4 million more, but the regret might also be zero (if E_1 rather than E_2 occurs), and it could not be worse than \$4 million (as it would be if A_2 were chosen and E_1 were to occur).

Actions	Events: E_1 = low level of demand and production	Events: E_2 = high level of demand and production	Row Maximum
A_1 = install small antipollution system	5 − 5 = 0	8 − 4 = 4	4 **Minimax regret**
A_2 = install large antipollution system	10 − 5 = 5	4 − 4 = 0	5

CRITICISMS OF NONPROBABILISTIC TECHNIQUES

When we survey the above solutions to our decision-making problems, we discover that the results differ depending on the criterion chosen. In our benefit-maximizing example, the maximin criterion suggests A_1 (the construction of a small plant), the maximax criterion suggests A_2 (the construction of a large plant), and the minimax-regret criterion suggests A_1 as well. Similarly different results were obtained in the cost-minimizing case as well. Such differences, however, should not surprise us. They merely reflect the underlying differences in decision-making philosophies that stress being careful, being daring, or minimizing future regret, respectively.

However, certain other problems arise with the above criteria that might make us think twice about applying them. We consider three among a longer list of such problems in the remainder of this section.

UNDUE SENSITIVITY TO IRRELEVANT FACTORS The results obtained by the use of these criteria are easily affected by irrelevant factors. Consider Table 23.2, and imagine a government offering a fixed subsidy of \$8 million, *regardless of the firm's action,* if demand should be weak. One would think that this incentive should not affect the firm's action, but under the maximin criterion it does: The E_1 column entries change from 8 and −2 to 16 and 6, the row minima change from 5 and −2 to 5 and 6, and the maximin action changes from A_1 to A_2.

Consider the same subsidy in the context of Table 23.3. The E_1 column entries (being costs) change from 5 and 10 to −3 and 2, the row maxima change from 8 and 10 to 8 and 4, and the minimax action changes from A_1 to A_2.

Although a fixed subsidy would not change the minimax-regret action, some other irrelevant factor easily might. Imagine that Table 23.2 contained a third possible action, A_3 = buying an established plant, with payoffs (in millions of dollars) of −5 and +20, respectively, for E_1 and E_2. The existence of this third alternative would change the Table 23.6 entries in the E_1 column from 0 and 10 to 0, 10, and 13, and it would change the E_2 column from 7 and 0 to 15, 8, and 0. Hence, the row maxima would become 15, 10, and 13, and the minimax-regret action would change from A_1 to A_2. But why should the mere existence of another (and rejected) alternative change the choice between the remaining alternatives?

UNDUE RELIANCE ON EXTREME VALUES Another factor that has worried decision makers is the fact that the above criteria ignore all payoffs except certain extreme values found in a given row. Consider again Table 23.2 and imagine that the 12 were changed to 12,000. Despite the drastic change, and the sudden possibility of making a profit of $12 *billion* by constructing a large plant, the maximin criterion would continue to counsel that action A_1 be taken and that a small plant be built in order to avoid a possible $2 million loss.

LACK OF CONSIDERATION FOR THE PROBABILITIES OF EVENTS All of the criteria ignore the probabilities of events. But, critics argue, even guesses could often be extremely helpful. If, in the example just cited (Table 23.2 with the 12 changed to 12,000), E_1 had a low probability and E_2 had a high probability, it would surely be foolish to apply the maximin criterion and forgo an almost certain $12 billion gain in order to avoid a highly unlikely $2 million loss. Indeed, many decision makers prefer the criteria discussed in the next sections because they do take probabilities into account.

23.4 Decision Making with Probabilities: Prior Analysis

Oftentimes a decision maker can develop fairly good estimates for the probabilities of alternative future events. Decision criteria that make use of such estimates include the *maximum-likelihood criterion,* the *maximization* (or *minimization*) *of expected monetary value,* the *minimization of expected opportunity loss* or *regret value,* and the *maximization of expected utility.* In this section, we will discuss the use of these criteria in **prior analysis.** This type of decision making under uncertainty employs probabilities, but only those available *prior to* gathering new experimental or sample evidence about the likelihood of alternative future events.

As noted in Section 8.10, *Revising Probabilities: Bayes' Theorem,* such probabilities are called *prior probabilities.* They are usually purely subjective and thus represent nothing but a personal degree of belief in the likelihood of some event. But they can also be objective and thus indicate the relative frequency with which the event in question is bound to occur if logic or past experience can be used as a guide. (Turn to Section 8.5 on page 289 to review the concepts of objective and subjective probability.)

MAXIMUM LIKELIHOOD

A decision maker using the **maximum-likelihood criterion** simply ignores all the events that might occur, except the most likely one, and selects the action that produces the optimal result (maximum benefit or minimum cost) associated with this most likely event. Table 23.8 on the next page, which is an adaptation of Table 23.1, illustrates the procedure.

Critics argue that using the maximum-likelihood criterion amounts to "playing ostrich" because it ignores so much that *might* happen. In this example, the best of all possible outcomes (12) is never even considered. In other cases, the preoccupation with the event of the highest probability might lead the decision maker to focus on an event with a probability of .1, while ignoring other events with a combined probability of .9 (but individual probabilities of less than .1).

TABLE 23.8 | Maximizing Benefit: The Maximum-Likelihood Criterion

This table shows the annual profits (in millions of dollars) associated with four possible action/event combinations. Given the assumed prior probabilities of the events, namely $p(E_1) = .7$ and $p(E_2) = .3$, the maximum-likelihood criterion leads a decision maker to focus entirely on the shaded E_1 column (because .7 is greater than .3) and to select the optimal result in that column (highlighted in red). Thus, A_1 is the action chosen by those who employ the maximum-likelihood criterion.

	Events	
Actions	E_1 = weak demand for new product $p(E_1) = .7$	E_2 = strong demand for new product $p(E_2) = .3$
A_1 = constructing a small plant	8	5
A_2 = constructing a large plant	−2	12

Proponents of this criterion, on the other hand, argue that people often do behave in precisely this fashion. They look at nothing but the most likely event, as evidenced, for example, in the famous *cobweb cycles* in agricultural and labor markets. Thus, farmers assume that the *most likely* future price of hogs is the current price. Hence, a low price in period 1 (because it is used as an indicator of a low price in period 2) discourages the raising of hogs in period 1 and leads to a shortage and an unexpectedly *high* price in period 2. This high price in period 2, in turn, encourages the raising of hogs in period 2 and leads to a surplus and an unexpectedly low price in period 3. And so it goes, low and high prices following one another eternally.[2]

EXPECTED MONETARY VALUE

A decision maker using the **expected-monetary-value criterion** determines an expected monetary value for each possible action and then selects the action with the optimal expected monetary value (the largest, if the objective is to maximize some benefit; the smallest, if the objective is to minimize some cost).

DEFINITION 23.6 The **expected monetary value** *(EMV)* of an action equals the sum of the weighted payoffs associated with that action, the weights being the probabilities of the alternative events that produce the various possible payoffs.

USING THE *EMV* CRITERION The following two example problems illustrate how we can use the expected-monetary-value criterion. Respectively, they deal with maximizing a benefit or minimizing a cost.

[2]For a more detailed discussion of agricultural and labor market cobweb cycles, see Heinz Kohler, *Intermediate Microeconomics: Theory and Applications,* 3rd ed. (Glenview, Ill.: Scott, Foresman and Company, 1990), pp. 192–195 and 371–373.

EXAMPLE PROBLEM 23.7

Consider the decision-making problem summarized by Table 23.8. Maximize the benefit by applying the *expected-monetary-value criterion.*

SOLUTION: See Table 23.9.

TABLE 23.9 | Maximizing Benefit: The Expected-Monetary-Value Criterion

This table shows the annual profits (in millions of dollars) associated with four possible action/event combinations. It also shows the expected monetary value of each possible action, based on the assumed prior probabilities of the events; namely, $p(E_1) = .7$ and $p(E_2) = .3$. Because the objective is to maximize benefit, the largest EMV is optimal. Thus, A_1 is the action chosen by those who employ the expected-monetary-value criterion.

	Events		
Actions	E_1 = weak demand for new product $p(E_1) = .7$	E_2 = strong demand for new product $p(E_2) = .3$	**Expected Monetary Value, *EMV***
A_1 = constructing a small plant	8	5	8(.7) + 5(.3) = **7.1** **Optimum**
A_2 = constructing a large plant	−2	12	−2(.7) + 12(.3) = 2.2

Note how a decision maker who consistently chooses A_1 when confronted with the type of situation given in Table 23.9 will, on average, gain \$7.1 million per year because \$8 million will be gained 70 percent of the time and \$5 million will be gained 30 percent of the time. In contrast, a consistent choice of nonoptimal A_2 would, in the long run, yield a gain of only \$2.2 million per year because \$2 million would be lost 70 percent of the time and \$12 million would be gained 30 percent of the time.

EXAMPLE PROBLEM 23.8

Review Example Problem 23.3. Minimize the cost by applying the *expected-monetary-value criterion*. Assume $p(E_1) = .7$ and $p(E_2) = .3$.

SOLUTION: See Table 23.10 on the next page.

Note how a decision maker who, when confronted with the type of situation given in Table 23.10, consistently chooses A_1 will, on average, incur costs of only \$5.9 million per year. In contrast, the nonoptimal choice of A_2 would, in the long run, produce costs of \$8.2 million per year.

FINDING PROBABILITIES FOR THE EMV CRITERION The probabilities used in the preceding two examples might be the decision maker's best guesses. It may well happen, however, that a decision maker has no idea about event probabilities whatsoever. In that case, many decision

TABLE 23.10 | Minimizing Cost: The Expected-Monetary-Value Criterion

This table shows the annual costs (in millions of dollars) associated with four possible action/event combinations. It also shows the expected monetary value of each possible action, based on the assumed prior probabilities of the events; namely, $p(E_1) = .7$ and $p(E_2) = .3$. Because the objective is to minimize cost, the smallest EMV is optimal. Thus, A_1 is the action chosen by those who employ the EMV criterion.

	Events		
Actions	E_1 = low level of demand and production $p(E_1) = .7$	E_2 = high level of demand and production $p(E_2) = .3$	**Expected Monetary Value, *EMV***
A_1 = install small antipollution system	5	8	5(.7) + 8(.3) = **5.9** **Optimum**
A_2 = install large antipollution system	10	4	10(.7) + 4(.3) = 8.2

theorists recommend assigning equal probabilities to all events. Given a list of collectively exhaustive and mutually exclusive events, the probability assigned to each then equals 1 divided by the number of such events. This procedure of assigning equal prior probabilities to all possible events (when absolutely nothing is known about the likelihood of occurrence of these events) is variously referred to as the **equal-likelihood criterion,** the **criterion of insufficient reason, Bayes' postulate,** or (because he popularized it, even though it was first suggested by Thomas Bayes) the **Laplace criterion.**

GRAPHICAL EXPOSITION The use of the expected-monetary-value criterion can also be depicted graphically, as in the decision tree of Figure 23.3. It is based on Figure 23.1 and, as the caption indicates, the decision-tree analysis leads to the same decision as Table 23.9. Because the graphical process of finding the optimal action involves starting at the terminal (ultimate payoff) points of the tree branches (at the "top" or right side of the tree) and then working backward along the branches to find expected monetary values for each fork, this type of graphical solution of a decision problem is called **backward induction.**

EXPECTED OPPORTUNITY LOSS

A decision maker using the **expected-opportunity-loss criterion** determines an expected opportunity loss, or expected regret value, for each possible action and then selects the action with the smallest of these values. This procedure *always* yields the same result as the expected-monetary-value criterion.

DEFINITION 23.7 The **expected opportunity loss *(EOL)*** or **expected regret value** of an action equals the sum of the weighted opportunity losses associated with that action, the weights being the probabilities of the alternative events that produce the various possible opportunity losses.

FIGURE 23.3 | A Decision Tree and the Expected-Monetary-Value Criterion

The application of the expected-monetary-value criterion is often depicted by means of a decision tree. Event probabilities are attached to each event branch. Then, by a process termed **backward induction,** *the ultimate payoff values appearing at the tips of the branches on the far right are translated, using these probabilities, into expected monetary values at each fork of the tree. (Here, the EMV values are $7.1 million at event point b, $2.2 million at event point c, and, ultimately, $7.1 million at action point a.) When maximizing benefit, a decision maker employing the EMV criterion will take the action leading to the highest EMV. (In this case, the decision maker will follow the branch from action point a to event point b.) By refusing to follow the alternative action branch (here from a to c) that leads to the lower EMV, the benefit-maximizing decision maker is said to "cut off" or "prune" the nonoptimal path through the tree. (Note the red lines suggesting a cut by the pruning shears.) This pruning leaves intact only the optimal path from a to b and beyond and makes the expected monetary value of the decision maker's action equal to $7.1 million as well.*

Note: *Branch pruning can take place only at action points, never at event points, because only the former are controlled by the decision maker.*

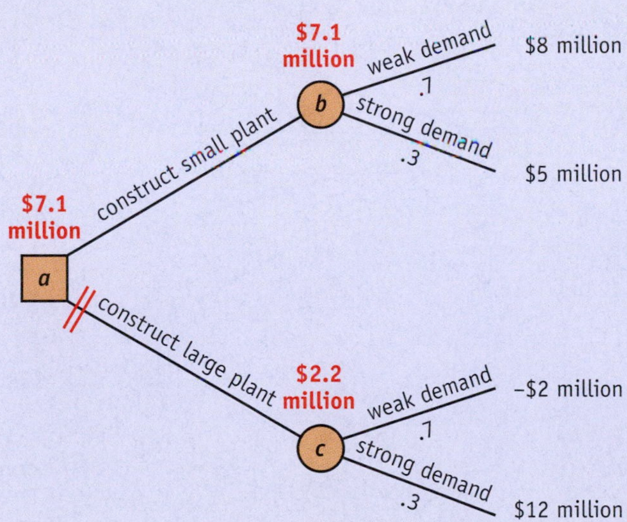

APPLICATION 23.1

THE DECISION TO SEED HURRICANES—A SECOND LOOK

Application 10.3 on page 414 employed the normal curve to analyze the decision to seed hurricanes. Decision-tree analysis can be employed with equal success and was, in fact, used in that decision. Figure 23.A on the next page is a copy of the government's analysis.

(continued)

Application 23.1 (continued)

FIGURE 23.A

The diagram is almost self-explanatory. The government, at action point a, can decide to seed or not to seed. Subsequently, at event points b or c, changes in wind speed will occur, with varying probabilities. The ultimate "payoff" is here measured in millions of dollars of property damage. Naturally, the government wants to minimize this cost. The branch from a to c is pruned. The decision is to go ahead and seed.

Can you figure out how the expected monetary values at b and c were calculated?

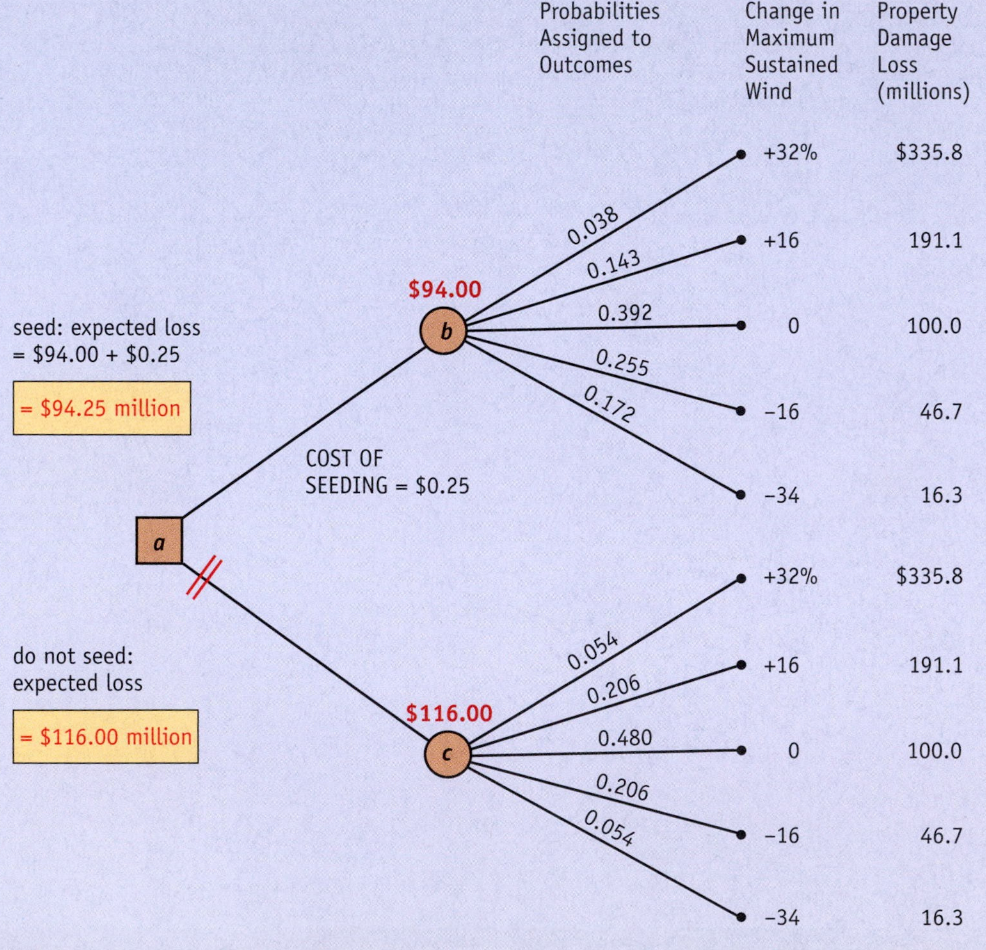

SOURCE: Adapted from R. A. Howard, J. E. Matheson, and D. W. North, "The Decision to Seed Hurricanes," *Science*, June 16, 1972, pp. 1191–1202. (This article is well worth reading, especially for its expanded discussion of the value of gathering additional information.)

USING THE *EOL* CRITERION The following two example problems illustrate how we can use the expected-opportunity-loss criterion. Respectively, they deal with maximizing a benefit or minimizing a cost.

EXAMPLE PROBLEM 23.9

Consider the decision-making problem summarized by Table 23.9. Solve it by applying the *expected-opportunity-loss criterion.*

SOLUTION: See Table 23.11.

TABLE 23.11 | Maximizing Benefit: The Expected-Opportunity-Loss Criterion

This table, based on Table 23.9, shows the opportunity-loss or regret values (in millions of dollars) associated with four possible action/event combinations. It also shows the expected opportunity loss for each possible action, based on the assumed prior probabilities of the events; namely, $p(E_1) = .7$ and $p(E_2) = .3$. The smallest EOL is optimal. Thus, A_1 is chosen by those who employ the expected-opportunity-loss criterion. It is no accident that this result is identical with that given by the expected-monetary-value criterion (Table 23.9).

Actions	Events: E_1 = weak demand for new product $p(E_1) = .7$	Events: E_2 = strong demand for new product $p(E_2) = .3$	Expected Opportunity Loss, *EOL*
A_1 = constructing a small plant	8 − 8 = 0	12 − 5 = 7	0(.7) + 7(.3) = **2.1** **Optimum**
A_2 = constructing a large plant	8 − (−2) = 10	12 − 12 = 0	10(.7) + 0(.3) = 7

Note how a decision maker who consistently chooses A_1 when confronted with the type of situation given in Table 23.11 will, on average, incur an opportunity loss of $2.1 million per year because that loss will be zero 70 percent of the time and equal to $7 million 30 percent of the time. In contrast, a consistent choice of nonoptimal A_2 would, in the long run, produce an opportunity loss of $7 million per year because such a loss would equal $10 million 70 percent of the time and be zero 30 percent of the time.

EXAMPLE PROBLEM 23.10

Consider the decision-making problem summarized by Table 23.10. Solve it by applying the *expected-opportunity-loss criterion.*

SOLUTION: See Table 23.12 on the next page.

TABLE 23.12 | Minimizing Cost: The Expected-Opportunity-Loss Criterion

This table, based on Table 23.10, shows the opportunity-loss or regret values (in millions of dollars) associated with four possible action/event combinations. It also shows the expected opportunity loss for each possible action, based on the assumed prior probabilities of the events; namely, $p(E_1) = .7$ and $p(E_2) = .3$. The smallest EOL is optimal; thus, A_1 is chosen by those who employ the expected-opportunity-loss criterion. It is no accident that this result is identical with that given by the expected-monetary-value criterion (Table 23.10).

	Events		
Actions	E_1 = low level of demand and production $p(E_1) = .7$	E_2 = high level of demand and production $p(E_2) = .3$	**Expected Opportunity Loss, *EOL***
A_1 = install small antipollution system	5 − 5 = 0	8 − 4 = 4	0(.7) + 4(.3) = **1.2** **Optimum**
A_2 = install large antipollution system	10 − 5 = 5	4 − 4 = 0	5(.7) + 0(.3) = 3.5

EXPECTED UTILITY

All of the decision-making criteria discussed so far have employed *monetary* outcome measures. Yet critics have argued that using money to measure outcomes is a mistake, that people will invariably take those actions that maximize their welfare or *utility,* and that actions that maximize monetary benefit or minimize monetary cost often do not coincide with those that maximize utility. We can use the situation depicted in Table 23.13 to illustrate what these critics have in mind.

Would the typical decision maker really be indifferent between actions A_1 (investing $100 million in vineyards) and A_2 (investing $100 million in the auto industry) just because their expected monetary values are equal? Critics argue that the decision maker would not be indifferent because A_2, unlike A_1, involves *risk.* Choosing A_2 over A_1 is equivalent to taking a gamble. It involves giving up a sure thing (a $15 million return from action A_1, regardless of which event occurs) for an uncertain thing (*either* a $25 million return if E_1 occurs *or* a $5 million return if E_2 occurs).

TYPES OF GAMBLES True enough, the gamble between A_1 and A_2 would be a **fair gamble** in the sense that the expected monetary value of what is given up precisely equals the expected monetary value of what is received. Consider how people who give up A_1 give up the certainty of receiving $15 million. They also know that they will receive, *on average,* $15 million from action A_2. However, if critics are right, and most people would *not* take this fair gamble, most people would be even less inclined to take an **unfair gamble.** In such a gamble, the expected monetary value of what is given up exceeds the expected monetary value of what is received. By changing all the entries of 15 in the A_1 row of Table 23.13 to 16, for example, action A_2 would be turned into an unfair gamble. Indeed, many people (critics assert) would even reject many a

TABLE 23.13 | Doubts about the Expected-Monetary-Value Criterion

This table shows the annual profits (in millions of dollars) associated with four possible action/event combinations. It also shows the expected monetary value of each possible action, based on the assumed prior probabilities of the events, namely $p(E_1) = p(E_2) = .5$. According to the EMV criterion, a decision maker would be indifferent between the two actions, but critics argue that most people would decisively opt for A_1.

Actions	Events		Expected Monetary Value, *EMV*
	E_1 = oil price rises moderately $p(E_1) = .5$	E_2 = oil price rises sharply $p(E_2) = .5$	
A_1 = investing $100 million in vineyards	15	15	15(.5) + 15(.5) = **15**
A_2 = investing $100 million in auto industry	25	5	25(.5) + 5(.5) = **15**

more-than-fair gamble in which the expected monetary value of what is given up is less than the expected monetary value of what is received. By changing all the entries of 15 in the A_1 row of Table 23.13 to 14, for example, action A_2 would be turned into a more-than-fair gamble.

THE ST. PETERSBURG PARADOX The apparent paradox of people refusing to take fair gambles was first solved some 250 years ago. A Swiss mathematician, Daniel Bernoulli (1700–1782), studied gamblers at the casinos of St. Petersburg, and he considered this game between two persons, A and B:

> A fair coin is tossed until heads appears. If heads appears on the first toss, A pays B \$1. If heads appears for the first time on the second toss, A pays B \$2. If heads appears first on the third toss, A pays B \$4. And so on, with A always paying $\$2^{n-1}$ at the *n*th toss if heads appears.

If playing this game is to be a *fair* gamble, what fee, Bernoulli asked, should B be willing to pay A for the privilege of playing this game? Because the player of a fair game is never asked to pay more than the expected monetary value of gain, this value can be calculated as suggested in Table 23.14 on the next page.

Given a probability of .5 for heads to appear on the first toss, the expected monetary value of gain is $\$1(.5) = \$.50$ if the game ends after the first toss. Given a probability of $(.5)^2 = .25$ for heads to appear first on the second toss, the expected monetary value of gain is $\$2(.5)^2 = \$2(.25) = \$.50$ if the game ends after the second toss. And so it goes. Thus, the expected monetary value of gain when playing this game is the sum of the expected monetary values of all possible outcomes, or the infinite series $\$.50 + \$.50 + \ldots + \$.50 = \infty$. Yet people are clearly not willing to pay an infinite sum of money for the privilege of playing this game, even though such a payment would make the gamble precisely fair.

SOLVING THE PARADOX We probably could solve the paradox by postulating that gamblers cannot possibly be convinced to take this game seriously. How could they be so gullible as to believe that payoff would actually be made should they be lucky enough to win a large sum? If

TABLE 23.14 | The St. Petersburg Game

The gain from playing the St. Petersburg game has an expected monetary value of infinity (equal to the sum of the last column of this table).

Toss Number (1)	Payoff if Heads First Appears at Given Toss (2)	Probability of Heads First Appearing at Given Toss (3)	Expected Monetary Value = Payoff × Probability (4) = (2) × (3)
1	$1	.5	$.50
2	2	$(.5)^2$	$.50
3	4	$(.5)^3$	$.50
4	8	$(.5)^4$	$.50
5	16	$(.5)^5$	$.50
.	.	.	.
.	.	.	.
.	.	.	.
			Sum: ∞

heads did not appear until the 44th toss, for example, the required payoff would equal more than the entire gross national income of the United States!

Bernoulli, however, had a different idea. He argued that people making decisions under uncertainty were not attempting to maximize expected *monetary* values, but maximized expected *utilities* instead. He thought that the **total utility of money,** the overall welfare people derived from the possession of a given quantity of money, was rising the more money people had. Yet, he also thought that the **marginal utility of money,** the change in total utility that was associated with a one-dollar change in the quantity of money, was declining the more money people had. Any person starting with $500, for example, would, therefore, place a smaller subjective value on gaining an extra sum than on losing an equal amount. Any game with an equal probability of gaining and losing a given amount was, therefore, fair in monetary terms but unfair in utility terms. The game's expected utility was negative. No wonder people refused to play it!

Figure 23.4 contains a hypothetical person's **utility-of-money function**—the relationship, that is, between alternative amounts of money the person might possess and the different utility totals associated with these amounts. In accordance with Bernoulli's postulate, the graph assumes that the *total* utility of money rises with greater amounts of it. (Note how the red line rises from 0 toward *C*.) The *marginal* utility of money, on the other hand (measured by the *slope* of the total utility curve) declines with greater amounts of money. (Note how the slope equals 8.22/300 between *B* and *A*, but only 5.92/300 between *A* and *C*.)

In Figure 23.4, the total utility of money, *U*, is related to the amount of money, $, by the equation $U = \sqrt{\$}$. Thus, a person with $500 is assumed to receive a total of $\sqrt{500} = 22.36$ *utils* (units of utility) from it (point *A*). The same person would, however, receive only 5.92 *extra* utils from an added $300 (when moving from *A* to *C*) but would lose 8.22 utils by a loss of $300

FIGURE 23.4 | The Utility of Money

This graph illustrates a person's utility function that is characterized by a declining marginal utility of money. In this example, the total utility of money, U, is related to the amount of money, \$, by the equation $U = \sqrt{\$}$. Other relationships are also possible.

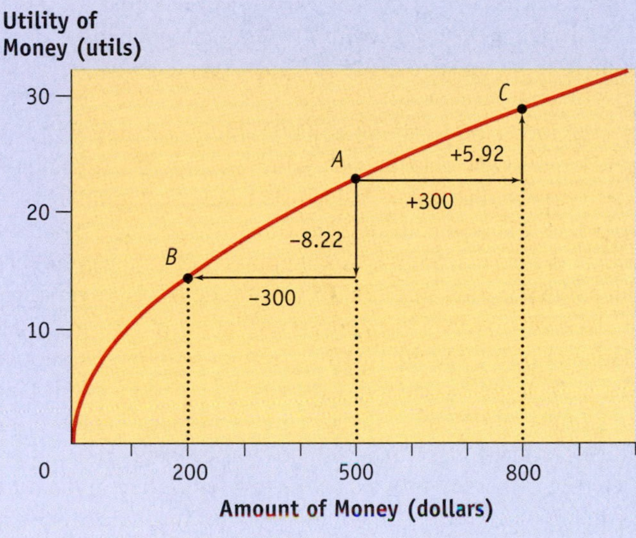

(when moving from *A* to *B*). Given this type of utility function, the St. Petersburg paradox is easily solved. While the expected *monetary value* of the game equals infinity, its expected *utility* equals

$$\begin{aligned} EU &= \sqrt{1}(.5) + \sqrt{2}(.5)^2 + \sqrt{4}(.5)^3 + \sqrt{8}(.5)^4 + \sqrt{16}(.5)^5 + \ldots \\ &= 1(1/2) + \sqrt{2}(1/4) + 2(1/8) + 2\sqrt{2}(1/16) + 4(1/32) + \ldots \\ &= 1/2 + \sqrt{2}(1/4) + 1/4 + \sqrt{2}(1/8) + 1/8 + \ldots \\ &= 1 + \sqrt{2}(1/2) = 1.707 \text{ utils} \end{aligned}$$

The equation $U = \sqrt{\$}$ implies $U^2 = \$$. Hence, an expected utility of 1.707 translates into a dollar equivalent of $(1.707)^2 = \$2.91$. This \$2.91, then, is the far-less-than-infinite amount that a person who maximized expected utility, and possessed the $U = \sqrt{\$}$ utility function, would pay for the privilege of playing the St. Petersburg game!

Someone else who also maximized expected utility, but possessed a different utility function, would act quite differently. This difference brings us to an important conclusion: Even if people maximize the expected utility rather than the expected monetary value of an action when facing uncertainty, we cannot predict their behavior without a knowledge of their utility functions. Indeed, the shape of these functions reveals important information about people's attitudes concerning the spread of possible outcomes of their action around the action's expected value. The extent of such spread (as from 15 down to 5 and up to 25 for action A_2 in Table 23.13) in fact measures the *risk* of an action, and people can view risk in one of three ways. They can be averse to it. They can be neutral toward it. They can seek it out.

RISK AVERSION Imagine that the investor whose choices were pictured in Table 23.13 possesses the type of utility function postulated by Bernoulli and illustrated in panel (a) of Figure 23.5. Action A_1, as we noted earlier, would bring the investor a profit of $15,000 a year, regardless of what happens to the price of oil. This amount of money is associated, according to point *B* on the utility function, with a total utility of 0*b*. Action A_2, on the other hand, would bring the investor, with equal probability, a profit of $5,000 a year *or* of $25,000 a year. As we can see from points *A* and *C*, respectively, the associated utilities equal 0*a* and 0*c*. *The expected* utility from an equally weighted $5,000 or $25,000 a year, however, equals the sum of half of 0*a* plus half of 0*c*. This sum is shown in the graph by utility 0*d*. It corresponds to point *D*, located on the dashed line connecting *A* and *C* and above the $15,000 expected *monetary* value of the $5,000 or $25,000 gamble.

Note: The expected utility of receiving $5,000 with a probability of .2 or $25,000 with a probability of .8 could similarly be read on dashed line *AC*, but at a point above the $5,000(.2) + $25,000(.8) = $21,000 expected monetary value of this different gamble.

Whenever a person in this way considers the utility (as at point *B*) of a certain prospect of money to be higher than the expected utility (as at point *D*) of an uncertain prospect of equal expected monetary value, the person is said to hold an attitude of **risk aversion.**

The attitude of risk aversion is always present when a person's marginal utility of money, shown here by the slope of utility function 0*ABC*, declines with larger amounts of money.

Risk aversion is, in fact, quite common. Consider how people do all kinds of things, small and large, to *escape* gambles. In many countries, they still place person-to-person calls instead of station-to-station calls. At airports, banks, and post offices, they prefer single lines feeding to many clerks to the chance of getting into a slow or fast line. They diversify their assets and do not "place all their eggs in one basket." They buy plenty of insurance. They reject fair gambles, as our risk-averse investor would by taking action A_1 (to gain utility 0*b*) rather than action A_2 (that has an equal expected monetary value but a smaller expected utility 0*d*).

RISK NEUTRALITY Let us imagine instead that panel (b) of Figure 23.5 were to illustrate our investor's utility function. In this case, the utility of action A_1, with its certain payoff of $15,000 a year, would equal 0*f*, corresponding to point *F*. Action A_2 would bring, according to points *E* and *G*, utility of 0*e* or 0*g*, and with equal probability. The expected utility of this gamble, however, would also equal 0*f*. (A straight line between *E* and *G* leads to point *F* above the $15,000 expected monetary value of the $5,000 or $25,000 gamble.)

Whenever a person, in the fashion of panel (b), point F, considers the utility of a certain prospect of money to be equal to the expected utility of an uncertain prospect of equal expected monetary value, the person is said to hold an attitude of **risk neutrality.** This attitude is always present when a person's marginal utility of money, shown here by the slope of utility function 0*EFG*, remains constant with larger amounts of money.

Risk neutrality is not very common. But those who advocate using the expected-monetary-value criterion implicitly assume risk neutrality. If all people were risk-neutral, our investor would be truly indifferent between actions A_1 and A_2 because, as we saw, their expected monetary values are equal. By the same token, a risk-neutral person would be willing to pay $100 for the privilege of taking each of the following fair gambles, because the expected monetary value of each of these is also $100:

- a 99 percent chance of getting $101.01 and a 1 percent chance of getting nothing
- a 50 percent chance of getting $101 and a 50 percent chance of getting $99
- a 1 percent chance of getting $10,000 and a 99 percent chance of getting nothing
- a 1 percent chance of getting $1 million, a 1 percent chance of losing $990,000, and a 98 percent chance of getting nothing

FIGURE 23.5 | Attitudes toward Risk

This set of graphs illustrates three basic attitudes toward risk: risk aversion in panel (a), risk neutrality in panel (b), and risk seeking in panel (c). These attitudes correspond, respectively, to declining, constant, and increasing marginal utilities of money.

(a) Risk Aversion

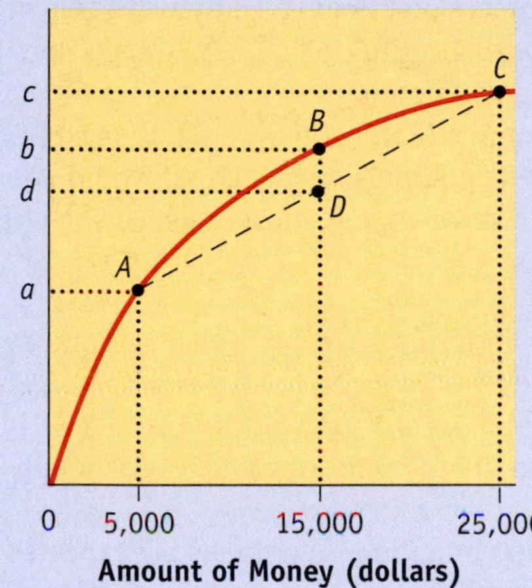

(b) Risk Neutrality

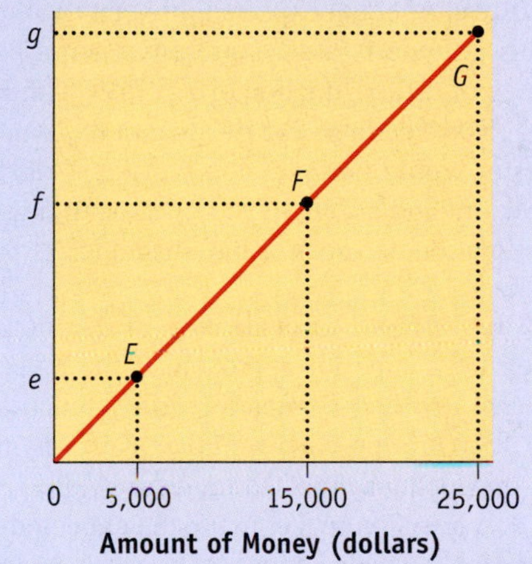

(c) Risk Seeking

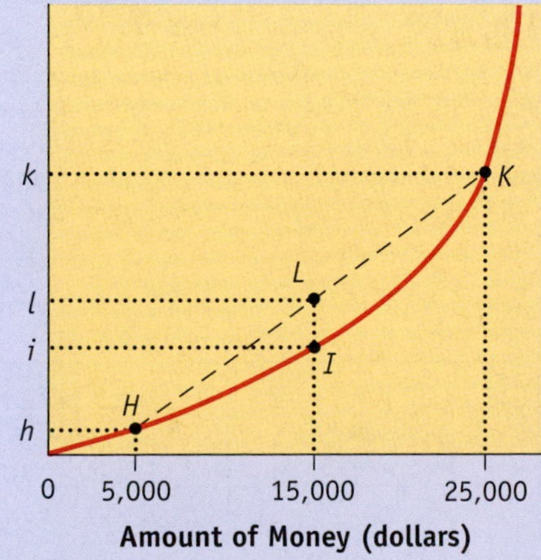

After thinking about it, you might pay the $100 price for the first two of these gambles. But do you have the sweepstakes mentality to go after the third? Are you ready for the Russian roulette of the last?

RISK SEEKING What if panel (c) of Figure 23.5 illustrated our investor's utility function? In this case, the utility of action A_1, with its certain payoff of $15,000 a year, would equal 0*i*, corresponding to point *I*. Action A_2 would bring, according to points *H* and *K*, utility of 0*h* or 0*k*, and with equal probability. By the now familiar procedure, we can establish the expected utility of this gamble as 0*l*, corresponding to point *L* on dashed line *HK*.

Whenever a person, in the fashion of panel (c), considers the utility (as at point *I*) of a certain prospect of money to be lower than the expected utility (as at point *L*) of an uncertain prospect of equal expected monetary value, the person is said to hold an attitude of **risk seeking.** This attitude is always present when a person's marginal utility of money, shown here by the slope of utility function 0*HIK,* rises with larger amounts of money.

Risk seeking, like risk neutrality, is not very common. If all people were risk seekers, our investor would prefer action A_2 to A_1. And all of us, like compulsive gamblers, would constantly seek out and accept huge riches-or-ruin gambles. In fact, of course, most of us have the opposite inclination and seek to buy insurance.

CONCLUSION An evaluation of decision outcomes in terms of utility rather than money may well be a superior approach. If the investor depicted in Table 23.13, for example, were risk-averse and had Bernoulli's utility function, the decision problem could be laid out as in Table 23.15. This approach would explain why the investor would prefer A_1 to A_2, even though A_1 and A_2 have equal expected monetary values.

A decision maker using the **expected-utility criterion,** thus, determines the expected utility for each possible action and then selects the action that maximizes expected utility. The **expected utility *(EU)*** of an action equals the sum of the weighted utilities associated with that action, the weights being the probabilities of the alternative events that produce the various possible utility payoffs.

TABLE 23.15 | Maximizing Expected Utility

This table, based on Table 23.13, shows the utility associated with four possible action/event combinations for a risk-averse person with a utility function of $U = \sqrt{\$}$. The table also shows the expected utility of each possible action, based on the assumed prior probabilities of the events; namely, $p(E_1) = p(E_2) = .5$. Because the objective is to maximize expected utility, the largest EU is optimal. Thus, A_1 is the action chosen by those who employ the expected-utility criterion.

	Events		
Actions	E_1 = oil price rises moderately $p(E_1) = .5$	E_2 = oil price rises sharply $p(E_2) = .5$	**Expected Utility, *EU***
A_1 = investing $100 million in vineyards	$\sqrt{15} = 3.87$	$\sqrt{15} = 3.87$	3.87(.5) + 3.87(.5) = **3.87 Optimum**
A_2 = investing $100 million in auto industry	$\sqrt{25} = 5$	$\sqrt{5} = 2.24$	5(.5) + 2.24(.5) = 3.62

WHEN DECISION ANALYSIS CAME OF AGE

A mere three decades ago, decision analysis was still an experimental management technique. The idea that a choice facing a decision maker could be expressed as a mathematical function of probability and utility numbers (that measured, respectively, the decision maker's uncertainties and value judgments) and that the best action was the one with the highest expected utility had just begun to move out of business schools and into practical application in the business world. By the early 1980s, however, decision making, with the help of quantitative models that incorporated personal judgment, had gained acceptance in many large corporations and government departments.

For example, the AIL Division of Cutler-Hammer, Inc., was once offered the opportunity to acquire the defense-market rights to a new flight-safety-system patent. The inventor claimed he had a strong patent position as well as technical superiority, but the market for the product depended on legislative action and was thus very uncertain. Management had to decide fast whether to purchase the rights to the new patent or to reject the offer. It used standard decision-tree techniques. Its initial analysis appears in Figure 23.B.

INITIAL ANALYSIS. The immediate choice (at action point *a*) was the purchase of a six-month option on the patent rights or rejection of the offer. Six months hence (at event point *b*), analysts judged, there was a 71 percent chance of exercising the option and a 29 percent chance of not doing so. Three years down the road (at event point *c*), there was a 15 percent chance of getting, and an 85 percent chance of not getting, a first defense contract. Five years down the road (at event point *d*), finally, there was a 25 percent chance of getting a second defense contract and a 75 percent chance

FIGURE 23.B

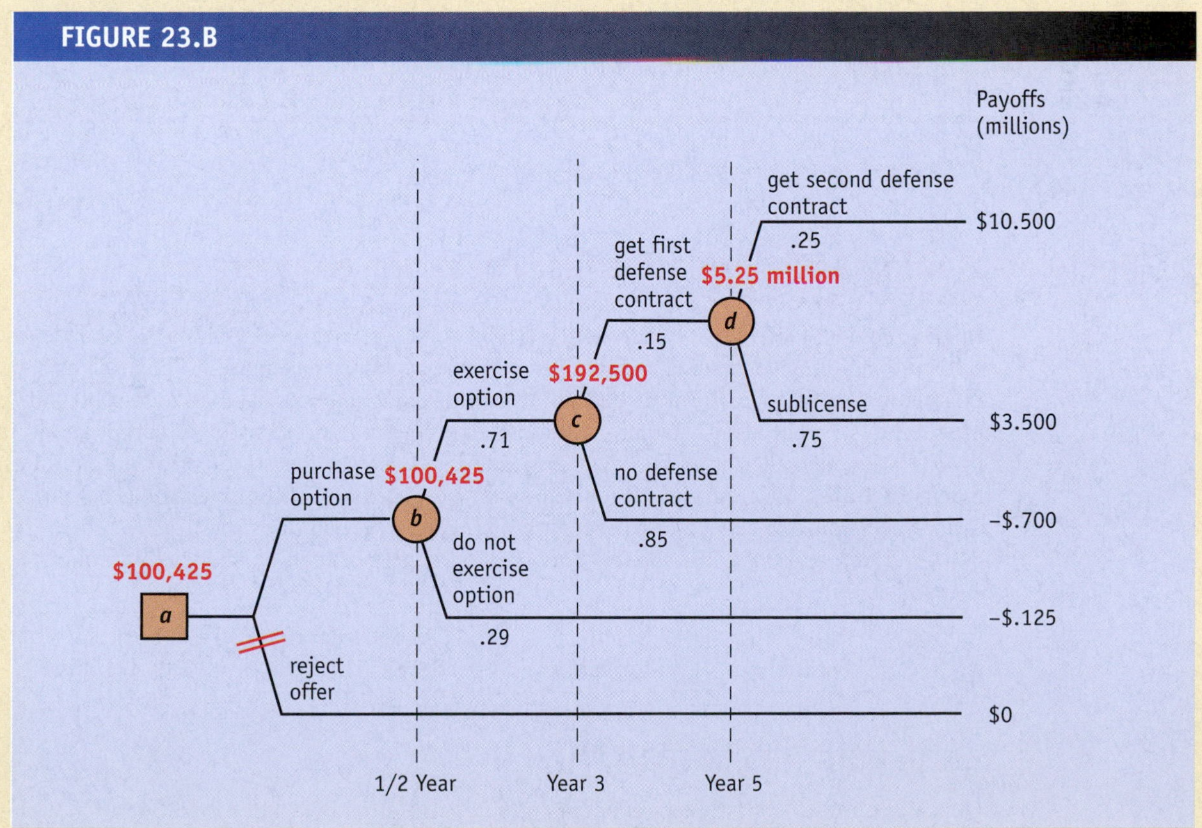

(continued)

Application 23.2 (continued)

of being able to sublicense. Thus, there were five possible outcomes. Using the technique of backward induction, company executives computed the expected monetary values given in red. The tree was pruned as shown. Purchasing the option was worth \$100,425. Rejecting the offer was worth \$0.

FURTHER ANALYSIS. Upon further analysis, however, management discovered a third possible action at *a*; namely, rejecting the offer and seeking a sublicense later on. That approach was shown to yield an expected value of \$49,800, about half of the \$100,425 expected monetary value of the option-purchase route. Nevertheless, being risk-averse, management chose the newly discovered third alternative. Its analysis showed the *EMV* of \$49,800 to be composed of a 94 percent chance of zero gain or loss and a 6 percent chance of gaining \$830,000. On the other hand, as we can figure from the diagram, the *EMV* of \$100,425 is provided by a riskier route composed of a 29 percent chance of losing \$125,000, a .71(85) = 60 percent chance of losing \$700,000, and a .71(15) = 11 percent chance of a positive return with an expectation of \$5.25 million. Thus, management effectively maximized *expected utility* rather than monetary value.

WIDE APPLICATIONS. Since that time long ago, many other companies have also used the decision-tree technique. Ford has decided in this way whether to produce its own tires (at the time, Ford executives could hardly foresee the Firestone debacle in 2000–2001) and whether to stop producing convertibles. Honeywell used the technique to decide whether to pursue certain new weapons programs. Pillsbury used it to determine whether to switch from a box to a bag for a certain grocery product (and whether it was worthwhile to make a market test of the issue). Southern Railway employed it to choose whether to electrify part of its system. Gulf Oil used it to decide whether to look for oil at certain sites. ITT used decision trees in deciding whether to make certain capital investments.

SOURCE: Adapted from Jacob W. Ulvila and Rex V. Brown, "Decision Analysis Comes of Age," *Harvard Business Review*, September–October 1982, pp. 130–141. For a fascinating discussion of the use of decision trees in legal disputes, see Samuel E. Bodily, "When Should You Go to Court?" *Harvard Business Review*, May–June 1981, pp. 103–113. Figure 23.B reprinted by permission of the *Harvard Business Review*.

23.5 Decision Making with Probabilities: Posterior Analysis

In the previous section, we discussed various forms of decision making that made use of prior probabilities concerning events over which a decision maker has no control. In contrast, **posterior analysis** is a form of decision making under uncertainty that starts out with prior probabilities, proceeds to gather additional experimental or sample evidence about event probabilities, and then uses this new evidence to transform the set of prior probabilities, by means of Bayes' theorem, into a revised set of posterior probabilities with the help of which a final decision is reached. The procedure of revising probabilities, first discussed in Section 8.10, *Revising Probabilities: Bayes' Theorem,* on page 322, can be sketched as follows:

Prior Probability	+	New Information	+	Application of Bayes' Theorem	=	Posterior Probability

GATHERING NEW INFORMATION

Consider our decision problem concerning the construction of either a small or a large plant to manufacture and sell a new product (Table 23.9 on page 1125). The decision maker's prior probabilities for the two possible events (E_1 = weak demand and E_2 = strong demand) were given as $p(E_1) = .7$ and $p(E_2) = .3$, but they might have been based on nothing but a hunch. Instead of proceeding with the analysis on that basis (as illustrated in Tables 23.9 and 23.11, or in

Figure 23.3), the decision maker might decide to gather new information about the event probabilities. The required research can take many different forms. In this particular case, the firm might conduct a consumer survey to gauge the likely strength of future demand. In other instances, other approaches might be more appropriate:

- obtaining a long-range weather forecast, perhaps, or a forecast of future prices and wages
- sampling inputs bought or output produced for quality
- building a pilot plant to test a new production process
- conducting a seismic test (that can indicate the likely presence of oil deposits)
- taking an aptitude test (that can indicate future job performance)
- even paying a bribe (that can provide inside information on the likely reaction of a TV network to a new pilot that might be offered to it by a filmmaker)

Unfortunately, none of this new information will be perfect. Even the best of aptitude tests will flunk some job applicants who later turn out to be superb, while passing others who later turn out to be incompetent. Even the best of seismic tests can deny the presence of oil in a field that is already producing oil, while confirming the presence of oil at a site that is later proven to be dry. Thus, the decision maker who wants to know about weak or strong demand for the new product will still have to contend with uncertainty, even if a consumer survey is conducted and a fancy market-research report is received. Indeed, the market-research firm's past record may be that indicated by Table 23.16.

TABLE 23.16 | The Past Record of a Market-Research Firm

This table shows the probabilities that a firm's market research will discover the true state of affairs about the demand for a new product. Based on past performance, the conditional probability is .9 that the firm's research result indicates weak demand when demand is in fact weak. It is .1 that the result indicates strong demand when demand is in fact weak. Similarly, the conditional probability is .2 that the firm's research result indicates weak demand when demand is in fact strong. It is .8 that the result indicates strong demand when demand is in fact strong.

	True State of Affairs	
Market-Research Result	E_1 = weak demand	E_2 = strong demand
R_1 = demand will be weak	$p(R_1 \mid E_1) = .9$	$p(R_1 \mid E_2) = .2$
R_2 = demand will be strong	$p(R_2 \mid E_1) = .1$	$p(R_2 \mid E_2) = .8$

As the caption explains, although the firm's record is not perfect, its "batting average" is quite impressive. We can place a fairly high degree of confidence in the research firm's reports. When it predicts weak demand, it is correct 90 percent of the time. When it predicts strong demand, it is correct 80 percent of the time.

APPLYING BAYES' THEOREM

Let us now suppose that our decision maker does consult the research firm and is given a report concerning the likely intensity of future demand. What happens next depends on the content of the report.

A REPORT OF WEAK DEMAND If the report indicates weak demand (the research result is R_1), the data contained in the first row of Table 23.16 come into play as *Bayes' theorem* is applied. According to Formula 8.K on page 323, the posterior probability of an event is computed as

$$p(\text{E}|\text{R}) = \frac{p(\text{E}) \times p(\text{R}|\text{E})}{p(\text{E}) \times p(\text{R}|\text{E}) + p(\overline{\text{E}}) \times p(\text{R}|\overline{\text{E}})}$$

where E denotes the event, $\overline{\text{E}}$ its complement, and R the research result.

In our case, therefore (using the above-noted prior probabilities and the data of Table 23.16),

$$p(\text{E}_1|\text{R}_1) = \frac{p(\text{E}_1) \times p(\text{R}_1|\text{E}_1)}{p(\text{E}_1) \times p(\text{R}_1|\text{E}_1) + p(\text{E}_2) \times p(\text{R}_1|\text{E}_2)} = \frac{.7(.9)}{.7(.9) + .3(.2)} = .91$$

and

$$p(\text{E}_2|\text{R}_1) = \frac{p(\text{E}_2) \times p(\text{R}_1|\text{E}_2)}{p(\text{E}_2) \times p(\text{R}_1|\text{E}_2) + p(\text{E}_1) \times p(\text{R}_1|\text{E}_1)} = \frac{.3(.2)}{.3(.2) + .7(.9)} = .09$$

A REPORT OF STRONG DEMAND What if the research firm's report had predicted a strong demand for the new product (the research result had been R_2)? In that case, an analogous set of calculations would have been performed:

$$p(\text{E}_1|\text{R}_2) = \frac{p(\text{E}_1) \times p(\text{R}_2|\text{E}_1)}{p\text{E}_1) \times p(\text{R}_2|\text{E}_1) + p(\text{E}_2) \times p(\text{R}_2|\text{E}_2)} = \frac{.7(.1)}{.7(.1) + .3(.8)} = .23$$

and

$$p(\text{E}_2|\text{R}_2) = \frac{p(\text{E}_2) \times p(\text{R}_2|\text{E}_2)}{p(\text{E}_2) \times p(\text{R}_2|\text{E}_2) + p(\text{E}_1) \times p(\text{R}_2|\text{E}_1)} = \frac{.3(.8)}{.3(.8) + .7(.1)} = .77$$

FINDING THE OPTIMAL STRATEGY

If our decision maker were risk-neutral and cared to maximize expected *monetary* value (which we will assume), an optimal strategy could now be mapped out with the help of these posterior probabilities. An **optimal strategy,** also called **Bayes' strategy,** is a complete plan specifying the actions to be taken at each available action point, if the expected (monetary or utility) payoff is to be the best one available. The procedure is illustrated in Figure 23.6.

Figure 23.6 illustrates the example discussed so far in which a decision maker, at action point *a*, has decided to make a consumer survey in order to gauge the likely intensity of future demand. This decision inevitably takes us to event point *b*. At event point *b*, the survey will predict either weak or strong future demand, taking us to either action point *c* or action point *d*. Once located at either *c* or *d*, the decision maker must then act and construct either a small plant or a large plant. As a result, one of the event points labeled *f* through *i* is reached, and chance will decide whether demand is in fact weak or strong. The right-hand column shows the payoffs, which are equal to those given throughout this chapter (starting with Table 23.1), but are reduced by an assumed $100,000 cost of taking the survey.

FIGURE 23.6 | Posterior Decision-Tree Analysis

This decision tree summarizes the development of an optimal strategy, while making use of posterior probabilities. (All dollar amounts are in millions.)

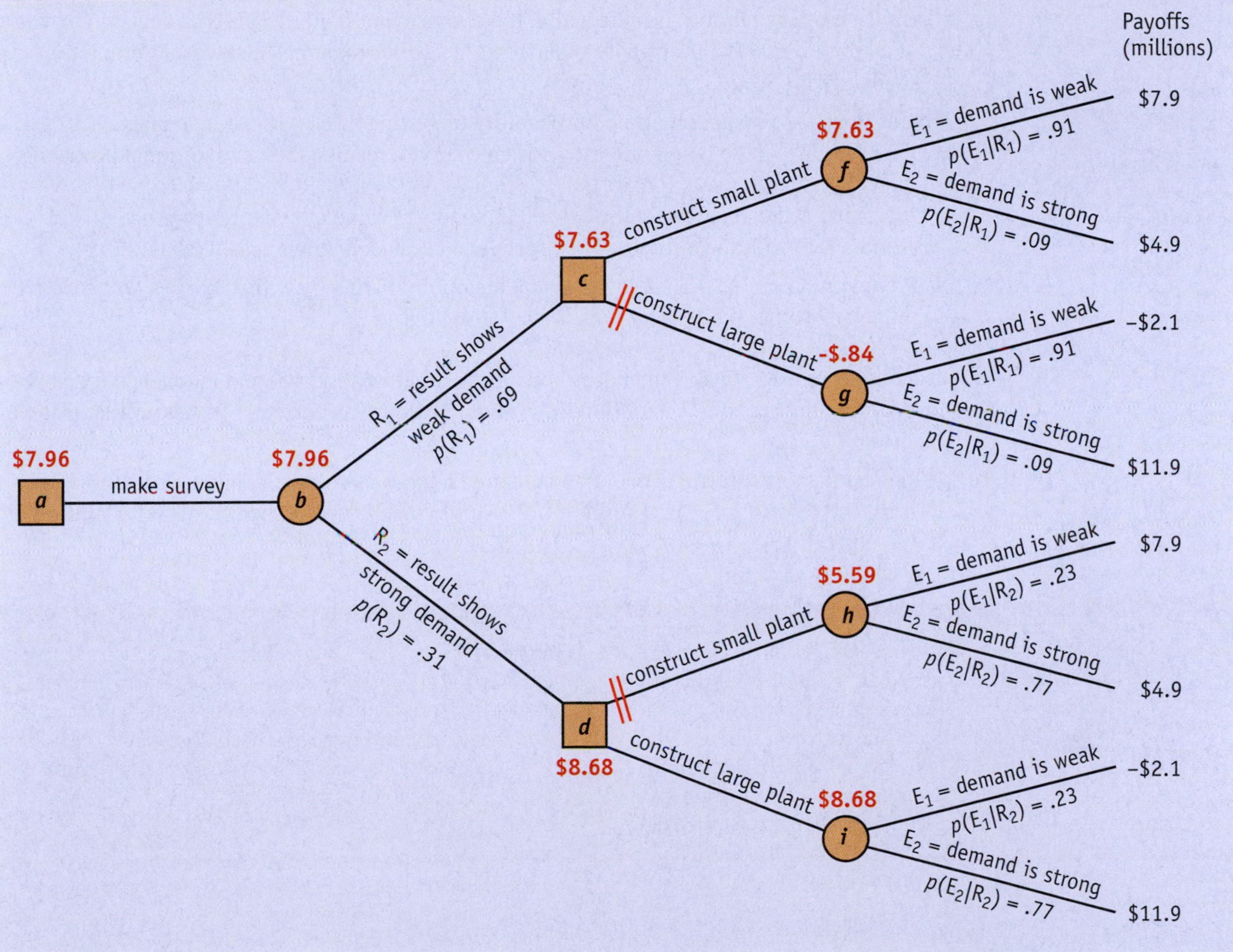

BACKWARD INDUCTION We can find the optimal strategy by using the process of backward induction and systematically examining each of the (encircled) event points in our graph.

Event point *f*. Given the conditional probabilities of $p(E_1|R_1) = .91$ and $p(E_2|R_1) = .09$ that were calculated above, the decision maker can calculate the expected monetary value at point *f* as \$7.9(.91) + \$4.9(.09) = \$7.63 (million). This number is highlighted in red above event point *f*.

Event point *g*. Given the same conditional probabilities as at *f*, the decision maker can calculate the expected monetary value at point *g* as −\$2.1(.91) + \$11.9(.09) = −\$.84 (million). This number is indicated in red above event point *g*. Surely, a decision maker at action point *c* would want to move toward *f* rather than *g*. Thus, we can prune the branch going from *c* to *g* (note the red cut) and carry the red *EMV* figure at *f* to *c*.

Event point *h*. The probabilities are now different as we assume having received a survey report indicating strong demand (R_2). Given the conditional probabilities calculated above, the decision maker can calculate the expected monetary value at point *h* as \$7.9(.23) + \$4.9(.77) = \$5.59 (million). This number is indicated in red above point *h*.

Event point *i*. Given the same conditional probabilities as at point *h*, the decision maker can calculate the expected monetary value at point *i* as −\$2.1(.23) + \$11.9(.77) = \$8.68 (million). This number is indicated in red above event point *i*. Surely, a decision maker at action point *d* would want to move toward *i* rather than *h*. Thus, we can prune the branch going from *d* to *h* (note the red cut) and carry the red *EMV* figure at *i* to *d*.

Event point *b*. The unconditional probability of getting survey result R_1 equals .7(.9) + .3(.2) = .69. There being only two possible survey results, the unconditional probability of getting survey result R_2 can, thus, be found quickly as $p(R_2) = 1 - p(R_1) = 1 - .69 = .31$. Thus, we can calculate the expected monetary value at event point *b* as \$7.63(.69) + \$8.68(.31) = \$7.96 (million). This figure can be placed above *b* as well as *a*.

Conclusion. Given that a survey is made, the optimal strategy, which carries an expected monetary value of \$7.96 million, is the following:

a. If the result shows weak demand, to construct a small plant (at *c*) and let chance (at *f*) determine the reward: of \$7.9 million if the survey result was correct, of \$4.9 million if it was incorrect

b. If the result shows strong demand, to construct a large plant (at *d*) and let chance (at *i*) determine the reward: of −\$2.1 million if the survey result was incorrect, of \$11.9 million if it was correct

The course of action just noted would be the best strategy, given the information available at the time. However, this information can change over time and, if it is not too late, the decision can be changed accordingly. Information can change as a result of some deliberate action taken by the decision maker, such as the making of a second, independent survey. It can also change as a result of some unpredicted event, such as a scandal that seriously hurts the firm's image. In the former case, new posterior probabilities can be calculated. In the latter case, the decision maker may wish to revise the prior probabilities as well.

EXAMPLE PROBLEM 23.11

To illustrate one of the contingencies just noted in the Caution box, imagine that a second (independent) survey were to confirm (rather than contradict) a report of weak demand obtained by a first report. How would this change the computations made earlier?

SOLUTION: The conditional probability of E_1, given the first R_1, which was shown to be .91, would then change to become the conditional probability of E_1, given the first R_1 *and* a second R_1^*, and would be calculated as

$$p(E_1|R_1 \text{ and } R_1^*) = \frac{p(E_1) \times p(R_1|E_1) \times p(R_1^*|E_1)}{p(E_1) \times p(R_1|E_1) \times p(R_1^*|E_1) + p(E_2) \times p(R_1|E_2) \times p(R_1^*|E_2)}$$

$$= \frac{.7(.9)(.9)}{.7(.9)(.9) + .3(.2)(.2)} = .98$$

Thus, as more and more information comes in, the posterior probability depends less and less on the prior probability. In this case, the prior .7 changed to .91 after the first survey, and we now see it change to .98 after the second. However, evidence can go either way; hence, a posterior probability can decline below the prior probability as well as rise above it.

23.6 The Value of Information

In the previous section, we made an implicit assumption: that it was worthwhile to the decision maker to spend $100,000 on a consumer survey. In fact, this assumption has been borne out, as we can see when comparing the expected monetary values of the optimal strategies that have emerged from prior analysis ($7.10 million in Figure 23.3) and posterior analysis ($7.96 million in Figure 23.6). Yet this result was a lucky circumstance. It is worth it to consider the issue systematically.

THE EXPECTED VALUE OF PERFECT INFORMATION

We begin by defining an important new concept:

DEFINITION 23.8 The **expected value of perfect information *(EVPI)*** is the maximum amount a decision maker can be expected to pay for obtaining perfect information about future events and, thus, for eliminating uncertainty completely.

The computation of the *EVPI* differs slightly, depending on the goal that is being pursued:

- When the objective is the maximization of some benefit, the *EVPI* equals the difference between the expected benefit when the optimal decision is made with perfect information and the expected benefit when that decision is made under uncertainty.
- When the objective is the minimization of some cost, the *EVPI* equals the difference between the expected cost when the optimal decision is made under uncertainty and the expected cost when that decision is made with perfect information.

Depending on whether the expected value of the optimal action under uncertainty is based on prior or posterior probabilities, we can also distinguish a **prior expected value of perfect information (prior *EVPI*)** and a **posterior expected value of perfect information (posterior *EVPI*).**

THE PRIOR *EVPI* Consider the case illustrated in Table 23.9 and Figure 23.3. The expected value of that decision under uncertainty equals $7.1 million. However, if someone offered our decision maker perfect information about the guaranteed occurrence of either E_1 or E_2, things would be different. If told that E_1 will occur with certainty, the decision maker would instantly take action A_1 and gain $8 million. If told that E_2 will occur with certainty, the decision maker would instantly take action A_2 and gain $12 million. There is a problem, however.

The purveyor of the perfect information may not reveal it until *after* being paid. Otherwise, the decision maker would have the information and could use it while paying nothing for it. To determine the expected value of a decision with perfect information, the decision maker must guess, before possessing the information, about the likelihood of receiving a report that E_1 will occur, $p(R_1)$, and of receiving a report that E_2 will occur, $p(R_2)$. Suppose that such prior probabilities, like $p(E_1)$ and $p(E_2)$ earlier, are also set to equal .7 and .3, respectively. Then the expected value of the decision with perfect information is $8(.7) + $12(.3) = $9.2 (million).

Given an expected value of the decision under uncertainty of \$7.1 million,

$$\text{prior } EVPI = \$9.2 - \$7.1 = \$2.1 \text{ million}$$

This amount is the maximum the decision maker would pay to the holder of perfect information for revealing it. Note that this figure also equals the expected opportunity loss of the optimal decision under uncertainty (Table 23.11). This equality of prior *EVPI* and *EOL* always holds, which explains why some decision makers prefer the expected-opportunity-loss criterion (Table 23.11) to the expected-monetary-value criterion (Table 23.9). The former automatically indicates the *EVPI*. Nevertheless, because the computations are less complicated, most decision makers use the *EMV* criterion that always points to the same optimal action.

THE POSTERIOR *EVPI* Now consider the case illustrated in Figure 23.6. The expected value of that decision under uncertainty equals \$7.96 million because this decision maker has the advantage of additional information (the survey result). Accordingly, we can determine

Application 23.3
The Value of Perfect Information: The Case of the U.S. Cattle Industry
http://www.harcourtcollege.com/business_stats/kohler/siteresources.html

$$\text{posterior } EVPI = \$9.20 - \$7.96 = \$1.24 \text{ million}$$

After having already paid \$100,000 for a survey of consumers, this decision maker would pay a purveyor of perfect information only this smaller maximum amount. Application 23.3, *The Value of Perfect Information: The Case of the U.S. Cattle Industry,* found on the Web site, provides an interesting real-world example.

THE EXPECTED VALUE OF SAMPLE INFORMATION

In fact, no one will ever be able to provide *perfect* information about future events. Decision makers, therefore, are much more interested in another concept to which we now turn:

DEFINITION 23.9 The **expected value of sample information *(EVSI)*** is the maximum amount that a decision maker can be expected to pay for obtaining admittedly imperfect information about future events and, thus, for reducing, rather than eliminating, uncertainty.

The computation of the *EVSI* differs slightly, depending on the goal that is being pursued:

- When the objective is the maximization of some benefit, the *EVSI* equals the difference between the expected benefit when the optimal decision is made with the sample information (and before paying for it) and the expected benefit when that decision is made without it.
- When the objective is the minimization of some cost, the *EVSI* equals the difference between the expected cost when the optimal decision is made without the sample information and the expected cost when that decision is made with it, but again before paying for it.

Consider our Figure 23.6 example. The optimal decision with the survey information is expected to yield \$7.96 million only *after* paying an assumed \$100,000 for conducting the survey. Hence, the expected gross benefit with survey information equals \$8.06 million. The optimal decision without the survey information (Figure 23.3) is expected to yield \$7.10 million. Hence,

$$EVSI = \$8.06 - \$7.10 = \$.96 \text{ million}$$

Our decision maker would pay a maximum of \$960,000 for the survey. Given that \$100,000 was paid in fact, we now know that a shrewd survey firm could have extracted an additional \$860,000 for its (imperfect) information.

THE EFFICIENCY OF SAMPLE INFORMATION

We noted on the preceding page that our decision maker, before obtaining any sample information, would place a maximum value of \$2.1 million on perfect information. But the expected value of inevitably imperfect sample information was just shown to equal \$.96 million. The ratio of the latter to the former, multiplied by 100, has a special name. It is called the **efficiency of sample information *(ESI)*.** Thus,

$$ESI = \frac{EVSI}{\text{prior } EVPI} \cdot 100$$

We can compute the *ESI* for our example as

$$ESI = \frac{EVSI}{\text{prior } EVPI} \cdot 100 = \frac{\$.96 \text{ million}}{\$2.10 \text{ million}} \cdot 100 = 45.7$$

This *ESI* value indicates that the consumer survey provided only 45.7 percent of what perfect information would have been worth. Some decision makers employ this type of efficiency rating to decide whether they should look for some other type of information. Presumably, they seek other information when the rating is low, but decide that the information is as good as one can hope to obtain when the rating is high. Naturally, what is "low" and what is "high" is a debatable point.

23.7 Preposterior Analysis

When decision makers are deciding the worth of obtaining additional (experimental or sample) information before proceeding to prior or posterior analysis, they are engaged in **preposterior analysis.** This analysis can be simple or complicated.

INFORMATION PRICED AT OR ABOVE PRIOR *EVPI* When new (and inevitably imperfect) information about future events is being offered to decision makers at a price equal to or above the (prior) expected value of perfect information, things are simple: It makes no sense to buy the information. It is then better to stick with prior analysis. In the above example, for instance, it would not be worthwhile to acquire assuredly imperfect information at a price of \$2.1 million or more because that sum equals the prior EVPI.

INFORMATION PRICED BELOW PRIOR *EVPI* When the new (and inevitably imperfect) information about future events is being offered at a price below the prior *EVPI,* however, things get complicated. It becomes necessary to determine how that price compares with the expected value of the sample information, *EVSI,* that is being offered. On that basis, we can decide to buy the information or proceed without it. In our above example, the information was offered, we assumed, for \$100,000, while being worth, we calculated, \$960,000. Hence, the decision to make the survey (a decision that was treated as a foregone conclusion in Figure 23.6) was validated in retrospect.

It is customary, however, to make the decision about possibly acquiring additional information in a more systematic way, either with the help of a decision tree (that now includes the choice between posterior and prior analysis) or in tabular form. The decision-tree approach is referred to as *extensive-form analysis.* The tabular approach is *normal-form analysis.*

FIGURE 23.7 | Preposterior Decision-Tree Analysis

This decision tree summarizes the development of an optimal strategy that includes the initial choice between engaging in prior analysis only or engaging in posterior analysis. Thus, the tree combines Figures 23.3 and 23.6. (All dollar amounts are in millions.)

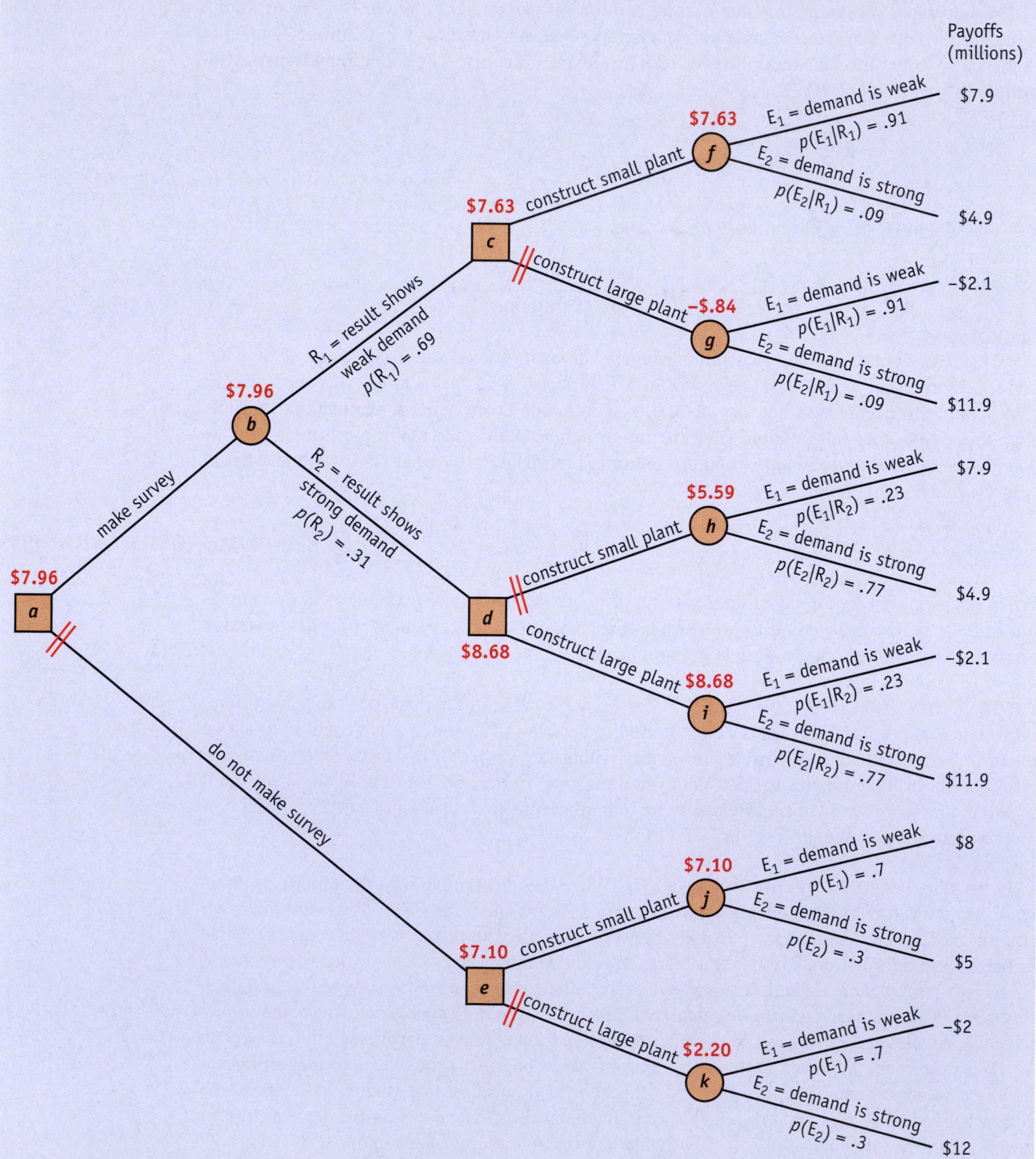

EXTENSIVE-FORM ANALYSIS

Figure 23.7 provides an example of **extensive-form analysis,** a form of preposterior analysis that uses backward induction on a decision tree to identify the optimal strategy. The lower branches of this particular tree—those emanating from action point *e*—correspond precisely to Figure 23.3 and illustrate prior analysis. The upper branches—those emanating from action point *a*—correspond to Figure 23.6 and illustrate posterior analysis.

The Figure 23.7 tree as a whole now depicts the initial choice (at *a*) of making or not making a survey. Because the former route leads to *b* (and an expected monetary value, *after* paying the $100,000 survey cost, of $7.96 million), while the latter route leads to *e* (and a lower expected monetary value of $7.10 million), the decision maker would prune the branch leading from *a* to e and beyond, as indicated here.

Thus, the optimal strategy is the following:

a. Do make a survey.

b. If the result shows weak demand, construct a small plant (and let chance at *f* determine the reward).

c. If the result shows strong demand, construct a large plant (and let chance at *i* determine the reward).

The difference between the expected monetary values at *b* and *e*, or $860,000, represents the *additional* amount (on top of the actual $100,000 survey cost) that the decision maker could pay for this information before "making a survey" and "not making a survey" would become a matter of indifference. Thus, the *EVSI* equals $960,000, as noted above. Therefore, we could show that the "make survey" branch, rather than the "do not make survey" branch, would be pruned from this decision tree if the survey cost exceeded this sum and equaled, say, $1 million, rather than $100,000.

NORMAL-FORM ANALYSIS

The normal form of preposterior analysis always leads to the same conclusion as the extensive form, but uses a different route to reach it. In **normal-form analysis,** we systematically compute an expected payoff value for every conceivable strategy and then select the strategy with the best of these values as the optimal strategy. As we can see by inspecting Figure 23.7, our example includes 6 potential strategies, which we can label S_1 through S_6. They are the following:

S_1: making a survey; then, given a report of weak demand, constructing a small plant and, given a report of strong demand, constructing a small plant as well

S_2: making a survey; then, given a report of weak demand, constructing a small plant and, given a report of strong demand, constructing a large plant

S_3: making a survey; then, given a report of weak demand, constructing a large plant and, given a report of strong demand, constructing a small plant

S_4: making a survey; then, given a report of weak demand, constructing a large plant and, given a report of strong demand, constructing a large plant as well

S_5: making no survey; constructing a small plant

S_6: making no survey; constructing a large plant

TABLE 23.17 | Calculation of Expected Payoff for Strategy S_1

First-Stage Event Probability (1)	Second-Stage Event Probability (2)	Joint Probability (3) = (1) × (2)	Payoff (millions of dollars) (4)	Weighted Payoff (millions of dollars) (5) = (3) × (4)
$p(R_1) = .69$	$p(E_1 \mid R_1) = .91$	.69(.91) = .63	7.9	.63(7.9) = 4.98
$p(R_1) = .69$	$p(E_2 \mid R_1) = .09$	.69(.09) = .06	4.9	.06(4.9) = .29
$p(R_2) = .31$	$p(E_1 \mid R_2) = .23$	.31(.23) = .07	7.9	.07(7.9) = .55
$p(R_2) = .31$	$p(E_2 \mid R_2) = .77$	.31(.77) = .24	4.9	.24(4.9) = 1.18
		1.00		**Expected Payoff: 7.00**

TABLE 23.18 | Calculation of Expected Payoff for Strategy S_6

Event Probability (1)	Payoff (millions of dollars) (2)	Weighted Payoff (millions of dollars) (3) = (1) × (2)
$p(E_1) = .7$	−2	.7(−2) = −1.4
$p(E_2) = .3$	12	.3(12) = 3.6
		Expected Payoff: 2.2

Tables 23.17 and 23.18, respectively, illustrate the computation of expected payoff values for strategies S_1 and S_6. A complete normal-form analysis, however, would require similar computations for all of the remaining possible strategies (S_2–S_5).

Observe the logic of Table 23.17. The first two rows indicate that a report of weak demand has a probability of .69 and that the subsequent construction of a small plant, which is what strategy S_1 requires in that case, can have two consequences: (1) that demand is in fact weak (which carries a conditional probability of .91) and a payoff of $7.9 million is received or (2) that demand is in fact strong (which carries a conditional probability of .09) and a payoff of $4.9 million is received. The last two rows indicate, similarly, that a report of strong demand has a probability of .31 and that the subsequent construction of a small plant, which is what strategy S_1 requires in that case as well, can also have two consequences: (1) that demand is in fact weak (which carries a conditional probability of .23) and a payoff of $7.9 million is received, or (2) that demand is in fact strong (which carries a conditional probability of .77) and a payoff of $4.9 million is received. The rest of the table is self-explanatory. So is the much simpler Table 23.18, which contains a normal-form analysis of strategy S_6.

Table 23.19, finally, summarizes our results for S_1 and S_6, along with those of similar calculations for the other strategies.

Given that S_2 has the highest expected value (highlighted in red), S_2 is the optimal strategy. This result corresponds precisely to the result of our extensive-form analysis (that is, to the portion of our Figure 23.7 decision tree that has *not* been pruned away). Note that, except for rounding error, the expected value of the optimal strategy has been found to be the same in the two forms of analysis.

TABLE 23.19 | Normal-Form Analysis: Summary

Strategy	Expected Payoff (millions of dollars)
S_1	7.00
S_2	**7.98**
S_3	1.12
S_4	2.10
S_5	7.10
S_6	2.20

PROS AND CONS

It is easy to see why most people prefer the extensive form of analysis: It is so much easier computationally. The pruning of the decision tree leaves only the optimal strategy behind and the expected values of all the nonoptimal strategies need not be computed at all.

There are occasions, however, when the manifold and detailed calculations produced by normal-form analysis come in handy. The most important of these occasions arises when a decision maker wants to determine how sensitive the selection of the optimal strategy is to the initial choice of prior probabilities, such as $p(E_1) = .7$ and $p(E_2) = .3$ in our example. Oftentimes, decision makers feel uncomfortable with probabilities based on subjective feelings and, therefore, want to test whether slight or moderate changes in these values would change the ultimate result. In our example, as Table 23.19 shows, there are three leading contenders for optimal strategy: S_1, S_2, and S_5.

What would have happened, a decision maker might wonder, if the prior probabilities had been $p(E_1) = p(E_2) = .5$ instead of $p(E_1) = .7$ and $p(E_2) = .3$? Would S_1 have become the optimal strategy? Or S_5? Or even S_4? To answer such questions, the systematic calculations of the normal-form analysis might be repeated with the new probability values.

APPLICATION 23.4

SEQUENTIAL SAMPLING

A logical extension of preposterior analysis emerged from the pioneering work of Abraham Wald (1902–1950). Wald recognized that if a decision maker (as in Figure 23.7) can make the choice of either gathering information or doing entirely without it before deciding upon a course of action, that decision maker surely also has the option, after getting information, to seek still more information, and still more after that, and so on, before making a final decision. In principle, the number of information-gathering stages could be infinite. The need to make a decision, of course, dictates an end to that process long before that. From this thought emerged the new technique of **sequential sampling,** in which the sample size is not fixed in advance, but a decision is made, after each bit of information is received, either to continue sampling or to put a stop to it.

Wald argued that much of traditional sampling was wasteful in that people were forever scrutinizing complete samples of fixed size even when an examination of the first few units in the sample already indicated the decision to be made. Wald showed how the sequential-sampling technique could replace traditional hypothesis testing. After each observation, a test statistic could be computed, and once it reached predetermined limits, the null hypothesis could be accepted or rejected. Depending on what the observations turned out to be, the statistician might make the decision to accept or to reject after only a few observations

(continued)

Application 23.4 (continued)

or after many. But the great advantage of the procedure was that, on average, it would require a smaller number of observations than a fixed-size sample required, while attaining the same probability of making a type I or type II error. This advantage is a crucial one, especially in the costly case of destructive sampling.

Tables are now available for carrying out various sequential-sampling plans. In the realm of industrial quality control, for example, such a table might state:

- the set of alternative hypotheses (such as "H_0: The proportion of defectives is .01 or less" and "H_A: The proportion of defectives is greater than .01")
- the probability of error (such as "The type I error probability of rejecting H_0 although it is true = .05" and "The type II error probability of accepting H_0 although it is false = .10")
- appropriate instructions depending on the number of items sampled so far (such as "Accept H_0 if the number of defectives is 5 or below," "Reject H_0 if the number of defectives is 20 or more," and "Inspect another unit")

23.8 The Great Controversy: Classical versus Bayesian Statistics

A great controversy erupted among statisticians in the early 1960s. It continues unabated to this day. As a result of the development of decision theory by Wald and others, more and more statisticians turned away from traditional, "classical" methods of analysis, which relied on *objective probabilities* exclusively and attempted to *make inferences.* Instead, they turned to Bayesian methods, which incorporated personal judgment in the form of *subjective probabilities* and attempted to *make decisions* in the face of uncertainty. The quarrel between the two camps turned out to be heated and is reminiscent of (and not entirely unrelated to) the Neyman-Pearson versus Fisher controversy noted in Chapter 13. The essence of the controversy can, perhaps, be seen most easily by an example.

AN EXAMPLE

Consider two urns, I and II, each containing 6 balls. The contents of the urns are as follows:

Urn I: 5 white balls and 1 black ball

Urn II: 1 white ball and 5 black balls

You are told all of the above, given one of the urns (but not told which), and asked to draw a ball from it at random. It turns out to be white. You are asked to determine the probability of the white ball having come from urn I. (If you prefer a less abstract example, just think of the urns as shipments of raw materials having come from two different suppliers. Think of the white and black balls as satisfactory and defective items contained in the shipments. And think of yourself as assessing the quality of items shipped. How likely is it, you may ask, that the satisfactory item you picked came from Supplier I?)

It is easy enough to state the answer in a general way. The probability that you drew from urn I, given that a white ball was drawn, or $p(\text{I}|\text{W})$, equals the ratio of the joint probability of encountering urn I and a white ball, or $p(\text{I } \textit{and} \text{ W})$, to the unconditional probability of drawing a white ball, $p(\text{W})$. Thus,

$$p(\text{I}|\text{W}) = \frac{p(\text{I } \textit{and} \text{ W})}{p(\text{W})} \tag{1}$$

According to the general multiplication law (Formula 8.I on page 312), $p(\text{I } \textit{and} \text{ W}) = p(\text{I}) \times p(\text{W}|\text{I})$; hence,

$$p(\text{I}|\text{W}) = \frac{p(\text{I}) \times p(\text{W}|\text{I})}{p(\text{W})} \tag{2}$$

The probability of drawing a white ball can occur in two mutually exclusive ways, by means of urn I or urn II:

$$p(\text{W}) = p(\text{I } \textit{and} \text{ W}) + p(\text{II } \textit{and} \text{ W}) \tag{3}$$

and this probability, in turn, equals

$$p(\text{W}) = p(\text{I}) \times p(\text{W}|\text{I}) + p(\text{II}) \times p(\text{W}|\text{II}) \tag{4}$$

Combining equations 2 and 4,

$$p(\text{I}|\text{W}) = \frac{p(\text{I}) \times p(\text{W}|\text{I})}{p(\text{I}) \times p(\text{W}|\text{I}) + p(\text{II}) \times p(\text{W}|\text{II})} \tag{5}$$

Equation 5 is our answer stated in general terms. Do we know enough to be specific? We know that $p(\text{W}|\text{I}) = (5/6)$ because urn I contains 6 balls, 5 of which are white. We also know that $p(\text{W}|\text{II}) = (1/6)$ because urn II contains 6 balls, 1 of which is white. But we know nothing else. The best we can say is:

$$p(\text{I}|\text{W}) = \frac{p(\text{I}) \times (5/6)}{p(\text{I}) \times (5/6) + p(\text{II}) \times (1/6)} \tag{6}$$

CLASSICAL CONCLUSION Classical statisticians, who like to rely on objective probabilities exclusively, would stop right here. They would despair of finding an answer unless someone supplied values for $p(\text{I})$ and $p(\text{II})$, the unconditional probabilities of being given urn I or urn II.

BAYESIAN CONCLUSION Bayesian statisticians do not give up as easily. Under most circumstances, they argue, people hold some degree of belief concerning all kinds of probabilities. And if they are totally ignorant on the matter (as, perhaps, in this case), they can always invoke Bayes' postulate and assume that $p(\text{I}) = p(\text{II}) = (1/2)$. In that case, the answer is

$$p(\text{I}|\text{W}) = \frac{(1/2) \times (5/6)}{(1/2) \times (5/6) + (1/2) \times (1/6)} = \frac{5}{6} \tag{7}$$

Notice that the answer has risen, as a result of picking a white ball, from a prior 1/2 to a posterior 5/6.

THE UNRESOLVED ISSUE

Classical statisticians are apt to reject all techniques that make use of subjective probabilities as nonsensical. They would, therefore, relegate to the ash heap most of the decision theory presented in this chapter. The legitimacy of subjective probability values, however, is not the only issue. The cardinal measurement of utilities (noted in this chapter's optional section) is seen as an equally weak link in the Bayesian analysis, for example.

The Bayesians are far from speechless, however. They argue that real-life people act precisely as modern decision theory suggests. People hold beliefs about various probabilities. They obtain new information. If it is not too costly, they revise their beliefs. Finally, they act. Indeed, say the Bayesians, if we rigidly stuck to the use of objective probabilities only, many problems, especially in business and economics, could not be solved at all. Moreover, as Bayesians, see it, even classical methods are riddled with *subjective* judgment and the claim of exclusive use of objective data is patently false. Consider, the Bayesians say, how the classical statistician's subjective judgment determines how a hypothesis is formulated, what kind of probability distribution is employed, what the maximum error probability is to be (almost without thought, the significance level is set at $\alpha = .05$ or .01), and what kinds of data are to be collected.

More likely than not, the controversy will be with us for some time to come.

Summary

1. *Decision theory* consists of a variety of methods that can be employed in the systematic analysis and solution of decision-making problems. Such problems arise because uncertainty exists about future events over which the decision maker has no control, but which are bound to influence the ultimate outcome of a decision.
2. Certain identical elements are present in every decision problem involving uncertainty. They include (a) mutually exclusive decision alternatives or *actions* that are available to the decision maker, (b) mutually exclusive future occurrences or *events* that will affect the outcome of any present action taken but that are not under the control of a decision maker, and (c) positive or negative net benefits or *payoffs* that are associated with each possible action/event combination and that are, thus, the joint outcome of choice and chance. Any decision-making situation in the context of uncertainty can be summarized with the help of a *payoff table*. It consists of a tabular listing of the payoffs associated with all possible combinations of actions and events. A *decision tree* provides an alternative summary.
3. When nothing is known about the likelihood of those alternative future events that are certain to affect the eventual outcome of a present decision, and when the decision maker does not even care to guess what the event probabilities might be, one of three decision criteria is commonly employed: *maximin* (or *minimax*), *maximax* (or *minimin*), or *minimax regret.*
   a. According to the *maximin criterion,* a decision maker who seeks to maximize some benefit identifies the minimum benefit associated with each possible action, finds the maximum among these minima, and chooses the action associated with this maximum of minima. The same criterion is called the *minimax criterion* when a decision maker seeks to minimize some cost. Such a decision maker identifies the maximum cost associated with each possible action, finds the minimum among these maxima, and chooses the action associated with this minimum of maxima.
   b. According to the *maximax criterion,* a decision maker who seeks to maximize some benefit identifies the maximum benefit associated with each possible action, finds the maximum among these maxima, and chooses the action associated with this maximum of maxima. The same criterion is called the *minimin criterion* when a decision maker seeks to minimize some cost. Such a decision maker identifies the minimum cost associated with each possible action, finds the minimum among these minima, and chooses the action associated with this minimum of minima.
   c. According to the *minimax-regret criterion,* a decision maker identifies the maximum regret value associated with each possible action, finds the minimum among these maxima, and chooses the action associated with this minimum of maximum regret values.

   The above criteria can be criticized for a number of reasons, including undue sensitivity of the results to irrelevant factors, undue reliance on extreme values, and a total lack of consideration for the probabilities of events.
4. A form of decision making under uncertainty that employs probabilities, but only those available prior to the gathering of new experimental or sample evidence about the

likelihood of alternative future events, is *prior analysis.* Once again, a number of alternative criteria can be employed.

a. According to the *maximum-likelihood criterion,* a decision maker simply ignores all the events that might occur except the most likely one and selects the action that produces the optimal result (maximum benefit or minimum cost) associated with this most likely event.

b. A decision maker using the *expected-monetary-value criterion* determines an expected monetary value for each possible action and selects the action with the optimal expected monetary value. The optimal *EMV* is the largest one available if the objective is to maximize some benefit. The optimal *EMV* is the smallest one available if the objective is to minimize some cost. This criterion is often employed with the help of a decision tree; expected monetary values are then computed (from ultimate payoff values and event-branch probabilities) for each fork of the tree by a process termed *backward induction.*

c. A decision maker using the *expected-opportunity-loss criterion* determines an expected opportunity loss for each possible action and selects the action with the smallest of these values. This criterion always yields the same result as the expected-monetary-value criterion.

d. Observation shows that people making decisions under uncertainty often fail to follow the *EMV* criterion. We can explain this fact by studying people's attitudes toward risk. For a *risk-averse* person, the *marginal utility of money* declines with larger amounts of money; for a *risk-neutral* person, it is constant; for a *risk-seeking* person, it rises. Except for the risk-neutral person, the optimization of expected monetary value does not produce maximum welfare. For the risk averter and the risk seeker, therefore, a different decision criterion is superior; namely, that of *maximizing expected utility.*

5. A form of decision making under uncertainty that starts out with prior probabilities, proceeds to gather additional experimental or sample evidence about event probabilities, and then uses this new evidence to transform the set of prior probabilities, by means of Bayes' theorem, into a revised set of posterior probabilities (with the help of which a final decision is reached) is *posterior analysis.*

6. The maximum amount a decision maker can be expected to pay for obtaining perfect information about future events—and, thus, for eliminating uncertainty completely—is called *the expected value of perfect information.* This *EVPI* always equals the expected opportunity loss of the optimal decision under uncertainty. The maximum amount a decision maker can be expected to pay for obtaining admittedly imperfect information about future events—and, thus, for reducing rather than eliminating uncertainty—is called the *expected value of sample information.* The ratio of this *EVSI* to the (prior) *EVPI,* multiplied by 100, measures the *efficiency of sample information,* or *ESI.*

7. A form of decision making under uncertainty that decides the worth of obtaining additional information before proceeding to prior and posterior analysis is *preposterior analysis.* We can perform this analysis by using either one of two alternative approaches that always yield the same result: (a) the decision-tree approach *(extensive-form analysis)* and (b) the tabular approach *(normal-form analysis).*

8. With the development of decision theory (and its widespread use of subjective probabilities), a great controversy among statisticians has emerged. Classicists wish to rely exclusively on objective probabilities and view statistics as a means to *making inferences.* Bayesians freely incorporate personal judgment by means of subjective probabilities and are apt to view statistics as a collection of techniques for *making decisions* in the face of uncertainty.

Key Terms

action branches
action point
actions
backward induction
Bayes' postulate
Bayes' strategy
criterion of insufficient reason
decision branches
decision fork
decision making under uncertainty
decision node
decision point
decision theory
decision tree
dominant action
efficiency of sample information *(ESI)*)
equal-likelihood criterion
event branches
event point
events
expected monetary value *(EMV)*
expected-monetary-value criterion
expected opportunity loss *(EOL)*
expected-opportunity-loss criterion
expected regret value
expected utility *(EU)*
expected-utility criterion
expected value of perfect information *(EVPI)*
expected value of sample information *(EVSI)*
extensive-form analysis
fair gamble

inadmissible action
Laplace criterion
marginal utility of money
maximax
maximin
maximum-likelihood criterion
minimax
minimax regret
minimin
more-than-fair gamble
normal-form analysis
opportunity loss *(OL)*
optimal strategy
payoffs
payoff table
posterior analysis
posterior expected value of perfect information (posterior *EVPI*)
preposterior analysis
prior analysis
prior expected value of perfect information (prior *EVPI*)
regret
regret table
risk aversion
risk neutrality
risk seeking
sequential sampling
state-of-nature branches
state-of-nature fork
state-of-nature node
state-of-nature point
states of nature
total utility of money
unfair gamble
utility-of-money function

Practice Problems

NOTE

Most statistical programs, including EXCEL or MINITAB, are not designed to help solve decision-making problems. However, you may wish to check out Arborist, a decision-tree program published by Texas Instruments.

SECTION 23.2 BASIC CONCEPTS

1. An airline is about to resume service after a lengthy strike. Its executives are considering three ways to win back customers: (1) issuing 40 percent discount coupons that can be freely used by anyone during the following 12 months, (2) issuing 40 percent discount coupons that can only be used by named recipients (and that would be mailed to the airline's best prior customers), and (3) making a statement on TV and simply hoping for the best. The executives believe that the profit consequences of each of these approaches will differ, depending on whether the next year brings a recession, as some suspect, or a continuation of last year's boom. In millions of dollars, the next-year profit predictions are −80 and +120 for (1), −120 and +150 for (2), and +32 and +60 for (3).

a. Set up a *payoff table* for this decision-making problem.

b. What would it take to make action (3) a *dominant action?*

c. Draw a decision tree.

2. A U.S. firm plans to enter a new market in China. The firm's executives are considering four alternatives: (1) building a plant in China, (2) hiring a Chinese sales force to sell U.S.-made products exported to China, (3) sending mail-order catalogues to Chinese consumers, and (4) teaming up with Chinese firms that would act as sales agents. The executives believe that the profit consequences of each of these approaches will differ, depending on whether demand turns out to be low, moderate, or huge. In millions of dollars, the next-year profit predictions are 2, 4, and 10 for (1); 3, 3, and 3 for (2); −5, −1, and +20 for (3); and −2, 0, and 30 for (4).

a. Set up a *payoff table* for this decision-making problem.

b. What would it take to make action (4) a *dominant action?*

c. Draw a decision tree.

3. The owners of a professional baseball team are considering two alternatives: (1) selling a strictly limited number of season tickets so as to have more individual tickets available, or (2) selling all the season tickets the fans will take, even at the risk of having no room left for would-be buyers of individual tickets. The owners believe that the profit consequences of each of these approaches will differ, depending on whether the team's record next season turns out to poor, average, or superb. In millions of dollars, the next-season profit predictions are −10, 0, and +30 for (1) and 0, +10, and +20 for (2).

a. Set up a *payoff table* for this decision-making problem.

b. What would it take to make action (2) a *dominant action?*

c. Draw a decision tree.

4. The executives of a pharmaceutical company are considering two alternative uses for the $300 million of cash they have on hand: (1) accelerating their cancer drug research or (2) opening a new division to produce nuclear medical devices. The executives believe that the profit consequences of each of these approaches will differ, depending on whether a certain breakthrough in cancer research is achieved or fails to materialize. In millions of dollars, the next-year profit predictions are +900 and −300 for (1) and +30 and +30 for (2).

a. Set up a *payoff table* for this decision-making problem.

b. What would it take to make action (2) a *dominant action?*

c. Draw a decision tree.

5. A promoter must make a decision about an upcoming rock concert: (1) renting an open-air stadium or (2) renting a giant auditorium in College Hall. The promoter believes that the profit consequences of each of these approaches will differ, depending on whether there is rain or no rain on the concert date. In thousands of dollars, the profit predictions are 100 and 500 for (1) and 200 and 200 for (2).

   a. Set up a *payoff table* for this decision-making problem.

   b. What would it take to make action (2) a *dominant action?*

   c. Draw a decision tree.

6. A manufacturer of aircraft engines is considering announcing next year's price. The current price could (1) be reduced, (2) be maintained, or (3) be raised. The manufacturer believes that the profit consequences of each of these approaches will differ, depending on whether the price of a similar engine produced by a major competitor will later be reduced, maintained, or raised in turn. In millions of dollars, the profit predictions are 10, 20, and 30 for (1); 0, 30, and 20 for (2); and −20, 40, and 60 for (3).

   a. Set up a *payoff table* for this decision-making problem.

   b. What would it take to make action (3) a *dominant action?*

   c. Draw a decision tree.

7. Someone has $10,000 to invest and receives this advice: (1) put it all into a mutual fund that invests in stock, (2) put it all into bonds that pay 10 percent interest per year, or (3) split the money in half and choose half (1) and half (2). Unfortunately, the mutual fund is expected to produce an annual return of 15 percent if the stock market goes up, of 5 percent if the stock market is unchanged, and of −15 percent if the stock market declines.

   a. Set up a *payoff table* for this decision-making problem.

   b. What would it take to make action (2) a *dominant action?*

   c. Draw a decision tree.

8. A fashion designer must commit resources now to produce (1) short, (2) medium, or (3) long skirts for the next season. Unfortunately, next year's fashion will be determined by the Paris fashion show 6 months from now, which will point to short, medium, or long as the way to go. Depending on what Paris says, the profit consequences, in millions of dollars, are 30, 10, and 1 for (1); 1, 30, and 2 for (2); and 0, 5, and 30 for (3).

   a. Set up a *payoff table* for this decision-making problem.

   b. What would it take to make action (3) a *dominant action?*

   c. Draw a decision tree.

SECTION 23.3 DECISION MAKING WITHOUT PROBABILITIES

9. Review Practice Problems 1–4. In each case, determine the best action under the criterion of

   a. maximin.

   b. maximax.

10. Review Practice Problems 5–8. In each case, determine the best action under the criterion of

    a. maximin.

    b. maximax.

11. Depending on whether future demand is low, moderate, or high, a real estate developer foresees profits (in millions of dollars) of 4, 5, or 6 from a small project; of 1, 6, or 10 from a medium-sized project; and of −5, 0, or 30 from a large project. Determine the best action under the criterion of

    a. maximin.

    b. maximax.

12. Depending on whether future demand is low, moderate, or high, a producer of aircraft ELTs (emergency locator transmitters) foresees profits (in thousands of dollars) of 15, 20, or 25 from a small production run; of 6, 20, or 35 from a medium-sized run; and of −10, 0, or 69 from a large run. Determine the best action under the criterion of

    a. maximin.

    b. maximax.

TABLE 23.20 | Actions, Events, and Payoffs

	Events					
Actions	E_1	E_2	E_3	E_4	E_5	E_6
A_1	0	−15	−35	−50	23	67
A_2	−15	−35	−50	23	67	102
A_3	−35	−50	23	67	102	139
A_4	−49	23	67	102	139	150
A_5	23	67	102	139	145	−100

13. Table 23.20 shows profits (in million dollars) that are associated with 5 actions and 6 events. Determine the best action under the criterion of

a. maximin.

b. maximax.

14. Consider Table 23.20 and assume the entries are costs. Determine the best action under the criterion of

a. minimax.

b. minimin.

c. minimax regret.

15. Reconsider Practice Problem 11, but now determine the best action under the criterion of minimax regret. Show your regret table.

16. Reconsider Practice Problem 12, but now determine the best action under the criterion of minimax regret. Show your regret table.

Section 23.4 Decision Making with Probabilities: Prior Analysis

17. Reconsider Table 23.20 and assume the following event probabilities: $p(E_1) = .1$, $p(E_2) = .2$, $p(E_3) = .3$, $p(E_4) = .1$, $p(E_5) = .05$, and $p(E_6) = .25$. Determine the best action under the *maximum-likelihood* criterion for

a. Practice Problem 13.

b. Practice Problem 14.

18. Assuming $p(E_1) = .7$ and $p(E_2) = .3$, determine the best action under the criterion of *maximum likelihood* for

a. Practice Problem 1.

b. Practice Problem 4.

c. Practice Problem 5.

19. Assuming $p(E_1) = .1$, $p(E_2) = .6$, and $p(E_3) = .3$, determine the best action under the criterion of *maximum likelihood* for

a. Practice Problem 2.

b. Practice Problem 3.

c. Practice Problem 6.

d. Practice Problem 7.

e. Practice Problem 8.

20. Reconsider Practice Problem 12. Determine the best action under the *expected-monetary-value* criterion, assuming $p(E_1) = .1$, $p(E_2) = .7$, and $p(E_3) = .2$.

21. The caption to Figure 23.A on page 1128 ends with a question. What is the answer?

22. Review Practice Problem 1. Assuming $p(E_1) = .7$ and $p(E_2) = .3$, determine the best action under the criterion of *expected monetary value.*

23. Review Practice Problem 2. Assuming $p(E_1) = .1$, $p(E_2) = .6$, and $p(E_3) = .3$, determine the best action under the criterion of *expected monetary value.*

24. An investor is thinking of buying a bankrupt private airport and its associated resort for \$5 million (which would involve an annual cost of \$500,000). An additional cost of \$200,000 per year is expected to run the new venture. At a contemplated landing fee of \$100, the probabilities that 6,000 planes, 7,000 planes, or 8,000 planes will land per year are .1, .5, and .4, respectively. Use a decision tree to determine the optimal action, given the desire to maximize *expected monetary value* and given the option not to make the investment at all.

25. An independent producer of TV films wants to market a new soap opera. The rights can be sold to a distributor for \$125 million now, or the program can be offered to a TV network for review with these possible results (in the judgment of the film producer): a 60 percent chance of rejection (which ruins all further chances of a sale to anyone and spells a \$30 million loss) or a 40 percent chance of getting a contract (which means a \$300 million profit). Use a decision tree to determine the optimal action, given the desire to maximize *expected monetary value.*

26. Review Practice Problem 25 and assume that the film producer wants to maximize *expected utility* rather than expected monetary value. Also assume that the producer's utility function is correctly described by $U = \sqrt{\$}$. Does this change the decision? (**Note:** For purposes of this exercise, convert negative dollar values into negative utility values by taking the square root of the absolute dollar values.)

27. In each of the following cases, determine whether the person is risk-averse, risk-neutral, or risk-seeking.

a. Someone is indifferent between getting \$1,000 with certainty or a taking gamble that provides \$5,000 with a probability of .2 and \$100 with a probability of .8.

b. Someone is indifferent between getting \$3,000 with certainty or a taking gamble that provides \$5,000 with a probability of .2 and \$100 with a probability of .8.

c. Someone prefers getting \$1,000 with certainty to taking *any* gamble that provides a lower *EMV.*

d. Someone prefers getting \$1,000 with certainty to taking *some but not all* gambles that provide a lower *EMV.*

SECTION 23.5 DECISION MAKING WITH PROBABILITIES: POSTERIOR ANALYSIS

28. Reconsider Practice Problem 25. Suppose that a consulting firm is willing to offer advice on the network's likely reaction for a \$1 million fee. The consulting firm's "track record" is given in Table 23.21. Use a decision tree to determine the optimal strategy if the film producer definitely decides to buy the advice and then to take the action (sell the rights or offer the film to the network) that maximizes *expected monetary value.*

TABLE 23.21 | Film Consultant's Track Record

Advice Given	Subsequent Events	
	E_1 = rejection	E_2 = contract offer
R_1 = network will reject	$p(R_1\|E_1) = .8$	$p(R_1\|E_2) = .3$
R_2 = network will offer contract	$p(R_2\|E_1) = .2$	$p(R_2\|E_2) = .7$

29. On page 1140, the text illustrates the computation of posterior probabilities on the basis of Formula 8.K. Confirm the results with alternative Formula 8.L (which can be reviewed on page 323).

30. On page 1130 of the text, in the discussion of event point *b* in Figure 23.6, "Posterior Decision-Tree Analysis," the unconditional probability of getting survey result R_2 is found indirectly as $p(R_2) = 1 - p(R_1) = 1 - .69 = .31$. Make a direct computation.

31. A firm has just produced 10 million copies of a new game for the Christmas market. It can sell the entire batch to a distributor for a net return of \$20 million in 6 months, or it can market the games on its own to individual buyers with a 40 percent chance of encountering weak demand (and getting a net return of \$2 million in 6 months) and a 60 percent chance of encountering strong demand (and getting a net return of \$40 million in 6 months). However, for a \$2 million fee, a consulting firm is offering advice on the likely demand situation. The consulting firm's track record is given in Table 23.22 on the next page. Use a decision tree to determine the optimal strategy if

a. the firm definitely decides to buy the advice and then to take the action (sell to distributor or market on its own) that maximizes *expected monetary value.*

b. the firm definitely decides to forgo the advice and then to take the action (sell to distributor or market on its own) that maximizes *expected monetary value.*

TABLE 23.22 | Toy Consultant's Track Record

Advice Given	Subsequent Events	
	E_1 = weak demand	E_2 = strong demand
R_1 = weak demand	$p(R_1 \mid E_1) = .7$	$p(R_1 \mid E_2) = .2$
R_2 = strong demand	$p(R_2 \mid E_1) = .3$	$p(R_2 \mid E_2) = .8$

32. A firm has just produced 10,000 personal computers. It can sell the entire batch to a distributor for a net return of $10 million in 6 months, or it can market the computers on its own to individual buyers with a 60 percent chance of encountering weak demand (and getting a net return of $2 million in 6 months) and a 40 percent chance of encountering strong demand (and getting a net return of $20 million in 6 months). However, for a $1 million fee, a consulting firm is offering advice on the likely demand situation. The consulting firm's track record is given in Table 23.23. Use a decision tree to determine the optimal strategy if

- **a.** the firm definitely decides to buy the advice and then to take the action (sell to distributor or market on its own) that maximizes *expected monetary value.*
- **b.** the firm definitely decides to forgo the advice and then to take the action (sell to distributor or market on its own) that maximizes *expected monetary value.*

TABLE 23.23 | Computer Consultant's Track Record

Advice Given	Subsequent Events	
	E_1 = weak demand	E_2 = strong demand
R_1 = weak demand	$p(R_1 \mid E_1) = .6$	$p(R_1 \mid E_2) = .1$
R_2 = strong demand	$p(R_2 \mid E_1) = .4$	$p(R_2 \mid E_2) = .9$

SECTION 23.6 THE VALUE OF INFORMATION

33. Review Practice Problem 28. Determine the (prior) expected value of perfect information.

34. Review Practice Problem 28. Determine the expected value of the sample information.

35. Review Practice Problem 28. Determine the efficiency of the sample information.

36. For the situation described in Practice Problem 31, determine

- **a.** the (prior) expected value of perfect information.
- **b.** the expected value of the sample information.
- **c.** the efficiency of the sample information.

37. For the situation described in Practice Problem 32, determine

- **a.** the (prior) expected value of perfect information.
- **b.** the expected value of the sample information.
- **c.** the efficiency of the sample information.

SECTION 23.7 PREPOSTERIOR ANALYSIS

38. Reread this chapter's discussion of Figure 23.7. Then redo the decision-tree analysis under the assumption that the survey costs $1 million rather than $100,000.

39. Conduct an extensive-form (preposterior) analysis for an oil company, given the following information: It can drill for oil on a given site now (and the prior probabilities of E_1 = finding oil or E_2 = not finding oil are considered equal) or it can sell its rights to the site for $10 million. If it drills and finds oil, a net payoff of \$100 million is expected. If no oil is found, that payoff equals −\$15 million. It can instead contract for a \$10 million seismic test. If the test predicts oil, it can drill (and get a net payoff of \$90 million if oil is in fact found and of −\$25 million if none is found) or it can sell the rights (for \$20 million). If the test predicts no oil, it can drill (and get a net payoff of \$90 million if oil is in fact found and of −\$25 million if none is found) or it can sell the rights for \$1 million. The "track record" of the seismic-test company is given in Table 23.24.

TABLE 23.24 | Seismic Test Company's Track Record

	Subsequent Events	
Report Issued	E_1 = oil is found	E_2 = oil is not found
R_1 = oil present	$p(R_1\|E_1) = .6$	$p(R_1\|E_2) = .2$
R_2 = no oil present	$p(R_2\|E_1) = .4$	$p(R_2\|E_2) = .8$

40. Consider the answer to Practice Problem 39. If no test is made, what is the (prior) expected value of perfect information, assuming $p(R_1) = p(E_1)$ and also that $p(R_2) = p(E_2)$?

41. Consider the answer to Practice Problem 39. What is the expected value of the sample information?

42. Text Table 23.19 on page 1149 gives expected payoffs for six different strategies, but the computation is shown only for strategies S_1 and S_6 (in Tables 23.17 and 23.18). Make a similar computation for S_2.

43. According to the text (page 1149), "the pruning of the decision tree [during extensive-form analysis] leaves only the optimal strategy behind and the expected values of all the nonoptimal strategies need not be computed at all." However, these values *could* be computed easily enough, even from a decision tree. Prove it, using Figure 23.7.

44. Review the situation described in Practice Problem 31 and conduct an extensive form of (preposterior) analysis: Should the firm buy the advice or make its decision without the advice?

45. Review the situation described in Practice Problem 31, but this time conduct a normal form of (preposterior) analysis.

46. Review the situation described in Practice Problem 32 and conduct an extensive form of (preposterior) analysis: Should the firm buy the advice or make its decision without the advice?

47. Review the situation described in Practice Problem 32, but this time conduct a normal form of (preposterior) analysis.

Section 23.8 The Great Controversy: Classical versus Bayesian Statistics

48. Review the Bayesian conclusion on page 1151 of the text. What would equation (7) be like if the original subjective probabilities had been different, such as $p(I) = 1/3$ and $p(II) = 2/3$?

49. It is important to appreciate the wider applications of the extended example found in Section 23.8. The urns, for instance, might represent two shipments of raw materials coming from different suppliers, while the white and black balls might represent satisfactory and defective items contained therein. To show your understanding, assess the likelihood of a randomly sampled item having come from supplier A rather than B, given that the item was defective and given the prior belief that A's shipments contain 10 percent defectives, while B's shipments contain 1 percent defectives.

50. It is important to appreciate the wider applications of the extended example found in Section 23.8. The urns, for instance, might represent the outputs of a plant that were produced during the day shift and night shift, respectively, while the white and black balls might represent satisfactory and defective items. To show your understanding, assess the likelihood of a randomly sampled item having come from the night shift rather than the day shift, given that the item was defective and given the prior belief that night shift output is 5 percent defective, while the day shift's output is 0.1 percent defective.

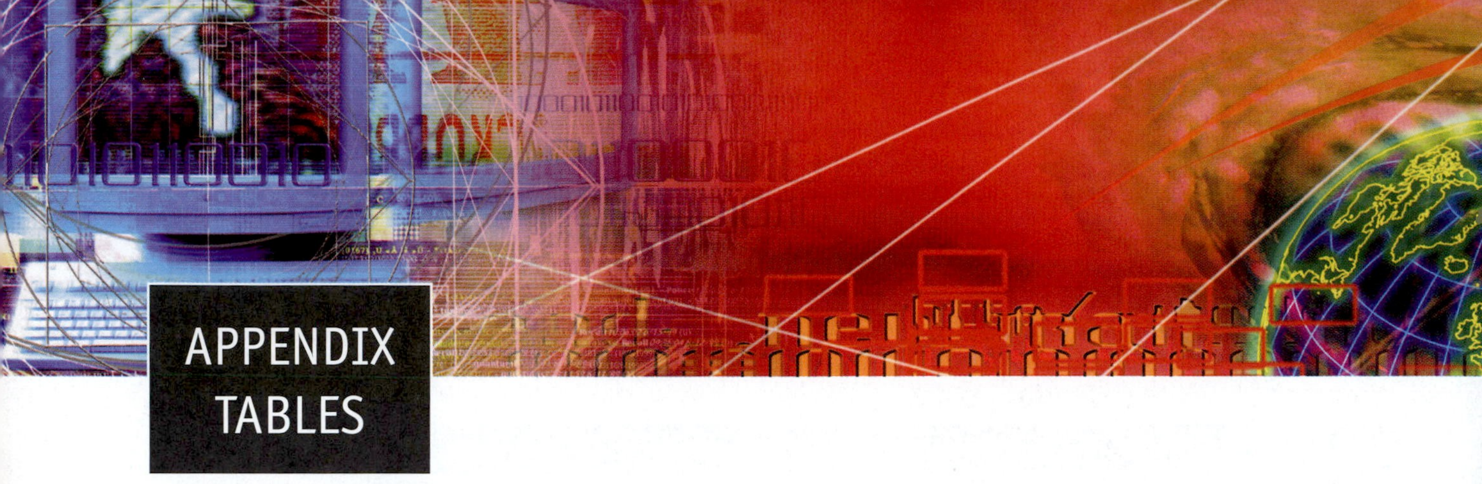

APPENDIX TABLES

Table A

Random Numbers

Table B

The Greek Alphabet

Table C

Binomial Probabilities for Individual Values of x

Table D

Binomial Probabilities for Cumulative Values of x

Table E

Exponential Functions

Table F

Poisson Probabilities for Individual Values of x

Table G

Poisson Probabilities for Cumulative Values of x

Table H

Standard Normal Curve Areas

Table I

Exponential Probabilities for Cumulative Values of x

Table J

Critical Normal Deviate Values for Statistical Estimation

Table K

Student t Distributions

Table L

Critical Normal Deviate Values for Hypothesis Testing

Table M

Chi-Square Distributions

Table N

F Distributions

Table O

Values of q_α in Tukey's *HSD* Test

Table P

Values of d_L and d_U for the Durbin-Watson Test

Table Q

Critical Values of D for the Kolmogorov-Smirnov Maximum Deviation Test for Goodness of Fit

Table R

Factors for Constructing $\overline{X}$ or R Control Charts

APPENDIX TABLE A | Random Numbers

71274	84346	75444	85690	35384	87841	97411	78698	46796	33552
64017	01373	14665	31891	80997	14321	47741	59980	87739	38174
43747	17686	11045	15549	52779	65135	00275	95434	36337	24041
59688	48689	41591	47042	83615	93034	25077	64835	67798	30547
95016	73467	11447	59500	94921	15166	69217	26267	11316	22651
65207	30591	65947	58339	00952	32111	45459	14986	57395	34492
34510	78657	08883	49489	85619	52912	01662	49854	78354	30631
56299	60624	91572	31734	18159	18927	31314	59682	41320	88602
02113	12579	86172	03819	69968	02616	72687	42699	04792	16510
00884	87979	45184	61572	20086	14498	29640	94263	90964	29278
89367	53577	97412	19603	57234	63055	49059	35761	72007	22751
99781	56740	42659	46617	21828	99831	45987	63450	66919	78252
92024	12100	76013	12587	86340	74880	79979	35906	38122	64917
82861	09215	87342	72789	76132	24468	93065	78968	03321	48081
11286	13011	67982	74101	44961	25468	14247	95934	50711	24492
68674	24686	14460	61242	92310	86810	87702	69811	53996	99517
24882	20749	94139	28785	74402	18561	79069	56838	30020	99707
21740	51134	39298	92203	66230	30636	58169	78982	50057	39908
46901	34825	28673	10404	97777	30782	04680	15319	84125	40937
92686	81702	74149	76326	01101	96278	90855	55145	89705	51199
98743	59366	94797	96803	69876	87533	19675	59246	65348	06606
11463	25619	38107	91053	58416	02720	86563	27443	99598	04074
76975	18636	54975	67422	57101	68857	35389	35641	34505	71552
67359	50379	81053	97357	00717	59504	34480	77127	23243	48682
34084	48031	27227	48912	10797	88917	93126	52945	79457	66528
94553	44441	83166	40056	73935	52103	13972	56781	31900	95037
20545	43211	34500	92233	53497	39401	78535	82360	57410	32060
05646	01152	13235	39168	69214	83852	00144	08105	94247	37189
54022	58295	96122	87620	74774	06884	81689	68392	25776	08748
32291	30700	32561	83579	94582	77930	06826	96855	97751	42664
66212	75061	65891	96896	15107	12985	97616	64241	08592	81036
98059	44951	23078	92793	80756	52799	20340	62969	81775	31065
23157	52179	24394	39833	89427	58771	26992	00649	25475	50888
28911	81929	91368	49372	43335	44465	43257	66893	34761	60423
85959	90369	02100	28727	83001	84166	20473	35305	38088	54795
34459	31400	58760	17157	73816	55527	54133	24605	56153	35354
04073	57781	36894	93000	57834	29343	98195	58425	97275	71392
22126	91330	95667	75737	36869	55209	41663	04943	59401	17039
10288	61685	25302	84097	13088	86840	04020	43046	01043	43157
75431	32853	72907	99432	65482	23011	70466	87386	67471	77629
90800	17425	28042	53770	98924	31863	84115	82488	23239	82185
19083	89475	05207	41284	83405	55825	31117	59821	96455	63796
10405	67911	77238	46262	42766	07215	02391	47316	78724	41170
34711	77325	99768	63455	44335	91028	27740	86163	81474	08159
73334	61941	16883	05012	63191	35763	60157	09617	25501	44989
79452	68381	71937	23274	60273	47091	82876	24641	03825	50894
13864	28746	32434	88325	99996	96130	39471	74020	56077	22133
73082	50271	83240	80065	09328	02940	41686	32758	89467	73553
43060	88221	35010	79829	71520	80453	95049	66352	77495	83256
15172	42061	33264	63832	48528	23258	13520	83222	45659	39074

APPENDIX TABLE B | The Greek Alphabet

alpha	A	α
beta	B	β
gamma	Γ	γ
delta	Δ	δ
epsilon	E	ε
zeta	Z	ζ
eta	H	η
theta	Θ	θ
iota	I	ι
kappa	K	κ
lambda	Λ	λ
mu	M	μ
nu	N	ν
xi	Ξ	ξ
omicron	O	o
pi	Π	π
rho	P	ρ
sigma	Σ	σ
tau	T	τ
upsilon	Y	υ
phi	Φ	φ
chi	X	χ
psi	Ψ	ψ
omega	Ω	ω

APPENDIX TABLE C | Binomial Probabilities for Individual Values of *x*

Entries in the table give the probability of x successes in n trials of a binomial experiment, where π is the probability of a success in one trial. For example, with n = 2 trials and π = .40, the probability of x = 2 successes is .1600. The table can also be read for probabilities in excess of .50, merely by rephrasing the question asked of it. Thus, with n = 2 trials and π = .80, the probability of x = 2 successes equals the probability of x = 0 failures, given π =.20, or .6400.

		Values of π									
n	*x*	.05	.10	.15	.20	.25	.30	.35	.40	.45	.50
1	0	.9500	.9000	.8500	.8000	.7500	.7000	.6500	.6000	.5500	.5000
	1	.0500	.1000	.1500	.2000	.2500	.3000	.3500	.4000	.4500	.5000
2	0	.9025	.8100	.7225	.6400	.5625	.4900	.4225	.3600	.3025	.2500
	1	.0950	.1800	.2550	.3200	.3750	.4200	.4550	.4800	.4950	.5000
	2	.0025	.0100	.0225	.0400	.0625	.0900	.1225	.1600	.2025	.2500
3	0	.8574	.7290	.6141	.5120	.4219	.3430	.2746	.2160	.1664	.1250
	1	.1354	.2430	.3251	.3840	.4219	.4410	.4436	.4320	.4084	.3750
	2	.0071	.0270	.0574	.0960	.1406	.1890	.2389	.2880	.3341	.3750
	3	.0001	.0010	.0034	.0080	.0156	.0270	.0429	.0640	.0911	.1250
4	0	.8145	.6561	.5220	.4096	.3164	.2401	.1785	.1296	.0915	.0625
	1	.1715	.2916	.3685	.4096	.4219	.4116	.3845	.3456	.2995	.2500
	2	.0135	.0486	.0975	.1536	.2109	.2646	.3105	.3456	.3675	.3750
	3	.0005	.0036	.0115	.0256	.0469	.0756	.1115	.1536	.2005	.2500
	4	.0000	.0001	.0005	.0016	.0039	.0081	.0150	.0256	.0410	.0625
5	0	.7738	.5905	.4437	.3277	.2373	.1681	.1160	.0778	.0503	.0312
	1	.2036	.3280	.3915	.4096	.3955	.3602	.3124	.2592	.2059	.1562
	2	.0214	.0729	.1382	.2048	.2637	.3087	.3364	.3456	.3369	.3125
	3	.0011	.0081	.0244	.0512	.0879	.1323	.1811	.2304	.2757	.3125
	4	.0000	.0004	.0022	.0064	.0146	.0284	.0488	.0768	.1128	.1562
	5	.0000	.0000	.0001	.0003	.0010	.0024	.0053	.0102	.0185	.0312
6	0	.7351	.5314	.3771	.2621	.1780	.1176	.0754	.0467	.0277	.0156
	1	.2321	.3543	.3993	.3932	.3560	.3025	.2437	.1866	.1359	.0938
	2	.0305	.0984	.1762	.2458	.2966	.3241	.3280	.3110	.2780	.2344
	3	.0021	.0146	.0415	.0819	.1318	.1852	.2355	.2765	.3032	.3125
	4	.0001	.0012	.0055	.0154	.0330	.0595	.0951	.1382	.1861	.2344
	5	.0000	.0001	.0004	.0015	.0044	.0102	.0205	.0369	.0609	.0938
	6	.0000	.0000	.0000	.0001	.0002	.0007	.0018	.0041	.0083	.0156
7	0	.6983	.4783	.3206	.2097	.1335	.0824	.0490	.0280	.0152	.0078
	1	.2573	.3720	.3960	.3670	.3115	.2471	.1848	.1306	.0872	.0547
	2	.0406	.1240	.2097	.2753	.3115	.3177	.2985	.2613	.2140	.1641
	3	.0036	.0230	.0617	.1147	.1730	.2269	.2679	.2903	.2918	.2734
	4	.0002	.0026	.0109	.0287	.0577	.0972	.1442	.1935	.2388	.2734
	5	.0000	.0002	.0012	.0043	.0115	.0250	.0466	.0774	.1172	.1641
	6	.0000	.0000	.0001	.0004	.0013	.0036	.0084	.0172	.0320	.0547
	7	.0000	.0000	.0000	.0000	.0001	.0002	.0006	.0016	.0037	.0078

(continued)

APPENDIX TABLE C (*continued*)

n	x	.05	.10	.15	.20	.25	.30	.35	.40	.45	.50
						Values of π					
8	0	.6634	.4305	.2725	.1678	.1001	.0576	.0319	.0168	.0084	.0039
	1	.2793	.3826	.3847	.3355	.2670	.1977	.1373	.0896	.0548	.0312
	2	.0515	.1488	.2376	.2936	.3115	.2965	.2587	.2090	.1569	.1094
	3	.0054	.0331	.0839	.1468	.2076	.2541	.2786	.2787	.2568	.2188
	4	.0004	.0046	.0185	.0459	.0865	.1361	.1875	.2322	.2627	.2734
	5	.0000	.0004	.0026	.0092	.0231	.0467	.0808	.1239	.1719	.2188
	6	.0000	.0000	.0002	.0011	.0038	.0100	.0217	.0413	.0703	.1094
	7	.0000	.0000	.0000	.0001	.0004	.0012	.0033	.0079	.0164	.0312
	8	.0000	.0000	.0000	.0000	.0000	.0001	.0002	.0007	.0017	.0039
9	0	.6302	.3874	.2316	.1342	.0751	.0404	.0207	.0101	.0046	.0020
	1	.2985	.3874	.3679	.3020	.2253	.1556	.1004	.0605	.0339	.0176
	2	.0629	.1722	.2597	.3020	.3003	.2668	.2162	.1612	.1110	.0703
	3	.0077	.0446	.1069	.1762	.2336	.2668	.2716	.2508	.2119	.1641
	4	.0006	.0074	.0283	.0661	.1168	.1715	.2194	.2508	.2600	.2461
	5	.0000	.0008	.0050	.0165	.0389	.0735	.1181	.1672	.2128	.2461
	6	.0000	.0001	.0006	.0028	.0087	.0210	.0424	.0743	.1160	.1641
	7	.0000	.0000	.0000	.0003	.0012	.0039	.0098	.0212	.0407	.0703
	8	.0000	.0000	.0000	.0000	.0001	.0004	.0013	.0035	.0083	.0176
	9	.0000	.0000	.0000	.0000	.0000	.0000	.0001	.0003	.0008	.0020
10	0	.5987	.3487	.1969	.1074	.0563	.0282	.0135	.0060	.0025	.0010
	1	.3151	.3874	.3474	.2684	.1877	.1211	.0725	.0403	.0207	.0098
	2	.0746	.1937	.2759	.3020	.2816	.2335	.1757	.1209	.0763	.0439
	3	.0105	.0574	.1298	.2013	.2503	.2668	.2522	.2150	.1665	.1172
	4	.0010	.0112	.0401	.0881	.1460	.2001	.2377	.2508	.2384	.2051
	5	.0001	.0015	.0085	.0264	.0584	.1029	.1536	.2007	.2340	.2461
	6	.0000	.0001	.0012	.0055	.0162	.0368	.0689	.1115	.1596	.2051
	7	.0000	.0000	.0001	.0008	.0031	.0090	.0212	.0425	.0746	.1172
	8	.0000	.0000	.0000	.0001	.0004	.0014	.0043	.0106	.0229	.0439
	9	.0000	.0000	.0000	.0000	.0000	.0001	.0005	.0016	.0042	.0098
	10	.0000	.0000	.0000	.0000	.0000	.0000	.0000	.0001	.0003	.0010
11	0	.5688	.3138	.1673	.0859	.0422	.0198	.0088	.0036	.0014	.0005
	1	.3293	.3835	.3248	.2362	.1549	.0932	.0518	.0266	.0125	.0054
	2	.0867	.2131	.2866	.2953	.2581	.1998	.1395	.0887	.0513	.0269
	3	.0137	.0710	.1517	.2215	.2581	.2568	.2254	.1774	.1259	.0806
	4	.0014	.0158	.0536	.1107	.1721	.2201	.2428	.2365	.2060	.1611
	5	.0001	.0025	.0132	.0388	.0803	.1321	.1830	.2207	.2360	.2256
	6	.0000	.0003	.0023	.0097	.0268	.0566	.0985	.1471	.1931	.2256
	7	.0000	.0000	.0003	.0017	.0064	.0173	.0379	.0701	.1128	.1611
	8	.0000	.0000	.0000	.0002	.0011	.0037	.0102	.0234	.0462	.0806
	9	.0000	.0000	.0000	.0000	.0001	.0005	.0018	.0052	.0126	.0269
	10	.0000	.0000	.0000	.0000	.0000	.0000	.0002	.0007	.0021	.0054
	11	.0000	.0000	.0000	.0000	.0000	.0000	.0000	.0000	.0002	.0005

(*continued*)

APPENDIX TABLE C (*continued*)

		Values of π									
n	*x*	.05	.10	.15	.20	.25	.30	.35	.40	.45	.50
12	0	.5404	.2824	.1422	.0687	.0317	.0138	.0057	.0022	.0008	.0002
	1	.3413	.3766	.3012	.2062	.1267	.0712	.0368	.0174	.0075	.0029
	2	.0988	.2301	.2924	.2835	.2323	.1678	.1088	.0639	.0339	.0161
	3	.0173	.0853	.1720	.2362	.2581	.2397	.1954	.1419	.0923	.0537
	4	.0021	.0213	.0683	.1329	.1936	.2311	.2367	.2128	.1700	.1208
	5	.0002	.0038	.0193	.0532	.1032	.1585	.2039	.2270	.2225	.1934
	6	.0000	.0005	.0040	.0155	.0401	.0792	.1281	.1766	.2124	.2256
	7	.0000	.0000	.0006	.0033	.0115	.0291	.0591	.1009	.1489	.1934
	8	.0000	.0000	.0001	.0005	.0024	.0078	.0199	.0420	.0762	.1208
	9	.0000	.0000	.0000	.0001	.0004	.0015	.0048	.0125	.0277	.0537
	10	.0000	.0000	.0000	.0000	.0000	.0002	.0008	.0025	.0068	.0161
	11	.0000	.0000	.0000	.0000	.0000	.0000	.0001	.0003	.0010	.0029
	12	.0000	.0000	.0000	.0000	.0000	.0000	.0000	.0000	.0001	.0002
13	0	.5133	.2542	.1209	.0550	.0238	.0097	.0037	.0013	.0004	.0001
	1	.3512	.3672	.2774	.1787	.1029	.0540	.0259	.0113	.0045	.0016
	2	.1109	.2448	.2937	.2680	.2059	.1388	.0836	.0453	.0220	.0095
	3	.0214	.0997	.1900	.2457	.2517	.2181	.1651	.1107	.0660	.0349
	4	.0028	.0277	.0838	.1535	.2097	.2337	.2222	.1845	.1350	.0873
	5	.0003	.0055	.0266	.0691	.1258	.1803	.2154	.2214	.1989	.1571
	6	.0000	.0008	.0063	.0230	.0559	.1030	.1546	.1968	.2169	.2095
	7	.0000	.0001	.0011	.0058	.0186	.0442	.0833	.1312	.1775	.2095
	8	.0000	.0000	.0001	.0011	.0047	.0142	.0336	.0656	.1089	.1571
	9	.0000	.0000	.0000	.0001	.0009	.0034	.0101	.0243	.0495	.0873
	10	.0000	.0000	.0000	.0000	.0001	.0006	.0022	.0065	.0162	.0349
	11	.0000	.0000	.0000	.0000	.0000	.0001	.0003	.0012	.0036	.0095
	12	.0000	.0000	.0000	.0000	.0000	.0000	.0000	.0001	.0005	.0016
	13	.0000	.0000	.0000	.0000	.0000	.0000	.0000	.0000	.0000	.0001
14	0	.4877	.2288	.1028	.0440	.0178	.0068	.0024	.0008	.0002	.0001
	1	.3593	.3559	.2539	.1539	.0832	.0407	.0181	.0073	.0027	.0009
	2	.1229	.2570	.2912	.2501	.1802	.1134	.0634	.0317	.0141	.0056
	3	.0259	.1142	.2056	.2501	.2402	.1943	.1366	.0845	.0462	.0222
	4	.0037	.0349	.0998	.1720	.2202	.2290	.2022	.1549	.1040	.0611
	5	.0004	.0078	.0352	.0860	.1468	.1963	.2178	.2066	.1701	.1222
	6	.0000	.0013	.0093	.0322	.0734	.1262	.1759	.2066	.2088	.1833
	7	.0000	.0002	.0019	.0092	.0280	.0618	.1082	.1574	.1952	.2095
	8	.0000	.0000	.0003	.0020	.0082	.0232	.0510	.0918	.1398	.1833
	9	.0000	.0000	.0000	.0003	.0018	.0066	.0183	.0408	.0762	.1222
	10	.0000	.0000	.0000	.0000	.0003	.0014	.0049	.0136	.0312	.0611
	11	.0000	.0000	.0000	.0000	.0000	.0002	.0010	.0033	.0093	.0222
	12	.0000	.0000	.0000	.0000	.0000	.0000	.0001	.0005	.0019	.0056
	13	.0000	.0000	.0000	.0000	.0000	.0000	.0000	.0001	.0002	.0009
	14	.0000	.0000	.0000	.0000	.0000	.0000	.0000	.0000	.0000	.0001

(*continued*)

APPENDIX TABLE C (*continued*)

		Values of π									
n	x	.05	.10	.15	.20	.25	.30	.35	.40	.45	.50
15	0	.4633	.2059	.0874	.0352	.0134	.0047	.0016	.0005	.0001	.0000
	1	.3658	.3432	.2312	.1319	.0668	.0305	.0126	.0047	.0016	.0005
	2	.1348	.2669	.2856	.2309	.1559	.0916	.0476	.0219	.0090	.0032
	3	.0307	.1285	.2184	.2501	.2252	.1700	.1110	.0634	.0318	.0139
	4	.0049	.0428	.1156	.1876	.2252	.2186	.1792	.1268	.0780	.0417
	5	.0006	.0105	.0449	.1032	.1651	.2061	.2123	.1859	.1404	.0916
	6	.0000	.0019	.0132	.0430	.0917	.1472	.1906	.2066	.1914	.1527
	7	.0000	.0003	.0030	.0138	.0393	.0811	.1319	.1771	.2013	.1964
	8	.0000	.0000	.0005	.0035	.0131	.0348	.0710	.1181	.1647	.1964
	9	.0000	.0000	.0001	.0007	.0034	.0116	.0298	.0612	.1048	.1527
	10	.0000	.0000	.0000	.0001	.0007	.0030	.0096	.0245	.0515	.0916
	11	.0000	.0000	.0000	.0000	.0001	.0006	.0024	.0074	.0191	.0417
	12	.0000	.0000	.0000	.0000	.0000	.0001	.0004	.0016	.0052	.0139
	13	.0000	.0000	.0000	.0000	.0000	.0000	.0001	.0003	.0010	.0032
	14	.0000	.0000	.0000	.0000	.0000	.0000	.0000	.0000	.0001	.0005
	15	.0000	.0000	.0000	.0000	.0000	.0000	.0000	.0000	.0000	.0000
16	0	.4401	.1853	.0743	.0281	.0100	.0033	.0010	.0003	.0001	.0000
	1	.3706	.3294	.2097	.1126	.0535	.0228	.0087	.0030	.0009	.0002
	2	.1463	.2745	.2775	.2111	.1336	.0732	.0353	.0150	.0056	.0018
	3	.0359	.1423	.2285	.2463	.2079	.1465	.0888	.0468	.0215	.0085
	4	.0061	.0514	.1311	.2001	.2252	.2040	.1553	.1014	.0572	.0278
	5	.0008	.0137	.0555	.1201	.1802	.2099	.2008	.1623	.1123	.0667
	6	.0001	.0028	.0180	.0550	.1101	.1649	.1982	.1983	.1684	.1222
	7	.0000	.0004	.0045	.0197	.0524	.1010	.1524	.1889	.1969	.1746
	8	.0000	.0001	.0009	.0055	.0197	.0487	.0923	.1417	.1812	.1964
	9	.0000	.0000	.0001	.0012	.0058	.0185	.0442	.0840	.1318	.1746
	10	.0000	.0000	.0000	.0002	.0014	.0056	.0167	.0392	.0755	.1222
	11	.0000	.0000	.0000	.0000	.0002	.0013	.0049	.0142	.0337	.0667
	12	.0000	.0000	.0000	.0000	.0000	.0002	.0011	.0040	.0115	.0278
	13	.0000	.0000	.0000	.0000	.0000	.0000	.0002	.0008	.0029	.0085
	14	.0000	.0000	.0000	.0000	.0000	.0000	.0000	.0001	.0005	.0018
	15	.0000	.0000	.0000	.0000	.0000	.0000	.0000	.0000	.0001	.0002
	16	.0000	.0000	.0000	.0000	.0000	.0000	.0000	.0000	.0000	.0000

(*continued*)

APPENDIX TABLE C (*continued*)

		Values of π									
n	*x*	.05	.10	.15	.20	.25	.30	.35	.40	.45	.50
17	0	.4181	.1668	.0631	.0225	.0075	.0023	.0007	.0002	.0000	.0000
	1	.3741	.3150	.1893	.0957	.0426	.0169	.0060	.0019	.0005	.0001
	2	.1575	.2800	.2673	.1914	.1136	.0581	.0260	.0102	.0035	.0010
	3	.0415	.1556	.2359	.2393	.1893	.1245	.0701	.0341	.0144	.0052
	4	.0076	.0605	.1457	.2093	.2209	.1868	.1320	.0796	.0411	.0182
	5	.0010	.0175	.0668	.1361	.1914	.2081	.1849	.1379	.0875	.0472
	6	.0001	.0039	.0236	.0680	.1276	.1784	.1991	.1839	.1432	.0944
	7	.0000	.0007	.0065	.0267	.0668	.1201	.1685	.1927	.1841	.1484
	8	.0000	.0001	.0014	.0084	.0279	.0644	.1134	.1606	.1883	.1855
	9	.0000	.0000	.0003	.0021	.0093	.0276	.0611	.1070	.1540	.1855
	10	.0000	.0000	.0000	.0004	.0025	.0095	.0263	.0571	.1008	.1484
	11	.0000	.0000	.0000	.0001	.0005	.0026	.0090	.0242	.0525	.0944
	12	.0000	.0000	.0000	.0000	.0001	.0006	.0024	.0081	.0215	.0472
	13	.0000	.0000	.0000	.0000	.0000	.0001	.0005	.0021	.0068	.0182
	14	.0000	.0000	.0000	.0000	.0000	.0000	.0001	.0004	.0016	.0052
	15	.0000	.0000	.0000	.0000	.0000	.0000	.0000	.0001	.0003	.0010
	16	.0000	.0000	.0000	.0000	.0000	.0000	.0000	.0000	.0000	.0001
	17	.0000	.0000	.0000	.0000	.0000	.0000	.0000	.0000	.0000	.0000
18	0	.3972	.1501	.0536	.0180	.0056	.0016	.0004	.0001	.0000	.0000
	1	.3763	.3002	.1704	.0811	.0338	.0126	.0042	.0012	.0003	.0001
	2	.1683	.2835	.2556	.1723	.0958	.0458	.0190	.0069	.0022	.0006
	3	.0473	.1680	.2406	.2297	.1704	.1046	.0547	.0246	.0095	.0031
	4	.0093	.0700	.1592	.2153	.2130	.1681	.1104	.0614	.0291	.0117
	5	.0014	.0218	.0787	.1507	.1988	.2017	.1664	.1146	.0666	.0327
	6	.0002	.0052	.0301	.0816	.1436	.1873	.1941	.1655	.1181	.0708
	7	.0000	.0010	.0091	.0350	.0820	.1376	.1792	.1892	.1657	.1214
	8	.0000	.0002	.0022	.0120	.0376	.0811	.1327	.1734	.1864	.1669
	9	.0000	.0000	.0004	.0033	.0139	.0386	.0794	.1284	.1694	.1855
	10	.0000	.0000	.0001	.0008	.0042	.0149	.0385	.0771	.1248	.1669
	11	.0000	.0000	.0000	.0001	.0010	.0046	.0151	.0374	.0742	.1214
	12	.0000	.0000	.0000	.0000	.0002	.0012	.0047	.0145	.0354	.0708
	13	.0000	.0000	.0000	.0000	.0000	.0002	.0012	.0045	.0134	.0327
	14	.0000	.0000	.0000	.0000	.0000	.0000	.0002	.0011	.0039	.0117
	15	.0000	.0000	.0000	.0000	.0000	.0000	.0000	.0002	.0009	.0031
	16	.0000	.0000	.0000	.0000	.0000	.0000	.0000	.0000	.0001	.0006
	17	.0000	.0000	.0000	.0000	.0000	.0000	.0000	.0000	.0000	.0001
	18	.0000	.0000	.0000	.0000	.0000	.0000	.0000	.0000	.0000	.0000

(*continued*)

APPENDIX TABLE C (*continued*)

n	x	.05	.10	.15	.20	.25	.30	.35	.40	.45	.50
		Values of π									
19	0	.3774	.1351	.0456	.0144	.0042	.0011	.0003	.0001	.0000	.0000
	1	.3774	.2852	.1529	.0685	.0268	.0093	.0029	.0008	.0002	.0000
	2	.1787	.2852	.2428	.1540	.0803	.0358	.0138	.0046	.0013	.0003
	3	.0533	.1796	.2428	.2182	.1517	.0869	.0422	.0175	.0062	.0018
	4	.0112	.0798	.1714	.2182	.2023	.1491	.0909	.0467	.0203	.0074
	5	.0018	.0266	.0907	.1636	.2023	.1916	.1468	.0933	.0497	.0222
	6	.0002	.0069	.0374	.0955	.1574	.1916	.1844	.1451	.0949	.0518
	7	.0000	.0014	.0122	.0443	.0974	.1525	.1844	.1797	.1443	.0961
	8	.0000	.0002	.0032	.0166	.0487	.0981	.1489	.1797	.1771	.1442
	9	.0000	.0000	.0007	.0051	.0198	.0514	.0980	.1464	.1771	.1762
	10	.0000	.0000	.0001	.0013	.0066	.0220	.0528	.0976	.1449	.1762
	11	.0000	.0000	.0000	.0003	.0018	.0077	.0233	.0532	.0970	.1442
	12	.0000	.0000	.0000	.0000	.0004	.0022	.0083	.0237	.0529	.0961
	13	.0000	.0000	.0000	.0000	.0001	.0005	.0024	.0085	.0233	.0518
	14	.0000	.0000	.0000	.0000	.0000	.0001	.0006	.0024	.0082	.0222
	15	.0000	.0000	.0000	.0000	.0000	.0000	.0001	.0005	.0022	.0074
	16	.0000	.0000	.0000	.0000	.0000	.0000	.0000	.0001	.0005	.0018
	17	.0000	.0000	.0000	.0000	.0000	.0000	.0000	.0000	.0001	.0003
	18	.0000	.0000	.0000	.0000	.0000	.0000	.0000	.0000	.0000	.0000
	19	.0000	.0000	.0000	.0000	.0000	.0000	.0000	.0000	.0000	.0000
20	0	.3585	.1216	.0388	.0115	.0032	.0008	.0002	.0000	.0000	.0000
	1	.3774	.2702	.1368	.0576	.0211	.0068	.0020	.0005	.0001	.0000
	2	.1887	.2852	.2293	.1369	.0669	.0278	.0100	.0031	.0008	.0002
	3	.0596	.1901	.2428	.2054	.1339	.0716	.0323	.0123	.0040	.0011
	4	.0133	.0898	.1821	.2182	.1897	.1304	.0738	.0350	.0139	.0046
	5	.0022	.0319	.1028	.1746	.2023	.1789	.1272	.0746	.0365	.0148
	6	.0003	.0089	.0454	.1091	.1686	.1916	.1712	.1244	.0746	.0370
	7	.0000	.0020	.0160	.0545	.1124	.1643	.1844	.1659	.1221	.0739
	8	.0000	.0004	.0046	.0222	.0609	.1144	.1614	.1797	.1623	.1201
	9	.0000	.0001	.0011	.0074	.0271	.0654	.1158	.1597	.1771	.1602
	10	.0000	.0000	.0002	.0020	.0099	.0308	.0686	.1171	.1593	.1762
	11	.0000	.0000	.0000	.0005	.0030	.0120	.0336	.0710	.1185	.1602
	12	.0000	.0000	.0000	.0001	.0008	.0039	.0136	.0355	.0727	.1201
	13	.0000	.0000	.0000	.0000	.0002	.0010	.0045	.0146	.0366	.0739
	14	.0000	.0000	.0000	.0000	.0000	.0002	.0012	.0049	.0150	.0370
	15	.0000	.0000	.0000	.0000	.0000	.0000	.0003	.0013	.0049	.0148
	16	.0000	.0000	.0000	.0000	.0000	.0000	.0000	.0003	.0013	.0046
	17	.0000	.0000	.0000	.0000	.0000	.0000	.0000	.0000	.0002	.0011
	18	.0000	.0000	.0000	.0000	.0000	.0000	.0000	.0000	.0000	.0002
	19	.0000	.0000	.0000	.0000	.0000	.0000	.0000	.0000	.0000	.0000
	20	.0000	.0000	.0000	.0000	.0000	.0000	.0000	.0000	.0000	.0000

SOURCE: The National Bureau of Standards, *Tables of the Binomial Probability Distribution,* Applied Mathematics Series, no. 6 (Washington, D.C.: U.S. Government Printing Office, 1949). The original contains probabilities for values of n up to 49 and for values of π in increments of .01. All entries were calculated by Formula 9.D.

APPENDIX TABLE D | Binomial Probabilities for Cumulative Values of x

Entries in this table give the probability of x or fewer successes in n trials of a binomial experiment, where π is the probability of a success in one trial. For example, with $n = 5$ trials and $\pi = .20$, the probability of two or fewer successes is .9421. (Probability values in blank spaces equal 1.0000).

		Values of π					
n	x	.05	.10	.20	.30	.40	.50
1	0	0.9500	0.9000	0.8000	0.7000	0.6000	0.5000
	1	1.0000	1.0000	1.0000	1.0000	1.0000	1.0000
2	0	0.9025	0.8100	0.6400	0.4900	0.3600	0.2500
	1	0.9975	0.9900	0.9600	0.9100	0.8400	0.7500
	2	1.0000	1.0000	1.0000	1.0000	1.0000	1.0000
3	0	0.8574	0.7290	0.5120	0.3430	0.2160	0.1250
	1	0.9927	0.9720	0.8960	0.7840	0.6480	0.5000
	2	0.9999	0.9990	0.9920	0.9730	0.9360	0.8750
	3	1.0000	1.0000	1.0000	1.0000	1.0000	1.0000
4	0	0.8145	0.6561	0.4096	0.2401	0.1296	0.0625
	1	0.9860	0.9477	0.8192	0.6517	0.4752	0.3125
	2	0.9995	0.9963	0.9728	0.9163	0.8208	0.6875
	3	1.0000	0.9999	0.9984	0.9919	0.9744	0.9375
	4		1.0000	1.0000	1.0000	1.0000	1.0000
5	0	0.7738	0.5905	0.3277	0.1681	0.0778	0.0313
	1	0.9774	0.9185	0.7373	0.5282	0.3370	0.1875
	2	0.9988	0.9914	0.9421	0.8369	0.6826	0.5000
	3	1.0000	0.9995	0.9933	0.9692	0.9130	0.8125
	4		1.0000	0.9997	0.9976	0.9898	0.9688
	5			1.0000	1.0000	1.0000	1.0000
6	0	0.7351	0.5314	0.2621	0.1176	0.0467	0.0156
	1	0.9672	0.8857	0.6554	0.4202	0.2333	0.1094
	2	0.9978	0.9841	0.9011	0.7443	0.5443	0.3438
	3	0.9999	0.9987	0.9830	0.9295	0.8208	0.6563
	4	1.0000	0.9999	0.9984	0.9891	0.9590	0.8906
	5		1.0000	0.9999	0.9993	0.9959	0.9844
	6			1.0000	1.0000	1.0000	1.0000
7	0	0.6983	0.4783	0.2097	0.0824	0.0280	0.0078
	1	0.9556	0.8503	0.5767	0.3294	0.1586	0.0625
	2	0.9962	0.9743	0.8520	0.6471	0.4199	0.2266
	3	0.9998	0.9973	0.9667	0.8740	0.7102	0.5000
	4	1.0000	0.9998	0.9953	0.9712	0.9037	0.7734
	5		1.0000	0.9996	0.9962	0.9812	0.9375
	6			1.0000	0.9998	0.9984	0.9922
	7				1.0000	1.0000	1.0000

(continued)

APPENDIX TABLE D (*continued*)

		Values of π					
n	*x*	.05	.10	.20	.30	.40	.50
8	0	0.6634	0.4305	0.1678	0.0576	0.0168	0.0039
	1	0.9428	0.8131	0.5033	0.2553	0.1064	0.0352
	2	0.9942	0.9619	0.7969	0.5518	0.3154	0.1445
	3	0.9996	0.9950	0.9437	0.8059	0.5941	0.3633
	4	1.0000	0.9996	0.9896	0.9420	0.8263	0.6367
	5		1.0000	0.9988	0.9887	0.9502	0.8555
	6			0.9999	0.9987	0.9915	0.9648
	7			1.0000	0.9999	0.9993	0.9961
	8				1.0000	1.0000	1.0000
9	0	0.6302	0.3874	0.1342	0.0404	0.0101	0.0020
	1	0.9288	0.7748	0.4362	0.1960	0.0705	0.0195
	2	0.9916	0.9470	0.7382	0.4628	0.2318	0.0898
	3	0.9994	0.9917	0.9144	0.7297	0.4826	0.2539
	4	1.0000	0.9991	0.9804	0.9012	0.7334	0.5000
	5		0.9999	0.9969	0.9747	0.9006	0.7461
	6		1.0000	0.9997	0.9957	0.9750	0.9102
	7			1.0000	0.9996	0.9962	0.9805
	8				1.0000	0.9997	0.9980
	9					1.0000	1.0000
10	0	0.5987	0.3487	0.1074	0.0282	0.0060	0.0010
	1	0.9139	0.7361	0.3758	0.1493	0.0464	0.0107
	2	0.9885	0.9298	0.6778	0.3828	0.1673	0.0547
	3	0.9990	0.9872	0.8791	0.6496	0.3823	0.1719
	4	0.9999	0.9984	0.9672	0.8497	0.6331	0.3770
	5	1.0000	0.9999	0.9936	0.9526	0.8338	0.6230
	6		1.0000	0.9991	0.9894	0.9452	0.8281
	7			0.9999	0.9999	0.9877	0.9453
	8			1.0000	1.0000	0.9983	0.9893
	9					0.9999	0.9990
	10					1.0000	1.0000
11	0	0.5688	0.3138	0.0859	0.0198	0.0036	0.0005
	1	0.8981	0.6974	0.3221	0.1130	0.0302	0.0059
	2	0.9848	0.9104	0.6174	0.3127	0.1189	0.0327
	3	0.9984	0.9815	0.8369	0.5696	0.2963	0.1133
	4	0.9999	0.9972	0.9496	0.7897	0.5328	0.2744
	5	1.0000	0.9997	0.9883	0.9218	0.7535	0.5000
	6		1.0000	0.9980	0.9784	0.9006	0.7256
	7			0.9998	0.9957	0.9707	0.8867
	8			1.0000	0.9994	0.9941	0.9673
	9				1.0000	0.9993	0.9941
	10					1.0000	0.9995
	11						1.0000

(*continued*)

APPENDIX TABLE D (*continued*)

		Values of π					
n	x	.05	.10	.20	.30	.40	.50
12	0	0.5404	0.2824	0.0687	0.0138	0.0022	0.0002
	1	0.8816	0.6590	0.2749	0.0850	0.0196	0.0032
	2	0.9804	0.8891	0.5583	0.2528	0.0834	0.0193
	3	0.9978	0.9744	0.7946	0.4925	0.2253	0.0730
	4	0.9998	0.9957	0.9274	0.7237	0.4382	0.1938
	5	1.0000	0.9995	0.9806	0.8821	0.6652	0.3872
	6		0.9999	0.9961	0.9614	0.8418	0.6128
	7		1.0000	0.9994	0.9905	0.9427	0.8062
	8			0.9999	0.9983	0.9847	0.9270
	9			1.0000	0.9998	0.9972	0.9807
	10				1.0000	0.9997	0.9968
	11					1.0000	0.9998
	12						1.0000
13	0	0.5133	0.2542	0.0550	0.0097	0.0013	0.0001
	1	0.8646	0.6213	0.2336	0.0637	0.0126	0.0017
	2	0.9755	0.8661	0.5017	0.2025	0.0579	0.0112
	3	0.9969	0.9658	0.7473	0.4206	0.1686	0.0461
	4	0.9997	0.9935	0.9009	0.6543	0.3530	0.1334
	5	1.0000	0.9991	0.9700	0.8346	0.5744	0.2905
	6		0.9999	0.9930	0.9376	0.7712	0.5000
	7		1.0000	0.9988	0.9818	0.9023	0.7095
	8			0.9998	0.9960	0.9679	0.8666
	9			1.0000	0.9993	0.9922	0.9539
	10				0.9999	0.9987	0.9888
	11				1.0000	0.9999	0.9983
	12					1.0000	0.9999
	13						1.0000
14	0	0.4877	0.2288	0.0440	0.0068	0.0008	0.0001
	1	0.8470	0.5846	0.1979	0.0475	0.0081	0.0009
	2	0.9699	0.8416	0.4481	0.1608	0.0398	0.0065
	3	0.9958	0.9559	0.6982	0.3552	0.1243	0.0287
	4	0.9996	0.9908	0.8702	0.5842	0.2793	0.0898
	5	1.0000	0.9985	0.9561	0.7805	0.4859	0.2120
	6		0.9998	0.9884	0.9067	0.6925	0.3953
	7		1.0000	0.9976	0.9685	0.8499	0.6047
	8			0.9996	0.9917	0.9417	0.7880
	9			1.0000	0.9983	0.9825	0.9102
	10				0.9998	0.9961	0.9713
	11				1.0000	0.9994	0.9935
	12					0.9999	0.9991
	13					1.0000	0.9999
	14						1.0000

(*continued*)

APPENDIX TABLE D (*continued*)

n	x	Values of π .05	.10	.20	.30	.40	.50
15	0	0.4633	0.2059	0.0352	0.0047	0.0005	0.0000
	1	0.8290	0.5490	0.1671	0.0353	0.0052	0.0005
	2	0.9638	0.8159	0.3980	0.1268	0.0271	0.0037
	3	0.9945	0.9444	0.6482	0.2969	0.0905	0.0176
	4	0.9994	0.9873	0.8358	0.5155	0.2173	0.0592
	5	0.9999	0.9978	0.9389	0.7216	0.4032	0.1509
	6	1.0000	0.9997	0.9819	0.8689	0.6098	0.3036
	7		1.0000	0.9958	0.9500	0.7869	0.5000
	8			0.9992	0.9848	0.9050	0.6964
	9			0.9999	0.9963	0.9662	0.8491
	10			1.0000	0.9993	0.9907	0.9408
	11				0.9999	0.9981	0.9824
	12				1.0000	0.9997	0.9963
	13					1.0000	0.9995
	14						1.0000
16	0	0.4401	0.1853	0.0281	0.0033	0.0003	0.0000
	1	0.8108	0.5147	0.1407	0.0261	0.0033	0.0003
	2	0.9571	0.7892	0.3518	0.0994	0.0183	0.0021
	3	0.9930	0.9316	0.5981	0.2459	0.0651	0.0106
	4	0.9991	0.9830	0.7982	0.4499	0.1666	0.0384
	5	0.9999	0.9967	0.9183	0.6598	0.3288	0.1051
	6	1.0000	0.9995	0.9733	0.8247	0.5272	0.2272
	7		0.9999	0.9930	0.9256	0.7161	0.4018
	8		1.0000	0.9985	0.9743	0.8577	0.5982
	9			0.9998	0.9929	0.9417	0.7728
	10			1.0000	0.9984	0.9809	0.8949
	11				0.9997	0.9951	0.9616
	12				1.0000	0.9991	0.9894
	13					0.9999	0.9979
	14					1.0000	0.9997
	15						1.0000
17	0	0.4181	0.1668	0.0225	0.0023	0.0002	0.0000
	1	0.7922	0.4818	0.1182	0.0193	0.0021	0.0001
	2	0.9497	0.7618	0.3096	0.0774	0.0123	0.0012
	3	0.9912	0.9174	0.5489	0.2019	0.0464	0.0064
	4	0.9988	0.9779	0.7582	0.3887	0.1260	0.0245
	5	0.9999	0.9953	0.8943	0.5968	0.2639	0.0717
	6	1.0000	0.9992	0.9623	0.7752	0.4478	0.1662
	7		0.9999	0.9891	0.8954	0.6405	0.3145
	8		1.0000	0.9974	0.9597	0.8011	0.5000
	9			0.9995	0.9873	0.9081	0.6855
	10			0.9999	0.9968	0.9652	0.8338
	11			1.0000	0.9993	0.9894	0.9283
	12				0.9999	0.9975	0.9755
	13				1.0000	0.9995	0.9936
	14					0.9999	0.9988
	15					1.0000	0.9999
	16						1.0000

(*continued*)

APPENDIX TABLE D (*continued*)

		Values of π					
n	*x*	.05	.10	.20	.30	.40	.50
18	0	0.3972	0.1501	0.0180	0.0016	0.0001	0.0000
	1	0.7735	0.4503	0.0991	0.0142	0.0013	0.0001
	2	0.9419	0.7338	0.2713	0.0600	0.0082	0.0007
	3	0.9891	0.9018	0.5010	0.1646	0.0328	0.0038
	4	0.9985	0.9718	0.7164	0.3327	0.0942	0.0154
	5	0.9998	0.9936	0.8671	0.5344	0.2088	0.0481
	6	1.0000	0.9988	0.9487	0.7217	0.3743	0.1189
	7		0.9998	0.9837	0.8593	0.5634	0.2403
	8		1.0000	0.9957	0.9404	0.7368	0.4073
	9			0.9991	0.9790	0.8653	0.5927
	10			0.9998	0.9939	0.9424	0.7597
	11			1.0000	0.9986	0.9797	0.8811
	12				0.9997	0.9942	0.9519
	13				1.0000	0.9987	0.9846
	14					0.9998	0.9962
	15					1.0000	0.9993
	16						0.9999
	17						1.0000
19	0	0.3774	0.1351	0.0144	0.0011	0.0001	0.0000
	1	0.7547	0.4203	0.0829	0.0104	0.0008	0.0000
	2	0.9335	0.7054	0.2369	0.0462	0.0055	0.0004
	3	0.9868	0.8850	0.4551	0.1332	0.0230	0.0022
	4	0.9980	0.9648	0.6733	0.2822	0.0696	0.0096
	5	0.9998	0.9914	0.8369	0.4739	0.1629	0.0318
	6	1.0000	0.9983	0.9324	0.6655	0.3081	0.0835
	7		0.9997	0.9767	0.8180	0.4878	0.1796
	8		1.0000	0.9933	0.9161	0.6675	0.3238
	9			0.9984	0.9674	0.8139	0.5000
	10			0.9997	0.9895	0.9115	0.6762
	11			0.9999	0.9972	0.9648	0.8204
	12			1.0000	0.9994	0.9884	0.9165
	13				0.9999	0.9969	0.9682
	14				1.0000	0.9994	0.9904
	15					0.9999	0.9978
	16					1.0000	0.9996
	17						1.0000

(continued)

APPENDIX TABLE D (*continued*)

n	x	Values of π .05	.10	.20	.30	.40	.50
20	0	0.3585	0.1216	0.0115	0.0008	0.0000	0.0000
	1	0.7358	0.3917	0.0692	0.0076	0.0005	0.0000
	2	0.9245	0.6769	0.2061	0.0355	0.0036	0.0002
	3	0.9841	0.8670	0.4114	0.1071	0.0160	0.0013
	4	0.9974	0.9568	0.6296	0.2375	0.0510	0.0059
	5	0.9997	0.9887	0.8042	0.4164	0.1256	0.0207
	6	1.0000	0.9976	0.9133	0.6080	0.2500	0.0577
	7		0.9996	0.9679	0.7723	0.4159	0.1316
	8		0.9999	0.9900	0.8867	0.5956	0.2517
	9		1.0000	0.9974	0.9520	0.7553	0.4119
	10			0.9994	0.9829	0.8725	0.5881
	11			0.9999	0.9949	0.9435	0.7483
	12			1.0000	0.9987	0.9790	0.8684
	13				0.9997	0.9935	0.9423
	14				1.0000	0.9984	0.9793
	15					0.9997	0.9941
	16					1.0000	0.9987
	17						0.9998
	18						1.0000
50	0	0.0769	0.0052	0.0000	0.0000	0.0000	0.0000
	1	0.2794	0.0338	0.0002	0.0000	0.0000	0.0000
	2	0.5405	0.1117	0.0013	0.0000	0.0000	0.0000
	3	0.7604	0.2503	0.0057	0.0000	0.0000	0.0000
	4	0.8964	0.4312	0.0185	0.0002	0.0000	0.0000
	5	0.9622	0.6161	0.0480	0.0007	0.0000	0.0000
	6	0.9882	0.7702	0.1034	0.0025	0.0000	0.0000
	7	0.9968	0.8779	0.1904	0.0073	0.0001	0.0000
	8	0.9992	0.9421	0.3073	0.0183	0.0002	0.0000
	9	0.9998	0.9755	0.4437	0.0402	0.0008	0.0000
	10	1.0000	0.9906	0.5836	0.0789	0.0022	0.0000
	11		0.9968	0.7107	0.1390	0.0057	0.0000
	12		0.9990	0.8139	0.2229	0.0133	0.0002
	13		0.9997	0.8894	0.3279	0.0280	0.0005
	14		0.9999	0.9393	0.4468	0.0540	0.0013
	15		1.0000	0.9692	0.5692	0.0955	0.0033
	16			0.9856	0.6839	0.1561	0.0077
	17			0.9937	0.7822	0.2369	0.0164
	18			0.9975	0.8594	0.3356	0.0325
	19			0.9991	0.9152	0.4465	0.0595
	20			0.9997	0.9522	0.5610	0.1013
	21			0.9999	0.9749	0.6701	0.1611
	22			1.0000	0.9877	0.7660	0.2399
	23				0.9944	0.8438	0.3359
	24				0.9976	0.9022	0.4439
	25				0.9991	0.9427	0.5561
	26				0.9997	0.9686	0.6641
	27				0.9999	0.9840	0.7601
	28				1.0000	0.9924	0.8389
	29					0.9966	0.8987
	30					0.9986	0.9405

(continued)

APPENDIX TABLE D *(continued)*

n	x	.05	.10	.20	.30	.40	.50
		Values of π					
	31					0.9995	0.9675
	32					0.9998	0.9836
	33					0.9999	0.9923
	34					1.0000	0.9967
	35						0.9987
	36						0.9995
	37						0.9998
	38						1.0000
100	0	0.0059	0.0000	0.0000	0.0000	0.0000	0.0000
	1	0.0371	0.0003	0.0000	0.0000	0.0000	0.0000
	2	0.1183	0.0019	0.0000	0.0000	0.0000	0.0000
	3	0.2578	0.0078	0.0000	0.0000	0.0000	0.0000
	4	0.4360	0.0237	0.0000	0.0000	0.0000	0.0000
	5	0.6160	0.0576	0.0000	0.0000	0.0000	0.0000
	6	0.7660	0.1172	0.0001	0.0000	0.0000	0.0000
	7	0.8720	0.2061	0.0003	0.0000	0.0000	0.0000
	8	0.9369	0.3209	0.0009	0.0000	0.0000	0.0000
	9	0.9718	0.4513	0.0023	0.0000	0.0000	0.0000
	10	0.9885	0.5832	0.0057	0.0000	0.0000	0.0000
	11	0.9957	0.7030	0.0126	0.0000	0.0000	0.0000
	12	0.9985	0.8018	0.0253	0.0000	0.0000	0.0000
	13	0.9995	0.8761	0.0469	0.0001	0.0000	0.0000
	14	0.9999	0.9274	0.0804	0.0002	0.0000	0.0000
	15	1.0000	0.9601	0.1285	0.0004	0.0000	0.0000
	16		0.9794	0.1923	0.0010	0.0000	0.0000
	17		0.9900	0.2712	0.0022	0.0000	0.0000
	18		0.9954	0.3621	0.0045	0.0000	0.0000
	19		0.9980	0.4602	0.0089	0.0000	0.0000
	20		0.9992	0.5595	0.0165	0.0000	0.0000
	21		0.9997	0.6540	0.0288	0.0000	0.0000
	22		0.9999	0.7389	0.0479	0.0001	0.0000
	23		1.0000	0.8109	0.0755	0.0003	0.0000
	24			0.8686	0.1136	0.0006	0.0000
	25			0.9125	0.1631	0.0012	0.0000
	26			0.9442	0.2244	0.0024	0.0000
	27			0.9658	0.2964	0.0046	0.0000
	28			0.9800	0.3768	0.0084	0.0000
	29			0.9888	0.4623	0.0148	0.0000
	30			0.9939	0.5491	0.0248	0.0000
	31			0.9969	0.6331	0.0398	0.0001
	32			0.9984	0.7107	0.0615	0.0002
	33			0.9993	0.7793	0.0913	0.0004
	34			0.9997	0.8371	0.1303	0.0009
	35			0.9999	0.8839	0.1795	0.0018

(continued)

APPENDIX TABLE D (*continued*)

		Values of π			
n	*x*	.20	.30	.40	.50
100	36	0.9999	0.9201	0.2386	0.0033
	37	1.0000	0.9470	0.3068	0.0060
	38		0.9660	0.3822	0.0105
	39		0.9790	0.4621	0.0176
	40		0.9875	0.5433	0.0284
	41		0.9928	0.6225	0.0443
	42		0.9960	0.6967	0.0666
	43		0.9979	0.7635	0.0967
	44		0.9989	0.8211	0.1356
	45		0.9995	0.8689	0.1841
	46		0.9997	0.9070	0.2421
	47		0.9999	0.9362	0.3086
	48		0.9999	0.9577	0.3822
	49		1.0000	0.9729	0.4602
	50			0.9832	0.5398
	51			0.9900	0.6178
	52			0.9942	0.6914
	53			0.9968	0.7579
	54			0.9983	0.8159
	55			0.9991	0.8644
	56			0.9996	0.9033
	57			0.9998	0.9334
	58			0.9999	0.9557
	59			1.0000	0.9716
	60				0.9824
	61				0.9895
	62				0.9940
	63				0.9967
	64				0.9982
	65				0.9991
	66				0.9996
	67				0.9998
	68				0.9999
	69				1.0000

SOURCE: For values of *n* up to 20, the National Bureau of Standards, *Tables of the Binomial Probability Distribution,* Applied Mathematics Series, no. 6 (Washington, D.C.: U.S. Government Printing Office, 1949); for $n = 50$ and $n = 100$, computed by the author.

APPENDIX TABLE E | Exponential Functions

μ	e^{μ}	$e^{-\mu}$	μ	e^{μ}	$e^{-\mu}$
0.00	1.0000	1.000000	3.00	20.086	.049787
0.10	1.1052	.904837	3.10	22.198	.045049
0.20	1.2214	.818731	3.20	24.533	.040762
0.30	1.3499	.740818	3.30	27.113	.036883
0.40	1.4918	.670320	3.40	29.964	.033373
0.50	1.6487	.606531	3.50	33.115	.030197
0.60	1.8221	.548812	3.60	36.598	.027324
0.70	2.0138	.496585	3.70	40.447	.024724
0.80	2.2255	.449329	3.80	44.701	.022371
0.90	2.4596	.406570	3.90	49.402	.020242
1.00	2.7183	.367879	4.00	54.598	.018316
1.10	3.0042	.332871	4.10	60.340	.016573
1.20	3.3201	.301194	4.20	66.686	.014996
1.30	3.6693	.272532	4.30	73.700	.013569
1.40	4.0552	.246597	4.40	81.451	.012277
1.50	4.4817	.223130	4.50	90.017	.011109
1.60	4.9530	.201897	4.60	99.484	.010052
1.70	5.4739	.182684	4.70	109.95	.009095
1.80	6.0496	.165299	4.80	121.51	.008230
1.90	6.6859	.149569	4.90	134.29	.007447
2.00	7.3891	.135335	5.00	148.41	.006738
2.10	8.1662	.122456	5.10	164.02	.006097
2.20	9.0250	.110803	5.20	181.27	.005517
2.30	9.9742	.100259	5.30	200.34	.004992
2.40	11.023	.090718	5.40	221.41	.004517
2.50	12.182	.082085	5.50	244.69	.004087
2.60	13.464	.074274	5.60	270.43	.003698
2.70	14.880	.067206	5.70	298.87	.003346
2.80	16.445	.060810	5.80	330.30	.003028
2.90	18.174	.055023	5.90	365.04	.002739
3.00	20.086	.049787	6.00	403.43	.002479

SOURCE: George F. Becker and C. E. Van Orstrand, *Smithsonian Mathematical Tables: Hyperbolic Functions* (Washington, D.C.: Smithsonian Institution, 1909), pp. 226–258.

Additional values for Appendix Table E can be found by interpolation or by noting this:

$$e = 2.71828 \qquad e^{\mu} = 2.71828^{\mu} \qquad e^{-\mu} = \frac{1}{e^{\mu}} = \frac{1}{2.71828^{\mu}}$$

With the help of logarithms, we can easily solve these expressions for any given μ. For example, if $\mu =$ 2.33 (a value not found in the table), we can write

$$e^{2.33} = 2.71828^{2.33}$$

$$\log e^{2.33} = 2.33(\log 2.71828) = 2.33(.434294) = 1.011905$$

$$e^{2.33} = \text{antilog } 1.011905 = 10.277976$$

$$e^{-2.33} = \frac{1}{10.277976} = .097295$$

APPENDIX TABLE F | Poisson Probabilities for Individual Values of x

Entries in this table give the probability of x occurrences for a Poisson process with a mean of μ. For example, when $\mu = 1.5$, the probability of $x = 4$ occurrences is .0471.

	Values of μ									
x	0.1	0.2	0.3	0.4	0.5	0.6	0.7	0.8	0.9	1.0
0	.9048	.8187	.7408	.6703	.6065	.5488	.4966	.4493	.4066	.3679
1	.0905	.1637	.2222	.2681	.3033	.3293	.3476	.3595	.3659	.3679
2	.0045	.0164	.0333	.0536	.0758	.0988	.1217	.1438	.1647	.1839
3	.0002	.0011	.0033	.0072	.0126	.0198	.0284	.0383	.0494	.0613
4	.0000	.0001	.0002	.0007	.0016	.0030	.0050	.0077	.0111	.0153
5	.0000	.0000	.0000	.0001	.0002	.0004	.0007	.0012	.0020	.0031
6	.0000	.0000	.0000	.0000	.0000	.0000	.0001	.0002	.0003	.0005
7	.0000	.0000	.0000	.0000	.0000	.0000	.0000	.0000	.0000	.0001

	Values of μ									
x	1.1	1.2	1.3	1.4	1.5	1.6	1.7	1.8	1.9	2.0
0	.3329	.3012	.2725	.2466	.2231	.2019	.1827	.1653	.1496	.1353
1	.3662	.3614	.3543	.3452	.3347	.3230	.3106	.2975	.2842	.2707
2	.2014	.2169	.2303	.2417	.2510	.2584	.2640	.2678	.2700	.2707
3	.0738	.0867	.0998	.1128	.1255	.1378	.1496	.1607	.1710	.1804
4	.0203	.0260	.0324	.0395	.0471	.0551	.0636	.0723	.0812	.0902
5	.0045	.0062	.0084	.0111	.0141	.0176	.0216	.0260	.0309	.0361
6	.0008	.0012	.0018	.0026	.0035	.0047	.0061	.0078	.0098	.0120
7	.0001	.0002	.0003	.0005	.0008	.0011	.0015	.0020	.0027	.0034
8	.0000	.0000	.0001	.0001	.0001	.0002	.0003	.0005	.0006	.0009
9	.0000	.0000	.0000	.0000	.0000	.0000	.0001	.0001	.0001	.0002

	Values of μ									
x	2.1	2.2	2.3	2.4	2.5	2.6	2.7	2.8	2.9	3.0
0	.1225	.1108	.1003	.0907	.0821	.0743	.0672	.0608	.0550	.0498
1	.2572	.2438	.2306	.2177	.2052	.1931	.1815	.1703	.1596	.1494
2	.2700	.2681	.2652	.2613	.2565	.2510	.2450	.2384	.2314	.2240
3	.1890	.1966	.2033	.2090	.2138	.2176	.2205	.2225	.2237	.2240
4	.0992	.1082	.1169	.1254	.1336	.1414	.1488	.1557	.1622	.1680
5	.0417	.0476	.0538	.0602	.0668	.0735	.0804	.0872	.0940	.1008
6	.0146	.0174	.0206	.0241	.0278	.0319	.0362	.0407	.0455	.0504
7	.0044	.0055	.0068	.0083	.0099	.0118	.0139	.0163	.0188	.0216
8	.0011	.0015	.0019	.0025	.0031	.0038	.0047	.0057	.0068	.0081
9	.0003	.0004	.0005	.0007	.0009	.0011	.0014	.0018	.0022	.0027
10	.0001	.0001	.0001	0002	.0002	.0003	.0004	.0005	.0006	.0008
11	.0000	.0000	.0000	.0000	.0000	.0001	.0001	.0001	.0002	.0002
12	.0000	.0000	.0000	.0000	.0000	.0000	.0000	.0000	.0000	.0001

(continued)

APPENDIX TABLE F (*continued*)

x	3.1	3.2	3.3	3.4	3.5	3.6	3.7	3.8	3.9	4.0
					Values of μ					
0	.0450	.0408	.0369	.0334	.0302	.0273	.0247	.0224	.0202	.0183
1	.1397	.1304	.1217	.1135	.1057	.0984	.0915	.0850	.0789	.0733
2	.2165	.2087	.2008	.1929	.1850	.1771	.1692	.1615	.1539	.1465
3	.2237	.2226	.2209	.2186	.2158	.2125	.2087	.2046	.2001	.1954
4	.1734	.1781	.1823	.1858	.1888	.1912	.1931	.1944	.1951	.1954
5	.1075	.1140	.1203	.1264	.1322	.1377	.1429	.1477	.1522	.1563
6	.0555	.0608	.0662	.0716	.0771	.0826	.0881	.0936	.0989	.1042
7	.0246	.0278	.0312	.0348	.0385	.0425	.0466	.0508	.0551	.0595
8	.0095	.0111	.0129	.0148	.0169	.0191	.0215	.0241	.0269	.0298
9	.0033	.0040	.0047	.0056	.0066	.0076	.0089	.0102	.0116	.0132
10	.0010	.0013	.0016	.0019	.0023	.0028	.0033	.0039	.0045	.0053
11	.0003	.0004	.0005	.0006	.0007	.0009	.0011	.0013	.0016	.0019
12	.0001	.0001	.0001	.0002	.0002	.0003	.0003	.0004	.0005	.0006
13	.0000	.0000	.0000	.0000	.0001	.0001	.0001	.0001	.0002	.0002
14	.0000	.0000	.0000	.0000	.0000	.0000	.0000	.0000	.0000	.0001

x	4.1	4.2	4.3	4.4	4.5	4.6	4.7	4.8	4.9	5.0
					Values of μ					
0	.0166	.0150	.0136	.0123	.0111	.0101	.0091	.0082	.0074	.0067
1	.0679	.0630	.0583	.0540	.0500	.0462	.0427	.0395	.0365	.0337
2	.1393	.1323	.1254	.1188	.1125	.1063	.1005	.0948	.0894	.0842
3	.1904	.1852	.1798	.1743	.1687	.1631	.1574	.1517	.1460	.1404
4	.1951	.1944	.1933	.1917	.1898	.1875	.1849	.1820	.1789	.1755
5	.1600	.1633	.1662	.1687	.1708	.1725	.1738	.1747	.1753	.1755
6	.1093	.1143	.1191	.1237	.1281	.1323	.1362	.1398	.1432	.1462
7	.0640	.0686	.0732	.0778	.0824	.0869	.0914	.0959	.1002	.1044
8	.0328	.0360	.0393	.0428	.0463	.0500	.0537	.0575	0614	.0653
9	.0150	.0168	.0188	.0209	.0232	.0255	.0280	.0307	.0334	.0363
10	.0061	.0071	.0081	.0092	.0104	.0118	.0132	.0147	.0164	.0181
11	.0023	.0027	.0032	.0037	.0043	.0049	.0056	.0064	.0073	.0082
12	.0008	.0009	.0011	.0014	.0016	.0019	.0022	.0026	.0030	.0034
13	.0002	.0003	.0004	.0005	.0006	.0007	.0008	.0009	.0011	.0013
14	.0001	.0001	.0001	.0001	.0002	.0002	.0003	.0003	.0004	.0005
15	.0000	.0000	.0000	.0000	.0001	.0001	.0001	.0001	.0001	.0002

(*continued*)

APPENDIX TABLE F *(continued)*

x	Values of μ 5.1	5.2	5.3	5.4	5.5	5.6	5.7	5.8	5.9	6.0
0	.0061	.0055	.0050	.0045	.0041	.0037	.0033	.0030	.0027	.0025
1	.0311	.0287	.0265	.0244	.0225	.0207	.0191	.0176	.0162	.0149
2	.0793	.0746	.0701	.0659	.0618	.0580	.0544	.0509	.0477	.0446
3	.1348	.1293	.1239	.1185	.1133	.1082	.1033	.0985	.0938	.0892
4	.1719	.1681	.1641	.1600	.1558	.1515	.1472	.1428	.1383	.1339
5	.1753	.1748	.1740	.1728	.1714	.1697	.1678	.1656	.1632	.1606
6	.1490	.1515	.1537	.1555	.1571	.1584	.1594	.1601	.1605	.1606
7	.1086	.1125	.1163	.1200	.1234	.1267	.1298	.1326	.1353	.1377
8	.0692	.0731	.0771	.0810	.0849	.0887	.0925	.0962	.0998	.1033
9	.0392	.0423	.0454	.0486	.0519	.0552	.0586	.0620	.0654	.0688
10	.0200	.0220	.0241	.0262	.0285	.0309	.0334	.0359	.0386	.0413
11	.0093	.0104	.0116	.0129	.0143	.0157	.0173	.0190	.0207	.0225
12	.0039	.0045	.0051	.0058	.0065	.0073	.0082	.0092	.0102	.0113
13	.0015	.0018	.0021	.0024	.0028	.0032	.0036	.0041	.0046	.0052
14	.0006	.0007	.0008	.0009	.0011	.0013	.0015	.0017	.0019	.0022
15	.0002	.0002	.0003	.0003	.0004	.0005	.0006	.0007	.0008	.0009
16	.0001	.0001	.0001	.0001	.0001	.0002	.0002	.0002	.0003	.0003
17	.0000	.0000	.0000	.0000	.0000	.0001	.0001	.0001	.0001	.0001

x	Values of μ 6.1	6.2	6.3	6.4	6.5	6.6	6.7	6.8	6.9	7.0
0	.0022	.0020	.0018	.0017	.0015	.0014	.0012	.0011	.0010	.0009
1	.0137	.0126	.0116	.0106	.0098	.0090	.0082	.0076	.0070	.0064
2	.0417	.0390	.0364	.0340	.0318	.0296	.0276	.0258	.0240	.0223
3	.0848	.0806	.0765	.0726	.0688	.0652	.0617	.0584	.0552	.0521
4	.1294	.1249	.1205	.1162	.1118	.1076	.1034	.0992	.0952	.0912
5	.1579	.1549	.1519	.1487	.1454	.1420	.1385	.1349	.1314	.1277
6	.1605	.1601	.1595	.1586	.1575	.1562	.1546	.1529	.1511	.1490
7	.1399	.1418	.1435	.1450	.1462	.1472	.1480	.1486	.1489	.1490
8	.1066	.1099	.1130	.1160	.1188	.1215	.1240	.1263	.1284	.1304
9	.0723	.0757	.0791	.0825	.0858	.0891	.0923	.0954	.0985	.1014
10	.0441	.0469	.0498	.0528	.0558	.0588	.0618	.0649	.0679	.0710
11	.0245	.0265	.0285	.0307	.0330	.0353	.0377	.0401	.0426	.0452
12	.0124	.0137	.0150	.0164	.0179	.0194	.0210	.0227	.0245	.0264
13	.0058	.0065	.0073	.0081	.0089	.0098	.0108	.0119	.0130	.0142
14	.0025	.0029	.0033	.0037	.0041	.0046	.0052	.0058	.0064	.0071
15	.0010	.0012	.0014	.0016	.0018	.0020	.0023	.0026	.0029	.0033
16	.0004	.0005	.0005	.0006	.0007	.0008	.0010	.0011	.0013	.0014
17	.0001	.0002	.0002	.0002	.0003	.0003	.0004	.0004	.0005	.0006
18	.0000	.0001	.0001	.0001	.0001	.0001	.0001	.0002	.0002	.0002
19	.0000	.0000	.0000	.0000	.0000	.0000	.0000	.0001	.0001	.0001

(continued)

APPENDIX TABLE F (*continued*)

x	7.1	7.2	7.3	7.4	7.5	7.6	7.7	7.8	7.9	8.0
					Values of μ					
0	.0008	.0007	.0007	.0006	.0006	.0005	.0005	.0004	.0004	.0003
1	.0059	.0054	.0049	.0045	.0041	.0038	.0035	.0032	.0029	.0027
2	.0208	.0194	.0180	.0167	.0156	.0145	.0134	.0125	.0116	.0107
3	.0492	.0464	.0438	.0413	.0389	.0366	.0345	.0324	.0305	.0286
4	.0874	.0836	.0799	.0764	.0729	.0696	.0663	.0632	.0602	.0573
5	.1241	.1204	.1167	.1130	.1094	.1057	.1021	.0986	.0951	.0916
6	.1468	.1445	.1420	.1394	.1367	.1339	.1311	.1282	.1252	.1221
7	.1489	.1486	.1481	.1474	.1465	.1454	.1442	.1428	.1413	.1396
8	.1321	.1337	.1351	.1363	.1373	.1382	.1388	.1392	.1395	.1396
9	.1042	.1070	.1096	.1121	.1144	.1167	.1187	.1207	.1224	.1241
10	.0740	.0770	.0800	.0829	.0858	.0887	.0914	.0941	.0967	.0993
11	.0478	.0504	.0531	.0558	.0585	.0613	.0640	.0667	.0695	.0722
12	.0283	.0303	.0323	.0344	.0366	.0388	.0411	.0434	.0457	.0481
13	.0154	.0168	.0181	.0196	.0211	.0227	.0243	.0260	.0278	.0296
14	.0078	.0086	.0095	.0104	.0113	.0123	.0134	.0145	.0157	.0169
15	.0037	.0041	.0046	.0051	.0057	.0062	.0069	.0075	.0083	.0090
16	.0016	.0019	.0021	.0024	.0026	.0030	.0033	.0037	.0041	.0045
17	.0007	.0008	.0009	.0010	.0012	.0013	.0015	.0017	.0019	.0021
18	.0003	.0003	.0004	.0004	.0005	.0006	.0006	.0007	.0008	.0009
19	.0001	.0001	.0001	.0002	.0002	.0002	.0003	.0003	.0003	.0004
20	.0000	.0000	.0001	.0001	.0001	.0001	.0001	.0001	.0001	.0002
21	.0000	.0000	.0000	.0000	.0000	.0000	.0000	.0000	.0001	.0001

x	8.1	8.2	8.3	8.4	8.5	8.6	8.7	8.8	8.9	9.0
					Values of μ					
0	.0003	.0003	.0002	.0002	.0002	.0002	.0002	.0002	.0001	.0001
1	.0025	.0023	.0021	.0019	.0017	.0016	.0014	.0013	.0012	.0011
2	.0100	.0092	.0086	.0079	.0074	.0068	.0063	.0058	.0054	.0050
3	.0269	.0252	.0237	.0222	.0208	.0195	.0183	.0171	.0160	.0150
4	.0544	.0517	.0491	.0466	.0443	.0420	.0398	.0377	.0357	.0337
5	.0882	.0849	.0816	.0784	.0752	.0722	.0692	.0663	.0635	.0607
6	.1191	.1160	.1128	.1097	.1066	.1034	.1003	.0972	.0941	.0911
7	.1378	.1358	.1338	.1317	.1294	.1271	.1247	.1222	.1197	.1171
8	.1395	.1392	.1388	.1382	.1375	.1366	.1356	.1344	.1332	.1318
9	.1256	.1269	.1280	.1290	.1299	.1306	.1311	.1315	.1317	.1318

(*continued*)

APPENDIX TABLE F (*continued*)

x	Values of μ 8.1	8.2	8.3	8.4	8.5	8.6	8.7	8.8	8.9	9.0
10	.1017	.1040	.1063	.1084	.1104	.1123	.1140	.1157	.1172	.1186
11	.0749	.0776	.0802	.0828	.0853	.0878	.0902	.0925	.0948	.0970
12	.0505	.0530	.0555	.0579	.0604	.0629	.0654	.0679	.0703	.0728
13	.0315	.0334	.0354	.0374	.0395	.0416	.0438	.0459	.0481	.0504
14	.0182	.0196	.0210	.0225	.0240	.0256	.0272	.0289	.0306	.0324
15	.0098	.0107	.0116	.0126	.0136	.0147	.0158	.0169	.0182	.0194
16	.0050	.0055	.0060	.0066	.0072	.0079	.0086	.0093	.0101	.0109
17	.0024	.0026	.0029	.0033	.0036	.0040	.0044	.0048	.0053	.0058
18	.0011	.0012	.0014	.0015	.0017	.0019	.0021	.0024	.0026	.0029
19	.0005	.0005	.0006	.0007	.0008	.0009	.0010	.0011	.0012	.0014
20	.0002	.0002	.0002	.0003	.0003	.0004	.0004	.0005	.0005	.0006
21	.0001	.0001	.0001	.0001	.0001	.0002	.0002	.0002	.0002	.0003
22	.0000	.0000	.0000	.0000	.0001	.0001	.0001	.0001	.0001	.0001

x	Values of μ 9.1	9.2	9.3	9.4	9.5	9.6	9.7	9.8	9.9	10
0	.0001	.0001	.0001	.0001	.0001	.0001	.0001	.0001	.0001	.0000
1	.0010	.0009	.0009	.0008	.0007	.0007	.0006	.0005	.0005	.0005
2	.0046	.0043	.0040	.0037	.0034	.0031	.0029	.0027	.0025	.0023
3	.0140	.0131	.0123	.0115	.0107	.0100	.0093	.0087	.0081	.0076
4	.0319	.0302	.0285	.0269	.0254	.0240	.0226	.0213	.0201	.0189
5	.0581	.0555	.0530	.0506	.0483	.0460	.0439	.0418	.0398	.0378
6	.0881	.0851	.0822	.0793	.0764	.0736	.0709	.0682	.0656	.0631
7	.1145	.1118	.1091	.1064	.1037	.1010	.0982	.0955	.0928	.0901
8	.1302	.1286	.1269	.1251	.1232	.1212	.1191	.1170	.1148	.1126
9	.1317	.1315	.1311	.1306	.1300	.1293	.1284	.1274	.1263	.1251
10	.1198	.1210	.1219	.1228	.1235	.1241	.1245	.1249	.1250	.1251
11	.0991	.1012	.1031	.1049	.1067	.1083	.1098	.1112	.1125	.1137
12	.0752	.0776	.0799	.0822	.0844	.0866	.0888	.0908	.0928	.0948
13	.0526	.0549	.0572	.0594	.0617	.0640	.0662	.0685	.0707	.0729
14	.0342	.0361	.0380	.0399	.0419	.0439	.0459	.0479	.0500	.0521
15	.0208	.0221	.0235	.0250	.0265	.0281	.0297	.0313	.0330	.0347
16	.0118	.0127	.0137	.0147	.0157	.0168	.0180	.0192	.0204	.0217
17	.0063	.0069	.0075	.0081	.0088	.0095	.0103	.0111	.0119	.0128
18	.0032	.0035	.0039	.0042	.0046	.0051	.0055	.0060	.0065	.0071
19	.0015	.0017	.0019	.0021	.0023	.0026	.0028	.0031	.0034	.0037
20	.0007	.0008	.0009	.0010	.0011	.0012	.0014	.0015	.0017	.0019
21	.0003	.0003	.0004	.0004	.0005	.0006	.0006	.0007	.0008	.0009
22	.0001	.0001	.0002	.0002	.0002	.0002	.0003	.0003	.0004	.0004
23	.0000	.0001	.0001	.0001	.0001	.0001	.0001	.0001	.0002	.0002
24	.0000	.0000	.0000	.0000	.0000	.0000	.0000	.0001	.0001	.0001

(*continued*)

APPENDIX TABLE F (*continued*)

	Values of μ									
x	11	12	13	14	15	16	17	18	19	20
0	.0000	.0000	.0000	.0000	.0000	.0000	.0000	.0000	.0000	.0000
1	.0002	.0001	.0000	.0000	.0000	.0000	.0000	.0000	.0000	.0000
2	.0010	.0004	.0002	.0001	.0000	.0000	.0000	.0000	.0000	.0000
3	.0037	.0018	.0008	.0004	.0002	.0001	.0000	.0000	.0000	.0000
4	.0102	.0053	.0027	.0013	.0006	.0003	.0001	.0001	.0000	.0000
5	.0224	.0127	.0070	.0037	.0019	.0010	.0005	.0002	.0001	.0001
6	.0411	.0255	.0152	.0087	.0048	.0026	.0014	.0007	.0004	.0002
7	.0646	.0437	.0281	.0174	.0104	.0060	.0034	.0018	.0010	.0005
8	.0888	.0655	.0457	.0304	.0194	.0120	.0072	.0042	.0024	.0013
9	.1085	.0874	.0661	.0473	.0324	.0213	.0135	.0083	.0050	.0029
10	.1194	.1048	.0859	.0663	.0486	.0341	.0230	.0150	.0095	.0058
11	.1194	.1144	.1015	.0844	.0663	.0496	.0355	.0245	.0164	.0106
12	.1094	.1144	.1099	.0984	.0829	.0661	.0504	.0368	.0259	.0176
13	.0926	.1056	.1099	.1060	.0956	.0814	.0658	.0509	.0378	.0271
14	.0728	.0905	.1021	.1060	.1024	.0930	.0800	.0655	.0514	.0387
15	.0534	.0724	.0885	.0989	.1024	.0992	.0906	.0786	.0650	.0516
16	.0367	.0543	.0719	.0866	.0960	.0992	.0963	.0884	.0772	.0646
17	.0237	.0383	.0550	.0713	.0847	.0934	.0963	.0936	.0863	.0760
18	.0145	.0256	.0397	.0554	.0706	.0830	.0909	.0936	.0911	.0844
19	.0084	.0161	.0272	.0409	.0557	.0699	.0814	.0887	.0911	.0888
20	.0046	.0097	.0177	.0286	.0418	.0559	.0692	.0798	.0866	.0888
21	.0024	.0055	.0109	.0191	.0299	.0426	.0560	.0684	.0783	.0846
22	.0012	.0030	.0065	.0121	.0204	.0310	.0433	.0560	.0676	.0769
23	.0006	.0016	.0037	.0074	.0133	.0216	.0320	.0438	.0559	.0669
24	.0003	.0008	.0020	.0043	.0083	.0144	.0226	.0328	.0442	.0557
25	.0001	.0004	.0010	.0024	.0050	.0092	.0154	.0237	.0336	.0446
26	.0000	.0002	.0005	.0013	.0029	.0057	.0101	.0164	.0246	.0343
27	.0000	.0001	.0002	.0007	.0016	.0034	.0063	.0109	.0173	.0254
28	.0000	.0000	.0001	.0003	.0009	.0019	.0038	.0070	.0117	.0181
29	.0000	.0000	.0001	.0002	.0004	.0011	.0023	.0044	.0077	.0125
30	.0000	.0000	.0000	.0001	.0002	.0006	.0013	.0026	.0049	.0083
31	.0000	.0000	.0000	.0000	.0001	.0003	.0007	.0015	.0030	.0054
32	.0000	.0000	.0000	.0000	.0001	.0001	.0004	.0009	.0018	.0034
33	.0000	.0000	.0000	.0000	.0000	.0001	.0002	.0005	.0010	.0020
34	.0000	.0000	.0000	.0000	.0000	.0000	.0001	.0002	.0006	.0012
35	.0000	.0000	.0000	.0000	.0000	.0000	.0000	.0001	.0003	.0007
36	.0000	.0000	.0000	.0000	.0000	.0000	.0000	.0001	.0002	.0004
37	.0000	.0000	.0000	.0000	.0000	.0000	.0000	.0000	.0001	.0002
38	.0000	.0000	.0000	.0000	.0000	.0000	.0000	.0000	.0000	.0001
39	.0000	.0000	.0000	.0000	.0000	.0000	.0000	.0000	.0000	.0001

SOURCE: Richard S. Burington and Donald C. May, *Handbook of Probability and Statistics with Tables* (Sandusky, Ohio: Handbook Publishers, 1953), pp. 259–262. All entries were calculated by Formula 9.H.

APPENDIX TABLE G | Poisson Probabilities for Cumulative Values of x

Entries in this table give the probability of x or fewer occurrences for a Poisson process with a mean of μ. For example, when $\mu = 2.9$, the probability of 4 or fewer occurrences is .8318.

	Values of μ									
x	0.1	0.2	0.3	0.4	0.5	0.6	0.7	0.8	0.9	1.0
0	0.9048	0.8187	0.7408	0.6703	0.6065	0.5488	0.4966	0.4493	0.4066	0.3679
1	0.9953	0.9825	0.9631	0.9384	0.9098	0.8781	0.8442	0.8088	0.7725	0.7358
2	0.9998	0.9989	0.9964	0.9921	0.9856	0.9769	0.9659	0.9526	0.9371	0.9197
3	1.0000	0.9999	0.9997	0.9992	0.9982	0.9966	0.9942	0.9909	0.9865	0.9810
4	1.0000	1.0000	1.0000	0.9999	0.9998	0.9996	0.9992	0.9986	0.9977	0.9963
5	1.0000	1.0000	1.0000	1.0000	1.0000	1.0000	0.9999	0.9998	0.9997	0.9994
6	1.0000	1.0000	1.0000	1.0000	1.0000	1.0000	1.0000	1.0000	1.0000	0.9999
7	1.0000	1.0000	1.0000	1.0000	1.0000	1.0000	1.0000	1.0000	1.0000	1.0000

	Values of μ									
x	1.1	1.2	1.3	1.4	1.5	1.6	1.7	1.8	1.9	2.0
0	0.3329	0.3012	0.2725	0.2466	0.2231	0.2019	0.1827	0.1653	0.1496	0.1353
1	0.6990	0.6626	0.6268	0.5918	0.5578	0.5249	0.4932	0.4628	0.4338	0.4060
2	0.9004	0.8795	0.8571	0.8335	0.8088	0.7834	0.7572	0.7306	0.7037	0.6767
3	0.9743	0.9662	0.9569	0.9463	0.9344	0.9212	0.9068	0.8913	0.8747	0.8571
4	0.9946	0.9923	0.9893	0.9857	0.9814	0.9763	0.9704	0.9636	0.9559	0.9473
5	0.9990	0.9985	0.9978	0.9968	0.9955	0.9940	0.9920	0.9896	0.9868	0.9834
6	0.9999	0.9997	0.9996	0.9994	0.9991	0.9987	0.9981	0.9974	0.9966	0.9955
7	1.0000	1.0000	0.9999	0.9999	0.9998	0.9997	0.9996	0.9994	0.9992	0.9989
8	1.0000	1.0000	1.0000	1.0000	1.0000	1.0000	0.9999	0.9999	0.9998	0.9998
9	1.0000	1.0000	1.0000	1.0000	1.0000	1.0000	1.0000	1.0000	1.0000	1.0000

	Values of μ									
x	2.1	2.2	2.3	2.4	2.5	2.6	2.7	2.8	2.9	3.0
0	0.1225	0.1108	0.1003	0.0907	0.0821	0.0743	0.0672	0.0608	0.0550	0.0498
1	0.3796	0.3546	0.3309	0.3084	0.2873	0.2674	0.2487	0.2311	0.2146	0.1991
2	0.6496	0.6227	0.5960	0.5697	0.5438	0.5184	0.4936	0.4695	0.4460	0.4232
3	0.8386	0.8194	0.7993	0.7787	0.7576	0.7360	0.7141	0.6919	0.6696	0.6472
4	0.9379	0.9275	0.9162	0.9041	0.8912	0.8774	0.8629	0.8477	0.8318	0.8153
5	0.9796	0.9751	0.9700	0.9643	0.9580	0.9510	0.9433	0.9349	0.9258	0.9161
6	0.9941	0.9925	0.9906	0.9884	0.9858	0.9828	0.9794	0.9756	0.9713	0.9665
7	0.9985	0.9980	0.9974	0.9967	0.9958	0.9947	0.9934	0.9919	0.9901	0.9881
8	0.9997	0.9995	0.9994	0.9991	0.9989	0.9985	0.9981	0.9976	0.9969	0.9962
9	0.9999	0.9999	0.9999	0.9998	0.9997	0.9996	0.9995	0.9993	0.9991	0.9989
10	1.0000	1.0000	1.0000	1.0000	0.9999	0.9999	0.9999	0.9998	0.9998	0.9997
11	1.0000	1.0000	1.0000	1.0000	1.0000	1.0000	1.0000	1.0000	0.9999	0.9999
12	1.0000	1.0000	1.0000	1.0000	1.0000	1.0000	1.0000	1.0000	1.0000	1.0000

(continued)

APPENDIX TABLE G *(continued)*

x	Values of μ 3.1	3.2	3.3	3.4	3.5	3.6	3.7	3.8	3.9	4.0
0	0.0450	0.0408	0.0369	0.0334	0.0302	0.0273	0.0247	0.0224	0.0202	0.0183
1	0.1847	0.1712	0.1586	0.1468	0.1359	0.1257	0.1162	0.1074	0.0992	0.0916
2	0.4012	0.3799	0.3594	0.3397	0.3208	0.3027	0.2854	0.2689	0.2531	0.2381
3	0.6248	0.6025	0.5803	0.5584	0.5366	0.5152	0.4942	0.4735	0.4533	0.4335
4	0.7982	0.7806	0.7626	0.7442	0.7254	0.7064	0.6872	0.6678	0.6484	0.6288
5	0.9057	0.8946	0.8829	0.8705	0.8576	0.8441	0.8301	0.8156	0.8006	0.7851
6	0.9612	0.9554	0.9490	0.9421	0.9347	0.9267	0.9182	0.9091	0.8995	0.8893
7	0.9858	0.9832	0.9802	0.9769	0.9733	0.9692	0.9648	0.9599	0.9546	0.9489
8	0.9953	0.9943	0.9931	0.9917	0.9901	0.9883	0.9863	0.9840	0.9815	0.9786
9	0.9986	0.9982	0.9978	0.9973	0.9967	0.9960	0.9952	0.9942	0.9931	0.9919
10	0.9996	0.9995	0.9994	0.9992	0.9990	0.9987	0.9984	0.9981	0.9977	0.9972
11	0.9999	0.9999	0.9998	0.9998	0.9997	0.9996	0.9995	0.9994	0.9993	0.9991
12	1.0000	1.0000	1.0000	0.9999	0.9999	0.9999	0.9999	0.9998	0.9998	0.9997
13	1.0000	1.0000	1.0000	1.0000	1.0000	1.0000	1.0000	1.0000	0.9999	0.9999
14	1.0000	1.0000	1.0000	1.0000	1.0000	1.0000	1.0000	1.0000	1.0000	1.0000

x	Values of μ 4.1	4.2	4.3	4.4	4.5	4.6	4.7	4.8	4.9	5.0
0	0.0166	0.0150	0.0136	0.0123	0.0111	0.0101	0.0091	0.0082	0.0074	0.0067
1	0.0845	0.0780	0.0719	0.0663	0.0611	0.0563	0.0518	0.0477	0.0439	0.0404
2	0.2238	0.2102	0.1974	0.1851	0.1736	0.1626	0.1523	0.1425	0.1333	0.1247
3	0.4142	0.3954	0.3772	0.3595	0.3423	0.3257	0.3097	0.2942	0.2793	0.2650
4	0.6093	0.5898	0.5704	0.5512	0.5321	0.5132	0.4946	0.4763	0.4582	0.4405
5	0.7693	0.7531	0.7367	0.7199	0.7029	0.6858	0.6684	0.6510	0.6335	0.6160
6	0.8786	0.8675	0.8558	0.8436	0.8311	0.8180	0.8046	0.7908	0.7767	0.7622
7	0.9427	0.9361	0.9290	0.9214	0.9134	0.9049	0.8960	0.8867	0.8769	0.8666
8	0.9755	0.9721	0.9683	0.9642	0.9597	0.9549	0.9497	0.9442	0.9382	0.9319
9	0.9905	0.9889	0.9871	0.9851	0.9829	0.9805	0.9778	0.9749	0.9717	0.9682
10	0.9966	0.9959	0.9952	0.9943	0.9933	0.9922	0.9910	0.9896	0.9880	0.9863
11	0.9989	0.9986	0.9983	0.9980	0.9976	0.9971	0.9966	0.9960	0.9953	0.9945
12	0.9997	0.9996	0.9995	0.9993	0.9992	0.9990	0.9988	0.9986	0.9983	0.9980
13	0.9999	0.9999	0.9998	0.9998	0.9997	0.9997	0.9996	0.9995	0.9994	0.9993
14	1.0000	1.0000	1.0000	0.9999	0.9999	0.9999	0.9999	0.9999	0.9998	0.9998
15	1.0000	1.0000	1.0000	1.0000	1.0000	1.0000	1.0000	1.0000	0.9999	0.9999
16	1.0000	1.0000	1.0000	1.0000	1.0000	1.0000	1.0000	1.0000	1.0000	1.0000

x	Values of μ 5.1	5.2	5.3	5.4	5.5	5.6	5.7	5.8	5.9	6.0
0	0.0061	0.0055	0.0050	0.0045	0.0041	0.0037	0.0033	0.0030	0.0027	0.0025
1	0.0372	0.0342	0.0314	0.0289	0.0266	0.0244	0.0224	0.0206	0.0189	0.0174
2	0.1165	0.1088	0.1016	0.0948	0.0884	0.0824	0.0768	0.0715	0.0666	0.0620
3	0.2513	0.2381	0.2254	0.2133	0.2017	0.1906	0.1801	0.1700	0.1604	0.1512
4	0.4231	0.4061	0.3895	0.3733	0.3575	0.3422	0.3272	0.3127	0.2987	0.2851

(continued)

APPENDIX TABLE G (*continued*)

x	5.1	5.2	5.3	5.4	5.5	5.6	5.7	5.8	5.9	6.0
					Values of μ					
5	0.5984	0.5809	0.5635	0.5461	0.5289	0.5119	0.4950	0.4783	0.4619	0.4457
6	0.7474	0.7324	0.7171	0.7017	0.6860	0.6703	0.6544	0.6384	0.6224	0.6063
7	0.8560	0.8449	0.8335	0.8217	0.8095	0.7970	0.7842	0.7710	0.7576	0.7440
8	0.9252	0.9181	0.9106	0.9026	0.8944	0.8857	0.8766	0.8672	0.8574	0.8472
9	0.9644	0.9603	0.9559	0.9512	0.9462	0.9409	0.9352	0.9292	0.9228	0.9161
10	0.9844	0.9823	0.9800	0.9775	0.9747	0.9718	0.9686	0.9651	0.9614	0.9574
11	0.9937	0.9927	0.9916	0.9904	0.9890	0.9875	0.9859	0.9840	0.9821	0.9799
12	0.9976	0.9972	0.9967	0.9962	0.9955	0.9949	0.9941	0.9932	0.9922	0.9912
13	0.9992	0.9990	0.9988	0.9986	0.9983	0.9980	0.9977	0.9973	0.9969	0.9964
14	0.9997	0.9997	0.9996	0.9995	0.9994	0.9993	0.9991	0.9990	0.9988	0.9986
15	0.9999	0.9999	0.9999	0.9998	0.9998	0.9998	0.9997	0.9996	0.9996	0.9995
16	1.0000	1.0000	1.0000	0.9999	0.9999	0.9999	0.9999	0.9999	0.9999	0.9998
17	1.0000	1.0000	1.0000	1.0000	1.0000	1.0000	1.0000	1.0000	1.0000	0.9999
18	1.0000	1.0000	1.0000	1.0000	1.0000	1.0000	1.0000	1.0000	1.0000	1.0000

x	8.1	8.2	8.3	8.4	8.5	8.6	8.7	8.8	8.9	9.0
					Values of μ					
0	0.0003	0.0003	0.0002	0.0002	0.0002	0.0002	0.0002	0.0002	0.0001	0.0001
1	0.0028	0.0025	0.0023	0.0021	0.0019	0.0018	0.0016	0.0015	0.0014	0.0012
2	0.0127	0.0118	0.0109	0.0100	0.0093	0.0086	0.0079	0.0073	0.0068	0.0062
3	0.0396	0.0370	0.0346	0.0323	0.0301	0.0281	0.0262	0.0244	0.0228	0.0212
4	0.0941	0.0887	0.0837	0.0789	0.0744	0.0701	0.0660	0.0621	0.0584	0.0550
5	0.1822	0.1736	0.1653	0.1573	0.1496	0.1422	0.1352	0.1284	0.1219	0.1157
6	0.3013	0.2896	0.2781	0.2670	0.2562	0.2457	0.2355	0.2256	0.2160	0.2068
7	0.4391	0.4254	0.4119	0.3987	0.3856	0.3728	0.3602	0.3478	0.3357	0.3239
8	0.5786	0.5647	0.5508	0.5369	0.5231	0.5094	0.4958	0.4823	0.4689	0.4557
9	0.7041	0.6915	0.6788	0.6659	0.6530	0.6400	0.6269	0.6137	0.6006	0.5874
10	0.8058	0.7955	0.7850	0.7743	0.7634	0.7522	0.7409	0.7294	0.7178	0.7060
11	0.8807	0.8731	0.8652	0.8571	0.8487	0.8400	0.8311	0.8220	0.8126	0.8030
12	0.9313	0.9261	0.9207	0.9150	0.9091	0.9029	0.8965	0.8898	0.8829	0.8758
13	0.9628	0.9595	0.9561	0.9524	0.9486	0.9445	0.9403	0.9358	0.9311	0.9262
14	0.9810	0.9791	0.9771	0.9749	0.9726	0.9701	0.9675	0.9647	0.9617	0.9585
15	0.9908	0.9898	0.9887	0.9875	0.9862	0.9847	0.9832	0.9816	0.9798	0.9780
16	0.9958	0.9953	0.9947	0.9941	0.9934	0.9926	0.9918	0.9909	0.9899	0.9889
17	0.9982	0.9979	0.9976	0.9973	0.9970	0.9966	0.9962	0.9957	0.9952	0.9947
18	0.9992	0.9991	0.9990	0.9989	0.9987	0.9985	0.9983	0.9981	0.9978	0.9976
19	0.9997	0.9996	0.9996	0.9995	0.9995	0.9994	0.9993	0.9992	0.9991	0.9989
20	0.9999	0.9999	0.9998	0.9998	0.9998	0.9997	0.9997	0.9997	0.9996	0.9996
21	1.0000	0.9999	0.9999	0.9999	0.9999	0.9999	0.9999	0.9999	0.9998	0.9998
22	1.0000	1.0000	1.0000	1.0000	1.0000	1.0000	1.0000	0.9999	0.9999	0.9999
23	1.0000	1.0000	1.0000	1.0000	1.0000	1.0000	1.0000	1.0000	1.0000	1.0000

(*continued*)

APPENDIX TABLE G (*continued*)

	Values of μ									
x	9.1	9.2	9.3	9.4	9.5	9.6	9.7	9.8	9.9	10.0
0	0.0001	0.0001	0.0001	0.0001	0.0001	0.0001	0.0001	0.0001	0.0001	0.0000
1	0.0011	0.0010	0.0009	0.0009	0.0008	0.0007	0.0007	0.0006	0.0005	0.0005
2	0.0058	0.0053	0.0049	0.0045	0.0042	0.0038	0.0035	0.0033	0.0030	0.0028
3	0.0198	0.0184	0.0172	0.0160	0.0149	0.0138	0.0129	0.0120	0.0111	0.0103
4	0.0517	0.0486	0.0456	0.0429	0.0403	0.0378	0.0355	0.0333	0.0312	0.0293
5	0.1098	0.1041	0.0987	0.0935	0.0885	0.0838	0.0793	0.0750	0.0710	0.0671
6	0.1978	0.1892	0.1808	0.1727	0.1650	0.1575	0.1502	0.1433	0.1366	0.1301
7	0.3123	0.3010	0.2900	0.2792	0.2687	0.2584	0.2485	0.2388	0.2294	0.2202
8	0.4426	0.4296	0.4168	0.4042	0.3918	0.3796	0.3676	0.3558	0.3442	0.3328
9	0.5742	0.5611	0.5479	0.5349	0.5218	0.5089	0.4960	0.4832	0.4705	0.4579
10	0.6941	0.6820	0.6699	0.6576	0.6453	0.6330	0.6205	0.6080	0.5955	0.5830
11	0.7932	0.7832	0.7730	0.7626	0.7520	0.7412	0.7303	0.7193	0.7081	0.6968
12	0.8684	0.8607	0.8529	0.8448	0.8364	0.8279	0.8191	0.8101	0.8009	0.7916
13	0.9210	0.9156	0.9100	0.9042	0.8981	0.8919	0.8853	0.8786	0.8716	0.8645
14	0.9552	0.9517	0.9480	0.9441	0.9400	0.9357	0.9312	0.9265	0.9216	0.9165
15	0.9760	0.9738	0.9715	0.9691	0.9665	0.9638	0.9609	0.9579	0.9546	0.9513
16	0.9878	0.9865	0.9852	0.9838	0.9823	0.9806	0.9789	0.9770	0.9751	0.9730
17	0.9941	0.9934	0.9927	0.9919	0.9911	0.9902	0.9892	0.9881	0.9869	0.9857
18	0.9973	0.9969	0.9966	0.9962	0.9957	0.9952	0.9947	0.9941	0.9935	0.9928
19	0.9988	0.9986	0.9985	0.9983	0.9980	0.9978	0.9975	0.9972	0.9969	0.9965
20	0.9995	0.9994	0.9993	0.9992	0.9991	0.9990	0.9989	0.9987	0.9986	0.9984
21	0.9998	0.9998	0.9997	0.9997	0.9996	0.9996	0.9995	0.9995	0.9994	0.9993
22	0.9999	0.9999	0.9999	0.9999	0.9998	0.9998	0.9998	0.9998	0.9997	0.9997
23	1.0000	1.0000	1.0000	0.9999	0.9999	0.9999	0.9999	0.9999	0.9999	0.9999
24	1.0000	1.0000	1.0000	1.0000	1.0000	1.0000	1.0000	1.0000	0.9999	0.9999
25	1.0000	1.0000	1.0000	1.0000	1.0000	1.0000	1.0000	1.0000	1.0000	1.0000

	Values of μ									
x	11.0	12.0	13.0	14.0	15.0	16.0	17.0	18.0	19.0	20.0
0	0.0000	0.0000	0.0000	0.0000	0.0000	0.0000	0.0000	0.0000	0.0000	0.0000
1	0.0002	0.0001	0.0000	0.0000	0.0000	0.0000	0.0000	0.0000	0.0000	0.0000
2	0.0012	0.0005	0.0002	0.0001	0.0000	0.0000	0.0000	0.0000	0.0000	0.0000
3	0.0049	0.0023	0.0011	0.0005	0.0002	0.0001	0.0000	0.0000	0.0000	0.0000
4	0.0151	0.0076	0.0037	0.0018	0.0009	0.0004	0.0002	0.0001	0.0000	0.0000
5	0.0375	0.0203	0.0107	0.0055	0.0028	0.0014	0.0007	0.0003	0.0002	0.0001
6	0.0786	0.0458	0.0259	0.0142	0.0076	0.0040	0.0021	0.0010	0.0005	0.0003
7	0.1432	0.0895	0.0540	0.0316	0.0180	0.0100	0.0054	0.0029	0.0015	0.0008
8	0.2320	0.1550	0.0998	0.0621	0.0374	0.0220	0.0126	0.0071	0.0039	0.0021
9	0.3405	0.2424	0.1658	0.1094	0.0699	0.0433	0.0261	0.0154	0.0089	0.0050
10	0.4599	0.3472	0.2517	0.1757	0.1185	0.0774	0.0491	0.0304	0.0183	0.0108
11	0.5793	0.4616	0.3532	0.2600	0.1847	0.1270	0.0847	0.0549	0.0347	0.0214
12	0.6887	0.5760	0.4631	0.3585	0.2676	0.1931	0.1350	0.0917	0.0606	0.0390
13	0.7813	0.6815	0.5730	0.4644	0.3632	0.2745	0.2009	0.1426	0.0984	0.0661
14	0.8540	0.7720	0.6751	0.5704	0.4656	0.3675	0.2808	0.2081	0.1497	0.1049
15	0.9074	0.8444	0.7636	0.6694	0.5681	0.4667	0.3714	0.2866	0.2148	0.1565

(*continued*)

APPENDIX TABLE G (*continued*)

	Values of μ									
x	11.0	12.0	13.0	14.0	15.0	16.0	17.0	18.0	19.0	20.0
16	0.9441	0.8987	0.8355	0.7559	0.6641	0.5660	0.4677	0.3750	0.2920	0.2211
17	0.9678	0.9370	0.8905	0.8272	0.7489	0.6593	0.5640	0.4686	0.3784	0.2970
18	0.9823	0.9626	0.9302	0.8826	0.8195	0.7423	0.6549	0.5622	0.4695	0.3814
19	0.9907	0.9787	0.9573	0.9235	0.8752	0.8122	0.7363	0.6509	0.5606	0.4703
20	0.9953	0.9884	0.9750	0.9521	0.9170	0.8682	0.8055	0.7307	0.6472	0.5591
21	0.9977	0.9939	0.9859	0.9711	0.9469	0.9108	0.8615	0.7991	0.7255	0.6437
22	0.9989	0.9969	0.9924	0.9833	0.9672	0.9418	0.9047	0.8551	0.7931	0.7206
23	0.9995	0.9985	0.9960	0.9907	0.9805	0.9633	0.9367	0.8989	0.8490	0.7875
24	0.9998	0.9993	0.9980	0.9950	0.9888	0.9777	0.9593	0.9317	0.8933	0.8432
25	0.9999	0.9997	0.9990	0.9974	0.9938	0.9869	0.9747	0.9554	0.9269	0.8878
26	1.0000	0.9999	0.9995	0.9987	0.9967	0.9925	0.9848	0.9718	0.9514	0.9221
27	1.0000	0.9999	0.9998	0.9994	0.9983	0.9959	0.9912	0.9827	0.9687	0.9475
28	1.0000	1.0000	0.9999	0.9997	0.9991	0.9978	0.9950	0.9897	0.9805	0.9657
29	1.0000	1.0000	1.0000	0.9999	0.9996	0.9989	0.9973	0.9940	0.9881	0.9782
30	1.0000	1.0000	1.0000	0.9999	0.9998	0.9994	0.9985	0.9967	0.9930	0.9865
31	1.0000	1.0000	1.0000	1.0000	0.9999	0.9997	0.9992	0.9982	0.9960	0.9919
32	1.0000	1.0000	1.0000	1.0000	0.9999	0.9999	0.9996	0.9990	0.9978	0.9953
33	1.0000	1.0000	1.0000	1.0000	1.0000	0.9999	0.9998	0.9995	0.9988	0.9973
34	1.0000	1.0000	1.0000	1.0000	1.0000	1.0000	0.9999	0.9997	0.9994	0.9985
35	1.0000	1.0000	1.0000	1.0000	1.0000	1.0000	0.9999	0.9999	0.9997	0.9992
36	1.0000	1.0000	1.0000	1.0000	1.0000	1.0000	1.0000	0.9999	0.9998	0.9996
37	1.0000	1.0000	1.0000	1.0000	1.0000	1.0000	1.0000	1.0000	0.9999	0.9998
38	1.0000	1.0000	1.0000	1.0000	1.0000	1.0000	1.0000	1.0000	1.0000	0.9999
39	1.0000	1.0000	1.0000	1.0000	1.0000	1.0000	1.0000	1.0000	1.0000	0.9999
40	1.0000	1.0000	1.0000	1.0000	1.0000	1.0000	1.0000	1.0000	1.0000	1.0000

SOURCE: Computed by the author.

APPENDIX TABLE H | Standard Normal Curve Areas

Entries in this table give the area under the curve between the mean and z standard deviations above the mean. For example, for z = 2.25, the area under the curve between the mean and z is .4878.

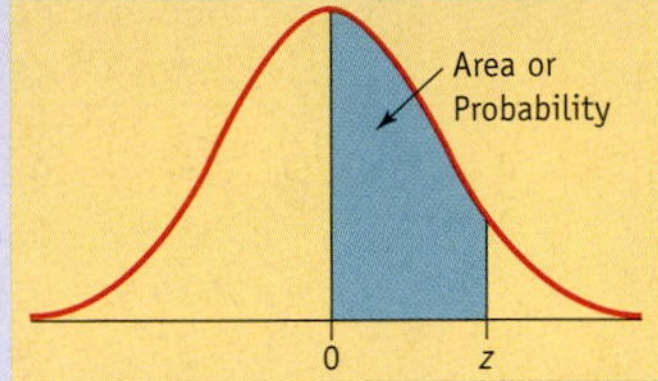

z	.00	.01	.02	.03	.04	.05	.06	.07	.08	.09
.0	.0000	.0040	.0080	.0120	.0160	.0199	.0239	.0279	.0319	.0359
.1	.0398	.0438	.0478	.0517	.0557	.0596	.0636	.0675	.0714	.0753
.2	.0793	.0832	.0871	.0910	.0948	.0987	.1026	.1064	.1103	.1141
.3	.1179	.1217	.1255	.1293	.1331	.1368	.1406	.1443	.1480	.1517
.4	.1554	.1591	.1628	.1664	.1700	.1736	.1772	.1808	.1844	.1879
.5	.1915	.1950	.1985	.2019	.2054	.2088	.2123	.2157	.2190	.2224
.6	.2257	.2291	.2324	.2357	.2389	.2422	.2454	.2486	.2518	.2549
.7	.2580	.2612	.2642	.2673	.2704	.2734	.2764	.2794	.2823	.2852
.8	.2881	.2910	.2939	.2967	.2995	.3023	.3051	.3078	.3106	.3133
.9	.3159	.3186	.3212	.3238	.3264	.3289	.3315	.3340	.3365	.3389
1.0	.3413	.3438	.3461	.3485	.3508	.3531	.3554	.3577	.3599	.3621
1.1	.3643	.3665	.3686	.3708	.3729	.3749	.3770	.3790	.3810	.3830
1.2	.3849	.3869	.3888	.3907	.3925	.3944	.3962	.3980	.3997	.4015
1.3	.4032	.4049	.4066	.4082	.4099	.4115	.4131	.4147	.4162	.4177
1.4	.4192	.4207	.4222	.4236	.4251	.4265	.4279	.4292	.4306	.4319
1.5	.4332	.4345	.4357	.4370	.4382	.4394	.4406	.4418	.4429	.4441
1.6	.4452	.4463	.4474	.4484	.4495	.4505	.4515	.4525	.4535	.4545
1.7	.4554	.4564	.4573	.4582	.4591	.4599	.4608	.4616	.4625	.4633
1.8	.4641	.4649	.4656	.4664	.4671	.4678	.4686	.4693	.4699	.4706
1.9	.4713	.4719	.4726	.4732	.4738	.4744	.4750	.4756	.4761	.4767
2.0	.4772	.4778	.4783	.4788	.4793	.4798	.4803	.4808	.4812	.4817
2.1	.4821	.4826	.4830	.4834	.4838	.4842	.4846	.4850	.4854	.4857
2.2	.4861	.4864	.4868	.4871	.4875	.4878	.4881	.4884	.4887	.4890
2.3	.4893	.4896	.4898	.4901	.4904	.4906	.4909	.4911	.4913	.4916
2.4	.4918	.4920	.4922	.4925	.4927	.4929	.4931	.4932	.4934	.4936
2.5	.4938	.4940	.4941	.4943	.4945	.4946	.4948	.4949	.4951	.4952
2.6	.4953	.4955	.4956	.4957	.4959	.4960	.4961	.4962	.4963	.4964
2.7	.4965	.4966	.4967	.4968	.4969	.4970	.4971	.4972	.4973	.4974
2.8	.4974	.4975	.4976	.4977	.4977	.4978	.4979	.4979	.4980	.4981
2.9	.4981	.4982	.4982	.4983	.4984	.4984	.4985	.4985	.4986	.4986
3.0	.4986	.4987	.4987	.4988	.4988	.4989	.4989	.4989	.4990	.4990
3.1	.4990	.4991	.4991	.4991	.4992	.4992	.4992	.4992	.4993	.4993
3.2	.4993	.4993	.4994	.4994	.4994	.4994	.4994	.4994	.4995	.4995
3.3	.4995	.4995	.4995	.4996	.4996	.4996	.4996	.4996	.4996	.4997
3.4	.4997	.4997	.4997	.4997	.4997	.4997	.4997	.4997	.4997	.4998
3.6	.4998	.4998	.4999	.4999	.4999	.4999	.4999	.4999	.4999	.4999
3.9	.5000									

SOURCE: The National Bureau of Standards, *Tables of Normal Probability Functions,* Applied Mathematics Series, no. 23 (Washington, D.C.: U.S. Government Printing Office, 1953). The original contains probabilities for values of z from 0 to 8.285, mostly in increments of .0001, and for areas from $\mu - z$ to $\mu + z$.

APPENDIX TABLE I | Exponential Probabilities for Cumulative Values of x

Entries in this table give the area under the curve between zero and x. For example, for $\lambda = 1.2$ and $x = .9$, the area under the curve is .6604, because in that case $\lambda x = 1.08$.

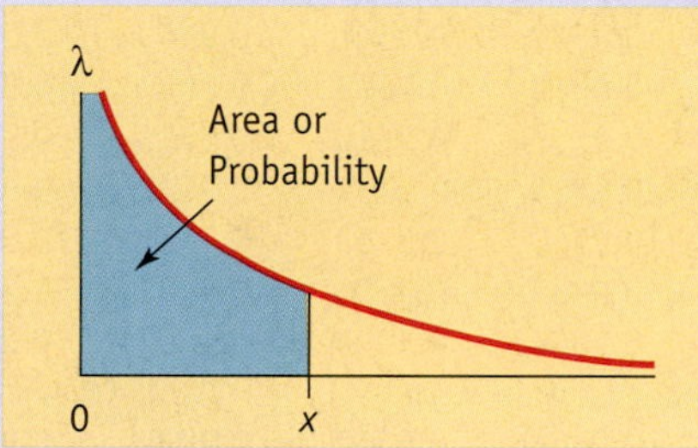

λx	.00	.01	.02	.03	.04	.05	.06	.07	.08	.09
0.0	0.0000	0.0100	0.0198	0.0296	0.0392	0.0488	0.0582	0.0676	0.0769	0.0861
0.1	0.0952	0.1042	0.1131	0.1219	0.1306	0.1393	0.1479	0.1563	0.1647	0.1730
0.2	0.1813	0.1894	0.1975	0.2055	0.2134	0.2212	0.2289	0.2366	0.2442	0.2517
0.3	0.2592	0.2666	0.2739	0.2811	0.2882	0.2953	0.3023	0.3093	0.3161	0.3229
0.4	0.3297	0.3363	0.3430	0.3495	0.3560	0.3624	0.3687	0.3750	0.3812	0.3874
0.5	0.3935	0.3995	0.4055	0.4114	0.4173	0.4231	0.4288	0.4345	0.4401	0.4457
0.6	0.4512	0.4566	0.4621	0.4674	0.4727	0.4780	0.4831	0.4883	0.4934	0.4984
0.7	0.5034	0.5084	0.5132	0.5181	0.5229	0.5276	0.5323	0.5370	0.5416	0.5462
0.8	0.5507	0.5551	0.5596	0.5640	0.5683	0.5726	0.5768	0.5810	0.5852	0.5893
0.9	0.5934	0.5975	0.6015	0.6054	0.6094	0.6133	0.6171	0.6209	0.6247	0.6284
1.0	0.6321	0.6358	0.6394	0.6430	0.6465	0.6501	0.6535	0.6570	0.6604	0.6638
1.1	0.6671	0.6704	0.6737	0.6770	0.6802	0.6834	0.6865	0.6896	0.6927	0.6958
1.2	0.6988	0.7018	0.7048	0.7077	0.7106	0.7135	0.7163	0.7192	0.7220	0.7247
1.3	0.7275	0.7302	0.7329	0.7355	0.7382	0.7408	0.7433	0.7459	0.7484	0.7509
1.4	0.7534	0.7559	0.7583	0.7607	0.7631	0.7654	0.7678	0.7701	0.7724	0.7746
1.5	0.7769	0.7791	0.7813	0.7835	0.7856	0.7878	0.7899	0.7920	0.7940	0.7961
1.6	0.7981	0.8001	0.8021	0.8041	0.8060	0.8080	0.8099	0.8118	0.8136	0.8155
1.7	0.8173	0.8191	0.8209	0.8227	0.8245	0.8262	0.8280	0.8297	0.8314	0.8330
1.8	0.8347	0.8363	0.8380	0.8396	0.8412	0.8428	0.8443	0.8459	0.8474	0.8489
1.9	0.8504	0.8519	0.8534	0.8549	0.8563	0.8577	0.8591	0.8605	0.8619	0.8633
2.0	0.8647	0.8660	0.8673	0.8687	0.8700	0.8713	0.8725	0.8738	0.8751	0.8763
2.1	0.8775	0.8788	0.8800	0.8812	0.8823	0.8835	0.8847	0.8858	0.8870	0.8881
2.2	0.8892	0.8903	0.8914	0.8925	0.8935	0.8946	0.8956	0.8967	0.8977	0.8987
2.3	0.8997	0.9007	0.9017	0.9027	0.9037	0.9046	0.9056	0.9065	0.9074	0.9084
2.4	0.9093	0.9102	0.9111	0.9120	0.9128	0.9137	0.9146	0.9154	0.9163	0.9171
2.5	0.9179	0.9187	0.9195	0.9203	0.9211	0.9219	0.9227	0.9235	0.9242	0.9250
2.6	0.9257	0.9265	0.9272	0.9279	0.9286	0.9293	0.9301	0.9307	0.9314	0.9321
2.7	0.9328	0.9335	0.9341	0.9348	0.9354	0.9361	0.9367	0.9373	0.9380	0.9386
2.8	0.9392	0.9398	0.9404	0.9410	0.9416	0.9422	0.9427	0.9433	0.9439	0.9444
2.9	0.9450	0.9455	0.9461	0.9466	0.9471	0.9477	0.9482	0.9487	0.9492	0.9497

(continued)

APPENDIX TABLE I *(continued)*

λx	.00	.01	.02	.03	.04	.05	.06	.07	.08	.09
3.0	0.9502	0.9507	0.9512	0.9517	0.9522	0.9526	0.9531	0.9536	0.9540	0.9545
3.1	0.9550	0.9554	0.9558	0.9563	0.9567	0.9571	0.9576	0.9580	0.9584	0.9588
3.2	0.9592	0.9596	0.9600	0.9604	0.9608	0.9612	0.9616	0.9620	0.9624	0.9627
3.3	0.9631	0.9635	0.9638	0.9642	0.9646	0.9649	0.9653	0.9656	0.9660	0.9663
3.4	0.9666	0.9670	0.9673	0.9676	0.9679	0.9683	0.9686	0.9689	0.9692	0.9695
3.5	0.9698	0.9701	0.9704	0.9707	0.9710	0.9713	0.9716	0.9718	0.9721	0.9724
3.6	0.9727	0.9729	0.9732	0.9735	0.9737	0.9740	0.9743	0.9745	0.9748	0.9750
3.7	0.9753	0.9755	0.9758	0.9760	0.9762	0.9765	0.9767	0.9769	0.9772	0.9774
3.8	0.9776	0.9779	0.9781	0.9783	0.9785	0.9787	0.9789	0.9791	0.9793	0.9796
3.9	0.9798	0.9800	0.9802	0.9804	0.9806	0.9807	0.9809	0.9811	0.9813	0.9815
4.0	0.9817	0.9834	0.9850	0.9864	0.9877	0.9889	0.9899	0.9909	0.9918	0.9926
5.0	0.9933	0.9939	0.9945	0.9950	0.9955	0.9959	0.9963	0.9967	0.9970	0.9973
6.0	0.9975	0.9978	0.9980	0.9982	0.9983	0.9985	0.9986	0.9988	0.9989	0.9990
7.0	0.9991	0.9992	0.9993	0.9993	0.9994	0.9994	0.9995	0.9995	0.9996	0.9996
8.0	0.9997	0.9997	0.9997	0.9998	0.9998	0.9998	0.9998	0.9998	0.9998	0.9999
9.0	0.9999	0.9999	0.9999	0.9999	0.9999	0.9999	0.9999	0.9999	0.9999	0.9999

SOURCE: Compiled by the author.

APPENDIX TABLE J | Critical Normal Deviate Values for Statistical Estimation

Given a confidence level of C = .80 (or 80 percent) the area between the mean and the upper tail is .40, which, according to Appendix Table H, is associated with a z value of 1.2817.

Note: *Some statisticians refer to the combined area of the two unshaded tails as α and, therefore, to the confidence level as $1 - \alpha$.*

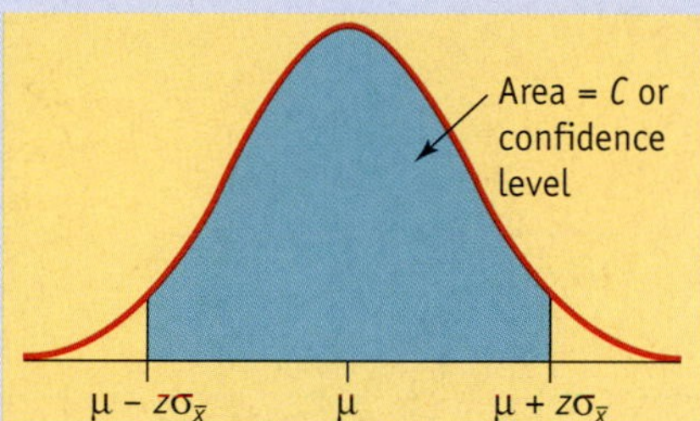

Confidence Level C	Normal Deviate z
.80	1.2817
.90	1.645
.95	1.96
.96	2.054
.97	2.17
.975	2.24
.98	2.3267
.99	2.575
.995	2.81
.996	2.88
.997	2.96
.998	3.08
.999	3.27

SOURCE: The National Bureau of Standards, *Tables of Normal Probability Functions,* Applied Mathematics Series, no. 23 (Washington, D.C.: U.S. Government Printing Office, 1953).

APPENDIX TABLE K | Student t Distributions

The following table provides the values of t_α that correspond to a given upper-tail area α and a specified number of degrees of freedom. For example, for an upper-tail area of $\alpha = .05$ and 9 degrees of freedom, the critical value of $t_\alpha = 1.833$.

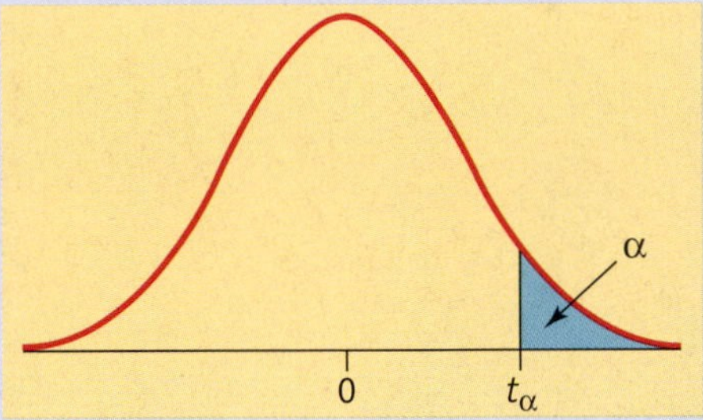

Degrees of Freedom	Critical Tail Areas (= α for one-tailed tests, = $\alpha/2$ for two-tailed tests)									
	.4	.25	.1	.05	.025	.01	.005	.0025	.001	.0005
1	.325	1.000	3.078	6.314	12.706	31.821	63.657	127.32	318.31	636.62
2	.289	.816	1.886	2.920	4.303	6.965	9.925	14.089	22.327	31.598
3	.277	.765	1.638	2.353	3.182	4.541	5.841	7.453	10.214	12.924
4	.271	.741	1.533	2.132	2.776	3.747	4.604	5.598	7.173	8.610
5	.267	.727	1.476	2.015	2.571	3.365	4.032	4.773	5.893	6.869
6	.265	.718	1.440	1.943	2.447	3.143	3.707	4.317	5.208	5.959
7	.263	.711	1.415	1.895	2.365	2.998	3.499	4.029	4.785	5.408
8	.262	.706	1.397	1.860	2.306	2.896	3.355	3.833	4.501	5.041
9	.261	.703	1.383	1.833	2.262	2.821	3.250	3.690	4.297	4.781
10	.260	.700	1.372	1.812	2.228	2.764	3.169	3.581	4.144	4.587
11	.260	.697	1.363	1.796	2.201	2.718	3.106	3.497	4.025	4.437
12	.259	.695	1.356	1.782	2.179	2.681	3.055	3.428	3.930	4.318
13	.259	.694	1.350	1.771	2.160	2.650	3.012	3.372	3.852	4.221
14	.258	.692	1.345	1.761	2.145	2.624	2.977	3.326	3.787	4.140
15	.258	.691	1.341	1.753	2.131	2.602	2.947	3.286	3.733	4.073
16	.258	.690	1.337	1.746	2.120	2.583	2.921	3.252	3.686	4.015
17	.257	.689	1.333	1.740	2.110	2.567	2.898	3.222	3.646	3.965
18	.257	.688	1.330	1.734	2.101	2.552	2.878	3.197	3.610	3.922
19	.257	.688	1.328	1.729	2.093	2.539	2.861	3.174	3.579	3.883
20	.257	.687	1.325	1.725	2.086	2.528	2.845	3.153	3.552	3.850
21	.257	.686	1.323	1.721	2.080	2.518	2.831	3.135	3.527	3.819
22	.256	.686	1.321	1.717	2.074	2.508	2.819	3.119	3.505	3.792
23	.256	.685	1.319	1.714	2.069	2.500	2.807	3.104	3.485	3.767
24	.256	.685	1.318	1.711	2.064	2.492	2.797	3.091	3.467	3.745
25	.256	.684	1.316	1.708	2.060	2.485	2.787	3.078	3.450	3.725
26	.256	.684	1.315	1.706	2.056	2.479	2.779	3.067	3.435	3.707
27	.256	.684	1.314	1.703	2.052	2.473	2.771	3.057	3.421	3.690
28	.256	.683	1.313	1.701	2.048	2.467	2.763	3.047	3.408	3.674
29	.256	.683	1.311	1.699	2.045	2.462	2.756	3.038	3.396	3.659
30	.256	.683	1.310	1.697	2.042	2.457	2.750	3.030	3.385	3.646
40	.255	.681	1.303	1.684	2.021	2.423	2.704	2.971	3.307	3.551
60	.254	.679	1.296	1.671	2.000	2.390	2.660	2.915	3.232	3.460
120	.254	.677	1.289	1.658	1.980	2.358	2.617	2.860	3.160	3.373
∞	.253	.674	1.282	1.645	1.960	2.326	2.576	2.807	3.090	3.291

(continued)

APPENDIX TABLE K (*continued*)

While a significance level α is associated with an upper-tail area α in an upper-tailed test, it is associated with an upper-tail as well as lower-tail area α/2 in a two-tailed test. The confidence level always equals C = 1 – α. Therefore, a significance level of, say, α = .05, goes with an upper-tail area of .05 in a one tailed test (C = .95), but with an upper-tail area of .025 in a two-tailed test (C = .95).

Confidence level	Critical Tail Areas (= α for one-tailed tests; $\alpha/2$ for two-tailed tests)									
$C = 1 - \alpha$	.4	.25	.1	.05	.025	.01	.005	.0025	.001	.0005
One-tailed test	.60	.75	.90	.95	.975	.99	.995	.9975	.999	.9995
Two-tailed test	.20	.50	.80	.90	.95	.98	.99	.995	.998	.999

SOURCE: E. S. Pearson and H. O. Hartley, *Biometrika Tables for Statisticians,* vol. 1 (Cambridge: Cambridge University Press, 1966), p. 146. Reprinted by permission of Biometrika Trustees.

APPENDIX TABLE L | Critical Normal Deviate Values for Hypothesis Testing

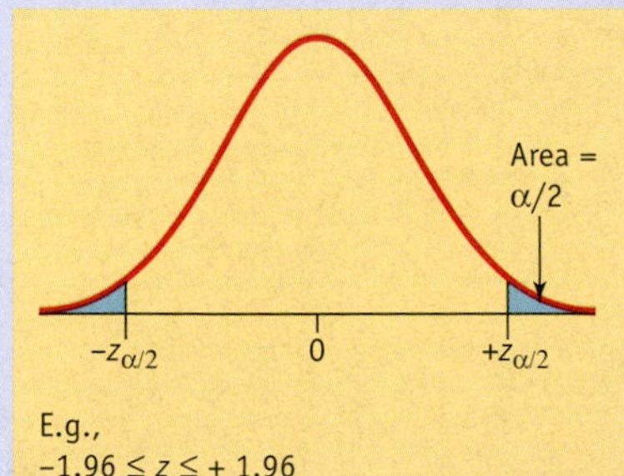

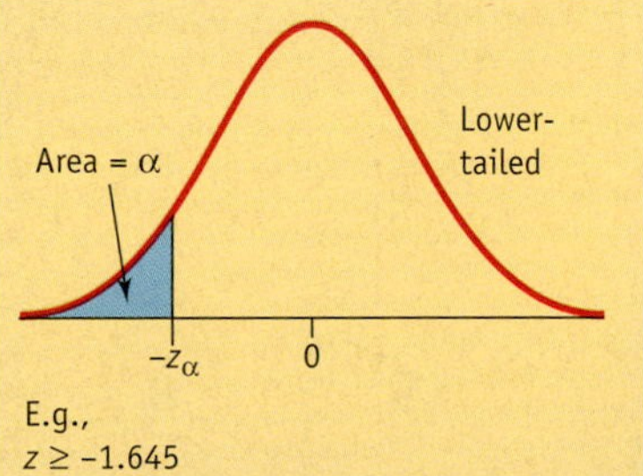

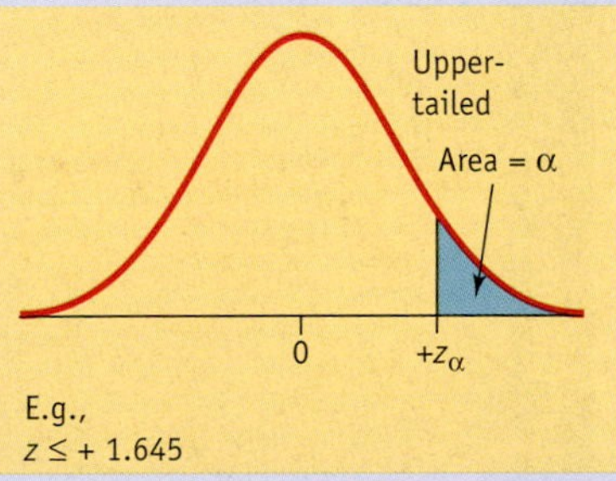

Two-Tailed Tests		One-Tailed Tests	
Significance Level α	Normal Deviate $z_{\alpha/2}$	Significance Level α	Normal Deviate z_α
.10	1.645	.10	1.2817
.05	1.96	.05	1.645
.025	2.24	.025	1.96
.01	2.575	.01	2.3267
.005	2.81	.005	2.575
.001	3.27	.001	3.08

SOURCE: The National Bureau of Standards, *Tables of Normal Probability Functions,* Applied Mathematics Series, no. 23 (Washington, D.C.: U.S. Government Printing Office, 1953).

APPENDIX TABLE M | Chi-Square Distributions

This table provides values of χ^2_α that correspond to a given upper-tail area, α, and a specified number of degrees of freedom. For example, for an upper-tail area of .05 and 4 degrees of freedom, the critical value of $\chi^2_{.05(4)}$ equals 9.488.

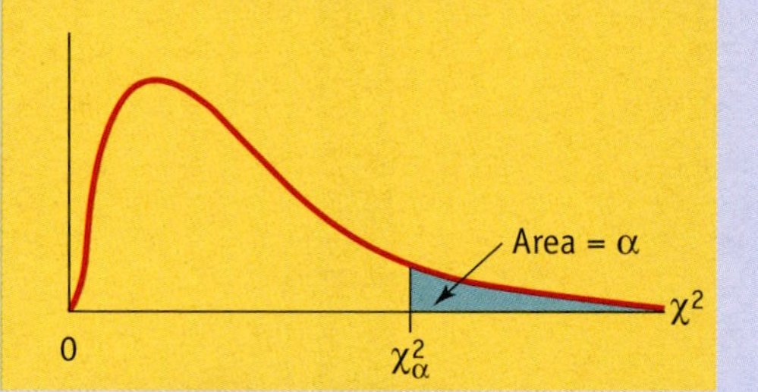

	Critical Values for Upper-Tail Area, α													
d.f.	.99	.98	.95	.90	.80	.70	.50	.30	.20	.10	.05	.02	.01	.001
1	$.0^3157$	$.0^3628$	.00393	.0158	.0642	.148	.455	1.074	1.642	2.706	3.841	5.412	6.635	10.827
2	.0201	.0404	.103	.211	.446	.713	1.386	2.408	3.219	4.605	5.991	7.824	9.210	13.815
3	.115	.185	.352	.584	1.005	1.424	2.366	3.665	4.642	6.251	7.815	9.837	11.345	16.266
4	.297	.429	.711	1.064	1.649	2.195	3.357	4.878	5.989	7.779	9.488	11.668	13.277	18.467
5	.554	.752	1.145	1.610	2.343	3.000	4.351	6.064	7.289	9.236	11.070	13.388	15.086	20.515
6	.872	1.134	1.635	2.204	3.070	3.828	5.348	7.231	8.558	10.645	12.592	15.033	16.812	22.457
7	1.239	1.564	2.167	2.833	3.822	4.671	6.346	8.383	9.803	12.017	14.067	16.622	18.475	24.322
8	1.646	2.032	2.733	3.490	4.594	5.527	7.344	9.524	11.030	13.362	15.507	18.168	20.090	26.125
9	2.088	2.532	3.325	4.168	5.380	6.393	8.343	10.656	12.242	14.684	16.919	19.679	21.666	27.877
10	2.558	3.059	3.940	4.865	6.179	7.267	9.342	11.781	13.442	15.987	18.307	21.161	23.209	29.588
11	3.053	3.609	4.575	5.578	6.989	8.148	10.341	12.899	14.631	17.275	19.675	22.618	24.725	31.264
12	3.571	4.178	5.226	6.304	7.807	9.034	11.340	14.011	15.812	18.549	21.026	24.054	26.217	32.909
13	4.107	4.765	5.892	7.042	8.634	9.926	12.340	15.119	16.985	19.812	22.362	25.472	27.688	34.528
14	4.660	5.368	6.571	7.790	9.467	10.821	13.339	16.222	18.151	21.064	23.685	26.873	29.141	36.123
15	5.229	5.985	7.261	8.547	10.307	11.721	14.339	17.322	19.311	22.307	24.996	28.259	30.578	37.697

(continued)

APPENDIX TABLE M *(continued)*

d.f.	Critical Values for Upper-Tail Area, α													
	.99	.98	.95	.90	.80	.70	.50	.30	.20	.10	.05	.02	.01	.001
16	5.812	6.614	7.962	9.312	11.152	12.624	15.338	18.418	20.465	23.542	26.296	29.633	32.000	39.252
17	6.408	7.255	8.672	10.085	12.002	13.531	16.338	19.511	21.615	24.769	27.587	30.995	33.409	40.790
18	7.015	7.906	9.390	10.865	12.857	14.440	17.338	20.601	22.760	25.989	28.869	32.346	34.805	42.312
19	7.633	8.567	10.117	11.651	13.716	15.352	18.338	21.689	23.900	27.204	30.144	33.687	36.191	43.820
20	8.260	9.237	10.851	12.443	14.578	16.266	19.337	22.775	25.038	28.412	31.410	35.020	37.566	45.315
21	8.897	9.915	11.591	13.240	15.445	17.182	20.337	23.858	26.171	29.615	32.671	36.343	38.932	46.797
22	9.542	10.600	12.338	14.041	16.314	18.101	21.337	24.939	27.301	30.813	33.924	37.659	40.289	48.268
23	10.196	11.293	13.091	14.848	17.187	19.021	22.337	26.018	28.429	32.007	35.172	38.968	41.638	49.728
24	10.856	11.992	13.848	15.659	18.062	19.943	23.337	27.096	29.553	33.196	36.415	40.270	42.980	51.179
25	11.524	12.697	14.611	16.473	18.940	20.867	24.337	28.172	30.675	34.382	37.652	41.566	44.314	52.620
26	12.198	13.409	15.379	17.292	19.820	21.792	25.336	29.246	31.795	35.563	38.885	42.856	45.642	54.052
27	12.879	14.125	16.151	18.114	20.703	22.719	26.336	30.319	32.912	36.741	40.113	44.140	46.963	55.476
28	13.565	14.847	16.928	18.939	21.588	23.647	27.336	31.391	34.027	37.916	41.337	45.419	48.278	56.893
29	14.256	15.574	17.708	19.768	22.475	24.577	28.336	32.461	35.139	39.087	42.557	46.693	49.588	58.302
30	14.953	16.306	18.493	20.599	23.364	25.508	29.336	33.530	36.250	40.256	43.773	47.962	50.892	59.703

NOTE: When the number of degrees of freedom (*d.f.*) exceeds 30, the χ^2 distribution can be approximated by the normal distribution, but the original Fisher/Yates table, nevertheless, provides values for up to 70 degrees of freedom.

SOURCE: Ronald A. Fisher and Frank Yates, *Statistical Tables for Biological, Agricultural and Medical Research*, 6th ed. (New York: Hafner, 1963), p. 47.

APPENDIX TABLE N | *F* Distributions

Entries in this table give F_α values, where α is the area or probability in the upper tail of the F distribution. For example, with 12 numerator degrees of freedom, 4 denominator degrees of freedom, and an $\alpha = .10$ area in the upper tail, $F_{.10} = 3.90$.

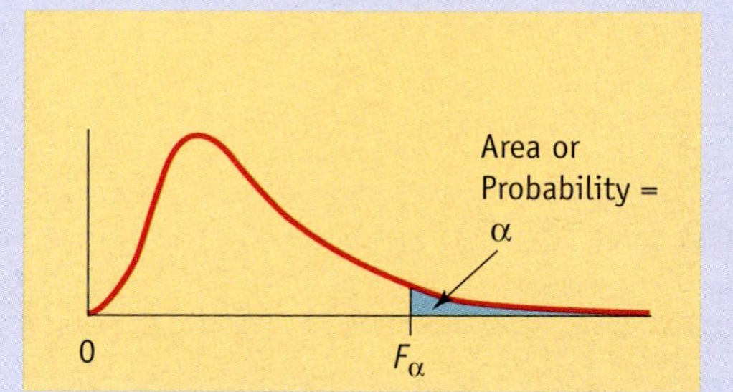

$F_{.10}$ Values

Denominator Degrees of Freedom	Numerator Degrees of Freedom: 1	2	3	4	5	6	7	8	9	10	12	15	20	24	30	40	60	120	∞
1	39.86	49.50	53.59	55.83	57.24	58.20	58.91	59.44	59.86	60.19	60.71	61.22	61.74	62.00	62.26	62.53	62.79	63.06	63.33
2	8.53	9.00	9.16	9.24	9.29	9.33	9.35	9.37	9.38	9.39	9.41	9.42	9.44	9.45	9.46	9.47	9.47	9.48	9.49
3	5.54	5.46	5.39	5.34	5.31	5.28	5.27	5.25	5.24	5.23	5.22	5.20	5.18	5.18	5.17	5.16	5.15	5.14	5.13
4	4.54	4.32	4.19	4.11	4.05	4.01	3.99	3.95	3.94	3.92	3.90	3.87	3.84	3.83	3.82	3.80	3.79	3.78	3.76
5	4.06	3.78	3.62	3.52	3.45	3.40	3.37	3.34	3.32	3.30	3.27	3.24	3.21	3.19	3.17	3.16	3.14	3.12	3.10
6	3.78	3.46	3.29	3.18	3.11	3.05	3.01	2.98	2.96	2.94	2.90	2.87	2.84	2.82	2.80	2.78	2.76	2.74	2.72
7	3.59	3.26	3.07	2.96	2.88	2.83	2.78	2.75	2.72	2.70	2.67	2.63	2.59	2.58	2.56	2.54	2.51	2.49	2.47
8	3.46	3.11	2.92	2.81	2.73	2.67	2.62	2.59	2.56	2.54	2.50	2.46	2.42	2.40	2.38	2.36	2.34	2.32	2.29
9	3.36	3.01	2.81	2.69	2.61	2.55	2.51	2.47	2.44	2.42	2.38	2.34	2.30	2.28	2.25	2.23	2.21	2.18	2.16
10	3.29	2.92	2.73	2.61	2.52	2.46	2.41	2.38	2.35	2.32	2.28	2.24	2.20	2.18	2.16	2.13	2.11	2.08	2.06
11	3.23	2.86	2.66	2.54	2.45	2.39	2.34	2.30	2.27	2.25	2.21	2.17	2.12	2.10	2.08	2.05	2.03	2.00	1.97
12	3.18	2.81	2.61	2.48	2.39	2.33	2.28	2.24	2.21	2.19	2.15	2.10	2.06	2.04	2.01	1.99	1.96	1.93	1.90
13	3.14	2.76	2.56	2.43	2.35	2.28	2.23	2.20	2.16	2.14	2.10	2.05	2.01	1.98	1.96	1.93	1.90	1.88	1.85
14	3.10	2.73	2.52	2.39	2.31	2.24	2.19	2.15	2.12	2.10	2.05	2.01	1.96	1.94	1.91	1.89	1.86	1.83	1.80
15	3.07	2.70	2.49	2.36	2.27	2.21	2.16	2.12	2.09	2.06	2.02	1.97	1.92	1.90	1.87	1.85	1.82	1.79	1.76
16	3.05	2.67	2.46	2.33	2.24	2.18	2.13	2.09	2.06	2.03	1.99	1.94	1.89	1.87	1.84	1.81	1.78	1.75	1.72
17	3.03	2.64	2.44	2.31	2.22	2.15	2.10	2.06	2.03	2.00	1.96	1.91	1.86	1.84	1.81	1.78	1.75	1.72	1.69
18	3.01	2.62	2.42	2.29	2.20	2.13	2.08	2.04	2.00	1.98	1.93	1.89	1.84	1.81	1.78	1.75	1.72	1.69	1.66
19	2.99	2.61	2.40	2.27	2.18	2.11	2.06	2.02	1.98	1.96	1.91	1.86	1.81	1.79	1.76	1.73	1.70	1.67	1.63
20	2.97	2.59	2.38	2.25	2.16	2.09	2.04	2.00	1.96	1.94	1.89	1.84	1.79	1.77	1.74	1.71	1.68	1.64	1.61

(continued)

APPENDIX TABLE N (*continued*)

Denominator Degrees of Freedom	$F_{.10}$ Values Numerator Degrees of Freedom																		
	1	2	3	4	5	6	7	8	9	10	12	15	20	24	30	40	60	120	∞
21	2.96	2.57	2.36	2.23	2.14	2.08	2.02	1.98	1.95	1.92	1.87	1.83	1.78	1.75	1.72	1.69	1.66	1.62	1.59
22	2.95	2.56	2.35	2.22	2.13	2.06	2.01	1.97	1.93	1.90	1.86	1.81	1.76	1.73	1.70	1.67	1.64	1.60	1.57
23	2.94	2.55	2.34	2.21	2.11	2.05	1.99	1.95	1.92	1.89	1.84	1.80	1.74	1.72	1.69	1.66	1.62	1.59	1.55
24	2.93	2.54	2.33	2.19	2.10	2.04	1.98	1.94	1.91	1.88	1.83	1.78	1.73	1.70	1.67	1.64	1.61	1.57	1.53
25	2.92	2.53	2.32	2.18	2.09	2.02	1.97	1.93	1.89	1.87	1.82	1.77	1.72	1.69	1.66	1.63	1.59	1.56	1.52
26	2.91	2.52	2.31	2.17	2.08	2.01	1.96	1.92	1.88	1.86	1.81	1.76	1.71	1.68	1.65	1.61	1.58	1.54	1.50
27	2.90	2.51	2.30	2.17	2.07	2.00	1.95	1.91	1.87	1.85	1.80	1.75	1.70	1.67	1.64	1.60	1.57	1.53	1.49
28	2.89	2.50	2.29	2.16	2.06	2.00	1.94	1.90	1.87	1.84	1.79	1.74	1.69	1.66	1.63	1.59	1.56	1.52	1.48
29	2.89	2.50	2.28	2.15	2.06	1.99	1.93	1.89	1.86	1.83	1.78	1.73	1.68	1.65	1.62	1.58	1.55	1.51	1.47
30	2.88	2.49	2.28	2.14	2.05	1.98	1.93	1.88	1.85	1.82	1.77	1.72	1.67	1.64	1.61	1.57	1.54	1.50	1.46
40	2.84	2.44	2.23	2.09	2.00	1.93	1.87	1.83	1.79	1.76	1.71	1.66	1.61	1.57	1.54	1.51	1.47	1.42	1.38
60	2.79	2.39	2.18	2.04	1.95	1.87	1.82	1.77	1.74	1.71	1.66	1.60	1.54	1.51	1.48	1.44	1.40	1.35	1.29
120	2.75	2.35	2.13	1.99	1.90	1.82	1.77	1.72	1.68	1.65	1.60	1.55	1.48	1.45	1.41	1.37	1.32	1.26	1.19
∞	2.71	2.30	2.08	1.94	1.85	1.77	1.72	1.67	1.63	1.60	1.55	1.49	1.42	1.38	1.34	1.30	1.24	1.17	1.00

Denominator Degrees of Freedom	$F_{.05}$ Values Numerator Degrees of Freedom																		
	1	2	3	4	5	6	7	8	9	10	12	15	20	24	30	40	60	120	∞
1	161.4	199.5	215.7	224.6	230.2	234.0	236.8	238.9	240.5	241.9	243.9	245.9	248.0	249.1	250.1	251.1	252.2	253.3	254.3
2	18.51	19.00	19.16	19.25	19.30	19.33	19.35	19.37	19.38	19.40	19.41	19.43	19.45	19.45	19.46	19.47	19.48	19.49	19.50
3	10.13	9.55	9.28	9.12	9.01	8.94	8.89	8.85	8.81	8.79	8.74	8.70	8.66	8.64	8.62	8.59	8.57	8.55	8.53
4	7.71	6.94	6.59	6.39	6.26	6.16	6.09	6.04	6.00	5.96	5.91	5.86	5.80	5.77	5.75	5.72	5.69	5.66	5.63
5	6.61	5.79	5.41	5.19	5.05	4.95	4.88	4.82	4.77	4.74	4.68	4.62	4.56	4.53	4.50	4.46	4.43	4.40	4.36
6	5.99	5.14	4.76	4.53	4.39	4.28	4.21	4.15	4.10	4.06	4.00	3.94	3.87	3.84	3.81	3.77	3.74	3.70	3.67
7	5.59	4.74	4.35	4.12	3.97	3.87	3.79	3.73	3.68	3.64	3.57	3.51	3.44	3.41	3.38	3.34	3.30	3.27	3.23
8	5.32	4.46	4.07	3.84	3.69	3.58	3.50	3.44	3.39	3.35	3.28	3.22	3.15	3.12	3.08	3.04	3.01	2.97	2.93
9	5.12	4.26	3.86	3.63	3.48	3.37	3.29	3.23	3.18	3.14	3.07	3.01	2.94	2.90	2.86	2.83	2.79	2.75	2.71
10	4.96	4.10	3.71	3.48	3.33	3.22	3.14	3.07	3.02	2.98	2.91	2.85	2.77	2.74	2.70	2.66	2.62	2.58	2.54
11	4.84	3.98	3.59	3.36	3.20	3.09	3.01	2.95	2.90	2.85	2.79	2.72	2.65	2.61	2.57	2.53	2.49	2.45	2.40
12	4.75	3.89	3.49	3.26	3.11	3.00	2.91	2.85	2.80	2.75	2.69	2.62	2.54	2.51	2.47	2.43	2.38	2.34	2.30
13	4.67	3.81	3.41	3.18	3.03	2.92	2.83	2.77	2.71	2.67	2.60	2.53	2.46	2.42	2.38	2.34	2.30	2.25	2.21
14	4.60	3.74	3.34	3.11	2.96	2.85	2.76	2.70	2.65	2.60	2.53	2.46	2.39	2.35	2.31	2.27	2.22	2.18	2.13
15	4.54	3.68	3.29	3.06	2.90	2.79	2.71	2.64	2.59	2.54	2.48	2.40	2.33	2.29	2.25	2.20	2.16	2.11	2.07
16	4.49	3.63	3.24	3.01	2.85	2.74	2.66	2.59	2.54	2.49	2.42	2.35	2.28	2.24	2.19	2.15	2.11	2.06	2.01
17	4.45	3.59	3.20	2.96	2.81	2.70	2.61	2.55	2.49	2.45	2.38	2.31	2.23	2.19	2.15	2.10	2.06	2.01	1.96
18	4.41	3.55	3.16	2.93	2.77	2.66	2.58	2.51	2.46	2.41	2.34	2.27	2.19	2.15	2.11	2.06	2.02	1.97	1.92

(*continued*)

$F_{.05}$ Values

Denominator Degrees of Freedom	Numerator Degrees of Freedom																		
	1	2	3	4	5	6	7	8	9	10	12	15	20	24	30	40	60	120	∞
19	4.38	3.52	3.13	2.90	2.74	2.63	2.54	2.48	2.42	2.38	2.31	2.23	2.16	2.11	2.07	2.03	1.98	1.93	1.88
20	4.35	3.49	3.10	2.87	2.71	2.60	2.51	2.45	2.39	2.35	2.28	2.20	2.12	2.08	2.04	1.99	1.95	1.90	1.84
21	4.32	3.47	3.07	2.84	2.68	2.57	2.49	2.42	2.37	2.32	2.25	2.18	2.10	2.05	2.01	1.96	1.92	1.87	1.81
22	4.30	3.44	3.05	2.82	2.66	2.55	2.46	2.40	2.34	2.30	2.23	2.15	2.07	2.03	1.98	1.94	1.89	1.84	1.78
23	4.28	3.42	3.03	2.80	2.64	2.53	2.44	2.37	2.32	2.27	2.20	2.13	2.05	2.01	1.96	1.91	1.86	1.81	1.76
24	4.26	3.40	3.01	2.78	2.62	2.51	2.42	2.36	2.30	2.25	2.18	2.11	2.03	1.98	1.94	1.89	1.84	1.79	1.73
25	4.24	3.39	2.99	2.76	2.60	2.49	2.40	2.34	2.28	2.24	2.16	2.09	2.01	1.96	1.92	1.87	1.82	1.77	1.71
26	4.23	3.37	2.98	2.74	2.59	2.47	2.39	2.32	2.27	2.22	2.15	2.07	1.99	1.95	1.90	1.85	1.80	1.75	1.69
27	4.21	3.35	2.96	2.73	2.57	2.46	2.37	2.31	2.25	2.20	2.13	2.06	1.97	1.93	1.88	1.84	1.79	1.73	1.67
28	4.20	3.34	2.95	2.71	2.56	2.45	2.36	2.29	2.24	2.19	2.12	2.04	1.96	1.91	1.87	1.82	1.77	1.71	1.65
29	4.18	3.33	2.93	2.70	2.55	2.43	2.35	2.28	2.22	2.18	2.10	2.03	1.94	1.90	1.85	1.81	1.75	1.70	1.64
30	4.17	3.32	2.92	2.69	2.53	2.42	2.33	2.27	2.21	2.16	2.09	2.01	1.93	1.89	1.84	1.79	1.74	1.68	1.62
40	4.08	3.23	2.84	2.61	2.45	2.34	2.25	2.18	2.12	2.08	2.00	1.92	1.84	1.79	1.74	1.69	1.64	1.58	1.51
60	4.00	3.15	2.76	2.53	2.37	2.25	2.17	2.10	2.04	1.99	1.92	1.84	1.75	1.70	1.65	1.59	1.53	1.47	1.39
120	3.92	3.07	2.68	2.45	2.29	2.17	2.09	2.02	1.96	1.91	1.83	1.75	1.66	1.61	1.55	1.50	1.43	1.35	1.25
∞	3.84	3.00	2.60	2.37	2.21	2.10	2.01	1.94	1.88	1.83	1.75	1.67	1.57	1.52	1.46	1.39	1.32	1.22	1.00

$F_{.025}$ Values

Denominator Degrees of Freedom	Numerator Degrees of Freedom																		
	1	2	3	4	5	6	7	8	9	10	12	15	20	24	30	40	60	120	∞
1	647.8	799.5	864.2	899.6	921.8	937.1	948.2	956.7	963.3	968.6	976.7	984.9	993.1	997.2	1001	1006	1010	1014	1018
2	38.51	39.00	39.17	39.25	39.30	39.33	39.36	39.37	39.39	39.40	39.41	39.43	39.45	39.46	39.46	39.47	39.48	39.49	39.50
3	17.44	16.04	15.44	15.10	14.88	14.73	14.62	14.54	14.47	14.42	14.34	14.25	14.17	14.12	14.08	14.04	13.99	13.95	13.90
4	12.22	10.65	9.98	9.60	9.36	9.20	9.07	8.98	8.90	8.84	8.75	8.66	8.56	8.51	8.46	8.41	8.36	8.31	8.26
5	10.01	8.43	7.76	7.39	7.15	6.98	6.85	6.76	6.68	6.62	6.52	6.43	6.33	6.28	6.23	6.18	6.12	6.07	6.02
6	8.81	7.26	6.60	6.23	5.99	5.82	5.70	5.60	5.52	5.46	5.37	5.27	5.17	5.12	5.07	5.01	4.96	4.90	4.85
7	8.07	6.54	5.89	5.52	5.29	5.12	4.99	4.90	4.82	4.76	4.67	4.57	4.47	4.42	4.36	4.31	4.25	4.20	4.14
8	7.57	6.06	5.42	5.05	4.82	4.65	4.53	4.43	4.36	4.30	4.20	4.10	4.00	3.95	3.89	3.84	3.78	3.73	3.67
9	7.21	5.71	5.08	4.72	4.48	4.32	4.20	4.10	4.03	3.96	3.87	3.77	3.67	3.61	3.56	3.51	3.45	3.39	3.33
10	6.94	5.46	4.83	4.47	4.24	4.07	3.95	3.85	3.78	3.72	3.62	3.52	3.42	3.37	3.31	3.26	3.20	3.14	3.08
11	6.72	5.26	4.63	4.28	4.04	3.88	3.76	3.66	3.59	3.53	3.43	3.33	3.23	3.17	3.12	3.06	3.00	2.94	2.88
12	6.55	5.10	4.47	4.12	3.89	3.73	3.61	3.51	3.44	3.37	3.28	3.18	3.07	3.02	2.96	2.91	2.85	2.79	2.72
13	6.41	4.97	4.35	4.00	3.77	3.60	3.48	3.39	3.31	3.25	3.15	3.05	2.95	2.89	2.84	2.78	2.72	2.66	2.60
14	6.30	4.86	4.24	3.89	3.66	3.50	3.38	3.29	3.21	3.15	3.05	2.95	2.84	2.79	2.73	2.67	2.61	2.55	2.49

(*continued*)

APPENDIX TABLE N (*continued*)

$F_{.025}$ Values

Denominator Degrees of Freedom	Numerator Degrees of Freedom																		
	1	2	3	4	5	6	7	8	9	10	12	15	20	24	30	40	60	120	∞
15	6.20	4.77	4.15	3.80	3.58	3.41	3.29	3.20	3.12	3.06	2.96	2.86	2.76	2.70	2.64	2.59	2.52	2.46	2.40
16	6.12	4.69	4.08	3.73	3.50	3.34	3.22	3.12	3.05	2.99	2.89	2.79	2.68	2.63	2.57	2.51	2.45	2.38	2.32
17	6.04	4.62	4.01	3.66	3.44	3.28	3.16	3.06	2.98	2.92	2.82	2.72	2.62	2.56	2.50	2.44	2.38	2.32	2.25
18	5.98	4.56	3.95	3.61	3.38	3.22	3.10	3.01	2.93	2.87	2.77	2.67	2.56	2.50	2.44	2.38	2.32	2.26	2.19
19	5.92	4.51	3.90	3.56	3.33	3.17	3.05	2.96	2.88	2.82	2.72	2.62	2.51	2.45	2.39	2.33	2.27	2.20	2.13
20	5.87	4.46	3.86	3.51	3.29	3.13	3.01	2.91	2.84	2.77	2.68	2.57	2.46	2.41	2.35	2.29	2.22	2.16	2.09
21	5.83	4.42	3.82	3.48	3.25	3.09	2.97	2.87	2.80	2.73	2.64	2.53	2.42	2.37	2.31	2.25	2.18	2.11	2.04
22	5.79	4.38	3.78	3.44	3.22	3.05	2.93	2.84	2.76	2.70	2.60	2.50	2.39	2.33	2.27	2.21	2.14	2.08	2.00
23	5.75	4.35	3.75	3.41	3.18	3.02	2.90	2.81	2.73	2.67	2.57	2.47	2.36	2.30	2.24	2.18	2.11	2.04	1.97
24	5.72	4.32	3.72	3.38	3.15	2.99	2.87	2.78	2.70	2.64	2.54	2.44	2.33	2.27	2.21	2.15	2.08	2.01	1.94
25	5.69	4.29	3.69	3.35	3.13	2.97	2.85	2.75	2.68	2.61	2.51	2.41	2.30	2.24	2.18	2.12	2.05	1.98	1.91
26	5.66	4.27	3.67	3.33	3.10	2.94	2.82	2.73	2.65	2.59	2.49	2.39	2.28	2.22	2.16	2.09	2.03	1.95	1.88
27	5.63	4.24	3.65	3.31	3.08	2.92	2.80	2.71	2.63	2.57	2.47	2.36	2.25	2.19	2.13	2.07	2.00	1.93	1.85
28	5.61	4.22	3.63	3.29	3.06	2.90	2.78	2.69	2.61	2.55	2.45	2.34	2.23	2.17	2.11	2.05	1.98	1.91	1.83
29	5.59	4.20	3.61	3.27	3.04	2.88	2.76	2.67	2.59	2.53	2.43	2.32	2.21	2.15	2.09	2.03	1.96	1.89	1.81
30	5.57	4.18	3.59	3.25	3.03	2.87	2.75	2.65	2.57	2.51	2.41	2.31	2.20	2.14	2.07	2.01	1.94	1.87	1.79
40	5.42	4.05	3.46	3.13	2.90	2.74	2.62	2.53	2.45	2.39	2.29	2.18	2.07	2.01	1.94	1.88	1.80	1.72	1.64
60	5.29	3.93	3.34	3.01	2.79	2.63	2.51	2.41	2.33	2.27	2.17	2.06	1.94	1.88	1.82	1.74	1.67	1.58	1.48
120	5.15	3.80	3.23	2.89	2.67	2.52	2.39	2.30	2.22	2.16	2.05	1.94	1.82	1.76	1.69	1.61	1.53	1.43	1.31
∞	5.02	3.69	3.12	2.79	2.57	2.41	2.29	2.19	2.11	2.05	1.94	1.83	1.71	1.64	1.57	1.48	1.39	1.27	1.00

$F_{.01}$ Values

Denominator Degrees of Freedom	Numerator Degrees of Freedom																		
	1	2	3	4	5	6	7	8	9	10	12	15	20	24	30	40	60	120	∞
1	4052	4999.5	5403	5625	5764	5859	5928	5981	6022	6056	6106	6157	6209	6235	6261	6287	6313	6339	6366
2	98.50	99.00	99.17	99.25	99.30	99.33	99.36	99.37	99.39	99.40	99.42	99.43	99.45	99.46	99.47	99.47	99.48	99.49	99.50
3	34.12	30.82	29.46	28.71	28.24	27.91	27.67	27.49	27.35	27.23	27.05	26.87	26.69	26.60	26.50	26.41	26.32	26.22	26.13
4	21.20	18.00	16.69	15.98	15.52	15.21	14.98	14.80	14.66	14.55	14.37	14.20	14.02	13.93	13.84	13.75	13.65	13.56	13.46
5	16.26	13.27	12.06	11.39	10.97	10.67	10.46	10.29	10.16	10.05	9.89	9.72	9.55	9.47	9.38	9.29	9.20	9.11	9.02
6	13.75	10.92	9.78	9.15	8.75	8.47	8.26	8.10	7.98	7.87	7.72	7.56	7.40	7.31	7.23	7.14	7.06	6.97	6.88
7	12.25	9.55	8.45	7.85	7.46	7.19	6.99	6.84	6.72	6.62	6.47	6.31	6.16	6.07	5.99	5.91	5.82	5.74	5.65
8	11.26	8.65	7.59	7.01	6.63	6.37	6.18	6.03	5.91	5.81	5.67	5.52	5.36	5.28	5.20	5.12	5.03	4.95	4.86
9	10.56	8.02	6.99	6.42	6.06	5.80	5.61	5.47	5.35	5.26	5.11	4.96	4.81	4.73	4.65	4.57	4.48	4.40	4.31
10	10.04	7.56	6.55	5.99	5.64	5.39	5.20	5.06	4.94	4.85	4.71	4.56	4.41	4.33	4.25	4.17	4.08	4.00	3.91
11	9.65	7.21	6.22	5.67	5.32	5.07	4.89	4.74	4.63	4.54	4.40	4.25	4.10	4.02	3.94	3.86	3.78	3.69	3.60
12	9.33	6.93	5.95	5.41	5.06	4.82	4.64	4.50	4.39	4.30	4.16	4.01	3.86	3.78	3.70	3.62	3.54	3.45	3.36

(continued)

APPENDIX TABLE N (*continued*)

Denominator Degrees of Freedom	$F_{.01}$ Values Numerator Degrees of Freedom																		
	1	2	3	4	5	6	7	8	9	10	12	15	20	24	30	40	60	120	∞
13	9.07	6.70	5.74	5.21	4.86	4.62	4.44	4.30	4.19	4.10	3.96	3.82	3.66	3.59	3.51	3.43	3.34	3.25	3.17
14	8.86	6.51	5.56	5.04	4.69	4.46	4.28	4.14	4.03	3.04	3.80	3.66	3.51	3.43	3.35	3.27	3.18	3.09	3.00
15	8.68	6.36	5.42	4.89	4.56	4.32	4.14	4.00	3.89	3.80	3.67	3.52	3.37	3.29	3.21	3.13	3.05	2.96	2.87
16	8.53	6.23	5.29	4.77	4.44	4.20	4.03	3.89	3.78	3.69	3.55	3.41	3.26	3.18	3.10	3.02	2.93	2.84	2.75
17	8.40	6.11	5.18	4.67	4.34	4.10	3.93	3.79	3.68	3.59	3.46	3.31	3.16	3.08	3.00	2.92	2.83	2.75	2.65
18	8.29	6.01	5.09	4.58	4.25	4.01	3.84	3.71	3.60	3.51	3.37	3.23	3.08	3.00	2.92	2.84	2.75	2.66	2.57
19	8.18	5.93	5.01	4.50	4.17	3.94	3.77	3.63	3.52	3.43	3.30	3.15	3.00	2.92	2.84	2.76	2.67	2.58	2.49
20	8.10	5.85	4.94	4.43	4.10	3.87	3.70	3.56	3.46	3.37	3.23	3.09	2.94	2.86	2.78	2.69	2.61	2.52	2.42
21	8.02	5.78	4.87	4.37	4.04	3.81	3.64	3.51	3.40	3.31	3.17	3.03	2.88	2.80	2.72	2.64	2.55	2.46	2.36
22	7.95	5.72	4.82	4.31	3.99	3.76	3.59	3.45	3.35	3.26	3.12	2.98	2.83	2.75	2.67	2.58	2.50	2.40	2.31
23	7.88	5.66	4.76	4.26	3.94	3.71	3.54	3.41	3.30	3.21	3.07	2.93	2.78	2.70	2.62	2.54	2.45	2.35	2.26
24	7.82	5.61	4.72	4.22	3.90	3.67	3.50	3.36	3.26	3.17	3.03	2.89	2.74	2.66	2.58	2.49	2.40	2.31	2.21
25	7.77	5.57	4.68	4.18	3.85	3.63	3.46	3.32	3.22	3.13	2.99	2.85	2.70	2.62	2.54	2.45	2.36	2.27	2.17
26	7.72	5.53	4.64	4.14	3.82	3.59	3.42	3.29	3.18	3.09	2.96	2.81	2.66	2.58	2.50	2.42	2.33	2.23	2.13
27	7.68	5.49	4.60	4.11	3.78	3.56	3.39	3.26	3.15	3.06	2.93	2.78	2.63	2.55	2.47	2.38	2.29	2.20	2.10
28	7.64	5.45	4.57	4.07	3.75	3.53	3.36	3.23	3.12	3.03	2.90	2.75	2.60	2.52	2.44	2.35	2.26	2.17	2.06
29	7.60	5.42	4.54	4.04	3.73	3.50	3.33	3.20	3.09	3.00	2.87	2.73	2.57	2.49	2.41	2.33	2.23	2.14	2.03
30	7.56	5.39	4.51	4.02	3.70	3.47	3.30	3.17	3.07	2.98	2.84	2.70	2.55	2.47	2.39	2.30	2.21	2.11	2.01
40	7.31	5.18	4.31	3.83	3.51	−3.29	3.12	2.99	2.89	2.80	2.66	2.52	2.37	2.29	2.20	2.11	2.02	1.92	1.80
60	7.08	4.98	4.13	3.65	3.34	3.12	2.95	2.82	2.72	2.63	2.50	2.35	2.20	2.12	2.03	1.94	1.84	1.73	1.60
120	6.85	4.79	3.95	3.48	3.17	2.96	2.79	2.66	2.56	2.47	2.34	2.19	2.03	1.95	1.86	1.76	1.66	1.53	1.38
∞	6.63	4.61	3.78	3.32	3.02	2.80	2.64	2.51	2.41	2.32	2.18	2.04	1.88	1.79	1.70	1.59	1.47	1.32	1.00

SOURCE: E. S. Pearson and H. O. Hartley, *Biometrika Tables for Statisticians* vol. 1 (Cambridge: Cambridge University Press, 1966), pp. 170-173. Reprinted by permission of Biometrika Trustees.

APPENDIX TABLE O | Values of q_α in Tukey's *HSD* Test

Error d.f.	α	k = Number of means or number of steps between ordered means										
		2	3	4	5	6	7	8	9	10	11	12
5	.05	3.64	4.60	5.22	5.67	6.03	6.33	6.58	6.80	6.99	7.17	7.32
	.01	5.70	6.98	7.80	8.42	8.91	9.32	9.67	9.97	10.24	10.48	10.70
6	.05	3.46	4.34	4.90	5.30	5.63	5.90	6.12	6.32	6.49	6.65	6.79
	.01	5.24	6.33	7.03	7.56	7.97	8.32	8.61	8.87	9.10	9.30	9.48
7	.05	3.34	4.16	4.68	5.06	5.36	5.61	5.82	6.00	6.16	6.30	6.43
	.01	4.95	5.92	6.54	7.01	7.37	7.68	7.94	8.17	8.37	8.55	8.71
8	.05	3.26	4.04	4.53	4.89	5.17	5.40	5.60	5.77	5.92	6.05	6.18
	.01	4.75	5.64	6.20	6.62	6.96	7.24	7.47	7.68	7.86	8.03	8.18
9	.05	3.20	3.95	4.41	4.76	5.02	5.24	5.43	5.59	5.74	5.87	5.98
	.01	4.60	5.43	5.96	6.35	6.66	6.91	7.13	7.33	7.49	7.65	7.78
10	.05	3.15	3.88	4.33	4.65	4.91	5.12	5.30	5.46	5.60	5.72	5.83
	.01	4.48	5.27	5.77	6.14	6.43	6.67	6.87	7.05	7.21	7.36	7.49
11	.05	3.11	3.82	4.26	4.57	4.82	5.03	5.20	5.35	5.49	5.61	5.71
	.01	4.39	5.15	5.62	5.97	6.25	6.48	6.67	6.84	6.99	7.13	7.25
12	.05	3.08	3.77	4.20	4.51	4.75	4.95	5.12	5.27	5.39	5.51	5.61
	.01	4.32	5.05	5.50	5.84	6.10	6.32	6.51	6.67	6.81	6.94	7.06
13	.05	3.06	3.73	4.15	4.45	4.69	4.88	5.05	5.19	5.32	5.43	5.53
	.01	4.26	4.96	5.40	5.73	5.98	6.19	6.37	6.53	6.67	6.79	6.90
14	.05	3.03	3.70	4.11	4.41	4.64	4.83	4.99	5.13	5.25	5.36	5.46
	.01	4.21	4.89	5.32	5.63	5.88	6.08	6.26	6.41	6.54	6.66	6.77
15	.05	3.01	3.67	4.08	4.37	4.59	4.78	4.94	5.08	5.20	5.31	5.40
	.01	4.17	4.84	5.25	5.56	5.80	5.99	6.16	6.31	6.44	6.55	6.66
16	.05	3.00	3.65	4.05	4.33	4.56	4.74	4.90	5.03	5.15	5.26	5.35
	.01	4.13	4.79	5.19	5.49	5.72	5.92	6.08	6.22	6.35	6.46	6.56
17	.05	2.98	3.63	4.02	4.30	4.52	4.70	4.86	4.99	5.11	5.21	5.31
	.01	4.10	4.74	5.14	5.43	5.66	5.85	6.01	6.15	6.27	6.38	6.48
18	.05	2.97	3.61	4.00	4.28	4.49	4.67	4.82	4.96	5.07	5.17	5.27
	.01	4.07	4.70	5.09	5.38	5.60	5.79	5.94	6.08	6.20	6.31	6.41
19	.05	2.96	3.59	3.98	4.25	4.47	4.65	4.79	4.92	5.04	5.14	5.23
	.01	4.05	4.67	5.05	5.33	5.55	5.73	5.89	6.02	6.14	6.25	6.34
20	.05	2.95	3.58	3.96	4.23	4.45	4.62	4.77	4.90	5.01	5.11	5.20
	.01	4.02	4.64	5.02	5.29	5.51	5.69	5.84	5.97	6.09	6.19	6.28

(continued)

APPENDIX TABLE O (*continued*)

Error d.f.	α	*k* = Number of means or number of steps between ordered means										
		2	3	4	5	6	7	8	9	10	11	12
24	.05	2.92	3.53	3.90	4.17	4.37	4.54	4.68	4.81	4.92	5.01	5.10
	.01	3.96	4.55	4.91	5.17	5.37	5.54	5.69	5.81	5.92	6.02	6.11
30	.05	2.89	3.49	3.85	4.10	4.30	4.46	4.60	4.72	4.82	4.92	5.00
	.01	3.89	4.45	4.80	5.05	5.24	5.40	5.54	5.65	5.76	5.85	5.93
40	.05	2.86	3.44	3.79	4.04	4.23	4.39	4.52	4.63	4.73	4.82	4.90
	.01	3.82	4.37	4.70	4.93	5.11	5.26	5.39	5.50	5.60	5.69	5.76
60	.05	2.83	3.40	3.74	3.98	4.16	4.31	4.44	4.55	4.65	4.73	4.81
	.01	3.76	4.28	4.59	4.82	4.99	5.13	5.25	5.36	5.45	5.53	5.60
120	.05	2.80	3.36	3.68	3.92	4.10	4.24	4.36	4.47	4.56	4.64	4.71
	.01	3.70	4.20	4.50	4.71	4.87	5.01	5.12	5.21	5.30	5.37	5.44
∞	.05	2.77	3.31	3.63	3.86	4.03	4.17	4.29	4.39	4.47	4.55	4.62
	.01	3.64	4.12	4.40	4.60	4.76	4.88	4.99	5.08	5.16	5.23	5.29

SOURCE: E. S. Pearson and H. O. Hartley, *Biometrika Tables for Statisticians,* vol. 1 (Cambridge: Cambridge University Press, 1966), pp. 192–193. Reprinted by permission of Biometrika Trustees.

APPENDIX TABLE P | Values of d_L and d_U for the Durbin-Watson Test

$\alpha = .05$

n	$m = 1$ d_L	$m = 1$ d_U	$m = 2$ d_L	$m = 2$ d_U	$m = 3$ d_L	$m = 3$ d_U	$m = 4$ d_L	$m = 4$ d_U	$m = 5$ d_L	$m = 5$ d_U
15	1.08	1.36	0.95	1.54	0.82	1.75	0.69	1.97	0.56	2.21
16	1.10	1.37	0.98	1.54	0.86	1.73	0.74	1.93	0.62	2.15
17	1.13	1.38	1.02	1.54	0.90	1.71	0.78	1.90	0.67	2.10
18	1.16	1.39	1.05	1.53	0.93	1.69	0.82	1.87	0.71	2.06
19	1.18	1.40	1.08	1.53	0.97	1.68	0.86	1.85	0.75	2.02
20	1.20	1.41	1.10	1.54	1.00	1.68	0.90	1.83	0.79	1.99
21	1.22	1.42	1.13	1.54	1.03	1.67	0.93	1.81	0.83	1.96
22	1.24	1.43	1.15	1.54	1.05	1.66	0.96	1.80	0.86	1.94
23	1.26	1.44	1.17	1.54	1.08	1.66	0.99	1.79	0.90	1.92
24	1.27	1.45	1.19	1.55	1.10	1.66	1.01	1.78	0.93	1.90
25	1.29	1.45	1.21	1.55	1.12	1.66	1.04	1.77	0.95	1.89
26	1.30	1.46	1.22	1.55	1.14	1.65	1.06	1.76	0.98	1.88
27	1.32	1.47	1.24	1.56	1.16	1.65	1.08	1.76	1.01	1.86
28	1.33	1.48	1.26	1.56	1.18	1.65	1.10	1.75	1.03	1.85
29	1.34	1.48	1.27	1.56	1.20	1.65	1.12	1.74	1.05	1.84
30	1.35	1.49	1.28	1.57	1.21	1.65	1.14	1.74	1.07	1.83
31	1.36	1.50	1.30	1.57	1.23	1.65	1.16	1.74	1.09	1.83
32	1.37	1.50	1.31	1.57	1.24	1.65	1.18	1.73	1.11	1.82
33	1.38	1.51	1.32	1.58	1.26	1.65	1.19	1.73	1.13	1.81
34	1.39	1.51	1.33	1.58	1.27	1.65	1.21	1.73	1.15	1.81
35	1.40	1.52	1.34	1.58	1.28	1.65	1.22	1.73	1.16	1.80
36	1.41	1.52	1.35	1.59	1.29	1.65	1.24	1.73	1.18	1.80
37	1.42	1.53	1.36	1.59	1.31	1.66	1.25	1.72	1.19	1.80
38	1.43	1.54	1.37	1.59	1.32	1.66	1.26	1.72	1.21	1.79
39	1.43	1.54	1.38	1.60	1.33	1.66	1.27	1.72	1.22	1.79
40	1.44	1.54	1.39	1.60	1.34	1.66	1.29	1.72	1.23	1.79
45	1.48	1.57	1.43	1.62	1.38	1.67	1.34	1.72	1.29	1.78
50	1.50	1.59	1.46	1.63	1.42	1.67	1.38	1.72	1.34	1.77
55	1.53	1.60	1.49	1.64	1.45	1.68	1.41	1.72	1.38	1.77
60	1.55	1.62	1.51	1.65	1.48	1.69	1.44	1.73	1.41	1.77
65	1.57	1.63	1.54	1.66	1.50	1.70	1.47	1.73	1.44	1.77
70	1.58	1.64	1.55	1.67	1.52	1.70	1.49	1.74	1.46	1.77
75	1.60	1.65	1.57	1.68	1.54	1.71	1.51	1.74	1.49	1.77
80	1.61	1.66	1.59	1.69	1.56	1.72	1.53	1.74	1.51	1.77
85	1.62	1.67	1.60	1.70	1.57	1.72	1.55	1.75	1.52	1.77
90	1.63	1.68	1.61	1.70	1.59	1.73	1.57	1.75	1.54	1.78
95	1.64	1.69	1.62	1.71	1.60	1.73	1.58	1.75	1.56	1.78
100	1.65	1.69	1.63	1.72	1.61	1.74	1.59	1.76	1.57	1.78

(continued)

APPENDIX TABLE P (*continued*)

	$\alpha = .025$									
	$m = 1$		$m = 2$		$m = 3$		$m = 4$		$m = 5$	
n	d_L	d_U	d_L	d_U	d_L	d_U	d_L	d_U	d_L	d_U
15	0.95	1.23	0.83	1.40	0.71	1.61	0.59	1.84	0.48	2.09
16	0.98	1.24	0.86	1.40	0.75	1.59	0.64	1.80	0.53	2.03
17	1.01	1.25	0.90	1.40	0.79	1.58	0.68	1.77	0.57	1.98
18	1.03	1.26	0.93	1.40	0.82	1.56	0.72	1.74	0.62	1.93
19	1.06	1.28	0.96	1.41	0.86	1.55	0.76	1.72	0.66	1.90
20	1.08	1.28	0.99	1.41	0.89	1.55	0.79	1.70	0.70	1.87
21	1.10	1.30	1.01	1.41	0.92	1.54	0.83	1.69	0.73	1.84
22	1.12	1.31	1.04	1.42	0.95	1.54	0.86	1.68	0.77	1.82
23	1.14	1.32	1.06	1.42	0.97	1.54	0.89	1.67	0.80	1.80
24	1.16	1.33	1.08	1.43	1.00	1.54	0.91	1.66	0.83	1.79
25	1.18	1.34	1.10	1.43	1.02	1.54	0.94	1.65	0.86	1.77
26	1.19	1.35	1.12	1.44	1.04	1.54	0.96	1.65	0.88	1.76
27	1.21	1.36	1.13	1.44	1.06	1.54	0.99	1.64	0.91	1.75
28	1.22	1.37	1.15	1.45	1.08	1.54	1.01	1.64	0.93	1.74
29	1.24	1.38	1.17	1.45	1.10	1.54	1.03	1.63	0.96	1.73
30	1.25	1.38	1.18	1.46	1.12	1.54	1.05	1.63	0.98	1.73
31	1.26	1.39	1.20	1.47	1.13	1.55	1.07	1.63	1.00	1.72
32	1.27	1.40	1.21	1.47	1.15	1.55	1.08	1.63	1.02	1.71
33	1.28	1.41	1.22	1.48	1.16	1.55	1.10	1.63	1.04	1.71
34	1.29	1.41	1.24	1.48	1.17	1.55	1.12	1.63	1.06	1.70
35	1.30	1.42	1.25	1.48	1.19	1.55	1.13	1.63	1.07	1.70
36	1.31	1.43	1.26	1.49	1.20	1.56	1.15	1.63	1.09	1.70
37	1.32	1.43	1.27	1.49	1.21	1.56	1.16	1.62	1.10	1.70
38	1.33	1.44	1.28	1.50	1.23	1.56	1.17	1.62	1.12	1.70
39	1.34	1.44	1.29	1.50	1.24	1.56	1.19	1.63	1.13	1.69
40	1.35	1.45	1.30	1.51	1.25	1.57	1.20	1.63	1.15	1.69
45	1.39	1.48	1.34	1.53	1.30	1.58	1.25	1.63	1.21	1.69
50	1.42	1.50	1.38	1.54	1.34	1.59	1.30	1.64	1.26	1.69
55	1.45	1.52	1.41	1.56	1.37	1.60	1.33	1.64	1.30	1.69
60	1.47	1.54	1.44	1.57	1.40	1.61	1.37	1.65	1.33	1.69
65	1.49	1.55	1.46	1.59	1.43	1.62	1.40	1.66	1.36	1.69
70	1.51	1.57	1.48	1.60	1.45	1.63	1.42	1.66	1.39	1.70
75	1.53	1.58	1.50	1.61	1.47	1.64	1.45	1.67	1.42	1.70
80	1.54	1.59	1.52	1.62	1.49	1.65	1.47	1.67	1.44	1.70
85	1.56	1.60	1.53	1.63	1.51	1.65	1.49	1.68	1.46	1.71
90	1.57	1.61	1.55	1.64	1.53	1.66	1.50	1.69	1.48	1.71
95	1.58	1.62	1.56	1.65	1.54	1.67	1.52	1.69	1.50	1.71
100	1.59	1.63	1.57	1.65	1.55	1.67	1.53	1.70	1.51	1.72

(*continued*)

APPENDIX TABLE P (*continued*)

	$\alpha = .01$									
	$m = 1$		$m = 2$		$m = 3$		$m = 4$		$m = 5$	
n	d_L	d_U	d_L	d_U	d_L	d_U	d_L	d_U	d_L	d_U
15	0.81	1.07	0.70	1.25	0.59	1.46	0.49	1.70	0.39	1.96
16	0.84	1.09	0.74	1.25	0.63	1.44	0.53	1.66	0.44	1.90
17	0.87	1.10	0.77	1.25	0.67	1.43	0.57	1.63	0.48	1.85
18	0.90	1.12	0.80	1.26	0.71	1.42	0.61	1.60	0.52	1.80
19	0.93	1.13	0.83	1.26	0.74	1.41	0.65	1.58	0.56	1.77
20	0.95	1.15	0.86	1.27	0.77	1.41	0.68	1.57	0.60	1.74
21	0.97	1.16	0.89	1.27	0.80	1.41	0.72	1.55	0.63	1.71
22	1.00	1.17	0.91	1.28	0.83	1.40	0.75	1.54	0.66	1.69
23	1.02	1.19	0.94	1.29	0.86	1.40	0.77	1.53	0.70	1.67
24	1.04	1.20	0.96	1.30	0.88	1.41	0.80	1.53	0.72	1.66
25	1.05	1.21	0.98	1.30	0.90	1.41	0.83	1.52	0.75	1.65
26	1.07	1.22	1.00	1.31	0.93	1.41	0.85	1.52	0.78	1.64
27	1.09	1.23	1.02	1.32	0.95	1.41	0.88	1.51	0.81	1.63
28	1.10	1.24	1.04	1.32	0.97	1.41	0.90	1.51	0.83	1.62
29	1.12	1.25	1.05	1.33	0.99	1.42	0.92	1.51	0.85	1.61
30	1.13	1.26	1.07	1.34	1.01	1.42	0.94	1.51	0.88	1.61
31	1.15	1.27	1.08	1.34	1.02	1.42	0.96	1.51	0.90	1.60
32	1.16	1.28	1.10	1.35	1.04	1.43	0.98	1.51	0.92	1.60
33	1.17	1.29	1.11	1.36	1.05	1.43	1.00	1.51	0.94	1.59
34	1.18	1.30	1.13	1.36	1.07	1.43	1.01	1.51	0.95	1.59
35	1.19	1.31	1.14	1.37	1.08	1.44	1.03	1.51	0.97	1.59
36	1.21	1.32	1.15	1.38	1.10	1.44	1.04	1.51	0.99	1.59
37	1.22	1.32	1.16	1.38	1.11	1.45	1.06	1.51	1.00	1.59
38	1.23	1.33	1.18	1.39	1.12	1.45	1.07	1.52	1.02	1.58
39	1.24	1.34	1.19	1.39	1.14	1.45	1.09	1.52	1.03	1.58
40	1.25	1.34	1.20	1.40	1.15	1.46	1.10	1.52	1.05	1.58
45	1.29	1.38	1.24	1.42	1.20	1.48	1.16	1.53	1.11	1.58
50	1.32	1.40	1.28	1.45	1.24	1.49	1.20	1.54	1.16	1.59
55	1.36	1.43	1.32	1.47	1.28	1.51	1.25	1.55	1.21	1.59
60	1.38	1.45	1.35	1.48	1.32	1.52	1.28	1.56	1.25	1.60
65	1.41	1.47	1.38	1.50	1.35	1.53	1.31	1.57	1.28	1.61
70	1.43	1.49	1.40	1.52	1.37	1.55	1.34	1.58	1.31	1.61
75	1.45	1.50	1.42	1.53	1.39	1.56	1.37	1.59	1.34	1.62
80	1.47	1.52	1.44	1.54	1.42	1.57	1.39	1.60	1.36	1.62
85	1.48	1.53	1.46	1.55	1.43	1.58	1.41	1.60	1.39	1.63
90	1.50	1.54	1.47	1.56	1.45	1.59	1.43	1.61	1.41	1.64
95	1.51	1.55	1.49	1.57	1.47	1.60	1.45	1.62	1.42	1.64
100	1.52	1.56	1.50	1.58	1.48	1.60	1.46	1.63	1.44	1.65

NOTE: The α levels are for one-tailed tests. For two-tailed tests, consult $\alpha/2$.

SOURCE: J. Durbin and G. S. Watson, "Testing for Serial Correlation in Least Squares Regression II," *Biometrika* 38 (June 1951), pp. 173–175. Reprinted by permission.

APPENDIX TABLE Q | Critical Values of D for the Kolmogorov-Smirnov Maximum Deviation Test for Goodness of Fit

This table provides critical values, D, that correspond to an upper-tail probability, α, of the test statistic, D. For example, for an upper-tail area of α = .05 and a sample of n = 10, the critical value of $D_a = .36866$. Thus, the probability is .05 that an observed value of $D \geq .36866$.

n	Critical Values for Upper-Tail Area, α .10	.05	.025	.01	.005
1	.90000	.95000	.97500	.99000	.99500
2	.68377	.77639	.84189	.90000	.92929
3	.56481	.63604	.70760	.78456	.82900
4	.49265	.56522	.62394	.68887	.73424
5	.44698	.50945	.56328	.62718	.66853
6	.41037	.46799	.51926	.57741	.61661
7	.38148	.43607	.48342	.53844	.57581
8	.35831	.40962	.45427	.50654	.54179
9	.33910	.38746	.43001	.47960	.51332
10	.32260	.36866	.40925	.45662	.48893
11	.30829	.35242	.39122	.43670	.46770
12	.29577	.33815	.37543	.41918	.44905
13	.28470	.32549	.36143	.40362	.43247
14	.27481	.31417	.34890	.38970	.41762
15	.26588	.30397	.33760	.37713	.40420
16	.25778	.29472	.32733	.36571	.39201
17	.25039	.28627	.31796	.35528	.38086
18	.24360	.27851	.30936	.34569	.37062
19	.23735	.27136	.30143	.33685	.36117
20	.23156	.26473	.29408	.32866	.35241
21	.22617	.25858	.28724	.32104	.34427
22	.22115	.25283	.28087	.31394	.33666
23	.21645	.24746	.27490	.30728	.32954
24	.21205	.24242	.26931	.30104	.32286
25	.20790	.23768	.26404	.29516	.31657
26	.20399	.23320	.25907	.28962	.31064
27	.20030	.22898	.25438	.28438	.30502
28	.19680	.22497	.24993	.27942	.29971
29	.19348	.22117	.24571	.27471	.29466
30	.19032	.21756	.24170	.27023	.28987
31	.18732	.21412	.23788	.26596	.28530
32	.18445	.21085	.23424	.26189	.28094
33	.18171	.20771	.23076	.25801	.27677
34	.17909	.20472	.22743	.25429	.27279
35	.17659	.20185	.22425	.25073	.26897
36	.17418	.19910	.22119	.24732	.26532
37	.17188	.19646	.21826	.24404	.26180
38	.16966	.19392	.21544	.24089	.25843
39	.16753	.19148	.21273	.23786	.25518
40	.16547	.18913	.21012	.23494	.25205

(continued)

APPENDIX TABLE Q (*continued*)

	Critical Values for Upper-Tail Area, α				
n	.10	.05	.025	.01	.005
41	.16349	.18687	.20760	.23213	.24904
42	.16158	.18468	.20517	.22941	.24613
43	.15974	.18257	.20283	.22679	.24332
44	.15796	.18053	.20056	.22426	.24060
45	.15623	.17856	.19837	.22181	.23798
46	.15457	.17665	.19625	.21944	.23544
47	.15295	.17481	.19420	.21715	.23298
48	.15139	.17302	.19221	.21493	.23059
49	.14987	.17128	.19028	.21277	.22828
50	.14840	.16959	.18841	.21068	.22604
51	.14697	.16796	.18659	.20864	.22386
52	.14558	.16637	.18482	.20667	.22174
53	.14423	.16483	.18311	.20475	.21968
54	.14292	.16332	.18144	.20289	.21768
55	.14164	.16186	.17981	.20107	.21574
56	.14040	.16044	.17823	.19930	.21384
57	.13919	.15906	.17669	.19758	.21199
58	.13801	.15771	.17519	.19590	.21019
59	.13686	.15639	.17373	.19427	.20844
60	.13573	.15511	.17231	.19267	.20673
61	.13464	.15385	.17091	.19112	.20506
62	.13357	.15263	.16956	.18960	.20343
63	.13253	.15144	.16823	.18812	.20184
64	.13151	.15027	.16693	.18667	.20029
65	.13052	.14913	.16567	.18525	.19877
66	.12954	.14802	.16443	.18387	.19729
67	.12859	.14693	.16322	.18252	.19584
68	.12766	.14587	.16204	.18119	.19442
69	.12675	.14483	.16088	.17990	.19303
70	.12586	.14381	.15975	.17863	.19167
71	.12499	.14281	.15864	.17739	.19034
72	.12413	.14183	.15755	.17618	.18903
73	.12329	.14087	.15649	.17498	.18776
74	.12247	.13993	.15544	.17382	.18650
75	.12167	.13901	.15442	.17268	.18528
76	.12088	.13811	.15342	.17155	.18408
77	.12011	.13723	.15244	.17045	.18290
78	.11935	.13636	.15147	.16938	.18174
79	.11860	.13551	.15052	.16832	.18060
80	.11787	.13467	.14960	.16728	.17949
81	.11716	.13385	.14868	.16626	.17840
82	.11645	.13305	.14779	.16526	.17732
83	.11576	.13226	.14691	.16428	.17627
84	.11508	.13148	.14605	.16331	.17523
85	.11442	.13072	.14520	.16236	.17421
86	.11376	.12997	.14437	.16143	.17321

(*continued*)

APPENDIX TABLE Q (*continued*)

n	Critical Values for Upper-Tail Area, α .10	.05	.025	.01	.005
87	.11311	.12923	.14355	.16051	.17223
88	.11248	.12850	.14274	.15961	.17126
89	.11186	.12779	.14195	.15873	.17031
90	.11125	.12709	.14117	.15786	.16938
91	.11064	.12640	.14040	.15700	.16846
92	.11005	.12572	.13965	.15616	.16755
93	.10947	.12506	.13891	.15533	.16666
94	.10889	.12440	.13818	.15451	.16579
95	.10833	.12375	.13746	.15371	.16493
96	.10777	.12312	.13675	.15291	.16408
97	.10722	.12249	.13606	.15214	.16324
98	.10668	.12187	.13537	.15137	.16242
99	.10615	.12126	.13469	.15061	.16161
100	.10563	.12067	.13403	.14987	.16081

NOTE: For larger samples, critical values can be computed as follows:

$\alpha = .10$	$\alpha = .05$	$\alpha = .025$	$\alpha = .01$	$\alpha = .005$
$\frac{1.22}{\sqrt{n}}$	$\frac{1.36}{\sqrt{n}}$	$\frac{1.48}{\sqrt{n}}$	$\frac{1.63}{\sqrt{n}}$	$\frac{1.73}{\sqrt{n}}$

SOURCE: Leslie H. Miller, "Table of Percentage Points of Kolmogorov Statistics," *Journal of the American Statistical Association,* 51 (1956), pp. 113–115. Reprinted by permission.

APPENDIX TABLE R | Factors for Constructing $\overline{X}$ or R Control Charts

Sample Size n	Charting Averages: d_2	Charting Averages: $A_2 = \frac{3}{d_2\sqrt{n}}$	Charting Ranges: d_3	Charting Ranges: $D_3 = 1 - 3\frac{d_3}{d_2}$ (but never < 0)	Charting Ranges: $D_4 = 1 + 3\frac{d_3}{d_2}$
2	1.128	1.880	.853	0	3.267
3	1.693	1.023	.888	0	2.574
4	2.059	.729	.880	0	2.282
5	2.326	.577	.864	0	2.114
6	2.534	.483	.848	0	2.004
7	2.704	.419	.833	.076	1.924
8	2.847	.373	.820	.136	1.864
9	2.970	.337	.808	.184	1.816
10	3.078	.308	.797	.223	1.777
11	3.173	.285	.787	.256	1.744
12	3.258	.266	.778	.283	1.717
13	3.336	.249	.770	.307	1.693
14	3.407	.235	.763	.328	1.672
15	3.472	.223	.756	.347	1.653
16	3.532	.212	.750	.363	1.637
17	3.588	.203	.744	.378	1.622
18	3.640	.194	.739	.391	1.608
19	3.689	.187	.734	.403	1.597
20	3.735	.180	.729	.415	1.585
21	3.778	.173	.724	.425	1.575
22	3.819	.167	.720	.434	1.566
23	3.858	.162	.716	.443	1.557
24	3.895	.157	.712	.451	1.548
25	3.931	.153	.708	.459	1.541

SOURCE: *ASTM Manual on Presentation of Data and Control Chart Analysis* (Philadelphia, PA: American Society for Testing and Materials, 1976), Table 27 of ASTM STP 15D. Reprinted with permission.

Name Index

Subject Index